CONTINUE THE ADVENTURE!
Pokémon Black Version 2 and Pokémon White Version 2 Volume 2:
The Official National Pokédex & Guide
THE OFFICIAL NATIONAL POKÉDEX AND GUIDE: VOLUME 2
POKÉDEX
Pokémon Black Version 2
Pokémon White Version 2
Includes...
The latest up-to-date National Pokédex, including newly revealed Pokémon
Tips and strategies on training and battle to help you master the games
Insider info on Pokémon moves and Abilities in the new games!
A spectacular full-color Pokémon poster!
AVAILABLE NOVEMBER 2012!
WWW.POKEMON.COM
D1536717

Two years have passed since the last adventure in the Unova region.

New Gym Leaders and a new Champion are waiting for new challengers.

If you intend to face the Ch

prepare you

battling you

against our

ampion of the Unova region,

urself by
ur Pokémon
s!

CONTENTS

Town and Route

Quick Index

By Route Number

Alphabetical by Name

Meet Pokémon with Hidden Abilities

Hidden Grotto Index

How to Register in the Unova Pokédex

A•C

D•F

G•I

J•L

M•O

P•R

S•T

U•V

W•X

Y•Z

Pokémon Black Version 2 and *Pokémon White Version 2* Unova Region Map

You can fly to the places marked with a bird Pokémon icon.

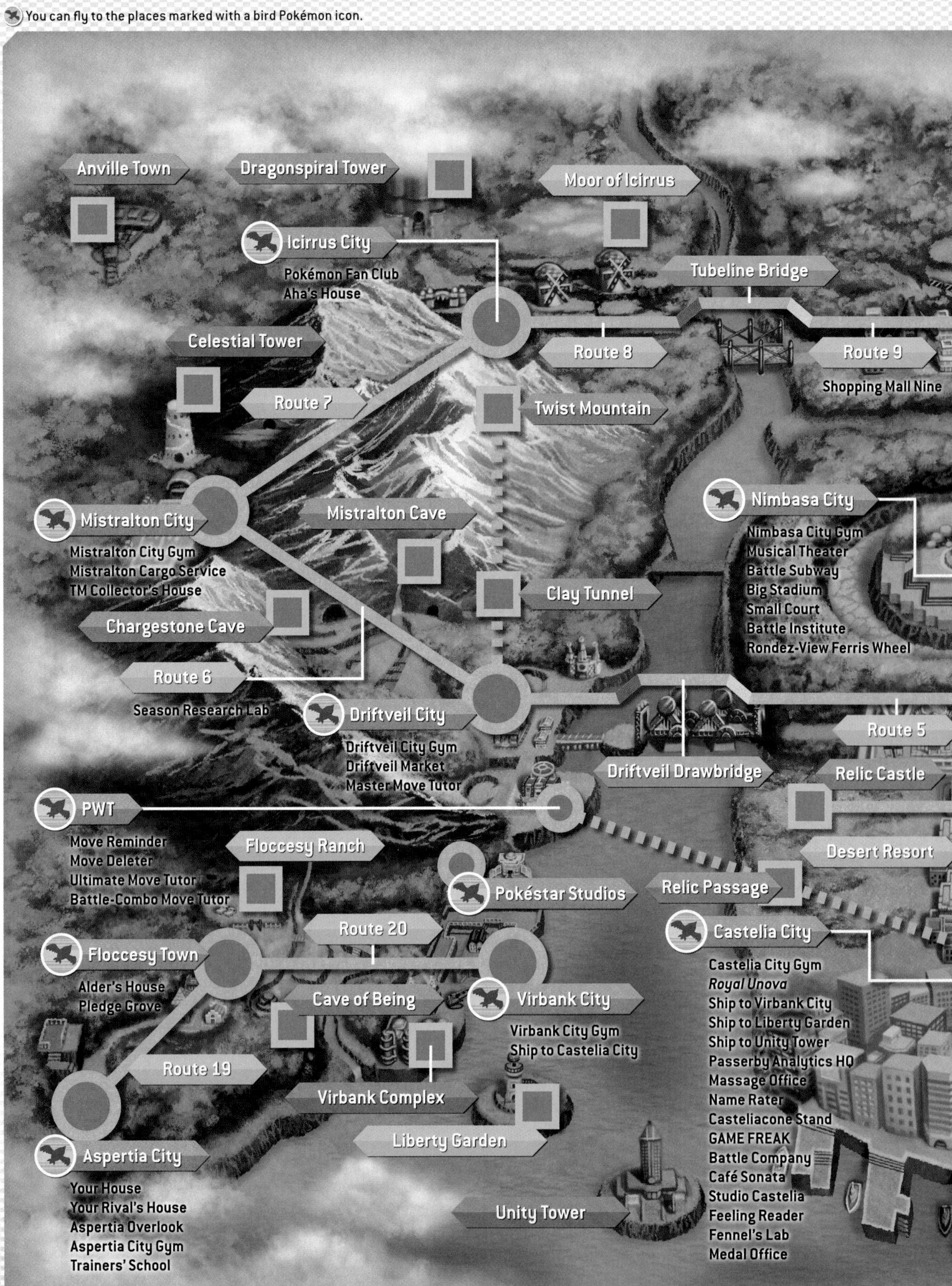
Anville Town
Dragonspiral Tower
Moor of Icirrus
Icirrus City
Pokémon Fan Club
Aha's House
Tubeline Bridge
Celestial Tower
Route 8
Route 9
Shopping Mall Nine
Route 7
Twist Mountain
Nimbasa City
Nimbasa City Gym
Musical Theater
Battle Subway
Big Stadium
Small Court
Battle Institute
Rondez-View Ferris Wheel
Mistralton City
Mistralton City Gym
Mistralton Cargo Service
TM Collector's House
Mistralton Cave
Clay Tunnel
Chargestone Cave
Route 6
Season Research Lab
Driftveil City
Driftveil City Gym
Driftveil Market
Master Move Tutor
Route 5
Driftveil Drawbridge
Relic Castle
PWT
Move Reminder
Move Deleter
Ultimate Move Tutor
Battle-Combo Move Tutor
Floccesy Ranch
Desert Resort
Pokéstar Studios
Relic Passage
Castelia City
Castelia City Gym
Royal Unova
Ship to Virbank City
Ship to Liberty Garden
Ship to Unity Tower
Passerby Analytics HQ
Massage Office
Name Rater
Casteliacone Stand
GAME FREAK
Battle Company
Café Sonata
Studio Castelia
Feeling Reader
Fennel's Lab
Medal Office
Route 20
Floccesy Town
Alder's House
Pledge Grove
Cave of Being
Virbank City
Virbank City Gym
Ship to Castelia City
Route 19
Virbank Complex
Liberty Garden
Aspertia City
Your House
Your Rival's House
Aspertia Overlook
Aspertia City Gym
Trainers' School
Unity Tower

This is the map of the Unova region, where your adventure awaits.
All of the cities, towns, routes, caves, and other important places are shown.

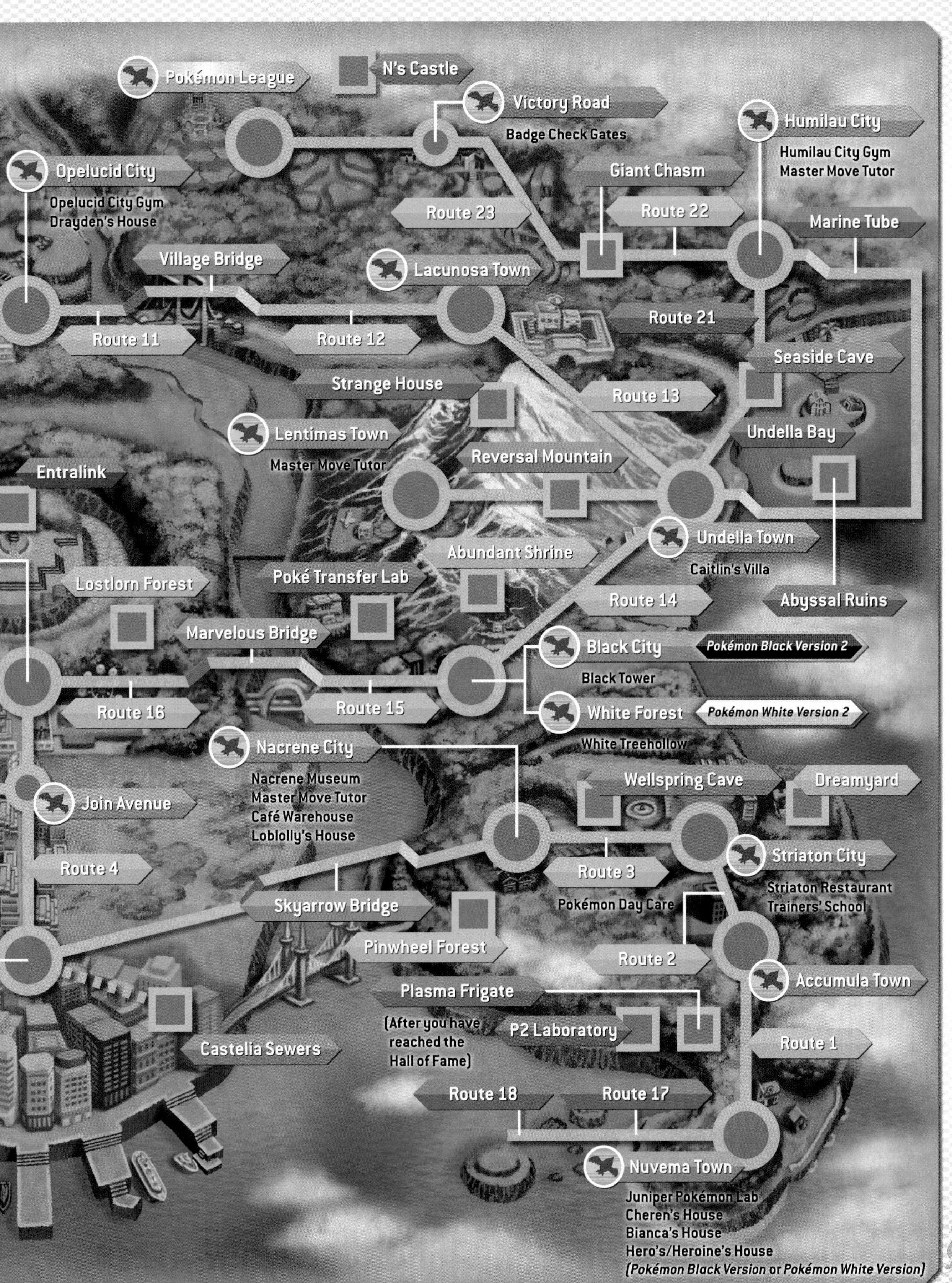

Pokémon Black Version 2 and *Pokémon White Version 2* Recommended Route

Below is the recommended route for your grand adventure through the Unova region. Check this guide when you want to know how much progress you have made so far, or when you aren't sure where to go next.

Step	Location	Page	Events
1	Aspertia City	p. 80	● Leave your room and answer Mom's questions ● Go to the Aspertia City Outlook with your rival ● Pick one of Snivy, Tepig, or Oshawott to be your partner in your adventure ● Receive a Pokédex from Bianca ● Have your first Pokémon battle with your rival ● Receive 10 Poké Balls from Bianca ● Receive Running Shoes from Mom ● Receive Town Maps from your rival's little sister
2	Route 19	p. 88	● Learn how to catch Pokémon from Bianca ● Meet Pokémon Trainer Alder
3	Floccesy Town	p. 90	● Alder tells you to go to Route 20
4	Route 20	p. 92	● Head north to Floccesy Ranch
5	Floccesy Ranch	p. 96	● Battle with your rival for the second time ● Give your rival a Town Map ● Search for the ranch owner's missing Herdier ● Encounter Team Plasma for the first time
6	Floccesy Town	p. 91	● Battle the students at Alder's house ● Receive a Medal Box from Mr. Medal
7	Route 19	p. 90	● Receive five Oran Berries from Alder
8	Aspertia City	p. 85	Gym Battle ❶ : Gym Leader Cheren ● Register Cheren, Bianca, and Professor Juniper in your Xtransceiver ● Talk with Professor Juniper on your Xtransceiver ● Receive the C-Gear from Bianca
9	Floccesy Town	p. 91	● Bianca adds the Habitat List to your Pokédex
10	Route 20	p. 95	● Head east to reach Virbank City
11	Virbank City	p. 98	● Explore the whole city before heading to the Virbank Complex
12	Virbank Complex	p. 102	● Listen to the foreman's request and battle with three Workers
13	Virbank City	p. 100	Gym Battle ❷ : Gym Leader Roxie
14	Pokéstar Studios	p. 104	● Watch Roxie's dad's debut film with him
15	Virbank City	p. 101	● Confront Team Plasma for the first time ● Receive HM01 Cut from Roxie
16	Route 20	p. 95	● Confront Team Plasma
17	Virbank City	p. 102	● Take the ship to Castelia City
18	Castelia City	p. 110	● Receive a Bicycle from a Harlequin
19	Liberty Garden	p. 116	● Explore the whole island before returning to Castelia City
20	Castelia City	p. 113	● Meet Iris in front of the Pokémon Gym ● Follow your rival to the Castelia Sewers
21	Castelia Sewers	p. 117	● Form a team with your rival to confront Team Plasma ● Meet the Castelia City Gym Leader—Burgh ● Receive HM04 Strength from your rival
22	Castelia City	p. 115	Gym Battle ❸ : Gym Leader Burgh ● Meet the mysterious figure—Colress
23	Route 4	*Pokémon Black Version 2* → p. 122 *Pokémon White Version 2* → p. 125	● Battle Colress for the first time
24	Desert Resort	p. 128	● Go through the desert to head for the Relic Castle
25	Relic Castle	p. 129	● Explore the whole castle before heading to Join Avenue
26	Join Avenue	p. 132	● Become the new manager at the request of the owner

Step	Location	Page	Tasks
27	Nimbasa City	p. 134	● Form a team with a city resident for a Multi Battle against the Subway Bosses—Emmet and Ingo ● Receive a Vs. Recorder from your battle partner ● Receive a Prop Case from the owner of the Pokémon Musical
28	Anville Town	p. 142	● Explore the whole town before returning to Nimbasa City
29	Route 16 Lostlorn Forest	p. 143	● Explore the whole area before returning to Nimbasa City
30	Nimbasa City	p. 138	Gym Battle 4 : Gym Leader Elesa ● Confront Team Plasma
31	Route 5	p. 145	● Receive HM02 Fly from Bianca ● Battle against Motorcyclist Charles
32	Driftveil Drawbridge	p. 147	● Go across the bridge to reach Driftveil City
33	Driftveil City	p. 148	● Meet a former Team Plasma member ● Battle with Rood at the ex-Team Plasma base ● Receive Zorua from Rood Gym Battle 5 : Gym Leader Clay
34	PWT (The Pokémon World Tournament)	p. 154	● Take part in the Driftveil Tournament ● Battle against your rival in the first round ● Battle against Cheren in the second round ● Battle against Colress in the final round ● Confront Team Plasma on the Plasma Frigate
35	Relic Passage	p. 159	● Go through the Relic Castle to reach the Castelia Sewers ● Use Fly to return to the PWT from Castelia City
36	Relic Castle	p. 131	● Catch Volcarona
37	Route 6	p. 161	● Receive HM03 Surf from Cheren ● Receive a Deerling with the Hidden Ability Serene Grace at the Season Research Lab
38	Mistralton Cave	p. 163	● Explore the whole cave before returning to Route 6
39	Chargestone Cave	p. 165	● Go through the cave to reach Mistralton City
40	Mistralton City	p. 168	● Meet Professor Juniper and Skyla
41	Route 7	p. 172	● Speak with the old man in the house to have Tornadus, Thundurus, and Landorus registered in your Pokédex
42	Celestial Tower	p. 174	● Speak to Professor Juniper on the first floor
43	Mistralton City	p. 170	Gym Battle 6 : Gym Leader Skyla ● Talk to Skyla at the Mistralton Cargo Service and board the airplane
44	Lentimas Town	p. 176	● Speak with Professor Juniper ● Explore every last corner of the town before heading to Reversal Mountain
45	Reversal Mountain	p. 177	● Go around the mountain to reach the Strange House
46	Strange House	p. 180	● Receive the Lunar Wing
47	Reversal Mountain	p. 178	● Form a team with Bianca to make it through the mountain
48	Undella Town	p. 181	● Battle with your rival for the third time ● Explore the whole town before heading to Undella Bay
49	Undella Bay	p. 184	● Explore the whole bay before returning to Undella Town
50	Route 13	p. 185	● Catch Cobalion
51	Lacunosa Town	p. 188	● Confront Team Plasma's Zinzolin
52	Route 12	p. 190	● Make your way to Village Bridge
53	Village Bridge	p. 191	● Make your way to Route 11
54	Route 11	p. 192	● Catch Virizion
55	Opelucid City	p. 194	● Explore the whole city before heading to Route 9
56	Route 9	p. 200	● Explore the whole route before returning to Opelucid City

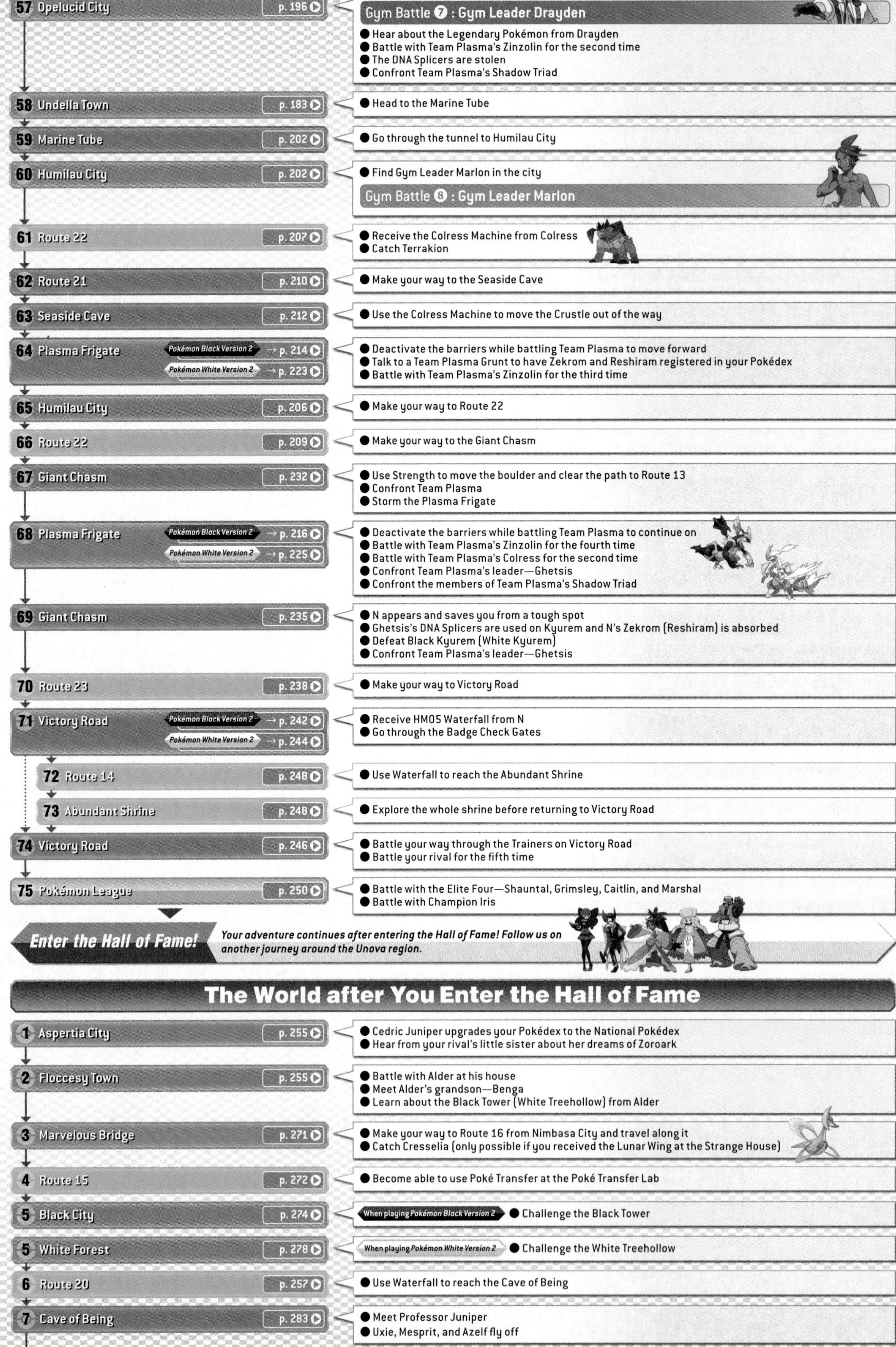

57 Opelucid City p. 196

Gym Battle 7 : Gym Leader Drayden

- Hear about the Legendary Pokémon from Drayden
- Battle with Team Plasma's Zinzolin for the second time
- The DNA Splicers are stolen
- Confront Team Plasma's Shadow Triad

58 Undella Town p. 183

- Head to the Marine Tube

59 Marine Tube p. 202

- Go through the tunnel to Humilau City

60 Humilau City p. 202

- Find Gym Leader Marlon in the city

Gym Battle 8 : Gym Leader Marlon

61 Route 22 p. 207

- Receive the Colress Machine from Colress
- Catch Terrakion

62 Route 21 p. 210

- Make your way to the Seaside Cave

63 Seaside Cave p. 212

- Use the Colress Machine to move the Crustle out of the way

64 Plasma Frigate Pokémon Black Version 2 → p. 214 / Pokémon White Version 2 → p. 223

- Deactivate the barriers while battling Team Plasma to move forward
- Talk to a Team Plasma Grunt to have Zekrom and Reshiram registered in your Pokédex
- Battle with Team Plasma's Zinzolin for the third time

65 Humilau City p. 206

- Make your way to Route 22

66 Route 22 p. 209

- Make your way to the Giant Chasm

67 Giant Chasm p. 232

- Use Strength to move the boulder and clear the path to Route 13
- Confront Team Plasma
- Storm the Plasma Frigate

68 Plasma Frigate Pokémon Black Version 2 → p. 216 / Pokémon White Version 2 → p. 225

- Deactivate the barriers while battling Team Plasma to continue on
- Battle with Team Plasma's Zinzolin for the fourth time
- Battle with Team Plasma's Colress for the second time
- Confront Team Plasma's leader—Ghetsis
- Confront the members of Team Plasma's Shadow Triad

69 Giant Chasm p. 235

- N appears and saves you from a tough spot
- Ghetsis's DNA Splicers are used on Kyurem and N's Zekrom (Reshiram) is absorbed
- Defeat Black Kyurem (White Kyurem)
- Confront Team Plasma's leader—Ghetsis

70 Route 23 p. 238

- Make your way to Victory Road

71 Victory Road Pokémon Black Version 2 → p. 242 / Pokémon White Version 2 → p. 244

- Receive HM05 Waterfall from N
- Go through the Badge Check Gates

72 Route 14 p. 248

- Use Waterfall to reach the Abundant Shrine

73 Abundant Shrine p. 248

- Explore the whole shrine before returning to Victory Road

74 Victory Road p. 246

- Battle your way through the Trainers on Victory Road
- Battle your rival for the fifth time

75 Pokémon League p. 250

- Battle with the Elite Four—Shauntal, Grimsley, Caitlin, and Marshal
- Battle with Champion Iris

Enter the Hall of Fame! *Your adventure continues after entering the Hall of Fame! Follow us on another journey around the Unova region.*

The World after You Enter the Hall of Fame

1 Aspertia City p. 255

- Cedric Juniper upgrades your Pokédex to the National Pokédex
- Hear from your rival's little sister about her dreams of Zoroark

2 Floccesy Town p. 255

- Battle with Alder at his house
- Meet Alder's grandson—Benga
- Learn about the Black Tower (White Treehollow) from Alder

3 Marvelous Bridge p. 271

- Make your way to Route 16 from Nimbasa City and travel along it
- Catch Cresselia (only possible if you received the Lunar Wing at the Strange House)

4 Route 15 p. 272

- Become able to use Poké Transfer at the Poké Transfer Lab

5 Black City p. 274

When playing *Pokémon Black Version 2*
- Challenge the Black Tower

5 White Forest p. 278

When playing *Pokémon White Version 2*
- Challenge the White Treehollow

6 Route 20 p. 257

- Use Waterfall to reach the Cave of Being

7 Cave of Being p. 283

- Meet Professor Juniper
- Uxie, Mesprit, and Azelf fly off

Step	Location	Page	Tasks
8	Clay Tunnel	p. 284	● Catch Regirock ● Unlock the Iceberg Chamber using Unova Link's Key System and catch Regice ● Unlock the Iron Chamber using Unova Link's Key System and catch Registeel
9	Twist Mountain	p. 288	● Put Regirock, Regice, and Registeel in your party to catch Regigigas
10	Undella Town	p. 260	● Receive HM06 Dive from your rival ● Battle with your rival for the sixth time ● Zinzolin gives you the key to deciphering the scripts found in the Abyssal Ruins ● Battle with Cynthia at Caitlin's Villa
11	Abyssal Ruins	p. 291	● Use Dive in Undella Bay to dive deep underwater ● Solve the puzzles to collect the items
12	Driftveil City	p. 262	● Battle with your rival for the seventh time (from this point on, you can battle him once a day)
13	Celestial Tower	p. 264	● Catch Mesprit
14	Route 23	p. 264	● Catch Azelf
15	Victory Road	p. 265	● Chase Zoroark and head for N's Castle
16	N's Castle	p. 294	● Battle with Pokémon Trainer N ● Receive the Dark Stone (Light Stone) from N ● Travel along Route 9 from Opelucid City and head for the Tubeline Bridge
17	Tubeline Bridge	p. 297	● Make your way to Route 8
18	Route 8 • Moor of Icirrus	p. 298	● Go through the moor to reach Icirrus City
19	Icirrus City	p. 301	● Confront the members of Team Plasma's Shadow Triad (from this point on, you can battle them every time the season changes)
20	Dragonspiral Tower	p. 305	● Meet Cedric Juniper and hear what he has to say ● Catch Zekrom (Reshiram) ● Hear about Kyurem from N
21	Giant Chasm	p. 265	● Catch Kyurem ● Receive the DNA Splicers
22	Skyarrow Bridge	p. 307	● Go through the gate in Castelia City ● Go across the bridge to reach Pinwheel Forest
23	Pinwheel Forest	p. 309	● Form a team with Cheren and explore the forest
24	Nacrene City	p. 312	● Catch Uxie ● Receive either a Cover Fossil or a Plume Fossil from Lenora ● Receive a Pokémon Egg from a woman
25	Route 3	p. 314	● Make your way to Wellspring Cave
26	Wellspring Cave	p. 317	● Explore the whole cave before returning to Route 3
27	Striaton City	p. 318	● Enjoy a battle with Cilan, Chili, or Cress at the Striaton Restaurant (from this point on, you can battle them once a day)
28	Dreamyard	p. 320	● Catch Latios (Latias)
29	Route 2	p. 322	● Make your way to Accumula Town
30	Accumula Town	p. 324	● Explore the whole city before heading to Route 1
31	Route 1	p. 326	● Use Surf to reach Route 17
32	Route 17 • Route 18 • P2 Laboratory	p. 328	● Meet Crasher Wake ● Receive the Magma Stone ● Battle with Colress for the third time on the Plasma Frigate (from this point on, you can battle him once a day)
33	Nuvema Town	p. 331	● Receive the Super Rod from Cedric Juniper ● Receive a Permit from Professor Juniper ◆ only possible if the number of Pokémon you have seen in your Pokédex has reached 297, not including Mythical Pokémon such as Victini, Keldeo, or Meloetta
34	Reversal Mountain	p. 267	● Set out from Lentimas Town ● Catch Heatran (only possible if you received the Magma Stone on Route 18)
35	Nature Preserve	p. 333	● If you have a Permit, you can fly here by airplane from Mistralton City ● Catch a Shiny Haxorus

Once you have visited every area, it is time for the grandest journey of all: completing the National Pokédex!

Pokémon Black Version 2 and Pokémon White Version 2

People and Places to Visit Daily

Trade Poké Balls

Where: Virbank Complex

Speak to the man and give him a Poké Ball. He'll give you a Great Ball in exchange.

p. 103

Take the *Royal Unova*

Where: Castelia City

Speak to the receptionist at the cruise ship dock in the evening. You can board the *Royal Unova*.

p. 111

Get ready for Pokémon battles

Where: GAME FREAK in Castelia City

You can battle Morimoto and Nishino on floor 22F of the GAME FREAK building. Look out! They will get even tougher after the Hall of Fame.

YES
NO
Oh! You've become strong! I can tell.
Do you want to have a battle with me?

p. 111

Buy Casteliacones

Where: Castelia City

You can buy a Casteliacone at the Casteliacone stand on Mode Street. You can choose to buy one or a dozen!

p. 111

Get five different Berries

Where: Studio Castelia

Show the Pokémon that is requested and receive one of the following Berries: Aspear, Cheri, Chesto, Pecha, or Rawst.

p. 111

Get a massage for your Pokémon

Where: Castelia City

In a building on the same street as the Gym, check the first floor for a woman. Speak with her, and she will give your Pokémon a massage, which will make the Pokémon more friendly.

p. 112

Receive an item at the experiment

Where: Castelia Sewers

Speak to the Scientist and she'll give you one of the following items: Potion, Super Potion, or Revive.

But I did manage to make a Potion.
Here, you can have it!

p. 119

Receive an item at the experiment

Where: Castelia Sewers (spring and summer only)

Speak to the Scientist and he'll give you one of the following items: Antidote, Full Heal, or Full Restore.

I created an Antidote. Here, take it!

p. 119

Take Wing!

Where: Route 4

A person wants to see a Pokémon of a certain stat value or higher. The Wing or Wings you'll receive in exchange will vary according to the stat and your Game Card.

have any Pokémon with a Speed of 57 or greater with you!

Pokémon Black Version 2 → p. 123
Pokémon White Version 2 → p. 126

Ride the Ferris wheel after a Pokémon battle

Where: Nimbasa City by the Ferris wheel

Defeat the Trainer in front of the Ferris wheel, and the Trainer will ride the Ferris wheel with you. The Trainer changes depending on the season and your gender.

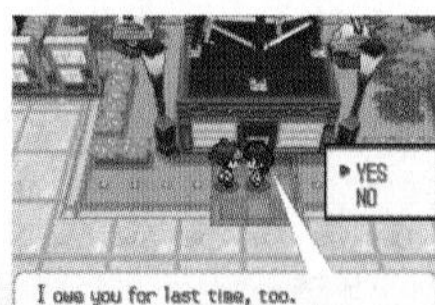

YES
NO
I owe you for last time, too.
You're gonna pay! You ready? Huh?

p. 137

Buy five different Berries

Where: Route 5

A woman will sell you the following Berries: Grepa, Hondew, Kelpsy, Pomeg, or Qualot. She sells five of the same Berry for 200.

p. 146

Receive a Heart Scale

Where: Driftveil City

On the first floor of the Driftveil Luxury Suites, you'll find a Lady. Show her a Pokémon with the move she wants to see, and she'll give you a Heart Scale.

p. 149

Receive five different Flutes

Where: Route 13

Keep going back and talking to this person to get all five Flutes. You can only get one of each kind.

p. 186

Receive four different Berries

Where: Lacunosa Town (Night and Late Night)

In a house on the high ground is a man who gives you one of the following Berries: Bluk, Leppa, Lum, or Pecha.

p. 189

Receive four different Props

Where: Opelucid City

West of the Pokémon Center is a house where you can get a Prop each day to a total of four.

p. 195

In the Unova region, you can visit certain places or people every day to receive an item or have a Pokémon battle. Check this list for recommendations.

Events colored ● are available after finishing the main story.

Receive two different items

Where: Shopping Mall Nine

On the first floor is a woman who asks you to shop for her. If you get her a Hyper Potion that day, you'll receive an Energy Root. If you give it to her the next day, you'll receive EnergyPowder.

p. 201

Receive a Pearl

Where: Humilau City

An elderly lady in a house asks you to walk her Mienfoo. If Mienfoo is happy, you'll receive a Pearl.

p. 204

Test yourself against Cynthia!

Where: Undella Town (spring only)

Visit Caitlin's Villa and you'll be able to challenge Cynthia! A word of warning: you can't battle her in summer, and she's not there in autumn or winter.

p. 182

Challenge your rival for a battle

Where: Ex-Team Plasma Base

After a battle in Undella Town, your rival appears in the ex-Team Plasma Base. Your mission, if you choose to accept it, is to battle him!

p. 262

Get access to shops

Where: Black City / White Forest

As you clear areas in Black Tower or White Treehollow, you'll gain access to shops where you can buy various items.

Pokémon Black Version 2 → p. 275

Pokémon White Version 2 → p. 279

Receive seven different Fossils

Where: Twist Mountain

Talk to the Worker on lower level 1, and every day you'll get a Fossil that you can have restored into a Pokémon. Even if you already received a particular Fossil, you can keep getting more day by day.

p. 290

Answer correctly to get a Medal

Where: Twist Mountain

The Heavy Machinery Pro will quiz you every day. He's in lower level 2. Complete five quizzes correctly, and you'll receive a Medal from Mr. Medal.

p. 290

Receive four different Rocks

Where: Route 8

A generous Parasol Lady will give you a Damp Rock in the morning, a Heat Rock in the afternoon, a Smooth Rock in the evening, and an Icy Rock at night (and in the late night).

p. 299

Receive two different items

Where: Aha's House

Go to Icirrus City and visit Aha's house. If you answer the quiz he gives you, you'll receive an Antidote for a correct answer. You can't lose, because a wrong answer nets you a Parlyz Heal.

p. 304

Stardust in your eyes

Where: Pinwheel Forest Entrance

Include a Fighting-type Pokémon in your party and check the challenge rock. You'll obtain one Stardust a day.

p. 311

Enjoy a Multi Battle

Where: Striaton Restaurant

Speak to Cilan, Chili, or Cress. You can team up with him for a Multi Battle against the other two!

p. 319

Win a Big Mushroom

Where: Striaton Restaurant

A woman asks you to guess which Pokémon is holding a Big Mushroom. If you guess correctly, she'll give you the Big Mushroom.

p. 319

Receive a Fluffy Tail

Where: Accumula Town

Show the woman a Pokémon that is 16'5" or taller, and you'll receive a Fluffy Tail. Even if you show her the same Pokémon every day, she'll still hand over a Fluffy Tail!

p. 324

Receive a Poké Doll

Where: Accumula Town

Show the boy a Pokémon that is 0'08" or shorter, and you'll receive a Poké Doll. Even if you show him the same Pokémon every day, he'll still give you a Poké Doll daily!

p. 324

Challenge Colress to a battle!

Where: Plasma Frigate at P2 Laboratory

The first time you challenge Colress, you'll find him in his room. After that, go to the north deck to battle him.

p. 331

Two Years Ago...

The events that threatened to destroy the Unova region

From *Pokémon Black Version* and *Pokémon White Version*

In Nuvema Town, a young teen dreamed of becoming a Pokémon Trainer.

One day, this hopeful dreamer received a large Gift Box from Professor Juniper, an authority on Pokémon research.

The professor's gift was a Pokémon.
It was the greatest gift the teen could ever have imagined.
Inside the Gift Box were three precious Pokémon—Snivy, Tepig, and Oshawott.
After selecting one of these three Pokémon, the dreamer—at last a real Trainer—said farewell to all that was familiar and set out on a journey of adventure and discovery.

The young Trainer had two great ambitions.
The first was to challenge the Pokémon League.
By doing so, the Trainer could become Champion of the Unova region.
The Trainer's second ambition was to catch every Pokémon and complete the Unova Pokédex.

The Trainer was not alone on this journey, however. Two childhood friends, Bianca and Cheren, also set out on the same path.
These friends taught the young Trainer the skills needed for Pokémon battle and the ways of catching new Pokémon.

Bianca: "Wow... You're gonna be an awesome Trainer someday, I can tell! No doubt!"

The Trainer took every opportunity to do battle, and the Pokémon that accompanied the young Trainer grew by leaps and bounds.
In what seemed like no time at all, the young Trainer and the Pokémon grew strong.

The rules dictate that, in order to challenge the Pokémon League,
a Trainer must defeat the Gym Leaders of the eight Pokémon Gyms in Unova.

And thus the young Trainer began journeying to the Gyms.

At the first Gym, this young Trainer saw victory over Cilan, Cress, or Chili of the Striaton City Gym.
At the second Gym, the young Trainer defeated Nacrene City Gym Leader Lenora.

During the course of this journey, however, an enemy appeared before the Trainer.
The enemy took the form of a group commanded by a stranger calling himself Ghetsis. This group was Team Plasma.
At the head of Team Plasma stood the Seven Sages, wise men gathered from across the world.
The members of Team Plasma were devoted to the one they called "king,"
and in his name, they wrought havoc across Unova, ever seeking to free Pokémon from their human Trainers.
Every time the Trainer encountered Team Plasma,
the meeting inevitably ended in battle, and the young Trainer constantly thwarted their hopes.

At the third Gym, the young Trainer was victorious over Burgh, the Castelia City Gym Leader.
The fourth Gym saw the young Trainer's defeat of Nimbasa City Gym Leader Elesa.

The young Trainer met a young man called simply "N."
This N was a Trainer of staggering talent.

N said, "I'll defeat the Champion and become unbeatable, unlike any other! I'll make all Trainers free their Pokémon!
If you want to be together with Pokémon,
your only hope is to collect the Badges from each area
and head for the Pokémon League!
Try and stop me there, if you dare!
If your conviction is not strong enough, you will never be able to defeat me."

The liberation of Pokémon...
The desire that Ghetsis professed as his, and
the dream that N held, were one and the same.
What connection could there be between Team Plasma and N?

At the fifth Gym, Driftveil City Gym Leader Clay crumbled before the young Trainer.
And at the sixth Gym, Mistralton City Gym Leader Skyla was brought low by the Trainer.
And, too, at the seventh Gym, it was Icirrus City Gym Leader Brycen's turn to fall to the Trainer.

On arriving at the top of Dragonspiral Tower, the Trainer found N together with Zekrom (Reshiram).

N said, "What do you think? How do you like the beautiful form of the Pokémon who appears before and fights beside the hero that will lead the way to a new world? Now, Zekrom (Reshiram) and I will head to the Pokémon League and defeat the Champion! This will be the last of the Pokémon battles that hurt Pokémon so. A world for Pokémon alone... It's finally going to be a reality."

The young Trainer knew that it was only a matter of time before N would appear as an enemy across a field of battle. And so the Trainer began training harder than ever before.

Finally, at the eighth Gym, the young Trainer overcame Opelucid City Gym Leader Iris.

Having exceeded all others, the young Trainer now proceeded to Victory Road, the greatest hurdle still ahead in the Unova region.

Putting everything on the line, the young Trainer challenged the Pokémon League. Victory remained with the young Trainer in each battle against the members of the Elite Four—Shauntal, Grimsley, Caitlin, and Marshal.

At last, all that remained was the battle against the Champion, Alder. But when he arrived, the Trainer found that Alder had already been defeated by N. A huge castle suddenly appeared, surrounding the Pokémon League. It was N's castle, which had been under construction for years in the earth beneath and around the Pokémon League. The young Trainer rushed into the castle to stop N and Team Plasma.

Deep within the castle sat N upon a throne. Beside him stood the Legendary Pokémon Zekrom (Reshiram). It was time at last for the climactic battle against N.

When the dust finally settled after the battle, N spoke: "I was beaten. Your ideals... Your feelings... They were stronger than mine, it seems..."

It was then that Team Plasma's leader—Ghetsis—appeared. Ghetsis said, "After all of that, do you think you're still worthy of sharing the name Harmonia with me? You good-for-nothing boy!"

"To start with, I spurred N into pursuing the truth. The reason we reawakened the Legendary Pokémon now was to give MY Team Plasma more power! Power to control the fearful masses! You lost to an ordinary Trainer! There is such a thing as being too stupid!"

Ghetsis never had any intention of freeing the Pokémon. He had been plotting to control the whole world, using Pokémon as his tools, while deceiving the people by hiding behind the false figurehead he had created in making N a king.

The young Trainer's Pokémon battle with Ghetsis began. Their fierce combat raged across the field of battle, sparks flew like embers. But for the young Trainer who believed wholeheartedly in Pokémon, a Trainer like Ghetsis, who only sought to use his Pokémon as tools, was no match. The Trainer scored a complete victory over Ghetsis.

After witnessing their battle, N spoke again: "It's about when I first met you in Accumula Town. I was shocked when I heard what your Pokémon was saying. I was shocked because that Pokémon said that it liked you. It said it wanted to be with you..."

"There's no way that a person like me, someone who understands only Pokémon— No, actually... I didn't understand them, either. No way I could measure up to you, when you had met so many Pokémon and were surrounded by friends..."

"You said you have a dream... That dream... Make it come true! Wonderful dreams and ideals give you the power to change the world! If anyone can, it's you! Well, then... Farewell!"

When the young Trainer returned to the Pokémon League, it was at last time to challenge Champion Alder. This was a true battle between two Trainers who believed in their Pokémon. The painful battle was waged hard and long. Yet the heart that believes most in its Pokémon will win in the end. Believing that, the young Trainer ordered the final blow. And Alder wished the young Trainer well. "Well done! You certainly are an unmatched talent!" The young Trainer had become Champion of all Unova.

Yet the journey was not over, and the young Trainer's adventures continued. Looker, a member of the International Police, requested that the Trainer aid his search for Team Plasma's Seven Sages. The Seven Sages were the leading figures of Team Plasma and leaving them free to roam might allow Team Plasma to rise again. Giallo, Rood, Gorm, Ryoku, Zinzolin, and Bronius, the remaining Seven Sages, had hidden themselves around the Unova region, and the young Trainer apprehended each, handing each one over to Looker.

But where had N gone? The question continued to plague the young Trainer. Looker had the answer: "A report has reached my ears of someone far from here. Indeed, this someone has spotted a person like N and a...dragon Pokémon."

And now, two years later, another young teen with dreams of becoming a Trainer is about to set out on a journey, a journey from Aspertia City...

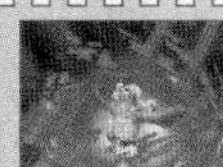

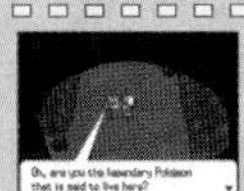

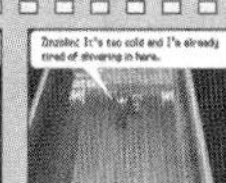
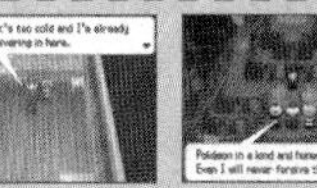

HERO

Boy

HEROINE

Girl

RIVAL

FRIEND

Your Childhood Friend

Rival

All right! Let's see how much stronger you've become! Come at me!

Experienced Pokémon Trainer

Bianca

Filling up the Pokédex is totally fun!

PROFESSOR

Aurea Juniper

Our world is a world where we live with Pokémon. Everyone! Keep that in mind as you pursue your dreams with your Pokémon!

PROFESSOR

Cedric Juniper

Are you meeting lots of Pokémon? There really are lots of Pokémon in the Unova region and the rest of the world! I made the Habitat List so people would know that!

SCIENTIST

Fennel

Hi there, Trainer! My name is Fennel. I'm researching Pokémon Trainers! The Game Sync is a vital part of that research!

MYSTERIOUS SCIENTIST

Colress

Is it possible to bring out their maximum power through the bond they share with their Trainers? Or is there some other, different method? I'd like to test my theory by battling with you.

TEAM PLASMA

Grunt (male)

What? Don't treat us like villains! And don't interfere with our plans to liberate Pokémon!

TEAM PLASMA

Grunt (female)

What's the big idea? This Pokémon I stole is useless!

TEAM PLASMA

Zinzolin

Once again, we will use the Legendary Dragon-type Pokémon and we will rule the Unova region! Curious Trainers, we shall not let you run around as you please!

GYM LEADER

Aspertia City

Cheren

A Leader Who Seeks the Right Path

Everyone has a different dream. Search for your life's purpose.

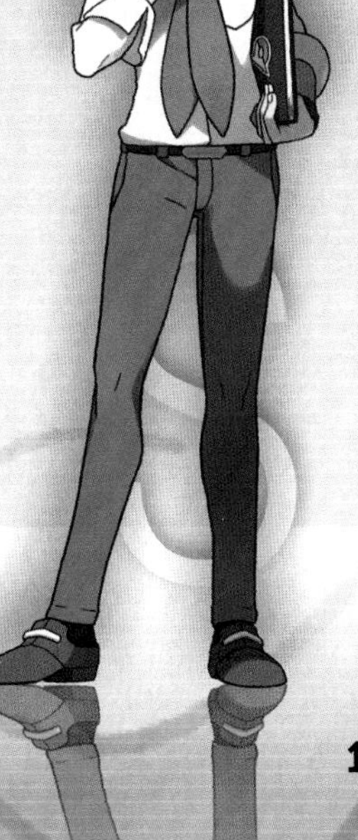

GYM LEADER

Virbank City

Roxie

A Little Poison in Your Days, A Little Poison on the Stage

It's kindness to say no for your friends and Pokémon, right?

GYM LEADER

Castelia City

Burgh

Premier Insect Artist

Umm... That's right. You! Use Bug-type Pokémon!

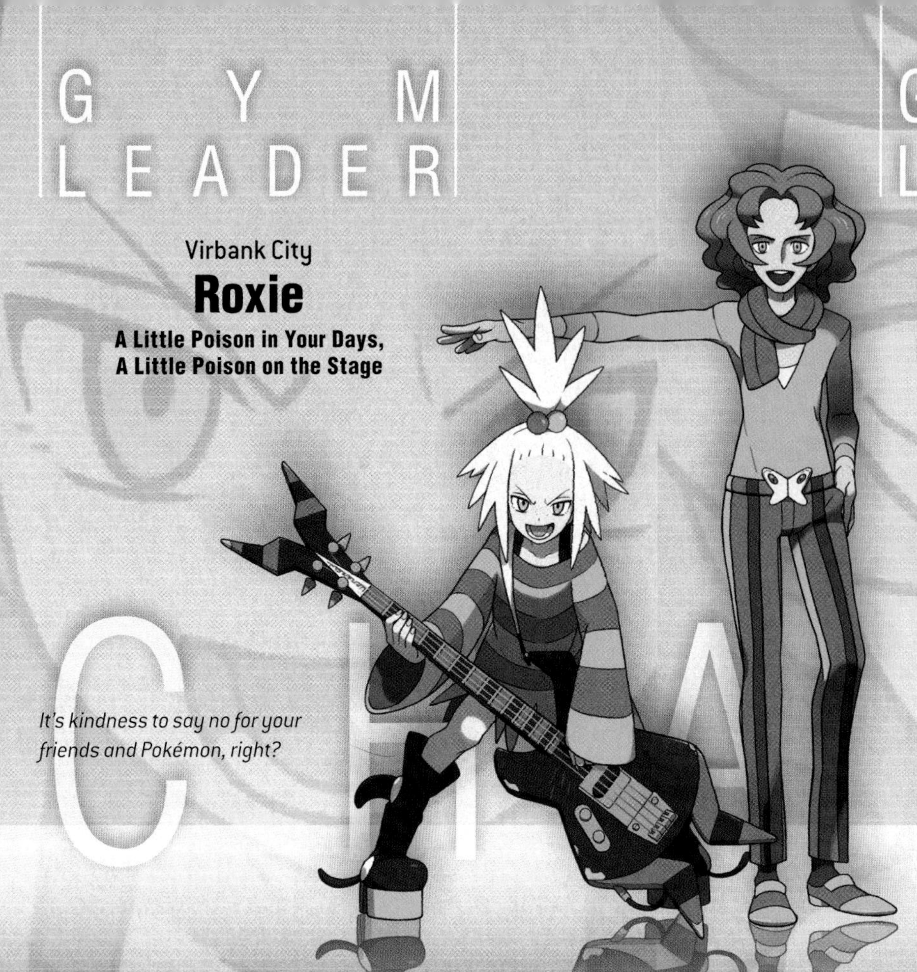

CHARA

GYM LEADER

Nimbasa City

Elesa

The Shining Beauty

If you shine with an inner light, all that surrounds you will be illuminated by it!

CHARA

GYM LEADER

Driftveil City

Clay

The Underground Boss

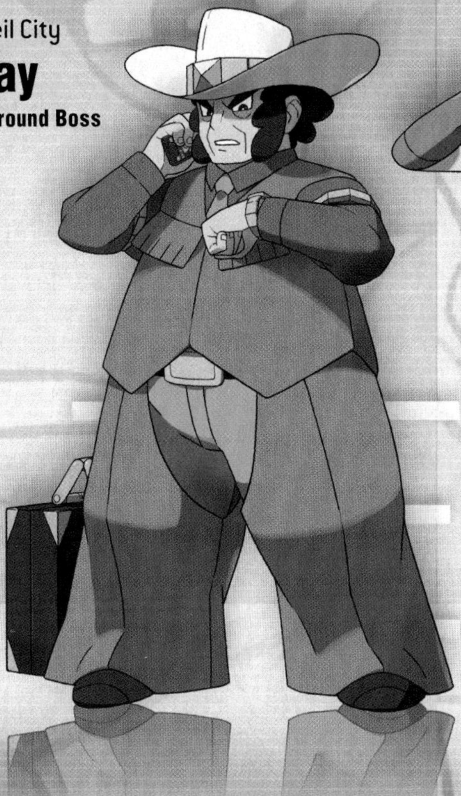

Don't lie to yerself!
It's best to live honestly.

GYM LEADER

Mistralton City

Skyla

The High-Flying Girl

Yearning makes you look up at the sky. To fly, go beyond yearning and take action!

CTERS

GYM LEADER

Opelucid City

Drayden

The Spartan Mayor

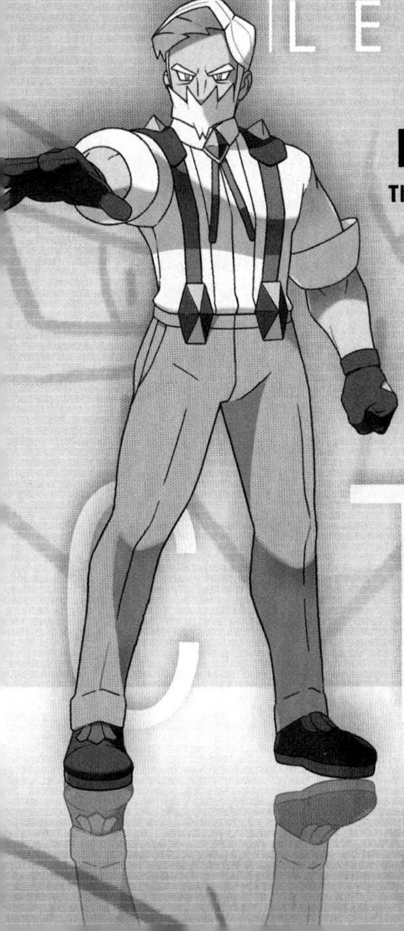

Sincere Trainer!
Be flexible!

GYM LEADER

Humilau City

Marlon

A Bigger Splash Than the Sea!

It's cliché to compare life to a rough sea, but don't be swept away!

CTERS

ELITE FOUR

Shauntal

ELITE FOUR

Grimsley

What will be determined here is which of us can absorb the opponent's light and shine... But who will decide that? It shall be I, Grimsley of the Elite Four.

That's part of a novel I'm writing. I want to write down the event that happened on that day...

ELITE FOUR

Caitlin

It's me who appeared when the flower opened up. You, standing over there... You look like a Pokémon Trainer with strength and kindness.

ELITE FOUR

Marshal

My name is Marshal. I am the No. 1 pupil of my mentor, Alder. In order to master the art of fighting, I've kept training.

CHAMPION

I really look forward to having serious battles with strong Trainers! I mean, come on! If I battle with people like that, not only will I get stronger, my Pokémon will, too!

Iris

POKÉMON TRAINER

N

I can't allow selfish humans to make Pokémon suffer!

TEAM PLASMA

Ghetsis

How fortunate for you! Few get to be the sole audience member for one of my speeches.

SUBWAY BOSS

Ingo

SUBWAY BOSS

Emmet

Battling in a different place will let me see different scenery, and I might learn something, too.
Follow the rules and drive safely! We're headed for victory! All aboard!
CHARACTERS

Pokémon Black Version 2 & Pokémon White Version 2: The Official Pokémon Unova Strategy Guide

Pokémon Trainer Handbook

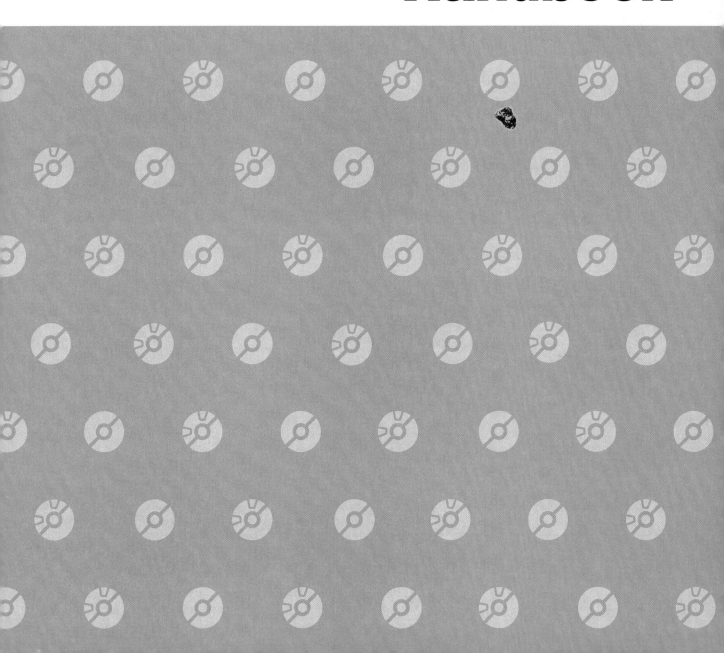

Catch Wild Pokémon

Find wild Pokémon

Wild Pokémon love nature, and their many different habitats include tall grass, caves, desert, wetlands, lakes, and rivers. They may also appear along with certain phenomena in the field, such as rustling grass and dust clouds. When you find a place where it looks like a Pokémon might appear, rush on over to check it out.

Main areas where you can find Pokémon

Tall Grass

Dark Grass

Cave

Desert

Water Surface

Fishing (after the Hall of Fame)

Special places where wild Pokémon appear

Rustling Grass

Dust Cloud

Flying Pokémon's Shadow

Rippling Water

Tip

Hidden Grotto Pokémon with Hidden Abilities

Uncommon Pokémon live in the Hidden Grottoes found between trees. The Pokémon found in Hidden Grottoes have Hidden Abilities.

Throw Poké Balls to catch Pokémon

When you discover a wild Pokémon, throw a Poké Ball to catch it. But a Pokémon won't just hop into the Poké Ball you've thrown. If it's still full of energy, it will escape from the Poké Ball. Use the following techniques to catch Pokémon.

Tips for catching Pokémon

1 Reduce HP

A Pokémon's HP is a measure of how tired it is. Use moves to attack a Pokémon and lower its HP. When the Pokémon's HP is lowered, even a little bit, it's easier to catch. When the HP bar is red, it means the Pokémon is weak. That's the time to throw a Poké Ball!

2 Inflict status conditions

Some Pokémon moves and Abilities inflict status conditions on their targets (p. 42). A Pokémon with a status condition, such as Poison or Paralysis, is easier to catch. Lower the target's HP and use status conditions to maximize your chances of success.

3 Use the right Poké Ball

Many different kinds of Poké Balls exist. Each kind of Poké Ball performs differently. They are each specialized for a certain use (p. 30). Always use a Poké Ball that's effective for the kind of Pokémon you want to catch. It's a basic Pokémon-catching principle.

Catching many Pokémon makes it easier to catch other Pokémon

Catching many wild Pokémon increases the likelihood of catching others. Sometimes, when you throw a Poké Ball, it will click shut after rocking only once and the Pokémon will be caught. This phenomenon is called a "critical capture." The more Pokémon you have caught, the more often this phenomenon occurs, so catch many Pokémon from the start of the game.

Critical captures

1. **A critical capture is a phenomenon where a Pokémon is caught after the Poké Ball rocks only once.**
2. **The more Pokémon you catch, the more likely you are to see this phenomenon.**
3. **If you catch more than 400 Pokémon, this phenomenon is much more likely to occur.**

Use the right Poké Ball for each Pokémon

Many different types of Poké Ball can be found in the Unova region. Each Poké Ball's special effects depend on factors such as Pokémon type or the location of the battle. Learn the best uses for each Poké Ball so you can use the right one for the Pokémon you're aiming to catch.

Basic Poké Balls

Poké Ball

The most basic device you can use to catch Pokémon.

● **How to make it available at Poké Marts:**

Sold from the beginning

Great Ball

Better at catching Pokémon than the Poké Ball.

● **How to make it available at Poké Marts:**

Obtain one Gym Badge

Ultra Ball

Better at catching Pokémon than the Great Ball.

● **How to make it available at Poké Marts:**

Obtain five Gym Badges

Master Ball

It is the ultimate ball that is sure to catch any wild Pokémon.

● **How to get one:**

Mistralton City (Professor Juniper), P2 Laboratory (Colress), etc.

Premier Ball

Same as a regular Poké Ball. Given as a bonus at Poké Marts.

● **How to get one:**

Buy 10 Poké Balls at one time

Poké Balls with special features

Quick Ball

Most effective when thrown right at the start of battle.

● **Poké Marts that carry this Ball:**

Opelucid City, Pokémon League, etc.

Timer Ball

The more turns that have elapsed in battle, the more effective it is.

● **Poké Marts that carry this Ball:**

Opelucid City, Pokémon League, etc.

Heal Ball

Restores a caught Pokémon's HP and status.

● **Poké Marts that carry this Ball:**

Virbank City, Castelia City, etc.

Dusk Ball

Good for catching Pokémon at night and in caves.

● **Poké Marts that carry this Ball:**

Driftveil City, Lentimas Town, etc.

Net Ball

Good for catching Bug- and Water-type Pokémon.

● **Poké Marts that carry this Ball:**

Virbank City, Castelia City, etc.

Dive Ball

Good for catching Pokémon that live in the water.

● **Poké Marts that carry this Ball:**

Undella Town, Humilau City

Nest Ball

The lower the Pokémon's level, the more effective it is.

● **Poké Marts that carry this Ball:**

Castelia City, Driftveil City, etc.

Luxury Ball

Your friendship with the caught Pokémon will grow faster (p. 36).

● **Poké Marts that carry this Ball:**

Undella Town, Humilau City, etc.

Repeat Ball

Good for catching Pokémon of a species you've caught before.

● **Poké Marts that carry this Ball:**

Victory Road, Pokémon League, etc.

Other ways to obtain Pokémon

The main way to get Pokémon is catching them in a Poké Ball, but there are many other ways to obtain Pokémon as well. Knowing all of the ways to obtain Pokémon is important for completing the Pokédex.

Other methods for obtaining Pokémon

Evolve them through battle

Pokémon build up Experience Points when they take part in battles. After getting a certain number of Experience Points, Pokémon will level up. Some Pokémon evolve at a certain level.

Evolve them by meeting certain conditions

Pokémon evolve in many different ways, such as by befriending their Trainer or having Stones with special powers used on them.

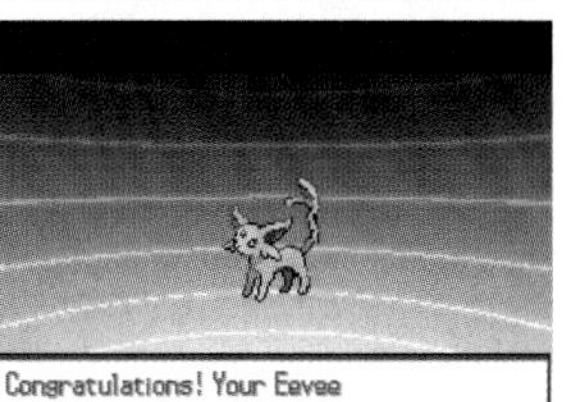

Congratulations! Your Eevee
evolved into Espeon!

Link Trade

Trade Pokémon with friends, family, and people all over the world. This way you both can get the Pokémon you want (p. 348).

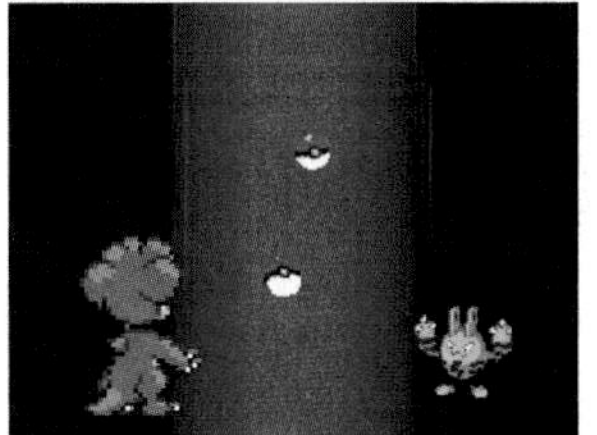

Get them through story events

Sometimes people you talk to during the story will entrust you with Pokémon. They are often kinds of Pokémon you won't encounter in the wild, so make sure to take them.

Trade with people in towns

Some people in towns will ask you to trade them a certain Pokémon. Many of these Pokémon are hard to find, so be sure to take them up on it.

Search for Legendary Pokémon

You basically only have one chance to catch a Legendary Pokémon. If you find one, do everything in your power to catch it.

A wild Cobalion appeared!

Get Pokémon Eggs from the Pokémon Day Care

Leave two Pokémon at the Pokémon Day Care and sometimes Eggs will be discovered (p. 343).

Your Pokémon was holding an Egg!

Restore Fossils

You may find ancient Pokémon Fossils during your adventure. Restore the Fossils to obtain a Pokémon.

Tip

N's Pokémon also appear

You may encounter Pokémon that the Pokémon Trainer N has released. N's Pokémon have a unique way of appearing. When you catch them, the OT's name is "N."

Catch a Pokémon when two wild Pokémon appear

There's a trick to catching Pokémon when two wild Pokémon appear in the dark grass. You can't throw a Poké Ball while battling two Pokémon. Knock out the Pokémon you don't want to catch, and leave the other Pokémon in battle. If you do this, your target will become the remaining Pokémon, so you can go ahead and throw a Poké Ball.

How to catch a Pokémon when two wild Pokémon appear in the dark grass

1. **Since you can't catch two Pokémon at once, decide which one you want to catch.**
2. **First, knock out the Pokémon you don't want to catch.**
3. **Throw Poké Balls to catch the Pokémon you're after.**

Catch Shiny Pokémon

Some Pokémon have a different color than others of the same species. When one of these Pokémon appears, a ring of light circles its body, so you'll know right away. The only thing different about these Pokémon is how they look, but they are extremely hard to find. If you see one, make sure to catch it and treasure it!

A ring of light appears with them

Examples of Shiny Pokémon

Use star Pokémon in battle

Have one of your Pokémon be the star of a Pokéstar Studios movie that has a strange ending, and that Pokémon will become a star Pokémon (p. 371). When a star Pokémon enters battle during your adventure or during a Link Battle, it will emit a special light. Make your favorite Pokémon a star at Pokéstar Studios and show it off to your friends!

Raise Pokémon by Battling

Pokémon grow stronger as they battle

Winning a battle gives Pokémon Experience Points. When they gain enough points, they'll level up and their stats—Attack, HP, and so forth—will increase. Have them battle to help them grow stronger.

As it gains Experience Points it will level up.

How Experience Points Work

▲ When your Pokémon defeats a Pokémon with a level that is higher than its own, it will get more Experience Points.
▼ When your Pokémon defeats a Pokémon with a level that is lower than its own, it will get fewer Experience Points.

Pokémon evolve by leveling up

Some Pokémon can evolve into new Pokémon with different names. There are several ways to evolve Pokémon, but the most basic method is through battling and earning Experience Points to level up.

Evolution Example: Sandile

Sandile

First Evolution

Krokorok

Second Evolution

Krookodile

Other evolution methods

Use special Stones

Special Stones, such as the Thunderstone, have the power to trigger Pokémon evolution instantly.

Strengthen your friendship

Take good care of a Pokémon and it will reward you by growing. Some Pokémon evolve if they level up while they're on friendly terms with you.

Link Trade

Some Pokémon evolve when they are traded to a friend, family member, or person somewhere in the world by Link Trade.

Fulfill certain conditions

Some Pokémon can be evolved under special conditions or at specific locations.

Pokémon use moves

Pokémon can learn all kinds of moves, which are useful both in battle and while traveling on your adventure. There are more than 500 different moves, each with its own unique effects. The maximum number of moves a Pokémon can know at one time is four. So think hard about which moves you want your Pokémon to know to bring out its unique characteristics.

Three fundamental kinds of moves

Attack Moves

These moves do damage by attacking the target. Some moves also inflict status conditions (p. 42).

Defense Moves

These moves can restore HP or cure status conditions. Some defense moves even leech an opponent's HP.

Status Moves

These moves strengthen the user or weaken an opponent. They're called status moves because they affect the status of Pokémon in battle.

Tip Use status moves to your advantage in battle

Status moves give you the upper hand by doing things such as raising your Pokémon's attacking power, or making it harder for your opponent to land moves. Use them to your advantage in battle!

How to teach new moves to Pokémon

Level them up

Pokémon can learn various moves at certain levels. Once they reach that level, they can learn the move.

Use a TM or HM

TMs and HMs are items that teach moves to Pokémon. You can use the same one over and over on different Pokémon.

Learn moves in exchange for Shards

Give the master Move Tutor a certain number of Shards found during your travels and he will teach you different moves.

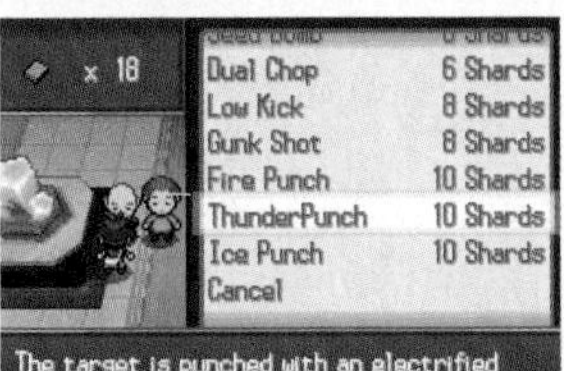

Have an expert teach them

Some people will teach your Pokémon moves, such as the ultimate moves for the starter Pokémon, battle-combo moves, and the strongest Dragon-type move.

Pokémon have different Abilities

Each Pokémon species has various Abilities. For instance, Purrloin can have the Limber or Unburden Abilities. Some Abilities take effect during battle, while other Abilities come in handy as you explore the region.

Triggered Abilities are visible

When a Pokémon's Ability is triggered in battle, messages appear for both your Pokémon and your opponent's Pokémon, so it's clear when an Ability activates.

Examples of Abilities and their effects

Ability **Pickup**

May pick up an item while it's in your party. The Pokémon's level determines what items you're likely to find (p. 437).

● **Pokémon with this Ability** Lillipup

Ability **Intimidate**

Lowers opponents' Attack by 1 when the Pokémon enters battle. This can reduce the amount of damage done by physical moves.

● **Pokémon with this Ability** Growlithe, Sandile, and others

Ability **Illuminate**

This Ability works when a Pokémon is the first one in the party. It makes it easier to encounter wild Pokémon.

● **Pokémon with this Ability** Starmie, Watchog, and others

Ability **Telepathy**

Prevents damage from an ally's moves. This Ability is useful in Double and Triple Battles.

● **Pokémon with this Ability** Elgyem, Beheeyem, and others

Tip: Have a Pokémon with Pickup in your party

A Pokémon with the Pickup Ability picks up items. It will pick up useful items like Potions or Great Balls, so put a Pokémon with this Ability in your party when you're low on prize money. Very rarely, it may even pick up a Nugget, which can be sold for a lot of prize money. Put a Lillipup with the Pickup Ability in your party, and you might cash in!

Put multiple Lillipup in your party, and you'll pick up a pile of items.

Tip: Use Hidden Abilities effectively in battle

Hidden Abilities are special Abilities of certain Pokémon, such as ones caught in Hidden Grottoes or befriended in the Pokémon Global Link. Pokémon with these Abilities are rarely seen, so when battling, you can use them to turn your opponent's expectations upside down and disrupt their tactics.

Bouffalant
Hidden Ability
Soundproof

Pelipper
Hidden Ability
Rain Dish

Pokémon and Trainers become friends

Friendship is the bond of affection and trust that can grow between a Pokémon and its Trainer. Keep a Pokémon happy and it will grow to like you, but a mistreated Pokémon will dislike you. Use the Xtransceiver to call Bianca and check how friendly you and your Pokémon are (p. 63).

How to improve your friendship with your Pokémon

Travel together	Put a Pokémon in your party and go on an adventure together.
Level it up	Battle with a Pokémon and have it level up.
Use stat-boosting items on it	Use items such as Protein or Zinc to boost base stats.
Use items on it during battles	Use items such as X Attack and X Defend during battles.
Teach it a new move with a TM	Use a TM or HM to teach it a new move.
Battle Gym Leaders with it	Use it in major battles, such as those with Gym Leaders.
Feed it Berries	Give it Berries, such as a Pomeg Berry or Grepa Berry.
Get it a massage	Take it to get a massage in Castelia City.
Use a Beauty Salon	Take it to a Beauty Salon in Join Avenue to get it groomed.
Give it Sweet Hearts	Give it Sweet Hearts obtained from the Feeling Check.
Go to a café	Take it to a café in Join Avenue.
Participate in the Pokémon Musical	Participate in the Pokémon Musical in Nimbasa City.

Bianca assesses your friendship

Bianca's Assessments

Friendship: High

- What great friends you are! It's so nice how you trust each other! It makes me kinda jealous!
- You two sure get along great! It looks like you are having fun being together! You seem bright and cheerful!
- You seem really close! You look so, so happy! It's enough to make me happy, too!
- You're starting to get to be friends. Just maybe, walking along the same path has made you understand one another.
- You still have room for improvement. How nice! I mean, you can become even better friends!
- You aren't getting along, are you? It's glaring at you with a look that's kinda scary.
- You aren't getting along, are you? It doesn't look like it's having fun even when you're together.

Friendship: Low

Tip: Give a Pokémon the Soothe Bell

When using one of the methods above to befriend your Pokémon, give it the Soothe Bell and you'll grow your friendship with it even more quickly. You can get the Soothe Bell in Nimbasa City.

Benefits of friendship

Pokémon evolve

Many species of Pokémon evolve when leveled up while they're on friendly terms with you.

They can learn many moves

You can teach your Pokémon moves, including the ultimate moves for the starter Pokémon, battle-combo moves, and the strongest Dragon-type move.

Some moves can be used as field moves

Some Pokémon moves can be used in the field to open up areas you couldn't reach before.

Field move examples

HM 01 Cut

Cuts down thin trees that are blocking your path, opening up room for you to pass.

● **How to get it:** Given to you by Roxie in Virbank City

HM 02 Fly

Whisks you through the air and back to any town or city you've already visited. You'll land in front of its Pokémon Center.

● **How to get it:** Given to you by Bianca on Route 5

HM 03 Surf

Lets you move freely on bodies of water, such as oceans and lakes, just as you would on land.

● **How to get it:** Given to you by Cheren on Route 6

HM 04 Strength

Unleashes enormous strength, pushing aside boulders that you normally couldn't budge.

● **How to get it:** Given to you by Hugh in Castelia Sewers

HM 05 Waterfall

Lets you climb waterfalls so you can see what's at the top.

● **How to get it:** Given to you by N on Victory Road

HM 06 Dive

Lets you dive into the deep ocean from dark patches in the water to explore the ocean bed.

● **How to get it:** Given to you by Hugh in Undella Town

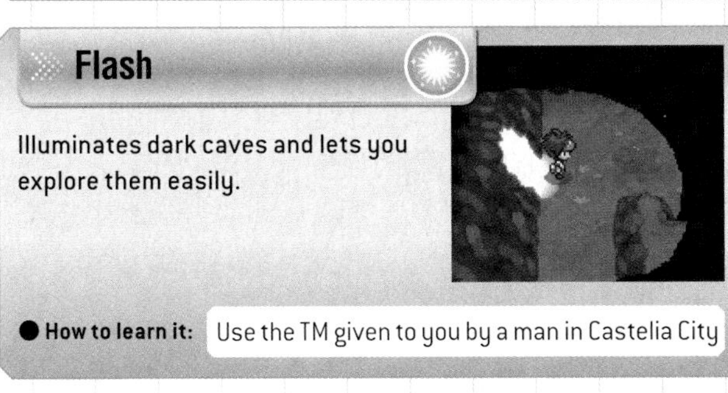

Flash

Illuminates dark caves and lets you explore them easily.

● **How to learn it:** Use the TM given to you by a man in Castelia City

Sweet Scent

Pokémon will appear more often when this is used in areas where wild Pokémon live.

● **How to learn it:** Certain Pokémon learn it by leveling up

Tip

Party Pokémon that know many HM Moves will make for smooth travels

Many Pokémon can learn multiple moves that help you in the field. If you have one or two of these Pokémon in your party, it will make getting around easier.

Ducklett

● **Recommended moves**

- Fly
- Surf
- Dive

Braviary

● **Recommended moves**

- Cut
- Fly
- Strength

Master Winning Battle Strategies

The 17 different types

Pokémon can be classified into 17 types, such as Normal, Fire, Water, or Grass. The matchups between these types are a key factor in determining a battle's outcome. Master all of the different types!

Examples of the 17 Pokémon types

Normal

Patrat and others

Fire

Tepig and others

Water

Oshawott and others

Grass

Snivy and others

Electric

Magnemite and others

Ice

Cubchoo and others

Fighting

Riolu and others

Poison

Zubat and others

Ground

Sandshrew and others

Flying

Pidove and others

Psychic

Woobat and others

Bug

Sewaddle and others

Rock

Roggenrola and others

Ghost

Litwick and others

Dragon

Druddigon and others

Dark

Purrloin and others

Steel

Klink and others

Both Pokémon and Pokémon moves have types

Both Pokémon and their moves have types. This Oshawott is typical of most Pokémon. Although it belongs to the Water type, it learns moves from other types as well.

Example: Oshawott

Pokémon type: Water

Type of the move Fury Cutter: Bug

The move's type is used when attacking

When Oshawott attacks Purrloin with Fury Cutter, look at Fury Cutter's type—the Bug type.

The Pokémon's type is used when defending

When Purrloin attacks Oshawott, look at Oshawott's type—the Water type.

Turn the tables by targeting a Pokémon's weakness

Types interact like a big game of rock-paper-scissors. For instance, Water is strong against Fire, but weak against Grass. If the attacking Pokémon's move type is strong against the defending Pokémon's type, the move does increased damage.

Types have good and bad matchups

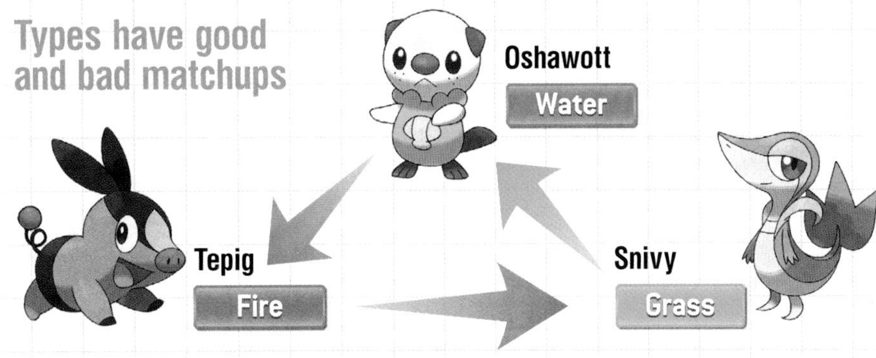

Good type matchups mean increased damage!

Bad type matchups mean reduced damage...

Exploit weaknesses to defeat even higher level opponents in one hit

Exploiting your opponent's weakness and using moves that have a type advantage is one of the most important strategies in a Pokémon battle. For example, by targeting the Lv. 40 Emboar's weakness, even a Lv. 30 Dewott can defeat it in just one hit!

Use type advantages to increase attack damage

Under the right conditions, your moves will do at least 50% more damage than usual. If you can keep dishing out that kind of damage, victory is sure to be within your reach.

How to increase damage

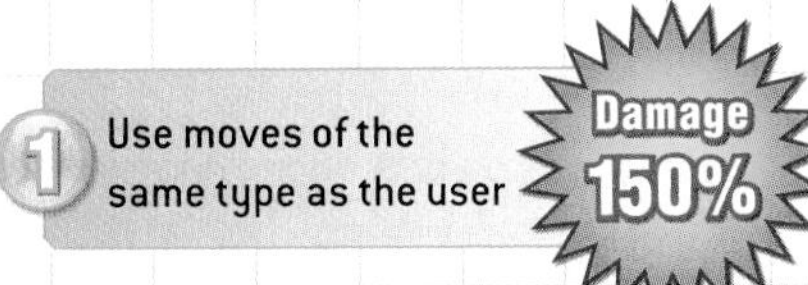

1 Use moves of the same type as the user
Damage 150%

Battle messages describe the damage range

Message	Matchup	Damage
It's super effective!	Good	2–4 times damage
It's not very effective...	Not good	Half damage or less
[No message]	Normal	Regular damage
It doesn't affect...	Bad	No damage
A critical hit!	-	2 times damage

Overall strength is the product of six stats

Each Pokémon's overall strength depends on individual stats, such as Attack or Defense. Six different stats indicate a Pokémon's proficiency in different areas. In order to defeat strong Pokémon, you'll need to understand how each stat works.

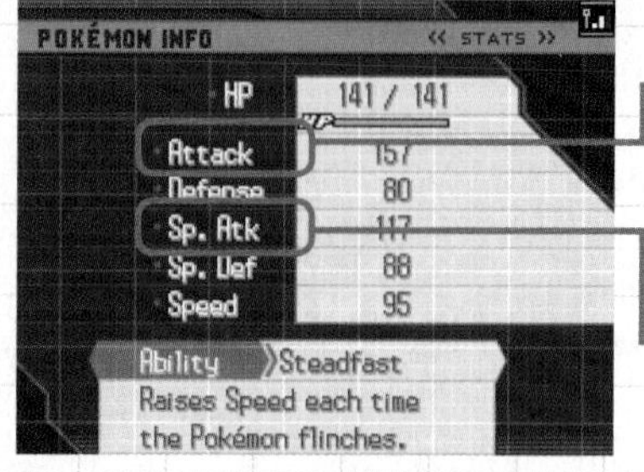

If the font is red, the stat will grow easily.

If the font is blue, the stat will not grow easily.

The six stats

HP

The Pokémon's health. If attacks reduce its HP to 0, the Pokémon faints.

Speed

The Pokémon's attack speed. The higher the number, the more likely the Pokémon will attack first.

Stats affecting physical moves

Attack

The higher this stat is, the more damage the Pokémon does with physical moves.

Defense

The higher this stat is, the less damage the Pokémon takes from physical moves.

Stats affecting special moves

Sp. Atk

The higher this stat is, the more damage the Pokémon does with special moves.

Sp. Def

The higher this stat is, the less damage the Pokémon takes from special moves.

Stats also affect the three kinds of moves

Moves belong to one of three kinds—physical, special, or status. There's an important connection between these kinds of moves and a Pokémon's stats. For example, a Pokémon with high Attack will do the most damage if it uses physical moves.

The three kinds of moves

Physical Moves

Most physical moves make direct contact with the target, such as Retaliate and Low Sweep.

Special Moves

Special moves are ones like Scald and Incinerate. Most moves that don't bring the user into direct contact with the target are special moves.

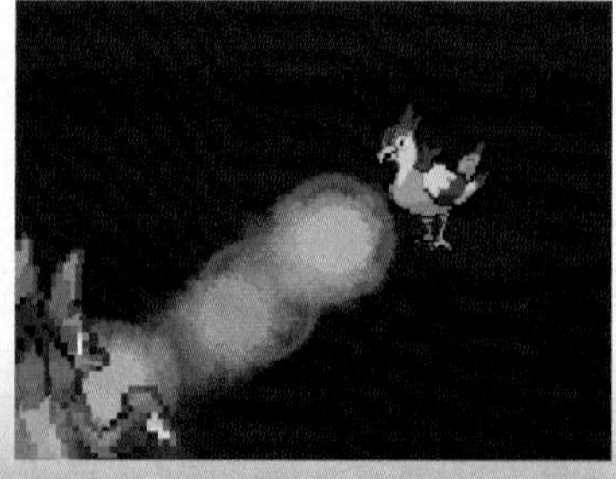

Status Moves

Moves like the weather-changing Rain Dance or moves that alter the user's or target's stats are considered status moves.

Pokémon have a Nature and a Characteristic

Each individual Pokémon has its own Nature and Characteristic. A Pokémon's Nature affects how its stats increase when it gains a level. A Pokémon's Characteristic indicates which stat will grow the most.

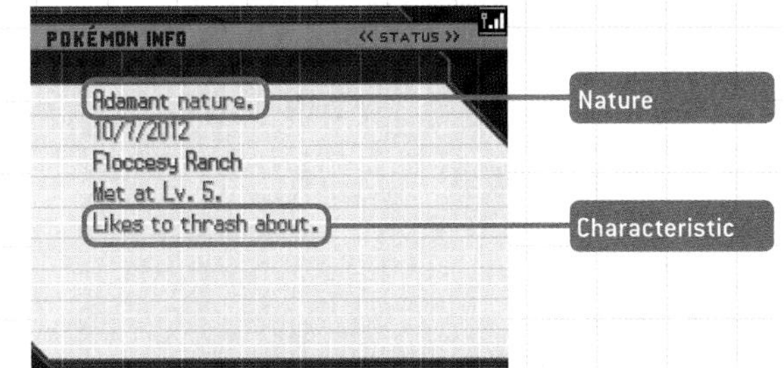

How Pokémon Natures affect stat growth

Nature	Attack	Defense	Speed	Sp. Atk	Sp. Def
Hardy					
Lonely	◎	▲			
Brave	◎		▲		
Adamant	◎			▲	
Naughty	◎				▲
Bold	▲	◎			
Docile					
Relaxed		◎	▲		
Impish		◎		▲	
Lax		◎			▲
Timid	▲		◎		
Hasty		▲	◎		
Serious					
Jolly			◎	▲	
Naive			◎		▲
Modest	▲			◎	
Mild		▲		◎	
Quiet			▲	◎	
Bashful					
Rash				◎	▲
Calm	▲				◎
Gentle		▲			◎
Sassy			▲		◎
Careful				▲	◎
Quirky					

◎ Gains more upon leveling up ▲ Gains less upon leveling up

How Pokémon Characteristics affect stat growth

HP grows most	Attack grows most	Defense grows most	Speed grows most	Sp. Attack grows most	Sp. Defense grows most
Loves to eat.	Proud of its power.	Sturdy body.	Likes to run.	Highly curious.	Strong willed.
Naps often.	Likes to thrash about.	Capable of taking hits.	Alert to sounds.	Mischievous.	Somewhat vain.
Often dozes off.	A little quick tempered.	Highly persistent.	Impetuous and silly.	Thoroughly cunning.	Strongly defiant.
Scatters things often.	Likes to fight.	Good endurance.	Somewhat of a clown.	Often lost in thought.	Hates to lose.
Likes to relax.	Quick tempered.	Good perseverance.	Quick to flee.	Very finicky.	Somewhat stubborn.

Raise stats at Dojos and Cafés located on Join Avenue

You can raise stats by utilizing the Dojos and Cafés that are located on Join Avenue (p. 133). Increase the popularity of such Dojos and Cafés on Join Avenue and you'll be able to raise stats even more. When you're raising a Pokémon for battle, be sure to visit Dojos and Cafés.

Use status conditions to gain an advantage

Pokémon can be affected by status conditions such as Sleep and Poison. These conditions can immobilize a Pokémon or eat away at its HP. Hit other Pokémon with moves that inflict status conditions.

Status conditions cause physical changes.

Status condition examples

Poison

The target's HP decreases each turn. This condition does not wear off on its own.

Paralysis

There's a 25% chance that the target can't attack. The target's Speed is also lowered. This condition does not wear off on its own.

Sleep

Excluding the use of specific moves, the target becomes unable to attack. This condition can wear off during battle.

Frozen

Excluding the use of specific moves, the target becomes unable to attack. This condition can wear off during battle.

Burned

The target's HP decreases each turn. The target's Attack is also lowered. This condition does not wear off on its own.

Confused

The target will sometimes attack itself. This condition can wear off during battle.

Infatuation

The target becomes infatuated by a Pokémon of the opposite gender and is unable to attack 50% of the time. Once the Pokémon that inflicted the Infatuation status is defeated, the condition will wear off.

Heal status conditions as soon as possible

If one of your Pokémon is affected by a status condition, heal it as soon as you can. By leaving a status condition alone, your Pokémon might lose HP each turn, or be unable to attack, putting you in a tricky position. Keep items that heal status conditions, such as Antidotes and Awakenings, on hand so that you can be ready to heal your Pokémon as soon as they are inflicted with a status condition.

Make good use of Pokémon Abilities

The Abilities a Pokémon can have differs depending on its species. Many Abilities can prove to be a great advantage in battle. Unlike Pokémon moves, Abilities take effect upon entering battle, or when hit by another Pokémon's attack, for example.

Abilities can affect the course of a battle and tip the odds in your favor.

Ability Levitate

Gives the Pokémon full immunity to all Ground-type moves.

● Pokémon with this Ability

Bronzong, Tynamo, etc.

Ability Natural Cure

Cures the Pokémon's status conditions when it switches out.

● Pokémon with this Ability

Starmie, Swablu, etc.

Ability Immunity

Protects the Pokémon against the Poison status condition.

● Pokémon with this Ability

Zangoose, etc.

Master Winning Battle Strategies

Give Pokémon items to hold

Each Pokémon can hold a single item. Give your Pokémon items that have an effect in battle to gain an advantage, or give them items that increase what you receive after a battle. It's always a good idea to give your Pokémon items to hold.

Examples of useful held items

Quick Claw
Allows the holder to attack first sometimes.

Scope Lens
Boosts the holder's critical-hit ratio.

BrightPowder
Lowers the accuracy of opponents.

Life Orb
Increases the power of moves by 30% at the cost of inflicting some damage on the user.

Amulet Coin
Doubles the prize money if the holding Pokémon is brought into battle at least once.

Lucky Egg
Gain 50% more Experience Points after a battle.

Weather affects how battles go

Certain Pokémon moves can change the weather during a battle. Weather conditions directly affect the power of a move. Pokémon Abilties, as well, can greatly affect the course of a battle. Sometimes weather conditions will play to your advantage, while at other times they will put you at a disadvantage. One strategy is to use certain moves that allow you to change the weather to your advantage.

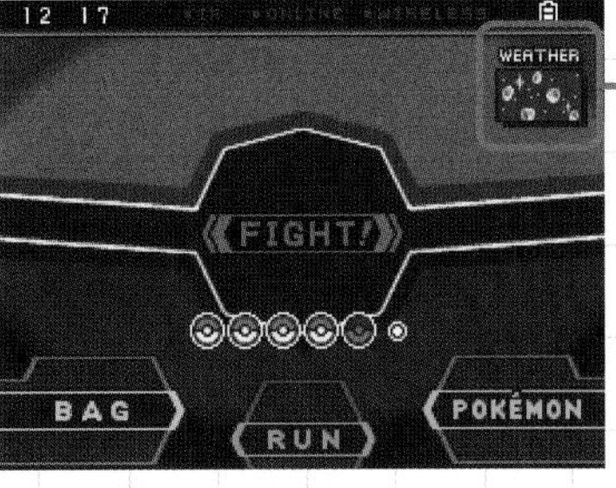

You can check the current weather condition on the Touch Screen.

Weather conditions and their effects

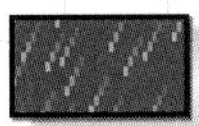

Rain

When the weather condition is Rain, the power of Water-type moves goes up and the power of Fire-type moves goes down.

Hail

When the weather condition is Hail, every Pokémon that doesn't belong to the Ice type takes damage every turn.

Sandstorm

When the weather condition is Sandstorm, every Pokémon that doesn't belong to the Ground, Rock, or Steel type takes damage every turn.

Sunny

When the weather condition is Sunny, the power of Fire-type moves goes up and the power of Water-type moves goes down.

Build a strong team that can defeat the Pokémon League

If you want to defeat the Pokémon League Champion after a long adventure in *Pokémon Black Version 2* or *Pokémon White Version 2*, you'll want to have more than just one strong Pokémon in your party. It's important to raise some support Pokémon to back up your main Pokémon.

Example: Building a team around Snivy

Snivy is weak against Fire-type moves. Therefore, it's a good idea to include the Water-type Pokémon Psyduck, whose Water-type moves are strong against Fire-type Pokémon, in your party. However, Psyduck, is weak against Electric-type moves. In order to back up Psyduck, it would be smart to include Sandile, who is strong against Electric-type Pokémon. Sandile is weak against Water-type moves, but Snivy's Grass-type moves can make short work of any Water-type Pokémon.

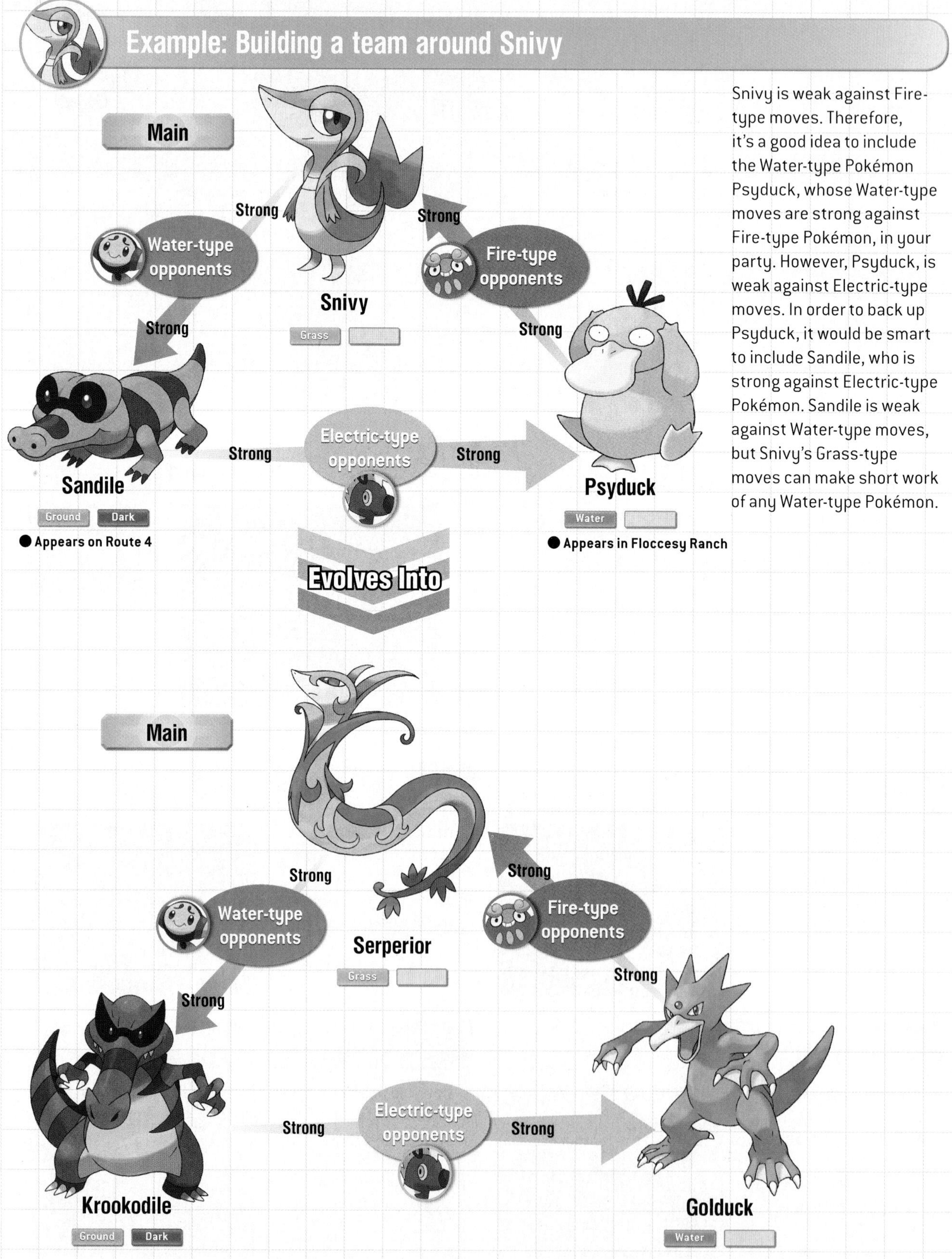

Example: Building a team around Tepig

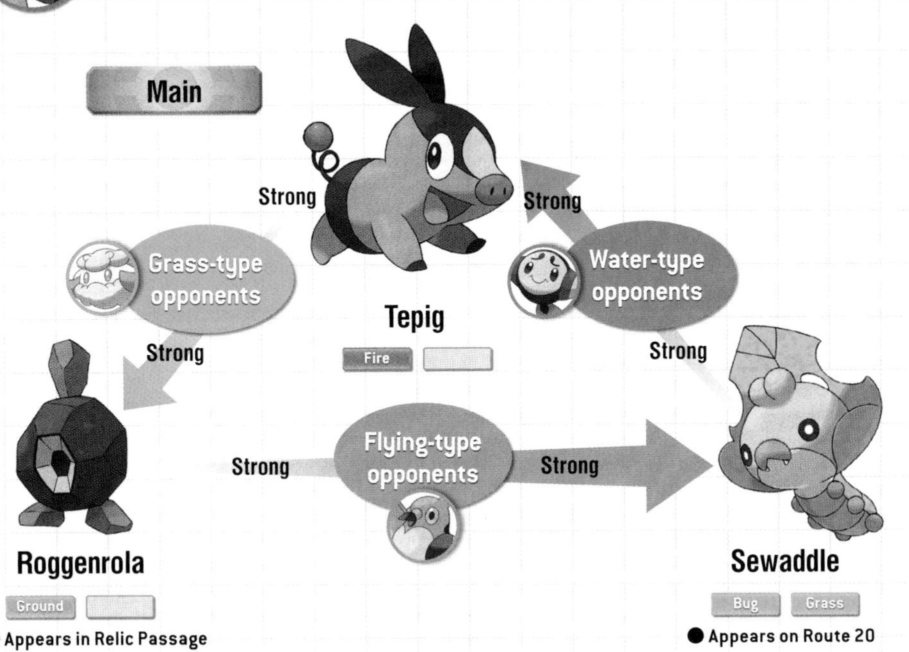

Tepig is weak against Water-type moves. Therefore, it's a good idea to include the Grass-type Pokémon Sewaddle, whose Grass-type moves are strong against Water-type Pokémon, in your party. However, Sewaddle, is weak against Flying-type moves. In order to back up Sewaddle, it would be smart to include Roggenrola who is strong against Flying-type Pokémon. Roggenrola is weak against Grass-type moves, but Tepig's Fire-type moves can make short work of any Grass-type Pokémon.

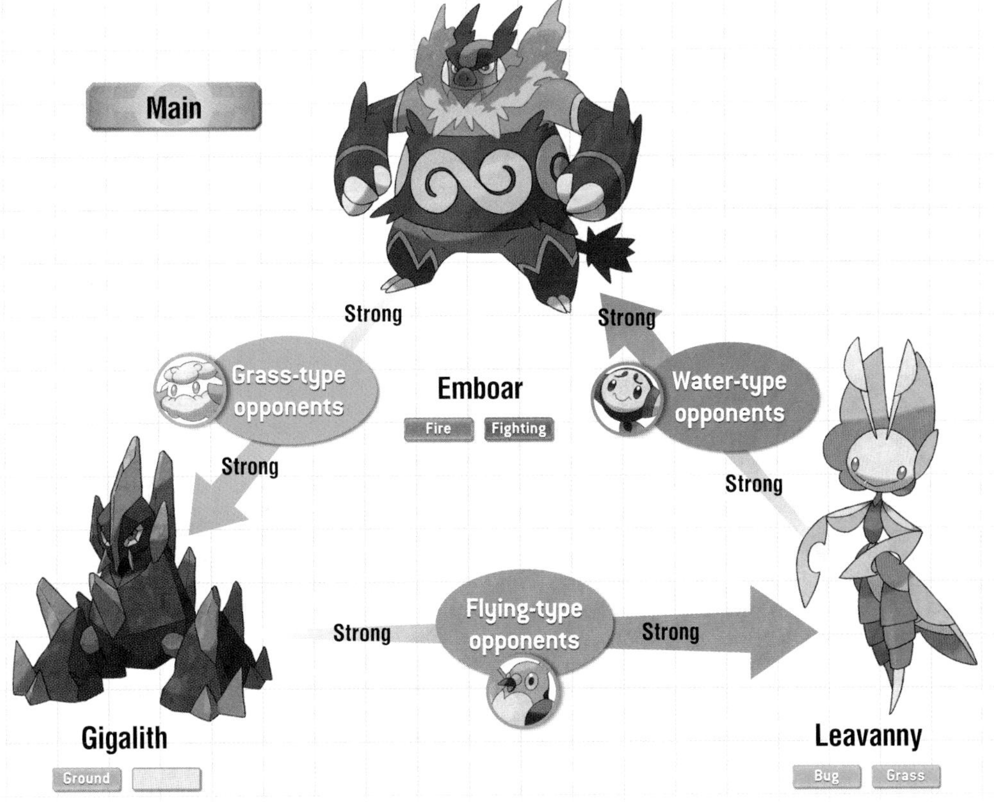

Example: Building a team around Oshawott

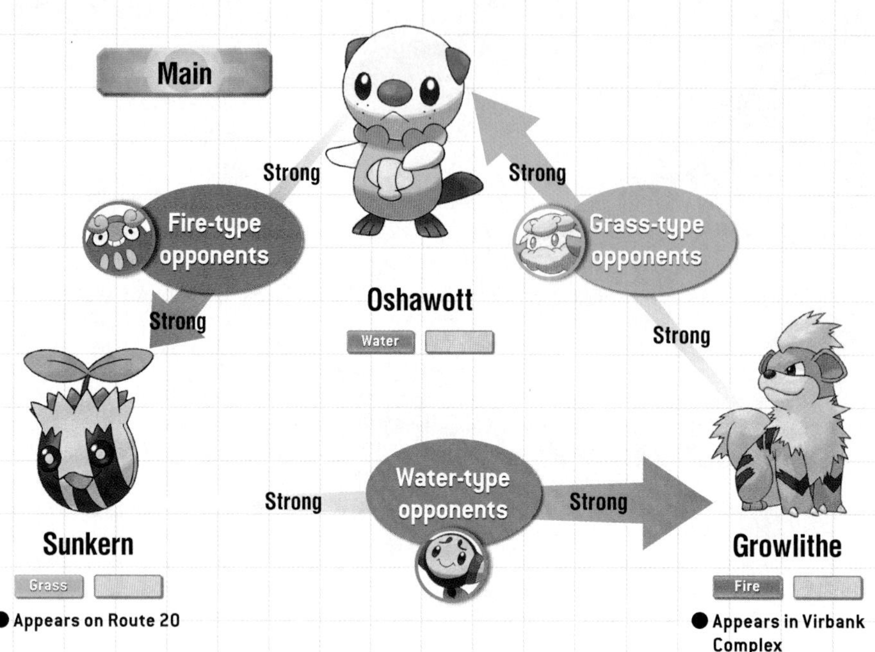

Oshawott is weak against Grass-type moves. Therefore, it's a good idea to include the Fire-type Pokémon Growlithe, whose Fire-type moves are strong against Grass-type Pokémon, in your party. However, Growlithe is weak against Water-type moves. In order to back up Growlithe, it would be smart to include Sunkern who is strong against Water-type Pokémon. Sunkern is weak against Fire-type moves, but Oshawott's Water-type moves can make short work of any Fire-type Pokémon.

Evolves Into

Main

Samurott

Water

Strong

Fire-type opponents

Strong

Strong

Grass-type opponents

Strong

Sunflora

Grass

Strong

Water-type opponents

Strong

Arcanine

Fire

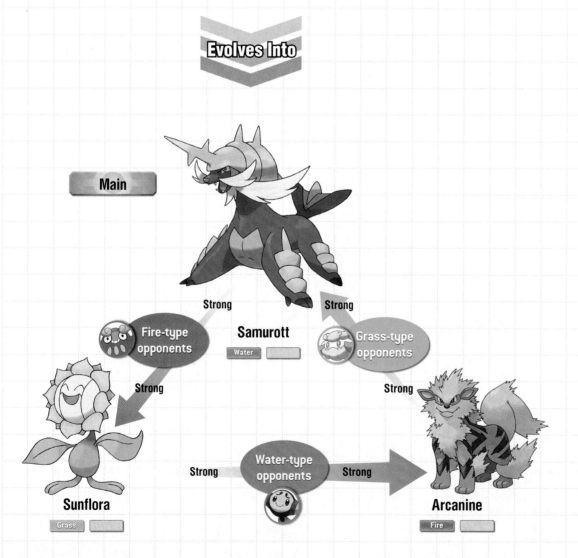

One strategy is to include Pokémon you catch during your journey in your party

In order to become the Champion, you'll need to build a powerful team. One way to do this is to include some of the rare and powerful Pokémon that you catch during your journey. Including even one of the four Pokémon shown below will greatly increase your team's strength.

Rare Pokémon that can be obtained before entering the Hall of Fame

Unova Pokédex No. 152

Zoroark

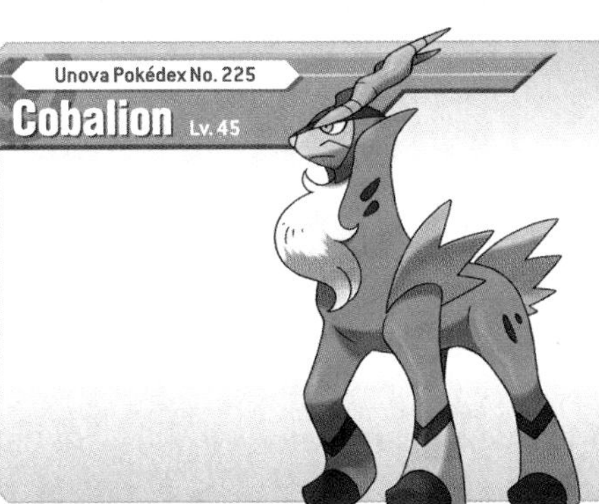

● Place to receive

Driftveil City (Zorua)

● Recommended moves

Move	Type
Night Daze	Dark
U-turn	Bug
Flamethrower	Fire
Aerial Ace	Flying

● Battle strategy

Raise the Zorua you can get in Driftveil City and evolve it into Zoroark. Have Zoroark learn moves of a variety of types so that it can take on any Pokémon your opponent may bring out.

Unova Pokédex No. 225

Cobalion Lv. 45

● Place to receive

Route 13

● Recommended moves

Move	Type
Iron Head	Steel
Thunder Wave	Electric
Volt Switch	Electric
Sacred Sword	Fighting

● Battle strategy

Cobalion belongs to the Steel type, so it's a good idea to use the Steel-type move Iron Head as your primary attack. Thunder Wave is also useful, as it can inflict the Paralysis status condition on your opponents.

Unova Pokédex No. 226

Terrakion Lv. 45

● Place to receive

Route 22

● Recommended moves

Move	Type
Rock Slide	Rock
Swords Dance	Normal
Sacred Sword	Fighting
X-Scissor	Bug

● Battle strategy

Terrakion belongs to the Rock type, so it's a good idea to use the Rock-type move Rock Slide as your primary attack. Swords Dance is also useful, as it raises the Attack stat, making Sacred Sword and X-Scissor even more damaging.

Unova Pokédex No. 227

Virizion Lv. 45

● Place to receive

Route 11

● Recommended moves

Move	Type
Giga Drain	Grass
Aerial Ace	Flying
X-Scissor	Bug
Sacred Sword	Fighting

● Battle strategy

A great strategy with Virizion is to use the Grass-type move Giga Drain to damage your opponents while regaining HP. Teach Virizion moves of a variety of types so it can go up against many different Pokémon.

How to raise the Pokémon in your party

Most people raise their Pokémon by battling with them. At the same time, Trainers want to use their highest level Pokémon in battle. Are there some tips for raising lower-level Pokémon as quickly as possible? Here are some techniques to help you build a strong team of Pokémon without needing to have them all participate in battle directly.

Effective Pokémon-raising techniques

Switch out the Pokémon after the battle begins

As long as a Pokémon appears in the battle for even one turn, it will receive Experience Points. You can use this to your advantage by putting a lower-level Pokémon in the lead position of your party and then switching it out for a more powerful Pokémon as soon as the battle begins.

Revive a fainted Pokémon before the battle ends

If a lower-level Pokémon faints during battle, switch in another Pokémon for it, and then use Revive on it. As long as you revive the fainted Pokémon before the battle ends, it will receive Experience Points.

Trade Pokémon with another Trainer

Pokémon that you obtain via Link Trades receive 50% more Experience Points than Pokémon obtained through regular means. Ask someone to trade you a Pokémon that you'd like to raise so you can get this Experience Point bonus.

When the mysterious Pokérus infects one of your Pokémon, that Pokémon can grow strong

Pokérus is a beneficial virus that can infect Pokémon. You can't see it, but the Pokémon Center receptionist will tell you if your Pokémon have it when you bring them in for healing. The effects of Pokérus cause a Pokémon's stats to increase at a faster rate, making it easier to train. After a few days, the Pokérus goes away, but its effects remain. Pokérus will not go away while a Pokémon is deposited in a PC Box. Pro tip: have lots of battles with a Pokémon with Pokérus in your party and it may transmit Pokérus to other party members.

Stats grow faster

This is your chance to train your Pokémon and make them good and strong!

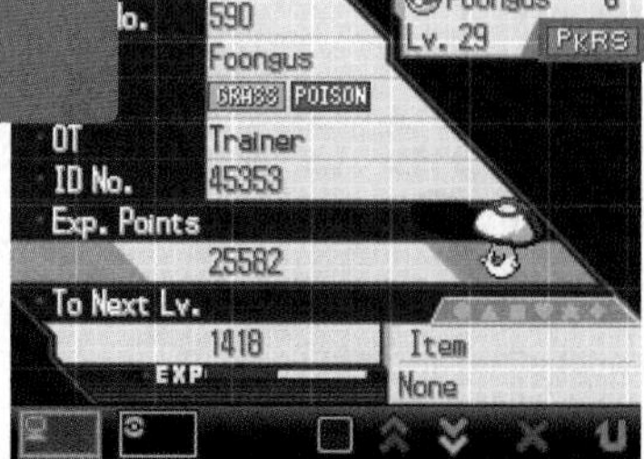

Pokérus goes away after one to four days

After Pokérus goes away, a smiley face will appear, indicating that the Pokémon is now immune to the virus and can no longer infect other Pokémon with Pokérus.

Raising Pokémon gets easier with a Lucky Egg or Exp. Share

Some special items enable you to raise both your lead Pokémon and a supporting Pokémon at the same time. Two such useful items are the Lucky Egg and Exp. Share. Give the Lucky Egg to your main Pokémon and the Exp. Share to a supporting Pokémon and watch your Pokémon grow!

How to use the Lucky Egg and Exp. Share

Lucky Egg

Gain more Experience Points than usual

The Lucky Egg is an item that gives 50% more Experience Points than usual. It is most effective if you have your main Pokémon hold it.

● How to get one

1. Meet Professor Juniper on the first floor of Celestial Tower.

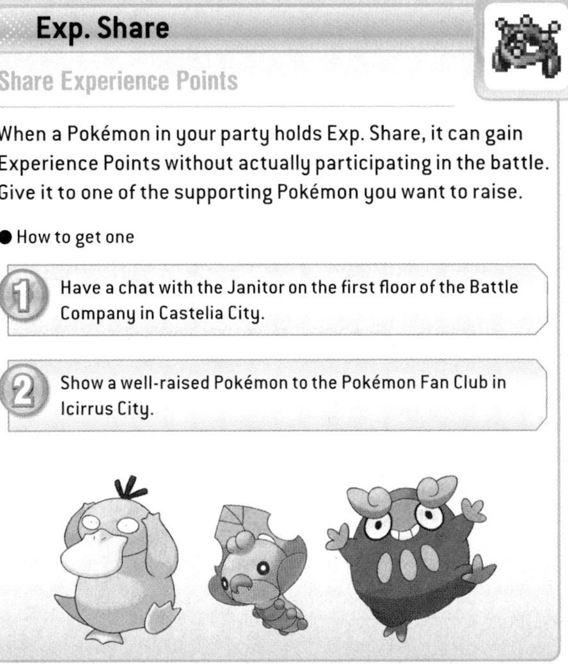

Exp. Share

Share Experience Points

When a Pokémon in your party holds Exp. Share, it can gain Experience Points without actually participating in the battle. Give it to one of the supporting Pokémon you want to raise.

● How to get one

1. Have a chat with the Janitor on the first floor of the Battle Company in Castelia City.
2. Show a well-raised Pokémon to the Pokémon Fan Club in Icirrus City.

Using both items together for maximum benefit

1 When one Exp. Share is held (and the levels of the Pokémon are the same)

This diagram shows what happens when your lead Pokémon holds a Lucky Egg and one Pokémon in your party holds an Exp. Share.

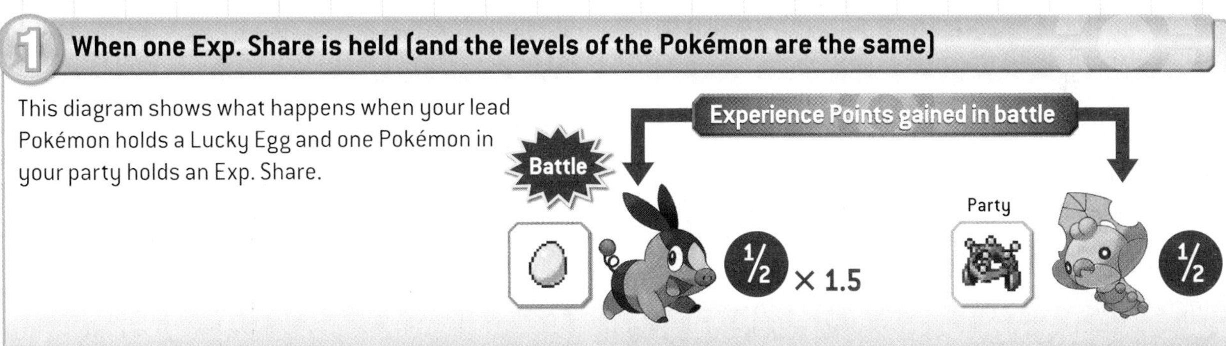

2 When two Exp. Shares are held (and the levels of the Pokémon are the same)

This diagram shows what happens when your lead Pokémon holds a Lucky Egg and two Pokémon in your party each hold an Exp. Share.

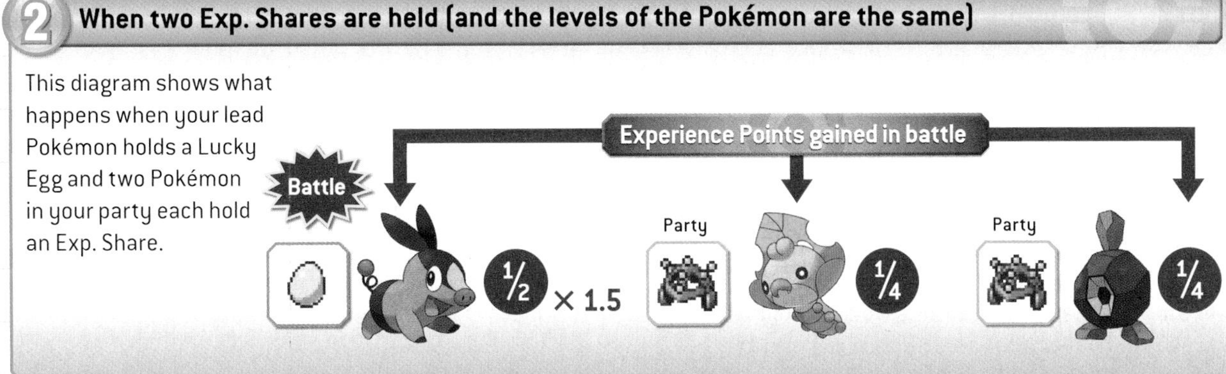

Learn the rules of Pokémon battles

Over the course of your adventures in *Pokémon Black Version 2* and *Pokémon White Version 2*, you'll experience the following four battle formats: Single Battle, Double Battle, Triple Battle, and Rotation Battle. It's important to learn the different rules and attributes of every format if you want to win.

Single Battle

Each side battles with one Pokémon at a time

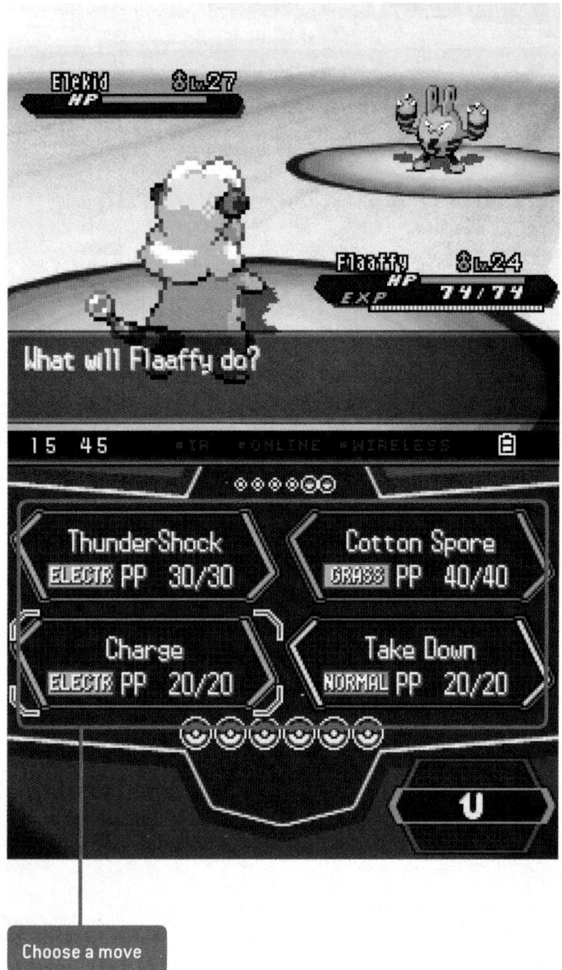

Choose a move

Each Pokémon Trainer sends out one Pokémon with which to battle. The straightforward nature of Single Battle, in which you focus on attacking and exploiting your opponent's weaknesses, is what makes this such a fun battle format. But if you want to become a Pokémon battle master, you need to think carefully about how to raise your Pokémon, what items to give them to hold, and much more. In Single Battle, you can get an explanation of a move if you press the A Button while holding down the L Button when choosing the move.

Double Battle

Each side battles with two Pokémon at a time

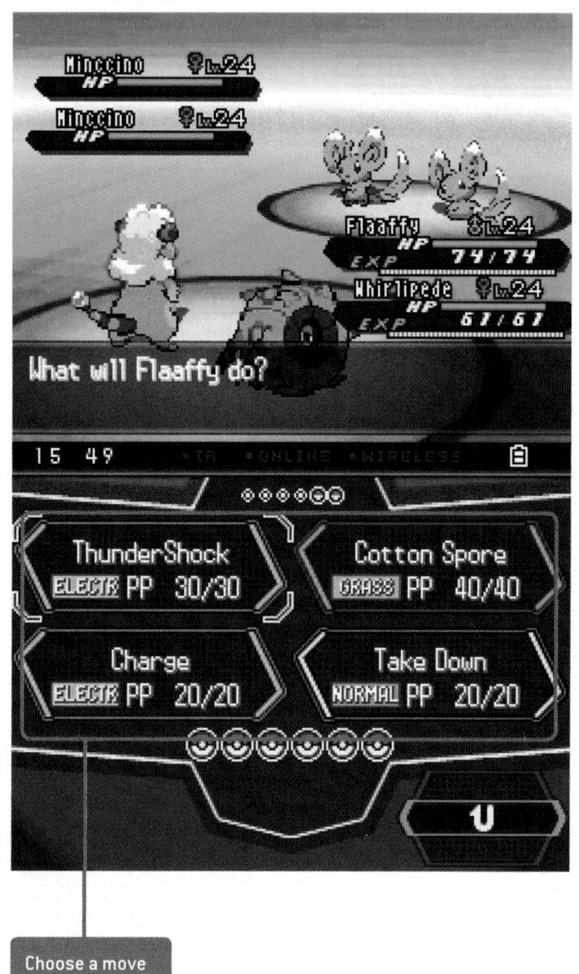

Choose a move

Each Pokémon Trainer sends out two Pokémon with which to battle. In Double Battles, attacks that can hit both of your opponent's Pokémon become very useful. Double Battles will require you to learn even more about moves and their effects than in Single Battles. It's important to come up with good ways to combine a Pokémon's moves, held item, and Ability in order to achieve victory in Double Battles.

Triple Battle

Each side battles with three Pokémon at a time

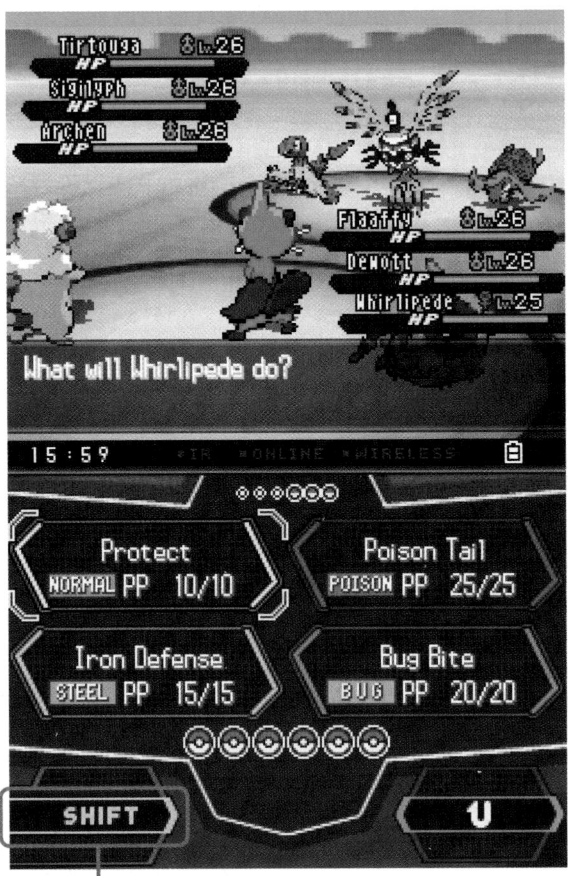

Swap the Pokémon in the middle with the Pokémon on the left or right side

Each Pokémon Trainer sends out three Pokémon with which to battle. The Pokémon in the middle can target any of the opposing Trainer's three Pokémon. The Pokémon on the left and right have a limited range. Each can target only the Pokémon directly in front of itself and the Pokémon in the middle, but not the Pokémon on the far side of its position. Triple Battles can be extremely demanding, as they require you to shift your Pokémon around in order to exploit your opponent's weaknesses.

Rotation Battle

In this evolved form of Single Battle format, each side battles with three Pokémon at a time

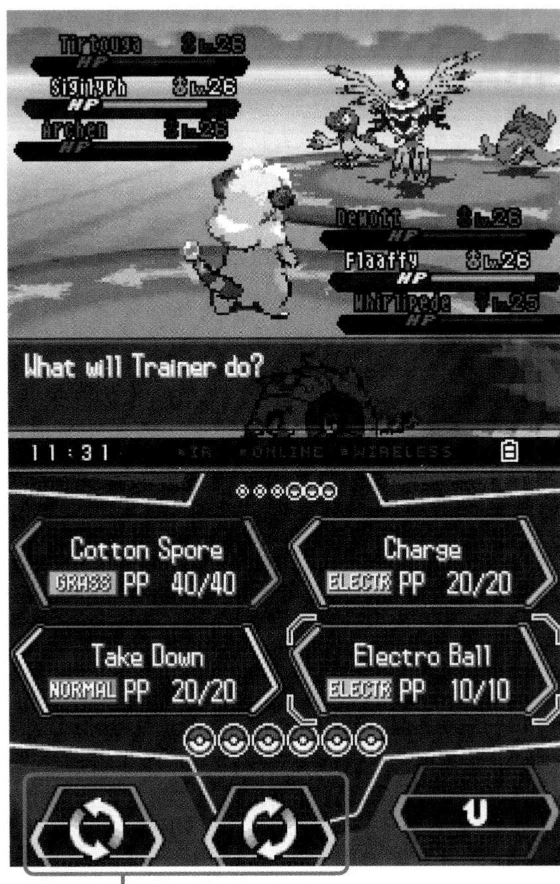

Rotate in one of the Pokémon from the back and use its attack that same turn

The Rotation Battle is an evolved form of the Single Battle format. Each Pokémon Trainer sends out three Pokémon with which to battle. Only one Pokémon can attack per turn, but you can choose to use a move from any of your Pokémon. What makes Rotation Battles unique is that Pokémon can move and attack on the same turn. For example, if you choose a move from a Pokémon in the back, it will rotate to the front and use its move on the same turn.

Using the Game Functions

How to use the game menus

Throughout your journey, you can press the X Button to show the main menu on the Touch Screen. Once you learn what the different options are and what information they contain, you'll have no problem finding your way.

Menu Screen

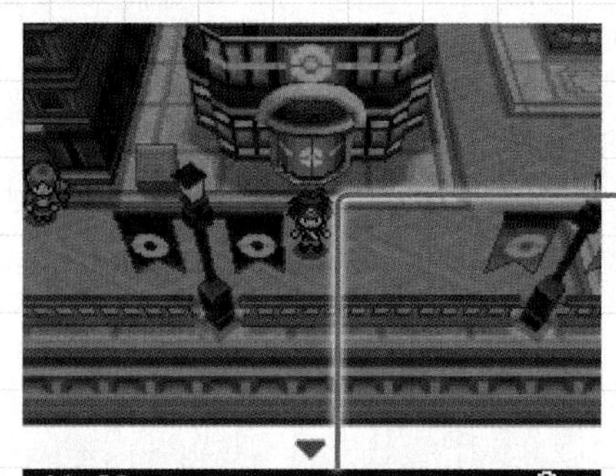

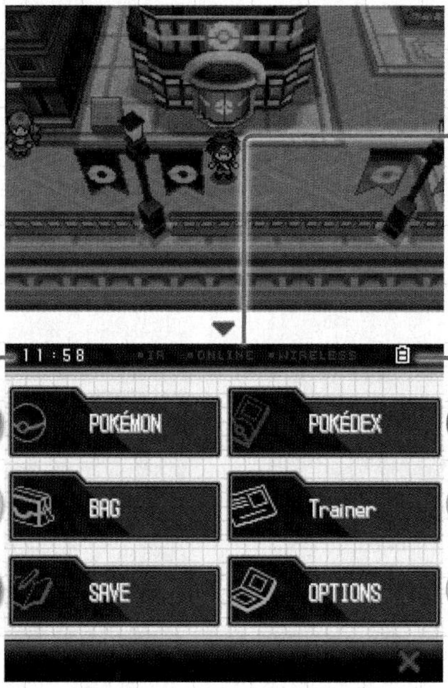

1 POKÉMON
2 POKÉDEX
3 BAG
4 Trainer
5 SAVE
6 OPTIONS

Communication Features

Communication features currently being used or available are shown.

Current time

Shows the current time, according to the clock feature of the system in the Nintendo DS family of systems.

Nintendo DS battery level

The mini-scale graph of the Nintendo DS battery status is shown.

Using the game functions

1 Pokémon

Displays the Pokémon currently in your party. You can also access detailed info on each.

2 Pokédex

A device that records Pokémon data, including how many you've seen and caught.

3 Bag

Stores the items you've collected. Open it to use the items inside.

4 Trainer Info

Shows how far you've come as a Trainer. You can check which Gym Badges have been obtained and other data.

5 Save

Tap here to save your game. Remember to save often.

6 Options

Adjust the gameplay options to your liking.

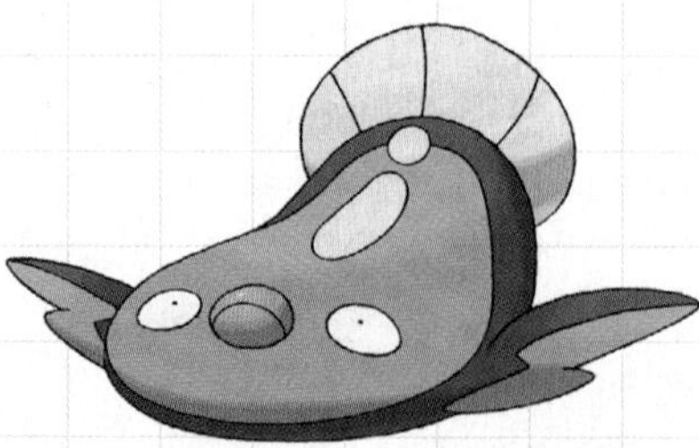

Pokémon

Tap "POKÉMON" on the menu to see a list of your current party Pokémon. You can also view more info about your Pokémon or use field moves, such as Fly or Flash. To use these field moves, just select a Pokémon, then the move.

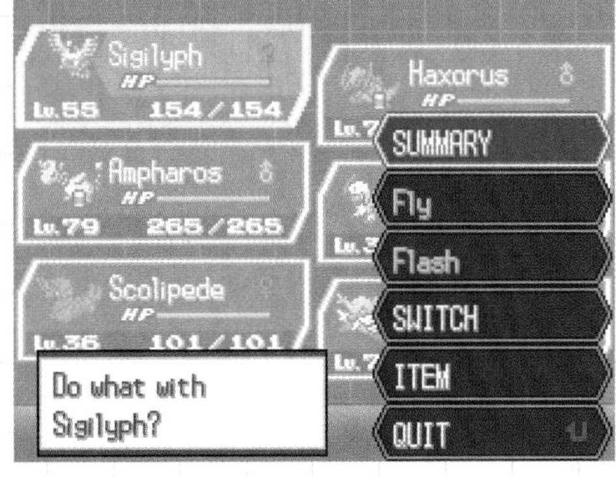

What you can do with the party Pokémon screen

SUMMARY

Shows where you caught the Pokémon, its moves, its stats, and more.

SWITCH

Move a Pokémon around in your lineup. The top-left Pokémon is the first Pokémon and the top-right Pokémon is the second Pokémon to join a battle.

ITEM

Lets you give a Pokémon an item to hold or take away its held item.

FIELD MOVE

Lets your Pokémon use a field move, such as Fly or Flash.

Pokémon data under "Summary"

Three pages of Pokémon data

From the party Pokémon screen, choose "SUMMARY" to view a Pokémon's info. There are three separate pages of info.

Trainer Memo and Info on the Pokémon

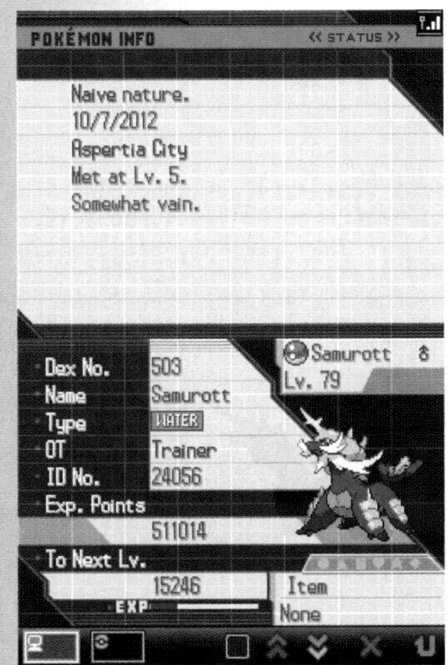

The top screen shows the Pokémon's Nature, Characteristic, and more. General information is on the lower screen.

Stats and Learned Moves

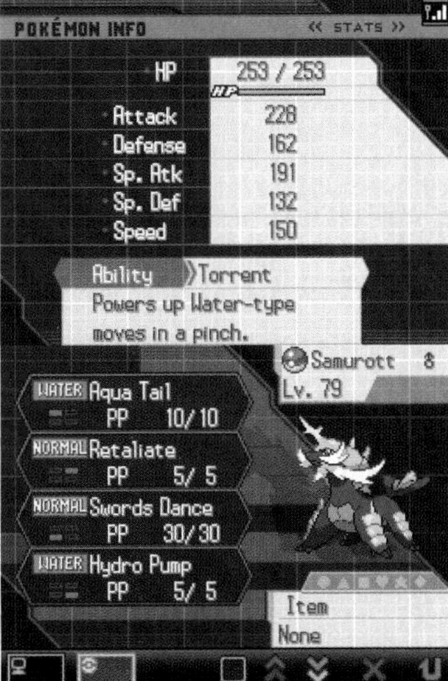

The top screen shows the Pokémon's stats and its Ability. The lower screen shows the moves it knows.

Ribbons (Pokémon taken from other regions only)

This is only for Pokémon caught in other regions or distributed by official Pokémon promotions. The lower screen shows any Ribbons it has earned.

Pokédex

The Pokédex is the device that automatically records Pokémon data. Whenever you encounter a Pokémon in the field or in a Trainer battle, it's added to your list of Pokémon seen. Once you obtain it, it's added to your list of Pokémon obtained.

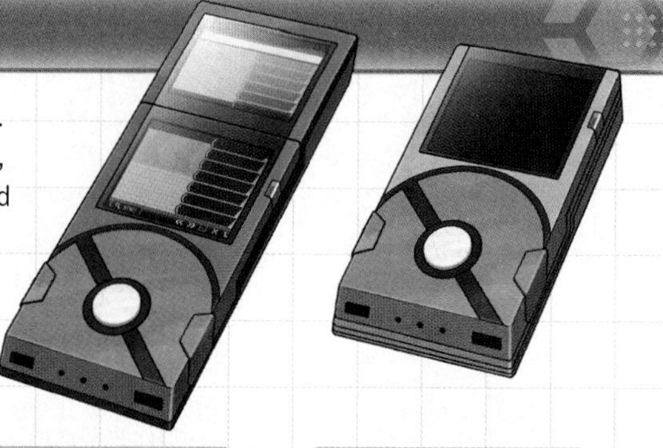

Boy's Pokédex

Girl's Pokédex

Pokédex screen

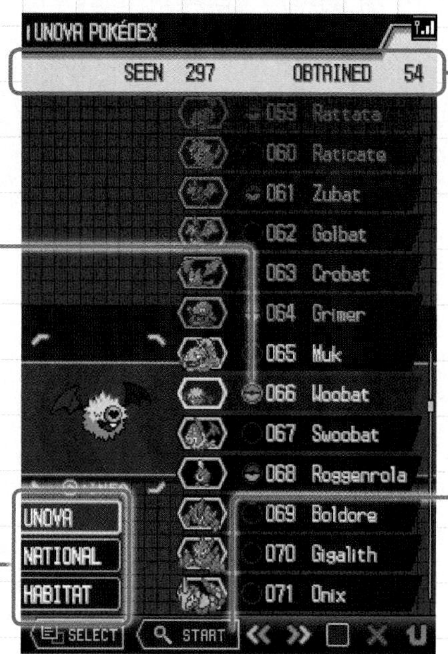

The number of Pokémon seen and Pokémon obtained

Icon to show it has been obtained

When you've obtained a Pokémon, it'll be registered in your Pokédex and the Poké Ball icon is shown

Switches among the Unova Pokédex, the National Pokédex, and the Habitat List

Search

You can narrow down the Pokémon you're looking for by Pokédex number, name, type, and more

Note: "National" appears after receiving the National Pokédex

How Pokédex entries are registered

1 No Pokédex data

Switches among the Unova Pokédex, the National Pokédex, and the Habitat List.

2 Name and Habitat recorded

When you see a Pokémon, its name and appearance are added to the Pokédex. Tap "AREA," and its Habitat is also displayed.

3 Detailed information added

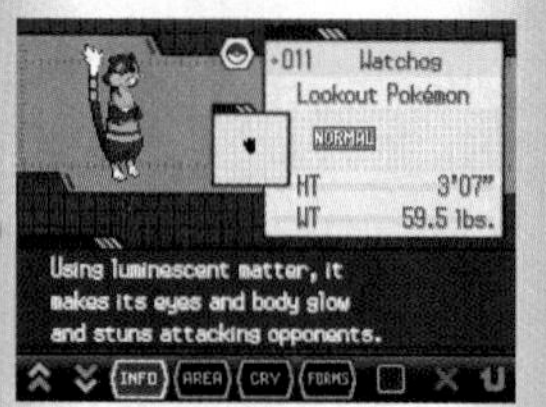

Once you obtain a Pokémon, the Pokédex records its type, size, description, and more. The Pokédex entry is now complete.

Check gender, form, and color differences

Tap "FORMS" to check gender and form differences. You can also check Shiny Pokémon you've obtained.

Complete the Habitat List!

The Habitat List is a new function introduced in *Pokémon Black Version 2* and *Pokémon White Version 2*. When you find or catch a Pokémon on a road, in a cave, or in a town or city, the Pokémon will be registered in the Habitat List for that location. When you complete the Habitat List, you'll get a stamp. As you catch Pokémon and get stamps, you'll get even closer to the completion of your Pokédex. Have fun seeing all the info on your Pokémon!

Habitat List screen

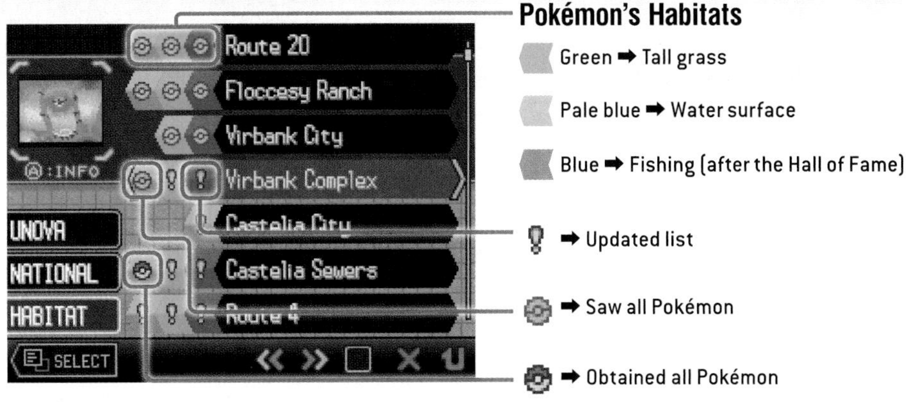

You can see Pokémon's Habitats with one glance

Pokémon Habitats are divided into three categories: tall grass / land / desert, water surface, and fishing. When Pokémon who appear in a certain place differ depending on the season, the pages for tall grass / land / desert and water surface are displayed by season.

Habitats by area

Tall grass / land / desert

Water surface

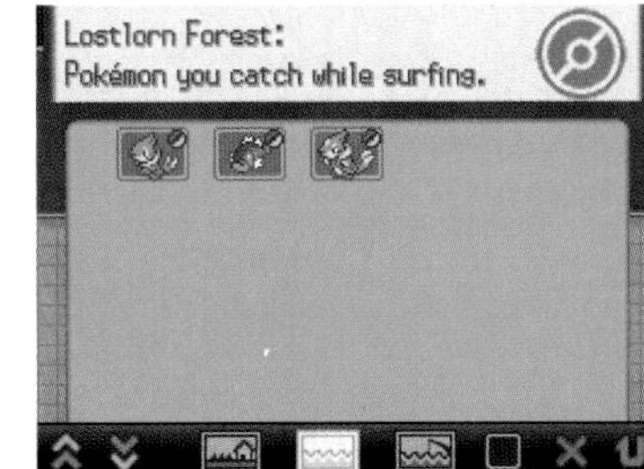

Fishing

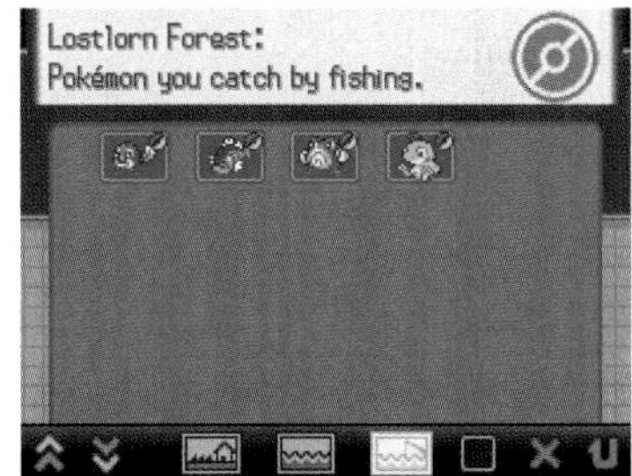

Complete the Habitat List and receive a stamp

There are two kinds of stamps for the Habitat List: a pale-colored stamp that you receive when you've seen all the Pokémon living in the place, and a dark-colored stamp that you receive when you've obtained all the Pokémon in the location.

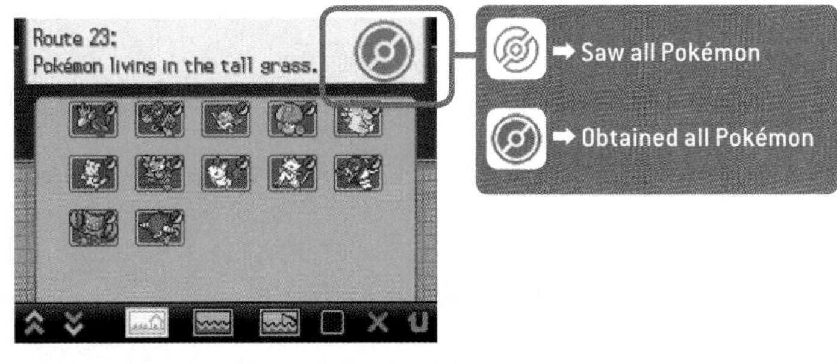

Bag

Your Bag is where you store the items you collect on your journey. The Bag has six Cases in total. Items are automatically sorted into each Case.

Boy's Bag

Girl's Bag

Contents of your Bag

Key Items Case

Stores important items acquired on your journey, like the Bicycle and the Dowsing Machine

Items Case

Store items for Pokémon to hold, evolution Stones, and more

Medicine Case

Store items that restore HP or PP, or cure status conditions

TMs & HMs Case

Store your TMs and HMs

Berries Case

Store your Berries as you obtain them on your journey

Free Space

Choose and store frequently used items in this Case.

Icons

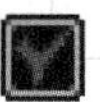 Registered to the Y Button

 Item effective when held by a Pokémon

 Poké Ball

 Mail

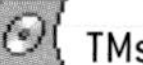 TMs

 HMs

New functions of your Bag

Free Space

It's a Case to store your favorite items for quick access. It has a search function and can be registered to the Y Button, too.

Sort

You can sort items in Cases so that you can find items easily. You can sort by type or name.

Tip: Register frequently used items and screens for quick access

Register frequently used items and screens by clicking the box. You can use them just by pressing the Y Button. This feature is very useful because you don't have to open screens for your Bag or Pokédex. Press "SELECT" to sort the contents registered to the Y Button.

Check the box

Press the Y Button

Trainer Info

Trainer Info covers your Trainer Card and the Gym Badges you obtain during your adventure. Tap the icon labeled with your name to access it at any time. Your Trainer Card records lots of information about your adventure, so don't forget to check it every so often. Show it to your friends and family to enjoy your adventure even more!

Trainer Card

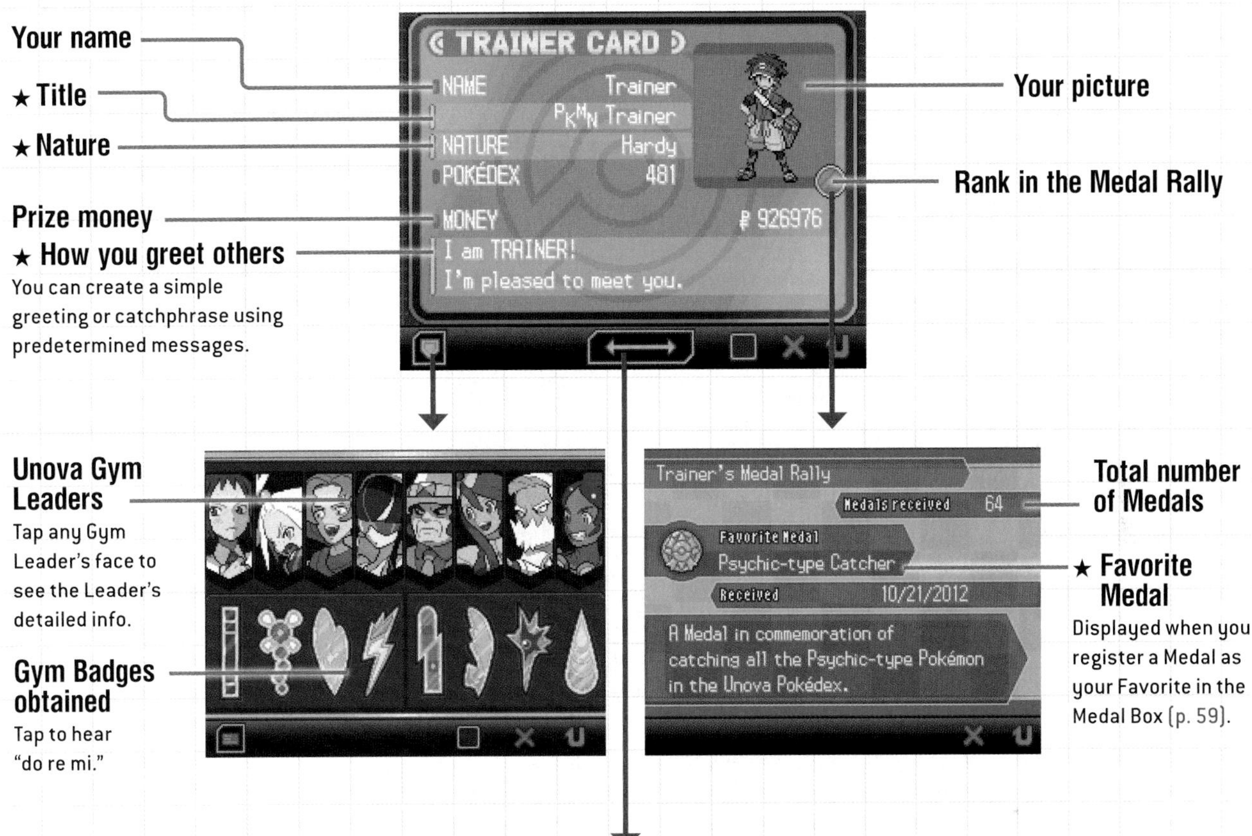

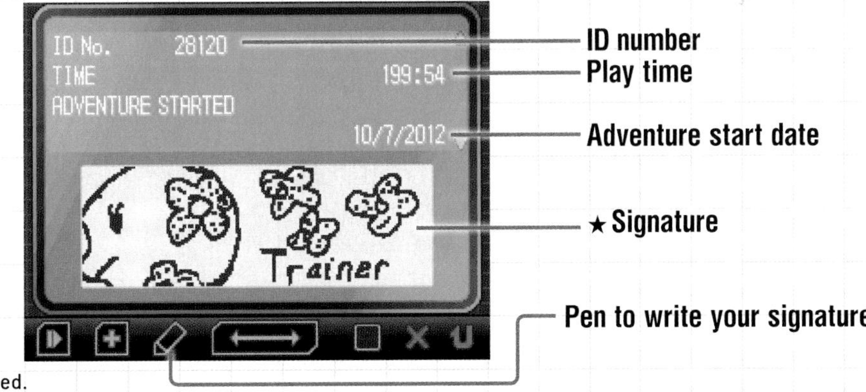

Those marked with a ★ can be customized.

Trainer Card Features

Tap to customize

You can personalize the information on your Trainer Card by tapping it. Remember that the information will be seen by other players through Tag Mode and the Union Room in a Pokémon Center. Customize it in a cool or funny way.

Upgrade your Trainer Card

After you've achieved big goals, such as defeating the Pokémon Champion, Iris, and entering the Hall of Fame, or shooting all 40 movies in Pokéstar Studios, your Trainer Card is upgraded and changes color. Meet these conditions and upgrade your Trainer Card.

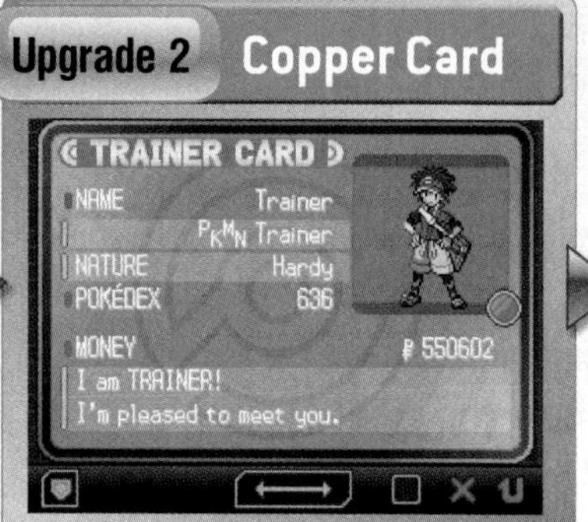

When playing *Pokémon Black Version 2*

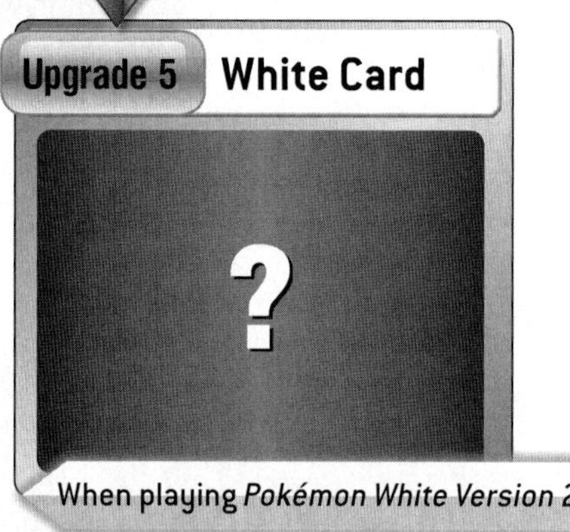

When playing *Pokémon White Version 2*

Conditions for upgrading your Trainer Card

These are the five conditions to upgrade your Trainer Card. Play *Pokémon Black Version 2* or *Pokémon White Version 2* thoroughly to get the pinnacle of Trainer Cards—the Black Card or White Card.

1. **Defeat the Champion and enter the Hall of Fame**
2. **Complete the National Pokédex**
3. **Shoot all 40 movies at Pokéstar Studios**
4. **Win the Champions Tournament in the PWT (Pokémon World Tournament)**
5. **Make your Black Level and White Level 30 or higher**

Medal Rally

Medals are rewards for those who put a lot of effort into various activities in *Pokémon Black Version 2* and *Pokémon White Version 2*. When you achieve certain results, Mr. Medal will give you Medals accordingly. There are 255 kinds of Medals.

The Medal Box is in your Bag

The Medal Box is in the Key Items Case of your Bag. When you get a new Medal, check the Medal Box.

Difference between Medals and Hint Medals

Medals

Medals are rewards for achieving certain conditions. Mr. Medal gives you your Medals at a Pokémon Center. Press the magnifier at the bottom left corner to display them by name.

Hint Medals

Hints to obtain Medals are written on Hint Medals. You also receive hints from Mr. Medal. Press the magnifier to display only Hint Medals.

Medal types

There are 255 Medals divided into five types. You can tell the type of Medal by the color.

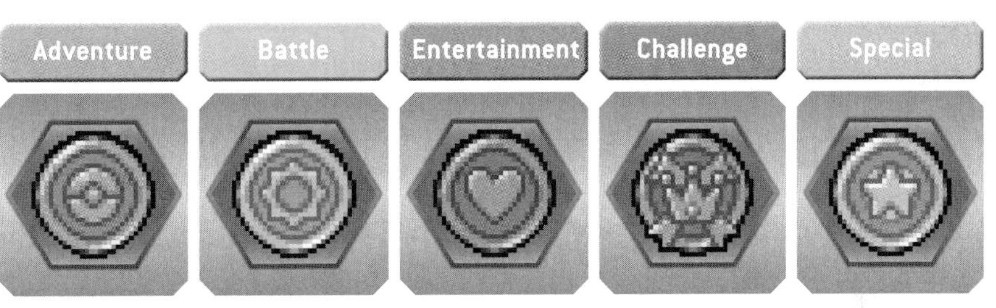

Tip

Ranks in the Medal Rally

Your rank goes up depending on the number of Medals you've obtained. The color of the Medal Box changes depending on your rank.

Number of Medals	Rank
0–49	Trainee rank
50–99	Rookie rank
100–149	Elite rank
150–199	Master rank
200 and up	Legend rank

You can find out your current rank at the Medal Office in Castelia City.

Tip

Register your Favorite Medal

Choose a Medal in the Medal Box and press the A Button to register it as your Favorite Medal. It will be displayed in your Trainer Card. Your Favorite Medal can be viewed through Tag Mode and the Union Room in a Pokémon Center. Choose the Medal you're most proud of as your Favorite Medal.

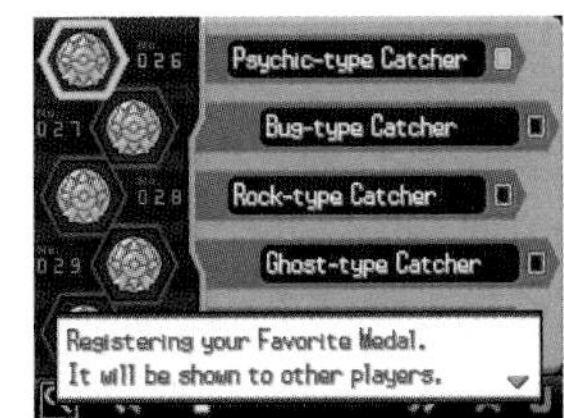

Check p. 448 for the Medal list.

Save

The Save menu lets you save your data when you want to quit in the middle of your *Pokémon Black Version 2* or *Pokémon White Version 2* game. When you save your data, you'll see the save screen shown below, where you can check details about your game.

Save screen

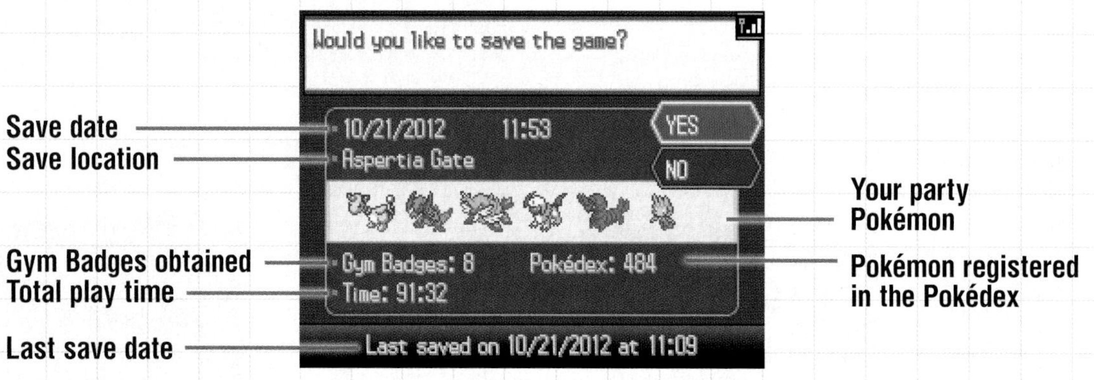

Save your game anytime

Before battling a Gym Leader

It's a good idea to save the game before battling a Gym Leader. If you lose and hadn't saved the game, you have to go through the Gym again. If you have saved the game, you can start over at the battle with the Gym Leader.

Before battling the Elite Four

It's a good idea to save the game before battling the Elite Four in the Pokémon League. You can choose the order to challenge the Elite Four. Save the data before taking stairs to one of the Elite Four's squares.

Before trying to catch a valuable Pokémon

When you see a Legendary Pokémon like Cobalion, Terrakion, or Virizion, it's a good idea to save the game before trying to catch it. That way, even if you make the Pokémon faint, you can try again.

How to delete your save data

If you want to delete your save data and start over, press Up on the +Control Pad, SELECT, and the B Button at the same time. Once you delete it, you cannot restore it. So please think carefully before deleting it.

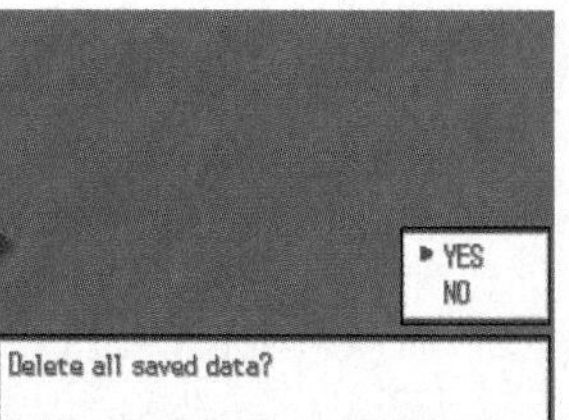

 Options

The Options menu lets you adjust game settings to suit your preferences, making it easier to play. For instance, if the game text scrolls too slowly, you can increase the speed. If there's a game feature you want to change, open the Options menu and adjust it to your liking.

Options menu

What you can do with the Options menu

1 Text Speed

Choose from slow, mid (middle), or fast text speeds.

2 Battle Scene

Choose whether you want to see animations when Pokémon use their moves and when they are affected by status conditions.

3 Battle Style

When you defeat one Pokémon on a team, you'll be asked whether you want to switch your own Pokémon. If you want to automatically stay with your current Pokémon, select "SET" to turn off these messages.

Shift

Pros

After defeating a Pokémon, you can switch to one better suited to the next opponent.

Cons

You'll be asked frequently if you want to switch Pokémon.

Set

Pros

Lets you keep battling with a single Pokémon (to focus on leveling it up).

Cons

In Set mode, you have to use up a turn to switch your Pokémon after defeating the target(s).

4 Sound

Choose between stereo and mono sound.

5 Save Before IR

You can choose to save the game before IR (Infrared Connection) is launched.

Get a handle on using these handy items

There are lots of items that are especially useful on your journey or in completing the Pokédex. Just a few of them, the Town Map, Dowsing Machine, and Xtransceiver, are highlighted below.

Town Map

It's the map of the entire Unova region, including its cities, towns, routes, caves, and bridges. Places you've visited are shown in gray, and they'll turn blue as you visit them. You can also see your current position. Tap the "+" icon to magnify.

Place Name

Info about the location

Places and facilities within that location

Places you have visited
★ You can use Fly to fly there.

Places you have not visited
★ You cannot use Fly to fly there.

Places you cannot go with the move Fly

Current Position

Zoom in on the Town Map
You can press SELECT to zoom in as well.

How to obtain the Town Map

In Aspertia City, your rival's sister gives the map to you.

Dowsing Machine

The Dowsing Machine can detect items that are hidden in caves and forests. Follow the arrow shown on the lower screen. You cannot pick up the item if you are standing right on top of it. Step aside, face the spot where you were, then press the A Button.

When the Touch Screen flashes, follow the arrow.

When you are on the spot where an item is, the dowsing bars will meet each other in the middle and the screen will flash. You can find many rare items, so you should have the Dowsing Machine activated as you take on your adventure.

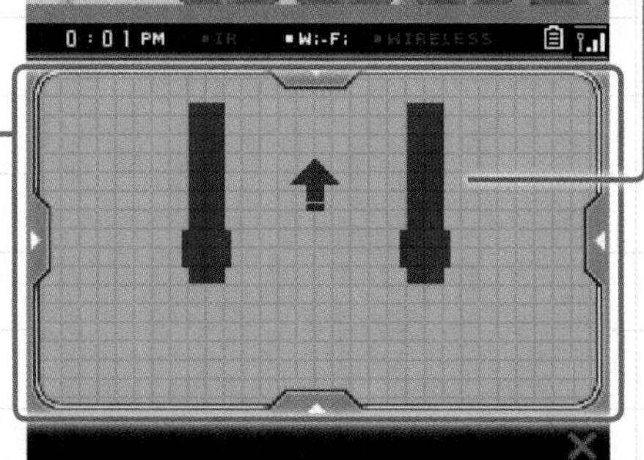

Dowsing Machine

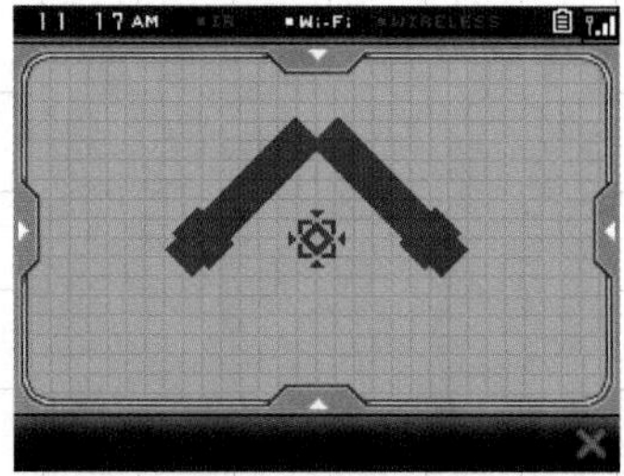

How to obtain the Dowsing Machine

In Castelia City, Bianca will give you the Dowsing Machine.

Xtransceiver

A high-tech transceiver with a camera function, it allows up to four-way calls. In *Pokémon Black Version 2* and *Pokémon White Version 2*, you can call some of the people you meet, such as Professor Juniper and your rival. They can check your progress with the Pokédex, tell you where to go next, and so on. Knowing who to give a call will help you through your adventure.

Professor Juniper

She tells you about your Pokédex.

Select "Tell me about evolution," and she'll talk about how to evolve Pokémon. Select "Check my Pokédex," and she'll check how complete your Pokédex is.

Rival

He tells you where to go next.

Select "Something up?" and you'll hear advice on your journey, such as where to go next. Talk to him when you don't know what to do.

Cheren

He'll tell you about the Pokémon in your party.

Select "Tell me about types," and he'll tell you about Pokémon weaknesses. Select "Tell me about Abilities," and he'll tell you about the effects of Abilities.

Mom

She'll tell you about your current location.

She'll tell you what's great about your current location, some tips, or exciting information.

Bianca

She tells you about your friendship with the Pokémon and their effort in your party.

Select "Please look at friendship," and she'll tell you about how much a Pokémon has grown close to you. Select "Please look at effort" and she'll tell you how much effort has been made.

Pokémon effort analysis

When there is room to make more effort
Trainer's [Pokémon name]...It seems like it can work a little harder.

When the effort values are full
Trainer's [Pokémon name]...It has worked really hard, hasn't it?

◆ "Please look at effort" becomes available after the Hall of Fame.

Town Shops and Services

Pokémon Center

Pokémon Centers are facilities that support Pokémon Trainers. Pokémon Centers in the Unova region are separated into two floors. The first floor has both the Poké Mart and the Pokémon Center where you can heal your Pokémon.

The second floor has three rooms where you can enjoy different communication features. Once you begin the Medal Rally, Mr. Medal will appear on the first floor.

2F Communications Area

In the Union Room, you can trade Pokémon, battle, and enjoy minigames with other nearby players. At the Wi-Fi Club, you can trade Pokémon and battle with friends that are far away. At the Global Terminal, you can trade Pokémon and battle with Trainers from all over the world.

1F Pokémon Center

If you speak to the person at the Pokémon Center's reception counter, you can heal the HP, PP, and status conditions of all the Pokémon in your party for free. Use the PC on the left side of the counter to deposit or withdraw Pokémon or organize the held items of your Pokémon. Also, you can use the Help option to view detailed explanations of how to play the game, complete with images.

1F Poké Mart

The Poké Mart sells a variety of items. The number of items you can buy from the upper clerk increases as you acquire more Gym Badges. The items sold by the upper clerk are the same no matter which Poké Mart you visit. The items sold by the lower clerk change depending on which town or city you are in.

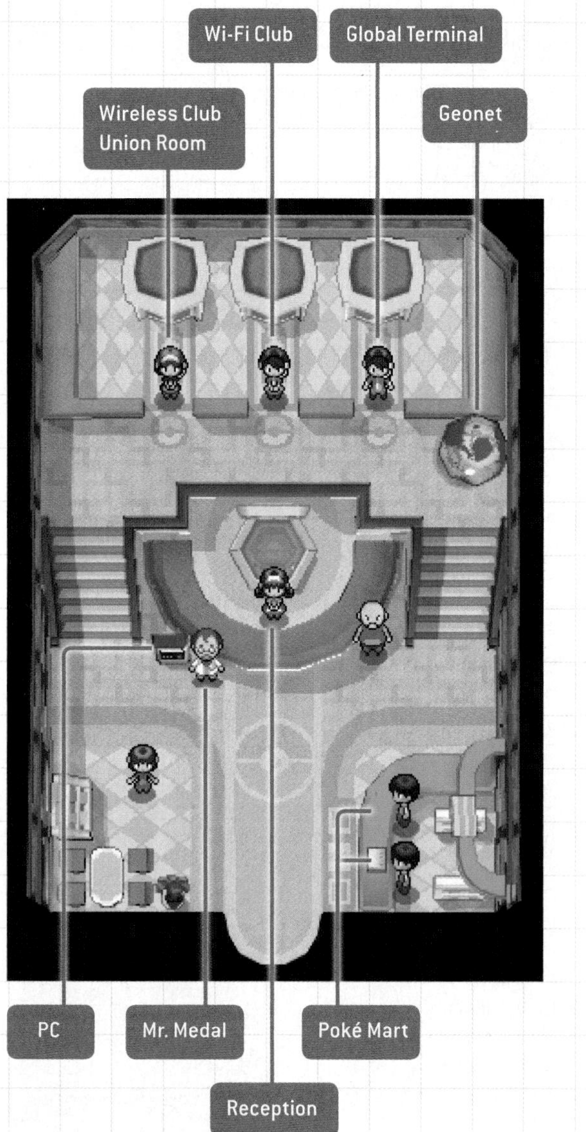

Poké Mart

This section lists the items sold in the Poké Mart. The list of items sold by the upper clerk is split up by the number of Gym Badges that are required. Check which items you can buy with your number of Gym Badges. The list of items sold by the lower clerk is split up by town or city. When you want to buy a Dusk Ball, for example, check this list to find out which town or city you need to visit.

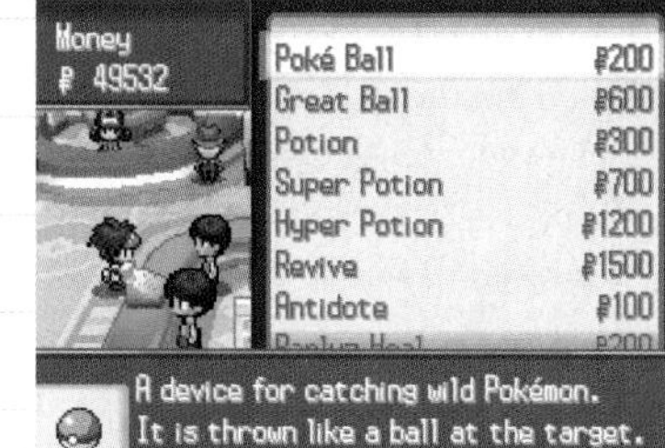

Items sold by the upper clerk (and conditions for sale)

Gym Badges: 0		Gym Badges: 1–2		Gym Badges: 3–4		Gym Badges: 5–6		Gym Badges: 7		Gym Badges: 8	
Poké Ball	200	Poké Ball	200	Poké Ball	200	Poké Ball	200	Poké Ball	200	Poké Ball	200
		Great Ball	600	Great Ball	600	Great Ball	600	Great Ball	600	Great Ball	600
						Ultra Ball	1,200	Ultra Ball	1,200	Ultra Ball	1,200
Potion	300	Potion	300	Potion	300	Potion	300	Potion	300	Potion	300
		Super Potion	700	Super Potion	700	Super Potion	700	Super Potion	700	Super Potion	700
				Hyper Potion	1,200	Hyper Potion	1,200	Hyper Potion	1,200	Hyper Potion	1,200
								Max Potion	2,500	Max Potion	2,500
										Full Restore	3,000
				Revive	1,500	Revive	1,500	Revive	1,500	Revive	1,500
		Antidote	100	Antidote	100	Antidote	100	Antidote	100	Antidote	100
		Parlyz Heal	200	Parlyz Heal	200	Parlyz Heal	200	Parlyz Heal	200	Parlyz Heal	200
		Awakening	250	Awakening	250	Awakening	250	Awakening	250	Awakening	250
		Burn Heal	250	Burn Heal	250	Burn Heal	250	Burn Heal	250	Burn Heal	250
		Ice Heal	250	Ice Heal	250	Ice Heal	250	Ice Heal	250	Ice Heal	250
						Full Heal	600	Full Heal	600	Full Heal	600
		Escape Rope	550	Escape Rope	550	Escape Rope	550	Escape Rope	550	Escape Rope	550
		Repel	350	Repel	350	Repel	350	Repel	350	Repel	350
				Super Repel	500	Super Repel	500	Super Repel	500	Super Repel	500
						Max Repel	700	Max Repel	700	Max Repel	700

Items sold by the lower clerk (excluding Mail)

Accumula Town	
Repeat Ball	1,000
Nest Ball	1,000
Quick Ball	1,000

Castelia City	
Heal Ball	300
Net Ball	1,000
Nest Ball	1,000

Driftveil City	
Net Ball	1,000
Nest Ball	1,000
Dusk Ball	1,000

Lentimas Town	
Heal Ball	300
Nest Ball	1,000
Dusk Ball	1,000

Nimbasa City	
TM73 Thunder Wave	10,000
TM74 Gyro Ball	10,000
TM16 Light Screen	30,000
TM33 Reflect	30,000

Undella Town	
Luxury Ball	1,000
Dive Ball	1,000

Opelucid City	
Dusk Ball	1,000
Timer Ball	1,000
Quick Ball	1,000

Humilau City	
Luxury Ball	1,000
Dive Ball	1,000
Net Ball	1,000

Victory Road	
Heal Ball	300
Net Ball	1,000
Nest Ball	1,000
Quick Ball	1,000
Dusk Ball	1,000
Timer Ball	1,000
Repeat Ball	1,000
Luxury Ball	1,000

Mistralton City	
TM07 Hail	50,000
TM11 Sunny Day	50,000
TM18 Rain Dance	50,000
TM37 Sandstorm	50,000

Pokémon League	
Heal Ball	300
Net Ball	1,000
Nest Ball	1,000
Quick Ball	1,000
Dusk Ball	1,000
Timer Ball	1,000
Repeat Ball	1,000
Luxury Ball	1,000

Icirrus City	
Dusk Ball	1,000
Timer Ball	1,000
Quick Ball	1,000

Virbank City	
Heal Ball	300
Net Ball	1,000

Lacunosa Town	
TM14 Blizzard	70,000
TM25 Thunder	70,000
TM38 Fire Blast	70,000

Striaton City	
TM04 Calm Mind	80,000
TM08 Bulk Up	80,000

Amanita's PC (Someone's PC)

The various boxes that can be accessed from the PC allow you to deposit Pokémon you've caught or withdraw them to take them on your adventure. After you talk to Amanita in Castelia City, the name of the PC becomes "Amanita's PC."

What you can do with Amanita's PC

Deposit Pokémon

Use this when you want to put Pokémon from your party into the PC Box. You can also release Pokémon.

Withdraw Pokémon

Use this to move Pokémon from your PC Box into your party. To use this function, you need space in your party.

Move Pokémon

You can deposit and withdraw Pokémon or move them from one PC Box to another.

Battle Box

You can put up to six Pokémon that you often use in battles into your Battle Box. The Pokémon in your Battle Box can be used for Link Battles, the PWT (p. 154), and the Battle Subway.

Move Items

You can organize the items held by your Pokémon. You can give an item held by one Pokémon to another or you can put the item into your Bag.

Tip: Use the new and improved PC Box

In *Pokémon Black Version 2* and *Pokémon White Version 2*, the PC Box has been greatly improved to be much easier to use. Tap the icons on the screen to switch between the Basic Mode, Relocate Mode, and Group Move Mode. Choose the best mode for the operation you wish to perform.

Switch modes to move your Pokémon into Boxes as you like

Basic Mode

Tap the Pokémon you wish to move and you can move it into the PC Boxes that are shown to the right.

Relocate Mode

Slide the Pokémon to the location where you wish to relocate it.

Group Move Mode

Circle the group of Pokémon you wish to move inside the dotted line to move them all at once.

Your PC

Use the PC with your name on it to store Mail held by a Pokémon received in a Link Trade. You can store up to 20 messages at a time. You can read the messages you stored at any time.

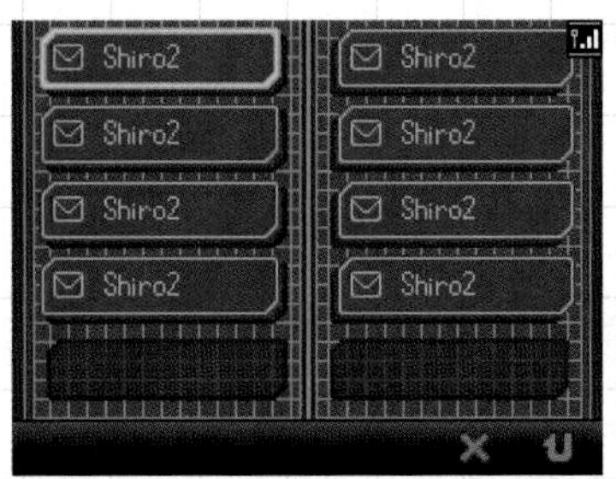

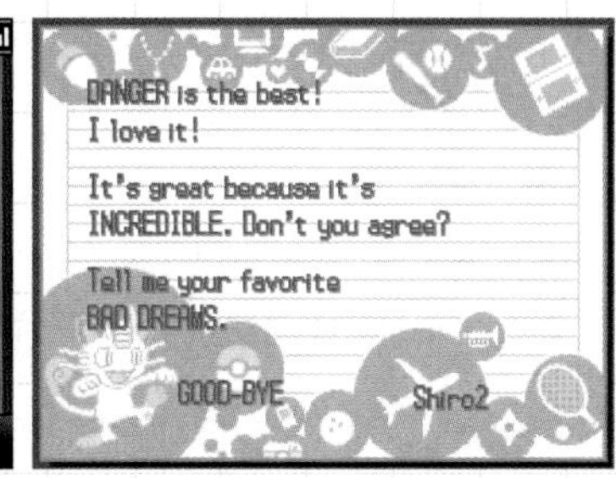

Tip: When trading, have your Pokémon hold Mail

It's fun to send messages along with the Pokémon you trade by giving them Mail when you're making a Link Trade. There are 12 different types of Mail and a variety of different paper options from which to choose. Visit the different Poké Marts across the region to collect all the different types of Mail (p. 448).

Professor's PC

Use the Professor's PC to check the completion level of your Pokédex. Turn it on, and you'll be connected with Professor Juniper, who will rate your Unova Pokédex's completion.

Tip: Complete the Unova Pokédex to receive rewards

Complete the Unova Pokédex, and you can receive a reward from Professor Juniper. Once you've completed the Unova Pokédex, go see Professor Juniper in Nuvema Town.

See 297 kinds of Pokémon in the Unova region		**Permit** Gain access to the Nature Preserve.
Catch 297 kinds of Pokémon in the Unova region		**Oval Charm** Find Eggs more easily.

◆ Not including Mythical Pokémon such as Victini, Keldeo, or Meloetta

Help

Help shows you important information about how to enjoy *Pokémon Black Version 2* and *Pokémon White Version 2*. Images accompany the various explanations, so it's easy to understand.

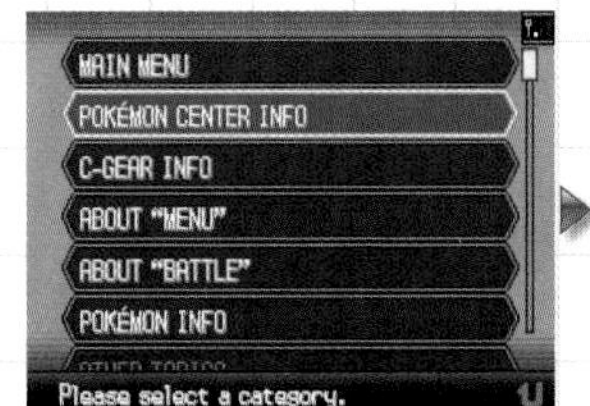

POKÉMON CENTER
You can restore your tired Pokémon and buy useful items. You'll find the PC where you can keep captured Pokémon.
You can hear Professor Juniper's evaluation of your Pokédex.
Visit 2F for Link Trade and Link Battle.

Communications Area

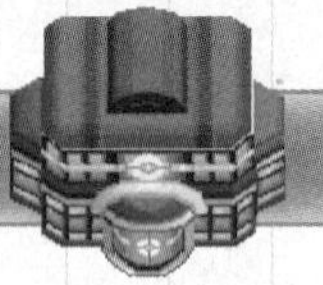

The Communications Area is on the second floor of the Pokémon Center. It has three rooms where you can enjoy different types of communication features. Each room can be enjoyed in its own way, so learn which room best matches what you want to do.

Union Room

Connectivity: DS Wireless Communications or Nintendo 3DS Local Play

Trade Pokémon or battle with nearby friends

Use DS Wireless Communications or Nintendo 3DS Local Play to connect with other nearby players to trade Pokémon or battle. You can use this room without any additional equipment.

What you can do:

Greetings

With Greetings, you can show off your Trainer Card to other players (p. 57).

Battle

Enjoy Single Battle, Double Battle, Triple Battle, Rotation Battle, or Multi Battle formats.

Trade

Each player selects three Pokémon candidates for trade to begin a Negotiation Trade.

Draw

Use powerful drawing tools to enjoy drawing with up to four other players.

Spin Trade

Up to five players can participate in this fun game of trading Pokémon Eggs. You can even receive Berries.

Wi-Fi Club

Connectivity: Nintendo Wi-Fi Connection

Trade Pokémon or battle with friends with whom you've exchanged Friend Codes

Utilizing a Nintendo Wi-Fi Connection, you can trade Pokémon and battle against Trainers who are far away from you. You need to have first registered each other's Friend Code in your Pal Pads in order to use this room.

What you can do:

Voice Chat

Talk to Trainers who aren't nearby. Voice Chat is automatically turned on when trading Pokémon or battling.

Xtransceiver

Enjoy video chat with friends who aren't nearby. Play two different types of minigames.

Battle

Enjoy Single Battle, Double Battle, Triple Battle, Rotation Battle, or Multi Battle formats.

Trade

Each player selects three Pokémon candidates for trade to begin a Negotiation Trade.

Global Terminal

Connectivity: Nintendo Wi-Fi Connection

Connect to the Internet to trade Pokémon or battle with Trainers from all over the world

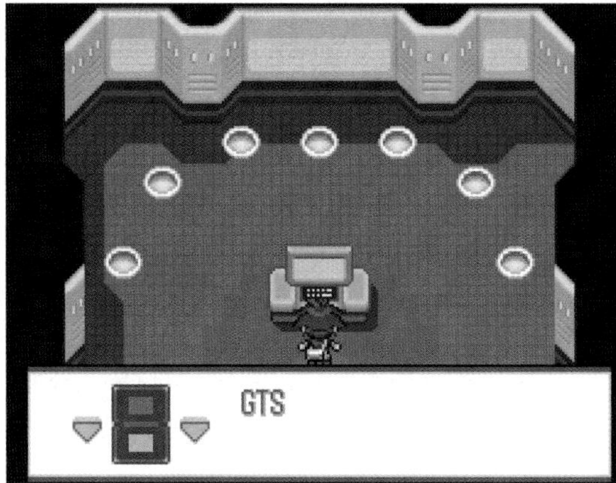

Utilizing Nintendo Wi-Fi Connection, you can trade Pokémon and battle against Trainers who are far away from you. You can meet other Pokémon fans from across the world in this room without exchanging Friend Codes.

What you can do:

Random Matchups

Enjoy Pokémon battles with Trainers from around the world. Choose between Free mode, in which an opponent is automatically found, or Rating mode, in which an opponent is chosen based on your Rating compared to other players.

GTS (Global Trade Station)

Have fun trading Pokémon with Trainers from across the world. There are two methods of trading over the GTS. One method lets you specify exactly which Pokémon you want, and the other, GTS Negotiation Trade, lets you set certain conditions for the type of Pokémon you are looking for (p. 350).

Musical Photo

View the photos you took at the end of a Pokémon Musical (p. 408).

Battle Videos

You can send, receive, and view Battle Videos, which are recordings of actual battles.

Geonet

Connectivity: Nintendo Wi-Fi Connection

Geonet is a high-tech globe that registers the location of Trainers with whom you have traded Pokémon over the GTS. Through playing Pokémon, you can feel connected to people from all over the world.

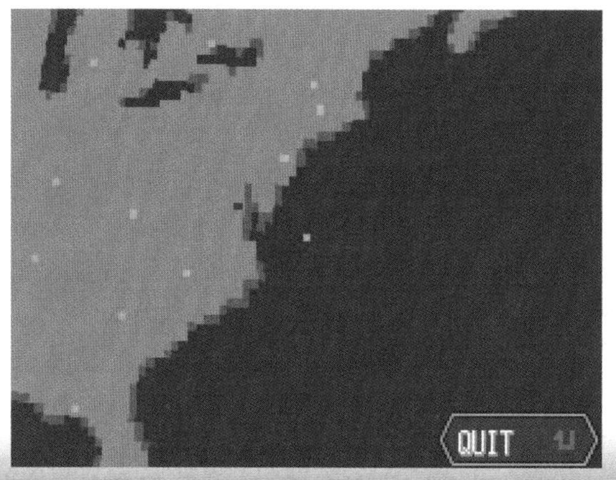

Tip

Register Friend Codes in your Pal Pad

In order to trade Pokémon and battle with a friend in the Wi-Fi Club, you first need to have registered each other's Friend Code in your Pal Pads. There are two ways to register Friend Codes.

How to register Friend Codes

1 Exchange using IR (Infrared Connection)

A method of trading using the Infrared Connection. With a few taps on the C-Gear, you can easily complete a trade.

2 Input manually

Open up your Pal Pad from the Key Items Case in your Bag and input your friend's name and his or her 12-digit Friend Code.

Route 20: Sunny Electric bulletin boards

Every gate has an electric bulletin board. When you want to read the announcements on the board, stand in front of it and press the A Button. The announcements on the electric bulletin board can be divided into three categories: weather, information, and breaking news. A total of five different types of announcement will be displayed on the board. The usefulness of these electric bulletin boards increases after entering the Hall of Fame, because information about mass outbreaks of rare Pokémon will begin to be announced.

Electric bulletin board info

Genre	Theme	Content
Weather	Date and Weather	When you go from a city with a gate to another city, information about the weather on that route will be displayed.
Information	Regional Information	Information about the place you are heading will be displayed, matching your progress in the story.
	Advertisements	Advertisements for the Poké Mart and Shopping Mall Nine are shown.
	Mass Outbreaks of Pokémon (after entering the Hall of Fame)	After entering the Hall of Fame, a mass outbreak—a large group of Pokémon appearing all at once—will occur somewhere once a day. Information about the mass outbreak location will be displayed.
Breaking News	News Bulletins	Defeat the Gym Leaders or the Champion through the course of the story, and that information will be shown here.

TV Shows

Cheren, I've heard that you traveled all over the Unova region.

You'll often find TVs inside houses. Stand in front of a TV and press the A Button to watch whatever's on! There are three categories of TV shows: shows about celebrities, shows about battles, and variety shows. So, learn more about the Gym Leaders, find out the latest about moves and items, and learn a wide variety of other useful information by watching TV.

TV Programs and their content

Program Genre	Content
Celebrity	Nancy and Chris appear in these programs. Watch shows such as "Pokémon Idol" and "Pokémon Idol Chat," and learn a bit more about the various Gym Leaders.
Battle	In the show "Moves for Living," you can learn detailed information about moves. In the "What's That?" show, you can learn a lot about items. You can learn a lot of new stuff, so don't miss these shows if you're into Pokémon battles.
Variety	A variety of unique shows are shown, such as "Personality Assessment and Horoscope," "PokéSports Spectacular," "The Pokémon Whisperer," and "PokéQuiz."

Pokémon Horoscopes

On the TV show "Personality Assessment and Horoscope," you can learn about the horoscope in the Unova region that corresponds with the month you were born. You can also learn about the lucky item for your horoscope.

Time and Seasons in Unova

Some Pokémon will only appear during certain seasons

The Unova region has four seasons: spring, summer, autumn, and winter. A season in Unova goes by at the beginning of every month in real time. Along with a change in season, the scenery across Unova will change. For example, the water level in the Castelia Sewers will change and snow will accumulate on Twist Mountain. Furthermore, time in the Unova region moves at the same speed as actual time, and each day has periods of morning, evening, night, and late night. The length of these times of day changes with the season.

Changes to the scenery in each season (Route 1)

Spring

Pink flower petals dance through the sky. Young buds are sprouting on the green trees.

Summer

The leaves of the trees have turned a dark, summery green, and yellow flowers dance through the sky.

Autumn

Autumn comes to the routes, as leaves float through the sky and the trees show brilliant autumn colors.

Winter

The ground turns white as if it has been covered in frost. The color of the ground fades, and dried leaves blow through the sky, so everything feels extra wintry.

Changes in time and the seasons

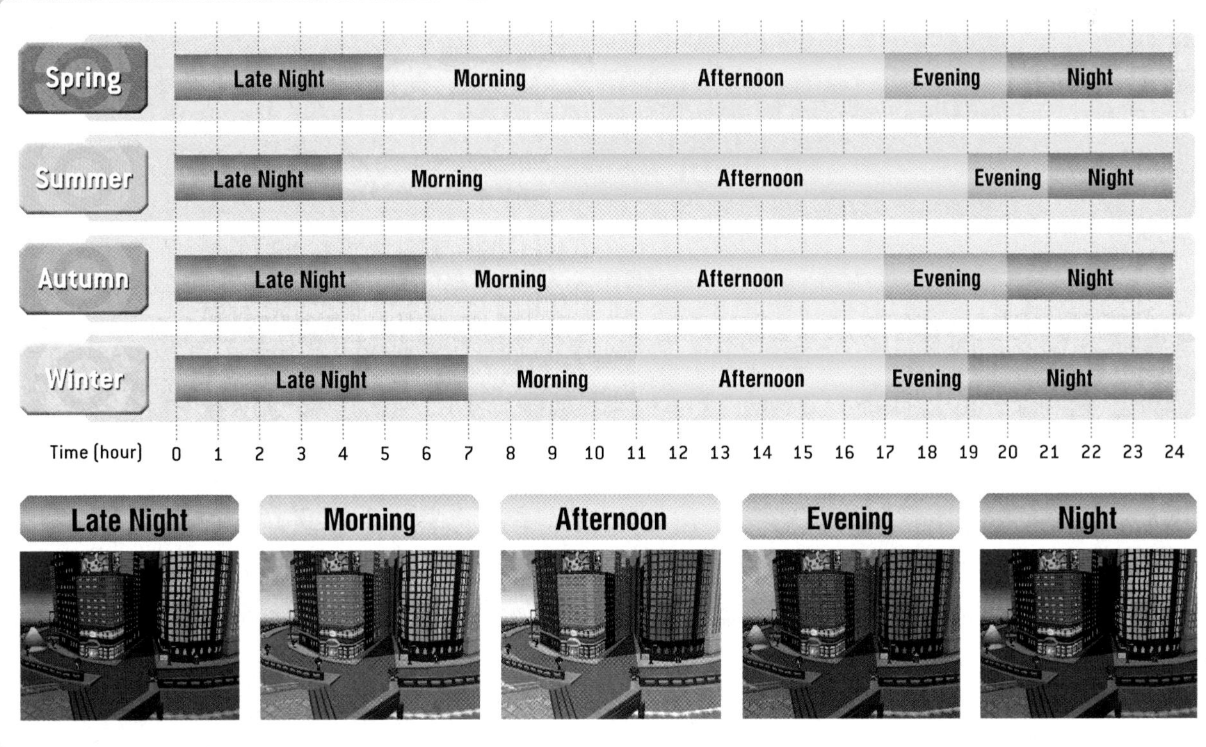

Unova Link

Unova Link enhances the *Pokémon Black Version 2* or *Pokémon White Version 2* experience by revealing deeper parts of the game. Select it from the main menu.

Unova Link ① Key System

The Key System uses Keys obtained through gameplay to change various parts of the game. Send your Keys to other players with IR (Infrared Connection). You can only send Keys you've obtained on your own, not Keys received from other players.

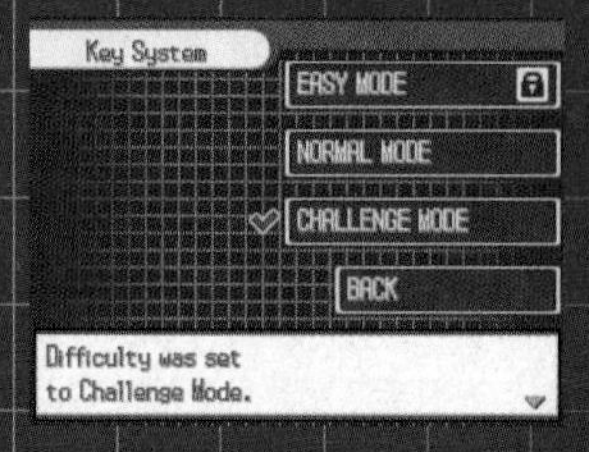

What the Key System can do

Set Difficulty

The difficulty level of *Pokémon Black Version 2* or *Pokémon White Version 2* can be set to one of three levels to adjust for the skill level of the player. Difficulty can even be changed after you've progressed through your adventure.

Easy Mode

This is a difficulty level for beginners. It makes Pokémon battles easier.

- Key needed and how to get it:

Easy Key
Get by entering the Hall of Fame in *Pokémon White Version 2*

Normal Mode

This difficulty level is for people who've played Pokémon before. It's the default difficulty level.

Challenge Mode

This is a difficulty level for advanced players. Battles become more difficult.

- Key needed and how to get it:

Challenge Key
Get by entering the Hall of Fame in *Pokémon Black Version 2*

Change City

You can switch between Black City and White Forest. This makes White Forest appear in *Pokémon Black Version 2* and Black City appear in *Pokémon White Version 2*.

Black City

This city appears in *Pokémon Black Version 2*. If you have the Tower Key, you can make this city appear in *Pokémon White Version 2* as well.

- Key needed and how to get it:

Tower Key
Obtained once you get past Area 5 in *Pokémon Black Version 2*'s Black Tower

White Forest

This city appears in *Pokémon White Version 2*. If you have the Treehollow Key, you can make this city appear in *Pokémon Black Version 2* as well.

- Key needed and how to get it:

Treehollow Key
Obtained once you get past Area 5 in *Pokémon White Version 2*'s White Treehollow

Mystery Door

This system is for catching Registeel and Regice. If you receive the Iron Key and the Iceberg Key, you can catch both.

Iron Chamber

If you have the Iron Key, you can go to the Iron Chamber and catch Registeel.

- Key needed and how to get it:

Iron Key
Get by catching Regirock in *Pokémon Black Version 2*

Iceberg Chamber

If you have the Iceberg Key, you can go to the Iceberg Chamber and catch Regice.

- Key needed and how to get it:

Iceberg Key
Get by catching Regirock in *Pokémon White Version 2*

Unova Link ② Memory Link

Memory Link is a system that lets you link to a saved game file from *Pokémon Black Version* and *Pokémon White Version* and see what happened in the two years between the previous games and *Pokémon Black Version 2* and *Pokémon White Version 2*. Link to the saved game file in one of two ways: DS Wireless Communications or Nintendo Wi-Fi Connection. You can link to a saved game file at any time during either adventure.

Were the words of the Pokémon in Accumula Town really true?

List of Memory Link events

Memory Link	Where	Content	How far you need to have played in *Pokémon Black Version* or *Pokémon White Version* to see the Memory Link event
A TRIPLE TEAM (p. 319)	Striaton City	Why the Striaton City Gym Leaders, Cilan, Cress, and Chili, closed the Gym...	Must have a Gym Badge
DIFFERENT BONES AND DREAMS (p. 313)	Nacrene City	Why was Clay Tunnel made? Lenora and Burgh are key.	Must have five Gym Badges
HEARTS' DESIRE (p. 304)	Icirrus City	Why did Brycen resign as Gym Leader and become a Pokéstar Studios actor? The shocking truth is...	Must have seen the end credits
A NEW LIGHT (p. 265)	Opelucid City	The story of how Drayden met Iris, the Champion, during his travels around the world.	Must have eight Gym Badges
TAKING IT TO THE NEXT LEVEL (p. 171)	Mistralton City	The reason that the always-cool Elesa changed her hair color. An unexpected facet of her personality is also revealed.	Must have six Gym Badges
WHITE AND BLACK (p. 150)	Driftveil City	A former member of Team Plasma, which was supposed to have disbanded, worries about whether he should go back. And N makes a decision.	Must have seen the end credits
FAREWELL, BELOVED SISTER (p. 136)	Nimbasa City's Musical Theater	The owner of the Musical Theater is handed a Prop Case someone left behind.	Must have the Prop Case
MEETING FRIENDS, SAYING GOOD-BYE (p. 83)	Aspertia City's Pokémon Center / anyone in the Unova region	The truth behind the appearance of Pokémon that were trained by N appearing in the Unova region.	Must have seen the end credits
(p. 313)	Nacrene City	Loblolly has become a Décor designer so famous, she has rabid fans.	Help Loblolly pick Décor
(p. 332)	Nuvema Town	The hero (heroine) of *Pokémon Black Version* or *Pokémon White Version*'s room is decorated with award certificates and trophies.	Obtain award certificates or trophies
(p. 332)	Nuvema Town	The name on the sign in front of the hero (heroine) of *Pokémon Black Version* or *Pokémon White Version*'s house is changed to that player's name.	—
(p. 327)	Route 1	After entering the Hall of Fame, you can challenge Bianca to a Pokémon battle.	Must have seen the end credits
(p. 260)	Route 5	After entering the Hall of Fame, you can challenge Cheren to a Pokémon battle.	Must have seen the end credits

Unova Link ③ NINTENDO 3DS LINK

NINTENDO 3DS LINK brings over Pokémon and items from the Nintendo 3DS download software *Pokémon Dream Radar*. Insert *Pokémon Black Version 2* or *Pokémon White Version 2* into your Nintendo 3DS system, and when you receive the research data that was sent, the Pokémon will be transferred.

Key Pokémon that can be brought from *Pokémon Dream Radar*

Tornadus
Therian Forme

Landorus
Therian Forme

Thundurus
Therian Forme

Nintendo 3DS game *Pokémon Dream Radar*

Pokémon DREAM RADAR

Catch the Pokémon found in a place called the Interdream Zone in this virtual shooting game. Fire at the Dream Clouds that float around in this space to find hiding Pokémon or discover items.

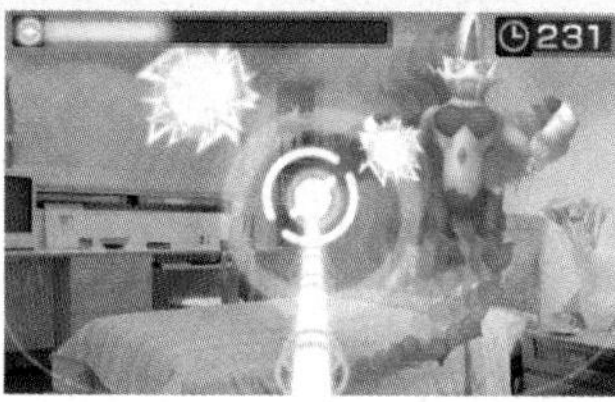

Game Information

Pokémon Dream Radar

- Publisher: The Pokémon Company
- Distributor: Nintendo
- Developer: Creatures Inc./ GAME FREAK inc.
- Platform: Nintendo 3DS
- Genre: Virtual Shooting
- Players: 1
- Connectivity: None
- Release Date: October 7, 2012 (Sunday)
- Rating: E

Professor Burnet

How to purchase this download software at the Nintendo eShop

Pokémon Dream Radar is only available as download software. It can be purchased when a Nintendo 3DS system is connected to the Internet and accesses the Nintendo eShop.

On the Nintendo 3DS HOME Menu, select Nintendo eShop.

You can search for this software by entering the keyword "Pokemon" into the search field. Tap "Purchase" on the purchase confirmation screen to buy the software.

When the download is complete, the software will be added to the HOME Menu.

How to play *Pokémon Dream Radar* Three Phases

Pokémon Dream Radar takes place in the Interdream Zone. The player is a member of a research lab, searching for Pokémon at the request of Professor Burnet. She is researching the Interdream Zone. The game is divided into three phases: a search phase, a battle phase, and an upgrade phase.

How *Pokémon Dream Radar* works

Search Phase

Shoot at Dream Clouds to search for Pokémon.

In this phase, you shoot a Beam at Dream Clouds. Then you collect the Pokémon, items, or balls of energy called Dream Orbs that come out of the clouds by shooting the Beam at them. Use Dream Orbs you collected by hitting them with the Beam to power up your equipment in the upgrade phase.

Battle Phase

Keep hitting the Pokémon with the Beam to catch it.

You catch Pokémon in this phase. Continue to hit the Pokémon with the Beam as it moves around. You can catch the Pokémon by hitting it with the Beam until the gauge in the upper left of the screen is full. If your time runs out, the Pokémon will get away.

Upgrade Phase

Prepare for your next search by upgrading your device.

In this phase, you upgrade your device. Use Dream Orbs to power up your Beam and make it easier to catch Pokémon. If you enhance your Visoscope, you can find more Dream Clouds. Also, as you gather Dream Orbs, more extensions will be developed for your device.

Items developed in the development lab

Items Developed	Dream Orbs Needed				Explanation
	Lv. 2	Lv. 3	Lv. 4	Lv. MAX	
Beam Upgrade	100	500	1,000	1,500	Raises the level of the Beam. This makes it easier to catch Pokémon.
Energy Upgrade	100	500	1,000	1,500	Raises the level of the Energy Pack. This increases the length of time you have to catch Pokémon.
Scope Upgrade	100	500	1,000	1,500	This increases the level of the Visoscope. The number of Dream Clouds you can find will go up.
Vortex Charge	100	-	-	-	Creates a vortex that pulls Pokémon to a place where they're easy to catch.
Dragnet Charge	50	-	-	-	Creates a net that slows down the movements of Pokémon for a short time.
Energy Recharge	50	-	-	-	Restores the energy used when catching a Pokémon.

◆ When you install a Vortex Charge, Dragnet Charge, or Energy Recharge, the number of Dream Orbs needed is displayed.

Visoscope Levels

Lv.	Dream Clouds Maximum Number
1	10
2	15
3	20
4	25
MAX	30

Search extensions

Extension	Dream Orbs Needed	Extension Function	Conditions for Use
Basic Extension	0	A balanced searching device.	Available from the start.
Retrieval Extension	100	This search extension makes it easier to find Pokémon.	It can be used after you've gathered 200 or more Dream Orbs.
Eureka Extension α	0	The alpha version of an extension for finding the mystery Poké-mon.	It can be used after you've gathered 400 or more Dream Orbs.
Dowsing Extension	100	This search extension reacts to Pokémon that are holding some-thing.	It can be used after you've caught Tornadus and gathered 200 or more Dream Orbs.
Eureka Extension β	0	The beta version of an extension for finding the mystery Pokémon.	It can be used after you've caught Tornadus and gathered 1,000 or more Dream Orbs.
Eureka Extension γ	0	The gamma version of an extension for finding the mystery Poké-mon.	It can be used after you've caught Thundurus and gathered 1,500 or more Dream Orbs.
Simulator α	400	This simulator was created to research Tornadus's traits.	Available after Landorus has been caught.
Simulator β	600	This simulator was created to research Thundurus's traits.	Available after Landorus has been caught.
Simulator γ	800	This simulator was created to research Landorus's traits.	Available after Landorus has been caught.

How to play *Pokémon Dream Radar* — Valuable Pokémon and items await

Catch Therian Forme Tornadus, Thundurus, and Landorus while upgrading your device. You will come across many other precious Pokémon and items.

Catching Pokémon and getting items in *Pokémon Dream Radar*

At the start of the game

Pokémon that can be found

Drifloon

Swablu

Munna

Sigilyph

Riolu

Items that can be found	
Red Shard	PP Up
Blue Shard	Leppa Berry
Yellow Shard	Revive
Green Shard	

You can catch Therian Forme Tornadus.

After you catch Therian Forme Tornadus

Pokémon that can be found

Shuckle

Igglybuff

Items that can be found
Max Revive
Sun Stone
Moon Stone

You can catch Therian Forme Thundurus.

After you catch Therian Forme Thundurus

Pokémon that can be found

Staryu

Bronzor

Porygon

Ralts

Items that can be found
Fire Stone
Water Stone
Thunderstone
Leaf Stone

You can catch Therian Forme Landorus.

After you catch Therian Forme Landorus (beating the game)

Pokémon that can be found

Smoochum

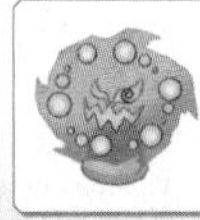
Spiritomb

Togepi

Rotom

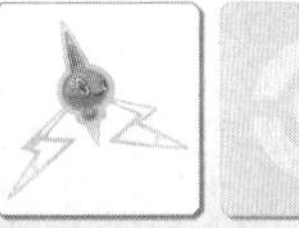

Items that can be found
Sacred Ash
Rare Candy

Items you can find with Simulator α

Item obtained by capturing Tornadus
Star Piece
Heart Scale
PP Up
Max Revive
Rare Candy
Life Orb

Items you can find with Simulator β

Item obtained by capturing Thundurus
Star Piece
Heart Scale
Rare Candy
Dawn Stone
King's Rock
Focus Sash

Items you can find with Simulator γ

Item obtained by capturing Landorus
Star Piece
Heart Scale
Rare Candy
Life Orb
Focus Sash
Eviolite

Pokémon Black Version 2 & Pokémon White Version 2: The Official Pokémon Unova Strategy Guide

Walkthrough

Walkthrough
Understanding Each Page

This walkthrough is mostly illustrated with the male main character from *Pokémon Black Version 2*, but the information applies equally to *Pokémon White Version 2* or either version of the game with the female main character.

Challenge the Gym Leaders of every city! Working together with your Pokémon is what makes you grow as a Trainer. As you and your Pokémon grow stronger, the world you know will expand!

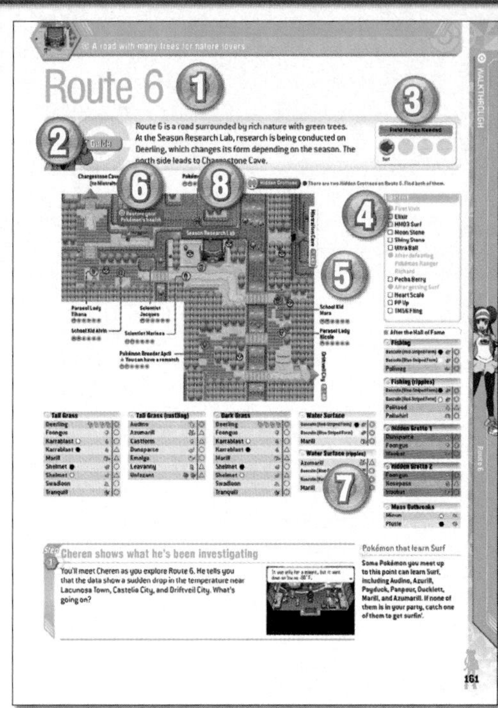

1 Location Name

2 Location Guide

Here's your guide to the special features of various locations!

3 Field Moves Needed

Check these icons to see what moves you need to access every area on the map and collect all the items.

 Cut
 Strength
 Surf
 Waterfall
 Dive
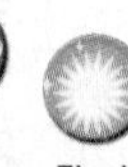  Flash

4 Items

This is your checklist of the items you can find by searching the area. At times, you must meet certain conditions to get an item, and those conditions are included. For cities and towns, you'll find the items sold by the lower clerks in the Poké Marts in Pokémon Centers.
Also listed are the items you can obtain in exchange for the BP you gain in the Battle Subway and in the PWT, along with the items that can be sold for great profit.

5 Trainers Waiting to Challenge You

Find out where you can encounter Pokémon Trainers who will challenge you if they spot you.
The Poké Balls beneath each Trainer's name indicate how many Pokémon that Trainer has in his or her party. Trainers who challenge you to a Triple Battle or Rotation Battle are also marked, as are those who can be challenged to rematches.

6 Restore Your Pokémon's Health

You'll sometimes find people in homes or places along routes that can restore your Pokémon's health. These locations are marked on each map. When Pokémon in your party are unwell, do your best to reach these spots and have your loyal Pokémon restored to full health.

7 Pokémon Encounters

See the Pokémon that appear in the area and the seasons in which they appear. This information is valuable in completing your Pokédex, and also comes in handy when trying to fill out the Habitat List. When there is a Hidden Grotto in the area, you'll be able to see which Pokémon appear there. Pokémon with N as the original Trainer are listed. (These Pokémon aren't displayed in the Habitat List, though. Neither are Pokémon appearing in Hidden Grottoes.)

● Pokémon Encounter Rate

◎	Frequent
○	Average
△	Rare
▲	Almost never

● Version Differences

⬢	Only appears in *Pokémon Black Version 2*
⬡	Only appears in *Pokémon White Version 2*

8 Hidden Grottoes

Hints will be displayed here if there are Hidden Grottoes in a particular location. If you press the A Button to investigate the entrance to a Hidden Grotto, you'll be able to enter it. You can find Pokémon and items inside Hidden Grottoes. Throw a Poké Ball to capture Pokémon there. These Pokémon have Hidden Abilities, so try hard to catch them when you can! After you capture a Pokémon in a Hidden Grotto, another will appear there

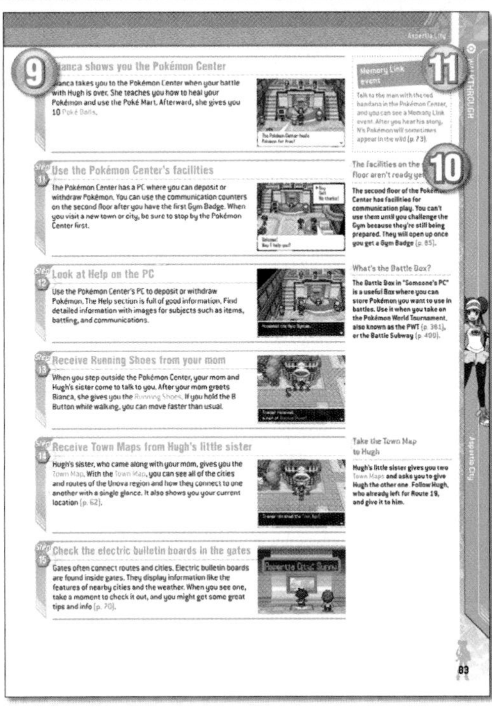

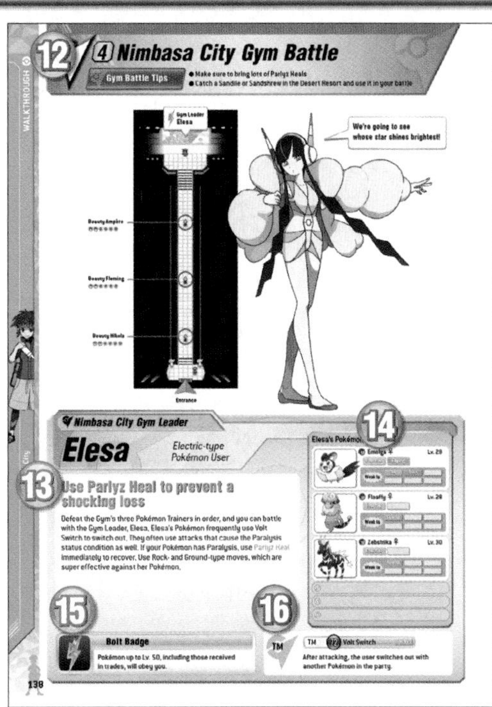

after a while, so be sure to revisit these locations. See the table of contents for an index of all the locations containing Hidden Grottoes.

9 Completion Guide

What do you need to move forward? Get step-by-step descriptions of key events in each city, route, or cave. If you follow these steps in order, you'll be able to complete the entire game! Combine this with the Recommended Route chart and your progress should be a breeze (p. 8).

 Extra Information

You want more hints? Get 'em right here! The info may include effective ways to use the items you receive or behind-the-scenes stories.

 Memory Link Activation Point

Using the Unova Link's Memory Link program, you may be able to witness link events that happened in various locations. Memory Link allows you to experience the events that occurred between the ending of *Pokémon Black Version* and *Pokémon White Version* and the beginning of *Pokémon Black Version 2* and *Pokémon White Version 2*. Don't miss out on using Memory Link to get the full story of the Unova region! A summary of Memory Link events can be found on p. 73.

 Gym Battle Preparation

A little preparation before attempting to challenge a Gym Leader will make it much easier to take home a win. The information in this section will help you prepare thoroughly. If at first you don't succeed, try, try again.

 Gym Battle Guide

Get some hints on the tricks of each Gym and the best ways to attack the weak points of each Gym Leader's Pokémon.

14 Gym Leader's Pokémon

Find out about the Pokémon that each Gym Leader will use in battle, including their weaknesses. This gives you the info you need to choose appropriate Pokémon and moves so you can target your opponent's weaknesses relentlessly!

 Gym Badge Received from the Gym Leader

Take a look at the Gym Badge you get for defeating a Gym Leader, plus the effects of the Gym Badge.

 TMs Received from the Gym Leader

Get an outline of the TMs you get for defeating Gym Leaders.

A city at the foot of high mountains where you can see all of Unova

Aspertia City

Aspertia City is located on the western edge of the Unova region. It's home to both you and your rival, Hugh. The Aspertia Outlook in the northern side of the city offers a fantastic view of the Unova region, spreading out to the north.

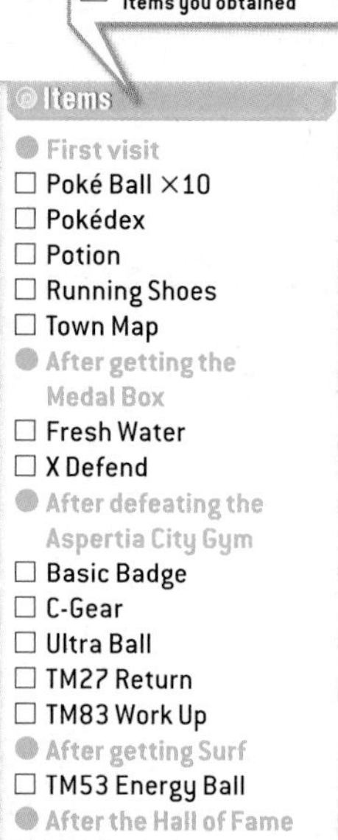

Items

- First visit
- ☐ Poké Ball ×10
- ☐ Pokédex
- ☐ Potion
- ☐ Running Shoes
- ☐ Town Map
- After getting the Medal Box
- ☐ Fresh Water
- ☐ X Defend
- After defeating the Aspertia City Gym
- ☐ Basic Badge
- ☐ C-Gear
- ☐ Ultra Ball
- ☐ TM27 Return
- ☐ TM83 Work Up
- After getting Surf
- ☐ TM53 Energy Ball
- After the Hall of Fame
- ☐ Max Revive

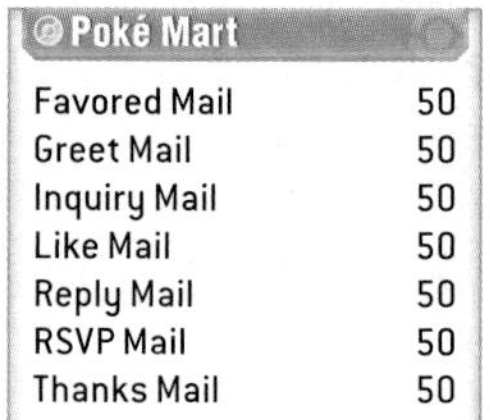

Poké Mart

Item	Price
Favored Mail	50
Greet Mail	50
Inquiry Mail	50
Like Mail	50
Reply Mail	50
RSVP Mail	50
Thanks Mail	50

Water Surface

Pokémon	Version	Rarity
Basculin (Blue-Striped Form)	○	◎
Basculin (Red-Striped Form)	●	◎

Water Surface (ripples)

Pokémon	Version	Rarity
Basculin (Blue-Striped Form)	●	◎
Basculin (Red-Striped Form)	○	◎

After the Hall of Fame

Fishing

Pokémon	Version	Rarity
Basculin (Blue-Striped Form)	○	◎
Basculin (Red-Striped Form)	●	◎
Goldeen		◎

Fishing (ripples)

Pokémon	Version	Rarity
Basculin (Blue-Striped Form)	●	◎
Basculin (Red-Striped Form)		◎
Goldeen		◎
Seaking		○

Step 1 Leave your room and answer your mom's questions

Walk from your room into the next, and your mom starts talking to you. She'll ask you if you want a Pokémon and a Pokédex, so answer "YES" to her questions to show your determination to go out on an adventure.

Do you want to have a Pokémon?
YES
NO

Your mom and Professor Juniper are old friends

At the end of the opening, there's a scene where your mom gets a call from Professor Juniper on the Xtransceiver. Professor Juniper and your mom are apparently old friends.

Step 2 Look for Bianca, Professor Juniper's assistant

Your mom tells you that Professor Juniper's assistant, a girl named Bianca, has come to meet you. Go out into the town and look for Bianca so you can get your Pokémon. You can tell it's her by her big hat.

The girl's name is Bianca. I was told you should look for a big, green hat!

Bianca appeared in *Pokémon Black Version* and *Pokémon White Version*

Bianca, who you meet in Aspertia City, went on an adventure with the main character of the previous game, *Pokémon Black Version* and *Pokémon White Version*. She has been working as Professor Juniper's assistant in the two years that have passed since her journey.

Check the TV in your room

TVs are placed in your room and in houses all over the region. Many different programs are shown on TV, like fun programs and programs that will help you during your adventure. If you see a TV during your adventure, be sure to check it out (p. 70)!

Check inside your Bag

Press the X Button to look in your Bag and check what's inside. The Bag already holds the Xtransceiver (p. 63) and a Pal Pad (p. 69). Both of them are very important items.

Search for Bianca with Hugh

Right after you leave your house, Hugh talks to you. He already has a Pokémon, but he wants a traveling partner. When you talk to him, he decides to help you look for Bianca.

Check your Trainer Card

Press the X Button and tap the player's name to look at your Trainer Card. There is a lot of information listed on the Trainer Card. Check it frequently (p. 57).

Meet Bianca at the Aspertia City Outlook

As you go toward the stairs to the Aspertia City Outlook, Hugh tells you he's sure that Bianca is there. From here, you go up alone and meet Bianca, who is wearing a big hat.

You can't go inside the Trainers' School yet

A Trainers' School is in the center of town, but you can't go inside until you have visited Floccesy Town (p. 90). Deep inside the Trainers' School is the Aspertia City Gym. Visit it later in your adventure.

Choose one of Bianca's Pokémon

Bianca asks if you'll help complete the Pokédex. After you accept this task, talk to her again. Bianca shows you a container with three Poké Balls inside. Choose one.

Save the Pokémon Center for later

You can't enter the Pokémon Center while walking around with Hugh and looking for Bianca. But you will be able to go inside after you receive a Pokémon and Pokédex from Bianca and battle Hugh.

You can receive only one Pokémon from Bianca

Receive a Pokémon from Bianca

After you receive a Pokémon from Bianca, you get the Pokédex. She tells you the Pokédex is a high-tech device that automatically registers the Pokémon you encounter (p. 54).

Nickname your Pokémon

Bianca asks if you want to nickname your Pokémon when you get it from her. Nicknaming your Pokémon with a name that has special meaning to you can make you feel even more attached to it. If you're not ready to nickname it yet, you can always name it later (p. 112).

Step 8 Hugh gets a Pokédex, too

As you walk down the stairs of the Aspertia City Outlook, Hugh starts talking. He asks Bianca if he can have a Pokédex, so he can learn about Pokémon and become stronger.

Hugh: Please give me
a Pokédex, too!

Be sure to save often

It's a good idea to save after Hugh receives the Pokédex from Bianca and before you battle with him. That way you get in the habit of saving often, such as before a big battle (p. 60).

Step 9 Your first Pokémon battle with Hugh

If you talk to Hugh or try to walk past him down the stairs, he will challenge you to a Pokémon battle. The battle takes place right after you receive your Pokémon, but its level is the same as Hugh's. Fight with everything you've got!

Hugh: Let's see how good
a Trainer you are!

The story continues even if you lose to Hugh

Usually, if all of the Pokémon in your party faint, you will be returned to the Pokémon Center. But even if you lose your first battle with Hugh, you won't be returned to the Pokémon Center, and your adventure will continue.

Battle with your rival, Hugh! 1

Hugh's Pokémon is a type your Pokémon is weak against, but it doesn't know any moves that are super effective against your Pokémon yet.

I raised this Pokémon from an Egg!

Hugh's Pokémon

If you chose Snivy:	If you chose Tepig:	If you chose Oshawott:
Tepig ♂ Lv. 5 — Fire	Oshawott ♂ Lv. 5 — Water	Snivy ♂ Lv. 5 — Grass
Weak to: Water, Ground, Rock	Weak to: Grass, Electric	Weak to: Fire, Ice, Poison, Flying, Bug

Step 10 Bianca shows you the Pokémon Center

Bianca takes you to the Pokémon Center when your battle with Hugh is over. She teaches you how to heal your Pokémon and use the Poké Mart. Afterward, she gives you 10 Poké Balls.

Memory Link event

Talk to the man with the red bandana in the Pokémon Center, and you can see a Memory Link event. After you hear his story, N's Pokémon will sometimes appear in the wild (p. 73).

Step 11 Use the Pokémon Center's facilities

The Pokémon Center has a PC where you can deposit or withdraw Pokémon. You can use the communication counters on the second floor after you have the first Gym Badge. When you visit a new town or city, be sure to stop by the Pokémon Center first.

The facilities on the second floor aren't ready yet!

The second floor of the Pokémon Center has facilities for communication play. You can't use them until you challenge the Gym because they're still being prepared. They will open up once you get a Gym Badge (p. 85).

Step 12 Look at Help on the PC

Use the Pokémon Center's PC to deposit or withdraw Pokémon. The Help section is full of good information. Find detailed information with images for subjects such as items, battling, and communications.

Accessed the Help System.

What's the Battle Box?

The Battle Box in "Someone's PC" is a useful Box where you can store Pokémon you want to use in battles. Use it when you take on the Pokémon World Tournament, also known as the PWT (p. 381), or the Battle Subway (p. 409).

Step 13 Receive Running Shoes from your mom

When you step outside the Pokémon Center, your mom and Hugh's sister come to talk to you. After your mom greets Bianca, she gives you the Running Shoes. If you hold the B Button while walking, you can move faster than usual.

Step 14 Receive Town Maps from Hugh's little sister

Hugh's sister, who came along with your mom, gives you the Town Map. With the Town Map, you can see all of the cities and routes of the Unova region and how they connect to one another with a single glance. It also shows you your current location (p. 62).

Trainer obtained the Town Map!

Take the Town Map to Hugh

Hugh's little sister gives you two Town Maps and asks you to give Hugh the other one. Follow Hugh, who already left for Route 19, and give it to him.

Step 15 Check the electric bulletin boards in the gates

Gates often connect routes and cities. Electric bulletin boards are found inside gates. They display information like the features of nearby cities and the weather. When you see one, take a moment to check it out, and you might get some great tips and info (p. 70).

Step 16 Follow Bianca to Route 19

When you're in front of the Pokémon Center, Bianca tells you she will show you how to catch Pokémon. After this, follow her to Route 19, which is right past the gate to the north (p. 88).

After obtaining the Medal Box — Visit the Trainers' School

When you visit the Trainers' School, the boy blocking the entrance moves to the left so you can go inside. Enter the Trainers' School, where the Gym Leader Cheren teaches. The Aspertia City Gym is deep inside.

After obtaining the Medal Box — Read about status conditions on the blackboard

Check the blackboard in the Trainers' School to learn about status conditions like Poison and Paralysis. Status conditions can have a big influence on how a battle turns out. Learn about what each one does (p. 42).

After obtaining the Medal Box — Use items in battle

The X Defend you get from talking to the boy in the Trainers' School raises Defense by 1 when it's used in battle. When you get items for battling, use them aggressively to turn the tide of battle in your favor.

After obtaining the Medal Box — Learn how to cancel evolution

A girl in the Trainers' School teaches you how to cancel evolution. Press the B Button during evolution to cancel. One reason to use this is if your Pokémon can learn powerful moves at a lower level.

After obtaining the Medal Box — Take on your first Gym battle!

At the back of the Trainers' School, you'll find the Aspertia City Gym. This is the first Gym you'll challenge in the Unova region. Restore your party Pokémon's HP in the Pokémon Center first. Then go into the Gym.

Cheren appeared in *Pokémon Black Version* and *Pokémon White Version*

Cheren, who you meet in Aspertia City, went on an adventure with the main character of the previous games, *Pokémon Black Version* and *Pokémon White Version*. In the two years since, he has attained real skill and became a Gym Leader.

Alder shows he has class

According to the woman in the Trainers' School, the original plan was to have Alder teach the class. Alder declined because he wanted to let a young person have the chance.

Learn type matchups

A boy in the Trainers' School teaches you that Normal-type Pokémon are weak to Fighting-type moves. To be effective in battle, you need to learn about type matchups (p. 38).

Clyde has a gift for you

Clyde stands near the entrance to the Gym in every city and always gives you Fresh Water before you challenge the Gym. It restores the HP of one Pokémon by 50 points. If your Pokémon's HP gets low during battle, use Fresh Water to restore it.

1 Aspertia City Gym Battle

Gym Battle Tips

- Make sure to bring lots of Potions
- Catching Riolu in Floccesy Ranch and battling with it will give you an advantage

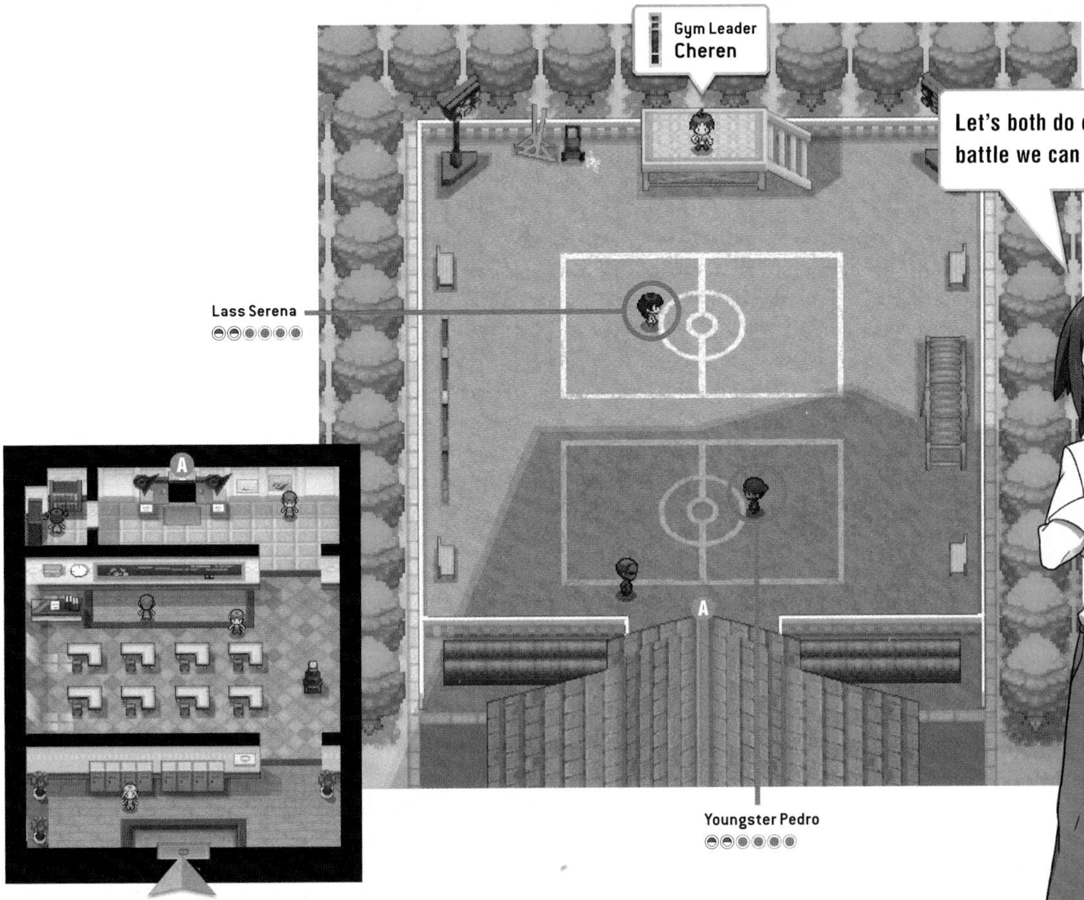

Gym Leader Cheren

Let's both do our best and have a battle we can be proud of!

Lass Serena

Youngster Pedro

Entrance

Aspertia City Gym Leader

Cheren

Normal-type Pokémon User

Use moves that deal massive damage to defeat him quickly

Defeat both Pokémon Trainers, and you can battle with the Gym Leader, Cheren. Both of Cheren's Pokémon are Normal type, so they are weak to Fighting-type moves. They use the move Work Up, which raises Attack and Sp. Atk, so defeat them quickly before your Pokémon is hit with a powerful attack. If you have a Riolu that knows the move Force Palm, you can attack their weak points for massive damage.

Cheren's Pokémon

Pokémon	Lv.	Type	Weak to
Patrat ♂	Lv. 11	Normal	Fighting
Lillipup ♂	Lv. 13	Normal	Fighting

Basic Badge

Pokémon up to Lv. 20, including those received in trades, will obey you.

TM 83 Work Up (Normal)

Raises the user's Attack and Sp. Atk by 1.

Bianca is waiting outside the Gym

Bianca was waiting outside the Gym, and she will approach you when you emerge victorious from the battle with Gym Leader Cheren. Bianca gives you TM27 Return, in honor of your victory.

This is from me!
It's the TM for the move Return.

Talk to the Gym Trainers after your Gym battle victory

After you defeat Cheren, talk to the other Trainers in the Gym. They talk about different things after you defeat the Gym Leader, so listen to what they each have to say.

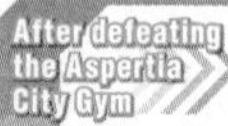

Talk to Professor Juniper

Cheren comes out of the Gym, and Cheren, Bianca, and Professor Juniper's info is registered on the Xtransceiver. Right after that, the Xtransceiver rings. It's Professor Juniper. It's your first conversation with the Professor.

Repel can be purchased now

After you've obtained the Aspertia City Gym Badge, you can buy Repel. Repel prevents wild Pokémon that are weaker than the Pokémon at the front of your party from appearing for 100 steps after its use.

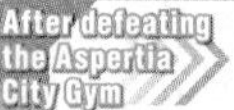

Get the most out of the Xtransceiver

Call Professor Juniper with the Xtransceiver to check how complete your Pokédex is. Or you can call Bianca and have her tell you how the friendship between you and a Pokémon is, or Cheren to have him tell you about your Pokémon's Abilities and type matchups (p. 38).

Repel can be used continuously

If you have another Repel in your Bag when you use Repel, a convenient feature asks you if you want to use another when the current one runs out. The same goes for Super Repel and Max Repel.

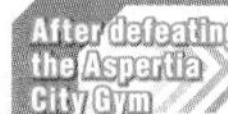

Use the C-Gear like a pro

After Hugh enters the Gym, Bianca gives you a C-Gear. The C-Gear is a device that makes it easy to use communication features such as Infrared Connection, DS Wireless Communications, and Nintendo Wi-Fi Connection. It's displayed on the Touch Screen.

Trainer obtained the C-Gear!

Tap "?" to read Help

Turn on the C-Gear and tap the question mark in the lower right of the screen to read the Help for the C-Gear. There is a detailed explanation of the function of each button on the C-Gear, so check it out if there's something you want to know.

After defeating the Aspertia City Gym — The second floor of the Pokémon Center opens

The second floor of the Pokémon Center, which was closed for preparation, is now open. You can now use the Union Room for wireless play, as well as the Wi-Fi Club and the Global Terminal, which use Nintendo Wi-Fi Connection (p. 69).

Welcome to the Pokémon Wireless Club Union Room.

A woman in the house has a gift for you

Talk to the woman in the house to the south of the gate after you get the Aspertia City Gym Badge. She's on the second floor, and she'll give you an Ultra Ball. She won't give it to you before you win at the Gym, so go get the item after your victory.

After defeating the Aspertia City Gym — Register your location on Geonet

The globe on the right side of the second floor, Geonet, is a high-tech device that lets you register where you live. Check it after trading Pokémon on the GTS and you'll see the home locations of the people you traded Pokémon with.

After defeating the Aspertia City Gym — Head for Floccesy Town and the next Gym

Bianca tells you there is also a Pokémon Gym in Virbank City, which is past Floccesy Town. That's your next objective. Floccesy Town is to the east, past Route 19 (p. 88).

Pokédex Completed — An award certificate decorates your wall

After completing the Pokédex, talk to the Game Director in the GAME FREAK building in Castelia City. You'll receive a sharp-looking award certificate that will decorate the wall on your room. You'll want to get both award certificates: one for the Unova Pokédex and one for the National Pokédex.

Collect items after getting Surf

Get HM03 Surf from Cheren on Route 6 before you come back here to collect items. Go east on the water surface to the south of your house, and you'll be able to scoop up some items.

Route 19

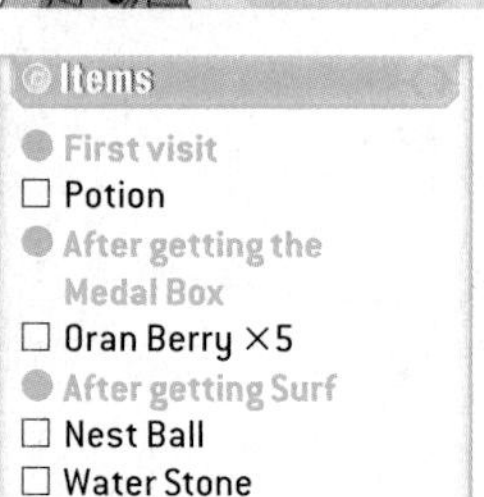

Route 19 is a short road that connects Aspertia City and Floccesy Town. It's located at the base of a mountain, so the north side of the route is lined with cliffs. Walk through the tall grass, and you'll encounter wild Pokémon.

Items

- First visit
- ☐ Potion
- After getting the Medal Box
- ☐ Oran Berry ×5
- After getting Surf
- ☐ Nest Ball
- ☐ Water Stone

Tall Grass	
Patrat	◎
Purrloin	◎

Tall Grass (rustling)	
Patrat	◎

Water Surface	
Basculin (Blue-Striped Form) ⬡	◎
Basculin (Red-Striped Form) ⬢	◎

Water Surface (ripples)	
Basculin (Blue-Striped Form) ⬢	◎
Basculin (Red-Striped Form) ⬡	◎

■ After entering the Hall of Fame

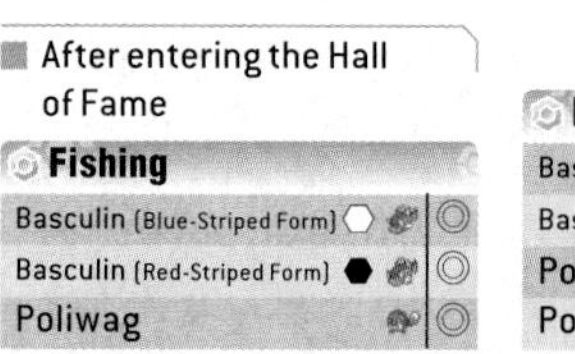

Fishing	
Basculin (Blue-Striped Form) ⬡	◎
Basculin (Red-Striped Form) ⬢	◎
Poliwag	◎

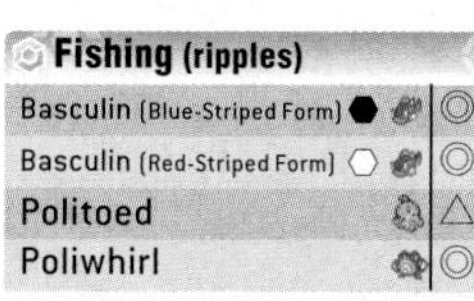

Fishing (ripples)	
Basculin (Blue-Striped Form) ⬢	◎
Basculin (Red-Striped Form) ⬡	◎
Politoed	△
Poliwhirl	◎

Step 1 Learn how to catch Pokémon

Bianca is waiting for you on Route 19. She'll demonstrate how to catch wild Pokémon by catching a wild Purrloin that is hiding in the tall grass. She also teaches you how to register it in the Pokédex (p. 54).

Use your Pokémon's moves to lower the HP of the Pokémon you want to catch.

Critical captures

Sometimes a Pokémon will be caught after you throw a Poké Ball and it rocks only once. This is called a critical capture. The more Pokémon you catch, the more often this phenomenon will occur (p. 29).

Step 2 Walk through the tall grass, and you'll encounter wild Pokémon

Use the Poké Ball that you received from Bianca in Aspertia City to catch a wild Pokémon in the tall grass. The Pokémon you caught will join your party, becoming a helpful partner on your adventure.

A wild Patrat appeared!

Heal your Pokémon in Aspertia City

When your Pokémon's HP drops from battles with wild Pokémon, go back to Aspertia City. Visit the Pokémon Center or go to your house and talk to your mom to fully restore your Pokémon's HP and PP.

Step 3 Check Trainer Tips signs

There's a Trainer Tips sign near the water on Route 19. Signs like this have lots of great information that will help you on your adventure. You'll find signs throughout the Unova region. When you see one, make sure to stop and read it!

Make an effort to talk to all the people you meet during your journey!

Check the sign to earn a Medal

After receiving the Medal Box, you can receive Medals by fulfilling various conditions (p. 448). Read the Trainer Tips sign, and you'll learn that there are two types of Medals you can get by reading lots of Trainer Tips signs.

Step 4 Collect items as you go

You'll find useful items throughout the Unova region, whether on various routes, inside caves, or elsewhere. Take time to explore every corner and gather all the items. Some items are in hard-to-reach locations that require the use of HMs.

Trainer found a Potion!

Jump down from the ledge for a shortcut

Head east along Route 19, and you'll come across a ledge. When traveling to Floccesy Town from Aspertia City, you can jump down from this ledge to skip the tall grass and reach your destination more quickly.

Step 5 Alder calls to you

While on your way to Floccesy Town, a man with red hair will call down to you from atop the northern cliff. He is named Alder and says he'll help train your Pokémon. He then leaves for Floccesy Town.

My name is Alder!

Two years ago, Alder was the Champion

Alder awaited the challenges of Trainers as the Unova region Champion two years ago. He has since retired to his residence in Floccesy Town.

Step 6 Head east for Floccesy Town

In order to reach the top of the cliff Alder was standing upon, you'll need the HM Surf. You can't reach the top just yet, so keep on heading east. Go after Alder and enter Floccesy Town (p. 90).

After obtaining the Medal Box — Receive Oran Berries from Alder

Enter Route 19 from Floccesy Town and Alder will call down to you from atop the northern cliff. Alder will descend from the cliff and give you some words of encouragement for your Aspertia City Gym battle, along with five Oran Berries.

Give Pokémon a Berry to hold

Give your Pokémon an Oran Berry, and it will recover 10 HP when its HP is reduced to half or less during battle. Unlike a Potion, you don't need to spend a turn to use it, so giving your Pokémon an Oran Berry to hold in battle can be a nice helping hand.

Return to Aspertia City

You'll learn from Alder that the Aspertia City Gym Leader has arrived, which means you can go challenge the Gym. Head west on Route 19 to return to Aspertia City (p. 80).

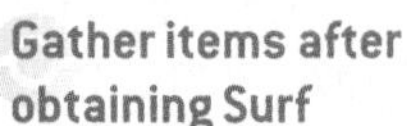

Gather items after obtaining Surf

Get HM03 Surf from Cheren on Route 6 before you come back here to collect items. There are two items that can only be obtained by traveling across the water.

The town is famous for a clock tower that tells of the town's beginnings

Floccesy Town

In little Floccesy Town, you can find Alder's house and a Pokémon Center. In the center of town, you'll also find the clock tower, for which the town is famous. Pledge Grove, which has a strong connection with the Mythical Pokémon Keldeo, is located at the north end of town.

Field Moves Needed

Alder's House

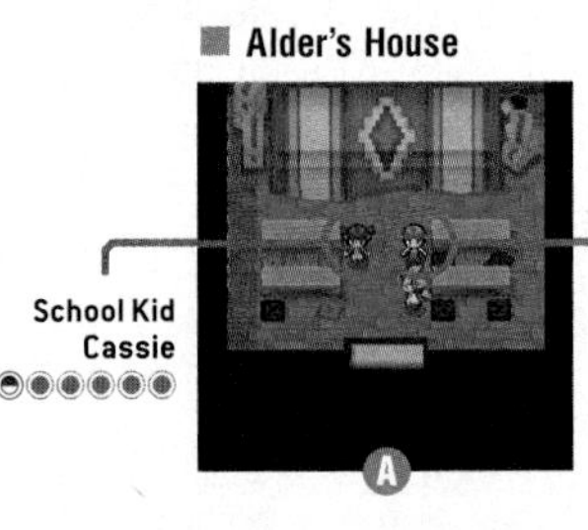

Items

- First visit
- ☐ Potion
- After visiting Floccesy Ranch
- ☐ Medal Box
- ☐ X Speed

Poké Mart (Lower Clerk)

Item	Price
Favored Mail	50
Greet Mail	50
Inquiry Mail	50
Like Mail	50
Reply Mail	50
RSVP Mail	50
Thanks Mail	50

Floccesy Town

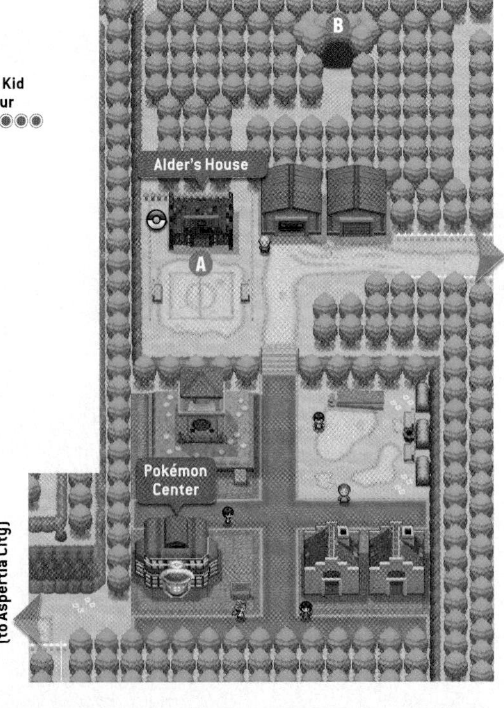

Pledge Grove

Step 1 Go after your rival and head to Route 20

When you run into Alder north of town, he'll ask you why you have two Town Maps. After hearing your explanation, he'll tell you that your rival was seen on Route 20. Go after your rival and head to Route 20 (p. 92).

You can't enter Alder's house at first

When you first visit Floccesy Town, Alder will be blocking the entrance to his house. You'll be able to enter his house after your visit to Floccesy Ranch, so don't worry about it right now.

After visiting Floccesy Ranch — Keep type matchups in mind when battling

After returning from Floccesy Ranch, you'll have to battle against Alder's students. Alder's students will use different Pokémon, depending on which Pokémon you chose at the beginning of your adventure. Keep type matchups in mind during this battle and switch out Pokémon as necessary.

After visiting Floccesy Ranch — Receive a Medal Box from Mr. Medal

After leaving Alder's house, you can receive a Medal Box from a man called Mr. Medal. With the Medal Box, you can participate in the Medal Rally competition, as well as obtain Medals during your adventure by fulfilling various conditions (p. 59).

After visiting Floccesy Ranch — Visit the Pokémon Center to start collecting Medals

The Medal Rally is a competition in which participants collect as many Medals as they can. Mr. Medal will give you Medals for which you've fulfilled the conditions. Not only that, but he'll give you Hint Medals, which have hints written on them about how to obtain proper Medals (p. 59).

Aim for 50 Medals

In the Medal Rally, you're assigned a Rank based on the number of Medals you've obtained. Aim for 50 Medals to advance your first Rank. There are 255 Medals in total to collect.

After visiting Floccesy Ranch — Return to Aspertia City for a Gym Battle

After Mr. Medal leaves, Alder shows up to inform you that the Aspertia City Gym Leader has arrived. It's time for your first Gym Battle! Take Route 19 to return to Aspertia City (p. 80).

After defeating the Aspertia City Gym — Bianca upgrades your Pokédex

On your way to Route 20, Bianca will catch up with you. She'll upgrade your Pokédex to add the Habitat List function (p. 55). Open up your Pokédex and take a look at this new function.

Complete the Habitat List

The Habitat List is a useful function that records the different wild Pokémon that appear in a location, such as on a route or in a cave. When you meet all of the possible Pokémon in a given a location, you'll get a stamp.

After defeating the Aspertia City Gym » Take Route 20 to go to Virbank City

Virbank City is located on the eastern end of Route 20. Up until now, a Hiker was blocking the road, but with your newly acquired Gym Badge in hand, you should be able to head on through toward Route 20.

When Keldeo is in your party » Keldeo can change Forms

With Keldeo in your party, head to the rock with the deeply cut marks on it inside Pledge Grove. Inspect the rock, and Keldeo will learn Secret Sword. As long as Keldeo knows this move, it will be in its Resolute Form.

About the special Pokémon, Keldeo

Keldeo is a Mythical Pokémon that can be received as a gift during special promotions. Its high Sp. Atk stat is one of its characteristics. Teach it special moves for maximum effectiveness.

In autumn, fallen leaves accumulate and hide the ground beneath

Route 20

Route 20 is a road that connects Floccesy Town and Virbank City. A river runs from the south all the way to Floccesy Ranch in the north. In autumn, fallen leaves cover the ground, changing the scenery dramatically.

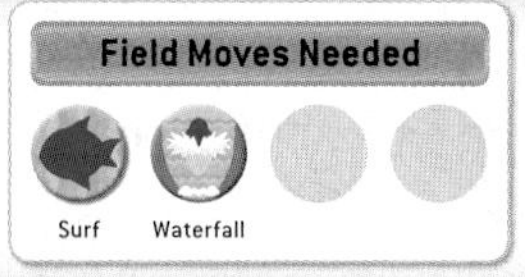

Spring Autumn Winter

Tall Grass	
Patrat	○
Pidove	○
Purrloin	○
Sewaddle	◎
Sunkern	△

Tall Grass (rustling)	
Audino	◎
Dunsparce	○

Dark Grass	
Patrat	○
Pidove	○
Purrloin	○
Sewaddle	○
Sunkern	△
Venipede	○

Mass Outbreaks	
Mr. Mime	⬡
Sudowoodo	⬢

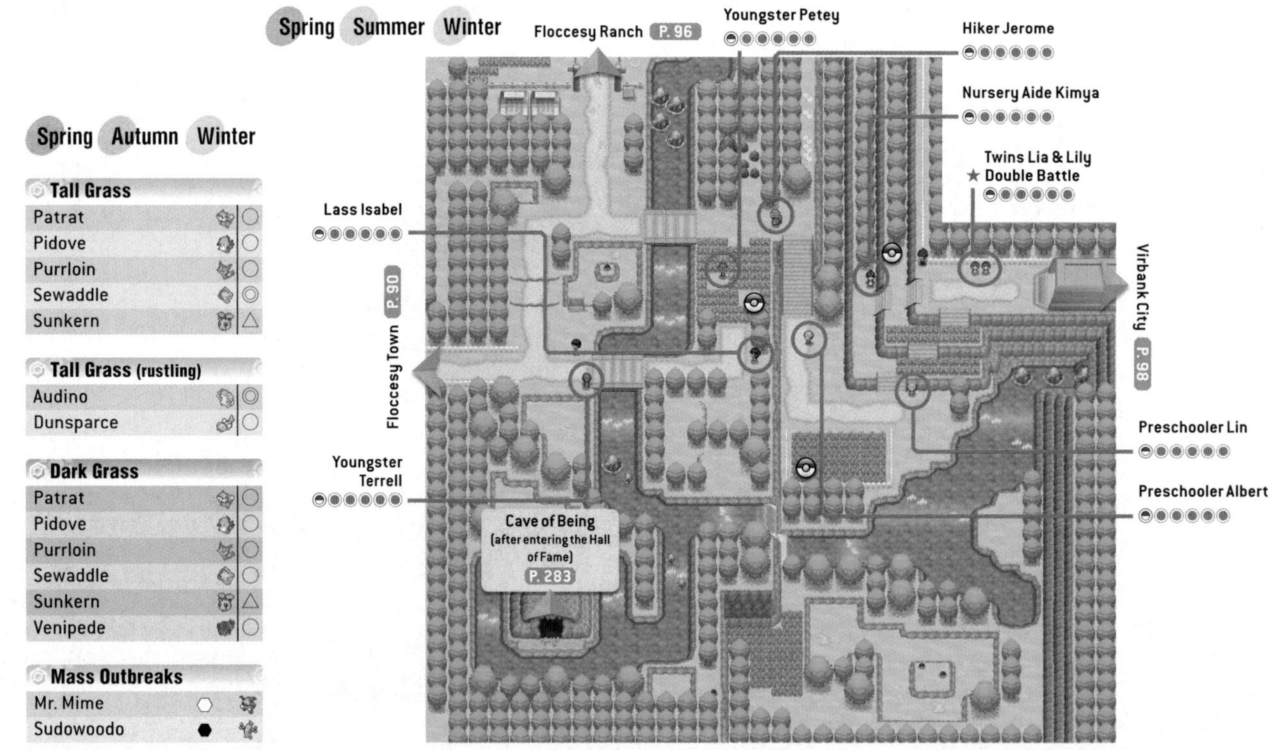

Items

- First visit
- ☐ Parlyz Heal
- ☐ Poké Ball (only in autumn)
- After defeating the Aspertia City Gym
- ☐ Antidote
- ☐ Dire Hit
- ☐ Great Ball ×3
- ☐ Pecha Berry ×3
- After getting Surf
- ☐ Max Revive (only in autumn)
- ☐ Rare Candy (only in autumn)
- After defeating Pokémon Ranger Leaf
- ☐ Sitrus Berry (only in autumn)
- After defeating Pokémon Ranger Bret
- ☐ Leppa Berry (only in autumn)
- After defeating Pokémon Ranger Malory
- ☐ Leppa Berry (only in autumn)
- After getting Waterfall
- ☐ Sticky Barb (only in autumn)
- After defeating Pokémon Ranger Naoko
- ☐ Sitrus Berry (only in autumn)

Sunkern
Grass
ABILITIES
● Chlorophyll
● Solar Power

Azurill
Normal
ABILITIES
● Thick Fat
● Huge Power

Venipede
Bug / Poison
ABILITIES
● Poison Point
● Swarm

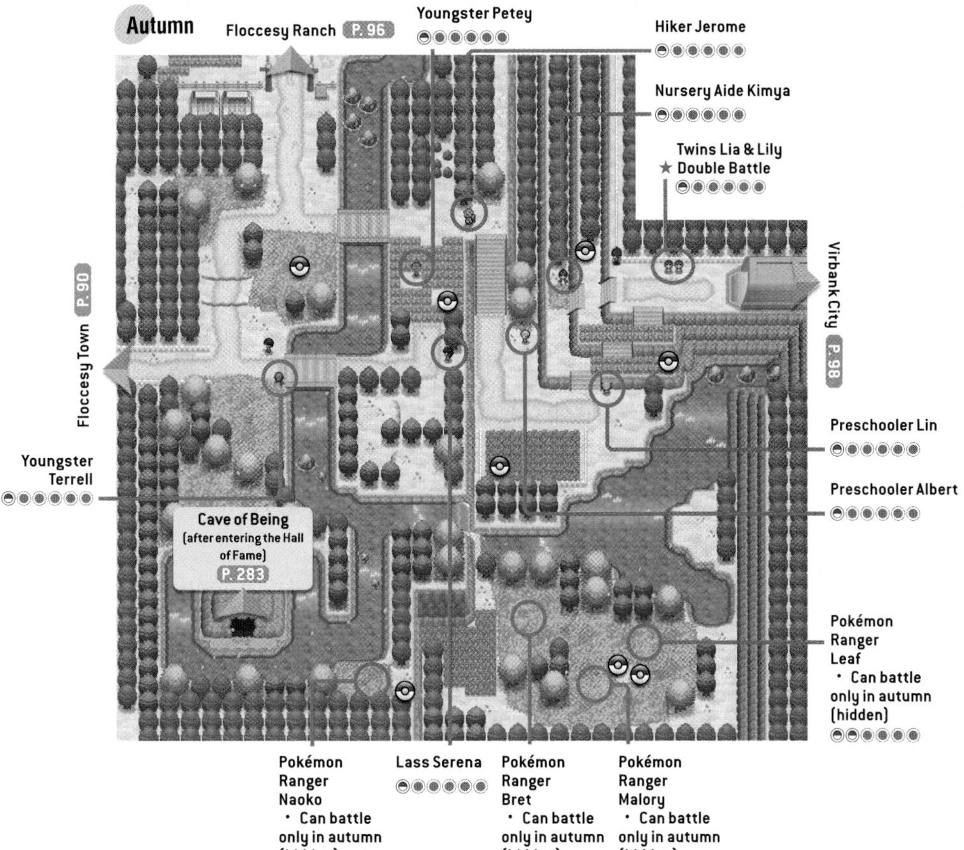

Summer

Tall Grass

Pokémon	Rarity
Patrat	○
Pidove	△
Purrloin	○
Sewaddle	◎
Sunkern	○

Tall Grass (rustling)

Pokémon	Rarity
Audino	◎
Dunsparce	○

Dark Grass

Pokémon	Rarity
Patrat	○
Pidove	△
Purrloin	○
Sewaddle	○
Sunkern	○
Venipede	○

Mass Outbreaks

Pokémon	Version
Mr. Mime	⬡
Sudowoodo	⬢

All Seasons

Water Surface

Pokémon	Rarity
Azurill	◎
Basculin (Blue-Striped Form) ⬡	◎
Basculin (Red-Striped Form) ⬢	◎

Water Surface (ripples)

Pokémon	Rarity
Azumarill	△
Basculin (Blue-Striped Form) ⬢	◎
Basculin (Red-Striped Form) ⬡	◎
Marill	◎

■ After the Hall of Fame

Fishing

Pokémon	Rarity
Basculin (Blue-Striped Form) ⬡	◎
Basculin (Red-Striped Form) ⬢	◎
Poliwag	◎

Fishing (ripples)

Pokémon	Rarity
Basculin (Blue-Striped Form) ⬢	◎
Basculin (Red-Striped Form) ⬡	◎
Politoed	△
Poliwhirl	◎

Step 1 Battle against Pokémon Trainers

When you meet the gaze of another Pokémon Trainer, he or she will challenge you to battle. Battle other Trainers as often as you can in order to make your Pokémon stronger. You'll also receive prize money each time you defeat a Trainer.

When eyes meet, it's time for battle

If you try to pass directly in front of a Pokémon Trainer, he or she will challenge you to battle. Walk behind Trainers when you want to avoid battle.

Step 2 You can't go to the east side of Route 20 yet

When you first come here looking for your rival, the stairs that lead to the east side of the route will be blocked by a Hiker. You'll need the Aspertia City Gym Badge to get past the Hiker and proceed to Virbank City.

Step 3 Head north to Floccesy Ranch

Your rival is nowhere to be seen on the west side of Route 20. He must have gone to Floccesy Ranch (p. 96), which is located to the north of Route 20. To get there, cross the bridge and head north.

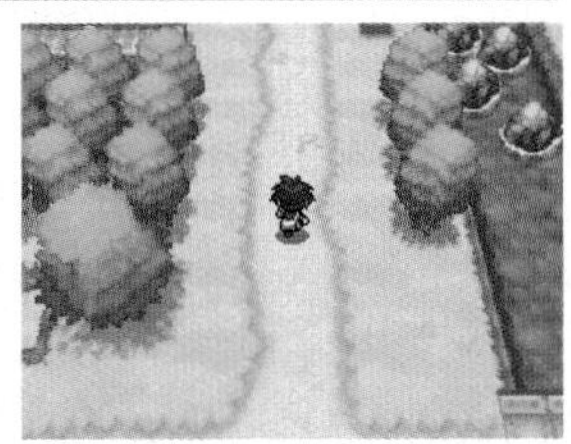

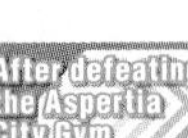

After defeating the Aspertia City Gym: If you see rustling grass, stop, look, and listen

After acquiring your first Gym Badge, you'll start seeing a strange phenomenon. When a single spot in the grass begins to rustle, hurry to it and enter the spot. You'll encounter a Pokémon that uniquely appears in rustling grass (p. 28).

A wild Audino appeared!

Defeat Audino to gain lots of Experience Points

When you encounter an Audino in the rustling grass and defeat it, you'll receive more Experience Points than from other Pokémon. These extra Experience Points will help you raise your Pokémon even more quickly.

After defeating the Aspertia City Gym: Travel to the east side of the route

On seeing your Aspertia City Gym Badge, the Hiker that was blocking the path will challenge you. Battle and defeat the Hiker, and you'll be able to move on to the east side of Route 20.

It's a rough world out there!
Here, I'll show you!

Heal up your Pokémon at Floccesy Ranch

When your Pokémon's HP and PP get low from battle, head over to Floccesy Ranch. Speak with the owner's wife, and she'll fully restore them.

After defeating the Aspertia City Gym: Cheren and your rival talk to you

Go down the steps and proceed eastward. Cheren and your rival will approach you from behind. Cheren tells you that in patches of tall grass, you'll sometimes encounter two Pokémon at the same time or run into higher-level Pokémon.

After defeating the Aspertia City Gym

In dark grass, two Pokémon can appear at the same time

You'll sometimes encounter two wild Pokémon when moving through patches of dark grass. This will trigger a Double Battle where the first two Pokémon in your party will appear in battle. If you want to catch one of the two wild Pokémon, you'll need to defeat the other first (p. 32).

Pokémon found in dark grass are higher level

Pokémon that can be found in patches of dark grass are of a higher level than those that are found in standard tall grass in the same area. Because of that, they'll be a bit more challenging to catch. Do your best to catch them so you can strengthen your party.

After defeating the Aspertia City Gym

Two Trainers, Double Battle

If your eyes meet those of a pair of Trainers, they will challenge you to a Double Battle. This will be your first Double Battle against other Trainers. Whenever two Trainers stand together, you'll have to face them in a Double Battle, so prepare yourself.

Strong and strong come together
to become...very strong!

Line up your party prior to battle

In a Double Battle, the first two Pokémon in your party will appear in battle. Check your party and make sure your second Pokémon is a strong one.

After defeating the Aspertia City Gym

Head east for Virbank City

Battle Trainers while making your way to the gate located to the east. Go through the gate to reach Virbank City, where the next Gym awaits (p. 98).

After facing Team Plasma in Virbank City

Teach the Team Plasma Grunt a lesson

Head west to chase after the Team Plasma Grunt. Climb the stairs in the center of the route and then head south to find the Team Plasma Grunt, who's hiding. Confront the Grunt to start a battle.

Yeesh! I really hate it when
people won't let things go!

Gather items after obtaining Surf

After receiving HM03 Surf from Cheren on Route 6, come back here in autumn to collect items. There are three items that can be obtained only by traveling across the water.

After facing Team Plasma in Virbank City

Go back to Virbank City

Defeat the Team Plasma Grunt, and your rival will appear. He has news that Team Plasma is traveling in some kind of ship. In order to get to Castelia City, which has a large port, first go back to Virbank City (p. 98).

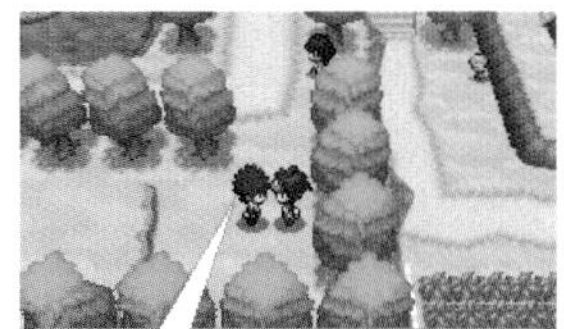

They must be moving around by boat!

Get Berries from Pokémon Rangers

After you get Surf, you can challenge the Pokémon Rangers Bret and Malory and defeat them to receive Leppa Berries. You can also battle against Leaf and Naoko to receive Sitrus Berries. It'll come in handy later to find them and get all the Berries.

After getting Surf

Battle against Pokémon Rangers

You can find four Pokémon Rangers hidden beneath piles of leaves in the southern part of Route 20 if you visit it during autumn. Approach one of the piles of leaves and a Pokémon Ranger will leap out and challenge you to a battle. 'Tis the season to find and battle all four of them.

I'll show you the Ranger spirit that
burns with a crimson flame!

Come back to the Cave of Being after entering the Hall of Fame

You can visit the Cave of Being in the south once you receive HM05 Waterfall from N on Victory Road. However, if you go there before entering the Hall of Fame, nothing will happen. Come back and visit it after entering the Hall of Fame (p. 283).

Floccesy Ranch

Guide

Floccesy Ranch came about naturally as Pokémon and people gathered in the area. The ranch is owned and operated by a husband and wife. A rich forest is located directly above Floccesy Ranch's northern boundaries.

Items

- ☐ Parlyz Heal
- ☐ Poké Ball
- ☐ Potion ×2
- ☐ TM21 Frustration
- ☐ X Attack

Hidden Grotto	
Dunsparce	△
Herdier	○
Marill	◎

Tall Grass	
Azurill	○
Lillipup	◎
Mareep	○
Patrat	○
Pidove	△
Psyduck	○
Riolu	△

Tall Grass (rustling)	
Audino	◎
Dunsparce	○

Janitor Orville
Youngster Kenny

Hidden Grottoes
● Floccesy Ranch has Hidden Grottoes. Find them all!

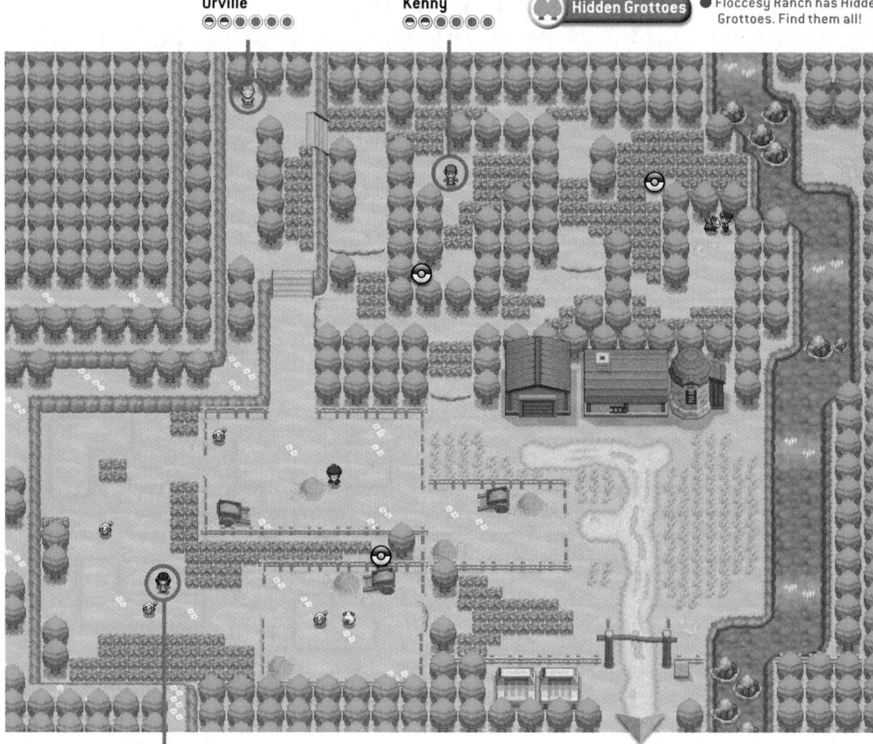

Lass Molly

Route 20 P. 92 (to Floccesy Town / Aspertia City)

Water Surface	
Azurill	◎
Basculin (Blue-Striped Form) ○	◎
Basculin (Red-Striped Form) ●	◎

Water Surface (ripples)	
Azumarill	△
Basculin (Blue-Striped Form) ●	◎
Basculin (Red-Striped Form) ○	◎
Marill	◎

■ After entering the Hall of Fame

Fishing	
Basculin (Blue-Striped Form) ○	◎
Basculin (Red-Striped Form) ●	◎
Poliwag	◎

Fishing (ripples)	
Basculin (Blue-Striped Form) ●	◎
Basculin (Red-Striped Form) ○	◎
Politoed	△
Poliwhirl	◎

Step 1 Your rival challenges you to battle

When you try to pass through the opening in the fence on the west side of Floccesy Ranch, your rival approaches you and challenges you to a Pokémon battle. Accept his challenge and show him you're already skilled in Pokémon battle.

Hugh: Oh! Nice!
You've come here to toughen up!

Battle with your rival! 2

Your rival still has only one Pokémon. He raised it up to Lv. 8, but it still doesn't know any moves that can exploit your Pokémon's weaknesses.

All right! Let's see how much stronger you've become! Come at me!

Rival's Pokémon

If you chose Snivy:

Tepig ♂ Lv. 8	Fire
Weak to	Water, Ground, Rock

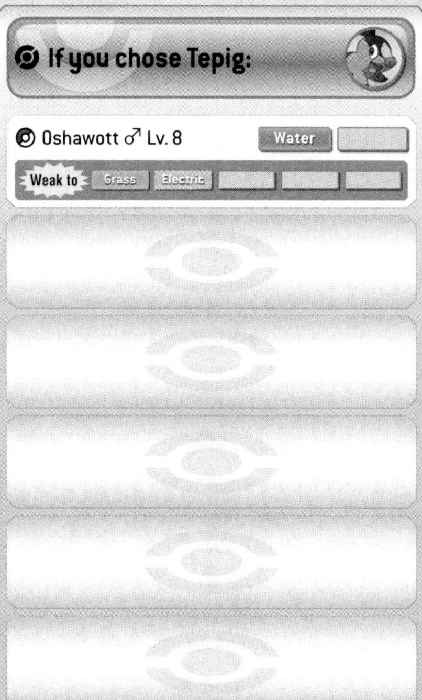

If you chose Tepig:

Oshawott ♂ Lv. 8	Water
Weak to	Grass, Electric

If you chose Oshawott:

Snivy ♂ Lv. 8	Grass
Weak to	Fire, Ice, Poison, Flying, Bug

Step 2 Search for the owner's Herdier

After giving your rival a Town Map, the owner of Floccesy Ranch approaches you and asks for your help in searching for his lost Herdier. Your rival gets angry at the owner for not acting worried in the slightest and runs off in search of Herdier.

Owner: By the way, you didn't happen to see a Herdier around here, did you?

Have the owner's wife heal your Pokémon

The owner's wife helps to run the ranch along with the owner. Talk to her, and she will bring your Pokémon back to perfect health. When your Pokémon's HP drops from battles against other Trainers or wild Pokémon, speak to her for a full recovery.

Step 3 Proceed while battling Pokémon Trainers

You'll find a Trainer waiting beyond the fence located on the west side of the Floccesy Ranch. You can also find two Trainers to battle in the forest to the north. Battle them to make your Pokémon stronger and then proceed through the forest to find Herdier.

Oh! I haven't seen you before! Would you mind sparring with me?

Your rival gets angry at the careless owner

The owner mentioned that one of his Pokémon had disappeared, but he didn't seem to be in much of a hurry to go look for it. Your rival grew very angry at the owner's careless attitude. Perhaps something happened in your rival's past that made him disposed to anger?

Step 4 Find a member of Team Plasma with Herdier

Deep inside the forest, you'll find a member of Team Plasma with Herdier. Your rival hurries off to notify the owner. The member of Team Plasma will throw TM21 Frustration at you and escape.

Step 5 Use TMs

TMs and HMs are items that teach moves to Pokémon. They don't go away after use, so you can use them as many times as you like. There are 95 in total. Teach a variety of moves to the Pokémon in your party (p. 432).

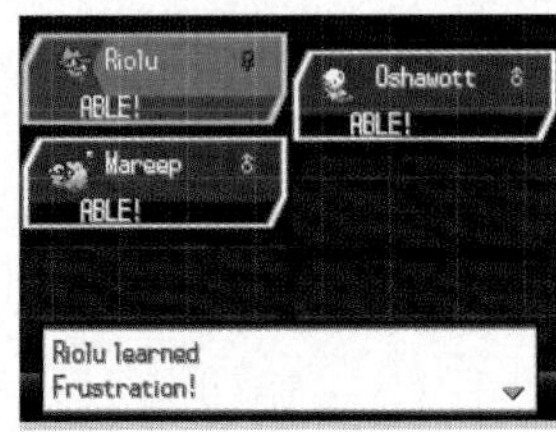

Step 6 Return to Floccesy Town

Now that you've handed off the Town Map to your rival and found the lost Herdier, it's time to return to Floccesy Town and have Alder help train your Pokémon. Head west on Route 20 to reach Floccesy Town (p. 90).

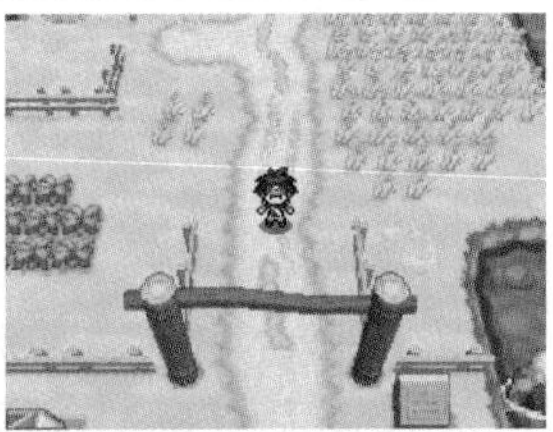

A city often covered by clouds and smoke, with very active residents

Virbank City

Virbank City is an industrial town with a massive crane near the water. It also has a Pokémon Center and is home to the Virbank City Gym. Not only that, but you can board a ship to Castelia City from the docks. You will also find the Virbank Complex to the south of the town.

Pokéstar Studios P. 104
Pokémon Center
Route 20 (to Floccesy Town) P. 92
Castelia City P. 106
Virbank City Gym
Virbank Complex P. 102

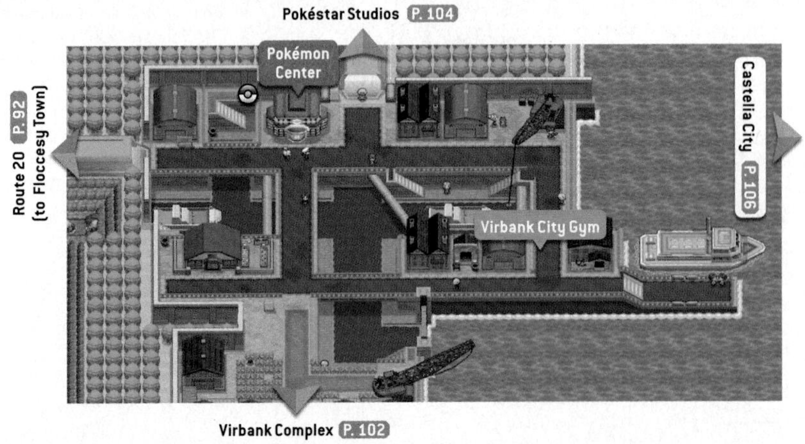

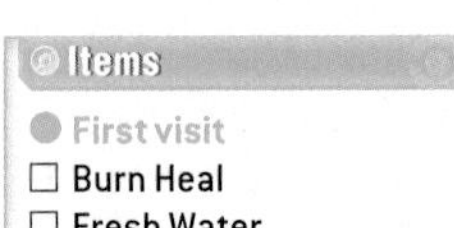

Items

- First visit
- ☐ Burn Heal
- ☐ Fresh Water
- ☐ Poké Ball ×5
- ☐ Poké Toy
- After defeating Virbank City Gym
- ☐ TM09 Venoshock
- ☐ Toxic Badge
- After visiting Pokéstar Studios
- ☐ HM01 Cut
- After getting Surf
- ☐ Rare Candy

Poké Mart (Lower Clerk)	
Favored Mail	50
Greet Mail	50
Inquiry Mail	50
Like Mail	50
Reply Mail	50
RSVP Mail	50
Thanks Mail	50
Heal Ball	300
Net Ball	1,000

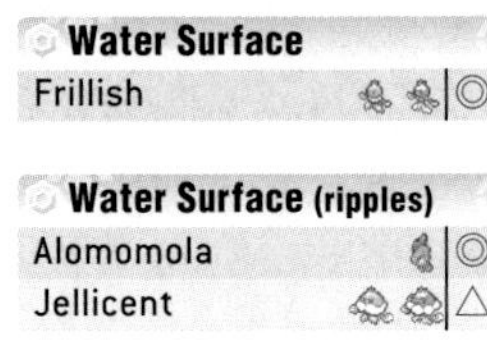

Water Surface	
Frillish	◎

Water Surface (ripples)	
Alomomola	◎
Jellicent	△

■ After entering the Hall of Fame

Fishing	
Finneon	◎
Krabby	◎
Qwilfish	△

Fishing (ripples)	
Kingler	○
Krabby	◎
Lumineon	◎

Step 1 Your mom gives you a call

Upon your arrival in Virbank City, your Xtransceiver rings. It's your mom checking in on you. She tells you that if you go to Virbank Complex at night, you can enjoy a nice view. Be sure to visit later on.

Step 2 The captain runs off to Pokéstar Studios

Go to the Pokémon Center and you'll run into Roxie, the Virbank City Gym Leader, who is talking with her father, Pop Roxie, who happens to be the ship's captain. He has decided to go to Pokéstar Studios to become an actor. Brushing off his daughter's desperate attempts to stop him, Pop Roxie sets off for Pokéstar Studios.

Step 3 Head over to the Virbank Complex before your gym battle

At this point, you can challenge the Virbank City Gym at any time, but it's a good idea to visit the Virbank Complex first (p. 102). Battle the wild Pokémon and Trainers there to make your Pokémon even stronger before your Gym battle.

Step 4 Challenge the Virbank City Gym

After you're finished in the Virbank Complex, it's time to challenge the Virbank City Gym. The Gym Leader, Roxie, uses Poison-type Pokémon. Remember to stock up on Antidotes at the Poké Mart before your battle.

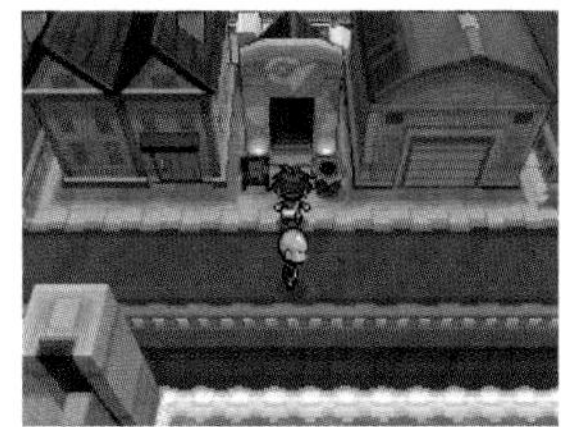

Choose your personality

You can decide what kind of personality you'll have in Unity Tower by answering the questions of a man inside the Pokémon Center. After trading Pokémon with an overseas player, you can visit Unity Tower by taking a ship from Castelia City (p. 113).

Without the captain, the ship can't leave port

The ship captain has gone off to Pokéstar Studios. Without the captain at the helm, you can't go to Castelia City. You'll need to first obtain the Virbank City Gym Badge and then visit Pokéstar Studios before you can take the ship to Castelia City.

Magnemite, who are immune to poison, inhabit the area

The Steel-type Pokémon Magnemite inhabit the Virbank Complex. Steel-type Pokémon are immune to poison, which would be an advantage in your upcoming Virbank City Gym battle (p. 463). Catching and raising one could be a smart play.

2 Virbank City Gym Battle

Gym Battle Tips

- Make sure to bring lots of Antidotes
- Catching Magnemite in the Virbank Complex and battling with it will give you an advantage

Get ready! I'm gonna knock some sense outta ya!

Virbank City Gym Leader

Roxie

Poison-type Pokémon User

If your Pokémon are poisoned, heal them quickly

Defeat both Pokémon Trainers and you can battle the Gym Leader, Roxie. Both of Roxie's Pokémon belong to the Poison type, but Whirlipede has even more weaknesses than Koffing. Use Fire- or Flying-type moves to exploit your opponents' weaknesses for a quick victory. If one of your Pokémon is poisoned when it gets hit by Venoshock, the move will do double damage. If your Pokémon gets poisoned, quickly use an Antidote to cure it.

Roxie's Pokémon

Pokémon	Lv.	Type	Weak to
Koffing ♀	Lv. 16	Poison	Ground◆, Psychic
Whirlipede ♀	Lv. 18	Bug, Poison	Fire, Flying, Psychic, Rock

Toxic Badge

Pokémon up to Lv. 30, including those received in trades, will obey you.

TM 09 Venoshock 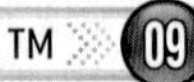 Poison

Does double damage when your opponent is inflicted with the poisoned or badly poisoned status conditions.

◆ The damage may change depending on the effects of this Pokémon's Ability.

Virbank City After winning the Gym battle

Get invited to Pokéstar Studios by the scout

After defeating Roxie, you'll be approached by a man at the entrance to the Gym. It turns out that he's a scout from Pokéstar Studios. Roxie overhears your conversation and, apparently thinking of her father, suddenly dashes out of the Gym.

I felt like you were something special
during your battle with Roxie.

Take a good look at the Gym's interior

The interior of the Virbank City Gym is like a rock club. A huge picture of Koffing can be seen on the stage, and there is an advertisement looking for new band members posted near the entrance.

Virbank City After winning the Gym battle

Head through the gate north of town to proceed to Pokéstar Studios

In order to get to Castelia City, you first need the captain of the ship to come back from Pokéstar Studios. Go through the gate located north of town and head to Pokéstar Studios to bring Pop Roxie back (p. 104).

After visiting Pokéstar Studios

Confront Team Plasma for the first time

After returning from Pokéstar Studios, head over to the docks and you'll see some members of Team Plasma standing in front of Roxie and your rival. It's time to challenge Team Plasma! Talk to the Grunt in the center and the battle will begin. It's time to show Team Plasma what you're made of.

Save before the battle

You will not enter the battle until you speak to the Team Plasma Grunt and select "YES." Make a point of saving before you say you're ready. If you don't do well in battle the first time, you can start over from right before the battle started (p. 60).

After visiting Pokéstar Studios

Receive HM01 Cut from Roxie

After suffering a sound defeat, the Team Plasma members run away as fast as they can. Before dashing off in pursuit, Roxie will give you HM01 Cut. It's her thanks for your help in chasing off Team Plasma.

After visiting Pokéstar Studios

Use HMs to teach moves to your Pokémon

Use HMs to teach your Pokémon some very handy moves. Moves learned from HMs often let you go to places on the field that you can't reach otherwise (p. 37). If you want to make your Pokémon forget one of these moves, talk to the Move Deleter, who can be found at the PWT.

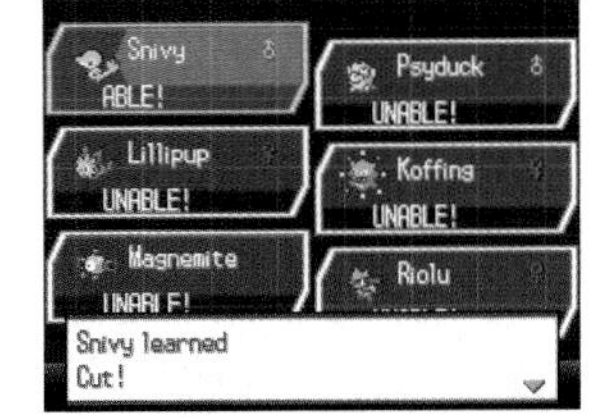

If none of them are in your party, go back and catch one

You can use HM01 Cut to cut down the small trees that sometimes block your path. However, the only Pokémon you have encountered up to this point who can learn this move are Patrat, Purrloin, Sewaddle, and Sunkern.

After visiting Pokéstar Studios

Go after your rival and head to Route 20

Where did the members of Team Plasma take off to? Roxie will ask you and your rival to search Route 20. Your rival will run off ahead, so head over to Route 20 to chase after him (p. 92).

After confronting Team Plasma on Route 20 — The ship captain returns from Pokéstar Studios

Pop Roxie has returned to the Virbank City docks after the movie he starred in didn't do well at all. He is feeling down, but Roxie cheers him up. He decides to return to his job as ship captain.

You can keep trying while you continue on as captain!

After confronting Team Plasma on Route 20 — Board the ship and set off for Castelia City

Enter the building at the docks and you'll find your rival waiting at the counter inside. Talk to him and he'll ask if you want to go to Castelia City. In order to track down Team Plasma, board the ship together and set off for Castelia City (p. 106).

YES
NO
Hugh: You're going to Castelia City, right?

Gather items after you get Surf

Get HM03 Surf from Cheren on Route 6 before you come back here to collect items. From the southern part of town, head north on the water surface to collect items.

A complex that is designed so Pokémon can work there easily

Virbank Complex

Virbank Complex is an industrial zone that contains a massive crane and tanks. You can travel across the raised walkways in between the tanks.

Entrance

Tall Grass

Pokémon	Version	Frequency
Elekid	○	○
Magby	●	○
Magnemite		○
Patrat		◎
Pidove		◎

Tall Grass (rustling)

Pokémon	Version	Frequency
Audino		◎

Water Surface

Pokémon	Version	Frequency
Frillish		◎

Water Surface (ripples)

Pokémon	Version	Frequency
Alomomola		◎
Jellicent		△

After entering the Hall of Fame

Fishing

Pokémon	Version	Frequency
Finneon		◎
Krabby		◎
Qwilfish		△

Fishing (ripples)

Pokémon	Version	Frequency
Kingler		○
Krabby		◎
Lumineon		◎

Inside

Tall Grass

Pokémon	Version	Frequency
Elekid	○	○
Growlithe		○
Koffing		○
Magby	●	○
Magnemite		○
Patrat		○

Tall Grass (rustling)

Pokémon	Version	Frequency
Audino		◎

Dark Grass

Pokémon	Version	Frequency
Elekid	○	○
Growlithe		○
Koffing		○
Magby	●	○
Magnemite		○
Patrat		○

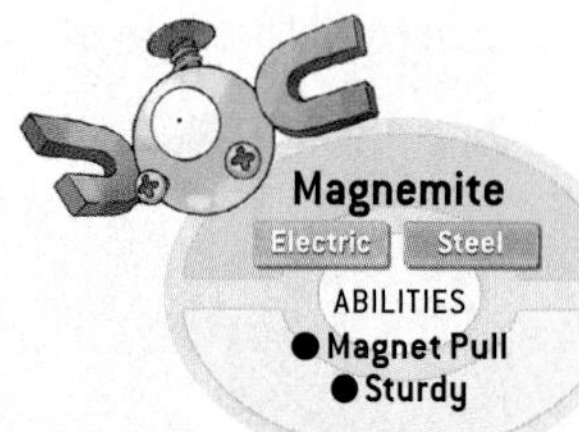

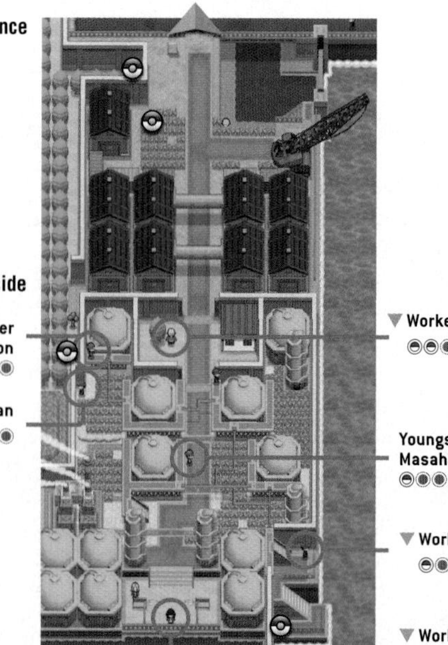

Items

- First visit
- ☐ Silk Scarf
- ☐ X Accuracy
- ☐ TM46 Thief
- After battling with the three Workers
- ☐ TM94 Rock Smash
- When the Habitat List is completed
- ☐ Great Ball ×5
- After speaking to the assistant three times
- ☐ Ether
- After obtaining Cut
- ☐ Super Potion

Step 1 Trade for a Great Ball daily

Go east as you enter Virbank Complex to go down the stairs to find a man. He trades your Poké Ball for a Great Ball. You can trade with him once a day, so talk to him every day.

Visit here at night or late night

In a Xtransceiver chat with your mom, she says to visit Virbank Complex at night or late night. The tanks and towers there are lit up, making for a beautiful night atmosphere.

Step 2 Give Pokémon items to hold

Here you can find a Silk Scarf. Have your Pokémon hold it, and the power of its Normal-type moves go up. You can really take advantage of this boost when you have a Normal-type Pokémon, such as Patrat or Lillipup, with Normal-type moves.

Trainer found a Silk Scarf!

Step 3 Fulfill a man's request to get his Workers fired up

Go south into Virbank Complex, and you'll see a man standing there. When you talk to him, he'll ask you to motivate three of his new Workers. Battle all three to get them fired up.

▸YES
NO
How about it?
Help a guy out, will ya?

Step 4 Challenge three Workers to a Pokémon battle

Enter the complex and take the stairs on the south side up to the surrounding path. Cross the raised walkway. The three Workers wait on the east end, north end, and west end of the raised walkways, so find them all and get them battling.

What? The foreman said so? OK, fine.
We just have to battle, right?

Step carefully on the raised walkway

If you take a step in the wrong direction on the raised walkway connecting tanks, you'll fall. You'll also fall if you stand still on the walkway for too long. Keep walking carefully on the raised walkways, and you'll make it to the end.

Step 5 Get the TM for Rock Smash from a man

Battle with the three Workers around Virbank Complex, then talk to the man again. To show his gratitude for getting his Workers fired up, he'll give you TM94 Rock Smash.

Comes in handy at Clay Tunnel

You'll need TM94 Rock Smash after the Hall of Fame when you want to enter Clay Tunnel (p. 284). Now's the time and place to get it.

Step 6 Get items by completing the Habitat List

Talk to the woman at the south end of the complex, and she'll ask you to complete the Virbank Complex Habitat List. Meet all the Pokémon here, and she'll give you five Great Balls as a reward.

Could you use it to show me what kind
of Pokémon live in this complex?

Complete the Habitat List!

Walk through the tall grass to meet Pokémon to complete the Habitat List of Virbank Complex.

Step 7 Chase after the assistant and talk to him three times

There is a knowledgeable assistant in front of a tower on the west side. Talk to him, and he'll move to the front of the smokestack on the south side. Chase after him and talk to him again. Then he'll move to a clearing on the south side. Talk to him once again. After you've listened to him talk three times, he'll give you an Ether.

Oh! My knowledge overflowed,
and it was overheard!

Catch Magnemite

Magnemite that appear in the tall grass are Steel-type Pokémon. Since they don't become poisoned, they have the upper hand against the Poison-type Pokémon at Virbank City Gym. Catch one here and raise it.

Step 8 Go back to Virbank City to challenge its Gym

Explore every corner of Virbank Complex to battle Pokémon Trainers and collect items before you go back to Virbank City (p. 98). If you haven't battled her yet, Roxie, the Gym Leader, is waiting for challengers at Virbank City Gym.

Collect an item after you get Cut

Come back after you receive HM01 Cut from Roxie for your victory at Virbank City Gym. Chop down a tree and walk a bit, and you'll find an item there.

Pokéstar Studios, where great movies are produced

Pokéstar Studios

Pokéstar Studios is a leisure facility where you can fulfill your dream of becoming a movie star with your Pokémon. There is a high-tech studio to shoot movies and a theater that can show up to eight movies at a time.

Field Moves Needed

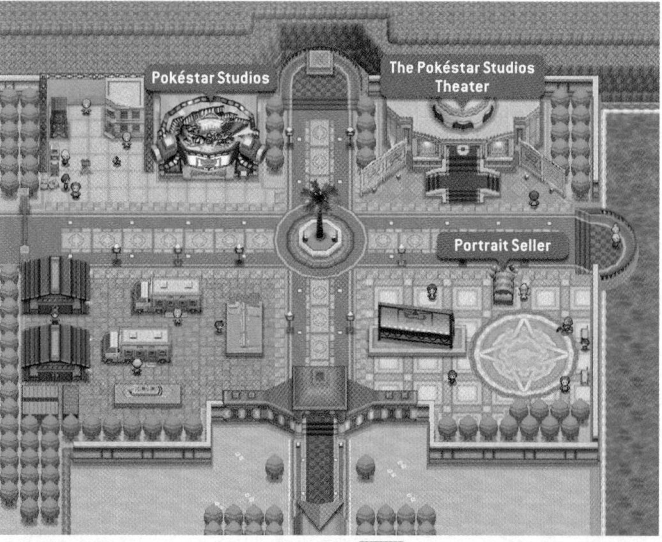

Step 1 Go for a tour at Pokéstar Studios, the movie capital

Go north through the gate, and the scout who talked to you at Virbank City will talk to you with the boss of Pokéstar Studios, Stu Deeoh. Let the scout guide you through Pokéstar Studios and its theater.

Step 2 Watch Pop Roxie's film with him

You'll find Pop Roxie at the theater. As you watch the movie he starred in, you'll notice that the movie isn't too good and the audience isn't impressed. Disappointed, Pop Roxie returns to Virbank City.

Step 3 Become an actor and star in a movie!

The scout invites you into the studio, where you'll costar with a famous actor, Brycen. Follow the movie scenario to complete making the movie. Do a good job, and you'll be able to take on new scenarios (p. 367).

Step 4 Follow Pop Roxie to return to Virbank City

Once Pop Roxie returns to Virbank City, you can take the ship to Castelia City. Go south through the gate to return to Virbank City (p. 98). After that, go south to where you can board the ship.

So many exhibits to see

Many unique items are on display on the plaza in front of the studios, such as a miniature model of the *Royal Unova* and a replica of Skyarrow Bridge done to 1/144 scale. Take your time and take a look around.

Familiar faces among the famous actors

Brycen used to be the Icirrus City Gym Leader two years ago, and Sabrina is a Gym Leader from the Kanto region. Now, they're famous actors. In some scenarios, you'll be costarring with them!

Portraits for sale

The Harlequin in front of the theater sells portraits. As your rank as a star goes up, your portrait will be sold, too.

A big city with skyscrapers piercing the clouds

Castelia City

Castelia City is filled with skyscrapers. It's the biggest city in the Unova region. It boasts the elegant cruise ship, the *Royal Unova*, and ships to Virbank City and Liberty Garden leave from the port.

Items

- First visit
- ☐ Amulet Coin
- ☐ Bicycle
- ☐ Charcoal
- ☐ Destiny Knot
- ☐ Dowsing MCHN
- ☐ Ether
- ☐ Exp. Share
- ☐ Guard Spec.
- ☐ Heart Scale
- ☐ Moomoo Milk
- ☐ Quick Claw
- ☐ Revive
- ☐ Scope Lens
- ☐ TM44 Rest
- ☐ TM45 Attract
- ☐ TM70 Flash
- After completing the Castelia Harlequin Hunt
- ☐ Rare Candy
- When your answer to the woman's question is Snivy
- ☐ Miracle Seed
- When your answer to the woman's question is Tepig
- ☐ Charcoal
- When your answer to the woman's question is Oshawott
- ☐ Mystic Water
- When your Pokédex's SEEN number is 40 Pokémon or more
- ☐ Eviolite
- After defeating Clemens in the Battle Company
- ☐ Quick Ball ×2
- After defeating Warren in the Battle Company
- ☐ Timer Ball ×5
- After you've answered all of the surveys at Passerby Analytics HQ
- ☐ Soda Pop
- After visiting the Castelia Sewers
- ☐ Fresh Water
- ☐ Miracle Seed
- After winning the Castelia City Gym challenge
- ☐ Insect Badge
- ☐ TM76 Struggle Bug
- After getting Surf
- ☐ BlackGlasses (spring and summer only)
- ☐ Repel (spring and summer only)

Poké Mart (Lower Clerk)

Item	Price
Favored Mail	50
Greet Mail	50
Inquiry Mail	50
Like Mail	50
Reply Mail	50
RSVP Mail	50
Thanks Mail	50
Heal Ball	300
Nest Ball	1,000
Net Ball	1,000

Casteliacones

Item	Price
Casteliacone	100

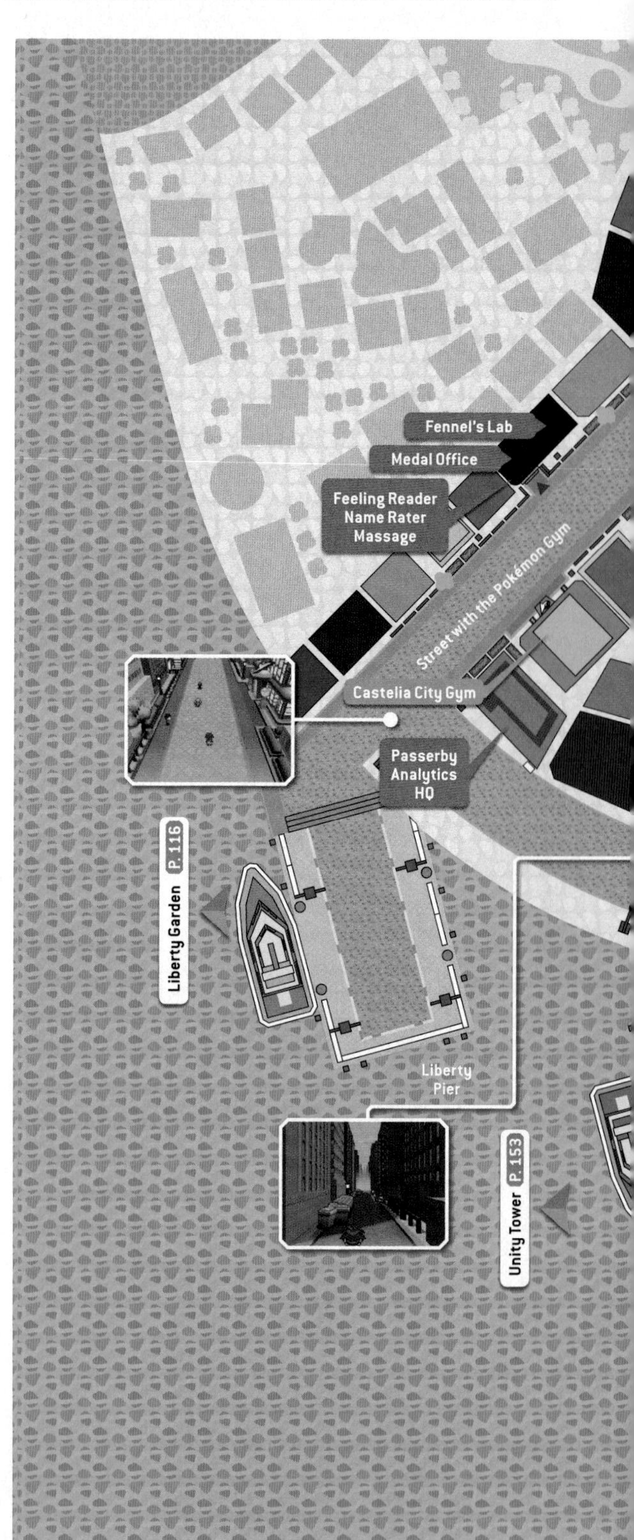

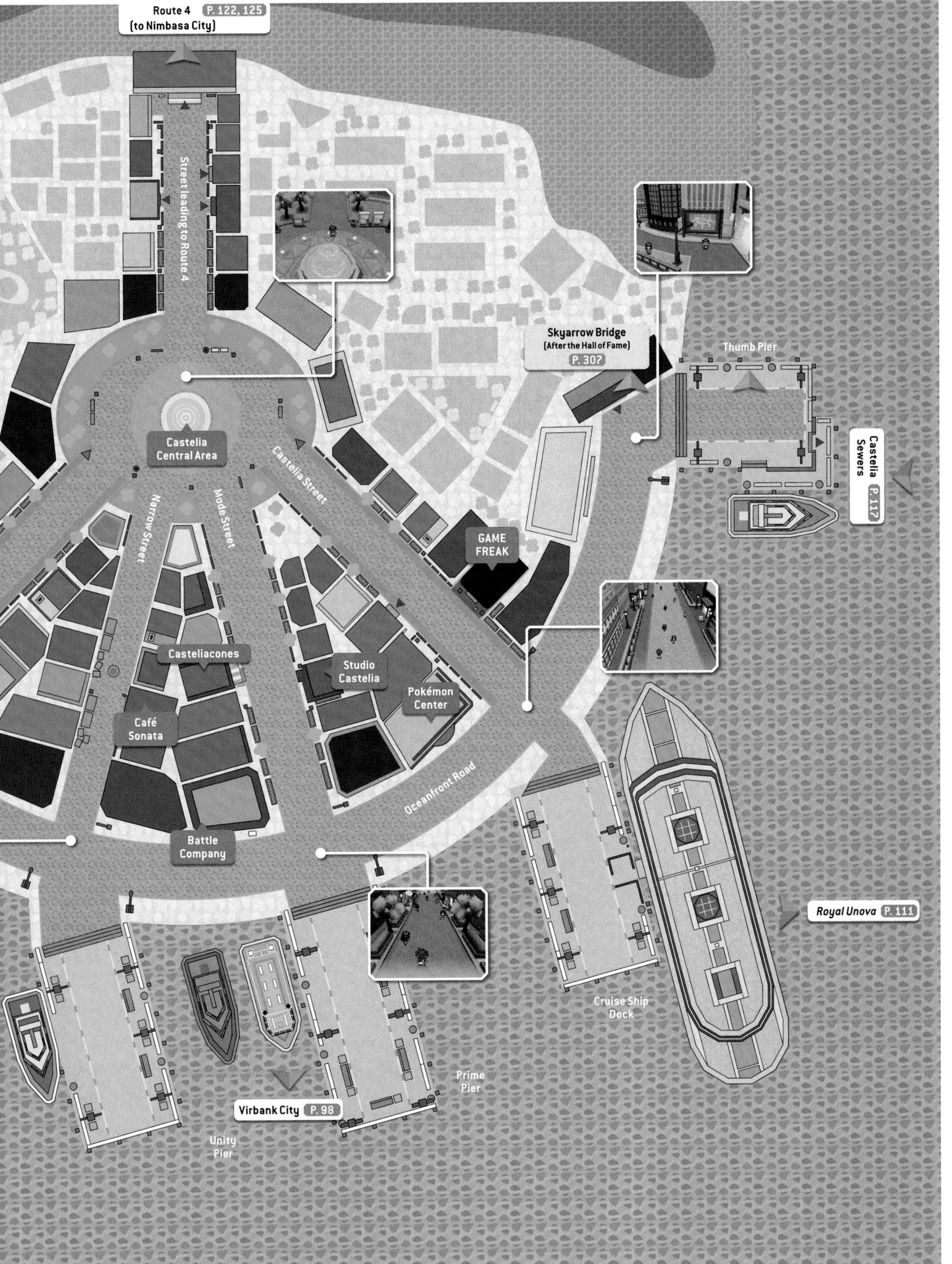

▲ Building entrances enable you to enter buildings.

Street with the Pokémon Gym

The building on the left

Narrow Street

Café Sonata

Mode Street

Studio Castelia

Castelia Street

The building on the left

The building on the right (GAME FREAK)

Oceanfront Road

Battle Company

Passerby Analytics HQ

Street leading to Route 4

The building on the left

11F

1F

The building on the right ①

47F

1F

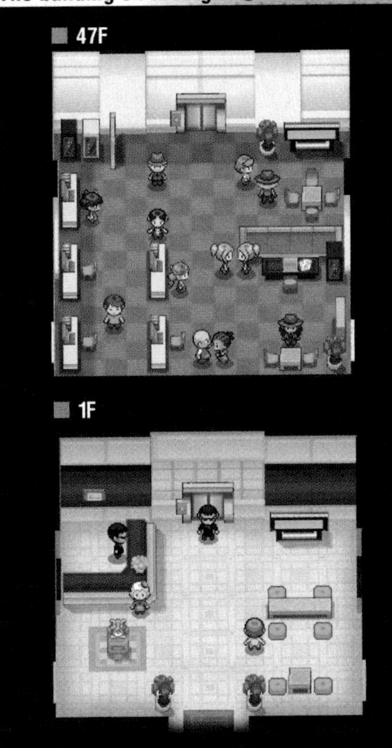

The building on the right ②

47F

1F

Reached via Castelia Sewers

Back Street

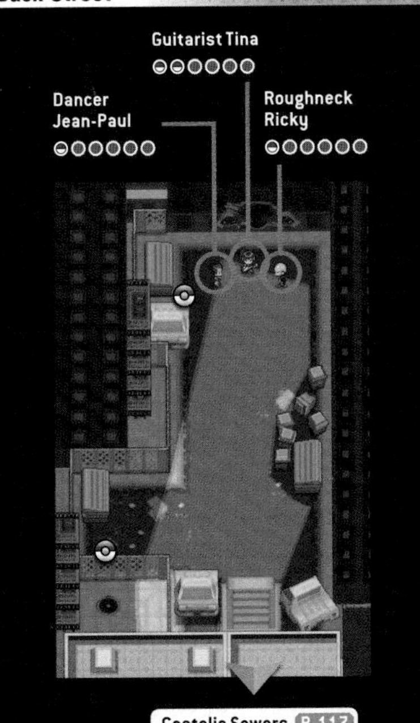

Castelia Sewers P. 117

Royal Unova

Castelia Sewers P. 117

Tall Grass

Pokémon	Version	Frequency
Buneary	⬢	◯
Cottonee	⬢	◎
Eevee		△
Petilil	⬡	◎
Pidove		◯
Rattata		◎
Skitty	⬡	◯

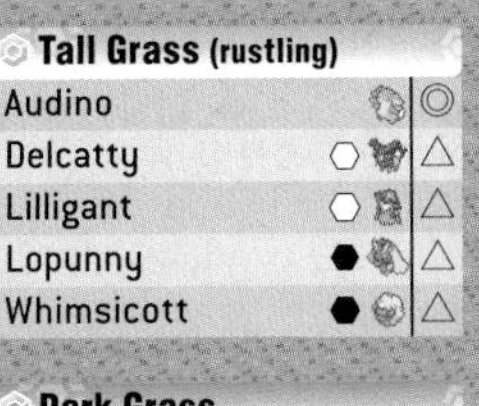

Tall Grass (rustling)

Pokémon	Version	Frequency
Audino		◎
Delcatty	⬡	△
Lilligant	⬡	△
Lopunny	⬢	△
Whimsicott	⬢	△

Dark Grass

Pokémon	Version	Frequency
Buneary	⬢	◯
Cottonee	⬢	◎
Eevee		△
Petilil	⬡	◎
Pidove		◯
Rattata		◎
Skitty	⬡	◯

Step 1 Register your rival in the Xtransceiver

When you get off the ship, your rival asks you to register him in your Xtransceiver. If you contact him, he'll tell you where you should go next on your journey. Contact him for advice when you're not sure where to go.

You can go back to Virbank City anytime

The ship to Virbank City is moored at Prime Pier. Remember you can go back to Virbank City anytime. Just speak to the captain.

Step 2 Get the Bicycle from a Harlequin

Head north from Prime Pier where you got off the ship, and you'll see a Harlequin. He'll give you the Bicycle. You can travel a lot faster by Bicycle than by running with the Running Shoes.

Move faster by Bicycle

The Bicycle is especially useful to speed up travel in Castelia City, which is a sprawling place. Register it to the Y Button so that you can get on and off it quickly (p. 56).

Step 3 Try the Castelia Harlequin Hunt

To complete the hunt, you'll need to speak to three Harlequins in different locations. They're in the Battle Company, Medal Office, and Passerby Analytics HQ. After speaking to them all, you can get a Rare Candy from the Harlequin at Prime Pier.

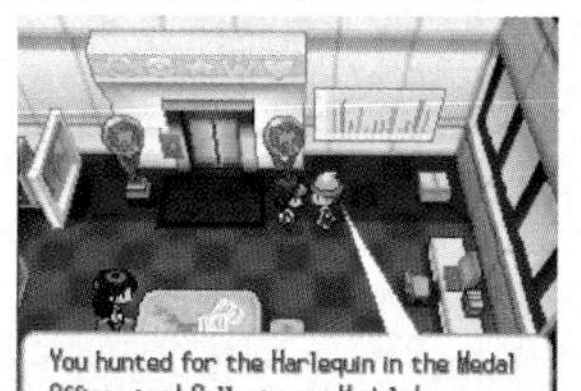

Battle Company is the place for battles

There are four Pokémon Trainers on the 47th floor, and one Trainer on the 55th floor, of the Battle Company. Battle all of them and make your Pokémon strong. Some Trainers give you an item after the battle is over.

Step 4 Get an Exp. Share at the Battle Company

When you enter the Battle Company on Mode Street, a Janitor speaks to you and gives you an Exp. Share. It's a very useful item that gives Experience Points to a Pokémon even when that Pokémon isn't used in battle (p. 49).

Get an item to power up moves

Speak to a woman on the first floor of the Battle Company. She will give you a Miracle Seed if your answer to her question is Snivy, a Charcoal if your answer is Tepig, or a Mystic Water if your answer is Oshawott.

Step 5 Skyarrow Bridge: You shall not pass

The gate on the east side of Castelia City leads to the Skyarrow Bridge. However, a Worker is blocking the entrance because his crew is inspecting the bridge to make sure it's strong enough. It will open after you enter the Hall of Fame (p. 255), and you'll be able to cross.

Step 6 Receive the Quick Claw from a woman

You can't cross the Skyarrow Bridge yet, but you can enter the gate on the Castelia City side. Speak to the woman by the entrance in this gate. She'll give you the Quick Claw, which can be very useful in battle.

Have a slow Pokémon hold the Quick Claw

Have a Pokémon hold the Quick Claw. Regardless of the Pokémon's Speed, it can attack first occasionally. No matter how slow the Pokémon is, it will have a chance to attack first.

Step 7 Take the *Royal Unova* in the evening

You can board the *Royal Unova* at the cruise ship dock in the evening for a fare of 1,000. If you defeat a certain number of Pokémon Trainers, you can get a prize. The challenge is different on different days of the week. Keep battling, and the ship will return to the port after a certain amount of time has passed.

Talk to the crew to get hints

Once you get on the *Royal Unova*, talk to the crew. They will tell you how many Pokémon Trainers you need to beat and give you hints on how many Trainers are in rooms with a red door or a blue door.

Number of Trainers per day and prizes

Day	Number of Trainers	Prize
Monday	Four people	Lava Cookie
Tuesday	Three people	Berry Juice
Wednesday	Four people	Lava Cookie
Thursday	Five people	Old Gateau
Friday	Four people	Lava Cookie
Saturday	Six people	RageCandyBar
Sunday	Seven people	Rare Candy

Step 8 Battle at GAME FREAK every day

In the GAME FREAK building, take the elevator up to the 22nd floor to visit the creators of *Pokémon Black Version 2* and *Pokémon White Version 2*. You can challenge the Trainers Morimoto and Nishino to battle once a day there.

Morimoto

Nishino

Step 9 Listen to the story of the Game Director

The Game Director on the north side of the GAME FREAK building asks you to show him your Pokédex when you've filled it up a lot. When you complete your Pokédex, show it to him. You'll receive a great award certificate (p. 337).

Combine a move with an item

On the 11th floor of the building on Castelia Street, a woman gives you TM44 Rest and advises you to have a Pokémon with the move Rest hold a Chesto Berry. That's because the Pokémon can wake up immediately after recovering its HP with the move.

Step 10 Buy a Casteliacone

You can buy Casteliacones once a day at Casteliacones on Mode Street. The Casteliacone can heal all status conditions. You can choose to buy one or a dozen. It costs only 100 per cone, so it's a good deal. Buy one or even a dozen every day.

There was a long line two years ago

Casteliacones were so popular two years ago that they were only available on Tuesdays in spring, summer, and autumn. Also, you were allowed to buy only one at a time. However, the boom seems to have passed, and now you can buy a Casteliacone every day.

Step 11 Get Berries by showing Pokémon

Talk to the guy in Studio Castelia. Every day he tells you he wants to paint a certain type of Pokémon. Show him the type of Pokémon he wants to see, and you can receive one of the following Berries: Cheri Berry, Chesto Berry, Pecha Berry, Rawst Berry, or Aspear Berry.

Step 12 Get TM70 Flash

Enter Narrow Street and continue down the road. A man in sunglasses pops out from behind a garbage bin and gives you TM70 Flash. If you teach Flash to a Pokémon, it can light up dark caves.

Register your favorite Pokémon

Talk to the girl in the Pokémon Center, and the first Pokémon in your party will be registered as your favorite Pokémon. The favorite Pokémon will be displayed in the ranking screen of the Vs. Recorder.

Step 13 Visit Passerby Analytics HQ

Talk to the leader, and he will appoint you as a statistician. Being a statistician lets you receive Passerby Survey requests. Speak to the blonde woman in the HQ, and answer the questionnaire. Then, you can have fun using Tag Mode with other Pokémon fans.

Step 14 Visit the Medal Office

The Medal Office is on the second floor of the building across from the Gym. There, you can learn how many Medals you have and your Medal rank. Visit the office when you've collected 50 Medals. They will hold a rank-up ceremony for you (p. 337).

The Medal Rally is a competition to
evaluate various activities of Trainers.

If you collect all 255 Medals...?

You can receive 255 Medals from Mr. Medal. After collecting all of them, visit the Medal Office. You'll see a wonderful event.

Step 15 Visit Fennel and Amanita's Lab

Fennel's Lab is on the third floor in the building across from the Gym. Fennel and her assistant tell you about Game Sync, and Amanita tells you about the Pal Pad and the PC Boxes.

Hi there, Trainer!
My name is Fennel.

The PC's name changes

Amanita is the person who manages the PC Boxes. After speaking to Amanita, the "Someone's PC" option in the PC menu changes to "Amanita's PC."

Step 16 Get a massage for your Pokémon

Talk to a woman on the first floor in the building across from the Gym, and she will give your Pokémon a massage. Having one of your Pokémon get a massage will make that Pokémon a little more friendly toward you! Pokémon massages are available once per day (p. 12).

Make your Pokémon more friendly

Some Pokémon evolve with high friendship. Also, some of the moves that Pokémon learn from people require high friendship to be learned. Have a Pokémon get a massage every day to make it more friendly toward you.

Step 17 Visit the Name Rater

The old man in the same building is the Name Rater. Talk to him, and he will change your Pokémon's nickname. However, you can change a Pokémon's nickname only when you are its original Trainer.

YES
NO
Want me to rate the nicknames
of your Pokémon?

Step 18 Have the Feeling Reader tell you your lucky person

The Feeling Reader is in the same building. Speak to him after taking Feeling Checks with two or more people with the C-Gear and he'll tell you your lucky person for the day.

Take Feeling Checks with a lot of friends

Feeling Check is a game to test your friendship. Access it by touching IR (Infrared Connection) on the C-Gear. You will receive one Sweet Heart if the result is 0 to 79, two Sweet Hearts if the result is 80 to 99, and three if it is 100.

Step 19 Receive an Amulet Coin from an old man

Enter the building on the left side of the street north of the Central Plaza, and speak to the old man on the first floor. He'll give you an Amulet Coin. It's an item that doubles a battle's prize money if the holding Pokémon joins in.

Go to Unity Tower

Take the ship from Unity Pier to go to Unity Tower. Players from other countries who have traded Pokémon over the GTS gather here. Trade Pokémon with a lot of players (p. 153).

Step 20 Receive an Eviolite from an assistant

Enter the building on the right of the street leading to Route 4 and speak to the Pokémon fanatic by the elevator on the first floor. If the "SEEN" number of your Pokédex is 40 or more, he'll give you an Eviolite.

Have a Pokémon hold an Eviolite

If held by a Pokémon that can still evolve, an Eviolite raises a Pokémon's Defense and Sp. Def by 50%. Give this item to a Pokémon that can still evolve, and it will last longer in battles.

Step 21 Bianca gives you the Dowsing Machine

When you enter the gate to Route 4, Bianca comes to speak to you and gives you the Dowsing Machine. It's an item that helps you find hidden items (p. 62). You can use it in many places around the Unova region.

Register the Dowsing Machine to the Y Button

The Dowsing Machine is an item you'll use often on roads and in caves. Register it to the Y Button for quick access. You'll find hidden items much more easily with the Dowsing Machine.

Step 22 Try Funfest Missions in the Entralink!

Funfest Missions are games where you have to achieve various goals. If you use wireless communications, you can play Funfest Missions with up to 100 people. As you continue on your adventure, you'll have more missions to play.

Add a Funfest Mission

Speak to the old man near the fountain in the Central Plaza. The Entralink Funfest Mission "Train with Martial Artists" will be added for you to play.

Step 23 Go to Liberty Garden

Head south from the street with the Castelia Gym to Liberty Pier, and you can take a ship to Liberty Garden. After traveling around Castelia City, take the ship and go to Liberty Garden (p. 116).

You cannot challenge the Gym yet

Clyde is standing in front of the Castelia Gym and tells you that the Gym Leader is not there. Then, Iris shows up. When you talk to her about Team Plasma, she tells you she might know of a place where suspicious people go to hide and leaves.

Chase Iris and head for the eastern pier

Head toward the east side of town. After passing the Pokémon Center, you'll see Iris. She tells you that Thumb Pier is a suspicious place, then heads further east. Chase her. Go south at the front of the gate to get to Thumb Pier.

Iris lives in Opelucid City

Opelucid City is where Iris and Drayden were Gym Leaders two years ago.

Head to the Castelia Sewers with your rival

At Thumb Pier, Iris explains that you can get into the Castelia Sewers. Your rival arrives and enters the sewers without a blink. Follow him (p. 117).

Catch Pokémon in the empty lot

After you meet Burgh in the Castelia Sewers, the person blocking the stairs disappears. Take the stairs, and you'll find an empty lot. Even though it's in the city, guess what? There's some tall grass. You know what to do! If not, read up on catching wild Pokémon (p. 28).

Pokémon are different depending on the version

The empty lot in Castelia City is where you can encounter wild Pokémon that you can find nowhere else. Don't miss getting Buneary in *Pokémon Black Version 2* and Skitty in *Pokémon White Version 2*.

Head west to challenge the Gym

After you meet Burgh in the Castelia Sewers, you can challenge the Castelia City Gym. Restore your Pokémon's health in the Pokémon Center, and head west to the street with the Castelia City Gym.

3 Castelia City Gym Battle

Gym Battle Tips

- A Pokémon holding a Quick Claw is raring to go!
- Catch a Zubat in the Castelia Sewers to get an advantage.

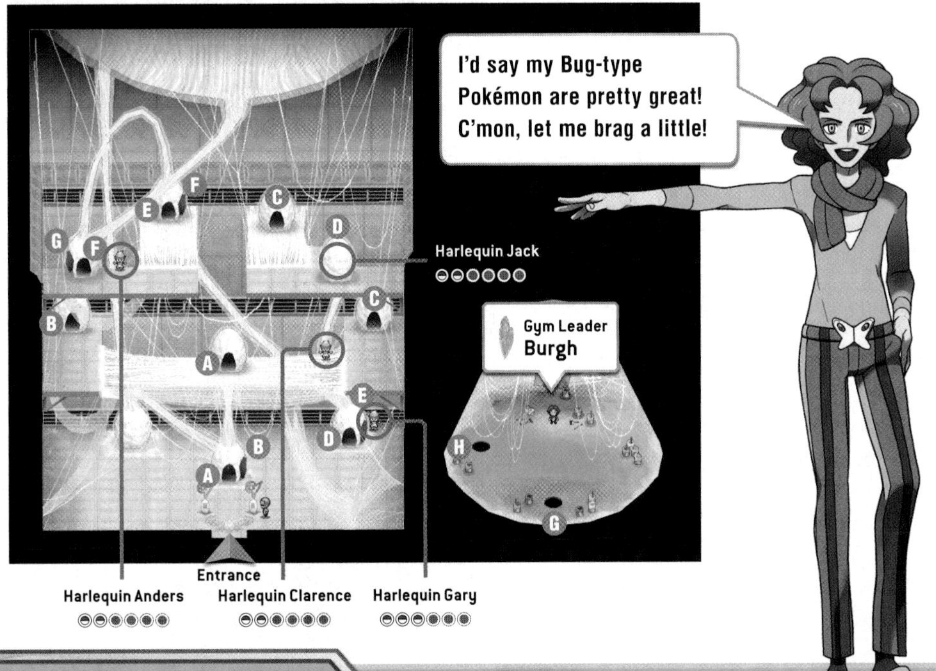

Castelia City Gym Leader

Burgh

Bug-type Pokémon User

First strike goes to the Pokémon holding a Quick Claw!

In the Gym, move from cocoon to cocoon and defeat four Pokémon Trainers to reach the spot where Burgh waits. Burgh's Pokémon try to strike first by using moves to affect their Speed. Outmaneuver him by giving your Pokémon a Quick Claw to hold, so they can attack first regardless of Speed. If you can get in a strong first strike with a Ground- or Fire-type move, you'll have a chance to defeat the opposing Pokémon before your Pokémon gets attacked.

Burgh's Pokémon

Pokémon	Level	Type	Weak to
Swadloon ♂	Lv. 22	Bug, Grass	Fire, Flying, Ice, Poison, Bug, Rock
Dwebble ♂	Lv. 22	Bug, Rock	Water, Rock, Steel
Leavanny ♂	Lv. 24	Bug, Grass	Fire, Flying, Ice, Poison, Bug, Rock

Insect Badge

Pokémon up to Lv. 40, including those received in trades, will obey you.

TM 76 Struggle Bug (Bug)

It lowers the target's Sp. Atk stat by one. Its effect is weaker when used against multiple Pokémon.

Head north to Route 4

After defeating the Gym Leader, head to Nimbasa City where the next Gym is. Nimbasa City is located at the north end of Route 4. Head to the Central Plaza to go north from Castelia City.

After beating the Castelia City Gym

The mysterious Colress speaks to you

▸YES
NO
by battling with you.
Do you find this acceptable?

The mysterious man you met in the Castelia Sewers talks to you in the Central Plaza. Having identified himself as Colress, he asks you to battle him for research purposes. Colress says he'll wait for you on Route 4 and then leaves.

Yes, yep, yeah, sure, OK!

When Colress challenges you, you could choose "No." Even if you do, the result will be the same. You'll end up battling him on Route 4 anyway!

Follow that mysterious man!

Colress left, saying he'd wait for you on Route 4. Don't keep him waiting! Head straight north from the Central Plaza, pass through the gate, and you'll be on Route 4 (p. 122, 125).

Beyond the stairs from the Castelia Sewers

Battle a group of three Pokémon Trainers

I'm gonna pay you back in spades!

In spring or summer, you can get to the back streets from the Castelia Sewers if you have a Pokémon that learned Surf (p. 162). Defeat the three Trainers there, and you'll get a Medal.

Use Fly to travel more freely

After you battle three Trainers in the back streets and collect items, use Fly to travel. You can reach places without having to pass through the Castelia Sewers.

An island symbol of hope for a world where humans and Pokémon live free

Liberty Garden

Liberty Garden is an island bought 200 years ago by a wealthy person who wished for a world where humans and Pokémon could live freely. In the lighthouse in the center of the island, you'll see a small room where it looks like a Pokémon had lived alone.

Step 1 Check everything out before returning to Castelia City

Take the ship at Liberty Pier in Castelia City, and you'll arrive at Liberty Garden. The only major thing on the island is the lighthouse. After you check everything, speak to the guy on the west dock, and set sail back to Castelia City (p. 106).

If you bring Victini

Victini is the Pokémon that was said to have lived alone in the lighthouse on this island. Visit Liberty Garden with Victini in your party, and something unexpected might happen.

Iron bars around the exits were dismantled, drawing curious Trainers

Castelia Sewers

The water level in the Castelia Sewers changes according to the seasons. As the water level rises in spring and summer or drops in autumn and winter, you can reach different places. Take the stairs, and you can get to the empty lot or the back streets.

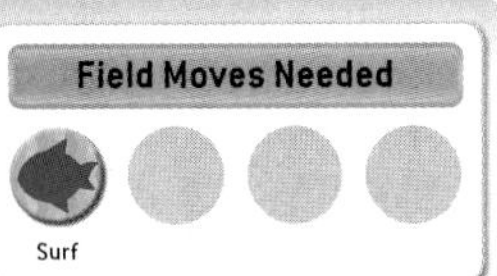

Spring Summer

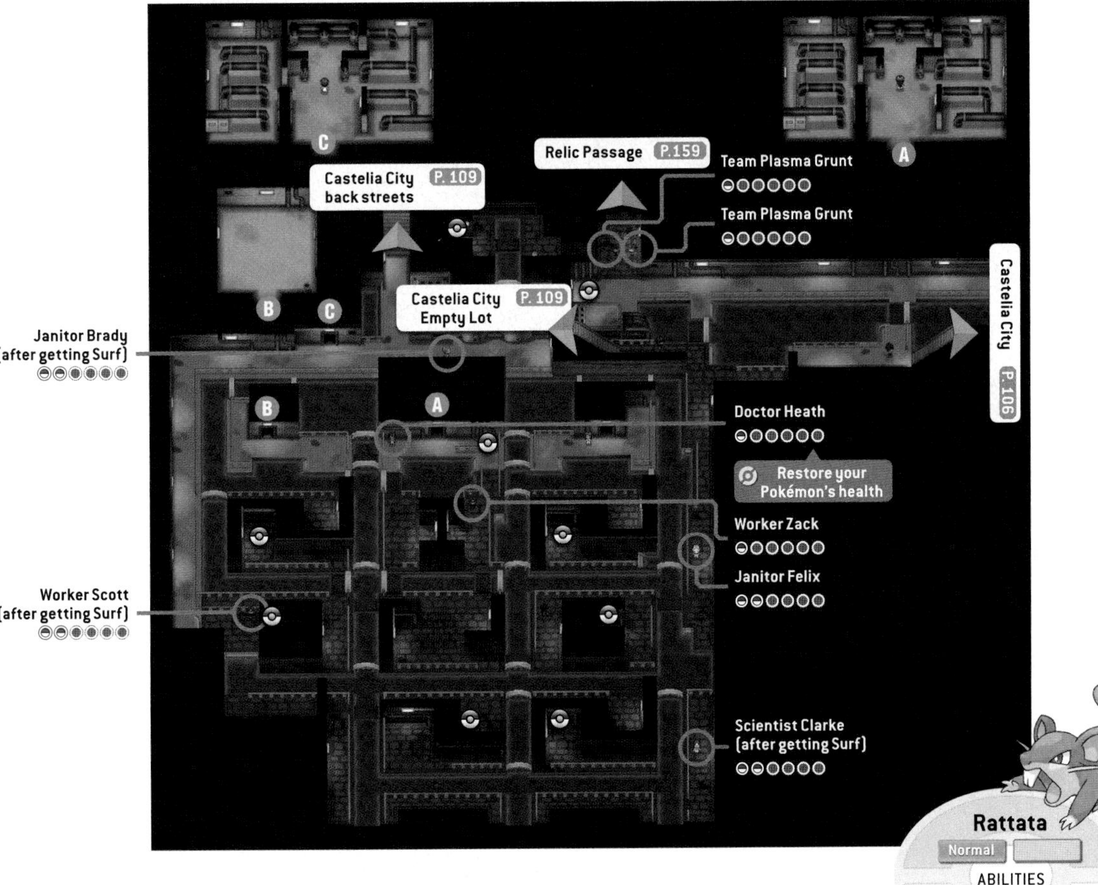

Rattata
Normal
ABILITIES
● Run Away
● Guts

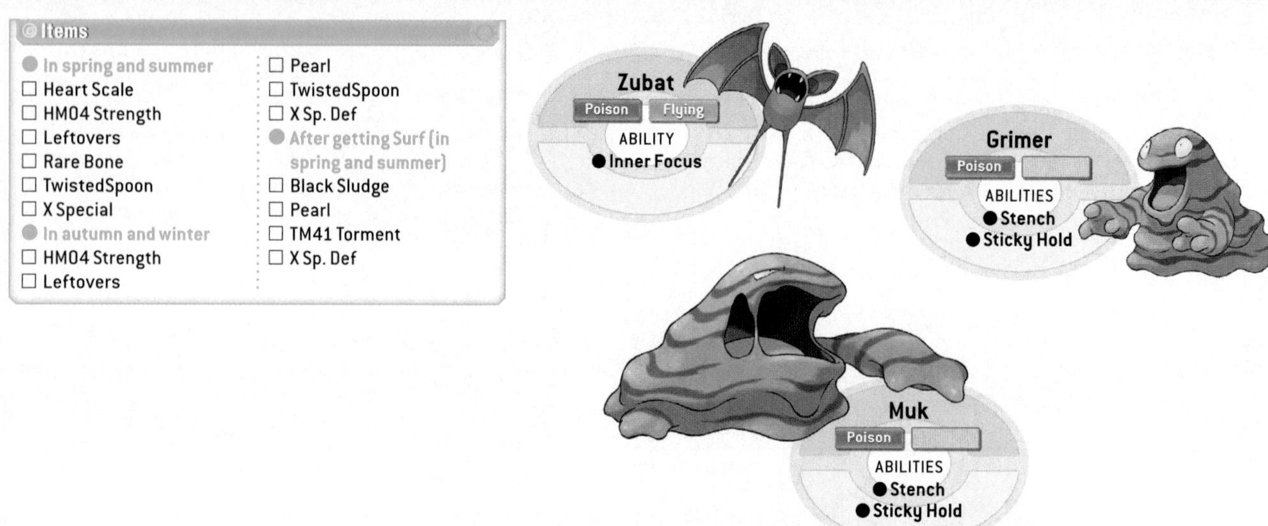

Items

- In spring and summer
- ☐ Heart Scale
- ☐ HM04 Strength
- ☐ Leftovers
- ☐ Rare Bone
- ☐ TwistedSpoon
- ☐ X Special
- In autumn and winter
- ☐ HM04 Strength
- ☐ Leftovers
- ☐ Pearl
- ☐ TwistedSpoon
- ☐ X Sp. Def
- After getting Surf (in spring and summer)
- ☐ Black Sludge
- ☐ Pearl
- ☐ TM41 Torment
- ☐ X Sp. Def

Autumn Winter

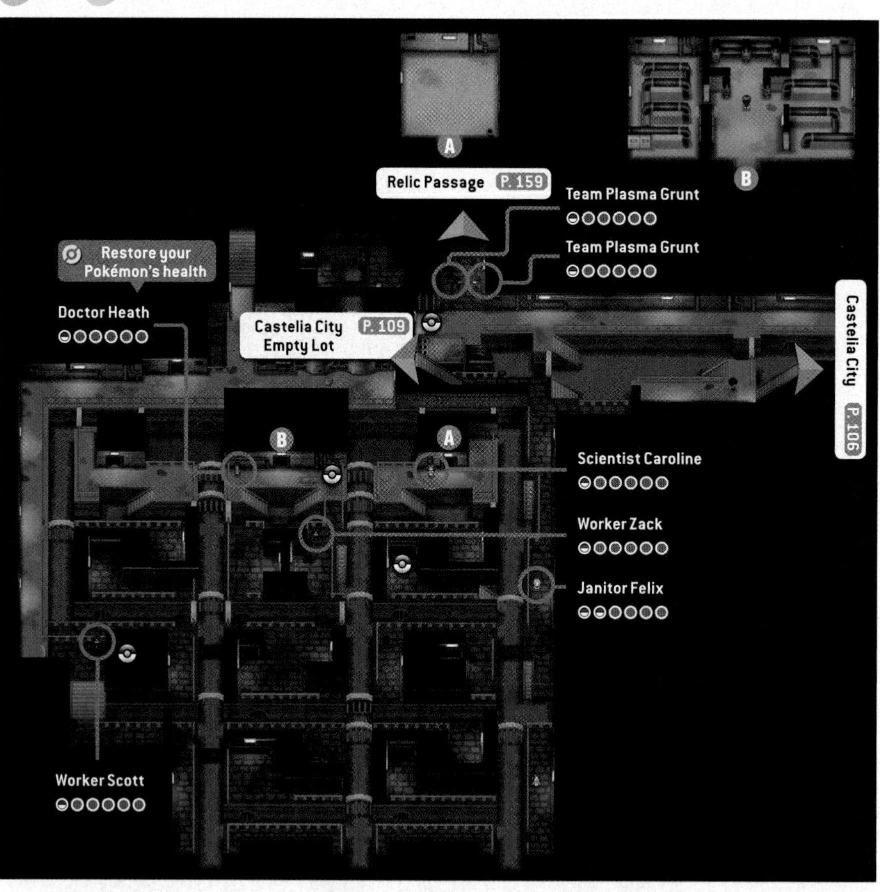

All Seasons

Sewers	
Grimer	◎
Rattata	◎
Zubat	◎

Spring Summer

Water Surface	
Grimer	◎

Water Surface (ripples)	
Grimer	◎
Muk	△

After the Hall of Fame

Fishing	
Grimer	◎

Fishing (ripples)	
Grimer	◎
Muk	○

Step 1 Explore the sewers with your rival

When you enter the Castelia Sewers, your rival suggests that you two search for Team Plasma together. Say "Yes" and you'll team up with him in battles against wild Pokémon. However, you'll still fight against Pokémon Trainers alone.

YES
NO
I'm counting on you, Trainer!
Are you ready to go?

Your rival restores your Pokémon's health

While you're with rival Hugh, he'll restore your Pokémon's health after a battle, even when they faint. Take advantage of this, and use Pokémon you want to train in battles.

Step 2 Two wild Pokémon will jump out

While you're with your rival, wild Pokémon always jump out in pairs. When you want to catch one of the Pokémon, make the other Pokémon faint first, and then throw a Poké Ball.

Someone is blocking the path

The stairs to the west from the entrance lead to the Empty Lot in Castelia City. At your first visit, a person is blocking it and you cannot take the stairs. After you beat Team Plasma and meet Burgh, you can take the stairs.

Step 3 The water level changes depending on the season

The water level in the Castelia Sewers changes throughout the year. The Pokémon Trainers you can battle and items you can get also change with the seasons. However, Team Plasma will be in the same place until you battle them.

Step 4 Have Doctor Heath heal your Pokémon

Doctor Heath is in front of the room where a Scientist is conducting experiments. If you defeat him, he'll restore your Pokémon's health. After that, he'll heal your Pokémon whenever you speak to him. If your Pokémon are hurt, have him heal them.

Before you go, let me give your Pokémon
a little booster shot!

Battle and heal

Doctors and Nurses restore your Pokémon's health when you defeat them. Speak to them to challenge them for battle, then enjoy the benefits of having health care on hand!

Step 5 Receive an item every day depending on the experiment result

Speak to the female Scientist in the room behind Doctor Heath. Depending on the result of her experiment, she'll give you one of the following items a day: Potion, Super Potion, or Revive. Visit her every day to get a free item.

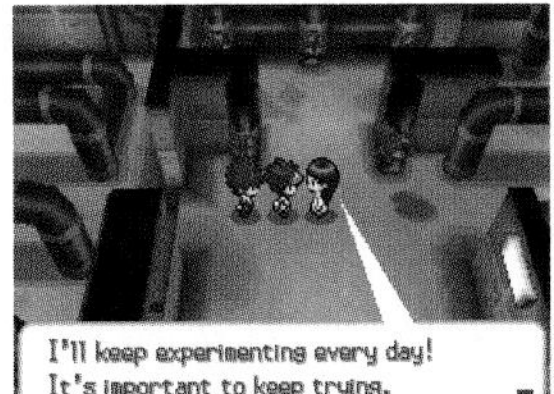

I'll keep experimenting every day!
It's important to keep trying.

Step 6 Team up with your rival to beat Team Plasma

From the entrance, head west and then north. You'll find two Team Plasma Grunts standing there. Team up with your rival and beat them. Then the grunts leave, saying they've got the Pokémon they need.

Team Plasma: Shaddap!
Hand over your Pokémon!

Have a Pokémon hold Leftovers

The Leftovers that you can obtain in the Castelia Sewers is an item that restores the holder's HP gradually every turn. If you let a Pokémon with high HP hold it, it makes the Pokémon even more resilient.

Step 7 Meet Castelia Gym Leader Burgh

Looking at the cave deep in the sewers, your rival tries to chase Team Plasma further, but Castelia Gym Leader Burgh shows up and stops him. Burgh tells you he didn't see any suspicious people.

Step 8 Receive HM Strength from your rival

Hugh gives you HM04 Strength as thanks. Then, he tells you he'll look for Team Plasma and leaves. From here on out, you'll be battling in the sewers without him.

Have a Pokémon learn Strength

Teach a Pokémon in your party Strength and it will be able to move boulders blocking roads and drop them in holes. Dunsparce, Psyduck, Riolu, Growlithe, Grimer, and more can learn the move.

Step 9 A mysterious man shows up

After your rival leaves, a mysterious man comes out from the cave in the back. The mysterious man in a white coat seems to have been watching you and your rival battling against Team Plasma. He praises the way you battled and leaves.

Step 10 You don't have to go to the cave leading further back

The cave where the mysterious man came out leads to the Relic Passage. However, the area you can access is limited because there are ledges ahead. When you visit the Relic Passage from the Pokémon World Tournament, you'll be able to explore the whole area (p. 159).

You could proceed to the Relic Passage

The area of the Relic Passage you can visit from the Castelia Sewers is limited, but you can still battle three Pokémon Trainers. Wild Pokémon also appear. Stop by the Relic Passage to train your Pokémon before the Gym battle.

Step 11 Take the stairs to go to the empty lot

After you defeat Team Plasma and meet Burgh, the person who was blocking the stairs will disappear. Now you can take the stairs, so you can move forward. Beyond the stairs, you'll find the empty lot (p. 114).

The only access is from the Castelia Sewers

You cannot go to the empty lot from Castelia City. In order to get there, you have to go through the Castelia Sewers. Regardless of the water level, you can reach the stairs, so you can go there in any season.

Step 12 Go back to Castelia City to challenge the Gym

Burgh has returned to the Castelia City Gym, so you can have your Gym battle now! Leave Team Plasma to your rival for now, and go back to Castelia City (p. 106). Leave the Castelia Sewers the way you came in, and you'll be in Castelia City.

Come back again in spring or summer

After getting HM03 Surf on Route 6, come back to the sewers in spring or summer. If you have a Pokémon who knows Surf, you can go to the area you couldn't visit before.

You cannot use Surf in autumn and winter

Because the water level decreases in autumn and winter, you cannot use Surf. After receiving HM03 Surf from Cheren on Route 6, visit the sewers again in spring or summer and get surfin'!

Collect items and battle

Only when you use Surf in spring or summer can you visit all the places in the Castelia Sewers. Make sure to visit the Castelia Sewers during these seasons to collect all the items and battle all of the Pokémon Trainers.

Receive an item every day depending on the experiment result

Speak to the male Scientist in the room in the north where you can go by using Surf. Depending on the result of his experiment, he'll give you one of the following items a day: Antidote, Full Heal, or Full Restore. Visit him every day in spring and summer.

After getting Surf

Take the stairs to go to the Back Street

You can reach the stairs in the far north by using Surf when the water level is high in spring or summer. Take the stairs, and you'll arrive at the Back Street in Castelia City (p. 109).

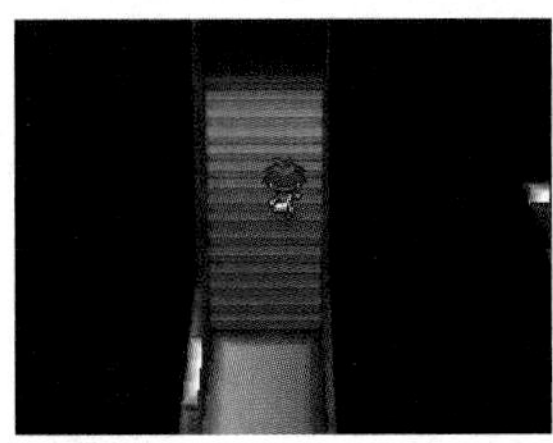

You cannot go from Castelia City

You can't reach the Back Street from Castelia City. You can visit there only in spring and summer, and you need Surf to reach it. It's difficult to get there, but you can leave easily by using Fly.

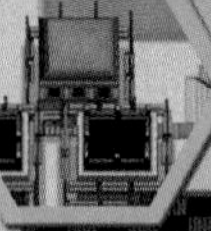

The route that was once covered in sand now has a lot of buildings

Route 4

When playing *Pokémon Black Version 2*

Two years ago, Route 4 was still buried in shifting sands. Thanks to the progress of technology, it's now lined with buildings. There are two exits to the north: the eastern exit leads to Join Avenue, and the western exit continues to the Desert Resort.

Items

- First visit
- ☐ Grip Claw
- ☐ Mystic Water
- ☐ Protein
- ☐ Sitrus Berry
- ☐ Stardust
- ☐ TM28 Dig
- ☐ Wide Lens
- If you correctly identify the Pokémon cry that is mimicked
- ☐ Poké Toy

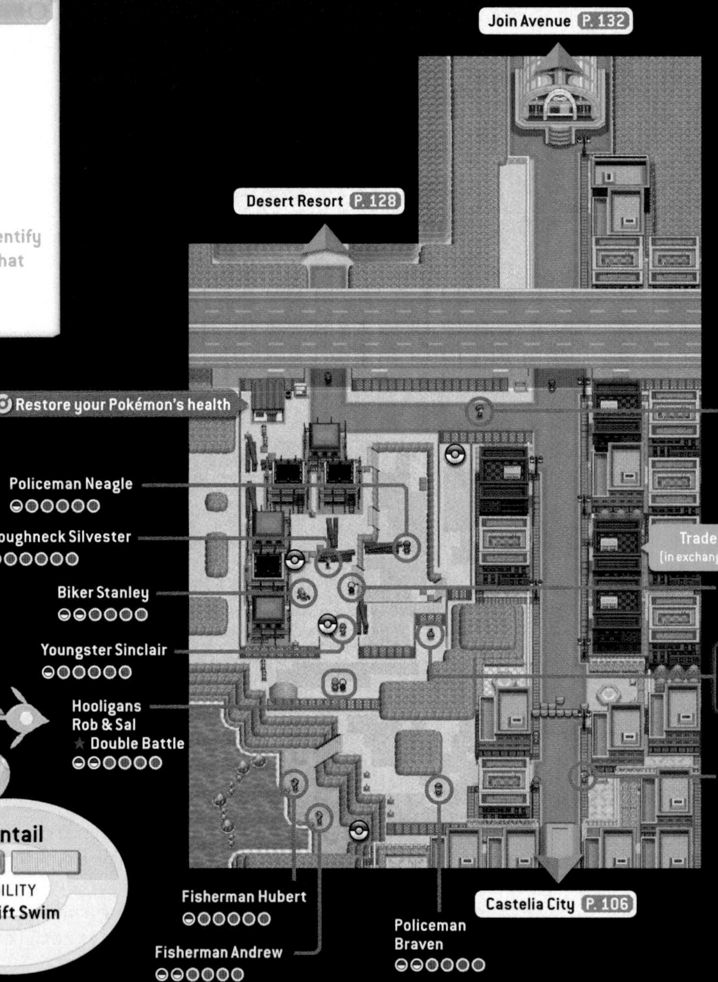

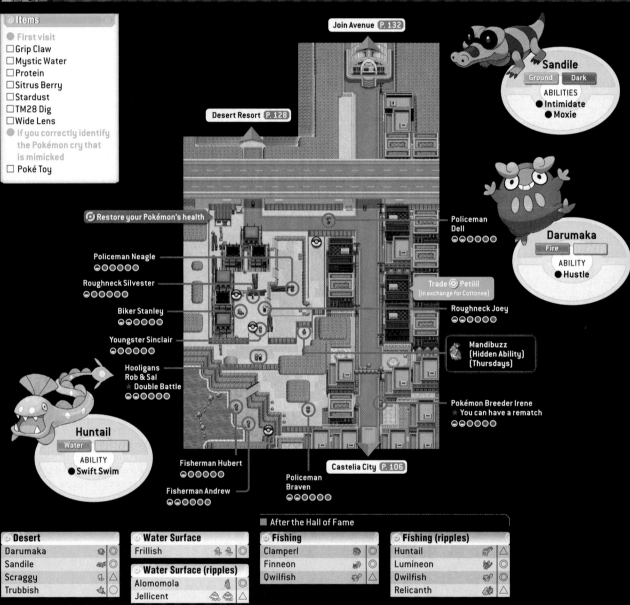

Join Avenue P. 132
Desert Resort P. 128
Castelia City P. 106

Restore your Pokémon's health

Policeman Neagle
Roughneck Silvester
Biker Stanley
Youngster Sinclair
Hooligans Rob & Sal ★ Double Battle
Fisherman Hubert
Fisherman Andrew
Policeman Braven
Policeman Dell
Trade Petilil (in exchange for Cottonee)
Roughneck Joey
Mandibuzz (Hidden Ability) (Thursdays)
Pokémon Breeder Irene ★ You can have a rematch

Sandile — Ground / Dark — ABILITIES: Intimidate, Moxie

Darumaka — Fire — ABILITY: Hustle

Huntail — Water — ABILITY: Swift Swim

Desert	
Darumaka	◎
Sandile	◎
Scraggy	△
Trubbish	○

Water Surface	
Frillish	◎

Water Surface (ripples)	
Alomomola	◎
Jellicent	△

After the Hall of Fame

Fishing	
Clamperl	◎
Finneon	◎
Qwilfish	△

Fishing (ripples)	
Huntail	△
Lumineon	◎
Qwilfish	◎
Relicanth	△

Step 1 Battle the Pokémon Breeder as often as you like

A Pokémon Breeder is located near the gate to Route 4. This Pokémon Breeder is a Trainer you can fight every time you visit this location. You don't even have to leave Route 4; simply going in and out of one of the buildings will allow you to challenge her to a rematch.

Having lots of battles is the best way to train a Pokémon quickly!

Step 2 Take up the challenge that Colress has thrown down

When you proceed north, you'll find Colress standing before you. As promised, he's waiting on Route 4 to battle you. The stone wall behind him blocks you from moving ahead, so you'll have to face him in battle if you want to continue your journey.

Pokémon appear in the dark sand

There is dark sand and light sand in desert areas. When you walk on the dark sand, Pokémon pop out. If you want to catch Pokémon, start by walking in areas with dark sand.

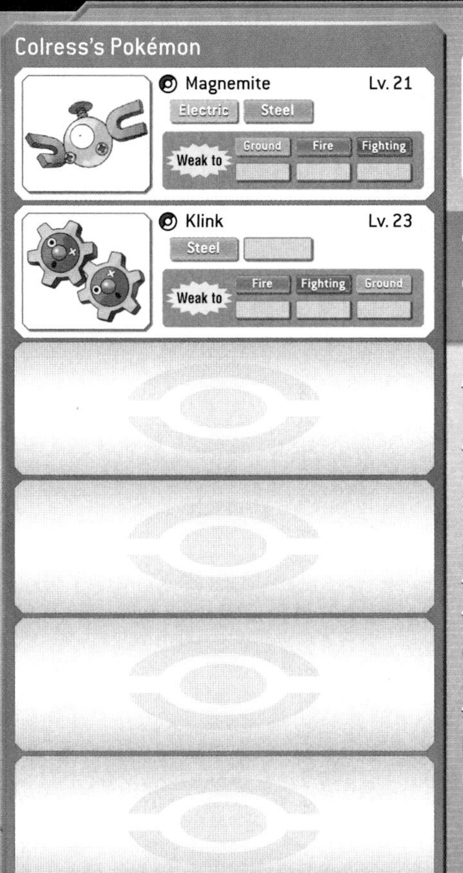

Colress's Pokémon

Pokémon	Lv.	Type	Weak to
Magnemite	Lv. 21	Electric, Steel	Ground, Fire, Fighting
Klink	Lv. 23	Steel	Fire, Fighting, Ground

Well then, I will test you to see if you're a Trainer who can bring out the hidden potential of Pokémon!

Take on Pokémon Trainer Colress! 1

Attack with Fire- and Ground-type moves

The Magnemite and Klink that Colress uses both have the same kinds of weaknesses. Magnemite is particularly weak to Ground-type moves and will take four times the regular amount of damage from any Ground-type attacks. Send out Pokémon that can use Fire-, Ground-, and Fighting-type moves to bring the battle to a quick end.

Step 3 Head north on the road that was blocked by Crustle

Before your battle with Colress, he kindly removed the stone-like Crustle that were blocking your path. He used a machine that excites Pokémon to wake the sleeping Crustle. After defeating Colress, continue to the north.

Use the Dowsing Machine to find items

There are many items waiting to be discovered in the sandy areas of Route 4. Use your Dowsing Machine to pinpoint these items' location. Search out items to build up your inventory (p. 62).

Step 4 Speak to the girl who focuses on Speed

Enter the building to the east and speak to the girl there, and she will name a particular Speed value. If you have a Pokémon in your party with the same Speed stat, you will receive five Health Wings. If your Pokémon has a Speed stat higher than the number she names, you will get one. You can visit her every day.

Step 5 Trade your Cottonee for a Petilil

In the building north of where you found the girl who focuses on Speed, another girl will ask you to trade Pokémon with her. If you give her your Cottonee, you can receive a Petilil. Cottonee can be caught around Castelia City.

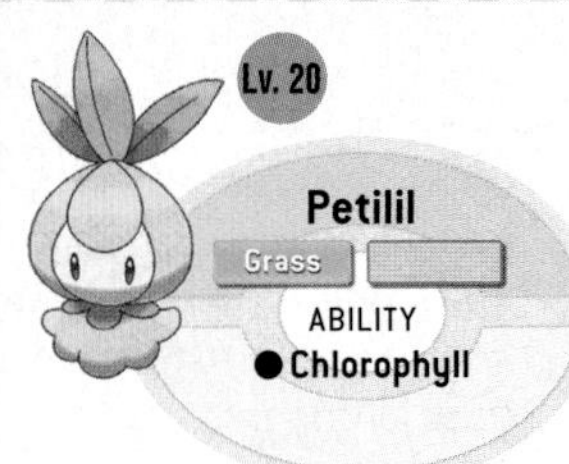

Step 6 Identify the cries of the Pokémon in your party

Try speaking to the girl in the building north of where you can trade Cottonee. She will imitate the cry of one of your party Pokémon. If you correctly identify which Pokémon it is, you can receive a Poké Toy.

You can try to identify her mimicry again and again

You will only get a reward the first time you correctly identify the Pokémon cry that the girl imitates. You can try your hand at her challenge every time you talk to her, though! Why not take a breather from your adventure sometimes and enjoy a fun quiz?

Step 7 Have a woman fully heal your Pokémon

Follow the newly paved road to the west. In the building that lies at the end of it, you'll find a woman who will heal your Pokémon. If your Pokémon have been injured during battles with wild Pokémon or other Trainers, be sure to stop by and talk to her.

Step 8 Battle a Mandibuzz every Thursday

A Mandibuzz with a special Hidden Ability will appear every Thursday beyond the sandy area that lies to the south of the paved road. When you talk to it, the battle begins. If you accidentally defeat it, it will appear again the next Thursday so you can challenge it again and again.

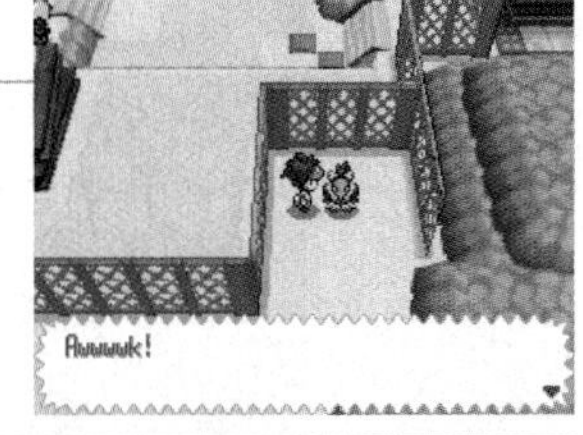

Step 9 Head north to reach the Desert Resort

Head north on the western arm of Route 4 and you can reach the Desert Resort. Stop by here to train your Pokémon for a bit before heading to Join Avenue (p. 132). Once you have explored as far as the Relic Castle, return to Route 4.

After visiting the Relic Castle: Head north to Join Avenue

When you return to Route 4, head east and then turn north at the intersection. You should arrive at the glittering, neon entrance to Join Avenue. Continue north and enter Join Avenue (p. 132).

Route 4

When playing *Pokémon White Version 2*

Route 4 has developed since the events of two years ago, but the discovery of archeological ruins put a halt to any construction plans. There are two exits to the north: the eastern exit leads to Join Avenue and the western exit leads to the Desert Resort.

Field Moves Needed

Items

- First visit
- ☐ BrightPowder
- ☐ Light Clay
- ☐ Mystic Water
- ☐ Protein
- ☐ Sitrus Berry
- ☐ Stardust
- ☐ TM28 Dig
- If you correctly identify the Pokémon cry that is mimicked
- ☐ Poké Toy

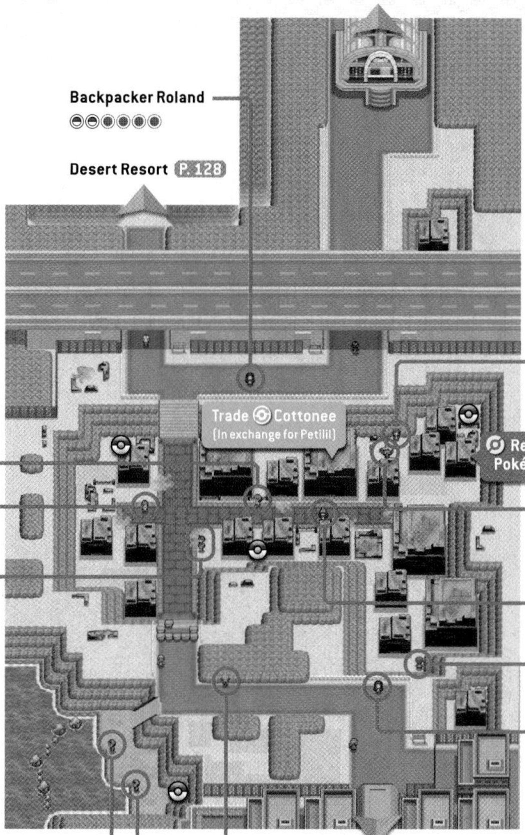

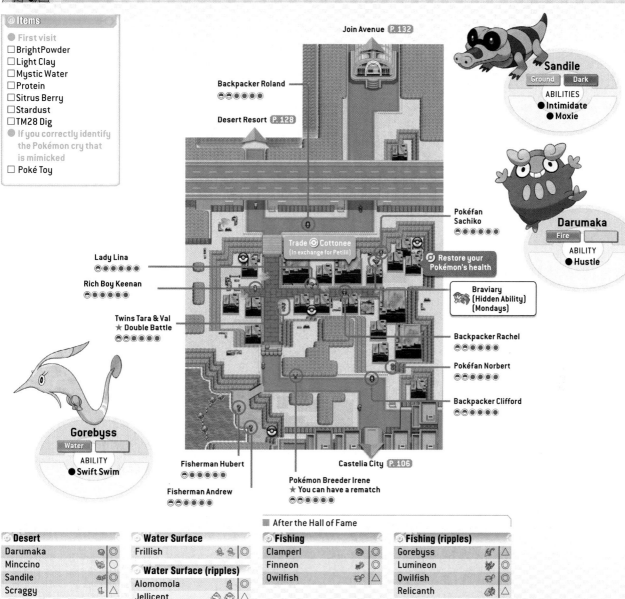

Join Avenue P. 132

Backpacker Roland

Desert Resort P. 128

Pokéfan Sachiko

Trade Cottonee (In exchange for Petilil)

Restore your Pokémon's health

Lady Lina

Rich Boy Keenan

Braviary (Hidden Ability) (Mondays)

Twins Tara & Val
★ Double Battle

Backpacker Rachel

Pokéfan Norbert

Backpacker Clifford

Fisherman Hubert

Castelia City P. 106

Fisherman Andrew

Pokémon Breeder Irene
★ You can have a rematch

Sandile
Ground / Dark
ABILITIES
● Intimidate
● Moxie

Darumaka
Fire
ABILITY
● Hustle

Gorebyss
Water
ABILITY
● Swift Swim

Desert	
Darumaka	◎
Minccino	○
Sandile	◎
Scraggy	△

Water Surface	
Frillish	◎

Water Surface (ripples)	
Alomomola	◎
Jellicent	△

After the Hall of Fame

Fishing	
Clamperl	◎
Finneon	◎
Qwilfish	△

Fishing (ripples)	
Gorebyss	△
Lumineon	◎
Qwilfish	◎
Relicanth	△

Step 1 Battle the Pokémon Breeder as often as you like

When you continue along the newly paved road, you will come across a Pokémon Breeder. This Pokémon Breeder is one Trainer that you can fight every time you visit this location. You don't even have to leave Route 4. Simply going in and out of one of the buildings will allow you to challenge her to a rematch.

Having lots of battles is the best way to train a Pokémon quickly!

There is always a sandstorm raging here

On Route 4, the weather is always a sandstorm during battles. Pokémon of any type other than Rock, Ground, or Steel will receive damage every turn. Keep an eye on your Pokémon's HP bar!

Step 2 Take up the challenge that Colress has thrown down

When you proceed to the west, you will find Colress standing before you. As promised, he is waiting on Route 4 to battle with you. The stone wall behind him blocks you from moving ahead. You will have to accept his challenge and face him in a Pokémon battle if you want to continue on your journey.

Pokémon appear in the dark sand

There is dark sand and light sand in desert areas. When you walk on the dark sand, Pokémon pop out. If you want to catch Pokémon, you should start by walking in areas with dark sand.

Colress's Pokémon

Pokémon	Lv.	Type	Weak to
Magnemite	Lv. 21	Electric, Steel	Ground, Fire, Fighting
Klink	Lv. 23	Steel	Fire, Fighting, Ground

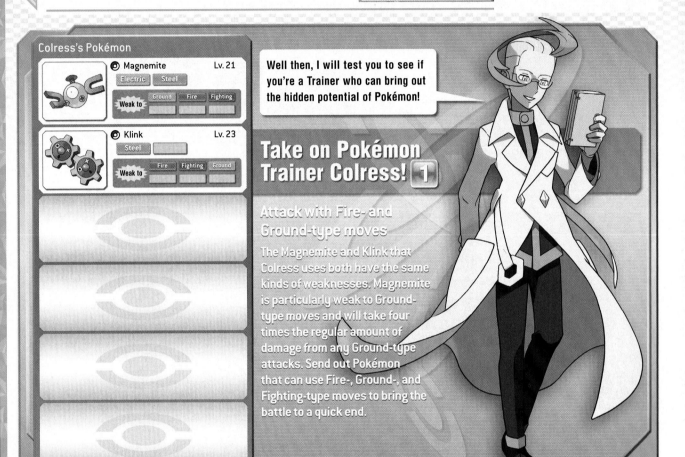

> Well then, I will test you to see if you're a Trainer who can bring out the hidden potential of Pokémon!

Take on Pokémon Trainer Colress! 1

Attack with Fire- and Ground-type moves

The Magnemite and Klink that Colress uses both have the same kinds of weaknesses. Magnemite is particularly weak to Ground-type moves and will take four times the regular amount of damage from any Ground-type attacks. Send out Pokémon that can use Fire-, Ground-, and Fighting-type moves to bring the battle to a quick end.

Step 3 Head north on the road that was blocked by Crustle

Before your battle with Colress, he kindly removed the stone-like Crustle that were blocking your path. He used a machine that excites Pokémon to wake the sleeping Crustle. After defeating Colress, continue to the north.

Use the Dowsing Machine to find items

There are many items waiting to be discovered in the sandy areas of Route 4. Use your Dowsing Machine to pinpoint these items' location. Search out items to build up your inventory (p. 62).

Step 4 Speak to the boy who focuses on Attack

Enter the building to the east and speak to the boy there, and he will name a particular Attack value. If you have a Pokémon in your party with the same Attack stat, you will receive five Swift Wings. If your Pokémon has an Attack stat higher than the number he names, you will get one. You can visit him every day.

Do you have a Pokémon whose Attack stat is the same as or higher than 97?

Step 5 Trade your Petilil for a Cottonee

In the building east of the one where you found the boy who focuses on Attack, another boy will ask you to trade Pokémon with him. If you give him your Petilil, you can receive a Cottonee. Petilil can be caught around Castelia City.

Step 6 Battle a Braviary every Monday

A Braviary with a special Hidden Ability will appear every Monday to the east of the building where you can trade Pokémon with the young boy. When you talk to it, the battle begins. If you accidentally defeat it, it will appear again the next Monday so you can challenge it again and again.

Step 7 Have the woman fully heal your Pokémon

In the building east of the area where Braviary appears, you'll find a woman who will heal your Pokémon if you speak to her. If your Pokémon have been injured during battles in the sandstorm, be sure to stop by here.

Hmm? Aren't you a bit tired?
Don't be shy. Take a rest!

Step 8 Identify the cries of the Pokémon in your party

Speak to the woman in the building that lies directly west of the one where you had your Pokémon healed. She will imitate the cry of one of your party Pokémon. If you correctly identify which Pokémon it is, you can receive a Poké Toy.

You can try to identify her mimicry again and again

You will only get a reward the first time you correctly identify the Pokémon cry that the girl imitates. You can try your hand at her challenge every time you talk to her, though! Why not take a breather from your adventure sometimes and enjoy a fun quiz?

Step 9 Head north to reach the Desert Resort

Head north on the western arm of Route 4 and you can reach the Desert Resort. Advance into the desert to train your Pokémon for a bit before heading to Join Avenue (p. 132). Once you have explored as far as the Relic Castle, return to Route 4.

After visiting the Relic Castle: Head north to Join Avenue

When you return to Route 4, head east and then turn north at the intersection. You should arrive at the glittering, neon entrance to Join Avenue. Continue north and enter Join Avenue (p. 132).

Desert Resort

Guide

The Desert Resort is a vast desert where a sandstorm always rages. At the back is the entrance to the Relic Castle. Two years ago, there were two entrances, but one of them has been buried in sand since then.

Field Moves Needed

Items

First visit

- ☐ Blue Shard
- ☐ Green Shard
- ☐ Heart Scale
- ☐ Max Ether
- ☐ Nugget
- ☐ Red Shard
- ☐ Soft Sand
- ☐ Stardust
- ☐ Yellow Shard

After defeating Pokémon Ranger Anja

- ☐ Rawst Berry

After defeating Pokémon Ranger Jaden

- ☐ Rawst Berry

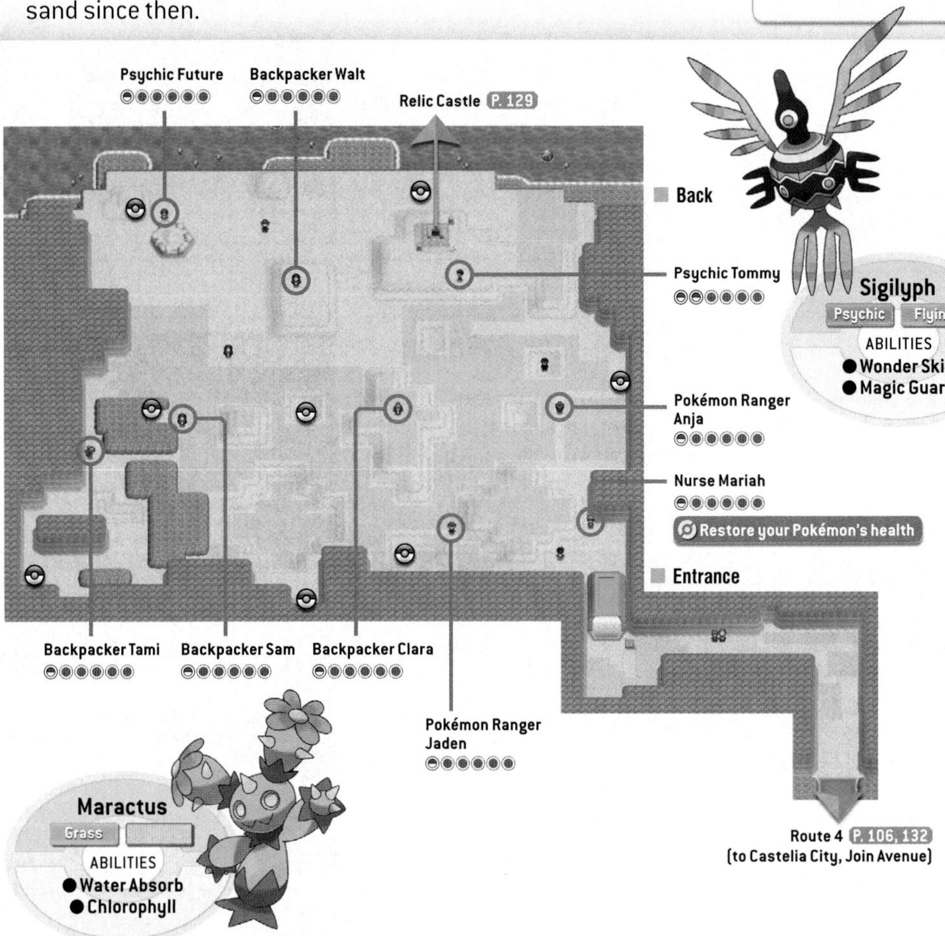

Psychic Future

Backpacker Walt

Relic Castle P. 129

Back

Psychic Tommy

Pokémon Ranger Anja

Nurse Mariah

Restore your Pokémon's health

Entrance

Backpacker Tami

Backpacker Sam

Backpacker Clara

Pokémon Ranger Jaden

Route 4 P. 106, 132
(to Castelia City, Join Avenue)

Sigilyph
Psychic / Flying
ABILITIES
- Wonder Skin
- Magic Guard

Sandshrew
Ground
ABILITY
- Sand Veil

Maractus
Grass
ABILITIES
- Water Absorb
- Chlorophyll

Entrance

Desert	
Darumaka	◎
Dwebble	○
Maractus	○
Sandile	◎
Sandshrew	○
Scraggy	◎

Back

Desert	
Darumaka	○
Dwebble	○
Maractus	○
Sandile	◎
Sandshrew	○
Sigilyph	○
Trapinch	△

N's Pokémon	
Darmanitan	Lv. 35
Darumaka	Lv. 22
Sandile	Lv. 22
Scraggy	Lv. 22
Sigilyph	Lv. 22

Mass Outbreaks
Hippowdon

Step 1 Have Nurse Mariah heal your Pokémon

Nurse Mariah is right where you go through the entrance gate. Defeat her in battle and then talk to her. She'll heal your Pokémon every time. If your Pokémon are hurt, have her heal them.

OK, let's get you all fixed up!
Just leave it up to me!

An endless sandstorm

The Desert Resort is always in the middle of a sandstorm. In a battle, Pokémon will lose HP every turn unless they are Rock, Ground, or Steel types. Heal your Pokémon as you explore.

Step 2 Proceed while battling Pokémon Trainers

There are nine Pokémon Trainers at the back of the desert. Collect the items there and battle them all. Your Pokémon will probably lose HP through battles or due to sandstorm, so heal your Pokémon often.

A desert is like one giant sandbox, right?
So come on, let's let our Pokémon play!

Step 3 Enter the Relic Castle in the northeast

Go to the back of the desert and go north towards the east side. You'll come to the entrance to the Relic Castle. You can explore 1F and B1F when you go inside this way. Before you move on, explore the Relic Castle (p. 129).

After visiting the Relic Castle Head for Join Avenue from Route 4

Explore the Relic Castle, but soon it'll be time to go back to challenging Gyms. Go south from the Desert Resort and you'll be back on Route 4 (p. 122, 125). From there, go to Join Avenue.

Use the Dowsing Machine to find items

This vast desert has many hidden items. Use the Dowsing Machine to find all the hidden items. Register the Dowsing Machine to the Y Button and you can use it anytime you want to (p. 62).

Get Berries from Pokémon Rangers

Defeat Anja and Jaden to receive Rawst Berries. Anja is at the back of the desert on the east side. Jaden is on the south side. Make sure you defeat them and get Rawst Berries.

Funfest Missions will be added

At the back of the desert, talk to the Pokémon Ranger on the north side. In *Pokémon Black Version 2*, "Get Rich Quick!" will be added. In *Pokémon White Version 2*, "Treasure Hunting!" will be added.

Ancient ruins with a glorious history, buried in the sand as time went by

Relic Castle

Guide

The Relic Castle is comprised of ancient ruins buried in sand. The first floor has quicksand. If you get caught in the sand, you'll fall to B1F. From the Relic Passage, you can go to the lowest floor, a place you cannot reach from the Desert Resort.

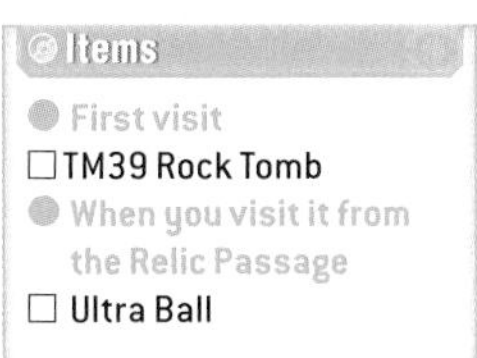

1F • B1F

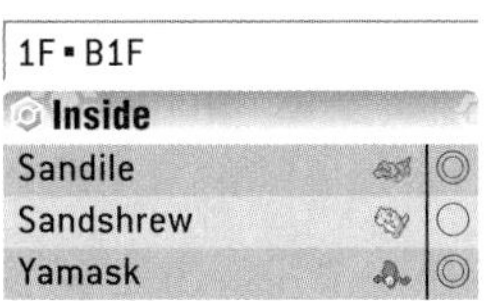

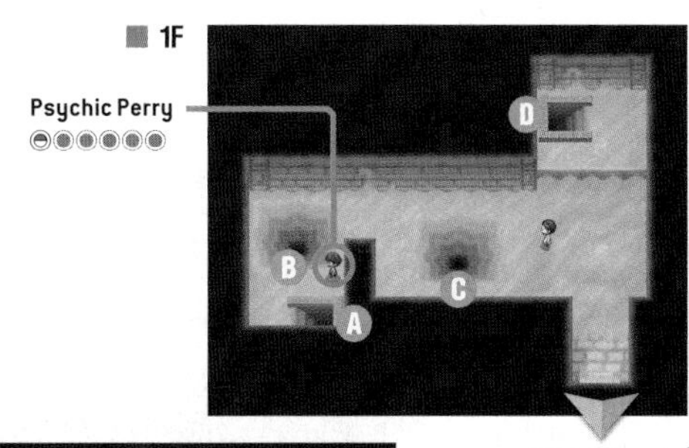

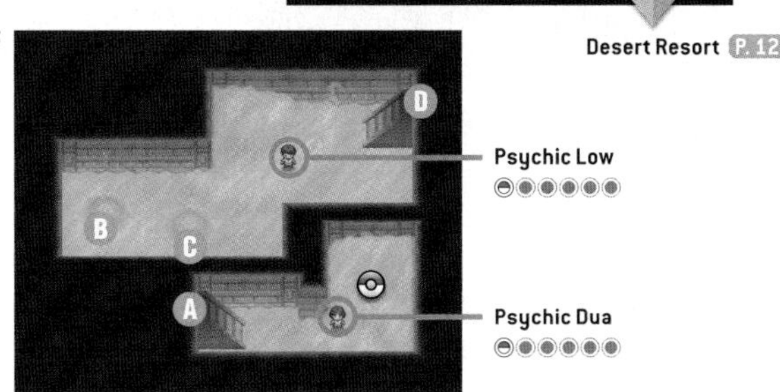

◆ You cannot go to the first floor from B and C on B1F.

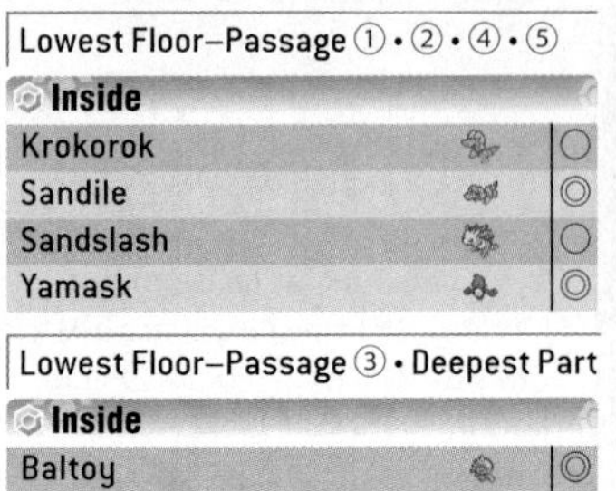

Lowest Floor–Passage ①・②・④・⑤	
Inside	
Krokorok	○
Sandile	◎
Sandslash	○
Yamask	◎

Lowest Floor–Passage ③・Deepest Part	
Inside	
Baltoy	◎

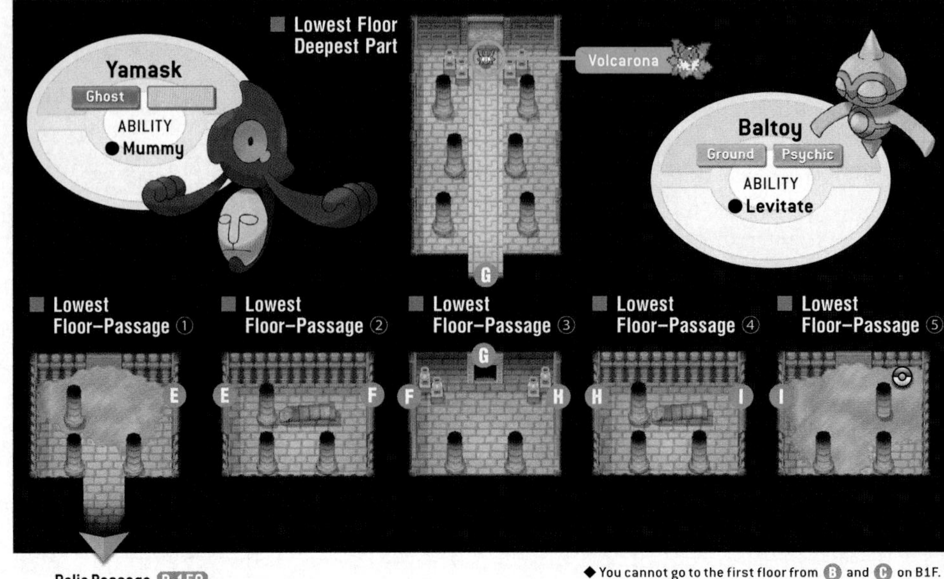

Relic Passage P. 159

◆ You cannot go to the first floor from B and C on B1F.

Step 1 Battle the Pokémon Trainer on the first floor

There are two areas of quicksand on the first floor. If you try to run through quicksand, you'll be caught and fall to the lower floor. Walk slowly around the quicksand to approach the Pokémon Trainer on the west side on the first floor and challenge him.

My Psychic-type Pokémon
just started making noises.

Step 2 Take the stairs to reach B1F

Take the stairs near the Pokémon Trainer on the first floor to go down to B1F. You'll arrive at a different place than if you fell through the quicksand. After you battle the Pokémon Trainer and collect the item, take the stairs you took earlier to go back to the first floor.

Just being here fills me
with magical power...

Step 3 Fall through quicksand to reach B1F

When you go back to the first floor, this time, fall through the quicksand to reach B1F. You'll reach the same place whichever quicksand you fall through. After battling the Pokémon Trainer on B1F, take the stairs to go back to the first floor.

It was a massive ruins two years ago

Two years ago, the Relic Castle was a massive ruins with six stories in the ground, multiple small rooms on the lowest floor, and the tower that reached through the ground. However, most of them have been buried in the past two years.

Step 4 Return to Route 4

There is another floor, the lowest floor in the Relic Castle, but from the Desert Resort entrance, you can only reach the first floor and B1F. Once you've battled the Pokémon Trainers and collected the items on these floors, go back to the Desert Resort (p. 128).

When you take the Relic Passage » Head east through the passage

Enter the Relic Castle from the Relic Passage, and you'll reach the lowest floor. Head east through the passage, and you'll find an item at the end of Passage ⑤. Once you have the item, go back two rooms to the west and head north from Passage ③.

Visit it from the PWT

You can enter the Relic Passage from the Castelia Sewers, too. However, you cannot reach the Relic Castle from that direction. When you visit the Pokémon World Tournament, take the Relic Passage to visit the lowest floor of the Relic Castle.

When you take the Relic Passage » Find Volcarona in the deepest room

Head north from Passage ③, and head to the deepest part on the lowest floor. Go north and you'll find Volcarona at the end. Talk to it to enter a battle with it. You can meet Volcarona only here, so make sure to catch it.

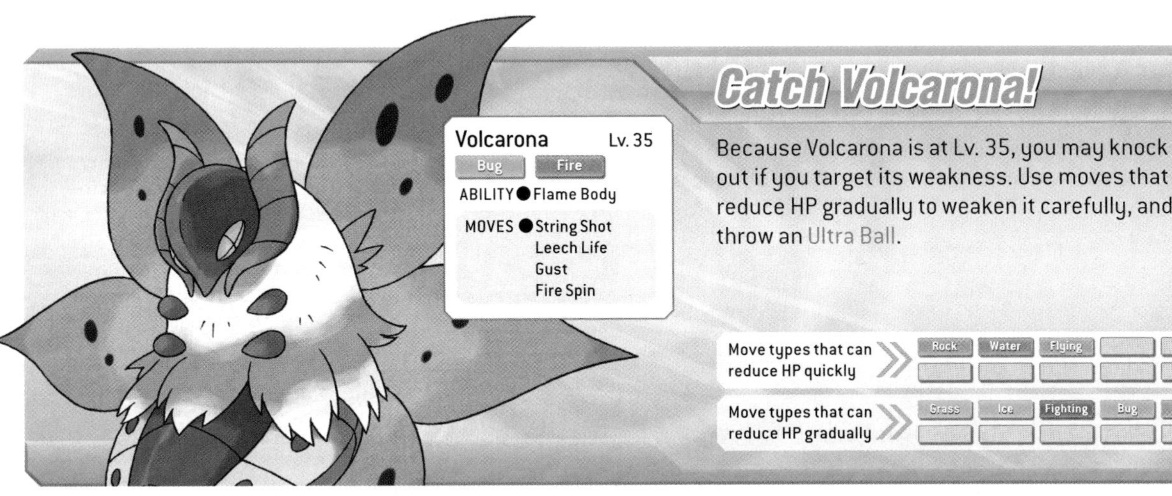

Catch Volcarona!

Volcarona Lv. 35

Bug / Fire

ABILITY ● Flame Body

MOVES ● String Shot, Leech Life, Gust, Fire Spin

Because Volcarona is at Lv. 35, you may knock it out if you target its weakness. Use moves that can reduce HP gradually to weaken it carefully, and then throw an Ultra Ball.

Move types that can reduce HP quickly	Rock	Water	Flying		
Move types that can reduce HP gradually	Grass	Ice	Fighting	Bug	Steel

When you take the Relic Passage » Go back to the Relic Passage

After collecting the item and catching Volcarona, you've done everything you can on the lowest floor of the Relic Castle. Head west from Passage ③ and then head south from Passage ① to go back to the Relic Passage (p. 159).

Join Avenue

Join Avenue is a big avenue with no shops at the beginning. You'll become the manager upon the owner's request, and as you invite visitors to start shops and recommend that people visit these shops, the avenue will grow as a place with lots of shops.

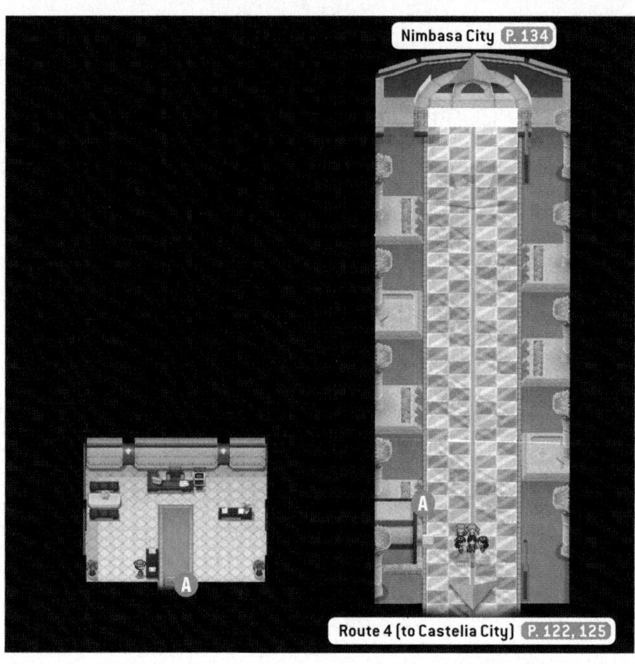

Step 1 Become a manager upon the owner's request

When you enter Join Avenue, the owner who is surrounded by his assistants speaks to you. He asks you to be the manager to develop the avenue. Become the manager, and develop an exciting avenue.

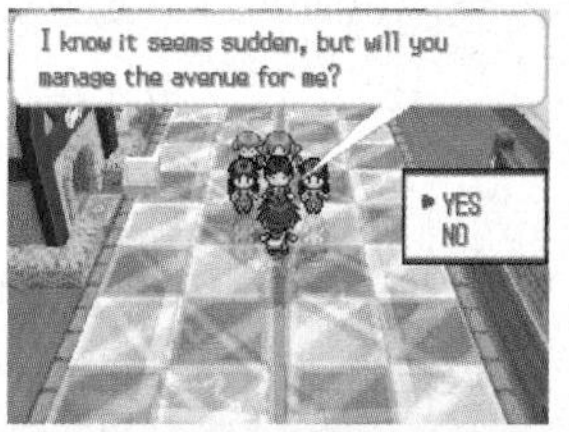

I know it seems sudden, but will you manage the avenue for me?
YES
NO

Learn a lot of things from the assistants

You're the manager of the avenue, and the assistants Jacci and Future are always at the office to help you. Speak to them when you want to change your title, favorite phrase, and more, or when you want to know info about the avenue.

Step 2 Answer the owner's questions

After accepting the owner's request, the owner will ask you your favorite phrase and what you say when you're moved. You can enter any words you want up to eight characters. The words will be communicated by Tag Mode, so choose words that make people happy.

Step 3 Find out how to develop the avenue

The owner leaves, but the assistants Jacci and Future will stay and tell you how to develop the avenue. Learn from them how to build shops and how to invite visitors to make the avenue lively.

Neat
Messy
Boss, what does your room look like?

Visitors come to the avenue even without using communication features

The key for attracting visitors to Join Avenue is using communication features. However, even without communicating with people, a few visitors will come to the avenue every day. So, even when you cannot communicate, you can still develop the avenue.

Step 4 Head north to Nimbasa City

The next destination is Nimbasa City, where the fourth Gym is. After learning how to develop the avenue from the assistants in Join Avenue, head straight north to go to Nimbasa City (p. 134).

Communicate with many people to develop Join Avenue

Increase the selection of products in shops

Join Avenue develops as you use communication features with more people. Invite visitors to be residents of the avenue, and you'll have more shops that are useful for your adventure and Pokémon training. Also when you recommend shops to visitors, shops and the avenue will be more popular and shops will have a wider selection of products. Use the various communication features and create your own avenue.

Have more shops on the avenue

Invite a visitor to be a resident, and he or she will build one of eight kinds of shops on the avenue. Nurseries won't be built until you enter the Hall of Fame and the avenue rank is 15 or more.

How to build shops

1. Talk to a visitor
2. Choose "Invite"
3. Choose "Make the person a resident"

Raise the ranks of the shops and the avenue

As you recommend shops to visitors, the shops and the avenue get more and more popular, and the shops' ranks go up. Recommend shops that visitors will like. If you recommend shops that they don't wish to visit, they'll leave.

How to rank up

1. Talk to a visitor
2. Choose "Recommend"
3. Choose a shop that the visitor wants

Boost the ranks of shops

When the popularity reaches a certain point, the shop's rank goes up, and more products will be available. The shop's rank goes up to 10.

Raise your avenue's rank

When the popularity reaches a certain point, the avenue's rank goes up, and you'll receive various rewards. The avenue's rank goes up to 100.

Use various communication features to attract visitors

Not only passersby using Tag Mode will visit your Join Avenue, but also people you traded with or battled via the C-Gear, people you talked to in the Union Room, and people you traded Pokémon with over the GTS.

Communication features that increase the number of visitors

1. Communication features of the C-Gear
2. Union Room
3. Global Terminal
4. Battle Subway

Nimbasa City

Nimbasa City is a huge city of leisure, with various facilities such as the Battle Subway, the Musical Theater, and an amusement park. The east of the city leads to Route 16, and the west leads to Route 5.

Field Moves Needed

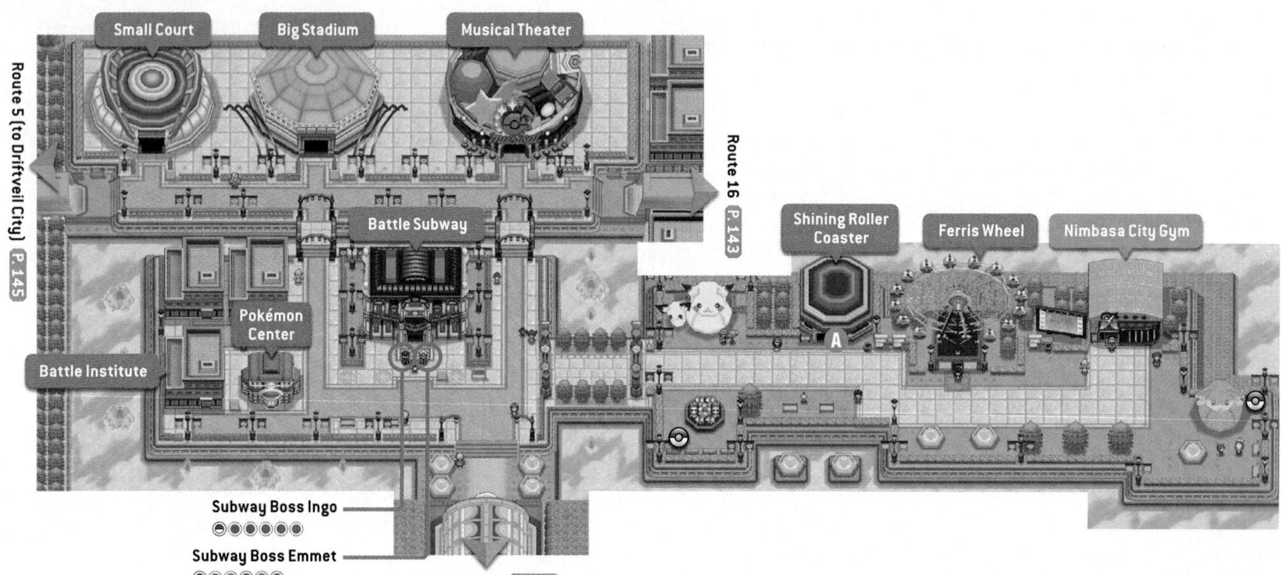

Items

First visit
- ☐ Dropped Item
- ☐ Fresh Water
- ☐ Macho Brace
- ☐ Parlyz Heal ×2
- ☐ Prop Case
- ☐ Red Shard ×10
- ☐ Sun Stone
- ☐ TM49 Echoed Voice
- ☐ Vs. Recorder

If your friendship with the Pokémon at the head of your party is strong
- ☐ Soothe Bell

After defeating the Nimbasa City Gym
- ☐ Bolt Badge
- ☐ TM72 Volt Switch

Exchange Service Corner at the Battle Subway (Left Clerk)

TM17 Protect	6 BP	TM48 Round	18 BP
TM20 Safeguard	6 BP	TM75 Swords Dance	18 BP
TM32 Double Team	6 BP	TM87 Swagger	18 BP
TM59 Incinerate	6 BP	TM88 Pluck	18 BP
TM31 Brick Break	12 BP	TM34 Sludge Wave	24 BP
TM79 Frost Breath	12 BP	TM51 Ally Switch	24 BP
TM89 U-turn	12 BP	TM60 Quash	24 BP
TM10 Hidden Power	18 BP	TM64 Explosion	24 BP
TM23 Smack Down	18 BP	TM77 Psych Up	24 BP

Shining Roller Coaster

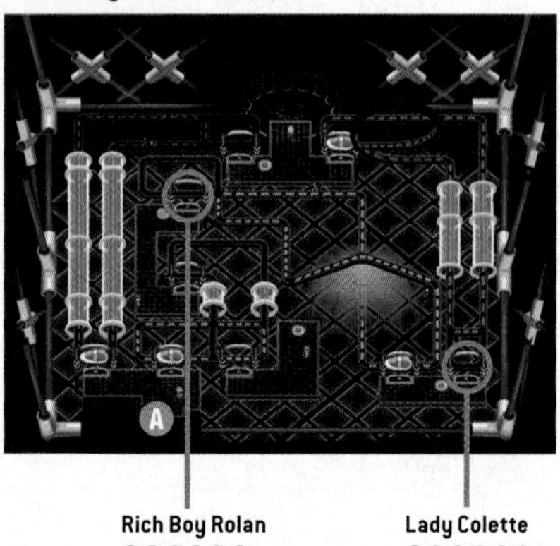

Poké Mart (Lower Clerk)

Item	Price
TM73 Thunder Wave	10,000
TM74 Gyro Ball	10,000
TM16 Light Screen	30,000
TM33 Reflect	30,000

Exchange Service Corner at the Battle Subway (Right Clerk)

Calcium	1 BP	Zoom Lens	12 BP
Carbos	1 BP	Absorb Bulb	16 BP
HP Up	1 BP	Cell Battery	16 BP
Iron	1 BP	Eject Button	16 BP
Protein	1 BP	Flame Orb	16 BP
Zinc	1 BP	Power Anklet	16 BP
Fire Stone	3 BP	Power Band	16 BP
Leaf Stone	3 BP	Power Belt	16 BP
Thunderstone	3 BP	Power Bracer	16 BP
Water Stone	3 BP	Power Herb	16 BP
Binding Band	8 BP	Power Lens	16 BP
Muscle Band	8 BP	Power Weight	16 BP
Razor Claw	8 BP	Red Card	16 BP
Razor Fang	8 BP	Toxic Orb	16 BP
Scope Lens	8 BP	White Herb	16 BP
Wide Lens	8 BP	Choice Band	24 BP
Wise Glasses	8 BP	Choice Scarf	24 BP
Air Balloon	12 BP	Choice Specs	24 BP
BrightPowder	12 BP	Focus Sash	24 BP
Focus Band	12 BP	Life Orb	24 BP
Iron Ball	12 BP	Rare Candy	24 BP

Step 1 Form a team to challenge Ingo and Emmet

When you enter the city, Subway Bosses Ingo and Emmet will be standing at the entry to the Battle Subway. Talk to the Pokémon Trainer in front of them. You'll be asked if you'd like to battle together. Do as requested and get ready for a Battle Subway Boss challenge!

This is an a-MAZ-ing opportunity! Would you PLEASE battle with me?

Your partner is the opposite gender of your player character

When you challenge Ingo and Emmet, you'll be paired up with Rosa if you're playing a boy character or with Nate if you're playing a girl character.

Everybody smile!
Check safety.
Aim for victory!
All aboard!

Challenge Subway Bosses Ingo and Emmet!

Together with your partner, land supereffective moves.

If you received Snivy from Bianca, your partner will send out Dewott; if you started with Tepig, your partner will send out Servine; and if you started with Oshawott, your partner will send out Pignite. Defeat one of the Pokémon with supereffective moves, and finish the other together with your partner's Pokémon.

Ingo's Pokémon

Pokémon	Lv.	Type	Weak to
Boldore ♂	Lv. 26	Rock	Water, Grass, Fighting, Ground, Steel

Emmet's Pokémon

Pokémon	Lv.	Type	Weak to
Gurdurr ♂	Lv. 26	Fighting	Flying, Psychic

Step 2 You score a Vs. Recorder!

After the battle, Ingo and Emmet go back to the Battle Subway. Your partner will give you a Vs. Recorder. It enables you to record a video of a battle in the Battle Subway or a Link Battle with a friend.

Trainer obtained the Vs. Recorder!

Step 3 Show how it's done in the Battle Subway

In the Battle Subway, you can get on a real winning streak. For every seven Trainers you defeat, you'll get Battle Points (BP). Exchange Battle Points for items useful in battles. The more Trainers you challenge, the more BP you can collect (p. 409).

The Battle Subway is the subway where Trainers see who's strongest!

Create your own style

Talk to the man at the Gear Station in the Battle Subway to set up how you want to introduce yourself. You can also register what you want to say when you win or lose a battle. Set up your style before you challenge the Battle Subway.

Step 4 Take the train to Anville Town

From the Battle Subway's Gear Station, you can take a train to Anville Town, a small town located at the west end of the Unova region (p. 142)!

Talk to the Depot Agent with Pansage

You'll hear from a girl at the Anville Town station that Pansage is missing. After that, the Depot Agent will appear with Pansage in front of Big Stadium. Talk to the agent about the girl (p. 142).

Step 5 Take on Pokémon battles at Big Stadium

Baseball, soccer, and football are played in Big Stadium. Which sport is played depends on the day. You can also enjoy battles with Pokémon Trainers on the field during practice. Visit there to train your Pokémon (p. 140).

Kids! Please cooperate with this practice session for my Pokémon!

Get a Soothe Bell

Talk to the old woman on 2F in a house to the north of the Battle Institute. If your lead Pokémon has high friendship, she'll give you a Soothe Bell. This item helps Pokémon grow friendlier more quickly.

Step 6 Court trouble with Pokémon battles at Small Court

Tennis and basketball are played in Small Court, which is west of Big Stadium. Tennis and basketball alternate, depending on the day. On the court during practices, you can get your share of Pokémon battles with athletes and Pokémon Trainers (p. 140).

The amount you sweat is a good indicator of how youthful you are!

What is a Shiny Pokémon?

You can hear about Shiny Pokémon in a house north of the Pokémon Center. Shiny Pokémon are the same as others when it comes to stats and such, but they are stupendously rare and parts of their bodies show different colors than normal. You can count yourself pretty lucky if you see one (p. 32).

Step 7 Get a Prop Case from the owner of the Musical Theater

When you enter the Musical Theater, the owner will talk to you. He'll give you a Prop Case, which you'll need to participate in the musical. You can use it to store Props to dress up your Pokémon.

Trainer obtained the Prop Case!

Memory Link event

Use Memory Link and the Musical Theater owner will give you the Prop Case from *Pokémon Black Version* or *Pokémon White Version* (p. 73).

Step 8 Your Pokémon take center stage in the Pokémon Musical

At the Pokémon Musical, dress up your Pokémon with Props so it can participate in a musical. When the show ends, you may receive a Prop. Participate in the musical many times, collect a lot of Props, and enjoy the fun of dressing up your Pokémon (p. 401).

Step 9 Get a Macho Brace

Go through the gate to Route 16 on the east side of the city, and speak to an Infielder waiting at the gate. He'll give you a Macho Brace. A Pokémon holding it in battle will grow stronger more quickly.

Trainer obtained a Macho Brace!

Macho Macho Brace

If you let a Pokémon hold a Macho Brace, the item reduces its Speed temporarily, but promotes faster growth of its base stats. If you want a Pokémon to be special in your land, start by giving it a Macho Brace.

Step

Head for Route 16 to train your Pokémon

Go to Route 16 before you challenge the Nimbasa City Gym (p. 143). There are 10 Pokémon Trainers there so you can train your Pokémon. Take time to explore every corner of Route 16 and Lostlorn Forest before you come back.

Visit the Battle Institute after the Hall of Fame

You can take a Battle Test in the Battle Institute. However, the test is available only after the Hall of Fame. Become the Pokémon League Champion and then come back here (p. 258).

Step

Get the Dropped Item at the amusement park

Visit the amusement park in the east side of the city, and get the Dropped Item, which you'll find just past the entrance toward the south end. The Trainer who dropped it will give you a call, and you'll be able to gradually build friendship with this person (p. 416).

The gender of your player character determines who you'll meet

The gender of the Trainer who lost the Dropped Item depends on the gender of your player character. If your player is a girl, the Trainer will be Curtis. If your player is a boy, the Trainer will be Yancy.

Step

Battle Trainers on the roller coaster

Go to the Shining Roller Coaster on the north side of the amusement park and proceed by pressing the switches to change the path. Talk to the woman in the back and you'll be able to challenge Elesa, the Leader of the Nimbasa City Gym.

Two years ago, it was a Gym

The Shining Roller Coaster used to be the Nimbasa City Gym. You can see Trainers such as Ladies and Rich Boys still waiting for challengers there.

Step

Battle against the Trainer in front of the Ferris wheel

There's a Pokémon Trainer in front of the Ferris wheel next to the roller coaster. After defeating the Trainer, you can ride the Ferris wheel together. The Trainer varies, depending on the season and the gender of your player character (p. 418).

Step 14

Challenge the Nimbasa City Gym

You can challenge the Gym after talking with the woman at the back of the Shining Roller Coaster. If Clyde is there blocking the entrance, go to the roller coaster first. Don't forget to heal your Pokémon at the Pokémon Center before you challenge the Gym.

4 Nimbasa City Gym Battle

Gym Battle Tips

- Make sure to bring lots of Parlyz Heals
- Catch a Sandile or Sandshrew in the Desert Resort and use it in your battle

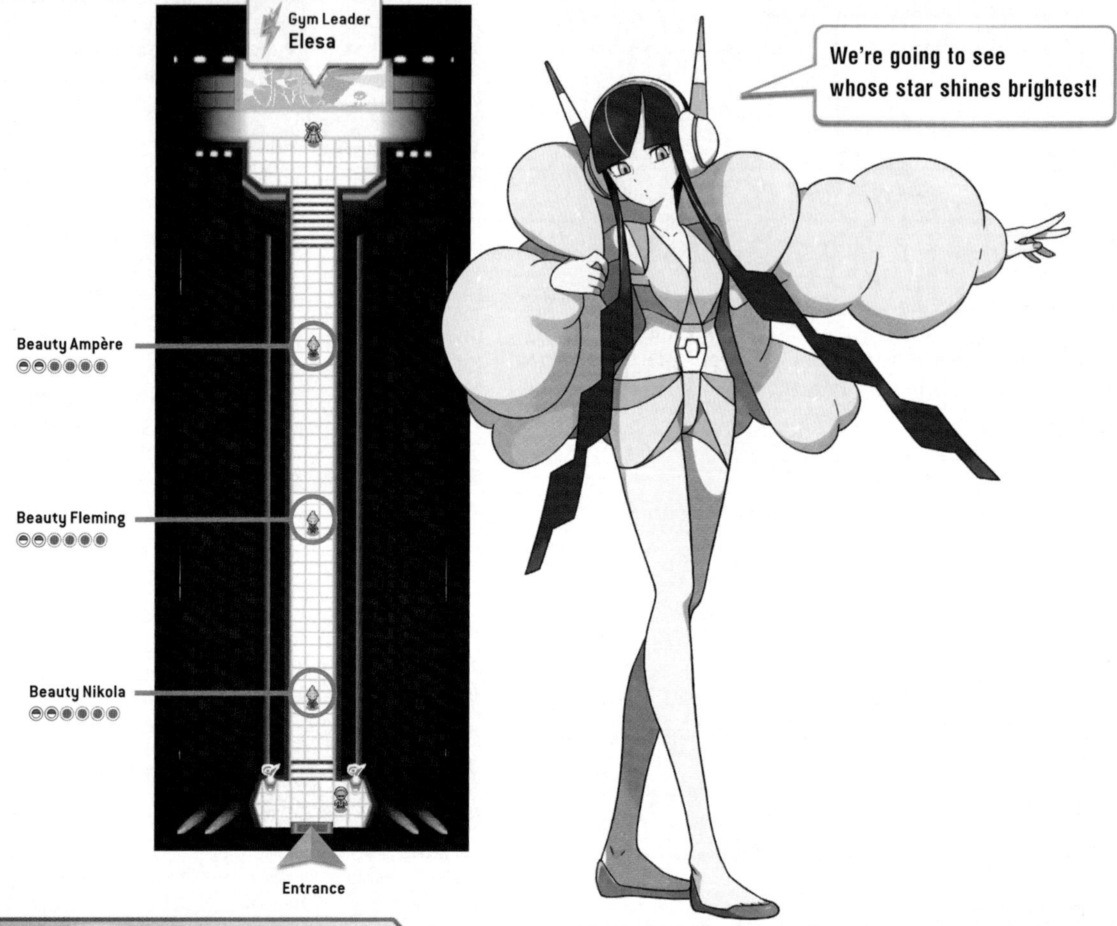

Nimbasa City Gym Leader

Elesa

Electric-type Pokémon User

Use Parlyz Heal to prevent a shocking loss

Defeat the Gym's three Pokémon Trainers in order, and you can battle with the Gym Leader, Elesa. Elesa's Pokémon frequently use Volt Switch to switch out. They often use attacks that cause the Paralysis status condition as well. If your Pokémon has Paralysis, use Parlyz Heal immediately to recover. Use Rock- and Ground-type moves, which are super effective against her Pokémon.

Elesa's Pokémon
Emolga ♀ Lv. 28
Electric Flying
Weak to Ice Rock
Flaaffy ♀ Lv. 28
Electric
Weak to Ground
Zebstrika ♀ Lv. 30
Electric
Weak to Ground

Bolt Badge

Pokémon up to Lv. 50, including those received in trades, will obey you.

TM 72 Volt Switch — Electric

After attacking, the user switches out with another Pokémon in the party.

After defeating the Nimbasa City Gym

Hugh and Team Plasma face off

When you walk towards the gate to Route 5, you run into Team Plasma and Hugh in front of Big Stadium. Hugh doesn't try to hide how angry he is with Team Plasma. The Team Plasma Grunts are also itching for a fight.

You're about to feel my rage!

Stop by the Pokémon Center before proceeding

A battle with Team Plasma awaits you when you go to where Hugh is after the Gym battle. Before meeting up with Hugh, make sure to stop by the Pokémon Center and restore any HP your party lost.

After defeating the Nimbasa City Gym

Teach the Team Plasma Grunts a lesson

Defeat the Team Plasma Grunt that stands right in front of you, blocking your way. Then talk to the Grunt in the bottom of the group or the Grunt in the center and a battle will start. When you defeat one Grunt, a battle will begin with the other Grunt right away. You will have to win against them in consecutive battles.

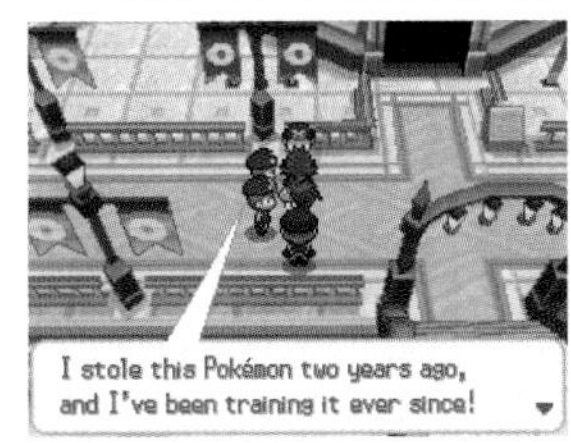

I stole this Pokémon two years ago,
and I've been training it ever since!

After defeating the Nimbasa City Gym

A sad incident haunts Hugh

The Team Plasma Grunts leave when you win, and then Hugh tells you about how Team Plasma stole his little sister's Purrloin five years ago. Hugh restores your Pokémon's HP and chases after Team Plasma.

I was only a little kid...
I couldn't do anything...

The reason for Hugh's rage becomes clear

All of Hugh's frustration for not being able to protect his sister's Purrloin has turned to anger, and since then he has been confronting Team Plasma. He decided he needs to get stronger to get Purrloin back, so he'll keep fighting until he does just that.

Take Route 5 to the next Gym

You've chased off Team Plasma for now, so continue on to the next Gym. The fifth Gym is in Driftveil City, which is just past Route 5. Go west toward Route 5 (p. 145).

Utilize Big Stadium and Small Court

Sports played at Big Stadium

Baseball

■ Days played

M Tu W Th F Sa Su

■ Time when you can battle

All day

Except for 2 to 4:59 p.m.

I'm a little bit strong.
I will work out!

Pokémon Trainers you can battle every day

Level	Pokémon Trainer	Item you can get
Level 1	Infielder Alex	Potion
	Infielder Connor	Potion
	Infielder Todd	Potion
Level 2	Infielder Alex	Super Potion
	Infielder Connor	Super Potion
	Infielder Todd	Super Potion
	Backers Ami & Eira	—
Level 3	Infielder Alex	Hyper Potion
	Infielder Connor	Hyper Potion
	Infielder Todd	Hyper Potion
	Backers Ami & Eira	—

Soccer

■ Days played

M Tu W Th F Sa Su

■ Time when you can battle

All day

Except for 2 to 3:59 p.m.

Join the training of
our Pokémon Eleven!

Pokémon Trainers you can battle every day

Level	Pokémon Trainer	Item you can get
Level 1	Striker Tony	Potion
	Striker Marco	Potion
	Striker Roberto	Potion
Level 2	Striker Tony	Super Potion
	Striker Marco	Super Potion
	Striker Roberto	Super Potion
	Backers Kay & Ali	—
Level 3	Striker Tony	Hyper Potion
	Striker Marco	Hyper Potion
	Striker Roberto	Hyper Potion
	Backers Kay & Ali	—

Football

■ Days played

M Tu W Th F Sa Su

■ Time when you can battle

All day

Except for 2 to 3:59 p.m.

Pokémon Trainers you can battle every day

Level	Pokémon Trainer	Item you can get
Level 1	Linebacker Dan	Potion
	Linebacker Bob	Potion
	Linebacker Jonah	Potion
Level 2	Linebacker Dan	Super Potion
	Linebacker Bob	Super Potion
	Linebacker Jonah	Super Potion
	Backers Hawk & Dar	—
Level 3	Linebacker Dan	Hyper Potion
	Linebacker Bob	Hyper Potion
	Linebacker Jonah	Hyper Potion
	Backers Hawk & Dar	—

Visit daily and train your Pokémon

Enjoy Pokémon battles at Nimbasa City's Big Stadium and Small Court. When you obtain more Gym Badges, the number of people to battle will increase and you'll get better items when you win. Visit every day and make your Pokémon stronger.

Levels

Level	Condition
Level 1	Obtain three Gym Badges
Level 2	Obtain five Gym Badges
Level 3	Obtain seven Gym Badges

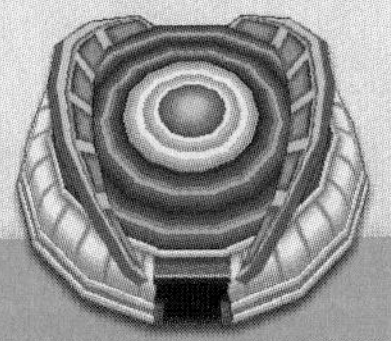

Sports played at Small Court

■ Days played

■ Time when you can battle

All day

Except for 10 to 10:59 a.m.

An elegant Smasher
has an elegant battle!

Pokémon Trainers you can battle every day

Level	Pokémon Trainer	Item you can get
Level 1	Smasher Elena	Potion
	Smasher Aspen	Potion
	Smasher Mari	Potion
Level 2	Smasher Elena	Super Potion
	Smasher Aspen	Super Potion
	Smasher Mari	Super Potion
	Backers Joe & Ross	—
Level 3	Smasher Elena	Hyper Potion
	Smasher Aspen	Hyper Potion
	Smasher Mari	Hyper Potion
	Backers Joe & Ross	—

■ Days played

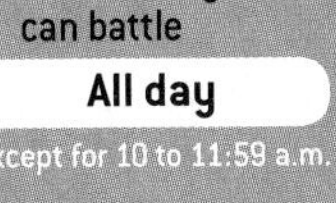

■ Time when you can battle

All day

Except for 10 to 11:59 a.m.

I'll improve by having a lot
of Pokémon battles!

Pokémon Trainers you can battle every day

Level	Pokémon Trainer	Item you can get
Level 1	Hoopster Bobby	Potion
	Hoopster John	Potion
	Hoopster Lamarcus	Potion
Level 2	Hoopster Bobby	Super Potion
	Hoopster John	Super Potion
	Hoopster Lamarcus	Super Potion
	Backers Masa & Yas	—
Level 3	Hoopster Bobby	Hyper Potion
	Hoopster John	Hyper Potion
	Hoopster Lamarcus	Hyper Potion
	Backers Masa & Yas	—

Tip

Use the items you received and keep battling

As you get more Gym Badges, the level of the Trainers in Big Stadium and Small Court increases. When you defeat a Trainer, you get a Potion at the first level, a Super Potion at the second, and a Hyper Potion at the third. You keep getting them as you win, so use them without any worries about wasting them.

Trainer obtained a Potion!

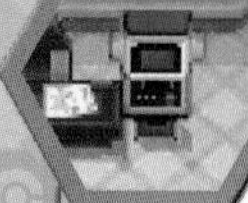

A city with a rail yard where trains park for an overhaul

Anville Town

Guide

Anville Town is a small town that can be reached by riding one of Nimbasa's Battle Subway trains. A turntable for changing the direction of trains sits in the center of town. On weekends, the town is bustling with tourists who have come to watch the trains that come on those days.

Field Moves Needed

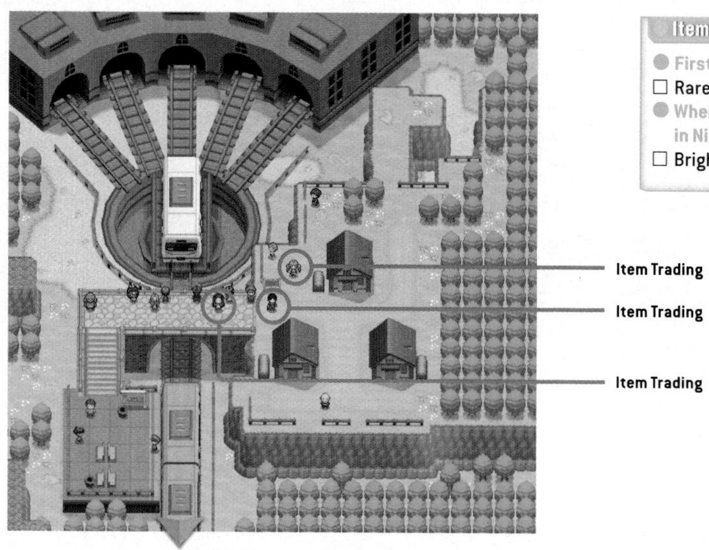

Items

- First visit
- ☐ Rare Candy
- When you find Pansage in Nimbasa City
- ☐ BrightPowder

Step 1 Talk to the girl on the platform

A girl will be standing right in front of you on the platform when you get off the train. When you talk to her, you'll find out that her Pansage got lost somewhere in Nimbasa City. When you return to Nimbasa City, do the right thing and look for her Pansage for her (p. 134).

Oh, Pansage...
Where could you be?

Find Pansage in Nimbasa City

After talking to the girl on the platform, talk to the station attendant with the Pansage in Nimbasa City. If you talk to the girl on the platform again once you've done that, she'll give you a BrightPowder as thanks.

Step 2 Get items for taking on the Battle Subway

You can get an item in a house on the eastern side of town, but what you get depends on the number of times you've battled in the Battle Subway. If you win seven battles in a row and then visit, it changes the types of items it's possible for you to receive. After each seven-win streak, there is one more item you can get.

Trainer obtained a Rare Candy!

Seven-win streaks increase the kinds of items you can receive

You can receive one of the following items: Rare Candy, Full Restore, Revive, Max Revive, Elixir, Protein, Iron, Calcium, Zinc, Carbos, or HP Up. Each seven-win streak you have will increase the variety of items it's possible to receive.

Step 3 Return to Nimbasa City after you've had a look around

Return to Nimbasa City once you're ready (p. 134). On the weekends, there are trains on the turntables, so many tourists come to visit, and the town is very lively. Some of the visitors trade items, so be sure to visit every weekend.

▸YES
NO
Would you like to board?

Trade items with the item traders

During the weekend a train will be on the turntable

On the weekend, trains come to the turntable, and many people who trade items also visit the town. You can trade: an Escape Rope for a Revive, a Star Piece for a PP Up, and 20 Poké Balls for a Full Restore.

YES
NO
Will you trade your 2 Escape Ropes for my 1 Revive?

A Funfest Mission is added

When you trade an item with a Backpacker, the Funfest Mission "Exciting Trading" will be added if you are playing *Pokémon Black Version 2* ("Exhilarating Trading" if you are playing *Pokémon White Version 2*).

Many who visit Nimbasa City drop by to take a break

Route 16 • Lostlorn Forest

Route 16 is a short route that connects Nimbasa City and Marvelous Bridge. Deep within a grove in the forest, there was the Lostlorn Forest, which was known as a place where everyone would get lost, at least until two years ago.

Field Moves Needed

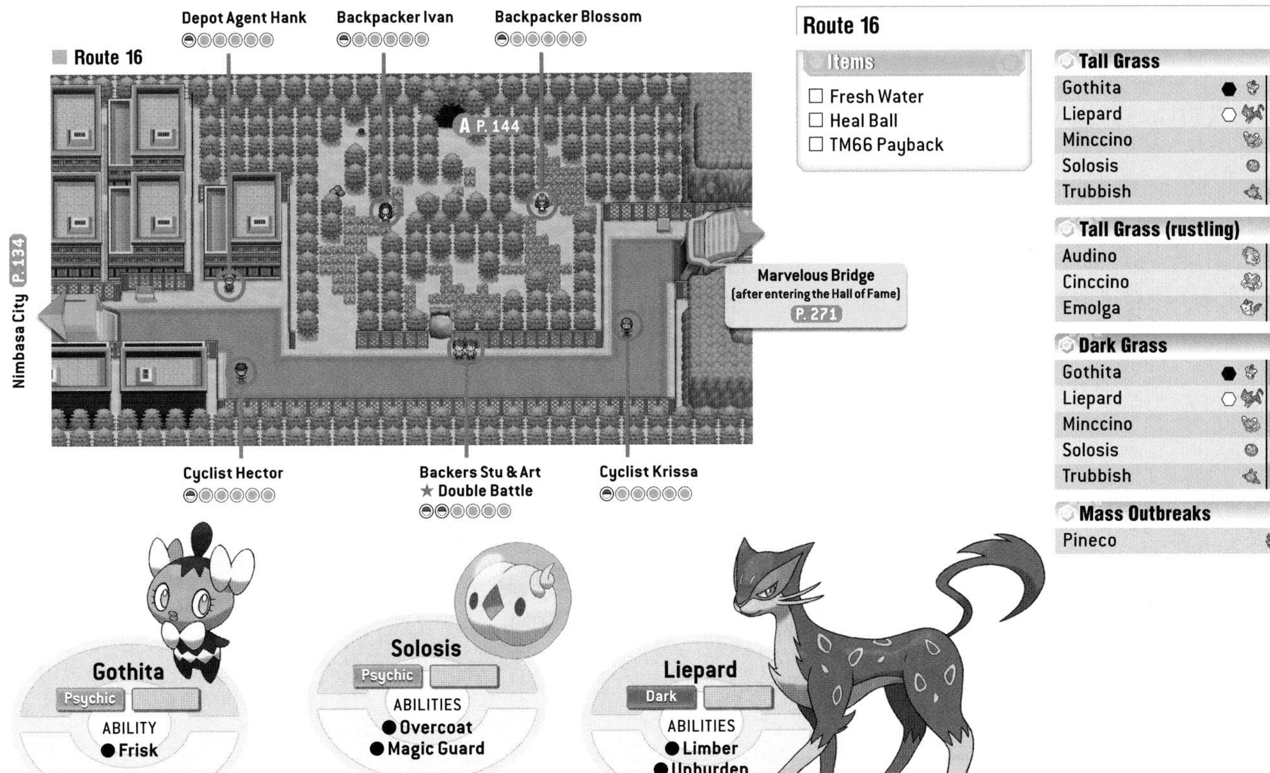

Route 16

Items

- ☐ Fresh Water
- ☐ Heal Ball
- ☐ TM66 Payback

Tall Grass		
Gothita	●	◎
Liepard	○	○
Minccino		◎
Solosis		◎
Trubbish		○

Tall Grass (rustling)		
Audino		◎
Cinccino		○
Emolga		△

Dark Grass		
Gothita	●	◎
Liepard	○	○
Minccino		◎
Solosis		◎
Trubbish		○

Mass Outbreaks	
Pineco	

Step 1 Proceed east while battling Trainers

Route 16 may be short, but seven Pokémon Trainers are waiting to battle you there. Two of them will even challenge you to a Double Battle. Battle with all of the Trainers here to be more prepared for your Nimbasa City Gym battle.

When I'm riding my Bicycle, don't you think I look stronger?

Until two years ago, this was a lush forest

Two years ago, Lostlorn Forest was a grove thick with trees. But this was only an illusion created by Zoroark, and it actually looked like the fantastic scene it is now.

■ Lostlorn Forest Hidden Grottoes ● Lostlorn Forest has Hidden Grottoes! Find them!

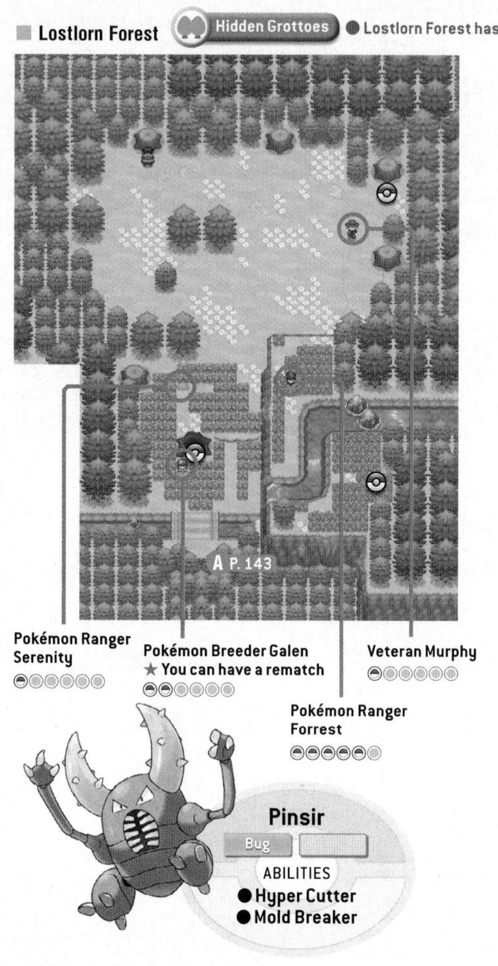

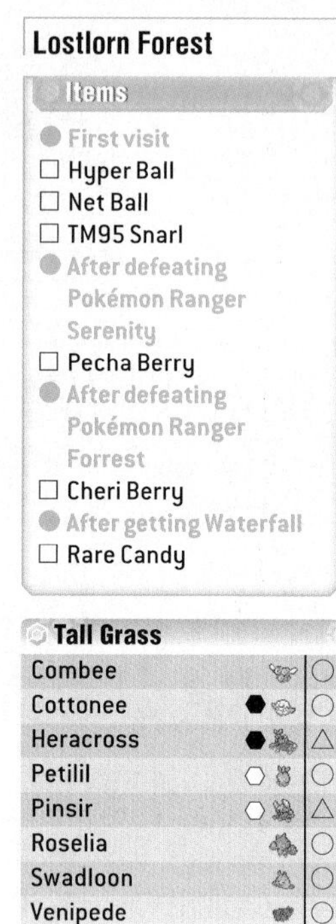

Lostlorn Forest

Items

- First visit
- ☐ Hyper Ball
- ☐ Net Ball
- ☐ TM95 Snarl
- After defeating Pokémon Ranger Serenity
- ☐ Pecha Berry
- After defeating Pokémon Ranger Forrest
- ☐ Cheri Berry
- After getting Waterfall
- ☐ Rare Candy

Tall Grass		
Combee		○
Cottonee	⬢	○
Heracross	⬢	△
Petilil	⬡	○
Pinsir	⬡	△
Roselia		○
Swadloon		○
Venipede		○

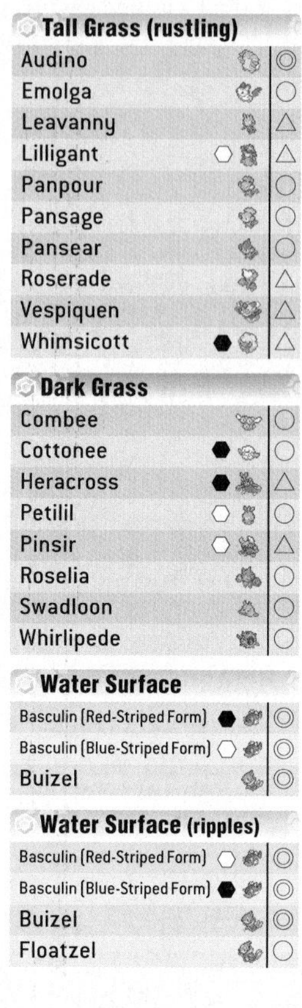

Tall Grass (rustling)		
Audino		◎
Emolga		○
Leavanny		△
Lilligant	⬡	△
Panpour		○
Pansage		○
Pansear		○
Roserade		△
Vespiquen		△
Whimsicott	⬢	△

Dark Grass		
Combee		○
Cottonee	⬢	○
Heracross	⬢	△
Petilil	⬡	○
Pinsir	⬡	△
Roselia		○
Swadloon		○
Whirlipede		○

Water Surface		
Basculin (Red-Striped Form)	⬢	◎
Basculin (Blue-Striped Form)	⬡	◎
Buizel		◎

Water Surface (ripples)		
Basculin (Red-Striped Form)	⬡	◎
Basculin (Blue-Striped Form)	⬢	◎
Buizel		◎
Floatzel		○

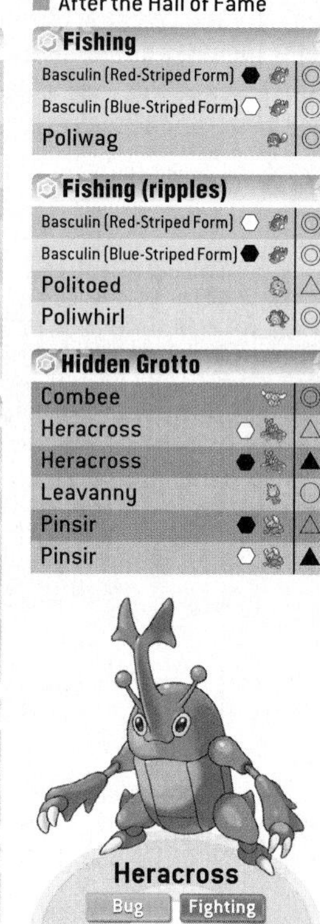

■ After the Hall of Fame

Fishing		
Basculin (Red-Striped Form)	⬢	◎
Basculin (Blue-Striped Form)	⬡	◎
Poliwag		◎

Fishing (ripples)		
Basculin (Red-Striped Form)	⬡	◎
Basculin (Blue-Striped Form)	⬢	◎
Politoed		△
Poliwhirl		◎

Hidden Grotto		
Combee		◎
Heracross	⬡	△
Heracross	⬢	▲
Leavanny		○
Pinsir	⬢	△
Pinsir	⬡	▲

Step 2 Explore the Lostlorn Forest

Go north through the dense clump of trees, and you will find Lostlorn Forest. Talk to the Backpacker deep within the clearing. He will tell you about Zoroark's visit two years ago and give you TM95 Snarl.

Step 3 The elevator to the Marvelous Bridge is out of order

If you go east on Route 16, you will enter the gate that connects to the Marvelous Bridge. But the elevator inside the gate isn't moving, so you can't go to the Marvelous Bridge. It will start working again after you enter the Hall of Fame.

Get Berries from Pokémon Rangers

When you defeat Pokémon Ranger Serenity you get a Pecha Berry, and when you defeat Forrest, you get a Cheri Berry. Serenity is hiding in a pile of leaves. Make sure to find them and get the Berries.

Step 4 Explore every last corner of the area before returning to Nimbasa City

Once you've seen every corner of Route 16 and Lostlorn Forest, head back to Nimbasa City. It's finally time to challenge the Nimbasa City Gym. Heal your Pokémon at the Pokémon Center and head to the Gym, which is in the eastern part of the city (p. 134).

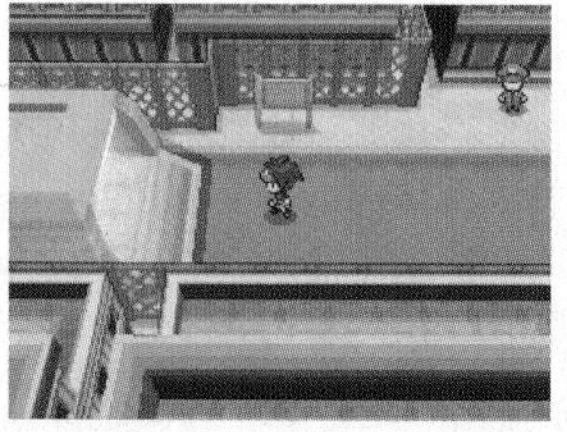

Come back after you get HM05 Waterfall

You can climb the waterfall in Lostlorn Forest once you receive HM05 Waterfall from N on Victory Road. Come back to battle with Pokémon Trainers and collect items.

Route 5

Route 5 is a short route. If you go east, it leads to Nimbasa City, and if you go west, it leads to the Driftveil Drawbridge. It's often lively because many Pokémon Trainers always gather here.

Field Moves Needed

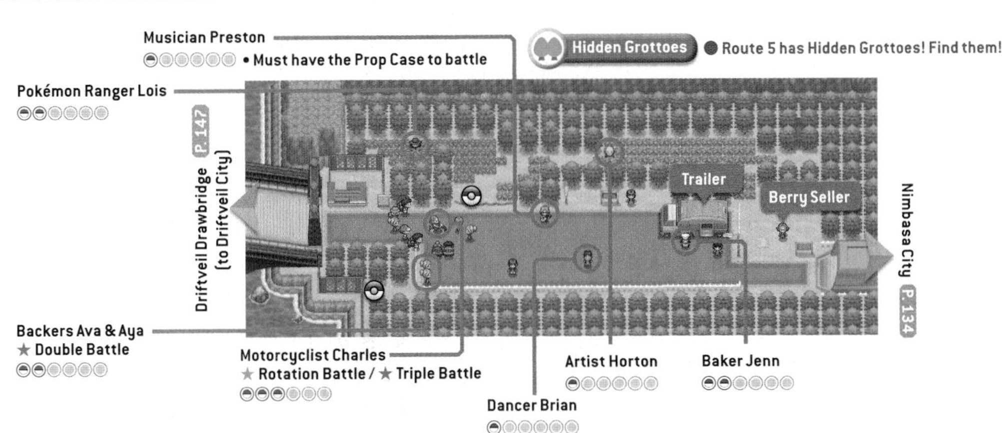

Items

- First visit
- ☐ HM02 Fly
- ☐ Hyper Potion
- ☐ Super Repel
- After defeating Pokémon Ranger Lois
- ☐ Cheri Berry

Props

- After defeating Musician Preston
- ☐ Electric Guitar

◆ If this prop is already in the Prop Case obtained in the Memory Link event, you can't get this prop.

Tall Grass	
Gothita	◎
Liepard	○
Minccino	◎
Solosis	◎
Trubbish	○

Tall Grass (rustling)	
Audino	◎
Cinccino	○
Emolga	△

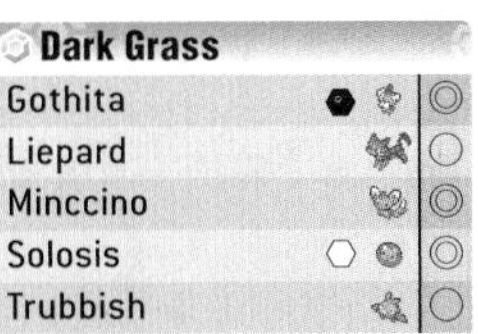

Dark Grass	
Gothita	◎
Liepard	○
Minccino	◎
Solosis	◎
Trubbish	○

Hidden Grotto	
Foongus	◎
Liepard	○
Minccino	△

Mass Outbreaks
Natu

Items the Maid in the trailer will buy

Items Case	Bought for
Aguav Berry	20
Apicot Berry	20
Aspear Berry	20
Babiri Berry	20
BalmMushroom	25,000
Belue Berry	500
Berry Juice	1,500
Big Mushroom	5,000
Bluk Berry	500
Casteliacone	2,000
Charti Berry	20
Cheri Berry	20
Chesto Berry	20
Chilan Berry	20
Chople Berry	20
Coba Berry	20
Colbur Berry	20

Items Case	Bought for
Cornn Berry	500
Custap Berry	30,000
Durin Berry	500
Enigma Berry	30,000
Figy Berry	20
Fresh Water	200
Ganlon Berry	20
Grepa Berry	20
Haban Berry	20
Hondew Berry	20
Honey	500
Iapapa Berry	20
Jaboca Berry	30,000
Kasib Berry	20
Kebia Berry	20
Kelpsy Berry	20
Lansat Berry	30,000

Items Case	Bought for
Lava Cookie	4,000
Leftovers	200
Lemonade	350
Leppa Berry	20
Liechi Berry	20
Lucky Egg	200
Lum Berry	20
Mago Berry	20
Magost Berry	500
Micle Berry	30,000
Moomoo Milk	500
Nanab Berry	500
Nomel Berry	500
Occa Berry	20
Old Gateau	4,000
Oran Berry	20
Pamtre Berry	500

Items Case	Bought for
Passho Berry	20
Payapa Berry	20
Pecha Berry	20
Persim Berry	20
Petaya Berry	20
Pinap Berry	500
Pomeg Berry	20
Qualot Berry	20
Rabuta Berry	500
RageCandyBar	6,000
Rare Candy	10,000
Rawst Berry	20
Razz Berry	500
Rindo Berry	20
Rowap Berry	30,000
Salac Berry	20
Shoal Salt	7,000

Items Case	Bought for
Shuca Berry	20
Sitrus Berry	20
Soda Pop	300
Spelon Berry	500
Starf Berry	30,000
Stick	200
Sweet Heart	100
Tamato Berry	20
Tanga Berry	20
TinyMushroom	500
Wacan Berry	20
Watmel Berry	500
Wepear Berry	500
Wiki Berry	20
Yache Berry	20

◆ **Motorcyclist Charles challenges you to a Rotation Battle in *Pokémon Black Version 2* or a Triple Battle in *Pokémon White Version 2*.**

Step 1 Receive Fly from Bianca

As you head west from Nimbasa City, Bianca calls out to you from behind. Bianca hands you HM02 Fly. You can use this HM to fly to any city you've visited before instantly.

Have your Pokémon learn Fly right away

Many Pokémon can learn Fly, including Pidove and Sigilyph. When you receive HM02 Fly from Bianca, have a Pokémon learn it immediately.

Step 2 Find Hidden Grottoes

Bianca tells you about the Hidden Grottoes in the Unova region. Hidden Grottoes are places reached through gaps between trees. When you go inside, you can meet Pokémon with Hidden Abilities. Sometimes there are also items inside.

Step 3 Buy Berries every day

On the eastern side of the route, near the gate, a woman sells Berries. She will sell the following Berries: Pomeg Berry, Kelpsy Berry, Qualot Berry, Hondew Berry, Grepa Berry. She sells five of the same type of Berry for 200. You can only buy one bunch of Berries per day.

Get a Berry from a Pokémon Ranger

Pokémon Ranger Lois waits at the northwestern part of Route 5. You get a Cheri Berry for defeating her, so take her on and get the Berry as a bonus.

Step 4 The Maid buys various foods

The Maid in the trailer will pay a lot for food. This includes items such as Berry Juice, Casteliacone, and other items with food-like names. Sell her many different items (p. 145).

Step 5 Battle with a Pokémon Trainer and get a Prop

If you defeat Musician Preston on Route 5, he will give you the Electric Guitar Prop. Props are used to decorate your Pokémon when they take part in Nimbasa City's Musical.

If you already have it, you can't get the Prop

If you already obtained the Prop Case from *Pokémon Black Version* or *Pokémon White Version* through Memory Link, you might already have the Electric Guitar Prop. If you do, you won't get the Prop even if you beat Preston.

Step 6 A man asks for help

As you continue west on Route 5, you encounter a big group of people. A man on a bike blocks the road and won't let you pass until you defeat him in battle. When you talk to the man with the blue hair, he asks for your help.

Step 7 Challenge Motorcyclist Charles to a battle

There's a man riding a motorcycle. His name... Charles. He will challenge you to a Rotation Battle in *Pokémon Black Version 2* or a Triple Battle in *Pokémon White Version 2*. Check the order of Pokémon in your party and battle (p. 51).

Visit after defeating the Nimbasa City Gym

If you visit this area before you get the Nimbasa City Gym Badge, you can't battle Charles and won't be able to continue to the Driftveil Drawbridge. Visit Route 5 after you win the Gym Badge.

Step 8 Head west to the Driftveil Drawbridge

The crowd disperses when you beat Motorcyclist Charles in battle, and you can proceed. Keep going west over the Driftveil Drawbridge (p. 147).

Driftveil Drawbridge

The Driftveil Drawbridge is a bridge that can be raised and lowered to allow boats to pass through the ocean that spreads beneath it. It links Driftveil City to Route 5, which leads to Nimbasa City.

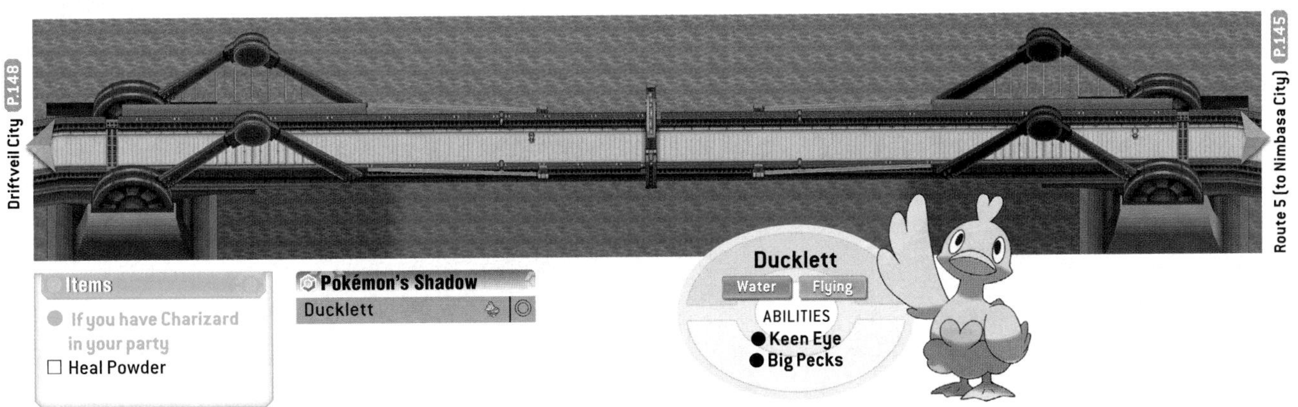

Items
- If you have Charizard in your party
- ☐ Heal Powder

Pokémon's Shadow

Ducklett

Ducklett
Water / Flying
ABILITIES
- Keen Eye
- Big Pecks

Step 1 Step or ride onto Pokémon's shadows to collect feathers

The shadows of winged Pokémon sometimes fall on the bridge. Step or ride onto these shadows to collect Wings. There are seven types, and six of them can be used to raise your Pokémon's base stats. Travel back and forth on bridges to collect lots of feathers!

Trainer found a Genius Wing!

Ducklett might swoop down on you

If you step on one of the shadows that appear on the bridge, a wild Ducklett sometimes swoops down to attack. This is the only place where you can encounter Ducklett. If you do meet one, be sure to catch it!

Wing types

Wing Name	Effect
Clever Wing	Slightly raises the base Sp. Defense stat of a Pokémon. Can be used until the stat reaches its maximum value.
Genius Wing	Slightly raises the base Sp. Attack stat of a Pokémon. Can be used until the stat reaches its maximum value.
Health Wing	Slightly raises the base HP stat of a Pokémon. Can be used until the stat reaches its maximum value.
Muscle Wing	Slightly raises the base Attack stat of a Pokémon. Can be used until the stat reaches its maximum value.
Pretty Wing	A pretty wing. Can be sold to the Poké Mart for 100 in prize money.
Resist Wing	Slightly raises the base Defense stat of a Pokémon. Can be used until the stat reaches its maximum value.
Swift Wing	Slightly raises the base Speed stat of a Pokémon. Can be used until the stat reaches its maximum value.

Step 2 Have a Charizard in your party and then talk to the boy

Near the center of the bridge, you'll find a young boy. If you speak to him while you have a Charizard in your party, he'll give you a Heal Powder to thank you for showing him a real Charizard. This item will make a Pokémon less friendly, but it cures all status conditions.

Trainer obtained a Heal Powder!

Charizard comes from another region

Charizard is a Pokémon native to the Kanto region. Bring it to your game through a Link Trade from *Pokémon Black Version* or *Pokémon White Version*, or use the Poké Transfer function that becomes available in previous games after entering the Hall of Fame.

Step 3 Cross the bridge to get to Driftveil City

If you continue straight west across the bridge, you'll arrive in Driftveil City, home to the next Gym (p. 148). The bridge is extremely long, but riding your Bicycle will help you race across it.

Funfest Missions will be added

Speak to the man who is standing beyond the entrance to the Driftveil Drawbridge. The Entralink Funfest Mission "Wings Falling on the Drawbridge" will be added for you to enjoy.

Driftveil City

Driftveil City is a port town that distributes a wide variety of goods. A market in the city sells items you can't get anywhere else in Unova. The city has developed considerably in the past two years and is now filled with large hotels.

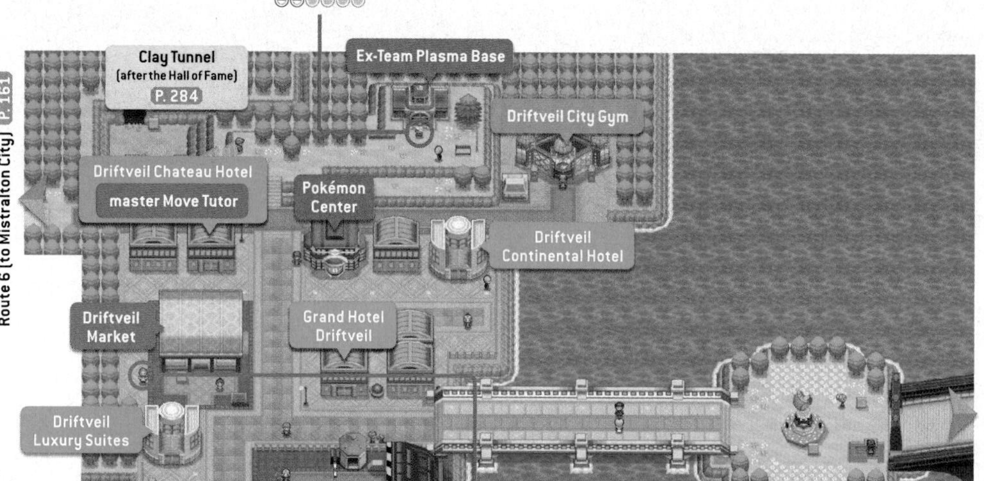

Items

- First visit
- ☐ Air Balloon
- ☐ Big Root
- ☐ Calcium
- ☐ Everstone
- ☐ Fresh Water
- ☐ Haban Berry
- ☐ Luxury Ball ×3
- ☐ TM63 Embargo
- When the number of Seen Pokémon in the Pokédex is over 70
- ☐ Shell Bell
- If you have Pokémon in your party of Lv. 30 or higher
- ☐ Expert Belt
- After winning at the Driftveil City Gym
- ☐ Quake Badge
- ☐ TM78 Bulldoze

Poké Mart (Lower Clerk)

Item	Price	Item	Price
BridgeMail D	50	RSVP Mail	50
Favored Mail	50	Thanks Mail	50
Greet Mail	50	Dusk Ball	1,000
Inquiry Mail	50	Nest Ball	1,000
Like Mail	50	Net Ball	1,000
Reply Mail	50		

Driftveil Market

Item	Price	Item	Price
☐ Heal Powder	450	☐ Luck Incense	9,600
☐ EnergyPowder	500	☐ Odd Incense	9,600
☐ Moomoo Milk	500	☐ Pure Incense	9,600
☐ Energy Root	800	☐ Rock Incense	9,600
☐ Revival Herb	2,800	☐ Rose Incense	9,600
☐ Full Incense	9,600	☐ Sea Incense	9,600
☐ Lax Incense	9,600	☐ Wave Incense	9,600

◆ **Motorcyclist Charles will challenge you to a Triple Battle in *Pokémon Black Version 2* or a Rotation Battle in *Pokémon White Version 2***

Step 1 Ex-Team Plasma member struggles for understanding

Once you enter the city, you will come across a former Team Plasma member trying to convince a current Team Plasma member to turn away from the path of evil. The Team Plasma member is unwilling to listen, however. After witnessing this scene, you will be invited by the ex-Team Plasma member to visit their base.

We were friends when we
were both in Team Plasma...

Changes in the weather

Driftveil City's weather changes depending on the date and season. Rain can fall during spring, summer, and autumn, and snow or hail will sometimes fall during winter. When you visit the city, observe the changes in weather.

Step 2 Visit the hotels to collect items

Unfortunately, you can't get a room for the night, but you can visit four grand hotels in Driftveil City. Try visiting each hotel to obtain a number of different items that people give to you or that have been dropped by guests.

Trainer obtained a Shell Bell!

Receive a Haban Berry from Axew

In the Grand Hotel Driftveil to the south of the Pokémon Center, examine the Axew on 19F, and it will give you the Haban Berry it's carrying in its mouth.

Step 3 Go shopping in the Driftveil Market

The Driftveil Market sells a number of items that you can't obtain anywhere else, such as Moomoo Milk, EnergyPowder, and Heal Powder. There are also nine different kinds of incense for sale, so be sure to stop by!

Buy heaps of Moomoo Milk

At the Driftveil Market, you can buy Moomoo Milk by the dozen! This is an item that can restore 100 HP, and each bottle costs 500. Buy in bulk and be ready for anything!

Step 4 Battle again with Motorcyclist Charles

On the west side of the market, you can meet Motorcyclist Charles again. This time, he will challenge you to a Triple Battle in *Pokémon Black Version 2* or a Rotation Battle in *Pokémon White Version 2*.

YES
NO
Its name... Triple Battle!
Want to learn about it?

Receive an Expert Belt

If you have a Lv. 30 or higher Pokémon in your party, the man wearing sunglasses in the Driftveil Market will give you an Expert Belt. This item will raise the power of moves when they are super effective.

Step 5 Receive a Heart Scale every day

Speak to the woman on the first floor of the Driftveil Luxury Suites, which are located to the south of the Driftveil Market. If you show her a Pokémon that knows the move she says, you can receive a Heart Scale. Speak to her every day to collect plenty of Heart Scales.

The reminder girl is at the PWT

You will need to give one Heart Scale to the reminder girl at the PWT to have her help your Pokémon to remember forgotten moves. Be sure to visit later when there is a move that you want your Pokémon to know for battle that it has forgotten (p. 382).

Step 6 Have the master Move Tutor teach you some moves

On the first floor of the Driftveil Chateau Hotel you can find a master Move Tutor. The master Move Tutor in Driftveil City is a maniac for Red Shards. If you give the master Move Tutor the number of Red Shards he asks for, you will be able to learn a number of different moves.

There are four master Move Tutors altogether

In addition to the one in Driftveil City, there is a master Move Tutor in Lentimas Town who wants Blue Shards (p. 176), one in Humilau City who wants Yellow Shards (p. 204), and one in Nacrene City who wants Green Shards (p. 313).

Red Shards needed for learning moves

Move you can learn	Number needed
Covet	2
Bug Bite	2
Drill Run	4
Bounce	4
Signal Beam	4

Move you can learn	Number needed
Iron Head	4
Super Fang	6
Uproar	6
Seed Bomb	6
Dual Chop	6

Move you can learn	Number needed
Low Kick	8
Gunk Shot	8
Fire Punch	10
ThunderPunch	10
Ice Punch	10

Red Shard

Step 7 The excavation site is still inaccessible

In the north of the city, a tunnel is being constructed under Clay's instruction. It's appropriately called Clay Tunnel. It hasn't been completed, so you can't enter it just yet. Try visiting again after you manage to enter the Hall of Fame [p. 255].

Construction on a shortcut
to Twist Mountain has started.

Step 8 Gym Leader Clay isn't in the Gym

If you visit the Driftveil Gym, you will find that the entrance is being blocked by someone. It seems that Clay is not in. Since you cannot challenge the Gym yet, take up the invitation you received when you first arrived in the city and head to the ex-Team Plasma base for a visit.

The Gym Leader, Clay, is currently
in the middle of something.

Step 9 Visit the ex-Team Plasma Base

When you visit the ex-Team Plasma base on the hill to the west of the gym, you will find an old man named Rood waiting at the entrance. Rood wishes to have a Pokémon battle to determine just what kind of person you are. Accept his challenge for battle.

Have five or fewer Pokémon in your party when you go

You can receive Zorua at the ex-Team Plasma Base. However, you will not be able to take Zorua with you if you don't have a space in your party. Before heading to the base, deposit Pokémon in the PC so that you have room in your party.

Step 10 Receive Zorua from Rood

Enter the house with your rival and Rood will explain how he and the other ex-Team Plasma members are repenting for their evil deeds two years ago. He will then ask you to look after a Pokémon for him and you will be given Zorua. It appears that Zorua's original Trainer was N.

Step 11 Head to the Gym to challenge Clay

While you were visiting the ex-Team Plasma base, Clay returned to the Gym. Now you can challenge him at the Driftveil City Gym. Have your Pokémon healed at the Driftveil Pokémon Center, then head for the Gym on the east side of the city.

Let me tell you, though,
Clay's tough!

Memory Link can be activated

After speaking with Rood at the ex-Team Plasma Base, leave the house and then go inside again to trigger a Memory Link event. See what happened when N returned to the base in secret (p. 73).

5 Driftveil City Gym Battle

Gym Battle Tips

- Have your Pokémon carry a Quick Claw
- Catch a Ducklett on the Driftveil Drawbridge to take the upper hand in battle

Entrance

Driftveil City Gym Leader

Clay

Ground-type Pokémon User

The best defense against his Bulldoze move is carrying a Quick Claw

You will travel along conveyor belts to reach Clay's location in the Gym. When you battle Clay, the Bulldoze move that his Pokémon use will lower your Pokémon's Speed by 1 without fail if it hits you. Have your Pokémon carry Quick Claws to give you the chance to attack first. If you attack with Pokémon using Water-type moves, your team will fight most efficiently—all of Clay's Pokémon are weak against those moves.

Clay's Pokémon

Pokémon	Level	Type	Weak to
Krokorok ♂	Lv. 31	Ground, Dark	Water, Grass, Ice, Fighting, Bug
Sandslash ♂	Lv. 31	Ground	Water, Grass, Ice
Excadrill ♂	Lv. 33	Ground, Steel	Fire, Water, Fighting, Ground

Quake Badge

Pokémon up to Lv. 60, including those received in trades, will obey you.

TM 78 Bulldoze

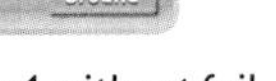

Ground

Lowers the target's Speed by 1 without fail. If it strikes multiple Pokémon, its power decreases.

Follow Clay out of the Gym

After defeating Gym Leader Clay, follow him out of the Gym and you will find your rival waiting for you. Clay will invite you and your rival to the Pokémon World Tournament (PWT) held south of the city.

Your rival already took on the Gym

Until Nimbasa City, you earned all of your Gym Badges before your rival, but your rival beat you to the punch in Driftveil City.

Hugh rages against Gym Leader Clay

Your rival criticizes Clay for allowing the ex-Team Plasma members to live in his city. Yet Clay warns your rival that if you only focus on what you think is right, you will end up prematurely rejecting all thoughts and opinions different than your own. Your rival does not seem convinced by this argument.

Follow your rival to the PWT

Clay tells you he will wait for you south of town and heads off. Knowing he'll gain some great experience at the PWT, your rival seems raring to go. Follow him as he leaves and make your way to the south of the city, where you can take part in the PWT (p. 381).

The former site of the Cold Storage

Two years ago, the southern part of Driftveil City was home to the Cold Storage. Now, two years later, the area has been reborn as the Pokémon World Tournament, a site where famous Trainers from around the world come to compete.

Follow Cheren to Route 6

Cheren tells you he has something to look into on Route 6. Follow him to find out more. Head north from the PWT site and at the end of the road, turn west to Route 6 (p. 161).

Players from around the world gather in Unity Tower

Players from other countries who have traded Pokémon gather in Unity Tower

This massive tower stands alone in the middle of the ocean. Once you trade Pokémon with a player from another country, you can go to Unity Tower by boarding the boat at the Unity Pier. The tower has 130 different floors, each representing a different country, and players from a particular country will gather on their country's floor. Enjoy chatting with up to five players on a floor, with up to 20 players in the entire tower.

Trade Pokémon with players from other countries

You must fulfill two conditions to go to Unity Tower. First, both you and the person you are trading Pokémon with must both be registered on Geonet. Second, you must trade with a player from another country to obtain a Pokémon from a foreign version of the game.

How to trade Pokémon with international players

GTS

Select "SEEK POKÉMON" and indicate the region where your trading partner lives. Search for a country using the first letter of the country's name.

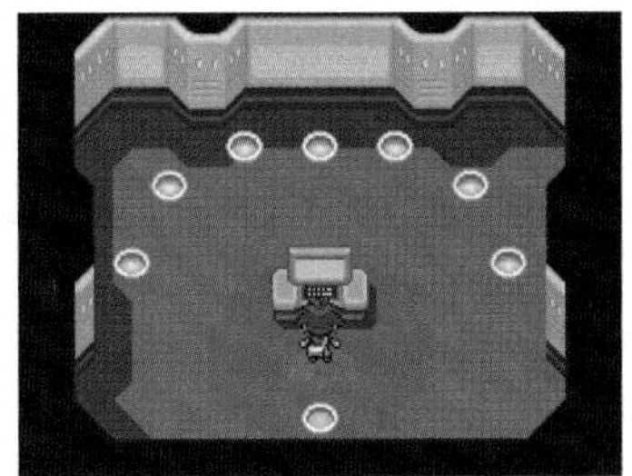

Union Room

You might be able to find an international player at special events or other places where a lot of Pokémon fans gather.

Wi-Fi Club

Register Friend Codes with a friend playing an international version of the games and trade Pokémon in the Wi-Fi Club.

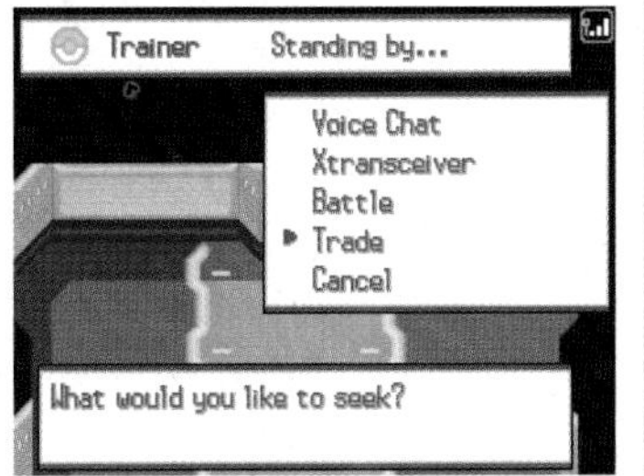

Meet the worldwide friends with whom you have traded Pokémon

Strike up a conversation with the players on each floor to hear about their country, the Pokémon you traded them, their hobbies, and more. Talk to every player that has gathered in the tower to hear all about the lives of international players.

Tower Floor

Pokédex

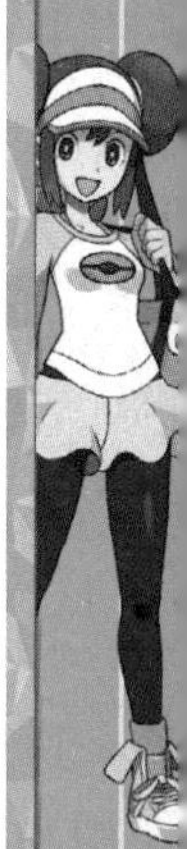

Pokémon World Tournament (PWT)

The Pokémon World Tournament (PWT) is a facility where famous Pokémon Trainers from every region gather to compete against one another tournament-style. You will find an entrance to the Relic Passage in the far western corner.

Field Moves Needed

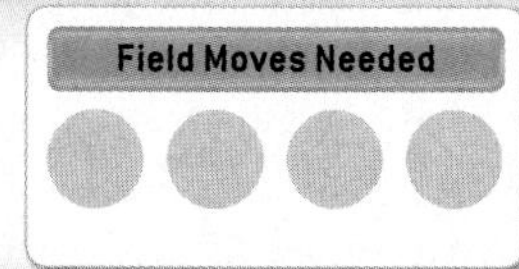

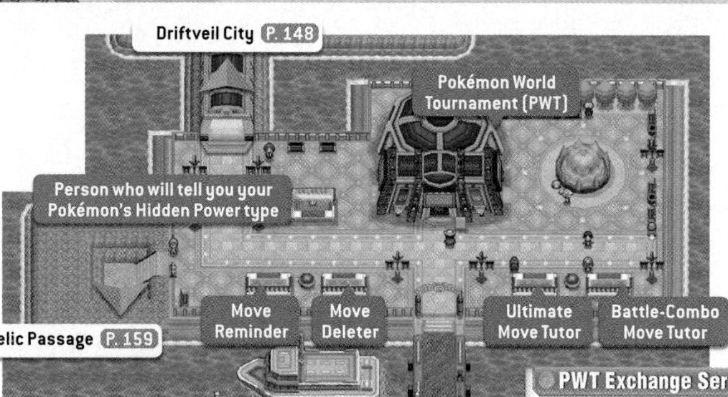

Items

- ☐ PP Up
- ☐ Rocky Helmet

PWT Exchange Service Corner (Left Clerk)

Item	BP	Item	BP
TM17 Protect	6 BP	TM48 Round	18 BP
TM20 Safeguard	6 BP	TM75 Swords Dance	18 BP
TM32 Double Team	6 BP	TM87 Swagger	18 BP
TM59 Incinerate	6 BP	TM88 Pluck	18 BP
TM31 Brick Break	12 BP	TM34 Sludge Wave	24 BP
TM79 Frost Breath	12 BP	TM51 Ally Switch	24 BP
TM89 U-turn	12 BP	TM60 Quash	24 BP
TM10 Hidden Power	18 BP	TM64 Explosion	24 BP
TM23 Smack Down	18 BP	TM77 Psych Up	24 BP

PWT Exchange Service Corner (Right Clerk)

Item	BP	Item	BP	Item	BP
Calcium	1 BP	Scope Lens	8 BP	Power Belt	16 BP
Carbos	1 BP	Wide Lens	8 BP	Power Bracer	16 BP
HP Up	1 BP	Wise Glasses	8 BP	Power Herb	16 BP
Iron	1 BP	Air Balloon	12 BP	Power Lens	16 BP
Protein	1 BP	BrightPowder	12 BP	Power Weight	16 BP
Zinc	1 BP	Focus Band	12 BP	Red Card	16 BP
Fire Stone	3 BP	Iron Ball	12 BP	Toxic Orb	16 BP
Leaf Stone	3 BP	Zoom Lens	12 BP	White Herb	16 BP
Thunderstone	3 BP	Absorb Bulb	16 BP	Choice Band	24 BP
Water Stone	3 BP	Cell Battery	16 BP	Choice Scarf	24 BP
Binding Band	8 BP	Eject Button	16 BP	Choice Specs	24 BP
Muscle Band	8 BP	Flame Orb	16 BP	Focus Sash	24 BP
Razor Claw	8 BP	Power Anklet	16 BP	Life Orb	24 BP
Razor Fang	8 BP	Power Band	16 BP	Rare Candy	24 BP

Step 1 The reminder girl will remind your Pokémon of a forgotten move

Give the reminder girl a Heart Scale, and she will help your Pokémon remember one move that it has forgotten. With her help, you'll even be able to use moves that your Pokémon knew at Lv. 1.

Step 2 Have the Move Deleter delete moves

The Move Deleter will make your Pokémon forget moves that they have learned. He can even make them forget a move that can't normally be forgotten, like an HM. When you want a Pokémon to forget a move, talk to the Move Deleter.

YES
NO
You've come to make me force your Pokémon to forget some moves?

Step 3 Learn the type of your Pokémon's Hidden Power move

Talk to the man in the booth to the west of the PWT, and he will be able to tell you what type your Pokémon's Hidden Power move will be. If you'd like to teach Hidden Power to any of your Pokémon, have him check them out!

Should I tell you what type of Hidden Power your Pokémon will learn?
YES
NO

Driftveil City Gym Badge required

Until you obtain a Driftveil City Gym Badge, you will find a man blocking the gate between Driftveil City and the PWT. Visit the PWT after you obtain the Quake Badge.

Step 4 Explore the Relic Passage

To the far west of the PWT is an entrance to the Relic Passage. If you fight the Trainers within the tunnel, your Pokémon will surely grow stronger. Before participating in the Pokémon World Tournament, try exploring the Relic Passage (p. 159).

After seeing everything, come right back

Once you have fully explored the Relic Passage, you will come out on the Castelia City side, in the Castelia Sewers. If you don't want to go all the way through and have an Escape Rope, you will be able to return to the PWT from the Castelia City side of the Relic Passage.

Step 5 Have your Pokémon learn the ultimate move

Speak to the old man at the ultimate Move Tutor booth, and he can teach Serperior, Emboar, or Samurott the ultimate move—but only if you have a very strong bond with your Pokémon.

Pokémon that can learn ultimate moves

In addition to the three Unova Pokémon, Venusaur, Charizard, Blastoise, Meganium, Typhlosion, Feraligatr, Sceptile, Blaziken, Swampert, Torterra, Infernape, and Empoleon can all learn the ultimate move from this tutor.

Ultimate moves that can be taught and the Pokémon that can learn them

Move	Type	Effect	Pokémon that can learn it
Frenzy Plant	Grass	A move with a power of 150. The user can't move during the next turn.	Serperior
Hydro Cannon	Water	A move with a power of 150. The user can't move during the next turn.	Samurott
Blast Burn	Fire	A move with a power of 150. The user can't move during the next turn. If the target is Frozen, it will be thawed.	Emboar

Serperior Emboar Samurott

Step 6 Have your Pokémon learn battle-combo moves

Talk to the man at the battle-combo move booth and you can have him teach battle-combo moves to any of the three Pokémon you received at the beginning of your adventure or their evolved forms. These moves will have additional effects if they are used on the same turn during a Double or Triple Battle.

▸YES
NO
Want me to teach it a battle-combo move?

Pokémon that can learn battle-combo moves

In addition to the Unova starter Pokémon, Bulbasaur, Charmander, Squirtle, Chikorita, Cyndaquil, Totodile, Treecko, Torchic, Mudkip, Turtwig, Chimchar, Piplup, and all of their evolved forms can learn battle-combo moves.

Battle-combo moves that can be taught and the Pokémon that can learn them

Move	Effect	Pokémon that can learn it
Grass Pledge	The power and effect change when used together with Water Pledge or Fire Pledge.	Snivy
	Power becomes 150 when combined with Water Pledge, and the opponent's Pokémon's Speed will be decreased for four turns.	Servine
	Power becomes 150 when combined with Fire Pledge, and all non-Fire types will be damaged every turn for four turns.	Serperior
Fire Pledge	The power and effect change when used together with Water Pledge or Grass Pledge.	Tepig
	Power becomes 150 when combined with Water Pledge, and your party's Pokémon's moves become more likely to have additional effects.	Pignite
	Power becomes 150 when combined with Grass Pledge, and all non-Fire types will be damaged every turn for four turns.	Emboar
Water Pledge	The power and effect change when used together with Fire Pledge or Grass Pledge.	Oshawott
	Power becomes 150 when combined with Fire Pledge, and your party's Pokémon's moves become more likely to have additional effects.	Dewott
	Power becomes 150 when combined with Grass Pledge, and the opponent's Pokémon's Speed will be decreased for four turns.	Samurott

Step 7 Clay and your rival are waiting at the entrance

Your rival stands beside Clay in front of the PWT. When you approach, Clay will hail you and proudly guide you into the elaborate tournament hall.

Step 8 Even Cheren comes at Clay's bidding

For some reason, Cheren is waiting at the PWT. Called by Clay, he has apparently come to take part in the tournament with you. Your rival and Cheren both head north to register as participants.

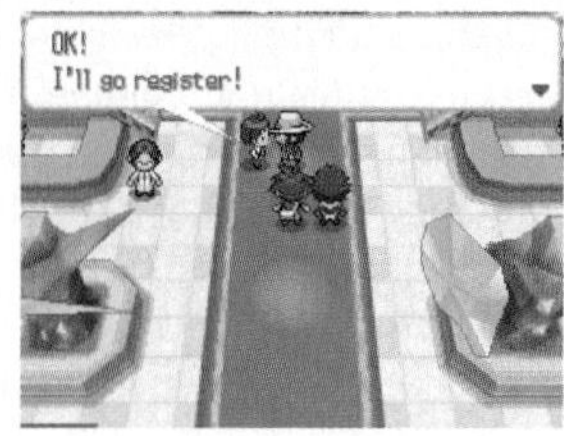

Cheren is reluctantly dragged along

When you meet him at the PWT, Cheren seems rather disgruntled about being dragged here when he was busy investigating something. Apparently Clay strong-armed him into coming to the PWT. Yet he quickly recovers his spirits and hurries off to register for the tournament.

Step 9 Register for the Driftveil Tournament

Proceed to the north and speak with the woman on the left, in the green hat. After selecting "Participate," select "Driftveil," and pick the Pokémon you will battle with. Finally, select "CONFIRM." Now you're ready to take part in the tournament.

Speak to the woman in the red hat after entering the Hall of Fame

The woman on the right, in the red hat, is in charge of registering people for the tournaments that open after you enter the Hall of Fame. Come speak to her after you have defeated the Champion and reached the Hall of Fame to try these tournaments.

Step 10 Win the Driftveil Tournament

You'll need three consecutive wins to win the tournament. Normally, your opponents in the second and third rounds are not decided ahead of time—but for your very first tournament, you'll face your rival in the first round, Cheren in the second round, and Colress in the final round.

No items allowed during battle

Once the tournament begins, you will not be able to use items. You will not even be able to select your Bag from the menu. If you wish to give your Pokémon an item to hold, you should do that before you register for the tournament.

Driftveil Tournament — First Round

Battle your rival!

It's time to go all out!

Quickly defeat the evolved forms of the three starter Pokémon

The first round of the Driftveil Tournament will be a match against your rival. He has three Pokémon now and will attack all of your weak points.

If you chose Snivy

Pokémon	Type	Weak to
Pignite ♂ Lv. 25	Fire / Fighting	Water, Ground, Flying, Psychic
Simipour ♂ Lv. 25	Water	Grass, Electric
Tranquill ♂ Lv. 25	Normal / Flying	Electric, Ice, Rock

If you chose Tepig

Pokémon	Type	Weak to
Dewott ♂ Lv. 25	Water	Grass, Electric
Simisage ♂ Lv. 25	Grass	Fire, Ice, Poison, Flying, Bug
Tranquill ♂ Lv. 25	Normal / Flying	Electric, Ice, Rock

If you chose Oshawott

Pokémon	Type	Weak to
Servine ♂ Lv. 25	Grass	Fire, Ice, Poison, Flying, Bug
Simisear ♂ Lv. 25	Fire	Water, Ground, Rock
Tranquill ♂ Lv. 25	Normal / Flying	Electric, Ice, Rock

Driftveil Tournament Second Round

Take on Cheren!

I'm glad I have the chance to go up against you again.

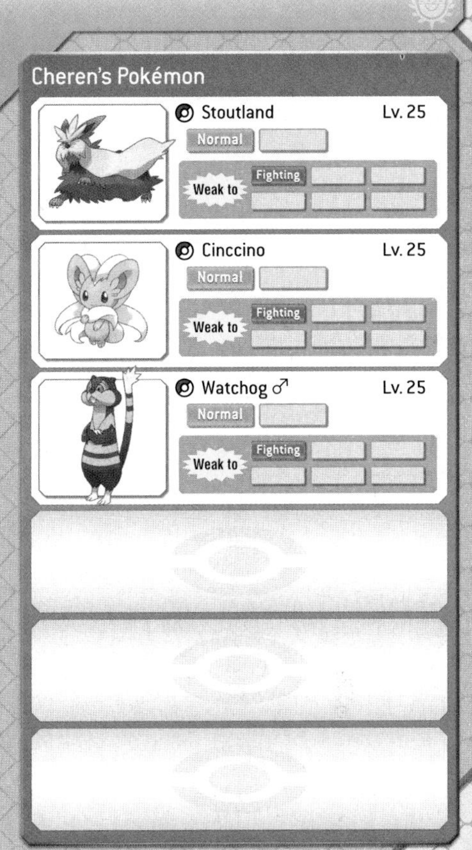

Cheren's Pokémon

Pokémon	Lv.	Type	Weak to
Stoutland	Lv. 25	Normal	Fighting
Cinccino	Lv. 25	Normal	Fighting
Watchog ♂	Lv. 25	Normal	Fighting

Put a quick end to this battle with Fighting-type moves

Cheren's Pokémon are all Normal type, so they all have the same weakness: Fighting-type moves. Using the Work Up move will raise your Pokémon's Attack and Sp. Atk, so if you can strike quickly at the opposing Pokémon's weak points, you may be able to defeat them before taking any damage.

Driftveil Tournament Final Round

Confront Colress!

I look forward to you teaching me that this is indeed true!

Colress's Pokémon

Pokémon	Lv.	Type	Weak to
Magneton	Lv. 25	Electric, Steel	Ground, Fire, Fighting
Elgyem	Lv. 25	Psychic	Bug, Ghost, Dark
Klink	Lv. 25	Steel	Fire, Fighting, Ground

If you strike the opponent's weaknesses, victory will be easily within your grasp

Among Colress's three Pokémon, Magneton and Klink have the same weaknesses. Defeat them quickly with Fire-, Ground-, or Fighting-type moves. Elgyem alone has different weaknesses. You'll be much more confident against it if you have Pokémon that know Bug-, Ghost-, or Dark-type moves.

Spot Team Plasma members outside the PWT

After receiving 1 BP for winning the tournament, head outside to see Team Plasma members passing nearby. When your rival moves to run after them, Colress tries to stop him, but he does not listen. He runs out of the area.

Head south and board the Plasma Frigate

Head south after your rival, and you will find a huge ship moored at the pier. Storm the ship together with your rival and Cheren. It turns out to be Team Plasma's base of operations. The three of you will immediately be surrounded by a great crowd of Team Plasma Grunts.

Defeat the crowd of Team Plasma Grunts

First, defeat two of the Grunts on your own. After that, you can team up with Cheren and then your rival to defeat pairs of Team Plasma Grunts. You'll be able to defeat all your enemies in no time that way.

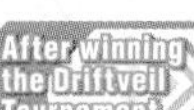

Confront a fired-up Zinzolin

Defeat the Team Plasma Grunts, and Zinzolin will appear from within the frigate. Zinzolin declares that Team Plasma will rule the Unova region. At Zinzolin's order, the Shadow Triad appear and whisk you and your allies away from the ship.

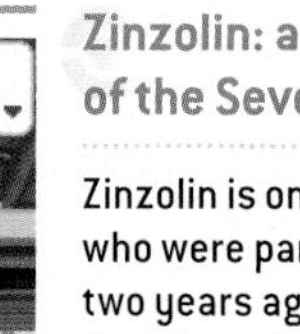

Return to Driftveil City

You and your allies will be left standing on the dock. Infuriated by this outcome, your rival runs off in a huff. Cheren also leaves to continue onward to Route 6. Return to Driftveil City to follow in Cheren's tracks (p. 148).

Challenge a variety of different tournaments

At the PWT, you can also take part in the Rental Tournament, where you battle with rental Pokémon, and the Mix Tournament, where you and your opponent swap Pokémon. The more tournaments you win, the more BP you can collect (p. 381).

Speak to Colress at the PWT hall

After winning the Driftveil Tournament, return to the PWT hall and you will find Colress. Speak to him and he will tell you that he plans to continue battling to prove his theories about bringing out the true power of Pokémon.

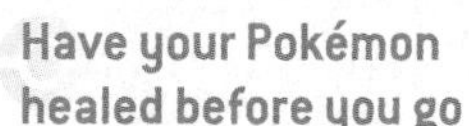

Have your Pokémon healed before you go

Heading south from the PWT and boarding Team Plasma's frigate will lead to a series of battles during which you cannot return to the city. Be sure to have your Pokémon healed at the Driftveil City Pokémon Center before you go.

Zinzolin: a former member of the Seven Sages

Zinzolin is one of the Seven Sages who were part of Team Plasma two years ago. Team Plasma was thought to have disbanded then, yet now they seem to be operating again for some new purpose.

Who are the mysterious Shadow Triad?

The Shadow Triad worked under Ghetsis when he was the head of Team Plasma two years ago. They appear with the speed and stealth of ninjas, and disappear again in much the same way. They claimed they would always be loyal servants of Ghetsis, so why are they cooperating with Zinzolin now?

Revisit after entering the Hall of Fame

After entering the Hall of Fame, the number of tournaments you can take part in at the PWT will greatly increase. These tournaments will become markedly more difficult, so winning them will be quite an ambitious aspiration. Take your time and conquer every last tournament!

Relic Passage

The Relic Passage is an underground cave that was recently discovered. It connects the Castelia Sewers and the PWT. It also leads to the lowest floor of the Relic Castle.

Items

First visit

- ☐ Escape Rope
- ☐ Hard Stone
- ☐ Max Repel
- ☐ Protein
- ☐ Rare Candy
- ☐ Rocky Helmet
- ☐ Ultra Ball

After getting Surf

- ☐ Big Pearl

The middle

Hiker Tobias

Psychic Tully

Psychic Ena

A

B

C

Relic Castle P. 129

Backpacker Annie

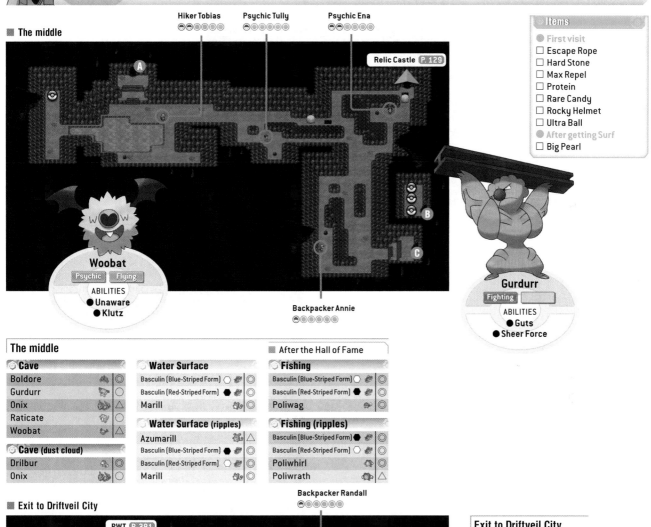

Woobat
Psychic / Flying
ABILITIES
● Unaware
● Klutz

Gurdurr
Fighting
ABILITIES
● Guts
● Sheer Force

The middle

Cave	
Boldore	◎
Gurdurr	○
Onix	△
Raticate	○
Woobat	△

Cave (dust cloud)	
Drilbur	◎
Onix	○

Water Surface	
Basculin (Blue-Striped Form) ○	◎
Basculin (Red-Striped Form) ●	◎
Marill	◎

Water Surface (ripples)	
Azumarill	△
Basculin (Blue-Striped Form) ●	◎
Basculin (Red-Striped Form) ○	◎
Marill	◎

After the Hall of Fame

Fishing	
Basculin (Blue-Striped Form) ○	◎
Basculin (Red-Striped Form) ●	◎
Poliwag	◎

Fishing (ripples)	
Basculin (Blue-Striped Form) ●	◎
Basculin (Red-Striped Form) ○	◎
Poliwhirl	◎
Poliwrath	△

Exit to Driftveil City

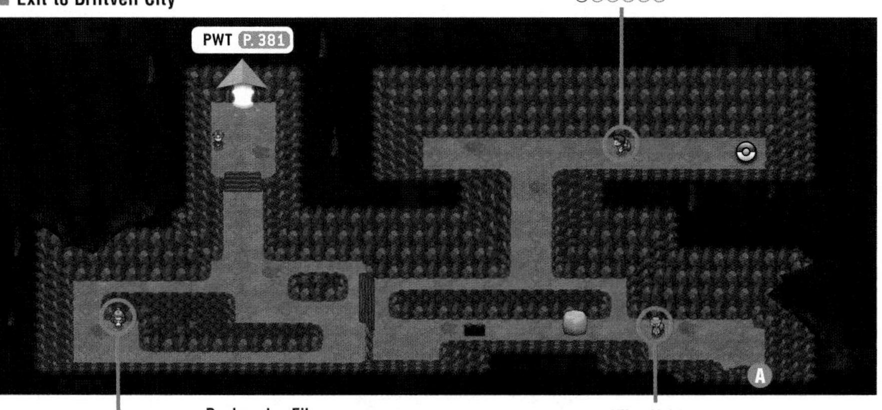

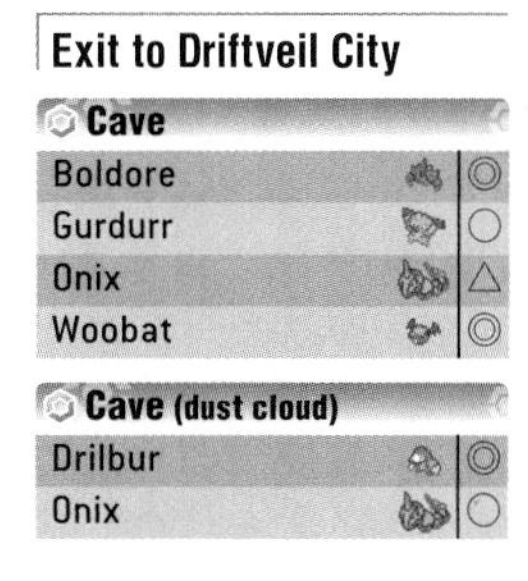

Exit to Driftveil City

Cave	
Boldore	◎
Gurdurr	○
Onix	△
Woobat	◎

Cave (dust cloud)	
Drilbur	◎
Onix	○

■ Exit to Castelia City

Exit to Castelia City

Cave	
Onix	◎
Rattata	○
Roggenrola	△
Timburr	◎
Woobat	◎

Cave (dust cloud)	
Drilbur	◎
Onix	○

Step 1 Battle Trainers in the tunnels

There are a total of 10 Pokémon Trainers waiting for you in the Relic Passage. Battle them and collect items as you proceed.

Hold up! Did you know this path was supposedly made ages and ages ago?

Get a new Funfest Mission

Speak to the Worker past the exit to Driftveil City. The Funfest Mission "Find Treasures!" will be added to your Entralink.

Step 2 The lowest floor of the Relic Castle

From the middle part of the passage, go east. You'll see an entrance on the north side of the dead end. Enter it and you'll be inside the Relic Castle. Have one of your Pokémon move the boulder with Strength to enter the Relic Castle (p. 129).

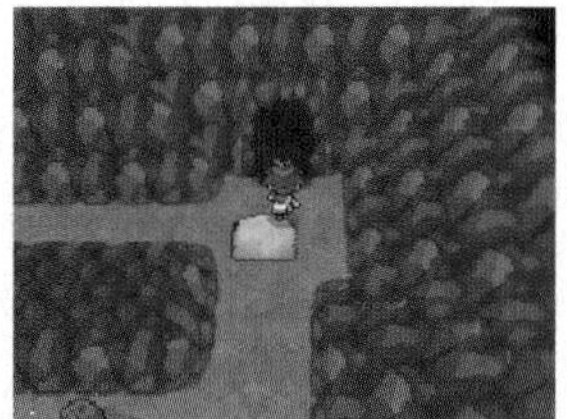

Explore the Relic Castle before you come back here

On the north side of the middle part of the passage is an entrance that leads to the Relic Castle's lowest floor, but it's a dead end. Go to collect items and catch Volcarona before you come back to the Relic Passage.

Step 3 Be careful around the ledges

There are ledges past the exit to Castelia City. If you jump over either of them, you won't be able to return to the middle passage or the exit to Driftveil City. Make sure to collect all the items before you jump over them to proceed.

Another way out

If you jump over the ledge at the exit to Castelia City, you can use an Escape Rope or have your Pokémon use Dig to return to the PWT.

Step 4 Use Fly to go back to the PWT

After you jump over the ledge at the exit to Castelia City and collect all the items there, go south to the Castelia Sewers. When you get to Castelia City, you can use Fly to go back to the PWT in an instant.

Come back after you get HM03 Surf

Get HM03 Surf from Cheren on Route 6 before you come back here to collect items. Go west on the water's surface in the middle passage to collect items.

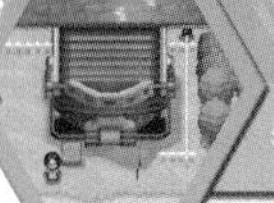

Route 6

Route 6 is a road surrounded by rich nature with green trees. At the Season Research Lab, research is being conducted on Deerling, which changes its form depending on the season. The north side leads to Chargestone Cave.

Field Moves Needed

Hidden Grottoes ● There are two Hidden Grottoes on Route 6. Find both of them.

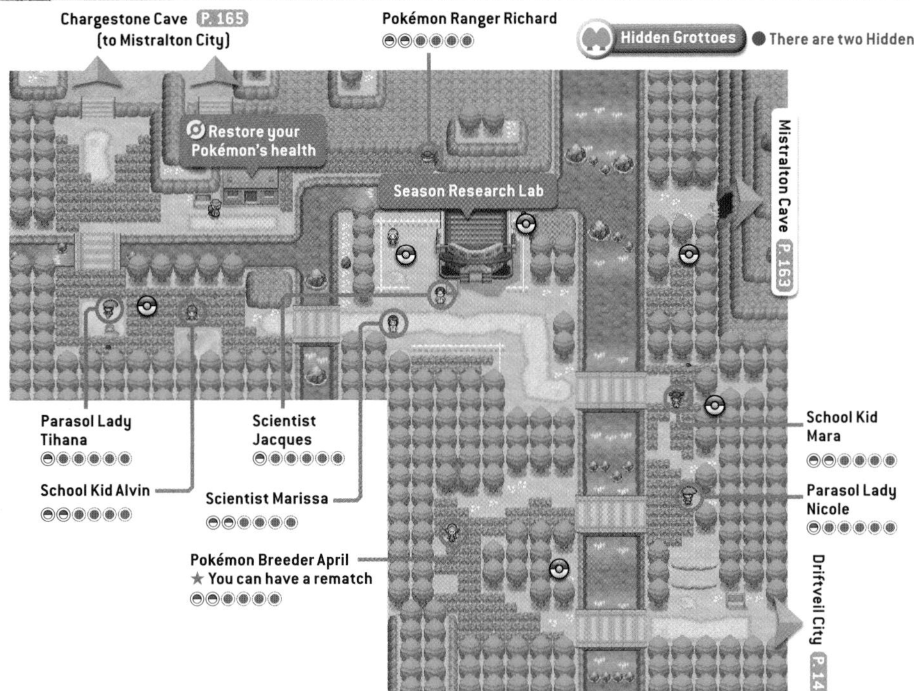

Items

- First Visit
- ☐ Elixir
- ☐ HM03 Surf
- ☐ Moon Stone
- ☐ Shiny Stone
- ☐ Ultra Ball
- After defeating Pokémon Ranger Richard
- ☐ Pecha Berry
- After getting Surf
- ☐ Heart Scale
- ☐ PP Up
- ☐ TM56 Fling

Tall Grass		
Deerling		◎
Foongus		○
Karrablast	○	○
Karrablast	●	△
Marill		△
Shelmet	●	○
Shelmet	○	△
Swadloon		○
Tranquill		○

Tall Grass (rustling)	
Audino	◎
Azumarill	△
Castform	△
Dunsparce	○
Emolga	○
Leavanny	△
Unfezant	△

Dark Grass		
Deerling		◎
Foongus		○
Karrablast	○	○
Karrablast	●	△
Marill		△
Shelmet	●	○
Shelmet	○	△
Swadloon		○
Tranquill		○

Water Surface		
Basculin (Red-Striped Form)	●	◎
Basculin (Blue-Striped Form)	○	◎
Marill		◎

Water Surface (ripples)		
Azumarill		△
Basculin (Blue-Striped Form)	●	◎
Basculin (Red-Striped Form)	○	◎
Marill		◎

After the Hall of Fame

Fishing		
Basculin (Red-Striped Form)	●	◎
Basculin (Blue-Striped Form)	○	◎
Poliwag		◎

Fishing (ripples)		
Basculin (Blue-Striped Form)	●	◎
Basculin (Red-Striped Form)	○	◎
Politoed		△
Poliwhirl		◎

Hidden Grotto 1	
Dunsparce	△
Foongus	◎
Woobat	○

Hidden Grotto 2	
Foongus	◎
Nosepass	△
Woobat	○

Mass Outbreaks	
Minun	○
Plusle	●

Step 1 Cheren shows what he's been investigating

You'll meet Cheren as you explore Route 6. He tells you that the data show a sudden drop in the temperature near Lacunosa Town, Castelia City, and Driftveil City. What's going on?

Pokémon that learn Surf

Some Pokémon you meet up to this point can learn Surf, including Audino, Azurill, Psyduck, Panpour, Ducklett, Marill, and Azumarill. If none of them is in your party, catch one of them to get surfin'.

Step 2 Receive HM03 Surf from Cheren

Cheren gives you HM03 Surf. He'll ask you to check on various things. Surf lets you travel over the surface of water, so use the HM to have a Pokémon in your party learn it.

Visit places Surf can take you

You can use Surf in many of the places you've visited already, such as Aspertia City, Route 19, and Route 20. Use Fly to go to these places and collect items.

Step 3 Get Deerling at the Season Research Lab

You can receive a Deerling with the Hidden Ability Serene Grace at the Season Research Lab. You cannot receive it if your party is full, so make an empty slot at Driftveil City Pokémon Center.

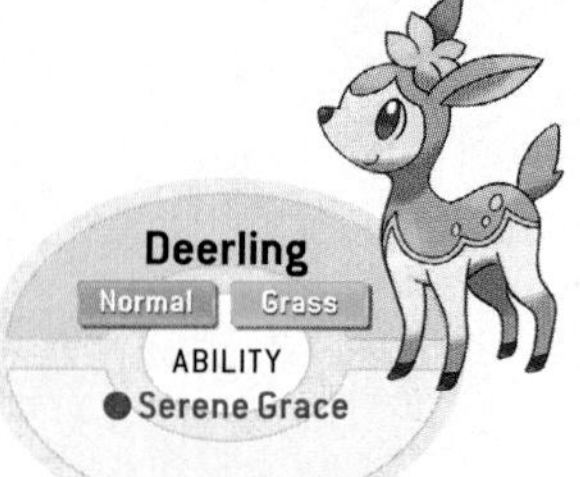

Step 4 Learn about the weather

When you have Pokémon in your party that can change the weather with its move or Ability, the Parasol Lady in the Season Research Lab will tell you about weather conditions in detail. You should listen to her and remember what she says to help you in battles.

Castform changes its form depending on the weather

Castform appears in the rustling grass on Route 6. This unique Pokémon changes its form and type depending on the weather. It turns into a Water type in rain, a Fire type when it's sunny, and an Ice type when it's hailing.

Step 5 Legendary Pokémon Cobalion appears

Head for Chargestone Cave and you'll see Cobalion along the way. It quickly disappears, though. Rood shows up right after that and tells you Cobalion will be a great asset if you can befriend it.

Get Berries from a Pokémon Ranger

Defeat Pokémon Ranger Richard to receive Pecha Berries. Richard stands through the tall grass to the east of the house where you can heal your Pokémon.

Step 6 Heal your Pokémon at the house

Talk to the woman in the house to the east of where you met Cobalion and she'll heal your Pokémon. You can visit there when your Pokémon get hurt during Trainer battles or against wild Pokémon.

Foongus will ambush you

When you check items on the ground on Route 6, a Foongus may pop out. The Foongus was pretending to be an item. You'll have no time to prepare yourself as it'll challenge you right away. Keep calm and battle.

Step 7 Go to Mistralton Cave

Use Surf by the house where you can heal your Pokémon and head east and you'll reach Mistralton Cave. Two years ago, the Legendary Pokémon Cobalion was found in this cave. Explore this cave before you proceed to Chargestone Cave (p. 163).

Step 8 Head for Chargestone Cave

Leave Mistralton Cave and head for Chargestone Cave. From the exit to Mistralton Cave, use Surf to go west and then north. Heal your Pokémon at the house and go north from there (p. 165).

Mistralton Cave

Mistralton Cave is located on Route 6. Two years ago, the Legendary Pokémon Cobalion was there. Now that Cobalion has left, this cave has mostly been forgotten by the people nearby.

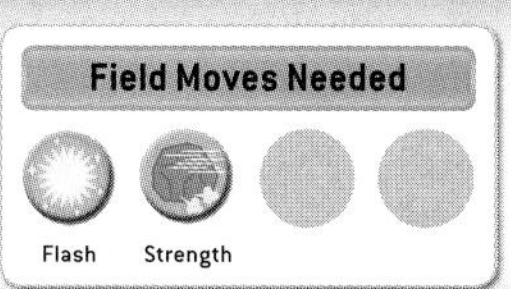

1F

Hiker Jebediah

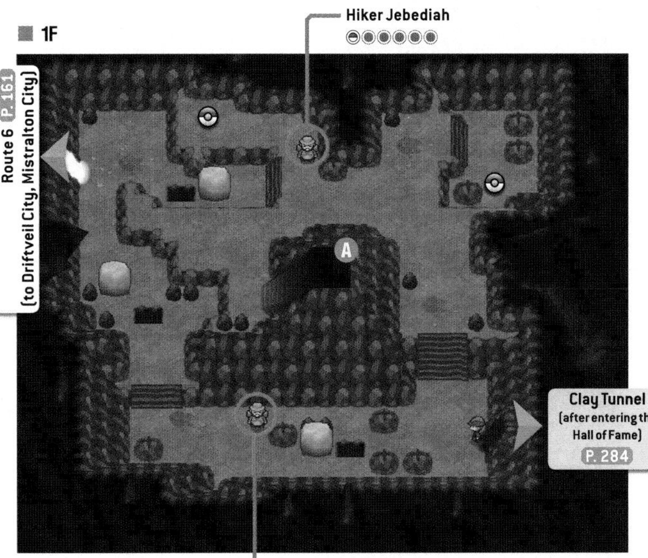

Route 6 P. 161 (to Driftveil City, Mistralton City)

Clay Tunnel (after entering the Hall of Fame) P. 284

Hiker Shelby

2F

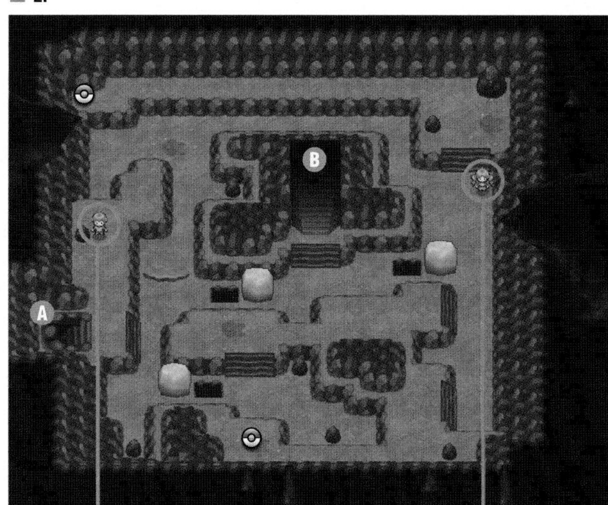

Ace Trainer Geoff

Ace Trainer Belle

3F

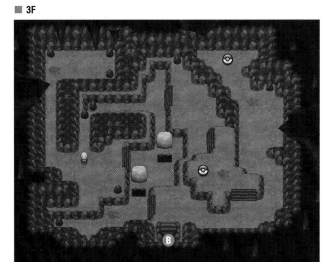

Items

- ☐ Blue Shard
- ☐ Dusk Ball
- ☐ Escape Rope
- ☐ Hyper Potion
- ☐ TM80 Rock Slide
- ☐ Yellow Shard

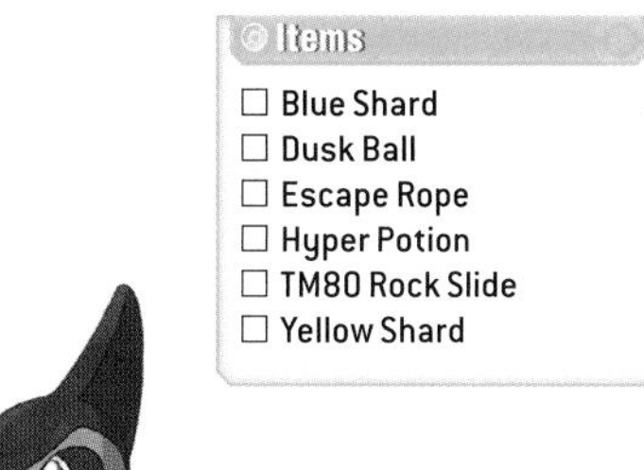

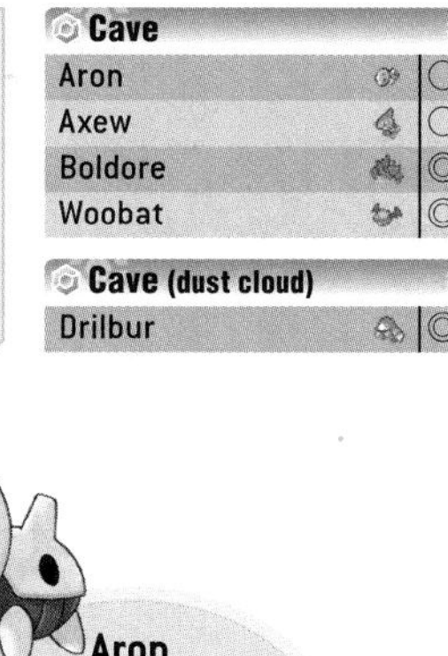

Cave	
Aron	○
Axew	○
Boldore	◎
Woobat	◎

Cave (dust cloud)	
Drilbur	◎

Axew
Dragon
ABILITIES
● Rivalry
● Mold Breaker

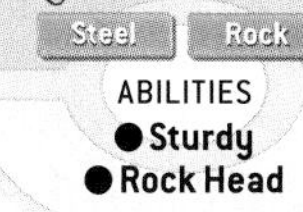

Aron
Steel | Rock
ABILITIES
● Sturdy
● Rock Head

Step 1 Brighten your surroundings with Flash

It's pitch black inside the cave—you can't see a step in front of you. Teach TM70 Flash to a Pokémon and use the move in the cave. The lit area expands, and it becomes easier to explore the cave.

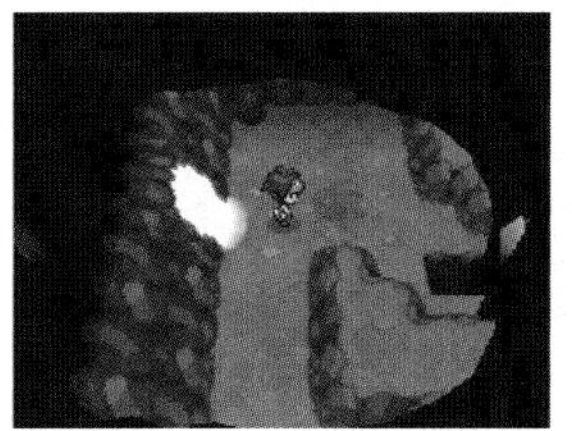

Get TM70 Flash

You get TM70 Flash from a sunglasses-wearing man who appears from behind a dumpster on Castelia City's Narrow Street. If you don't have it yet, visit Castelia City (p. 106).

Step 2 Use Strength to move boulders out of your way

Inside the cave, big boulders block your way forward. Use the HM Strength to move the boulders and push them into nearby holes. Now you can walk over the holes. Continue to move boulders as you make your way deeper into the cave.

Step 3 A man blocks the entrance to the Clay Tunnel

You can find an entrance to the Clay Tunnel on the east side of 1F. However, a man is blocking the entrance, and you can't go through (p. 284). He will not move until you enter the Hall of Fame, so ignore the tunnel for now and continue on.

Step 4 Move boulders to make a shortcut

You will see a big boulder to the west of Hiker Jebediah on the north side of 1F. Push this boulder into the hole, and it will create a shortcut. The next time you visit, you'll be able to go directly to floor 2F.

Step 5 Proceed while battling Pokémon Trainers

In Mistralton Cave, two Pokémon Trainers are exploring 1F and two more are on 2F. Battle them while you aim for 3F, the highest floor. If you use Strength to push boulders and reach the staircase at the center of 2F, you can finally reach 3F.

Step 6 Listen to the story of the man on 3F

There aren't any Pokémon Trainers on 3F, just an old man on the western side of the cave. When you talk to him, he tells you he's been searching for the Legendary Pokémon Cobalion for decades.

Cobalion resents humans

Long ago, Cobalion, Terrakion, and Virizion rescued Pokémon from a fire caused by a war between humans. From that point on, they've refused to associate with humans.

Two years ago Cobalion lived here

Two years ago, Cobalion lived on the third floor of Mistralton Cave, and you could encounter it here. Cobalion, which appears before you on Route 6, can be encountered again on Route 13 (p. 185).

Step 7 Explore every corner to collect items

When you push all of the boulders into the holes in Mistralton Cave, check out every corner. Collect items as you make your way around each floor, making sure not to miss anything.

Step 8 Leave the cave and return to Route 6

Once you've explored all of Mistralton Cave, go back to your journey to be the Pokémon Champion. Use the exit on the west side of 1F and return to Route 6, then proceed west (p. 161).

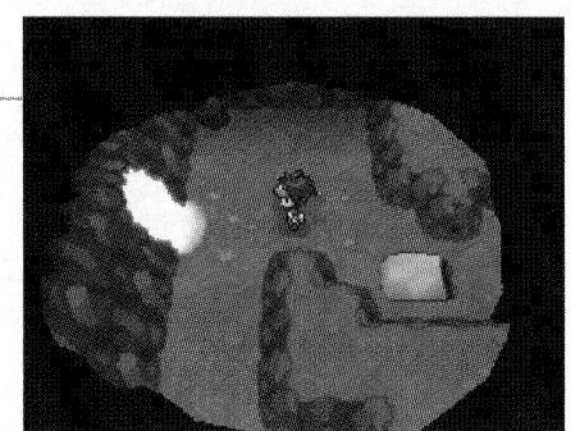

Chargestone Cave

Chargestone Cave is a cave that connects Mistralton City and Route 6, which leads north from Driftveil City. Chargestone Cave is where electrically charged stones seem to wait around every corner. These stones block many of the pathways through the cave.

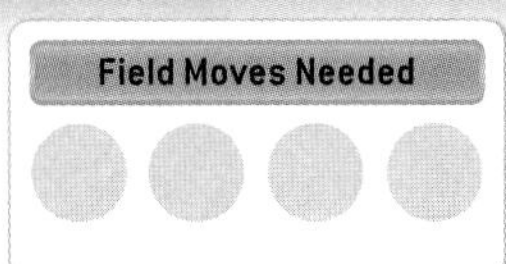

■ 1F

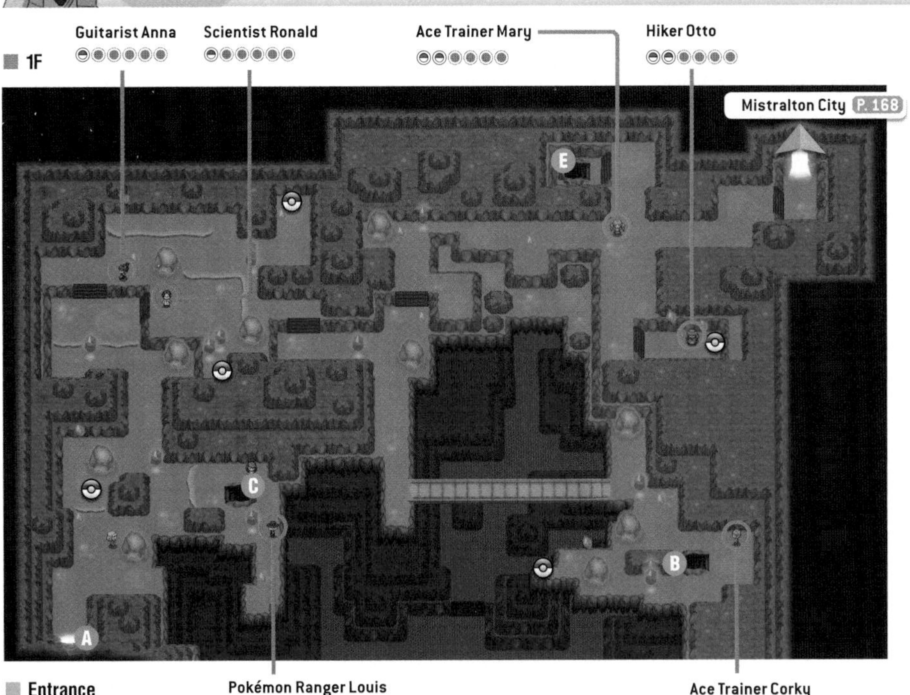

■ Entrance

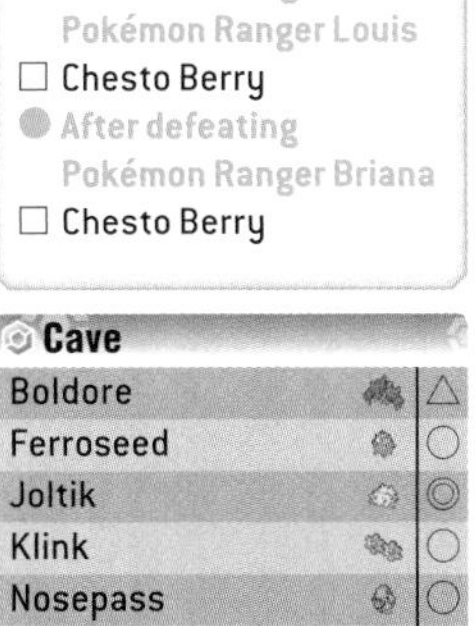

Items

- First Visit
- ☐ Big Nugget
- ☐ Carbos
- ☐ Escape Rope
- ☐ Full Heal
- ☐ Hyper Potion
- ☐ Iron
- ☐ Magnet
- ☐ Max Repel
- ☐ Metal Coat
- ☐ Nugget
- ☐ Revive
- ☐ Thunderstone
- After defeating Pokémon Ranger Louis
- ☐ Chesto Berry
- After defeating Pokémon Ranger Briana
- ☐ Chesto Berry

Cave	
Boldore	△
Ferroseed	○
Joltik	◎
Klink	○
Nosepass	○
Tynamo	△

Cave (dust cloud)	
Drilbur	◎

■ B1F

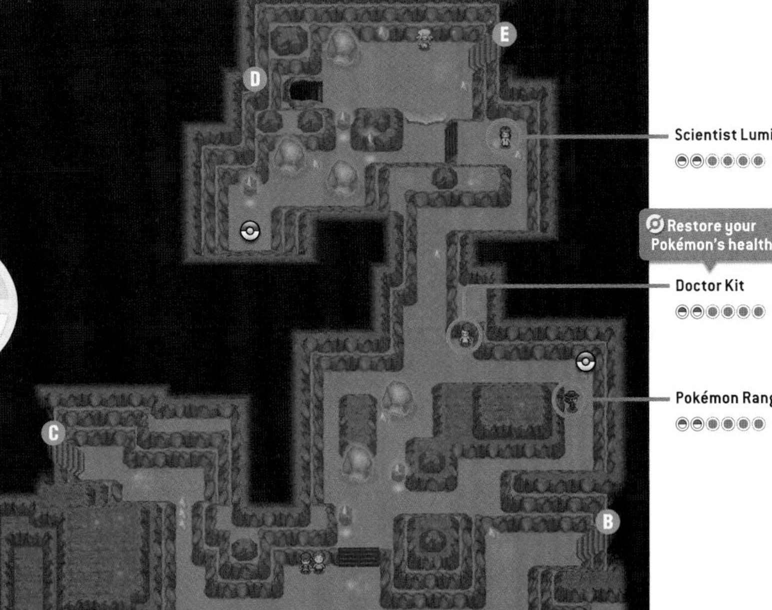

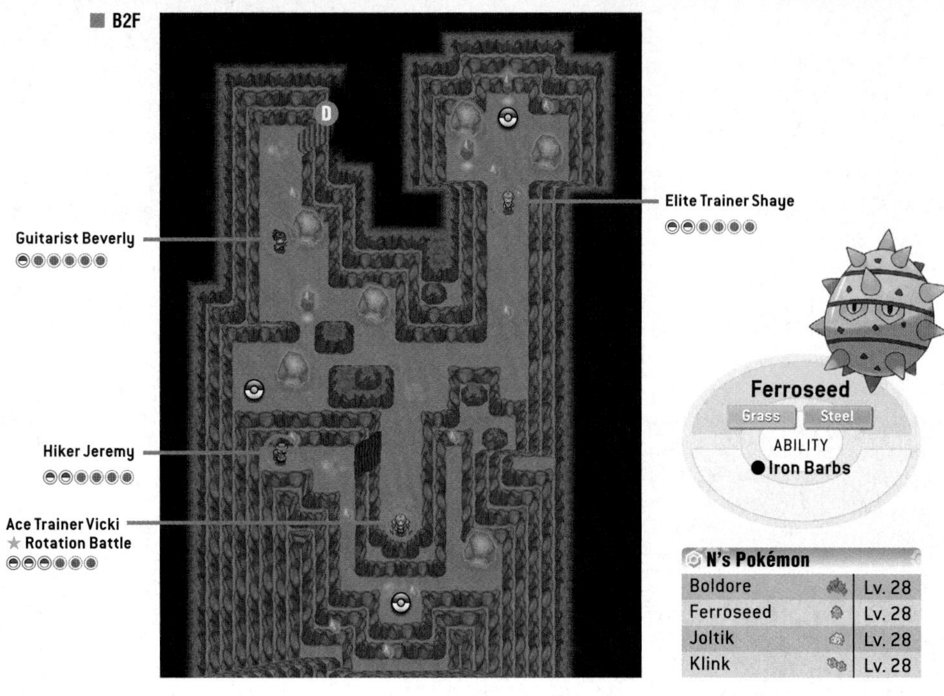

N's Pokémon	
Boldore	Lv. 28
Ferroseed	Lv. 28
Joltik	Lv. 28
Klink	Lv. 28

Step 1 Bianca tells you that you can move the floating stones

Go inside from Route 6 and head north. Bianca will speak to you and tell you that you can push and move the blue stones. When you get stuck, find a stone you can move.

If you push the floating stones,
they move!

Step 2 Continue into the cave while pushing stones

Clear the way forward by moving the stones blocking the path. The stones are electrically charged, so they will stick to boulders. If you try to push a stone in a direction with no boulders, it won't move. And if you accidentally push a stone in the wrong direction, you can head to another floor and it will return to where it was before.

You can only proceed after defeating the Driftveil City Gym

You can visit here without the Driftveil City Gym Badge, but Bianca will be on the bridge blocking the way. Get the Gym Badge and win the PWT before you visit here so you can proceed.

Step 3 You hear a voice on the bridge

Follow the path on 1F, and go over the bridge. You'll hear someone's voice. The voice says, "I have to go in order to save Pokémon and protect the very friend that I have to stop!" The person leaves without giving you a chance to see who it is.

Step 4 A Trainer challenges you to a Triple Battle

Go over a bridge, head east, and you'll be challenged for a Triple Battle. Be sure to check the order of your Pokémon before you take on the challenge.

Behold the destructive force created by my three prized Pokémon!

Step 5 Have Doctor Kit heal your Pokémon

Go down the stairs to B1F and go north. You'll meet Doctor Kit. Defeat him in Pokémon battle and afterward talk to him. He'll heal your Pokémon every time you talk to him. If your Pokémon are hurt, go over to him to heal up before moving on.

I may have lost the prize, but I'll still make your Pokémon healthy and hearty!

Step 6 Speak to Bianca and she reveals what she's up to

You'll meet Bianca at the dead end on the north side of B1F. Speak to her and she'll tell you that Professor Juniper requested her to research Tynamo and she came here since Tynamo live in Chargestone Cave.

I'm researching a Pokémon called Tynamo!

Step 7 A Trainer challenges you to a Rotation Battle

Go down to B2F and head south. You'll meet a Pokémon Trainer who'll challenge you to a Rotation Battle. Check the order of your Pokémon before you start the battle.

My three beloved Pokémon will make their debut in a perfect, weaving triangle.

Step 8 From the exit, head for Mistralton City

Explore every corner of Chargestone Cave before you go find Bianca on B1F. Head west from there, and go up the stairs to go back to 1F. Head east and go through the exit in the north side, and you'll be in Mistralton City (p. 168).

Funfest Missions will be added

Speak to the Lady on 1F, and in *Pokémon Black Version 2*, "Find Mysterious Ores!" will be added. In *Pokémon White Version 2*, "Find Shining Ores!" will be added for you to play.

It's all about the Nugget

Speak to the Nugget man and Nugget boy on B1F to receive a Nugget and a Big Nugget. The Gentleman at Icirrus City will buy them for 10,000 and 30,000 respectively (p. 301).

Tynamo appears in two spots

Bianca is researching Tynamo, a Pokémon that evolves twice. It appears in Chargestone Cave, as well as Seaside Cave 1F.

Mistralton City

Half of Mistralton City is taken up by a runway. Vegetables harvested around this runway are transported all over the world. If you go north, you'll enter Route 7, which leads to the Celestial Tower.

Field Moves Needed

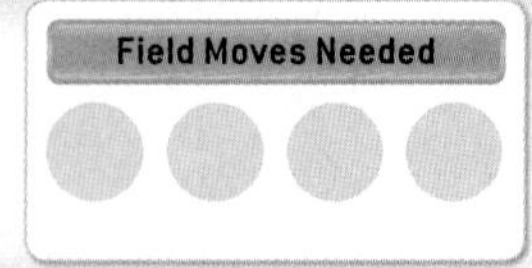

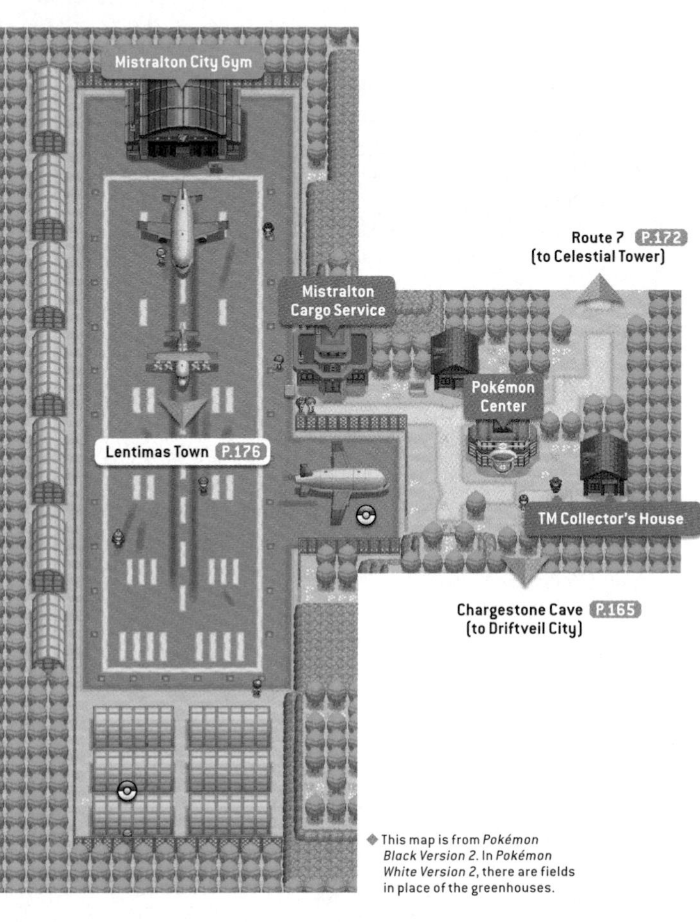

◆ This map is from *Pokémon Black Version 2*. In *Pokémon White Version 2*, there are fields in place of the greenhouses.

Items

- First visit
  - ☐ Fresh Water
  - ☐ Master Ball
  - ☐ Max Repel
  - ☐ Sharp Beak
  - ☐ TM58 Sky Drop
- Given depending on the number of TMs you currently have
  - ☐ HP Up x6
- If you have a Flying- or Psychic-type Pokémon in your party
  - ☐ Net Ball x5
- After defeating the Mistralton City Gym
  - ☐ Jet Badge
  - ☐ TM40 Aerial Ace
  - ☐ TM62 Acrobatics

Poké Mart (Lower Clerk)

Item	Price
TM07 Hail	50,000
TM11 Sunny Day	50,000
TM18 Rain Dance	50,000
TM37 Sandstorm	50,000

The Pokémon Breeder buys these items

Item	Price
Damp Mulch	1,000
Growth Mulch	1,000
Stable Mulch	1,000
Gooey Mulch	1,000

Step 1 Get HP Up from the TM Collector

Talk to the woman in the center of the house to the east of the Pokémon Center. She'll give you an HP Up when the number of TMs you have reaches 10, 20, 35, 50, and 70, plus one more when you've collected all of the TMs.

Thank you! I was thrilled to see them!

Step 2 Professor Juniper gives you the Master Ball

If you walk north on the western side of the Pokémon Center, Professor Juniper will talk to you. She thanks you for accepting the Pokédex. Then she evaluates your Pokédex and gives you the Master Ball.

Trainer obtained a Master Ball!

The ultimate Poké Ball

The Master Ball will always catch any Pokémon, so it's the ultimate Poké Ball. It can never be purchased in a shop, but you can win one in Join Avenue's Raffle Shop, where it's the top prize.

Meet the Mistralton City Gym Leader, Skyla

Skyla, the Mistralton City Gym Leader, joins you while you're talking to Professor Juniper. Professor Juniper had asked Skyla to fly her somewhere in her plane, but Professor Juniper leaves for Celestial Tower instead.

Trade Sweet Hearts for Heart Scales

The woman in Mistralton Cargo Service gives you a Heart Scale if you give her 10 Sweet Hearts. But there's a sweet deal from February 14 to March 14—you can get a Heart Scale for five Sweet Hearts.

YES
NO
Will you trade 10 Sweet Hearts for my Heart Scale?

Remember moves with Heart Scales

The reminder girl at the PWT can help your Pokémon remember a move it has forgotten if you give her Heart Scales. Keep collecting Heart Scales so you'll have plenty available if you rethink your Pokémon's moves.

Help the Worker at Mistralton Cargo Service

Talk to the man at the counter in the east side of the Mistralton Cargo Service when you have a Flying- or Psychic-type Pokémon in your party. He will give you five Net Balls as thanks for helping him carry luggage.

A Funfest Mission is added

Head to the runway on the west side of town and talk to the Backpacker on the southern side of the strip. The Entralink Funfest Mission "Big Harvest of Berries" is added.

The Pokémon Breeder buys Mulch

You will find a Pokémon Breeder wearing a bandana on the southern side of the runway. He'll pay a lot for each of the four types of Mulch. Once you get your hands on some Mulch, sell it to this Pokémon Breeder.

I work on a farm in Mistralton City.
So I need lots of Mulch! So much Mulch!

How do you get Mulch?

Four types of Mulch can be found in Hidden Grottoes. They can also be purchased at the Flower Shop in Join Avenue (p. 132). The version of the game the owner of the store came from determines what kinds of Mulch are sold at the shop.

Step 7 Follow Professor Juniper to Celestial Tower

Skyla says you can challenge the Gym or follow Professor Juniper to Celestial Tower. Pass through Route 7 (p. 172) and head to Celestial Tower to train your Pokémon.

Why visit Celestial Tower?

Stopping by Celestial Tower before going to the Gym is the best way to toughen up your Pokémon team a little before taking on the Gym. Battle all the Trainers on Route 7 and in Celestial Tower.

Challenge the Mistralton City Gym

Take Route 7 back to Mistralton City from Celestial Tower. First, stop by the Pokémon Center and heal your Pokémon. When you're all ready to go, head to the runway to the west, then go north, and you'll reach the Mistralton City Gym.

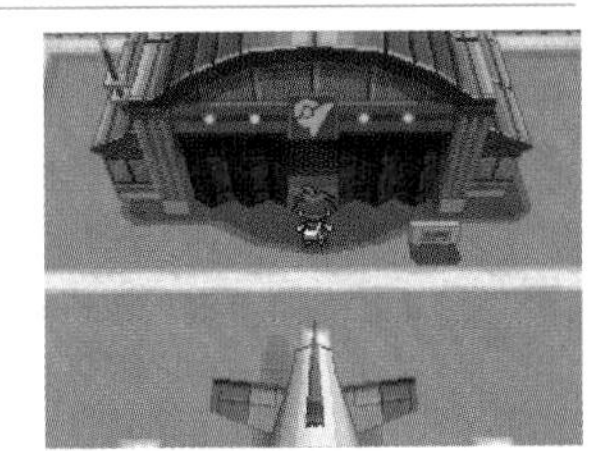

6 Mistralton City Gym Battle

Gym Battle Tips

- Teach a Pokémon in your party TM84 Rock Slide
- Battling with Boldore or Joltik, which can be caught in Chargestone Cave, can give you an advantage

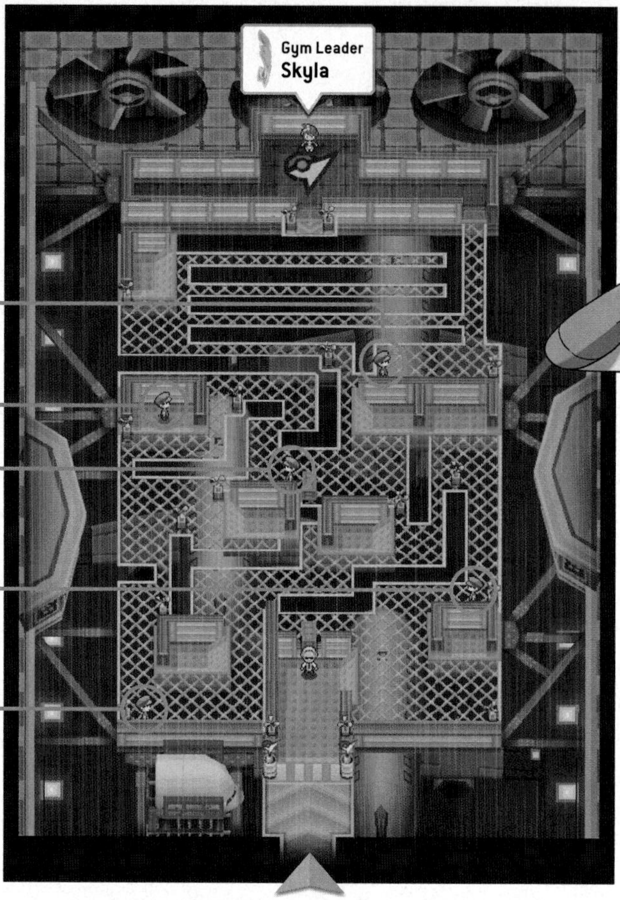

Gym Leader Skyla

Pilot Chase

Pilot Elron

Pilot Ewing

Pilot Flynn

Pilot Winslow

Entrance

You're a tough Trainer who can face the wind and not get blown off your feet!

Mistralton City Gym Leader

Skyla

Flying-type Pokémon User

Electric- or Rock-type moves deal massive damage

Sometimes a strong wind blows through the Gym, so move when the wind stops. When an exclamation point appears over your head, hide behind a wall and wait for the wind to stop again. Repeat this process as you make your way to Skyla. Skyla's Pokémon attack with moves that do the most possible damage to your Pokémon. Swap out your Pokémon depending on which Pokémon you're facing to protect your Pokémon's weak points. Strike Skyla's Pokémon's weak points with Electric- or Rock-type moves.

Skyla's Pokémon

Pokémon	Lv.	Type	Weak to
Swoobat ♀	Lv. 37	Psychic, Flying	Electric, Ice, Rock, Ghost, Dark
Skarmory ♀	Lv. 37	Steel, Flying	Fire, Electric
Swanna ♀	Lv. 39	Water, Flying	Electric, Rock

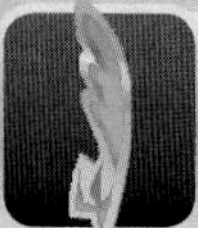

Jet Badge

Pokémon up to Lv. 70, including those received in trades, will obey you.

TM 62 Acrobatics Flying

If the user isn't holding an item, this attack's power is doubled.

After beating the Mistralton City Gym — Professor Juniper returns from Celestial Tower

Just as you emerge victorious from the Gym, Professor Juniper returns from Celestial Tower. Professor Juniper is heading to Mistralton Cargo Service to ride an airplane. Follow her into Mistralton Cargo Service.

If you go to the Gym first, the Professor won't be there

If you defeat the Mistralton City Gym before you go to Celestial Tower, Professor Juniper won't be there. To meet Professor Juniper in Celestial Tower, pass through Route 7 (p. 172) and head there first.

After beating the Mistralton City Gym — Search for the boy's buried treasure

Visit the house north of the Pokémon Center after you beat the Gym. If you go to the southern end of the runway after talking to the boy in that house, you can get TM40 Aerial Ace. The boy hid it in a field.

Aerial Ace always hits its target!
I hope it comes in handy!

Memory Link event

You'll see Skyla standing in front of the Gym after you've defeated her. Talk to her, and a Memory Link event will start. You can listen to a friendly chat between Skyla and Elesa (p. 73).

Bianca comes to the Cargo Service

Professor Juniper and Skyla are waiting when you enter Mistralton Cargo Service. Talk to Skyla. Just as you're about to board the plane, Bianca comes running into the Cargo Service. She's accompanying you to Lentimas Town.

You guys! Wait, wait, wait, wait!
Hff...pff...I want to fly, too!

Fly to Lentimas Town by plane

Professor Juniper's destination is Opelucid City. The seventh Gym is also there. You can't reach it solely on foot, so fly to Lentimas Town by plane, and go the rest of the way on foot (p. 176).

Speedy transport for vegetables or passengers

Two years ago, Mistralton City's planes were cargo planes that carried vegetables, but not passengers. Now, they fly people to many different places.

Route 7

Route 7 is thick with patches of tall grass. There are raised walkways everywhere, so you can use them to avoid walking through the tall grass. Celestial Tower is directly north, while the eastern part of the route goes to Twist Mountain.

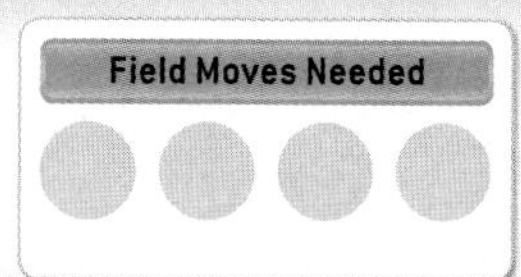

Hidden Grottoes

Route 7 has Hidden Grottoes. Find them!

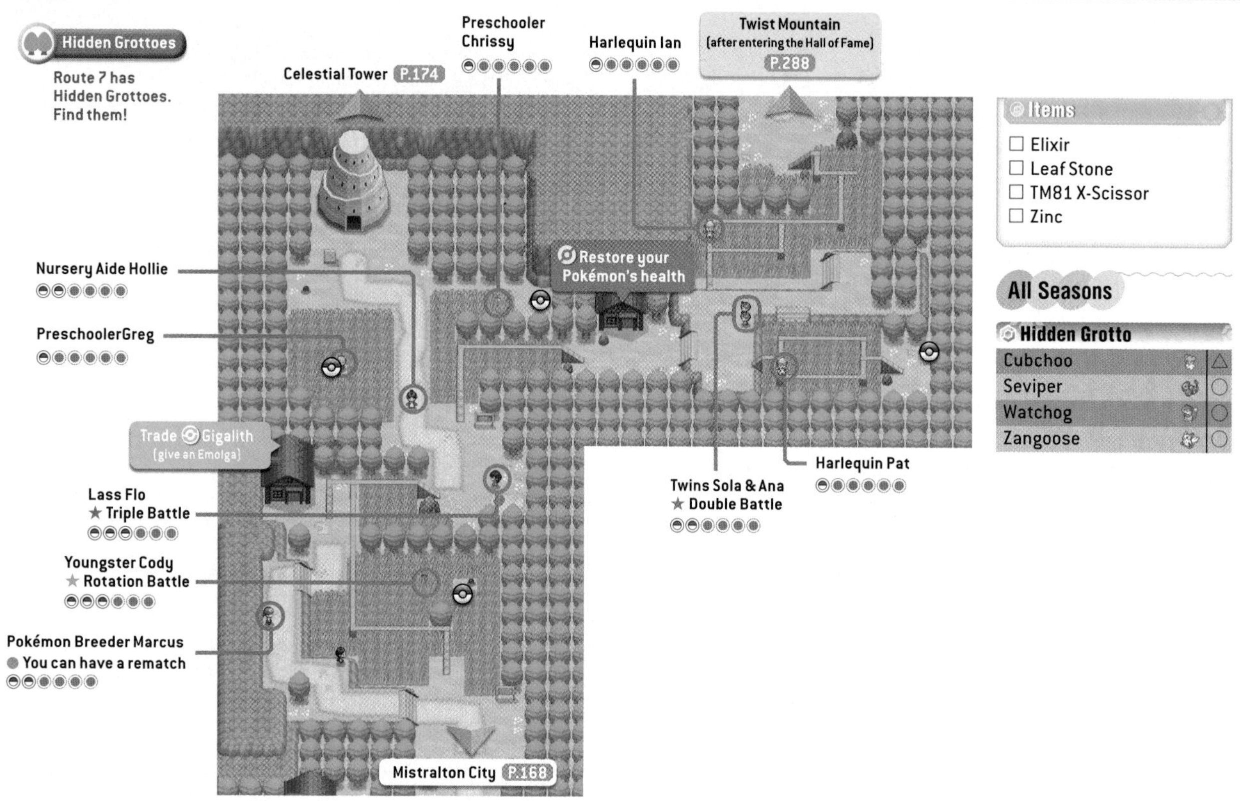

Items

- ☐ Elixir
- ☐ Leaf Stone
- ☐ TM81 X-Scissor
- ☐ Zinc

All Seasons

Hidden Grotto	
Cubchoo	△
Seviper	○
Watchog	○
Zangoose	○

Spring Summer Autumn

Tall Grass	
Deerling	○
Foongus	△
Seviper	△
Tranquill	◎
Watchog	○
Zangoose	△
Zebstrika	○

Tall Grass (rustling)	
Audino	◎
Emolga	○
Unfezant	△

Dark Grass	
Deerling	○
Foongus	△
Seviper	△
Tranquill	◎
Watchog	○
Zangoose	△
Zebstrika	○

Mass Outbreaks
Furret

Winter

Tall Grass	
Cubchoo	○
Deerling	○
Foongus	△
Seviper	△
Tranquill	○
Watchog	○
Zangoose	△
Zebstrika	○

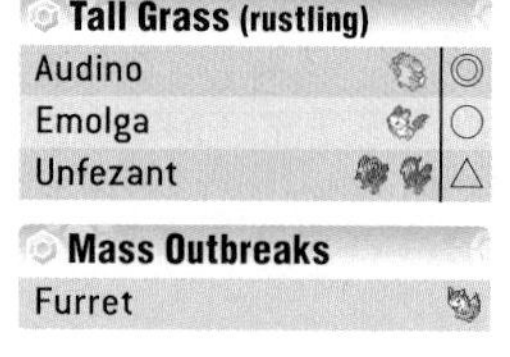

Tall Grass (rustling)	
Audino	◎
Emolga	○
Unfezant	△

Mass Outbreaks
Furret

Dark Grass	
Cubchoo	○
Deerling	○
Foongus	△
Seviper	△
Tranquill	○
Watchog	○
Zangoose	△
Zebstrika	○

Step 1 Watch your step when crossing the raised walkways

Take one wrong step on the raised walkways, and you'll fall into the tall grass they cross over. You'll also fall if you stand still on the walkway for too long. Proceed carefully over the raised walkways without stopping.

Go in and out of the house for a rematch

The Pokémon Breeder at the western side of the route can be battled over and over. After you battle him, you can simply go in and out of the nearby house to battle him again.

Step 2 Trade the Hiker an Emolga for a Gigalith

In the house on the western side of the route, a Hiker offers to trade Pokémon. If you give him an Emolga, he will give you a Gigalith. Emolga can be caught in the rustling grass in Routes 5, 6, and 7.

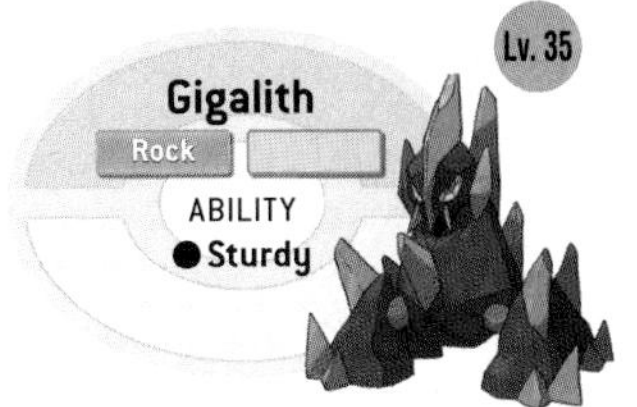

Step 3 Heal your Pokémon at the house

Talk to the girl in front of the television in the house on the east side of the route and she will restore your Pokémon's health. Stop by and get your Pokémon healed when they're low on HP from battles with Trainers or wild Pokémon.

Rest for just a moment now!

Be prepared for Triple Battles and Rotation Battles

The battle with Youngster Cody will be a Rotation Battle, and the battle with Lass Flo will be a Triple Battle. Check the Pokémon in your party before the battle and prepare for two types of battles.

Step 4 Register Tornadus, Thundurus, and Landorus in the Pokédex

Speak with the old man in the same house to have Tornadus, Thundurus, and Landorus registered in your Pokédex. The old man tells you he's seen the three of them, but they looked completely different.

These three don't appear in the wild

Tornadus, Thundurus, and Landorus don't appear in the wild in *Pokémon Black Version 2* or *Pokémon White Version 2*. You can catch them in *Pokémon Black Version*, *Pokémon White Version*, or *Pokémon Dream Radar* and bring them over.

Step 5 Your mom calls on the Xtransceiver

When you head east of the house on the route, your Xtransceiver will ring. Your mom's calling. She ends the call by telling you to make sure to go to the Pokémon Center right away if your Pokémon are hurt. She's always concerned about you.

Your mom used to work at a Pokémon Center

During your conversation on the Xtransceiver, your mom tells you she worked in the reception area at Pokémon Centers. She visited many different places and worked by healing people's Pokémon.

Step 6 You can't enter Twist Mountain yet

The entrance to Twist Mountain is at the north end of the route on the east side. But a burly man is standing in front of the entrance and won't let anyone through. Part of Twist Mountain has collapsed, and it's not safe to go inside. You can pass after you enter the Hall of Fame (p. 255).

The inside collapsed, and you can't get through!

Marshal is one of the Elite Four

The man standing in front of the entrance to Twist Mountain is Marshal, one of the Pokémon League's Elite Four. He uses Fighting-type Pokémon and is a pupil of the former Champion, Alder. You'll battle him later in your journey.

Step 7 Go north to reach Celestial Tower

Celestial Tower, where Professor Juniper headed, is directly north of Mistralton City. When you return from Twist Mountain, head west and then north. Go inside the tower (p. 174).

After visiting Celestial Tower: Go back to Mistralton City to challenge the Gym

After you've met Professor Juniper in Celestial Tower and had a look at everything, it's time to take on the Mistralton City Gym! Head back to Route 7 and go west to return to Mistralton City (p. 168). You can also use Fly from the top of the tower.

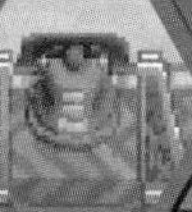

A tall tower with a large bell whose tones are said to purify the spirit

Celestial Tower

Celestial Tower is a five-story tower built as a memorial to lost Pokémon. A bell whose tones are said to comfort their spirits is placed on the top of the tower at the fifth floor.

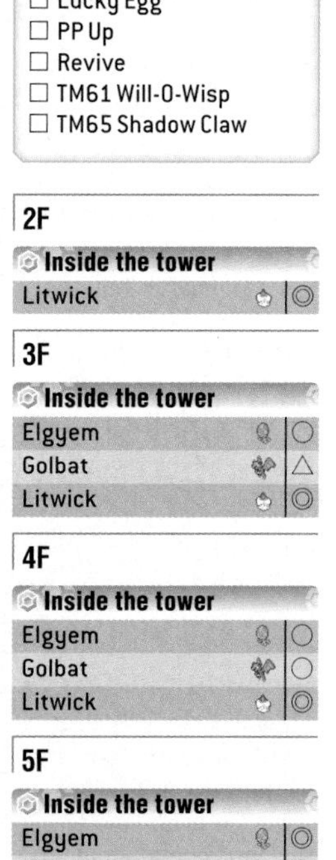

Items

- ☐ Hyper Potion
- ☐ Lucky Egg
- ☐ PP Up
- ☐ Revive
- ☐ TM61 Will-O-Wisp
- ☐ TM65 Shadow Claw

2F

Inside the tower	
Litwick	◎

3F

Inside the tower	
Elgyem	○
Golbat	△
Litwick	◎

4F

Inside the tower	
Elgyem	○
Golbat	○
Litwick	◎

5F

Inside the tower	
Elgyem	◎
Golbat	○
Litwick	◎

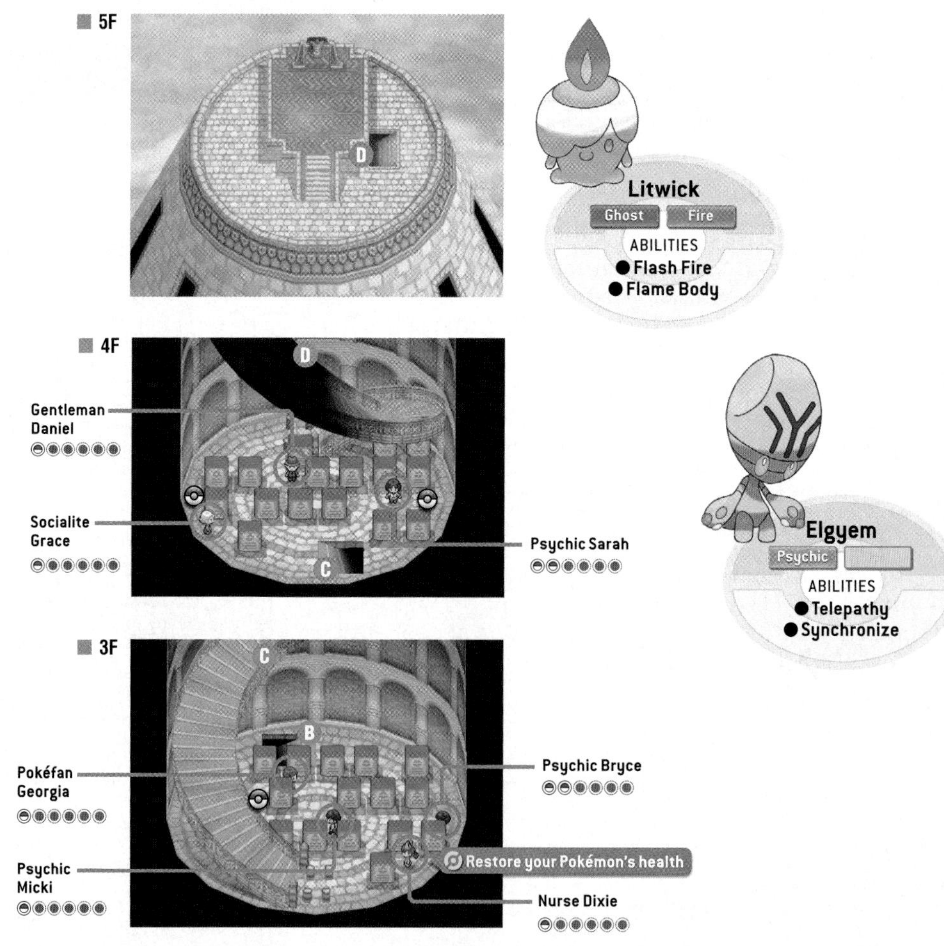

■ 2F

B

Pokéfan Jude

A

Psychic Joyce

School Kid Alberta

■ 1F

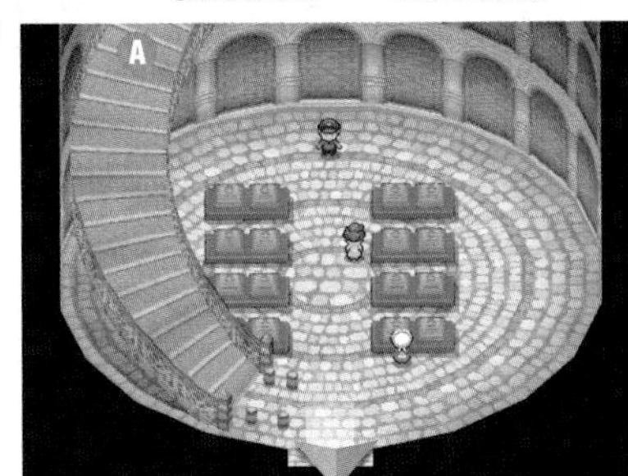

Route 7 (to Mistralton City) P.172

Step 1 Get the Lucky Egg from Professor Juniper

When you go inside, Professor Juniper is on the first floor. She suggests that you try using an item and hands you the Lucky Egg. Give it to the first Pokémon in your party. Once you've received the item, head up to explore the rest of the tower.

Step 2 Have Nurse Dixie heal your Pokémon on 3F

Nurse Dixie is waiting on the west side of the third floor. After you defeat her in a Pokémon battle, she will heal all of your Pokémon. Talk to her again if your Pokémon need healing!

Step 3 Ring the bell on the fifth floor

Climb the stairs in the center of the fifth floor and a bell will be right in front of you. The sound of this bell is said to soothe the resting spirits of Pokémon. Stand before the bell, press the A Button to ring it, and listen to its pure tone.

Step 4 Go back to Mistralton City to challenge the Gym

Return to Mistralton City and take on the Gym (p. 168). To walk there, go down to the first floor, proceed south on Route 7, and you will reach Mistralton City. You can also return to the city by using Fly from the top of the tower.

An item that gives you 50% more Exp. Points

When a Pokémon holds the Lucky Egg, it gets 50% more experience points in battle. If the Pokémon at the front of the party holds this item, it will level up more quickly (p. 49).

Carry a lot of Burn Heal

Wild Litwick are very common in Celestial Tower. If your Pokémon battles a Litwick with the Flame Body Ability, it might get burned. Be sure to stock up on Burn Heal at the Poké Mart before you visit the tower.

Save up money with the Amulet Coin

The Gentleman and Socialite on the fourth floor give you a lot of prize money when you defeat them in battle. Have the Pokémon at the front of your party hold an Amulet Coin so you get twice the prize money.

Lentimas Town

Lentimas Town is a small town with a Pokémon Center and a runway. A master Move Tutor who's obsessed with Blue Shards lives here. On the east side of town is the expansive Reversal Mountain.

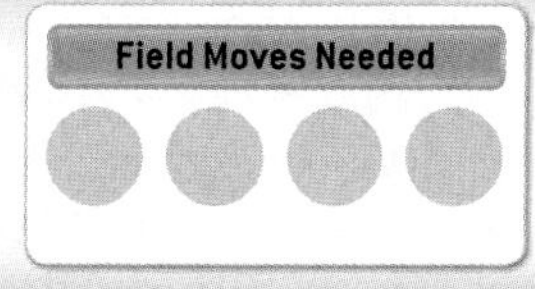

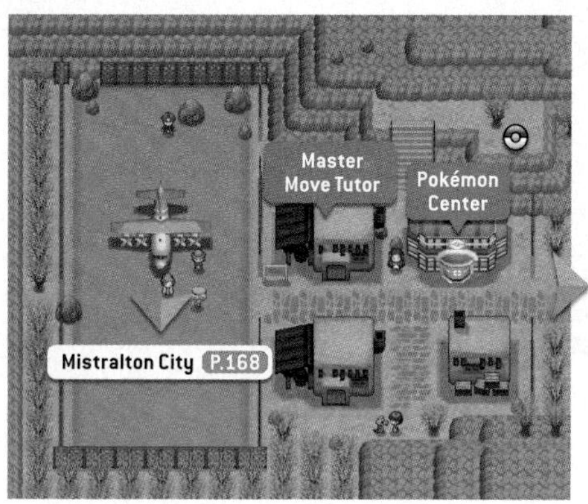

Items

- ☐ Fire Stone
- ☐ Spell Tag
- ☐ TM57 Charge Beam

Poké Mart

Item	Price
Favored Mail	50
Greet Mail	50
Inquiry Mail	50
Like Mail	50
Reply Mail	50
RSVP Mail	50
Thanks Mail	50
Heal Ball	300
Dusk Ball	1,000
Nest Ball	1,000

Step 1 Listen to Professor Juniper's story

When you get off of the plane, Professor Juniper tells you why she brought you along. She wants you to ask Opelucid City's Drayden about the Legendary Dragon-type Pokémon. Accept the task and set off to meet Drayden.

I want you to go to Opelucid City and hear what Drayden has to say.

Return to Mistralton City by plane

A plane is sitting on the runway. If you talk to the woman by the plane, you can board it and return to Mistralton City. You can also return to the city by using Fly.

Step 2 Learn from a master Move Tutor

A master Move Tutor lives in a house to the west of the Pokémon Center. The Move Tutor in Lentimas Town is obsessed with Blue Shards. He will teach a variety of moves for a certain number of Blue Shards.

Listen to the story of Zekrom and Reshiram from two years before

Two years ago, the Unova region's Legendary Dragon-type Pokémon, Zekrom and Reshiram, each recognized a different Pokémon Trainer as the hero and followed its chosen Trainer. Professor Juniper thinks there's no way Team Plasma can use them.

Moves you can learn and how many Blue Shards you need

Move you can learn	Blue Shards needed
Iron Defense	2
Last Resort	2
Magnet Rise	4
Magic Coat	4
Block	6
Electroweb	6

Move you can learn	Blue Shards needed
Hyper Voice	6
Icy Wind	6
Iron Tail	6
Aqua Tail	8
Earth Power	8
Foul Play	8

Move you can learn	Blue Shards needed
Zen Headbutt	8
Dark Pulse	10
Dragon Pulse	10
Gravity	10
Superpower	10

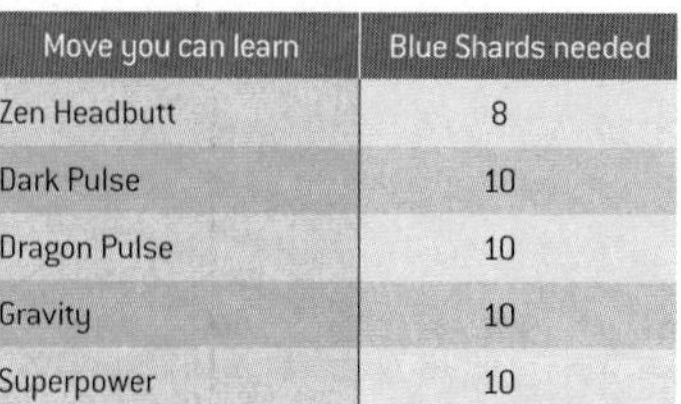

Blue Shard

Step 3 Head east to Reversal Mountain

To get to Opelucid City, you have to pass through Reversal Mountain. Bianca is already on her way there to do research. Follow Bianca, and continue to Reversal Mountain (p. 177).

Reversal Mountain

Reversal Mountain is a volcano so old there are records of eruptions even from long, long ago. It looks slightly different in *Pokémon Black Version 2* and *Pokémon White Version 2*. The exit leads to Undella Town.

When playing *Pokémon Black Version 2*

Lentimas Town entrance | Passage | Center | Undella Town Side Entrance

Black Belt Corey ★ Rotation Battle
Backpacker Kumiko
Hiker Jared
Ace Trainer Ray
Ace Trainer Cora
Hiker Markus
Backpacker Kiyo
Restore your Pokémon's health
Pokémon Ranger Eliza
Doctor Derek
Battle Girl Chan ★ Triple Battle

Undella Town P.181

Outside (same in both versions)

Strange House P.180

Lentimas Town P.176

Cyclist Jeremiah
Cyclist Adelaide

B1F ①

Pokémon Ranger Lewis

B1F ②

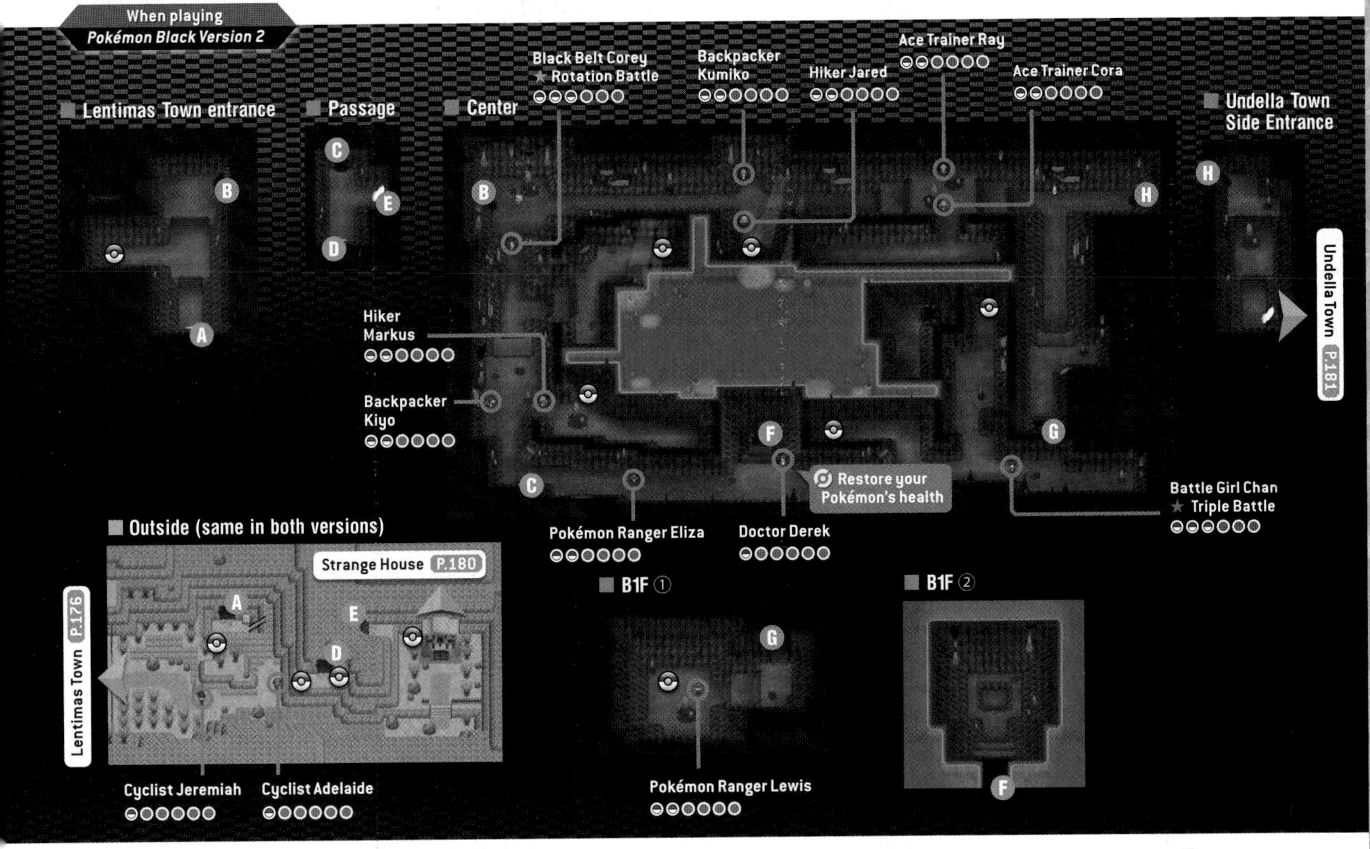

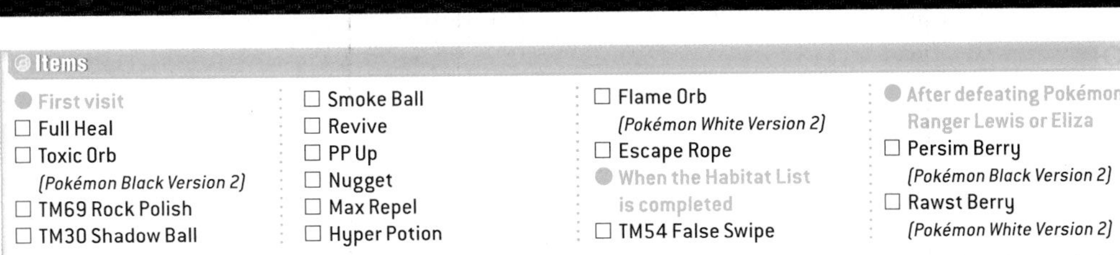

Items

● First visit
- ☐ Full Heal
- ☐ Toxic Orb *(Pokémon Black Version 2)*
- ☐ TM69 Rock Polish
- ☐ TM30 Shadow Ball
- ☐ Smoke Ball
- ☐ Revive
- ☐ PP Up
- ☐ Nugget
- ☐ Max Repel
- ☐ Hyper Potion
- ☐ Flame Orb *(Pokémon White Version 2)*
- ☐ Escape Rope

● When the Habitat List is completed
- ☐ TM54 False Swipe

● After defeating Pokémon Ranger Lewis or Eliza
- ☐ Persim Berry *(Pokémon Black Version 2)*
- ☐ Rawst Berry *(Pokémon White Version 2)*

Outside

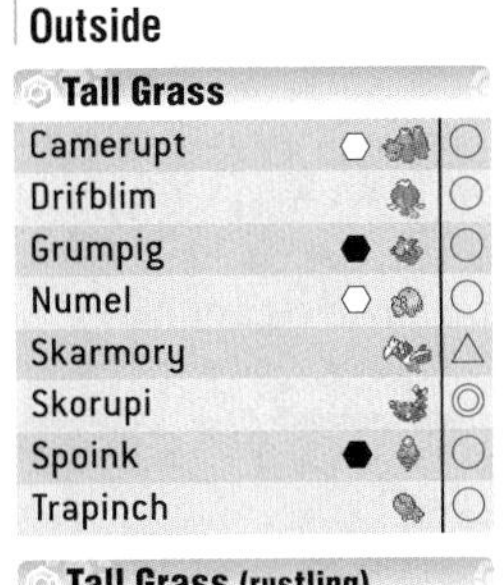

Tall Grass

Pokémon	Version	Frequency
Camerupt	⬡	○
Drifblim		○
Grumpig	⬢	○
Numel	⬡	○
Skarmory		△
Skorupi		◎
Spoink	⬢	○
Trapinch		○

Tall Grass (rustling)

Pokémon	Version	Frequency
Audino		◎

Dark Grass

Pokémon	Version	Frequency
Camerupt	⬡	◎
Drifblim		○
Grumpig	⬢	◎
Skarmory		○
Skorupi		◎
Vibrava		△

Mass Outbreaks

Pokémon	Version	Frequency
Cacturne		

All Areas

Cave

Pokémon	Version	Frequency
Boldore		○
Camerupt	⬡	△
Grumpig	⬢	△
Numel	⬡	○
Skorupi		○
Spoink	⬢	○
Woobat		◎

Cave (dust cloud)

Pokémon	Version	Frequency
Excadrill		◎

B1F ①

Cave

Pokémon	Version	Frequency
Boldore		○
Camerupt	⬡	○
Grumpig	⬢	○
Numel	⬡	△
Skorupi		○
Spoink	⬢	△
Woobat		◎

Cave (dust cloud)

Pokémon	Version	Frequency
Excadrill		◎

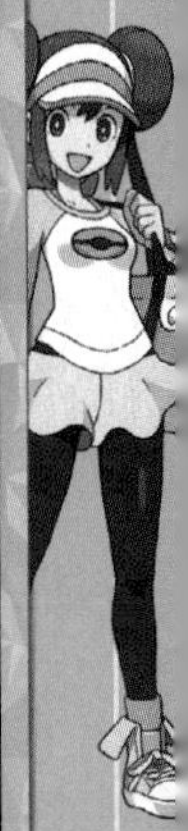

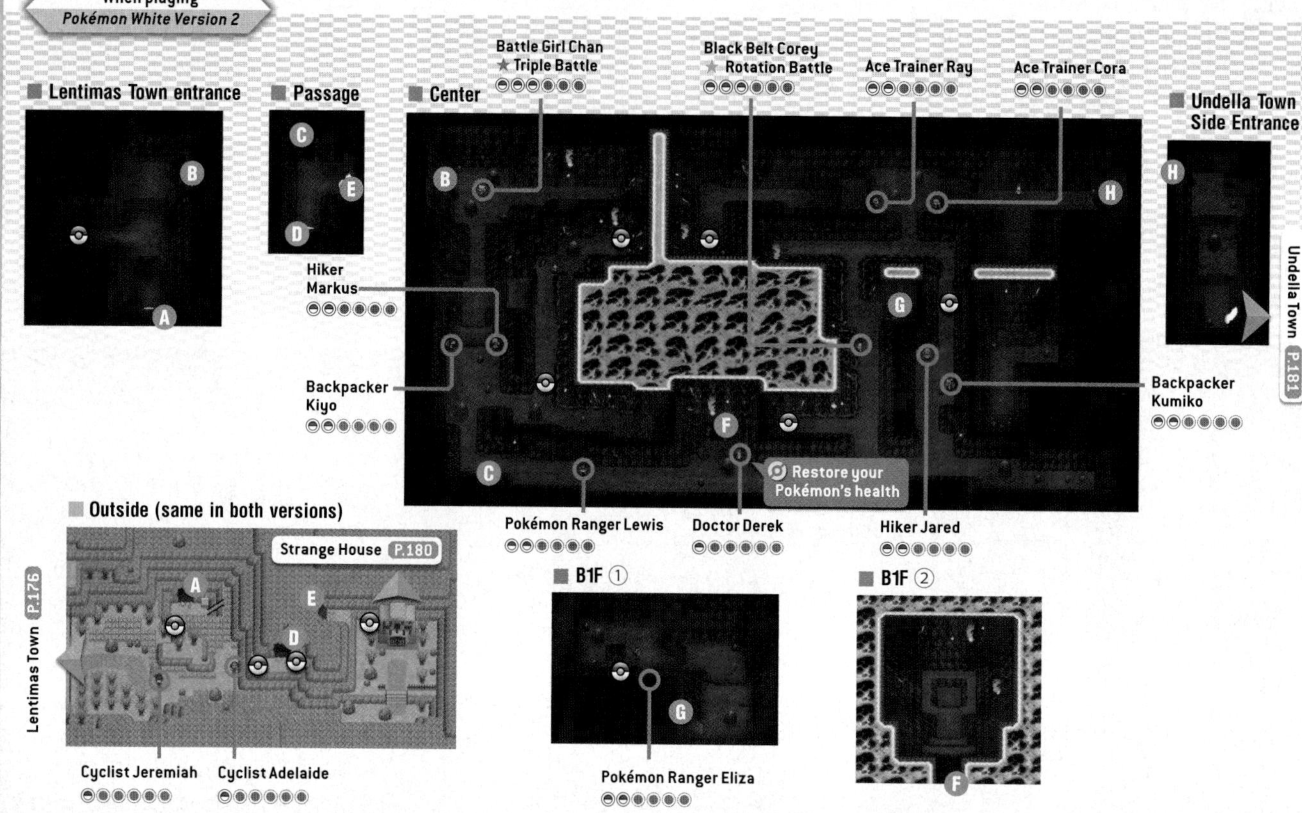

Step 1 Head east to the Strange House

Head east from Lentimas Town, and you'll arrive outside Reversal Mountain. You can see the entrance to the volcano, but first, head straight east to go to the Strange House at the east end (p. 180).

Train your Pokémon in the Strange House

There are 13 Pokémon Trainers in Reversal Mountain. It's a great idea to go to the Strange House first to train your Pokémon a little more.

Step 2 Go into Reversal Mountain

After exploring the Strange House, head back to the west. You might want to return to Lentimas Town to restore your Pokémon's health at the Pokémon Center first. Then, take the stairs to the north and enter Reversal Mountain.

Step 3 Explore the cave with Bianca

Proceed to the center, and you'll run into Bianca, who will ask you to travel with her. You'll team up with her when you battle wild Pokémon and Pokémon Trainers who challenge you simultaneously.

But the wild Pokémon here are really tough, and I'm having trouble with them!

Bianca restores your Pokémon's health

While you're with Bianca, she'll restore your Pokémon's health after a battle, even if they faint. Take advantage of this, and use Pokémon you want to train in battles.

Step 4 Have Doctor Derek heal your Pokémon

Doctor Derek is in front of the stairs to B1F ②. If you defeat him, he'll restore your Pokémon's health every time you speak to him. While you're with Bianca, you don't have to worry, but when you visit the mountain alone, ask him for help.

All right, here I go!
Life force to the max!

Bianca has a lot to say

While you travel with Bianca, you can turn around to talk to her. She has a lot of stories to tell you while she's healing your Pokémon!

Step 5 Team up with Bianca for Double Battle

In places where two Pokémon Trainers are facing each other, you'll team up with Bianca for a Multi Battle. Bianca will use her Musharna to battle. Work together to win!

Get Berries from Pokémon Rangers

Defeat Pokémon Rangers Lewis and Eliza, and you can receive a Persim Berry and a Rawst Berry. Lewis and Eliza are in the Center area or on B1F ①. Their positions switch between the two versions.

Step 6 Complete the Habitat List to get a useful TM

Speak to the Scientist in the east. He'll ask you to show him your Habitat List for Reversal Mountain. If you've seen all the Pokémon that live in the area, he'll give you TM54 False Swipe as a reward.

C'mon, tell me what kind of Pokémon
live in Reversal Mountain!

Have you seen Trapinch?

If you're having trouble filling the Habitat List for Reversal Mountain, you might be missing a Trapinch. None of the Pokémon Trainers in the mountain has one, so meeting it in the tall grass outside is the only way to register it to your Pokédex.

Step 7 Explore every corner to collect items

While you're with Bianca, she can heal your Pokémon every time you talk to her. Make the most of this convenient healing, and explore every corner of Reversal Mountain. After collecting all the items, head to the exit on the Undella Town side.

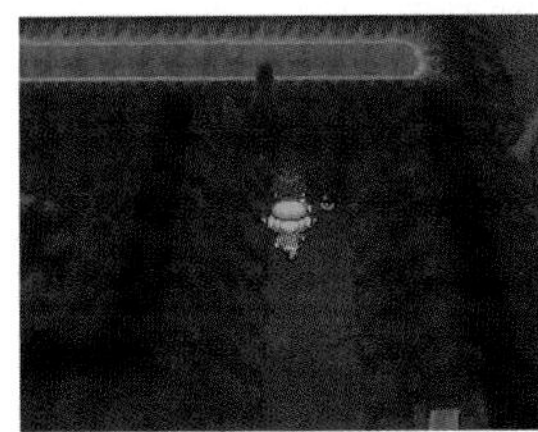

Be prepared for a Triple Battle and a Rotation Battle

You'll battle Black Belt Corey in a Rotation Battle, and Battle Girl Chan in a Triple Battle. Check the order of your party Pokémon before these battles, and aim for victory (p. 51).

Step 8 Leave Bianca, and head to Undella Town

Head south to the exit to Undella Town. When you are about to leave, Bianca tells you she wants to keep exploring. If you're ready to go, say your farewells, and head east to Undella Town (p. 181).

▸YES
NO
What do you want to do?
Should we say bye for now?

What is a Magma Stone?

Speak to Backpacker Kiyo after defeating him, and he'll tell you a story about a Magma Stone. It's an item related to the Legendary Pokémon Heatran in the Sinnoh region. You can catch Heatran on Route 18 in the Unova region, too (p. 328).

Strange House

The Strange House is located outside of Reversal Mountain. It's said that a sad incident happened here sometime in the past. Inside the house, a ghost appears, and furniture moves around on its own.

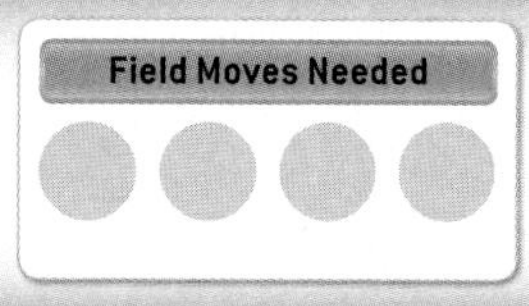

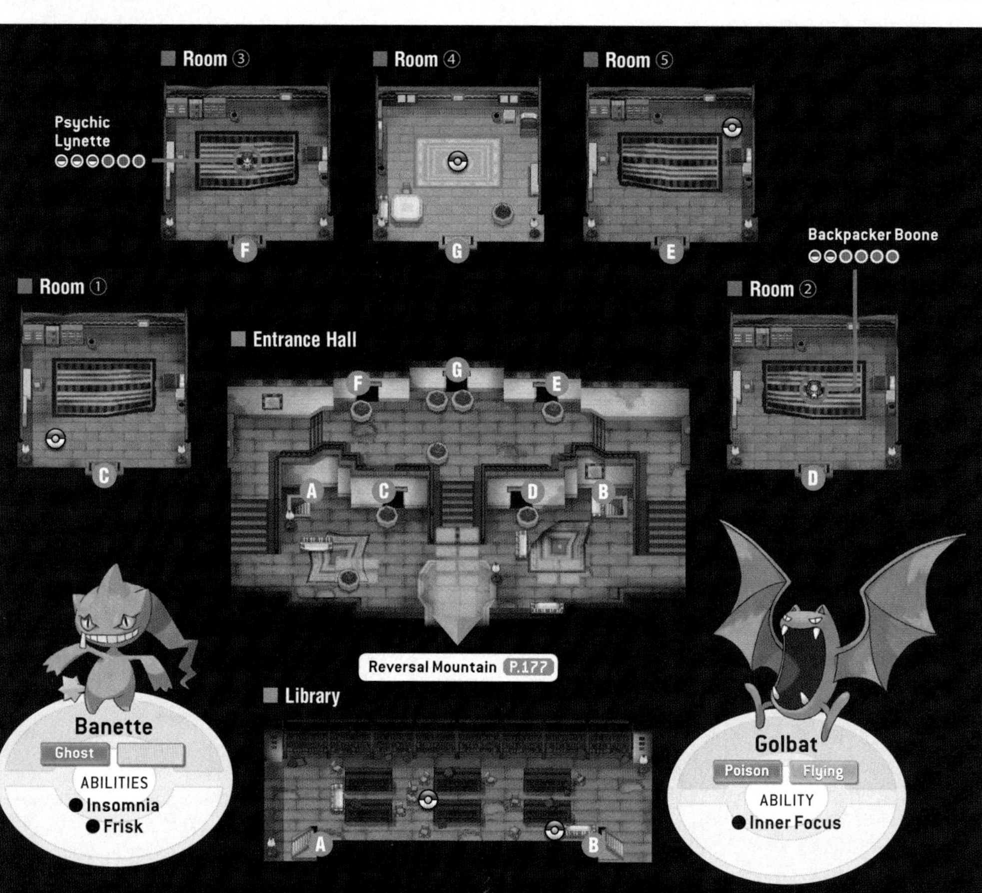

Items

- ☐ Dusk Stone
- ☐ Full Heal
- ☐ Lunar Wing
- ☐ Rare Candy
- ☐ Spell Tag

Entrance Hall・Library

Inside		
Banette		○
Duosion	⬡	△
Golbat		○
Gothita	⬢	○
Gothorita	⬢	△
Litwick		◎
Raticate		○
Solosis	⬡	○

Rooms ①・②・③・④・⑤

Inside		
Banette		○
Duosion	⬡	○
Golbat		○
Gothita	⬢	○
Gothorita	⬢	○
Litwick		○
Raticate		○
Solosis	⬡	○

Step 1 It's a strange place where furniture moves when you enter another room

Inside the building, stairs going up and down and entrances connect rooms, but most of them are blocked by furniture. First, go down to the library from the stairs on the west side, which is the only way to go at first. When you do, furniture moves, and you can move to other places.

You could start over by going outside

Inside the Strange House, you may not be able to move around because paths are blocked by furniture. When that happens, just exit the house. Moving around will be easier when you start over.

Step 2 You meet a ghost girl here and there

When you walk around the house, a ghost girl appears from time to time. It seems she was trapped in a dark dream and passed away in her sleep. You'll encounter the ghost girl three times.

Step 3 Get a Lunar Wing in the middle room

Take stairs at the Entrance Hall to go upstairs, and enter Room ④ in the middle. You'll find a Lunar Wing in the center of the room. When you get the item, the ghost girl appears and asks you to return it to a Pokémon someday.

Step 4 Return to Reversal Mountain

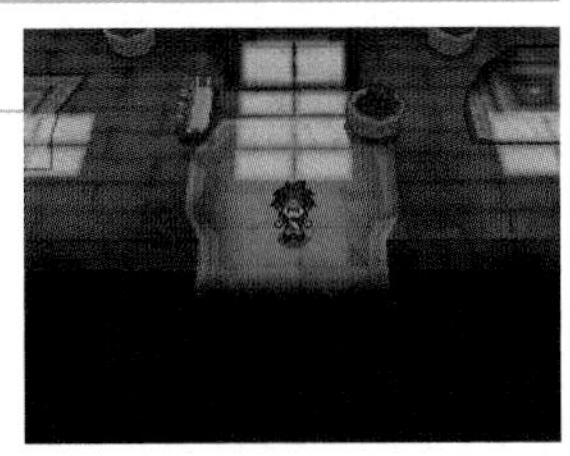

Once you've obtained the Lunar Wing, the search in the Strange House is complete. Leave the house, and head west to go back to Lentimas Town. Restore your Pokémon's health and enter Reversal Mountain (p. 177).

Go to the Marvelous Bridge after the Hall of Fame

If you have a Lunar Wing, you can meet Cresselia when you visit the Marvelous Bridge after entering the Hall of Fame (p. 271). Cresselia is the one that you have to return the Lunar Wing to!

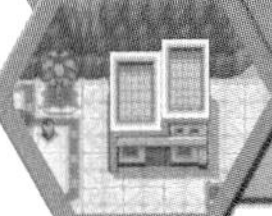

A summer retreat with a beach full of people who enjoy summer vacations

Undella Town

Guide

Undella Town is a good place to beat the heat, and many villas line the beach. Heading north of town leads to Route 13, and south leads to Route 14. The Marine Tube connected to Humilau City is scheduled to open very soon.

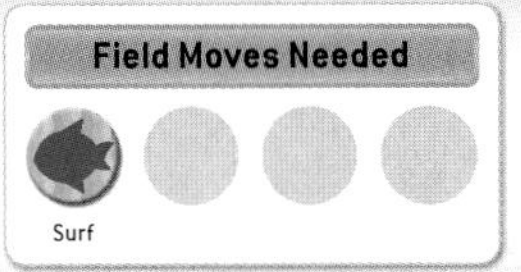

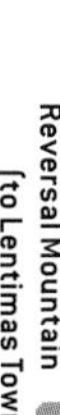

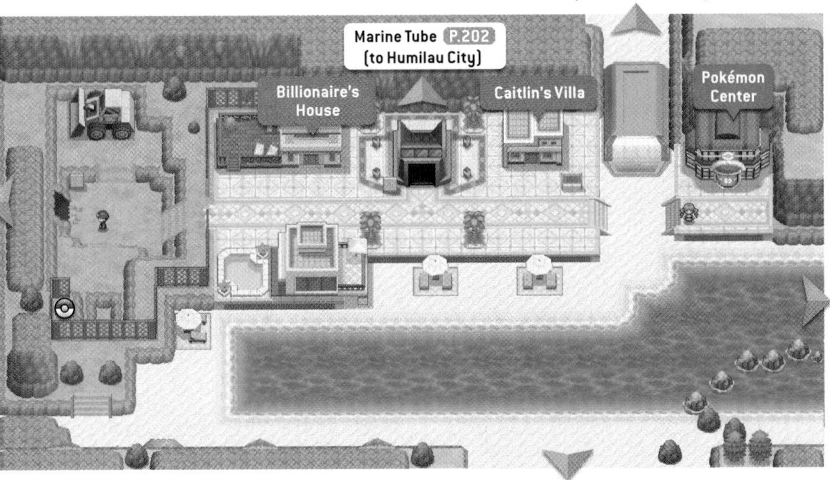

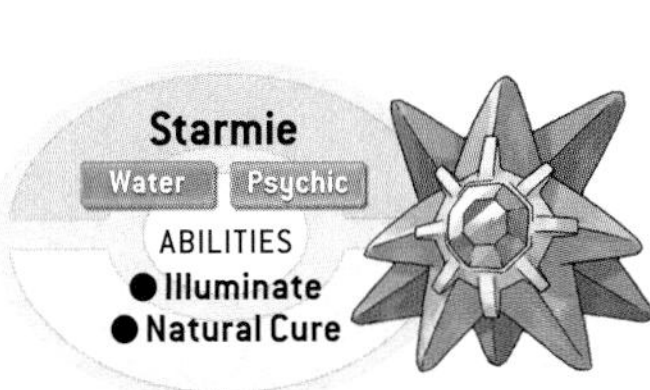

Items

- First visit
  - ☐ Berry Juice
  - ☐ Prism Scale
- After the Hall of Fame
  - ☐ HM06 Dive

Poké Mart (Lower Clerk)

Item	Price
Favored Mail	50
Greet Mail	50
Inquiry Mail	50
Like Mail	50
Reply Mail	50
RSVP Mail	50
Thanks Mail	50
Dive Ball	1,000
Luxury Ball	1,000

Water Surface

Pokémon		
Basculin (Blue-Striped Form)	○	△
Basculin (Red-Striped Form)	●	△
Frillish		◎
Staryu		◎

Water Surface (ripples)

Pokémon		
Basculin (Red-Striped Form)	○	△
Basculin (Blue-Striped Form)	●	△
Jellicent		◎
Starmie		△
Staryu		◎

After the Hall of Fame

Fishing

Pokémon	
Luvdisc	◎
Shellder	◎

Fishing (ripples)

Pokémon	
Cloyster	△
Luvdisc	◎
Shellder	◎

Items the billionaire will buy

Item	Price
Black Flute	8,000
Blue Flute	7,000
Red Flute	7,500
Relic Band	100,000
Relic Copper	1,000
Relic Crown	300,000
Relic Gold	10,000
Relic Silver	5,000
Relic Statue	200,000
Relic Vase	50,000
White Flute	8,000
Yellow Flute	7,500

Step 1 Sell your rare items to the billionaire

The billionaire in the house on the west side of the Marine Tube buys rare items. He will pay a high price for the Flutes you get from a man on Route 13 and the ancient items you get in the Abyssal Ruins.

Do you have such a rare item?
Do you?

He was living with his family in a large mansion two years ago

The billionaire in the house lived in a large mansion in Undella Town two years ago. His family seems to have moved to another town, so he's living here alone now.

Step 2 You cannot pass the Marine Tube yet

When you first visit Undella Town, the Marine Tube hasn't been opened yet because Janitors are working hard to clean it. The Marine Tube will open after defeating the Opelucid City Gym Leader.

Sorry, I'll be finished with the cleaning
soon. Please wait until then!

Step 3 Drop by Caitlin's Villa

Caitlin's Villa is on the east side of the Marine Tube. Caitlin is one of the Elite Four in the Pokémon League. Visit the villa after entering the Hall of Fame and you can meet Cynthia, the Champion in the Sinnoh region. Enjoy a Pokémon battle with Cynthia to test your might as a Trainer (p. 261).

This villa belongs to Caitlin, one of the
Pokémon League's Elite Four.

Step 4 Your rival challenges you to battle

When you head east from Caitlin's Villa and get close to the gate to Route 13, your rival catches up and talks to you. It's the first battle with him since you battled in the PWT. He's much stronger now, so get ready for a more serious battle this time!

Let's see how well we've
raised our Pokémon!

Restore your Pokémon's health before approaching the gate

When you get close to the gate to Route 13, your rival will challenge you to battle. Go to the Pokémon Center before approaching the gate and make sure to restore your Pokémon's health before the battle.

Battle with your rival! 3

His Pokémon have leveled up quite a bit since the two of you battled at Floccesy Ranch. Also, his first Pokémon is now fully evolved.

Let's see how well we've raised our Pokémon!

Hugh's Pokémon

If you chose Snivy:

Pokémon	Type	Weak to
Unfezant ♂ Lv. 39	Normal, Flying	Electric, Ice, Rock
Simipour ♂ Lv. 39	Water	Grass, Electric
Emboar ♂ Lv. 41	Fire, Fighting	Water, Ground, Flying, Psychic

If you chose Tepig:

Pokémon	Type	Weak to
Unfezant ♂ Lv. 39	Normal, Flying	Electric, Ice, Rock
Simisage ♂ Lv. 39	Grass	Fire, Ice, Poison, Flying, Bug
Samurott ♂ Lv. 41	Water	Grass, Electric

If you chose Oshawott:

Pokémon	Type	Weak to
Unfezant ♂ Lv. 39	Normal, Flying	Electric, Ice, Rock
Simisear ♀ Lv. 39	Fire	Water, Ground, Rock
Serperior ♂ Lv. 41	Grass	Fire, Ice, Poison, Flying, Bug

Hugh leaves after checking your strength

After you defeat Hugh, he seems quite satisfied about your strength. He tells you Team Plasma will run screaming when they see the two of you. He reaffirms his determination to rescue his sister's Purrloin and leaves.

If we're this strong, Team Plasma will run screaming when they see us!

Explore Undella Bay

Before heading to Route 13 to go to Opelucid City, visit Undella Bay, east of Undella Town (p. 184). After seeing everything and battling all the Pokémon Trainers, return to Undella Town.

Go to Route 14 later

Because Route 14 to the south of Undella Town has several waterfalls, you can't explore it fully if you don't have a way to climb them. It's better to go there after getting HM05 Waterfall (p. 248).

Buy a lot of Ultra Balls

On Route 13, where you're going next, you will be able to meet the Legendary Pokémon Cobalion. Buy plenty of Ultra Balls at the Poké Mart before you leave so you have a better chance of catching it.

A Funfest Mission is added

Speak to the man wearing sunglasses in the Pokémon Center. The Funfest Mission "Shocking Shopping!" will be added to your Entralink for you to play.

Take Route 13 to head to Opelucid City

Go through Undella Town's north gate, and you'll arrive on Route 13 (p. 185), which leads to Opelucid City.

Enter the Marine Tube

Return to Undella Town after defeating the Opelucid City Gym Leader. The Marine Tube you couldn't pass before is open now. Go through the tunnel to reach Humilau City, where the last Gym is (p. 202).

There's a woman who wants to be first

When you enter the Marine Tube, you'll meet a woman who wants to be the first person to go through it. After it's open, she's still standing in the same place. Did she manage to be the first one through?

Undella Bay

Undella Bay is a stretch of ocean where visitors to Undella Town often come to sunbathe. The swimmable area is actually quite restricted, due to the rocky shoals and small islands that surround the area. On the ocean floor, the Abyssal Ruins hold many secrets.

Field Moves Needed

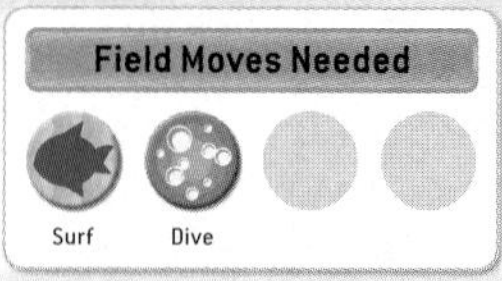

Items

- ☐ Draco Plate
- ☐ Splash Plate

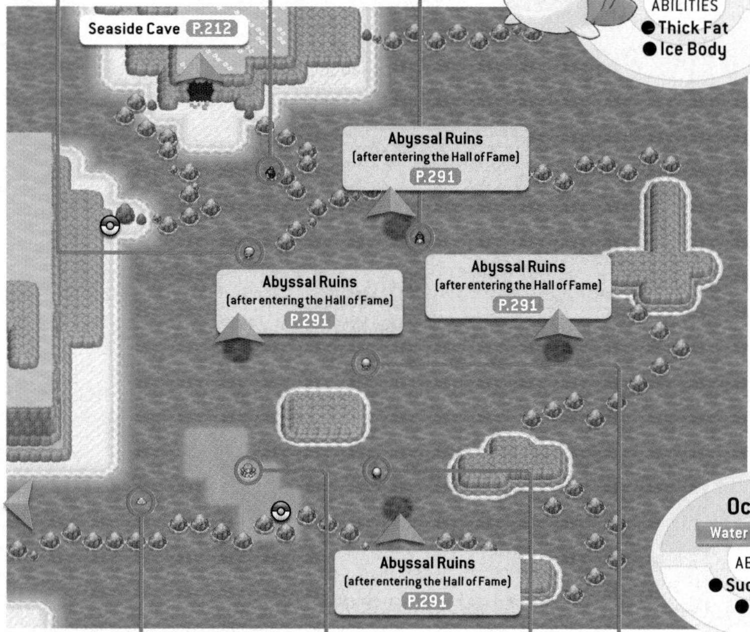

Map labels: Swimmer ♂ Matt; Swimmer ♀ Arissa; Swimmer ♀ Mitzi; Seaside Cave P.212; Abyssal Ruins (after entering the Hall of Fame) P.291; Abyssal Ruins (after entering the Hall of Fame) P.291; Abyssal Ruins (after entering the Hall of Fame) P.291; Abyssal Ruins (after entering the Hall of Fame) P.291; Undella Town P.181; Ace Trainer Summer; Swimmer ♂ Tim; Swimmer ♂ Bart

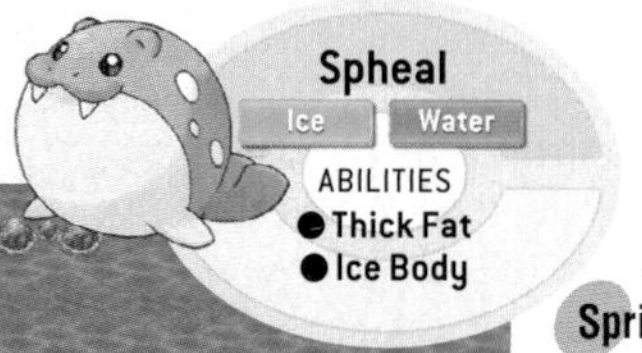

Jellicent ♂ (Hidden Ability) ● Mondays in *Pokémon Black Version 2*

Jellicent ♀ (Hidden Ability) ● Thursdays in *Pokémon White Version 2*

Spheal — Ice / Water — ABILITIES: ● Thick Fat ● Ice Body

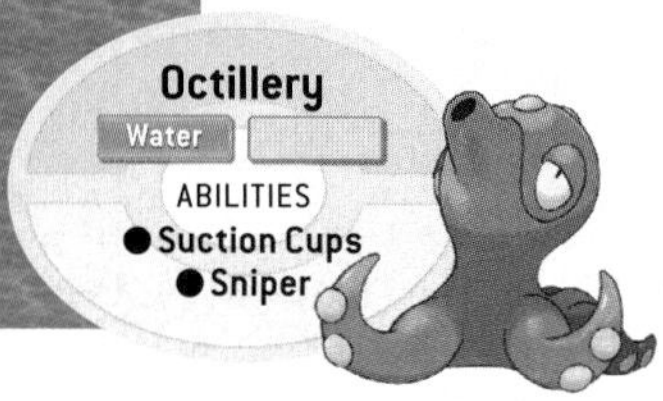

Octillery — Water — ABILITIES: ● Suction Cups ● Sniper

Spring Summer Autumn

Water Surface	
Frillish	◎
Mantyke	◎
Remoraid	△

Water Surface (ripples)	
Jellicent	◎
Mantine	△
Wailmer	◎
Wailord	△

Winter

Water Surface	
Frillish	◎
Remoraid	△
Spheal	◎

Water Surface (ripples)	
Sealeo	◎
Wailmer	◎
Wailord	△
Walrein	△

All Seasons

■ After the Hall of Fame

Fishing	
Chinchou	◎
Remoraid	◎

Fishing (ripples)	
Chinchou	◎
Lanturn	△
Octillery	△
Remoraid	◎

Step 1 Battle Jellicent on Mondays (Thursdays)

A Jellicent with a special Hidden Ability appears in Undella Bay. A male (♂) Jellicent appears on Mondays in *Pokémon Black Version 2*, and a female (♀) Jellicent appears on Thursdays in *Pokémon White Version 2*. If you accidentally defeat this Jellicent, another will appear the next week.

Step 2 Still too early to explore the ocean floor

There are four dark spots in the waters of Undella Bay. These are points where you can explore underwater using HM06 Dive. Unfortunately, you can't do that at this point in the game. You will be able to explore the Abyssal Ruins at the bottom of the ocean after entering the Hall of Fame (p. 255).

It's a deep part of the sea, but a Pokémon may be able to dive down.

Get Dive after entering the Hall of Fame

If you visit Undella Town after entering the Hall of Fame, your rival will give you HM06 Dive. Using Dive will allow you to check out the Abyssal Ruins (p. 291).

Step 3 Proceed while battling Pokémon Trainers

At the north end of Undella Bay lies the entrance to the Seaside Cave. A man is standing just inside the entrance, however, and prevents you from going any further. Instead of going in, thoroughly explore the area while battling the many Trainers who await you out on the open sea.

Seeing a Pokémon use its best moves against another Pokémon

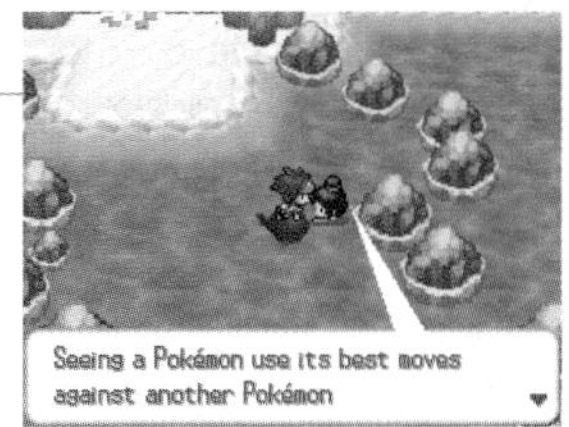

Step 4 Return to Undella Town

Since you cannot enter the Seaside Cave now, you cannot reach any other area from Undella Bay. Once you have explored the bay, return to Undella Town to head for Route 13 (p. 185).

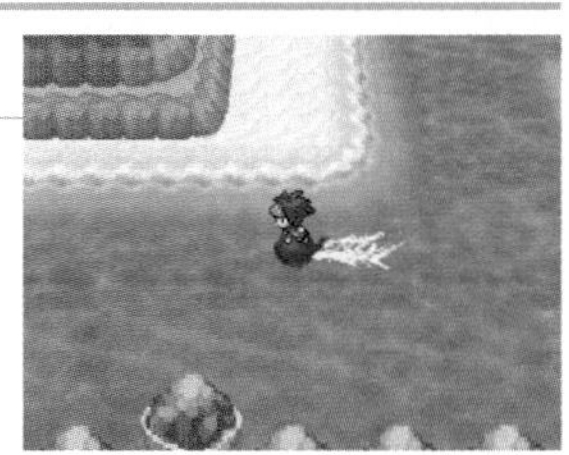

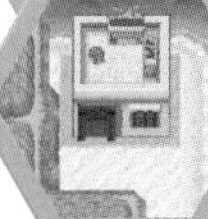

This seaside route is famous for sandbars that cross the ocean

Route 13

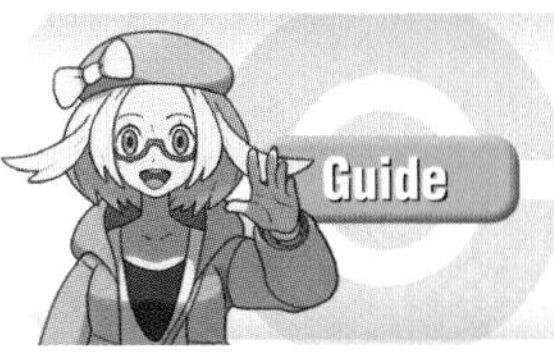

Guide

Route 13 has a lot of natural beauty, such as ocean beaches and greenery. At its northernmost reaches lies the mysterious Giant Chasm. Head west along the route to reach Lacunosa Town.

Field Moves Needed

Cut · Surf · Strength

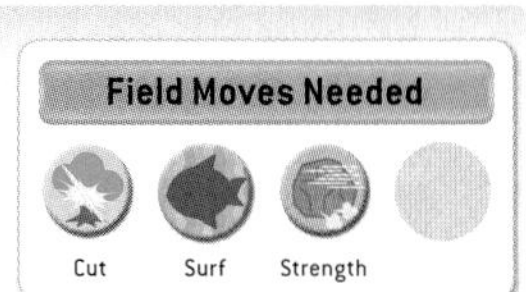

Items

First visit

- ☐ Blue Shard
- ☐ Luxury Ball
- ☐ Max Ether
- ☐ Max Repel
- ☐ Power Band *(Pokémon White Version 2)*
- ☐ Power Lens *(Pokémon Black Version 2)*
- ☐ Red Shard
- ☐ Star Piece
- ☐ TM29 Psychic
- ☐ Ultra Ball

After defeating Pokémon Ranger Dianne

- ☐ Sitrus Berry

After defeating Pokémon Ranger Daryl

- ☐ Sitrus Berry

In the area reachable from the Giant Chasm

- ☐ Hyper Potion

Tall Grass	
Absol	◯
Drifblim	◯
Lunatone	◯
Pelipper	◯
Solrock	◯
Tangela	◯

Tall Grass (rustling)	
Audino	◎
Emolga	◯
Tangrowth	△

Dark Grass	
Absol	◯
Drifblim	◯
Lunatone	◯
Pelipper	◯
Solrock	◯
Tangela	◯

Mass Outbreaks
Swellow

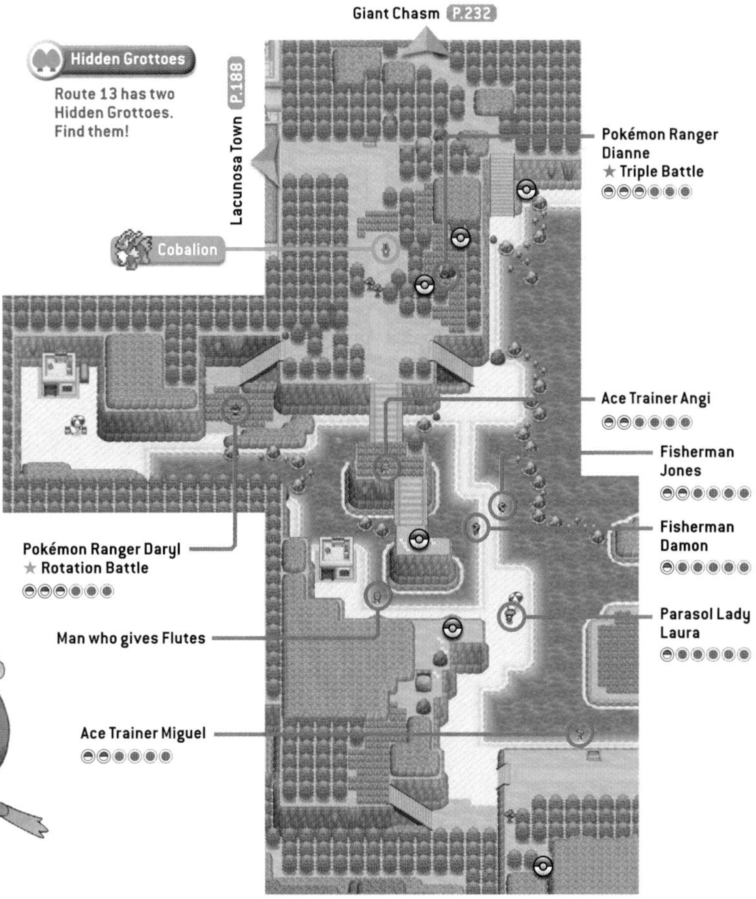

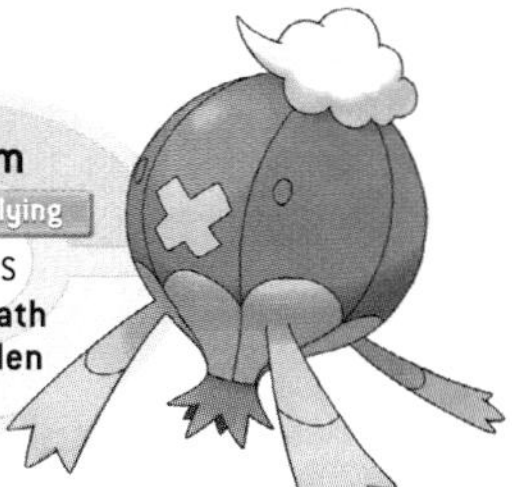

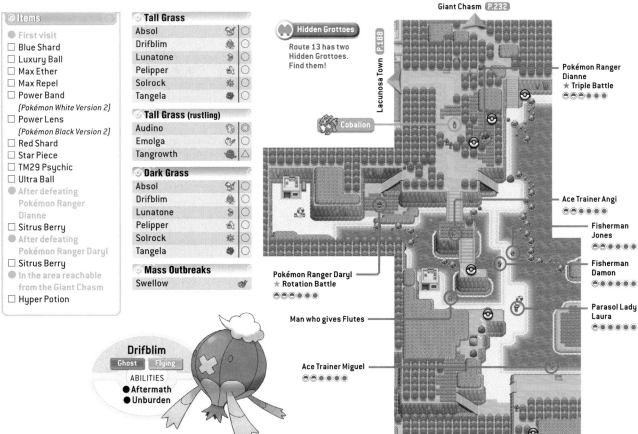

Giant Chasm P.232
Hidden Grottoes
Route 13 has two Hidden Grottoes. Find them!
Lacunosa Town P.188
Cobalion
Pokémon Ranger Dianne
★ Triple Battle
Ace Trainer Angi
Fisherman Jones
Fisherman Damon
Pokémon Ranger Daryl
★ Rotation Battle
Parasol Lady Laura
Man who gives Flutes
Ace Trainer Miguel

Drifblim

Ghost · Flying

ABILITIES

- Aftermath
- Unburden

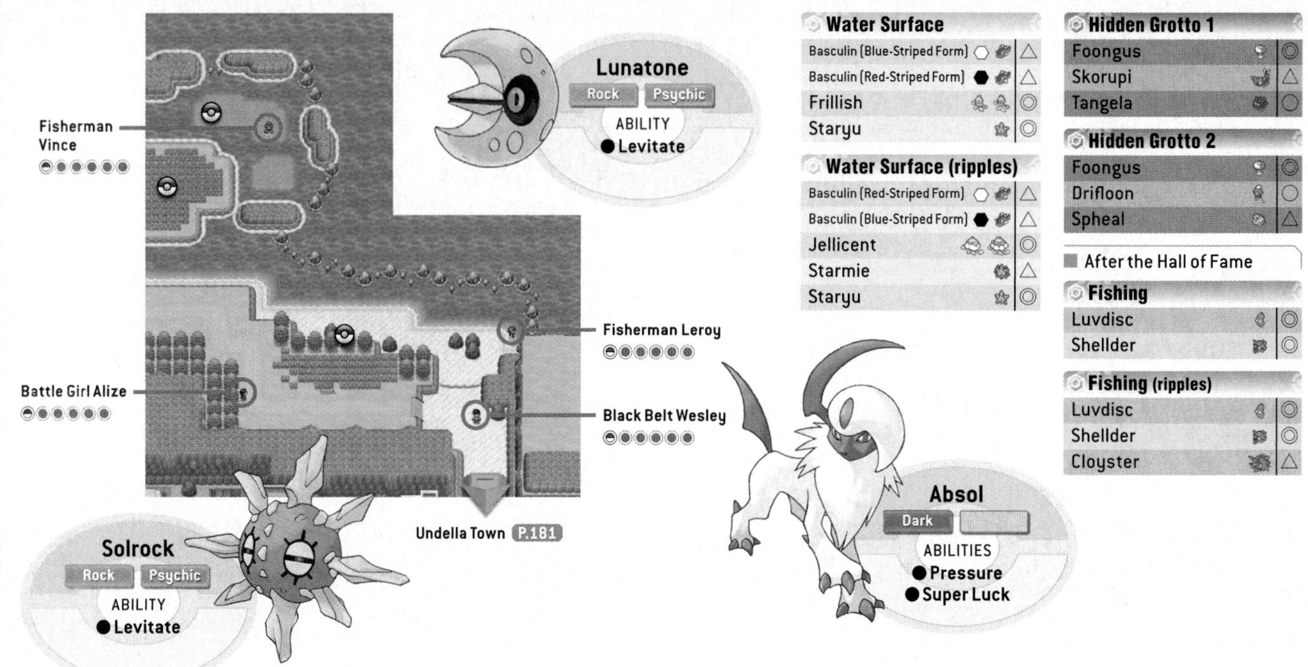

Water Surface		
Basculin (Blue-Striped Form)	○	△
Basculin (Red-Striped Form)	●	△
Frillish		◎
Staryu		◎

Water Surface (ripples)		
Basculin (Red-Striped Form)	○	△
Basculin (Blue-Striped Form)	●	△
Jellicent		◎
Starmie		△
Staryu		◎

Hidden Grotto 1	
Foongus	◎
Skorupi	△
Tangela	○

Hidden Grotto 2	
Foongus	◎
Drifloon	○
Spheal	△

■ After the Hall of Fame

Fishing	
Luvdisc	◎
Shellder	◎

Fishing (ripples)	
Luvdisc	◎
Shellder	◎
Cloyster	△

Step 1 Proceed while battling Trainers

Continue westward, battling Pokémon Trainers you pass by, and you will reach a high area at the end of the path. After going up the stairs, collect the item that can be reached by moving a rock using Strength. Once you have it, go back down the stairs and head north along the sandy beach.

Be prepared for Triple Battles and Rotation Battles

You will have a Rotation Battle against Pokémon Ranger Daryl and a Triple Battle against Pokémon Ranger Dianne. Check your party Pokémon before these battles begin and aim for victory (p. 51).

Step 2 Receive a Flute every day from the man

When the beach route forks north and west, take the west route. Once a day, you can speak to the man standing at the water's edge partway down the beach and receive a Flute. There are five kinds of Flute in total. You can head down to the beach and speak to him every day.

Step 3 Discover the Legendary Pokémon Cobalion

Make it across the beaches to the high ground. In the opening behind the trees you can cut down with Cut, you will discover Cobalion. It almost seems as if it was waiting here for you to come. If you try to speak to it, you will be drawn into battle. Now's your chance to catch it!

Get Berries from Pokémon Rangers

Defeat Daryl and Dianne to receive a Sitrus Berry from each of them. Daryl waits to the west of where you can find Cobalion and Dianne to the east.

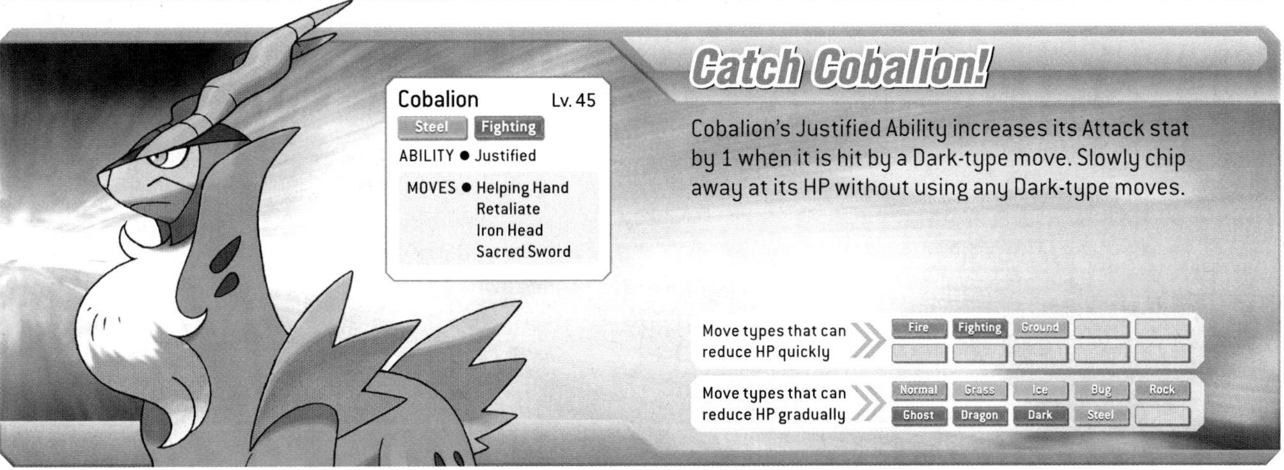

Catch Cobalion!
Cobalion Lv. 45
Steel
Fighting
ABILITY ● Justified
MOVES ● Helping Hand
Retaliate
Iron Head
Sacred Sword
Cobalion's Justified Ability increases its Attack stat by 1 when it is hit by a Dark-type move. Slowly chip away at its HP without using any Dark-type moves.
Move types that can reduce HP quickly
Fire
Fighting
Ground
Move types that can reduce HP gradually
Normal
Grass
Ice
Bug
Rock
Ghost
Dragon
Dark
Steel

Step 4 The path north is blocked for now

If you continue north of the area where you found Cobalion, you will see a boulder that can be pushed with Strength. However, a hole lies between you and the boulder so you cannot reach it from this side. You must approach the boulder from the Giant Chasm side. Remember to move it when you later reach the other side.

Step 5 Go west to reach Lacunosa Town

To the west of the boulder is the edge of Lacunosa Town. Opelucid City, home to the next Pokémon Gym, lies even farther west beyond the town. Stop in at Lacunosa Town to begin with (p. 188).

Use Strength to move boulders

When you visit the Giant Chasm, leave through the cave's south exit and continue south. Follow the path and you will arrive at the junction with Route 13. Use Strength to push the boulder at the end of the path and drop it into the hole.

After searching the Giant Chasm

Create a shortcut between Lacunosa Town and Giant Chasm

If you drop the boulder into the hole, you'll be able to easily return to Lacunosa Town from the Giant Chasm. When your Pokémon get injured from the battles in the Giant Chasm, have them healed at the Pokémon Center in Lacunosa Town.

Have Cobalion in your party

Cobalion joins you at Lv. 45, so as soon as you catch it, put it in your party. Cobalion is a strong ally that will be an asset in battle.

Receive an item at the house

Visit the house that lies on the far western edge of Route 13 and speak to the girl inside. In *Pokémon Black Version 2*, she will give you a Power Lens, while in *Pokémon White Version 2*, she will hand you a Power Band.

Lacunosa Town

The people of Lacunosa Town believe in an old legend that tells of a monster that attacks at night, and so even now they never leave their homes after dark. The west edge of the town is connected to Route 12.

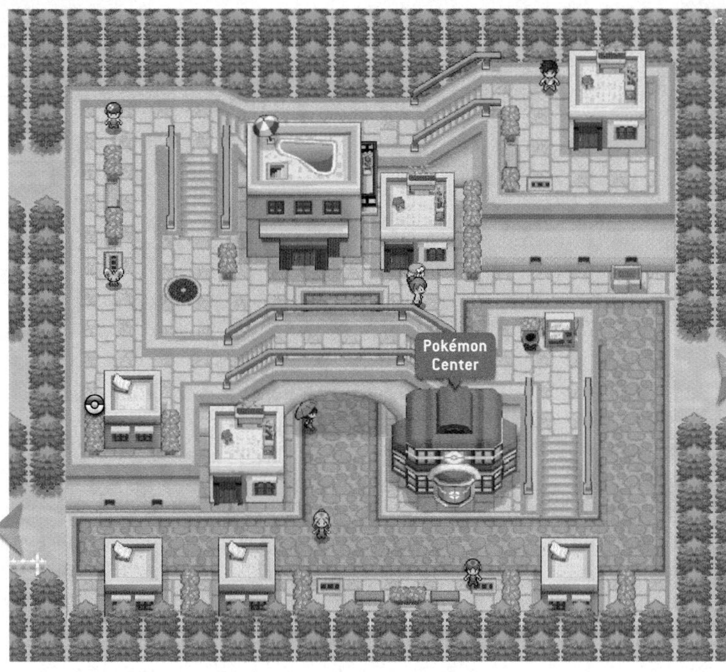

Items

- ☐ Full Heal
- ☐ Metronome

Poké Mart (Lower Clerk)

TM14 Blizzard	70,000
TM25 Thunder	70,000
TM38 Fire Blast	70,000

Step 1 Meet Professor Juniper and Bianca

Enter the town and head south, and Professor Juniper and Bianca will call out to you. Professor Juniper shows you to the house of a certain old woman who lives in the town. Apparently there is something she wants you to hear before you continue on your way to Opelucid City.

Step 2 Listen to the old woman's story

The old woman tells you of a legend that says the Giant Chasm was formed when a meteorite containing a Pokémon crashed into the planet. At night, that Pokémon would attack humans and Pokémon alike, appearing along with a chill wind that felt like it could freeze someone to the bone.

A really scary Pokémon was
hidden inside that meteorite...

The true meaning of the town's name?

When you hear about the wall built around the town to protect it from the monstrous Pokémon, Professor Juniper tells you that those surrounding walls might have been the reason for the town's name: lacunosus clouds resemble a net or fence.

Step 3 Learn about Zekrom (Reshiram) from Professor Juniper

After hearing the old woman's tale, Professor Juniper tells you about the Legendary Dragon-type Pokémon Zekrom (Reshiram). She thinks there is some link between it and the fearsome Pokémon in the legends of Lacunosa Town.

By the way, Trainer,
do you remember the story of Zekrom?
YES
NO

Different tales for different versions

The Legendary Pokémon that Professor Juniper will tell you about varies depending on which version of the game you are playing. In *Pokémon Black Version 2*, she tells you about Zekrom, while in *Pokémon White Version 2*, she speaks of Reshiram.

Step 4 Receive a Berry every night

Sometime during the night or late night, take the stairs in the north part of town to visit the house that lies to the east [p. 188]. If you speak to the businessman inside, he will give you a Pecha Berry, a Bluk Berry, a Lum Berry, or a Leppa Berry every day.

Step 5 Work together with your rival to defeat Zinzolin

When you head west from the Pokémon Center, you will run into your rival. Then, Team Plasma's Zinzolin appears before you both. After hearing Team Plasma's plans, Hugh snaps and asks for your help in battle. Combine your strength and take on Zinzolin.

YES
NO
Trainer! Give me a hand!
You ready?

Learn about your party Pokémon from past Gym battles

If you speak to the woman in the Pokémon Center, she will tell you which Pokémon you had in your party when you received each of your Gym Badges. You can look back and reflect on which Pokémon you used to battle against the Gym Leaders of Unova.

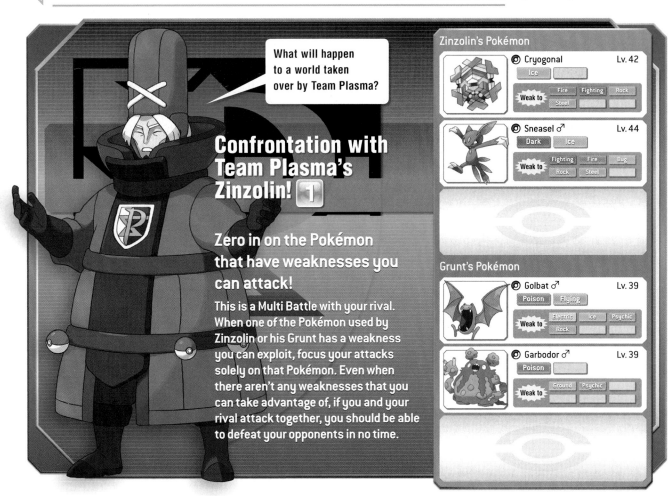

What will happen to a world taken over by Team Plasma?

Confrontation with Team Plasma's Zinzolin! 1

Zero in on the Pokémon that have weaknesses you can attack!

This is a Multi Battle with your rival. When one of the Pokémon used by Zinzolin or his Grunt has a weakness you can exploit, focus your attacks solely on that Pokémon. Even when there aren't any weaknesses that you can take advantage of, if you and your rival attack together, you should be able to defeat your opponents in no time.

Zinzolin's Pokémon

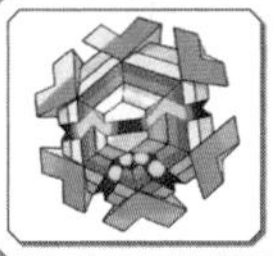

Pokémon	Lv.	Type	Weak to
Cryogonal	Lv. 42	Ice	Fire, Fighting, Rock, Steel
Sneasel ♂	Lv. 44	Dark, Ice	Fighting, Fire, Bug, Rock, Steel

Grunt's Pokémon

Pokémon	Lv.	Type	Weak to
Golbat ♂	Lv. 39	Poison, Flying	Electric, Ice, Psychic, Rock
Garbodor ♂	Lv. 39	Poison	Ground, Psychic

Step 6 Go after your rival and head to Route 12

When you defeat Zinzolin and the Team Plasma Grunt, they will leave. Your rival runs after them in a hurry. Head west out of town and continue to Route 12 to reach your destination in Opelucid City [p. 194].

Buy plenty of Ultra Balls before you go

From Route 12, you will be continuing on to Route 11. There you will be able to meet the Legendary Pokémon Virizion. Buy plenty of Ultra Balls at the Poké Mart before you leave, so that you can be certain to catch it.

Route 12

Route 12 is a short route, made up of grassy fields that stretch over gently sloping hill and rises. It links Lacunosa Town to the east and Village Bridge to the west.

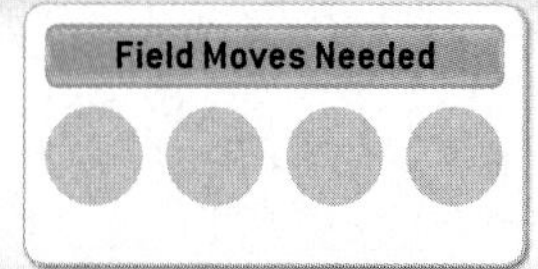

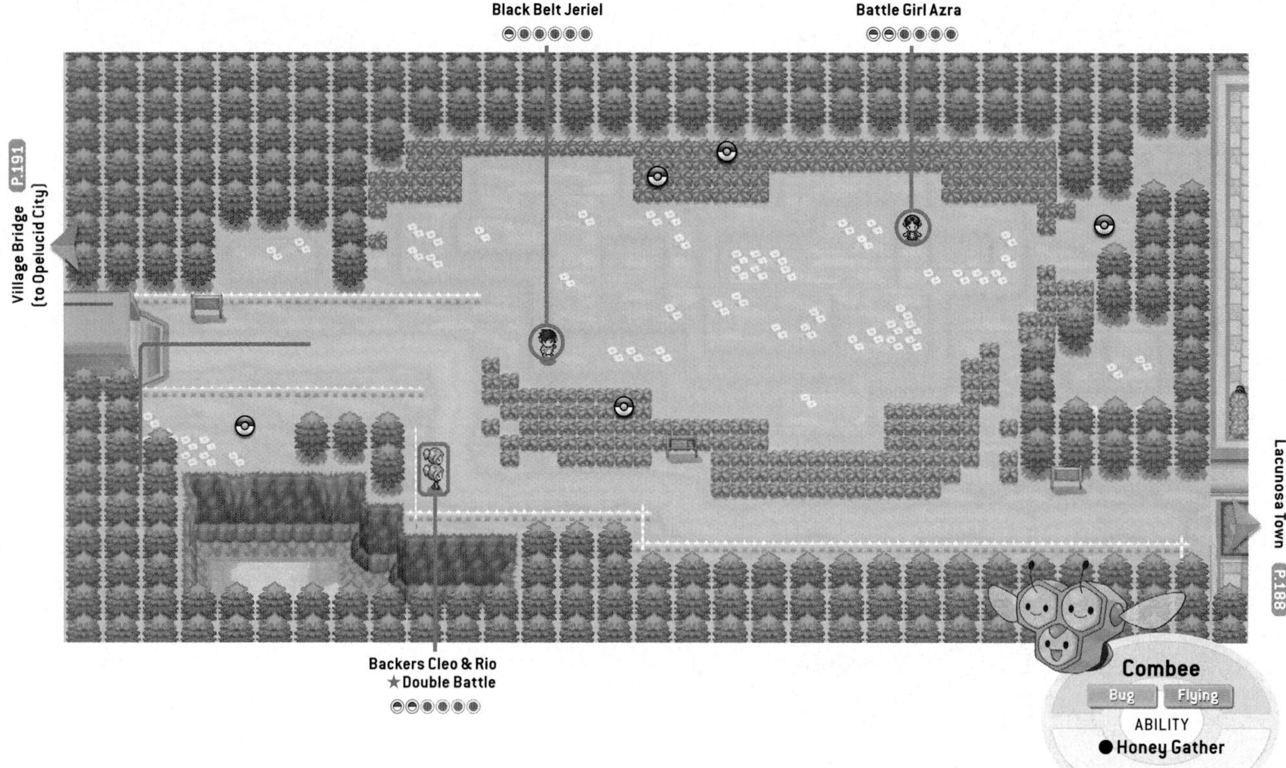

Combee
Bug / Flying
ABILITY
● Honey Gather

Items

- ☐ Green Shard
- ☐ Max Potion
- ☐ PP Up
- ☐ Timer Ball
- ☐ Yellow Shard

Tall Grass		
Combee		○
Heracross	⬢	○
Pinsir	⬡	○
Roselia		○
Sewaddle		○
Tranquill		○

Tall Grass (rustling)	
Audino	◎
Dunsparce	○
Emolga	○
Leavanny	△
Roserade	△
Unfezant	△
Vespiquen	△

Dark Grass		
Combee		○
Heracross	⬢	○
Pinsir	⬡	○
Roselia		○
Sewaddle		○
Tranquill		○

Mass Outbreaks
Doduo

Step 1 Head west for Village Bridge

Route 12 is a short route, but you can find four Trainers and five items among its gentle slopes. Take part in Pokémon battles and gather items as you make your way west to Village Bridge [p. 191].

That's why you're going to have to use two Pokémon against us!

Capture rarely seen Pokémon

Combee, Vespiquen, Heracross, and Pinsir do not appear in the wild anywhere but here and Lostlorn Forest. Catch some to register them in your Pokédex.

Village Bridge

Village Bridge spans a wide river and is lined with homes along its edges. Just as its name implies, it is indeed a bridge that is also a village. It connects Route 12, which leads to Lacunosa Town, with Route 11, which continues on to Opelucid City.

Field Moves Needed

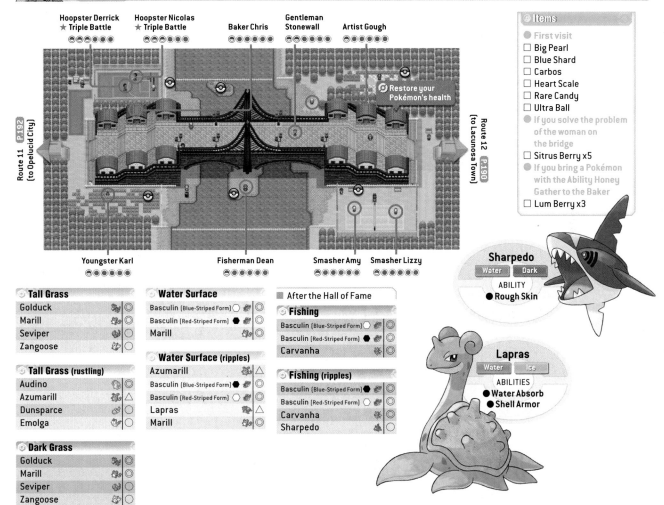

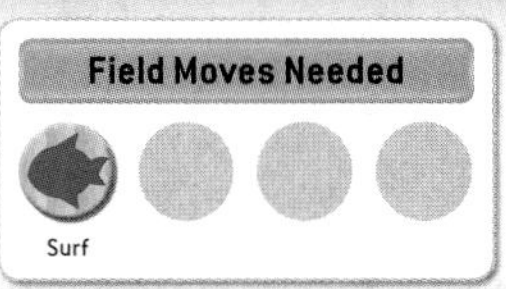

Hoopster Derrick ★ Triple Battle
Hoopster Nicolas ★ Triple Battle
Baker Chris
Gentleman Stonewall
Artist Gough
Restore your Pokémon's health
Route 11 (to Opelucid City) P.192
Route 12 (to Lacunosa Town) P.190
Youngster Karl
Fisherman Dean
Smasher Amy
Smasher Lizzy

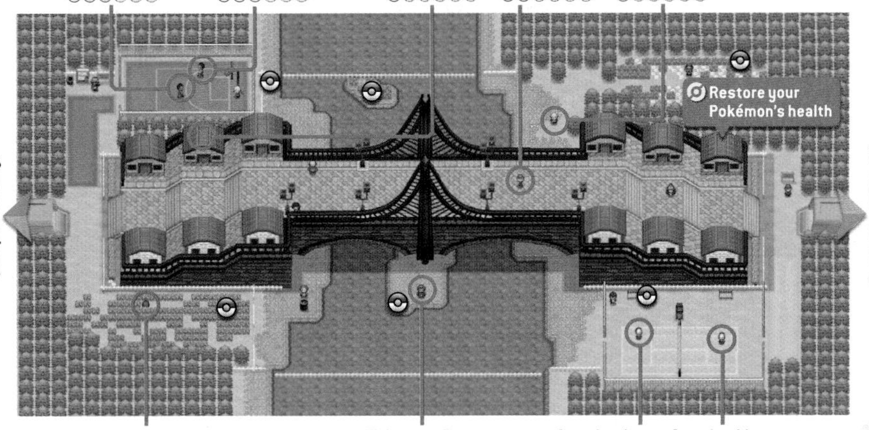

Items

- First visit
- ☐ Big Pearl
- ☐ Blue Shard
- ☐ Carbos
- ☐ Heart Scale
- ☐ Rare Candy
- ☐ Ultra Ball
- If you solve the problem of the woman on the bridge
- ☐ Sitrus Berry x5
- If you bring a Pokémon with the Ability Honey Gather to the Baker
- ☐ Lum Berry x3

Tall Grass	
Golduck	◎
Marill	◎
Seviper	○
Zangoose	○

Tall Grass (rustling)	
Audino	◎
Azumarill	△
Dunsparce	○
Emolga	○

Dark Grass	
Golduck	◎
Marill	◎
Seviper	○
Zangoose	○

Water Surface	
Basculin (Blue-Striped Form) ○	◎
Basculin (Red-Striped Form) ●	○
Marill	◎

Water Surface (ripples)	
Azumarill	△
Basculin (Blue-Striped Form) ●	○
Basculin (Red-Striped Form) ○	◎
Lapras	△
Marill	◎

After the Hall of Fame

Fishing	
Basculin (Blue-Striped Form) ○	◎
Basculin (Red-Striped Form) ●	◎
Carvanha	◎

Fishing (ripples)	
Basculin (Blue-Striped Form) ●	◎
Basculin (Red-Striped Form) ○	◎
Carvanha	◎
Sharpedo	○

Sharpedo
Water Dark
ABILITY
● Rough Skin

Lapras
Water Ice
ABILITIES
● Water Absorb
● Shell Armor

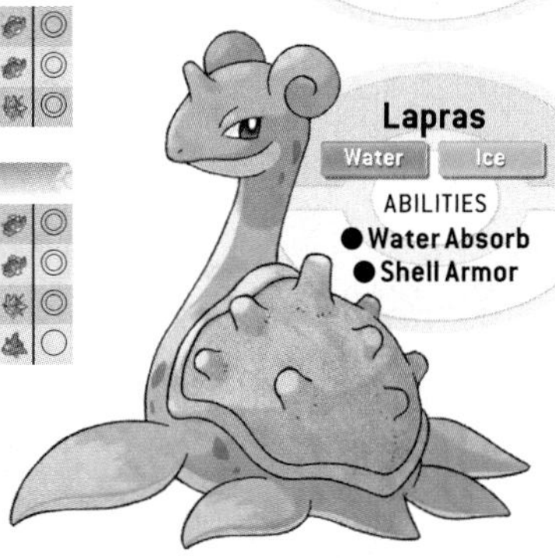

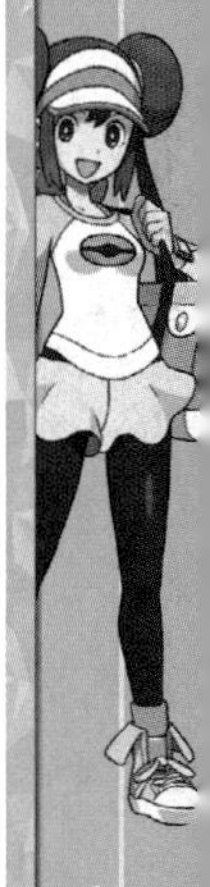

Step 1 Heal your Pokémon at the house

Make your way up and over the bridge, stopping in at the house farthest to the east. If you speak to the woman inside, she will fully heal your Pokémon. Since there is no Pokémon Center on Village Bridge, you should have her help you whenever you need your Pokémon healed.

Oh, your Pokémon look pretty tired.
Don't be shy. Take a nice long rest!

Step 2 A Gentleman challenges you to battle

Continue west over the bridge, and a Gentleman will suddenly stop you from going any further. He says he's trying to set a record for getting the most wins in a row, and he challenges you to battle with him. Accept his proposal.

YES
NO
I've got a 999-win streak.
Be my battle opponent!

The winning streak that stops at 999

The Gentleman who challenges you to battle on the bridge won 999 battles in a row before meeting you. Your battle puts an end to that streak, but it doesn't deter him from aiming for that magical 1,000 again.

Step 3 Show the Baker a Combee

After you battle her, the Baker in the second house from the west end of the bridge will ask you to show her a Pokémon with the Ability Honey Gather. Have a Combee in your party when you speak to her, and you will receive three Lum Berries.

Step 4 Go through the gate to the west and enter Route 11

Explore and battle the Pokémon Trainers on Village Bridge as you make your way west. Beyond the gate to the west is Route 11 (p. 192). Your next destination, Opelucid City, waits for you even farther west along Route 11.

Help the woman with her problem

Enter the room under the west side of the bridge, and the woman inside will chase you out. When that happens, speak to the woman who is standing on the bridge directly above that room. To thank you for clearing up the mystery of the voice she could hear from under the bridge, she will give you five Sitrus Berries.

Triple Battles with Hoopsters

The Hoopsters that are playing just north of the gate to Route 11 will challenge you to Triple Battles. Check the order of your party Pokémon before these battles begin.

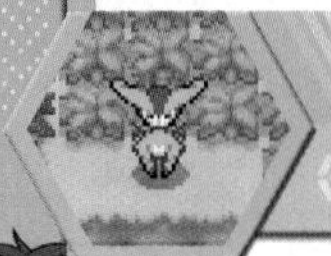

Limpid streams carved beautiful scenery on this road

Route 11

Route 11 is a short, paved road that runs over the river flowing down from the waterfall. Once you go through the gate at the west end, you will arrive in Opelucid City, home to the seventh Pokémon Gym.

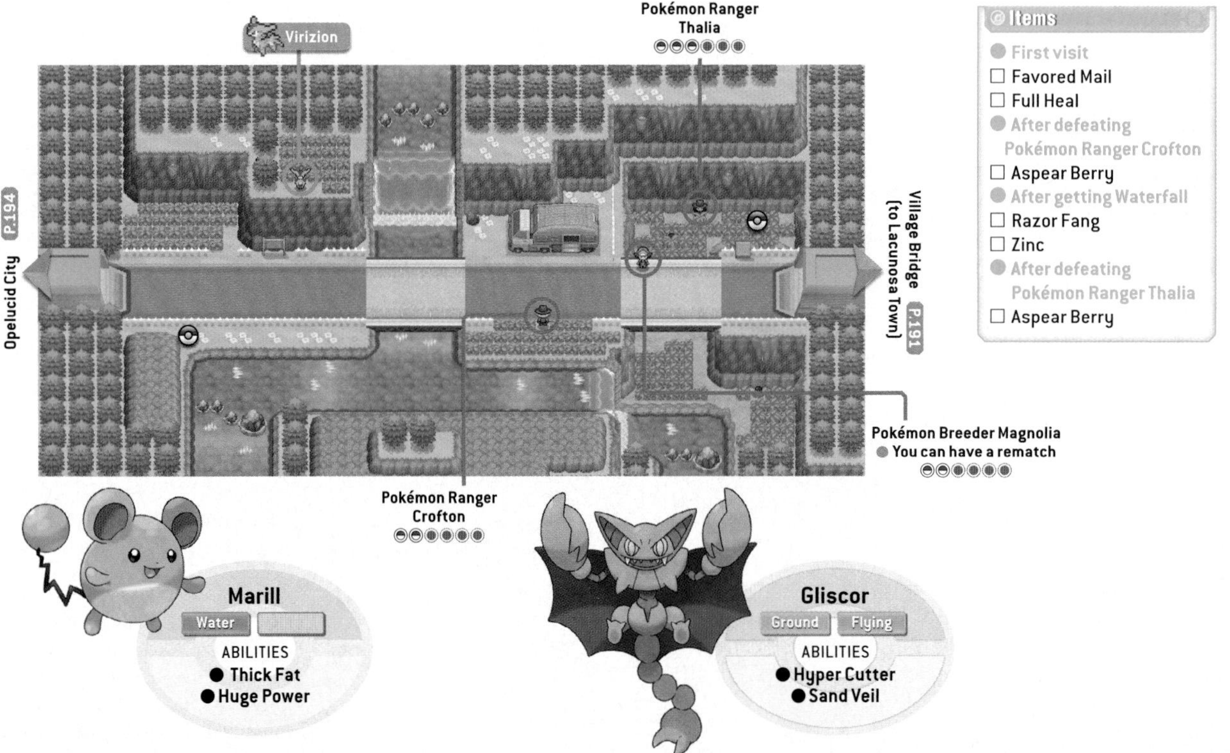

Items

First visit
- ☐ Favored Mail
- ☐ Full Heal

After defeating Pokémon Ranger Crofton
- ☐ Aspear Berry

After getting Waterfall
- ☐ Razor Fang
- ☐ Zinc

After defeating Pokémon Ranger Thalia
- ☐ Aspear Berry

Tall Grass		
Amoonguss		△
Gligar		○
Golduck		○
Karrablast	⬡	○
Karrablast	⬢	△
Marill		○
Seviper		○
Shelmet	⬢	○
Shelmet	⬡	△
Zangoose		○

Tall Grass (rustling)	
Audino	◎
Azumarill	△
Emolga	○
Gliscor	△

Mass Outbreaks
Masquerain

Dark Grass		
Amoonguss		△
Gligar		○
Golduck		○
Karrablast	⬡	○
Karrablast	⬢	△
Marill		○
Seviper		○
Shelmet	⬢	○
Shelmet	⬡	△
Zangoose		○

Water Surface		
Basculin (Red-Striped Form)	⬢	◎
Basculin (Blue-Striped Form)	⬡	◎
Buizel		◎

Water Surface (ripples)		
Buizel		◎
Basculin (Blue-Striped Form)	⬢	◎
Basculin (Red-Striped Form)	⬡	◎
Floatzel		○

■ After the Hall of Fame

Fishing		
Goldeen		◎
Basculin (Red-Striped Form)	⬢	◎
Basculin (Blue-Striped Form)	⬡	◎

Fishing (ripples)		
Goldeen		◎
Basculin (Blue-Striped Form)	⬢	◎
Basculin (Red-Striped Form)	⬡	◎
Seaking		○

Step 1 Proceed west while battling Pokémon Trainers

Continue westward while battling Trainers. You can also battle Pokémon Breeder Magnolia again and again. You don't have to leave Route 11; just going in and out of the trailer is enough to trigger a new battle.

Get Berries from Pokémon Rangers

Defeat Pokémon Ranger Crofton in front of the trailer and you will receive an Aspear Berry. Defeat Pokémon Ranger Thalia after learning Waterfall and you will receive another Aspear Berry.

Step 2 The Legendary Pokémon Virizion shows itself

When you make it to the western end of Route 11, Virizion will suddenly leap down from the cliff to the north. Just as was true with Cobalion, it seems to have been waiting for you to come. If you try to speak to it, you will be drawn into battle. Make sure to catch it.

Add Virizion to your party

Virizion will be a powerful ally for you in your adventure. As soon as you catch it, put it in your party and have it help you in battle. Virizion is a stout ally and an immediate asset.

Catch Virizion!

Virizion Lv. 45
Grass Fighting
ABILITY ● Justified
MOVES ● Helping Hand, Retaliate, Giga Drain, Sacred Sword

Even if you work hard to chip away at its HP, Virizion can quickly recover with its Giga Drain ability. You should still use moves of the types that won't do too much damage, though, to slowly lower its HP without the risk of knocking it out.

Move types that can reduce HP quickly	Flying	Fire	Ice	Poison	Psychic
Move types that can reduce HP gradually	Water	Grass	Electric	Ground	Rock
	Dark				

Step 3 Pass through the western gate to reach Opelucid City

There are other places to explore along Route 11, but you will need the HM05 Waterfall to reach all of them. Since you don't have it yet, continue west and go through the gate to reach Opelucid City (p. 194).

Come back after you get Waterfall

You will be able to climb the waterfall once you receive HM05 Waterfall from N on Victory Road. Come back again to battle with Pokémon Trainers and collect items once you have it.

Opelucid City

Drayden, the Gym Leader of Opelucid City, is also its mayor. On the surface, the city looks completely different in *Pokémon Black Version 2* compared to *Pokémon White Version 2*, but they both have the same basic outline.

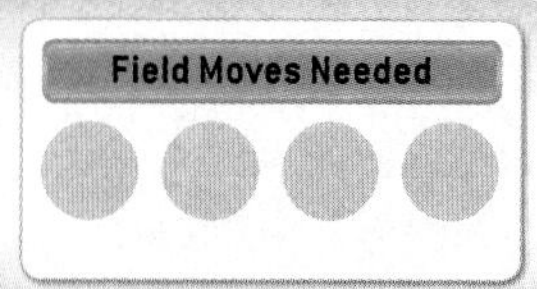

When playing
Pokémon Black Version 2

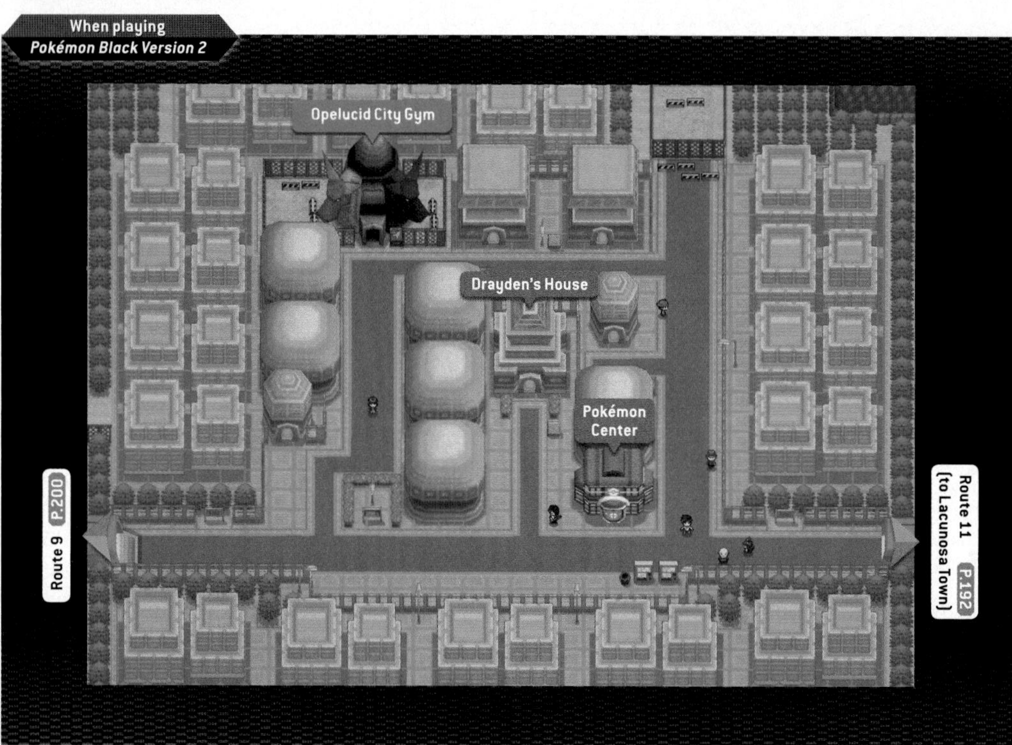

When playing
Pokémon White Version 2

Opelucid City Gym
Drayden's House
Pokémon Center
Route 9 P.200
Route 11 [to Lacunosa Town] P.192

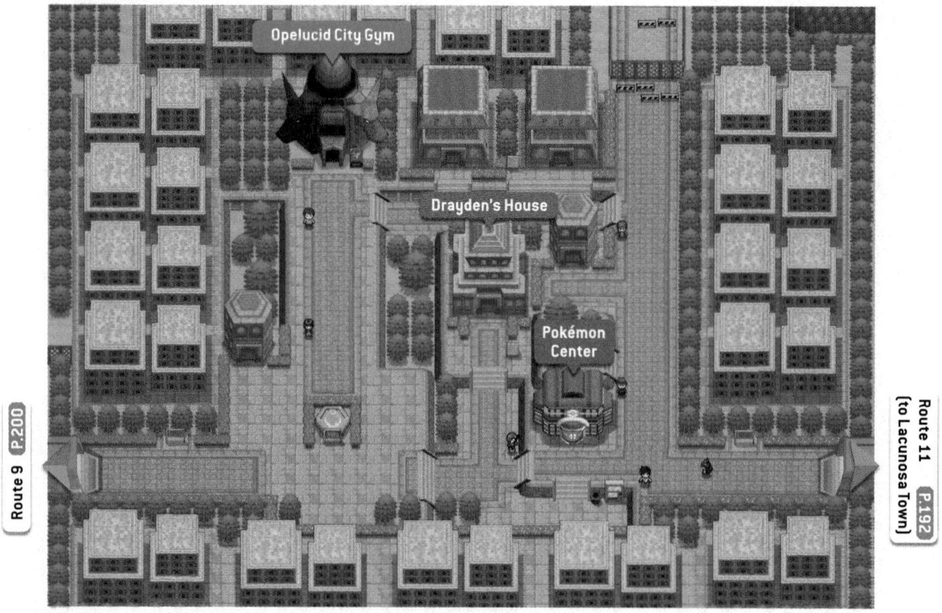

Items

- First visit
- ☐ Float Stone
- ☐ Fresh Water
- ☐ Ring Target
- ☐ Smoke Ball
- After defeating the Opelucid City Gym
- ☐ Legend Badge
- ☐ TM82 Dragon Tail

Props

- ☐ Big Bag
- ☐ Fluffy Beard
- ☐ Gift Box
- ☐ Scarlet Hat

◆ If this Prop is already in the Prop Case obtained in the Memory Link event, you can't get this Prop.

Poké Mart (Lower Clerk)

Item	Price
BridgeMail V	50
Favored Mail	50
Greet Mail	50
Inquiry Mail	50
Like Mail	50
Reply Mail	50
RSVP Mail	50
Thanks Mail	50
Dusk Ball	1,000
Quick Ball	1,000
Timer Ball	1,000

Step 1 Reunited with Iris from Castelia City

Iris, who you met in Castelia City, will call out to you when you enter the city and head west. After she shows you where to find the Gym, she recommends that you go to Route 9 before taking on the Gym Leader. Take Iris's good advice!

Step 2 Get Props from the old man

Speak to the old man in the house that lies west of the Trainer Tips sign, and he will give you one Prop for the Pokémon Musical each day. He will give you four different Props in total. Stop by four days in a row to get them all.

Step 3 Go to Route 9 to level up your Pokémon

You can challenge the Opelucid City Gym at once, of course, but a better choice is to follow Iris's advice and head for Route 9 first (p. 200). You can battle seven Trainers on Route 9, so that's seven more rungs in the ladder of building strong Pokémon.

Step 4 Take on the Opelucid City Gym Battle

After returning from Route 9, it's finally time for your Opelucid City Gym battle. Heal your Pokémon at the Pokémon Center and make your way to the Gym. You can reach it by heading directly north from the Trainer Tips sign.

Iris is Drayden's granddaughter!

Iris is the granddaughter of Gym Leader Drayden, though apparently they're not related by blood. Two years ago, Iris herself was the Gym Leader of Opelucid City (in *Pokémon White Version* only).

Receive items from the townspeople

Talk to the townspeople on the second floor of Drayden's house and in the houses to the east of the Opelucid City Gym to receive items. Visit all of the homes, talk to the people, and load up on items.

Listen to the Tympole choir

There are five Tympole on the second floor of the house just north of the Pokémon Center. If you have a Tympole in your party when you talk to the man there, you'll have an amazing opportunity to hear six Tympole singing in harmony. Don't miss this rare chance (p. 420).

Try your hand at a guessing game

Two houses east of the Opelucid City Gym, you'll find the site where the Battle House was two years ago. On the second floor, you can enjoy a game where you have to guess which child said the same thing as the little boy.

7 Opelucid City Gym Battle

Gym Battle Tips
- Learn Dual Chop and Ice Punch in Driftveil City
- Learn Icy Wind and Dragon Pulse in Lentimas Town

When playing *Pokémon Black Version 2*

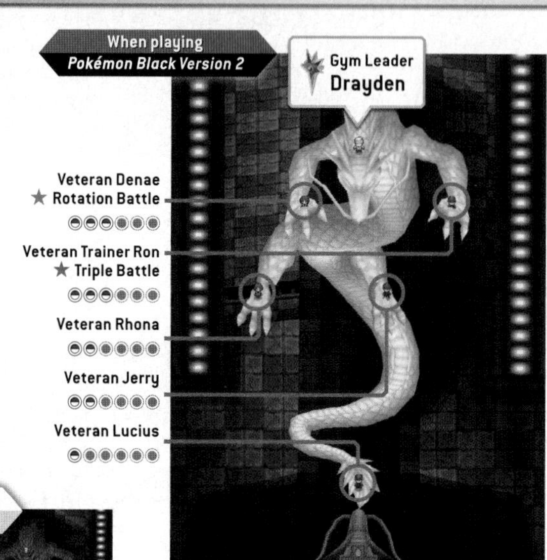

Perhaps you can show me that future, the way Iris has?

When playing *Pokémon White Version 2*

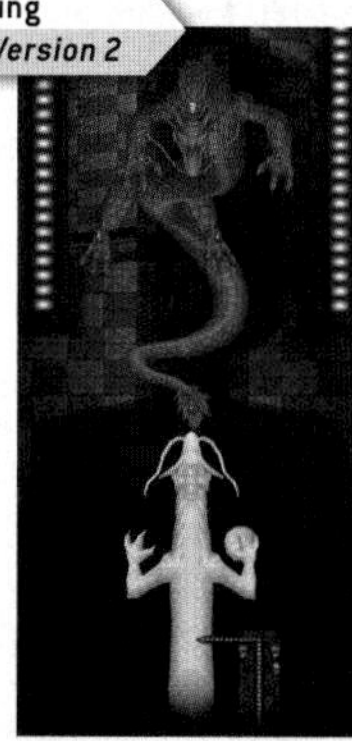

◆ The Trainers you will battle are the same.

Entrance

Opelucid City Gym Leader

Drayden

Dragon-type Pokémon User

Strike all of your opponents in their weak spot with Ice-type moves

You'll have to defeat the Trainers on either the right or the left side of the dragon statue to make your way up to where Drayden waits. Drayden's Pokémon are all Dragon-type Pokémon. If you also use Dragon-type Pokémon, you will be able to deal great damage, but you will also take great damage. Try using Pokémon that have learned Ice-type moves from the master Move Tutors.

Drayden's Pokémon

Pokémon	Lv.	Type	Weak to
Druddigon ♂	Lv. 46	Dragon	Ice, Dragon
Flygon ♂	Lv. 46	Ground, Dragon	Ice, Dragon
Haxorus ♂	Lv. 48	Dragon	Ice, Dragon

Legend Badge

Pokémon up to Lv. 80, including those received in trades, will obey you.

TM 82 Dragon Tail — Dragon

After damaging the opponent, this move will automatically end a battle against a Pokémon in the wild. When battling against a Trainer, it will force the opposing Pokémon to switch out after inflicting damage on it.

After defeating the Opelucid City Gym

Hear about the Legendary Pokémon at Drayden's house

When you leave the Gym, you will be shown to Drayden's home. There Drayden will tell you the tale of Zekrom and Reshiram, the legend of the other Dragon-type Pokémon, Kyurem, and the story behind the DNA Splicers that have been passed down in his family for generations.

But here's what's been bothering me...
Could there be one more dragon Pokémon?

After defeating the Opelucid City Gym

Team Plasma covers the whole city in ice

Team Plasma's frigate suddenly appears in the sky and releases an icy cannon blast, freezing the whole city solid. Zinzolin appears before Drayden and demands that he hand over the DNA Splicers. Drayden refuses, but Zinzolin will not give up that easily.

You can still use the Pokémon Center

The city may be covered in ice, but you can still use the Pokémon Center. Make your way through the icy streets by sliding until you strike an obstacle. You'll have to think carefully about your path to make your way to the entrance of the Pokémon Center.

After defeating the Opelucid City Gym

Find the three Grunts in the city and defeat them

Zinzolin sends his Grunts out into the city to search for the DNA Splicers. You will find these Grunts to the east of the Pokémon Center, and to both the south and the east of the Gym. Search them out and defeat them all.

Don't think about it too much.
It's easier that way!

After defeating the Opelucid City Gym

The battle with Zinzolin comes at last

After defeating the three Team Plasma Grunts, head for the Opelucid City Gym. Zinzolin is standing before its entrance. If you try to speak to him, you will be drawn into battle. Go to the Pokémon Center and have your Pokémon healed before speaking with him.

Zinzolin hates cold climates

Zinzolin hates being cold. The whole time he is in Opelucid City, he will keep griping about how cold he is. Yet for some reason, he hid inside a freezing cold storage unit when he was up to no good two years ago...

Oh, for crying out loud...I didn't expect to have to fight hampered by cold like this.

Battle Team Plasma's Zinzolin! 2

Strike your opponent's weaknesses for a quick way to victory

Zinzolin's Pokémon will use Confuse Ray to confuse your Pokémon and will reduce the damage his Pokémon take with Light Screen. If the battle drags on too long, you might find it difficult to win. Use Fire- and Fighting-type moves to strike at his Pokémon's weaknesses and quickly bring the battle to an end.

Zinzolin's Pokémon

Pokémon	Lv.	Type	Weak to
Cryogonal	Lv. 46	Ice	Fire, Fighting, Rock, Steel
Cryogonal	Lv. 46	Ice	Fire, Fighting, Rock, Steel
Weavile ♂	Lv. 48	Dark, Ice	Fighting, Fire, Bug, Rock, Steel

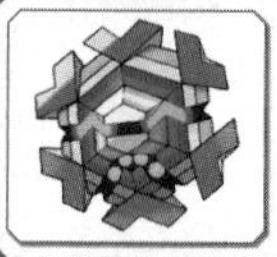

After the battle with Zinzolin — Drayden fully heals your Pokémon for you

When you defeat Zinzolin, Drayden will appear. He heals your Pokémon for you as thanks for protecting his treasure from Team Plasma. It seems that the DNA Splicers he had hidden away are still safe.

Drayden: You're even better than I hoped. Thanks to you, we drove them off.

After the battle with Zinzolin — The DNA Splicers are stolen by the Shadow Triad

Drayden retrieves the DNA Splicers from the Gym to check that they are still fine. At that moment, the Shadow Triad appears and steals the DNA Splicers from Drayden. Follow after them as they try to flee.

The treasure is hidden within the Gym

The DNA Splicers are hidden somewhere within the Opelucid City Gym. Apparently that is why Drayden had the Gym renovated. Unfortunately, the Shadow Triad tricks him and ends up stealing the DNA Splicers regardless.

After the battle with Zinzolin

One of the Shadow Triad fled to the east

As you proceed east, you'll encounter one of the Shadow Triad standing in front of the gate to Route 11. A battle starts as soon as you get close. Do everything in your power to get the DNA Splicers back.

Use Fighting-type moves for a decisive victory

The Shadow Triad's Pokémon are all weak to Fighting-type moves. In fact, Pawniard will take four times the normal amount of damage! Even if your Pokémon's levels are slightly lower than theirs, target their weaknesses, and you can defeat them with a single blow.

Shadow Triad Pokémon

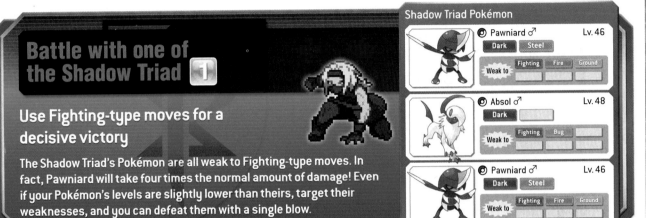

Pokémon	Lv.	Type	Weak to
Pawniard ♂	Lv. 46	Dark, Steel	Fighting, Fire, Ground
Absol ♂	Lv. 48	Dark	Fighting, Bug
Pawniard ♂	Lv. 46	Dark, Steel	Fighting, Fire, Ground

After the battle with the Shadow

Sensing danger, Cheren comes running

Even though you defeated one of the Shadow Triad, you didn't manage to recover the DNA Splicers. Cheren rushes to the scene. He tells you that Team Plasma must be close to Humilau City, because it has the lowest temperature in the Unova region now.

I have a good idea of where Team Plasma is hiding.

After the battle with the Shadow

Head to Humilau City

Make your way to Humilau City to protect Pokémon from Team Plasma. You can reach Humilau City through the Marine Tube in Undella Town, so Undella Town is your next destination (p. 181).

Route 9

Route 9 is a paved road that cuts through a wooded area. On the north side is Shopping Mall Nine, which boasts the greatest variety of goods in Unova.

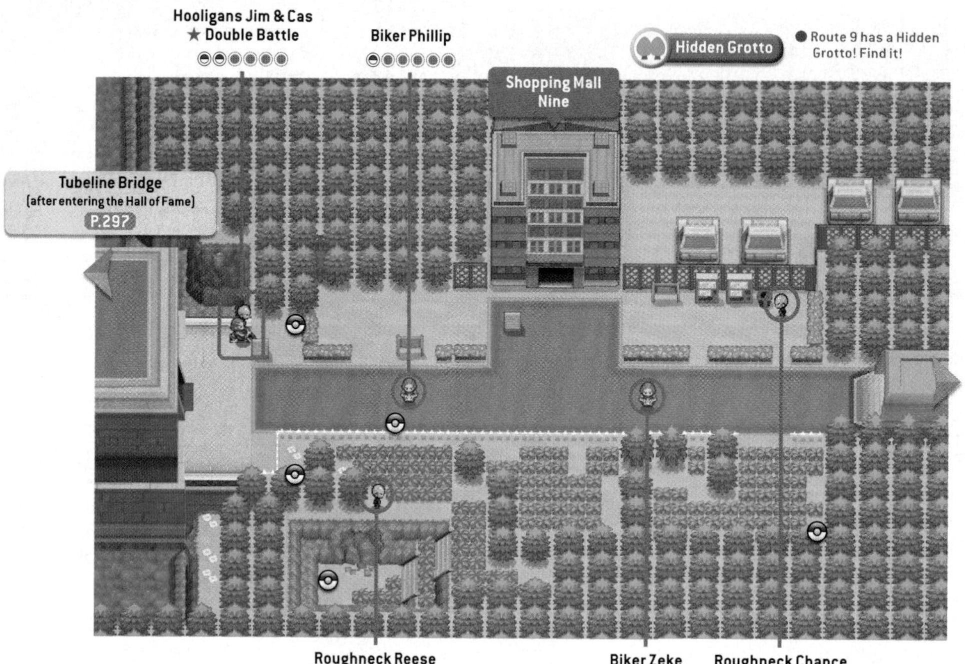

Items

- ☐ Elixir
- ☐ HP Up
- ☐ Iron
- ☐ Nugget
- ☐ Poké Doll
- ☐ Quick Ball

Tall Grass

Pokémon	Version	Rate
Duosion	○	○
Garbodor		○
Gothorita	●	○
Liepard		○
Minccino		◎
Muk		△
Pawniard		○

Tall Grass (rustling)

Pokémon	Rate
Audino	◎
Cinccino	△
Emolga	○
Gothitelle	△
Reuniclus	△

Dark Grass

Pokémon	Version	Rate
Duosion	○	○
Garbodor		○
Gothorita	●	○
Liepard		○
Minccino		◎
Muk		△
Pawniard		○

Hidden Grotto

Pokémon	Rate
Bouffalant	△
Garbodor	○
Liepard	◎
Muk	○

Mass Outbreaks

Pokémon
Swalot

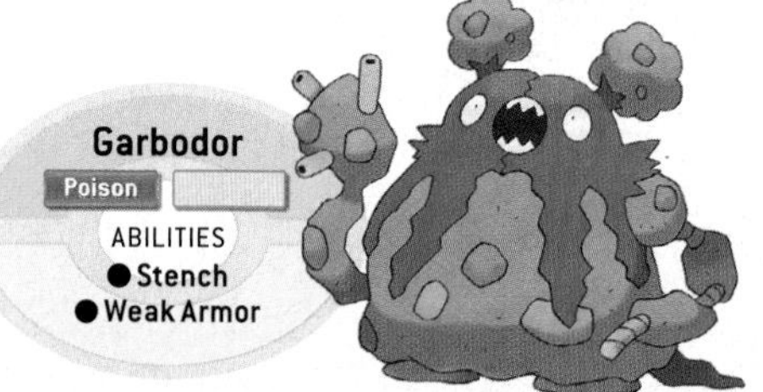

Step 1 You'll want to do more than window-shop

Go west on Route 9 to Shopping Mall Nine. This convenient mall has a great selection of items, including some you can't find in Poké Marts, so be sure to spend, spend, spend (p. 201)!

Special evening deals just for you

Special evening deals are available on the first floor of Shopping Mall Nine. In the evenings, talk to the Waitress on the east side of the floor. You can buy items such as Poké Balls at a special discount.

Step 2 Change Rotom's forms in the warehouse

At the back of Shopping Mall Nine, you'll be able to walk casually into a warehouse packed with cardboard boxes containing appliances. If you visit this room with Rotom in your party, you can change its form.

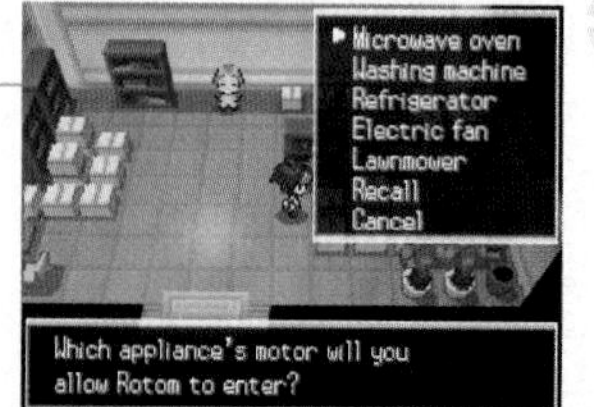

Get Rotom in a Pokémon trade

Someone will trade you a Rotom for a Ditto on Route 15, which is only accessible after you enter the Hall of Fame. You can catch Ditto in Crater Forest in the Giant Chasm (p. 232).

Step 3 A daily shopping request from a Lady

Talk to the Lady on the first floor of Shopping Mall Nine, and she'll ask you to buy her a Hyper Potion. If you bring her one that day, she'll give you an Energy Root. If you wait and bring it to her the next day, she'll give you EnergyPowder.

YES
NO
a Hyper Potion for me?
I'll give you the money for it.

Step 4 Return to Opelucid City for a Gym Battle

Once you're done battling with the Pokémon Trainers on the route and in the mall and collecting items, it's finally time for your seventh Gym battle. Go east through the gate to return to Opelucid City (p. 194).

The Tubeline Bridge is a dead end

The west end of Route 9 is connected to the Tubeline Bridge. Currently, an experiment to see how many people can stand on the Tubeline Bridge bridge is underway, so a person at the gate will stop you. Visit it after entering the Hall of Fame.

A little ice won't stop the shopping

When Team Plasma attacks Opelucid City and freezes it solid, Route 9 is also covered in ice. But if you slide over the icy ground, you can still get into the mall to do your shopping. Gnarly!

Stock up at Shopping Mall Nine

Buy items you can't get anywhere else

Shopping Mall Nine sells a variety of items on each of its three floors. Some items that are indispensable for raising Pokémon, such as Protein and Iron, can only be purchased here.

Floor Guide

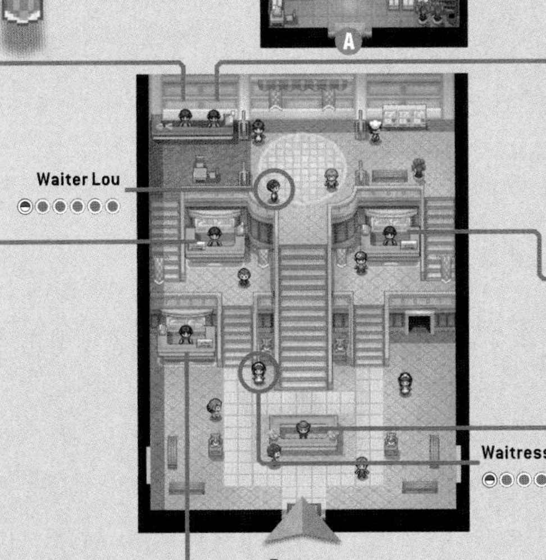

Counter on the left side of 3F

Items	Price
Calcium	9,800
Carbos	9,800
HP Up	9,800
Iron	9,800
Protein	9,800
Zinc	9,800

Counter on the left side of 2F

Items	Price
Favored Mail	50
Greet Mail	50
Inquiry Mail	50
Like Mail	50
Reply Mail	50
RSVP Mail	50
Thanks Mail	50
Poké Ball	200
Heal Ball	300
Great Ball	600
Dusk Ball	1,000
Nest Ball	1,000
Net Ball	1,000
Quick Ball	1,000
Timer Ball	1,000
Ultra Ball	1,200

Counter on the right side of 3F

Items	Price
X Sp. Def	350
X Special	350
X Speed	350
X Attack	500
X Defend	550
Dire Hit	650
Guard Spec.	700
X Accuracy	950

Counter on the right side of 2F

Items	Price
TM15 Hyper Beam	90,000
TM68 Giga Impact	90,000

Information

Counter on 1F

Items	Price	Items	Price
Antidote	100	Escape Rope	550
Parlyz Heal	200	Full Heal	600
Awakening	250	Max Repel	700
Burn Heal	250	Super Potion	700
Ice Heal	250	Poké Toy	1,000
Potion	300	Hyper Potion	1,200
Repel	350	Revive	1,500
Super Repel	500	Max Potion	2,500

An undersea tunnel built using cutting-edge technology

Marine Tube

Guide The Marine Tube is an undersea tunnel built with cutting-edge technology. The route has a transparent dome covering it so you can see the various Pokémon that live in the ocean.

Field Moves Needed

Items

- First visit
- ☐ TM42 Facade
- If you have a Pokémon holding the item Poison Barb
- ☐ Black Sludge

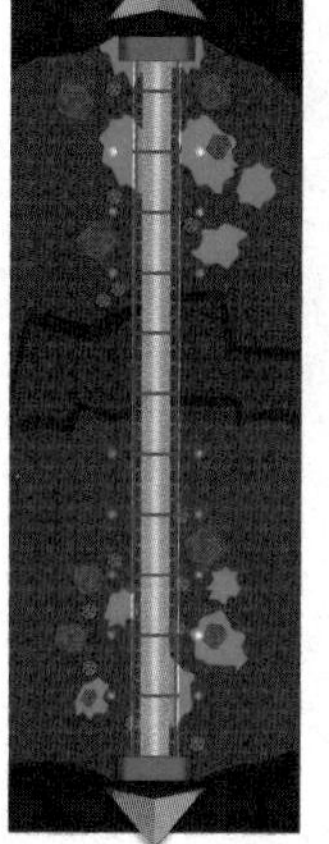

Step 1 Go through the tunnel to Humilau City

Enter the Marine Tube from Undella Town and head straight north while watching Pokémon swim elegantly through the ocean. When you leave the Marine Tube, you will arrive in Humilau City.

Have a Pokémon hold the Poison Barb

Talk to a woman in the tube when you have a Pokémon in your party that's holding the Poison Barb, and she'll give you Black Sludge. If a Poison-type Pokémon holds this item, its HP is restored during battle.

Step 2 Watch Wailord's noble swimming

Wailord appears between 3 p.m. and 4 p.m. every afternoon. When Wailord shows itself, it swims over and under the Marine Tube. If you see this, you'll get the Wailord Watcher Medal.

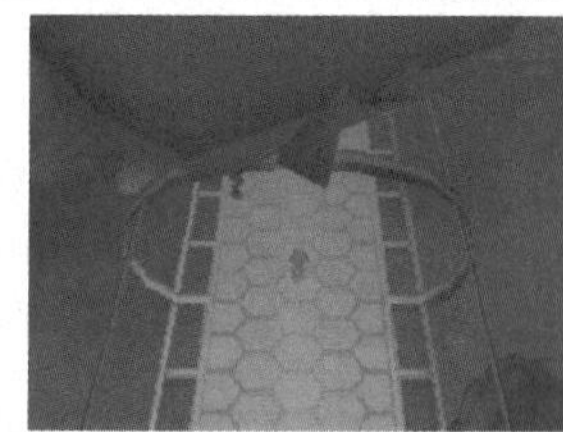

A resort city where buildings float in the waves and look like islands

Humilau City

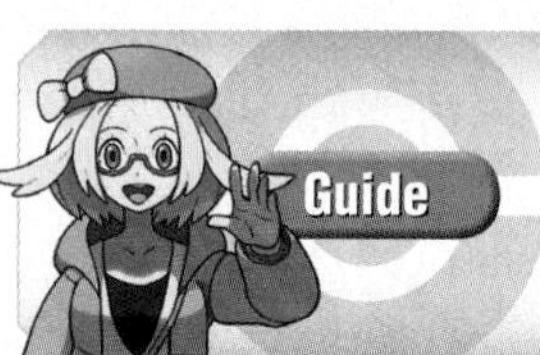

Guide Humilau City is a resort town with a tropical atmosphere. It's surrounded by the ocean and the homes of the city are built on top of wooden bridges. The city is connected to Route 22 in the west and to Route 21 in the south.

Field Moves Needed

Surf

Items

- First visit
- ☐ Fresh Water
- ☐ Heart Scale
- ☐ Protein
- ☐ Shell Bell
- If you talk to the Nurse while you have Luvdisc in your party
- ☐ Heart Scale x5
- After beating the Humilau City Gym
- ☐ TM55 Scald
- ☐ Wave Badge
- When the request is fulfilled at Celestial Tower after entering the Hall of Fame
- ☐ Revive

Poké Mart (Lower Clerk)	
Favored Mail	50
Greet Mail	50
Inquiry Mail	50
Like Mail	50
Reply Mail	50
RSVP Mail	50
Thanks Mail	50
Dive Ball	1,000
Luxury Ball	1,000
Net Ball	1,000

Water Surface	
Basculin (Blue-Striped Form)	△
Basculin (Red-Striped Form)	△
Frillish	◎
Staryu	◎

Water Surface (ripples)	
Basculin (Blue-Striped Form)	△
Basculin (Red-Striped Form)	△
Corsola	◎
Jellicent	◎
Starmie	△

■ After entering the Hall of Fame

Fishing	
Luvdisc	◎
Shellder	◎

Fishing (ripples)	
Cloyster	△
Luvdisc	◎
Shellder	◎

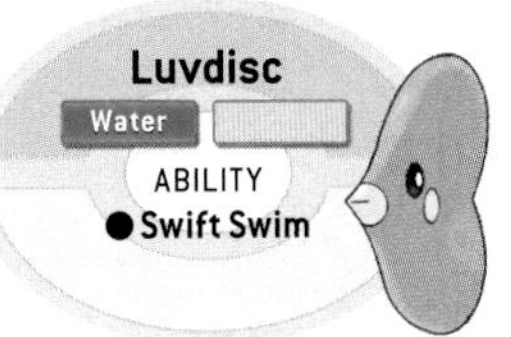

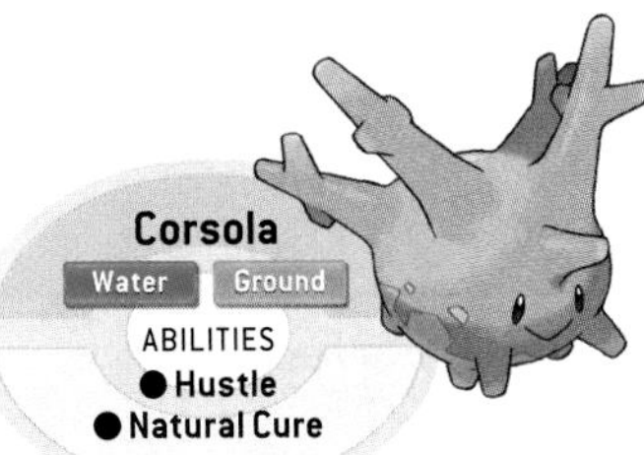

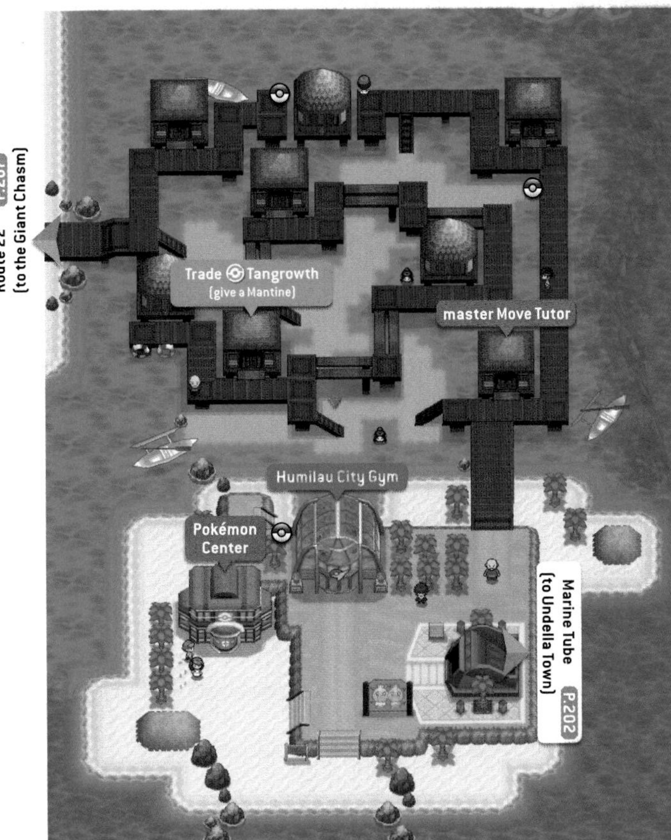

Step 1 Hugh is waiting by the exit

Hugh is waiting by the exit when you emerge from the Marine Tube. When you approach him, he tells you to defeat the Gym Leader first. Take his advice and head for the Humilau City Gym.

So you should focus on defeating the Gym Leader first!

Step 2 The Gym Leader, Marlon, pops out of the sea

Head to the pier to go look for the Gym Leader. As you walk north, a man will pop out of the ocean suddenly. It's the Gym Leader, Marlon. After you meet him, you can challenge the Humilau City Gym.

Step 3 Have a master Move Tutor teach your Pokémon moves

A master Move Tutor lives in the house directly to the north of the entrance to the Marine Tube. This Move Tutor is obsessed with yellow shards. If you give him the necessary number of Yellow Shards, he will teach your Pokémon a move.

Play with the face board

To the south of the Marine Tube entrance is a face board. Stand to the north of the board and peek through the face hole. Very rarely, a face-board super fan appears and takes your picture. When your picture is taken, you receive the Face Board Memorial Medal.

Where is Marlon from?

Humilau City's Gym Leader, Marlon, is a sunny guy with a unique way of speaking. The way he speaks is different from the way people in the Unova region speak.

Get some respect at the Pokémon Center

Talk to the man in the Pokémon Center when you have a Pokémon in your party that knows Surf. He can't swim, so he gives you some serious props on your achievement.

Moves you can learn and how many Yellow Shards you need

Move you can learn	Yellow Shards needed
Bind	2
Snore	2
Heal Bell	4
Knock Off	4
Roost	6

Move you can learn	Yellow Shards needed
Synthesis	6
Role Play	8
Sky Attack	8
Drain Punch	10
Giga Drain	10

Move you can learn	Yellow Shards needed
Heat Wave	10
Pain Split	10
Tailwind	10

Yellow Shard

Step 4 Trade the man a Mantine for a Tangrowth

In a house to the north of the Humilau City Gym, a man offers to trade Pokémon. If you give him a Mantine, he'll give you a Tangrowth. You can catch Mantine in Undella Bay, though you won't see them in winter.

YES
NO
If you have one, trade my Tangrowth for your Mantine. OK?

Step 5 Take Mienfoo on a daily walk

Talk to the old lady in the house on the western edge of town, and once a day she will ask you to take her Mienfoo on a walk. If you accept and walk around the house with it for a while, she will give you a Pearl.

YES
NO
Hey, you!
Would you walk with my dear Mienfoo?

Check on Mienfoo

If you agree to walk Mienfoo for the lady, check on it while you are walking to see how it's doing. Its gait is a little awkward at first, but it starts to step more lightly. When you see a satisfied "!" pop over its head, talk to the lady.

Step 6 The house is where the Heart Scales are

A Nurse with a Stunfisk lives in the house on the eastern edge of the city. Put a Luvdisc in your party and talk to the Nurse. She likes flat Pokémon, so when you have it with you, she'll give you five Heart Scales.

Trainer obtained Heart Scales!

Reel in a Luvdisc

Luvdisc is caught by fishing. But you don't get the Super Rod until after you enter the Hall of Fame. If you use Link Trade, you can bring a Luvdisc here before you enter the Hall of Fame.

Step 7 Take on the Humilau City Gym

After you've visited all of the houses, it's time for your final Gym battle. Have a look at your party Pokémon and items. If it seems like you're ready to go, head to the Humilau City Gym. It's just east of the Pokémon Center.

A Funfest Mission is added

Talk to the old man in the house west of the one with the man who trades Pokémon. The Entralink Funfest Mission "Memory Training!" will be added for you to play.

8 Humilau City Gym Battle

Gym Battle Tips

- Learn Seed Bomb and ThunderPunch in Driftveil City
- Catch Virizion on Route 11 and put it in your party

Humilau City Gym Leader

Marlon

Water-type Pokémon User

Watch out for burns! Grass- and Electric-type moves are your best choice

When you jump on one of the floating lily pads inside the Gym, it will move in the direction you're facing until it runs into an obstacle. Use these lily pads to move through the Gym and reach Marlon. Watch out: Marlon's Pokémon use Scald! It's a Water-type move that can inflict the Burned status condition. If your Pokémon get burned, quickly use Burn Heal or Full Heal to heal them. Marlon's Pokémon are weak against Grass- and Electric-type moves, so use these for an advantage.

Marlon's Pokémon

Pokémon	Level	Type	Weak to
Carracosta ♂	Lv. 49	Water, Rock	Grass◆, Electric◆, Fighting◆, Ground◆
Wailord ♂	Lv. 49	Water	Grass, Electric
Jellicent ♂	Lv. 51	Water, Ghost	Grass, Electric, Ghost, Dark

Wave Badge

All traded Pokémon, regardless of level, will obey you.

TM 55 Scald — Water

Has a 30% chance to inflict the Burned status condition on the opponent.

◆ The damage may change depending on the effects of this Pokémon's Ability.

Go after Team Plasma and head to Route 22

Your rival is waiting outside the Gym. Marlon shows up, too, but he doesn't appear to be interested in Team Plasma. Hugh asks you to search Route 22, so head to the west of town to get there (p. 207).

With information from Colress, head to Route 21

You run into Colress again on Route 22 and he tells you there's something of interest in Seaside Cave on Route 21. Go to the beach south of town, and use Surf on the water to proceed to Route 21 (p. 210).

Stock up on Full Restores

Cheren will tell you that the Plasma Frigate is headed for the Giant Chasm. Before proceeding, be sure to visit the Poké Mart in Humilau City and stock up on as many Full Restores as you can.

Take Route 22 to the Giant Chasm

The Plasma Frigate took off from Route 21 and headed for the Giant Chasm. Chase after it. The Giant Chasm can be entered from the west side of Route 22. First, head to Route 22 (p. 207).

Marlon refuses to help

Marlon makes the ocean his home and follows a policy of "the ocean accepts all rivers." As a result, he doesn't seem bothered by Team Plasma's wrongdoings. He refuses to help track down Team Plasma and just walks away.

Buy lots of Ultra Balls

After the Gym battle, you'll head to Route 22, where you will encounter the Legendary Pokémon Terrakion. Buy plenty of Ultra Balls at the Poké Mart in advance so you'll have a better chance of catching it.

Route 22

Guide

The uneven and complex terrain of Route 22 makes it almost maze-like in its structure. Raised walkways connect some of the elevated terrain. Route 22 connects Humilau City to the east and the Giant Chasm to the west.

Field Moves Needed

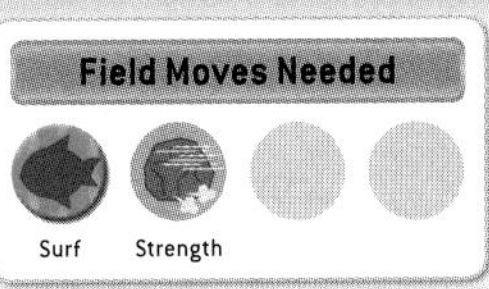

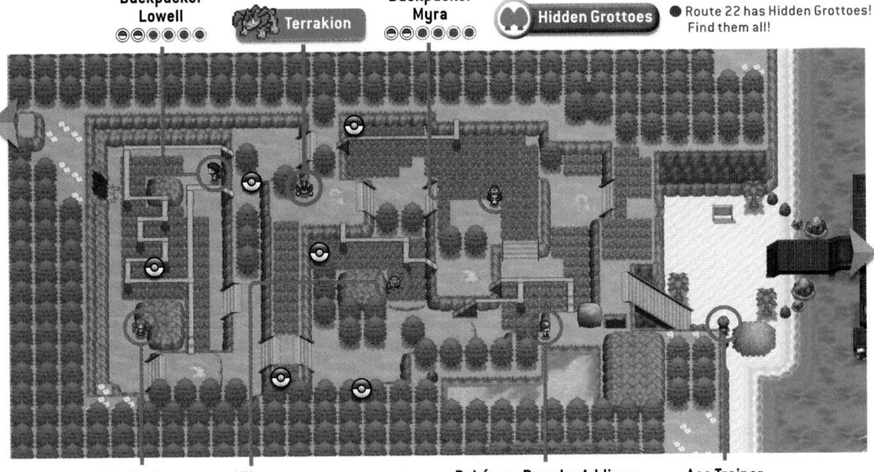

Items

- ☐ Calcium
- ☐ Colress Machine
- ☐ Max Potion
- ☐ Poison Barb
- ☐ PP Up
- ☐ Rare Candy
- ☐ Red Shard

Tall Grass

Pokémon	Frequency
Amoonguss	○
Delibird	△
Golduck	○
Lunatone	○
Marill	○
Mienfoo	○
Pelipper	○
Solrock	○

Tall Grass (rustling)

Pokémon	Frequency
Audino	◎
Azumarill	△
Emolga	○

Dark Grass

Pokémon	Frequency
Amoonguss	○
Delibird	△
Golduck	○
Lunatone	○
Marill	○
Mienfoo	○
Pelipper	○
Solrock	○

■ After entering the Hall of Fame

Fishing

Pokémon	Version	Frequency
Basculin (Blue-Striped Form)	⬡	◎
Basculin (Red-Striped Form)	⬢	◎
Goldeen		◎

Fishing (ripples)

Pokémon	Version	Frequency
Basculin (Blue-Striped Form)	⬢	◎
Basculin (Red-Striped Form)	⬡	◎
Goldeen		◎
Seaking		○

Water Surface

Pokémon	Version	Frequency
Basculin (Blue-Striped Form)	⬡	◎
Basculin (Red-Striped Form)	⬢	◎
Marill		◎

Water Surface (ripples)

Pokémon	Version	Frequency
Azumarill		△
Basculin (Blue-Striped Form)	⬢	◎
Basculin (Red-Striped Form)	⬡	◎
Marill		◎

Hidden Grottoes

Pokémon	Frequency
Amoonguss	◎
Mienfoo	△
Pelipper	○

Mass Outbreaks

Pokémon	Version
Ariados	⬢
Ledian	⬡

Step 1 A hole blocks your way

When heading west from Humilau City, climb the stairs and you'll find a gaping hole in the ground a bit to the south. There's a boulder that can plug the hole on the other side, but you can't push it from here. Head north after climbing the stairs.

Step 2 Proceed while battling Pokémon Trainers

Proceed west and battle the Pokémon Trainers along the way. You'll see raised walkways connecting the elevated terrain, but you will be blocked by trees or ledges and won't be able to use them yet. Keep heading west.

I might be lost right now, but I'll battle you anyway!

Watch out for Amoonguss in disguise!

When you inspect items on the ground, you may get more than you bargained for! Some of these items are actually Amoonguss lying in wait to battle you.

Step 3 Approach Terrakion and Colress will appear

You can find Terrakion on the elevated terrain west of the Backpacker Myra. Approach it and Colress will appear. Colress tells you that you're going to need the strength to protect your Pokémon if you intend to battle Team Plasma.

you must have the power to protect your own Pokémon!

Step 4 Receive the Colress Machine from Colress

Colress gives you the Colress Machine. He says that it's ineffective for battling Pokémon, but that you may find it useful for something. He then mentions that he saw something in Seaside Cave that reminded him of when you met on Route 4 and leaves.

Trainer obtained the Colress MCHN!

It proved helpful on Route 4, too

The Colress Machine has the same effect as the machine that was used on Route 4 to wake the sleeping Crustle. You'll find a place in Seaside Cave where a Crustle is blocking the way.

Step 5 The Legendary Pokémon Terrakion is waiting

When Colress leaves, catch Terrakion. It is standing on a raised area. Just like Cobalion and Virizion, it seems like Terrakion was waiting for you. If you speak to it, you will be drawn into battle. Be ready to catch it.

Catch Terrakion!

Terrakion Lv. 45

Rock | Fighting

ABILITY ● Justified

MOVES ● Helping Hand, Retaliate, Rock Slide, Sacred Sword

Terrakion comes at you with powerful attacks, such as Rock Slide and Sacred Sword. Weaken Terrakion by wearing down its HP little by little while restoring your own Pokémon's HP.

Move types that can reduce HP quickly	Water	Grass	Fighting	Ground	Psychic
	Steel				
Move types that can reduce HP gradually	Normal	Fire	Poison	Bug	Rock
	Dark				

Step 6 Proceed across the raised walkways

Raised walkways stretch south from the raised ground where you found Terrakion. Cross the walkways, but be careful: one misplaced step sends you tumbling down. Also, if you stand still on the walkway for too long, you'll fall. Continue to make your way east without stopping.

Add Terrakion to your party

Terrakion's stats are comparatively high, so it's a powerful ally. If you catch it, put it in your party. It should be an immediate force on your team.

Step 7 Move boulders to make a shortcut

A boulder you can move with Strength sits right by Pokémon Breeder Addison, who you can battle every time you visit. Push the boulder into the hole. Next time you visit, you can continue to the western side of Route 22 without walking through the tall grass.

Step 8 Collect items

On Route 22, many items lie in hard-to-see places, such as in the shade of trees or in tall grass. Explore every corner and collect items. Some items can't be obtained unless you use Surf.

Step 9 Find the entrance to the Giant Chasm

Proceed south from Terrakion's location and then continue west. There you'll find the entrance to the Giant Chasm, which you'll visit later. For now, keep on chasing Team Plasma.

Step 10 Use Fly to go back to Humilau City

Colress tells you that there is something in the Seaside Cave that's found past Route 21. To get there, use Fly to momentarily return to Humilau City and then continue to Route 21 (p. 206).

After investigating the Plasma Frigate: Continue into the Giant Chasm

Aim for the Giant Chasm, which is where Team Plasma is going (p. 232). If you pushed the boulder on the east side of the route into the hole during your last visit, there will be a shortcut. Walk over the raised walkways, and you can get to the west side quickly without having to pass through the tall grass.

Route 21

Guide

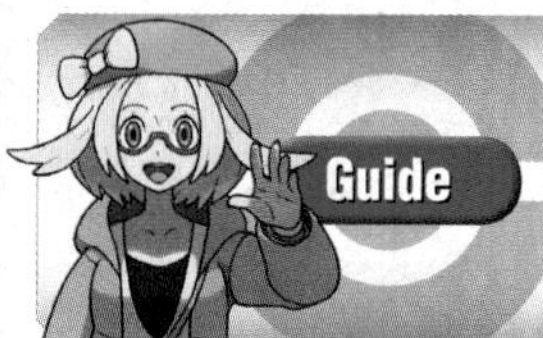

Route 21 is a short sea route that connects Humilau City to Seaside Cave. Pass between the rocks and small islands while battling Pokémon Trainers.

Field Moves Needed

Surf

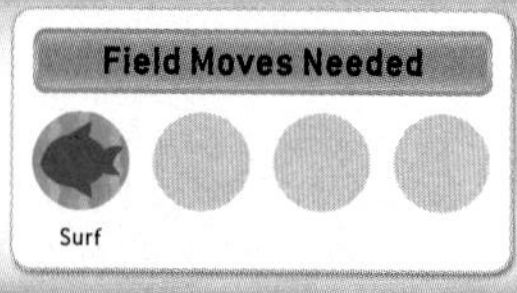

Humilau City P. 202
Swimmer ♀ Desiree
Swimmer ♀ Kaoru
Swimmer ♂ Harold
Swimmer ♂ Kyle
Plasma Frigate P. 214, 223
Seaside Cave P. 212
Seaside Cave P. 212
Black Belt Kenneth
Fisherman Kenzo
Doctor Braid
Restore your Pokémon's health

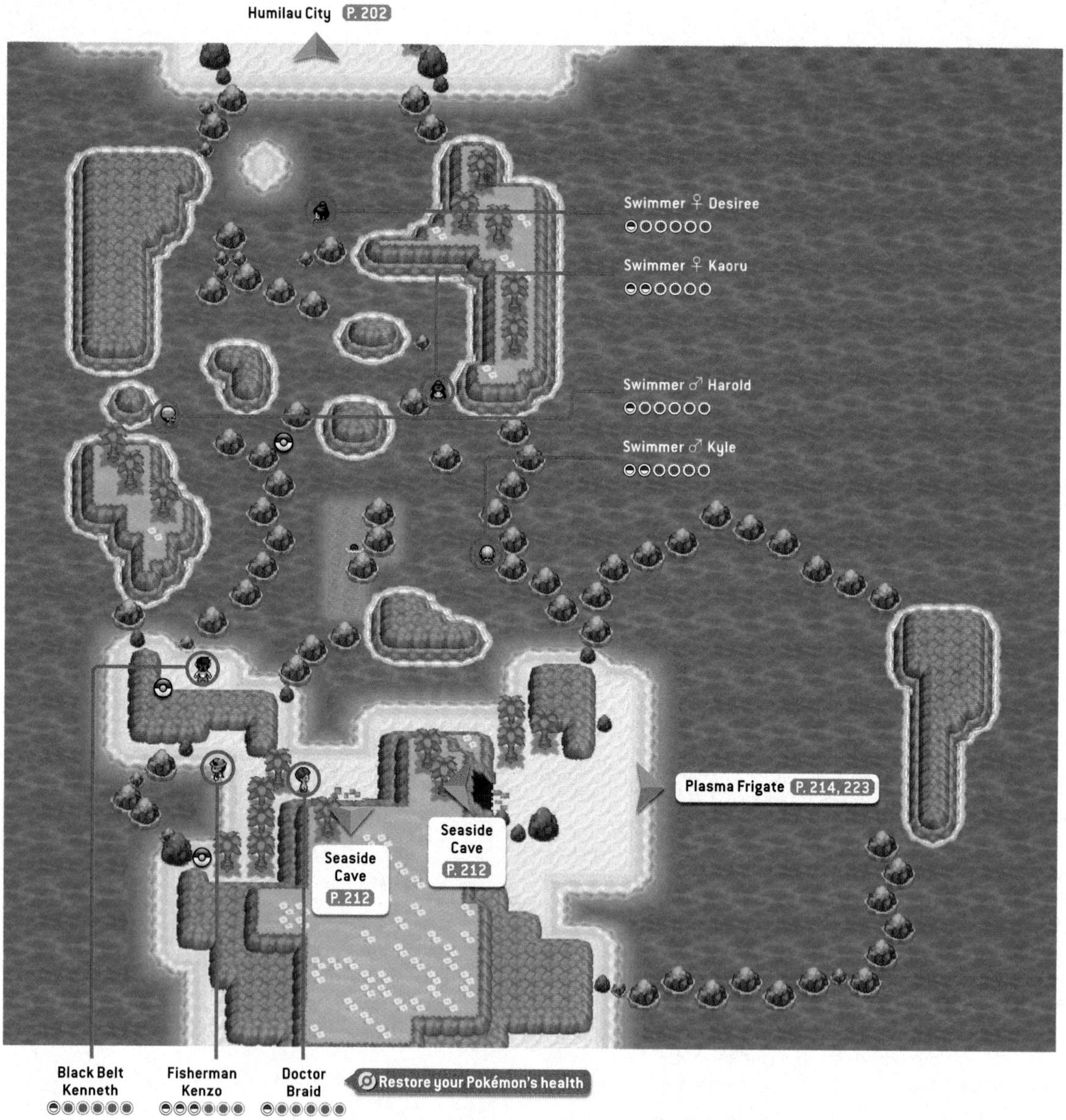

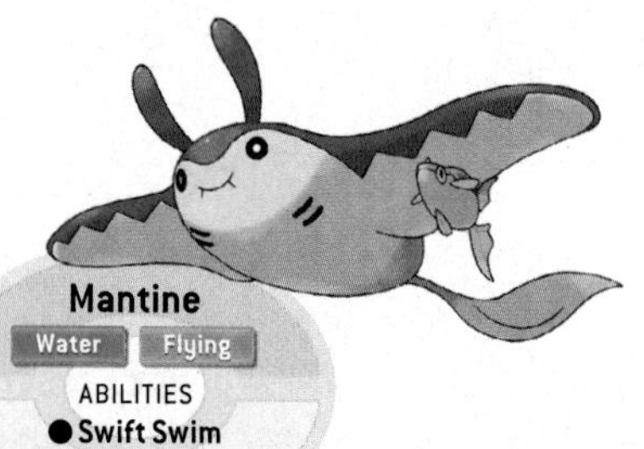

Items

- ☐ Big Pearl
- ☐ PP Up

Water Surface

Frillish	◎
Mantyke	◎
Remoraid	△

Water Surface (ripples)

Alomomola	◎
Jellicent	◎
Mantine	△

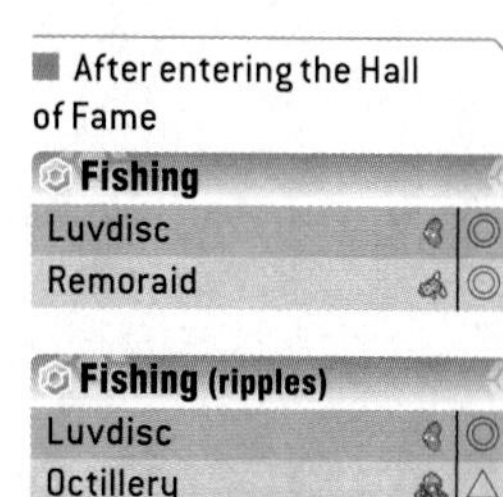

■ After entering the Hall of Fame

Fishing

Luvdisc	◎
Remoraid	◎

Fishing (ripples)

Luvdisc	◎
Octillery	△
Remoraid	◎

Mantine

Water | Flying

ABILITIES
- Swift Swim
- Water Absorb

Step 1 Make your way south while battling Trainers

Use Surf to head south. The rocks and islets form a natural route, so it's a straightforward trip over the water. Battle the swimming Pokémon Trainers as you make your way through the route.

Step 2 Have Doctor Braid heal your Pokémon

You can see Seaside Cave when you arrive at the beach to the south. Doctor Braid is standing by the entrance. After you defeat him in battle, talk to him. He'll heal your Pokémon every time you talk to him, so take advantage of Braid's ability to care for your Pokémon.

Swimmers use Water-type Pokémon

Swimmer ♂ and Swimmer ♀ will both come at you with their Water-type Pokémon. They must have befriended the Pokémon that live in the water while they were swimming around.

Step 3 Continue south into Seaside Cave

Battle with the Trainer on the beach to the west, pick up items, and explore Route 21. When you've seen everything, have Doctor Braid fix up your Pokémon, and then you can head into Seaside Cave (p. 212).

After exploring Seaside Cave: Storm the Plasma Frigate

When you exit the cave to the beach on the east side, you'll find Team Plasma's ship, the Plasma Frigate. It's the same one that you boarded before at the PWT. Right then, Marlon makes a grand entrance and lowers the ship's gangplank for you to board the ship (p. 214, 223).

Marlon sticks to his principles

Marlon isn't interested in Team Plasma, but he still helps you and Hugh. He can't decide whether Team Plasma is evil, but he explains that he believes in helping people when they're in trouble.

Seaside Cave

Seaside Cave passes through a large rock. The passage was opened up by erosion from wind and waves, as well as the power of Pokémon. The south exit leads to Undella Bay.

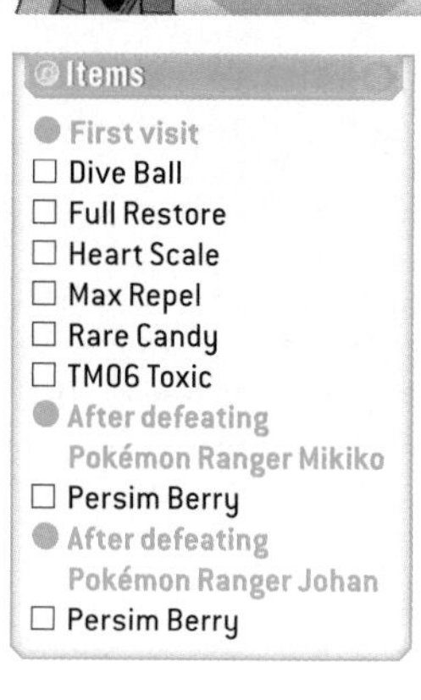

Items

- First visit
- ☐ Dive Ball
- ☐ Full Restore
- ☐ Heart Scale
- ☐ Max Repel
- ☐ Rare Candy
- ☐ TM06 Toxic
- After defeating Pokémon Ranger Mikiko
- ☐ Persim Berry
- After defeating Pokémon Ranger Johan
- ☐ Persim Berry

1F

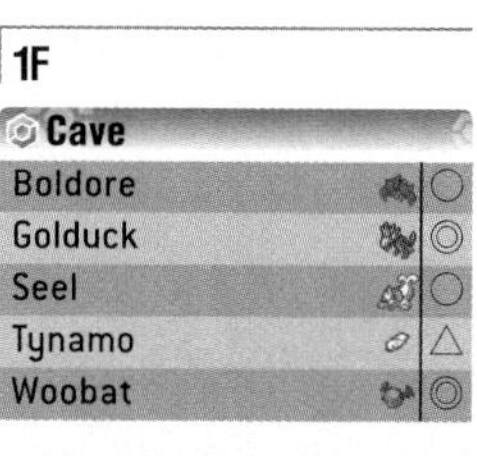

Cave	
Boldore	○
Golduck	◎
Seel	○
Tynamo	△
Woobat	◎

Cave (dust cloud)	
Excadrill	◎

Water Surface	
Frillish	◎
Seel	◎

Water Surface (ripples)	
Dewgong	○
Jellicent	◎
Seel	◎

After entering the Hall of Fame

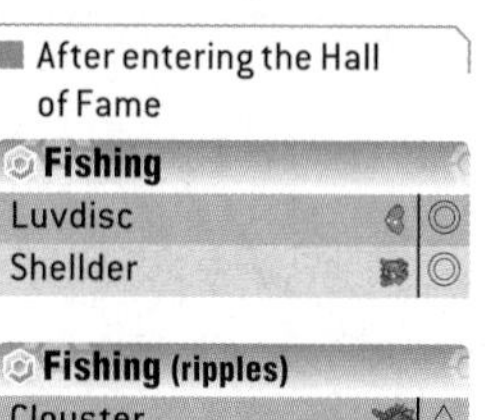

Fishing	
Luvdisc	◎
Shellder	◎

Fishing (ripples)	
Cloyster	△
Luvdisc	◎
Shellder	◎

1F

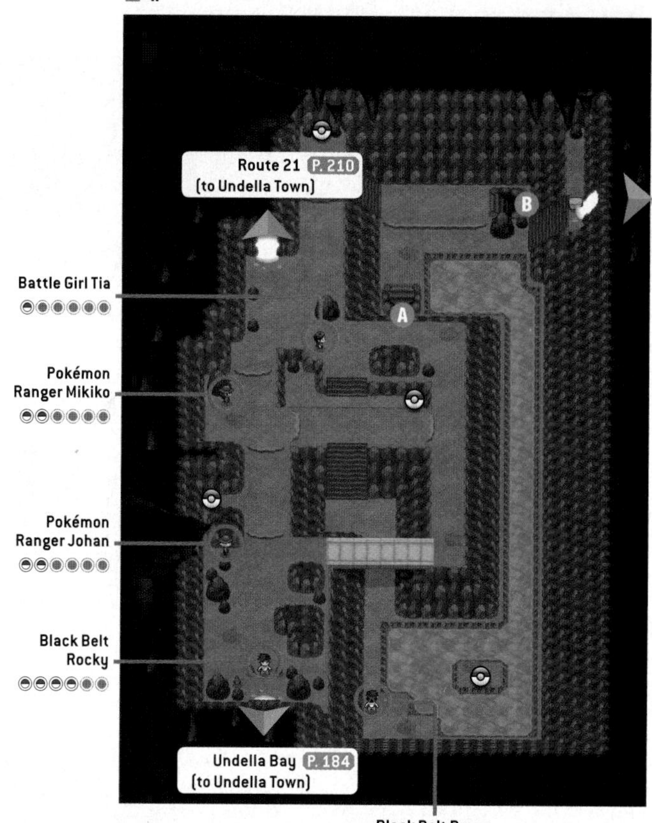

B1F

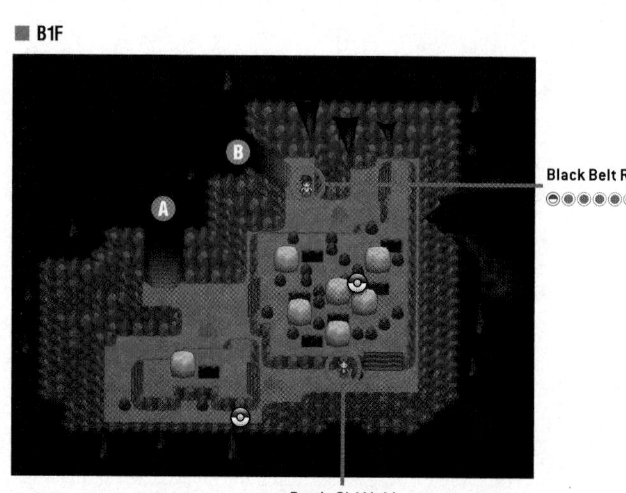

B1F

Cave	
Boldore	◎
Eelektrik	△
Golduck	◎
Shuckle	△
Woobat	◎

Cave (dust cloud)	
Excadrill	◎

Proceed while battling Pokémon Trainers

Four Pokémon Trainers are lined up on the west side of the first floor. Battle them while heading south. If you go south on the west side, ledges will prevent you from heading back, but you can use the bridge to the east to go back to the entrance. Take time to pick up items as you go.

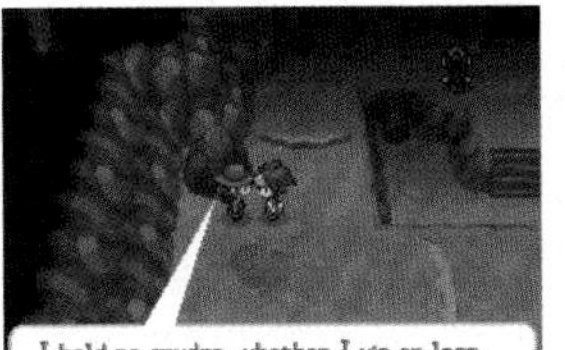

Now you, too, can come from Undella Town

When you defeat Black Belt Rocky on the west side of the first floor, he and his Roggenrola will leave, and the entrance leading to Undella Bay will be opened. Now you can also enter the cave from Undella Bay.

Use the Colress Machine on the rock blocking the way

Move north over the water using Surf on the east side of the first floor. At the top of the stairs, a rock will be blocking the exit. Press the A Button when you're standing next to the rock. The Colress Machine will energize the "rock," revealing it to be a Crustle—that attacks you!

Step 4 Leave the cave for the eastern side of Route 21

When you're victorious against the energized Crustle, you can go out though the east exit. Once you're done looking around in the cave and on B1F, head east to Route 21 (p. 211).

Get Berries from Pokémon Rangers

You can get a Persim Berry from Pokémon Rangers Mikiko and Johan. Mikiko and Johan are standing on the west side of the first floor. Don't be afraid to battle them and get Berries.

Catch Crustle

Use the Colress Machine to energize the Crustle, and when it attacks you, you can catch it. If you haven't caught one yet, make sure not to knock it out. You want to catch it and get a complete registration in the Pokédex.

Plasma Frigate

The Plasma Frigate is Team Plasma's hideout. It can do more than sail the ocean blue—it can extend its wings and fly through the blue sky, too. With the power of the Legendary Dragon-type Pokémon Kyurem, it can launch ice that never melts from its cannon.

Field Mov

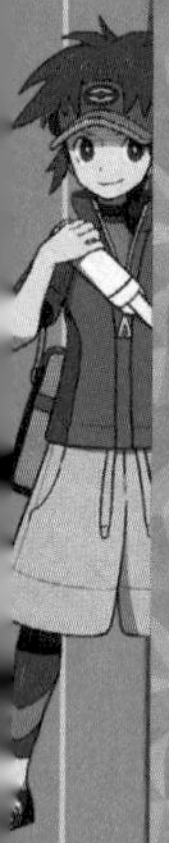

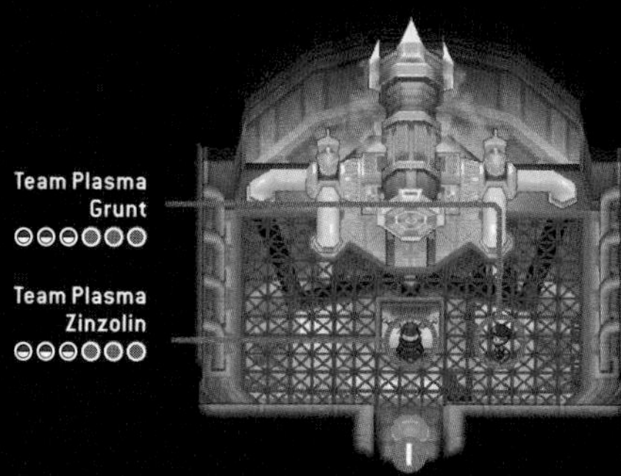

North Entrance

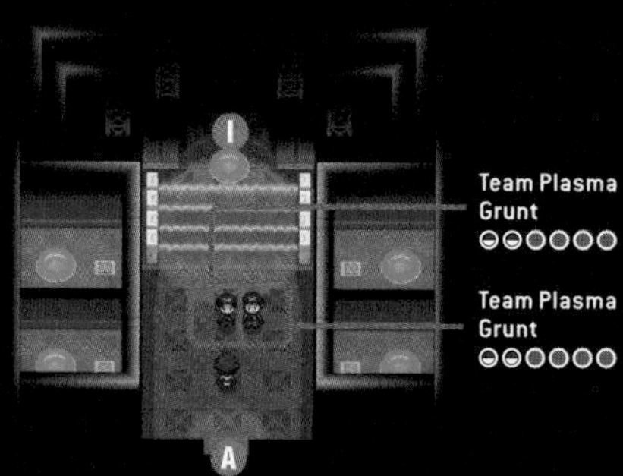

Items

- First visit
- ☐ Magmarizer
- ☐ Revive
- ☐ TM67 Retaliate
- After visiting the Giant Chasm
- ☐ Max Elixir
- ☐ Max Revive
- ☐ Plasma Card
- ☐ Power Band
- ☐ Zinc

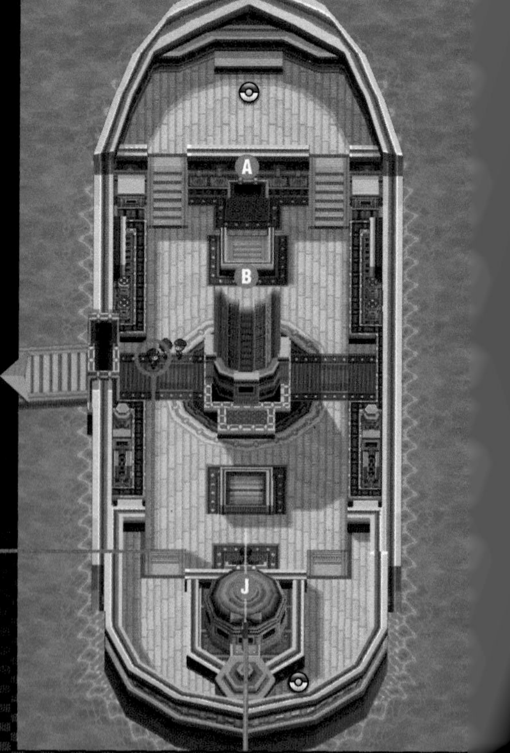

Team Plasma Grunt

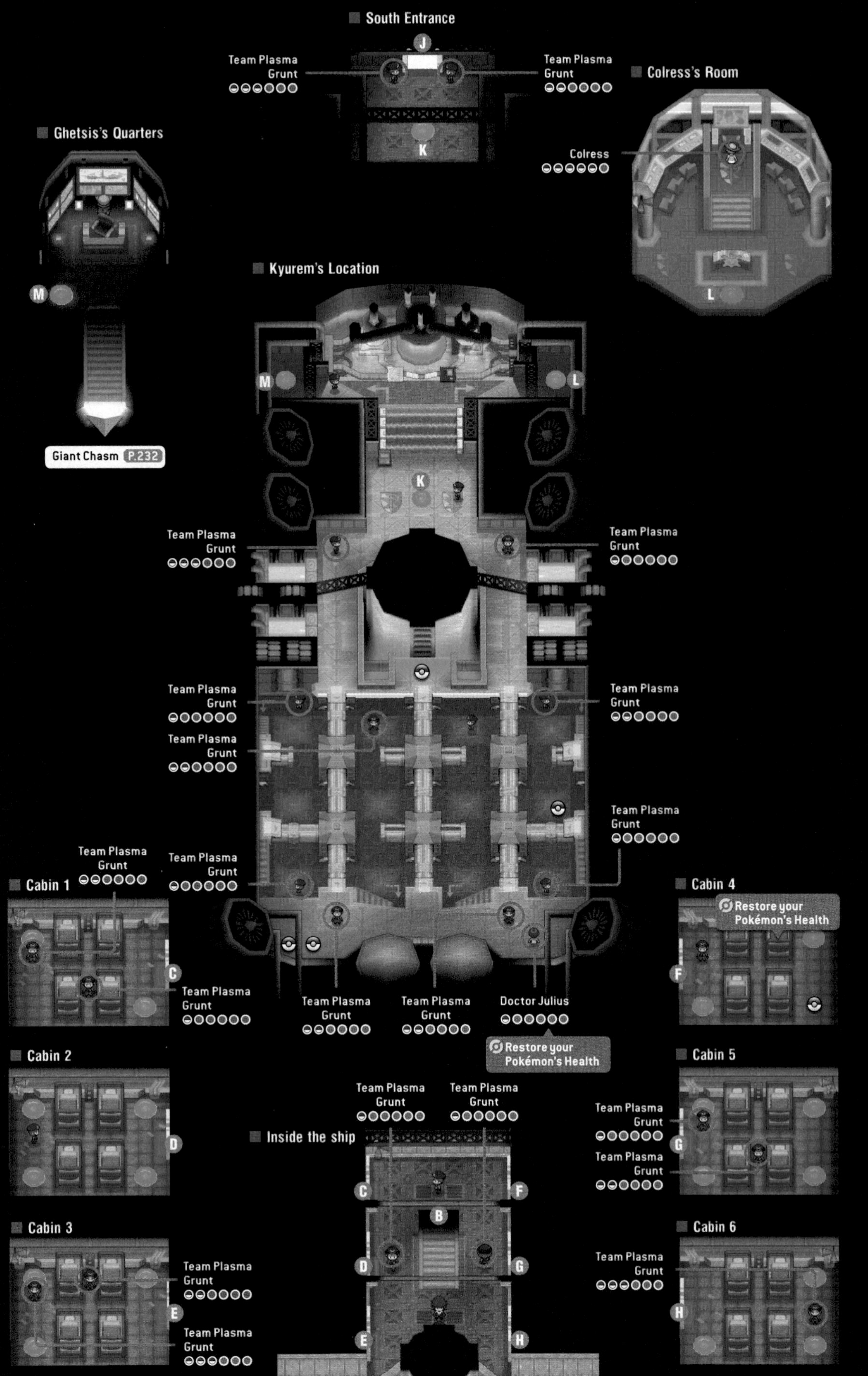
South Entrance
Team Plasma Grunt
Team Plasma Grunt
J
K
Colress's Room
Colress
L
Ghetsis's Quarters
M
Giant Chasm P.232
Kyurem's Location
M
L
K
Team Plasma Grunt
Team Plasma Grunt
Team Plasma Grunt
Team Plasma Grunt
Team Plasma Grunt
Team Plasma Grunt
Team Plasma Grunt
Cabin 1
Team Plasma Grunt
C
Team Plasma Grunt
Team Plasma Grunt
Team Plasma Grunt
Doctor Julius
Restore your Pokémon's Health
Cabin 4
Restore your Pokémon's Health
F
Cabin 2
D
Cabin 5
Team Plasma Grunt
Team Plasma Grunt
G
Team Plasma Grunt
Team Plasma Grunt
Inside the ship
C
F
B
D
G
E
H
Cabin 3
Team Plasma Grunt
E
Team Plasma Grunt
Cabin 6
Team Plasma Grunt
H

Step 1 Defeat Team Plasma with your rival

Hit the deck on ship, and Team Plasma Grunts will challenge you. Teach them a lesson they won't soon forget. Your rival will enter the ship through the north entrance chasing some cowardly Team Plasma Grunts. Follow him, and you'll enter the ship with him from the north entrance.

At first, you can't go inside the ship

You and your rival have to defeat the two Grunts at the north entrance before you can go inside the ship. Check whether the north entrance is blocked with a barrier, then go inside the ship.

Step 2 Step on red switches to deactivate barriers

At the north entrance, two Grunts are blocking the way. Challenge them for a Multi Battle with your rival. After you defeat them, step on four switches, two on each side, to deactivate the barrier at the back.

Listen to info from the ex-Team Plasma member

Go down from the deck, and you'll be spoken to by an ex-Team Plasma member who has infiltrated the Plasma Frigate. He'll tell you how to deactivate the barriers.

Step 3 Use the warp panels to step on four switches

Return to the deck, then go down again to explore all six cabins and step on warp panels. You'll eventually reach the red switch located near the north exit. Step on all four switches to deactivate the barrier.

Step 4 Check the bed to heal your Pokémon

Check the bed in cabin 4 on the east side of the ship and you can heal your Pokémon. You'll face many battles against Team Plasma Grunts in the Plasma Frigate. The bed will be your secret hideaway for restoring your Pokémon after they take hits in battle.

Step 5 Register Reshiram and Zekrom in your Pokédex

Go west inside the ship to cabin 2 and speak to Team Plasma at the back of the room. You'll be able to register the Legendary Pokémon Reshiram and Zekrom, which are said to have formed the Unova region, to your Pokédex.

Step 6 When you've warped out, you'll encounter Zinzolin and Kyurem

Deactivate the barrier at the north entrance and proceed. When you step on the warp panel, Zinzolin will be waiting for you. You'll see that Kyurem is trapped behind him and Zinzolin challenges you. Give the battle everything you've got!

Your rival's Pokémon is his evolved starter

In the Multi Battle against Zinzolin, your rival sends out his evolved starter Pokémon. Your rival will send out Emboar if you received Snivy, Samurott if you received Tepig, and Serperior if you received Oshawott.

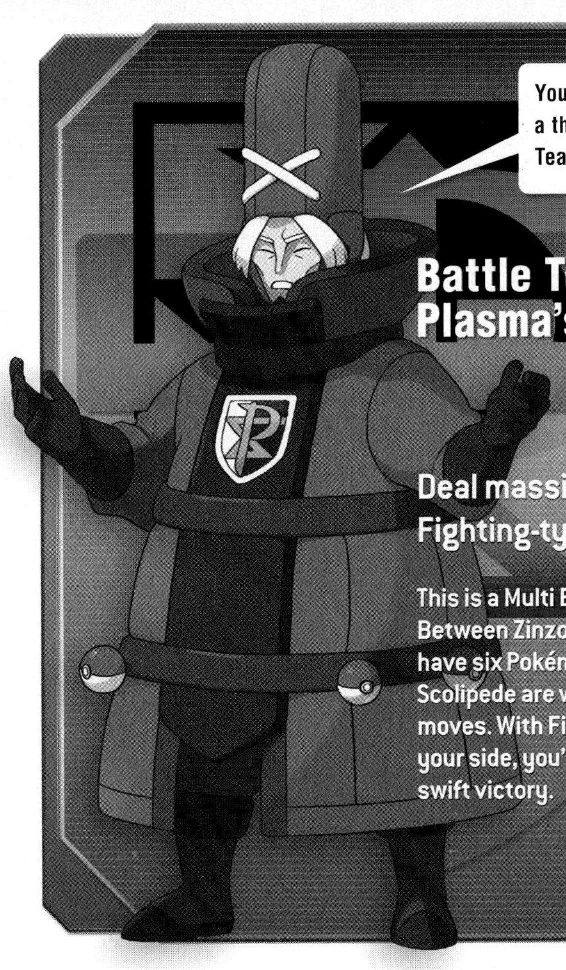

You could become a threat to Team Plasma.

Battle Team Plasma's Zinzolin! 3

Deal massive damage with Fighting-type Pokémon

This is a Multi Battle with your rival. Between Zinzolin and the Grunt, you'll have six Pokémon to face. All but Scolipede are weak to Fighting-type moves. With Fighting-type Pokémon on your side, you'll cruise to a swift victory.

Zinzolin's Pokémon

Pokémon	Lv.	Type	Weak to
Cryogonal	Lv. 48	Ice	Fire, Fighting, Rock, Steel
Cryogonal	Lv. 48	Ice	Fire, Fighting, Rock, Steel
Weavile ♂	Lv. 50	Dark, Ice	Fighting, Fire, Bug, Rock, Steel

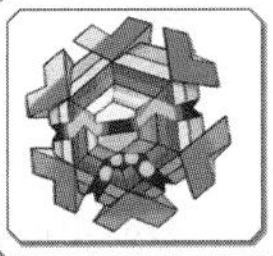

Grunt's Pokémon

Pokémon	Lv.	Type	Weak to
Liepard ♂	Lv. 45	Dark	Fighting, Bug
Watchog ♂	Lv. 45	Normal	Fighting
Scolipede ♂	Lv. 45	Bug, Poison	Fire, Flying, Psychic, Rock

Step 7 The Shadow Triad forces you off the ship

Although you bring Zinzolin to defeat, you're unable to retrieve the DNA Splicers. Zinzolin orders the Shadow Triad to appear and force you off the ship. After this, the Plasma Frigate flies away.

I'll let you take care of them, Shadow Triad!

Step 8 Use Fly to get back to Humilau City

Cheren will come to Route 21 and tell you that the Plasma Frigate headed for the Giant Chasm. To reach Route 22, you'll have to get back to Humilau City first (p. 206).

Why is Purrloin so important to your rival?

Your rival has been looking for his sister's Purrloin that was taken away. It's the Purrloin that his late grandfather caught for his sister. That's the reason he's putting all his effort into getting it back.

After visiting the Giant Chasm — The barrier blocks the way north

Get aboard the Plasma Frigate, take the south entrance, and head past the warp panels for the room where Kyurem is imprisoned. A barrier prevents you from reaching the north side. To deactivate it, you'll need a password and the Card Key.

More valuable nuggets of info from the ex-Team Plasma member

When you warp to the room where Kyurem is imprisoned, the ex-Team Plasma member gives you the scoop on how the rooms are structured and how to proceed.

After visiting the Giant Chasm — To proceed, step on switches to connect pipes

South of the room where Kyurem is imprisoned lies a pipe maze. Step on the switch above the pipe, and the pipe will extend or retract to allow you to go to different places. Stepping on these switches is your way forward.

After visiting the Giant Chasm — Battle everyone to obtain password clues

You'll hear password clues as you defeat Team Plasma. There are five clues in total. Defeat the Grunts to the south of the room where Kyurem is imprisoned to hear them all. With all five clues, you'll be able to figure out the password.

You're strong, so I'll tell you this. A hint for the password is...

The password is different in every adventure

The password to deactivate the barrier is different every time. It may consist of numbers or letters. Gather all the clues so you can figure out the password.

After visiting the Giant Chasm — Doctor Julius will heal your Pokémon

South of the room where Kyurem is imprisoned, you'll meet Doctor Julius. Defeat him in battle, and he'll heal your Pokémon whenever you ask. If your Pokémon are hurt, get the Doctor on the job!

You can't use the bed in the cabin

The stairs leading to the inside of the ship are blocked when you visit the Plasma Frigate through the Giant Chasm, so you won't be able to use the bed to heal your Pokémon.

After visiting the Giant Chasm — Obtain the Plasma Card

Defeat the female Grunt on the floor below the pipe maze to obtain the Plasma Card. She's at the back of the second row from the west. You'll need the Plasma Card as well as the password to deactivate the barrier, so make sure to get them both.

After visiting the Giant Chasm — Check the device and enter the password

Once you've obtained the password clues and the Plasma Card, check the device in front of the barrier. You'll see the password-entering display. Figure out the password from the clues and enter it. The barrier will be deactivated if the password is correct.

How to enter the password

Use the keyboard displayed on the Touch Screen to enter the password. It might be easiest to use the stylus. You could use the +Control Pad and the A Button to enter it instead.

After visiting the Giant Chasm

Approach Kyurem and Zinzolin will halt you

Deactivate the barrier and proceed. You'll find Kyurem in a cage in front of you. Approach Kyurem and Zinzolin will appear to stop you. This is the last battle against Zinzolin. You must defeat him no matter what to thwart his ambition.

You don't have the sense to know
when to quit, it seems.

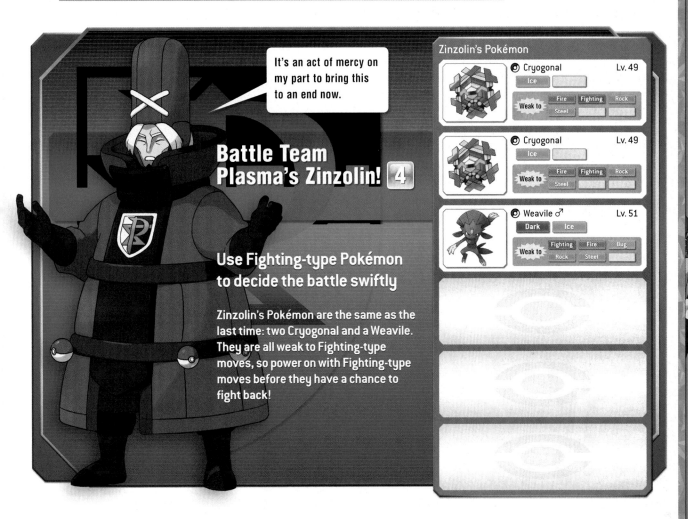

It's an act of mercy on my part to bring this to an end now.

Battle Team Plasma's Zinzolin! 4

Use Fighting-type Pokémon to decide the battle swiftly

Zinzolin's Pokémon are the same as the last time: two Cryogonal and a Weavile. They are all weak to Fighting-type moves, so power on with Fighting-type moves before they have a chance to fight back!

Zinzolin's Pokémon

Pokémon	Lv.	Type	Weak to
Cryogonal	Lv. 49	Ice	Fire, Fighting, Rock, Steel
Cryogonal	Lv. 49	Ice	Fire, Fighting, Rock, Steel
Weavile ♂	Lv. 51	Dark, Ice	Fighting, Fire, Bug, Rock, Steel

After the battle with Zinzolin

Go west to the warp panel

When you defeat Zinzolin, he makes some idle threats and then takes off. Pay no attention to him and just proceed. You can go east or west past Kyurem. Go east to take the warp panel first.

At first, you can't go west

You'll be stopped by Team Plasma if you try to pass Kyurem and go west. Who's on the west side of the ship? Go to Colress's room on the east side first and then you can go to the west side.

Colress has been waiting for you

Past the warp panel, you'll encounter Colress. As you may have guessed, he's a Team Plasma member. Apparently, he joined Team Plasma to research how to maximize a Pokémon's potential. Challenge him to battle!

Well now! Tell me if you have the answer I desire or not!

Team Plasma Battle Colress! 2

Use Fire- and Ground-type moves to attack

Colress's Pokémon are weak to Fire- and Ground-type moves, except for Beheeyem. Beheeyem will use powerful moves, such as Psychic and Energy Ball. Use Bug-, Ghost-, or Dark-type moves for supereffective damage and defeat it quickly.

Colress's Pokémon

Pokémon	Lv.	Type	Weak to
Magneton	Lv. 50	Electric, Steel	Ground, Fire, Fighting
Magnezone	Lv. 50	Electric, Steel	Ground, Fire, Fighting
Beheeyem ♂	Lv. 50	Psychic	Bug, Ghost, Dark
Metang	Lv. 50	Steel, Psychic	Fire, Ground
Klinklang	Lv. 52	Steel	Fire, Fighting, Ground

After the battle with Colress

First, defeat Colress, and then hear him out

Defeat Colress and he'll recognize your strengths. The question remains: when it comes to maximizing Pokémon's hidden power, which is stronger, Team Plasma's scientific approach, or the bond Pokémon share with their Trainers? He suggests you find out for yourself by using the warp panel on the other side.

You're a very strong Trainer indeed!
So let me ask you this!

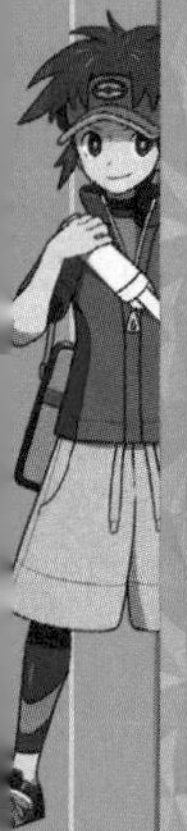

Go west in front of Kyurem

Leave Colress's room and head west. This time, you'll be able to reach the warp panel without Grunts interfering. Who's in the room on this side? You're about to find out...

Find out who's pulling the strings

Where do you warp to? You'll end up in Ghetsis's room. Ghetsis is frothing with fury at Colress for losing to you. You're about to find out that behind Team Plasma's evil deeds is the mastermind...called Ghetsis.

Defeated two years ago, but once again a threat

Ghetsis did many bad things to try to take over the Unova region two years ago. He departed after his defeat, but he's on the move again to fulfill his desire to rule the Unova region!

After the battle with Colress

Face the Shadow Triad's challenge

It seems that Ghetsis is planning to use Kyurem to rule the Unova region and force every person and Pokémon to buckle under to his reign. Out of nowhere, the Shadow Triad appears and challenges you.

Battle the First Shadow 2

The first of the triad

Use Fighting-type moves to steal the victory

In the first battle, you'll face two Pawniard and an Absol. Use Fighting-type moves, which are supereffective against all three of them. If you can muster some supereffective moves, you may be able to deny them the chance to counterattack, bringing this challenge to a swift conclusion.

Shadow Triad Pokémon

Pokémon	Lv.	Type	Weak to
Pawniard ♂	Lv. 49	Dark, Steel	Fighting, Fire, Ground
Pawniard ♂	Lv. 49	Dark, Steel	Fighting, Fire, Ground
Absol ♂	Lv. 51	Dark	Fighting, Bug

Battle the Second Shadow 2

The second of the triad

Fighting, Ghost, and Dark-type moves are effective

In the second battle against Shadow, you'll face two Pawniard and a Banette. Use Fighting-type moves against Pawniard, as you can deal four times the regular damage. Use Ghost- or Dark-type moves against Banette.

Shadow Triad Pokémon

Pokémon	Lv.	Type	Weak to
Pawniard ♂	Lv. 49	Dark, Steel	Fighting, Fire, Ground
Pawniard ♂	Lv. 49	Dark, Steel	Fighting, Fire, Ground
Banette ♂	Lv. 51	Ghost	Ghost, Dark

Battle the Third Shadow 2

The third of the triad

With Fighting- and Fire-type, land supereffective moves

In the third battle against Shadow, you'll face two Pawniard and an Accelgor. Use Fighting-type moves against Pawniard. Again, you can deal four times the regular damage. Fire-, Flying-, and Rock-type moves are effective against Accelgor.

Shadow Triad Pokémon

Pokémon	Lv.	Type	Weak to
Pawniard ♂	Lv. 49	Dark / Steel	Fighting, Fire, Ground
Pawniard ♂	Lv. 49	Dark / Steel	Fighting, Fire, Ground
Accelgor ♂	Lv. 51	Bug	Fire, Flying, Rock

After the battle with the Shadow Triad

Finally, the return of your rival's sister's Purrloin

Defeat all the members of the Shadow Triad, and Purrloin will finally be returned to your rival. It has evolved into Liepard and only listens to the Shadow Triad, but on the bright side, your rival's wish has finally come true.

After the battle with the Shadow Triad

South, south, south to the Giant Chasm

Ghetsis has vanished. While you were battling the Shadow Triad, he seems to have fled to the Giant Chasm. Give chase! Take the stairs to the south of the room, and you'll be able to reach the Giant Chasm (p. 235).

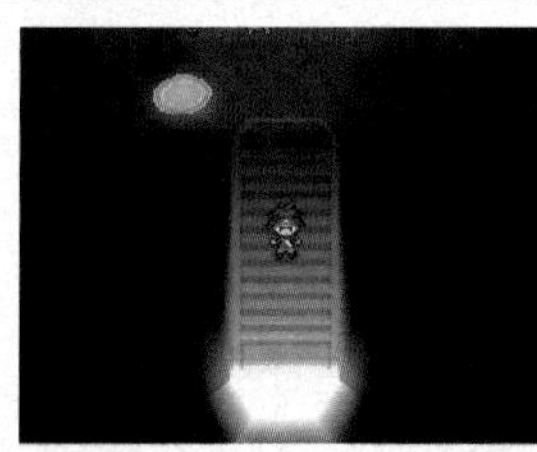

Have Doctor Julius heal your Pokémon

If your combat against the Shadow Triad damaged your Pokémon, return to the room where Kyurem is. At the dead end on the south side is Doctor Julius. Speak to him and have him heal your Pokémon.

Plasma Frigate

When playing *Pokémon White Version 2*

The Plasma Frigate is Team Plasma's hideout. Not only can it sail on the ocean, but it can also extend its wings to fly through the sky. With the power of the Legendary Dragon-type Pokémon Kyurem, it can launch ice that never melts from its cannon.

Field Moves Needed

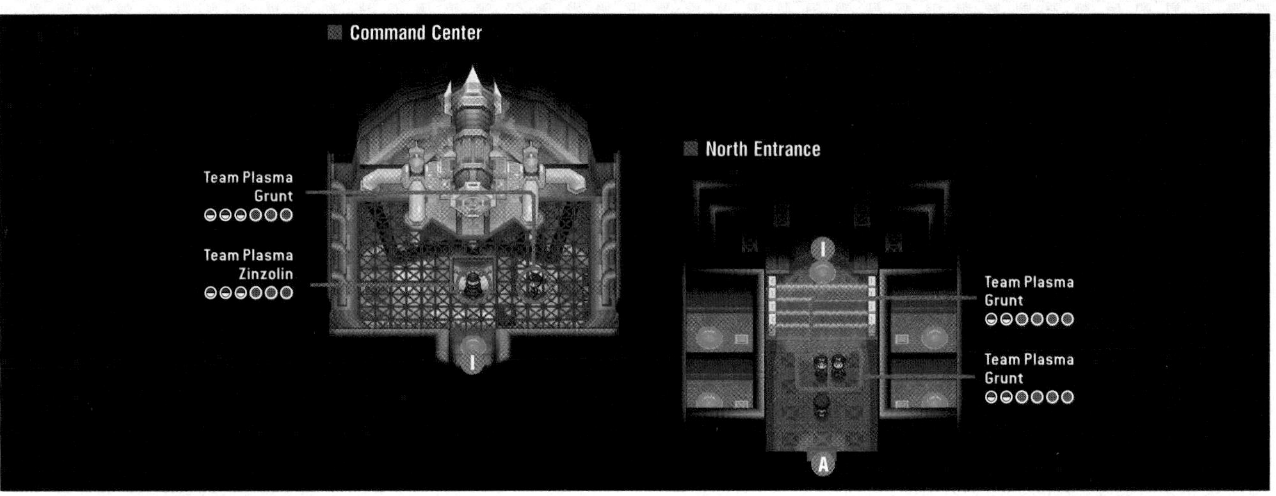

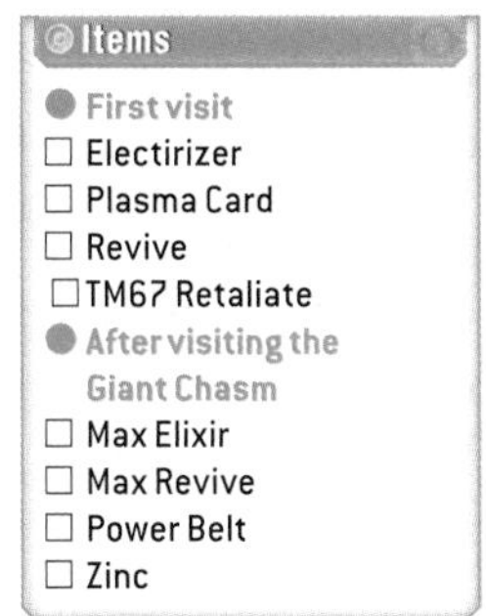

Items

- First visit
- ☐ Electirizer
- ☐ Plasma Card
- ☐ Revive
- ☐ TM67 Retaliate
- After visiting the Giant Chasm
- ☐ Max Elixir
- ☐ Max Revive
- ☐ Power Belt
- ☐ Zinc

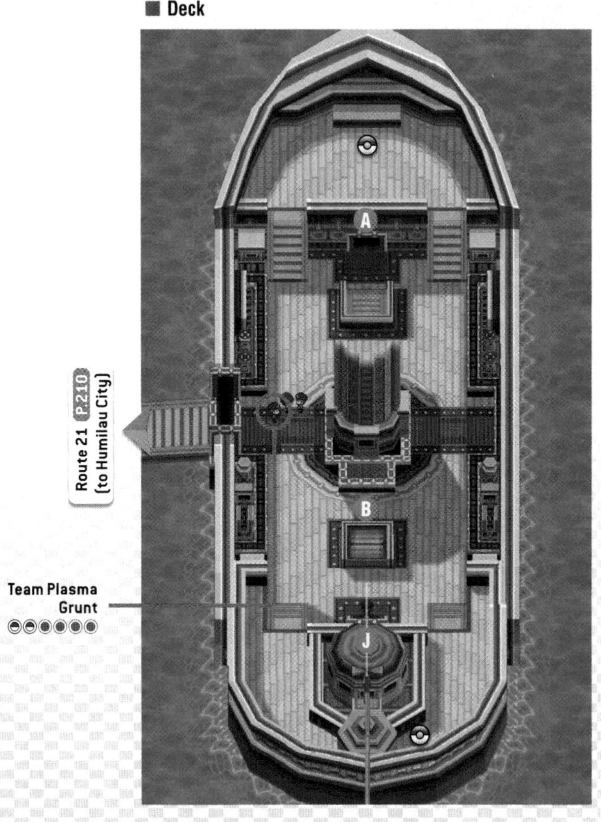

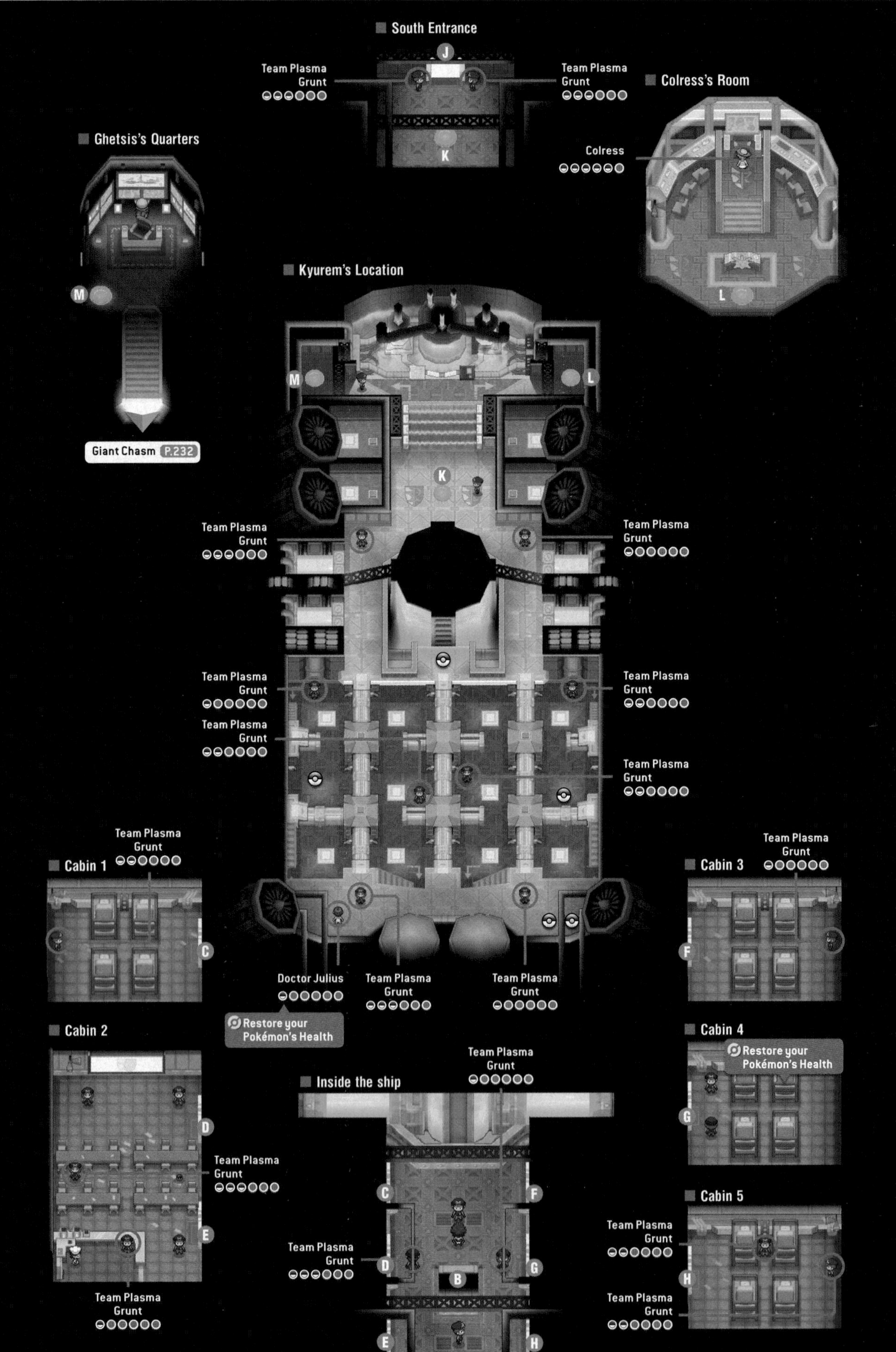
South Entrance
J
Team Plasma Grunt
Team Plasma Grunt
K
Colress's Room
Colress
L
Ghetsis's Quarters
M
Giant Chasm P.232
Kyurem's Location
M
L
K
Team Plasma Grunt
Team Plasma Grunt
Team Plasma Grunt
Team Plasma Grunt
Team Plasma Grunt
Team Plasma Grunt
Team Plasma Grunt
Cabin 1
C
Cabin 3
Team Plasma Grunt
F
Doctor Julius
Team Plasma Grunt
Team Plasma Grunt
Restore your Pokémon's Health
Cabin 2
D
Team Plasma Grunt
E
Team Plasma Grunt
Inside the ship
Team Plasma Grunt
C
F
Team Plasma Grunt
D
B
G
E
H
Cabin 4
Restore your Pokémon's Health
G
Cabin 5
Team Plasma Grunt
H
Team Plasma Grunt

Step 1 Defeat Team Plasma with your rival

When you board the ship, two Team Plasma Grunts will challenge you. After you beat them, your rival will enter the ship through the north door, chasing the Team Plasma Grunts as they run away. Follow him through the north entrance.

In the beginning, you cannot go inside the ship

You and Hugh will have to defeat the two Grunts together and get past the north entrance before you can go inside the ship. Unfortunately, the north entrance is blocked by a barrier. You'll need to look elsewhere to remove it.

Step 2 A barrier blocks the way

At the north entrance, two Grunts are blocking the way. Challenge them in a Multi Battle with your rival. After the battle, you'll find out that you need the Plasma Card as well as the password to deactivate the barrier that now blocks your path.

A former Team Plasma member gives you the scoop

Go down from the deck, and you'll meet a former member of Team Plasma who has infiltrated the Plasma Frigate. He'll tell you how to deactivate the ship's barriers.

Step 3 Battle everyone to obtain the password clues

Go back on the deck, then go down to explore all five cabins. Defeat the Team Plasma Grunts there and obtain password clues. There are five password clues altogether. Collect them all.

The password is different in every adventure

The password to deactivate the barrier is different every time. The password may consist of numbers or letters. Gather all the clues and figure out the password yourself.

Step 4 Check the bed to heal your Pokémon

Check the bed in cabin 4 on the east side of the ship and you can heal your Pokémon. You'll face many battles against Team Plasma Grunts in the Plasma Frigate. Use the bed to heal your Pokémon as they get hurt.

Step 5 Obtain the Plasma Card

Go west inside the ship to cabin 2, and speak to a female Grunt in the middle of the room. Defeat her and obtain the Plasma Card. You'll need the Plasma Card as well as the password to deactivate the barrier. Make sure to get them both.

Step 6 Register Reshiram and Zekrom in your Pokédex

Inside cabin 2, speak to the Team Plasma member on the north side of the room. You'll be able to register the Legendary Pokémon Reshiram and Zekrom, which are said to have formed the Unova region, in your Pokédex.

Step 7 Check the device and enter the password

Once you've obtained the password clues and the Plasma Card, check the device in front of the barrier. You'll see the password entering display. Figure out the password from the clues and enter it. The barrier will be deactivated if the password is correct.

Enter the password carefully

Enter the password using the keyboard displayed on the Touch Screen. Use the stylus to enter it carefully so you won't make a mistake. You can also use the +Control Pad and the A Button to enter it.

Step 8 After warping, you'll encounter Zinzolin and Kyurem

Deactivate the barrier at the north entrance and proceed. When you step on the warp panel, Zinzolin will be waiting for you. You see that Kyurem is trapped behind him and Zinzolin challenges you to a battle. Give it everything you've got.

Your rival's Pokémon is his evolved starter

In the Multi Battle against Zinzolin, your rival sends out his evolved starter Pokémon. Your rival will send out Emboar if you received Snivy, Samurott if you received Tepig, and Serperior if you received Oshawott.

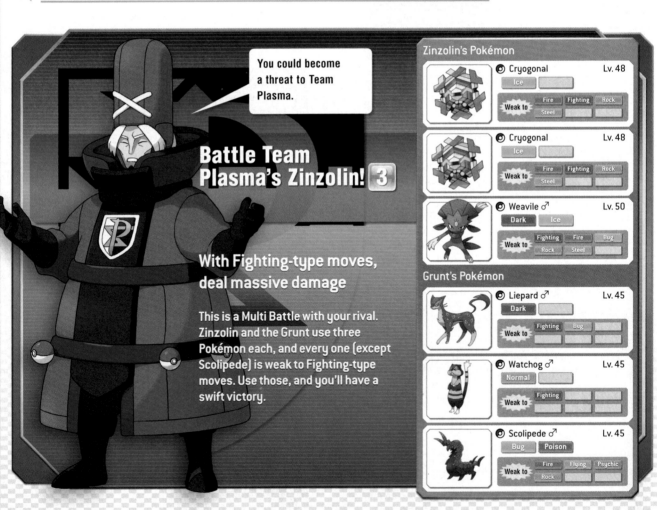

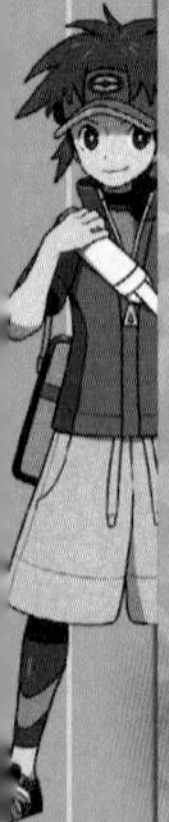

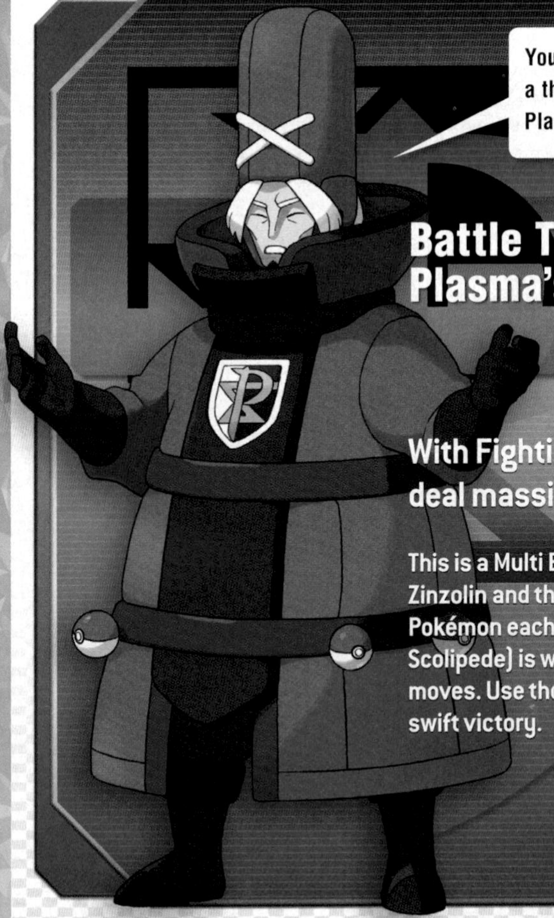

You could become a threat to Team Plasma.

Battle Team Plasma's Zinzolin! 3

With Fighting-type moves, deal massive damage

This is a Multi Battle with your rival. Zinzolin and the Grunt use three Pokémon each, and every one (except Scolipede) is weak to Fighting-type moves. Use those, and you'll have a swift victory.

Zinzolin's Pokémon

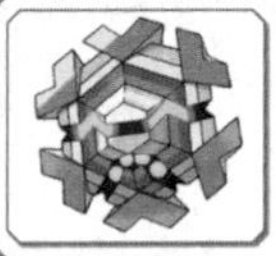

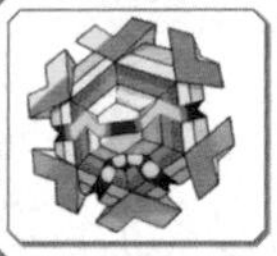

Pokémon	Lv.	Type	Weak to
Cryogonal	Lv. 48	Ice	Fire, Fighting, Rock, Steel
Cryogonal	Lv. 48	Ice	Fire, Fighting, Rock, Steel
Weavile ♂	Lv. 50	Dark, Ice	Fighting, Fire, Bug, Rock, Steel

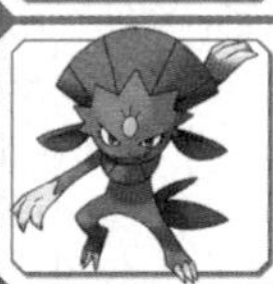

Grunt's Pokémon

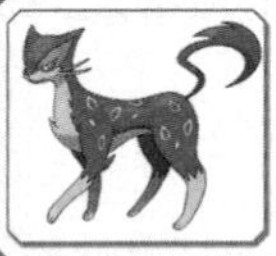

Pokémon	Lv.	Type	Weak to
Liepard ♂	Lv. 45	Dark	Fighting, Bug
Watchog ♂	Lv. 45	Normal	Fighting
Scolipede ♂	Lv. 45	Bug, Poison	Fire, Flying, Psychic, Rock

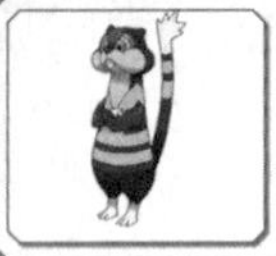

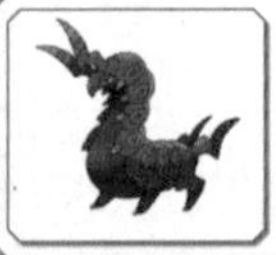

Step 9 The Shadow Triad forces you off the ship

After you defeat Zinzolin, however, you fail to retrieve the DNA Splicers. Zinzolin orders the Shadow Triad to appear and make you get off the ship. After that, the Plasma Frigate flies away into the air.

Why is your rival looking for Purrloin?

Your rival has been looking for his sister's Purrloin that was taken away. He finally tells you that his late grandfather caught the Purrloin for his sister, and that's why he's putting all his effort into getting it back.

Step 10 Use Fly to go back to Humilau City

Cheren will come to Route 21 and tell you that the Plasma Frigate headed for the Giant Chasm. To get to Route 22, you'll have to go back to Humilau City first (p. 206).

After visiting the Giant Chasm: Step on red switches to deactivate barriers

Get on board the Plasma Frigate, take the south entrance, and head for the room past the warp panels where Kyurem is imprisoned. A barrier blocks you from going farther north. To deactivate the barrier, you'll have to step on four switches, two on each side.

Oh! I nearly forgot to tell you!
This floor is a maze of pipes.

More information from the former Team Plasma member

When you warp out to the room where Kyurem is imprisoned, the former member of Team Plasma will speak to you again. He tells you how the rooms are structured and how to proceed.

After visiting the Giant Chasm: Step on the switches and connect pipes to proceed

South of the room where Kyurem is imprisoned is a pipe maze. Step on the switch over a pipe, and the pipe will extend or retract to allow you to go to different places. Step on these switches to proceed.

After visiting the Giant Chasm: Use the warp panels to step on four switches

On the floor below the pipe maze are warp panels, which will eventually lead you to the red switches that deactivate the barrier blocking the room where Kyurem is. Step on all four switches to deactivate the barrier.

A barrier was deactivated!

After visiting the Giant Chasm: Doctor Julius will heal your Pokémon

To the south of the room where Kyurem is imprisoned is Doctor Julius. If you talk to him after defeating him in a Pokémon battle, he'll heal your Pokémon every time. If your Pokémon are hurt, come see Doctor Julius.

No rest for the weary

The stairway leading to the inside of the ship is blocked when you visit the Plasma Frigate through the Giant Chasm. The cabin full of beds is inside, so you can't use them to rest and heal your Pokémon.

After visiting the Giant Chasm

Approach Kyurem and Zinzolin will stop you

Deactivate the barrier and proceed. You'll find Kyurem in the cage in front of you. Approach Kyurem and Zinzolin will come up from behind to stop you. This is the last battle against Zinzolin. You must defeat him no matter what to thwart his ambition.

You don't have the sense to know when to quit, it seems.

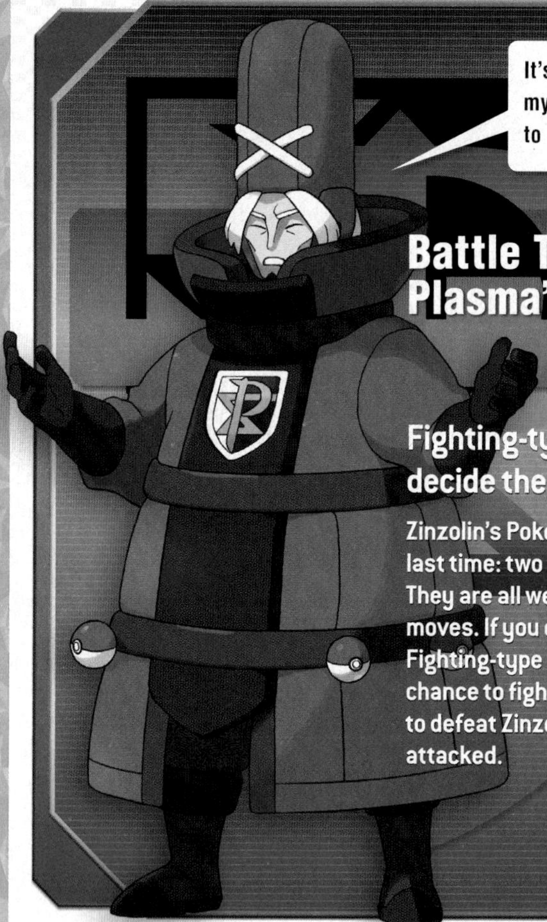

It's an act of mercy on my part to bring this to an end now.

Battle Team Plasma's Zinzolin! 4

Fighting-type moves can decide the battle swiftly

Zinzolin's Pokémon are the same as the last time: two Cryogonal and a Weavile. They are all weak to Fighting-type moves. If you can attack his team with Fighting-type moves before they have a chance to fight back, you might be able to defeat Zinzolin without even getting attacked.

Zinzolin's Pokémon

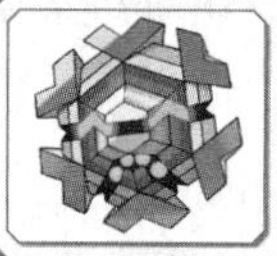

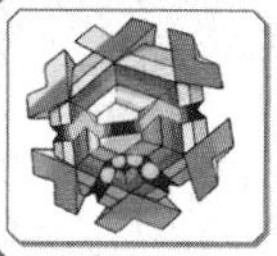

Pokémon	Lv.	Type	Weak to
Cryogonal	Lv. 49	Ice	Fire, Fighting, Rock, Steel
Cryogonal	Lv. 49	Ice	Fire, Fighting, Rock, Steel
Weavile ♂	Lv. 51	Dark, Ice	Fighting, Fire, Bug, Rock, Steel

After the battle with Zinzolin

Go east to take the warp panel

When you defeat Zinzolin, he'll make some vague threats and leave. Pay no attention to him. Just proceed. You can go east or west past Kyurem. Go east to take the warp panel first.

In the beginning, you cannot go west

Team Plasma will stop you if you try to go west past Kyurem. Who's on the west side of the ship? Go to Colress's room on the east side first and then you can go to the west side.

After the battle with Zinzolin

Colress has been waiting for you

Past the warp panel, Colress is waiting for you. As you may have guessed, he is a member of Team Plasma. Apparently, he joined Team Plasma to research how to bring out the full power of Pokémon. Challenge Colress.

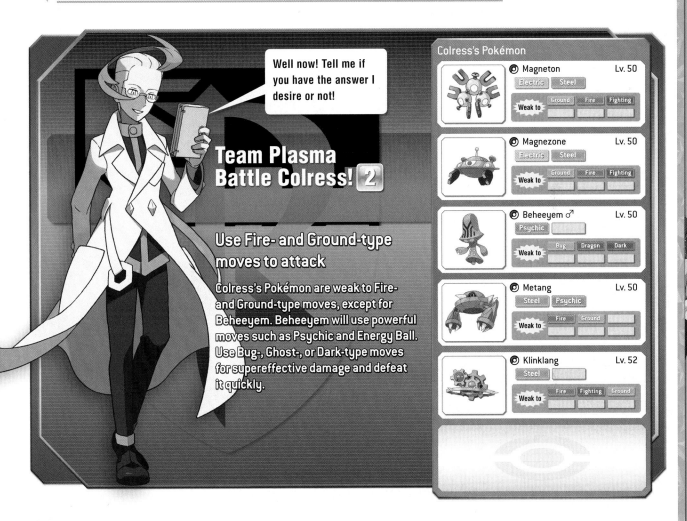

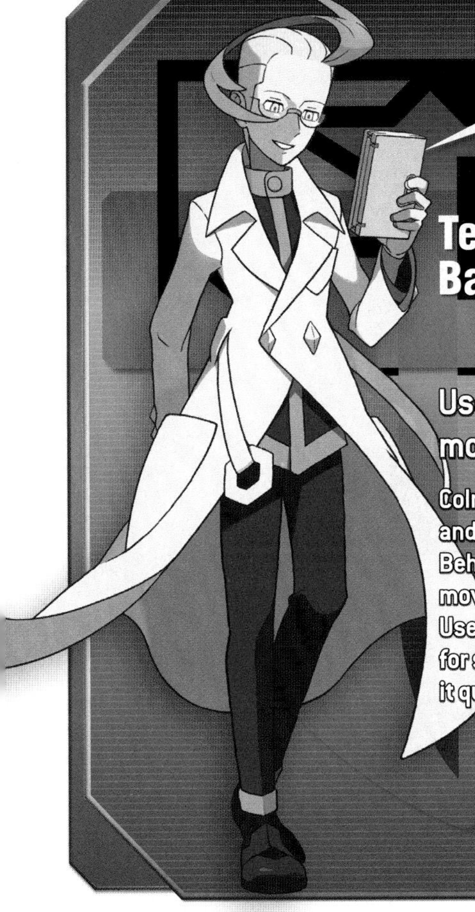

Well now! Tell me if you have the answer I desire or not!

Team Plasma Battle Colress! 2

Use Fire- and Ground-type moves to attack

Colress's Pokémon are weak to Fire- and Ground-type moves, except for Beheeyem. Beheeyem will use powerful moves such as Psychic and Energy Ball. Use Bug-, Ghost-, or Dark-type moves for supereffective damage and defeat it quickly.

Colress's Pokémon

Pokémon	Lv.	Type	Weak to
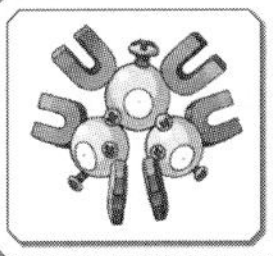 Magneton	Lv. 50	Electric, Steel	Ground, Fire, Fighting
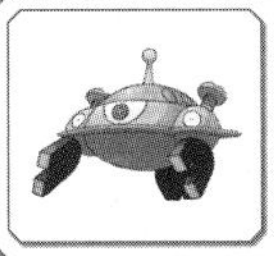 Magnezone	Lv. 50	Electric, Steel	Ground, Fire, Fighting
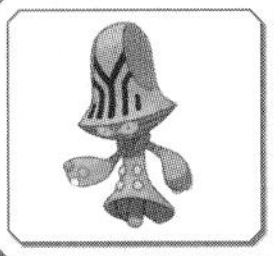 Beheeyem ♂	Lv. 50	Psychic	Bug, Dragon, Dark
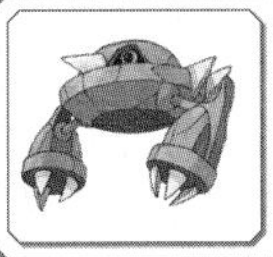 Metang	Lv. 50	Steel, Psychic	Fire, Ground
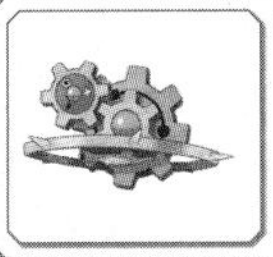 Klinklang	Lv. 52	Steel	Fire, Fighting, Ground

After the battle with Colress

Listen to what Colress has to say after you defeat him

Defeat Colress and he'll recognize your strengths. Which method is better at drawing forth the power hidden in Pokémon: Team Plasma's science or the bond with their Trainers? He suggests that you find out yourself by taking the warp panel on the other side.

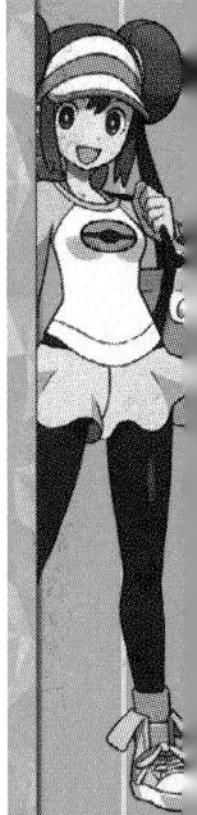

Go west in front of Kyurem

Head west after leaving Colress's room. You'll be able to reach the warp panel without getting stopped by Grunts this time. Who's in the room on this side? Step on the warp panel to find out...

The true leader of Team Plasma: none other than Ghetsis!

When you step on the warp panel, you'll find yourself in the presence of the man who's been behind Team Plasma's schemes the whole time: it's Ghetsis! He's furious that Colress lost to you, but his ambitious plans are still in motion...

Still pulling the strings, even after his defeat two years ago

Ghetsis did many bad things during his attempt to rule the Unova region two years ago. He was defeated by a powerful Trainer and got away, but he's back to fulfill his desire to rule.

After the battle with Colress

Take on the Shadow Triad's challenge

It seems Ghetsis is planning to use Kyurem to rule the Unova region and force every person and Pokémon to submit to his reign! At his command, the Shadow Triad appears out of nowhere and challenges you.

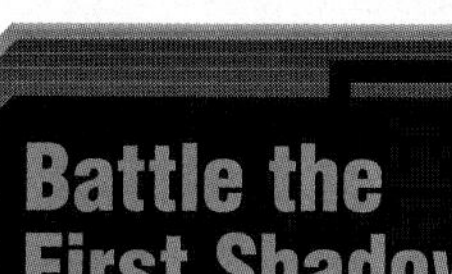

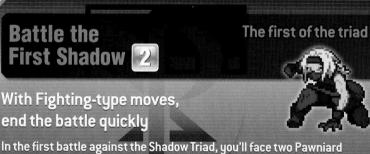

Battle the First Shadow 2

The first of the triad

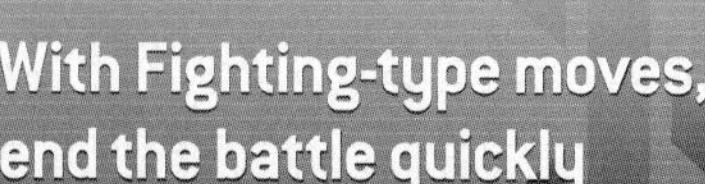

With Fighting-type moves, end the battle quickly

In the first battle against the Shadow Triad, you'll face two Pawniard and an Absol. Use Fighting-type moves, which are supereffective against all of them. Use supereffective moves that give no chance of counterattack for a swift victory.

Shadow Triad Pokémon

Pokémon	Lv.	Type	Weak to
Pawniard ♂	Lv. 49	Dark, Steel	Fighting, Fire, Ground
Pawniard ♂	Lv. 49	Dark, Steel	Fighting, Fire, Ground
Absol ♂	Lv. 51	Dark	Fighting, Bug

Battle the Second Shadow 2

The second of the triad

Fighting-, Ghost-, and Dark-type moves are effective

In the second battle against the Shadow Triad, you'll face two Pawniard and a Banette. Use Fighting-type moves against Pawniard, which deal four times the regular damage! They don't work against Banette, though—you'll have to switch to Ghost- or Dark-type moves.

Battle the Third Shadow 2

The third of the triad

With Fighting- and Fire-type moves, land supereffective damage

In the third battle against the Shadow Triad, you'll face two Pawniard and an Accelgor. Use Fighting-type moves against Pawniard, which again deal four times the regular damage! Fire-, Flying-, and Rock-type moves are a good choice against Accelgor.

After battling the Shadow Triad: Finally, your rival reclaims his sister's Pokémon

Defeat all three members of the Shadow Triad, and they will finally return the Pokémon your rival has been looking for! His sister's Purrloin has evolved into a Liepard, and it only listens to the Shadow Triad, but your rival's wish has finally come true.

After battling the Shadow Triad: Make your way south to the Giant Chasm

When the battle ends, Ghetsis has disappeared. He must have headed for the Giant Chasm while you were distracted. Go after him! Take the stairs to the south of the room and you'll be able to go to the Giant Chasm (p. 235).

Have Doctor Julius heal your Pokémon

Your Pokémon have probably been hurt in the battles against the Shadow Triad. Go back to the room where Kyurem is. At the dead end on the south side is Doctor Julius. Speak to him and have your Pokémon healed.

Giant Chasm

The Giant Chasm is a crater-shaped cave, with a verdant forest covering the floor of the crater. The residents of Lacunosa Town fear the monster hiding here. You can go to Route 23 from the west side of the cave.

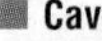

Cave

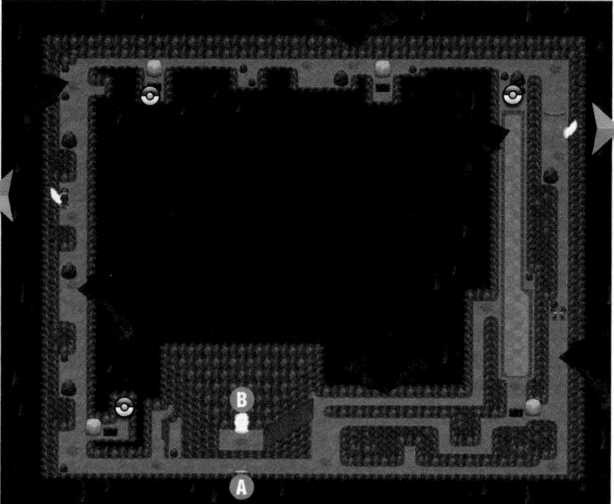

Route 23 P.238 (to Pokémon League)

Route 22 P.207 (to Humilau City)

Entrance

Route 13 P.185 (to Lacunosa Town)

Clefairy
Normal
ABILITIES
● Cute Charm
● Magic Guard

Items

First visit
- ☐ Max Repel
- ☐ Max Revive
- ☐ Moon Stone
- ☐ Razor Claw
- ☐ Star Piece
- ☐ TM13 Ice Beam
- ☐ Yellow Shard

After visiting the Plasma Frigate
- ☐ Carbos
- ☐ PP Up
- ☐ Star Piece
- ☐ Sun Stone
- ☐ TM03 Psyshock

After the Hall of Fame
- ☐ DNA Splicers

Entrance

Tall Grass	
Clefairy	○
Delibird	△
Lunatone	○
Pelipper	○
Solrock	○
Tangela	◎
Vanillish	○

Tall Grass (rustling)	
Audino	◎
Clefable	△
Tangrowth	△
Vanilluxe	△

Dark Grass	
Clefairy	○
Delibird	△
Lunatone	○
Pelipper	○
Solrock	○
Tangela	◎
Vanillish	○

Cave / Cave Depths

Cave	
Clefairy	○
Delibird	△
Lunatone	○
Piloswine	○
Sneasel	○
Solrock	○
Vanillish	○

Cave (dust cloud)	
Excadrill	◎

Water Surface	
Basculin (Blue-Striped Form) ○	◎
Basculin (Red-Striped Form) ●	◎
Seel	◎

Water Surface (ripples)	
Basculin (Blue-Striped Form) ●	◎
Basculin (Red-Striped Form) ○	◎
Dewgong	○
Seel ○	◎

After the Hall of Fame

Fishing	
Basculin (Blue-Striped Form) ○	◎
Basculin (Red-Striped Form) ●	◎
Poliwag	◎

Fishing (ripples)	
Basculin (Blue-Striped Form) ●	◎
Basculin (Red-Striped Form) ○	◎
Poliwhirl	◎
Poliwrath	△

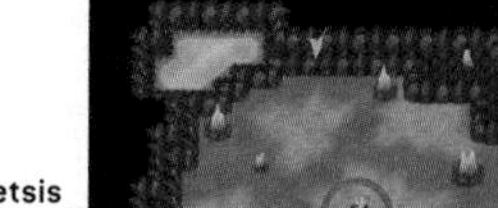

● Crater Forest at the Giant Chasm has a Hidden Grotto. Find it!

Cave Depths ②

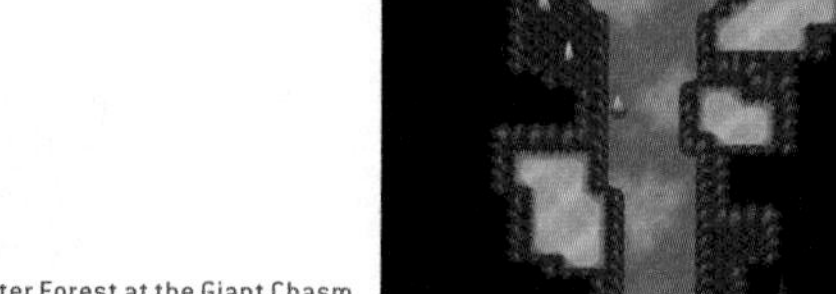

Cave Depths ①

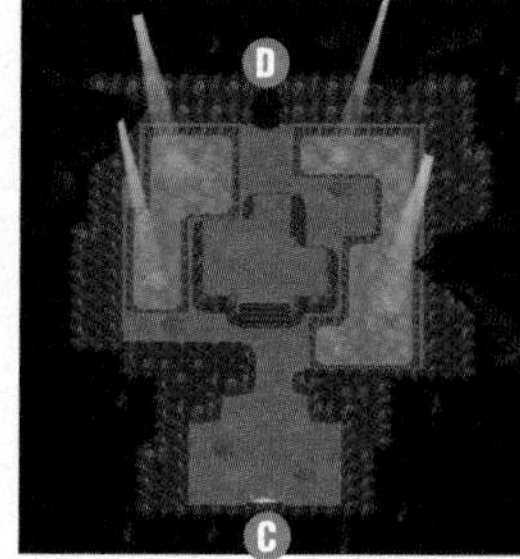

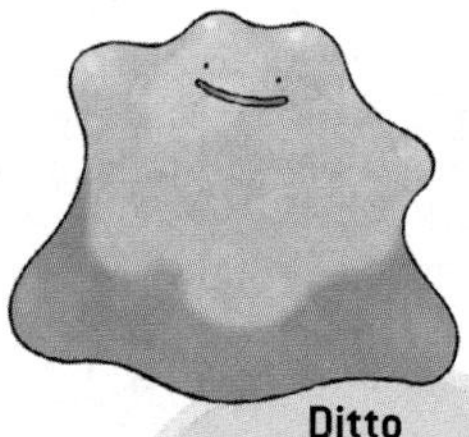

Ditto
Normal
ABILITY
● Limber

■ Crater Forest

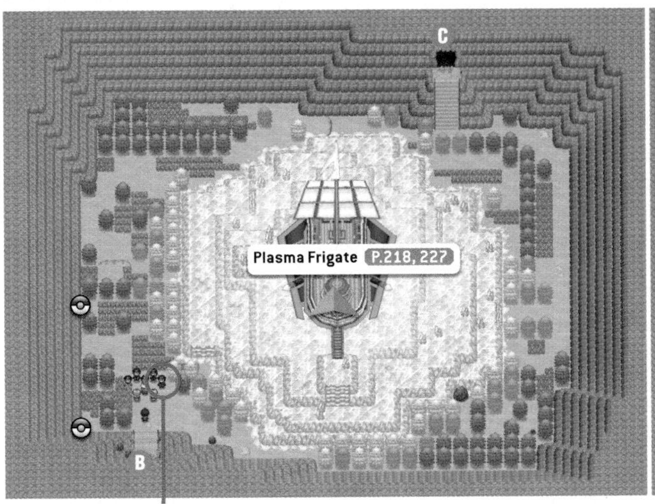

Team Plasma Grunt

■ Crater Forest (after battling Ghetsis)

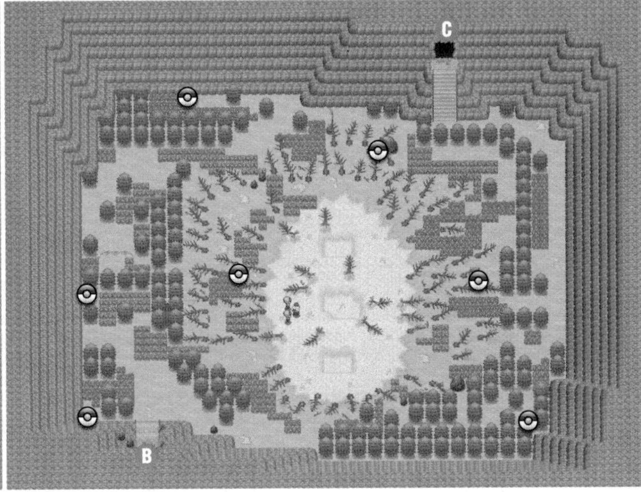

Crater Forest

Tall Grass	
Clefairy	○
Delibird	△
Ditto	○
Lunatone	○
Metang	○
Piloswine	◎
Solrock	○

Tall Grass (rustling)	
Audino	◎
Clefable	△
Mamoswine	△
Metagross	△

Dark Grass	
Clefairy	○
Delibird	△
Ditto	○
Lunatone	○
Metang	○
Piloswine	◎
Solrock	○

Hidden Grotto	
Clefairy	◎
Ditto	△
Metang	○
Sneasel	○

Step 1 Your rival appears when you enter the cave

Enter the cave, head south, and you'll encounter some members of Team Plasma. Your rival will show up and attempt to battle Team Plasma, but an ex-member of Team Plasma, acting as a spy, will use his wits to chase Team Plasma off. After this, continue south.

An ex-member of Team Plasma will help you out

Just like on the Plasma Frigate, an ex-member of Team Plasma will help you out here. While your rival was suspicious at first, it looks like he's starting to come around to them.

Step 2 Go outside and push the boulder using Strength

First, use Strength to move the boulders found inside the cave so you can pick up items. In the cave, head south as far as you can and then west, and you'll find an exit that leads to Route 13. Then, follow Route 13, and move the boulder found on the route (p. 187).

A shortcut to Lacunosa Town opens up

Fill the hole on Route 13 with the boulder to create a shortcut from the Giant Chasm to Lacunosa Town. When you need to heal your Pokémon or stock up on items, head back to Lacunosa Town.

Step 3 You can't get to Route 23 yet

Head west as far as you can go and then proceed north to find the exit that leads outside. However, some members of Team Plasma are blocking the exit. It leads to Route 23, but you can't get outside with Team Plasma blocking the way. Instead, keep exploring the cave for now.

Step 4 After collecting all the items, move on to Crater Forest

Explore every nook and cranny of the cave to collect all of the items. When you're done, head back to the south part of the cave. From the area that leads back to the entrance, go north and descend the stairs to find a hole that leads to Crater Forest. From there, venture north to Crater Forest.

Step 5 Rood is trying to convince members of Team Plasma

In Crater Forest, you'll encounter Rood, who used to be a member of Team Plasma. Rood is trying to explain to the members of Team Plasma that Ghetsis's real plan is to take over the Unova region, and that his talk about liberating Pokémon is nothing more than an excuse. Unfortunately, none of the members of Team Plasma seem to believe him.

Learn about your rival's missing Pokémon

Rood informs you that one of the Shadow Triad has the Purrloin that your rival has been searching for. In thanks, your rival promises to help Rood absolve his guilt.

Step 6 Defeat the members of Team Plasma who won't listen

Rood's attempt to avoid conflict by convincing the Team Plasma members of their misguided beliefs is a failure. You and your rival will have to battle the Team Plasma Grunts and defeat them.

We're going to crush you
along with the traitors!

Step 7 Rood gives you a Max Revive

Defeat the Team Plasma Grunts, and Rood will give you a Max Revive. Use it on a Pokémon that fainted to recover its HP and PP fully. It can't be purchased at Poké Marts, so choose the best time to use it.

Trainer obtained Max Revives!

Step 8 Move across the ice-covered ground and board the Plasma Frigate

After you defeat some of the Grunts, more will come to challenge you. However, Rood will take them on for you. Slide across the ice-covered ground to make your way to the Plasma Frigate and get on board (p. 218, 227).

Proceed carefully across the frozen ground

On the ice, you'll continue sliding in the direction you moved until you hit an obstacle. You can't change direction as you slide. Examine your surroundings and think carefully about which direction you need to go in order to reach your goal.

After investigating the Plasma Frigate

From the northern entrance, proceed to the deepest part of the area

Exit Ghetsis's cabin on the Plasma Frigate to reach the southern part of Crater Forest. From there, slide north across the ice, and then head east to descend from the mountain of ice. Head north and climb the stairs to enter the deepest part of the area.

You can collect the items later

There are lots of items for you to find in Crater Forest. However, as long as the Plasma Frigate is around, you won't be able to get some of them. You can come back and collect all of the items after you defeat Ghetsis, so ignore them for now and proceed deeper into the area.

After investigating the Plasma Frigate

Ghetsis is attempting to cover the Unova region in ice!

Enter the cave and proceed to Cave Depths② to find Ghetsis standing in the center of the area. Ghetsis proclaims that from this location, he'll summon Kyurem and cover the entire Unova region in ice. This means big trouble for the Unova region!

I'll freeze you solid right here
so you can watch my glorious ascent!

After investigating the Plasma Frigate

N and Zekrom (Reshiram) come to help

Kyurem unleashes the move Glaciate, but something blasts it away. It's N, flying down from the sky on the back of Zekrom (Reshiram) to save you from disaster! N sensed the pain Kyurem was enduring and has come to help.

After investigating the Plasma Frigate

Kyurem fuses with Zekrom (Reshiram)

Ghetsis had predicted that N would show up. He pulls out the DNA Splicers and uses them to fuse Kyurem with Zekrom (Reshiram). Use all the strength you've got to defeat Black Kyurem (White Kyurem)!

You can't catch Kyurem

Due to the disrupting signals Ghetsis emits from his cane, you can't catch the Kyurem that is fused with Zekrom (Reshiram). Using all your Trainer skills in battle against Kyurem is the only way to save it!

When playing *Pokémon Black Version 2*

Defeat Black Kyurem!

Kyurem Lv. 55

Dragon | Ice

ABILITY ● Teravolt

MOVES ● DragonBreath, Slash, Fusion Bolt, Freeze Shock

Weak to: Fighting, Rock, Dragon, Steel

Black Kyurem will do its best to thrash you with powerful attacks. It's a good idea to use Pokémon that can reduce the damage taken. Fire-, Ice-, and Steel-type Pokémon take only half damage from Ice-type moves.

Defeat White Kyurem!

When playing *Pokémon White Version 2*

White Kyurem has high Sp. Atk. Its Ice Burn and Fusion Flare moves can inflict massive damage. Use a Fire- or Water-type Pokémon in the battle and it will only take half damage.

Kyurem	Lv. 55
Type	Dragon, Ice
ABILITY	Turboblaze
MOVES	DragonBreath, Slash, Fusion Flare, Ice Burn
Weak to	Fighting, Rock, Dragon, Steel

After defeating Kyurem — An enraged Ghetsis challenges you to battle

Defeat Black Kyurem (White Kyurem), and it will separate back into Zekrom (Reshiram) and Kyurem. Kyurem will then vanish. Enraged after suddenly having his ambitions thwarted, Ghetsis comes directly at you, looking for a battle.

But first, I'll take down this disgusting Trainer with my own hand!

After defeating Kyurem — Sensing trouble, N heals your Pokémon

Right before Ghetsis starts the battle, N will heal all your Pokémon. Even if your Pokémon were injured in the battle against Black Kyurem (White Kyurem), they'll be fully recovered for the next battle. Don't hold back for this battle!

N: ...!

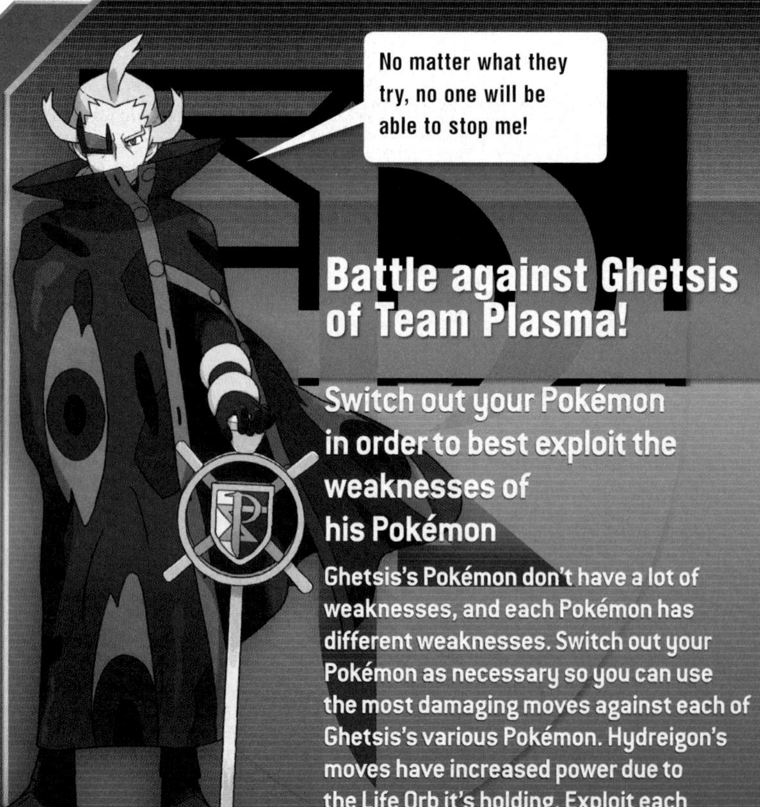

No matter what they try, no one will be able to stop me!

Battle against Ghetsis of Team Plasma!

Switch out your Pokémon in order to best exploit the weaknesses of his Pokémon

Ghetsis's Pokémon don't have a lot of weaknesses, and each Pokémon has different weaknesses. Switch out your Pokémon as necessary so you can use the most damaging moves against each of Ghetsis's various Pokémon. Hydreigon's moves have increased power due to the Life Orb it's holding. Exploit each Pokémon's weakness to the best of your ability. To your victory!

Ghetsis's Pokémon

Pokémon	Lv.	Type	Weak to
Cofagrigus ♂	Lv. 50	Ghost	Ghost, Dark
Seismitoad ♂	Lv. 50	Water, Ground	Grass
Drapion ♂	Lv. 50	Poison, Dark	Ground
Eelektross ♂	Lv. 50	Electric	Ground◆
Toxicroak ♂	Lv. 50	Poison, Fighting	Psychic, Ground, Flying
Hydreigon ♂	Lv. 52	Dark, Dragon	Ice, Fighting, Bug, Dragon

◆The damage may change depending on the effects of this Pokémon's Ability.

After defeating Ghetsis

The Shadow Triad takes Ghetsis away

Even after being defeated utterly, Ghetsis is still rambling on about his ambitions. However, Team Plasma is no more. Ghetsis appears to have lost his senses, and the Shadow Triad takes him away. At this moment, your conflict with Team Plasma is finally over.

After defeating Ghetsis

N and Zekrom (Reshiram) depart

N tells you to head to the Pokémon League before climbing aboard Zekrom (Reshiram) and flying away. Just then, your rival arrives. He's there to make sure that the battle with Team Plasma is truly over.

After defeating Ghetsis

Your rival will tell you how to get to Route 23

After talking to your rival about the Pokémon League, he gives you some words of encouragement. He then tells you that you can reach Route 23 through the cave in the Giant Chasm, so back there you go to take on the Pokémon League!

Victory Road and the Pokémon League are just past there!

Your rival decides to go home

Your rival has been with you throughout this journey. Now that he's recovered his sister's lost Purrloin, he's going back to Aspertia City to return it to her.

Gather items in Crater Forest

When you leave the depths of the cave and enter Crater Forest, you'll discover that the Plasma Frigate has already departed. When you first visited this area, you weren't able to obtain certain items because the Plasma Frigate was in the way. Now that it's gone, get busy gathering the goods.

After defeating Ghetsis

It may be a good idea to head back to Lacunosa Town

If you want to recover your Pokémon and do some shopping at the Poké Mart, head back to Lacunosa Town before continuing your adventure. If you filled the hole on Route 13 by pushing the boulder into it, you can quickly return to Lacunosa Town.

You can heal your Pokémon on Route 23

Soon after entering Route 23, you'll find a house where you can get your Pokémon all fixed up. If you don't have to pick up any items at the Poké Mart, head straight for Route 23.

Leave the cave and head to Route 23

The Pokémon League is located at the end of Victory Road, which can be reached by going through Route 23. In order to challenge the Elite Four and the Champion, first make your way to Route 23 (p. 238).

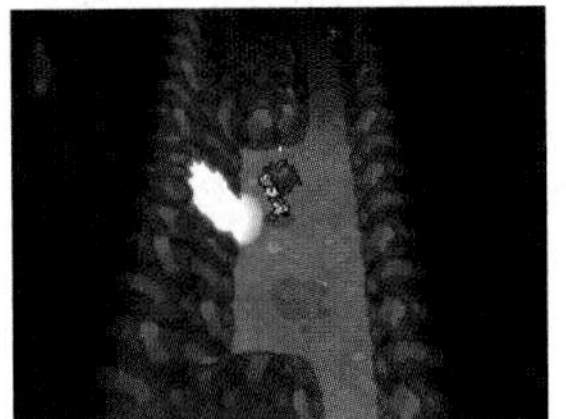

Route 23

Route 23 is a long road stretching from east to west. On the east side, the path meanders alongside a river, running between the water and the cliff face. At the western end, small paths wend throughout the labyrinthine stand of trees. Continue north and you'll arrive at Victory Road.

Items

- First visit
- ☐ Calcium
- ☐ Full Heal
- ☐ Green Shard
- ☐ Heart Scale
- ☐ HP Up
- ☐ Iron
- ☐ Max Potion
- ☐ Repeat Ball
- ☐ Star Piece
- ☐ TM05 Roar
- ☐ TM12 Taunt
- ☐ TM35 Flamethrower
- After defeating Pokémon Ranger Steve
- ☐ Sitrus Berry
- After defeating Pokémon Ranger Lena
- ☐ Sitrus Berry

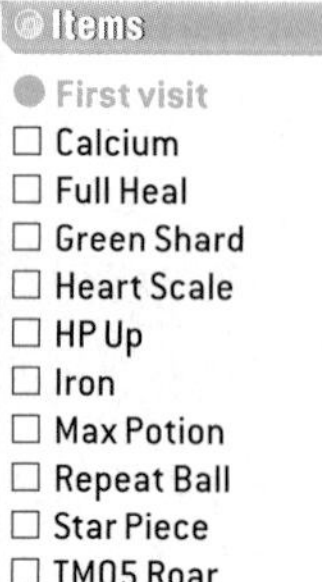

Tall Grass		
Amoonguss		○
Bouffalant		○
Gligar		○
Golduck		○
Mienfoo		○
Rufflet	⬡	△
Sawk	⬢	○
Throh	⬡	○
Vullaby	⬢	△

Tall Grass (rustling)		
Audino		◎
Emolga		○
Gliscor		△
Sawk	⬡	△
Throh	⬢	△

Dark Grass		
Amoonguss		○
Bouffalant		○
Golduck		○
Gligar		○
Mienshao		○
Rufflet	⬡	△
Sawk	⬢	○
Throh	⬡	○
Vullaby	⬢	△

Hidden Grottoes	
Absol	○
Gligar	△
Golduck	○
Seviper	○
Zangoose	○

Water Surface		
Basculin (Blue-Striped Form)	⬡	◎
Basculin (Red-Striped Form)	⬢	◎
Buizel		◎

Water Surface (ripples)		
Basculin (Blue-Striped Form)	⬢	◎
Basculin (Red-Striped Form)	⬡	◎
Buizel		◎
Floatzel		○

After the Hall of Fame

Fishing		
Basculin (Blue-Striped Form)	⬡	◎
Basculin (Red-Striped Form)	⬢	◎
Poliwag		◎

Fishing (ripples)		
Basculin (Blue-Striped Form)	⬢	◎
Basculin (Red-Striped Form)	⬡	◎
Poliwhirl		◎
Poliwrath		△

Hidden Grotto

Route 23 has a Hidden Grotto. Find it!

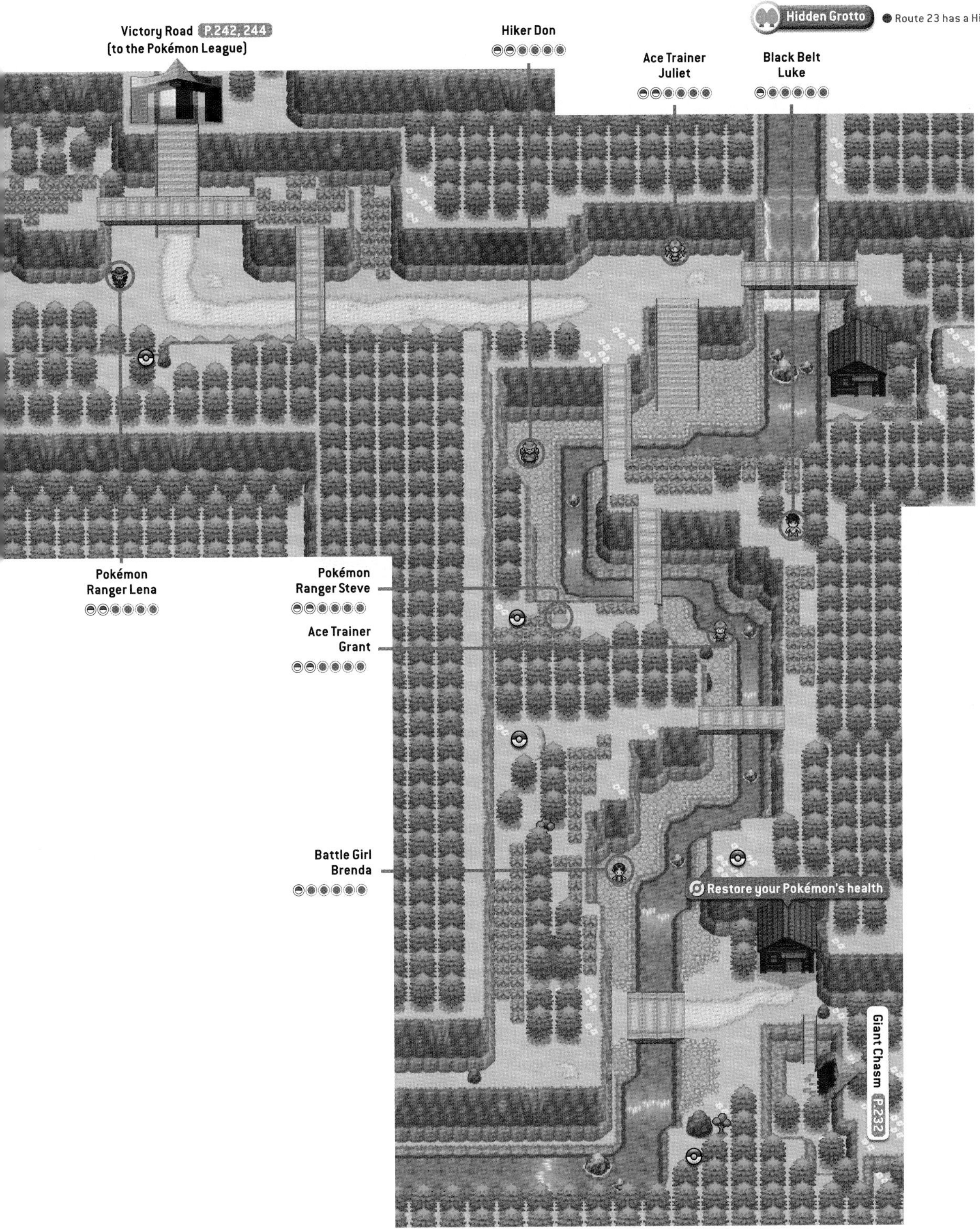

Victory Road P.242, 244
(to the Pokémon League)

Hiker Don

Ace Trainer Juliet

Black Belt Luke

Pokémon Ranger Lena

Pokémon Ranger Steve

Ace Trainer Grant

Battle Girl Brenda

Restore your Pokémon's health

Giant Chasm P.232

Step 1 Heal your Pokémon at the house

Enter the house situated at the top of the stairs to the north. If you speak to the woman inside, she'll fully heal your Pokémon. If you're visiting Route 23 immediately following your battle with Ghetsis, it's a great opportunity to get your Pokémon back in condition.

Yes! The team of you and your Pokémon can go as far as you want!

Step 2 Follow the river road along the valley

Go across the bridge west of the house and follow the river road northward. Battle Trainers along the way until you reach the end of the path and a great stairway at the northern end of it. Climb the stairs and make your way up to the cliff tops.

Step 3 After exploring the cliffs, turn west

When you make it up onto the cliffs, travel across the bridges to continue south. Now you can explore the river road from above, all the way from Victory Road to the Giant Chasm. Investigate every last corner before returning to the northern end and then head west.

Get Berries from Pokémon Rangers

Pokémon Ranger Steve, who hides among the fallen leaves on the eastern cliff, and Pokémon Ranger Lena, who waits before the stairs to Victory Road, will both give you Sitrus Berries if you beat them in battle.

Step 4 Use Strength to move boulders

Head west and arrive at an area where there are six boulders that you can move using Strength. Dropping all the boulders into their holes will make it much easier to go back and forth to the main route. Think carefully about which boulders should go into which holes before you start moving them.

Step 5 Weave through the maze of trees to battle Trainers

A stand of trees fills the western reaches of Route 23, creating a natural maze. Explore every last corner of it as you remove obstacles with Cut, battle the Trainers that wait among the trees, and gather items.

Step 6 Use Strength on boulders to make shortcuts

Among the boulders that can be moved using Strength on the south side of the maze, you'll find some that can only be moved after making it through the maze itself. Use Surf to go across the water surface and head up and down the area to drop all the boulders into their holes.

Step 7 Complete your exploration of the area before you turn east

The western side of Route 23 is a maze-like stretch of trees, so it can be hard to tell if you have been everywhere. Check the map (p. 238) as you go along, so you can see whether you've battled all the Trainers and collected all the items.

Step 8 Head north to Victory Road

Return to the spot where you found Pokémon Ranger Lena and turn north. When you climb up the long staircase, you'll find yourself before Victory Road's Badge Check Gates. Work up your courage and storm through the last hurdle before the Pokémon League (p. 242, 244).

Train your Pokémon by fighting everyone

On your way, the only places to train your Pokémon before taking on the Pokémon League are here on Route 23 and Victory Road. In order to make your Pokémon as strong as possible, do your best to fight all the Trainers you can find.

The old man in the house was once a contender

At the north end of the path that follows alongside the river on the east side of Route 23, you'll find a small house. Speak with the old man inside, and he'll give you TM35 Flamethrower. Apparently, he once challenged the Pokémon League himself!

Victory Road

When playing *Pokémon Black Version 2*

Victory Road is the last hurdle before the Pokémon League. Only those who have eight Gym Badges can go there. As many as 25 Trainers are waiting in the intricate landscape of caves, a grove, and a waterfall.

Items

- First visit
- ☐ Dragon Fang
- ☐ Dragon Scale
- ☐ Escape Rope
- ☐ Full Restore x2
- ☐ HM05 Waterfall
- ☐ Max Elixir
- ☐ Max Repel x2
- ☐ Max Revive
- ☐ PP Max
- ☐ PP Up
- ☐ Rare Candy
- ☐ Star Piece
- ☐ TM01 Hone Claws
- ☐ TM24 Thunderbolt
- ☐ TM93 Wild Charge
- ☐ Ultra Ball x2
- After defeating Pokémon Ranger Eddie
- ☐ Cheri Berry
- After defeating Pokémon Ranger Elle
- ☐ Rawst Berry

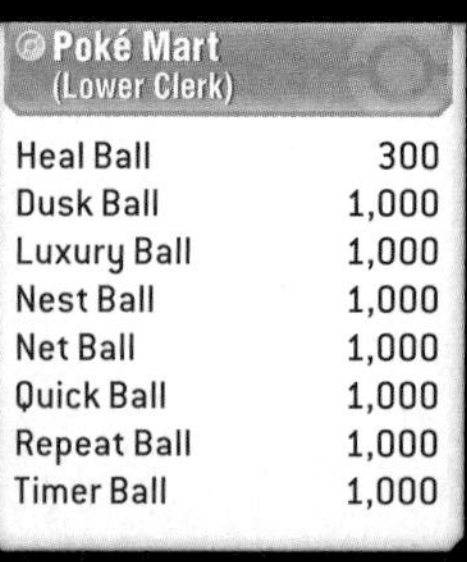

Poké Mart (Lower Clerk)	
Heal Ball	300
Dusk Ball	1,000
Luxury Ball	1,000
Nest Ball	1,000
Net Ball	1,000
Quick Ball	1,000
Repeat Ball	1,000
Timer Ball	1,000

Grove

Tall Grass	
Cottonee	◎
Roselia	◎

Tall Grass (rustling)	
Audino	◎
Dunsparce	○
Roserade	△
Whimsicott	△

Dark Grass	
Cottonee	◎
Roselia	◎

Cave 1F

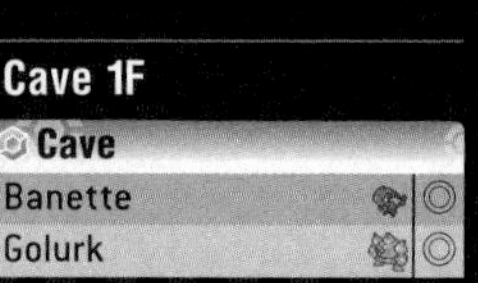
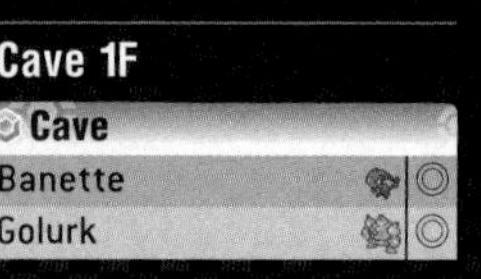

Cave	
Banette	◎
Golurk	◎

Cave 1F / 2F Back

Water Surface	
Basculin (Red-Striped Form)	◎
Marill	◎

Water Surface (ripples)	
Azumarill	△
Basculin (Blue-Striped Form)	◎
Marill	◎

After the Hall of Fame

Fishing	
Basculin (Red-Striped Form)	◎
Poliwag	◎

Fishing (ripples)	
Basculin (Blue-Striped Form)	◎
Poliwhirl	◎
Poliwrath	△

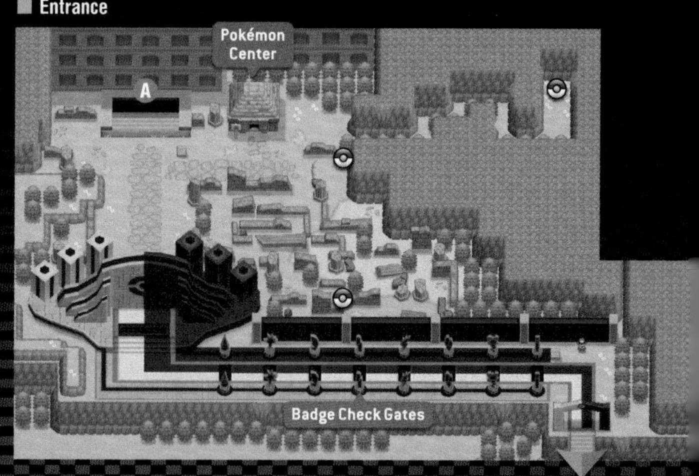

Route 23 P.238 (to Lacunosa Town)

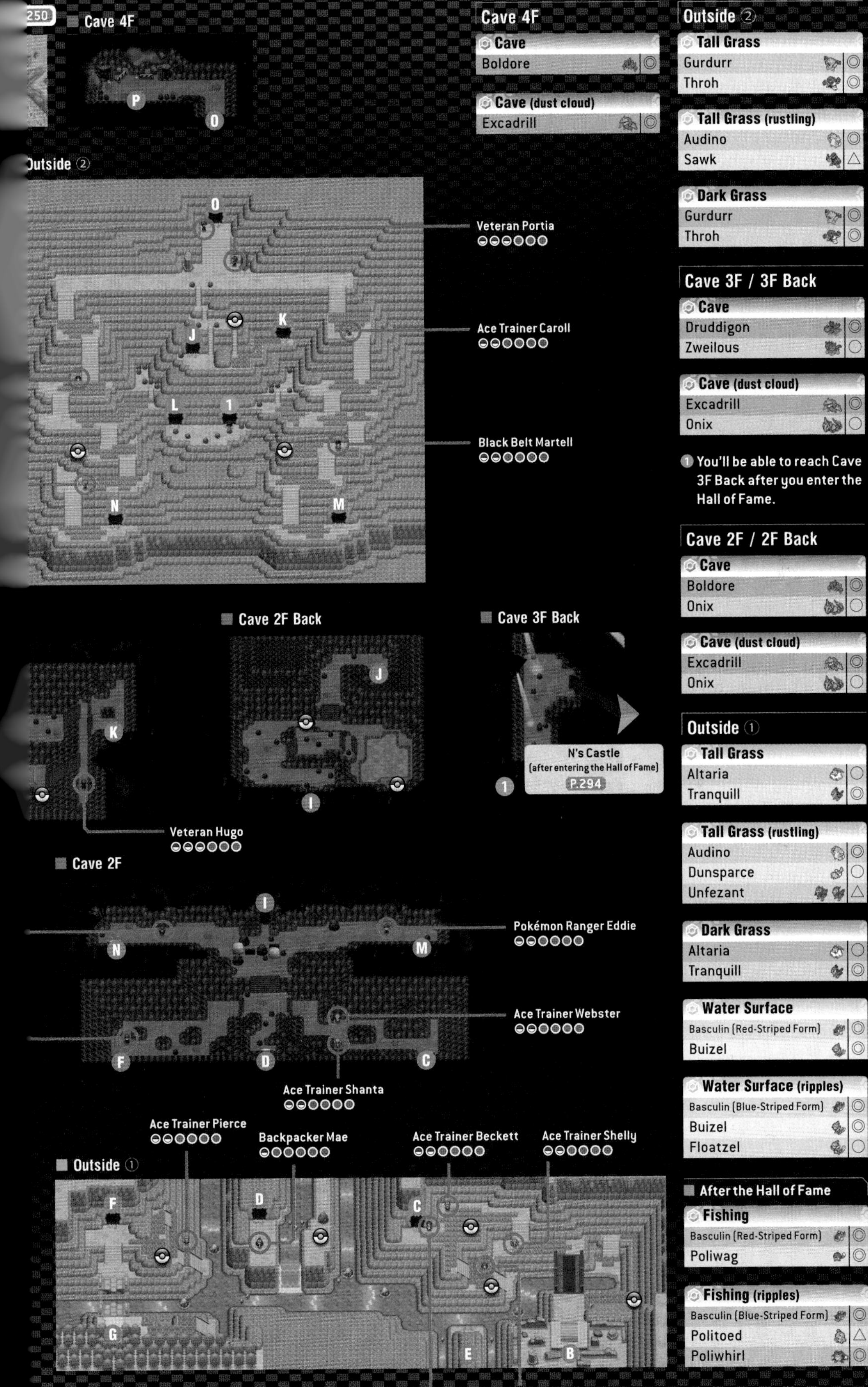

Cave 4F

Cave	
Boldore	◎

Cave (dust cloud)	
Excadrill	◎

Outside ②

Tall Grass	
Gurdurr	◎
Throh	◎

Tall Grass (rustling)	
Audino	◎
Sawk	△

Dark Grass	
Gurdurr	◎
Throh	◎

Cave 3F / 3F Back

Cave	
Druddigon	◎
Zweilous	○

Cave (dust cloud)	
Excadrill	◎
Onix	○

1 You'll be able to reach Cave 3F Back after you enter the Hall of Fame.

Cave 2F / 2F Back

Cave	
Boldore	◎
Onix	○

Cave (dust cloud)	
Excadrill	◎
Onix	○

Outside ①

Tall Grass	
Altaria	○
Tranquill	◎

Tall Grass (rustling)	
Audino	◎
Dunsparce	○
Unfezant	△

Dark Grass	
Altaria	○
Tranquill	◎

Water Surface	
Basculin (Red-Striped Form)	◎
Buizel	◎

Water Surface (ripples)	
Basculin (Blue-Striped Form)	◎
Buizel	◎
Floatzel	○

After the Hall of Fame

Fishing	
Basculin (Red-Striped Form)	◎
Poliwag	◎

Fishing (ripples)	
Basculin (Blue-Striped Form)	◎
Politoed	△
Poliwhirl	◎

Victory Road

When playing *Pokémon White Version 2*

Victory Road is the last hurdle before the Pokémon League. Only those who have eight Gym Badges can go there. As many as 25 Trainers are waiting in the intricate landscape of caves, a grove, and a waterfall.

Items

- First visit
- ☐ Dragon Fang
- ☐ Dragon Scale
- ☐ Escape Rope
- ☐ Full Restore x2
- ☐ HM05 Waterfall
- ☐ Max Elixir
- ☐ Max Repel x2
- ☐ Max Revive
- ☐ PP Max
- ☐ PP Up
- ☐ Rare Candy
- ☐ Star Piece
- ☐ TM01 Hone Claws
- ☐ TM24 Thunderbolt
- ☐ TM93 Wild Charge
- ☐ Ultra Ball x2
- After defeating Pokémon Ranger Elle
- ☐ Rawst Berry
- After defeating Pokémon Ranger Eddie
- ☐ Cheri Berry

Poké Mart (Lower Clerk)

Item	Price
Heal Ball	300
Dusk Ball	1,000
Luxury Ball	1,000
Nest Ball	1,000
Net Ball	1,000
Quick Ball	1,000
Repeat Ball	1,000
Timer Ball	1,000

Grove

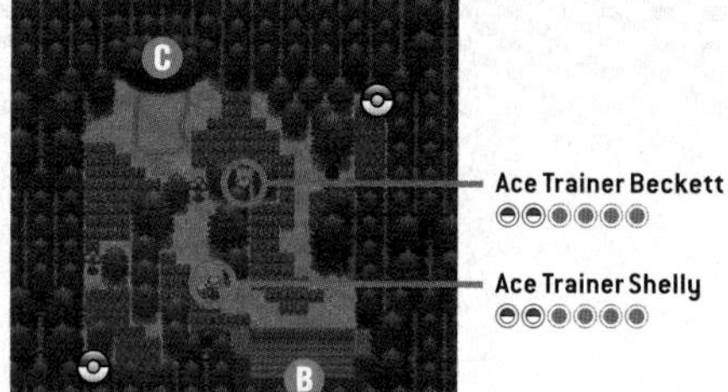

Cave 1F

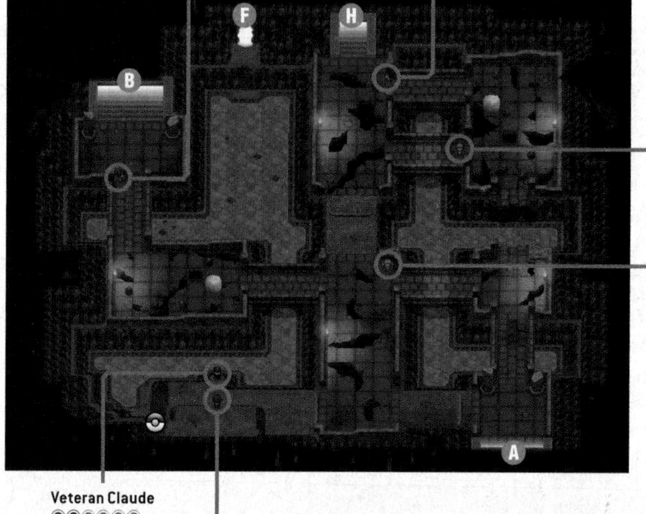

Entrance

Route 23 P.238 (to Lacunosa Town)

Tall Grass

Pokémon	Rarity
Petilil	◎
Roselia	◎

Tall Grass (rustling)

Pokémon	Rarity
Audino	◎
Dunsparce	○
Lilligant	△
Roserade	△

Dark Grass

Pokémon	Rarity
Petilil	◎
Roselia	◎

Cave 1F

Cave

Pokémon	Rarity
Banette	◎
Golurk	◎

Cave 1F / 2F Back

Water Surface

Pokémon	Rarity
Basculin (Blue-Striped Form)	◎
Marill	◎

Water Surface (ripples)

Pokémon	Rarity
Azumarill	△
Basculin (Red-Striped Form)	◎
Marill	◎

After the Hall of Fame

Fishing

Pokémon	Rarity
Basculin (Blue-Striped Form)	◎
Poliwag	◎

Fishing (ripples)

Pokémon	Rarity
Basculin (Red-Striped Form)	◎
Poliwhirl	◎
Poliwrath	△

Pokémon League P.250

Exit

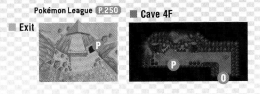

Cave 4F

Outside ②

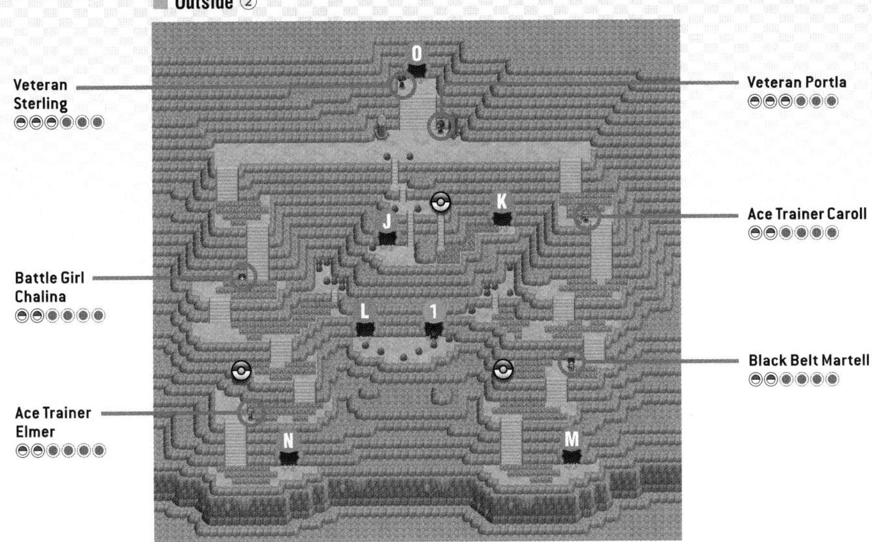

Cave 3F

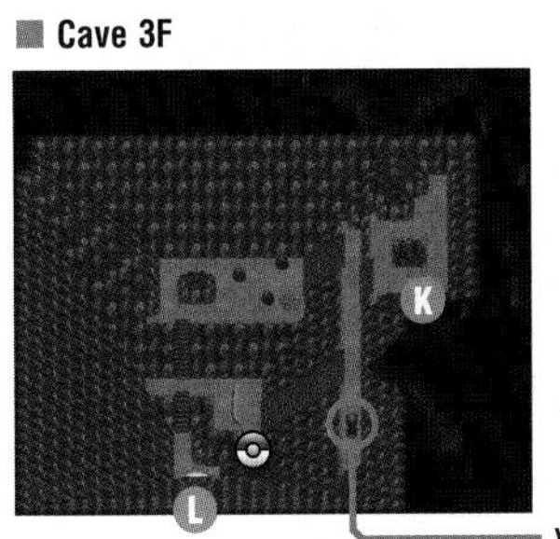

Cave 2F Back

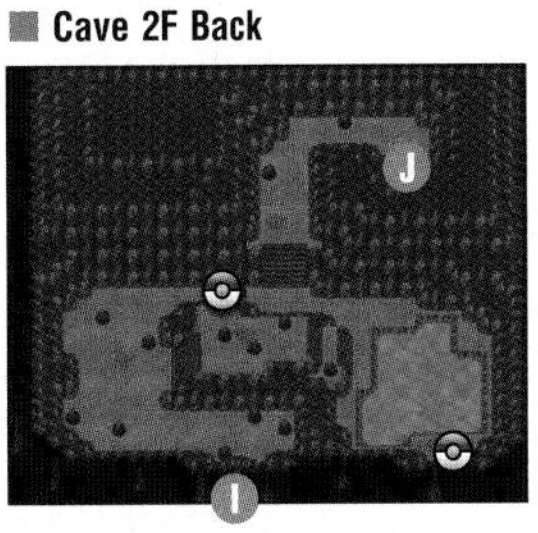

Cave 3F Back

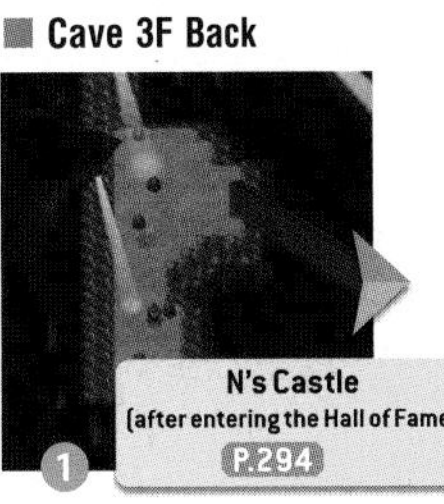

Cave 2F

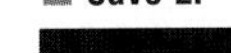

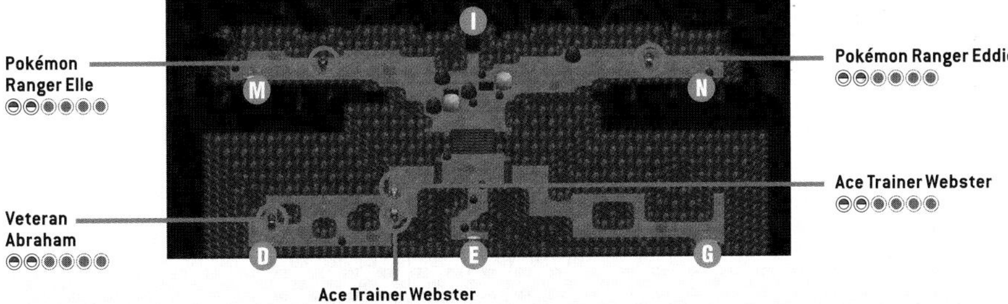

Restore your Pokémon's health

Outside ①

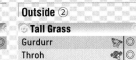

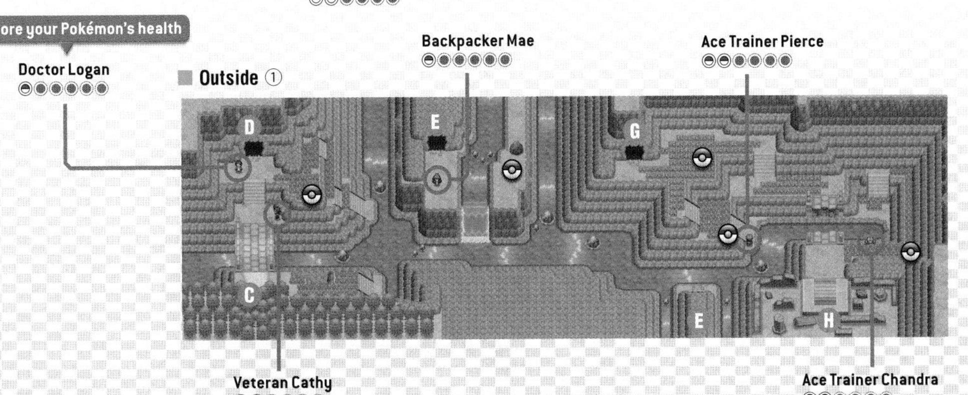

Cave 4F

Cave	
Boldore	◎

Cave (dust cloud)	
Excadrill	◎

Outside ②

Tall Grass	
Gurdurr	◎
Throh	◎

Tall Grass (rustling)	
Audino	◎
Sawk	△

Dark Grass	
Gurdurr	◎
Throh	◎

Cave 3F / 3F Back

Cave	
Druddigon	◎
Zweilous	○

Cave (dust cloud)	
Excadrill	◎
Onix	○

① You'll be able to reach Cave 3F Back after you enter the Hall of Fame.

Cave 2F / 2F Back

Cave	
Boldore	◎
Onix	○

Cave (dust cloud)	
Excadrill	◎
Onix	○

Outside ①

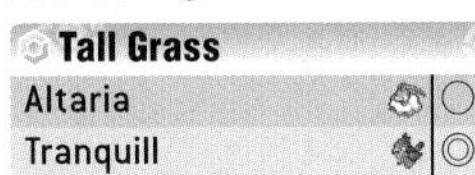

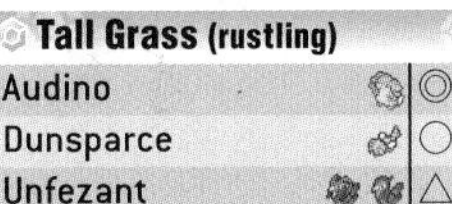

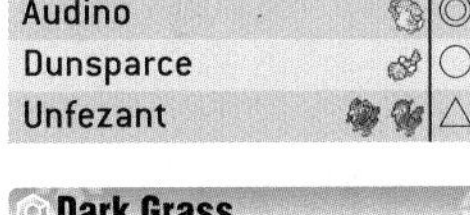

Tall Grass	
Altaria	○
Tranquill	◎

Tall Grass (rustling)	
Audino	◎
Dunsparce	○
Unfezant	△

Dark Grass	
Altaria	○
Tranquill	◎

Water Surface	
Basculin (Blue-Striped Form)	◎
Buizel	◎

Water Surface (ripples)	
Basculin (Red-Striped Form)	◎
Buizel	◎
Floatzel	○

After the Hall of Fame

Fishing	
Basculin (Blue-Striped Form)	◎
Poliwag	◎

Fishing (ripples)	
Basculin (Red-Striped Form)	◎
Politoed	△
Poliwhirl	◎

Victory Road (Pokémon White Version 2)

Step 1 Receive HM05 Waterfall from N

At the entrance to the Badge Check Gates, N meets up with you and hands over HM05 Waterfall. Teach the move to a Pokémon, and you can climb up and down waterfalls on Victory Road or in other places. It's cooler than cool!

Reach places with Waterfall

Once you teach a Pokémon Waterfall, visit waterfalls and see what you can pick up. Route 20, Lostlorn Forest, and Route 11, which you've already seen, have waterfalls. Also, visit Route 14 and the Abundant Shrine (p. 248).

Step 2 Go through the Badge Check Gates

Head west and go on through the Badge Check Gates. Every time you go through a gate, the lights will light up. When all eight gates are lit up, the huge door at the back will open, enabling you to proceed.

Step 3 Restore your Pokémon's health at the Pokémon Center

There is a Pokémon Center on the east side of the stairs leading to Cave 1F. Your Pokémon probably sustained some damage during your explorations on Route 23. Restore your Pokémon's HP in the Pokémon Center, then off you go to Cave 1F.

Rare Candy raises a Pokémon's level

Trainers on Victory Road are pretty strong, so you might want to use a Rare Candy to raise your Pokémon's level in advance. The best time to use a Rare Candy is right after the Pokémon levels up.

Step 4 Keep battling Trainers while going straight for the exit

As many as 25 Trainers make Victory Road a cauldron of combat. If you want to battle all the Trainers, you'll need to explore every corner. The routes are different in *Pokémon Black Version 2* and *Pokémon White Version 2*.

Zoroark blocks the path

You can't see what's beyond Zoroark until you enter the Hall of Fame. Become the Pokémon League Champion and then come back (p. 243, 245).

Step 5 Your rival halts you in your tracks

After exploring every corner and battling Trainers galore, make your move to Cave 4F. As you head west to the exit, your rival calls to you. He challenges you to battle that could make your Pokémon even stronger.

Get Berries from Pokémon Rangers

When you defeat Pokémon Ranger Eddie, you get a Cheri Berry. When you defeat Pokémon Ranger Elle, you get a Rawst Berry. Visit Cave 2F so you don't miss out on challenging them and getting Berries.

Battle your rival! 4

He's added a Bouffalant to his party since your battle in Undella Town and he now has four Pokémon. Their levels have increased by 16.

I'll battle with you before you take on the Pokémon League.

Hugh's Pokémon

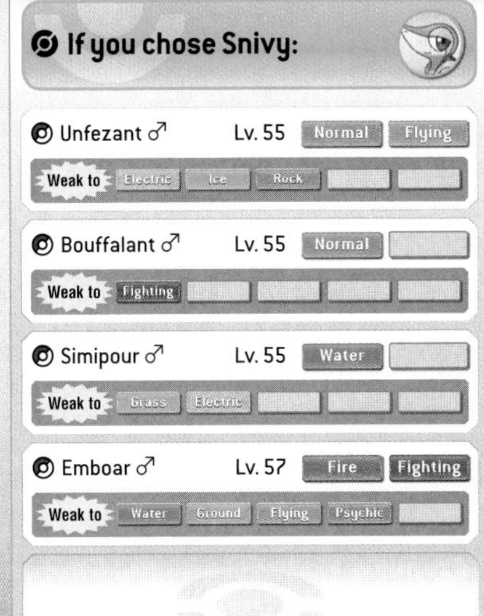

If you chose Snivy:

Pokémon	Lv.	Type	Weak to
Unfezant ♂	Lv. 55	Normal, Flying	Electric, Ice, Rock
Bouffalant ♂	Lv. 55	Normal	Fighting
Simipour ♂	Lv. 55	Water	Grass, Electric
Emboar ♂	Lv. 57	Fire, Fighting	Water, Ground, Flying, Psychic

If you chose Tepig:

Pokémon	Lv.	Type	Weak to
Unfezant ♂	Lv. 55	Normal, Flying	Electric, Ice, Rock
Bouffalant ♂	Lv. 55	Normal	Fighting
Simisage ♂	Lv. 55	Grass	Fire, Ice, Poison, Flying, Bug
Samurott ♂	Lv. 57	Water	Grass, Electric

If you chose Oshawott:

Pokémon	Lv.	Type	Weak to
Unfezant ♂	Lv. 55	Normal, Flying	Electric, Ice, Rock
Bouffalant ♂	Lv. 55	Normal	Fighting
Simisear ♂	Lv. 55	Fire	Water, Ground, Rock
Serperior ♂	Lv. 57	Grass	Fire, Ice, Poison, Flying, Bug

Step 6 North to the Pokémon League

After you defeat your rival, he'll give you TM24 Thunderbolt as thanks for finally achieving the objective of the journey. Now your destination, the Pokémon League, is just around the corner. Journey northward to reach the Pokémon League (p. 250).

Thunderbolt is worth learning

The move Thunderbolt is an Electric-type special move with a power of 95. Many Electric-type Pokémon can learn the move. It'll prove very useful in the Pokémon League, so teach the move to your Pokémon.

Route 14 • Abundant Shrine

Route 14, which lies south of Undella Town, runs east to west alongside rivers and waterfalls. Above the waterfalls and far to the west lies the Abundant Shrine, the only remaining sign that there once was a village here.

Abundant Shrine

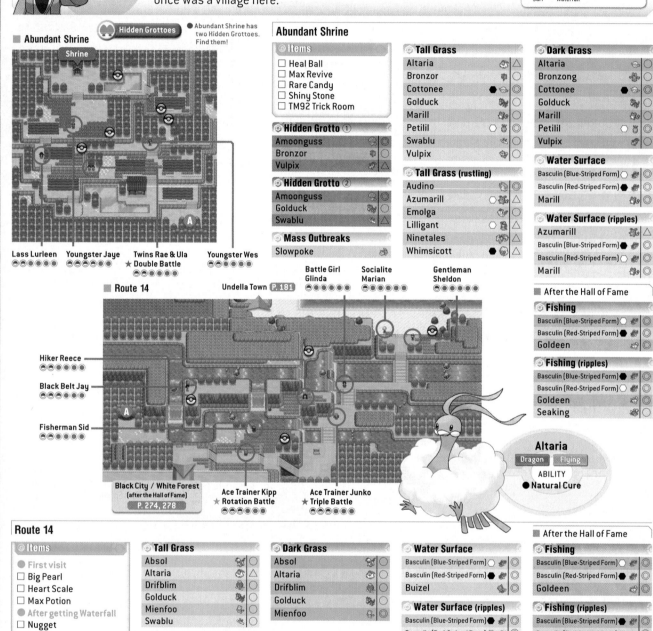

Hidden Grottoes

● Abundant Shrine has two Hidden Grottoes. Find them!

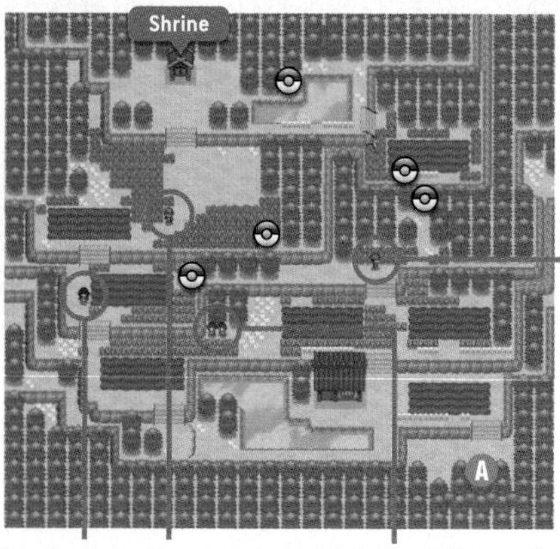

Shrine

Lass Lurleen ●●●●●●
Youngster Jaye ●●●●●●
Twins Rae & Ula ★ Double Battle ●●●●●●
Youngster Wes ●●●●●●

Abundant Shrine

Items

- ☐ Heal Ball
- ☐ Max Revive
- ☐ Rare Candy
- ☐ Shiny Stone
- ☐ TM92 Trick Room

Hidden Grotto ①

Pokémon	
Amoonguss	◎
Bronzor	○
Vulpix	△

Hidden Grotto ②

Pokémon	
Amoonguss	◎
Golduck	○
Swablu	△

Mass Outbreaks

Pokémon
Slowpoke

Tall Grass

Pokémon	
Altaria	△
Bronzor	○
Cottonee ●	◎
Golduck	○
Marill	◎
Petilil ○	◎
Swablu	◎
Vulpix	○

Tall Grass (rustling)

Pokémon	
Audino	◎
Azumarill ○	△
Emolga	○
Lilligant ○	△
Ninetales	△
Whimsicott ●	△

Dark Grass

Pokémon	
Altaria	○
Bronzong	○
Cottonee ●	◎
Golduck	○
Marill	◎
Petilil ○	◎
Vulpix	○

Water Surface

Pokémon	
Basculin (Blue-Striped Form) ○	◎
Basculin (Red-Striped Form) ●	◎
Marill	◎

Water Surface (ripples)

Pokémon	
Azumarill	△
Basculin (Blue-Striped Form) ●	◎
Basculin (Red-Striped Form) ○	◎
Marill	◎

After the Hall of Fame

Fishing

Pokémon	
Basculin (Blue-Striped Form) ○	◎
Basculin (Red-Striped Form) ●	◎
Goldeen	◎

Fishing (ripples)

Pokémon	
Basculin (Blue-Striped Form) ●	◎
Basculin (Red-Striped Form) ○	◎
Goldeen	◎
Seaking	○

Route 14

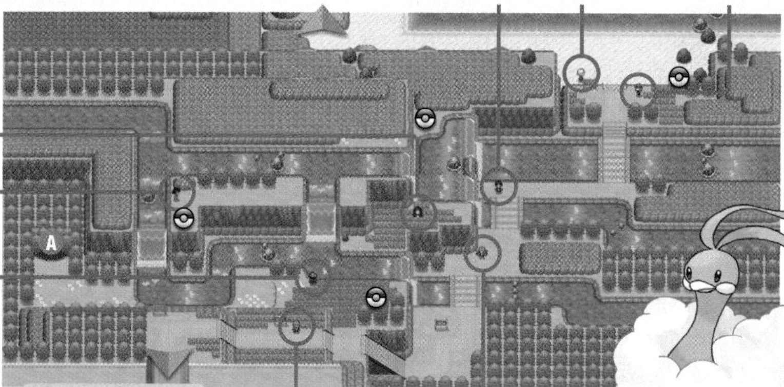

Undella Town P. 181

Battle Girl Glinda ●●●●●●
Socialite Marian ●●●●●●
Gentleman Sheldon ●●●●●●
Hiker Reece ●●●●●●
Black Belt Jay ●●●●●●
Fisherman Sid ●●●●●●
Black City / White Forest (after the Hall of Fame) P. 274, 278
Ace Trainer Kipp ★ Rotation Battle ●●●●●●
Ace Trainer Junko ★ Triple Battle ●●●●●●

Altaria
Dragon / Flying
ABILITY
● Natural Cure

Route 14

Items

- ● First visit
- ☐ Big Pearl
- ☐ Heart Scale
- ☐ Max Potion
- ● After getting Waterfall
- ☐ Nugget

Tall Grass

Pokémon	
Absol	○
Altaria	△
Drifblim	○
Golduck	○
Mienfoo	○
Swablu	○

Tall Grass (rustling)

Pokémon	
Audino	◎
Emolga	○

Dark Grass

Pokémon	
Absol	○
Altaria	○
Drifblim	○
Golduck	○
Mienfoo	◎

Water Surface

Pokémon	
Basculin (Blue-Striped Form) ○	◎
Basculin (Red-Striped Form) ●	◎
Buizel	◎

Water Surface (ripples)

Pokémon	
Basculin (Blue-Striped Form) ●	◎
Basculin (Red-Striped Form) ○	◎
Buizel	◎
Floatzel	○

After the Hall of Fame

Fishing

Pokémon	
Basculin (Blue-Striped Form) ○	◎
Basculin (Red-Striped Form) ●	◎
Goldeen	◎

Fishing (ripples)

Pokémon	
Basculin (Blue-Striped Form) ●	◎
Basculin (Red-Striped Form) ○	◎
Goldeen	◎
Seaking	○

Step 1 Head south from Undella Town for a visit

Use Surf from the southern part of Undella Town to cross the ocean, or navigate the long expanse of beach to make your way south. You'll arrive at Route 14. If you continue further south, you'll be able to explore all that Route 14 has to offer.

It's hard to see far through the thick mist

Route 14 is bathed in the spray of the waterfalls, so many parts are covered in a thick mist. It can be hard to see what lies around you through the haze. Be observant, so you don't miss any items as you explore the area.

Proceed south while battling Pokémon Trainers

First, visit all the areas you can reach without the use of Waterfall. Traverse the bridges spanning the river as you battle Trainers, and you'll see a staircase at the southern end of the path. Go upstairs and continue west.

Be ready for Triple Battles and Rotation Battles

Ace Trainer Junko will challenge you to a Triple Battle, while Ace Trainer Kipp asks for a Rotation Battle. Check the order of the Pokémon in your party before battling them.

You can't go through the western gate yet

At the western end of the stairs, there's a gate that leads to Black City (White Forest). However, seven old men block your way through the gate. Visit Black City (White Forest) after entering the Hall of Fame (p. 274, 278).

Today, we're dancing for no reason. ♪
Someday, we'll disappear for no reason.

Use Waterfall to explore the west

Go back along the path you traveled and make your way to the river. Use Surf to travel west and you'll reach a waterfall. If you use Waterfall to climb the rapids, you'll be able to explore the western side of Route 14. Explore everything there is to see above the waterfalls.

Go to the Abundant Shrine from the far western reach

Use Waterfall to reach the western edge of Route 14. Amid the trees at the base of the farthest waterfall to the west, you'll find the entrance to the Abundant Shrine. Go inside to explore the natural landscape of the Abundant Shrine.

A Funfest Mission is added

Speak with the Pokémon Breeder on the north side of the Abundant Shrine area. The Funfest Mission "Mulch Collector!" will be added for you to play.

Learn about Landorus from the children

In the Abundant Shrine area, the children will all gather together to trade stories about Tornadus, Thundurus, and Landorus flying through the sky in different Formes. A little girl tells you of a shrine to Landorus here in this abandoned village.

So you know what Landorus is like
when it means business, huh?

A shrine to Landorus

Examine the shrine with Landorus that you can get with *Pokémon Dream Radar* in your party. You'll receive the Reveal Glass, which will allow Tornadus, Thundurus, and Landorus to change Formes.

Step 7: Capture Pokémon you can't find anywhere else

As you battle Trainers and collect items, take the opportunity to catch Vulpix, Ninetales, Bronzor, and Bronzong, and register them in your Pokédex. These four Pokémon cannot be found anywhere other than the Abundant Shrine.

A wild Vulpix appeared!

Use Fly to return to Victory Road

Once you've explored the Abundant Shrine, resume your journey to become the Pokémon Champion. If you use Fly, you'll be able to fly straight back to Victory Road (p. 246).

Pokémon League

The Pokémon League is the greatest trial for those who aim for the pinnacle of the world of Pokémon Trainers. By defeating the Elite Four, you'll earn the chance for a battle against the Unova region's Champion.

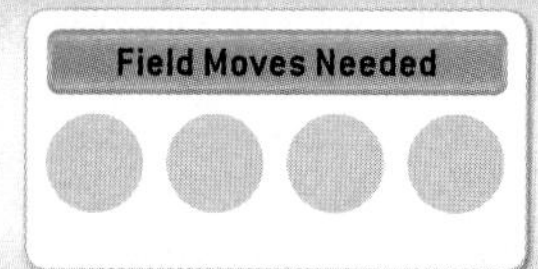

Grimsley's Room

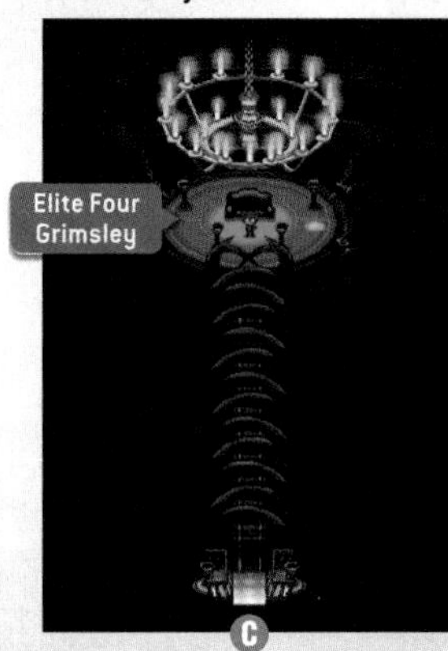

Caitlin's Room

Shauntal's Room

The Elite Four's Plaza

Marshal's Room

Entrance

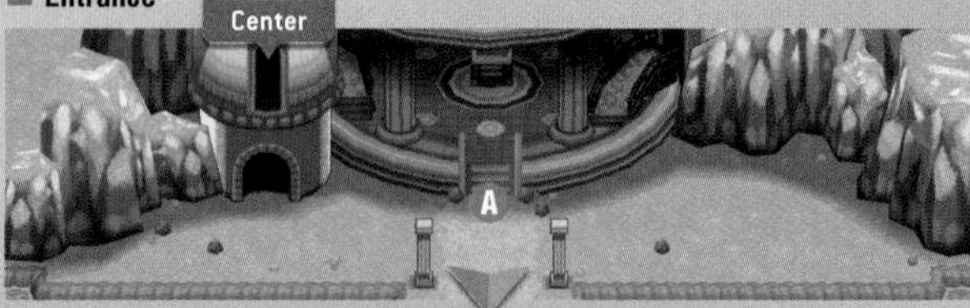

Victory Road P.242, 244

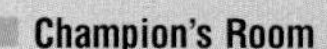

Champion's Room

Underground

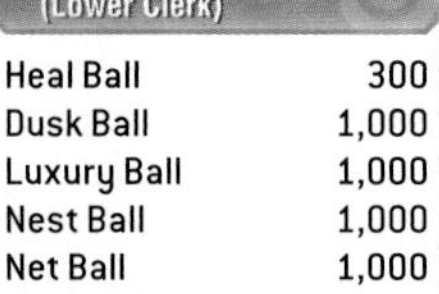

Poké Mart
(Lower Clerk)

Item	Price
Heal Ball	300
Dusk Ball	1,000
Luxury Ball	1,000
Nest Ball	1,000
Net Ball	1,000
Quick Ball	1,000
Repeat Ball	1,000
Timer Ball	1,000

Step 1 Be prepared for your battle against the Elite Four and the Champion

Once you begin your challenge, you won't be able to leave the Pokémon League until you defeat the Elite Four and the Champion. If you're defeated along the way, you'll have to start over. Use the five techniques below to take your victory.

Examine the statue after defeating the Elite Four

After you defeat all four members of the Elite Four, visit the statue in the center of the Elite Four's plaza. Check the plaque on the shining statue, and you can go underground. Once underground, head north and you'll see a building on top of the plateau. The Champion waits inside.

Defeat the Elite Four with help from these techniques

5 Techniques

Technique 1 Examine your party with an expert eye

Take a look at the moves the Pokémon in your party know. It's important that they know moves that will be effective against the Pokémon used by the Elite Four and the Champion. In addition to using TMs, enlist the help of the master Move Tutor to teach your Pokémon moves that can exploit the weaknesses of your opponents' Pokémon.

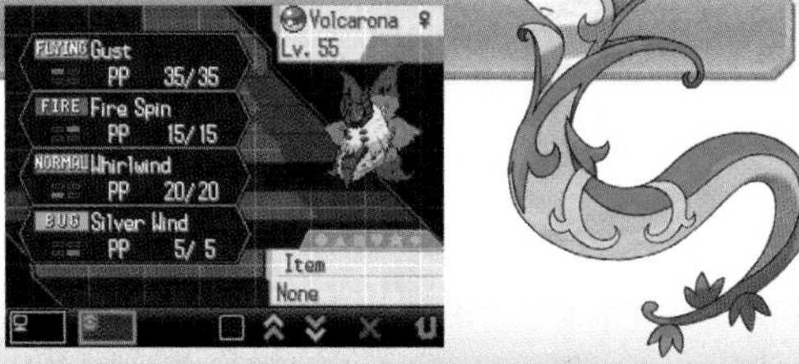

Technique 2 Give Pokémon items to hold in battle

Give your Pokémon items that are useful in battle if they aren't already holding some. For example, if one of your Pokémon has a low Speed stat, give it a Quick Claw to hold. If it has moves with low accuracy ratings, give it a Wide Lens.

Technique 3 Stock up on healing items

Healing items are, of course, important during actual battles, but you'll also want to have plenty on hand to restore your injured Pokémon's HP and recover any status conditions after each battle. Ensure you have plenty of Full Restores, which restore a Pokémon's HP and recover status conditions at the same time, as well as Revives, which can recover a fainted Pokémon, before you begin your challenge. Don't hold back on using PP-restoring items, either.

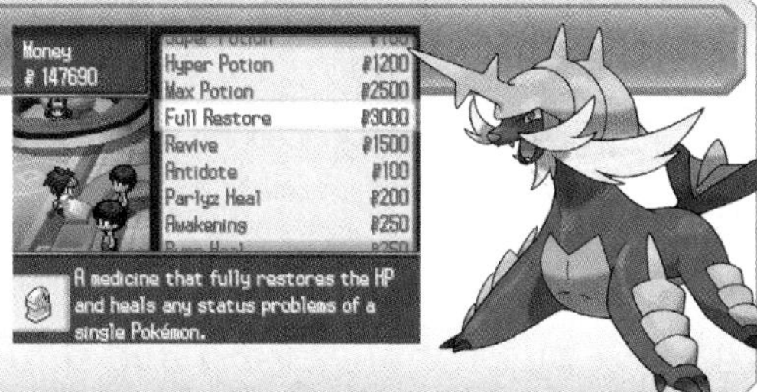

Technique 4 Save the most challenging opponent for last

Each of the Elite Four specializes in one of the following types: Ghost, Dark, Psychic, or Fighting. The order in which you challenge them is up to you. Take a look at your party and decide which opponents will be easiest. Make them your first battles. By defeating the easiest opponents first, your Pokémon will be able to become just a little bit stronger before you have to face your most difficult opponent.

Shauntal Grimsley Caitlin Marshal

Technique 5 Use Rare Candies to level up your Pokémon

If you are having trouble against even the first member of the Elite Four you choose to challenge, try raising the levels of the Pokémon in your party using Rare Candies. The higher a Pokémon's level, the stronger it becomes. You can obtain more Rare Candies even after you enter the Hall of Fame, so don't worry about using up all of the ones you have at this point.

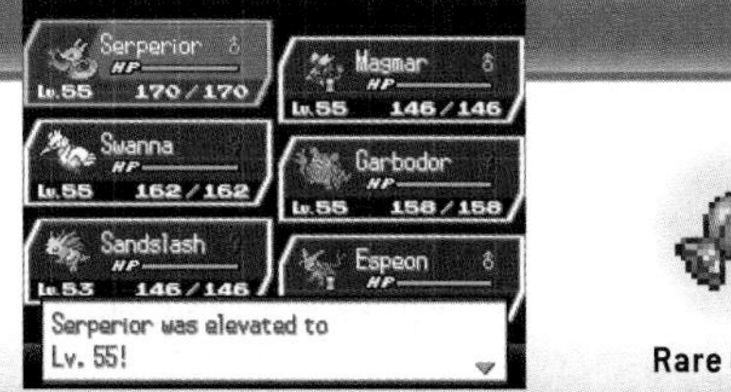

Rare Candy

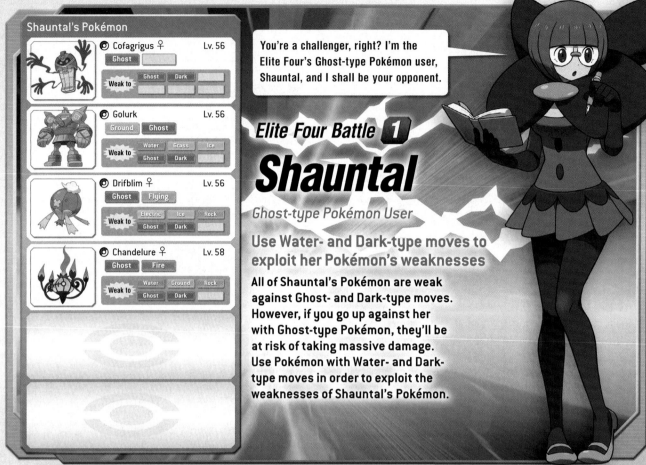

Shauntal's Pokémon

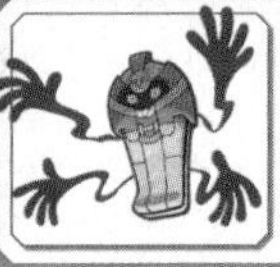

Pokémon	Lv.	Type	Weak to
Cofagrigus ♀	Lv. 56	Ghost	Ghost, Dark
Golurk	Lv. 56	Ground, Ghost	Water, Grass, Ice, Ghost, Dark
Drifblim ♀	Lv. 56	Ghost, Flying	Electric, Ice, Rock, Ghost, Dark
Chandelure ♀	Lv. 58	Ghost, Fire	Water, Ground, Rock, Ghost, Dark

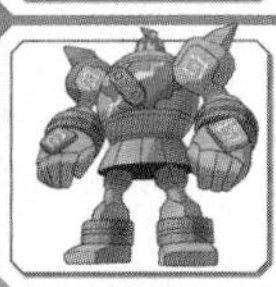

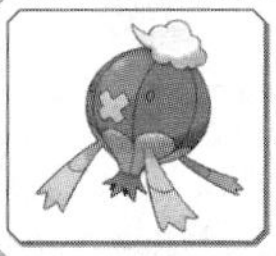

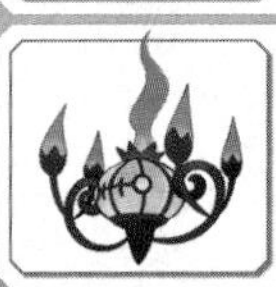

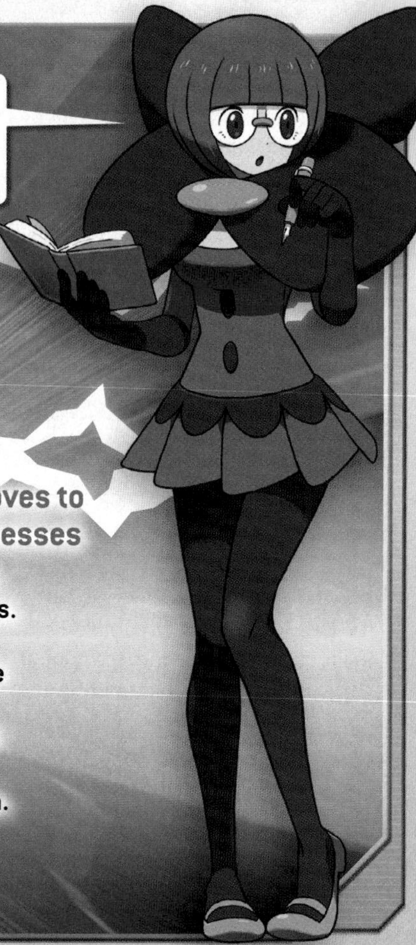

You're a challenger, right? I'm the Elite Four's Ghost-type Pokémon user, Shauntal, and I shall be your opponent.

Elite Four Battle 1

Shauntal

Ghost-type Pokémon User

Use Water- and Dark-type moves to exploit her Pokémon's weaknesses

All of Shauntal's Pokémon are weak against Ghost- and Dark-type moves. However, if you go up against her with Ghost-type Pokémon, they'll be at risk of taking massive damage. Use Pokémon with Water- and Dark-type moves in order to exploit the weaknesses of Shauntal's Pokémon.

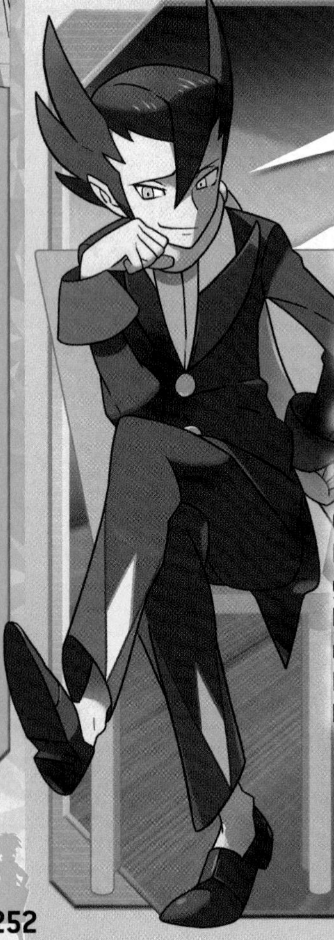

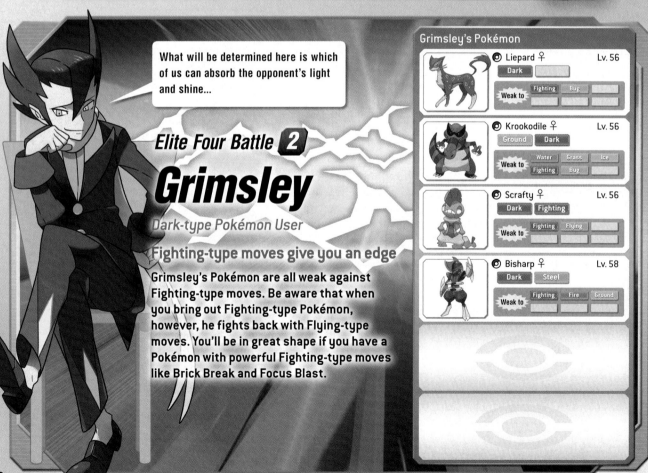

What will be determined here is which of us can absorb the opponent's light and shine...

Elite Four Battle 2

Grimsley

Dark-type Pokémon User

Fighting-type moves give you an edge

Grimsley's Pokémon are all weak against Fighting-type moves. Be aware that when you bring out Fighting-type Pokémon, however, he fights back with Flying-type moves. You'll be in great shape if you have a Pokémon with powerful Fighting-type moves like Brick Break and Focus Blast.

Grimsley's Pokémon

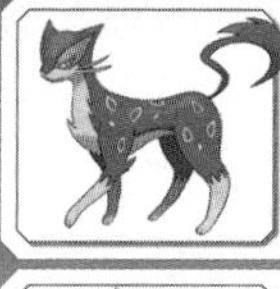

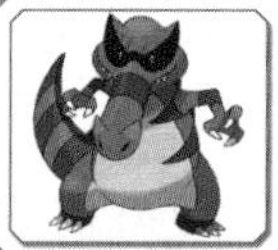

Pokémon	Lv.	Type	Weak to
Liepard ♀	Lv. 56	Dark	Fighting, Bug
Krookodile ♀	Lv. 56	Ground, Dark	Water, Grass, Ice, Fighting, Bug
Scrafty ♀	Lv. 56	Dark, Fighting	Fighting, Flying
Bisharp ♀	Lv. 58	Dark, Steel	Fighting, Fire, Ground

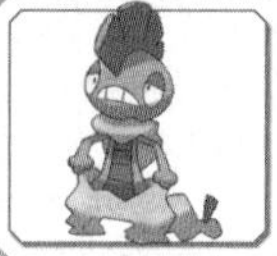

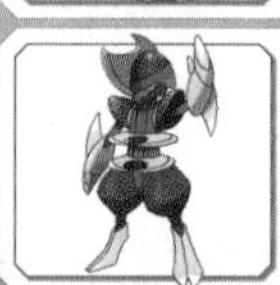

It's me who appeared when the flower opened up.

Elite Four Battle 3

Caitlin

Psychic-type Pokémon User

Use Dark-type Pokémon to gain the advantage

All of Caitlin's Pokémon are weak to Ghost- and Dark-type moves. If you use a Dark-type Pokémon, it can brush off the Psychic-type moves that Caitlin's Pokémon use. Not only that, but Dark-type Pokémon do 50% more damage when using Dark-type moves against Caitlin's Pokémon.

Caitlin's Pokémon

Pokémon	Level	Type	Weak to
Musharna ♀	Lv. 56	Psychic	Bug, Ghost, Dark
Reuniclus ♀	Lv. 56	Psychic	Bug, Ghost, Dark
Sigilyph ♀	Lv. 56	Psychic, Flying	Electric, Ice, Rock, Ghost, Dark
Gothitelle ♀	Lv. 58	Psychic	Bug, Ghost, Dark

Marshal's Pokémon

Pokémon	Level	Type	Weak to
Throh ♂	Lv. 56	Fighting	Flying, Psychic
Mienshao ♂	Lv. 56	Fighting	Flying, Psychic
Sawk ♂	Lv. 56	Fighting	Flying, Psychic
Conkeldurr ♂	Lv. 58	Fighting	Flying, Psychic

In order to master the art of fighting, I've kept training.

Elite Four Battle 4

Marshal

Fighting-type Pokémon User

Flying- and Psychic-type moves are the keys to victory

All of Marshal's Pokémon are weak to Flying- and Psychic-type moves. However, in order to cover these weaknesses, he will use Rock- and Dark-type moves. Catch Marshal off guard by teaching Flying-type moves like Aerial Ace to a Pokémon that doesn't belong to the Flying type.

Champion Battle

Iris

Dragon-type Pokémon User

Know what? I really look forward to having serious battles with strong Trainers!

Iris's Pokémon

Pokémon	Lv.	Type	Weak to
Hydreigon ♀	Lv. 57	Dark, Dragon	Ice, Fighting, Bug, Dragon
Aggron ♀	Lv. 57	Steel, Rock	Fighting, Ground, Water
Lapras ♀	Lv. 57	Water, Ice	Grass, Electric, Fighting, Rock
Druddigon ♀	Lv. 57	Dragon	Ice, Dragon
Archeops ♂	Lv. 57	Rock, Flying	Water, Electric, Ice, Rock, Steel
Haxorus ♀	Lv. 59	Dragon	Ice, Dragon

Switch out your Pokémon as necessary to best exploit your opponent's weakness

Iris has three Dragon-type Pokémon in her party. Each of them has a high attack power, which means they can easily dish out lots of damage. You'll need to take them out quickly, so bring a Pokémon that knows Ice-type moves like Ice Beam and Ice Punch. Ice-type moves are also effective against Archeops. Use Fighting-type moves against Aggron and Lapras to home in on their weaknesses.

Teach Ice Beam to a Pokémon?

Get TM13 Ice Beam in the Giant Chasm and teach it to your Pokémon. You can teach one of your Pokémon Ice Punch by giving 10 Red Shards to the master Move Tutor in Driftveil City.

Defeat the Champion and enter the Hall of Fame!

By defeating Champion Iris, you'll enter the Hall of Fame, marking the completion of a major goal of your journey. However, your adventure is not over yet. After the end credits, in which scenes of your adventure will appear, you'll once again set out from Aspertia City on a new journey.

Your Adventure after the Hall of Fame

While tracking Legendary Pokémon, return to familiar places for more exploration

Continue your adventures in the Unova region! After being returned to your home in Aspertia City, you'll now be able to reach areas that were not accessible before you entered the Hall of Fame. Run through all of the various areas in the Unova region, catching Legendary Pokémon and encountering Pokémon from other regions.

Aspertia City — Cedric upgrades your Pokédex

After you leave your room, Cedric will arrive at your home. He's a friend of your mother's. Cedric will upgrade your Pokédex, enabling you to register Pokémon from the National Pokédex.

It's Professor Juniper's dad

Cedric is Professor Juniper's dad. Both father and daughter are researching Pokémon. Cedric lives in Nuvema Town, where you can visit him later (p. 331).

Aspertia City — Hear from your rival's little sister about her strange dream

When you leave your house, your rival and his little sister will talk to you. Your rival's little sister says that she had a dream in which Zoroark was calling for you on Victory Road. Pay another visit to Victory Road later on (p. 265).

These days, I've been having
dreams about a Pokémon.

Get a special item from your mom

After Cedric leaves, you can receive a Max Revive from your mom. This is a very special item that can't be purchased at Poké Marts. Use it wisely.

Aspertia City — Mass outbreaks of Pokémon will occur

After you have entered the Hall of Fame, mass outbreaks of Pokémon sometimes occur in one area of the Unova region at a time. Find out the location of the mass outbreak by checking electric bulletin boards. It's up to you to check them daily so you can go catch the Pokémon.

Look at your Trainer Card

When you meet certain conditions, your Trainer Card gets upgraded, and its color changes. Entering the Hall of Fame is one of these conditions. When your Trainer Card gets upgraded, show it off to your friends (p. 58).

Floccesy Town — Battle the former Champion, Alder

Visit Alder's house in Floccesy Town. If you speak to him, he'll challenge you to a Pokémon battle. Say yes, and the battle will begin. Take a moment to check the Pokémon in your party before you decide whether to battle.

New wallpaper is now available

After entering the Hall of Fame, check Amanita's PC and you'll find a new wallpaper for your PC Boxes that commemorates your entrance into the Hall of Fame. Check "SPECIAL" on the menu.

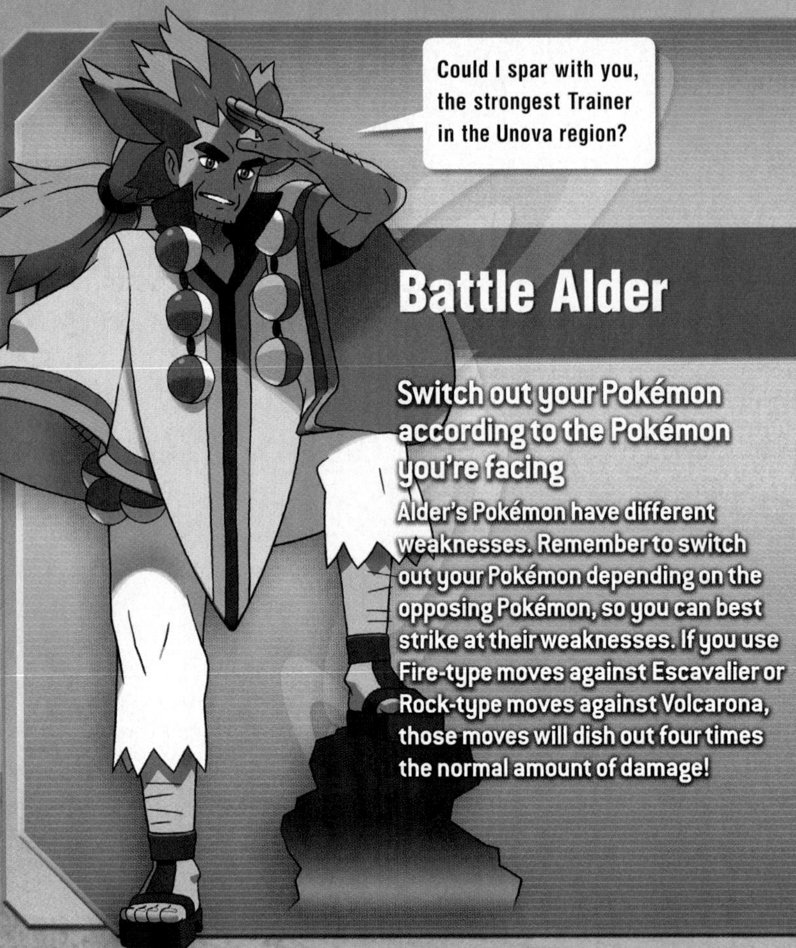

Could I spar with you, the strongest Trainer in the Unova region?

Battle Alder

Switch out your Pokémon according to the Pokémon you're facing

Alder's Pokémon have different weaknesses. Remember to switch out your Pokémon depending on the opposing Pokémon, so you can best strike at their weaknesses. If you use Fire-type moves against Escavalier or Rock-type moves against Volcarona, those moves will dish out four times the normal amount of damage!

Alder's Pokémon

Pokémon	Level	Type	Weak to
Accelgor ♂	Lv. 60	Bug	Fire, Flying, Rock
Bouffalant ♂	Lv. 60	Normal	Fighting
Conkeldurr ♂	Lv. 60	Fighting	Flying, Psychic
Escavalier ♂	Lv. 60	Bug, Steel	Fire
Braviary ♂	Lv. 60	Normal, Flying	Electric, Ice, Rock
Volcarona ♂	Lv. 62	Bug, Fire	Rock, Water, Flying

Floccesy Town

Challenge the Black Tower (White Treehollow)

Once you defeat Alder, his grandson Benga shows up. After meeting Benga, you'll be able to challenge him inside the Black Tower of Black City or the White Treehollow of White Forest (p. 276, 280).

If you'd like, you should take the challenge as well.

It's a dungeon that can be played over and over again

The Black Tower (White Treehollow) is a dungeon where your opponents change each time you enter. A battle against Benga awaits those who can make their way to Area 10. Gather your strongest Pokémon and give it a try.

Receive a Shiny Pokémon from Benga

After completing Area 10 of the Black Tower (White Treehollow), visit Alder's house. Players of *Pokémon Black Version 2* will receive a Shiny Gible, and players of *Pokémon White Version 2* will receive a Shiny Dratini.

Take good care of it!

Shiny Gible

Shiny Dratini

Route 20 Check out the Cave of Being

Head to the east side of Route 20 and then use Surf to travel westward across the water. Climb the waterfull and you'll be on your way to the Cave of Being. If you visit the cave after entering the Hall of Fame, you'll be able to encounter the Legendary Pokémon Uxie, Mesprit, and Azelf, so don't pass up this extraordinary opportunity (p. 283).

Castelia City GAME FREAK's Morimoto and Nishino get stronger

Oh! You've become strong! I can tell.
Do you want to have a battle with me?
▶YES
NO

On the 22nd floor of the GAME FREAK building in Castelia City, you can battle against Morimoto and Nishino once per day. They've also gotten a lot stronger. Come back here every day for challenging battles against Pokémon of Lv. 76 to 78.

Transfer over some strong Pokémon

Morimoto and Nishino have very high-level Pokémon. If it doesn't look like you can take them on with the Pokémon in your party, it might be a good idea to use Poké Transfer to transfer over some of the stronger Pokémon you have in other Pokémon series games (p. 282).

Castelia City Receive an Eevee from Amanita

Hey, that's right!
I have a bunch of Eevee!

Have five or fewer Pokémon in your party and visit the third floor of the building on the same street as the Castelia City Gym. Talk to Amanita, and she'll give you an Eevee with the Hidden Ability Anticipation.

Castelia City Trainers aboard the *Royal Unova* will really put you through a workout

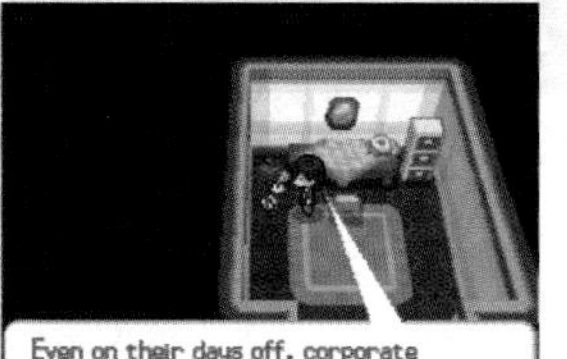

Even on their days off, corporate
warriors are ready for battle! Let's go!

The *Royal Unova*, which can be boarded from Castelia City, is a ship on which you can enjoy Pokémon battles every day. The rules haven't changed since before you entered the Hall of Fame (p. 111), but the Trainers' Pokémon are now much stronger and provide an increased challenge.

The Casteliacone store is super popular

Visit the Casteliacone store and you'll find a long line of customers. A rumor got out that the person who defeated the Champion bought a Casteliacone, and they became super popular. They're talking about you! It takes a bit of time to buy one, but they won't sell out, so don't worry.

Nimbasa City Challenge the Battle Institute

You can now put yourself on the line with Battle Tests at Nimbasa City's Battle Institute. In Battle Tests, you battle against five Trainers and you are assigned a rank at the end based on your results (p. 258). Bring your strongest Pokémon and give it a try.

Nimbasa City Visit Big Stadium and Small Court

A lot of sports started
as Gentlemen's games!

After entering the Hall of Fame, visit Big Stadium and Small Court in Nimbasa City and you'll find lots more Trainers to battle. The levels of their Pokémon have gotten a lot higher, too. Visit every day and make your Pokémon stronger (p. 259).

Take a Battle Test in the Battle Institute

Test how good you really are in battle

The Battle Institute in Nimbasa City allows you to take a Battle Test after you enter the Hall of Fame. Take it on with your well-trained Pokémon and your skill in raising them will be evaluated. Aim for the Master Rank!

How the Battle Test works

1 Choose your Pokémon

Now, please choose the Pokémon you would like to battle with.

Choose Pokémon from your party or Battle Box: three for Single Battles, four for Double Battles. You can't use more than one Pokémon with the same Pokédex number and no two Pokémon can hold the same item.

2 Battle five Trainers

After each battle, your Pokémon will be healed. Even if you lose a battle, the Battle Test will continue until you've battled all five Trainers.

3 See the results

How you battled against these five Trainers will be evaluated, and the result will be determined. Your results are displayed as points and as a rank.

Ranks are based on the number of points

Rank	Points Received
Master Rank	Over 6,000 points
Elite Rank	Over 5,000 points
Hyper Rank	Over 4,000 points
Super Rank	Over 3,000 points
Normal Rank	Over 2,000 points
Novice Rank	Over 1,000 points
Trainee Rank	Less than 1,000 points

Tip: Tips for getting a high score

There are tricks to getting a high score in a Battle Test. If you take the test while keeping these six points in mind, you should be able to get a high score and a better rank.

Tips for getting a high score

1. Don't let your Pokémon faint
2. Defeat your opponent in as few turns as possible
3. Win with a lot of HP remaining
4. Use a variety of moves
5. Hit opposing Pokémon with supereffective moves
6. Switch your Pokémon

Collect Medals by taking the test

If you take the Battle Test repeatedly, you can get four different Medals. Take the test 50 times or more to get all of these Medals!

Check p. 448 for the Medal list.

Tip: Download more Battle Tests

Be on the lookout. You can download more Battle Tests when they are distributed at official Pokémon events.

YES
NO
Would you like to download a special Battle Test?

◆ Check the official Pokémon website for details about official events.

After the Hall of Fame: Battle in Big Stadium and Small Court

Battle tougher opponents and get cool stuff!

Nimbasa City's Big Stadium and Small Court are powered up after you enter the Hall of Fame. The number of Pokémon Trainers you can battle each day increases, their Pokémon are at higher levels, and you receive great items for defeating these Trair

Trainers you can battle in Big Stadium

Day	Pokémon Trainer	Number	Item you can get
M Th Su	Infielder	3	Iron
	Backers (F)	1 Group	—
	Backers (M)	1 Group	—
	Random	3	Depends on opponent
Tu F	Striker	3	Carbos
	Backers (F)	1 Group	—
	Backers (M)	1 Group	—
	Random	3	Depends on opponent
W Sa	Linebacker	3	Protein
	Backers (M)	1 Group	—
	Backers (F)	1 Group	—
	Random	3	Depends on opponent

Trainers you can battle in Small Court

Day	Pokémon Trainer	Number	Item you can get
M W F Su	Smasher	3	Zinc
	Backers (M)	1 Group	—
	Backers (F)	1 Group	—
	Random	3	Depends on opponent
Tu Th Sa	Hoopster	3	Calcium
	Backers (M)	1 Group	—
	Backers (F)	1 Group	—
	Random	3	Depends on opponent

Trainers you can battle randomly

Pokémon Trainer	Item you can get
Ace Trainer (F)	PP Up
Ace Trainer (M)	PP Up
Artist	Ultra Ball
Backpacker (F)	Max Repel
Backpacker (M)	Max Repel
Baker	Moomoo Milk
Battle Girl	Energy Root
Black Belt	Energy Root
Clerk ♀	Ultra Ball
Clerk ♂	Ultra Ball
Clerk ♂	Ultra Ball
Dancer	Ultra Ball
Depot Agent	Ultra Ball
Doctor	Max Revive
Fisherman	Dive Ball
Gentleman	Nugget
Harlequin	Ultra Ball
Hiker	Red Shard
Janitor	Green Shard
Lady	Pearl
Lass	Ultra Ball
Maid	Ultra Ball
Musician	Ultra Ball
Nurse	Full Restore
Nursery Aide	Rare Candy
Parasol Lady	Ultra Ball

Pokémon Trainer	Item you can get
Pilot	Quick Ball
Pokéfan (F)	Max Potion
Pokéfan (M)	Max Potion
Pokémon Breeder (F)	Rare Candy
Pokémon Breeder (M)	Rare Candy
Pokémon Ranger (F)	Max Repel
Pokémon Ranger (M)	Max Repel
Policeman	Ultra Ball
Preschooler (F)	Poké Doll
Preschooler (M)	Poké Toy
Psychic (F)	Ultra Ball
Psychic (M)	Ultra Ball
Rich Boy	Stardust
Roughneck	Dusk Ball
School Kid (F)	Ultra Ball
School Kid (M)	Ultra Ball
Scientist (F)	Ether
Scientist (M)	Ether
Socialite	Big Pearl
Veteran (F)	PP Max
Veteran (M)	PP Max
Waiter	Moomoo Milk
Waitress	Moomoo Milk
Worker	Blue Shard
Worker	Yellow Shard
Youngster	Ultra Ball

Nimbasa City

The Judge shows up in the Battle Subway

After the Hall of Fame, the Judge shows up in the Battle Subway in Nimbasa City. Speak to him, and he'll size up the potential of a Pokémon in your party. Have him help you when you're deciding which Pokémon to train.

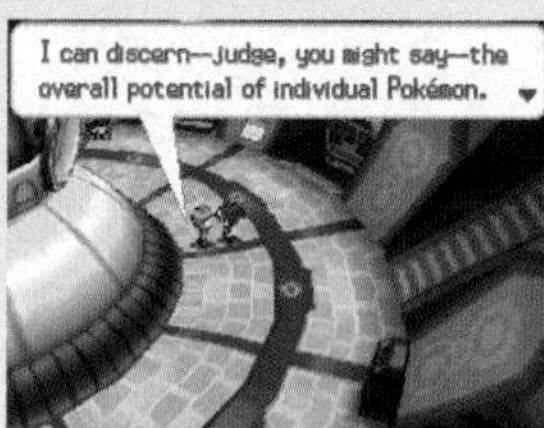

I can discern—Judge, you might say—the overall potential of individual Pokémon.

Memory Link can be activated

When you enter Nimbasa City from Route 5 and head west, you'll meet Cheren. Cheren challenges you to battle. Enjoy the battle with Cheren's strong Pokémon team (p. 73).

Driftveil City

Now you can visit the cave where you couldn't go before

Remember the tunnel that was under construction in the north part of Driftveil City? Once you enter the Hall of Fame, the construction is finished, and you can go through the tunnel. This is Clay Tunnel, which connects Driftveil City and Twist Mountain (p. 284).

PWT

Challenge the Unova Leaders Tournament

In the PWT, you can battle Gym Leaders and Champions from other regions. The woman with the red hat is in charge of registration. First, challenge the Unova Leaders Tournament and face off against the local Gym Leaders (p. 382).

Victory unlocks more tournaments

After you win the Unova Leaders Tournament, you can battle Gym Leaders from Kanto, Johto, Hoenn, and Sinnoh in tournaments.

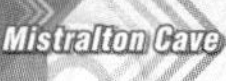

The man who was blocking the entrance disappears

A man was blocking the entrance on the east side of Mistralton Cave's first floor. Now that he's disappeared, you can explore the entrance he was blocking. When you go inside, you'll discover it leads to Clay Tunnel (p. 284).

Undella Town

Receive HM06 Dive

In Undella Town, your rival is standing in front of the gate that leads to Route 13. Speak to him and he'll give you HM06 Dive. If you use Dive, you can go to the Abyssal Ruins.

Trainer obtained an HM06 Dive!

Use Dive to explore the ruins

Teach Dive to a Pokémon in your party. Many Water-type Pokémon can learn the move. After you teach the move to your Pokémon, you can head to the Abyssal Ruins from Undella Bay (p. 291).

Your rival challenges you to battle

Your rival challenges you to battle after he gives you the HM. Choose "YES" to battle. If you need to restore your Pokémon's health first, choose "NO." Prepare for the battle, and speak to him again when you're ready.

▶YES
NO
Let's see who are Aspertia's strongest Pokémon!

Battle your rival! 5

He's added Flygon and Eelektross to his party and now he has six Pokémon. They are seven levels higher than the last time you battled.

What?!
It isn't like I came here because I heard rumors about Cynthia being here.

Hugh's Pokémon

If you chose Snivy:

Pokémon	Lv.	Type	Weak to
Unfezant ♂	Lv. 62	Normal, Flying	Electric, Ice, Rock
Bouffalant ♂	Lv. 62	Normal	Fighting
Flygon ♂	Lv. 62	Ground, Dragon	Ice, Dragon
Eelektross ♂	Lv. 62	Electric	Ground◆
Simipour ♂	Lv. 62	Water	Grass, Electric
Emboar ♂	Lv. 64	Fire, Fighting	Water, Ground, Flying, Psychic

If you chose Tepig:

Pokémon	Lv.	Type	Weak to
Unfezant ♂	Lv. 62	Normal, Flying	Electric, Ice, Rock
Bouffalant ♂	Lv. 62	Normal	Fighting
Flygon ♂	Lv. 62	Ground, Dragon	Ice, Dragon
Eelektross ♂	Lv. 62	Electric	Ground◆
Simisage ♂	Lv. 62	Grass	Fire, Ice, Poison, Flying, Bug
Samurott ♂	Lv. 64	Water	Grass, Electric

If you chose Oshawott:

Pokémon	Lv.	Type	Weak to
Unfezant ♂	Lv. 62	Normal, Flying	Electric, Ice, Rock
Bouffalant ♂	Lv. 62	Normal	Fighting
Flygon ♂	Lv. 62	Ground, Dragon	Ice, Dragon
Eelektross ♂	Lv. 62	Electric	Ground◆
Simisear ♂	Lv. 62	Fire	Water, Ground, Rock
Serperior ♂	Lv. 64	Grass	Fire, Ice, Poison, Flying, Bug

◆ The damage may change depending on the effects of this Pokémon's Ability.

Undella Town — Zinzolin gives you papers about the ancient scripts

After the battle with your rival, Zinzolin suddenly appears from behind. To atone for his bad deeds, Zinzolin gives you Ghetsis's papers. Thanks to the papers, you can read the ancient scripts in the Abyssal Ruins (p. 291).

Trainer is now able to read
the Abyssal Ruins script!

Undella Town — Meet Cynthia in Caitlin's Villa

Visit Caitlin's Villa in Undella Town, where you can meet Cynthia, the Champion of the Sinnoh region, who challenges you to a battle! Come prepared—as you'd expect from a Champion, Cynthia is a very experienced Trainer, and her Pokémon are extremely strong.

You can see Cynthia in the spring and summer

The first time you meet Cynthia, you can battle with her regardless of the season. After that, you can only battle her once a day during the spring. She spends her summers in the villa, too, but she doesn't like to battle in the summer. Other Gym Leaders visit the villa to hang out, too.

In order to get to know each other better as Pokémon Trainers, I would like our Pokémon to have a match.

Battle Cynthia

Switch Pokémon to target the opposing Pokémon's weaknesses

Cynthia's Pokémon will attack your Pokémon's weaknesses. If you restore your Pokémon's health immediately when they take damage, and keep switching to target her team's weaknesses, you could beat even Cynthia. However, her Spiritomb has no weaknesses, so you'll have to attack it with powerful moves.

Cynthia's Pokémon

Pokémon	Lv.	Type	Weak to
 Spiritomb ♀	Lv. 76	Ghost, Dark	
 Milotic ♀	Lv. 76	Water	Grass, Electric
 Glaceon ♀	Lv. 76	Ice	Fire, Fighting, Rock, Steel
 Lucario ♂	Lv. 76	Fighting, Steel	Fire, Fighting, Rock
 Togekiss ♂	Lv. 76	Normal, Flying	Electric, Ice, Rock
 Garchomp ♀	Lv. 78	Dragon, Ground	Ice, Dragon

Undella Town › Go to the Abyssal Ruins

Now that you have Dive, you can go to the Abyssal Ruins. Surf out into Undella Bay, east of Undella Town, and use Dive in a patch of darker water to reach the Abyssal Ruins (p. 291).

Show the Relic Crown to Zinzolin

Get the Relic Crown in the innermost part of the Abyssal Ruins, and speak to Zinzolin in Undella Town. After giving you a Big Pearl as thanks, Zinzolin leaves Undella Town.

Driftveil City › Battle with your rival in the ex-Team Plasma Base

After the battle with your rival in Undella Town, visit the ex-Team Plasma Base in Driftveil City. As Hugh promised Rood, he seems to visit the place to help the former Team Plasma members absolve their guilt. Speak to him if you'd like to battle.

You can battle with Hugh every day

You can battle your rival in the ex-Team Plasma Base in Driftveil City once a day. Visit him every day to battle and train your Pokémon.

Battle your rival! 6

His Pokémon team is the same as when you battled in Undella Town, but their levels have gone up by three. After this battle, their levels will stay the same.

Hugh's Pokémon

If you chose Snivy:

Pokémon	Lv.	Type	Weak to
Unfezant ♂	Lv. 65	Normal / Flying	Electric, Ice, Rock
Bouffalant ♂	Lv. 65	Normal	Fighting
Flygon ♂	Lv. 65	Ground / Dragon	Ice, Dragon
Eelektross ♂	Lv. 65	Electric	Ground◆
Simipour ♂	Lv. 65	Water	Grass, Electric
Emboar ♂	Lv. 67	Fire / Fighting	Water, Ground, Flying, Psychic

If you chose Tepig:

Pokémon	Lv.	Type	Weak to
Unfezant ♂	Lv. 65	Normal / Flying	Electric, Ice, Rock
Bouffalant ♂	Lv. 65	Normal	Fighting
Flygon ♂	Lv. 65	Ground / Dragon	Ice, Dragon
Eelektross ♂	Lv. 65	Electric	Ground◆
Simisage ♂	Lv. 65	Grass	Fire, Ice, Poison, Flying, Bug
Samurott ♂	Lv. 67	Water	Grass, Electric

If you chose Oshawott:

Pokémon	Lv.	Type	Weak to
Unfezant ♂	Lv. 65	Normal / Flying	Electric, Ice, Rock
Bouffalant ♂	Lv. 65	Normal	Fighting
Flygon ♂	Lv. 65	Ground / Dragon	Ice, Dragon
Eelektross ♂	Lv. 65	Electric	Ground◆
Simisear ♂	Lv. 65	Fire	Water, Ground, Rock
Serperior ♂	Lv. 67	Grass	Fire, Ice, Poison, Flying, Bug

◆ The damage may change depending on the effects of this Pokémon's Ability.

Humilau City — Accept a couple's request

There's a couple staying in a house in Humilau City. Speak to the man, and he'll ask you to ring Celestial Tower's bell so the sound will make him and his wife happy. Accept his request and head to Celestial Tower.

A Funfest Mission is added

Speak to the man in the Pokémon Center in Humilau City. The Funfest Mission "Where Are Fluttering Hearts?" will be added to the Entralink for you to play.

Celestial Tower — Battle a woman on each floor

When you visit Celestial Tower, a different woman is blocking the stairs on each floor. You'll have to battle each one before you can ring the bell. These women seem to have something to do with the man who sent you here.

If you want to ring the bell,
you'll have to battle with me!

Go to Celestial Tower from Mistralton City

Celestial Tower is at the north end of Route 7. The shortest way to get there is to use Fly to go to Mistralton City and then take Route 7 north.

Celestial Tower — Mesprit shows up when you check the mysterious presence

Go to the fifth floor of Celestial Tower after visiting the Cave of Being on Route 20, and Mesprit will show up. Mesprit is a Legendary Pokémon from the Sinnoh region. Make sure to catch it.

Kyauun!

Catch Mesprit!

Mesprit Lv. 65
Psychic
ABILITY ● Levitate
MOVES ● Future Sight, Charm, Extrasensory, Copycat

Mesprit lowers your Pokémon's Attack by using the move Charm. Use Fighting-type physical moves to lower Mesprit's HP into the red gradually, without making it faint.

Move types that can reduce HP quickly	Bug	Ghost	Dark
Move types that can reduce HP gradually	Fighting	Psychic	

Celestial Tower — Ring the bell on the fifth floor

When you reach the fifth floor of Celestial Tower after battling the women along the way, ring the bell in the center to fulfill the man's request. Could the sound of the bell really reach the couple in far-off Humilau City?

The sound of the bell reverberates through the area...

You can use Fly on the fifth floor

After ringing the bell on the fifth floor of Celestial Tower, you can use Fly to return to Humilau City immediately.

Humilau City — Speak to the man in Humilau City

Go back to Humilau City and speak to the man who sent you to ring the bell. He's surprised to hear about the women who challenged you in Celestial Tower. He says he and his wife haven't heard the sound of the bell yet, but he gives you a Revive as thanks anyway.

Oh, you! As for the sound of the bell, I don't think I've heard it yet...

Route 23 — Azelf shows up when you check the mysterious presence

Go to the plateau on the west side of Route 23 after visiting the Cave of Being on Route 20, and Azelf will show up. Azelf is a Legendary Pokémon from the Sinnoh region. Make sure to catch it.

Kyuuun!

Uxie shows up in Nacrene City

Azelf, Mesprit, and Uxie make up a trio of Legendary Pokémon from Sinnoh. After visiting the Cave of Being, you can meet Uxie in Nacrene City and try to catch it (p. 314).

Catch Azelf!

Azelf Lv. 65
Psychic
ABILITY ● Levitate
MOVES ● Future Sight, Nasty Plot, Extrasensory, Last Resort

Because Azelf raises its Sp. Atk by using the move Nasty Plot, it can be dangerous if you take too much time to catch it. Wear it down quickly with Bug-, Ghost-, or Dark-type moves.

Move types that can reduce HP quickly	Bug, Ghost, Dark
Move types that can reduce HP gradually	Fighting, Psychic

Victory Road — Chase after Zoroark and head for N's Castle

Visit Victory Road from the Pokémon League. Go down the stairs in the center of the Outside ②, and you'll see Zoroark. If you follow Zoroark, it will guide you to N's Castle. Go inside the castle (p. 294).

Opelucid City — Learn the strongest Dragon-type move from Drayden

Visit Drayden in Opelucid City and speak to him. Drayden can teach the strongest Dragon-type move, Draco Meteor, to one of your Dragon-type Pokémon if it has a strong bond with you.

YES
NO
Would you like your Pokémon to learn that move?

Memory Link can be activated

Speak to Drayden in front of his house and a Memory Link event will happen. Listen to the heartwarming conversation between Drayden and Iris (p. 73).

Giant Chasm — Visit from Dragonspiral Tower

Listen to N's story about Kyurem after catching Zekrom (Reshiram) in Dragonspiral Tower and visit the Giant Chasm. Going to Lacunosa Town using Fly is the shortest way to go there.

Giant Chasm — Kyurem appears at the deepest part

Go into the cave from Route 13 (p. 232). Proceed from Crater Forest to the Cave's Deepest Part ①, and go even further to reach the Cave's Deepest Part ②. You'll find Kyurem in the center. Speak to it for a battle, and take this opportunity to catch it!

Ghetsis's cane is broken

Ghetsis's cane has been left at the Cave's Deepest Part ② in the Giant Chasm. Previously, its signals disrupted the function of Poké Balls, but now that it's broken, you have the chance to catch Kyurem!

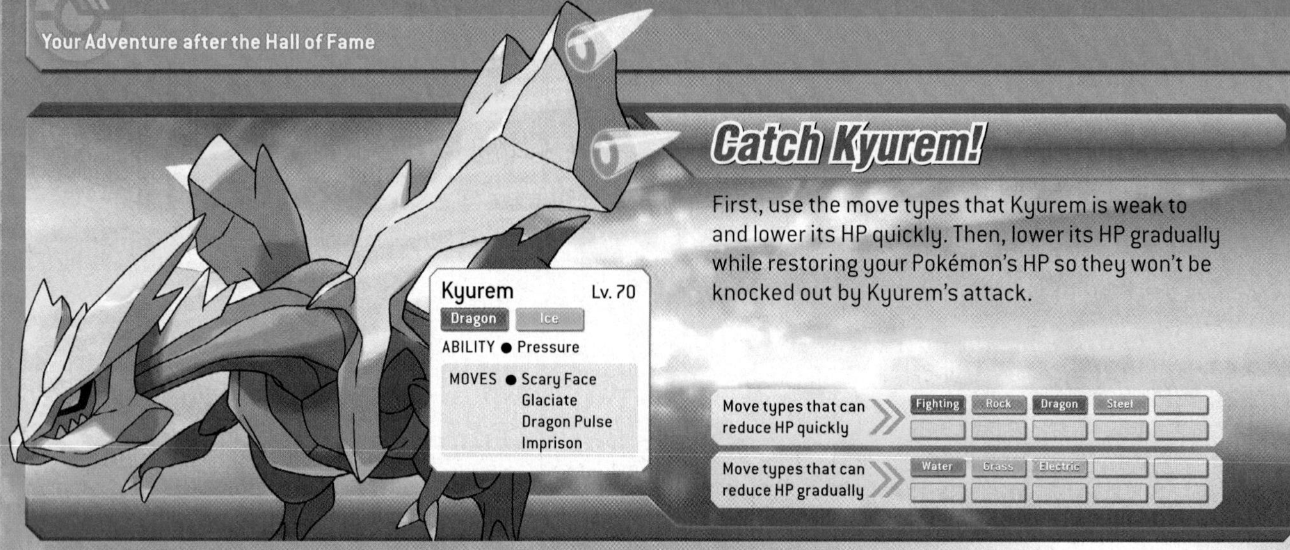

Catch Kyurem!

First, use the move types that Kyurem is weak to and lower its HP quickly. Then, lower its HP gradually while restoring your Pokémon's HP so they won't be knocked out by Kyurem's attack.

Move types that can reduce HP quickly	Fighting	Rock	Dragon	Steel	
Move types that can reduce HP gradually	Water	Grass	Electric		

Giant Chasm — Get the DNA Splicers

After you catch Kyurem, you'll discover an item on the ground where Kyurem was standing: the DNA Splicers! They must have fallen to the ground during your battle.

Giant Chasm — DNA Splicers make Absofusion possible

With both Kyurem and Zekrom (Reshiram) in your party, you can use the DNA Splicers. Choose Kyurem, then Zekrom (Reshiram). Absofusion will fuse the two together into Black Kyurem (White Kyurem).

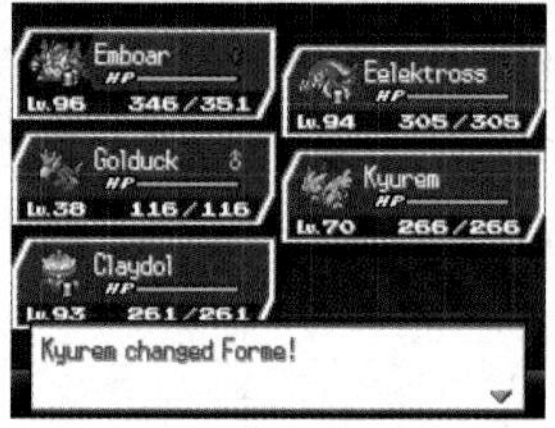

Giant Chasm — Fly to Castelia City to head for Nuvema Town

After you catch Kyurem, Cheren and Bianca show up. Bianca asks you to show your Pokédex to Professor Juniper. Fly to Castelia City on your way to Nuvema Town (p. 106).

New wallpapers have been added

Open Amanita's PC after catching Kyurem. You'll find new wallpapers for your PC Boxes under the "SPECIAL" option.

Reversal Mountain

Get a Magma Stone in advance

After getting a Magma Stone on Route 18 (p. 329), use Fly to go to Lentimas Town and visit Reversal Mountain. Heatran appears on B1F ②. When you approach and speak to it, you'll be drawn into battle.

Gwogobo gwobobobo!

Reach Route 18 from Route 1

To get to Route 18, travel over water from Route 1, go through the gate, and you'll arrive on Route 17. Route 18 is beyond the west end of Route 17. Visit there on the way to Nuvema Town (p. 328).

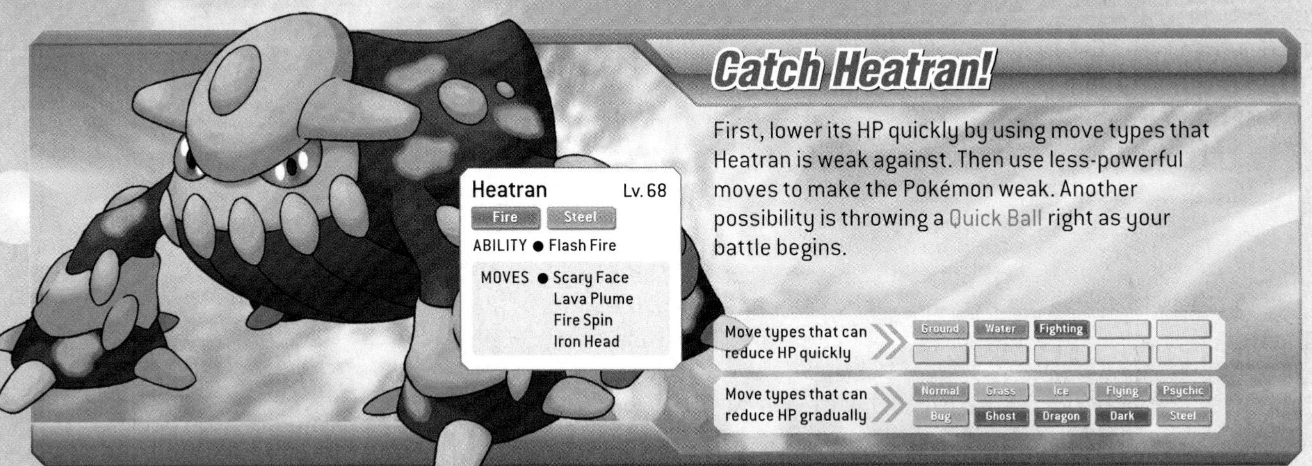

Catch Heatran!

Heatran Lv. 68

Fire / Steel

ABILITY ● Flash Fire

MOVES ● Scary Face, Lava Plume, Fire Spin, Iron Head

First, lower its HP quickly by using move types that Heatran is weak against. Then use less-powerful moves to make the Pokémon weak. Another possibility is throwing a Quick Ball right as your battle begins.

Move types that can reduce HP quickly	Ground	Water	Fighting		
Move types that can reduce HP gradually	Normal	Grass	Ice	Flying	Psychic
	Bug	Ghost	Dragon	Dark	Steel

Village Bridge

Show the desired Pokémon to a Hip Wader

A member of the Hip Waders has come back to Village Bridge and wants to see the Pokémon you caught. Show him the Pokémon he wants to see, and he'll give you five Dive Balls. Try to catch what he wants after getting a Super Rod.

Speak to the Fisherman on Route 8 first

A member of the Hip Waders is on Route 8. Visit Route 8 after getting a Super Rod. Speak to him, and he'll go back to Village Bridge where his house is (p. 300).

Pokémon League

Battle the Elite Four, who have become even stronger

The Elite Four and the Champion of the Pokémon League will get even stronger after you enter the Hall of Fame. They will have more Pokémon, and their Pokémon's levels will increase significantly. Fill your party with superior Pokémon and challenge them.

"The woman who uses Ghost types,
and the woman who uses Ground types.

Challenge the Pokémon League as many times as you like

When you meet a certain condition, such as defeating the Champion with one type of Pokémon or just one Pokémon, you'll receive a Medal. There are 19 possible Medals to get in the Pokémon League (p. 451).

I absolutely love writing about the close bonds between the Trainers and the Pokémon that I've competed against.

Elite Four Battle 1

Shauntal

Ghost-type Pokémon User

Use Ghost- or Dark-type moves to target the weaknesses of all six of them

Shauntal has added Froslass and Mismagius to her party. All six of them are weak to Ghost and Dark types. But look out... If you use Ghost-type Pokémon, she'll attack their weaknesses, too. Use Pokémon who have learned Dark-type moves.

Shauntal's Pokémon

Pokémon	Lv.	Type	Weak to
Cofagrigus ♀	Lv. 72	Ghost	Ghost, Dark
Golurk	Lv. 72	Ground, Ghost	Water, Grass, Ice, Ghost, Dark
Froslass ♀	Lv. 72	Ice, Ghost	Fire, Rock, Ghost, Dark, Steel
Mismagius ♀	Lv. 72	Ghost	Ghost, Dark
Drifblim ♀	Lv. 72	Ghost, Flying	Electric, Ice, Rock, Ghost, Dark
Chandelure ♀	Lv. 74	Ghost, Fire	Water, Ground, Rock, Ghost, Dark

Grimsley's Pokémon

Pokémon	Lv.	Type	Weak to
Liepard ♀	Lv. 72	Dark	Fighting, Bug
Krookodile ♀	Lv. 72	Ground, Dark	Water, Grass, Ice, Fighting, Bug
Scrafty ♀	Lv. 72	Dark, Fighting	Fighting, Flying
Honchkrow ♀	Lv. 72	Dark, Flying	Electric, Ice, Rock
Houndoom ♀	Lv. 72	Dark, Fire	Water, Fighting, Ground, Rock
Bisharp ♀	Lv. 74	Dark, Steel	Fighting, Fire, Ground

It's more important to master the cards you're holding than to complain about the ones your opponents were dealt.

Elite Four Battle 2

Grimsley

Dark-type Pokémon User

Use Fighting-type moves—except against Honchkrow

Grimsley has added Honchkrow and Houndoom to his party. Except for Honchkrow, they're all weak to Fighting-type moves. Use powerful moves like Brick Break and Focus Blast. And to target Honchkrow's weaknesses, use Electric-, Ice-, and Rock-type moves.

Caitlin's Pokémon

Pokémon	Type	Lv.	Weak to
Musharna ♀	Psychic	Lv. 72	Bug, Ghost, Dark
Sigilyph ♀	Psychic, Flying	Lv. 72	Electric, Ice, Rock, Ghost, Dark
Gallade ♂	Psychic, Fighting	Lv. 72	Flying, Ghost
Reuniclus ♀	Psychic	Lv. 72	Bug, Ghost, Dark
Gothitelle ♀	Psychic	Lv. 72	Bug, Ghost, Dark
Metagross	Steel, Psychic	Lv. 74	Fire, Ground

What I look for in my opponent is superb strength...

Elite Four Battle 3

Caitlin

Psychic-type Pokémon User

Use Ghost- and Fire-type moves

Caitlin has added Metagross and Gallade to her party. Except for Metagross, you can strike all of their weaknesses with Ghost-type moves. Use moves like Shadow Ball and Shadow Claw. For Metagross, Fire- and Ground-type moves are effective.

I thank you deeply for the chance for another round of combat against you.

Elite Four Battle 4

Marshal

Fighting-type Pokémon User

Flying-type moves are effective, except against Lucario

Marshal has added Lucario and Medicham to his party. Except for Lucario, they're weak to Flying-type moves. Have a Pokémon that's not holding an item use Acrobatics, and the power will be doubled. To target Lucario's weaknesses, use Fire-, Fighting-, or Ground-type moves.

Marshal's Pokémon

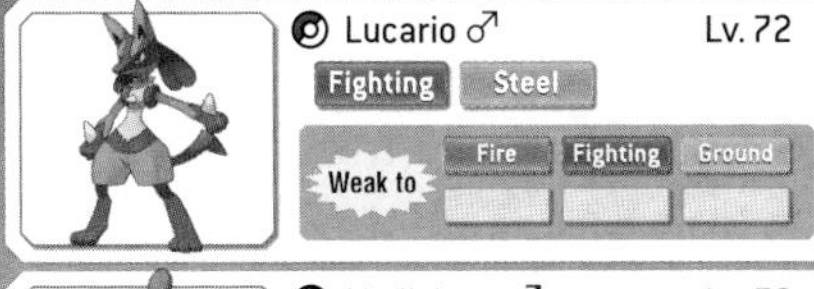

Pokémon	Type	Lv.	Weak to
Throh ♂	Fighting	Lv. 72	Flying, Psychic
Lucario ♂	Fighting, Steel	Lv. 72	Fire, Fighting, Ground
Medicham ♂	Fighting, Psychic	Lv. 72	Flying, Ghost
Mienshao ♂	Fighting	Lv. 72	Flying, Psychic
Sawk ♂	Fighting	Lv. 72	Flying, Psychic
Conkeldurr ♂	Fighting	Lv. 74	Flying, Psychic

Champion Battle

Iris

Dragon-type Pokémon User

The Trainers who come here are Trainers who desire victory with every fiber of their being!

Iris's Pokémon

Pokémon	Lv.	Type	Weak to
 Hydreigon ♀	Lv. 76	Dark, Dragon	Ice, Fighting, Bug, Dragon
 Aggron ♀	Lv. 76	Steel, Rock	Fighting, Ground, Water
 Lapras ♀	Lv. 76	Water, Ice	Grass, Electric, Fighting, Rock
 Druddigon ♀	Lv. 76	Dragon	Ice, Dragon
 Archeops ♂	Lv. 76	Rock, Flying	Water, Electric, Ice, Rock, Steel
 Haxorus ♀	Lv. 78	Dragon	Ice, Dragon

Defeat strong Dragon-type Pokémon as quickly as possible

Her Pokémon are 19 levels higher than they were before the Hall of Fame. The three Dragon-type Pokémon unleash powerful attacks. Defeat them quickly with Ice-type moves, such as Ice Beam and Blizzard. You can strike Archeops's weakness with Ice-type moves, too. When Aggron and Lapras join the battle, switch Pokémon to use moves to target their weaknesses.

You need two DS systems to play with Poké Transfer!

The levels of Iris's Pokémon are high, and many of them are Dragon-type Pokémon with high stats. If you can't win, you might want to bring strong Pokémon from other Game Cards using Link Trade or Poké Transfer.

When you defeat the Champion, you'll start from Aspertia City again

When you defeat the Champion Iris, you'll enter the Hall of Fame again, and you and your party Pokémon will be recorded for posterity by the device deep in the Pokémon League. The next time you start *Pokémon Black Version 2* or *Pokémon White Version 2*, you'll restart from Aspertia City.

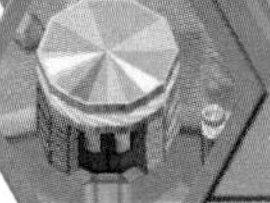

Marvelous Bridge

Marvelous Bridge is a bridge of great beauty. It connects Route 16, which leads to Nimbasa City, and Route 15, which leads to Black City (White Forest). Looking out from the bridge, it's ocean as far as the eye can see.

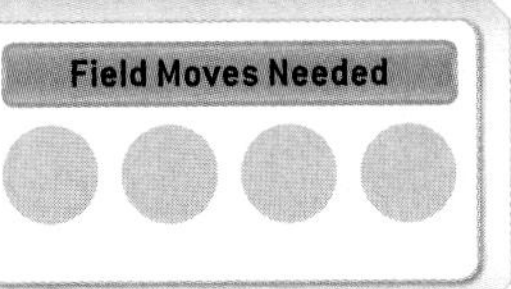

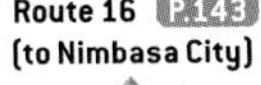

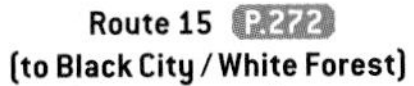

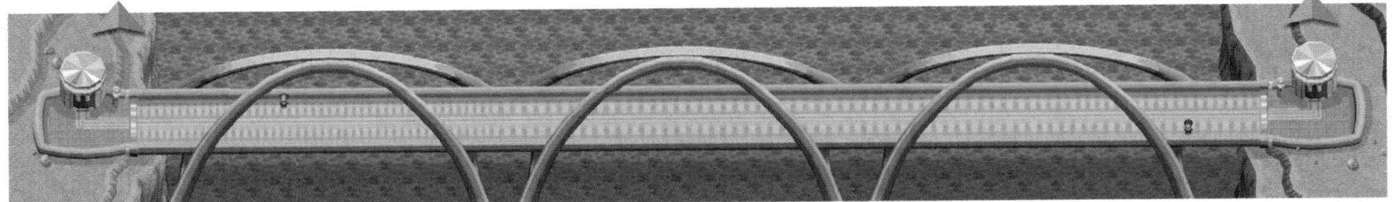

Magikarp Seller	
Magikarp	500

Pokémon Shadows
Swanna

Step 1 When 500 in cool cash gets you a Magikarp

Talk to the man over to the east on the Route 16 side. He'll be glad to sell you a Magikarp for 500 in prize money. Magikarp also appear as wild Pokémon in the Nature Preserve (p. 333). So you could catch it there instead and save your 500 for a rainy day.

Cross the bridge from Nimbasa City

Visit Marvelous Bridge from Nimbasa City via the east gate of Nimbasa City to Route 16. Keep going east and you'll arrive at Marvelous Bridge.

Step 2 Head east to Route 15

Head straight east and take the elevator at the end. Ride the elevator down and keep going east. Once you get through the gate, you're at Route 15, which leads to Black City (White Forest) (p. 272).

Step on shadows to get Wings

You'll see bird Pokémon shadows on Marvelous Bridge. Step on the shadows, and you can get seven types of Wings (p. 271). Watch out for fowl play, though: wild Swanna sometimes jump out!

If you have the Lunar Wing — Cresselia swoops down from the sky

If you obtained the Lunar Wing in the Strange House (p. 181), it will start shining when you proceed to the east side of the bridge. Hold the Lunar Wing high, and Cresselia will swoop down. Speak to it and then catch it!

A ghost girl appears occasionally

If you visit the bridge before catching Cresselia, you may be able to see a ghost girl once in a while. After you catch Cresselia, she won't appear anymore.

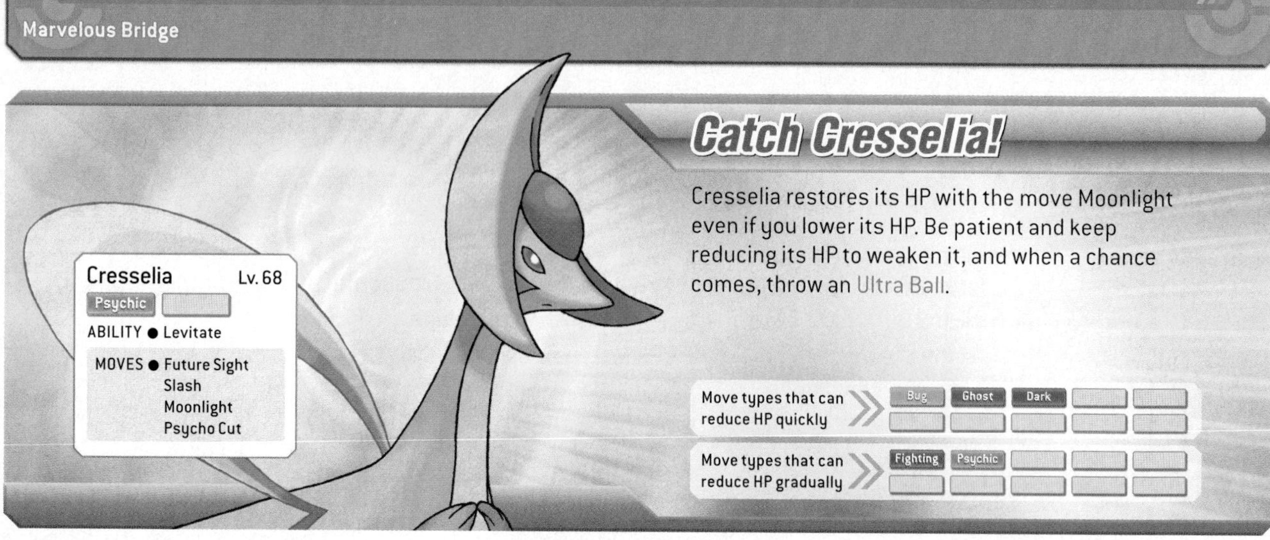

Cresselia Lv. 68
Psychic
ABILITY ● Levitate
MOVES ● Future Sight
Slash
Moonlight
Psycho Cut
Move types that can reduce HP quickly
Bug
Ghost
Dark
Move types that can reduce HP gradually
Fighting
Psychic

Catch Cresselia!

Cresselia restores its HP with the move Moonlight even if you lower its HP. Be patient and keep reducing its HP to weaken it, and when a chance comes, throw an Ultra Ball.

A road whose sharp cliffs may scare some people off

Route 15

Route 15 is characterized by its sheer cliffs. This is where you'll find the Poké Transfer Lab, where you can bring Pokémon over from other regions. The east side is connected to Black City (White Forest).

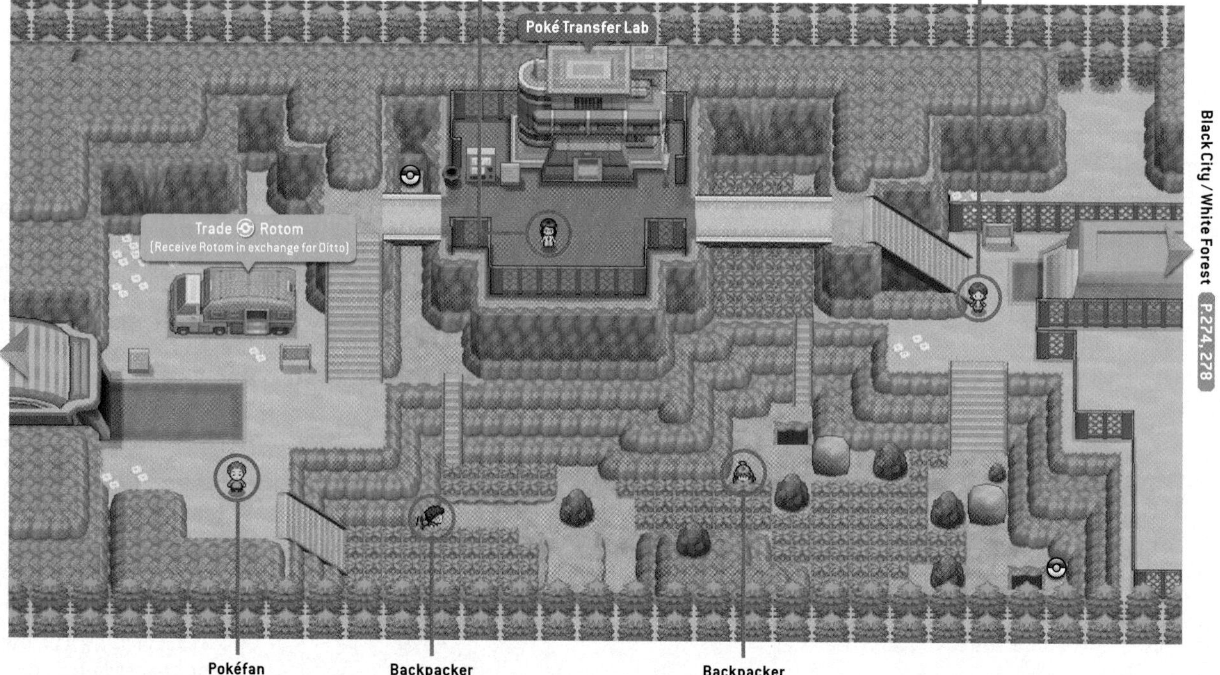

Items
☐ Max Potion
☐ TM26 Earthquake

Tyranitar
Rock / Dark
ABILITY
● Sand Stream

Tall Grass		
Gligar		○
Pupitar		○
Sandslash		◎
Sawk	●	○
Scrafty		○
Throh	○	○

Tall Grass (rustling)		
Audino		◎
Emolga		○
Gliscor		△
Sawk	○	△
Throh	●	△
Tyranitar		△

Dark Grass		
Gligar		○
Pupitar		○
Sandslash		◎
Sawk	●	○
Scrafty		○
Throh	○	○

Mass Outbreaks
Fearow

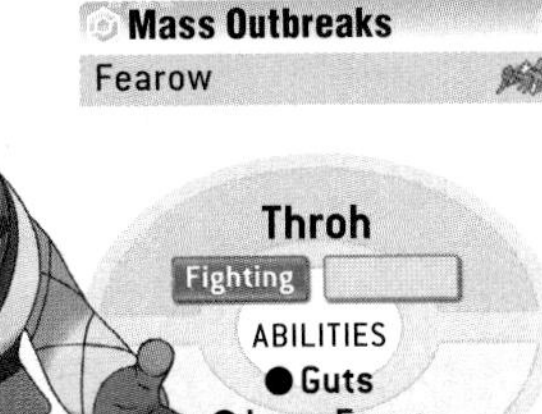

Sawk
Fighting
ABILITIES
● Sturdy
● Inner Focus

Throh
Fighting
ABILITIES
● Guts
● Inner Focus

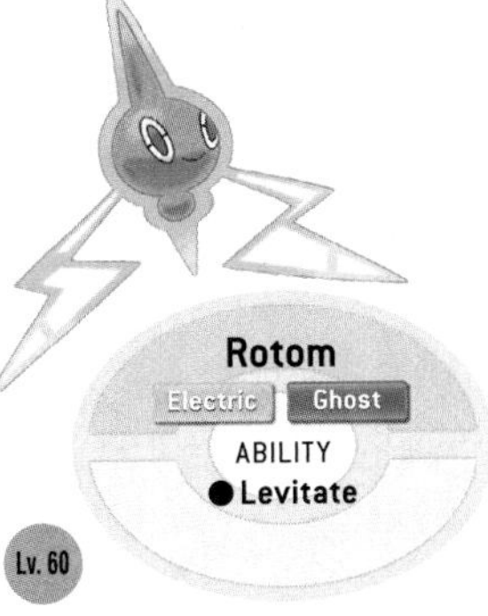

Rotom
Electric / Ghost
ABILITY
● Levitate
Lv. 60

Step 1 Give the woman a Ditto to receive a Rotom

On the west side of Route 15, you'll see a woman in a parked camper. She'll ask you to trade Pokémon. Give her a Ditto and she'll give you a Rotom. You can catch a Ditto in the Crater Forest in the Giant Chasm.

▸YES
NO
I would be very happy if you would trade my Rotom for your Ditto.

Step 2 Use Poké Transfer in the Poké Transfer Lab

In the Poké Transfer Lab, you can bring Pokémon over from *Pokémon Diamond, Pearl, Platinum, HeartGold*, and *SoulSilver Versions* using Poké Transfer. Bring over well-trained Pokémon to have them help you in your adventure (p. 282).

device, you may be able to bring Pokémon here from other regions.

Step 3 Get TM26 Earthquake

Use Strength to move the boulder on the east side of Route 15 and drop it in the hole. You can get TM26 Earthquake beyond it. Earthquake is a Ground-type move with a power of 100.

Trainer found a TM26 Earthquake!

Step 4 Head to Black City (White Forest)

Once you've seen everything, head east. Go through the gate at the end, and you'll arrive at Black City (p. 274) in *Pokémon Black Version 2*, and White Forest (p. 278) in *Pokémon White Version 2*.

Change Rotom's forms on Route 9

Once you have a Rotom, put it in your party and take it to Shopping Mall Nine on Route 9. If you check the cardboard boxes in the warehouse on the first floor, you can cause it to change its form (p. 200).

Pokémon can't be returned

Before you bring them over, realize that Pokémon brought from a different region via Poké Transfer can't be returned to the region they came from. Another thing to keep in mind: you can't transfer Pokémon that know HMs.

Black City

When playing *Pokémon Black Version 2*

Black City, a city in *Pokémon Black Version 2*, takes its place as a skyscraper-filled, modern metropolis. At the north end of town, you'll find the Black Tower, which is a dungeon that can be played over and over.

Route 14 P.248 (to Undella Town)

Black Tower

Pokémon Center

A store that sells evolution items will open here

Route 15 P.272 (to Nimbasa City)

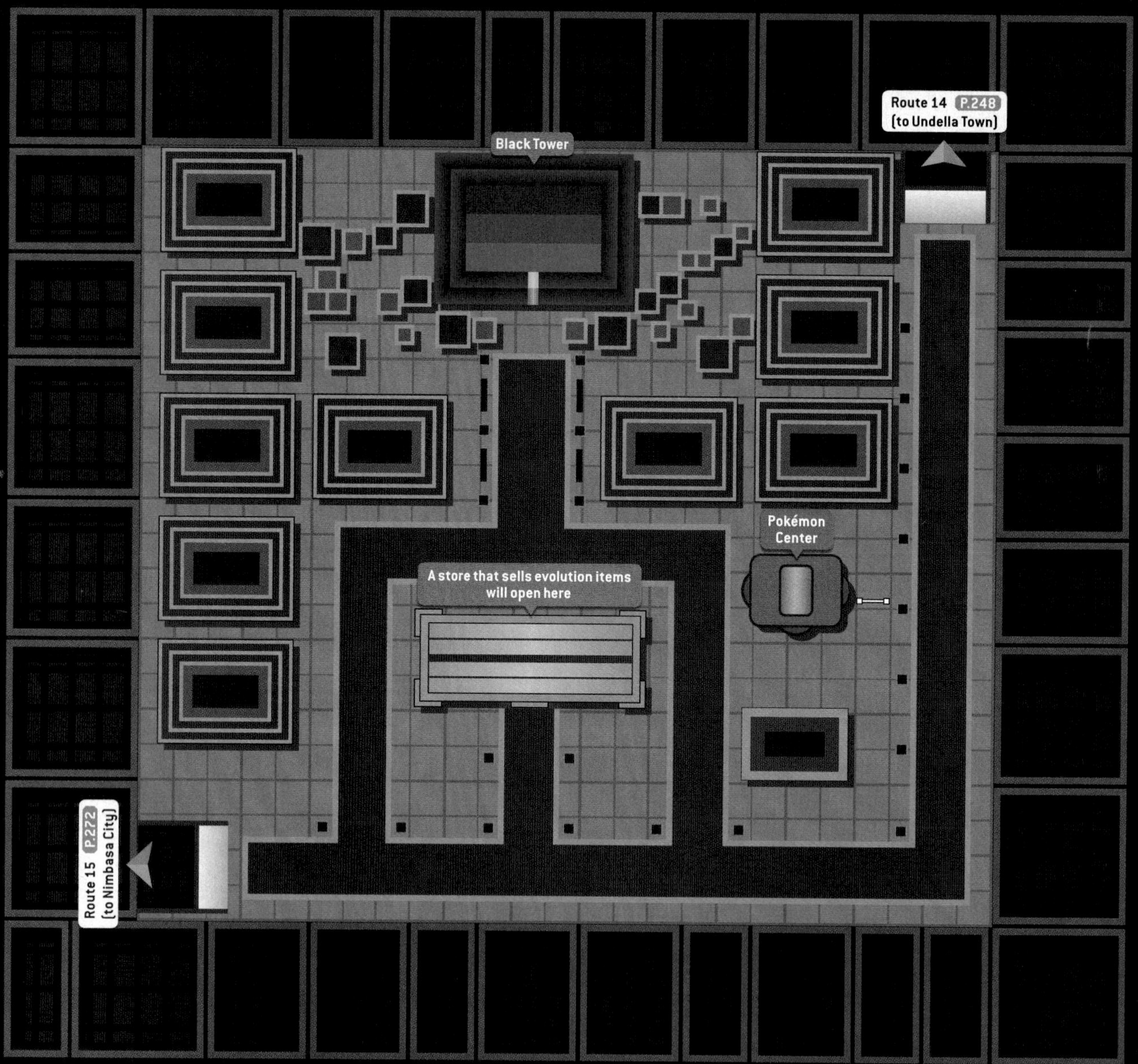

Poké Mart (Lower Clerk)	
BridgeMail M	50
Favored Mail	50
Greet Mail	50
Inquiry Mail	50
Like Mail	50
Reply Mail	50
RSVP Mail	50
Thanks Mail	50

Step 1 Challenge the Black Tower

After meeting Benga in Floccesy Town, you'll be able to challenge the Black Tower. Inside the Black Tower, you need to find and defeat the Boss Trainers of each area (p. 276). Whenever you enter the tower, the opponents will change, so you'll be able to play it as many times as you like.

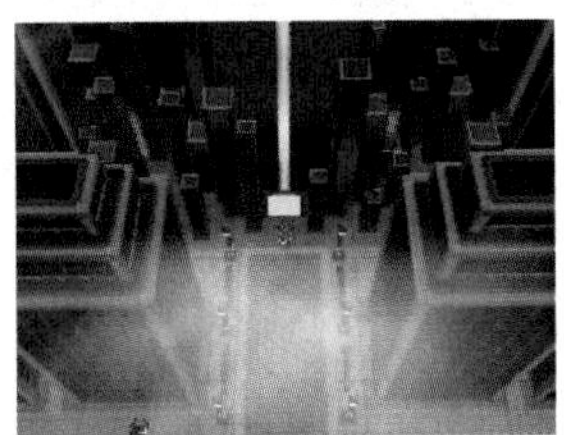

Step 2 Clear the areas to increase the number of shops

Clearing areas in the Black Tower causes new shops to open (p. 277). The shops sell items that can't be obtained anywhere else, giving you a great reason to clear the areas. Keep in mind that the shops have limited stock, so you can only buy items once per day.

Step 3 Get the Tower Key after clearing Area 5

After clearing Area 5, you'll receive the Tower Key. If you send it to a friend playing *Pokémon White Version 2*, your friend can use this Key to turn his or her White Forest into Black City (p. 72).

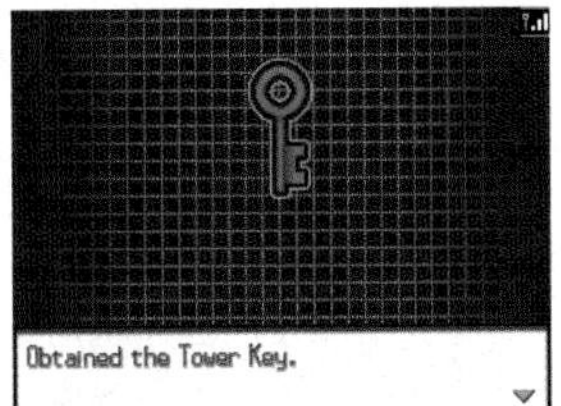

Send it to a friend with Unova Link

Use Unova Link to send the Tower Key to a friend playing *Pokémon White Version 2* by selecting "SEND AND RECEIVE KEYS" in the Key System settings.

Step 4 Complete Area 10 and get a Shiny Pokémon

After you defeat Benga, the Boss Trainer of Area 10, head back to Floccesy Town. Go see Benga in Alder's house and you can receive a Shiny Gible (p. 256).

Shiny Gible

Challenge the Black Tower and aim for Area 10

The map changes every time you enter the dungeon

The Trainers you encounter in the Black Tower in Black City change each time you enter it. Battle these Trainers while making your way through the various areas. Defeat the Boss Trainer at the end of each area to advance. There are 10 areas, each one more challenging than the previous.

The best thing to do when you're sick of schoolwork is to have a Pokémon battle!
At the top of the tower in Area 10, Alder's grandson, Benga, awaits you!

How to get the most out of the Black Tower

Unlike other battling facilities, such as the PWT or the Battle Subway, you'll gain Exp. Points and prize money from defeating the Trainers in the Black Tower. The more you battle there, the more you can increase your Pokémon's strength. However, you can't use your Bag, so you won't be able to heal HP or status conditions with items after a battle. If one of your Pokémon becomes low on HP, don't push it. Switch it out for another Pokémon.

The basic rules

1. You receive Exp. Points and prize money by defeating other Trainers
2. You can't use your Bag (the option disappears from the menu)
3. You can quit midway by leaving via the elevator, or by selecting "RETIRE" from the menu
4. You can save during your challenge
5. The Pokémon used by Trainers you encounter will not be registered in your Pokédex

How to clear an area

Search for the gate Trainer

I'll give you a hint.
The gate Trainer is male.

Defeat Trainers in the area, and they'll give you hints about where to find the gate Trainer who controls the door to the Boss Trainer's room.

Defeat the gate Trainer

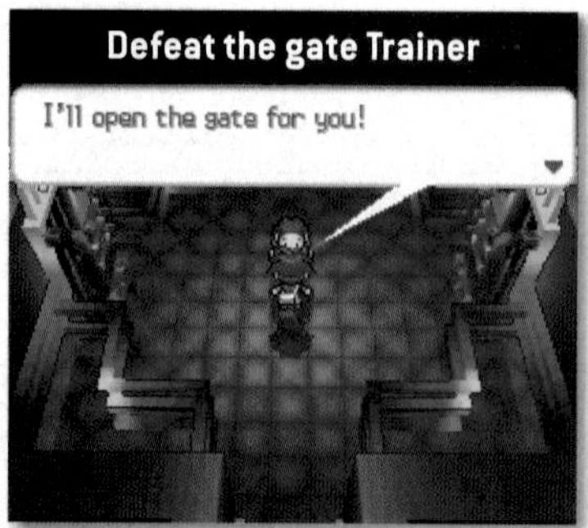

I'll open the gate for you!

Defeat the gate Trainer, and the door to the Boss Trainer's room will open, allowing you to challenge him or her.

Defeat the Boss Trainer

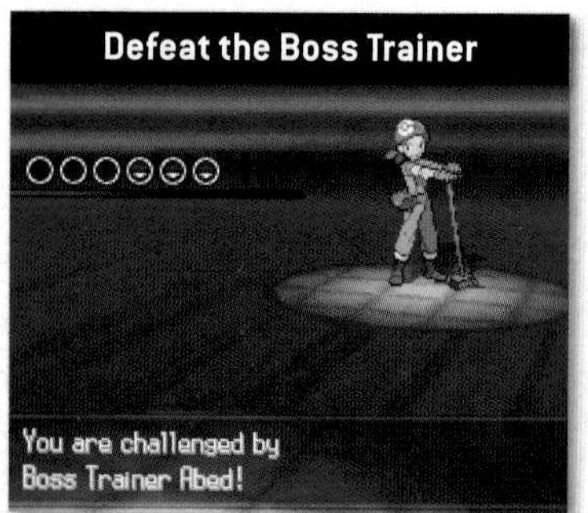

Defeat the Boss Trainer to clear the area. You'll automatically return to the entrance.

Defeat the Boss Trainers to clear an area

Defeat the Boss Trainer of an area, and you can receive a reward at the entrance. Also, the next time you start your challenge, you'll be able to choose a more difficult area. Clear the areas and make your way to Area 10 at the top, where Benga waits.

Please accept this prize in honor of your accomplishment!

Rewards

Items	Quantity
Calcium	Areas 1–3 ▼ One of a single item Areas 4–5 ▼ Two of a single item
Carbos	
HP Up	
Iron	
Protein	
Zinc	
Clever Wing	Areas 6–7 ▼ One of a single item Areas 8–9 ▼ Two of a single item
Genius Wing	
Health Wing	
Muscle Wing	
Rare Candy	
Resist Wing	
Swift Wing	
Grepa Berry	Area 10 ▼ One of a single item
Hondew Berry	
Kelpsy Berry	
Pomeg Berry	
Qualot Berry	
Rare Candy	
Tamato Berry	

Tip: Doctors heal your Pokémon

Defeat each area's Doctor. They will heal your Pokémon fully if you first win against them in battle. It's a one-time-only courtesy, so if none of your Pokémon requires aid, you can refuse the Doctor's services. You can then go back to the Doctor at a later time and get your Pokémon healed then.

YES
NO
Your Pokémon look tired...
Shall I recover them?

Clear areas to open up shops in Black City

By clearing areas in the Black Tower, new shops open in Black City. At each of the different shops, you can purchase items only once per day. Come back every day to do some shopping. The items sold differ between weekdays (Monday through Friday) and weekends (Saturday and Sunday).

How to unlock the shops and the items they sell

Shop location (conditions for opening)	Items sold Monday–Friday	Items sold Saturday–Sunday	Price
Top-left shop (clear Area 2)	Thunderstone	Protector	10,000
Top-right shop (clear Area 5)	Fire Stone	Metal Coat	20,000
Bottom-left shop (clear Area 8)	Dusk Stone	Up-Grade	40,000
Bottom-right shop (clear Area 10)	Dawn Stone	Dubious Disc	60,000

Thunderstone

Fire Stone

Dusk Stone

Dawn Stone

Keep trying until you get all of the Medals from Mr. Medal

You can obtain up to 12 Medals in the Black Tower. Some of the Medals can be obtained by clearing areas with a small number of steps or a small number of battles. Take on Unova's Challenge.

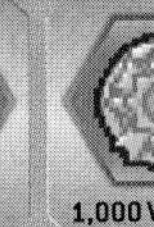

Tower Junior | Tower Master | 20 Victories | 50 Victories | 100 Victories | 1,000 Victories

Undefeated: Easy | Undefeated: Hard | Pinpoint: Easy | Pinpoint: Hard | Quick Clear: Easy | Quick Clear: Hard

Check p. 448 for the Medal list. 

White Forest

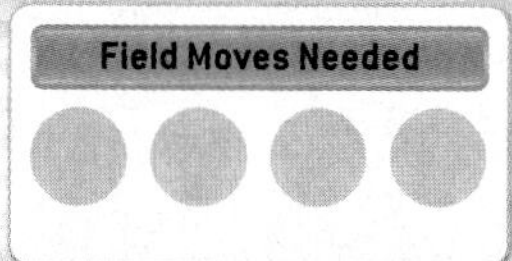

White Forest is a forest in *Pokémon White Version 2*. Giant trees grow throughout the forest, which is an area of natural beauty. In the center, you'll find the White Treehollow, a dungeon that can be played over and over.

Field Moves Needed

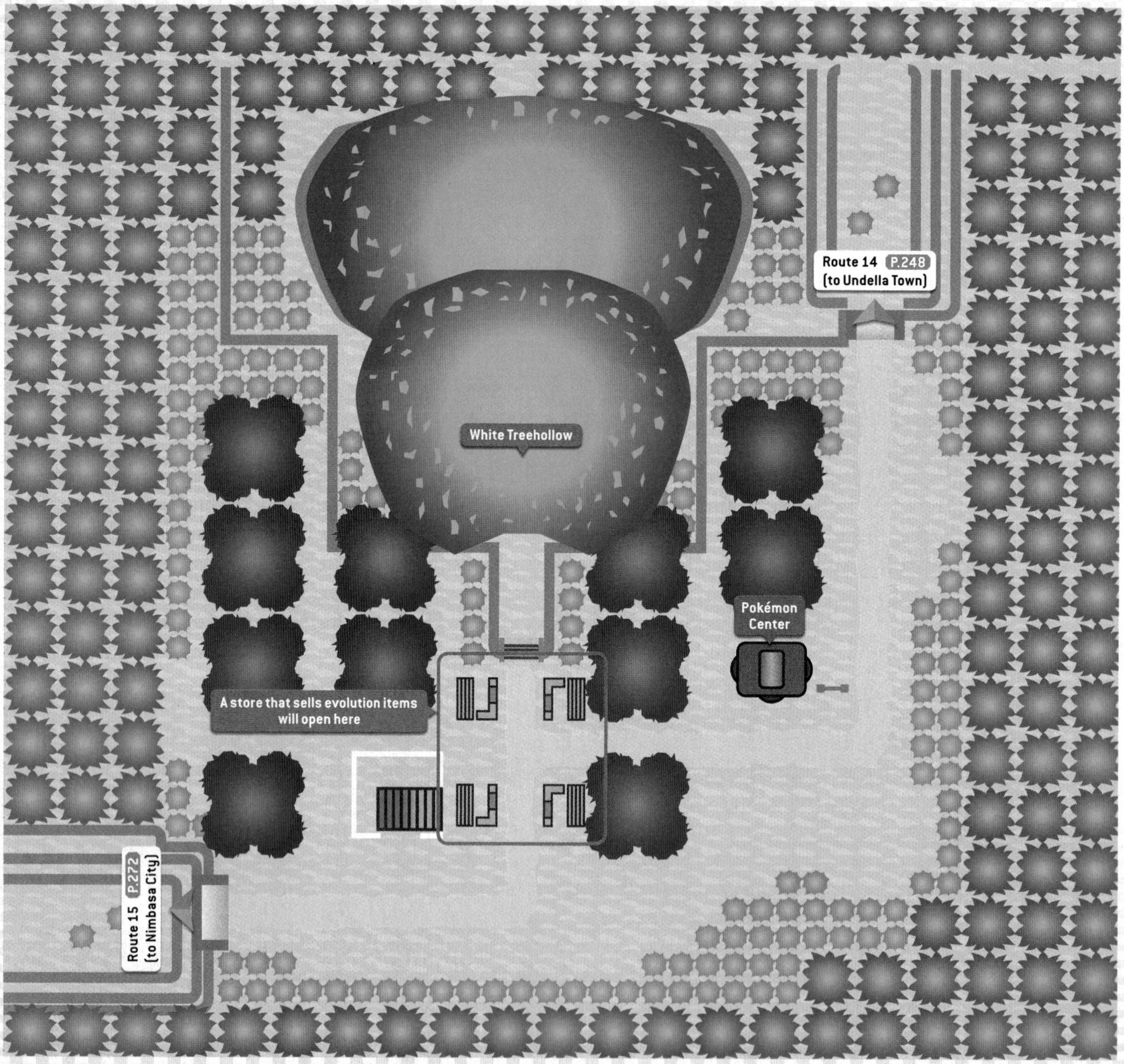

White Treehollow

Route 14 P.248
(to Undella Town)

Pokémon Center

A store that sells evolution items will open here

Route 15 P.272
(to Nimbasa City)

Poké Mart (Lower Clerk)	
BridgeMail M	50
Favored Mail	50
Greet Mail	50
Inquiry Mail	50
Like Mail	50
Reply Mail	50
RSVP Mail	50
Thanks Mail	50

Step 1 Challenge the White Treehollow

After meeting Benga in Floccesy Town, you'll be able to challenge the White Treehollow. Inside the White Treehollow, you'll need to find and defeat the Boss Trainers of each area (p. 280). Whenever you enter, the opponents will change, so you'll be able to play it as many times as you like.

Step 2 Clear the areas to increase the number of shops

Clearing the areas in the White Treehollow causes new shops to open (p. 281). Each of these shops carries items that can't be obtained elsewhere, so clear the areas and open up all of them. However, the shops are limited in that you can only buy items once per day.

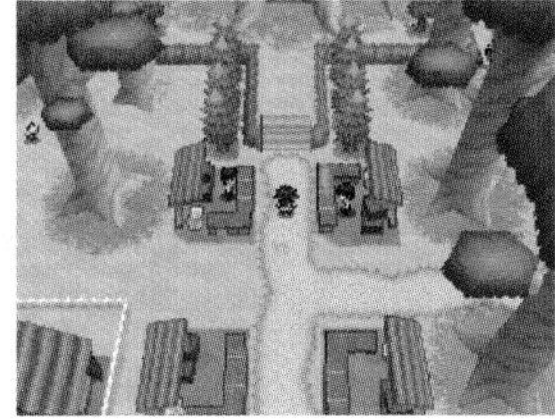

Step 3 Get the Treehollow Key after clearing Area 5

After completing Area 5, you'll receive the Treehollow Key. If you send it to a friend playing *Pokémon Black Version 2*, your friend can use this Key to turn his or her Black City into White Forest (p. 72).

Send it to your friend using Unova Link

You can send the Treehollow Key to a friend playing *Pokémon Black Version 2* using Unova Link by selecting "SEND AND RECEIVE KEYS" under Key System settings.

Step 4 Complete Area 10 and you can receive a Shiny Pokémon

After you defeat Benga, the Boss Trainer of Area 10, head back to Floccesy Town. Go see Benga in Alder's house and you can receive a Shiny Dratini (p. 256).

Shiny Dratini

Challenge the White Treehollow and aim for Area 10

The map changes every time you enter the dungeon

The Trainers you encounter in the White Treehollow in White Forest change each time you enter it. Battle these Trainers while making your way through the various areas. Defeat the Boss Trainer at the end of each area to advance. There are 10 areas, each one more challenging than the previous.

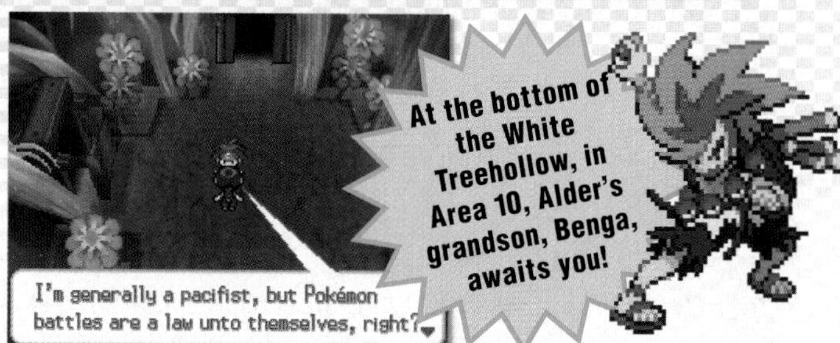

I'm generally a pacifist, but Pokémon battles are a law unto themselves, right?
At the bottom of the White Treehollow, in Area 10, Alder's grandson, Benga, awaits you!

How to get the most out of the White Treehollow

Unlike other battling facilities, such as the PWT or the Battle Subway, you'll gain Exp. Points and prize money from defeating the Trainers in the White Treehollow. The more you battle there, the more you can increase your Pokémon's strength. However, you can't use your Bag, so you won't be able to heal HP or status conditions with items after a battle. If one of your Pokémon becomes low on HP, don't push it. Switch it out for another Pokémon.

The basic rules

1. You receive Exp. Points and prize money by defeating other Trainers
2. You can't use your Bag (the option disappears from the menu)
3. You can quit midway by leaving via the elevator, or by selecting "RETIRE" from the menu
4. You can save during your challenge
5. The Pokémon used by Trainers you encounter will not be registered in your Pokédex

How to clear an area

Search for the gate Trainer

Keep this a secret, but the gate Trainer is female.

Defeat Trainers in the area, and they'll give you hints about where to find the gate Trainer who controls the door to the Boss Trainer's room.

Defeat the gate Trainer

I'd say you're good enough.
I'll open up the gate!

Defeat the gate Trainer, and the door to the Boss Trainer's room will open, allowing you to challenge him or her.

Defeat the Boss Trainer

You are challenged by Boss Trainer Abigail!

Defeat the Boss Trainer to clear the area. You'll automatically return to the entrance.

Defeat the Boss Trainers to clear an area

Defeat the Boss Trainer of an area, and you can receive a reward at the entrance. Also, the next time you start your challenge, you'll be able to choose a more difficult area. Clear the areas and make your way to Area 10 at the bottom, where Benga waits.

Rewards

Items	Quantity
Calcium	Areas 1–3 ▼ One of a single item Areas 4–5 ▼ Two of a single item
Carbos	
HP Up	
Iron	
Protein	
Zinc	
Clever Wing	Areas 6–7 ▼ One of a single item Areas 8–9 ▼ Two of a single item
Genius Wing	
Health Wing	
Muscle Wing	
Rare Candy	
Resist Wing	
Swift Wing	
Grepa Berry	Area 10 ▼ One of a single item
Hondew Berry	
Kelpsy Berry	
Pomeg Berry	
Qualot Berry	
Rare Candy	
Tamato Berry	

Tip — **Nurses heal your Pokémon**

There is a Nurse in each area who will bring your Pokémon to complete health once if you first win against the Nurse in battle. If none of your Pokémon requires aid, you can refuse the Nurse's services. You can then go back to the Nurse at a later time and get your Pokémon healed then.

Clear areas to open up shops in White Forest

By clearing the areas in the White Treehollow, new shops open in White Forest. At each of the different shops, you can purchase items only once per day. Come back every day to do some shopping. The items sold differ between weekdays (Monday through Friday) and weekends (Saturday and Sunday).

How to unlock the shops and the items they sell

Shop location (conditions for opening)	Items sold Monday–Friday	Items sold Saturday–Sunday	Price
Top-left shop (clear Area 2)	Leaf Stone	DeepSeaTooth	1,000
Top-right shop (clear Area 5)	Water Stone	DeepSeaScale	2,000
Bottom-left shop (clear Area 8)	Shiny Stone	Dragon Scale	4,000
Bottom-right shop (clear Area 10)	Oval Stone	King's Rock	6,000

Leaf Stone

Water Stone

Shiny Stone

Oval Stone

Keep trying until you get all of the Medals from Mr. Medal

You can obtain up to 12 Medals in the White Treehollow. Some of the Medals can be obtained by clearing areas with a small number of steps or a small number of battles. Take on Unova's Challenge.

Treehollow Junior · Treehollow Master · 20 Victories · 50 Victories · 100 Victories · 1,000 Victories

Undefeated: Easy · Undefeated: Hard · Pinpoint: Easy · Pinpoint: Hard · Quick Clear: Easy · Quick Clear: Hard

Check p. 448 for the Medal list.

Transfer Pokémon with Poké Transfer

Transfer Pokémon from other games using wireless communications

Poké Transfer is a device that transfers Pokémon from other Pokémon series games to your *Pokémon Black Version 2* or *Pokémon White Version 2* game. You can use it in the Poké Transfer Lab on Route 15. You will need two systems in the Nintendo DS family of systems to use Poké Transfer. Borrow a friend's system to use Poké Transfer and bring your Pokémon over from other games.

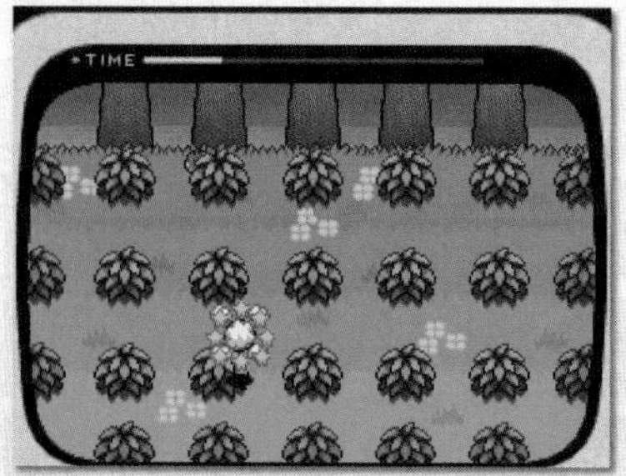

Games compatible with Poké Transfer in *Pokémon Black Version 2* and *Pokémon White Version 2*

Pokémon can be brought over from these Nintendo DS Pokémon games

Pokémon games that use Poké Transfer (Nintendo DS Pokémon games)

You can transfer up to six Pokémon at a time from another Nintendo DS Pokémon game

With Poké Transfer, you can transfer up to six Pokémon at one go. After you've chosen the six Pokémon to transfer, you'll get to play a minigame. On the Touch Screen, use the stylus to pull the bowstring. Release the bowstring to launch Poké Balls at the Pokémon that are hiding in the tall grass on the top screen. Hit all the Pokémon, and the game ends. The Pokémon you caught in the game will be sent to your PC Box in your *Pokémon Black Version 2* or *Pokémon White Version 2* game. You can use Poké Transfer as many times as you want every day.

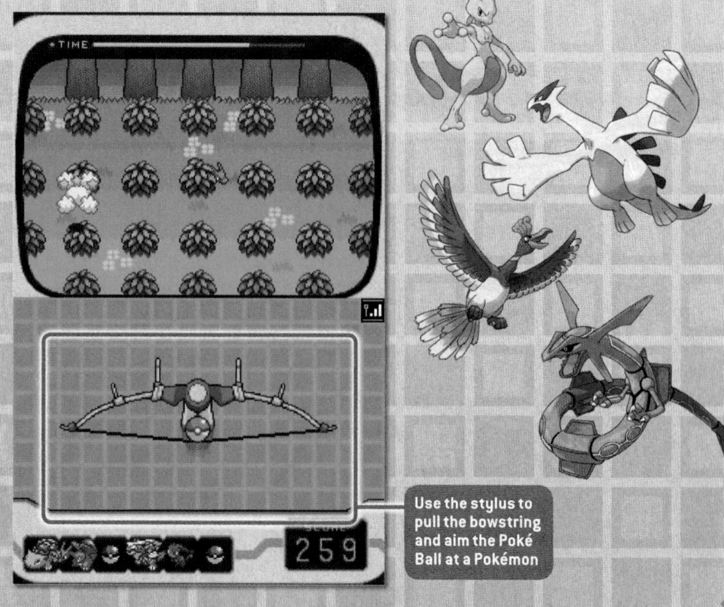

Use the stylus to pull the bowstring and aim the Poké Ball at a Pokémon

Cave of Being

The Cave of Being is a small cave that can be reached by climbing the waterfall located in the southern part of Route 20. It's said that the deepest part of the cave connects to the Sinnoh region.

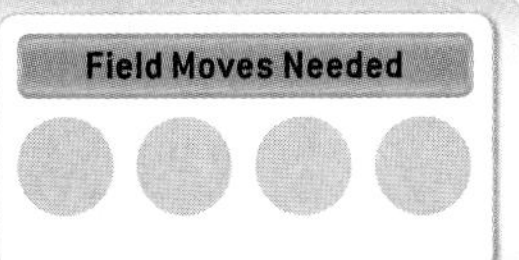

Route 20 P.92
(to Floccesy Town)

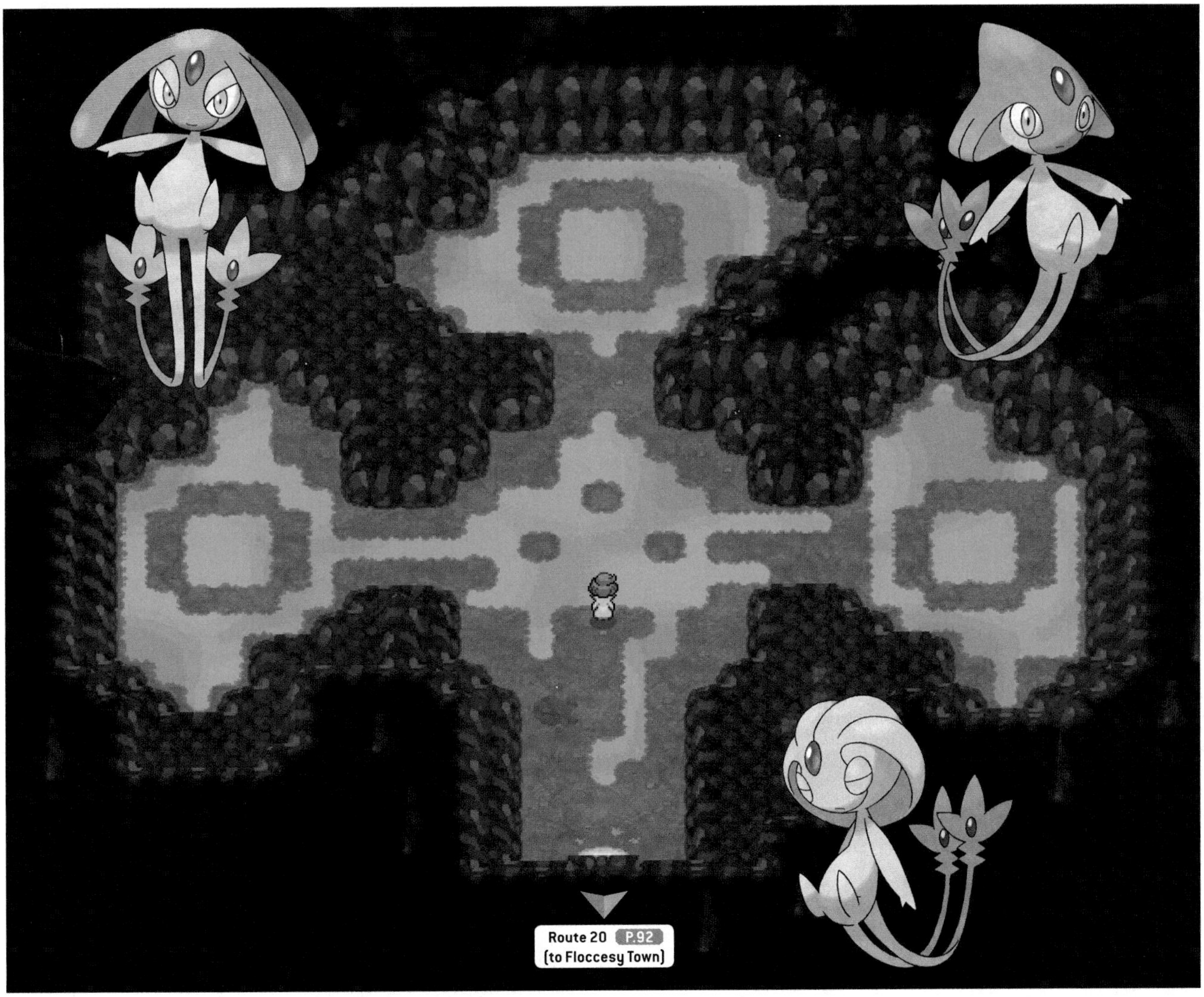

Step 1 Travel far and wide to catch all three

Go inside and Uxie, Mesprit, and Azelf will appear and then fly away. In order to catch them, you'll need to travel to Celestial Tower (p. 264), Route 23 (p. 264), and Nacrene City (p. 314).

Three Legendary Pokémon from the Sinnoh region

There are three famous lakes in the Sinnoh region: Lake Verity, Lake Valor, and Lake Acuity. Uxie, Mesprit, and Azelf each inhabits one of the lakes.

Clay Tunnel

Clay Tunnel is a tunnel created by Clay's constant mining. It connects Driftveil City, Mistralton Cave, and Twist Mountain. Deep inside, you'll discover the mysterious Underground Ruins.

Field Moves Needed

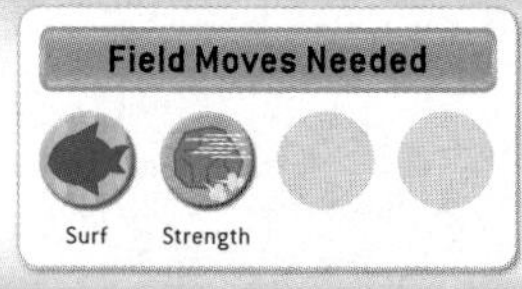

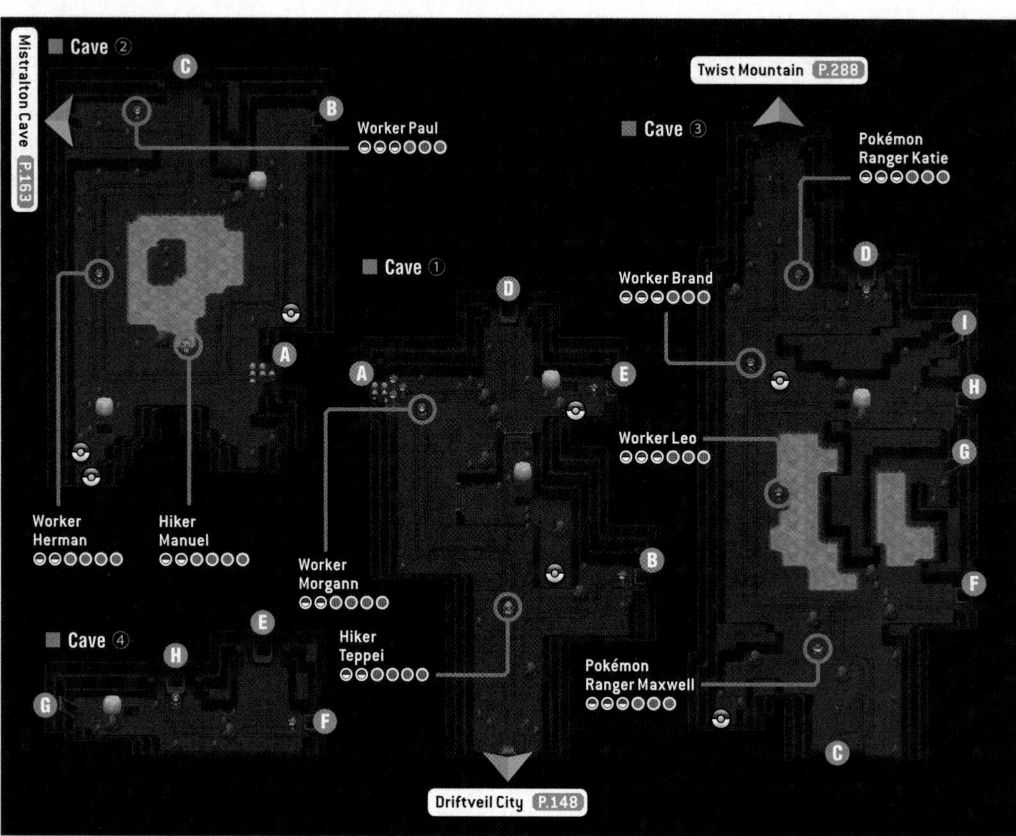

Items

- First visit
- ☐ Green Shard
- ☐ HP Up
- ☐ Max Revive
- ☐ Metal Coat
- ☐ Nugget
- ☐ Rare Bone
- ☐ Red Shard
- After defeating Pokémon Ranger Maxwell
- ☐ Lum Berry
- After defeating Pokémon Ranger Katie
- ☐ Lum Berry

Cave	
Boldore	◎
Durant	○
Lairon	○
Nosepass	○
Onix	△
Woobat	○

Cave (dust cloud)	
Excadrill	◎
Onix	○
Steelix	△

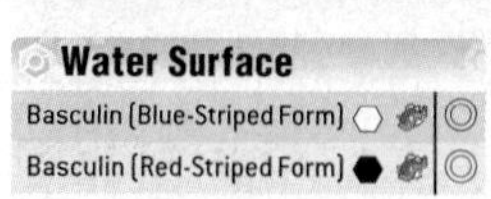

Water Surface	
Basculin (Blue-Striped Form) ◯	◎
Basculin (Red-Striped Form) ●	◎

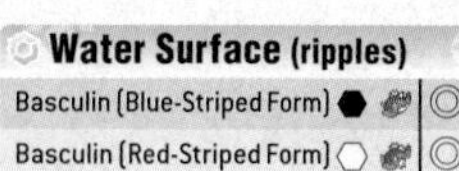

Water Surface (ripples)	
Basculin (Blue-Striped Form) ●	◎
Basculin (Red-Striped Form) ◯	◎

Fishing	
Basculin (Blue-Striped Form) ◯	◎
Basculin (Red-Striped Form) ●	◎
Poliwag	◎

Fishing (ripples)	
Basculin (Blue-Striped Form) ●	◎
Basculin (Red-Striped Form) ◯	◎
Poliwhirl	◎
Poliwrath	△

Step 1 Enter Clay Tunnel from Driftveil City

From the Pokémon Center in Driftveil City, head north and you'll come across the entrance to Clay Tunnel. You couldn't go inside before entering the Hall of Fame, but now the tunnel has finally been completed, so now you can. Take the stairs down from the raised area.

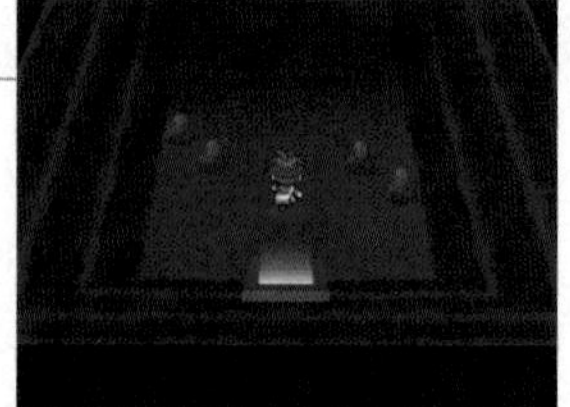

Step 2 Bring a Pokémon that knows Rock Smash

A group of Workers has gathered on the west side of cave ①. They're having trouble with a boulder that they can't seem to move. If you have a Pokémon that knows Rock Smash in your party, talk to them and you'll be able to open the way up to cave ②.

Wait a minute! Do you have a Pokémon that's learned Rock Smash?

You don't need Rock Smash

Even without a Pokémon that knows Rock Smash, you can proceed to cave ②. All you have to do is take the mining cart that can be found to the east of Hiker Teppei, who is located at the south end of cave ①.

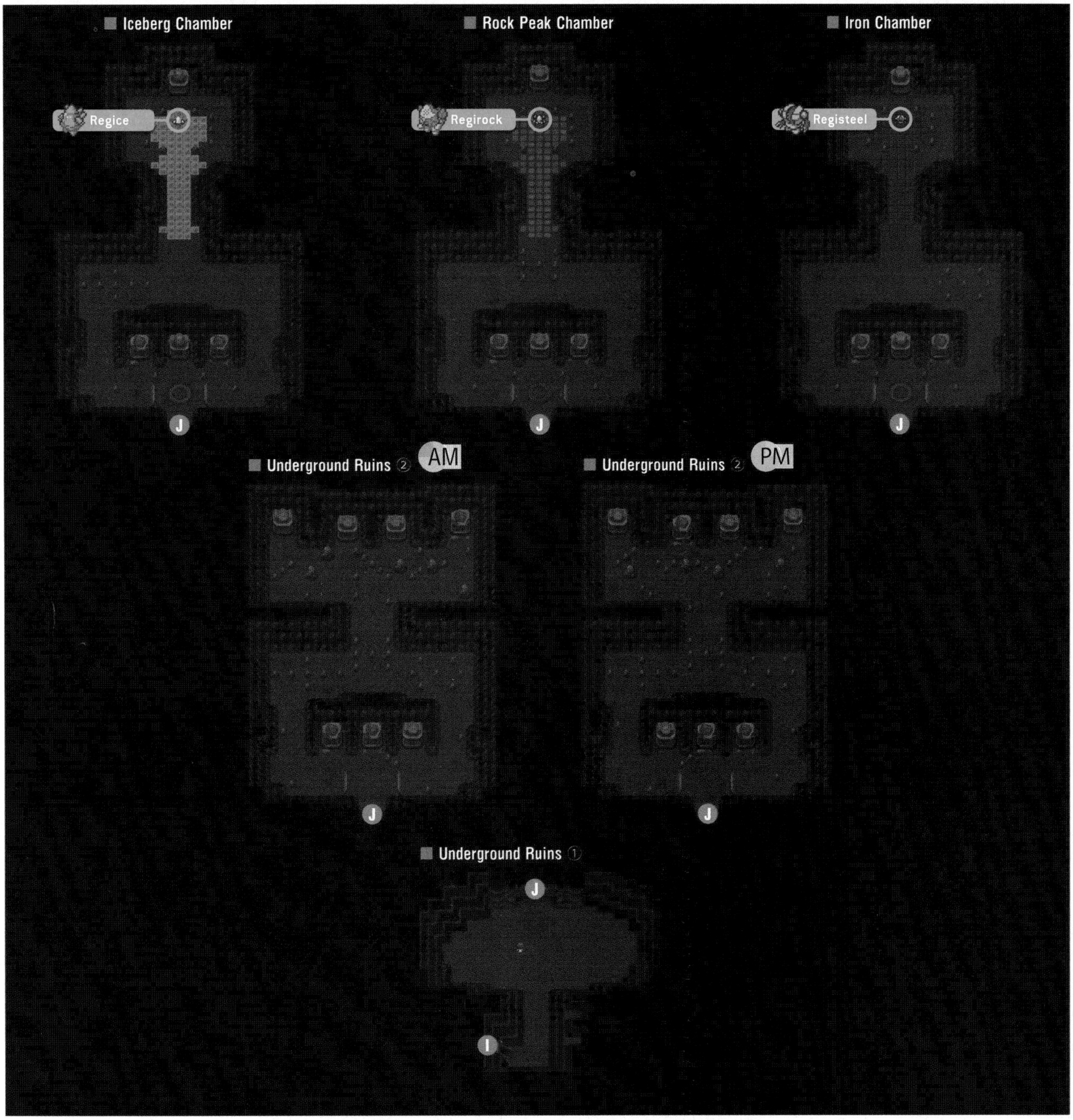

Iceberg Chamber
Regice

Rock Peak Chamber
Regirock

Iron Chamber
Registeel

Underground Ruins ② AM

Underground Ruins ② PM

Underground Ruins ①

Step 3 It connects to Mistralton Cave

Go to the northern end of cave ② and you'll find an entrance to Mistralton Cave on the western side. Before entering the Hall of Fame, there was a man blocking the way. However, now that you've entered the Hall of Fame, the man is gone and you can pass through.

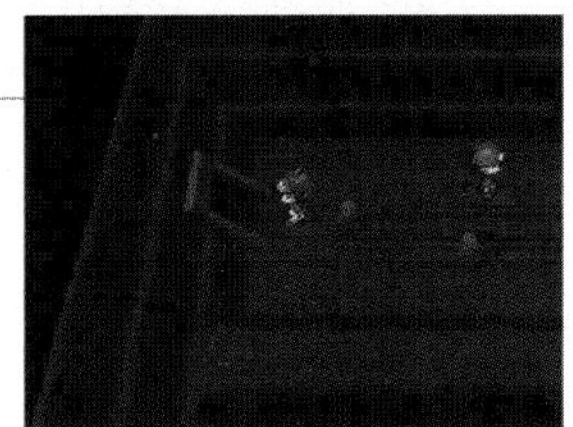

Step 4 Take the mining cart to go deeper into the tunnel

Proceed north through cave ② and head for cave ③. From here, you'll take a mining cart. Talk to the Worker in front of the mining cart to hop aboard and take it to the northern side of cave ①.

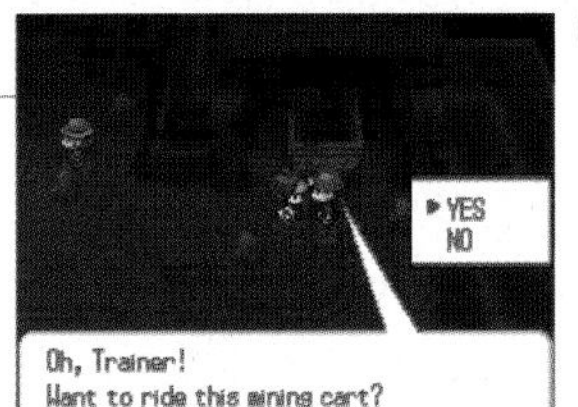

YES
NO
Oh, Trainer!
Want to ride this mining cart?

Apparently the soil in the tunnel is similar to that in the Hoenn region

According to one of the Workers, the soil in Clay Tunnel resembles that of the Hoenn region. Could this have something to do with the location of Regirock, Regice, and Registeel?

Step 5 Use Strength to move boulders and create shortcuts

You'll find boulders throughout Clay Tunnel that can be moved by using Strength. If you push all the boulders into the holes, you'll be able to move around more quickly. If you find a boulder while exploring, take a second to push it into a hole.

Get Berries from Pokémon Rangers

Defeat the Pokémon Rangers Maxwell and Katie to receive Lum Berries. You can find Maxwell at the southern end of cave ③. Katie is at the northern end. Defeat both of them to get Berries.

Step 6 Arrive at the Underground Ruins

Take a mining cart from the eastern side of the cave and travel further eastward (③). You'll arrive at Underground Ruins ①. The music will change suddenly, signifying your arrival. Proceed north to enter Underground Ruins ②.

Step 7 Examine a statue for hints about where to find the switch

In the northern half of Underground Ruins ②, you'll find four statues. Examine the statue that is located second from the far right for a hint. There are two variations to Underground Ruins ② depending on the time of day. Visiting it during both variations to get both hints is recommended.

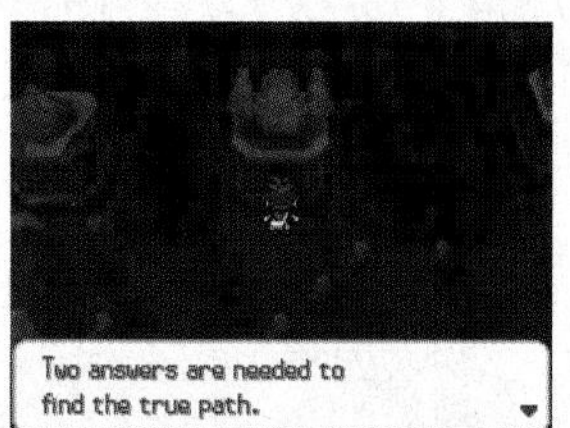

Wondering what "when the moon is in the sky" and "when the sun is in the sky" mean?

Underground Ruins ② changes depending on whether the time is A.M. or P.M. The 12 hours from 12:00 A.M. are considered "when the sun is in the sky," and the 12 hours from 12:00 P.M. are considered "when the moon is in the sky." Check the area out during both times.

Put the two hints together

Once you've got both hints from Underground Ruins ②, put them together. That will tell you where to find the switch in Underground Ruins ①.

Step 8 Push the switch on the ground and go to Rock Peak Chamber

Once you've obtained both hints, go back to Underground Ruins ① and push the switch. The "eyeball" mentioned in the hint was actually the circular pattern in front of the door. By pressing the switch, Underground Ruins ② will change into Rock Peak Chamber.

Step 9 Go deeper in to find Regirock

Head north after you press the switch in the Underground Ruins ①. Underground Ruins ② will transform into Rock Peak Chamber, and you'll find Regirock if you venture deeper inside. When you try to speak to it, you'll be drawn into battle. Catch it!

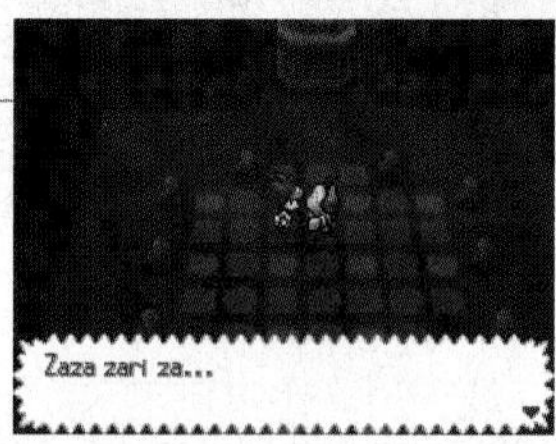

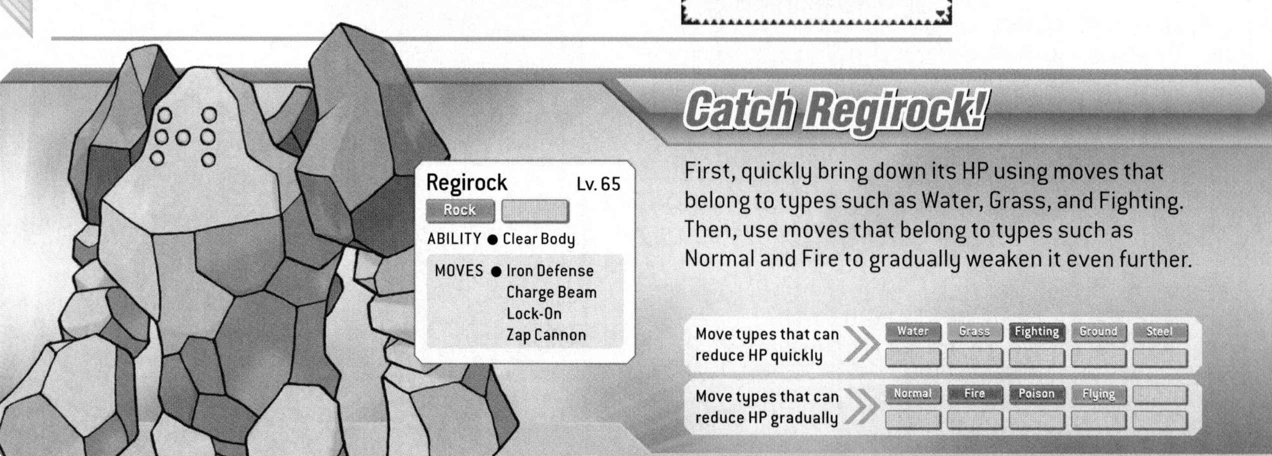

Catch Regirock!

Regirock Lv. 65
Rock
ABILITY ● Clear Body
MOVES ● Iron Defense, Charge Beam, Lock-On, Zap Cannon

First, quickly bring down its HP using moves that belong to types such as Water, Grass, and Fighting. Then, use moves that belong to types such as Normal and Fire to gradually weaken it even further.

Move types that can reduce HP quickly	Water	Grass	Fighting	Ground	Steel
Move types that can reduce HP gradually	Normal	Fire	Poison	Flying	

Step 10 Get the Iron Key (Iceberg Key)

By defeating Regirock, you'll receive the Iron Key in *Pokémon Black Version 2*, and the Iceberg Key in *Pokémon White Version 2*. Don't forget you can also change your Unova Link Key System settings [p. 72].

After changing to Iron Chamber in Key System Settings: Go deeper in to find Registeel

Change Mystery Door to Iron Chamber under the Key System settings in Unova Link, and Underground Ruins ② will turn into Iron Chamber. Go deeper in and you'll find Registeel. Speak to it and catch it.

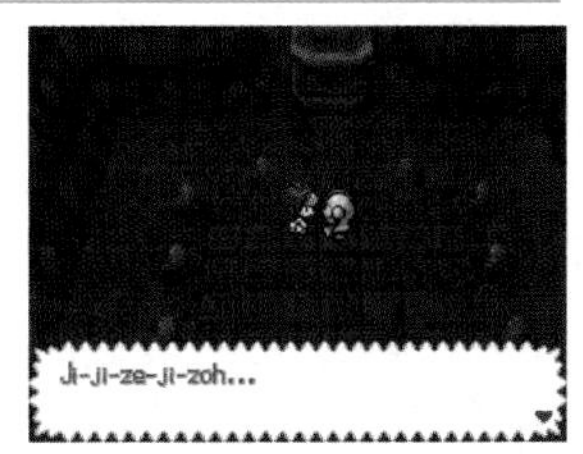

Change your settings from the title screen

You can change your Key System Settings from the title screen. Select "Key System" under "Unova Link" and then select "Key System Settings" to open the Mystery Door. From there, you can choose the room with which to connect.

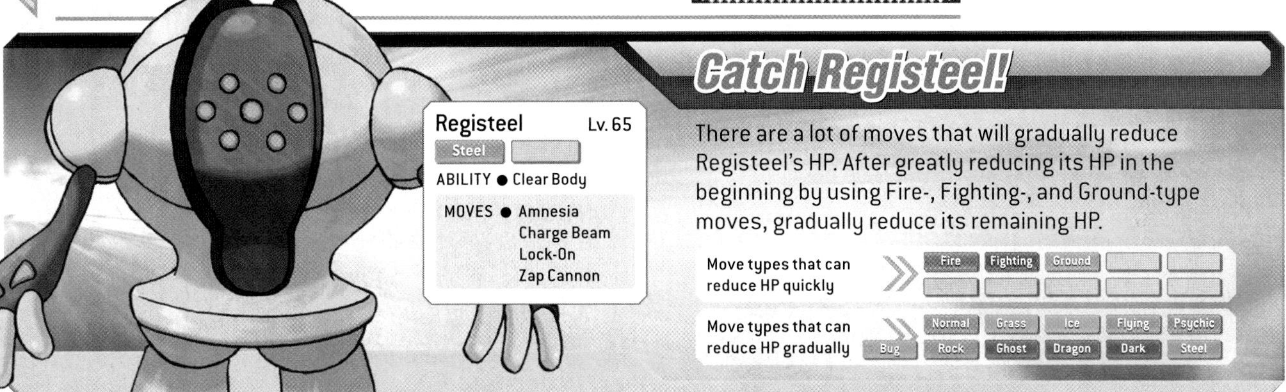

Catch Registeel!

Registeel Lv. 65
Steel
ABILITY ● Clear Body
MOVES ● Amnesia, Charge Beam, Lock-On, Zap Cannon

There are a lot of moves that will gradually reduce Registeel's HP. After greatly reducing its HP in the beginning by using Fire-, Fighting-, and Ground-type moves, gradually reduce its remaining HP.

Move types that can reduce HP quickly	Fire, Fighting, Ground
Move types that can reduce HP gradually	Normal, Grass, Ice, Flying, Psychic, Bug, Rock, Ghost, Dragon, Dark, Steel

After changing to Iceberg Chamber in Key System Settings: Go deeper in to find Regice

Change Mystery Door to Iceberg Chamber under the Key System settings of Unova Link, and Underground Ruins ② will turn into Iceberg Chamber. Go deeper in and you'll find Regice. Approach it and speak to it. Now all you have to do is catch it.

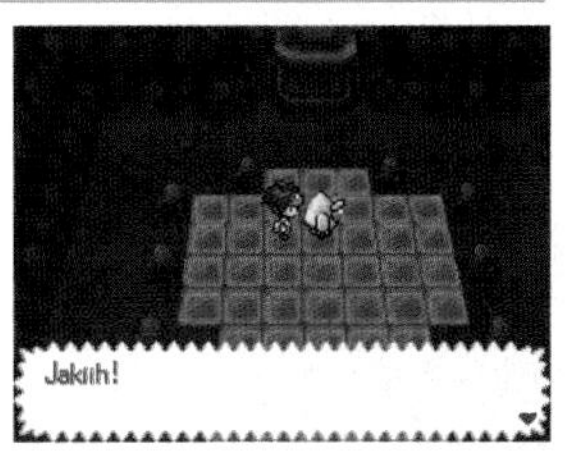

Trade keys using Unova Link

The Key you receive after catching Regirock is different between *Pokémon Black Version 2* and *Pokémon White Version 2*. Choose "SEND AND RECEIVE KEYS" from Unova Link to trade keys with a friend who is playing the other version of the game.

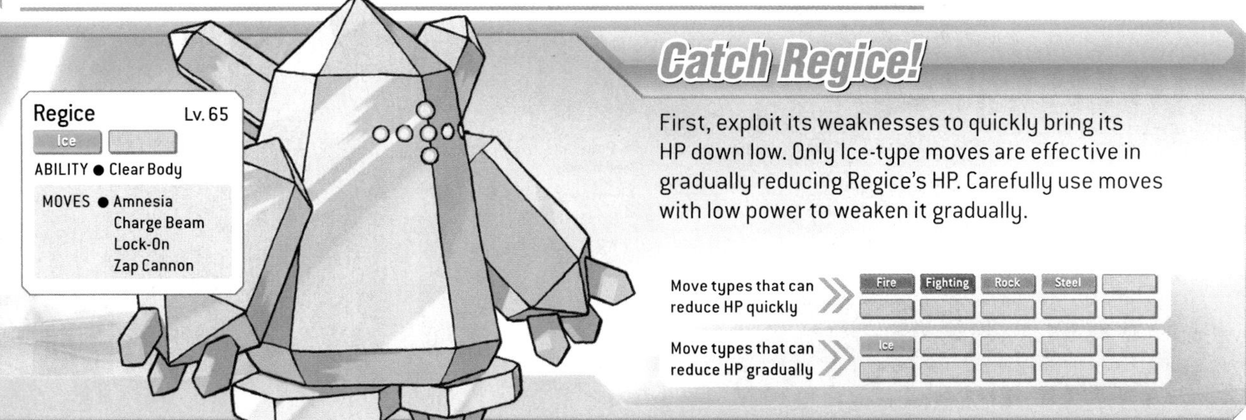

Catch Regice!

Regice Lv. 65
Ice
ABILITY ● Clear Body
MOVES ● Amnesia, Charge Beam, Lock-On, Zap Cannon

First, exploit its weaknesses to quickly bring its HP down low. Only Ice-type moves are effective in gradually reducing Regice's HP. Carefully use moves with low power to weaken it gradually.

Move types that can reduce HP quickly	Fire, Fighting, Rock, Steel
Move types that can reduce HP gradually	Ice

Step 11 Take Clay Tunnel to Twist Mountain

Head straight north from cave ③ and you'll reach Twist Mountain. Just like Clay Tunnel, there are many areas in Twist Mountain that were inaccessible to you before entering the Hall of Fame. Northward you go to Twist Mountain [p. 288]!

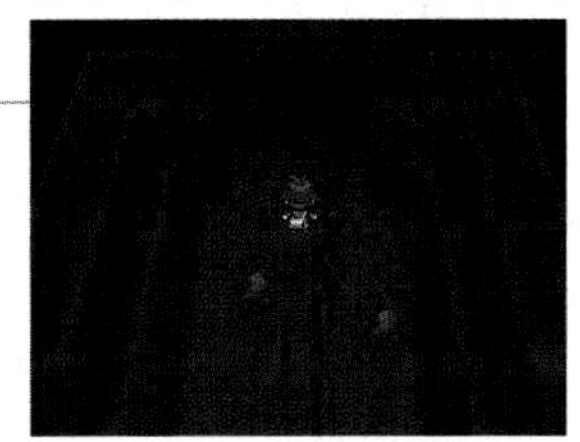

Twist Mountain

Twist Mountain is a mine with caves designed to make it easy to extract minerals from the mountain. From "outside" in the middle, you can go to different levels: upper, middle, lower, and lowest. At the lowest level is a room with a statue of Regigigas.

Items

All Seasons
- ☐ Dusk Stone
- ☐ Float Stone
- ☐ Full Restore
- ☐ Rare Bone
- ☐ Red Shard
- ☐ TM71 Stone Edge
- ☐ TM90 Substitution
- ☐ TM91 Flash Cannon

When the season is spring, summer, or autumn
- ☐ Dusk Ball

When the season is winter
- ☐ Big Nugget
- ☐ Eject Button

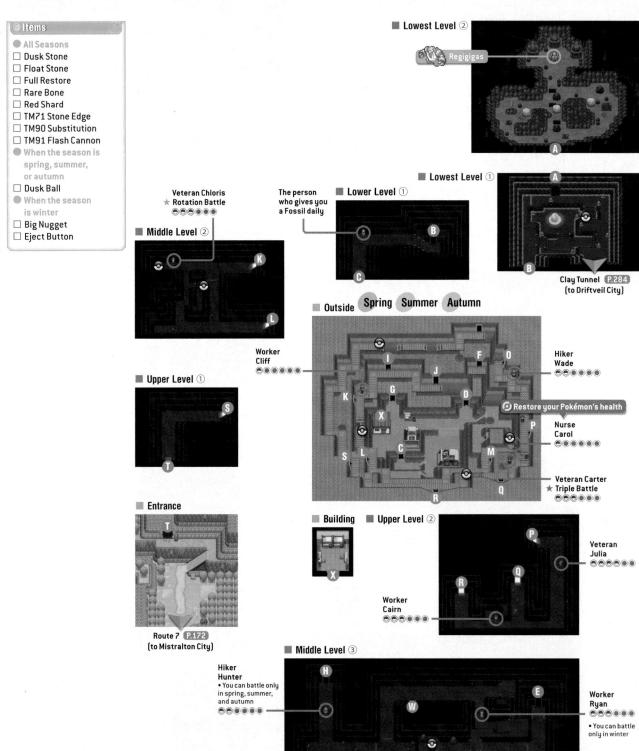

Lowest Level ②

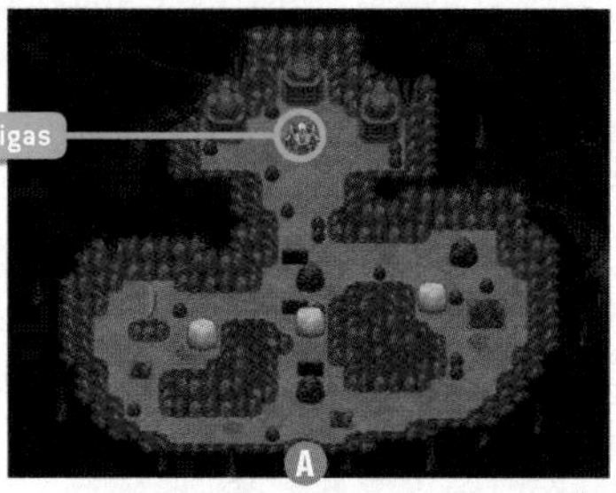

Regigigas

A

Lowest Level ①

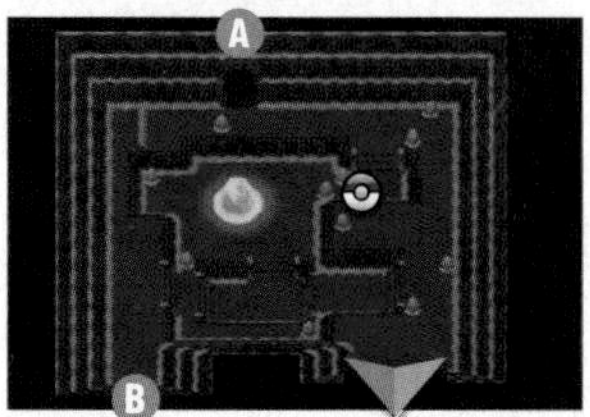

A, B

Clay Tunnel P.284 (to Driftveil City)

Lower Level ①

The person who gives you a Fossil daily

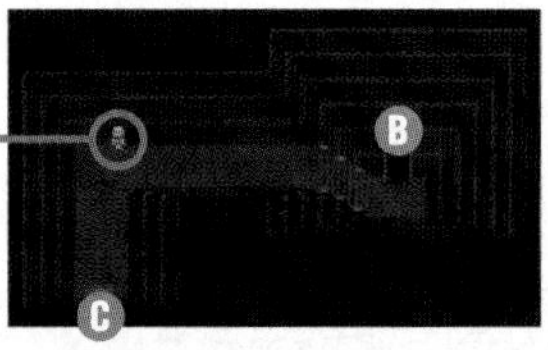

B, C

Middle Level ②

Veteran Chloris ★ Rotation Battle

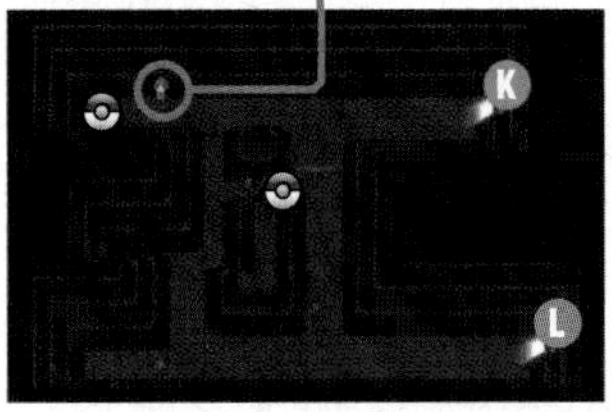

K, L

Outside Spring Summer Autumn

Worker Cliff

Hiker Wade

Restore your Pokémon's health

Nurse Carol

Veteran Carter ★ Triple Battle

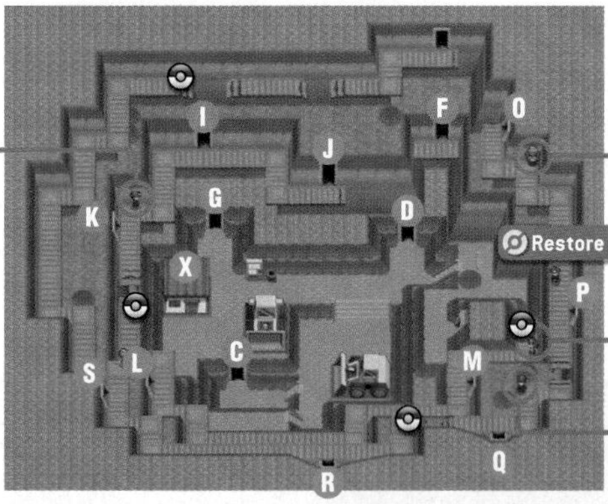

I, F, O, J, K, G, D, X, P, C, S, L, M, R, Q

Upper Level ①

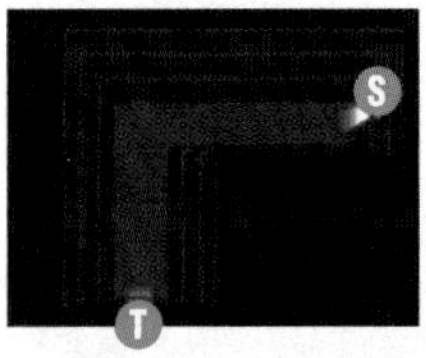

S, T

Entrance

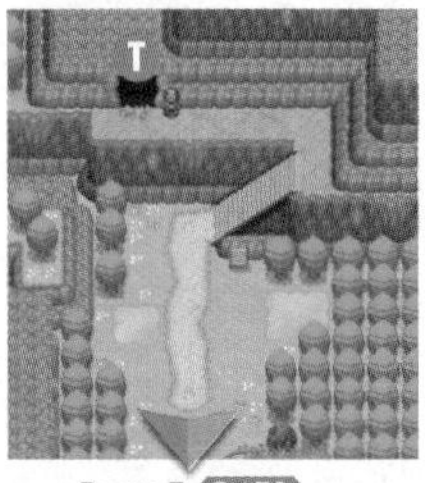

T

Route 7 P.172 (to Mistralton City)

Building

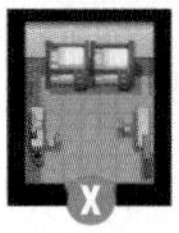

X

Upper Level ②

P, Q, R

Veteran Julia

Worker Cairn

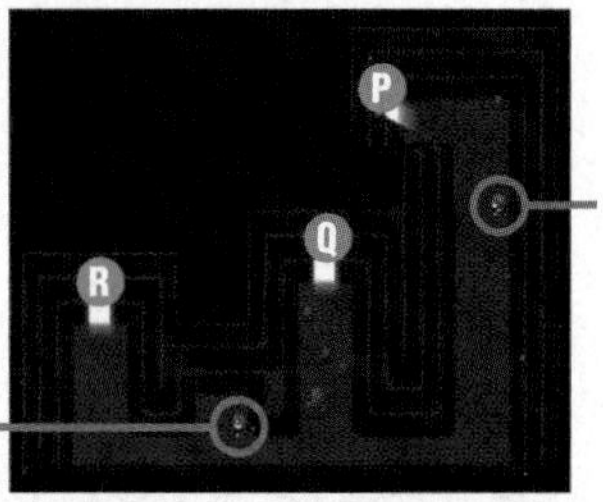

Middle Level ③

Hiker Hunter
- You can battle only in spring, summer, and autumn

Worker Ryan
- You can battle only in winter

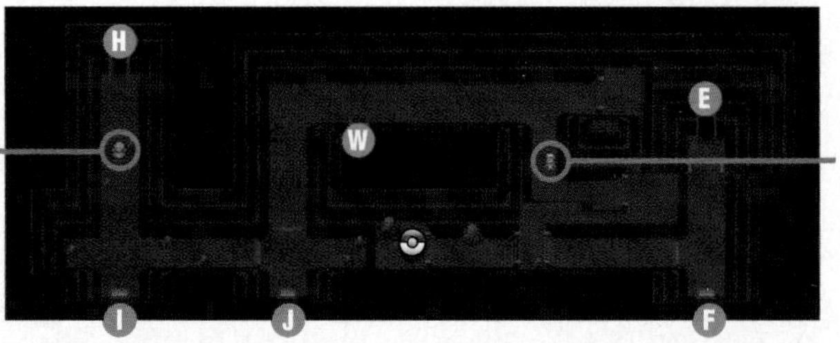

H, E, W, I, J, F

■ Middle Level ④ Spring Summer Autumn

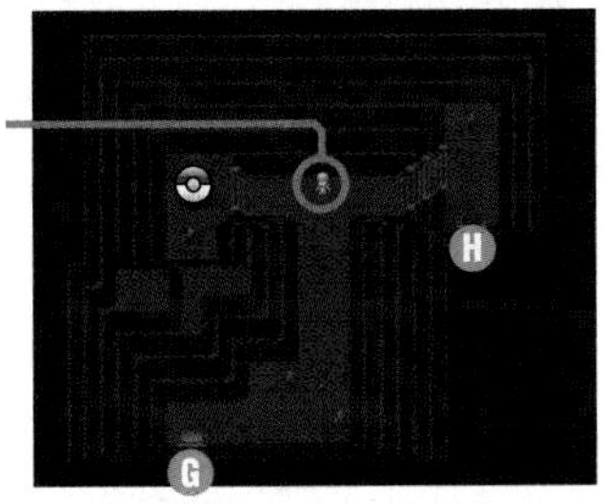

Worker
Victor
G
H

■ Upper Level ④ Winter

W
V

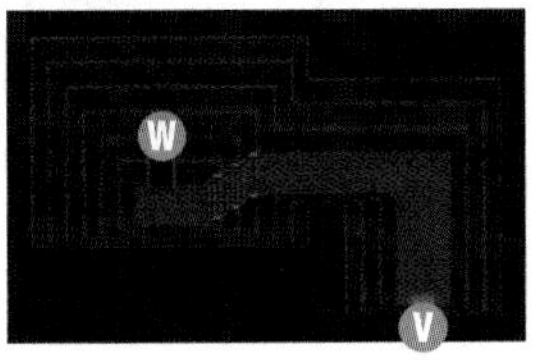

■ Lower Level ②

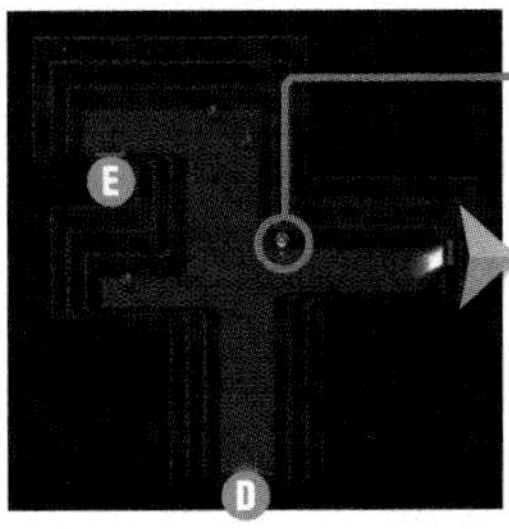

Heavy Machinery Pro
Icirrus City P.301
E
D

■ Upper Level ③

Worker
Gus
O
N

■ Outside Winter

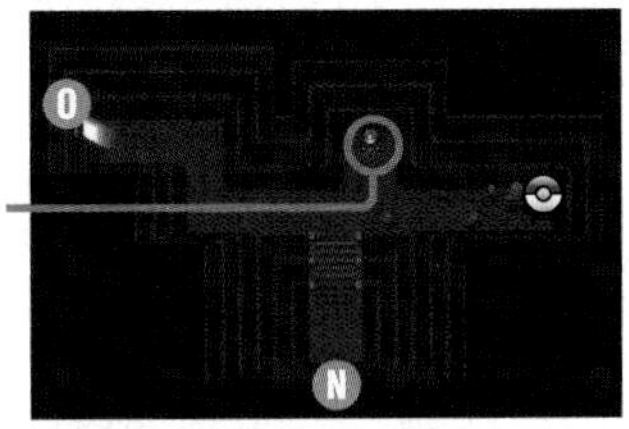

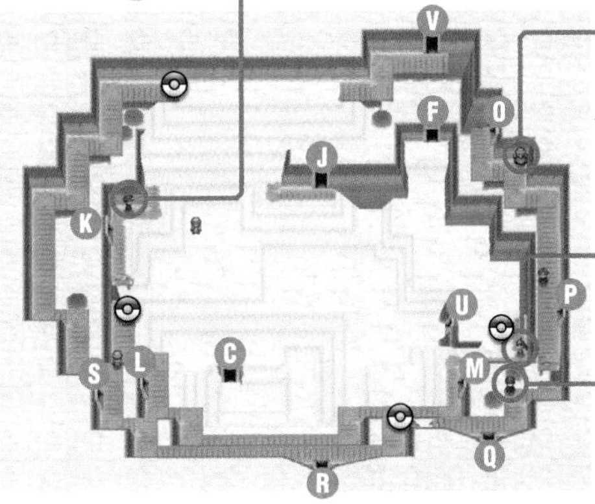

Worker
Cliff
Hiker
Wade
Restore your Pokémon's health
Nurse
Carol
Veteran Carter
★ Triple Battle
V
F
O
J
K
P
U
C
S
L
M
Q
R

■ Middle Level ①

N
M
Worker
Patton

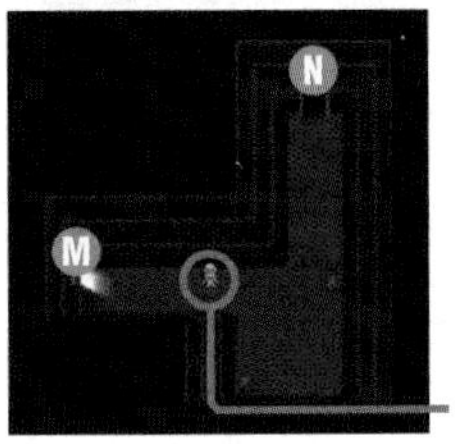

■ Lowest Level ③ (Only accessible in Winter)

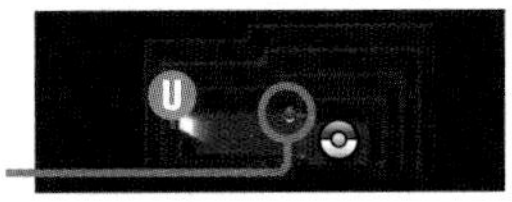

Veteran
Zach
U

Spring Autumn

Cave	
Beartic	○
Boldore	◎
Cryogonal	△
Durant	○
Gurdurr	○
Heatmor	△
Onix	△
Woobat	○

Summer

Cave	
Beartic	△
Boldore	○
Cryogonal	△
Durant	○
Gurdurr	○
Heatmor	○
Onix	△
Woobat	○

Winter

Cave	
Beartic	○
Boldore	○
Cryogonal	○
Durant	○
Gurdurr	○
Heatmor	△
Onix	△
Woobat	○

All Seasons

Cave (dust cloud)	
Excadrill	◎
Onix	○
Steelix	△

Step 1 Check the statue of Regigigas

To catch Regigigas at Twist Mountain, have Regirock, Regice, and Registeel in your party. Check the "statue" of Regigigas in Lowest Level ②, and it'll challenge you. Now all you've got left to do is catch it.

...Zut zutt!

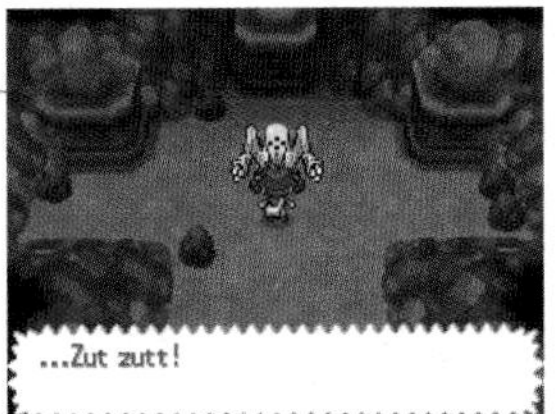

You can evolve Eevee into Glaceon

Lowest Level ① has an ice-covered rock. Level up Eevee near it to evolve it into Glaceon.

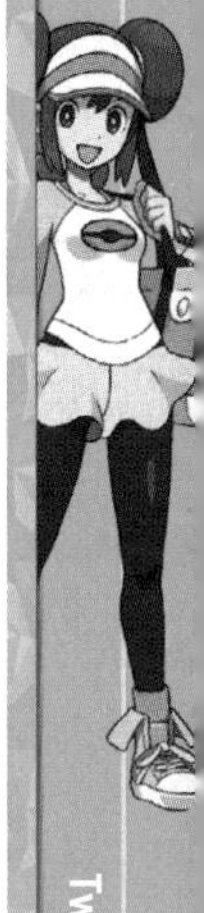

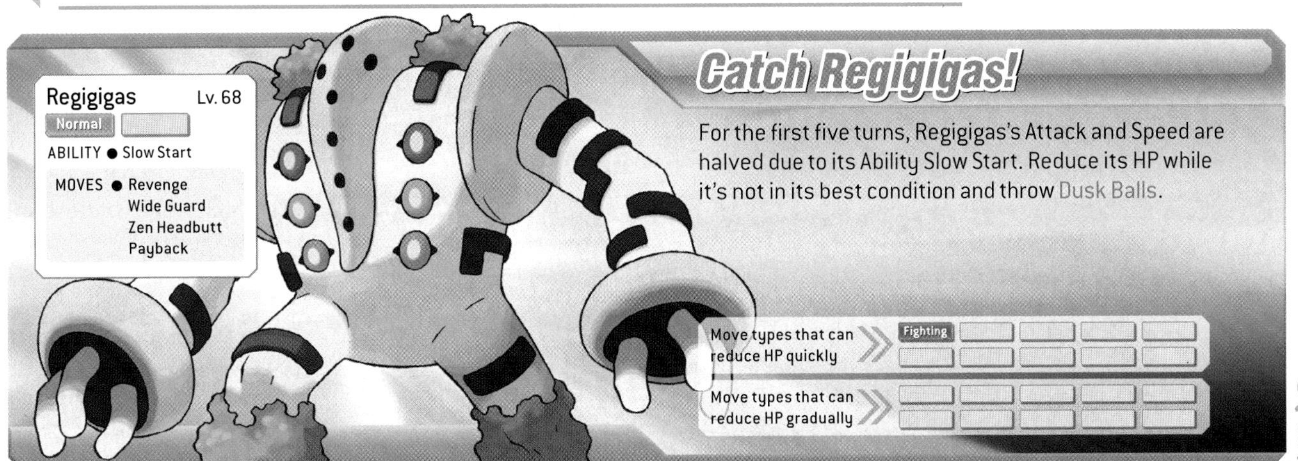

Regigigas Lv. 68
Normal
ABILITY ● Slow Start
MOVES ● Revenge
Wide Guard
Zen Headbutt
Payback

Catch Regigigas!

For the first five turns, Regigigas's Attack and Speed are halved due to its Ability Slow Start. Reduce its HP while it's not in its best condition and throw Dusk Balls.

Move types that can reduce HP quickly	Fighting
Move types that can reduce HP gradually	

Step 2 Receive a Fossil daily

There's a Worker in Lower Level ①. Talk to him, and you can get one Pokémon Fossil per day. Athough he may give you the same Fossil as the ones you already have, talk to him daily so you can eventually receive all seven different Fossils to complete your Pokédex.

Go to Nacrene Museum

After you obtain a Pokémon Fossil, visit Nacrene City. Speak to the woman at the Nacrene Museum reception, and she'll restore the Pokémon (p. 313).

Pokémon you can restore from Fossils

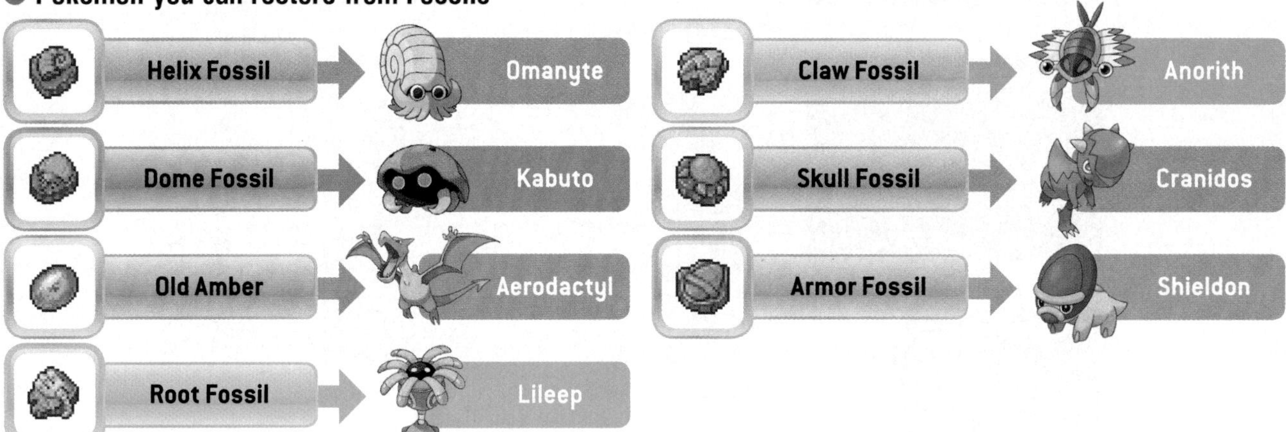

Fossil	Pokémon
Helix Fossil	Omanyte
Dome Fossil	Kabuto
Old Amber	Aerodactyl
Root Fossil	Lileep
Claw Fossil	Anorith
Skull Fossil	Cranidos
Armor Fossil	Shieldon

Step 3 Answer the Heavy Machinery Pro's quiz daily

At the intersection in Lower Level ②, you'll find the Heavy Machinery Pro. He gives you a quiz a day on heavy machinery. Talk to him and answer all his questions correctly. Answer correctly five times, and you'll receive a Medal from Heavy Machinery Pro.

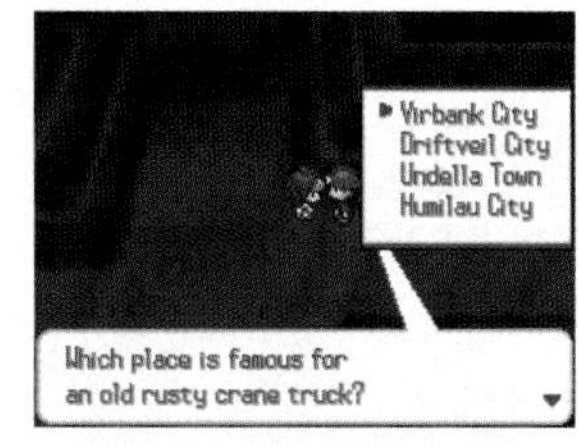

Visit Icirrus City another time

If you go east in Lower Level ②, you'll reach Icirrus City (p. 301). You can get out of Twist Mountain that way if you've visited there already. If you haven't, you should leave Twist Mountain toward Route 7 as you'll have to visit there later on the way to another place.

Step 4 Proceed while battling Pokémon Trainers

There are many Trainers waiting for you in Twist Mountain. Some of them, you can battle only in spring, summer, and autumn. There is also a Trainer you can battle only during winter. Explore every corner to battle all of the Trainers there.

When I am surrounded by rocks, my spirit goes up!!

Be ready for Triple Battles and Rotation Battles

Veteran Carter will challenge you to a Triple Battle outside. Veteran Chloris will challange you to a Rotation Battle in Middle Level ②. Check the order of the Pokémon in your party before battling them.

Step 5 Have Nurse Carol heal your Pokémon

On the east side outside is Nurse Carol. Defeat her in a Pokémon battle and then talk to her. She'll heal your Pokémon every time you do. Twist Mountain is very large, so you should talk to her often to heal your Pokémon.

That's your love of Pokémon!
Here's my love of Pokémon!

Step 6 Head for Route 7 from the top floor

Walk along the walls outside to reach Upper Level ① and then head south to exit Twist Mountain. Go south from the entrance, and you'll reach Route 7. Once you've explored every place in Twist Mountain, go back to your post–Hall of Fame adventuring.

Visit again when the season has changed

During winter, Twist Mountain is covered in snow, and you can reach places you couldn't during spring, summer, or autumn. Visit again during winter to collect items and battle Pokémon Trainers.

Abyssal Ruins

The Abyssal Ruins is said to be the tomb of an ancient king. After you've traveled through the tomb for a while, a torrent of water will wash you out of it. Only a few can decipher the ancient letters carved on the stones there.

Field Moves Needed

Top floor

Items on the top floor

- ☐ Relic Crown

3F

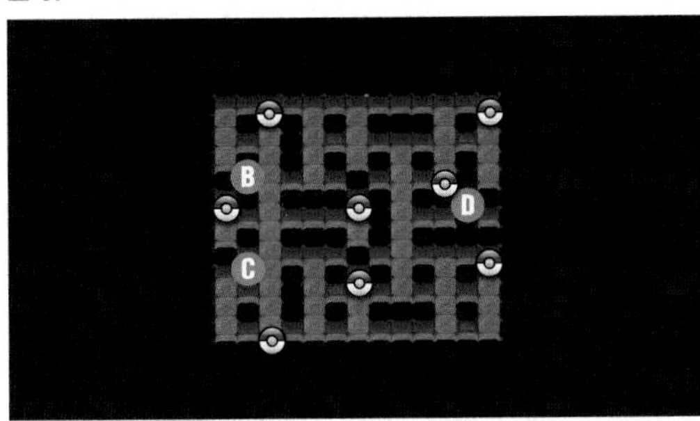

Items on the third floor

- ☐ Relic Band x3
- ☐ Relic Gold
- ☐ Relic Silver
- ☐ Relic Statue
- ☐ Relic Vase x2

2F

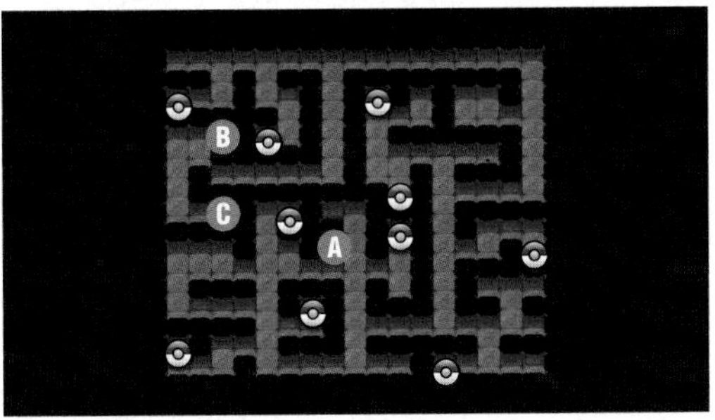

Items on the second floor

- ☐ Relic Band x2
- ☐ Relic Copper x2
- ☐ Relic Gold x3
- ☐ Relic Silver x2
- ☐ Relic Statue
- ☐ Relic Vase

1F

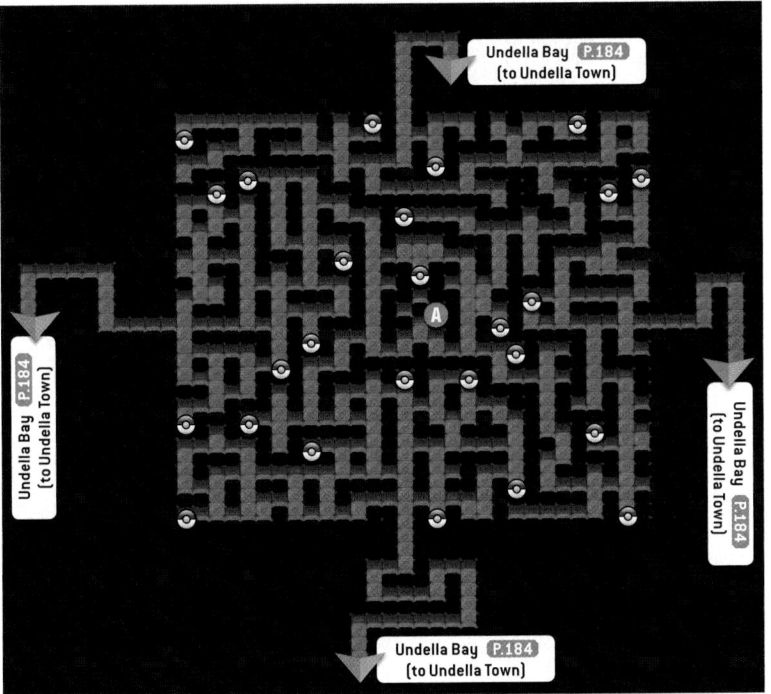

Items on the first floor

- ☐ Dread Plate
- ☐ Earth Plate
- ☐ Fist Plate
- ☐ Flame Plate
- ☐ Icicle Plate
- ☐ Insect Plate
- ☐ Iron Plate
- ☐ Meadow Plate
- ☐ Mind Plate
- ☐ Relic Copper x4
- ☐ Relic Gold x3
- ☐ Relic Silver x3
- ☐ Relic Statue
- ☐ Relic Vase
- ☐ Sky Plate
- ☐ Spooky Plate
- ☐ Stone Plate
- ☐ Toxic Plate
- ☐ Zap Plate

Step 1 Use Surf from Undella Town to head east

When you visit Undella Town, use Surf from the front or the east side of its Pokémon Center to head east on the water surface. When you reach Undella Bay, continue east to find a patch of darker water.

Visit here after you've met Zinzolin

Battle your rival at Undella Town, and Zinzolin appears after the battle to give you some papers. These help you decipher the ancient scripts (p. 261). You should get these papers before you visit the Abyssal Ruins.

Step 2 Use Dive to explore underwater

Press the A Button when you're in a patch of darker water, and you can go underwater using Dive. While underwater, continue to press UP on the +Control Pad, and you can enter the Abyssal Ruins. When you release the +Control Pad, you return to the surface.

There are four entrances to the ruins

All four entrances are connected inside the ruins. You'll return to the surface after a certain number of steps, so you can't explore the whole place in a single trip. Explore from each entrance to collect items.

Step 3 A torrent of water will wash you out of the ruins

When you enter the Abyssal Ruins, you'll hear a switch being pushed. If you travel a certain number of steps from this point, a torrent of water will automatically return you to the water's surface. In other words, you have limited time to search through the Abyssal Ruins.

Step 4 Reach the stone in the center of 1F taking the shortest path

To go to the second floor, head for the stone in the middle of 1F. If you don't take a direct route, you'll be sent back to the surface. Check the map (p. 291) to take the shortest route to reach the stone. Check the stone, and you'll be able to proceed to 2F.

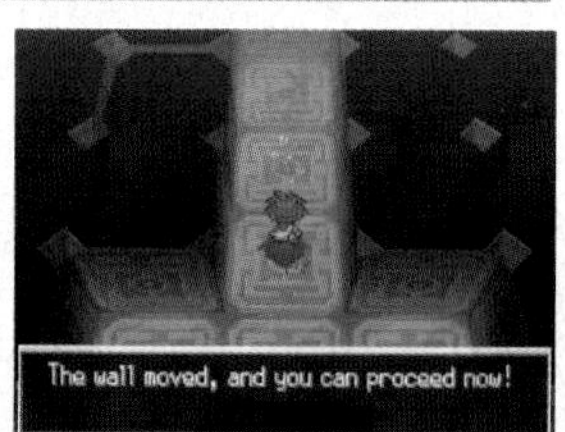

The wall moved, and you can proceed now!

Various Plates to obtain

On the first floor of the Abyssal Ruins, you can obtain 14 of 16 different types of Plates. Have Arceus hold one of them for Type Shift. Visit many times to obtain as many Plates as you can.

Step 5 Use Flash at the stone on the west side of 2F

To get to the third floor from the second floor, head for a stone on the west side. Among all the purple stones, find the one with the side you cannot see from anywhere on the entire second floor. Use Flash in front of this stone to proceed to 3F.

Step 6 Use Strength at the stone on the east side of 3F

To get to the top floor from the third floor, head for a stone on the east side. Among all the purple stones, find the one whose side you cannot see from anywhere on the entire third floor. Use Strength in front of the stone to proceed to the top floor.

Step 7 Get the Relic Crown on the top floor

Collect the item placed in the middle of the floor when you reach the top floor. The Relic Crown can be obtained only at the Abyssal Ruins. The billionaire in Undella Town buys it for a staggering 300,000.

Step 8 Return to Undella Town

You cannot collect all the items on the first floor in the Abyssal Ruins in a single visit. Explore many times to collect items little by little and venture deeper into the ruins. Once you've collected all the items, return to Undella Town.

Decipher the ancient scripts

The ancient scripts are written in code language. There is a rule to decipher for each floor. Talk to Zinzolin at Undella Town every time you reach a new floor. He'll give you clues to decipher the scripts.

The billionaire who will buy items from you

The billionaire in the house in Undella Town buys items, and he'll pay handsomely for them, including the Relic Crown (p. 182). You won't be able to sell those 14 Plates to him, though.

N's Castle

N's Castle is the former base of Team Plasma and appeared just once two years ago. It was built to surround the Pokémon League, but it fell into disrepair after the great battle two years ago. Yet one part of the ruins still remains.

Items

- ☐ Dark Stone (in *Pokémon Black Version 2*)
- ☐ Light Stone (in *Pokémon White Version 2*)
- ☐ Luxury Ball
- ☐ Protein
- ☐ TM50 Overheat

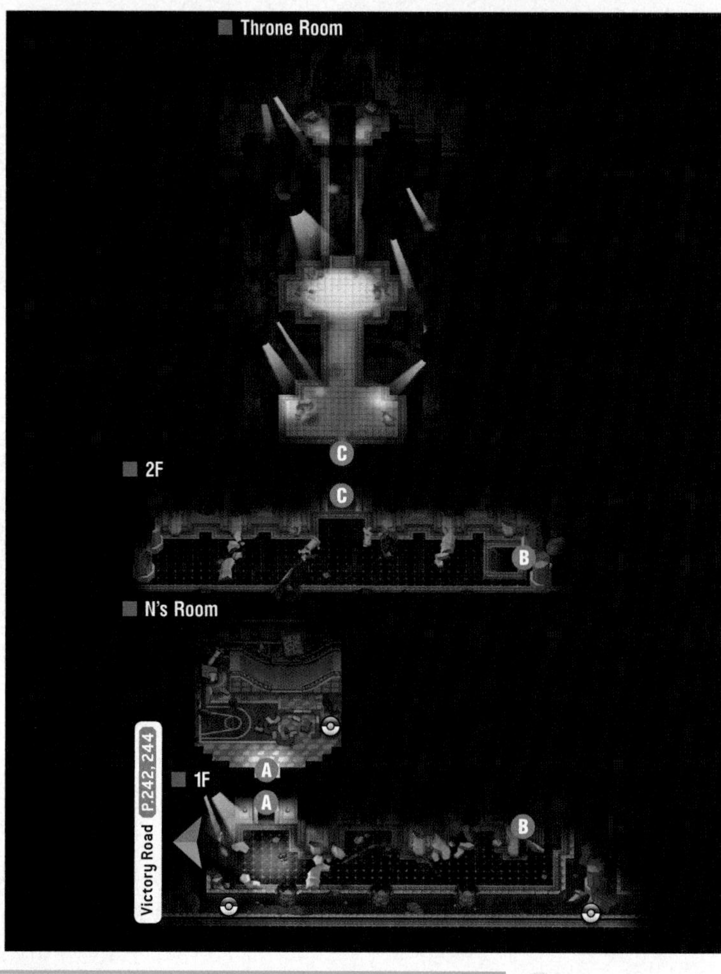

Step 1 Meet N in the crumbling remains of the castle

If you chase after Zoroark on Victory Road, you eventually arrive at N's Castle. When you go inside, you will find N waiting for you. He asks you to lead him into the deepest part of the castle. Agree to take him there.

YES
NO
Take me to the deepest chamber of this castle!

Listen to the sad tale in N's room

When you enter N's room, he will tell you the sad tale of his childhood. Then he leaves the room in silence. Perhaps he is affected by the memories of his painful past, and waits for you in the hall outside.

Step 2 Make your way to the second floor while collecting items

Once you accept N's request to guide him through the castle, he follows you wherever you wander. Collect items as you make your way up to the second floor and toward the Throne Room to the north.

Step 3 N challenges you to battle in the sunlit chamber

As you head north through the deepest part of the castle, N stops and challenges you to a battle in a room flooded with sunlight. In *Pokémon Black Version 2*, you will battle Zekrom. In *Pokémon White Version 2*, your opponent will be Reshiram.

If you say no, you can save your game

If you refuse N's request for a battle, he will wait until you are ready to begin. If you want to save your game before the battle, tell N no the first time and save your game before speaking to him again.

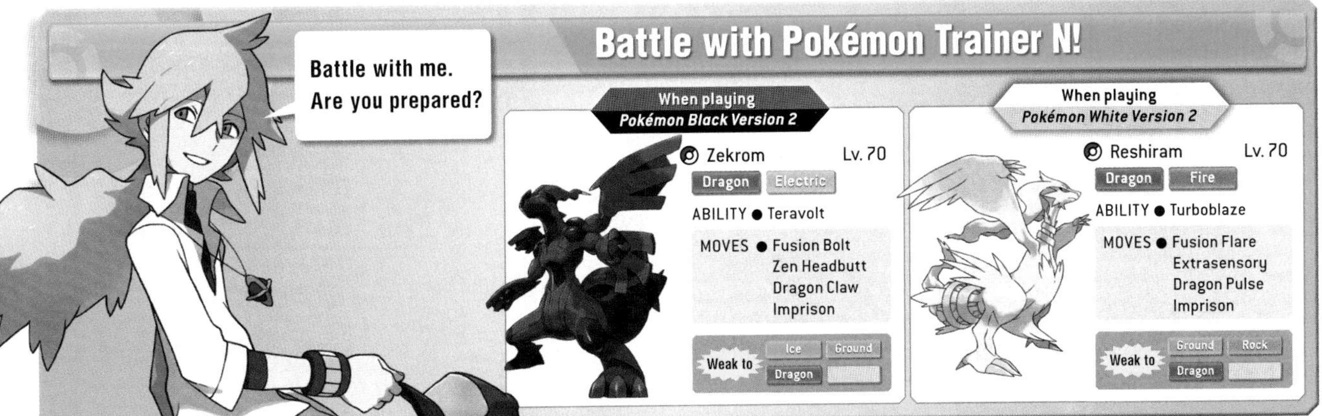

Battle with Pokémon Trainer N!

When playing *Pokémon Black Version 2*

Zekrom Lv. 70
Dragon Electric
ABILITY ● Teravolt
MOVES ● Fusion Bolt, Zen Headbutt, Dragon Claw, Imprison
Weak to: Ice, Ground, Dragon

When playing *Pokémon White Version 2*

Reshiram Lv. 70
Dragon Fire
ABILITY ● Turboblaze
MOVES ● Fusion Flare, Extrasensory, Dragon Pulse, Imprison
Weak to: Ground, Rock, Dragon

Step 4 Obtain the Dark Stone (Light Stone)

After N says his farewells, Zekrom (Reshiram) is transformed into the Dark Stone (Light Stone). N says he will entrust the Dark Stone (Light Stone) to you, and he leaves it in your hands when he goes.

I'll entrust you
with this Dark Stone!

Step 5 Return outside through the Victory Road

Once you have received the Dark Stone (Light Stone) from N, exit the castle and return to Victory Road. After you're out of the cave and back outside, use Fly to move more quickly.

Who is the Trainer that N searches for?

N says he will go in search of the Pokémon Trainer he met two years ago to thank him. Could he mean the main character from *Pokémon Black Version* or *Pokémon White Version*?

Step 6 Head for Dragonspiral Tower

Follow N's advice and head for Dragonspiral Tower. Use Fly to go to Opelucid City, then head west to Route 9 and even farther west to Tubeline Bridge (p. 297).

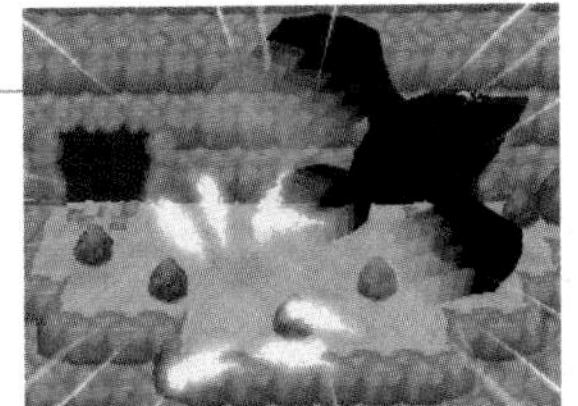

Head to a new destination from Tubeline Bridge

An area that was closed off before entering the Hall of Fame now links Tubeline Bridge and Dragonspiral Tower. Since it will be your first time visiting this new area, explore every corner as you go.

Step 7 When the seasons change, visit N's Castle again

You can battle N in his castle again. There are three conditions you will have to fulfill, though. You must capture Kyurem in the Giant Chasm, meet N at the Nimbasa City Ferris wheel on a Friday, and the season must have changed since your first battle with N.

N: How surprising...
I didn't expect you'd come here.

Hear tales of the past from N

After entering the Hall of Fame, you will be able to meet N every Friday if you go to the Ferris wheel in Nimbasa City. Speak to him and you can ride the Ferris wheel together. During the ride, N will share with you his memories from the events two years ago (p. 419).

Battle Pokémon Trainer N!

The formula for understanding other Trainers...You're OK with a Pokémon battle, right?

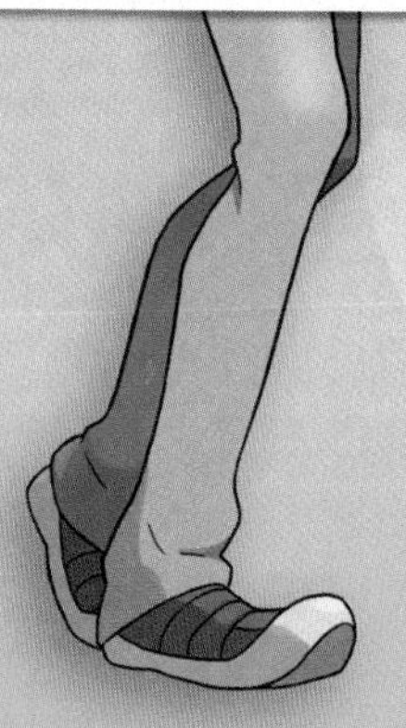

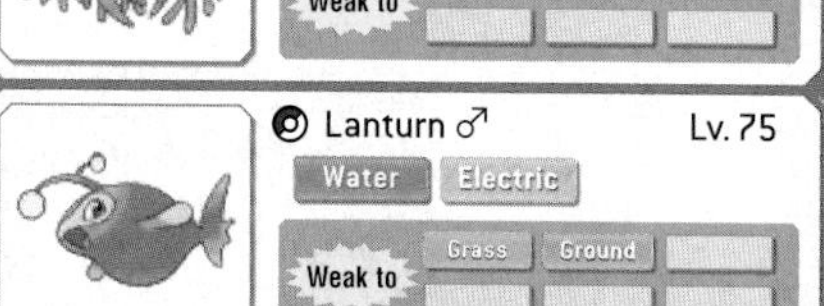

N's Pokémon (spring)

Pokémon	Lv.	Type	Weak to
Politoed ♂	Lv. 77	Water	Grass, Electric
Omastar ♂	Lv. 75	Rock, Water	Grass, Electric, Fighting, Ground
Kabutops ♂	Lv. 75	Rock, Water	Grass, Electric, Fighting, Ground
Starmie	Lv. 75	Water, Psychic	Grass, Electric, Bug, Ghost, Dark
Tentacruel ♂	Lv. 75	Water, Poison	Electric, Ground, Psychic
Lanturn ♂	Lv. 75	Water, Electric	Grass, Ground

N's Pokémon (summer)

Pokémon	Lv.	Type	Weak to
Ninetales ♀	Lv. 77	Fire	Water, Ground, Rock
Arcanine ♂	Lv. 75	Fire	Water, Ground, Rock
Rapidash ♂	Lv. 75	Fire	Water, Ground, Rock
Shiftry ♂	Lv. 75	Grass, Dark	Bug, Fire, Ice, Fighting, Poison, Flying
Ninjask ♂	Lv. 75	Bug, Flying	Rock, Fire, Electric, Ice, Flying
Leafeon ♀	Lv. 75	Grass	Fire, Ice, Poison, Flying, Bug

N's party Pokémon change depending on the season

You can have rematches against N in his castle, but the Pokémon in his party will greatly differ depending on the season. All of his Pokémon are incredibly strong, and they are at or above Lv. 75. But that's what makes the battle all the more exciting!

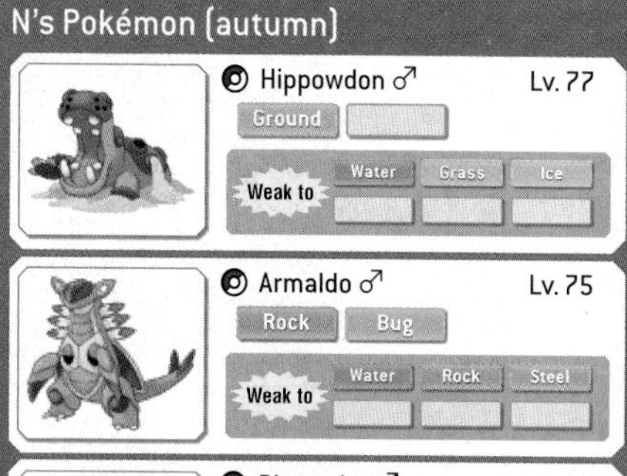

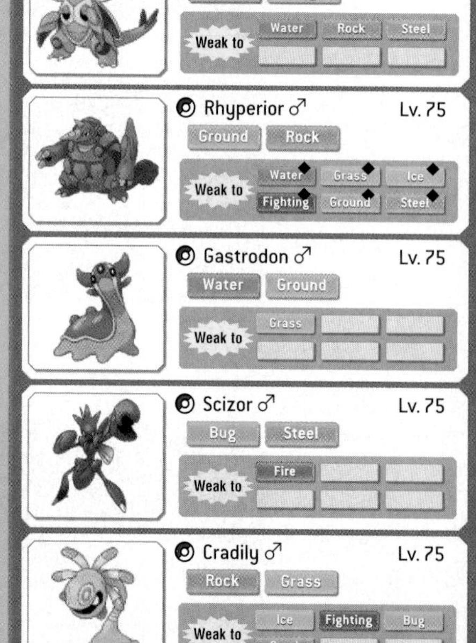

N's Pokémon (autumn)

Pokémon	Lv.	Type	Weak to
Hippowdon ♂	Lv. 77	Ground	Water, Grass, Ice
Armaldo ♂	Lv. 75	Rock, Bug	Water, Rock, Steel
Rhyperior ♂	Lv. 75	Ground, Rock	Water◆, Grass◆, Ice◆, Fighting◆, Ground◆, Steel◆
Gastrodon ♂	Lv. 75	Water, Ground	Grass
Scizor ♂	Lv. 75	Bug, Steel	Fire
Cradily ♂	Lv. 75	Rock, Grass	Ice, Fighting, Bug, Steel

N's Pokémon (winter)

Pokémon	Lv.	Type	Weak to
Abomasnow ♂	Lv. 77	Grass, Ice	Fire, Fighting, Poison, Flying, Bug, Rock, Steel
Glaceon ♀	Lv. 75	Ice	Fire, Fighting, Rock, Steel
Vanilluxe ♂	Lv. 75	Ice	Fire, Fighting, Rock, Steel
Cloyster ♂	Lv. 75	Water, Ice	Grass, Electric, Fighting, Rock
Mamoswine ♂	Lv. 75	Ice, Ground	Fire◆, Water, Grass, Fighting, Steel
Froslass ♀	Lv. 75	Ice, Ghost	Fire, Rock, Ghost, Dark, Steel

◆ The damage may change depending on the effects of this Pokémon's Ability.

Tubeline Bridge

The Tubeline Bridge connects Route 8 and Route 9. It's made of steel and is very sturdy. Even when a subway train passes directly below it, it won't budge an inch.

Items

- ☐ EnergyPowder
- ☐ TM34 Flame Charge

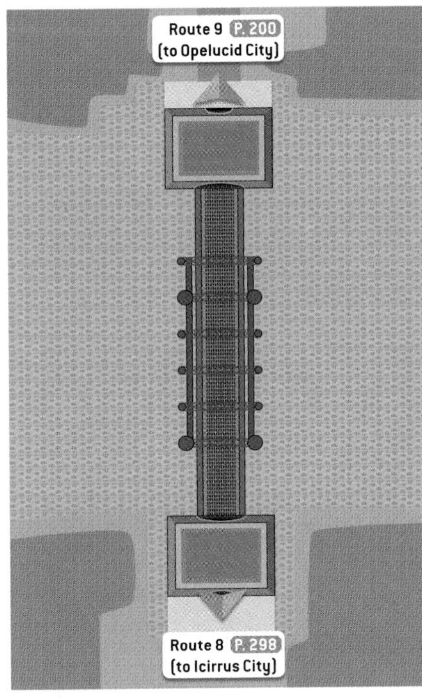

Step 1 How sturdy is the bridge? It can hold 4,934 people!

Head west from Route 9 to enter. Before you entered the Hall of Fame, you couldn't cross the bridge because a test was being conducted to determine how many people it could hold. Talk to the person at the gate, and you'll learn that 4,934 people were able to stand on the bridge at the same time. Try to imagine that scene!

Step 2 A woman complains about the noise

Near the entrance of the Tubeline Bridge, you'll find a woman who seems very frustrated about the loud noise. The level of the noise will increase the more you speak with her. There are four levels: 70 decibels, 80 decibels, 100 decibels, and 120 decibels.

Step 3 Talk to the running Battle Girl

As you proceed south on the bridge, you will find a Battle Girl running around. Talk to her to receive TM43 Flame Charge. It's a Fire-type move that also raises the user's Speed stat by one stage.

The sturdiest in Unova

There are lots of bridges in the Unova region, but the Tubeline Bridge is probably the sturdiest of them all. The bridge can take quite a load, whether heavy motorbikes roar across it, subway trains pass below it, or even if nearly 5,000 people stand on it at the same time.

Bring a Pokémon with the Soundproof Ability

Talk to the woman on the bridge when you have a Pokémon in your party with the Soundproof Ability, and she'll discover something interesting about her surroundings.

Step 4 Only one Biker remains

Two years ago, a large group of Bikers who called themselves the breakneck team would gather on the Tubeline Bridge every Friday night. However, now only one of them remains. He sadly talks about the Biker golden age of two years ago.

We were riding our motorbikes
to our hearts' content...

Step 5 Head south for Route 8

Head south on the Tubeline Bridge and enter the gate. Once inside the gate, head west and you will reach Route 8, which leads to Dragonspiral Tower.

It rains a lot here, and the marshy swamp holds many Pokémon

Route 8 • Moor of Icirrus

Route 8 is covered in marshes and water. Constant rain means the route is always mucky. To the north is the Moor of Icirrus, where a marsh has formed from water that has collected in uneven ground. Go south and you'll reach Icirrus City.

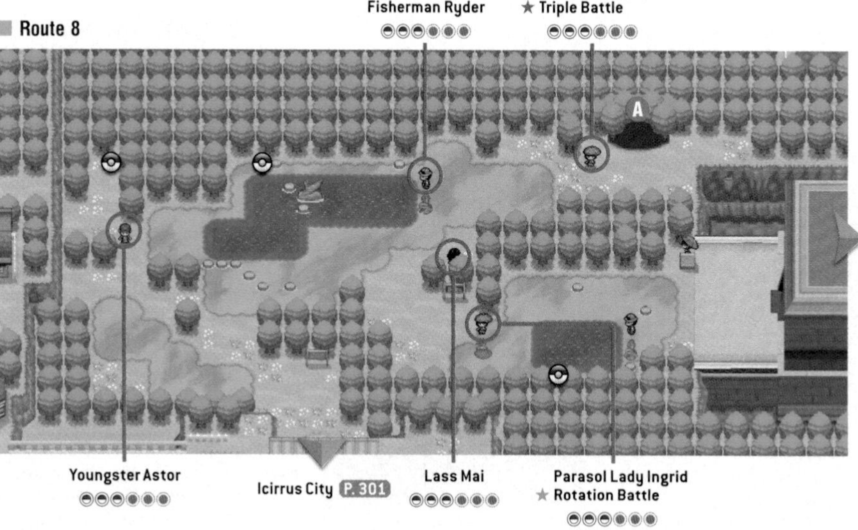

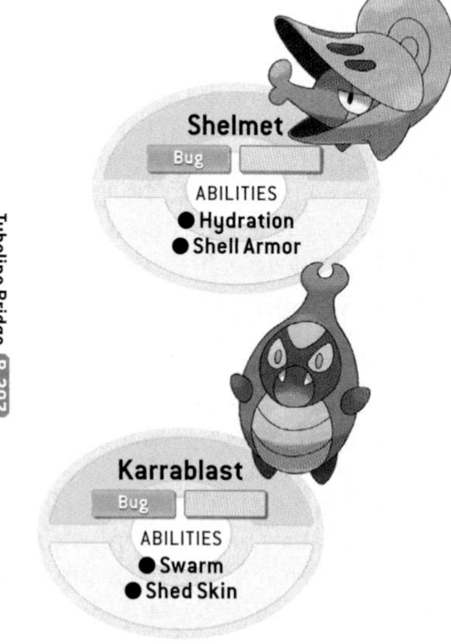

Route 8

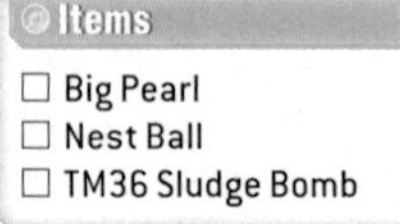

Items

- ☐ Big Pearl
- ☐ Nest Ball
- ☐ TM36 Sludge Bomb

Spring Summer Autumn

Wetlands		
Croagunk		○
Karrablast	⬡	○
Karrablast	⬢	△
Palpitoad		◎
Shelmet	⬢	○
Shelmet	⬡	△
Stunfisk		○

◆ In winter, the wetlands freeze and Pokémon don't appear.

Mass Outbreaks
Quagsire

All Seasons

Water Surface	
Palpitoad	◎
Stunfisk	◎

Water Surface (ripples)	
Palpitoad	◎
Seismitoad	△
Stunfisk	◎

Fishing	
Barboach	◎
Stunfisk	◎

Fishing (ripples)	
Barboach	◎
Stunfisk	◎
Whiscash	○

Moor of Icirrus

Items

- First visit
- ☐ Green Shard
- ☐ Heart Scale
- ☐ TM84 Poison Jab
- After defeating Pokémon Ranger Parker
- ☐ Lum Berry
- After defeating Pokémon Ranger Elaine
- ☐ Lum Berry
- In spring, summer, and autumn
- ☐ Full Heal
- ☐ Rare Candy

Wetlands

Pokémon		
Croagunk		○
Karrablast	⬡	○
Karrablast	⬢	△
Palpitoad		◎
Shelmet	⬢	○
Shelmet	⬡	△
Stunfisk		○

◆ In winter, the wetlands freeze and Pokémon don't appear.

Water Surface

Pokémon	
Stunfisk	◎

Water Surface (ripples)

Pokémon	
Seismitoad	△
Stunfisk	◎

Fishing

Pokémon	
Barboach	◎
Stunfisk	◎

Fishing (ripples)

Pokémon	
Barboach	◎
Stunfisk	◎
Whiscash	○

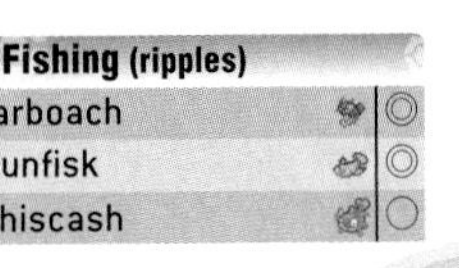

Stunfisk
Ground / Electric
ABILITIES
● Static
● Limber

Whiscash
Water / Ground
ABILITIES
● Oblivious
● Anticipation

■ Moor of Icirrus

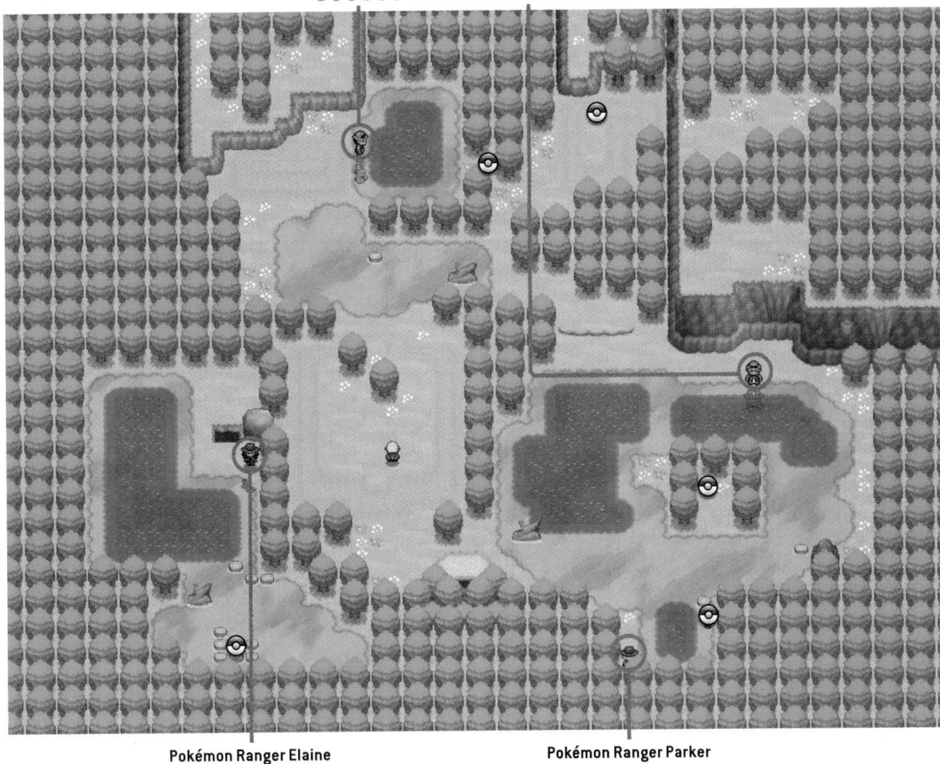

Step 1 Receive an item every day from the Parasol Lady

A lady on the eastern side of Route 8 will give you an item once per day. You can receive a different kind of rock from her depending on the time of day. In the morning, she will give you a Damp Rock. In the afternoon, she will give you a Heat Rock. In the evening, she will give you a Smooth Rock. At night, she will give you an Icy Rock.

Learn about fishing rods from an expert

Talk to the Fisherman on the eastern side of Route 8. If you don't have a Super Rod already, the Fisherman will mention Professor Juniper in Nuvema Town. That's a hint that you can receive a Super Rod from Professor Juniper's dad, Cedric (p. 332).

Step 2 Walk through the wetlands and you'll encounter wild Pokémon

On Route 8 and in the Moor of Icirrus, you'll find murky wetlands. Walk through these wetlands and you'll encounter wild Pokémon. However, during winter, the wetlands will be frozen over and Pokémon will not appear.

Explore the Moor of Icirrus

The Moor of Icirrus, north of Route 8, is covered in wetlands and water. Explore every last corner of the area while battling against other Pokémon Trainers, capturing wild Pokémon, and collecting items.

Knowing oneself, knowing the other, and knowing the surroundings...

Be ready for Triple Battles and Rotation Battles

Parasol Lady Ingrid on the eastern side of Route 8 will challenge you to a Rotation Battle, and Parasol Lady Tyra at the entrance of the Moor of Icirrus will challenge you to a Triple Battle. Check the order of the Pokémon in your party before battling them.

Step 4 Learn about Cobalion, Terrakion, and Virizion from the old man

You can learn about Cobalion, Terrakion, and Virizion from the old man in the Moor of Icirrus. He tells you a story about how these three Pokémon teamed up to take care of a young Pokémon after it was separated from its parents during a forest fire.

Who is the mysterious Pokémon in the man's story?

The young Pokémon in the old man's story is the Mythical Pokémon Keldeo! Like its three Legendary Pokémon caretakers, Keldeo has the Justified Ability.

Return to Route 8 after checking everything

To see everything in the Moor of Icirrus, you need the HMs Surf and Strength. Once you've used these HMs to explore thoroughly, return to Route 8.

Get Berries by defeating Pokémon Rangers

Get Lum Berries by defeating Pokémon Rangers Parker and Elaine in battles. Both Rangers are in the Moor of Icirrus. Lum Berries are very useful, so seek out these Rangers and defeat them!

Proceed west while battling Pokémon Trainers

When you return to Route 8 from the Moor of Icirrus, head straight west through the wetlands. After battling Youngster Astor in the west, head south from his location.

My Pokémon are gonna steam you out!

Step 7 Head south for Icirrus City

If you head south from where you found Youngster Astor, you'll arrive at Icirrus City. Up until two years ago, Icirrus City had its own Gym. What could have changed?

Talk to the member of the Hip Waders

After obtaining a Super Rod, talk to the Fisherman on the eastern side of Route 8. He'll tell you he's a member of a fishing team called the Hip Waders, and if you want to learn more about them, you'll have to come visit him at his home on Village Bridge. Then he leaves.

Visit the Hip Wader's house on Village Bridge

To join the Hip Waders, you'll need to visit the Fisherman on Village Bridge, in the third house from the right. Every day he'll declare a certain Pokémon as the "Official Hip Waders Catch of the Day." Catch that Pokémon and show it to him, and you can earn a reward (p. 267)!

Icirrus City

In Icirrus City, you will find the Pokémon Fan Club, as well as Aha's House, where you can take on a quiz challenge once per day. Brycen, who served as a Gym Leader in this city two years ago, now works as an actor at Pokéstar Studios.

Items

- First visit
  - ☐ Black Belt
  - ☐ PP Up
- When you show a Lv. 25–49 Pokémon to the chairman of the Pokémon Fan Club
  - ☐ Exp. Share
- When you show a Lv. 50–98 Pokémon to the chairman of the Pokémon Fan Club
  - ☐ Cleanse Tag
- When you show a Lv. 99 Pokémon to the chairman of the Pokémon Fan Club
  - ☐ King's Rock
- In winter
  - ☐ Max Elixir

Poké Mart (Lower Clerk)

Item	Price
BridgeMail T	50
Favored Mail	50
Greet Mail	50
Inquiry Mail	50
Like Mail	50
Reply Mail	50
RSVP Mail	50
Thanks Mail	50
Dusk Ball	1,000
Quick Ball	1,000
Timer Ball	1,000

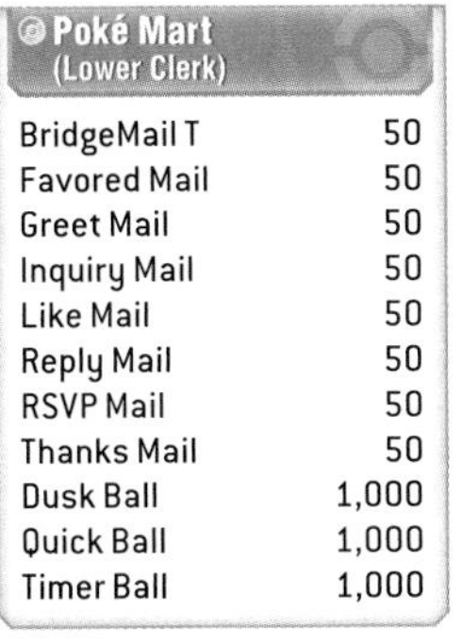

Croagunk
Poison / Fighting
ABILITIES
● Anticipation
● Dry Skin

Seismitoad
Water / Ground
ABILITIES
● Swift Swim
● Poison Touch

Spring Summer Autumn

Wetlands

Pokémon	Rate
Croagunk	○
Karrablast	○
Karrablast	△
Palpitoad	◎
Shelmet	○
Shelmet	△
Stunfisk	○

◆ In winter, the wetlands freeze and Pokémon don't appear.

All Seasons

Water Surface

Pokémon	Rate
Stunfisk	◎

Water Surface (ripples)

Pokémon	Rate
Seismitoad	△
Stunfisk	◎

Fishing

Pokémon	Rate
Barboach	◎
Stunfisk	◎

Fishing (ripples)

Pokémon	Rate
Barboach	◎
Stunfisk	◎
Whiscash	○

Spring Summer Autumn

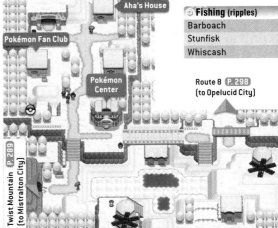

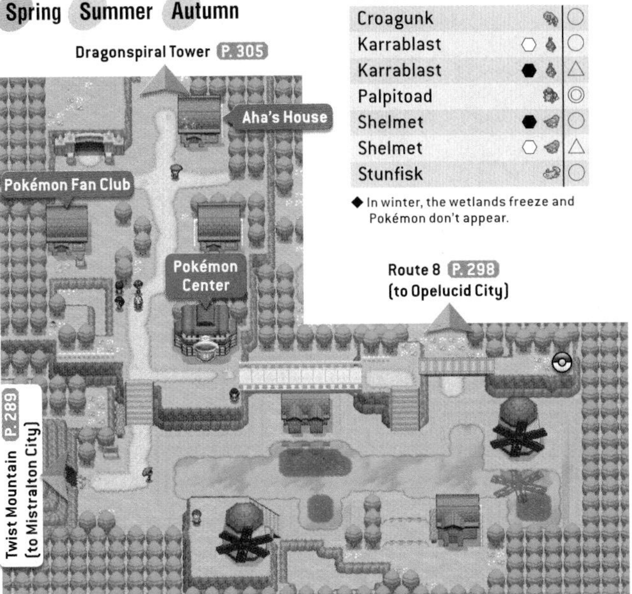

Winter

Dragonspiral Tower P. 305
Aha's House
Pokémon Fan Club
Pokémon Center
Route 8 P. 298 (to Opelucid City)
Twist Mountain P. 289 (to Mistralton City)

Items the old gentleman in the Pokémon Center will buy

Items	Price
Blue Shard	200
Bug Gem	200
Dark Gem	200
Dragon Gem	200
Electric Gem	200
Fighting Gem	200
Fire Gem	200
Flying Gem	200
Ghost Gem	200
Grass Gem	200
Green Shard	200
Ground Gem	200
Ice Gem	200
Normal Gem	200
Poison Gem	200
Psychic Gem	200
Red Shard	200
Rock Gem	200
Steel Gem	200
Water Gem	200
Yellow Shard	200
Hard Stone	500
Damp Rock	1,000
Everstone	1,000
Float Stone	1,000
Heat Rock	1,000
Icy Rock	1,000
Smooth Rock	1,000
Pearl	1,400
Oval Stone	1,500
Stardust	2,000
Dawn Stone	3,000
Dusk Stone	3,000
Fire Stone	3,000
Leaf Stone	3,000
Moon Stone	3,000
Odd Keystone	3,000
Shiny Stone	3,000
Sun Stone	3,000
Thunderstone	3,000
Water Stone	3,000
Shoal Shell	7,000
Big Pearl	7,500
Star Piece	9,800
Nugget	10,000
Pearl String	25,000
Big Nugget	30,000
Comet Shard	60,000

Step 1 Hear the story of the Legendary Pokémon

If you speak to the girl in front of the Pokémon Center, she'll tell you about a Legendary Dragon-type Pokémon. In *Pokémon Black Version 2*, it will be Zekrom, while in *Pokémon White Version 2*, you'll hear about Reshiram.

Step 2 Sell many different items, including unusual ones

The Gentleman in the Pokémon Center will buy items from you, such as the various Gems, Shards, and Stones. He's the only person in the game who will buy Pearl Strings and Comet Shards. Bring 'em when you got 'em.

Don't you have an adorable ore that shakes my core?

Step 3 No one expects the Shadow Triad

Head east from the Pokémon Center. If you follow the path to its end, the Shadow Triad will accost you. The Triad challenges you to a series of battles: Single Battle, Triple Battle, and Rotation Battle.

YES
NO
That's why we won't forgive you. Battle us!

Receive a Black Belt at the Pokémon Center

Speak to the Battle Girl in the Pokémon Center, and you can receive a Black Belt. If you have a Pokémon hold it, this item will increase the power of its Fighting-type moves. With battles against the Shadow Triad coming up, that's pretty handy.

You can quit between battles

After defeating the first or second member of the Shadow Triad, you'll be asked if you want to fight the next member. If you say no, the Shadow Triad will vanish. If you're not up to facing another battle, select "No" and come back again later.

Battle the Shadow Triad! 3

First Battle

Rumble to victory with Fighting-type moves

The first member of the Shadow Triad will challenge you to a Single Battle. The Shadow Triad member's Pokémon are all weak to Fighting-type moves. With the right Pokémon, you can deal four times the usual damage to Bisharp. Strike its weak points to bring a quick end to this battle.

Shadow Triad Pokémon

Pokémon	Lv.	Type	Weak to
Bisharp ♂	Lv. 65	Dark / Steel	Fighting, Fire, Ground
Bisharp ♂	Lv. 65	Dark / Steel	Fighting, Fire, Ground
Absol ♂	Lv. 67	Dark	Fighting, Bug

Battle the Shadow Triad! 3

Second Battle

Keep a Pokémon with Fighting-type moves in the center position

The second member of the Shadow Triad will challenge you to a Triple Battle. Place a Pokémon that can use Fighting-type moves in the center to put a quick stop to the Bisharp on either side of the Shadow's team. Fire-, Flying-, and Rock-type moves are effective against Accelgor.

Shadow Triad Pokémon

Pokémon	Lv.	Type	Weak to
Bisharp ♂	Lv. 65	Dark / Steel	Fighting, Fire, Ground
Accelgor ♂	Lv. 67	Bug	Fire, Flying, Rock
Bisharp ♂	Lv. 65	Dark / Steel	Fighting, Fire, Ground

Battle the Shadow Triad! 3

Third Battle

Fire- and Ground-type moves burn through Banette's weak points

The third member of the Shadow Triad will challenge you to a Rotation Battle. The Fighting-type moves that are so effective against Bisharp will have no effect on Banette. But, if you have Fire- and Ground-type moves in your arsenal, you'll be able to deal damage even when your opponent is Banette.

Shadow Triad Pokémon

Pokémon	Level	Type	Weak to
Bisharp ♂	Lv. 65	Dark / Steel	Fighting, Fire, Ground
Bisharp ♂	Lv. 65	Dark / Steel	Fighting, Fire, Ground
Banette ♂	Lv. 67	Ghost	Ghost, Dark

Step 4 Battle the Shadow Triad every season

When your battle ends, the Shadow Triad disappears without a word. Yet this is not the last that you might see of them. You can return to battle them once each season. When the seasons change, stop by Icirrus City for a rematch!

Step 5 Listen to the song of the four dancers

West of the Pokémon Center, four men and women are dancing in a circle. If you speak to each one of them, you'll learn that they're singing about a Legendary Dragon-type Pokémon. Talk to each dancer to hear all of the lines of the song.

Truth! Ideals!
Two dragons!

Step 6 Get three items from the Pokémon Fan Club Chairman

At the Pokémon Fan Club, if you show the Club Chairman a Pokémon you've raised well, you'll receive an item. Showing a Pokémon that has gained 25 to 49 levels gets you an Exp. Share, while 50 to 98 levels gets you a Cleanse Tag. And finally, Pokémon raised 99 levels will get you a King's Rock.

Step 7 Learn how friendly your Pokémon feel toward you

If you speak to the woman in the Pokémon Fan Club, she can tell you how friendly your Pokémon feel toward you. Select a Pokémon in your party and check its friendliness (p. 36).

YES
NO
Shall I check how friendly your Pokémon
is toward you?

Brycen is making a splash as an actor

Brycen, who was the Gym Leader in Icirrus City two years ago, has now become an epic movie star. He's best known for the Brycen-Man series, including Brycen-Man and Brycen-Man Strikes Back.

The former Icirrus City Gym is pretty cool

North of the Pokémon Fan Club is the building that housed the Icirrus City Gym two years ago. Why not check it out? Slide across the icy floors to make your way forward. If you step on the switches to change the positions of the walls, you'll be able to reach the deepest part of the Gym. Once you've made it all the way to the back of the Gym, head outside again.

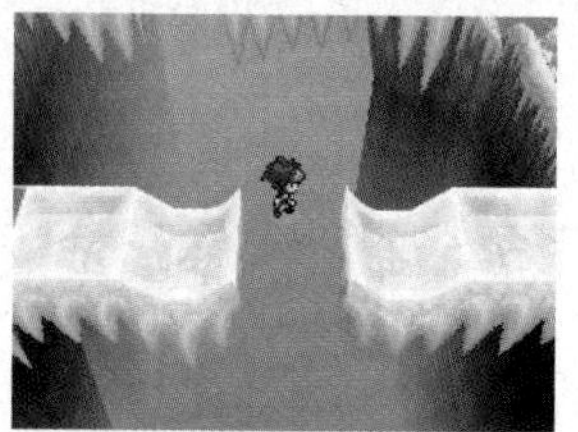

Memory Link event

Speak to Brycen in the former Icirrus City Gym to trigger a Memory Link event. Hear the tale of why Brycen decided to make a comeback as an actor (p. 73).

Receive a prize every day in the quiz

In Aha's House, you can take his simple quiz once a day. Aha will pose questions, so use the hints Wye gives you to answer them. You'll receive an Antidote for a correct answer and a Parlyz Heal for a wrong answer. It's like you can't lose!

An entrance on the west side of town leads to Twist Mountain

The cavern entrance at the west side of town leads to Twist Mountain (p. 289). Right beyond the entrance is a Heavy Machinery Pro who will quiz you each day with a single question. When you want to meet him, it's easiest to go from Icirrus City.

Head north to Dragonspiral Tower

Northward on the path west of the Pokémon Center leads to your next destination: Dragonspiral Tower. There, you'll be able to capture Zekrom (Reshiram). Buy plenty of Ultra Balls before you go.

Snow piles up, transforming the landscape

When winter rolls around, Icirrus City is always covered in snow. The hollows that litter the landscape will be filled with dense snow, so you can reach places that you could not go to in spring, summer, or autumn. It's your chance to nab that item waiting to the south of the Pokémon Fan Club.

In winter, meet the mysterious residents of the house

Inside the house, which can be reached only in the winter, you'll find a man and a woman. These two were once members of Team Magma and Team Aqua—former evildoers in the Hoenn region.

Listen to different music in the house to the south

When the snow falls, it fills the hollows in the ground, enabling you to enter the house in the south of Icirrus City. The sound designer is inside. Speak to him and he'll perform the music from Route 10 in *Pokémon Black Version* and *Pokémon White Version*!

Dragonspiral Tower

Dragonspiral Tower is said to be the oldest tower in the Unova region. It is believed to have a deep connection with the Legendary Pokémon Zekrom and Reshiram.

1F Outside

Spring Summer Autumn

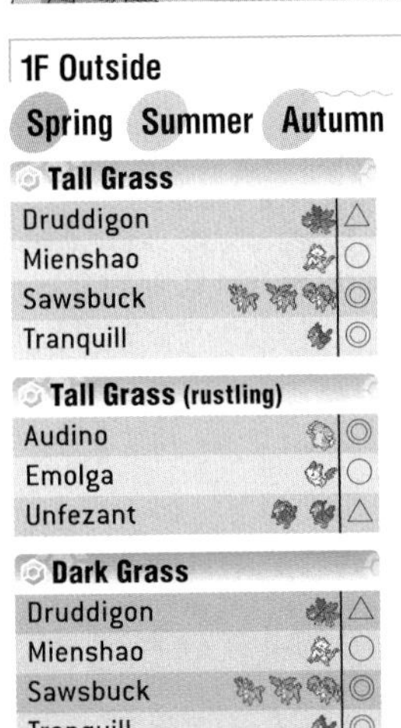

Tall Grass	
Druddigon	△
Mienshao	○
Sawsbuck	◎
Tranquill	◎

Tall Grass (rustling)	
Audino	◎
Emolga	○
Unfezant	△

Dark Grass	
Druddigon	△
Mienshao	○
Sawsbuck	◎
Tranquill	◎

Winter

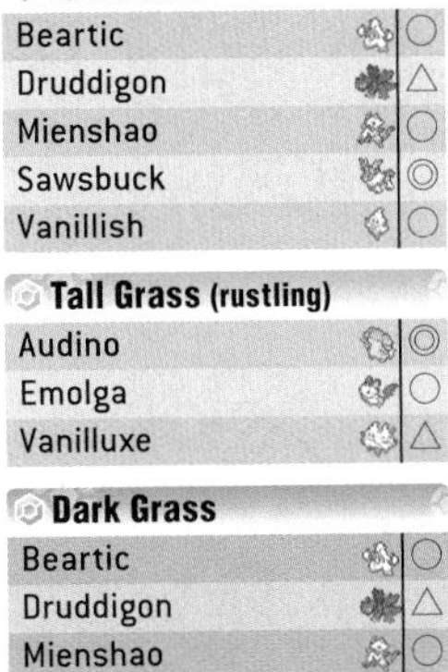

Tall Grass	
Beartic	○
Druddigon	△
Mienshao	○
Sawsbuck	◎
Vanillish	○

Tall Grass (rustling)	
Audino	◎
Emolga	○
Vanilluxe	△

Dark Grass	
Beartic	○
Druddigon	△
Mienshao	○
Sawsbuck	◎
Vanillish	○

All Seasons

Water Surface	
Basculin (Blue-Striped Form)	◎
Basculin (Red-Striped Form)	◎

Water Surface (ripples)	
Basculin (Blue-Striped Form)	◎
Basculin (Red-Striped Form)	◎

Fishing	
Basculin (Blue-Striped Form)	◎
Basculin (Red-Striped Form)	◎
Dratini	◎

Fishing (ripples)	
Basculin (Blue-Striped Form)	◎
Basculin (Red-Striped Form)	◎
Dragonair	△
Dragonite	▲
Dratini	◎

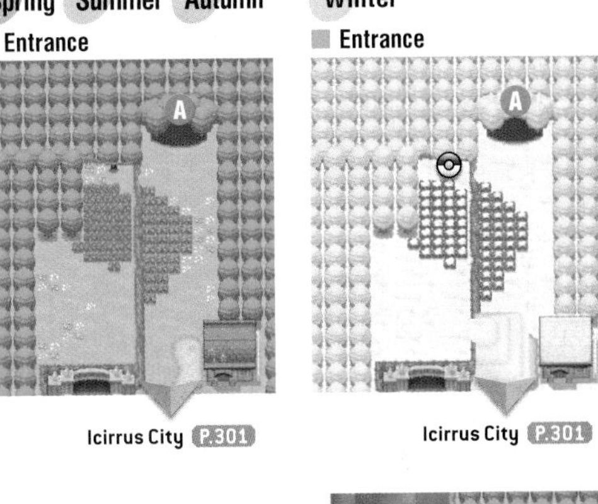

Entrance

Spring Summer Autumn

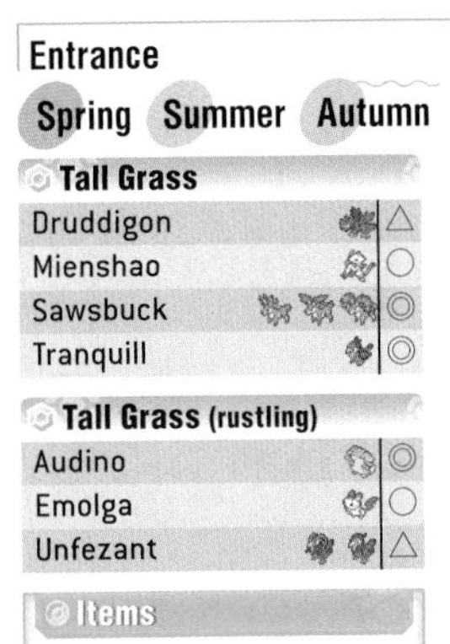

Tall Grass	
Druddigon	△
Mienshao	○
Sawsbuck	◎
Tranquill	◎

Tall Grass (rustling)	
Audino	◎
Emolga	○
Unfezant	△

Winter

Tall Grass	
Beartic	○
Mienshao	◎
Sawsbuck	◎
Vanillish	○

Tall Grass (rustling)	
Audino	◎
Emolga	○
Vanilluxe	△

Dark Grass	
Beartic	○
Mienfoo	▲
Mienshao	◎
Sawsbuck	◎
Vanillish	○

Items

First visit

- ☐ Adamant Orb
- ☐ Carbos
- ☐ Comet Shard
- ☐ Elixir
- ☐ Griseous Orb
- ☐ Lustrous Orb
- ☐ Max Revive
- ☐ Old Gateau
- ☐ PP Max
- ☐ Protein
- ☐ Shiny Stone
- ☐ TM02 Dragon Claw
- ☐ Ultra Ball

In winter

- ☐ NeverMeltIce

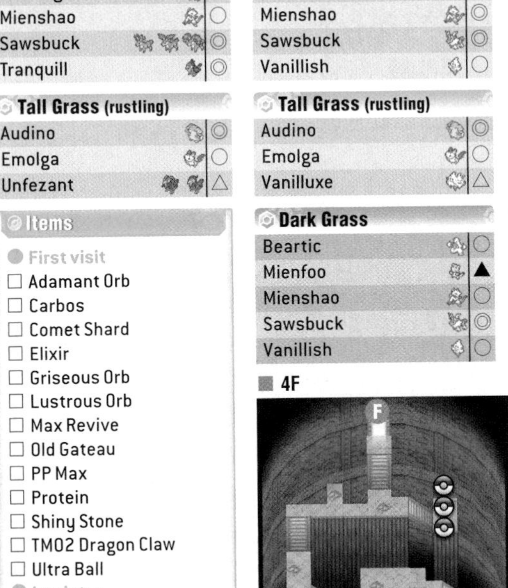

2F

Inside the tower	
Golurk	◎

1F

Inside the tower	
Druddigon	◎
Golurk	◎
Mienshao	○

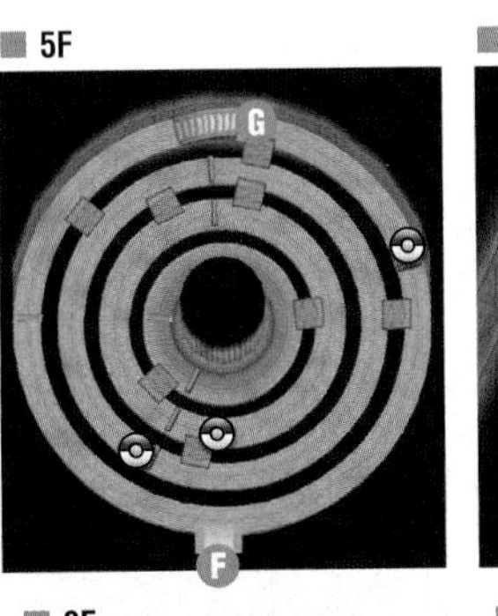

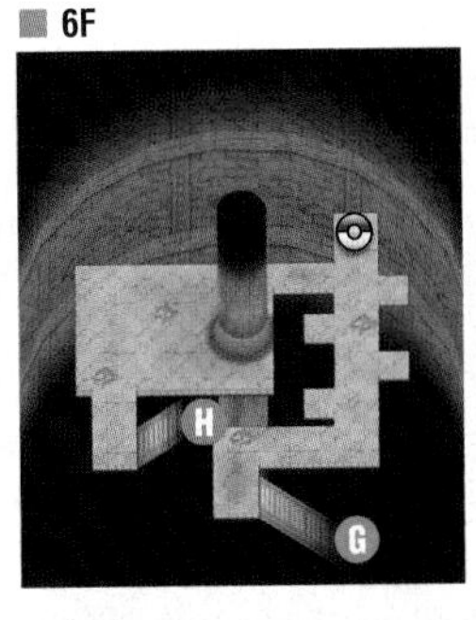

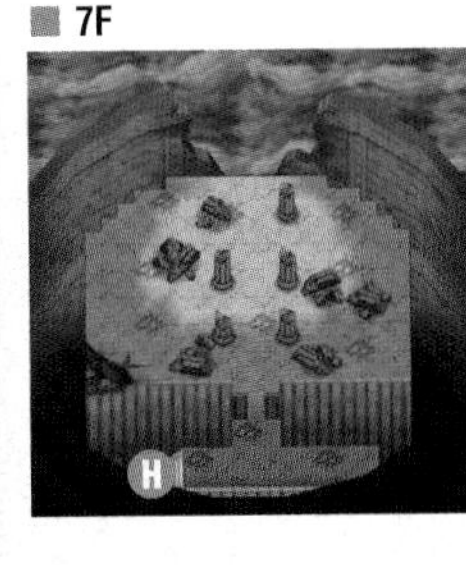

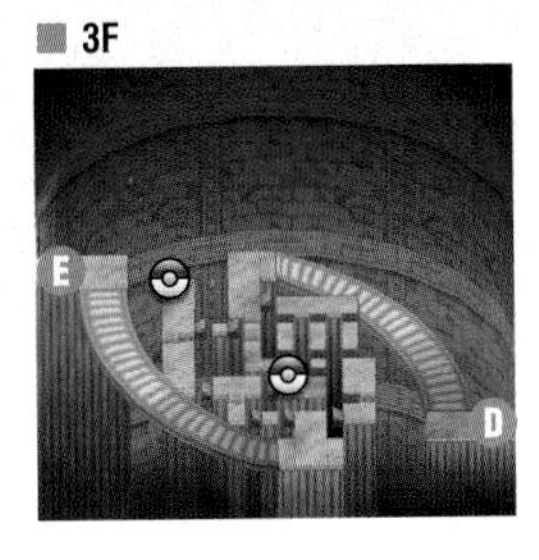

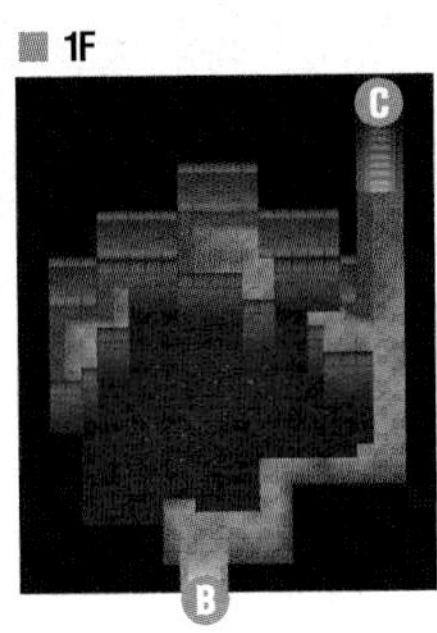

Step 1 Get an Old Gateau from Cedric

Head north from the entrance and then go to 1F Outside and you'll run into Cedric. After telling you about the relationship between Dragonspiral Tower and the Legendary Dragon-type Pokémon, he will give you an Old Gateau. It's an item that cures all status conditions.

Learn about the history of the Unova region

Cedric tells you about the history of Dragonspiral Tower. He explains that it has towered over the land since long before Unova was founded and that a Legendary Dragon-type Pokémon once waited at the top for the appearance of a person seeking the truth.

Step 2 Climb the tower while collecting items

You find no Trainers inside Dragonspiral Tower, and wild Pokémon appear only on 1F and 2F. Climb the tower and pick up any items you find on the ground. Your goal is to reach 7F—the top of the tower.

Collect items during winter

On the western side of the entrance to Dragonspiral Tower, you will see a raised area with items to collect. You can't reach these items except during winter. In winter, the snow piles up and you can reach the raised area.

Step 3 The Dark Stone (Light Stone) responds

Once you reach 7F, head deeper inside. The tower will shake, and the Dark Stone (Light Stone) inside your Bag will wriggle. Take the Dark Stone (Light Stone) out of your Bag.

Step 4 Zekrom (or Reshiram) appears

The Dark Stone (Light Stone) absorbs the surrounding aura, turning into an intense power and causing Zekrom (Reshiram) to appear. If you speak to it, you will be drawn into battle. Make sure to catch it.

When playing
Pokémon Black Version 2
Catch Zekrom!
Zekrom Lv. 70
Dragon Electric
ABILITY ● Teravolt
MOVES ● Fusion Bolt
Zen Headbutt
Dragon Claw
Imprison
First, exploit its weaknesses to quickly bring its HP down low. Next, work on gradually reducing Zekrom's HP while making sure to recover your Pokémon so they don't faint from Zekrom's powerful attacks.
Move types that can reduce HP quickly
Ice Ground Dragon
Move types that can reduce HP gradually
Fire Water Grass Electric Flying
Steel

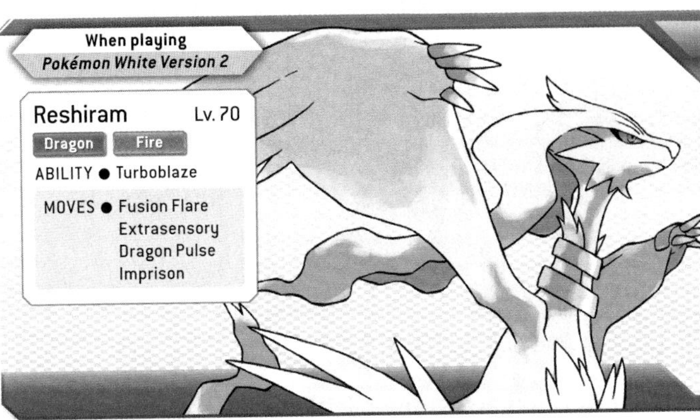

When playing
Pokémon White Version 2
Reshiram Lv. 70
Dragon Fire
ABILITY ● Turboblaze
MOVES ● Fusion Flare
Extrasensory
Dragon Pulse
Imprison

Catch Reshiram!

First, exploit its weaknesses to quickly bring its HP down low. Reshiram's moves are powerful, so keep the HP of your Pokémon up while you gradually reduce Reshiram's HP.

Move types that can reduce HP quickly	Ground	Rock	Dragon		
Move types that can reduce HP gradually	Fire	Grass	Electric	Bug	Steel

Step 5 N appears and talks to you

After you catch Zekrom (Reshiram), N will appear and talk to you. He tells you Kyurem has returned to the Giant Chasm. After telling you this, he leaves.

Go to the Giant Chasm!
Kyurem has returned.

Step 6 Head for the Giant Chasm

Head for the Giant Chasm to catch Kyurem (p. 265). You can use Fly from 7F of Dragonspiral Tower. Fly to Lacunosa Town and proceed to Route 13.

Set out from Humilau City if you didn't plug the hole with the boulder

If you didn't plug the hole between the Giant Chasm and Route 13 with the boulder, then fly to Humilau City (p. 202). From there, head to Route 22 and onwards to the Giant Chasm.

The biggest, longest bridge in Unova has four supporting towers

Skyarrow Bridge

The Skyarrow Bridge is the longest bridge in the Unova region. It connects Pinwheel Forest to Castelia City. The bridge has two levels: cars and trucks drive on the lower level, and people can cross above them.

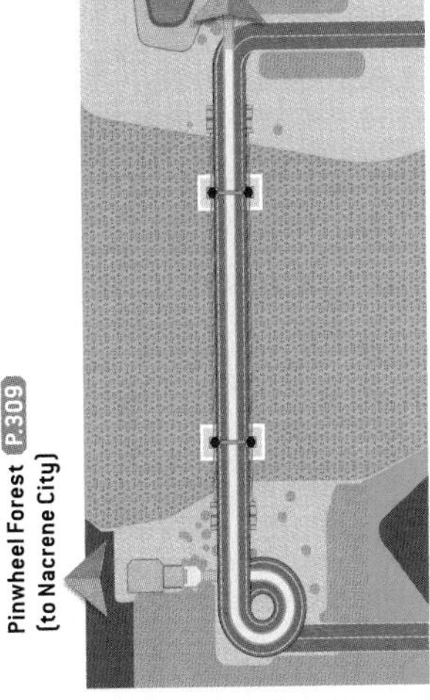

Step 1 Visit the Skyarrow Bridge by traveling east through Castelia City

Use Fly to travel to Castelia City and then head east from the Pokémon Center. Go inside the gate at the end and head south to reach the Skyarrow Bridge. From there, proceed south.

Meet a lady from Goldenrod City

A lady you encounter in the middle of the bridge speaks in the dialect of Goldenrod City in the faraway Johto region.

Step 2 Chase after the runner

I'm 100% rehydrated!
I feel better now! Thank you!

As you cross, you'll encounter a thirsty man who's running across the bridge. Give him some Fresh Water. Afterward, you can meet the same runner if you visit the Driftveil Drawbridge, the Tubeline Bridge, Village Bridge, Marvelous Bridge, and the Marine Tube in that order.

Quench the runner's thirst

If you give the runner Fresh Water on each bridge, you can encounter him once more on the Skyarrow Bridge, and he will give you a bottle of Moomoo Milk in gratitude.

Step 3 Enjoy the scenery

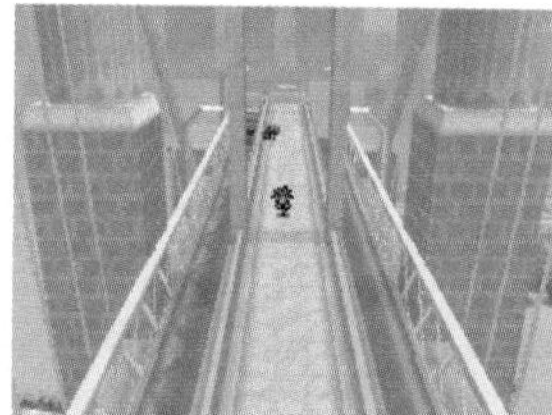

The beautiful Skyarrow Bridge is the longest bridge in the Unova region. The ocean stretches out in both directions, and you have a great view of the Castelia City skyline to the north. Enjoy the beautiful scenery while you make your way south.

Step 4 A man is selling Fresh Water

Near the midpoint of the bridge, you'll run into a man offering to sell Fresh Water for 300. This isn't a very good deal, but if you want some, say yes, and he'll thank you for your generosity. If you don't want to buy it, you'll have to say no twice—he's a persistent salesman!

Step 5 Go through the gate to reach Pinwheel Forest

Keep heading south and then follow the big curve and enter the gate at the end. On the other side, you'll arrive at Pinwheel Forest. Nacrene City is beyond the forest.

You can go through hollows of fallen trees, too

Pinwheel Forest

Pinwheel Forest is a lush forest where the trees have grown in so densely that not much light gets in. Follow the road south and east to reach the brighter entrance area, which leads to Nacrene City.

Hidden Grottoes ● Pinwheel Forest has several Hidden Grottoes. Find them all!

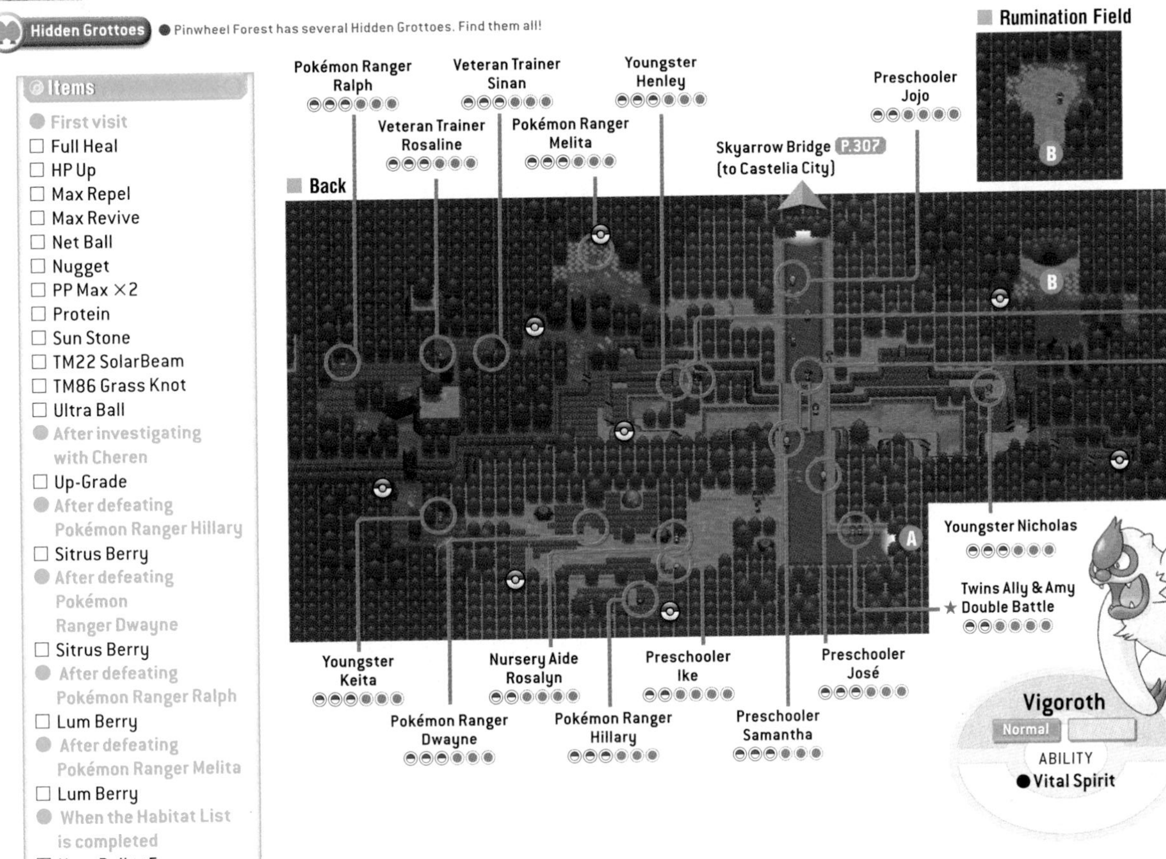

Items

- First visit
- ☐ Full Heal
- ☐ HP Up
- ☐ Max Repel
- ☐ Max Revive
- ☐ Net Ball
- ☐ Nugget
- ☐ PP Max ×2
- ☐ Protein
- ☐ Sun Stone
- ☐ TM22 SolarBeam
- ☐ TM86 Grass Knot
- ☐ Ultra Ball
- After investigating with Cheren
- ☐ Up-Grade
- After defeating Pokémon Ranger Hillary
- ☐ Sitrus Berry
- After defeating Pokémon Ranger Dwayne
- ☐ Sitrus Berry
- After defeating Pokémon Ranger Ralph
- ☐ Lum Berry
- After defeating Pokémon Ranger Melita
- ☐ Lum Berry
- When the Habitat List is completed
- ☐ Nest Ball ×5

Forest

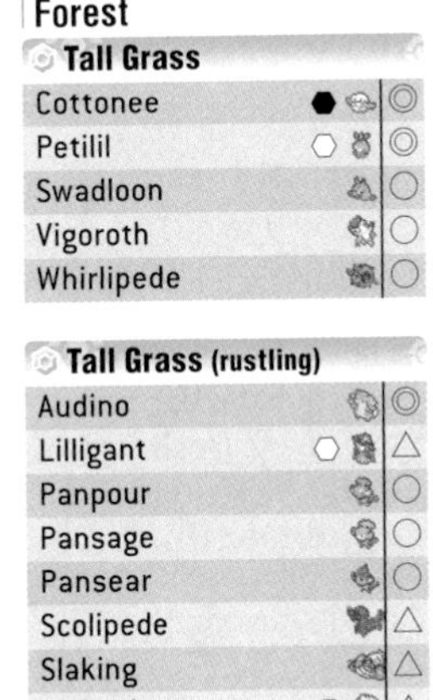

Tall Grass

Pokémon	Version	Frequency
Cottonee	●	◎
Petilil	○	◎
Swadloon		○
Vigoroth		○
Whirlipede		○

Tall Grass (rustling)

Pokémon	Version	Frequency
Audino		◎
Lilligant	○	△
Panpour		○
Pansage		○
Pansear		○
Scolipede		△
Slaking		△
Whimsicott	●	△

Dark Grass

Pokémon	Version	Frequency
Cottonee	●	◎
Petilil	○	◎
Swadloon		○
Vigoroth		○
Whirlipede		○

Hidden Grotto

Pokémon	Version	Frequency
Amoonguss		◎
Beedrill	●	○
Breloom		○
Butterfree	○	○
Murkrow		△

Water Surface

Pokémon	Version	Frequency
Basculin (Blue-Striped Form)	○	◎
Basculin (Red-Striped Form)	●	◎
Marill		◎

Water Surface (ripples)

Pokémon	Version	Frequency
Azumarill		△
Basculin (Blue-Striped Form)	●	◎
Basculin (Red-Striped Form)	○	◎
Marill		◎

Fishing

Pokémon	Version	Frequency
Basculin (Blue-Striped Form)	○	◎
Basculin (Red-Striped Form)	●	◎
Goldeen		◎

Fishing (ripples)

Pokémon	Version	Frequency
Basculin (Blue-Striped Form)	●	◎
Basculin (Red-Striped Form)	○	◎
Goldeen		◎
Seaking		○

Entrance

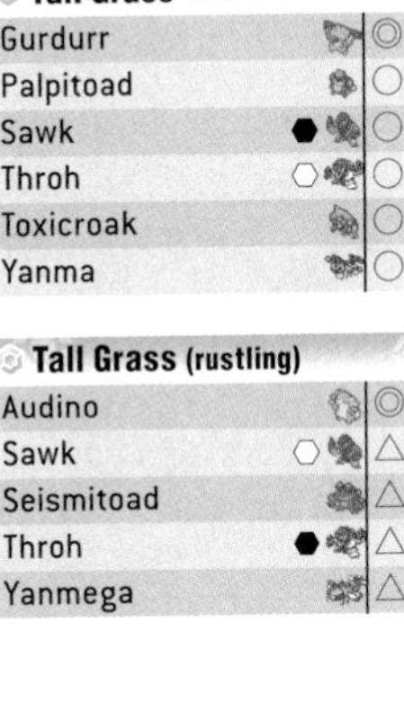

Tall Grass

Pokémon	Version	Frequency
Gurdurr		◎
Palpitoad		○
Sawk	●	○
Throh	○	○
Toxicroak		○
Yanma		○

Tall Grass (rustling)

Pokémon	Version	Frequency
Audino		◎
Sawk	○	△
Seismitoad		△
Throh	●	△
Yanmega		△

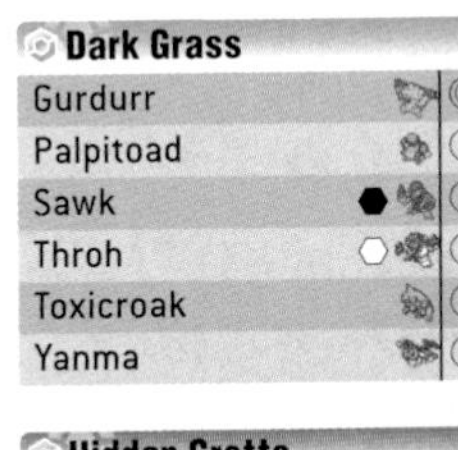

Dark Grass

Pokémon	Version	Frequency
Gurdurr		◎
Palpitoad		○
Sawk	●	○
Throh	○	○
Toxicroak		○
Yanma		○

Hidden Grotto

Pokémon	Version	Frequency
Bagon		○
Hariyama	●	◎
Hariyama	○	△
Medicham	●	△
Medicham	○	◎
Poliwhirl		△

N's Pokémon

Pidove	Lv. 13
Timburr	Lv. 13
Tympole	Lv. 13

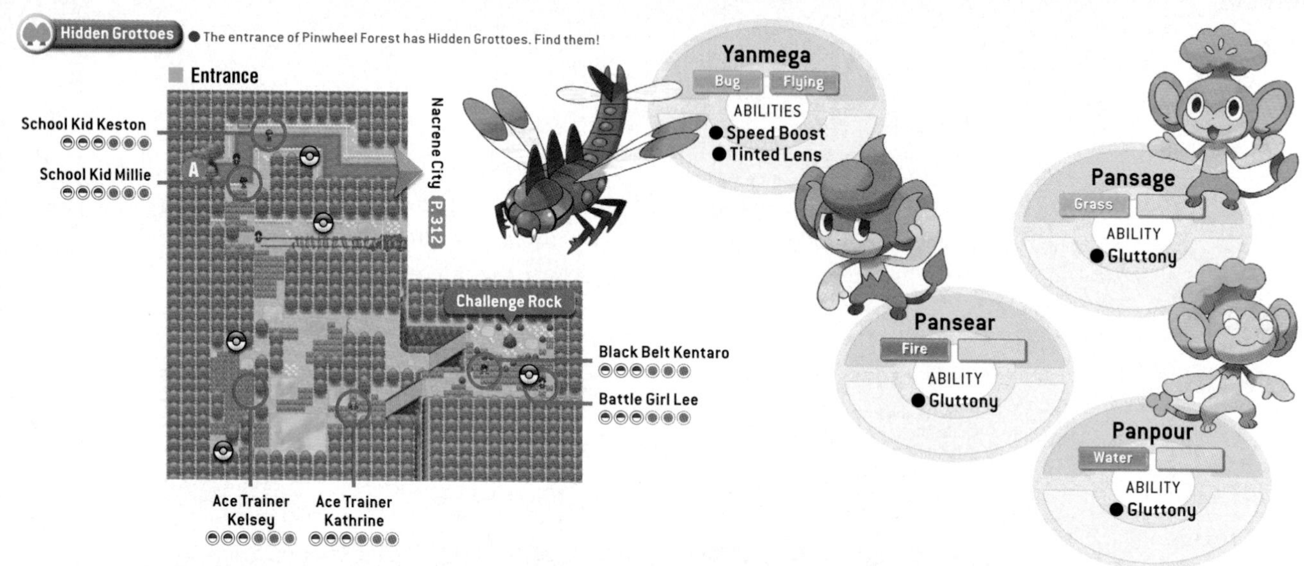

Step 1 The paved road leads south

Go through the Skyarrow Bridge gate, and you'll arrive in Pinwheel Forest. You'll find yourself on a paved road that leads south when you enter the area. But first, you'll have to get past Preschooler Jojo!

And you know, having Pokémon battles is even more fun!

What's the Unova Spartan Marathon?

On the paved road, you'll run into a man who tells you he is going to race in the Unova Spartan Marathon. It's a grueling event that requires its participants to run all the way around the Unova region clockwise, starting from Nimbasa City—without healing their Pokémon!

Step 2 You can't get through the fence yet

Just before the bridge above the river, you'll see a break in the fence on the eastern side of the road. Beyond the break is another path that leads deeper into the forest. However, before you meet with Cheren in Pinwheel Forest, a man will be standing there, preventing you from passing through. Try coming back later.

The legendary Pokémon...
Is it true it was really beyond here?

Use the Dowsing Machine to search out items

There are lots of hidden items off the road in Pinwheel Forest. Use your Dowsing Machine to find all the hidden items.

Step 3 Search the forest with Cheren

Cross the bridge and head south to find Cheren. He came here on information that members of Team Plasma were spotted in the area. Search the forest with him. If you get into battles during your search, Cheren will heal your Pokémon after each battle.

Could you help me look for them?
YES
NO

Evolve Eevee into Leafeon

In the eastern part of the forest, you'll find a boulder covered in moss. Level up Eevee near it to evolve it into Leafeon.

Step 4 Meet Gorm, formerly of Team Plasma

Continue along the path while battling against other Trainers. Eventually you will run into Gorm, who was one of the Seven Sages of Team Plasma two years ago. Don't worry, though—he's not up to anything this time. He's just here to reminisce about the past.

What did we believe in that made us try to steal the Dragon Skull?

A former villain

Gorm was behind the theft of the Dragon Skull from the Nacrene Museum two years ago. He was arrested by the International Police, along with most of the other Sages.

Step 5 Receive an Up-Grade from Cheren

Cheren's search concludes when Gorm leaves. As thanks for helping him, Cheren gives you an Up-Grade. If you give this Up-Grade to a Porygon and then Link Trade it, it will evolve into Porygon2.

Trainer obtained an Up-Grade!

Step 6 The break in the fence is clear

After you receive the item from Cheren, the man who was standing at the break in the fence will go away. Make your way back to the paved road and head north until you reach the break in the fence on the eastern side of the path. From there, you can explore the eastern part of the forest.

Step 7 Explore every corner to collect items

In the eastern part of the forest, you will find Rumination Field, where Virizion lived two years ago. You will also gain access to the river that runs below the bridge you crossed earlier. Explore every corner of Pinwheel Forest to collect items. After you're finished exploring, head west to go back to the paved road.

Step 8 Complete the Habitat List for a prize

Talk to the Scientist at the southern end of the forest and you'll be asked to show her your Habitat List for Pinwheel Forest. If you've encountered all of the land-dwelling Pokémon in this area, she'll give you five Nest Balls as a reward.

Step 9 Proceed east through the Pinwheel Forest entrance area

Go as far south as you can on the paved road and then head east. You'll leave the dense forest and enter the brighter entrance area. You'll find a break in the fence as you take the paved road eastwards. If you want to see everything in the area, you'll have to head south from the break in the fence.

Step 10 Proceed while battling Pokémon Trainers

Explore the southern part of the entrance area while battling against Pokémon Trainers and gathering items. Go as far south as you can and then head east. You'll find some stairs to a raised area.

Hey, Trainer! Let's have a refreshing battle and blow away all my troubles!

Step 11 Smash the challenge rock every day

On the raised area, you'll find the challenge rock. If you have a Fighting-type Pokémon in your party, you can smash the rock once per day. To smash it, examine the rock. Why perform this ritual? You can get a Stardust every day.

YES
NO
Would you like to have Terrakion smash the rock?

Step 12 Head east for Nacrene City

After you're finished exploring the southern part of the entrance area, head north to go back to the paved road. From there, travel east along the road to Nacrene City. Nacrene City was home to a Pokémon Gym two years ago (p. 312).

Get Berries from Pokémon Rangers

There are four Pokémon Rangers in Pinwheel Forest who will give you helpful Berries if you defeat them! Hillary and Dwayne give you Sitrus Berries, and Ralph and Melita offer Lum Berries. Seek out these Rangers and challenge them!

Learn about Virizion

The Pokémon Ranger standing in Rumination Field tells you a story about Virizion. He says that when Team Plasma began their acts of villainy, people heard a sad cry coming from the area and saw a green Pokémon running like the wind.

Having trouble? Look for Yanmega

Yanmega is key to completing the Habitat List for Pinwheel Forest. No Pokémon Trainers have it in their parties, so meeting it in tall grass is the only way to register it to your Pokédex.

Fighting-type Pokémon smash!

In order to smash the challenge rock, you'll need a Fighting-type Pokémon in your party. If you don't have one with you, visit the Pokémon Center in Nacrene City and add one of yours to your party.

Nacrene City

Nacrene City is a creative project that was constructed from disused warehouses. You'll find unique locations in Nacrene City, such as a museum and the house of Loblolly, the furniture artisan. Head east to Route 3, which leads to Striaton City.

Field Moves Needed

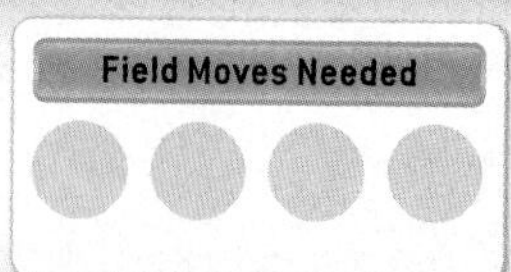

Items

- First visit
  - ☐ Cover Fossil / Plume Fossil
  - ☐ Pokémon Egg
- When you talk to a Café Warehouse patron on Sunday
  - ☐ Grubby Hanky
- Only when you returned the item to its owner on Thursday and then talked to the Waitress again on Sunday
  - ☐ Fluffy Tail

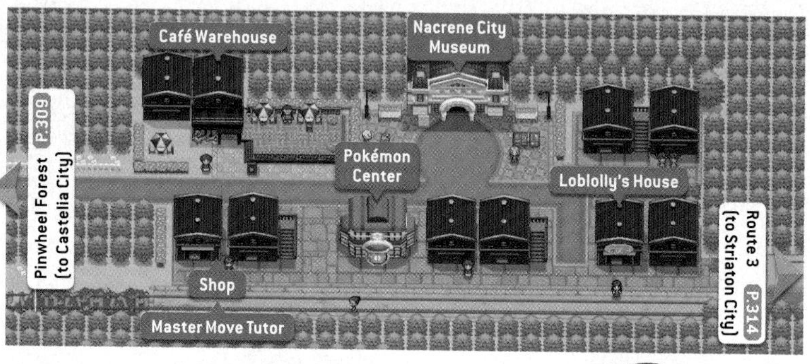

Poké Mart (Lower Clerk)

Item	Price
BridgeMail S	50
Favored Mail	50
Greet Mail	50
Inquiry Mail	50
Like Mail	50
Reply Mail	50
RSVP Mail	50
Thanks Mail	50

Shop

Item	Price
X Sp. Def	350
X Special	350
X Speed	350
X Attack	500
X Defend	550
Dire Hit	650
Guard Spec.	700
X Accuracy	950

Tirtouga
Water / Rock
ABILITIES
- Solid Rock
- Sturdy

Archen
Rock / Flying
ABILITY
- Defeatist

Step 1 Café Warehouse's Wednesday special and Saturday special

Café Warehouse has specials on Wednesdays and Saturdays. Speak to the Waitress on these days. She'll give you a Soda Pop on Wednesdays and a Lemonade on Saturdays.

Our café has a special on Wednesdays!
Here, have a Soda Pop!

Step 2 Return the lost item to the customer

Visit Café Warehouse on Sunday and talk to the Waitress by the table in back, and she'll entrust you with the Grubby Hanky. Visit again on Thursday and return it to the customer who lost it. After you've returned it, come back on Sunday to tell the Waitress. She'll give you a Fluffy Tail.

Different regulars show up every day

A certain regular customer will come to Café Warehouse each day. Each one brings a Pokémon he or she likes and spends the day in the seat by the table on the west side. On Sunday, the regular customer is a Waitress.

Step 3 Visit the Nacrene Museum

Enter the Nacrene Museum, which is to the east of Café Warehouse. The assistant director, Hawes, will greet you when you go inside. Lenora, the director and former Gym Leader, hurries over to you as Hawes shows you around the museum.

Welcome! I'm Hawes, the assistant director.

Sometimes you'll meet Uxie in front of the museum

If you have visited the Cave of Being prior to Nacrene City, you'll encounter Uxie in front of the Nacrene Museum. Make sure you're prepared to catch it (p. 314).

Step 4 Lenora gives you a Fossil

Lenora will give you either the Cover Fossil or the Plume Fossil. When it's restored, the Cover Fossil becomes Tirtouga, and the Plume Fossil becomes Archen. Pick whichever one you want!

Step 5 Restore Pokémon from Fossils

Talk to the receptionist on the east side of the entrance to the Nacrene Museum. You can have a Pokémon Fossil, such as a Fossil given to you by the Worker in Twist Mountain or the one you received from Lenora, turned back into a living Pokémon. Restored Pokémon will all be at Lv. 25.

▶YES
NO
You have a Fossil, don't you?
Shall I turn it back into a Pokémon?

Memory Link event

Climb the stairs at the back of the Nacrene Museum and talk to Lenora. A Memory Link event will start. Listen to Lenora and Burgh talk about bones (p. 73).

Step 6 Stop by Loblolly's house

Loblolly designs the Décor items you can place in your home in the Pokémon Dream World at the Pokémon Global Link (PGL). If you use Game Sync after choosing Décor, new Décor will be added to the Dream Catalogue.

My name is Loblolly.
I'm a designer of Décor items.

Memory Link event

If you've added Loblolly's Décor in the saved game file you linked to with Memory Link, Loblolly will now be a famous designer. Her house will be bustling with fans (p. 73).

Step 7 Have a master Move Tutor teach your Pokémon moves

A master Move Tutor lives on the first floor of a house to the west of the Pokémon Center. This Move Tutor really likes Green Shards. If you give him the necessary number of Green Shards, he'll teach your Pokémon a move.

Deoxys changes Formes

Check the meteorite displayed on the west side of the Nacrene Museum with Deoxys in your party to change its Forme.

Moves available for Green Shards

Moves	Green Shards
Gastro Acid	6
Worry Seed	6
After You	8
Helping Hand	8
Magic Room	8
Spite	8
Wonder Room	8
Outrage	10

Moves	Green Shards
Recycle	10
Stealth Rock	10
Trick	10
Endeavor	12
Skill Swap	12
Sleep Talk	12
Snatch	12

Green Shard

Step 8 Receive a Pokémon Egg from a woman

Talk to the woman in the gate leading to Route 3, and she will give you a Pokémon Egg if you have space in your party! Walk around with the Egg, and it will hatch eventually.

Hatch Happiny from an Egg

Happiny hatches from the Egg the woman gives you! Happiny doesn't appear in the wild, so make sure to get the Egg and register Happiny in the Pokédex.

Step 9 Go through the gate and head for Route 3

Once you've seen everything you want to see in Nacrene City, go east through the gate to Route 3. There are 10 Pokémon Trainers to battle on Route 3, so it's a good idea to stop by the Pokémon Center before you head out.

Meet Uxie at the museum

Pass by the front of the Nacrene Museum after visiting the Cave of Being on Route 20, and you will encounter Uxie. Uxie is a Legendary Pokémon from the Sinnoh region. Take this opportunity to catch it!

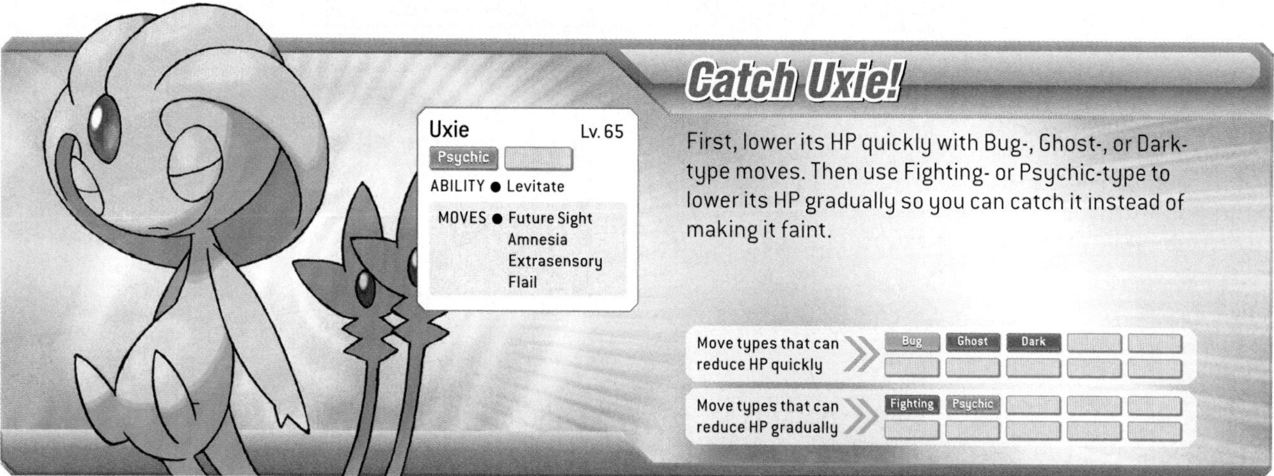

Catch Uxie!
Uxie Lv. 65
Psychic
ABILITY ● Levitate
MOVES ● Future Sight
Amnesia
Extrasensory
Flail
First, lower its HP quickly with Bug-, Ghost-, or Dark-type moves. Then use Fighting- or Psychic-type to lower its HP gradually so you can catch it instead of making it faint.
Move types that can reduce HP quickly
Bug
Ghost
Dark
Move types that can reduce HP gradually
Fighting
Psychic

A long and winding road with lots of ponds and tall grass

Route 3

Route 3 is a long route that connects Nacrene City to Striaton City. Along it, you'll find the Pokémon Day Care, which helps you raise Pokémon and discover Eggs.

Tall Grass	
Herdier	○
Purrloin	○
Tranquill	◎
Watchog	○
Yanma	○
Zebstrika	○

Tall Grass (rustling)	
Audino	◎
Stoutland	△
Unfezant	△
Yanmega	△

Mass Outbreaks	
Illumise	⬡
Volbeat	⬢

Dark Grass	
Herdier	○
Purrloin	○
Tranquill	◎
Watchog	○
Yanma	○
Zebstrika	○

Hidden Grotto 1	
Manectric	○
Pachirisu	◎
Zebstrika	△

Hidden Grotto 2	
Bibarel	◎
Lombre	△
Venonat	○

Water Surface		
Basculin (Blue-Striped Form)	⬡	◎
Basculin (Red-Striped Form)	⬢	◎
Corphish		◎

Water Surface (ripples)		
Basculin (Blue-Striped Form)	⬢	○
Basculin (Red-Striped Form)	⬡	○
Corphish		◎
Crawdaunt		○

Fishing		
Basculin (Blue-Striped Form)	⬡	◎
Basculin (Red-Striped Form)	⬢	◎
Goldeen		◎

Fishing (ripples)		
Basculin (Blue-Striped Form)	⬢	◎
Basculin (Red-Striped Form)	⬡	◎
Goldeen		◎
Seaking		○

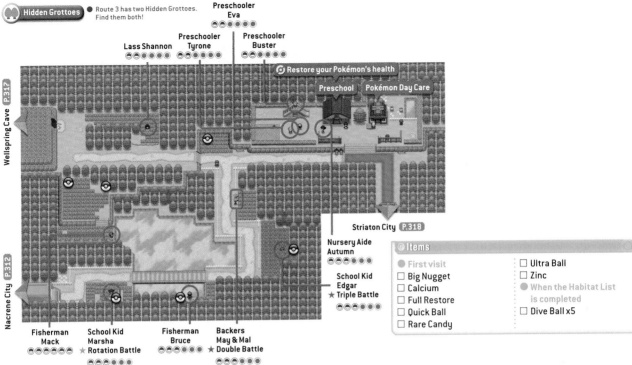

Hidden Grottoes ● Route 3 has two Hidden Grottoes. Find them both!

Preschooler Eva
Preschooler Tyrone
Preschooler Buster
Lass Shannon
Restore your Pokémon's health
Preschool
Pokémon Day Care
Wellspring Cave P.317
Striaton City P.318
Nacrene City P.312
Nursery Aide Autumn
School Kid Edgar ★ Triple Battle
Fisherman Mack
School Kid Marsha ★ Rotation Battle
Fisherman Bruce
Backers May & Mal ★ Double Battle

Items

First visit	
☐ Big Nugget	☐ Ultra Ball
☐ Calcium	☐ Zinc
☐ Full Restore	When the Habitat List is completed
☐ Quick Ball	☐ Dive Ball x5
☐ Rare Candy	

Step 1 Go north while battling Pokémon Trainers

Route 3 is long. Ten Pokémon Trainers are waiting to have a Pokémon battle on this route. Battle all the Trainers you meet while heading east, and then follow the route north.

Behold the strength I have perfected through Triple Battle!

Be prepared for Triple Battles and Rotation Battles

School Kid Marsha, in the western part of Route 3, challenges you to a Rotation Battle. School Kid Edgar, who's standing in the dark grass, challenges you to a Triple Battle. Check the order of the Pokémon in your party before battling them.

Step 2 Use Surf to reach another Trainer

You can travel over water by using Surf from the bridge you cross when you're heading east from Nacrene City. A Fisherman is waiting for you across the water, so use Surf to challenge him. You can also find items in the tall grass around him.

Step 3 Complete the Habitat List for a prize

The boy standing at the fork in the road to the north asks to see the Habitat List for Route 3 when you talk to him. Meet all the Pokémon on this route, and he'll give you 5 Dive Balls as thanks.

If you fill up the Habitat List, I'd like you to tell me!

Look for Yanmega in the rustling grass

Yanmega is key to completing the Habitat List for Route 3. No Pokémon Trainers have it in their parties, so encountering it in rustling grass is the only way to register it in your Pokédex.

Step 4 Go west to visit Wellspring Cave

The road stretches out east and west from the fork. Go west for now. Head north when you reach the rocks, and you'll find the entrance to Wellspring Cave (p. 317).

Explore the cave, then return to Route 3

Wellspring Cave is a dead end. After you've battled the Pokémon Trainers and picked up the items inside, return to Route 3.

Step 5 Have your Pokémon's health restored in the preschool

If you head east from the fork in the road, you'll find a preschool. The woman in charge will heal your Pokémon if you talk to her, so keep her in mind after tough battles!

They don't seem to be healthy.
Let them rest here a little bit!

The Pokémon in the preschool

You'll find Pansage, Pansear, and Panpour inside the preschool, playing with the children. According to a little girl, they were a gift from the former Striaton City Gym Leaders: Cilan, Chili, and Cress.

Step 6 Leave your Pokémon at the Pokémon Day Care

The Pokémon Day Care specializes in raising Pokémon for busy Trainers. If you leave a Pokémon there for a while and then take it back, you'll probably find that it's at a higher level now. This service costs money, but it's a great way to raise your Pokémon without battling (p. 340).

₽ 474320
I'm the Day-Care Lady.
We can raise Pokémon for you.

Pokémon Eggs are sometimes found

If you leave two Pokémon at the Day Care together, sometimes a Pokémon Egg will be found. Try leaving many different Pokémon at the Day Care.

Step 7 Talk to the boy while riding your Bicycle

The boy in front of the Pokémon Day Care apparently loves Bicycles. Talk to him while you're riding your Bicycle, and he'll think you're super cool!

Go! Go! People who ride Bicycles
are so cool!

Learn how to hatch Eggs quickly

The woman in the preschool will tell you about the Flame Body Ability. If a Pokémon with this Ability is in your party, any Eggs you're traveling with will hatch more quickly (p. 347).

Step 8 Head south for Striaton City

Striaton City is just south of the Pokémon Day Care. Two years ago, this city was home to an unusual Pokémon Gym with three Gym Leaders! Have a look and see what it's like now (p. 318).

Wellspring Cave

⊙ This underwater pool grew from rainwater soaking into the ground

Wellspring Cave is a small cave on the western side of Route 3. Rainwater that has soaked into the ground wells up to form pools of water on both 1F and B1F.

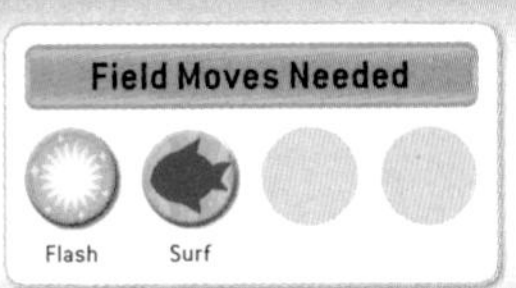

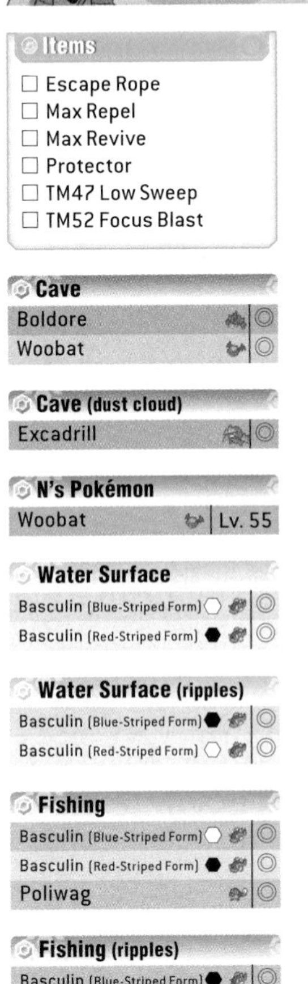

Items

- ☐ Escape Rope
- ☐ Max Repel
- ☐ Max Revive
- ☐ Protector
- ☐ TM47 Low Sweep
- ☐ TM52 Focus Blast

Cave	
Boldore	◎
Woobat	◎

Cave (dust cloud)	
Excadrill	◎

N's Pokémon	
Woobat	Lv. 55

Water Surface	
Basculin (Blue-Striped Form) ○	◎
Basculin (Red-Striped Form) ●	◎

Water Surface (ripples)	
Basculin (Blue-Striped Form) ●	◎
Basculin (Red-Striped Form) ○	◎

Fishing	
Basculin (Blue-Striped Form) ○	◎
Basculin (Red-Striped Form) ●	◎
Poliwag	◎

Fishing (ripples)	
Basculin (Blue-Striped Form) ●	◎
Basculin (Red-Striped Form) ○	◎
Poliwhirl	◎
Poliwrath	△

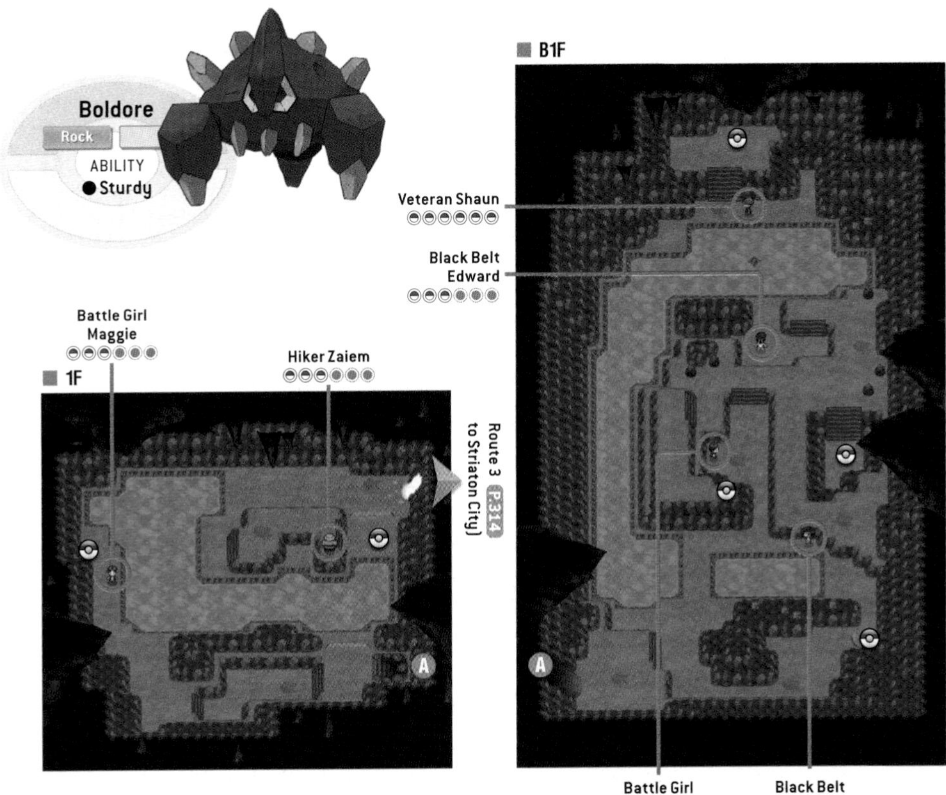

Step 1 Collect items while you make your way through the cave

Make your way deeper into Wellspring Cave while battling against other Trainers and collecting items. You'll need Surf to reach B1F.

Step 2 Use Flash to light up B1F

It's pitch black in B1F, and you won't be able to see even one step ahead. Bring a Pokémon that knows the move Flash and use it once you enter B1F. Flash will brighten up your surroundings so you can explore the cave.

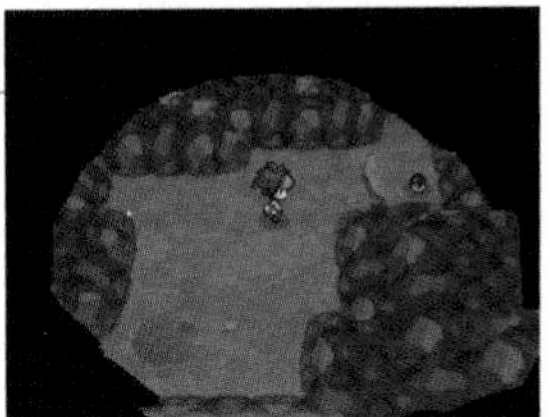

Flash can be taught using a TM

If you don't have a Pokémon in your party that knows how to use Flash, you can use a TM to teach the move. Because it's not an HM, your Pokémon can forget it easily when you don't need it anymore.

Step 3 Watch out for the strong Veteran

In the northern part of B1F, you'll encounter Veteran Shaun, who will challenge you with a full party of six strong Pokémon. This unusual battle should prove to be quite a challenge!

These Pokémon were born
on the same day and raised together!

Step 4 After you're finished exploring, head back to Route 3

After battling against all six Pokémon Trainers and gathering all of the items, you will have completed your exploration of Wellspring Cave. Go back to Route 3 and make your way to Striaton City.

Use an Escape Rope for a quick exit

Once you've finished exploring B1F of Wellspring Cave, use the Escape Rope that can be obtained on 1F. This useful item will pop you back to the cave's entrance on Route 3, so you don't have to retrace your steps. The Pokémon move Dig does the same thing!

Entry stairs built in memory of a former home in a snowier climate

Striaton City

The west side of Striaton City holds a lovely garden with a fountain, while a Trainers' School and some apartment buildings fill the eastern part of the city. The former Gym is now Striaton Restaurant.

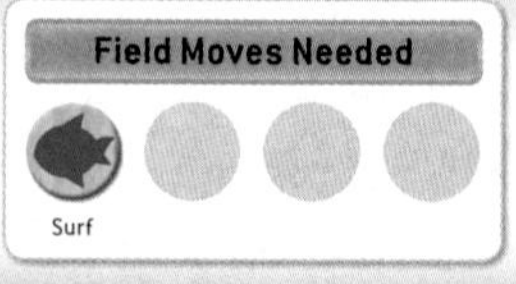

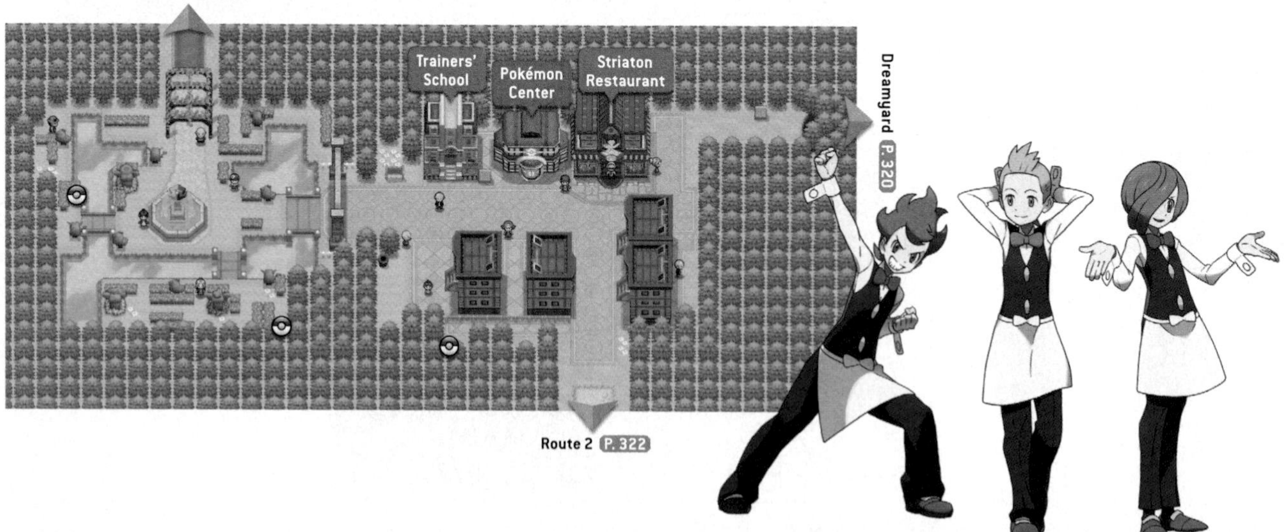

Items

First visit
- ☐ Big Pearl
- ☐ Dusk Ball
- ☐ Great Ball
- ☐ Max Elixir
- ☐ Timer Ball
- ☐ Up-Grade
- ☐ Yellow Shard

After acing the boy's quiz in the Trainers' School
- ☐ Persim Berry

When you talk to the woman when Shaymin is in your party
- ☐ Gracidea

Poké Mart (Lower Clerk)

Item	Price
TM04 Calm Mind	80,000
TM08 Bulk Up	80,000

Water Surface
Basculin (Blue-Striped Form) ○
Basculin (Red-Striped Form) ●
Corphish

Fishing
Basculin (Blue-Striped Form) ○
Basculin (Red-Striped Form) ●
Goldeen

Water Surface (ripples)
Basculin (Blue-Striped Form) ●
Basculin (Red-Striped Form) ○
Crawdaunt

Fishing (ripples)
Basculin (Blue-Striped Form) ●
Basculin (Red-Striped Form) ○
Goldeen
Seaking

Step 1 A boy in the Trainers' School gives you a quiz

Talk to the boy standing near the left wall of the classroom in the Trainers' School to take a quiz about status conditions. If you get both of his questions right, he'll give you a Persim Berry.

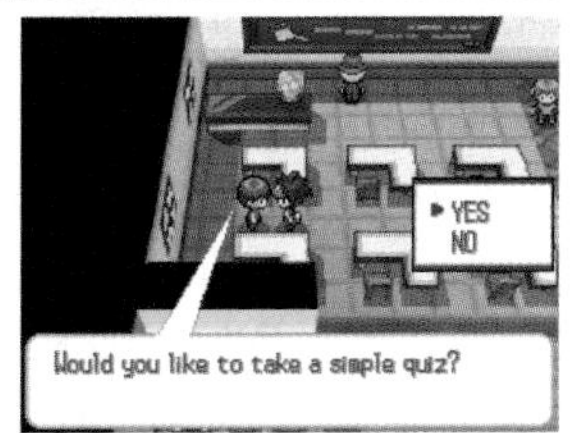

Step 2 Give some advice and have a battle

On the other side of the classroom, a man is trying to figure out how to make Ground-type moves hit Pokémon with the Levitate Ability. Give him some advice, and he'll challenge you to a battle.

A Funfest Mission is added

Enter the apartment building to the south of the Trainers' School and talk to the girl on the first floor. The Entralink Funfest Mission "Rock-Paper-Scissors Competition!" will be added for you to play.

Step 3 Learn about the Gracidea flower

Talk to the woman in the Pokémon Center, and she will tell you about the Gracidea. If you have Shaymin in your party and don't yet have a Gracidea, she will give one to you on the spot.

Bring Shaymin into your game

If you have received the Mythical Pokémon Shaymin in a different game, you can perform a Link Trade or use Poké Transfer to bring it into your game.

Step 4 Have a Multi Battle in Striaton Restaurant

You'll find former Gym Leaders Cilan, Chili, and Cress in Striaton Restaurant. Talk to one of the three brothers, and he'll team up with you for a Multi Battle against the other two! You can do this once a day.

Memory Link trigger point

Talk to Cilan, Chili, or Cress in Striaton Restaurant twice, and a Memory Link event will occur. Listen to their story about training for a new beginning (p. 73).

Step 5 Win a Big Mushroom by participating in the stage show

Talk to the lady on the stage in Striaton Restaurant, and you can participate in a minigame to win an item. You have to guess which Pokémon is holding a Big Mushroom. If you guess correctly, you get the item!

The Pokémon that appear in the show change each time

Pansear, Pansage, and Panpour can appear in the minigame. The one that appears will change each time you play.

Step 6 Visit the Dreamyard

Head east from Striaton Restaurant to visit the Dreamyard (p. 320). The Dreamyard isn't connected to any other areas, so go back to Striaton City after you're finished exploring.

A mysterious Pokémon is nearby

Visit the first floor of the apartment building to the south of the Pokémon Center, and you'll hear that people have been feeling a mysterious Pokémon's presence in the Dreamyard. This mysterious Pokémon is Latios (Latias).

Step 7 Head south for Route 2

After exploring the Dreamyard, head south from Striaton Restaurant to reach Route 2 (p. 322). There are six Pokémon Trainers for you to battle, so it's a good idea to heal your Pokémon first.

Take in a Stunfisk night

An unusual thing happens in Striaton City's garden on summer nights: a large school of Stunfisk gathers near the fountain. Take a stroll through the garden at night (or late night) and check out the illuminated bridge and the dancing Stunfisk!

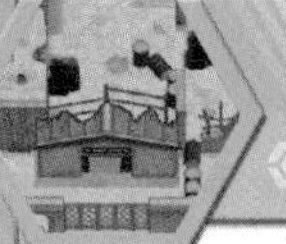

A plant site used as a playground for children and Pokémon

Dreamyard

The Dreamyard is an abandoned factory site that has been turned into a playground for children. There's a rumor going around Striaton City that a mysterious Pokémon's presence has been felt in the area recently.

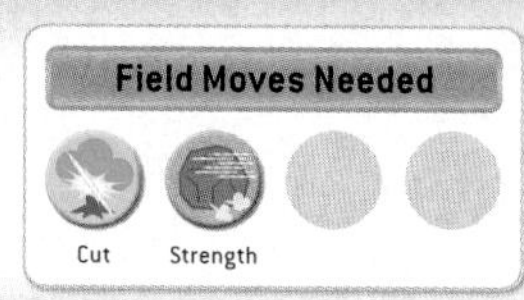

Items

- First visit
- ☐ Dawn Stone
- ☐ HP Up
- ☐ Iron
- ☐ Moon Stone
- ☐ Rare Candy
- ☐ Reaper Cloth
- ☐ TM85 Dream Eater
- ☐ Ultra Ball
- After catching Latios (Latias)
- ☐ Soul Dew

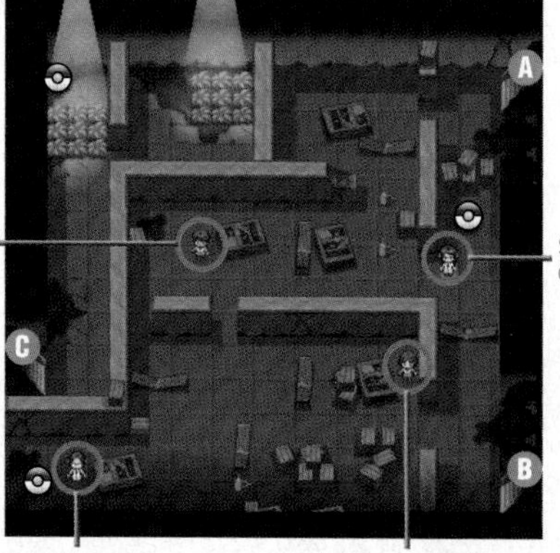

Outside

Tall Grass	
Golbat	○
Jigglypuff	○
Liepard	○
Munna	○
Raticate	○
Watchog	○

Tall Grass (rustling)	
Audino	◎
Crobat	△
Dunsparce	○
Musharna	△
Wigglytuff	△

Dark Grass	
Golbat	○
Jigglypuff	○
Liepard	○
Munna	○
Raticate	○
Watchog	○

Mass Outbreaks
Hypno

Underground

Dark Grass	
Golbat	○
Jigglypuff	○
Liepard	○
Munna	○
Raticate	○
Watchog	○

Step 1 Latios (Latias) appears, then flies off

When you enter the Dreamyard, Latios will appear in front of you if you are playing *Pokémon Black Version 2*, and Latias will appear in front of you if you are playing *Pokémon White Version 2*. It will then fly off. It will repeat this multiple times as you explore the Dreamyard.

It won't fly off to another area

Latios (Latias) will fly off soon after appearing in front of you. Don't worry, though. It won't leave the Dreamyard. If you fully explore the Dreamyard, you will be able to battle it.

Step 2 Proceed underground to battle Pokémon Trainers

Save your battle against Latios (Latias) for later and proceed underground for now. You'll find four Trainers there and then three more when you go back outside on the other end. Make your way through the area while collecting items and battling these Trainers.

Some Trainers require an indirect approach

Some Pokémon Trainers in the underground room will turn around and run away when you approach them. Wait around a corner and talk to them from the side when they approach, and you'll be able to battle them.

Step 3 Use Strength to move the boulder

Find the stairs to the south of the underground room and take them outside. Head north from there and use Strength to move the boulder you find. Plugging the hole with the boulder will open up a shortcut that lets you quickly get to the underground room from Striaton City.

Step 4 Head east across the top of the building and Latios (Latias) will finally stop

Enter the building on the northern side and collect the items you find inside. Climb the stairs and head west to pick up an item, then east. Go as far as you can and Latios (Latias) will stop. Talk to it to enter a battle.

Save right before the battle

Before you talk to Latios (Latias), be sure to save so you can try again in case you accidentally cause the Pokémon to faint.

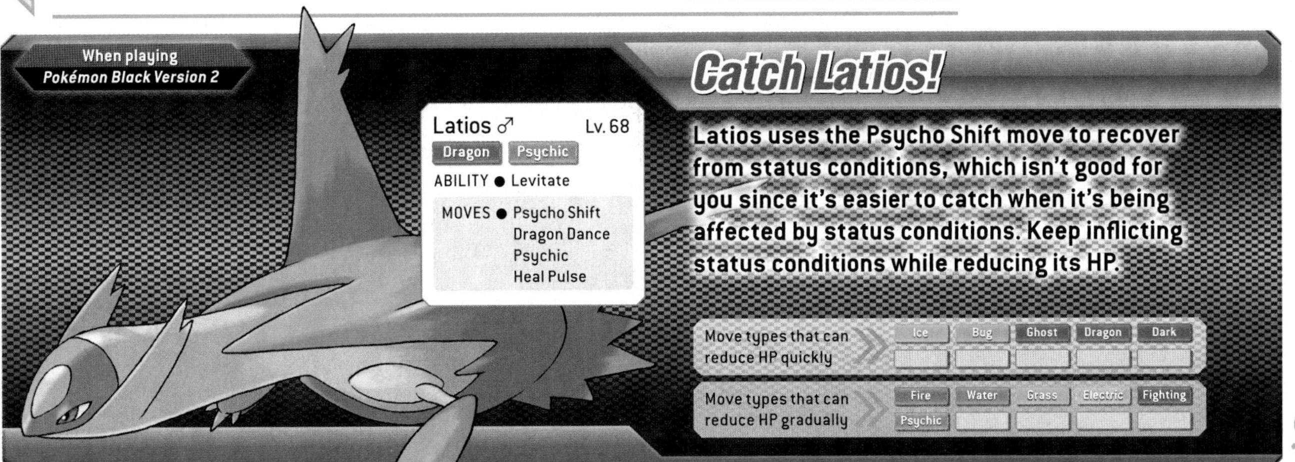

When playing *Pokémon Black Version 2*

Catch Latios!

Latios ♂ Lv. 68

Dragon | Psychic

ABILITY ● Levitate

MOVES ● Psycho Shift, Dragon Dance, Psychic, Heal Pulse

Latios uses the Psycho Shift move to recover from status conditions, which isn't good for you since it's easier to catch when it's being affected by status conditions. Keep inflicting status conditions while reducing its HP.

Move types that can reduce HP quickly	Ice	Bug	Ghost	Dragon	Dark
Move types that can reduce HP gradually	Fire	Water	Grass	Electric	Fighting
	Psychic				

Catch Latias!

First, exploit its weaknesses to quickly bring its HP down low. Latias uses the Charm move to lower your Pokémon's Attack stat by two stages. Weaken it gradually by using Fire- and Fighting-type physical moves.

Move types that can reduce HP quickly	Ice	Bug	Ghost	Dragon	Dark
Move types that can reduce HP gradually	Fire	Water	Grass	Electric	Fighting
	Psychic				

Step 5 Get Soul Dew

Catch Latios (Latias) and the Soul Dew will appear on the ground, so be sure to pick it up. When Latios or Latias holds this item, it will increase the holder's Special Attack and Special Defense stats by 50%.

Step 6 Head west to return to Striaton City

After you battle against all seven Trainers, collect all of the items, and catch Latios (Latias), your exploration of the Dreamyard will be over. Head back to Striaton City and make your way to Route 2 (p. 320).

A pastoral road where Trainers can challenge one another

Route 2

Route 2 connects Accumula Town and Striaton City. Cilan, Chili, and Cress of Striaton Restaurant often visit the route to help train Pokémon Trainers.

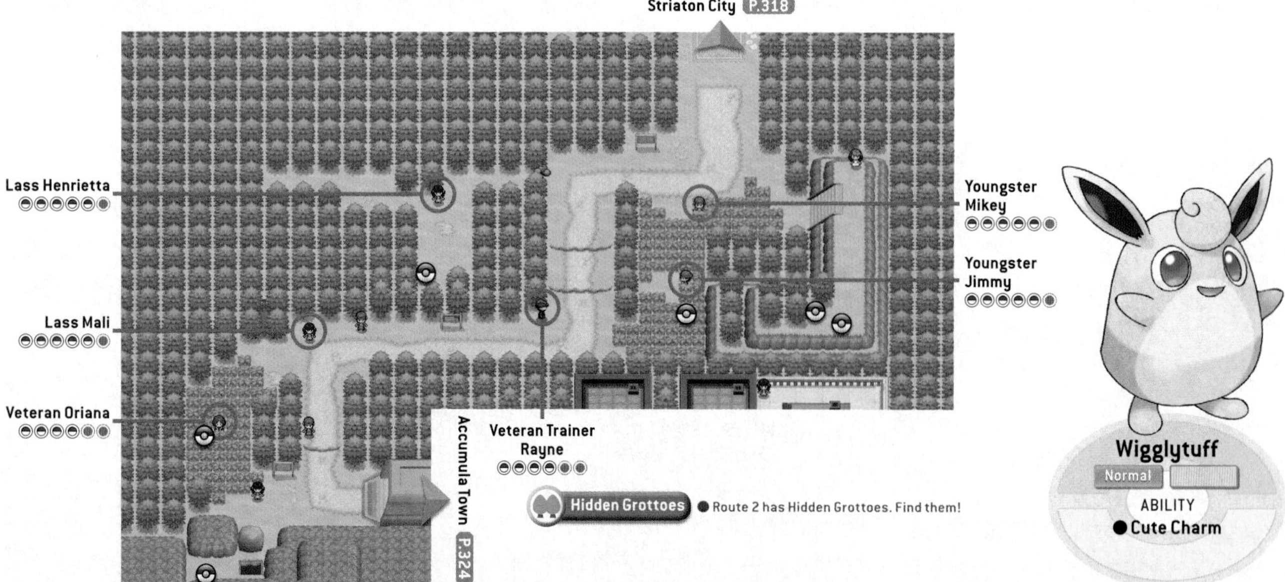

Wigglytuff
Normal
ABILITY
● Cute Charm

Items

First visit
- ☐ Calcium
- ☐ Carbos
- ☐ Full Heal
- ☐ Max Revive
- ☐ Repeat Ball
- ☐ Ultra Ball

When you have a Pokémon with the Solid Rock Ability in your party
- ☐ Dawn Stone

Tall Grass	
Herdier	◎
Jigglypuff	○
Lickitung	○
Liepard	○
Watchog	◎

Tall Grass (rustling)	
Audino	◎
Dunsparce	○
Lickilicky	△
Stoutland	△
Wigglytuff	△

Hidden Grotto	
Granbull	△
Nidoran ♀	○
Nidoran ♂	○
Watchog	◎

N's Pokémon	
Purrloin	Lv. 7

Herdier
Normal
ABILITIES
- Intimidate
- Sand Rush

Step 1 Proceed south while battling Trainers

After taking Route 2 from Striaton City, head south along the path. Along the way, you'll encounter six Trainers. Fight, fight, fight, fight, fight, fight while making your way south to the exit.

Beedrill! Volbeat!
Go, my beastly Bug-type Pokémon!

Trainers on Route 2 have lots of Pokémon

Expect these Trainers to test you thoroughly! Each one has a party of four or five Pokémon.

Step 2 Show off a Pokémon with the Solid Rock Ability

A woman on the raised area on Route 2 wants to see a Pokémon with the Solid Rock Ability. Put a Pokémon with the Solid Rock Ability in your party and talk to her to receive a Dawn Stone.

Solid Rock... Like a hard rock...
Hard rock?!

Which Pokémon have the Solid Rock Ability?

Pokémon such as Camerupt, Rhyperior, Tirtouga, and Carracosta have the Solid Rock Ability. If you have one of these in your PC, visit the Striaton City Pokémon Center to add it to your party.

Step 3 Use Strength to move a boulder and get an item

Head south as far as you can on Route 2, and you'll find a boulder that can be moved by using Strength. Use Strength to plug the hole with the boulder, then pick up the item just beyond it.

Step 4 Go through the gate to visit Accumula Town

Head east through the gate at the southern end of Route 2, and you'll reach Accumula Town, which is located between Striaton City and Nuvema Town (p. 324).

Accumula Town

Accumula Town is a small town between Route 2, which leads to Striaton City, and Route 1, which leads to Nuvema Town. Because of its many hills, the town offers some great views.

Items

- First visit
- ☐ BalmMushroom
- ☐ Poké Ball ×10
- If you answered the Snivy quiz correctly
- ☐ Grass Gem
- If you answered the Tepig quiz correctly
- ☐ Fire Gem
- If you answered the Oshawott quiz correctly
- ☐ Water Gem
- If you showed Kricketot and Whismur to the lady playing the piano
- ☐ Metronome

Poké Mart (Lower Clerk)

Item	Price	Item	Price
Favored Mail	50	RSVP Mail	50
Greet Mail	50	Thanks Mail	50
Inquiry Mail	50	Nest Ball	1,000
Like Mail	50	Quick Ball	1,000
Reply Mail	50	Repeat Ball	1,000

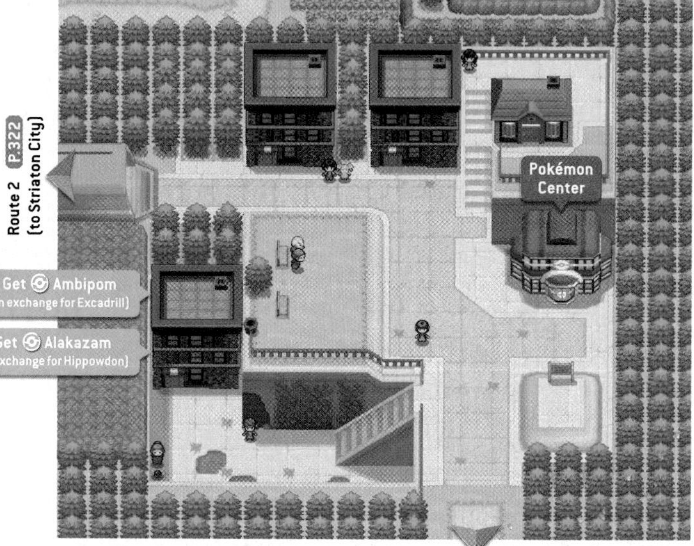

Step 1 Play Pokémon rock-paper-scissors

Talk to the girl you find on the second floor of the apartment building directly east of the gate. You can play a game of Pokémon rock-paper-scissors using the Grass, Fire, and Water types. The type with the advantage wins.

Step 2 Take on a quiz based off your first Pokémon

Talk to the dark-haired girl to participate in a quiz based on the Pokémon you picked at the start of your adventure. Answer correctly twice, and depending on the Pokémon's type, you will receive a Grass Gem, Fire Gem, or Water Gem.

Well, then I'll quiz you about Tepig!
Is Tepig's height 1'08"?
YES
NO

Step 3 Show off a Pokémon taller than 17 feet every day

The girl at the top of the stairs to the west of the Pokémon Center wants to see a Pokémon that is over 17 feet tall. Put a very tall Pokémon in your party and talk to her to receive a Fluffy Tail. You can show her a Pokémon once per day.

Which Pokémon are taller than 17 feet?

Pokémon taller than 17 feet include Onix and Steelix. There are other Pokémon that fit this description, too, so be on the lookout for tall Pokémon.

Step 4 Show off a Pokémon shorter than eight inches every day

The boy at the bottom of the stairs to the south of the Pokémon Center wants to see a Pokémon that is shorter than eight inches. Put a very short Pokémon in your party and talk to him to receive a Poké Doll. You can show him a Pokémon once per day.

Which Pokémon are shorter than eight inches?

Pokémon shorter than eight inches include Azurill, Budew, and Foongus. There are other Pokémon that fit this description, too, so be sure to keep an eye out.

Show Kricketot to the woman who is in a slump

Speak to the woman in the house on top of the hill. She has been stuck in a slump for some time and is feeling worried. Try speaking to her with Kricketot in your party. Kricketot is not native to the Unova region, so you will need to bring it from another region using Poké Transfer (p. 282).

Dedelee dun dun dun dum! ♪
It sounds just like a xylophone!

Show the still-troubled woman your Whismur

Even after you show her your Kricketot, it seems that the woman is still feeling troubled. This time, try speaking to her with Whismur in your party. Whismur is also not native to the Unova region. Once the woman is finally knocked out of her slump, she will give you a Metronome.

It's wonderfully pianissimo!
It reverberates like a sweet murmur!

Trade your Excadrill for an Ambipom

You will be invited to trade Pokémon with the woman on the first floor of the apartment down the stairs. Give the woman your Excadrill and you can receive an Ambipom. Excadrill appears in dust clouds inside caves like Reversal Mountain.

YES
NO
I'll trade you my Ambipom
for your Excadrill!

Have a Pokémon battle against the Excadrill you traded

After you trade Excadrill for Ambipom, come back and speak to the woman again, and she will ask you to battle her so she can show you how Excadrill has grown. Take on her challenge. Excadrill will have leveled up since you traded it.

YES
NO
Hey! If it's all right with you,
would you have a Pokémon battle with me?

Trade the same woman your Hippowdon for Alakazam

After you battle against the Excadrill you traded, the woman will ask you to make another trade with her. If you give her a Hippowdon, you can receive Alakazam. Hippowdon can be found in mass outbreaks in the Desert Resort.

YES
NO
I'll trade you my Alakazam!
C'mon, let's trade Pokémon!

Have a Pokémon battle against the Hippowdon you traded

After you trade Hippowdon for Alakazam, come back and speak to the woman again and she will ask you to battle her to show you how Hippowdon has grown. When you battle her, Hippowdon will have leveled up since you traded it.

The Hippowdon I got from you
has become really strong!

Take Kricketot and Whismur with you when you go

You can catch Kricketot in *Pokémon Platinum Version* and Whismur in *Pokémon HeartGold Version* or *Pokémon SoulSilver Version*. Use Poké Transfer to bring them to your game.

Out of the dumps with livelier music

After you've shown the woman living on the hill your Kricketot and Whismur, try speaking to her again. A lovely piano strain will be added to the background music. If you speak to the man standing in front of the drums nearby as well, you'll be able to enjoy a truly rich song.

Bringing Hippowdon to you

Hippowdon can be caught during mass outbreaks in the Desert Resort, but you never know when a mass outbreak will occur. Using Poké Transfer to bring one from *Pokémon Platinum Version* is another option.

Step 11 You can't take the item near the old woman

There is an old woman standing in front of the apartment building where you traded your Pokémon. An item is lying on the ground beside her, but even if you examine it, you won't be able to take it... What's going on?

My cute little Foongus looks just like a Poké Ball!

Step 12 Continue south and head for Route 1

Once you have explored all of Accumula Town, turn south to head for Route 1. From Route 1, you can continue onto Route 17 or 18. Once you have stocked up on healing items from the Pokémon Center, set out on the road again.

A small road by the shore, where you can enjoy the changing seasons

Route 1

Route 1 links Accumula Town and Nuvema Town. You can feel the changing of the seasons here, with flower petals blowing in the spring breeze and rustling leaves dancing on the crisp autumn wind. To the west, the road continues on Route 17.

Field Moves Needed

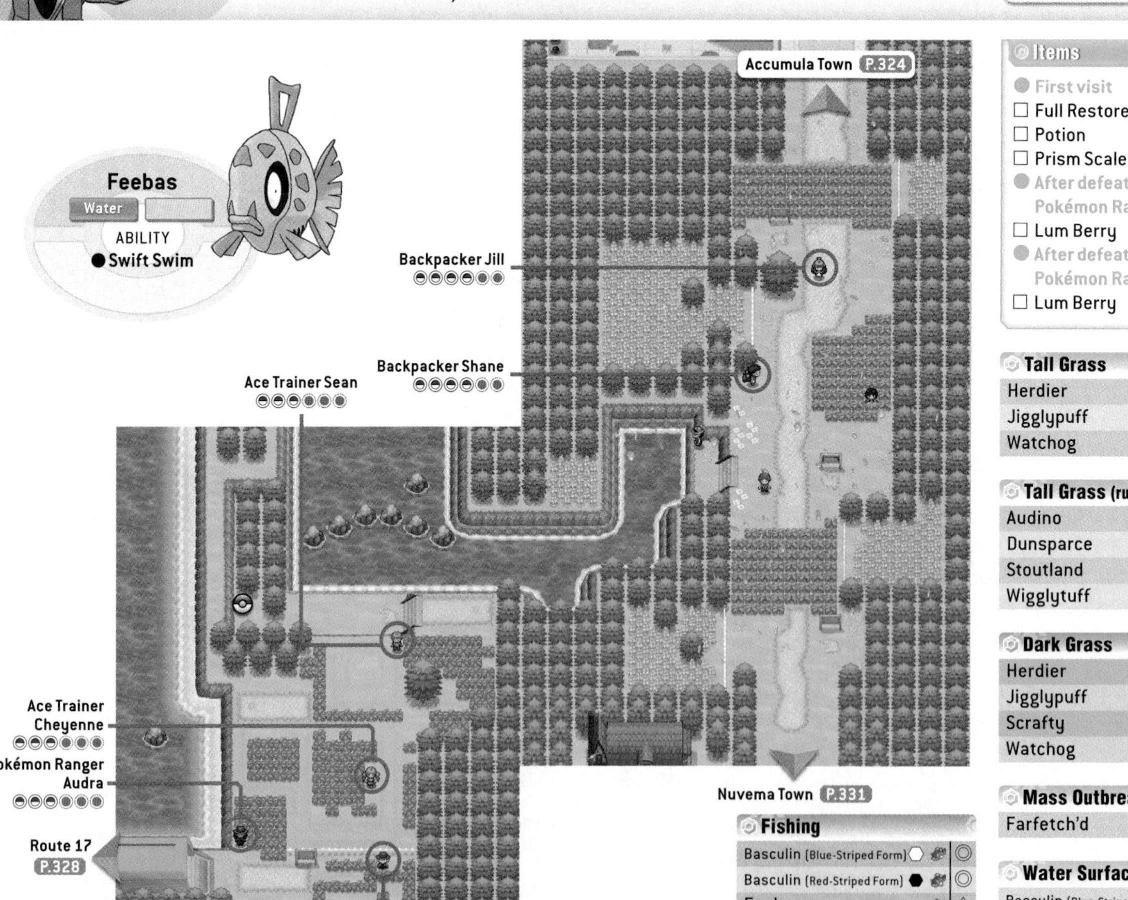

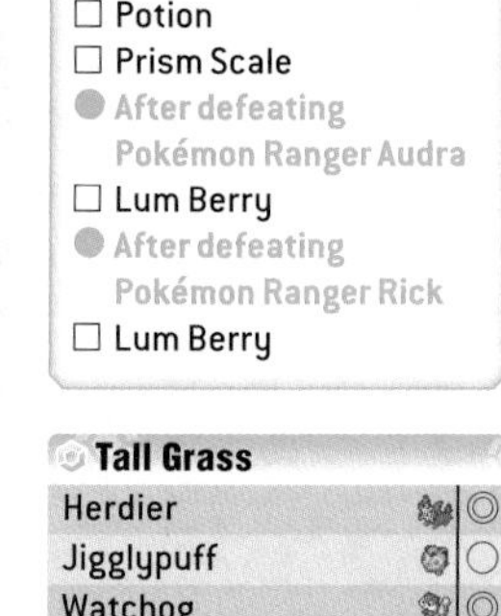

Items

- First visit
- ☐ Full Restore
- ☐ Potion
- ☐ Prism Scale
- After defeating Pokémon Ranger Audra
- ☐ Lum Berry
- After defeating Pokémon Ranger Rick
- ☐ Lum Berry

Tall Grass	
Herdier	◎
Jigglypuff	○
Watchog	◎

Tall Grass (rustling)	
Audino	◎
Dunsparce	○
Stoutland	△
Wigglytuff	△

Dark Grass	
Herdier	◎
Jigglypuff	○
Scrafty	○
Watchog	◎

Mass Outbreaks
Farfetch'd

Fishing	
Basculin (Blue-Striped Form) ⬡	◎
Basculin (Red-Striped Form) ⬢	◎
Feebas	△

Fishing (ripples)	
Basculin (Blue-Striped Form) ⬢	◎
Basculin (Red-Striped Form) ⬡	◎
Feebas	◎
Milotic	△

Water Surface	
Basculin (Blue-Striped Form) ⬡	◎
Basculin (Red-Striped Form) ⬢	◎

Water Surface (ripples)	
Basculin (Blue-Striped Form) ⬢	◎
Basculin (Red-Striped Form) ⬡	◎

Proceed south while battling Pokémon Trainers

Once you enter Route 1 from Accumula Town, head south along the path. There are two Trainers on the east side of Route 1. Fight them as you make your way down to the Trainer Tips sign.

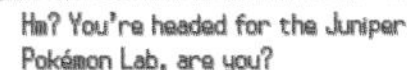

Use Surf to continue west

Head west from the Trainer Tips sign and get a glimpse of the blue water off the shore. Use Surf to continue west and go ashore on the open bit of land to the south. There are four Trainers in this area. They'd be glad of a battle before you move on.

Get Berries from Pokémon Rangers

Defeat Audra and Rick to receive Lum Berries. They are waiting to the east of the gate that leads to Route 17.

Pass through the gate en route to Route 17

Continue south, battling Trainers and collecting items, until you reach the gate at the end of the path. Go west through the gate, and you'll arrive at Route 17 (p. 328).

Return to Route 1 after checking everything

After you explore every last corner of Route 17, including Route 18 and the P2 Laboratory, your survey of the area will be complete. Next, return to Route 1 and turn to Nuvema Town.

Go south to reach Nuvema Town

When you return to Route 1 from Route 17, use Surf to head back to the east side of the path. Turn south at the Trainer Tips sign, and you'll be able to reach Nuvema Town, where Professor Juniper lives (p. 331).

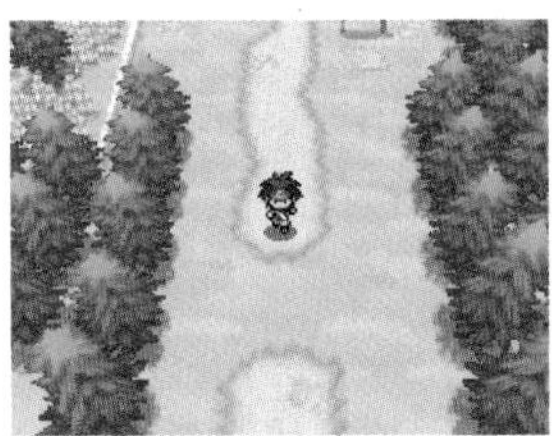

Memory Link event

If you follow Route 1 to the south, Bianca will call out to you just before you enter Nuvema Town. She'll challenge you to a Pokémon battle. You might really have to stretch against Bianca's strong Pokémon (p. 73).

The fast current here makes it difficult to surf

Route 17 • Route 18 • P2 Laboratory

Route 17 stretches across the sea to the west of Route 1. You can't always proceed freely, due to the strong ocean currents. At the west end of the path, you'll find Route 18, while the P2 Laboratory is located to the north. The Plasma Frigate is moored beside the P2 Laboratory.

Field Moves Needed

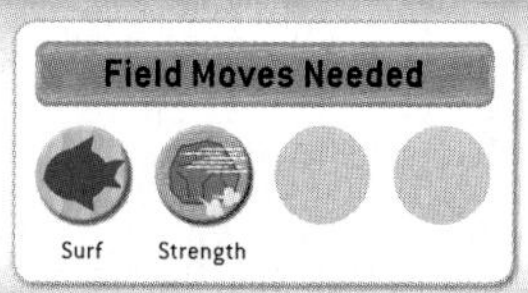

Hidden Grotto ● Route 18 has a Hidden Grotto. Find it!

Items

Route 17
- ☐ Blue Shard
- ☐ Dive Ball
- ☐ Pearl String
- ☐ Star Piece
- ☐ TM19 Telekinesis
- ☐ Zinc

Route 18
- ☐ Iron
- ☐ Magma Stone
- ☐ PP Max

P2 Laboratory
- ☐ Dubious Disc

Plasma Frigate
After beating Colress
- ☐ Master Ball

Items you can sell at the prefab house

Item	Price
Rare Bone	10,000

Route 17

Water Surface

Pokémon	
Frillish	◎

Water Surface (ripples)

Pokémon	
Alomomola	◎
Jellicent	△

Fishing

Pokémon	
Finneon	◎
Horsea	◎

Fishing (ripples)

Pokémon	
Horsea	◎
Kingdra	△
Lumineon	◎
Seadra	△

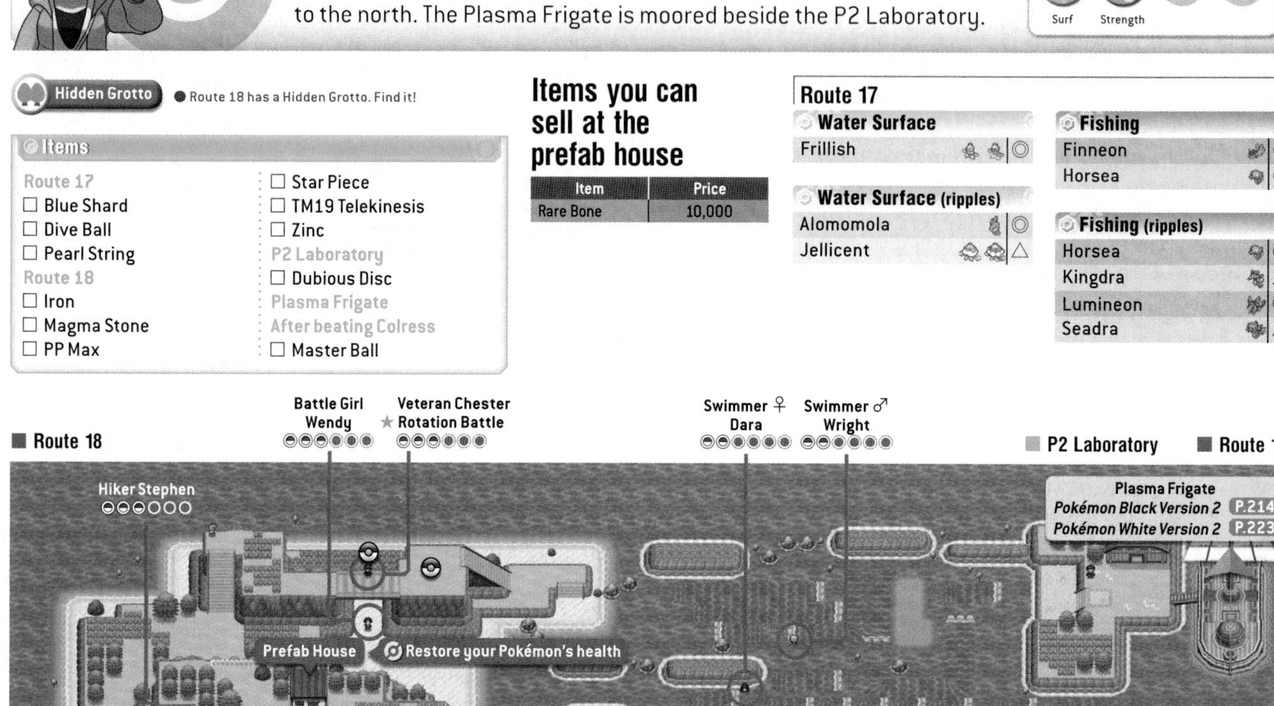

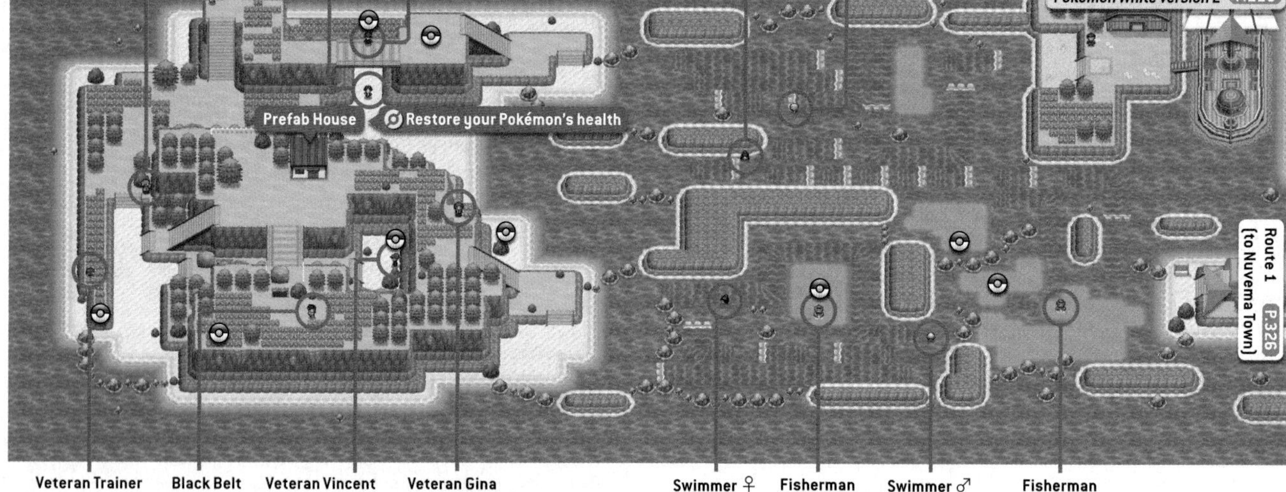

Route 18

Tall Grass

Pokémon		
Carnivine		○
Crustle		○
Sawk	●	○
Scrafty		◎
Throh	○	○
Tropius		○
Watchog		○

Tall Grass (rustling)

Pokémon		
Audino		◎
Dunsparce		○
Sawk	○	△
Throh	●	△

Mass Outbreaks

Pokémon
Hoppip

Dark Grass

Pokémon		
Carnivine		○
Crustle		○
Sawk	●	○
Scrafty		◎
Throh	○	○
Tropius		○
Watchog		○

Hidden Grotto

Pokémon	
Chatot	○
Corsola	○
Dragonite	△
Kingler	○

Water Surface

Pokémon	
Frillish	◎

Water Surface (ripples)

Pokémon	
Alomomola	◎
Jellicent	△

Fishing

Pokémon	
Corsola	△
Finneon	◎
Horsea	◎

Fishing (ripples)

Pokémon	
Horsea	◎
Kingdra	△
Lumineon	◎
Seadra	△

P2 Laboratory

Tall Grass

Pokémon	
Herdier	○
Klang	○
Magneton	○
Scrafty	○
Watchog	○
Weezing	○

Tall Grass (rustling)

Pokémon	
Audino	◎
Klinklang	△
Magnezone	△
Stoutland	△

Water Surface

Pokémon	
Frillish	◎

Water Surface (ripples)

Pokémon	
Alomomola	◎
Jellicent	△

Fishing

Pokémon	
Finneon	◎
Horsea	◎

Fishing (ripples)

Pokémon	
Kingdra	△
Lumineon	△
Qwilfish	◎
Seadra	◎

Step 1 Ride the wild waves to make your way forward

Once you pass through the gate from Route 1, use Surf to set out on the sea. The area is filled with strong currents that flow in only one direction, but to the west of the shoals are two currents that lead onward. If you ride on the lower current, you will be able to reach Route 18.

Be ready for Triple Battles and Rotation Battles

Veteran Trainer Gina on Route 18 will take you on in a Triple Battle, while Veteran Trainer Chester will challenge you to a Rotation Battle. Check the order of the Pokémon in your party and be prepared before battling them.

Step 2 Have the girl in the prefab house heal your Pokémon

Continue north on Route 18 and you will find a small prefab house. If you speak to the girl inside, she will heal your Pokémon. Stop by the prefab house and get your Pokémon healed when they're hurt in battles with Trainers or wild Pokémon.

Aren't your Pokémon a bit tired?
Here, don't be shy! Let them rest!

Use the Dowsing Machine to search out items

Many items are hidden in Route 17, Route 18, and the P2 Laboratory. Use the Dowsing Machine to search out and obtain all of the hidden items (p. 62).

Step 3 Have your Rare Bones bought from you

A man in sunglasses is standing against the wall at the back of the prefab house. If you speak to him, he will buy your Rare Bones from you. You will get more for them here than at a Poké Mart, so if you want to sell some Rare Bones, be sure to come here.

What's up?
Did you find something cool for me?

Step 4 Meet Crasher Wake from the Sinnoh region

Go west from the prefab house and go down to the beach, then turn north. At the northern tip of the island, you will find the masked man Crasher Wake. In fact, he is the Gym Leader of Pastoria City in the Sinnoh region. He stands staring out to sea and singing, then hurries off in a rush.

The ring is my rolling sea. ♪
The towering waves shaped me.

Crasher Wake will appear at the PWT

Crasher Wake says he is going to Driftveil City and then leaves. He is headed for the PWT. If you take part in the Sinnoh Leaders Tournament, you will be able to meet Crasher Wake again (p. 382).

Step 5 Obtain the Magma Stone

Head east from the spot where you met Crasher Wake. Cross the bridge where you meet Veteran Chester and you will find the Magma Stone. This is a very important item that you will need to meet Heatran.

Trainer found Magma Stone!

You can meet Heatran at Reversal Mountain

If you go to Reversal Mountain after obtaining the Magma Stone, Heatran will appear before you (p. 267). Be sure to visit the mountain later so you can catch Heatran.

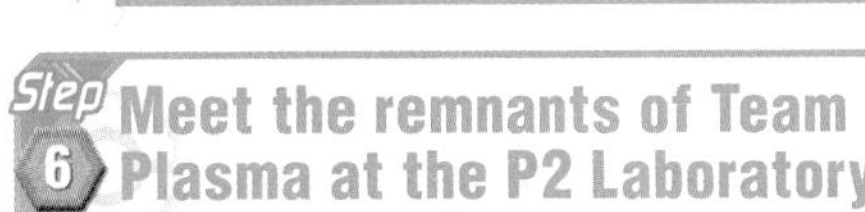

Step 6 Meet the remnants of Team Plasma at the P2 Laboratory

If you ride the currents from the north part of Route 18, you can continue east and reach the P2 Laboratory. Once you come ashore, you will find one of the remaining members of Team Plasma. What could they be doing here? Once you've collected the items from the building to the north, continue east.

I guess I'm the only one
who can change myself...

Step 7 The Plasma Frigate is moored here

Head east from the building and you'll find the Plasma Frigate moored beside the island. Inside are a number of Team Plasma grunts. Colress apparently gave them permission to stay here as long as they intend to bring out their Pokémon's potential by treating them well.

I knew that Ghetsis
was using me...

Step 8 Check the beds on board to heal your Pokémon

Descend belowdecks and enter cabin 4 on the east side of the ship. Check the bed there and your Pokémon will be fully healed. The bed that will allow your Pokémon to rest and heal is in the same room as when you visited before entering the Hall of Fame.

Have your Pokémon healed before battling Colress

In Colress's room on the Plasma Frigate, you can have a Pokémon battle with Colress. If you plan to battle with him, go to cabin 4 first and have your Pokémon fully healed.

Step 9 Colress waits for you beyond the warp panel

Enter the Plasma Frigate from the southern entrance and proceed into the warp panel area. You can warp into the room where Kyurem was. From there, head north, and at the end of the hall turn to the east. Take the warp panel to the east and you will be able to warp to Colress's room.

Step 10 Accept Colress's battle challenge

When you enter Colress's room, you will find him standing in the center. It seems that he has been continuing his research, and so, wishing to measure your Pokémon's strength, he challenges you to battle again. The number and levels of Colress's Pokémon have both increased, making this a challenging battle.

Be sure to save your game before speaking to him

If you speak to Colress in his room, you will be drawn into battle. If you wish to save your game before the battle, be sure to do it before you approach Colress.

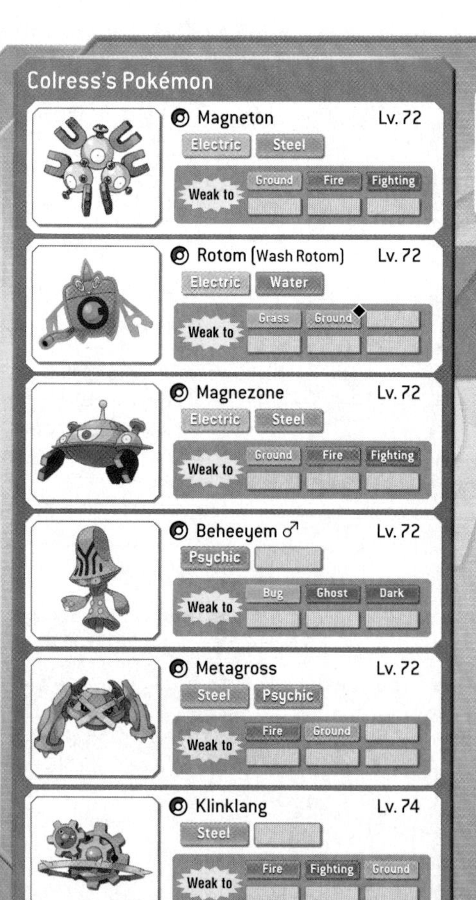

Colress's Pokémon

Pokémon	Lv.	Type	Weak to
Magneton	Lv. 72	Electric, Steel	Ground, Fire, Fighting
Rotom (Wash Rotom)	Lv. 72	Electric, Water	Grass, Ground◆
Magnezone	Lv. 72	Electric, Steel	Ground, Fire, Fighting
Beheeyem ♂	Lv. 72	Psychic	Bug, Ghost, Dark
Metagross	Lv. 72	Steel, Psychic	Fire, Ground
Klinklang	Lv. 74	Steel	Fire, Fighting, Ground

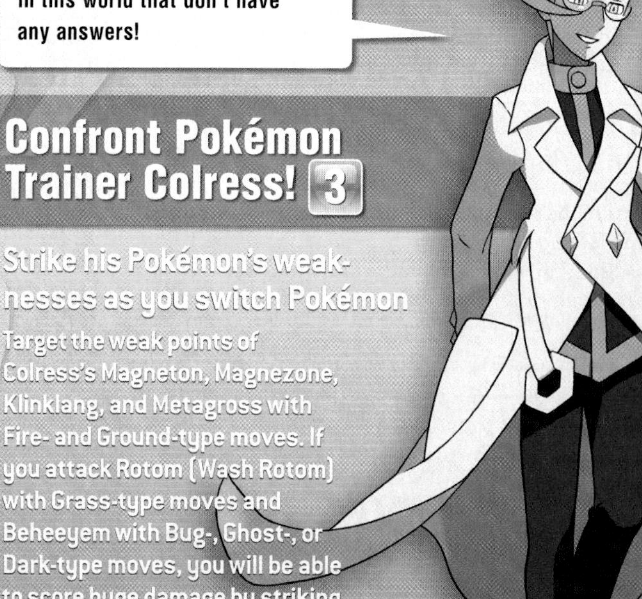

There are far more questions in this world that don't have any answers!

Confront Pokémon Trainer Colress! 3

Strike his Pokémon's weaknesses as you switch Pokémon

Target the weak points of Colress's Magneton, Magnezone, Klinklang, and Metagross with Fire- and Ground-type moves. If you attack Rotom (Wash Rotom) with Grass-type moves and Beheeyem with Bug-, Ghost-, or Dark-type moves, you will be able to score huge damage by striking their weaknesses.

◆ The damage may change depending on the effects of this Pokémon's Ability.

Step 11 Receive a Master Ball from Colress

If you win in your battle against Colress, he will reward you with a Master Ball. The Master Ball will catch any Pokémon without fail, so it is the ultimate Poké Ball. Why not try using one when trying to catch a Legendary Pokémon?

Battle with Colress every day

You can battle Colress once a day on the Plasma Frigate. After you fight him the first time, he will change locations. From the second battle onward, you will be able to fight him on the front of the deck. You will only receive a Master Ball the first time you battle him, though.

Step 12 Avoid the currents to reach Route 18

Leave the Plasma Frigate and set out again from the water beside the P2 Laboratory. You can travel through the space between the strong currents. When you make your way west, you will arrive at the beach in the middle of Route 18, an area you could not reach from Route 17.

Step 13 Explore every corner and collect items

When you arrive at the sandy beach from Route 18, battle the Pokémon Trainer there and collect items. The Crustle that appear in the dark grass in this area are the only Pokémon that hold Rare Bones.

Step 14 Return to Route 1 via Route 17

Once you have explored all of Route 18, including the parts you couldn't reach from Route 17, hit the water again to return to Route 17. Go again through the gate to the east and you will be back on Route 1 (p. 327).

A rural town whose sea breezes give the sense of something coming

Nuvema Town

Nuvema Town is the easternmost town in the Unova region. The town is home to Juniper Pokémon Lab, where Professor Juniper researches Pokémon origins. Cheren and Bianca are originally from Nuvema Town.

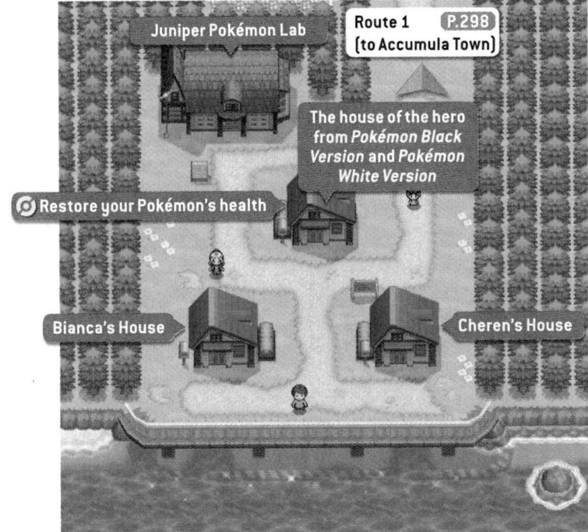

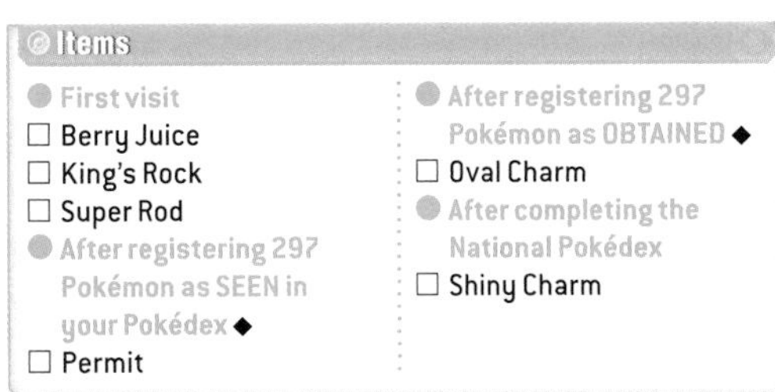

Items

First visit
- ☐ Berry Juice
- ☐ King's Rock
- ☐ Super Rod

After registering 297 Pokémon as SEEN in your Pokédex ◆
- ☐ Permit

After registering 297 Pokémon as OBTAINED ◆
- ☐ Oval Charm

After completing the National Pokédex
- ☐ Shiny Charm

◆ Not including Mythical Pokémon such as Victini, Keldeo, or Meloetta.

Step 1 Visit the house of the hero from *Pokémon Black Version* and *Pokémon White Version*

To the south of Juniper Pokémon Lab, you'll find the childhood home of the hero from *Pokémon Black Version* and *Pokémon White Version*. Venture inside, and you'll be able to meet the hero's mother. She'll heal your Pokémon, too!

Memory Link trigger point

If you have used Memory Link, the house's name plate will display the name of the player from *Pokémon Black Version* or *Pokémon White Version*. Furthermore, any trophies and certificates earned by the player in the previous game will decorate his or her room (p. 73).

Step 2 Visit Cheren and Bianca's houses, too

From the hero's house, head south to find both Cheren's house and Bianca's house. The eastern house is Cheren's, and the western house is Bianca's. Speak with their parents to hear stories about Cheren and Bianca.

Step 3 Visit Juniper Pokémon Lab

You'll find Professor Juniper in Juniper Pokémon Lab. Talk to her and she'll check the completeness of your Pokédex. Visit often to have her check both your SEEN and OBTAINED Pokémon numbers.

Receive an item from Cheren's father

Talk to Cheren's father, and he will give you a Berry Juice. It's a thank-you gift for being the first Trainer to challenge his son in a Gym battle.

Step 4 Receive a Super Rod from Cedric Juniper

You'll also find Cedric Juniper in the lab. Talk to Cedric, and he'll give you a Super Rod. Use it on the surface of water, and press the A Button when an exclamation mark appears. This will let you reel in a water-dwelling Pokémon!

Step 5 Receive a Permit from Professor Juniper

Once you've encountered every single Pokémon in the Unova Pokédex, talk to Professor Juniper, and she'll give you a Permit as a reward. With this item, you can visit the uncharted Nature Preserve area.

Step 6 Head to the Nature Preserve from Mistralton City

What sorts of Pokémon await you in the Nature Preserve? To find out, use Fly to travel to Mistralton City. There, you can board an airplane for the Nature Preserve.

Get your National Pokédex evaluated, too

Cedric Juniper will evaluate the completeness of your National Pokédex. He'll check how many Pokémon you have registered, and give you hints for how to complete your Pokédex.

After completing the Unova Pokédex: Receive an Oval Charm from Professor Juniper

Once you've caught every single Pokémon in the Unova Pokédex, talk to Professor Juniper, and she'll give you an Oval Charm as a reward. When you have this incredible item, it becomes much easier to find Pokémon Eggs at the Day Care.

Next, have your OBTAINED number evaluated

After you receive the Permit from Professor Juniper, she will evaluate the OBTAINED number in your Unova Pokédex. Have her check how many Pokémon you've caught.

After completing the National Pokédex

Receive a Shiny Charm from Professor Juniper

Once you've caught every single Pokémon in the National Pokédex, talk to Professor Juniper, and she'll give you a Shiny Charm as a reward. When you have this amazing item, it becomes easier to find Shiny Pokémon in caves and tall grass.

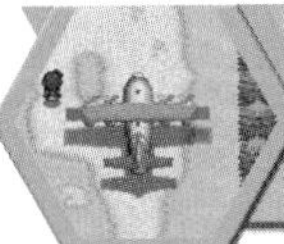

A Pokémon preserve located in a place far away from the Unova region

Nature Preserve

The Nature Preserve is far away from the Unova region, so you can only get there by plane. It was established as a preserve for Pokémon, and it's home to many kinds of Pokémon that you won't find anywhere else.

Field Moves Needed

Items

- ☐ Big Nugget
- ☐ Max Potion
- ☐ Rare Candy

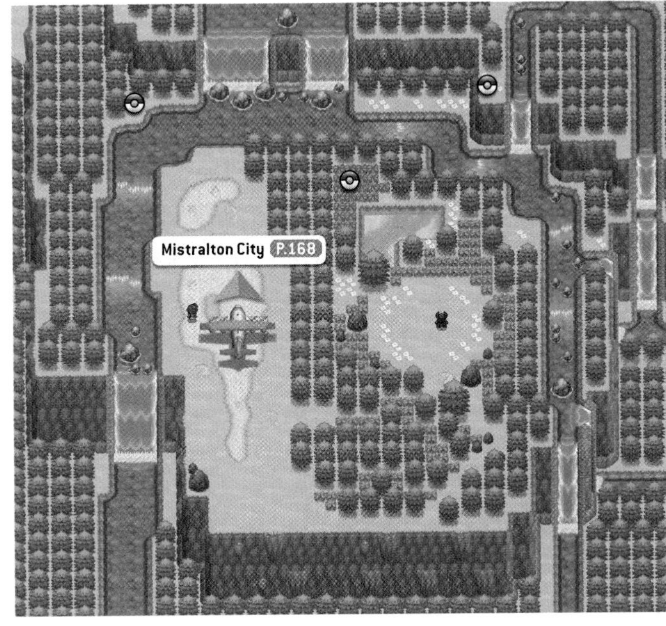

Tall Grass	
Altaria	○
Fraxure	○
Girafarig	○
Golduck	○
Kecleon	△
Noctowl	○
Nuzleaf	◎

Tall Grass (rustling)	
Audino	◎
Dunsparce	○
Shiftry	△

Dark Grass	
Altaria	○
Fraxure	○
Girafarig	○
Golduck	○
Kecleon	△
Noctowl	○
Nuzleaf	◎

Water Surface	
Basculin (Blue-Striped Form) ⬡	◎
Basculin (Red-Striped Form) ⬢	◎
Buizel	◎

Water Surface (ripples)	
Basculin (Blue-Striped Form) ⬢	◎
Basculin (Red-Striped Form) ⬡	◎
Buizel	◎
Floatzel	△

Fishing	
Basculin (Blue-Striped Form) ⬡	◎
Basculin (Red-Striped Form) ⬢	◎
Magikarp	◎

Fishing (ripples)	
Basculin (Blue-Striped Form) ⬢	◎
Basculin (Red-Striped Form) ⬡	◎
Gyarados	○
Magikarp	◎

Step 1 Board a plane at Mistralton Cargo Service

Once you arrive in Mistralton City, head over to Mistralton Cargo Service. Talk to the receptionist at the center counter. She will take notice of your Permit and invite you to board a plane piloted by Skyla headed for the Nature Preserve.

The Nature Preserve is not in the Unova region

The Nature Preserve is in a place far away from the Unova region, so it won't show up on your Town Map. You also won't be able to use Fly to visit it.

Step 2 Catch rare Pokémon

In the tall grass of the Nature Preserve, you will encounter Pokémon such as Noctowl, Nuzleaf, Girafarig, Kecleon, and Shiftry, all of whom cannot be found in the Unova region. Walk through the tall grass and catch Pokémon to bring you one step closer to completing your Pokédex.

Step 3 Catch the Shiny Haxorus

After you get off the plane, head south and make your way east along the narrow pathway through the trees. From there, head north until you reach a clearing in the forest. In the center of the clearing, you'll find a Haxorus of a different color. It will battle you if you speak to it. Catch it if you can!

It's a Shiny Haxorus!

This Haxorus in the Nature Preserve is Shiny, which means part of its body is differently colored from other Haxorus. Its stats are the same, though (p. 32).

Step 4 Talk to Skyla to return to the Unova region

Catch wild Pokémon and collect items while exploring the Nature Preserve. After you are finished exploring, speak to Skyla and you can return to Mistralton City. You can't leave by using Fly.

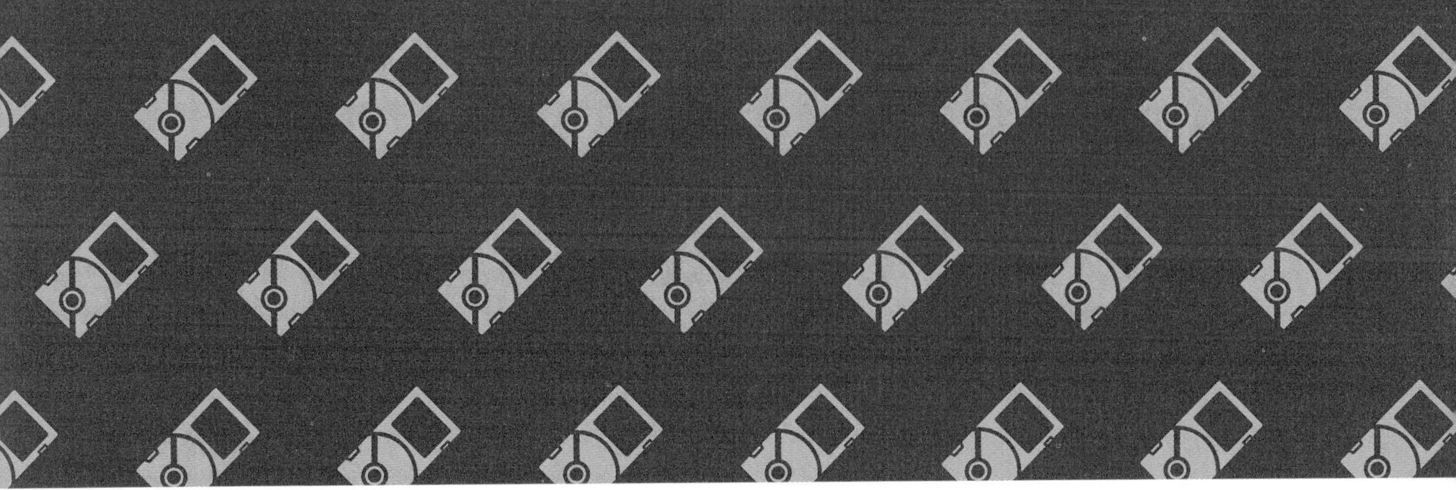

Unova Pokédex Challenge

Take the Unova Pokédex Challenge

Complete the Unova region Pokédex by catching 297 kinds of Pokémon

In the world of *Pokémon Black Version 2* and *Pokémon White Version 2*, the number of wild Pokémon species in the Unova region has increased from two years earlier. The Unova Pokédex has also changed—now 300 different Pokémon can be registered! You must register 297 Pokémon species to complete the Unova Pokédex, so take on the challenge!

When you're done, this number will be 297

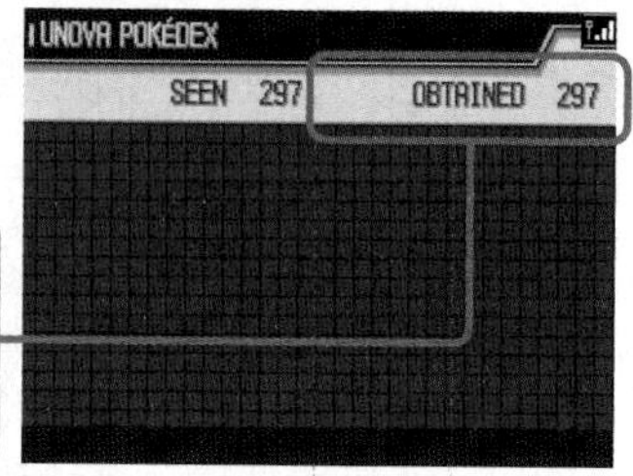

Pokémon not needed to complete the Unova Pokédex

Of the 300 Pokémon that can be registered in the Unova Pokédex, three of them don't need to be registered to complete it. The Mythical Pokémon Victini, Keldeo, and Meloetta can only be obtained through special distribution events, so they aren't required.

Victini

Keldeo

Meloetta

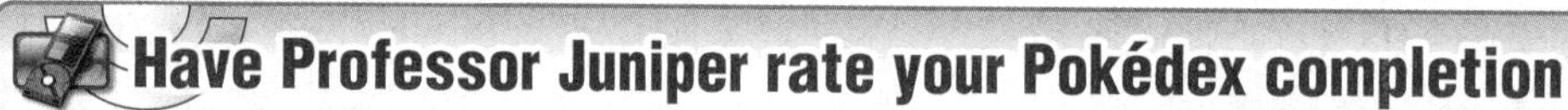

Have Professor Juniper rate your Pokédex completion

Professor Juniper provides a lot of support as you complete the Unova Pokédex. The professor tells you how complete your Unova Pokédex is. She gives advice on completing your Pokédex along with words of support.

How to have Professor Juniper rate your Pokédex

1. Call her on the Xtransceiver and ask her to "Check my Pokédex"

2. Go to Juniper Pokémon Lab in Nuvema Town and talk to her

Tip

Professor Juniper gives you gifts

When you complete the Pokédex, Professor Juniper will give you a special gift. When the number of Seen Pokémon reaches 297, she gives you the Permit so you can go to the Nature Preserve. When the number of Obtained Pokémon reaches 297, she gives you the Oval Charm, which makes it easier for Pokémon Eggs to be discovered at the Day Care.

You need *Pokémon Black Version* or *Pokémon White Version* to complete the Unova Pokédex

You can find most of the Pokémon you need to complete the Unova Pokédex in *Pokémon Black Version 2* or *Pokémon White Version 2*. Some Pokémon—including Tornadus, Thundurus, and Landorus—must be brought over from one of the previous games, *Pokémon Black Version* or *Pokémon White Version*.

Also, some Pokémon are easier to catch in *Pokémon Black* or *Pokémon White*, so put your previous games to good use! Don't forget, you can also catch Tornadus, Thundurus, and Landorus in *Pokémon Dream Radar* and transfer them to *Pokémon Black Version 2* or *Pokémon White Version 2*.

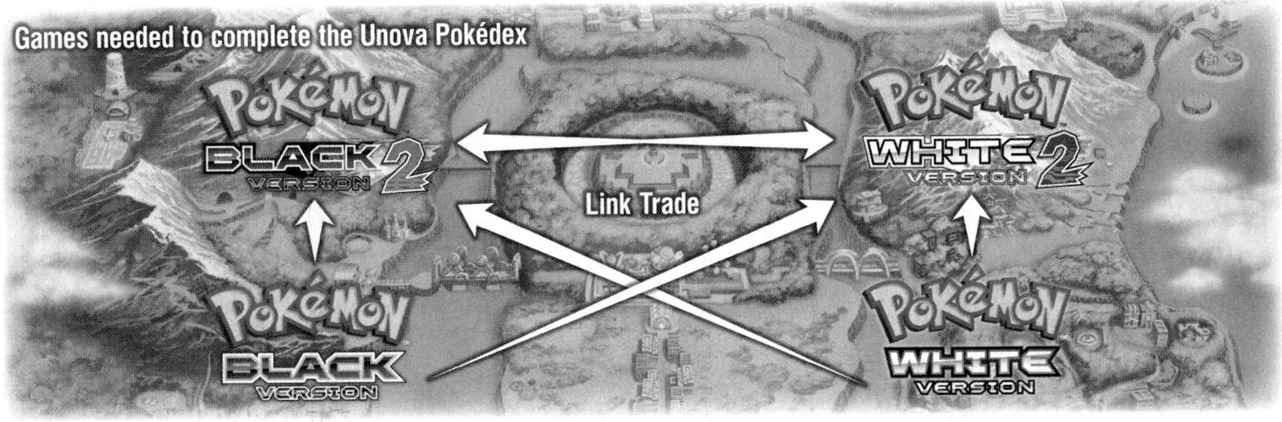

Receive Medals from Mr. Medal

When you meet certain conditions while catching all of the Unova region's Pokémon, you can get Medals from Mr. Medal. There are 18 different Medals in all. The Medals you get while catching Pokémon will encourage you to complete the Pokédex!

Check p. 448 for the Medal list.

Receive an award certificate from the Game Director

When you complete the Unova Pokédex, you can get a stately award certificate from Game Director in Castelia City's GAME FREAK building. The award certificate will be posted on the wall of your room, so you can look at it and remember this great achievement whenever you like.

Castelia City GAME FREAK

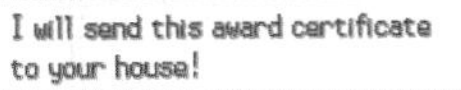

I will send this award certificate to your house!

Your room in Aspertia City

It's an award for completing the Unova Pokédex!

Unova Pokédex Completion Tip 1

Catch wild Pokémon

Master these techniques to increase your capture rate

The simplest way to fill out your Pokédex is to look for wild Pokémon and catch them with Poké Balls. Mastering the following techniques will ensure you always get the Pokémon you're after!

A wild Tyranitar appeared!

Catching Technique 1

Push the Pokémon's HP into the red

You could just fling your Poké Ball at a wild Pokémon, but there's a good chance the Pokémon will pop right back out! You probably won't catch it if it's still full of energy, so use attacks to lower its HP. Once it's weakened, you have a much better chance of sealing the deal.

What will Foongus do?

Lower its HP until the bar is red

When the Pokémon has just a few HP left, your odds of a successful catch are higher.

Catching Technique 2 Inflict status conditions on wild Pokémon

Use Pokémon moves to inflict status conditions. Some status conditions make a Pokémon much easier to catch. That's not all it takes, of course. If you inflict a status condition and lower the Pokémon's HP, you'll maximize your chances of making the catch.

Status conditions that aid in capture

Sleep (Easiest to Catch)
The target cannot attack. Wears off on its own after several turns.
● Some moves that cause Sleep status
Sing, Hypnosis

Frozen (Easiest to Catch)
The target cannot attack. Wears off on its own after several turns.
● Some moves that cause Frozen status
Powder Snow, Ice Beam

Paralysis
Lowers Speed, and each turn there's a 25% chance that the target can't attack. Does not wear off on its own.
● Some moves that cause Paralysis status
Thunder Wave, Lick

Poison
The target's HP decreases each turn. Does not wear off on its own.
● Some moves that cause Poison status
PoisonPowder, Poison Gas

Burned
Lowers Attack, and decreases HP each turn. Does not wear off on its own.
● Some moves that cause Burned status
Will-O-Wisp, Scald

◆ Some moves can be used when Asleep or Frozen.

Catching Technique 3 Catching many Pokémon makes it easier to catch other Pokémon

Catching many wild Pokémon increases the likelihood of catching others. Sometimes, when you throw a Poké Ball, it will click shut after rocking only once, and the Pokémon will be caught. This phenomenon is called a "critical capture."

Critical captures

1. **A Pokémon is caught after the Poké Ball rocks only once.**
2. **The more Pokémon you catch, the more likely this is to happen.**

Catching Technique 4 Catching many Pokémon makes it easier to catch other Pokémon

Certain Pokémon moves and Abilities come in handy for finding and catching wild Pokémon. Use these moves and Abilities to increase your chances of catching the Pokémon you're after.

Examples of useful moves for catching Pokémon

Sweet Scent
Use this in a place where wild Pokémon appear, such as tall grass or a cave, and wild Pokémon will certainly appear.

● Pokémon that can use this move
Roselia, Combee, Tropius, and others

False Swipe
Always leaves at least 1 HP remaining, even if the damage should knock the Pokémon out. Useful for lowering HP as far as it will go without causing the Pokémon to faint.

● Pokémon that can use this move
Gligar, Zangoose, and others

Super Fang
Use this to halve your target's HP. Keep using it over and over until you minimize your target's HP.

● Pokémon that can use this move
Rattata, Patrat, and others

Examples of useful Abilities for catching wild Pokémon

Illuminate
If the lead Pokémon has this Ability, you'll encounter wild Pokémon more often.

● Pokémon with this Ability
Staryu, Starmie, Watchog, and others

Sticky Hold
An Ability that excels at attracting Pokémon to your fishing line.

Landed a Pokémon!

● Pokémon with this Ability
Grimer, Trubbish, Accelgor, and others

Cute Charm
An Ability that's good at attracting Pokémon of the opposite gender.

● Pokémon with this Ability
Clefairy, Delcatty, Lopunny, and others

Catching Technique 5 Add a helpful Pokémon to your party

There are some Pokémon whose move sets are practically custom-made for catching wild Pokémon. Use these Pokémon to increase your chances of catching a wild Pokémon.

Example 1 Watchog's Moves

● Mainly Appears at

Route 7

Watchog's Illuminate Ability makes it easy to encounter wild Pokémon. It also learns Super Fang at Lv. 22. Give the reminder girl in the PWT area a Heart Scale to have it remember Hypnosis (p. 154). Teach it Thunder Wave with TM73.

Move Super Fang — Normal

Halves the target's HP.

Move Hypnosis — Psychic

Inflicts Sleep status on the target.

Move Thunder Wave — Electric

Inflicts Paralysis status.

Example 2 Leavanny's Moves

● How to Obtain

Catch Swadloon in Lostlorn Forest and level it up with high friendship.

Before Swadloon evolves into Leavanny, it knows GrassWhistle from Lv. 1, and after it evolves, you can use TM54 to teach it False Swipe. Use False Swipe to reduce the wild Pokémon's HP to 1, and inflict Sleep status with GrassWhistle. This puts wild Pokémon in the easiest-to-catch state, so throw a Poké Ball.

Move False Swipe — Normal

Always leaves 1 HP, even if the damage would have made the target faint.

Move GrassWhistle — Grass

Inflicts Sleep status on the target.

Example 3 Bisharp's Moves

● How to Obtain

Level up a Pawniard caught on Route 9 to Lv. 52.

Bisharp can learn TM54 False Swipe and TM73 Thunder Wave. Use False Swipe to reduce the wild Pokémon's HP to 1, and inflict Paralysis with Thunder Wave. This leaves any wild Pokémon in an easy-to-catch state.

Move False Swipe — Normal

Always leaves 1 HP, even if the damage would have made the target faint.

Move Thunder Wave — Electric

Inflicts Paralysis status.

Unova Pokédex Completion Tip 2

Catch Pokémon on the water or by fishing

Use the HM Surf or the Super Rod

Plenty of Pokémon live in the water, and you'll encounter them while using Surf to move over the water's surface. Also, after you enter the Hall of Fame, you can use fishing to catch some Pokémon that live in the water.

Unova Pokédex Completion Tip 3

Catch Specially Appearing Wild Pokémon

Pokémon special appearances

Some of the Unova region's Pokémon appear along with a special natural phenomenon. Many of these Pokémon are not usually seen. If you see one of these phenomena, rush right to it and see what Pokémon is there!

A wild Tangrowth appeared!

Special Pokémon appearances

Rustling Grass

Occurs in the light-green tall grass, not the dark grass. Step on the rustling grass and a Pokémon will appear.

Dust Cloud

If the lead Pokémon has this Ability, you'll encounter wild Pokémon more often.

Flying Pokémon Shadows

You may see these shadows on the Driftveil Drawbridge and Marvelous Bridge. Step on a shadow and a Pokémon will appear, or you will get an item.

Ripples in Water

Occurs on the water's surface. Surf over it, or cast your fishing line into that spot, and a Pokémon will appear.

Unova Pokédex Completion Tip 4

Obtain Pokémon through Evolution

Give Pokémon Experience Points by putting them in battle

Many kinds of Pokémon must be registered in the Unova Pokédex through evolution, so take advantage of the following techniques to level up Pokémon effectively. Many Pokémon evolve through leveling up. Here are a few tricks for leveling up your Pokémon more easily.

Congratulations! Your Flaaffy evolved into Ampharos!

Recommended ways to level up Pokémon

1 Put it into battle, then switch it out immediately

The most basic way to train a low-level Pokémon is to put it in battle at the start, then withdraw it immediately. Just by being in battle for that moment, it will receive a share of the Experience Points you earn.

Flaaffy, switch out! Come back!

2 Have the first Pokémon in your party hold the Lucky Egg

A Pokémon that holds the Lucky Egg will receive 50% more Experience Points. Have the first Pokémon in your party hold it. You'll get this item from Professor Juniper in Celestial Tower.

Flaaffy gained a boosted 837 Exp. Points!

3 Have one of your party Pokémon hold the Exp. Share

The Exp. Share gives a portion of the Experience Points earned in a battle to the Pokémon that holds it, even if that Pokémon didn't participate in the battle. You receive it in the Battle Company in Castelia City.

Flaaffy gained 186 Exp. Points!

4 Use the Pokémon Day Care to level up your Pokémon

Leaving a Pokémon in the Pokémon Day Care is also an effective way to raise levels. When you come to reclaim your Pokémon after you've continued on your adventure, the Pokémon's level will be higher.

By level, your Buneary has grown by about 6.

5 Use a Rare Candy to raise a Pokémon's level

Rare Candy raises a Pokémon's level by one. It's especially useful for Pokémon that require a lot of Experience Points to level up.

Flaaffy was elevated to Lv. 30!

4 Defeat many wild Audino

When you encounter an Audino in the rustling grass and defeat it, you'll receive more Experience Points than you would for defeating other Pokémon.

What will Flaaffy do?

Unova Pokédex Completion Tip 5

Using Stones to Evolve Pokémon

 Stones trigger an instant evolution

Some Pokémon evolve from the power contained within special stones. Eight types of evolution stone appear in *Pokémon Black Version 2* and *Pokémon White Version 2*. When you get a stone, use it on a Pokémon you want to evolve.

Main ways to get stones

 **Leaf Stone**
Route 7 / Exchange for 3 BP in the PWT or Battle Subway

 **Fire Stone**
Lentimas Town / Exchange for 3 BP in the PWT or Battle Subway

 **Water Stone**
Route 19 / Exchange for 3 BP in the PWT or Battle Subway

 **Thunderstone**
Chargestone Cave / Exchange for 3 BP in the PWT or Battle Subway

 **Moon Stone**
Route 6 / Giant Chasm's Crater Forest

 **Sun Stone**
Nimbasa City / Giant Chasm

 **Shiny Stone**
Route 6 / Abundant Shrine

 **Dusk Stone**
Strange House / Twist Mountain

Unova Pokédex Completion Tip 6

Evolve Pokémon through Friendship

 Make your Pokémon happy

Friendship is the bond of affection and trust that can grow between a Pokémon and its Trainer. Some Pokémon evolve by being leveled up with high friendship. If you do things that make the Pokémon happy, it will grow to like you. One recommended way to increase a Pokémon's friendship is have it hold the Soothe Bell, which you can obtain in Nimbasa City.

See page 36 for ways to increase a Pokémon's friendship.

Unova Pokédex Completion Tip 7

Obtain Pokémon by Restoring Fossils

 Restore the Fossils you obtain during your adventure

In Nacrene City, which you can visit after you enter the Hall of Fame, Lenora gives you the Cover Fossil or the Plume Fossil. Restore this Fossil to obtain a Pokémon. You can only get one of these two, so Link Trade to get the other Pokémon and register it in your Pokédex.

Restoring Pokémon from Fossils

1 Receive a Fossil from Lenora in Nacrene City

When you visit the Nacrene Museum in Nacrene City, Lenora will talk to you and give you a Fossil.

2 Restore Fossils in the Nacrene Museum

If you talk to the receptionist at Nacrene Museum when you have a Fossil, it can be turned into a Pokémon right away.

Unova Pokédex Completion Tip 8

Trade with people in towns to get Pokémon

Some Pokémon can only be obtained this way

In towns and houses, there are people waiting to trade Pokémon. You can get a Petilil (which usually only appears in *Pokémon Black 2*), a Cottonee (which usually only appears in *Pokémon White 2*), or a Gigalith (which you can usually only get by evolving a Boldore in a Link Trade). Trading with people in towns is a shortcut to completing your Pokédex.

Pokémon trades that help you complete the Unova Pokédex

Pokémon Received	Pokémon to Trade / How to Obtain	Location of Trader	Difference in Game Version
Petilil	Cottonee (catch in Castelia City empty lot)	Girl in building on Route 4	(*Pokémon Black Version 2*)
Cottonee	Petilil (catch in Castelia City empty lot)	Boy in building on Route 4	(*Pokémon White Version 2*)
Gigalith	Emolga (catch in Route 16 / rustling grass)	Hiker in building on Route 7	—
Tangrowth	Mantine (catch on Route 21 / rippling water)	Man in a house in Humilau City	—

Unova Pokédex Completion Tip 9

Get Special Pokémon During Your Adventure

Put all of your Pokémon-catching techniques to use

Some of the Pokémon you encounter during the story are known as Legendary Pokémon, because there's only one of each. Cobalion, Terrakion, and Virizion are all Legendary Pokémon, as are Reshiram and Zekrom. Zekrom can only be obtained in *Pokémon Black 2* and Reshiram can only be obtained in *Pokémon White 2*, so you'll need to Link Trade to get the other and complete your Unova Pokédex.

Rarely seen Pokémon needed to complete the Unova Pokédex

Zorua

Get it from the former Team Plasma member Rood in Driftveil City (p. 150). It was N's partner, so the name of the original Trainer is N. You can evolve it into Zoroark.

Volcarona

Catch it in the deepest room on the lowest floor of the Relic Castle (p. 131). The Relic Castle can be reached through the Relic Passage. If you leave it in the Pokémon Day Care and an Egg is discovered, you can hatch it and register Larvesta.

Cobalion

After you see it jump out of the tall grass on Route 6, you'll encounter it again as you head north on Route 13. This time, you have the chance to catch it (p. 186)!

Terrakion

It's on a hill as you head west on Route 22. Talk to it after you finish talking to Colress. Your chance to catch it has come (p. 208)!

Virizion

As you head west on Route 11, it will jump down from a ledge. Talk to it, and you will get a chance to catch it (p. 193).

Reshiram

When you defeat N in battle in N's Castle and receive the Light Stone, it will appear in Dragonspiral Tower and you can catch it *(Pokémon White Version 2)* (p. 306).

Zekrom

When you defeat N in battle in N's Castle and receive the Dark Stone, it will appear in Dragonspiral Tower and you can catch it *(Pokémon Black Version 2)* (p. 306).

See page 454 if you accidentally defeat one of these Pokémon.

Unova Pokédex Completion Tip 10

Obtain Pokémon by Hatching Eggs

Obtain earlier evolutionary forms with Pokémon Eggs

Leave two Pokémon at the Pokémon Day Care on Route 3, and sometimes an Egg will be discovered. Many Pokémon species in the Unova Pokédex can be obtained by hatching them from Eggs. Use these steps to discover Eggs and get the Pokémon you're after.

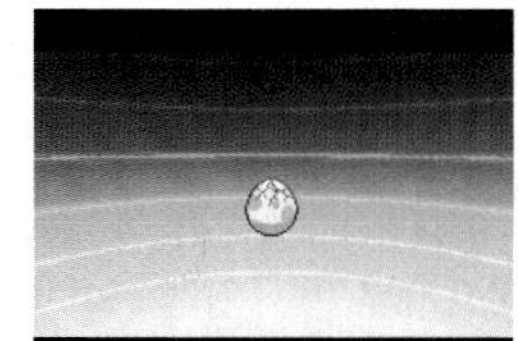

Steps leading to Egg discovery

1 Deposit Pokémon

₽158490
Fine, we'll raise your Tyranitar for a while.

Try leaving two Pokémon of opposite gender.

2 Take the Egg

If the male and female Pokémon left at the Day Care get along well, an Egg will be discovered.

3 Hatch the Egg

Larvitar hatched from the Egg!

Put the Egg in your party and carry it around on your adventure. Eventually, a Pokémon will hatch from the Egg.

The man at the Pokémon Day Care will give you clues to whether an Egg will be found

When you leave two Pokémon at the Pokémon Day Care, the old man tells you how well they get along. His words also reveal how likely it is that an Egg will be discovered.

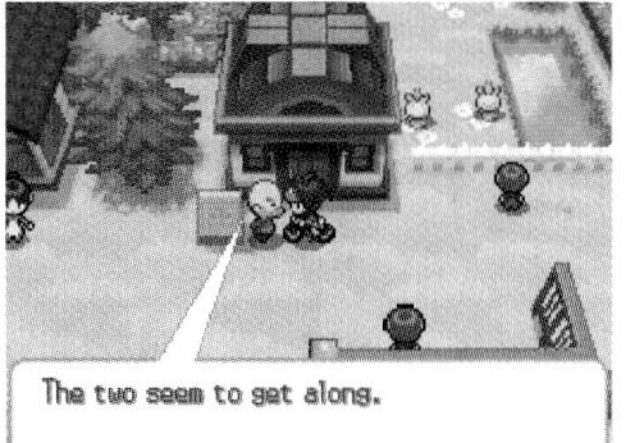

The Day Care Couple will raise Pokémon left at the Pokémon Day Care, and although these Pokémon's levels will increase, they will not evolve. To trigger evolution, you'll have to raise the Pokémon's level while it's in your party.

The old man's messages

#	Message	Likelihood
1	The two seem to get along very well!	Eggs are likely to be found
2	The two seem to get along.	
3	The two don't really seem to like each other much.	Eggs are harder to find
4	The two prefer to play with other Pokémon more than with each other.	Eggs will not be found

Get Medals for hatching Eggs

As you hatch Pokémon Eggs, Mr. Medal will give you Medals depending on your achievements. You can get four different Medals for hatching Eggs. The Hatching Aficionado Medal is given to players who hatch an amazing 100 Eggs!

Egg Beginner

Egg Breeder

Egg Elite

Hatching Aficionado

Check p. 448 for the Medal list.

How to Discover Eggs 1 Learn how to pair up Pokémon and find Eggs

To find Eggs, you can leave two Pokémon of the same species but opposite genders at the Pokémon Day Care. This is the simplest method. You can also pair off Pokémon by Egg Group. You can find an Egg from two different species of Pokémon if they have opposite genders and the same Egg Group, like Nosepass and Vanilluxe to the right.

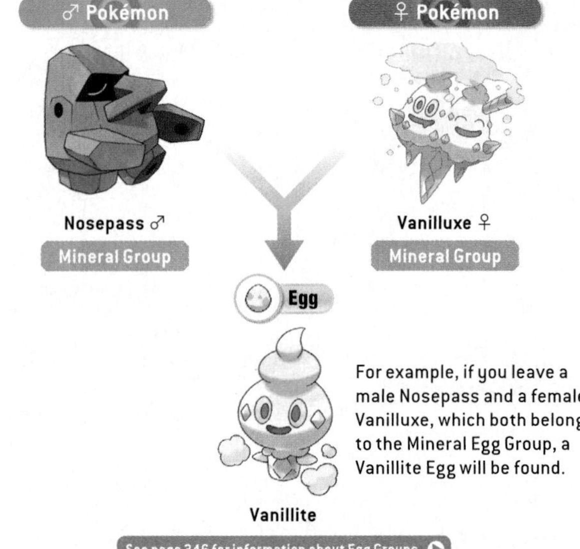

For example, if you leave a male Nosepass and a female Vanilluxe, which both belong to the Mineral Egg Group, a Vanillite Egg will be found.

See page 346 for information about Egg Groups.

How to get Eggs

1. **If you leave two Pokémon of opposite genders from the same Egg Group, an Egg will be found.**
2. **The Pokémon that hatches from the Egg is either the same species as the female or an earlier evolutionary form.**
3. **The hatched Pokémon is almost always in its initial evolutionary stage.**

How to Discover Eggs 2 With Ditto, you can find almost any kind of Egg

Some Pokémon's gender is unknown. Also, some Pokémon species have only one gender. Under normal circumstances, you can't find Eggs for these Pokémon. But leave one together with a Ditto, and you'll find an Egg after all! You can catch Ditto in Crater Forest at the bottom of the Giant Chasm (p. 223). Ditto can be a big help when you want more Eggs!

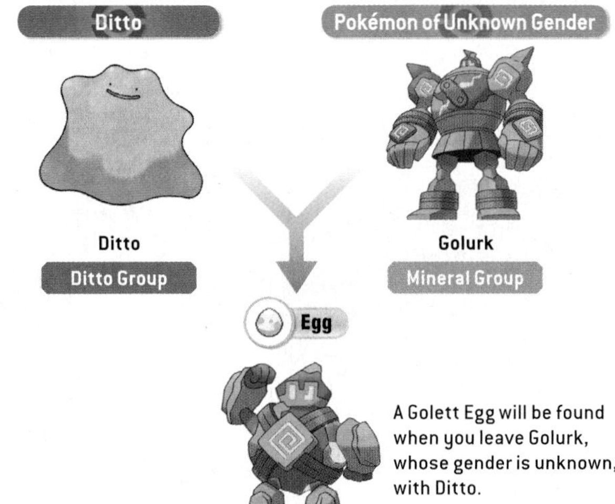

A Golett Egg will be found when you leave Golurk, whose gender is unknown, with Ditto.

Places where wild Ditto appear

Giant Chasm Crater Forest

Egg Move Rules 1 Have a Pokémon inherit moves

The two Pokémon you leave at the Pokémon Day Care can pass on a move they have learned to a Pokémon that hatches from an Egg. Usually, a newly hatched Pokémon only knows Lv. 1 moves. However, if both the Pokémon you left at the Day Care have learned a move that the hatched Pokémon can learn by leveling up, the hatched Pokémon will know that move. Check the following rules for details.

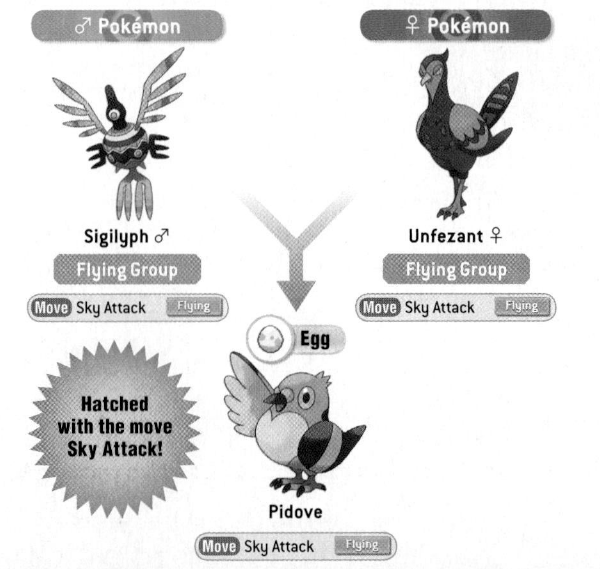

Info about inheriting moves

1. **If both Pokémon at the Pokémon Day Care know the same level-up move, the hatched Pokémon may know that level-up move.**
2. **A move that the male Pokémon knows and that the hatched Pokémon could learn from a TM can be passed on.**

Egg Move Rules 2 Teach your Pokémon Egg Moves

Pokémon may hatch from Eggs already knowing moves that they usually can't learn. These moves are called Egg Moves. For example, Mamoswine can't learn the move Icicle Crash by leveling up. But if the male Pokémon left at the Pokémon Day Care is a Beartic that knows Icicle Crash, the Swinub that hatches from the Egg might know the move Icicle Crash. Because many Egg Moves are so unexpected, you can surprise an opposing Trainer in battle.

♂ Pokémon
Beartic ♂
Field Group
Move Icicle Crash Ice

♀ Pokémon
Mamoswine ♀
Field Group

Egg
A Swinub with the Egg Move Icicle Crash hatches!
Swinub
Move Icicle Crash Ice

Inheriting Egg Moves

A move that the male Pokémon knows and that the hatched Pokémon can learn as an Egg Move can be passed on.

Ability Info 1 Either of the two Abilities can be inherited

You don't know which Ability a Pokémon will have until it hatches. For example, Seismitoad can have either the Swift Swim or Hydration Ability. Sometimes when you leave a female Seismitoad with the Swift Swim Ability at the Pokémon Day Care, the Egg that hatches will be a Tympole with the Hydration Ability.

♂ Pokémon
Pelipper ♂
Water Group 1
Ability Keen Eye

♀ Pokémon
Seismitoad ♀
Water Group 1
Ability Swift Swim

Egg
Tympole
Ability Swift Swim

Egg
Tympole
Ability Hydration

Abilities of hatched Pokémon

When the female Pokémon has two possible Abilities, the hatched Pokémon could have either one.

◆ The Ability of a Pokémon hatched from an Egg is more likely to be the Ability of the female Pokémon left at Pokémon Day Care.

Ability Info 2 Hidden Abilities can be inherited

If you leave a female Pokémon with a Hidden Ability at the Pokémon Day Care, you may find an Egg that hatches into a Pokémon with the same Ability. For Example, Liepard can have the Hidden Ability Prankster. If you discover an Egg when you leave a female Liepard with the Prankster Ability at the Pokémon Day Care, you may find an Egg of a Purrloin with Limber, Unburden, or the same Hidden Ability, Prankster.

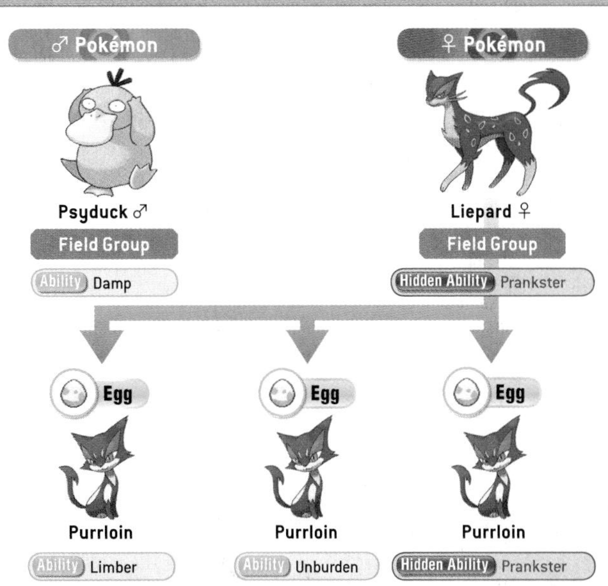

Hidden Ability rules

When the female Pokémon at the Pokémon Day Care has a Hidden Ability, you can sometimes hatch a Pokémon with a Hidden Ability.

◆ The Ability of a Pokémon hatched from an Egg is more likely to be the Ability of the female Pokémon left at the Day Care.

Pokémon Egg Groups

◆ Pokémon that belong to two Egg Groups are written in red.

Grass Group

- 001 Bulbasaur
- 002 Ivysaur
- 003 Venusaur
- 043 Oddish
- 044 Gloom
- 045 Vileplume
- 046 Paras
- 047 Parasect
- 069 Bellsprout
- 070 Weepinbell
- 071 Victreebel
- 102 Exeggcute
- 103 Exeggutor
- 114 Tangela
- 152 Chikorita
- 153 Bayleef
- 154 Meganium
- 182 Bellossom
- 187 Hoppip
- 188 Skiploom
- 189 Jumpluff
- 191 Sunkern
- 192 Sunflora
- 270 Lotad
- 271 Lombre
- 272 Ludicolo
- 273 Seedot
- 274 Nuzleaf
- 275 Shiftry
- 285 Shroomish
- 286 Breloom
- 315 Roselia
- 331 Cacnea
- 332 Cacturne
- 357 Tropius
- 387 Turtwig
- 388 Grotle
- 389 Torterra
- 407 Roserade
- 420 Cherubi
- 421 Cherrim
- 455 Carnivine
- 459 Snover
- 460 Abomasnow
- 465 Tangrowth
- 495 Snivy
- 496 Servine
- 497 Serperior
- 546 Cottonee
- 547 Whimsicott
- 548 Petilil
- 549 Lilligant
- 556 Maractus
- 590 Foongus
- 591 Amoonguss
- 597 Ferroseed
- 598 Ferrothorn

Bug Group

- 010 Caterpie
- 011 Metapod
- 012 Butterfree
- 013 Weedle
- 014 Kakuna
- 015 Beedrill
- 046 Paras
- 047 Parasect
- 048 Venonat
- 049 Venomoth
- 123 Scyther
- 127 Pinsir
- 165 Ledyba
- 166 Ledian
- 167 Spinarak
- 168 Ariados
- 193 Yanma
- 204 Pineco
- 205 Forretress
- 207 Gligar
- 212 Scizor
- 213 Shuckle
- 214 Heracross
- 265 Wurmple
- 266 Silcoon
- 267 Beautifly
- 268 Cascoon
- 269 Dustox
- 283 Surskit
- 284 Masquerain
- 290 Nincada
- 291 Ninjask
- 313 Volbeat
- 314 Illumise
- 328 Trapinch
- 329 Vibrava
- 330 Flygon
- 401 Kricketot
- 402 Kricketune
- 412 Burmy
- 413 Wormadam
- 414 Mothim
- 415 Combee
- 416 Vespiquen
- 451 Skorupi
- 452 Drapion
- 469 Yanmega
- 472 Gliscor
- 540 Sewaddle
- 541 Swadloon
- 542 Leavanny
- 543 Venipede
- 544 Whirlipede
- 545 Scolipede
- 557 Dwebble
- 558 Crustle
- 588 Karrablast
- 589 Escavalier
- 595 Joltik
- 596 Galvantula
- 616 Shelmet
- 617 Accelgor
- 632 Durant
- 636 Larvesta
- 637 Volcarona

Flying Group

- 016 Pidgey
- 017 Pidgeotto
- 018 Pidgeot
- 021 Spearow
- 022 Fearow
- 041 Zubat
- 042 Golbat
- 083 Farfetch'd
- 084 Doduo
- 085 Dodrio
- 142 Aerodactyl
- 163 Hoothoot
- 164 Noctowl
- 169 Crobat
- 176 Togetic
- 177 Natu
- 178 Xatu
- 198 Murkrow
- 227 Skarmory
- 276 Taillow
- 277 Swellow
- 278 Wingull
- 279 Pelipper
- 333 Swablu
- 334 Altaria
- 396 Starly
- 397 Staravia
- 398 Staraptor
- 430 Honchkrow
- 441 Chatot
- 468 Togekiss
- 519 Pidove
- 520 Tranquill
- 521 Unfezant
- 527 Woobat
- 528 Swoobat
- 561 Sigilyph
- 566 Archen
- 567 Archeops
- 580 Ducklett
- 581 Swanna
- 627 Rufflet
- 628 Braviary
- 629 Vullaby
- 630 Mandibuzz

Human-Like Group

- 063 Abra
- 064 Kadabra
- 065 Alakazam
- 066 Machop
- 067 Machoke
- 068 Machamp
- 096 Drowzee
- 097 Hypno
- 106 Hitmonlee
- 107 Hitmonchan
- 122 Mr. Mime
- 124 Jynx
- 125 Electabuzz
- 126 Magmar
- 237 Hitmontop
- 296 Makuhita
- 297 Hariyama
- 302 Sableye
- 307 Meditite
- 308 Medicham
- 313 Volbeat
- 314 Illumise
- 327 Spinda
- 331 Cacnea
- 332 Cacturne
- 390 Chimchar
- 391 Monferno
- 392 Infernape
- 427 Buneary
- 428 Lopunny
- 448 Lucario
- 453 Croagunk
- 454 Toxicroak
- 466 Electivire
- 467 Magmortar
- 532 Timburr
- 533 Gurdurr
- 534 Conkeldurr
- 538 Throh
- 539 Sawk
- 574 Gothita
- 575 Gothorita
- 576 Gothitelle
- 605 Elgyem
- 606 Beheeyem
- 619 Mienfoo
- 620 Mienshao
- 624 Pawniard
- 625 Bisharp

Monster Group

- 001 Bulbasaur
- 002 Ivysaur
- 003 Venusaur
- 004 Charmander
- 005 Charmeleon
- 006 Charizard
- 007 Squirtle
- 008 Wartortle
- 009 Blastoise
- 029 Nidoran♀
- 032 Nidoran♂
- 033 Nidorino
- 034 Nidoking
- 079 Slowpoke
- 080 Slowbro
- 104 Cubone
- 105 Marowak
- 108 Lickitung
- 111 Rhyhorn
- 112 Rhydon
- 115 Kangaskhan
- 131 Lapras
- 143 Snorlax
- 152 Chikorita
- 153 Bayleef
- 154 Meganium
- 158 Totodile
- 159 Croconaw
- 160 Feraligatr
- 179 Mareep
- 180 Flaaffy
- 181 Ampharos
- 199 Slowking
- 246 Larvitar
- 247 Pupitar
- 248 Tyranitar
- 252 Treecko
- 253 Grovyle
- 254 Sceptile
- 258 Mudkip
- 259 Marshtomp
- 260 Swampert
- 293 Whismur
- 294 Loudred
- 295 Exploud
- 304 Aron
- 305 Lairon
- 306 Aggron
- 357 Tropius
- 387 Turtwig
- 388 Grotle
- 389 Torterra
- 408 Cranidos
- 409 Rampardos
- 410 Shieldon
- 411 Bastiodon
- 443 Gible
- 444 Gabite
- 445 Garchomp
- 459 Snover
- 460 Abomasnow
- 463 Lickilicky
- 464 Rhyperior
- 610 Axew
- 611 Fraxure
- 612 Haxorus
- 621 Druddigon

Fairy Group

- 025 Pikachu
- 026 Raichu
- 035 Clefairy
- 036 Clefable
- 039 Jigglypuff
- 040 Wigglytuff
- 113 Chansey
- 176 Togetic
- 183 Marill
- 184 Azumarill
- 187 Hoppip
- 188 Skiploom
- 189 Jumpluff
- 209 Snubbull
- 210 Granbull
- 242 Blissey
- 285 Shroomish
- 286 Breloom
- 300 Skitty
- 301 Delcatty
- 303 Mawile
- 311 Plusle
- 312 Minun
- 315 Roselia
- 351 Castform
- 361 Snorunt
- 362 Glalie
- 407 Roserade
- 417 Pachirisu
- 420 Cherubi
- 421 Cherrim
- 468 Togekiss
- 478 Froslass
- 489 Phione
- 490 Manaphy
- 531 Audino
- 546 Cottonee
- 547 Whimsicott

Dragon Group

- 004 Charmander
- 005 Charmeleon
- 006 Charizard
- 023 Ekans
- 024 Arbok
- 116 Horsea
- 117 Seadra
- 129 Magikarp
- 130 Gyarados
- 147 Dratini
- 148 Dragonair
- 149 Dragonite
- 230 Kingdra
- 252 Treecko
- 253 Grovyle
- 254 Sceptile
- 333 Swablu
- 334 Altaria
- 336 Seviper
- 349 Feebas
- 350 Milotic
- 371 Bagon
- 372 Shelgon
- 373 Salamence
- 443 Gible
- 444 Gabite
- 445 Garchomp
- 559 Scraggy
- 560 Scrafty
- 610 Axew
- 611 Fraxure
- 612 Haxorus
- 621 Druddigon
- 633 Deino
- 634 Zweilous
- 635 Hydreigon

Mineral Group

- 074 Geodude
- 075 Graveler
- 076 Golem
- 081 Magnemite
- 082 Magneton
- 095 Onix
- 100 Voltorb
- 101 Electrode
- 137 Porygon
- 185 Sudowoodo
- 208 Steelix
- 233 Porygon2
- 292 Shedinja
- 299 Nosepass
- 337 Lunatone
- 338 Solrock
- 343 Baltoy
- 344 Claydol
- 361 Snorunt
- 362 Glalie
- 374 Beldum
- 375 Metang
- 376 Metagross
- 436 Bronzor
- 437 Bronzong
- 462 Magnezone
- 474 Porygon-Z
- 476 Probopass
- 478 Froslass
- 524 Roggenrola
- 525 Boldore
- 526 Gigalith
- 557 Dwebble
- 558 Crustle
- 562 Yamask
- 563 Cofagrigus
- 568 Trubbish
- 569 Garbodor
- 582 Vanillite
- 583 Vanillish
- 584 Vanilluxe
- 597 Ferroseed
- 598 Ferrothorn
- 599 Klink
- 600 Klang
- 601 Klinklang
- 615 Cryogonal
- 622 Golett
- 623 Golurk

Field Group

- 019 Rattata
- 020 Raticate
- 023 Ekans
- 024 Arbok
- 025 Pikachu
- 026 Raichu
- 027 Sandshrew
- 028 Sandslash
- 029 Nidoran♀
- 032 Nidoran♂
- 033 Nidorino
- 034 Nidoking
- 037 Vulpix
- 038 Ninetales
- 050 Diglett
- 051 Dugtrio
- 052 Meowth
- 053 Persian
- 054 Psyduck
- 055 Golduck
- 056 Mankey
- 057 Primeape
- 058 Growlithe
- 059 Arcanine
- 077 Ponyta
- 078 Rapidash
- 083 Farfetch'd
- 086 Seel
- 087 Dewgong
- 111 Rhyhorn
- 112 Rhydon
- 128 Tauros
- 133 Eevee
- 134 Vaporeon
- 135 Jolteon
- 136 Flareon
- 155 Cyndaquil
- 156 Quilava
- 157 Typhlosion
- 161 Sentret
- 162 Furret
- 179 Mareep
- 180 Flaaffy
- 181 Ampharos
- 190 Aipom
- 194 Wooper
- 195 Quagsire
- 196 Espeon
- 197 Umbreon
- 203 Girafarig
- 206 Dunsparce
- 209 Snubbull
- 210 Granbull
- 215 Sneasel
- 216 Teddiursa
- 217 Ursaring
- 220 Swinub
- 221 Piloswine
- 225 Delibird
- 228 Houndour
- 229 Houndoom
- 231 Phanpy
- 232 Donphan
- 234 Stantler
- 235 Smeargle
- 241 Miltank
- 255 Torchic
- 256 Combusken

No.	Pokémon
257	Blaziken
261	Poochyena
262	Mightyena
263	Zigzagoon
264	Linoone
273	Seedot
274	Nuzleaf
275	Shiftry
287	Slakoth
288	Vigoroth
289	Slaking
293	Whismur
294	Loudred
295	Exploud
300	Skitty
301	Delcatty
303	Mawile
309	Electrike
310	Manectric
320	Wailmer
321	Wailord
322	Numel
323	Camerupt
324	Torkoal
325	Spoink
326	Grumpig
327	Spinda
335	Zangoose
336	Seviper
352	Kecleon
359	Absol
363	Spheal
364	Sealeo
365	Walrein
390	Chimchar
391	Monferno
392	Infernape
393	Piplup
394	Prinplup
395	Empoleon
399	Bidoof
400	Bibarel
403	Shinx
404	Luxio
405	Luxray
417	Pachirisu
418	Buizel
419	Floatzel
424	Ambipom
427	Buneary
428	Lopunny
431	Glameow
432	Purugly
434	Stunky
435	Skuntank
448	Lucario
449	Hippopotas
450	Hippowdon
461	Weavile
464	Rhyperior
470	Leafeon
471	Glaceon
473	Mamoswine
495	Snivy
496	Servine
497	Serperior
498	Tepig
499	Pignite
500	Emboar
501	Oshawott
502	Dewott
503	Samurott
504	Patrat
505	Watchog
506	Lillipup
507	Herdier
508	Stoutland
509	Purrloin
510	Liepard
511	Pansage
512	Simisage
513	Pansear
514	Simisear
515	Panpour
516	Simipour
517	Munna
518	Musharna
522	Blitzle
523	Zebstrika
527	Woobat
528	Swoobat
529	Drilbur
530	Excadrill
551	Sandile
552	Krokorok
553	Krookodile
554	Darumaka
555	Darmanitan
559	Scraggy
560	Scrafty
570	Zorua
571	Zoroark
572	Minccino
573	Cinccino
585	Deerling
586	Sawsbuck
587	Emolga
613	Cubchoo
614	Beartic
619	Mienfoo
620	Mienshao
626	Bouffalant
631	Heatmor

Amorphous Group

No.	Pokémon
088	Grimer
089	Muk
092	Gastly
093	Haunter
094	Gengar
109	Koffing
110	Weezing
200	Misdreavus
202	Wobbuffet
218	Slugma
219	Magcargo
280	Ralts
281	Kirlia
282	Gardevoir
316	Gulpin
317	Swalot
351	Castform
353	Shuppet
354	Banette
355	Duskull
356	Dusclops
358	Chimecho
422	Shellos
423	Gastrodon
425	Drifloon
426	Drifblim
429	Mismagius
442	Spiritomb
475	Gallade
477	Dusknoir
479	Rotom
562	Yamask
563	Cofagrigus
577	Solosis
578	Duosion
579	Reuniclus
592	Frillish
593	Jellicent
602	Tynamo
603	Eelektrik
604	Eelektross
607	Litwick
608	Lampent
609	Chandelure
618	Stunfisk

Water Group 1

No.	Pokémon
007	Squirtle
008	Wartortle
009	Blastoise
054	Psyduck
055	Golduck
060	Poliwag
061	Poliwhirl
062	Poliwrath
079	Slowpoke
080	Slowbro
086	Seel
087	Dewgong
116	Horsea
117	Seadra
131	Lapras
138	Omanyte
139	Omastar
140	Kabuto
141	Kabutops
147	Dratini
148	Dragonair
149	Dragonite
158	Totodile
159	Croconaw
160	Feraligatr
183	Marill
184	Azumarill
186	Politoed
194	Wooper
195	Quagsire
199	Slowking
222	Corsola
223	Remoraid
224	Octillery
225	Delibird
226	Mantine
230	Kingdra
258	Mudkip
259	Marshtomp
260	Swampert
270	Lotad
271	Lombre
272	Ludicolo
278	Wingull
279	Pelipper
283	Surskit
284	Masquerain
341	Corphish
342	Crawdaunt
349	Feebas
350	Milotic
363	Spheal
364	Sealeo
365	Walrein
366	Clamperl
367	Huntail
368	Gorebyss
369	Relicanth
393	Piplup
394	Prinplup
395	Empoleon
399	Bidoof
400	Bibarel
418	Buizel
419	Floatzel
422	Shellos
423	Gastrodon
489	Phione
490	Manaphy
535	Tympole
536	Palpitoad
537	Seismitoad
564	Tirtouga
565	Carracosta
580	Ducklett
581	Swanna
594	Alomomola
618	Stunfisk

Water Group 2

No.	Pokémon
118	Goldeen
119	Seaking
129	Magikarp
130	Gyarados
170	Chinchou
171	Lanturn
211	Qwilfish
223	Remoraid
224	Octillery
318	Carvanha
319	Sharpedo
320	Wailmer
321	Wailord
339	Barboach
340	Whiscash
369	Relicanth
370	Luvdisc
456	Finneon
457	Lumineon
550	Basculin
594	Alomomola

Water Group 3

No.	Pokémon
072	Tentacool
073	Tentacruel
090	Shellder
091	Cloyster
098	Krabby
099	Kingler
120	Staryu
121	Starmie
138	Omanyte
139	Omastar
140	Kabuto
141	Kabutops
222	Corsola
341	Corphish
342	Crawdaunt
345	Lileep
346	Cradily
347	Anorith
348	Armaldo
451	Skorupi
452	Drapion
564	Tirtouga
565	Carracosta
566	Archen
567	Archeops

Ditto Group

No.	Pokémon
132	Ditto

No Eggs Discovered Group

No.	Pokémon
030	Nidorina
031	Nidoqueen
144	Articuno
145	Zapdos
146	Moltres
150	Mewtwo
151	Mew
172	Pichu
173	Cleffa
174	Igglybuff
175	Togepi
201	Unown
236	Tyrogue
238	Smoochum
239	Elekid
240	Magby
243	Raikou
244	Entei
245	Suicune
249	Lugia
250	Ho-Oh
251	Celebi
298	Azurill
360	Wynaut
377	Regirock
378	Regice
379	Registeel
380	Latias
381	Latios
382	Kyogre
383	Groudon
384	Rayquaza
385	Jirachi
386	Deoxys
406	Budew
433	Chingling
438	Bonsly
439	Mime Jr.
440	Happiny
446	Munchlax
447	Riolu
458	Mantyke
480	Uxie
481	Mesprit
482	Azelf
483	Dialga
484	Palkia
485	Heatran
486	Regigigas
487	Giratina
488	Cresselia
491	Darkrai
492	Shaymin
493	Arceus
494	Victini
638	Cobalion
639	Terrakion
640	Virizion
641	Tornadus
642	Thundurus
643	Reshiram
644	Zekrom
645	Landorus
646	Kyurem
647	Keldeo
648	Meloetta

Tip: Hatch Eggs with the effect of an Ability

Add a Pokémon with the Flame Body or Magma Armor Ability to your party when you have an Egg. The effect of the Ability makes the Egg hatch much faster.

Litwick

Ability: Flame Body

Volcarona

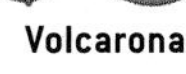

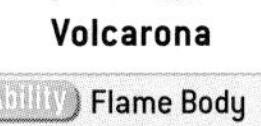

Ability: Flame Body

Camerupt

Ability: Magma Armor

Tip: It's easier to hatch a Shiny Pokémon if you trade with someone in another country

If you trade Pokémon with a player in a different country by using the GTS, leave the Pokémon you received in the Pokémon Day Care to find an Egg (p. 348). The odds of this Egg hatching a Shiny Pokémon are slightly higher.

Shiny Amoonguss

Shiny Tentacool

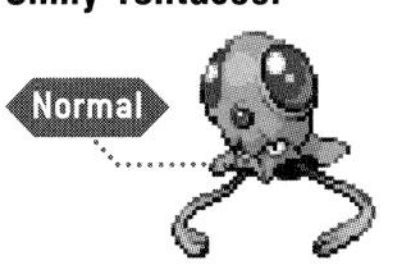

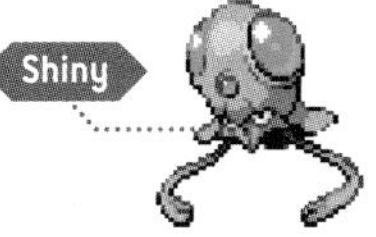

Unova Pokédex Completion Tip 11

Link Trade to get Pokémon

Use Link Trades to Complete the Unova Pokédex

Using the communications features in *Pokémon Black Version 2* and *Pokémon White Version 2*, you can trade Pokémon with your family and friends or players all over the world. These communications features can help you complete the Unova Pokédex more quickly. There are three different ways to Link Trade: IR (infrared), Wireless, and Online (Nintendo Wi-Fi Connection).

Communication methods available in *Pokémon Black Version 2* and *Pokémon White Version 2*

IR (Infrared)

This is the easiest way to trade Pokémon with Pokémon players around you. It's a simple method where each participant offers a Pokémon for trade.

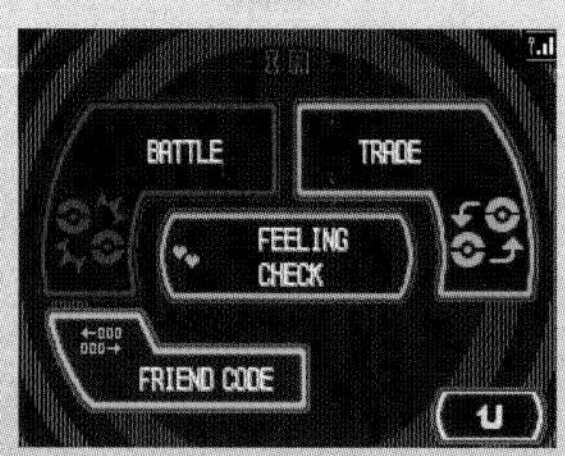

WIRELESS

Choose a trading partner from multiple friends or family members up to 30 feet away from you in this trading method. In this Negotiation Trade, each person offers three candidate Pokémon.

ONLINE

You can trade Pokémon with far away friends and other Pokémon players using Nintendo Wi-Fi Connection. In this Negotiation Trade, each person offers three candidate Pokémon.

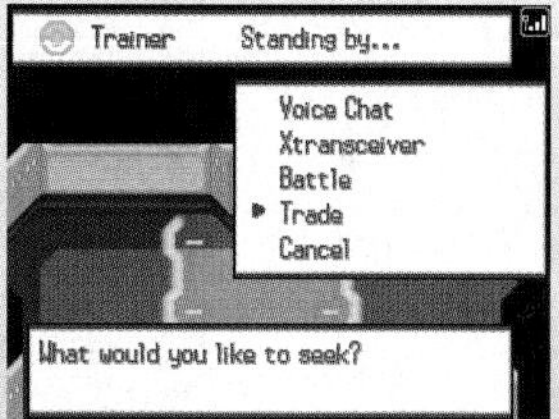

Some Pokémon evolve when you Link Trade them while they hold items

Some species of Pokémon evolve when you Link Trade them. There are also species of Pokémon that evolve when you Link Trade them while they are holding items. Both kinds will be needed to complete the Unova Pokédex, so be on the lookout for these evolution items.

Obtain items that evolve Pokémon when held during trade

Electirizer

Plasma Frigate (*Pokémon White Version 2* only)

Magmarizer

Plasma Frigate (*Pokémon Black Version 2* only)

Tip

The difference between Link Trades and Negotiation Trades

In conventional Pokémon trades, you and your trading partner must pick the Pokémon to trade in advance. In Negotiation Trades, each of you offers up to three Pokémon to trade and trade while conferring with each other.

Normal Trade

Negotiation Trade

Use communication features to get the Pokémon you're after

Link Trades are an easy way to get the Pokémon you want. Cooperating with friends to complete the Pokédex makes the process much more fun. Even better, Pokémon obtained in Link Trades level up more quickly, because they get 50% more Experience Points when used in battle. If you want to register a certain Pokémon, one way to do it is trade for its previous evolution and level it up yourself.

How Link Trading Pokémon works

IR (Infrared)

This is the easiest way to trade Pokémon with Pokémon players around you. It's a simple method where each participant offers a Pokémon for trade.

Tap IR on the C-Gear

Tap "TRADE"

Select a Pokémon to trade

Receive the Pokémon

WIRELESS

Wireless trades are conducted in the Union Room in the Pokémon Center 2F. Choose a trading partner from the people in the Union Room. The trading style is Negotiation Trade.

Enter the Union Room

Talk to a Friend

Negotiate

Receive the Pokémon

ONLINE

You can trade Pokémon with your friends using the Nintendo Wi-Fi Connection in the Wi-Fi Club in the Pokémon Center 2F. Only people you've traded Friend Codes with can trade with you. The trading style is Negotiation Trade.

Enter the Wi-Fi Club

Talk to a Friend

Negotiate

Receive the Pokémon

GTS (Wi-Fi) Trade Pokémon worldwide using GTS

The Global Trade Station (GTS) is a system for trading Pokémon with Pokémon fans worldwide. Use the GTS by going to the Global Terminal in the Pokémon Center 2F. There are four ways to trade Pokémon in all. Learn how each one works and choose a method that fits your goals.

Ways to Trade Pokémon on GTS

1 Select Pokémon to deposit

Deposit a Pokémon and then decide the conditions for the trade. If there is a Pokémon that meets your conditions, the trade will go through.

Select Pokémon to deposit

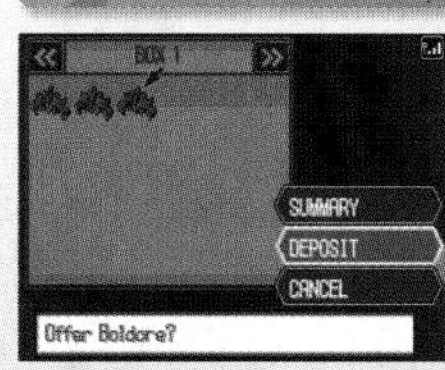

Choose a Pokémon to trade from your party or PC Box. It will be deposited in the GTS.

Decide what kind of Pokémon you want

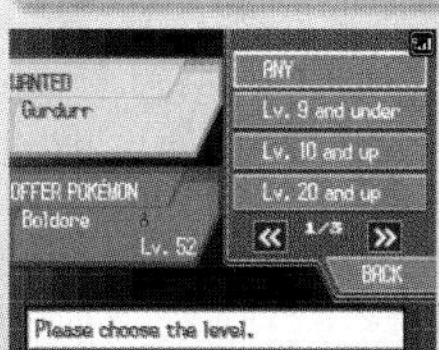

Decide what kind of Pokémon you want to trade the deposited Pokémon for. You can specify its gender and its level. You can also choose "ANY" or "EITHER" for some conditions.

Receive the Pokémon

After some time has passed, try accessing the GTS. When the trade is successful, you'll receive the Pokémon.

2 Seek Pokémon

Decide the species, level, etc. of the Pokémon you want. People who are offering Pokémon that meet those conditions will be displayed.

Choose the Pokémon you want

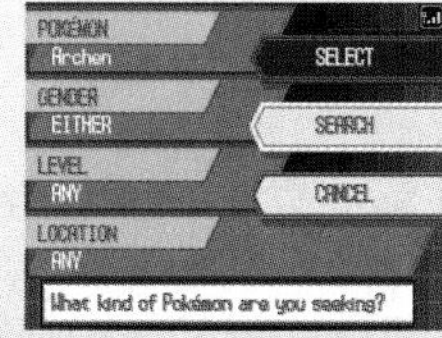

Search for a trading partner by entering what kind of Pokémon you want by its gender, etc.

Select a person to trade with

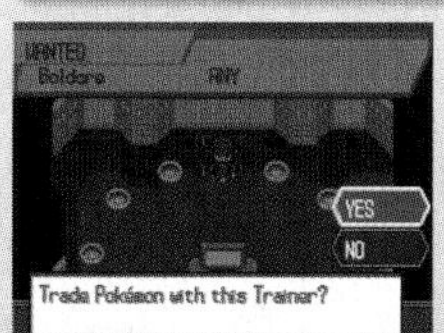

People who have deposited Pokémon that meet the trading conditions in the GTS are displayed. If there are many people, choose one.

Receive the Pokémon

When you pick a trading partner, choose the Pokémon they want and the trade will begin immediately.

Tip: Check the locations of people you've traded with on Geonet

Geonet is the high-tech globe in the Pokémon Center 2F. When you register, the place you live and the locations of people you've traded Pokémon with on the GTS are displayed. It even shows players from other countries.

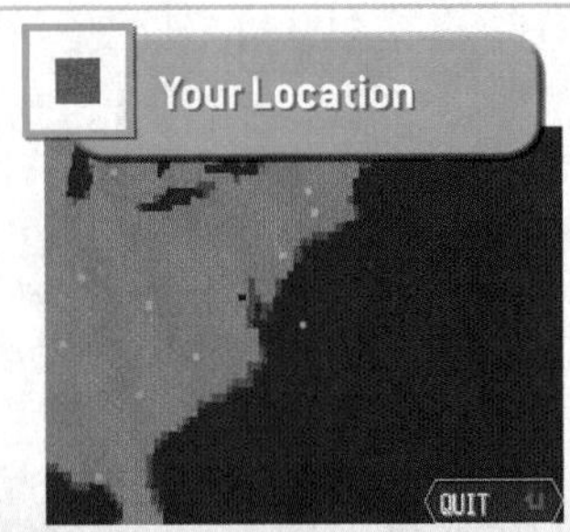

GTS Negotiation Trade Methods

1 Trade with Anyone

You can use Negotiation Trades on the GTS. You select Pokémon using general keywords like "COOL."

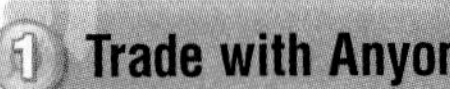

Decide on the trade conditions

Select the conditions for "WANT" and "HAVE." You can choose keywords, such as "COOL" and "CUTE."

Negotiate

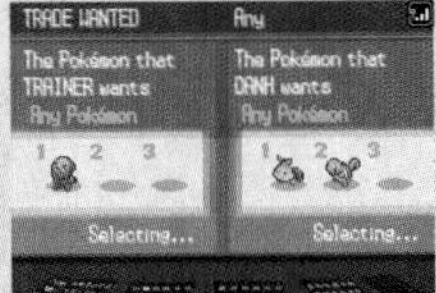

A trading partner who meets your requirements is found. When the trading partner is displayed, the Negotiation Trade begins.

Receive the Pokémon

When the trade is successful the Pokémon you traded for will come to you. Your new Pokémon will be put in your party or the PC Box.

2 TRADE RENDEZVOUS

Use this feature to Negotiation Trade with someone you've traded with before.

Select a person to trade with

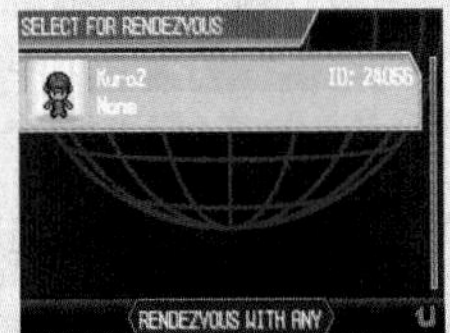

After you've selected Trade Rendezvous, a list of people to trade with will be displayed. Choose the person you want to trade with.

Select a person to trade with

Negotiate with your trading partner.

Who's on your Trade Rendezvous list?

- People you've traded with through IR
- People you've traded with at the Wi-Fi Club
- People you've traded with in the Union Room
- People you've traded with through the GTS or through GTS Negotiations

Tip: When you Link Trade globally, it has many benefits

When you get a Pokémon from a different language version of the game by using the GTS, check the Pokédex. The Pokémon's page is displayed in the language of your trading partner's game. Also, Pokémon from international versions get even more Experience Points, so they're easier to level up and evolve.

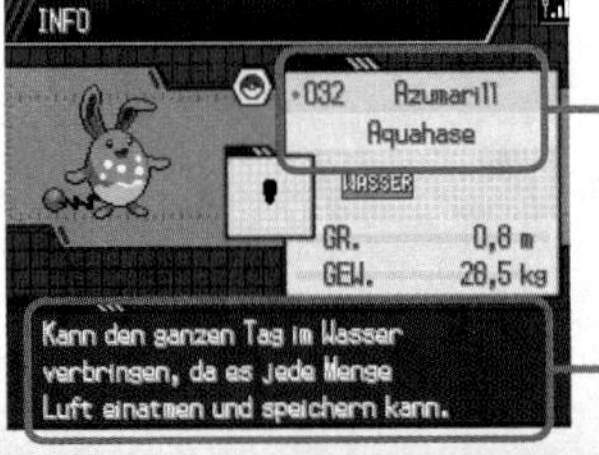

How to Register Pokémon in the Unova Pokédex

Most Pokémon can be registered with *Pokémon Black Version 2* and *Pokémon White Version 2*

This section tells you how to register all of the Pokémon in *Pokémon Black Version 2* and *Pokémon White Version 2's* Unova Pokédex. You can find most of the Pokémon you need to complete the Unova Pokédex in *Pokémon Black Version 2* or *Pokémon White Version 2*. Use this guide and you'll be able to tell at a glance which Pokémon must be brought over from *Pokémon Black Version* or *Pokémon White Version* using a Link Trade.

Unova Pokédex No. 000

Victini

Main ways to register in the Unova Pokédex

It was given out in special distribution events. Check www.pokemon.com to find out if any Pokémon are currently being distributed.

Unova Pokédex No. 001

Snivy

Main ways to register in the Unova Pokédex

Version	
Pokémon Black Version 2	Get from Bianca at the beginning of your adventure
Pokémon White Version 2	Get from Bianca at the beginning of your adventure
Pokémon Black Version	
Pokémon White Version	

Unova Pokédex No. 002

Servine

Main ways to register in the Unova Pokédex

Version	
Pokémon Black Version 2	Level up Snivy to Lv. 17
Pokémon White Version 2	Level up Snivy to Lv. 17
Pokémon Black Version	
Pokémon White Version	

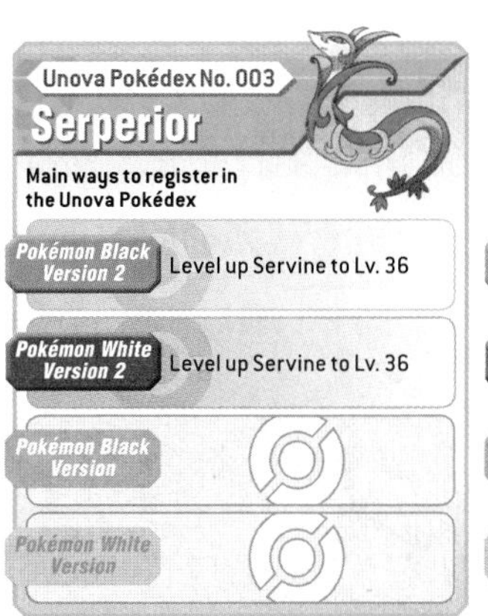

Unova Pokédex No. 003

Serperior

Main ways to register in the Unova Pokédex

Version	
Pokémon Black Version 2	Level up Servine to Lv. 36
Pokémon White Version 2	Level up Servine to Lv. 36
Pokémon Black Version	
Pokémon White Version	

Unova Pokédex No. 004

Tepig

Main ways to register in the Unova Pokédex

Version	
Pokémon Black Version 2	Get from Bianca at the beginning of your adventure
Pokémon White Version 2	Get from Bianca at the beginning of your adventure
Pokémon Black Version	
Pokémon White Version	

Unova Pokédex No. 005

Pignite

Main ways to register in the Unova Pokédex

Version	
Pokémon Black Version 2	Level up Tepig to Lv. 17
Pokémon White Version 2	Level up Tepig to Lv. 17
Pokémon Black Version	
Pokémon White Version	

Unova Pokédex No. 006

Emboar

Main ways to register in the Unova Pokédex

Version	
Pokémon Black Version 2	Level up Pignite to Lv. 36
Pokémon White Version 2	Level up Pignite to Lv. 36
Pokémon Black Version	
Pokémon White Version	

Unova Pokédex No. 007

Oshawott

Main ways to register in the Unova Pokédex

Version	
Pokémon Black Version 2	Get from Bianca at the beginning of your adventure
Pokémon White Version 2	Get from Bianca at the beginning of your adventure
Pokémon Black Version	
Pokémon White Version	

Unova Pokédex No. 008

Dewott

Main ways to register in the Unova Pokédex

Version	
Pokémon Black Version 2	Level up Oshawott to Lv. 17
Pokémon White Version 2	Level up Oshawott to Lv. 17
Pokémon Black Version	
Pokémon White Version	

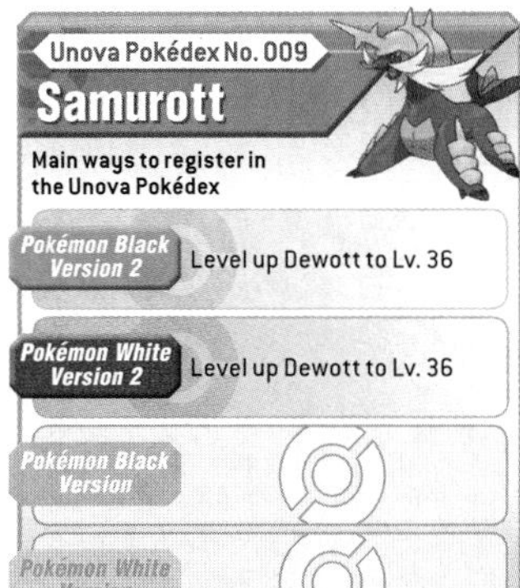

Unova Pokédex No. 009

Samurott

Main ways to register in the Unova Pokédex

Version	
Pokémon Black Version 2	Level up Dewott to Lv. 36
Pokémon White Version 2	Level up Dewott to Lv. 36
Pokémon Black Version	
Pokémon White Version	

Tip

Bring Pokémon from *Pokémon Black Version* and *Pokémon White Version*

Some Pokémon in the Unova Pokédex cannot be found unless an Egg is discovered at the Pokémon Day Care. Also, some Pokémon only appear in either *Pokémon Black Version* or *Pokémon White Version*. These species of Pokémon may be easier to register in the Pokédex if you bring them over in a Link Trade.

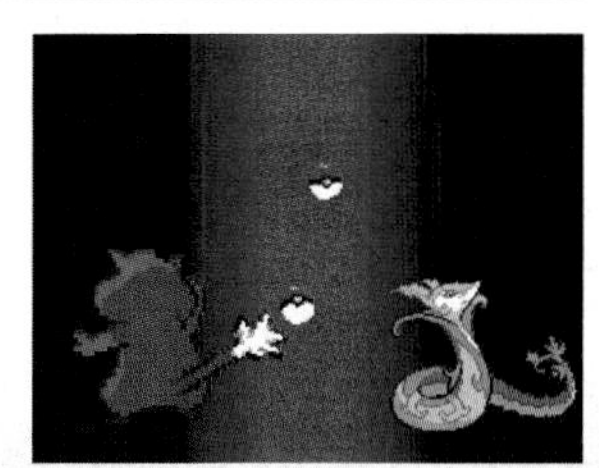

UNOVA POKÉDEX CHALLENGE

How to Register Pokémon in the Unova Pokédex

Unova Pokédex No.	Pokémon	Pokémon Black Version 2	Pokémon White Version 2	Pokémon Black Version	Pokémon White Version
010	Patrat	Route 19	Route 19		
011	Watchog	Route 7	Route 7		
012	Purrloin	Route 19	Route 19		
013	Liepard	Route 16	Route 16		
014	Pidove	Route 20	Route 20		
015	Tranquill	Route 6	Route 6		
016	Unfezant	Route 6 (rustling grass)	Route 6 (rustling grass)		
017	Sewaddle	Route 20	Route 20		
018	Swadloon	Lostlorn Forest	Lostlorn Forest		
019	Leavanny	Lostlorn Forest (rustling grass)	Lostlorn Forest (rustling grass)		
020	Sunkern	Route 20	Route 20		
021	Sunflora	Use Sun Stone on Sunkern	Use Sun Stone on Sunkern		
022	Lillipup	Floccesy Ranch	Floccesy Ranch		
023	Herdier	Route 3	Route 3		
024	Stoutland	Route 3 (rustling grass)	Route 3 (rustling grass)		
025	Mareep	Floccesy Ranch	Floccesy Ranch		
026	Flaaffy	Level up Mareep to Lv. 15	Level up Mareep to Lv. 15		
027	Ampharos	Level up Flaaffy to Lv. 30	Level up Flaaffy to Lv. 30		
028	Psyduck	Floccesy Ranch	Floccesy Ranch		
029	Golduck	Route 14	Route 14		

Unova Pokédex No. 030 Azurill

Main ways to register in the Unova Pokédex

Version	Location
Pokémon Black Version 2	Floccesy Ranch
Pokémon White Version 2	Floccesy Ranch
Pokémon Black Version	
Pokémon White Version	

Unova Pokédex No. 031 Marill

Main ways to register in the Unova Pokédex

Version	Location
Pokémon Black Version 2	Route 6
Pokémon White Version 2	Route 6
Pokémon Black Version	
Pokémon White Version	

Unova Pokédex No. 032 Azumarill

Main ways to register in the Unova Pokédex

Version	Location
Pokémon Black Version 2	Route 6 (rustling grass)
Pokémon White Version 2	Route 6 (rustling grass)
Pokémon Black Version	
Pokémon White Version	

Unova Pokédex No. 033 Riolu

Main ways to register in the Unova Pokédex

Version	Location
Pokémon Black Version 2	Floccesy Ranch
Pokémon White Version 2	Floccesy Ranch
Pokémon Black Version	
Pokémon White Version	

Unova Pokédex No. 034 Lucario

Main ways to register in the Unova Pokédex

Version	Location
Pokémon Black Version 2	Level up Riolu with high friendship in the morning, afternoon, or evening
Pokémon White Version 2	Level up Riolu with high friendship in the morning, afternoon, or evening
Pokémon Black Version	
Pokémon White Version	

Unova Pokédex No. 035 Dunsparce

Main ways to register in the Unova Pokédex

Version	Location
Pokémon Black Version 2	Route 20 (rustling grass)
Pokémon White Version 2	Route 20 (rustling grass)
Pokémon Black Version	
Pokémon White Version	

Unova Pokédex No. 036 Audino

Main ways to register in the Unova Pokédex

Version	Location
Pokémon Black Version 2	Route 20 (rustling grass)
Pokémon White Version 2	Route 20 (rustling grass)
Pokémon Black Version	
Pokémon White Version	

Unova Pokédex No. 037 Pansage

Main ways to register in the Unova Pokédex

Version	Location
Pokémon Black Version 2	Lostlorn Forest (rustling grass)
Pokémon White Version 2	Lostlorn Forest (rustling grass)
Pokémon Black Version	
Pokémon White Version	

Unova Pokédex No. 038 Simisage

Main ways to register in the Unova Pokédex

Version	Location
Pokémon Black Version 2	Use Leaf Stone on Pansage
Pokémon White Version 2	Use Leaf Stone on Pansage
Pokémon Black Version	
Pokémon White Version	

Unova Pokédex No. 039 Pansear

Main ways to register in the Unova Pokédex

Version	Location
Pokémon Black Version 2	Lostlorn Forest (rustling grass)
Pokémon White Version 2	Lostlorn Forest (rustling grass)
Pokémon Black Version	
Pokémon White Version	

Unova Pokédex No. 040 Simisear

Main ways to register in the Unova Pokédex

Version	Location
Pokémon Black Version 2	Use Fire Stone on Pansear
Pokémon White Version 2	Use Fire Stone on Pansear
Pokémon Black Version	
Pokémon White Version	

Unova Pokédex No. 041 Panpour

Main ways to register in the Unova Pokédex

Version	Location
Pokémon Black Version 2	Lostlorn Forest (rustling grass)
Pokémon White Version 2	Lostlorn Forest (rustling grass)
Pokémon Black Version	
Pokémon White Version	

Unova Pokédex No. 042 Simipour

Main ways to register in the Unova Pokédex

Version	Location
Pokémon Black Version 2	Use Water Stone on Panpour
Pokémon White Version 2	Use Water Stone on Panpour
Pokémon Black Version	
Pokémon White Version	

Unova Pokédex No. 043 Venipede

Main ways to register in the Unova Pokédex

Version	Location
Pokémon Black Version 2	Lostlorn Forest
Pokémon White Version 2	Lostlorn Forest
Pokémon Black Version	
Pokémon White Version	

Unova Pokédex No. 044 Whirlipede

Main ways to register in the Unova Pokédex

Version	Location
Pokémon Black Version 2	Lostlorn Forest (dark grass)
Pokémon White Version 2	Lostlorn Forest (dark grass)
Pokémon Black Version	
Pokémon White Version	

Unova Pokédex No. 045 Scolipede

Main ways to register in the Unova Pokédex

Version	Location
Pokémon Black Version 2	Deep in the Pinwheel Forest (rustling grass)
Pokémon White Version 2	Deep in the Pinwheel Forest (rustling grass)
Pokémon Black Version	
Pokémon White Version	

Unova Pokédex No. 046 Koffing

Main ways to register in the Unova Pokédex

Version	Location
Pokémon Black Version 2	Virbank Complex (inside)
Pokémon White Version 2	Virbank Complex (inside)
Pokémon Black Version	
Pokémon White Version	

Unova Pokédex No. 047 Weezing

Main ways to register in the Unova Pokédex

Version	Location
Pokémon Black Version 2	P2 Laboratory
Pokémon White Version 2	P2 Laboratory
Pokémon Black Version	
Pokémon White Version	

Unova Pokédex No. 048 Magnemite

Main ways to register in the Unova Pokédex

Version	Location
Pokémon Black Version 2	Virbank Complex Entrance
Pokémon White Version 2	Virbank Complex Entrance
Pokémon Black Version	
Pokémon White Version	

Unova Pokédex No. 049 Magneton

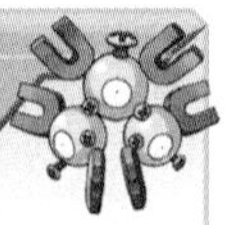

Main ways to register in the Unova Pokédex

Version	Location
Pokémon Black Version 2	P2 Laboratory
Pokémon White Version 2	P2 Laboratory
Pokémon Black Version	
Pokémon White Version	

Unova Pokédex No. 050

Magnezone

Main ways to register in the Unova Pokédex

Version	Method
Pokémon Black Version 2	P2 Laboratory (rustling grass)
Pokémon White Version 2	P2 Laboratory (rustling grass)
Pokémon Black Version	
Pokémon White Version	

Unova Pokédex No. 051

Growlithe

Main ways to register in the Unova Pokédex

Version	Method
Pokémon Black Version 2	Virbank Complex (inside)
Pokémon White Version 2	Virbank Complex (inside)
Pokémon Black Version	
Pokémon White Version	

Unova Pokédex No. 052

Arcanine

Main ways to register in the Unova Pokédex

Version	Method
Pokémon Black Version 2	Use Fire Stone on Growlithe
Pokémon White Version 2	Use Fire Stone on Growlithe
Pokémon Black Version	
Pokémon White Version	

Unova Pokédex No. 053

Magby

Main ways to register in the Unova Pokédex

Version	Method
Pokémon Black Version 2	Virbank Complex entrance
Pokémon White Version 2	Link Trade or use Poké Transfer
Pokémon Black Version	
Pokémon White Version	When Vincent is in White Forest

Unova Pokédex No. 054

Magmar

Main ways to register in the Unova Pokédex

Version	Method
Pokémon Black Version 2	Level up Magby to Lv. 30
Pokémon White Version 2	Link Trade or use Poké Transfer
Pokémon Black Version	
Pokémon White Version	

Unova Pokédex No. 055

Magmortar

Main ways to register in the Unova Pokédex

Version	Method
Pokémon Black Version 2	Link Trade Magmar while it holds the Magmarizer
Pokémon White Version 2	Link Trade Magmar while it holds the Magmarizer
Pokémon Black Version	
Pokémon White Version	

Unova Pokédex No. 056

Elekid

Main ways to register in the Unova Pokédex

Version	Method
Pokémon Black Version 2	Link Trade or use Poké Transfer
Pokémon White Version 2	Virbank Complex entrance
Pokémon Black Version	
Pokémon White Version	When Robbie is in White Forest

Unova Pokédex No. 057

Electabuzz

Main ways to register in the Unova Pokédex

Version	Method
Pokémon Black Version 2	Link Trade or use Poké Transfer
Pokémon White Version 2	Level up Elekid to Lv. 30
Pokémon Black Version	
Pokémon White Version	

Unova Pokédex No. 058

Electivire

Main ways to register in the Unova Pokédex

Version	Method
Pokémon Black Version 2	Link Trade Electabuzz while it holds the Electirizer
Pokémon White Version 2	Link Trade Electabuzz while it holds the Electirizer
Pokémon Black Version	
Pokémon White Version	

Unova Pokédex No. 059

Rattata

Main ways to register in the Unova Pokédex

Version	Method
Pokémon Black Version 2	Castelia Sewers
Pokémon White Version 2	Castelia Sewers
Pokémon Black Version	
Pokémon White Version	

Unova Pokédex No. 060

Raticate

Main ways to register in the Unova Pokédex

Version	Method
Pokémon Black Version 2	Relic Passage (middle)
Pokémon White Version 2	Relic Passage (middle)
Pokémon Black Version	
Pokémon White Version	

Unova Pokédex No. 061

Zubat

Main ways to register in the Unova Pokédex

Version	Method
Pokémon Black Version 2	Castelia Sewers
Pokémon White Version 2	Castelia Sewers
Pokémon Black Version	
Pokémon White Version	

Unova Pokédex No. 062

Golbat

Main ways to register in the Unova Pokédex

Version	Method
Pokémon Black Version 2	Celestial Tower 4F
Pokémon White Version 2	Celestial Tower 4F
Pokémon Black Version	
Pokémon White Version	

Unova Pokédex No. 063

Crobat

Main ways to register in the Unova Pokédex

Version	Method
Pokémon Black Version 2	Dreamyard (rustling grass)
Pokémon White Version 2	Dreamyard (rustling grass)
Pokémon Black Version	
Pokémon White Version	

Unova Pokédex No. 064

Grimer

Main ways to register in the Unova Pokédex

Version	Method
Pokémon Black Version 2	Castelia Sewers
Pokémon White Version 2	Castelia Sewers
Pokémon Black Version	
Pokémon White Version	

Unova Pokédex No. 065

Muk

Main ways to register in the Unova Pokédex

Version	Method
Pokémon Black Version 2	Castelia Sewers (rippling water)
Pokémon White Version 2	Castelia Sewers (rippling water)
Pokémon Black Version	
Pokémon White Version	

Unova Pokédex No. 066

Woobat

Main ways to register in the Unova Pokédex

Version	Method
Pokémon Black Version 2	Relic Passage exit to Driftveil City
Pokémon White Version 2	Relic Passage exit to Driftveil City
Pokémon Black Version	
Pokémon White Version	

Unova Pokédex No. 067

Swoobat

Main ways to register in the Unova Pokédex

Version	Method
Pokémon Black Version 2	Level up Woobat with high friendship
Pokémon White Version 2	Level up Woobat with high friendship
Pokémon Black Version	
Pokémon White Version	

Unova Pokédex No. 068

Roggenrola

Main ways to register in the Unova Pokédex

Version	Method
Pokémon Black Version 2	Relic Passage exit to Castelia City
Pokémon White Version 2	Relic Passage exit to Castelia City
Pokémon Black Version	
Pokémon White Version	

Unova Pokédex No. 069

Boldore

Main ways to register in the Unova Pokédex

Version	Method
Pokémon Black Version 2	Relic Passage exit to Driftveil City
Pokémon White Version 2	Relic Passage exit to Driftveil City
Pokémon Black Version	
Pokémon White Version	

Unova Pokédex No. 070 — Gigalith

Main ways to register in the Unova Pokédex

- **Pokémon Black Version 2**: Trade an Emolga with a Hiker in the house on Route 7
- **Pokémon White Version 2**: Trade an Emolga with a Hiker in the house on Route 7
- Pokémon Black Version
- Pokémon White Version

Unova Pokédex No. 071 — Onix

Main ways to register in the Unova Pokédex

- **Pokémon Black Version 2**: Relic Passage exit to Driftveil City
- **Pokémon White Version 2**: Relic Passage exit to Driftveil City
- Pokémon Black Version
- Pokémon White Version

Unova Pokédex No. 072 — Steelix

Main ways to register in the Unova Pokédex

- **Pokémon Black Version 2**: Clay Tunnel (dust cloud)
- **Pokémon White Version 2**: Clay Tunnel (dust cloud)
- Pokémon Black Version
- Pokémon White Version

Unova Pokédex No. 073 — Timburr

Main ways to register in the Unova Pokédex

- **Pokémon Black Version 2**: Relic Passage exit to Castelia City
- **Pokémon White Version 2**: Relic Passage exit to Castelia City
- Pokémon Black Version
- Pokémon White Version

Unova Pokédex No. 074 — Gurdurr

Main ways to register in the Unova Pokédex

- **Pokémon Black Version 2**: Relic Passage exit to Driftveil City
- **Pokémon White Version 2**: Relic Passage exit to Driftveil City
- Pokémon Black Version
- Pokémon White Version

Unova Pokédex No. 075 — Conkeldurr

Main ways to register in the Unova Pokédex

- **Pokémon Black Version 2**: Link Trade Gurdurr
- **Pokémon White Version 2**: Link Trade Gurdurr
- Pokémon Black Version
- Pokémon White Version

Unova Pokédex No. 076 — Drilbur

Main ways to register in the Unova Pokédex

- **Pokémon Black Version 2**: Relic Passage Exit to Driftveil City (dust cloud)
- **Pokémon White Version 2**: Relic Passage Exit to Driftveil City (dust cloud)
- Pokémon Black Version
- Pokémon White Version

Unova Pokédex No. 077 — Excadrill

Main ways to register in the Unova Pokédex

- **Pokémon Black Version 2**: Reversal Mountain Entrance (dust cloud)
- **Pokémon White Version 2**: Reversal Mountain Entrance (dust cloud)
- Pokémon Black Version
- Pokémon White Version

Unova Pokédex No. 078 — Skitty

Main ways to register in the Unova Pokédex

- **Pokémon Black Version 2**: Link Trade or use Poké Transfer
- **Pokémon White Version 2**: Castelia City empty lot
- Pokémon Black Version
- Pokémon White Version

Unova Pokédex No. 079 — Delcatty

Main ways to register in the Unova Pokédex

- **Pokémon Black Version 2**: Link Trade or use Poké Transfer to get Skitty, then use Moon Stone on it
- **Pokémon White Version 2**: Castelia City empty lot (rustling grass)
- Pokémon Black Version
- Pokémon White Version

Unova Pokédex No. 080 — Buneary

Main ways to register in the Unova Pokédex

- **Pokémon Black Version 2**: Castelia City empty lot
- **Pokémon White Version 2**: Link Trade or use Poké Transfer
- Pokémon Black Version
- Pokémon White Version

Unova Pokédex No. 081 — Lopunny

Main ways to register in the Unova Pokédex

- **Pokémon Black Version 2**: Castelia City empty lot (rustling grass)
- **Pokémon White Version 2**: Link Trade or use Poké Transfer to get Buneary, then level it up with high friendship
- Pokémon Black Version
- Pokémon White Version

Unova Pokédex No. 082 — Cottonee

Main ways to register in the Unova Pokédex

- **Pokémon Black Version 2**: Castelia City empty lot
- **Pokémon White Version 2**: Trade a Petilil with a boy on Route 4
- Pokémon Black Version
- Pokémon White Version

Unova Pokédex No. 083 — Whimsicott

Main ways to register in the Unova Pokédex

- **Pokémon Black Version 2**: Castelia City empty lot (rustling grass)
- **Pokémon White Version 2**: Use Sun Stone on Cottonee
- Pokémon Black Version
- Pokémon White Version

Unova Pokédex No. 084 — Petilil

Main ways to register in the Unova Pokédex

- **Pokémon Black Version 2**: Trade a Cottonee with a girl on Route 4
- **Pokémon White Version 2**: Castelia City empty lot
- Pokémon Black Version
- Pokémon White Version

Unova Pokédex No. 085 — Lilligant

Main ways to register in the Unova Pokédex

- **Pokémon Black Version 2**: Use Sun Stone on Petilil
- **Pokémon White Version 2**: Castelia City empty lot (rustling grass)
- Pokémon Black Version
- Pokémon White Version

Unova Pokédex No. 086 — Munna

Main ways to register in the Unova Pokédex

- **Pokémon Black Version 2**: Dreamyard
- **Pokémon White Version 2**: Dreamyard
- Pokémon Black Version
- Pokémon White Version

Unova Pokédex No. 087 — Musharna

Main ways to register in the Unova Pokédex

- **Pokémon Black Version 2**: Dreamyard (rustling grass)
- **Pokémon White Version 2**: Dreamyard (rustling grass)
- Pokémon Black Version
- Pokémon White Version

Unova Pokédex No. 088 — Cleffa

Main ways to register in the Unova Pokédex

- **Pokémon Black Version 2**: Leave a pair of Clefairy at the Pokémon Day Care, then hatch any Egg found
- **Pokémon White Version 2**: Leave a pair of Clefairy at the Pokémon Day Care, then hatch any Egg found
- Pokémon Black Version
- Pokémon White Version

Unova Pokédex No. 089 — Clefairy

Main ways to register in the Unova Pokédex

- **Pokémon Black Version 2**: Giant Chasm Cave
- **Pokémon White Version 2**: Giant Chasm Cave
- Pokémon Black Version
- Pokémon White Version

Main ways to register in the Unova Pokédex

Unova Pokédex No.	Pokémon	Pokémon Black Version 2	Pokémon White Version 2	Pokémon Black Version	Pokémon White Version
090	Clefable	Giant Chasm entrance (rustling grass)	Giant Chasm entrance (rustling grass)		
091	Eevee	Castelia City empty lot	Castelia City empty lot		
092	Vaporeon	Use Water Stone on Eevee	Use Water Stone on Eevee		
093	Jolteon	Use Thunderstone on Eevee	Use Thunderstone on Eevee		
094	Flareon	Use Fire Stone on Eevee	Use Fire Stone on Eevee		
095	Espeon	Level up Eevee with high friendship in the morning, afternoon, or evening	Level up Eevee with high friendship in the morning, afternoon, or evening		
096	Umbreon	Level up Eevee with high friendship at night or late night	Level up Eevee with high friendship at night or late night		
097	Leafeon	Level up Eevee near the moss-covered rock in Pinwheel Forest	Level up Eevee near the moss-covered rock in Pinwheel Forest		
098	Glaceon	Level up Eevee near the ice-covered rock in Twist Mountain	Level up Eevee near the ice-covered rock in Twist Mountain		
099	Sandile	Route 4	Route 4		
100	Krokorok	Relic Castle (lowest floor passages ①②④⑤)	Relic Castle (lowest floor passages ①②④⑤)		
101	Krookodile	Level up Krokorok to Lv. 40	Level up Krokorok to Lv. 40		
102	Darumaka	Route 4	Route 4		
103	Darmanitan	Level up Darumaka to Lv. 35	Level up Darumaka to Lv. 35		
104	Basculin	Aspertia City (water surface)	Aspertia City (water surface)		
105	Trubbish	Route 4	Route 16		
106	Garbodor	Route 9	Route 9		
107	Minccino	Route 16	Route 4		
108	Cinccino	Route 16 (rustling grass)	Route 16 (rustling grass)		
109	Rufflet	Link Trade	Route 23		Route 10

Unova Pokédex No. 110

Braviary

Main ways to register in the Unova Pokédex

Pokémon Black Version 2	Level up Rufflet obtained by Link Trade to Lv. 54
Pokémon White Version 2	Route 4 (Monday only)
Pokémon Black Version	
Pokémon White Version	

Unova Pokédex No. 111

Vullaby

Main ways to register in the Unova Pokédex

Pokémon Black Version 2	Route 23
Pokémon White Version 2	Link Trade
Pokémon Black Version	Route 10
Pokémon White Version	

Unova Pokédex No. 112

Mandibuzz

Main ways to register in the Unova Pokédex

Pokémon Black Version 2	Route 4 (Thursday only)
Pokémon White Version 2	Level up Vullaby obtained by Link Trade to Lv. 54
Pokémon Black Version	
Pokémon White Version	

Unova Pokédex No. 113

Sandshrew

Main ways to register in the Unova Pokédex

Pokémon Black Version 2	Desert Resort Entrance
Pokémon White Version 2	Desert Resort Entrance
Pokémon Black Version	
Pokémon White Version	

Unova Pokédex No. 114

Sandslash

Main ways to register in the Unova Pokédex

Pokémon Black Version 2	Relic Castle (lowest floor passages ①②④⑤)
Pokémon White Version 2	Relic Castle (lowest floor passages ①②④⑤)
Pokémon Black Version	
Pokémon White Version	

Unova Pokédex No. 115

Dwebble

Main ways to register in the Unova Pokédex

Pokémon Black Version 2	Desert Resort Entrance
Pokémon White Version 2	Desert Resort Entrance
Pokémon Black Version	
Pokémon White Version	

Unova Pokédex No. 116

Crustle

Main ways to register in the Unova Pokédex

Pokémon Black Version 2	Use Colress Machine in Seaside Cave, then catch it
Pokémon White Version 2	Use Colress Machine in Seaside Cave, then catch it
Pokémon Black Version	
Pokémon White Version	

Unova Pokédex No. 117

Scraggy

Main ways to register in the Unova Pokédex

Pokémon Black Version 2	Route 4
Pokémon White Version 2	Route 4
Pokémon Black Version	
Pokémon White Version	

Unova Pokédex No. 118

Scrafty

Main ways to register in the Unova Pokédex

Pokémon Black Version 2	Route 15
Pokémon White Version 2	Route 15
Pokémon Black Version	
Pokémon White Version	

Unova Pokédex No. 119

Maractus

Main ways to register in the Unova Pokédex

Pokémon Black Version 2	Desert Resort Entrance
Pokémon White Version 2	Desert Resort Entrance
Pokémon Black Version	
Pokémon White Version	

Unova Pokédex No. 120

Sigilyph

Main ways to register in the Unova Pokédex

Pokémon Black Version 2	Desert Resort Back
Pokémon White Version 2	Desert Resort Back
Pokémon Black Version	
Pokémon White Version	

Unova Pokédex No. 121

Trapinch

Main ways to register in the Unova Pokédex

Pokémon Black Version 2	Desert Resort Back
Pokémon White Version 2	Desert Resort Back
Pokémon Black Version	
Pokémon White Version	

Unova Pokédex No. 122

Vibrava

Main ways to register in the Unova Pokédex

Pokémon Black Version 2	Reversal Mountain Outside (dark grass)
Pokémon White Version 2	Reversal Mountain Outside (dark grass)
Pokémon Black Version	
Pokémon White Version	

Unova Pokédex No. 123

Flygon

Main ways to register in the Unova Pokédex

Pokémon Black Version 2	Level up Vibrava to Lv. 45
Pokémon White Version 2	Level up Vibrava to Lv. 45
Pokémon Black Version	
Pokémon White Version	

Unova Pokédex No. 124

Yamask

Main ways to register in the Unova Pokédex

Pokémon Black Version 2	Relic Castle 1F
Pokémon White Version 2	Relic Castle 1F
Pokémon Black Version	
Pokémon White Version	

Unova Pokédex No. 125

Cofagrigus

Main ways to register in the Unova Pokédex

Pokémon Black Version 2	Level up Yamask to Lv. 34
Pokémon White Version 2	Level up Yamask to Lv. 34
Pokémon Black Version	
Pokémon White Version	

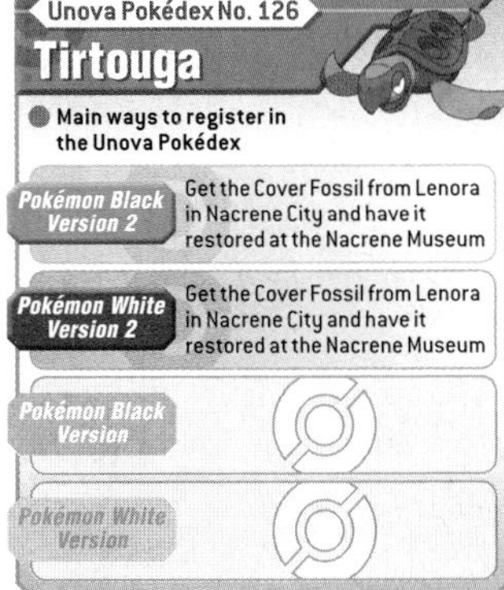

Unova Pokédex No. 126

Tirtouga

Main ways to register in the Unova Pokédex

Pokémon Black Version 2	Get the Cover Fossil from Lenora in Nacrene City and have it restored at the Nacrene Museum
Pokémon White Version 2	Get the Cover Fossil from Lenora in Nacrene City and have it restored at the Nacrene Museum
Pokémon Black Version	
Pokémon White Version	

Unova Pokédex No. 127

Carracosta

Main ways to register in the Unova Pokédex

Pokémon Black Version 2	Level up Tirtouga to Lv. 37
Pokémon White Version 2	Level up Tirtouga to Lv. 37
Pokémon Black Version	
Pokémon White Version	

Unova Pokédex No. 128

Archen

Main ways to register in the Unova Pokédex

Pokémon Black Version 2	Get the Plume Fossil from Lenora in Nacrene City and have it restored at the Nacrene Museum.
Pokémon White Version 2	Get the Plume Fossil from Lenora in Nacrene City and have it restored at the Nacrene Museum.
Pokémon Black Version	
Pokémon White Version	

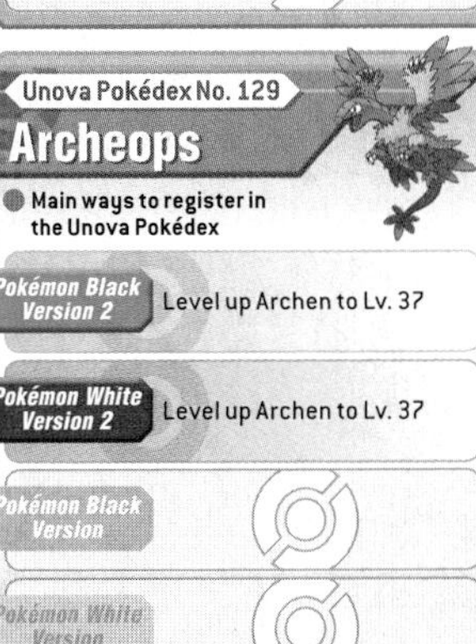

Unova Pokédex No. 129

Archeops

Main ways to register in the Unova Pokédex

Pokémon Black Version 2	Level up Archen to Lv. 37
Pokémon White Version 2	Level up Archen to Lv. 37
Pokémon Black Version	
Pokémon White Version	

Unova Pokédex No.	Pokémon	Pokémon Black Version 2	Pokémon White Version 2	Pokémon Black Version	Pokémon White Version
130	Klink	Chargestone Cave 1F	Chargestone Cave 1F		
131	Klang	P2 Laboratory	P2 Laboratory		
132	Klinklang	P2 Laboratory (rustling grass)	P2 Laboratory (rustling grass)		
133	Budew	Catch Roselia or Roserade, leave them at the Pokémon Day Care, find an Egg, and hatch it	Catch Roselia or Roserade, leave them at the Pokémon Day Care, find an Egg, and hatch it		
134	Roselia	Lostlorn Forest	Lostlorn Forest		
135	Roserade	Lostlorn Forest (rustling grass)	Lostlorn Forest (rustling grass)		
136	Gothita	Route 16	Link Trade	Route 16	
137	Gothorita	Strange House Room ①	Level up Gothita obtained by Link Trade to Lv. 32	Route 9	
138	Gothitelle	Route 9 (rustling grass)	Level up Gothorita obtained by Link Trade to Lv. 41	Route 9 (rustling grass)	
139	Solosis	Link Trade	Route 16		Route 16
140	Duosion	Level up Solosis obtained by Link Trade to Lv. 32	Strange House Room ①		Route 9
141	Reuniclus	Level up Duosion obtained by Link Trade to Lv. 41	Route 9 (rustling grass)		Route 9 (rustling grass)
142	Combee	Lostlorn Forest	Lostlorn Forest		
143	Vespiquen	Lostlorn Forest (rustling grass)	Lostlorn Forest (rustling grass)		
144	Emolga	Route 16 (rustling grass)	Route 16 (rustling grass)		
145	Heracross	Lostlorn Forest	Lostlorn Forest (Hidden Grotto)		
146	Pinsir	Lostlorn Forest (Hidden Grotto)	Lostlorn Forest		
147	Blitzle	Catch Zebstrika, leave them at the Pokémon Day Care, find an Egg, and hatch it	Catch Zebstrika, leave them at the Pokémon Day Care, find an Egg, and hatch it	Route 3	Route 3
148	Zebstrika	Route 7	Route 7		
149	Buizel	Lostlorn Forest (water surface)	Lostlorn Forest (water surface)		

Unova Pokédex No. 150

Floatzel

Main ways to register in the Unova Pokédex

Pokémon Black Version 2	Lostlorn Forest (rippling water)
Pokémon White Version 2	Lostlorn Forest (rippling water)
Pokémon Black Version	
Pokémon White Version	

Unova Pokédex No. 151

Zorua

Main ways to register in the Unova Pokédex

Pokémon Black Version 2	Receive from Rood in Driftveil City
Pokémon White Version 2	Receive from Rood in Driftveil City
Pokémon Black Version	
Pokémon White Version	

Unova Pokédex No. 152

Zoroark

Main ways to register in the Unova Pokédex

Pokémon Black Version 2	Level up Zorua to Lv. 30
Pokémon White Version 2	Level up Zorua to Lv. 30
Pokémon Black Version	
Pokémon White Version	

Unova Pokédex No. 153

Ducklett

Main ways to register in the Unova Pokédex

Pokémon Black Version 2	Driftveil Drawbridge (Pokémon shadows)
Pokémon White Version 2	Driftveil Drawbridge (Pokémon shadows)
Pokémon Black Version	
Pokémon White Version	

Unova Pokédex No. 154

Swanna

Main ways to register in the Unova Pokédex

Pokémon Black Version 2	Marvelous Bridge (Pokémon shadows)
Pokémon White Version 2	Marvelous Bridge (Pokémon shadows)
Pokémon Black Version	
Pokémon White Version	

Unova Pokédex No. 155

Karrablast

Main ways to register in the Unova Pokédex

Pokémon Black Version 2	Route 6
Pokémon White Version 2	Route 6
Pokémon Black Version	
Pokémon White Version	

Unova Pokédex No. 156

Escavalier

Main ways to register in the Unova Pokédex

Pokémon Black Version 2	Link Trade Shelmet for Karrablast
Pokémon White Version 2	Link Trade Shelmet for Karrablast
Pokémon Black Version	
Pokémon White Version	

Unova Pokédex No. 157

Shelmet

Main ways to register in the Unova Pokédex

Pokémon Black Version 2	Route 6
Pokémon White Version 2	Route 6
Pokémon Black Version	
Pokémon White Version	

Unova Pokédex No. 158

Accelgor

Main ways to register in the Unova Pokédex

Pokémon Black Version 2	Link Trade Karrablast for Shelmet
Pokémon White Version 2	Link Trade Karrablast for Shelmet
Pokémon Black Version	
Pokémon White Version	

Unova Pokédex No. 159

Deerling

Main ways to register in the Unova Pokédex

Pokémon Black Version 2	Route 6
Pokémon White Version 2	Route 6
Pokémon Black Version	
Pokémon White Version	

Unova Pokédex No. 160

Sawsbuck

Main ways to register in the Unova Pokédex

Pokémon Black Version 2	Dragonspiral Tower Entrance
Pokémon White Version 2	Dragonspiral Tower Entrance
Pokémon Black Version	
Pokémon White Version	

Unova Pokédex No. 161

Foongus

Main ways to register in the Unova Pokédex

Pokémon Black Version 2	Route 6
Pokémon White Version 2	Route 6
Pokémon Black Version	
Pokémon White Version	

Unova Pokédex No. 162

Amoonguss

Main ways to register in the Unova Pokédex

Pokémon Black Version 2	Route 11
Pokémon White Version 2	Route 11
Pokémon Black Version	
Pokémon White Version	

Unova Pokédex No. 163

Castform

Main ways to register in the Unova Pokédex

Pokémon Black Version 2	Route 6 (rustling grass)
Pokémon White Version 2	Route 6 (rustling grass)
Pokémon Black Version	
Pokémon White Version	

Unova Pokédex No. 164

Nosepass

Main ways to register in the Unova Pokédex

Pokémon Black Version 2	Chargestone Cave 1F
Pokémon White Version 2	Chargestone Cave 1F
Pokémon Black Version	
Pokémon White Version	

Unova Pokédex No. 165

Probopass

Main ways to register in the Unova Pokédex

Pokémon Black Version 2	Level up Nosepass in Chargestone Cave
Pokémon White Version 2	Level up Nosepass in Chargestone Cave
Pokémon Black Version	
Pokémon White Version	

Unova Pokédex No. 166

Aron

Main ways to register in the Unova Pokédex

Pokémon Black Version 2	Mistralton Cave 1F
Pokémon White Version 2	Mistralton Cave 1F
Pokémon Black Version	
Pokémon White Version	

Unova Pokédex No. 167

Lairon

Main ways to register in the Unova Pokédex

Pokémon Black Version 2	Clay Tunnel
Pokémon White Version 2	Clay Tunnel
Pokémon Black Version	
Pokémon White Version	

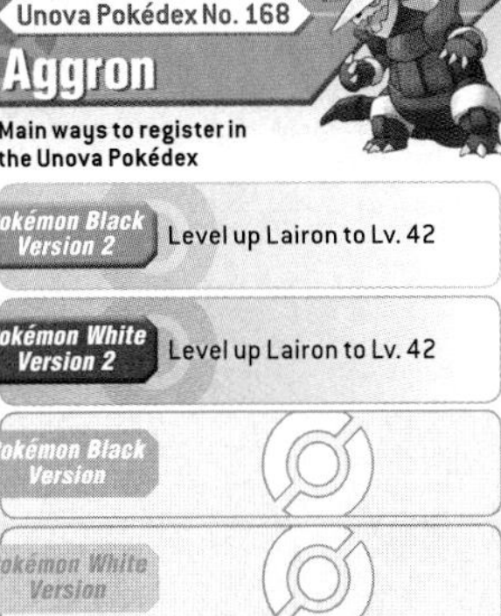

Unova Pokédex No. 168

Aggron

Main ways to register in the Unova Pokédex

Pokémon Black Version 2	Level up Lairon to Lv. 42
Pokémon White Version 2	Level up Lairon to Lv. 42
Pokémon Black Version	
Pokémon White Version	

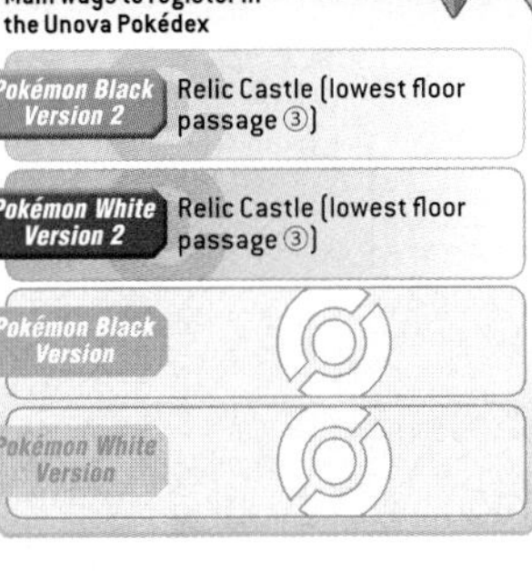

Unova Pokédex No. 169

Baltoy

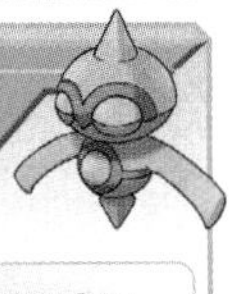

Main ways to register in the Unova Pokédex

Pokémon Black Version 2	Relic Castle (lowest floor passage ③)
Pokémon White Version 2	Relic Castle (lowest floor passage ③)
Pokémon Black Version	
Pokémon White Version	

Unova Pokédex No. 170

Claydol

Main ways to register in the Unova Pokédex

Version	Method
Pokémon Black Version 2	Level up Baltoy to Lv. 36
Pokémon White Version 2	Level up Baltoy to Lv. 36
Pokémon Black Version	
Pokémon White Version	

Unova Pokédex No. 171

Larvesta

Main ways to register in the Unova Pokédex

Version	Method
Pokémon Black Version 2	Catch Volcarona and leave it at the Pokémon Day Care to find an Egg and then hatch it
Pokémon White Version 2	Catch Volcarona and leave it at the Pokémon Day Care to find an Egg and then hatch it
Pokémon Black Version	Hatch the Egg received on Route 18
Pokémon White Version	Hatch the Egg received on Route 18

Unova Pokédex No. 172

Volcarona

Main ways to register in the Unova Pokédex

Version	Method
Pokémon Black Version 2	Relic Castle (lowest floor—deepest part)
Pokémon White Version 2	Relic Castle (lowest floor—deepest part)
Pokémon Black Version	
Pokémon White Version	

Unova Pokédex No. 173

Joltik

Main ways to register in the Unova Pokédex

Version	Method
Pokémon Black Version 2	Chargestone Cave 1F
Pokémon White Version 2	Chargestone Cave 1F
Pokémon Black Version	
Pokémon White Version	

Unova Pokédex No. 174

Galvantula

Main ways to register in the Unova Pokédex

Version	Method
Pokémon Black Version 2	Level up Joltik to Lv. 36
Pokémon White Version 2	Level up Joltik to Lv. 36
Pokémon Black Version	
Pokémon White Version	

Unova Pokédex No. 175

Ferroseed

Main ways to register in the Unova Pokédex

Version	Method
Pokémon Black Version 2	Chargestone Cave 1F
Pokémon White Version 2	Chargestone Cave 1F
Pokémon Black Version	
Pokémon White Version	

Unova Pokédex No. 176

Ferrothorn

Main ways to register in the Unova Pokédex

Version	Method
Pokémon Black Version 2	Level up Ferroseed to Lv. 40
Pokémon White Version 2	Level up Ferroseed to Lv. 40
Pokémon Black Version	
Pokémon White Version	

Unova Pokédex No. 177

Tynamo

Main ways to register in the Unova Pokédex

Version	Method
Pokémon Black Version 2	Chargestone Cave 1F
Pokémon White Version 2	Chargestone Cave 1F
Pokémon Black Version	
Pokémon White Version	

Unova Pokédex No. 178

Eelektrik

Main ways to register in the Unova Pokédex

Version	Method
Pokémon Black Version 2	Seaside Cave B1F
Pokémon White Version 2	Seaside Cave B1F
Pokémon Black Version	
Pokémon White Version	

Unova Pokédex No. 179

Eelektross

Main ways to register in the Unova Pokédex

Version	Method
Pokémon Black Version 2	Use Thunderstone on Eelektrik
Pokémon White Version 2	Use Thunderstone on Eelektrik
Pokémon Black Version	
Pokémon White Version	

Unova Pokédex No. 180

Frillish

Main ways to register in the Unova Pokédex

Version	Method
Pokémon Black Version 2	Undella Town (water surface)
Pokémon White Version 2	Undella Town (water surface)
Pokémon Black Version	
Pokémon White Version	

Unova Pokédex No. 181

Jellicent

Main ways to register in the Unova Pokédex

Version	Method
Pokémon Black Version 2	Undella Town (rippling water)
Pokémon White Version 2	Undella Town (rippling water)
Pokémon Black Version	
Pokémon White Version	

Unova Pokédex No. 182

Alomomola

Main ways to register in the Unova Pokédex

Version	Method
Pokémon Black Version 2	Virbank City (rippling water)
Pokémon White Version 2	Virbank City (rippling water)
Pokémon Black Version	
Pokémon White Version	

Unova Pokédex No. 183

Axew

Main ways to register in the Unova Pokédex

Version	Method
Pokémon Black Version 2	Mistralton Cave 1F
Pokémon White Version 2	Mistralton Cave 1F
Pokémon Black Version	
Pokémon White Version	

Unova Pokédex No. 184

Fraxure

Main ways to register in the Unova Pokédex

Version	Method
Pokémon Black Version 2	Nature Preserve
Pokémon White Version 2	Nature Preserve
Pokémon Black Version	
Pokémon White Version	

Unova Pokédex No. 185

Haxorus

Main ways to register in the Unova Pokédex

Version	Method
Pokémon Black Version 2	Level up Fraxure to Lv. 48
Pokémon White Version 2	Level up Fraxure to Lv. 48
Pokémon Black Version	
Pokémon White Version	

Unova Pokédex No. 186

Zangoose

Main ways to register in the Unova Pokédex

Version	Method
Pokémon Black Version 2	Route 7
Pokémon White Version 2	Route 7
Pokémon Black Version	
Pokémon White Version	

Unova Pokédex No. 187

Seviper

Main ways to register in the Unova Pokédex

Version	Method
Pokémon Black Version 2	Route 7
Pokémon White Version 2	Route 7
Pokémon Black Version	
Pokémon White Version	

Unova Pokédex No. 188

Elgyem

Main ways to register in the Unova Pokédex

Version	Method
Pokémon Black Version 2	Celestial Tower 3F
Pokémon White Version 2	Celestial Tower 3F
Pokémon Black Version	
Pokémon White Version	

Unova Pokédex No. 189

Beheeyem

Main ways to register in the Unova Pokédex

Version	Method
Pokémon Black Version 2	Level up Elgyem to Lv. 42
Pokémon White Version 2	Level up Elgyem to Lv. 42
Pokémon Black Version	
Pokémon White Version	

Unova Pokédex No. 190 Litwick

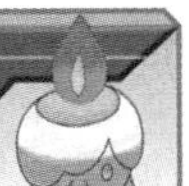

Main ways to register in the Unova Pokédex

Version	
Pokémon Black Version 2	Celestial Tower 2F
Pokémon White Version 2	Celestial Tower 2F
Pokémon Black Version	
Pokémon White Version	

Unova Pokédex No. 191 Lampent

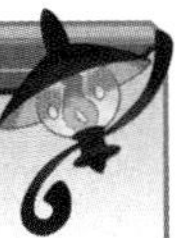

Main ways to register in the Unova Pokédex

Version	
Pokémon Black Version 2	Level up Litwick to Lv. 41
Pokémon White Version 2	Level up Litwick to Lv. 41
Pokémon Black Version	
Pokémon White Version	

Unova Pokédex No. 192 Chandelure

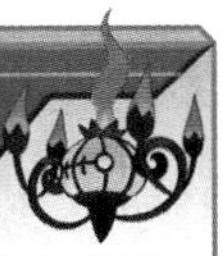

Main ways to register in the Unova Pokédex

Version	
Pokémon Black Version 2	Use Dusk Stone on Lampent
Pokémon White Version 2	Use Dusk Stone on Lampent
Pokémon Black Version	
Pokémon White Version	

Unova Pokédex No. 193 Heatmor

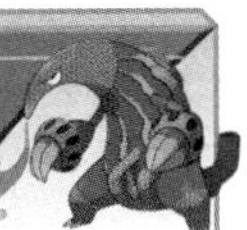

Main ways to register in the Unova Pokédex

Version	
Pokémon Black Version 2	Twist Mountain
Pokémon White Version 2	Twist Mountain
Pokémon Black Version	
Pokémon White Version	

Unova Pokédex No. 194 Durant

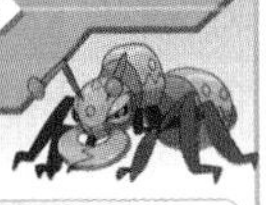

Main ways to register in the Unova Pokédex

Version	
Pokémon Black Version 2	Clay Tunnel
Pokémon White Version 2	Clay Tunnel
Pokémon Black Version	
Pokémon White Version	

Unova Pokédex No. 195 Cubchoo

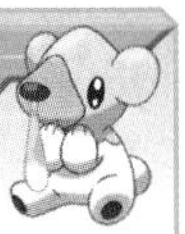

Main ways to register in the Unova Pokédex

Version	
Pokémon Black Version 2	Route 7 (winter only)
Pokémon White Version 2	Route 7 (winter only)
Pokémon Black Version	
Pokémon White Version	

Unova Pokédex No. 196 Beartic

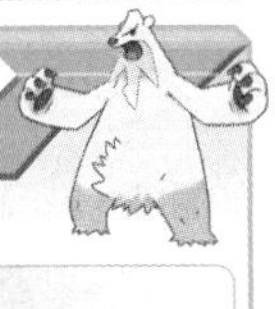

Main ways to register in the Unova Pokédex

Version	
Pokémon Black Version 2	Twist Mountain
Pokémon White Version 2	Twist Mountain
Pokémon Black Version	
Pokémon White Version	

Unova Pokédex No. 197 Cryogonal

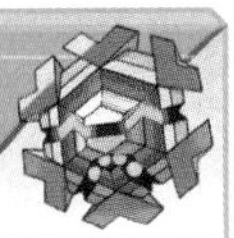

Main ways to register in the Unova Pokédex

Version	
Pokémon Black Version 2	Twist Mountain
Pokémon White Version 2	Twist Mountain
Pokémon Black Version	
Pokémon White Version	

Unova Pokédex No. 198 Tornadus

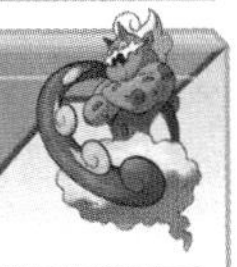

Main ways to register in the Unova Pokédex

Version	
Pokémon Black Version 2	Link Trade
Pokémon White Version 2	Link Trade
Pokémon Black Version	After the encounter on Route 7, it starts moving through the Unova region
Pokémon White Version	

Unova Pokédex No. 199 Thundurus

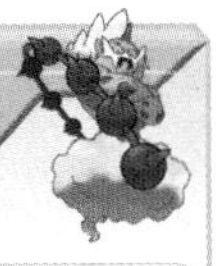

Main ways to register in the Unova Pokédex

Version	
Pokémon Black Version 2	Link Trade
Pokémon White Version 2	Link Trade
Pokémon Black Version	
Pokémon White Version	After the encounter on Route 7, it starts moving through the Unova region

Unova Pokédex No. 200 Landorus

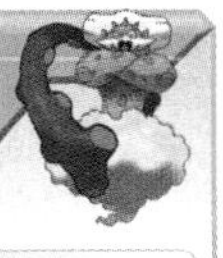

Main ways to register in the Unova Pokédex

Version	
Pokémon Black Version 2	Link Trade
Pokémon White Version 2	Link Trade
Pokémon Black Version	Add Tornadus and Thundurus to your party and go to the Abundant Shrine
Pokémon White Version	Add Tornadus and Thundurus to your party and go to the Abundant Shrine

Unova Pokédex No. 201 Skorupi

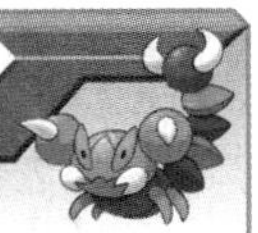

Main ways to register in the Unova Pokédex

Version	
Pokémon Black Version 2	Reversal Mountain Outside
Pokémon White Version 2	Reversal Mountain Outside
Pokémon Black Version	
Pokémon White Version	

Unova Pokédex No. 202 Drapion

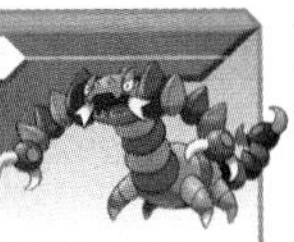

Main ways to register in the Unova Pokédex

Version	
Pokémon Black Version 2	Level up Skorupi to Lv. 40
Pokémon White Version 2	Level up Skorupi to Lv. 40
Pokémon Black Version	
Pokémon White Version	

Unova Pokédex No. 203 Skarmory

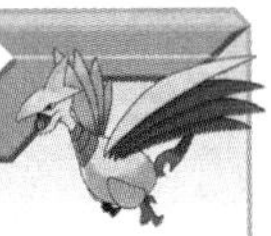

Main ways to register in the Unova Pokédex

Version	
Pokémon Black Version 2	Reversal Mountain Outside
Pokémon White Version 2	Reversal Mountain Outside
Pokémon Black Version	
Pokémon White Version	

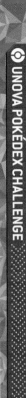

Unova Pokédex No. 204 Numel

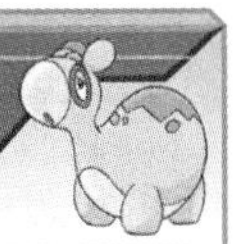

Main ways to register in the Unova Pokédex

Version	
Pokémon Black Version 2	Link Trade or use the Poké Transfer
Pokémon White Version 2	Reversal Mountain Outside
Pokémon Black Version	
Pokémon White Version	

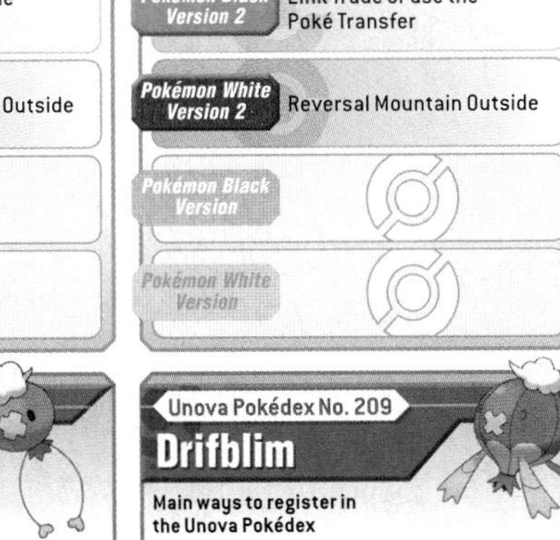

Unova Pokédex No. 205 Camerupt

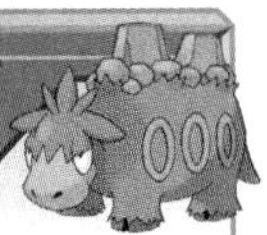

Main ways to register in the Unova Pokédex

Version	
Pokémon Black Version 2	Link Trade or use the Poké Transfer
Pokémon White Version 2	Reversal Mountain Outside
Pokémon Black Version	
Pokémon White Version	

Unova Pokédex No. 206 Spoink

Main ways to register in the Unova Pokédex

Version	
Pokémon Black Version 2	Reversal Mountain Outside
Pokémon White Version 2	Link Trade or use the Poké Transfer
Pokémon Black Version	
Pokémon White Version	

Unova Pokédex No. 207 Grumpig

Main ways to register in the Unova Pokédex

Version	
Pokémon Black Version 2	Reversal Mountain Outside
Pokémon White Version 2	Link Trade or use the Poké Transfer to get Spoink, then level it up to Lv. 32
Pokémon Black Version	
Pokémon White Version	

Unova Pokédex No. 208 Drifloon

Main ways to register in the Unova Pokédex

Version	
Pokémon Black Version 2	Route 13 Hidden Grotto
Pokémon White Version 2	Route 13 Hidden Grotto
Pokémon Black Version	
Pokémon White Version	

Unova Pokédex No. 209 Drifblim

Main ways to register in the Unova Pokédex

Version	
Pokémon Black Version 2	Reversal Mountain Outside
Pokémon White Version 2	Reversal Mountain Outside
Pokémon Black Version	
Pokémon White Version	

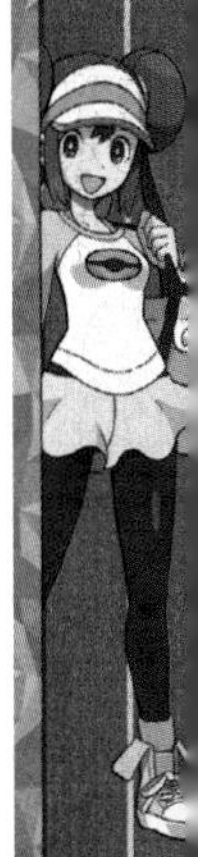

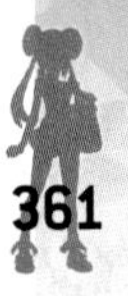

Unova Pokédex No. 210
Shuppet
Main ways to register in the Unova Pokédex

Version	Location
Pokémon Black Version 2	Catch Banette and leave it at the Pokémon Day Care to find an Egg and then hatch it
Pokémon White Version 2	Catch Banette and leave it at the Pokémon Day Care to find an Egg and then hatch it
Pokémon Black Version	
Pokémon White Version	

Unova Pokédex No. 211
Banette
Main ways to register in the Unova Pokédex

Version	Location
Pokémon Black Version 2	Strange House Entrance
Pokémon White Version 2	Strange House Entrance
Pokémon Black Version	
Pokémon White Version	

Unova Pokédex No. 212
Wingull
Main ways to register in the Unova Pokédex

Version	Location
Pokémon Black Version 2	Catch Pelipper and leave it at the Pokémon Day Care to find an Egg and then hatch it
Pokémon White Version 2	Catch Pelipper and leave it at the Pokémon Day Care to find an Egg and then hatch it
Pokémon Black Version	Route 13 (water surface)
Pokémon White Version	Route 13 (water surface)

Unova Pokédex No. 213
Pelipper
Main ways to register in the Unova Pokédex

Version	Location
Pokémon Black Version 2	Route 13
Pokémon White Version 2	Route 13
Pokémon Black Version	
Pokémon White Version	

Unova Pokédex No. 214
Lunatone
Main ways to register in the Unova Pokédex

Version	Location
Pokémon Black Version 2	Route 13
Pokémon White Version 2	Route 13
Pokémon Black Version	
Pokémon White Version	

Unova Pokédex No. 215
Solrock
Main ways to register in the Unova Pokédex

Version	Location
Pokémon Black Version 2	Route 13
Pokémon White Version 2	Route 13
Pokémon Black Version	
Pokémon White Version	

Unova Pokédex No. 216
Absol
Main ways to register in the Unova Pokédex

Version	Location
Pokémon Black Version 2	Route 13
Pokémon White Version 2	Route 13
Pokémon Black Version	
Pokémon White Version	

Unova Pokédex No. 217
Tangela
Main ways to register in the Unova Pokédex

Version	Location
Pokémon Black Version 2	Route 13
Pokémon White Version 2	Route 13
Pokémon Black Version	
Pokémon White Version	

Unova Pokédex No. 218
Tangrowth
Main ways to register in the Unova Pokédex

Version	Location
Pokémon Black Version 2	Route 13 (rustling grass)
Pokémon White Version 2	Route 13 (rustling grass)
Pokémon Black Version	
Pokémon White Version	

Unova Pokédex No. 219
Mienfoo
Main ways to register in the Unova Pokédex

Version	Location
Pokémon Black Version 2	Route 22
Pokémon White Version 2	Route 22
Pokémon Black Version	
Pokémon White Version	

Unova Pokédex No. 220
Mienshao
Main ways to register in the Unova Pokédex

Version	Location
Pokémon Black Version 2	Route 23 (dark grass)
Pokémon White Version 2	Route 23 (dark grass)
Pokémon Black Version	
Pokémon White Version	

Unova Pokédex No. 221
Gligar
Main ways to register in the Unova Pokédex

Version	Location
Pokémon Black Version 2	Route 11
Pokémon White Version 2	Route 11
Pokémon Black Version	
Pokémon White Version	

Unova Pokédex No. 222
Gliscor
Main ways to register in the Unova Pokédex

Version	Location
Pokémon Black Version 2	Route 11 (rustling grass)
Pokémon White Version 2	Route 11 (rustling grass)
Pokémon Black Version	
Pokémon White Version	

Unova Pokédex No. 223
Pawniard
Main ways to register in the Unova Pokédex

Version	Location
Pokémon Black Version 2	Route 9
Pokémon White Version 2	Route 9
Pokémon Black Version	
Pokémon White Version	

Unova Pokédex No. 224
Bisharp
Main ways to register in the Unova Pokédex

Version	Location
Pokémon Black Version 2	Level up Pawniard to Lv. 52
Pokémon White Version 2	Level up Pawniard to Lv. 52
Pokémon Black Version	
Pokémon White Version	

Unova Pokédex No. 225
Cobalion
Main ways to register in the Unova Pokédex

Version	Location
Pokémon Black Version 2	Route 13
Pokémon White Version 2	Route 13
Pokémon Black Version	
Pokémon White Version	

Unova Pokédex No. 226
Terrakion
Main ways to register in the Unova Pokédex

Version	Location
Pokémon Black Version 2	Route 22
Pokémon White Version 2	Route 22
Pokémon Black Version	
Pokémon White Version	

Unova Pokédex No. 227
Virizion
Main ways to register in the Unova Pokédex

Version	Location
Pokémon Black Version 2	Route 11
Pokémon White Version 2	Route 11
Pokémon Black Version	
Pokémon White Version	

Unova Pokédex No. 228
Tympole
Main ways to register in the Unova Pokédex

Version	Location
Pokémon Black Version 2	Catch Palpitoad or Seismitoad and leave it at the Pokémon Day Care to find an Egg and then hatch it
Pokémon White Version 2	Catch Palpitoad or Seismitoad and leave it at the Pokémon Day Care to find an Egg and then hatch it
Pokémon Black Version	Pinwheel Forest Entrance
Pokémon White Version	Pinwheel Forest Entrance

Unova Pokédex No. 229
Palpitoad
Main ways to register in the Unova Pokédex

Version	Location
Pokémon Black Version 2	Route 8 (spring/summer/autumn only)
Pokémon White Version 2	Route 8 (spring/summer/autumn only)
Pokémon Black Version	
Pokémon White Version	

Unova Pokédex No. 230
Seismitoad
Main ways to register in the Unova Pokédex
Pokémon Black Version 2: Route 8 (rippling water)
Pokémon White Version 2: Route 8 (rippling water)
Pokémon Black Version
Pokémon White Version
Unova Pokédex No. 231
Stunfisk
Main ways to register in the Unova Pokédex
Pokémon Black Version 2: Route 8 (water surface)
Pokémon White Version 2: Route 8 (water surface)
Pokémon Black Version
Pokémon White Version
Unova Pokédex No. 232
Shuckle
Main ways to register in the Unova Pokédex
Pokémon Black Version 2: Seaside Cave B1F
Pokémon White Version 2: Seaside Cave B1F
Pokémon Black Version
Pokémon White Version
Unova Pokédex No. 233
Mantyke
Main ways to register in the Unova Pokédex
Pokémon Black Version 2: Route 21 (water surface)
Pokémon White Version 2: Route 21 (water surface)
Pokémon Black Version
Pokémon White Version
Unova Pokédex No. 234
Mantine
Main ways to register in the Unova Pokédex
Pokémon Black Version 2: Route 21 (rippling water)
Pokémon White Version 2: Route 21 (rippling water)
Pokémon Black Version
Pokémon White Version
Unova Pokédex No. 235
Remoraid
Main ways to register in the Unova Pokédex
Pokémon Black Version 2: Undella Bay (water surface)
Pokémon White Version 2: Undella Bay (water surface)
Pokémon Black Version
Pokémon White Version
Unova Pokédex No. 236
Octillery
Main ways to register in the Unova Pokédex
Pokémon Black Version 2: Undella Bay (cast into rippling water with the Super Rod)
Pokémon White Version 2: Undella Bay (cast into rippling water with the Super Rod)
Pokémon Black Version
Pokémon White Version
Unova Pokédex No. 237
Corsola
Main ways to register in the Unova Pokédex
Pokémon Black Version 2: Humilau City (rippling water)
Pokémon White Version 2: Humilau City (rippling water)
Pokémon Black Version
Pokémon White Version
Unova Pokédex No. 238
Staryu
Main ways to register in the Unova Pokédex
Pokémon Black Version 2: Undella Town (water surface)
Pokémon White Version 2: Undella Town (water surface)
Pokémon Black Version
Pokémon White Version
Unova Pokédex No. 239
Starmie
Main ways to register in the Unova Pokédex
Pokémon Black Version 2: Undella Town (rippling water)
Pokémon White Version 2: Undella Town (rippling water)
Pokémon Black Version
Pokémon White Version
Unova Pokédex No. 240
Wailmer
Main ways to register in the Unova Pokédex
Pokémon Black Version 2: Undella Bay (rippling water)
Pokémon White Version 2: Undella Bay (rippling water)
Pokémon Black Version
Pokémon White Version
Unova Pokédex No. 241
Wailord
Main ways to register in the Unova Pokédex
Pokémon Black Version 2: Undella Bay (rippling water)
Pokémon White Version 2: Undella Bay (rippling water)
Pokémon Black Version
Pokémon White Version
Unova Pokédex No. 242
Lapras
Main ways to register in the Unova Pokédex
Pokémon Black Version 2: Village Bridge (rippling water)
Pokémon White Version 2: Village Bridge (rippling water)
Pokémon Black Version
Pokémon White Version
Unova Pokédex No. 243
Spheal
Main ways to register in the Unova Pokédex
Pokémon Black Version 2: Undella Bay (water surface in winter)
Pokémon White Version 2: Undella Bay (water surface in winter)
Pokémon Black Version
Pokémon White Version
Unova Pokédex No. 244
Sealeo
Main ways to register in the Unova Pokédex
Pokémon Black Version 2: Undella Bay (rippling water in winter)
Pokémon White Version 2: Undella Bay (rippling water in winter)
Pokémon Black Version
Pokémon White Version
Unova Pokédex No. 245
Walrein
Main ways to register in the Unova Pokédex
Pokémon Black Version 2: Undella Bay (rippling water in winter)
Pokémon White Version 2: Undella Bay (rippling water in winter)
Pokémon Black Version
Pokémon White Version
Unova Pokédex No. 246
Swablu
Main ways to register in the Unova Pokédex
Pokémon Black Version 2: Route 14
Pokémon White Version 2: Route 14
Pokémon Black Version
Pokémon White Version
Unova Pokédex No. 247
Altaria
Main ways to register in the Unova Pokédex
Pokémon Black Version 2: Route 14
Pokémon White Version 2: Route 14
Pokémon Black Version
Pokémon White Version
Unova Pokédex No. 248
Vulpix
Main ways to register in the Unova Pokédex
Pokémon Black Version 2: Abundant Shrine
Pokémon White Version 2: Abundant Shrine
Pokémon Black Version
Pokémon White Version
Unova Pokédex No. 249
Ninetales
Main ways to register in the Unova Pokédex
Pokémon Black Version 2: Abundant Shrine (rustling grass)
Pokémon White Version 2: Abundant Shrine (rustling grass)
Pokémon Black Version
Pokémon White Version

Unova Pokédex No. 250 — Bronzor

Main ways to register in the Unova Pokédex	
Pokémon Black Version 2	Abundant Shrine
Pokémon White Version 2	Abundant Shrine
Pokémon Black Version	
Pokémon White Version	

Unova Pokédex No. 251 — Bronzong

Main ways to register in the Unova Pokédex	
Pokémon Black Version 2	Abundant Shrine (dark grass)
Pokémon White Version 2	Abundant Shrine (dark grass)
Pokémon Black Version	
Pokémon White Version	

Unova Pokédex No. 252 — Sneasel

Main ways to register in the Unova Pokédex	
Pokémon Black Version 2	Giant Chasm Cave
Pokémon White Version 2	Giant Chasm Cave
Pokémon Black Version	
Pokémon White Version	

Unova Pokédex No. 253 — Weavile

Main ways to register in the Unova Pokédex	
Pokémon Black Version 2	Have Sneasel hold the Razor Claw and level it up at night or late night
Pokémon White Version 2	Have Sneasel hold the Razor Claw and level it up at night or late night
Pokémon Black Version	
Pokémon White Version	

Unova Pokédex No. 254 — Delibird

Main ways to register in the Unova Pokédex	
Pokémon Black Version 2	Route 22
Pokémon White Version 2	Route 22
Pokémon Black Version	
Pokémon White Version	

Unova Pokédex No. 255 — Vanillite

Main ways to register in the Unova Pokédex	
Pokémon Black Version 2	Catch Vanillish or Vanilluxe, leave them at the Pokémon Day Care, find an Egg, and hatch it
Pokémon White Version 2	Catch Vanillish or Vanilluxe, leave them at the Pokémon Day Care, find an Egg, and hatch it
Pokémon Black Version	Cold Storage Area
Pokémon White Version	Cold Storage Area

Unova Pokédex No. 256 — Vanillish

Main ways to register in the Unova Pokédex	
Pokémon Black Version 2	Giant Chasm Cave
Pokémon White Version 2	Giant Chasm Cave
Pokémon Black Version	
Pokémon White Version	

Unova Pokédex No. 257 — Vanilluxe

Main ways to register in the Unova Pokédex	
Pokémon Black Version 2	Giant Chasm Entrance (rustling grass)
Pokémon White Version 2	Giant Chasm Entrance (rustling grass)
Pokémon Black Version	
Pokémon White Version	

Unova Pokédex No. 258 — Swinub

Main ways to register in the Unova Pokédex	
Pokémon Black Version 2	Catch Piloswine, leave them at the Pokémon Day Care, find an Egg, and hatch it
Pokémon White Version 2	Catch Piloswine, leave them at the Pokémon Day Care, find an Egg, and hatch it
Pokémon Black Version	
Pokémon White Version	

Unova Pokédex No. 259 — Piloswine

Main ways to register in the Unova Pokédex	
Pokémon Black Version 2	Giant Chasm
Pokémon White Version 2	Giant Chasm
Pokémon Black Version	
Pokémon White Version	

Unova Pokédex No. 260 — Mamoswine

Main ways to register in the Unova Pokédex	
Pokémon Black Version 2	Giant Chasm Crater Forest (rustling grass)
Pokémon White Version 2	Giant Chasm Crater Forest (rustling grass)
Pokémon Black Version	
Pokémon White Version	

Unova Pokédex No. 261 — Ditto

Main ways to register in the Unova Pokédex	
Pokémon Black Version 2	Giant Chasm Crater Forest
Pokémon White Version 2	Giant Chasm Crater Forest
Pokémon Black Version	
Pokémon White Version	

Unova Pokédex No. 262 — Beldum

Main ways to register in the Unova Pokédex	
Pokémon Black Version 2	Catch Metang or Metagross, leave them at the Pokémon Day Care, find an Egg, and hatch it
Pokémon White Version 2	Catch Metang or Metagross, leave them at the Pokémon Day Care, find an Egg, and hatch it
Pokémon Black Version	
Pokémon White Version	

Unova Pokédex No. 263 — Metang

Main ways to register in the Unova Pokédex	
Pokémon Black Version 2	Giant Chasm Crater Forest
Pokémon White Version 2	Giant Chasm Crater Forest
Pokémon Black Version	
Pokémon White Version	

Unova Pokédex No. 264 — Metagross

Main ways to register in the Unova Pokédex	
Pokémon Black Version 2	Giant Chasm Crater Forest (rustling grass)
Pokémon White Version 2	Giant Chasm Crater Forest (rustling grass)
Pokémon Black Version	
Pokémon White Version	

Unova Pokédex No. 265 — Seel

Main ways to register in the Unova Pokédex	
Pokémon Black Version 2	Seaside Cave 1F
Pokémon White Version 2	Seaside Cave 1F
Pokémon Black Version	
Pokémon White Version	

Unova Pokédex No. 266 — Dewgong

Main ways to register in the Unova Pokédex	
Pokémon Black Version 2	Seaside Cave 1F (rippling water)
Pokémon White Version 2	Seaside Cave 1F (rippling water)
Pokémon Black Version	
Pokémon White Version	

Unova Pokédex No. 267 — Throh

Main ways to register in the Unova Pokédex	
Pokémon Black Version 2	Route 23 (rustling grass)
Pokémon White Version 2	Route 23
Pokémon Black Version	
Pokémon White Version	

Unova Pokédex No. 268 — Sawk

Main ways to register in the Unova Pokédex	
Pokémon Black Version 2	Route 23
Pokémon White Version 2	Route 23 (rustling grass)
Pokémon Black Version	
Pokémon White Version	

Unova Pokédex No. 269 — Bouffalant

Main ways to register in the Unova Pokédex	
Pokémon Black Version 2	Route 23
Pokémon White Version 2	Route 23
Pokémon Black Version	
Pokémon White Version	

Unova Pokédex No. 270

Druddigon

Main ways to register in the Unova Pokédex

Version	Method
Pokémon Black Version 2	Victory Road Cave 3F
Pokémon White Version 2	Victory Road Cave 3F
Pokémon Black Version	
Pokémon White Version	

Unova Pokédex No. 271

Golett

Main ways to register in the Unova Pokédex

Version	Method
Pokémon Black Version 2	Catch Golurk, leave them at the Pokémon Day Care, find an Egg, and hatch it
Pokémon White Version 2	Catch Golurk, leave them at the Pokémon Day Care, find an Egg, and hatch it
Pokémon Black Version	Dragonspiral Tower 1F
Pokémon White Version	Dragonspiral Tower 1F

Unova Pokédex No. 272

Golurk

Main ways to register in the Unova Pokédex

Version	Method
Pokémon Black Version 2	Victory Road Cave 1F
Pokémon White Version 2	Victory Road Cave 1F
Pokémon Black Version	
Pokémon White Version	

Unova Pokédex No. 273

Deino

Main ways to register in the Unova Pokédex

Version	Method
Pokémon Black Version 2	Catch Zweilous, leave them at the Pokémon Day Care, find an Egg, and hatch it
Pokémon White Version 2	Catch Zweilous, leave them at the Pokémon Day Care, find an Egg, and hatch it
Pokémon Black Version	Victory Road 1F
Pokémon White Version	Victory Road 1F

Unova Pokédex No. 274

Zweilous

Main ways to register in the Unova Pokédex

Version	Method
Pokémon Black Version 2	Victory Road Cave 3F
Pokémon White Version 2	Victory Road Cave 3F
Pokémon Black Version	
Pokémon White Version	

Unova Pokédex No. 275

Hydreigon

Main ways to register in the Unova Pokédex

Version	Method
Pokémon Black Version 2	Level up Zweilous to Lv. 64
Pokémon White Version 2	Level up Zweilous to Lv. 64
Pokémon Black Version	
Pokémon White Version	

Unova Pokédex No. 276

Slakoth

Main ways to register in the Unova Pokédex

Version	Method
Pokémon Black Version 2	Catch Vigoroth or Slaking, leave them at the Pokémon Day Care, find an Egg, and hatch it
Pokémon White Version 2	Catch Vigoroth or Slaking, leave them at the Pokémon Day Care, find an Egg, and hatch it
Pokémon Black Version	
Pokémon White Version	

Unova Pokédex No. 277

Vigoroth

Main ways to register in the Unova Pokédex

Version	Method
Pokémon Black Version 2	Deep in the Pinwheel Forest
Pokémon White Version 2	Deep in the Pinwheel Forest
Pokémon Black Version	
Pokémon White Version	

Unova Pokédex No. 278

Slaking

Main ways to register in the Unova Pokédex

Version	Method
Pokémon Black Version 2	Deep in the Pinwheel Forest (rustling grass)
Pokémon White Version 2	Deep in the Pinwheel Forest (rustling grass)
Pokémon Black Version	
Pokémon White Version	

Unova Pokédex No. 279

Corphish

Main ways to register in the Unova Pokédex

Version	Method
Pokémon Black Version 2	Route 3 (water surface)
Pokémon White Version 2	Route 3 (water surface)
Pokémon Black Version	
Pokémon White Version	

Unova Pokédex No. 280

Crawdaunt

Main ways to register in the Unova Pokédex

Version	Method
Pokémon Black Version 2	Route 3 (rippling water)
Pokémon White Version 2	Route 3 (rippling water)
Pokémon Black Version	
Pokémon White Version	

Unova Pokédex No. 281

Igglybuff

Main ways to register in the Unova Pokédex

Version	Method
Pokémon Black Version 2	Catch Jigglypuff or Wigglytuff, leave them at the Pokémon Day Care, find an Egg, and hatch it
Pokémon White Version 2	Catch Jigglypuff or Wigglytuff, leave them at the Pokémon Day Care, find an Egg, and hatch it
Pokémon Black Version	
Pokémon White Version	

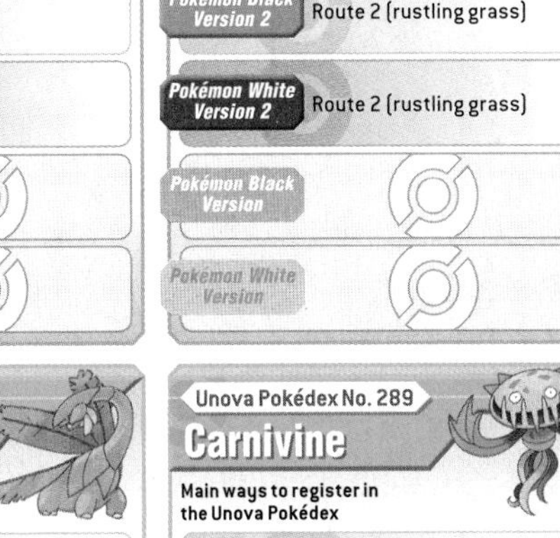

Unova Pokédex No. 282

Jigglypuff

Main ways to register in the Unova Pokédex

Version	Method
Pokémon Black Version 2	Dreamyard
Pokémon White Version 2	Dreamyard
Pokémon Black Version	
Pokémon White Version	

Unova Pokédex No. 283

Wigglytuff

Main ways to register in the Unova Pokédex

Version	Method
Pokémon Black Version 2	Dreamyard (rustling grass)
Pokémon White Version 2	Dreamyard (rustling grass)
Pokémon Black Version	
Pokémon White Version	

Unova Pokédex No. 284

Lickitung

Main ways to register in the Unova Pokédex

Version	Method
Pokémon Black Version 2	Route 2
Pokémon White Version 2	Route 2
Pokémon Black Version	
Pokémon White Version	

Unova Pokédex No. 285

Lickilicky

Main ways to register in the Unova Pokédex

Version	Method
Pokémon Black Version 2	Route 2 (rustling grass)
Pokémon White Version 2	Route 2 (rustling grass)
Pokémon Black Version	
Pokémon White Version	

Unova Pokédex No. 286

Yanma

Main ways to register in the Unova Pokédex

Version	Method
Pokémon Black Version 2	Pinwheel Forest Entrance
Pokémon White Version 2	Pinwheel Forest Entrance
Pokémon Black Version	
Pokémon White Version	

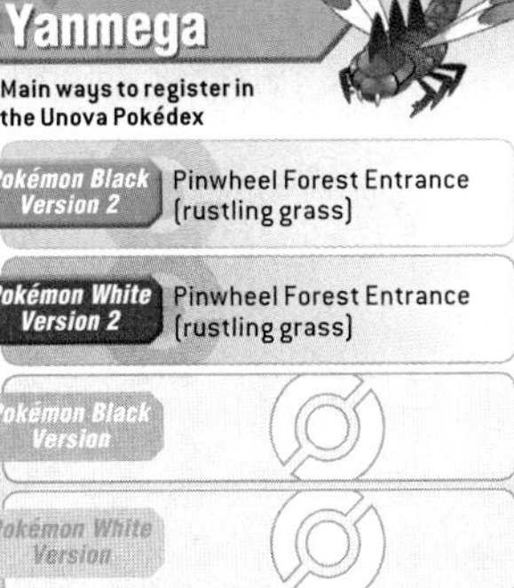

Unova Pokédex No. 287

Yanmega

Main ways to register in the Unova Pokédex

Version	Method
Pokémon Black Version 2	Pinwheel Forest Entrance (rustling grass)
Pokémon White Version 2	Pinwheel Forest Entrance (rustling grass)
Pokémon Black Version	
Pokémon White Version	

Unova Pokédex No. 288

Tropius

Main ways to register in the Unova Pokédex

Version	Method
Pokémon Black Version 2	Route 18
Pokémon White Version 2	Route 18
Pokémon Black Version	
Pokémon White Version	

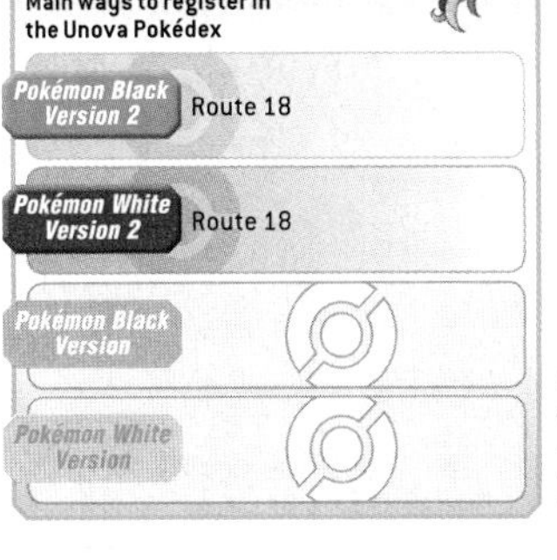

Unova Pokédex No. 289

Carnivine

Main ways to register in the Unova Pokédex

Version	Method
Pokémon Black Version 2	Route 18
Pokémon White Version 2	Route 18
Pokémon Black Version	
Pokémon White Version	

Unova Pokédex No. 290

Croagunk

Main ways to register in the Unova Pokédex

Pokémon Black Version 2	Route 8 (spring/summer/autumn only)
Pokémon White Version 2	Route 8 (spring/summer/autumn only)
Pokémon Black Version	
Pokémon White Version	

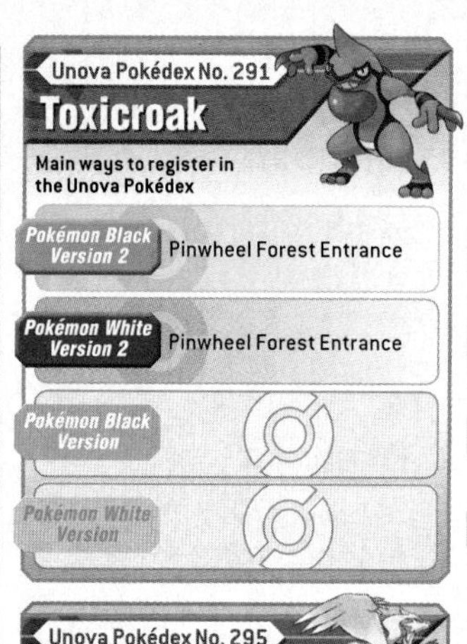

Unova Pokédex No. 291

Toxicroak

Main ways to register in the Unova Pokédex

Pokémon Black Version 2	Pinwheel Forest Entrance
Pokémon White Version 2	Pinwheel Forest Entrance
Pokémon Black Version	
Pokémon White Version	

Unova Pokédex No. 292

Larvitar

Main ways to register in the Unova Pokédex

Pokémon Black Version 2	Catch Pupitar or Tyranitar, leave them at the Pokémon Day Care, find an Egg, and hatch it
Pokémon White Version 2	Catch Pupitar or Tyranitar, leave them at the Pokémon Day Care, find an Egg, and hatch it
Pokémon Black Version	
Pokémon White Version	

Unova Pokédex No. 293

Pupitar

Main ways to register in the Unova Pokédex

Pokémon Black Version 2	Route 15
Pokémon White Version 2	Route 15
Pokémon Black Version	
Pokémon White Version	

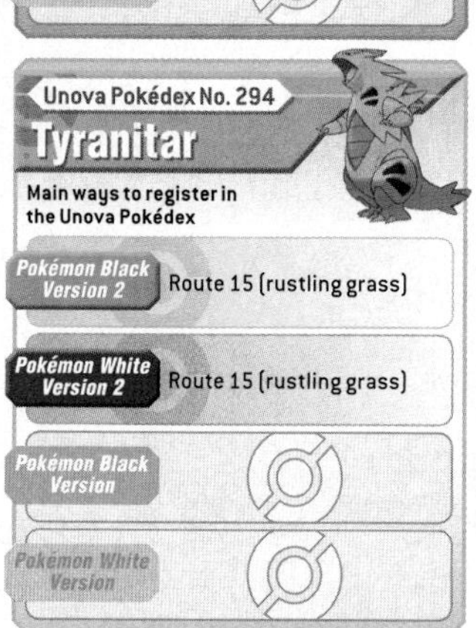

Unova Pokédex No. 294

Tyranitar

Main ways to register in the Unova Pokédex

Pokémon Black Version 2	Route 15 (rustling grass)
Pokémon White Version 2	Route 15 (rustling grass)
Pokémon Black Version	
Pokémon White Version	

Unova Pokédex No. 295

Reshiram

Main ways to register in the Unova Pokédex

Pokémon Black Version 2	Link Trade
Pokémon White Version 2	Dragonspiral Tower
Pokémon Black Version	N's Castle
Pokémon White Version	

Unova Pokédex No. 296

Zekrom

Main ways to register in the Unova Pokédex

Pokémon Black Version 2	Dragonspiral Tower
Pokémon White Version 2	Link Trade
Pokémon Black Version	
Pokémon White Version	N's Castle

Unova Pokédex No. 297

Kyurem

Main ways to register in the Unova Pokédex

Pokémon Black Version 2	Giant Chasm Deepest Part (after the Hall of Fame)
Pokémon White Version 2	Giant Chasm Deepest Part (after the Hall of Fame)
Pokémon Black Version	
Pokémon White Version	

Unova Pokédex No. 298

Keldeo

Main ways to register in the Unova Pokédex

Keldeo Ordinary Form can be obtained during special distribution periods. Check www.pokemon.com to find out if any Pokémon are currently being distributed.

Unova Pokédex No. 299

Meloetta

Main ways to register in the Unova Pokédex

Meloetta Aria Forme can be obtained during special distribution periods. Check www.pokemon.com to find out if any Pokémon are currently being distributed.

Unova Pokédex No. 300

Genesect

Main ways to register in the Unova Pokédex

Genesect can be obtained during special distribution periods. Check www.pokemon.com to find out if any Pokémon are currently being distributed.

Pokéstar Studios

Shoot Fantastic Movies at Pokéstar Studios

Play the Lead Role in Filming Blockbuster Movies!

Pokéstar Studios is a fabulous location where you can shoot all kinds of movies. You'll be the star of the show! Polish your performance and you'll get new scripts. There are 40 movies to star in. Make each one a masterpiece!

Become a Star at Pokéstar Studios

Pokéstar Studios  Pokéstar Studios is located to the north of Virbank City

You'll find Pokéstar Studios north of Virbank City. After your first visit, you can use Fly to return anytime you want. Pokéstar Studios has studios where you can shoot scripts, as well as theaters to screen the resulting movies. The posters near the theaters change depending on which movies are playing.

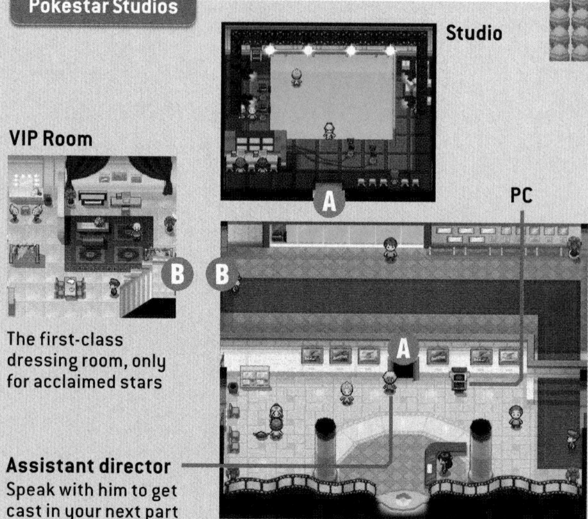

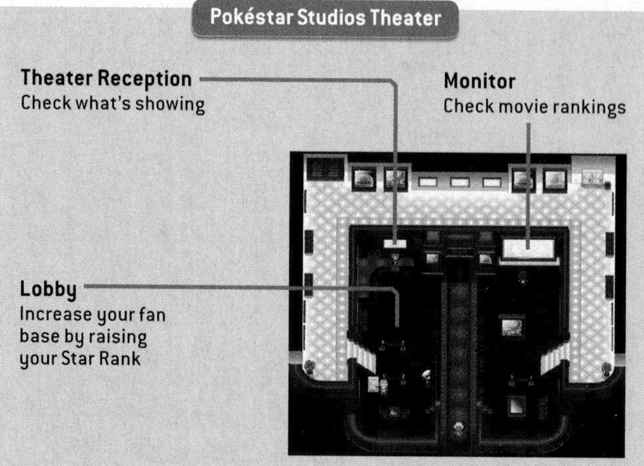

Pokéstar Studios ② Give an effective performance and the audience will tell you if you hit the mark

The two activities of Pokéstar Studios are shooting and screening movies. Shooting a movie means you'll act in a movie following the script received from the studio. Screening a movie means watching the completed film. The audience will give you its reaction to your performance.

Pokéstar Studios step-by-step

Step ① Select a script

When you want to act in a movie, talk to the assistant director to select a script. Your costar is usually a rental Pokémon.

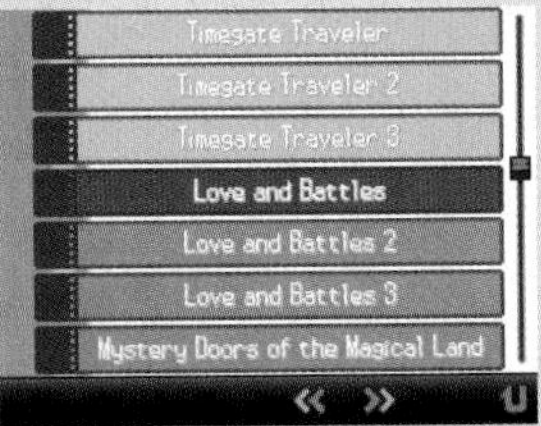

Step ② Act in the movie

Follow the script for a successful shoot. Your choices of the lines you speak and the moves your Pokémon make will determine the movie's plot.

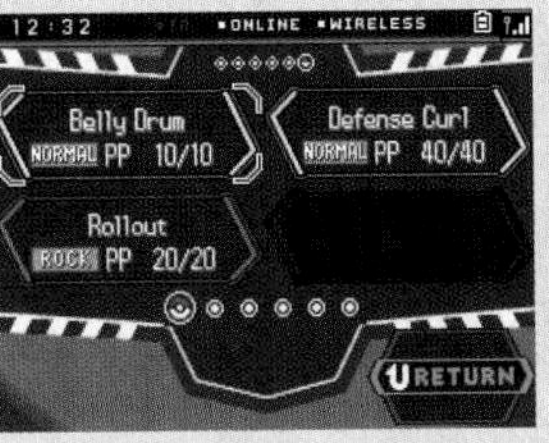

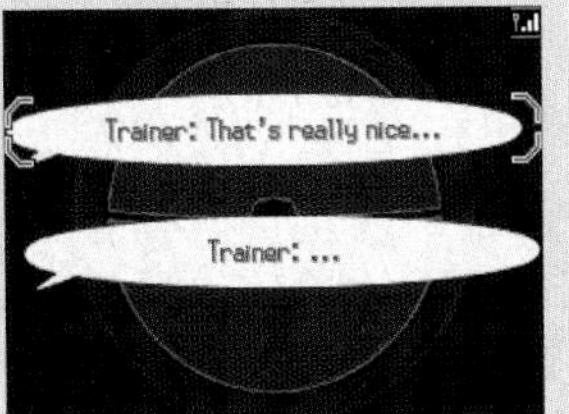

Step ③ Screen the movie in the theater

Completed movies can be screened right away at the theaters. You won't have to do anything while you watch movies. Just sit back and enjoy different stories and endings. After you've watched it completely through once, you can press the B Button to stop rolling the movie on subsequent viewings.

Step ④ Pay attention to your reviews

You'll have more fans waiting for you at the theaters as your Star Rank goes up. Your admirers may even give you items.

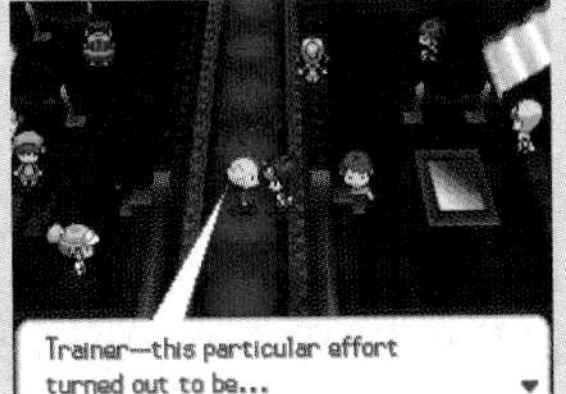

Trainer—this particular effort turned out to be...

This is from a very moved Policeman!
Oh, it's a present, not a bribe!

Tip: The stunning conclusion!

There are three possible endings: happy, sad, or weird, based on how you act. After you achieve a happy ending, your Pokémon can costar in the same script.

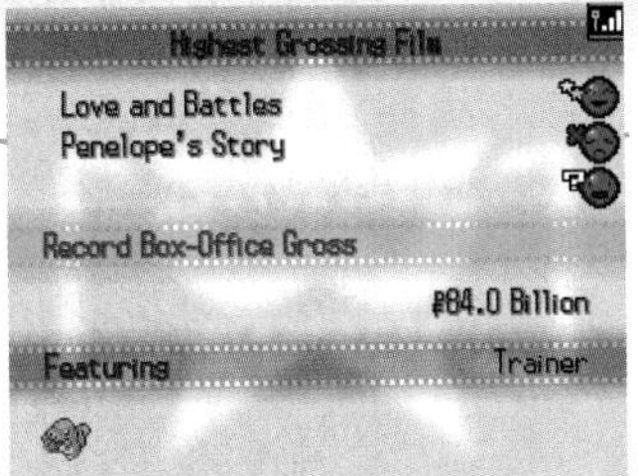

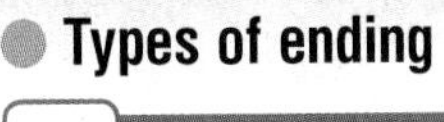

Types of ending

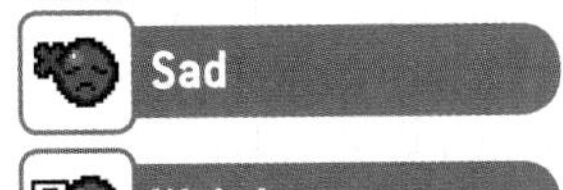

- Happy
- Sad
- Weird

Pokéstar Studios 3 Choose moves for your Pokémon and choose the lines you'll say

Shooting requires you to follow the script, select Pokémon moves, and choose your own lines. The scripts will provide clues. Use those clues to guess the correct moves and lines to complete the movie with a happy ending.

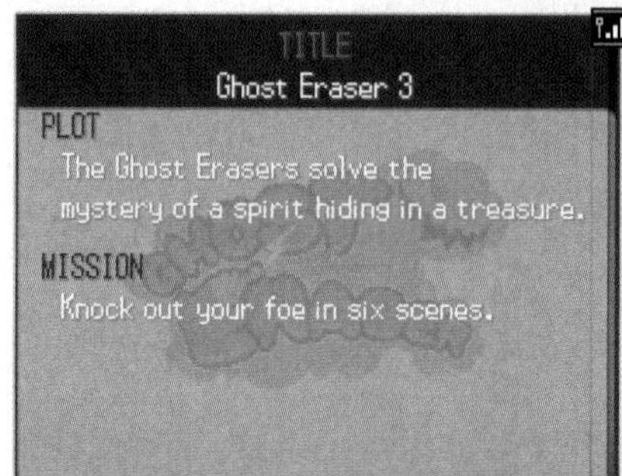

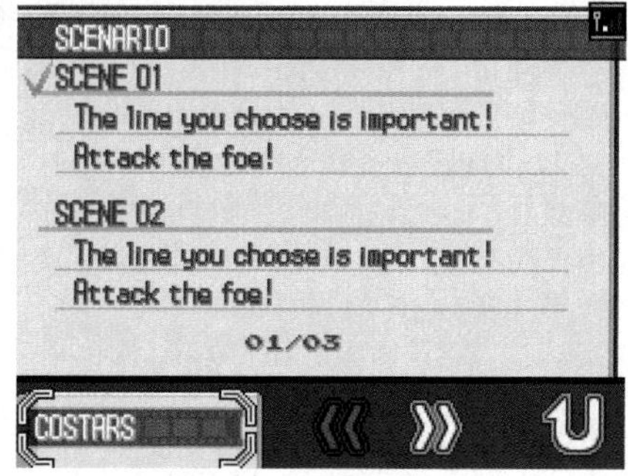

Shooting step-by-step

Choose a move

Choose a line

Check the director's comments

Tip: The storyline and the director's character are important clues when choosing your lines.

To film a happy ending, you'll have to choose the right lines. But this might not be so easy. Seemingly good lines are often wrong. Each director has his or her own preferences. Use your understanding of them to guess which line is most preferred.

Sergeo Pokémonski

Takashi Pokémi

John Pokénter

Sydney Pokémet

David Pokénch

Pokéstar Studios 4 In the theater, enjoy the story and the audience's reaction

Have fun watching your movie roll. During a movie shooting, some of the storyline is held back. When you screen the completed movie, you'll see the whole story. It's your chance to be involved in the drama and surprises on screen. Remember to keep an eye on the audience reaction, as the pros do.

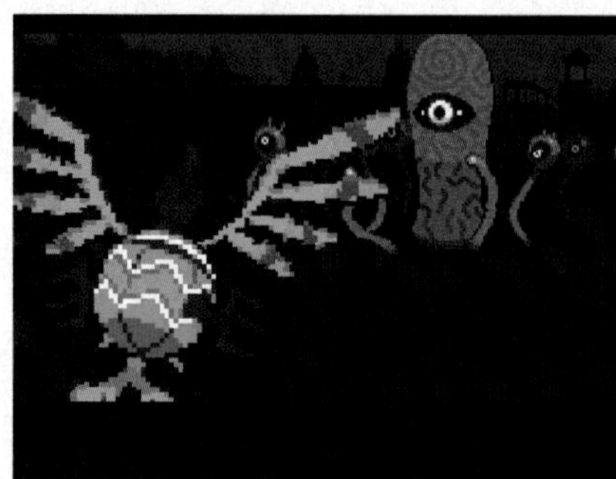

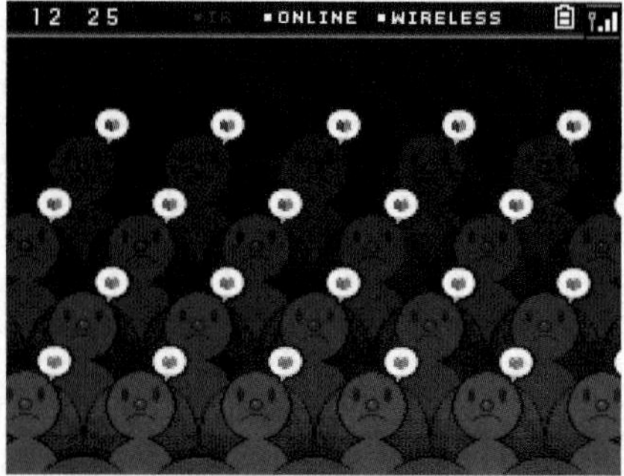

Pokéstar Studios 5 Show your star quality and you'll discover rank has its privileges

As your Star Rank goes up, people at Pokéstar Studios treat you with a certain respect. You'll be given new scripts, and your movies will become more popular. Based on the popularity of your movies, your fans will shower you with various gifts.

That last one was entertaining!
Your movies never miss!

Your rank

Type of Ending	Star Rank
Weird	Improves a lot
Happy	Improves slightly
Sad	Improves a fraction

Items from your fans

Fans	Items You May Receive			
	Improved Items ← → Standard Items			
Type 1	Pretty Wing	Lava Cookie ×5	Lemonade ×5	Fresh Water
Type 2	Max Revive	Hyper Potion ×5	Berry Juice	Potion
Type 3	Nugget	Moomoo Milk ×5	Escape Rope	Favored Mail
Type 4	Star Piece	Old Gateau ×5	RageCandyBar	Sweet Heart
Type 5	Full Restore	Big Pearl	Energy Root	EnergyPowder

Pokéstar Studios 6 Your Pokémon shines and becomes a star!

Each of your Pokémon also has its Star Rank. As its Star Rank goes up, the Box-Office Gross of that movie goes up, too. Star Pokémon will display additional special effects in battle. These effects occur during normal battles in your adventure and in Link Battles as well.

Pokémon rank

Type of Ending	Star Rank
Weird	Your Pokémon becomes a star
Happy	Improves moderately
Sad	Decreases

Pokéstar Studios 7 Play your part like a movie star, earn glowing reviews, and be richly rewarded!

Pokéstar Studios rewards you in many ways. Plus, there's a slew of Medals you could get from Mr. Medal. When you successfully reach happy endings in all 40 movies, a bronze statue will appear in Pokéstar Studios, and you'll be allowed to use the exclusive VIP Room, which only the few and the proud can enter.

Bronze Statue

You are the true star
of Pokéstar Studios!

VIP Room

From now on, only you have
permission to use this room freely!

New Face Hero

Hero Movie Star

Cop Movie Master

UFO Movie Master

Monster Movie Master

Sci-Fi Movie Master

Romantic Movie Star

Fantasy Movie Master

Comedic Movie Star

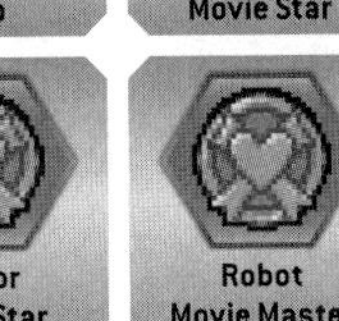

Horror Movie Star

Robot Movie Master

Ghost Movie Master

Hero Ending

Popular Movie Star

Masterpiece Star

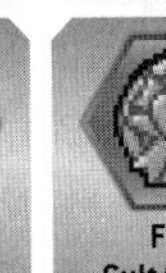
Blockbuster Star

First Cult Classic

Cult Classic Star

Check p. 448 for the Medal list.

Pokéstar Studios—All 40 Movies

◆ Note: Some movies are slightly different if you're playing as a girl.

Brycen-Man

MISSION: Knock out an opponent in every scene.

COSTARS

Pawniard ♂ Lv. 15 (Dark / Steel) ●ITEM None ●ABILITY Defiant

●MOVES	Type		
Brick Break	Fighting		
Aerial Ace	Flying		

Vullaby ♀ Lv. 13 (Dark / Steel) ●ITEM None ●ABILITY Big Pecks

●MOVES	Type		
Faint Attack	Dark		
Air Slash	Flying		

Hint: Choose moves that can target the weaknesses of Pawniard and Vullaby and knock them out with one hit.

SCENARIO

SCENE	SCENARIO
SCENE 01	Use a move Dark type is weak to!
SCENE 02	Use a move Flying type is weak to!

Brycen-Man Strikes Back

MISSION: Last for five scenes. Don't knock out your foe.

COSTARS

Honchkrow ♂ Lv. 34 (Dark / Flying) ●ITEM Scope Lens ●ABILITY Super Luck

●MOVES	Type		
Astonish	Ghost	Wing Attack	Flying
Thief	Dark		

Scrafty ♂ Lv. 34 (Dark / Fighting) ●ITEM Wide Lens ●ABILITY Shed Skin

●MOVES	Type		
Fire Punch	Fire	Hi Jump Kick	Fighting
Bulk Up	Fighting		

Hint: Avoid choosing an attack move so you won't beat Honchkrow. Instead, choose moves to protect your Pokémon.

SCENARIO

SCENE	SCENARIO
SCENE 01	The line you choose is important!
	The Lucario Kid: Out of MY way!
	The Lucario Kid: Why would I?
	The Lucario Kid: Bathroom?
SCENE 02	Protect yourself from your foe's attack!
SCENE 03	Protect yourself from your foe's attack! The line you choose is important!
	The Lucario Kid: You want what?
	The Lucario Kid: Bathroom, right?
	The Lucario Kid: So suspicious!
SCENE 04	Protect yourself from your foe's attack!
SCENE 05	Protect yourself from your foe's attack!

Brycen-Man Strikes Back 2

MISSION: Knock out SFX Prop H1 in 15 scenes. Ignoring other foes is OK.

COSTARS

Prop H1 ♂ Lv. 56 (Dark / Psychic) ●ITEM Eject Button ●ABILITY Levitate

●MOVES	Type		
U-turn	Bug	Night Shade	Ghost
Psychic	Psychic	Ice Beam	Ice

Zoroark ♂ Lv. 54 (Dark) ●ITEM Focus Sash ●ABILITY Illusion

●MOVES	Type		
Flamethrower	Fire	U-turn	Bug
Night	Dark	Focus Blast	Fighting

Mandibuzz ♀ Lv. 54 (Dark / Flying) ●ITEM Eject Button ●ABILITY Big Pecks

●MOVES	Type		
U-turn	Bug	Dark Pulse	Dark
Mirror Move	Flying	Air Slash	Flying

Hint: Knock out Zoroark and Vullaby quickly by targeting their weaknesses so Brycen-Man will use Prop H1 in early scenes.

SCENARIO

SCENE	SCENARIO
SCENE 01	The line you choose is important!!
	The Lucario Kid: I'll win easily!
	The Lucario Kid: Am I done for?
	The Lucario Kid: I must do this!
	The Lucario Kid: Better run...?
SCENE 02	Determine the SFX Prop's type!
SCENE 03	Pay attention to your foe's switches!
SCENE 04	The line you choose is important!
	The Lucario Kid: Are you OK?
	The Lucario Kid: Now's my chance.
	The Lucario Kid: Take this!
	The Lucario Kid: ...
SCENE 05	Pay attention to your foe's switches!
SCENE 06	Deliver a decisive blow!
SCENE 07	Deliver a decisive blow!
SCENE 08	Deliver a decisive blow!
SCENE 09	Deliver a decisive blow!
SCENE 10	Deliver a decisive blow!
SCENE 11	Deliver a decisive blow!
SCENE 12	Deliver a decisive blow!
SCENE 13	Deliver a decisive blow!
SCENE 14	Deliver a decisive blow!
SCENE 15	Deliver a decisive blow!

Full Metal Cop

MISSION: Let your Pokémon be knocked out in five scenes.

COSTARS

Heracross ♂ Lv. 20 (Bug / Fighting) ●ITEM None ●ABILITY Swarm

●MOVES	Type		
Horn Attack	Normal		
Tackle	Normal		

Hint: To let your Pokémon be knocked out, you must avoid defeating your foe's Pokémon. Choose a move that won't target its weaknesses.

SCENARIO

SCENE	SCENARIO
SCENE 01	Use a move with low power! The line you choose is important!
	The Sneasel Ninja: I won't lose!
	The Sneasel Ninja: I'll surrender.
SCENE 02	Use a move with low power!
SCENE 03	Use a move with low power!
SCENE 04	Throw the battle!
SCENE 05	Throw the battle!

Full Metal Cop 2

MISSION: Let your Pokémon be knocked out in eight scenes.

COSTARS

Sawk ♂ Lv. 30 (Fighting) ●ITEM Toxic Orb ●ABILITY Sturdy

●MOVES	Type		
Counter	Fighting		
Endure	Normal		

Hint: To let your Pokémon be knocked out, you must avoid defeating your foe's Pokémon. Pay attention to Sawk's moves and Ability.

SCENARIO

SCENE	SCENARIO
SCENE 01	Raise your stats! The line you choose is important!
	The Sneasel Ninja: Stop bluffing!
	The Sneasel Ninja: Cool!
SCENE 02	Attack your foe!
SCENE 03	Throw the battle!
SCENE 04	Throw the battle!
SCENE 05	Throw the battle!
SCENE 06	Throw the battle!
SCENE 07	Throw the battle!
SCENE 08	Throw the battle!

Tip

Brycen is now an actor

Brycen was the Icirrus City Gym Leader in *Pokémon Black Version* and *Pokémon White Version*. He went back to acting because he wanted people to see bonds between humans and Pokémon through his movies.

Full Metal Cop 3

MISSION Let all of your Pokémon be knocked out in 10 scenes.

COSTARS

Sewaddle ♀ Lv. 30 (Bug / Grass)
● ITEM: None ● ABILITY: Chlorophyll

● MOVES	Type		
Flail	Normal		
Endure	Normal		

Hint Your costar Sewaddle is not a strong Pokémon. To have it defeat all of your Pokémon, you'll need to strengthen Sewaddle's moves.

SCENARIO

SCENE	SCENARIO
SCENE 01	Use the weather! The line you choose is important! *The Sneasel Ninja: I see...* *The Sneasel Ninja: Bring it!*
SCENE 02	Use a move the foe's type is weak to!
SCENE 03	Throw the battle!
SCENE 04	Throw the battle!
SCENE 05	Throw the battle!
SCENE 06	Throw the battle!
SCENE 07	Throw the battle!
SCENE 08	Throw the battle!
SCENE 09	Throw the battle!
SCENE 10	Throw the battle!

Full Metal Cop 4

MISSION Let all of your Pokémon be knocked out in 20 scenes.

COSTARS

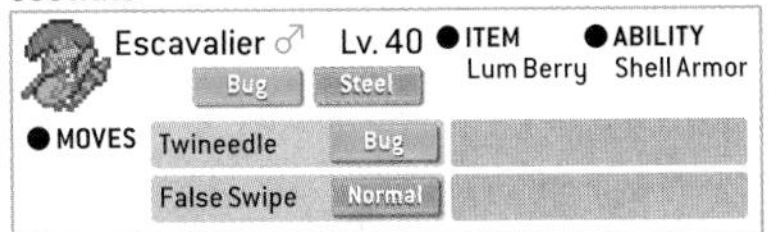

Escavalier ♂ Lv. 40 (Bug / Steel)
● ITEM: Lum Berry ● ABILITY: Shell Armor

● MOVES	Type		
Twineedle	Bug		
False Swipe	Normal		

Hint You have five Sneasel and one Weavile. When your Pokémon is knocked out, choose a Sneasel with a move that suits the script.

SCENARIO

SCENE	SCENARIO
SCENE 01	Raise your foe's stats!
SCENE 02	Use a move with low power!
SCENE 03	Use a move with low power!
SCENE 04	Use a move with low power!
SCENE 05	Use a move with low power!
SCENE 06	Move after your foe!
SCENE 07	Throw the battle!
SCENE 08	Throw the battle!
SCENE 09	Throw the battle!
SCENE 10	Throw the battle!
SCENE 11	Throw the battle!
SCENE 12	Throw the battle!
SCENE 13	Throw the battle!
SCENE 14	Throw the battle!
SCENE 15	Throw the battle!
SCENE 16	Throw the battle!
SCENE 17	Throw the battle!
SCENE 18	Throw the battle!
SCENE 19	Throw the battle!
SCENE 20	Throw the battle!

Invader

MISSION Knock out Elgyem in seven scenes. Don't knock out any other Pokémon.

COSTARS

Roggenrola ♂ Lv. 38 (Rock)
● ITEM: None ● ABILITY: Sturdy

● MOVES	Type	● MOVES	Type
Harden	Normal	Rock Blast	Rock
Sand-Attack	Ground		

Elgyem ♂ Lv. 32 (Psychic)
● ITEM: None ● ABILITY: Telepathy

● MOVES	Type	● MOVES	Type
Psybeam	Psychic	Hidden Power	Normal
Charge Beam	Electric		

Hint You can't knock out Roggenrola, so use a move that switches Roggenrola with Elgyem.

SCENARIO

SCENE	SCENARIO
SCENE 01	Switch your opponent's Pokémon!
SCENE 02	Use a move the foe's type is weak to! The line you choose is important! *You: I can't stand it! Run!* *You: I'll block it here!* *You: What can I do?*
SCENE 03	Use a move the foe's type is weak to!
SCENE 04	Use a move the foe's type is weak to!
SCENE 05	Deliver a decisive blow!
SCENE 06	Deliver a decisive blow!
SCENE 07	Deliver a decisive blow!

Invaders 2

MISSION Knock out SFX Prop U1 with Zap Cannon. Don't knock it out with any other move.

COSTARS

Prop U1 Lv. 38 (Flying / Electric)
● ITEM: BrightPowder ● ABILITY: Levitate

● MOVES	Type	● MOVES	Type
Counter	Fighting	BubbleBeam	Water
Recover	Normal	Signal Beam	Bug

Hint Use a move to raise the accuracy so you can knock out Prop U1 using Zap Cannon, which has low accuracy.

SCENARIO

SCENE	SCENARIO
SCENE 01	Ensure your attack is on target! The line you choose is important! *You: On it!* *You: Eh? What?* *You: Urk. Don't flip out...*
SCENE 02	Make sure you hit the foe!
SCENE 03	Ensure your attack is on target!
SCENE 04	Make sure you hit the foe!
SCENE 05	Ensure your attack is on target!
SCENE 06	Make sure you hit the foe!
SCENE 07	Deliver a decisive blow!
SCENE 08	Deliver a decisive blow!
SCENE 09	Deliver a decisive blow!

Invaders 3

MISSION Knock out Beheeyem in seven scenes. Don't knock out any other foes.

COSTARS

Ferroseed ♀ Lv. 52 (Grass / Steel)
● ITEM: Chesto Berry ● ABILITY: Iron Barbs

● MOVES	Type	● MOVES	Type
Spikes	Ground	Leech Seed	Grass
Iron Defense	Steel	Pin Missile	Bug

Beheeyem ♂ Lv. 40 (Psychic)
● ITEM: Chesto Berry ● ABILITY: Telepathy

● MOVES	Type	● MOVES	Type
Headbutt	Normal	Charge Beam	Electric
Rock Slide	Rock	Thunderbolt	Electric

Hint Use a move to drag Beheeyem into the battle so you won't beat Ferroseed. Use the items you took from the foe.

SCENARIO

SCENE	SCENARIO
SCENE 01	Steal the foe's item!
SCENE 02	Switch your opponent's Pokémon! The line you choose is important! *You: Is that so...?* *You: Whatever...* *You: NO!!* *You: You're serious—*
SCENE 03	Use the foe's item!
SCENE 04	Use the foe's item!
SCENE 05	Use the foe's item!
SCENE 06	Deliver a decisive blow!
SCENE 07	Deliver a decisive blow!

Invaders 4

MISSION Knock out SFX Prop U2 in 10 scenes. Don't knock out the other foe.

COSTARS

Emolga ♀ Lv. 62 (Electric / Flying)
● ITEM: Iron Ball ● ABILITY: Static

● MOVES	Type	● MOVES	Type
Volt Switch	Electric	Pursuit	Dark
Quick Attack	Normal	Light Screen	Psychic

Prop U2 Lv. 47 (Psychic / Electric)
● ITEM: Leftovers ● ABILITY: Levitate

● MOVES	Type	● MOVES	Type
Ice Beam	Ice	Hyper Beam	Normal
Dark Pulse	Dark	Flamethrower	Fire

Hint Prop U2's Ability is Levitate, so Ground-type moves won't hit it. Be resourceful to make these moves hit it.

SCENARIO

SCENE	SCENARIO
SCENE 01	Pay attention to your foe's item!
SCENE 02	Switch your Pokémon!
SCENE 03	Switch your Pokémon! The line you choose is important! *You: Sure, that makes sense.* *You: You're making a mistake!* *You: No! There's another way!* *You: We humans are awesome!*
SCENE 04	Switch your Pokémon!
SCENE 05	Don't be afraid to make sacrifices! Pay attention to your foe's item!
SCENE 06	Use a move the foe is weak to!
SCENE 07	Use a move the foe is weak to!
SCENE 08	Use a move the foe is weak to!
SCENE 09	Deliver a decisive blow!
SCENE 10	Deliver a decisive blow!

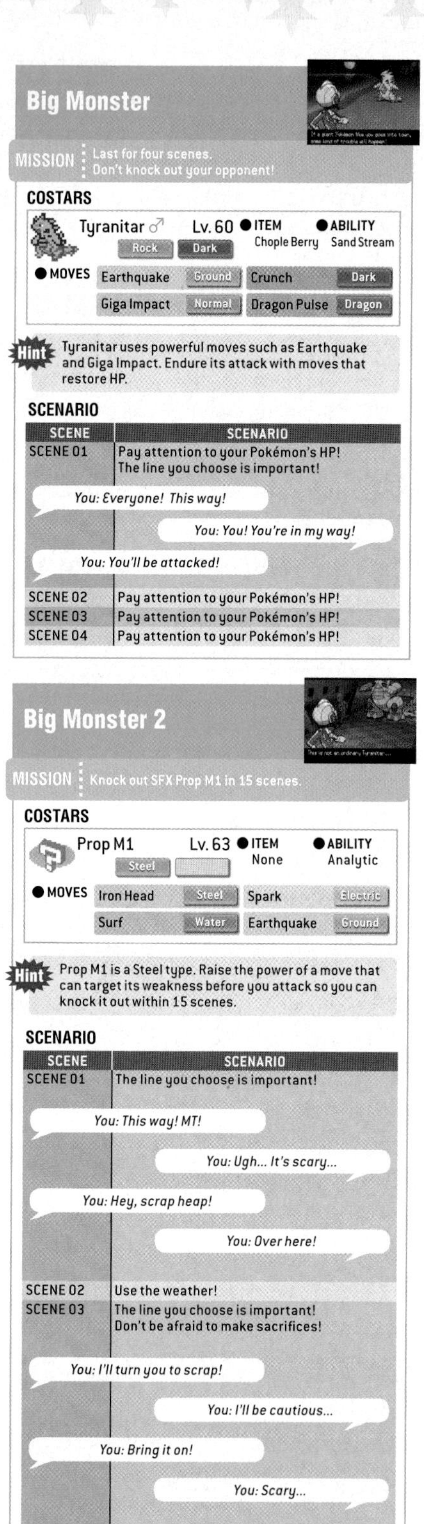

Big Monster

MISSION: Last for four scenes. Don't knock out your opponent!

COSTARS

Pokémon	Type	Lv.	ITEM	ABILITY
Tyranitar ♂	Rock / Dark	Lv. 60	Chople Berry	Sand Stream

MOVES: Earthquake (Ground), Crunch (Dark), Giga Impact (Normal), Dragon Pulse (Dragon)

Hint Tyranitar uses powerful moves such as Earthquake and Giga Impact. Endure its attack with moves that restore HP.

SCENARIO

SCENE	SCENARIO
SCENE 01	Pay attention to your Pokémon's HP! The line you choose is important! *You: Everyone! This way!* *You: You! You're in my way!* *You: You'll be attacked!*
SCENE 02	Pay attention to your Pokémon's HP!
SCENE 03	Pay attention to your Pokémon's HP!
SCENE 04	Pay attention to your Pokémon's HP!

Big Monster 2

MISSION: Knock out SFX Prop M1 in 15 scenes.

COSTARS

Pokémon	Type	Lv.	ITEM	ABILITY
Prop M1	Steel	Lv. 63	None	Analytic

MOVES: Iron Head (Steel), Spark (Electric), Surf (Water), Earthquake (Ground)

Hint Prop M1 is a Steel type. Raise the power of a move that can target its weakness before you attack so you can knock it out within 15 scenes.

SCENARIO

SCENE	SCENARIO
SCENE 01	The line you choose is important! *You: This way! MT!* *You: Ugh... It's scary...* *You: Hey, scrap heap!* *You: Over here!*
SCENE 02	Use the weather!
SCENE 03	The line you choose is important! Don't be afraid to make sacrifices! *You: I'll turn you to scrap!* *You: I'll be cautious...* *You: Bring it on!* *You: Scary...*
SCENE 04	Use a move the foe's type is weak to!
SCENE 05	Use a move the foe's type is weak to!
SCENE 06	Deliver a decisive blow!
SCENE 07	Deliver a decisive blow!
SCENE 08	Deliver a decisive blow!
SCENE 09	Deliver a decisive blow!
SCENE 10	Deliver a decisive blow!
SCENE 11	Deliver a decisive blow!
SCENE 12	Deliver a decisive blow!
SCENE 13	Deliver a decisive blow!
SCENE 14	Deliver a decisive blow!
SCENE 15	Deliver a decisive blow!

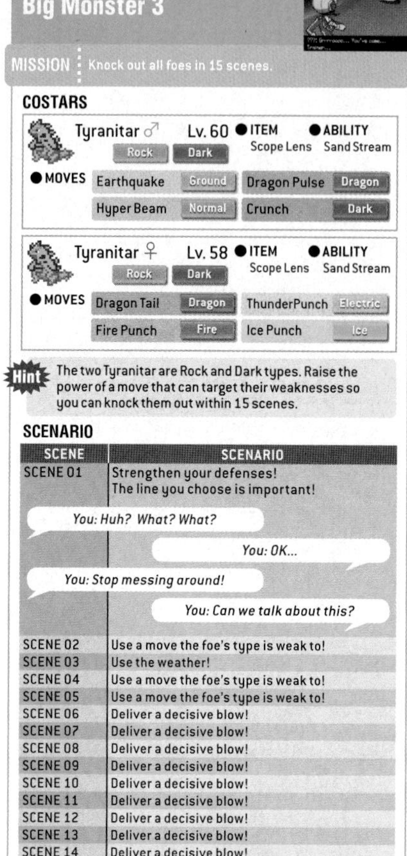

Big Monster 3

MISSION: Knock out all foes in 15 scenes.

COSTARS

Pokémon	Type	Lv.	ITEM	ABILITY
Tyranitar ♂	Rock / Dark	Lv. 60	Scope Lens	Sand Stream
Tyranitar ♀	Rock / Dark	Lv. 58	Scope Lens	Sand Stream

Tyranitar ♂ MOVES: Earthquake (Ground), Dragon Pulse (Dragon), Hyper Beam (Normal), Crunch (Dark)

Tyranitar ♀ MOVES: Dragon Tail (Dragon), ThunderPunch (Electric), Fire Punch (Fire), Ice Punch (Ice)

Hint The two Tyranitar are Rock and Dark types. Raise the power of a move that can target their weaknesses so you can knock them out within 15 scenes.

SCENARIO

SCENE	SCENARIO
SCENE 01	Strengthen your defenses! The line you choose is important! *You: Huh? What? What?* *You: OK...* *You: Stop messing around!* *You: Can we talk about this?*
SCENE 02	Use a move the foe's type is weak to!
SCENE 03	Use the weather!
SCENE 04	Use a move the foe's type is weak to!
SCENE 05	Use a move the foe's type is weak to!
SCENE 06	Deliver a decisive blow!
SCENE 07	Deliver a decisive blow!
SCENE 08	Deliver a decisive blow!
SCENE 09	Deliver a decisive blow!
SCENE 10	Deliver a decisive blow!
SCENE 11	Deliver a decisive blow!
SCENE 12	Deliver a decisive blow!
SCENE 13	Deliver a decisive blow!
SCENE 14	Deliver a decisive blow!
SCENE 15	Deliver a decisive blow!

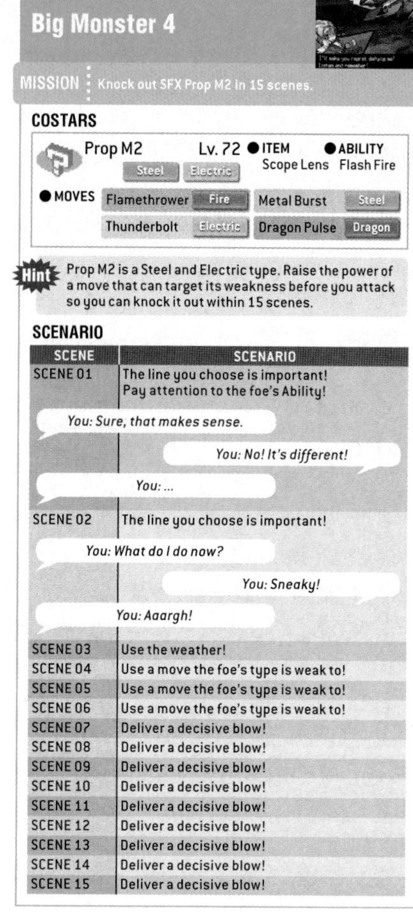

Big Monster 4

MISSION: Knock out SFX Prop M2 in 15 scenes.

COSTARS

Pokémon	Type	Lv.	ITEM	ABILITY
Prop M2	Steel / Electric	Lv. 72	Scope Lens	Flash Fire

MOVES: Flamethrower (Fire), Metal Burst (Steel), Thunderbolt (Electric), Dragon Pulse (Dragon)

Hint Prop M2 is a Steel and Electric type. Raise the power of a move that can target its weakness before you attack so you can knock it out within 15 scenes.

SCENARIO

SCENE	SCENARIO
SCENE 01	The line you choose is important! Pay attention to the foe's Ability! *You: Sure, that makes sense.* *You: No! It's different!* *You: ...*
SCENE 02	The line you choose is important! *You: What do I do now?* *You: Sneaky!* *You: Aaargh!*
SCENE 03	Use the weather!
SCENE 04	Use a move the foe's type is weak to!
SCENE 05	Use a move the foe's type is weak to!
SCENE 06	Use a move the foe's type is weak to!
SCENE 07	Deliver a decisive blow!
SCENE 08	Deliver a decisive blow!
SCENE 09	Deliver a decisive blow!
SCENE 10	Deliver a decisive blow!
SCENE 11	Deliver a decisive blow!
SCENE 12	Deliver a decisive blow!
SCENE 13	Deliver a decisive blow!
SCENE 14	Deliver a decisive blow!
SCENE 15	Deliver a decisive blow!

Tip: Find special events

Certain moves trigger special events in some of the scripts. Some of these events delve deeper into the story and others have unexpected results. Try to find them all.

Examples of special events

Brycen-Man Strikes Back 2

If you use the move Thief, Brycen-Man will say in disgust, "You use that move... and call yourself a hero of justice?"

Big Monster 4

These MTs are for sale.
There's a whole series of them.

Serizawa talks about how he got the Mecha Tyranitar. The surprising story will be revealed!

Tip: Break the box-office records

The box-office gross of a movie will be recorded after it's shown. The type of movie, the kind of ending, and so on determine the box-office record, and the best one will be recorded.

Box-office sales No. 1

Things that determine the box-office sales

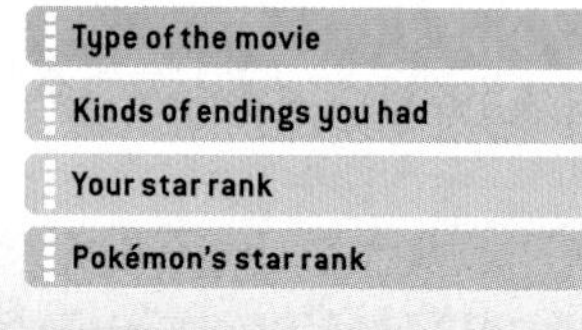

- Type of the movie
- Kinds of endings you had
- Your star rank
- Pokémon's star rank

Timegate Traveler

MISSION Knock out SFX Prop T1 in four scenes.

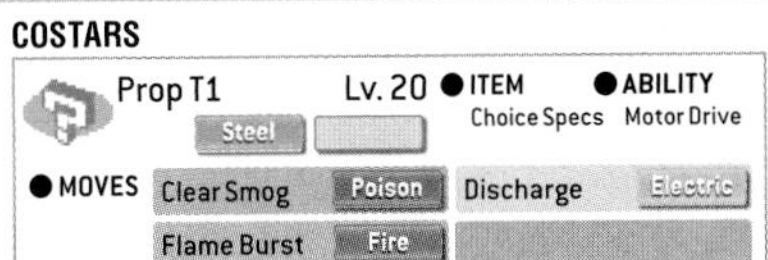

COSTARS

Costar	Type	Lv.	ITEM	ABILITY
Prop T1	Steel	Lv. 20	Choice Specs	Motor Drive

MOVES	Type	MOVES	Type
Clear Smog	Poison	Discharge	Electric
Flame Burst	Fire		

Hint Knocking out Prop T1 in four scenes is a difficult thing to do. Use a move to steal its item and raise your stats.

SCENARIO

SCENE	SCENARIO
SCENE 01	Steal the foe's item!
SCENE 02	Attack the foe!
SCENE 03	Attack the foe!
SCENE 04	Deliver a decisive blow!

Timegate Traveler 2

MISSION Last for five scenes. Don't knock out SFX Prop K1.

COSTARS

Costar	Type	Lv.	ITEM	ABILITY
Prop K1 ♂	Fighting	Lv. 30	Rocky Helmet	Huge Power

MOVES	Type	MOVES	Type
Focus Punch	Fighting	Taunt	Dark
Mach Punch	Fighting		

Hint If you choose the wrong move, your Duosion will be knocked out. Use moves to protect your Duosion well.

SCENARIO

SCENE	SCENARIO
SCENE 01	Protect yourself from attacks! The line you choose is important *Professor (you): Help!* *Professor (you): Can we talk?* *Professor (you): I'm not lying!*
SCENE 02	Change your foe's Ability
SCENE 03	Pay attention to your Pokémon's HP!
SCENE 04	Withstand your foe's attack!
SCENE 05	Withstand your foe's attack!

Timegate Traveler 3

MISSION Knock out SFX Prop T1 with Thunder. Don't knock it out with any other move.

COSTARS

Costar	Type	Lv.	ITEM	ABILITY
Prop K1 ♂	Fighting	Lv. 40	Red Card	Huge Power

MOVES	Type	MOVES	Type
Hammer Arm	Fighting	Mach Punch	Fighting
Jump Kick	Fighting		

Costar	Type	Lv.	ITEM	ABILITY
Prop T1	Steel	Lv. 50	Wide Lens	Motor Drive

MOVES	Type	MOVES	Type
Signal Beam	Bug	Overheat	Fire
Icicle Crash	Ice		

Hint The accuracy of the move Thunder is low. Use a move to change the weather to make sure Thunder hits the target.

SCENARIO

SCENE	SCENARIO
SCENE 01	Steal the foe's item! The line you choose is important *Professor (you): All your fault!* *Professor (you): You're wrong!* *Professor (you): I'll change it!*
SCENE 02	Change your foe's Ability
SCENE 03	Make sure you hit the foe!
SCENE 04	Make sure you hit the foe!
SCENE 04	Make sure you hit the foe!

Love and Battles

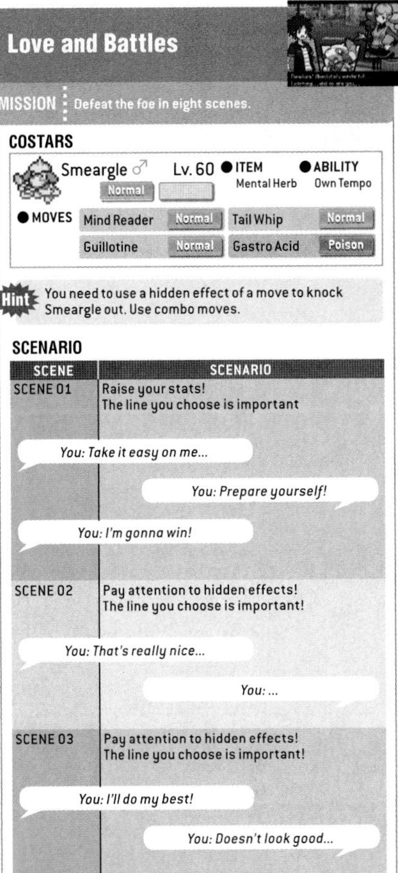

MISSION Defeat the foe in eight scenes.

COSTARS

Costar	Type	Lv.	ITEM	ABILITY
Smeargle ♂	Normal	Lv. 60	Mental Herb	Own Tempo

MOVES	Type	MOVES	Type
Mind Reader	Normal	Tail Whip	Normal
Guillotine	Normal	Gastro Acid	Poison

Hint You need to use a hidden effect of a move to knock Smeargle out. Use combo moves.

SCENARIO

SCENE	SCENARIO
SCENE 01	Raise your stats! The line you choose is important *You: Take it easy on me...* *You: Prepare yourself!* *You: I'm gonna win!*
SCENE 02	Pay attention to hidden effects! The line you choose is important! *You: That's really nice...* *You: ...*
SCENE 03	Pay attention to hidden effects! The line you choose is important! *You: I'll do my best!* *You: Doesn't look good...*
SCENE 04	Use hidden effects! Attack your foe!
SCENE 05	Use hidden effects! Attack your foe!
SCENE 06	Deliver a decisive blow!
SCENE 07	Deliver a decisive blow!
SCENE 08	Deliver a decisive blow!

Love and Battles 2

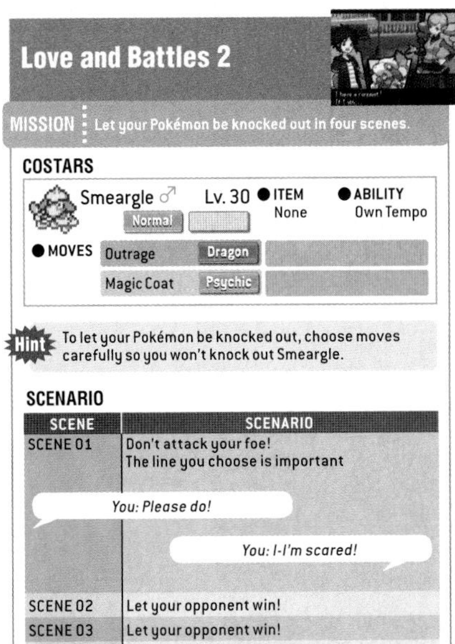

MISSION Let your Pokémon be knocked out in four scenes.

COSTARS

Costar	Type	Lv.	ITEM	ABILITY
Smeargle ♂	Normal	Lv. 30	None	Own Tempo

MOVES	Type	MOVES	Type
Outrage	Dragon		
Magic Coat	Psychic		

Hint To let your Pokémon be knocked out, choose moves carefully so you won't knock out Smeargle.

SCENARIO

SCENE	SCENARIO
SCENE 01	Don't attack your foe! The line you choose is important *You: Please do!* *You: I-I'm scared!*
SCENE 02	Let your opponent win!
SCENE 03	Let your opponent win!
SCENE 04	Let your opponent win!

Tip: Why is the studio green?

Some people might be surprised to find out that while movies have colorful images, the studio is totally green. It's because the images of the movies are created in CG. The green screen is perfect to create vivid images by superimposing the characters, Pokémon, or the background. This method is used in real movie shooting. In Pokéstar Studios, CG composition is done right after shooting and the movie is screened immediately. The technology is very impressive.

Studio

Your costar is called R1 in the studio. It looks like a green board.

Theater

In the finished movie, CG is added on R1, and it appears as Robot F-00.

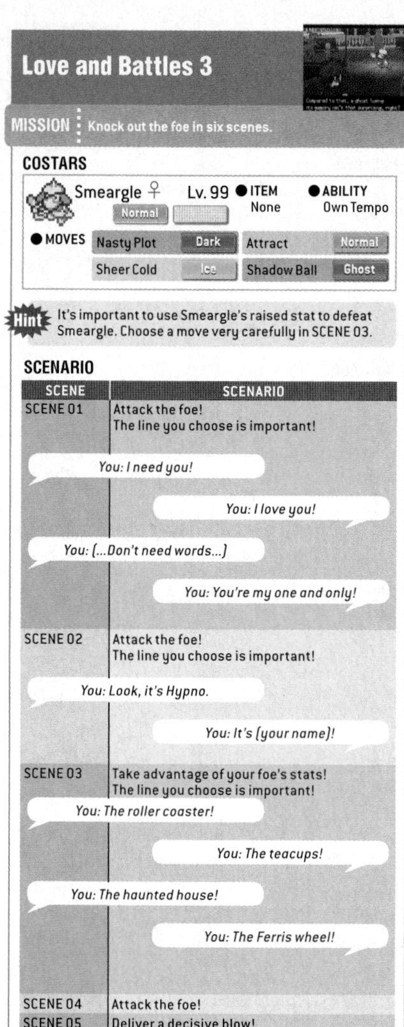

Love and Battles 3

MISSION: Knock out the foe in six scenes.

COSTARS

Pokémon	Type	Lv.	ITEM	ABILITY
Smeargle ♀	Normal	99	None	Own Tempo

MOVES	Type	MOVES	Type
Nasty Plot	Dark	Attract	Normal
Sheer Cold	Ice	Shadow Ball	Ghost

Hint It's important to use Smeargle's raised stat to defeat Smeargle. Choose a move very carefully in SCENE 03.

SCENARIO

SCENE	SCENARIO
SCENE 01	Attack the foe! The line you choose is important!
	You: I need you!
	You: I love you!
	You: (...Don't need words...)
	You: You're my one and only!
SCENE 02	Attack the foe! The line you choose is important!
	You: Look, it's Hypno.
	You: It's (your name)!
SCENE 03	Take advantage of your foe's stats! The line you choose is important!
	You: The roller coaster!
	You: The teacups!
	You: The haunted house!
	You: The Ferris wheel!
SCENE 04	Attack the foe!
SCENE 05	Deliver a decisive blow!
SCENE 06	Deliver a decisive blow!

Tip: Enjoy the VIP room

When you finish all 40 movies with happy endings, you'll be able to enter the VIP room, which is only available for special stars. In the VIP room, you'll be pampered by many people. Congratulations, superstar!

VIP treatment

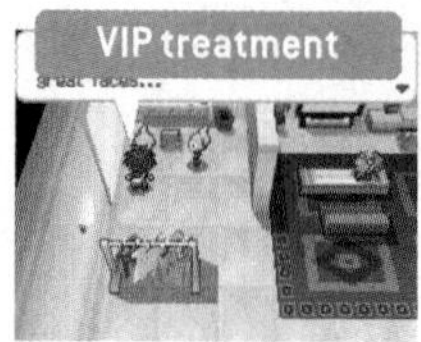

Your personal makeup artist is waiting for you.

Bodyguard power!

A bodyguard keeps a strict eye on who can enter. You'll be told that the VIP room once belonged to Brycen.

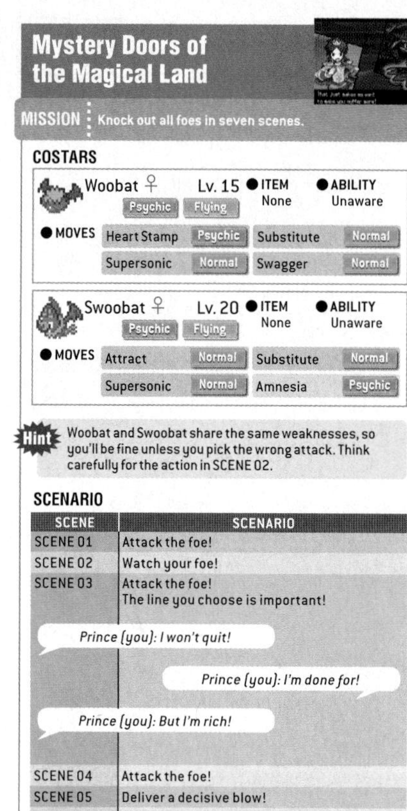

Mystery Doors of the Magical Land

MISSION: Knock out all foes in seven scenes.

COSTARS

Pokémon	Type	Lv.	ITEM	ABILITY
Woobat ♀	Psychic / Flying	15	None	Unaware

MOVES	Type	MOVES	Type
Heart Stamp	Psychic	Substitute	Normal
Supersonic	Normal	Swagger	Normal

Pokémon	Type	Lv.	ITEM	ABILITY
Swoobat ♀	Psychic / Flying	20	None	Unaware

MOVES	Type	MOVES	Type
Attract	Normal	Substitute	Normal
Supersonic	Normal	Amnesia	Psychic

Hint Woobat and Swoobat share the same weaknesses, so you'll be fine unless you pick the wrong attack. Think carefully for the action in SCENE 02.

SCENARIO

SCENE	SCENARIO
SCENE 01	Attack the foe!
SCENE 02	Watch your foe!
SCENE 03	Attack the foe! The line you choose is important!
	Prince (you): I won't quit!
	Prince (you): I'm done for!
	Prince (you): But I'm rich!
SCENE 04	Attack the foe!
SCENE 05	Deliver a decisive blow!
SCENE 06	Deliver a decisive blow!
SCENE 07	Deliver a decisive blow!

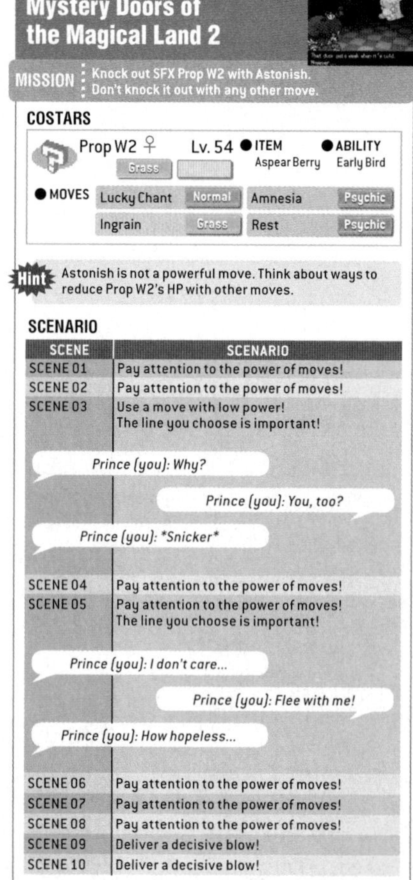

Mystery Doors of the Magical Land 2

MISSION: Knock out SFX Prop W2 with Astonish. Don't knock it out with any other move.

COSTARS

Pokémon	Type	Lv.	ITEM	ABILITY
Prop W2 ♀	Grass	54	Aspear Berry	Early Bird

MOVES	Type	MOVES	Type
Lucky Chant	Normal	Amnesia	Psychic
Ingrain	Grass	Rest	Psychic

Hint Astonish is not a powerful move. Think about ways to reduce Prop W2's HP with other moves.

SCENARIO

SCENE	SCENARIO
SCENE 01	Pay attention to the power of moves!
SCENE 02	Pay attention to the power of moves!
SCENE 03	Use a move with low power! The line you choose is important!
	Prince (you): Why?
	Prince (you): You, too?
	*Prince (you): *Snicker**
SCENE 04	Pay attention to the power of moves!
SCENE 05	Pay attention to the power of moves! The line you choose is important!
	Prince (you): I don't care...
	Prince (you): Flee with me!
	Prince (you): How hopeless...
SCENE 06	Pay attention to the power of moves!
SCENE 07	Pay attention to the power of moves!
SCENE 08	Pay attention to the power of moves!
SCENE 09	Deliver a decisive blow!
SCENE 10	Deliver a decisive blow!

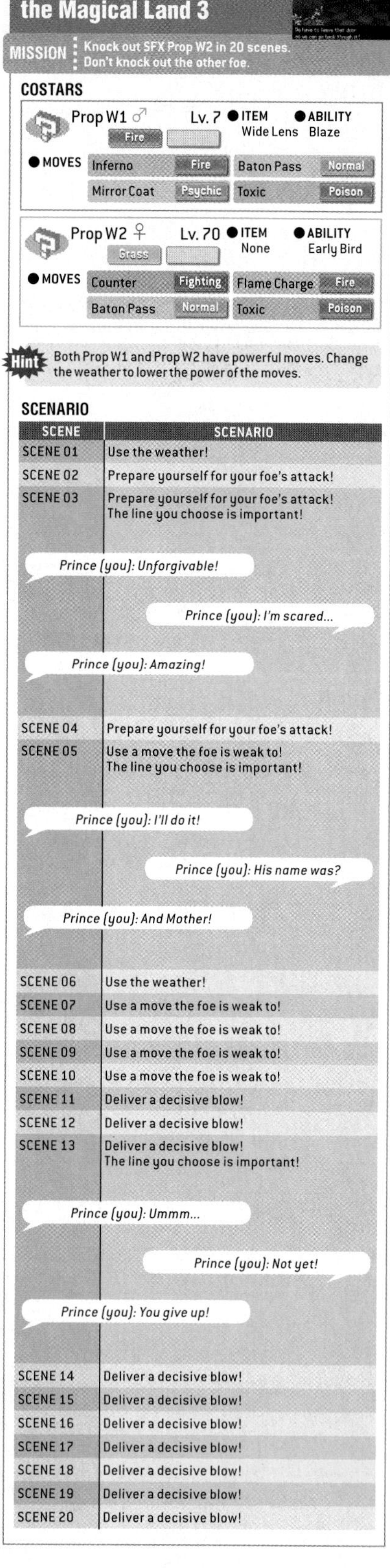

Mystery Doors of the Magical Land 3

MISSION: Knock out SFX Prop W2 in 20 scenes. Don't knock out the other foe.

COSTARS

Pokémon	Type	Lv.	ITEM	ABILITY
Prop W1 ♂	Fire	7	Wide Lens	Blaze

MOVES	Type	MOVES	Type
Inferno	Fire	Baton Pass	Normal
Mirror Coat	Psychic	Toxic	Poison

Pokémon	Type	Lv.	ITEM	ABILITY
Prop W2 ♀	Grass	70	None	Early Bird

MOVES	Type	MOVES	Type
Counter	Fighting	Flame Charge	Fire
Baton Pass	Normal	Toxic	Poison

Hint Both Prop W1 and Prop W2 have powerful moves. Change the weather to lower the power of the moves.

SCENARIO

SCENE	SCENARIO
SCENE 01	Use the weather!
SCENE 02	Prepare yourself for your foe's attack!
SCENE 03	Prepare yourself for your foe's attack! The line you choose is important!
	Prince (you): Unforgivable!
	Prince (you): I'm scared...
	Prince (you): Amazing!
SCENE 04	Prepare yourself for your foe's attack!
SCENE 05	Use a move the foe is weak to! The line you choose is important!
	Prince (you): I'll do it!
	Prince (you): His name was?
	Prince (you): And Mother!
SCENE 06	Use the weather!
SCENE 07	Use a move the foe is weak to!
SCENE 08	Use a move the foe is weak to!
SCENE 09	Use a move the foe is weak to!
SCENE 10	Use a move the foe is weak to!
SCENE 11	Deliver a decisive blow!
SCENE 12	Deliver a decisive blow!
SCENE 13	Deliver a decisive blow! The line you choose is important!
	Prince (you): Ummm...
	Prince (you): Not yet!
	Prince (you): You give up!
SCENE 14	Deliver a decisive blow!
SCENE 15	Deliver a decisive blow!
SCENE 16	Deliver a decisive blow!
SCENE 17	Deliver a decisive blow!
SCENE 18	Deliver a decisive blow!
SCENE 19	Deliver a decisive blow!
SCENE 20	Deliver a decisive blow!

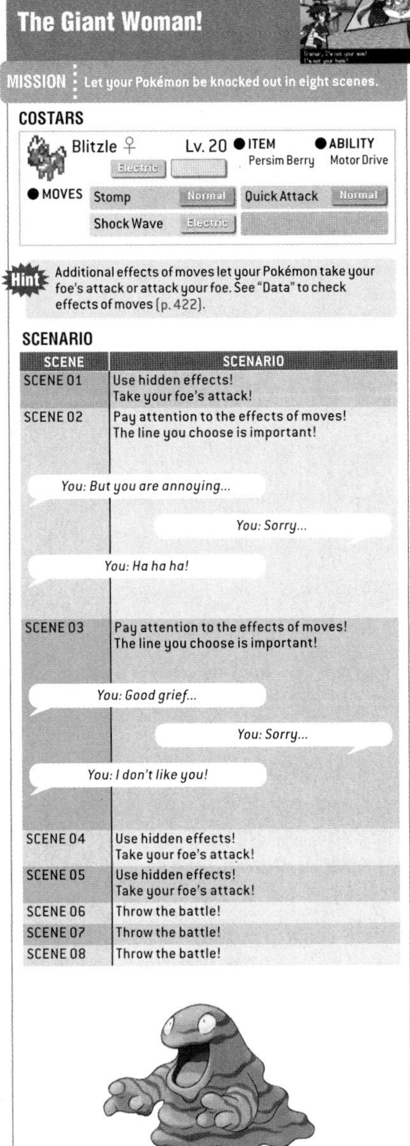

The Giant Woman!

MISSION Let your Pokémon be knocked out in eight scenes.

COSTARS

Pokémon	Type	Lv.	ITEM	ABILITY
Blitzle ♀	Electric	Lv. 20	Persim Berry	Motor Drive

MOVES	Type		Type
Stomp	Normal	Quick Attack	Normal
Shock Wave	Electric		

Hint Additional effects of moves let your Pokémon take your foe's attack or attack your foe. See "Data" to check effects of moves (p. 422).

SCENARIO

SCENE	SCENARIO
SCENE 01	Use hidden effects! Take your foe's attack!
SCENE 02	Pay attention to the effects of moves! The line you choose is important! *You: But you are annoying...* *You: Sorry...* *You: Ha ha ha!*
SCENE 03	Pay attention to the effects of moves! The line you choose is important! *You: Good grief...* *You: Sorry...* *You: I don't like you!*
SCENE 04	Use hidden effects! Take your foe's attack!
SCENE 05	Use hidden effects! Take your foe's attack!
SCENE 06	Throw the battle!
SCENE 07	Throw the battle!
SCENE 08	Throw the battle!

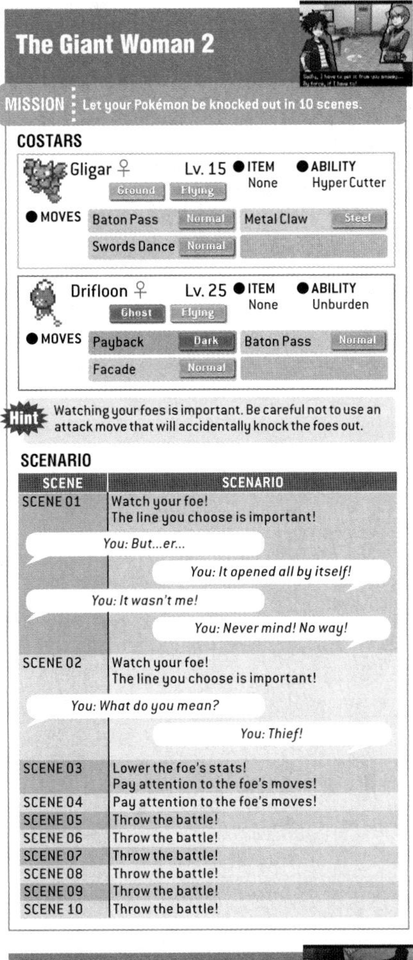

The Giant Woman 2

MISSION Let your Pokémon be knocked out in 10 scenes.

COSTARS

Pokémon	Type	Lv.	ITEM	ABILITY
Gligar ♀	Ground / Flying	Lv. 15	None	Hyper Cutter

MOVES	Type		Type
Baton Pass	Normal	Metal Claw	Steel
Swords Dance	Normal		

Pokémon	Type	Lv.	ITEM	ABILITY
Drifloon ♀	Ghost / Flying	Lv. 25	None	Unburden

MOVES	Type		Type
Payback	Dark	Baton Pass	Normal
Facade	Normal		

Hint Watching your foes is important. Be careful not to use an attack move that will accidentally knock the foes out.

SCENARIO

SCENE	SCENARIO
SCENE 01	Watch your foe! The line you choose is important! *You: But...er...* *You: It opened all by itself!* *You: It wasn't me!* *You: Never mind! No way!*
SCENE 02	Watch your foe! The line you choose is important! *You: What do you mean?* *You: Thief!*
SCENE 03	Lower the foe's stats! Pay attention to the foe's moves!
SCENE 04	Pay attention to the foe's moves!
SCENE 05	Throw the battle!
SCENE 06	Throw the battle!
SCENE 07	Throw the battle!
SCENE 08	Throw the battle!
SCENE 09	Throw the battle!
SCENE 10	Throw the battle!

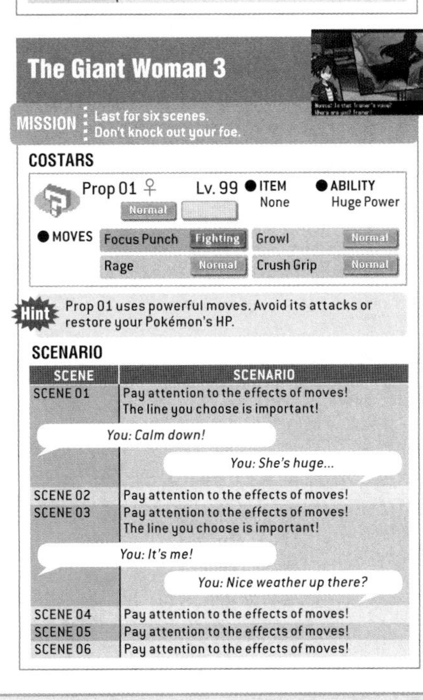

The Giant Woman 3

MISSION Last for six scenes. Don't knock out your foe.

COSTARS

Pokémon	Type	Lv.	ITEM	ABILITY
Prop 01 ♀	Normal	Lv. 99	None	Huge Power

MOVES	Type		Type
Focus Punch	Fighting	Growl	Normal
Rage	Normal	Crush Grip	Normal

Hint Prop 01 uses powerful moves. Avoid its attacks or restore your Pokémon's HP.

SCENARIO

SCENE	SCENARIO
SCENE 01	Pay attention to the effects of moves! The line you choose is important! *You: Calm down!* *You: She's huge...*
SCENE 02	Pay attention to the effects of moves!
SCENE 03	Pay attention to the effects of moves! The line you choose is important! *You: It's me!* *You: Nice weather up there?*
SCENE 04	Pay attention to the effects of moves!
SCENE 05	Pay attention to the effects of moves!
SCENE 06	Pay attention to the effects of moves!

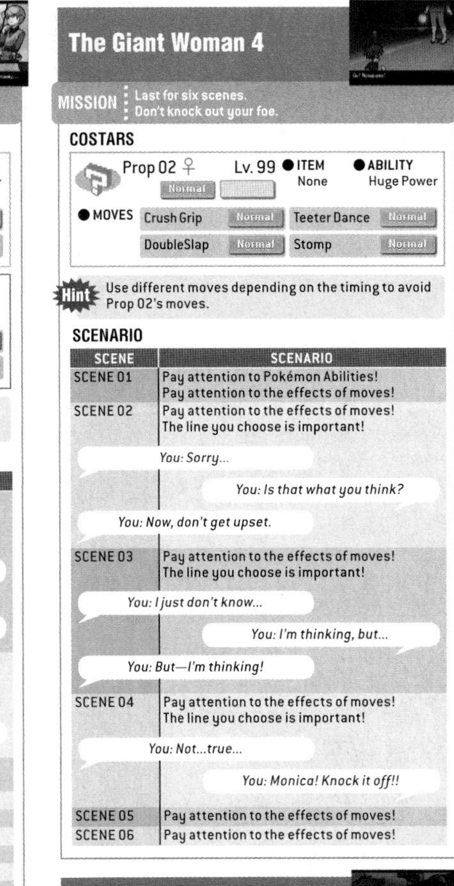

The Giant Woman 4

MISSION Last for six scenes. Don't knock out your foe.

COSTARS

Pokémon	Type	Lv.	ITEM	ABILITY
Prop 02 ♀	Normal	Lv. 99	None	Huge Power

MOVES	Type		Type
Crush Grip	Normal	Teeter Dance	Normal
DoubleSlap	Normal	Stomp	Normal

Hint Use different moves depending on the timing to avoid Prop 02's moves.

SCENARIO

SCENE	SCENARIO
SCENE 01	Pay attention to Pokémon Abilities! Pay attention to the effects of moves!
SCENE 02	Pay attention to the effects of moves! The line you choose is important! *You: Sorry...* *You: Is that what you think?* *You: Now, don't get upset.*
SCENE 03	Pay attention to the effects of moves! The line you choose is important! *You: I just don't know...* *You: I'm thinking, but...* *You: But—I'm thinking!*
SCENE 04	Pay attention to the effects of moves! The line you choose is important! *You: Not...true...* *You: Monica! Knock it off!!*
SCENE 05	Pay attention to the effects of moves!
SCENE 06	Pay attention to the effects of moves!

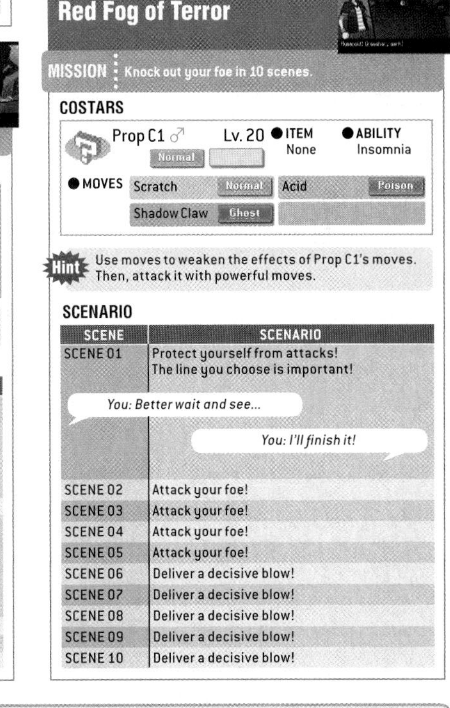

Red Fog of Terror

MISSION Knock out your foe in 10 scenes.

COSTARS

Pokémon	Type	Lv.	ITEM	ABILITY
Prop C1 ♂	Normal	Lv. 20	None	Insomnia

MOVES	Type		Type
Scratch	Normal	Acid	Poison
Shadow Claw	Ghost		

Hint Use moves to weaken the effects of Prop C1's moves. Then, attack it with powerful moves.

SCENARIO

SCENE	SCENARIO
SCENE 01	Protect yourself from attacks! The line you choose is important! *You: Better wait and see...* *You: I'll finish it!*
SCENE 02	Attack your foe!
SCENE 03	Attack your foe!
SCENE 04	Attack your foe!
SCENE 05	Attack your foe!
SCENE 06	Deliver a decisive blow!
SCENE 07	Deliver a decisive blow!
SCENE 08	Deliver a decisive blow!
SCENE 09	Deliver a decisive blow!
SCENE 10	Deliver a decisive blow!

Tip

Unlocking some scripts requires special conditions

When your movie has a happy ending, the script for the sequel will usually be added. However, some scripts won't be added unless you meet special conditions.

There's a present for you today—
a new script!

Scripts with special conditions

Title	Condition
Brycen-Man Strikes Back	Enter the Hall of Fame and have a happy ending in the previous title
Full Metal Cop	The box-office sales exceed 500 billion
Big Monster	Enter the Hall of Fame
Love and Battles	Enter the Hall of Fame
The Giant Woman!	The Star Rank goes up by one
Everlasting Memories	The Star Rank goes up by two
Ghost Eraser	After entering the Hall of Fame
Brycen-Man Strikes Back Harder	Have happy endings in all other movies

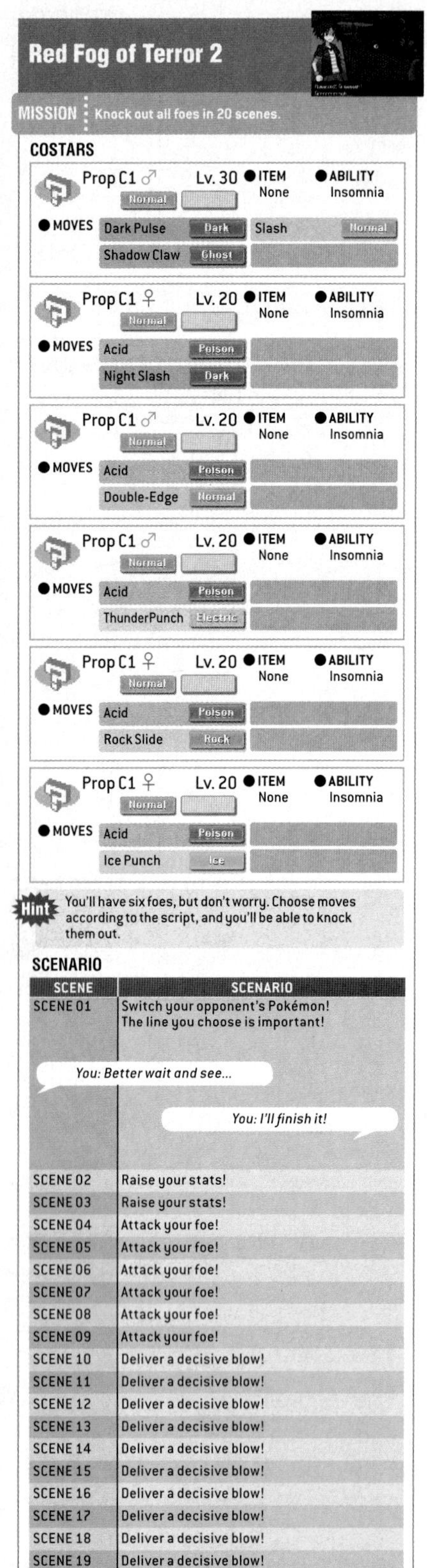

Red Fog of Terror 2

MISSION: Knock out all foes in 20 scenes.

COSTARS

Costar	Type	Lv.	Item	Ability	Moves
Prop C1 ♂	Normal	Lv. 30	None	Insomnia	Dark Pulse (Dark), Slash (Normal), Shadow Claw (Ghost)
Prop C1 ♀	Normal	Lv. 20	None	Insomnia	Acid (Poison), Night Slash (Dark)
Prop C1 ♂	Normal	Lv. 20	None	Insomnia	Acid (Poison), Double-Edge (Normal)
Prop C1 ♂	Normal	Lv. 20	None	Insomnia	Acid (Poison), ThunderPunch (Electric)
Prop C1 ♀	Normal	Lv. 20	None	Insomnia	Acid (Poison), Rock Slide (Rock)
Prop C1 ♀	Normal	Lv. 20	None	Insomnia	Acid (Poison), Ice Punch (Ice)

Hint You'll have six foes, but don't worry. Choose moves according to the script, and you'll be able to knock them out.

SCENARIO

SCENE	SCENARIO
SCENE 01	Switch your opponent's Pokémon! The line you choose is important! *You: Better wait and see...* / *You: I'll finish it!*
SCENE 02	Raise your stats!
SCENE 03	Raise your stats!
SCENE 04	Attack your foe!
SCENE 05	Attack your foe!
SCENE 06	Attack your foe!
SCENE 07	Attack your foe!
SCENE 08	Attack your foe!
SCENE 09	Attack your foe!
SCENE 10	Deliver a decisive blow!
SCENE 11	Deliver a decisive blow!
SCENE 12	Deliver a decisive blow!
SCENE 13	Deliver a decisive blow!
SCENE 14	Deliver a decisive blow!
SCENE 15	Deliver a decisive blow!
SCENE 16	Deliver a decisive blow!
SCENE 17	Deliver a decisive blow!
SCENE 18	Deliver a decisive blow!
SCENE 19	Deliver a decisive blow!
SCENE 20	Deliver a decisive blow!

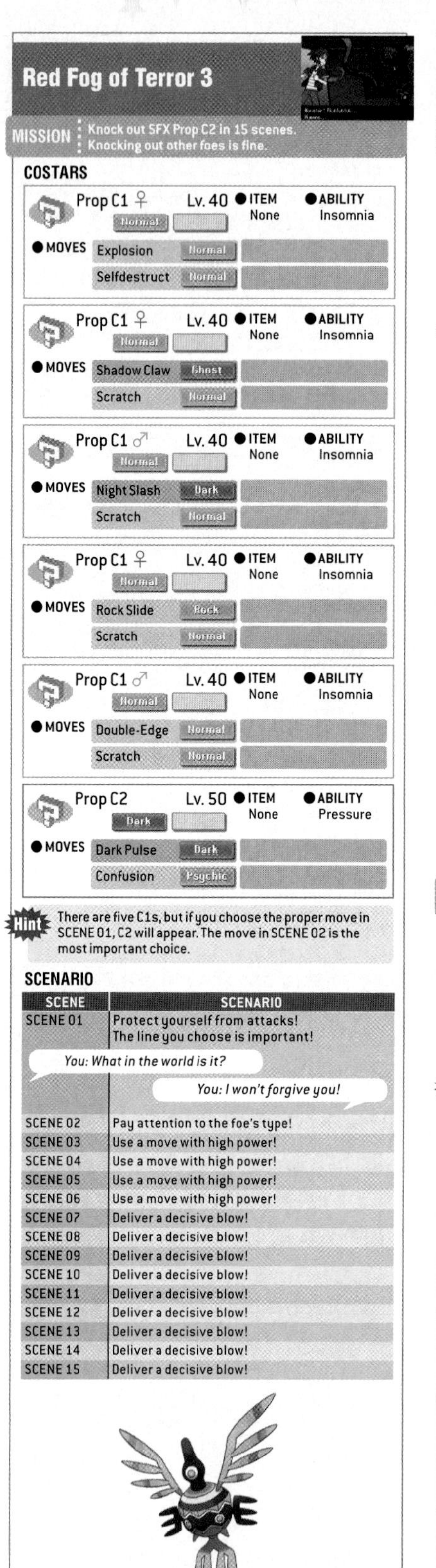

Red Fog of Terror 3

MISSION: Knock out SFX Prop C2 in 15 scenes. Knocking out other foes is fine.

COSTARS

Costar	Type	Lv.	Item	Ability	Moves
Prop C1 ♀	Normal	Lv. 40	None	Insomnia	Explosion (Normal), Selfdestruct (Normal)
Prop C1 ♀	Normal	Lv. 40	None	Insomnia	Shadow Claw (Ghost), Scratch (Normal)
Prop C1 ♂	Normal	Lv. 40	None	Insomnia	Night Slash (Dark), Scratch (Normal)
Prop C1 ♀	Normal	Lv. 40	None	Insomnia	Rock Slide (Rock), Scratch (Normal)
Prop C1 ♂	Normal	Lv. 40	None	Insomnia	Double-Edge (Normal), Scratch (Normal)
Prop C2	Dark	Lv. 50	None	Pressure	Dark Pulse (Dark), Confusion (Psychic)

Hint There are five C1s, but if you choose the proper move in SCENE 01, C2 will appear. The move in SCENE 02 is the most important choice.

SCENARIO

SCENE	SCENARIO
SCENE 01	Protect yourself from attacks! The line you choose is important! *You: What in the world is it?* / *You: I won't forgive you!*
SCENE 02	Pay attention to the foe's type!
SCENE 03	Use a move with high power!
SCENE 04	Use a move with high power!
SCENE 05	Use a move with high power!
SCENE 06	Use a move with high power!
SCENE 07	Deliver a decisive blow!
SCENE 08	Deliver a decisive blow!
SCENE 09	Deliver a decisive blow!
SCENE 10	Deliver a decisive blow!
SCENE 11	Deliver a decisive blow!
SCENE 12	Deliver a decisive blow!
SCENE 13	Deliver a decisive blow!
SCENE 14	Deliver a decisive blow!
SCENE 15	Deliver a decisive blow!

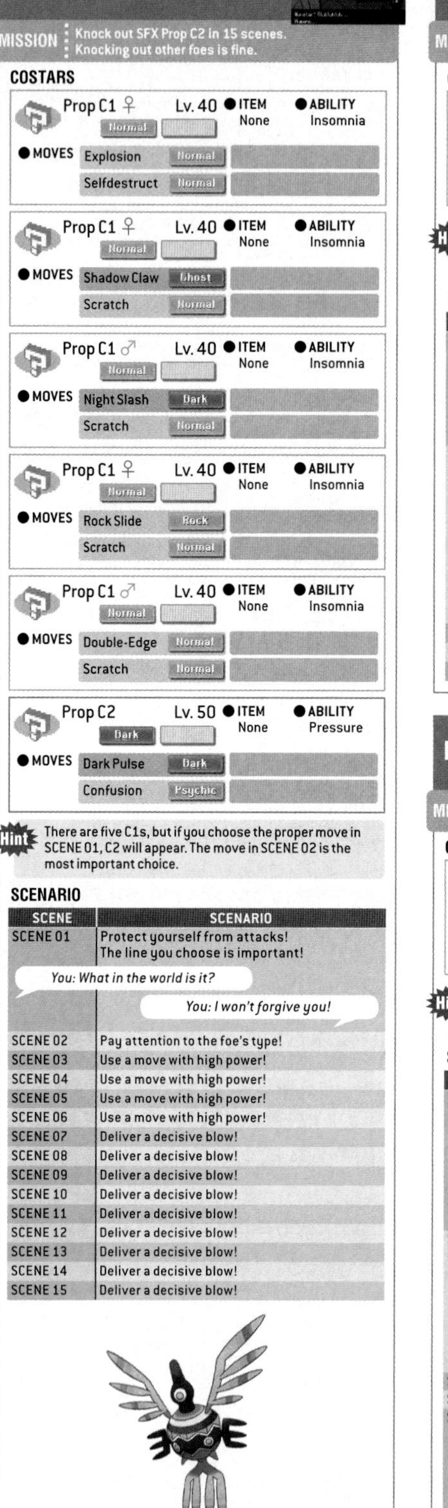

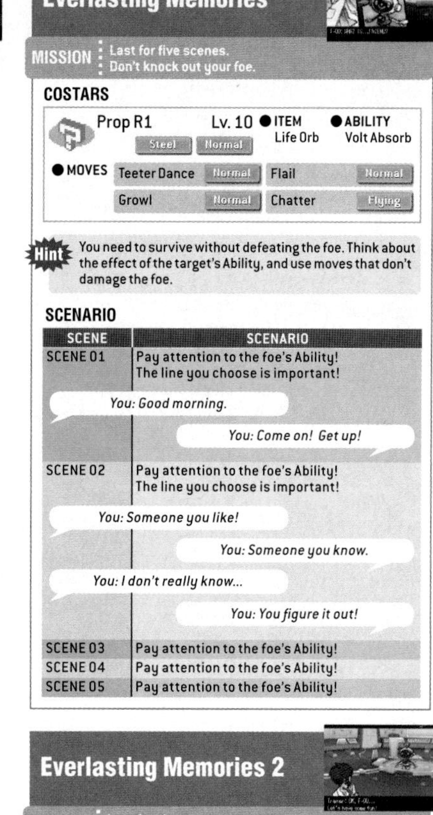

Everlasting Memories

MISSION: Last for five scenes. Don't knock out your foe.

COSTARS

Costar	Type	Lv.	Item	Ability	Moves
Prop R1	Steel / Normal	Lv. 10	Life Orb	Volt Absorb	Teeter Dance (Normal), Flail (Normal), Growl (Normal), Chatter (Flying)

Hint You need to survive without defeating the foe. Think about the effect of the target's Ability, and use moves that don't damage the foe.

SCENARIO

SCENE	SCENARIO
SCENE 01	Pay attention to the foe's Ability! The line you choose is important! *You: Good morning.* / *You: Come on! Get up!*
SCENE 02	Pay attention to the foe's Ability! The line you choose is important! *You: Someone you like!* / *You: Someone you know.* / *You: I don't really know...* / *You: You figure it out!*
SCENE 03	Pay attention to the foe's Ability!
SCENE 04	Pay attention to the foe's Ability!
SCENE 05	Pay attention to the foe's Ability!

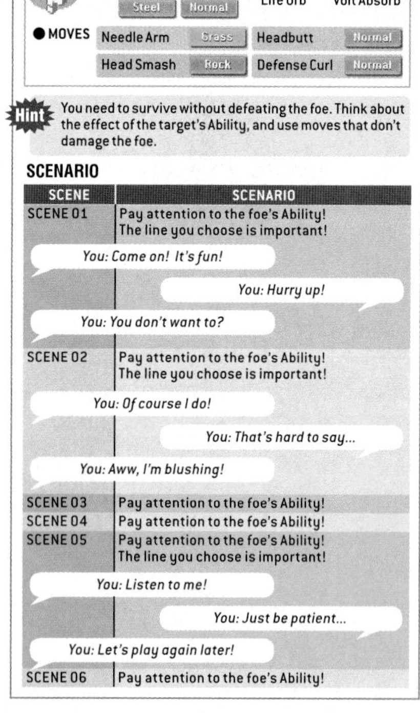

Everlasting Memories 2

MISSION: Last for six scenes. Don't knock out your foe.

COSTARS

Costar	Type	Lv.	Item	Ability	Moves
Prop R1	Steel / Normal	Lv. 58	Life Orb	Volt Absorb	Needle Arm (Grass), Headbutt (Normal), Head Smash (Rock), Defense Curl (Normal)

Hint You need to survive without defeating the foe. Think about the effect of the target's Ability, and use moves that don't damage the foe.

SCENARIO

SCENE	SCENARIO
SCENE 01	Pay attention to the foe's Ability! The line you choose is important! *You: Come on! It's fun!* / *You: Hurry up!* / *You: You don't want to?*
SCENE 02	Pay attention to the foe's Ability! The line you choose is important! *You: Of course I do!* / *You: That's hard to say...* / *You: Aww, I'm blushing!*
SCENE 03	Pay attention to the foe's Ability!
SCENE 04	Pay attention to the foe's Ability!
SCENE 05	Pay attention to the foe's Ability! The line you choose is important! *You: Listen to me!* / *You: Just be patient...* / *You: Let's play again later!*
SCENE 06	Pay attention to the foe's Ability!

Tip: Sabrina is now an actor

Sabrina, the Gym Leader of Saffron City in the Kanto region, has become an actor. She also participates in the PWT as a Pokémon Trainer.

Everlasting Memories 3

MISSION Knock out SFX Prop R2 with Blizzard. Don't knock it out with any other move.

COSTARS

Pokémon	Type	Lv.	ITEM	ABILITY
Prop R2	Steel / Normal	Lv. 52	None	Reckless

MOVES	Type	MOVES	Type
Wild Charge	Electric	Iron Head	Steel
Psychic	Psychic	Flare Blitz	Fire

Hint The accuracy of the move Blizzard is low. Use combo moves to raise Blizzard's accuracy.

SCENARIO

SCENE	SCENARIO
SCENE 01	Use the weather! The line you choose is important! *You: It's just the truth...* *You: You're just jealous...* *You: I'm sorry...* *You: It's my fault...*
SCENE 02	Determine the effect of moves! The line you choose is important! *You: Are you OK?!* *You: Is it broken?!* *You: It's gone berserk!*
SCENE 03	Determine effects and choose moves!
SCENE 04	Determine effects and choose moves!
SCENE 05	Determine effects and choose moves!
SCENE 06	Determine effects and choose moves!
SCENE 07	Deliver a decisive blow!
SCENE 08	Deliver a decisive blow!
SCENE 09	Deliver a decisive blow!

Everlasting Memories 4

MISSION Knock out SFX Prop R1 in nine scenes.

COSTARS

Pokémon	Type	Lv.	ITEM	ABILITY
Prop R1	Steel / Normal	Lv. 60	Persim Berry	Volt Absorb

MOVES	Type	MOVES	Type
Thrash	Normal	Perish Song	Normal
Hammer Arm	Fighting	Iron Head	Steel

Hint Choose moves that can withstand Prop R1's powerful attacks and turn the tide quickly.

SCENARIO

SCENE	SCENARIO
SCENE 01	Prepare yourself for your foe's attack!
SCENE 02	Lower your foe's stats! The line you choose is important! *You: I can't do it!* *You: Wahhhhh!* *You: F-00...* *You: No! I can't do it!*
SCENE 03	Use your foe's attack!
SCENE 04	Use your foe's attack!
SCENE 05	Deliver a decisive blow!
SCENE 06	Deliver a decisive blow!
SCENE 07	Deliver a decisive blow!
SCENE 08	Deliver a decisive blow!
SCENE 09	Deliver a decisive blow!

Ghost Eraser

MISSION Knock out an opponent in every scene.

COSTARS

Pokémon	Type	Lv.	ITEM	ABILITY
Gastly ♂	Ghost / Poison	Lv. 30	None	Levitate

MOVES	Type	MOVES	Type
Destiny Bond	Ghost	Sludge	Poison
Curse	Ghost	Will-O-Wisp	Fire

Pokémon	Type	Lv.	ITEM	ABILITY
Haunter ♂	Ghost / Poison	Lv. 30	None	Levitate

MOVES	Type	MOVES	Type
Destiny Bond	Ghost	Sludge Bomb	Poison
Mean Look	Normal	Will-O-Wisp	Fire

Pokémon	Type	Lv.	ITEM	ABILITY
Gengar ♂	Ghost / Poison	Lv. 30	None	Levitate

MOVES	Type	MOVES	Type
Destiny Bond	Ghost	Focus Blast	Fighting
Lick	Ghost	Will-O-Wisp	Fire

Hint Gastly, Haunter, and Gengar share the same weaknesses. Target their weaknesses and beat them one after another.

SCENARIO

SCENE	SCENARIO
SCENE 01	Use a move the foe's type is weak to! The line you choose is important! *Vigoroth: You afraid of something?* *Vigoroth: So, are you...angry?* *Vigoroth: Worried about something?*
SCENE 02	Use a move the foe's type is weak to! The line you choose is important! *Vigoroth: I am—a Ghost Eraser!* *Vigoroth: I'll mourn your passing.* *Vigoroth: I'll ask the ghosts!* *Vigoroth: You're both liars!*
SCENE 03	Use a move the foe's type is weak to!

Ghost Eraser 2

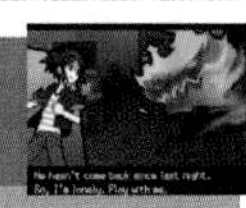

MISSION Knock out an opponent in every scene.

COSTARS

Pokémon	Type	Lv.	ITEM	ABILITY
Cacturne ♀	Grass / Dark	Lv. 50	None	Sand Veil

MOVES	Type	MOVES	Type
Destiny Bond	Ghost	Swagger	Normal
SolarBeam	Grass	Focus Blast	Fighting

Pokémon	Type	Lv.	ITEM	ABILITY
Qwilfish ♀	Water / Poison	Lv. 42	None	Poison Point

MOVES	Type	MOVES	Type
Destiny Bond	Ghost	Thunder Wave	Electric
Sludge Bomb	Poison	Explosion	Normal

Pokémon	Type	Lv.	ITEM	ABILITY
Kirlia ♀	Psychic	Lv. 50	None	Synchronize

MOVES	Type	MOVES	Type
Destiny Bond	Ghost	Hypnosis	Psychic
Calm Mind	Psychic	Psychic	Psychic

Hint Cacturne, Qwilfish, and Kirlia are all of different types, but your Vigoroth has moves to target their weaknesses.

SCENARIO

SCENE	SCENARIO
SCENE 01	Use a move the foe's type is weak to! The line you choose is important! *Vigoroth: Was he ashamed?* *Vigoroth: Did someone beat him?* *Vigoroth: Did he get tired of it?*
SCENE 02	Use a move the foe's type is weak to! The line you choose is important! *Vigoroth: Were they bullying him?* *Vigoroth: Was he a bad guy?* *Vigoroth: Were they jealous?* *Vigoroth: Lies! All lies!*
SCENE 03	Use a move the foe's type is weak to!

Ghost Eraser 3

MISSION Knock out your foe in six scenes.

COSTARS

Pokémon	Type	Lv.	ITEM	ABILITY
Golurk	Ground / Ghost	Lv. 75	None	Iron Fist

MOVES	Type	MOVES	Type
Focus Punch	Fighting	Double Team	Normal
Protect	Normal	Earthquake	Ground

Hint Use attacks that target Golurk's weaknesses. Slaking's Ability allows it to attack only every other turn, so you'll have to be patient.

SCENARIO

SCENE	SCENARIO
SCENE 01	The line you choose is important! Attack the foe! *Slaking: I'm a Ghost Eraser!* *Slaking: I'll mourn your passing.* *Slaking: I'm Slaking!* *Slaking: Who do I look like?*
SCENE 02	The line you choose is important! Attack the foe! *Slaking: Money!* *Slaking: Love!* *Slaking: Power!* *Slaking: I don't need anything!*
SCENE 03	The line you choose is important! Attack the foe! *Slaking: Myself, of course!* *Slaking: I'm Slaking!*
SCENE 04	Deliver a decisive blow!
SCENE 05	The line you choose is important! Deliver a decisive blow! *Slaking: Evil spirit!* *Slaking: The Majin of Mayhem!* *Slaking: I don't know!* *Slaking: A human!*
SCENE 06	Deliver a decisive blow!

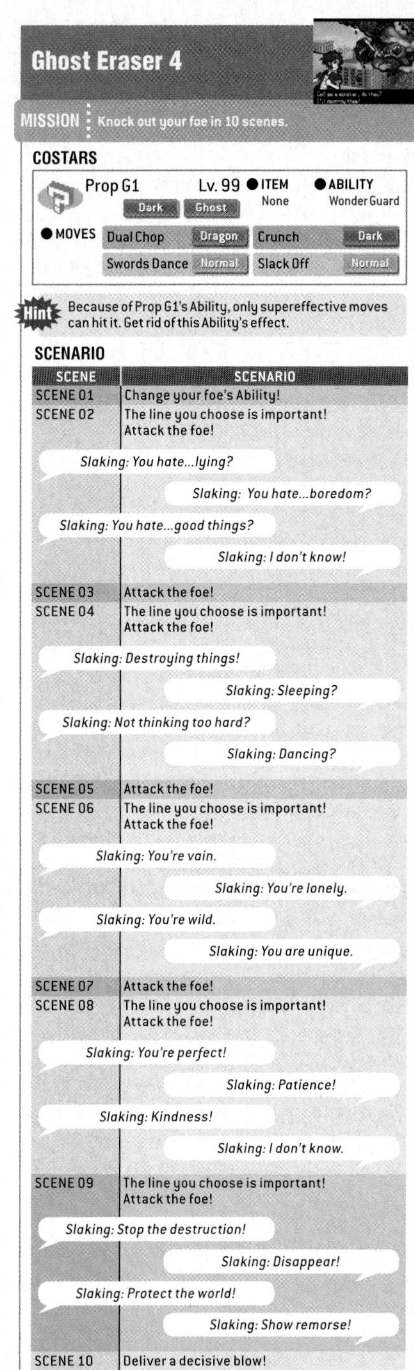

Ghost Eraser 4

MISSION: Knock out your foe in 10 scenes.

COSTARS

Pokémon	Type	Lv.	ITEM	ABILITY
Prop G1	Dark / Ghost	Lv. 99	None	Wonder Guard

MOVES: Dual Chop (Dragon), Crunch (Dark), Swords Dance (Normal), Slack Off (Normal)

Hint: Because of Prop G1's Ability, only supereffective moves can hit it. Get rid of this Ability's effect.

SCENARIO

SCENE	SCENARIO
SCENE 01	Change your foe's Ability!
SCENE 02	The line you choose is important! Attack the foe! *Slaking: You hate...lying?* *Slaking: You hate...boredom?* *Slaking: You hate...good things?* *Slaking: I don't know!*
SCENE 03	Attack the foe!
SCENE 04	The line you choose is important! Attack the foe! *Slaking: Destroying things!* *Slaking: Sleeping?* *Slaking: Not thinking too hard?* *Slaking: Dancing?*
SCENE 05	Attack the foe!
SCENE 06	The line you choose is important! Attack the foe! *Slaking: You're vain.* *Slaking: You're lonely.* *Slaking: You're wild.* *Slaking: You are unique.*
SCENE 07	Attack the foe!
SCENE 08	The line you choose is important! Attack the foe! *Slaking: You're perfect!* *Slaking: Patience!* *Slaking: Kindness!* *Slaking: I don't know.*
SCENE 09	The line you choose is important! Attack the foe! *Slaking: Stop the destruction!* *Slaking: Disappear!* *Slaking: Protect the world!* *Slaking: Show remorse!*
SCENE 10	Deliver a decisive blow!

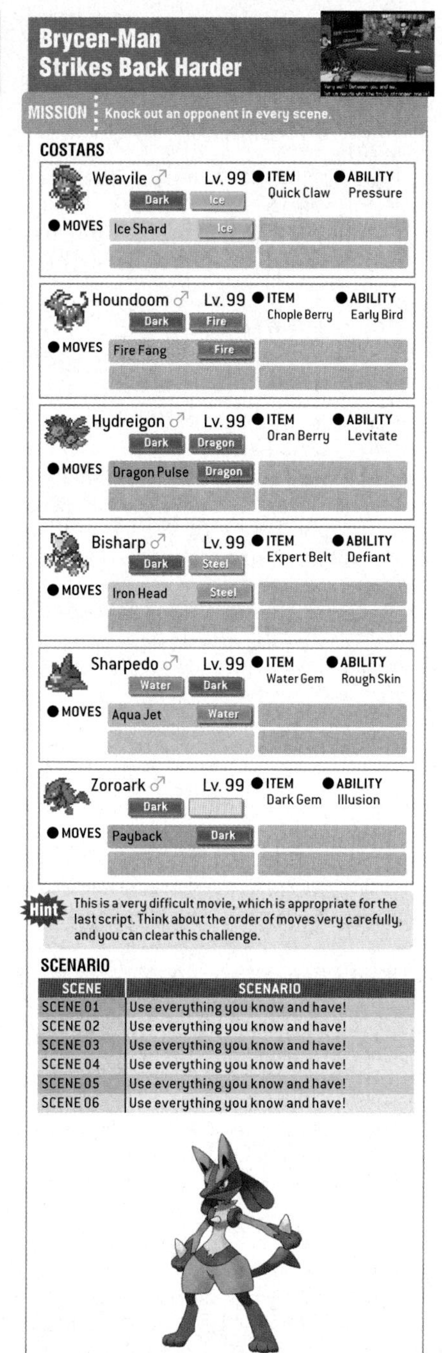

Brycen-Man Strikes Back Harder

MISSION: Knock out an opponent in every scene.

COSTARS

Pokémon	Type	Lv.	ITEM	ABILITY	MOVES
Weavile ♂	Dark / Ice	Lv. 99	Quick Claw	Pressure	Ice Shard (Ice)
Houndoom ♂	Dark / Fire	Lv. 99	Chople Berry	Early Bird	Fire Fang (Fire)
Hydreigon ♂	Dark / Dragon	Lv. 99	Oran Berry	Levitate	Dragon Pulse (Dragon)
Bisharp ♂	Dark / Steel	Lv. 99	Expert Belt	Defiant	Iron Head (Steel)
Sharpedo ♂	Water / Dark	Lv. 99	Water Gem	Rough Skin	Aqua Jet (Water)
Zoroark ♂	Dark	Lv. 99	Dark Gem	Illusion	Payback (Dark)

Hint: This is a very difficult movie, which is appropriate for the last script. Think about the order of moves very carefully, and you can clear this challenge.

SCENARIO

SCENE	SCENARIO
SCENE 01	Use everything you know and have!
SCENE 02	Use everything you know and have!
SCENE 03	Use everything you know and have!
SCENE 04	Use everything you know and have!
SCENE 05	Use everything you know and have!
SCENE 06	Use everything you know and have!

Tip: Make all 40 movies with happy endings, and you'll receive acclaim

If you get a happy ending in Brycen-Man Strikes Back Harder, a special ceremony will be held. To recognize your achievement in making all 40 movies into huge hits, all the staff members will fill the streets of Pokéstar Studios to praise you. Plus, they'll build a bronze statue on the studio lot to honor you!

Trainer, congratulations!

Now listen!
I was the director of your debut!

PWT

Pokémon World Tournament

Pokémon World Tournament

Aim for the Top at the PWT

Win your way through a series of grueling battles against the greatest Trainers of each region!

The Pokémon World Tournament (PWT) is a huge tournament-style competition in which the Pokémon Trainers of the world can test themselves against the best. Here you can battle not only the strongest Trainers in the Unova region, but also the Gym Leaders and Champions of all of the regions in the Pokémon series!

Guide to the PWT system

PWT Basics 1 The PWT is located south of Driftveil City

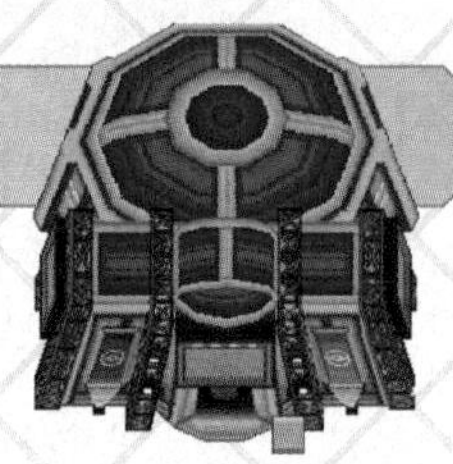

Head south from Driftveil City. If you wish to take part in the PWT, visit the large building in the center of the area. Register for the tournaments inside. Then get battling! When you win, you can exchange the BP you gain for cool items at the Exchange Service Corner.

PWT Lobby

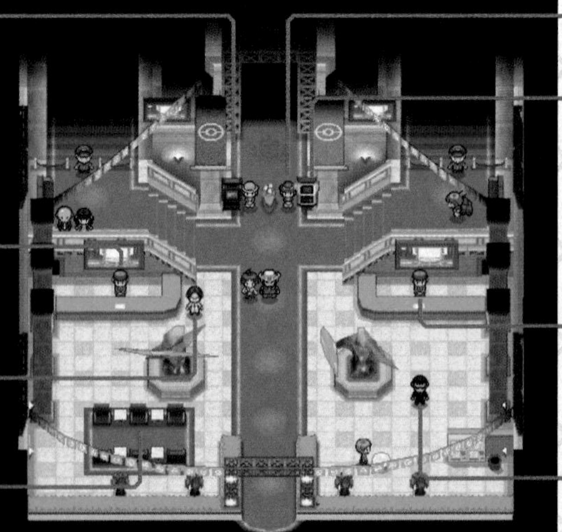

Records

Here you can check the number of wins you have had in the tournaments. You can also download tournaments using your wireless connection.

Exchange Service Corner Left clerk

Man who explains about BP

Lobby

After you take part in and win a tournament, the other Trainers who battled in the tournament with you will gather here in the lobby.

Reception Area

PC

You can use the PC in the building to change the Pokémon in your party without having to visit a Pokémon Center.

Exchange Service Corner Right clerk

Man who tells you about Trainers

This guy tells you about the Gym Leaders who take part in the tournaments, including their profiles and some rumors about them.

PWT Basics 2 The more you win, the more tournaments you can challenge

The number of tournaments you can take part in will increase as you fulfill certain requirements. If you win the World Leaders Tournament 10 times, for example, you will be able to challenge the Champions Tournament, where all of the Pokémon League Champions will be waiting for you.

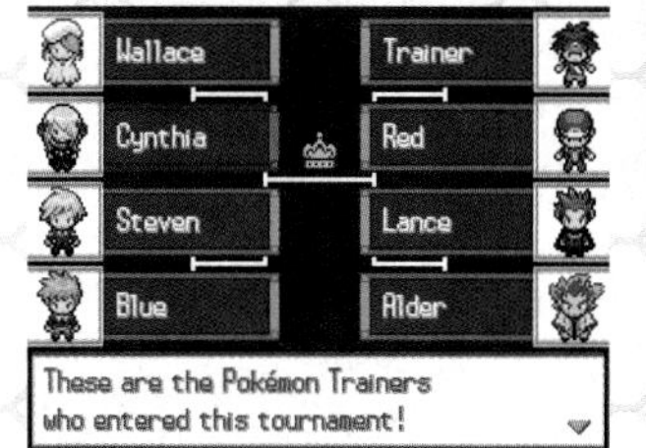

Step-by-Step PWT Tournaments

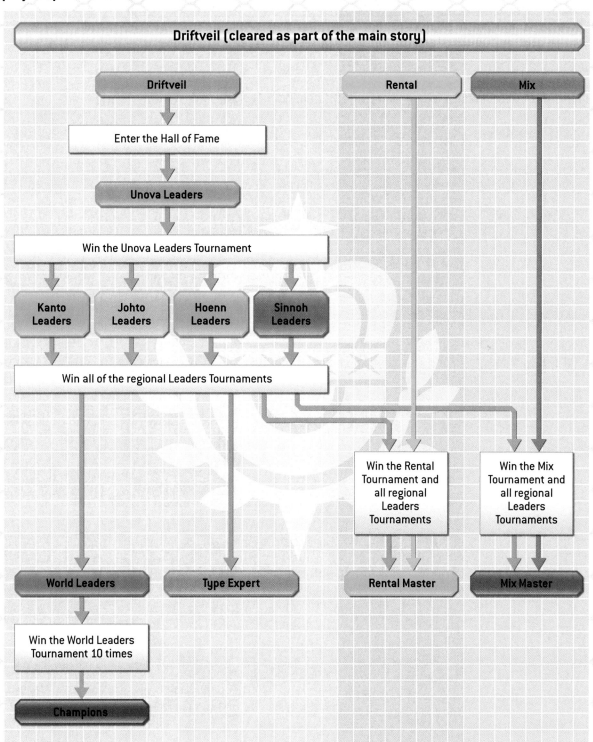

Driftveil (cleared as part of the main story)

- **Driftveil** → Enter the Hall of Fame → **Unova Leaders** → Win the Unova Leaders Tournament → **Kanto Leaders** / **Johto Leaders** / **Hoenn Leaders** / **Sinnoh Leaders** → Win all of the regional Leaders Tournaments
  - → **World Leaders** → Win the World Leaders Tournament 10 times → **Champions**
  - → **Type Expert**
- **Rental** + Win all of the regional Leaders Tournaments → Win the Rental Tournament and all regional Leaders Tournaments → **Rental Master**
- **Mix** + Win all of the regional Leaders Tournaments → Win the Mix Tournament and all regional Leaders Tournaments → **Mix Master**

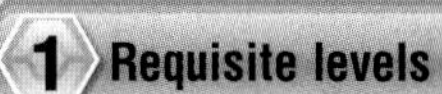 Learn the rules of each tournament

The PWT is a battle tournament with eight participants to determine who can make it to the end and seize the victory. When you register for a tournament, you'll be able to freely choose which of the four battle styles you prefer: Single, Double, Triple, or Rotation. You can obtain more BP when you win a tournament of Triple or Rotation Battles.

Rules for the Driftveil / Unova Leaders Tournaments

1 Requisite levels
- Can take part at any level. During the tournament, all of your Pokémon will temporarily become Lv. 25 (or Lv. 50 in the Unova Leaders Tournament).
- When your part in the tournament is over, they will return to their usual levels.

2 Battle rules
- Battle tournament where you defeat three opponents to win the tournament.
- Pokémon will be healed after each battle.

3 Eligible Pokémon
- Any Pokémon can participate.

Rules for other tournaments (other than Driftveil / Unova Leaders)

1 Participation Level
- Can take part at any level. During the tournament, all of your Pokémon will temporarily become Lv. 50.
- When your part in the tournament is over, they'll return to their usual levels.

2 Battle rules
- Battle tournament where you defeat three opponents to win the tournament.
- Pokémon will be healed after each battle.

3 Eligible Pokémon
- You cannot have two or more of the same Pokémon participate in a tournament.
- In Type Expert Tournaments, only Pokémon with the same type as the tournament can participate.

4 Ineligible Pokémon

Ineligible Pokémon are Mewtwo, Mew, Ho-Oh, Lugia, Celebi, Kyogre, Groudon, Rayquaza, Jirachi, Deoxys, Palkia, Dialga, Giratina, Phione, Manaphy, Darkrai, Shaymin, Arceus, Victini, Reshiram, Zekrom, Kyurem, Keldeo, Meloetta, and Eggs.

5 Item limitations
- The items held by your Pokémon must all be different.
- Pokémon holding Soul Dew cannot take part in the tournaments.

6 Move limitations
- Pokémon who know the move Sky Drop cannot take part in the tournaments.

Special rules for Mix / Mix Master Tournaments

In Mix and Mix Master Tournaments, you and your opponent will switch one party Pokémon (two in the case of a Triple Battle) before the battle begins. Once the battle ends, the switched Pokémon will return to their respective Trainers.

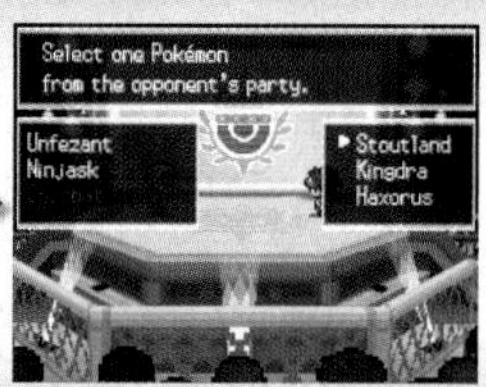

Special rules for Rental / Rental Master Tournaments

In Rental and Rental Master Tournaments, you will not battle with your own Pokémon, but with Pokémon that the PWT has readied for your use.

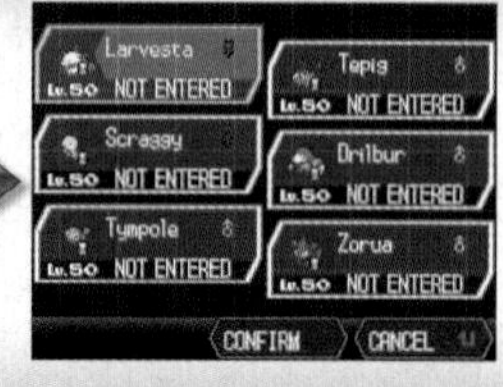

Special rules for Type Expert Tournaments

You participate by having three to six Pokémon of the same type in your party. However, you cannot use two or more of the same Pokémon.

PWT Basics 4 Exchange the BP (Battle Points) you win for items

The BP you receive in return for winning a tournament can be exchanged for a variety of items at the Exchange Service Counter. In most tournaments, you'll receive between one and three BP for winning; however, in the challenging World Leaders and Champions Tournaments, the fewer of your Pokémon that are knocked out, the more BP you will receive. Using the Triple Battle format, you can receive up to 18 BP if you win without having a single Pokémon faint in these tournaments.

BP awarded in each tournament

Tournament Name	Single Battle	Double Battle	Triple Battle	Rotation Battle
Driftveil	1 BP	1 BP	2 BP	2 BP
Unova Leaders	1 BP	1 BP	2 BP	2 BP
Kanto Leaders	2 BP	2 BP	3 BP	3 BP
Johto Leaders	2 BP	2 BP	3 BP	3 BP
Hoenn Leaders	2 BP	2 BP	3 BP	3 BP
Sinnoh Leaders	2 BP	2 BP	3 BP	3 BP
Type Expert	2 BP	2 BP	3 BP	3 BP

Tournament Name	Single Battle	Double Battle	Triple Battle	Rotation Battle
World Leaders	3–9 BP	3–12 BP	3–18 BP	3–12 BP
Champions	3–9 BP	3–12 BP	3–18 BP	3–12 BP
Rental	1 BP	1 BP	2 BP	2 BP
Rental Master	2 BP	2 BP	3 BP	3 BP
Mix	1 BP	1 BP	2 BP	2 BP
Mix Master	2 BP	2 BP	3 BP	3 BP

Items availabe at the Exchange Service Counter

Left clerk

Prize	Necessary BP
TM17 Protect	6 BP
TM20 Safeguard	6 BP
TM32 Double Team	6 BP
TM59 Incinerate	6 BP
TM31 Brick Break	12 BP
TM79 Frost Breath	12 BP
TM89 U-turn	12 BP
TM10 Hidden Power	18 BP
TM23 Smack Down	18 BP
TM48 Round	18 BP
TM75 Swords Dance	18 BP
TM87 Swagger	18 BP
TM88 Pluck	18 BP
TM34 Sludge Wave	24 BP
TM51 Ally Switch	24 BP
TM60 Quash	24 BP
TM64 Explosion	24 BP
TM77 Psych Up	24 BP

Right clerk

Prize	Necessary BP
Calcium	1 BP
Carbos	1 BP
HP Up	1 BP
Iron	1 BP
Protein	1 BP
Zinc	1 BP
Fire Stone	3 BP
Leaf Stone	3 BP
Thunderstone	3 BP
Water Stone	3 BP
Binding Band	8 BP
Muscle Band	8 BP
Razor Claw	8 BP
Razor Fang	8 BP
Scope Lens	8 BP

Prize	Necessary BP
Wide Lens	8 BP
Wise Glasses	8 BP
Air Balloon	12 BP
BrightPowder	12 BP
Focus Band	12 BP
Iron Ball	12 BP
Zoom Lens	12 BP
Absorb Bulb	16 BP
Cell Battery	16 BP
Eject Button	16 BP
Flame Orb	16 BP
Power Anklet	16 BP
Power Band	16 BP
Power Belt	16 BP
Power Bracer	16 BP

Prize	Necessary BP
Power Herb	16 BP
Power Lens	16 BP
Power Weight	16 BP
Red Card	16 BP
Toxic Orb	16 BP
White Herb	16 BP
Choice Band	24 BP
Choice Scarf	24 BP
Choice Specs	24 BP
Focus Sash	24 BP
Life Orb	24 BP
Rare Candy	24 BP

PWT Basics 5 Receive Medals from Mr. Medal

You can receive a total of 13 different Medals in the PWT. The World's Mightiest Medal can be received if you can manage to beat the fearsome competition in the Champions Tournament. The All Types Champ Medal will be yours if you win against all 17 types of the Type Expert Tournament. These two Medals are very difficult to obtain, so do your best and aim for a complete Medal collection!

Driftveil Mightiest

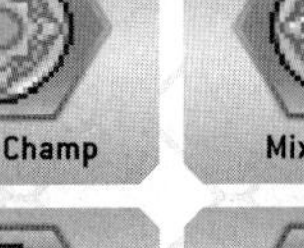
Rental Champ

Mix Champ

Unova Mightiest

Kanto Mightiest

Johto Mightiest

Hoenn Mightiest

Sinnoh Mightiest

Mightiest Leader

World's Mightiest

Rental Master

Mix Master

All Types Champ

Check p. 448 for the entire Medal list.

PWT challenger list

Driftveil

Cheren

Pokémon	Lv.	Type	Weak to
Stoutland	Lv. 25	Normal	Fighting
Zangoose	Lv. 25	Normal	Fighting
Cinccino	Lv. 25	Normal	Fighting
Watchog	Lv. 25	Normal	Fighting
Cinccino	Lv. 25	Normal	Fighting
Watchog	Lv. 25	Normal	Fighting

Roxie

Pokémon	Lv.	Type	Weak to
Scolipede	Lv. 25	Bug, Poison	Fire, Flying, Psychic, Rock
Seviper	Lv. 25	Poison	Ground, Psychic
Garbodor	Lv. 25	Poison	Ground, Psychic
Golbat	Lv. 25	Poison, Flying	Electric, Ice, Psychic, Rock
Garbodor	Lv. 25	Poison	Ground, Psychic
Golbat	Lv. 25	Poison, Flying	Electric, Ice, Psychic, Rock

Burgh

Pokémon	Lv.	Type	Weak to
Leavanny	Lv. 25	Bug, Grass	Fire, Flying, Ice, Poison, Bug, Rock
Vespiquen	Lv. 25	Bug, Flying	Rock, Fire, Electric, Ice, Flying
Crustle	Lv. 25	Bug, Rock	Water, Rock, Steel
Escavalier	Lv. 25	Bug, Steel	Fire
Crustle	Lv. 25	Bug, Rock	Water, Rock, Steel
Escavalier	Lv. 25	Bug, Steel	Fire

Elesa

Pokémon	Lv.	Type	Weak to
Zebstrika	Lv. 25	Electric	Ground
Flaaffy	Lv. 25	Electric	Ground
Galvantula	Lv. 25	Bug, Electric	Fire, Rock
Emolga	Lv. 25	Electric, Flying	Ice, Rock
Galvantula	Lv. 25	Bug, Electric	Fire, Rock
Emolga	Lv. 25	Electric, Flying	Ice, Rock

Driftveil (continued)

Clay

Pokémon	Lv.	Type	Weak to
Excadrill	Lv. 25	Ground, Steel	Fire, Water, Fighting, Ground
Claydol	Lv. 25	Ground, Psychic	Water, Grass, Ice, Bug, Ghost, Dark
Krokorok	Lv. 25	Ground, Dark	Water, Grass, Ice, Fighting, Bug
Palpitoad	Lv. 25	Water, Ground	Grass
Krokorok	Lv. 25	Ground, Dark	Water, Grass, Ice, Fighting, Bug
Palpitoad	Lv. 25	Water, Ground	Grass

Mix

Cheren

Pokémon	Lv.	Type	Weak to
Stoutland	Lv. 50	Normal	Fighting
Zangoose	Lv. 50	Normal	Fighting
Cinccino	Lv. 50	Normal	Fighting
Watchog	Lv. 50	Normal	Fighting
Cinccino	Lv. 50	Normal	Fighting
Watchog	Lv. 50	Normal	Fighting

Roxie

Pokémon	Lv.	Type	Weak to
Scolipede	Lv. 50	Bug, Poison	Fire, Flying, Psychic, Rock
Seviper	Lv. 50	Poison	Ground, Psychic
Garbodor	Lv. 50	Poison	Ground, Psychic
Golbat	Lv. 50	Poison, Flying	Electric, Ice, Psychic, Rock
Garbodor	Lv. 50	Poison	Ground, Psychic
Golbat	Lv. 50	Poison, Flying	Electric, Ice, Psychic, Rock

Burgh

Pokémon	Lv.	Type	Weak to
Leavanny	Lv. 50	Bug, Grass	Fire, Flying, Ice, Poison, Bug, Rock
Vespiquen	Lv. 50	Bug, Flying	Rock, Fire, Electric, Ice, Flying
Crustle	Lv. 50	Bug, Rock	Water, Rock, Steel
Escavalier	Lv. 50	Bug, Steel	Fire
Crustle	Lv. 50	Bug, Rock	Water, Rock, Steel
Escavalier	Lv. 50	Bug, Steel	Fire

Mix (continued)

Elesa

Pokémon	Lv.	Type	Weak to
Zebstrika	Lv. 50	Electric	Ground
Flaaffy	Lv. 50	Electric	Ground
Galvantula	Lv. 50	Bug / Electric	Fire, Rock
Emolga	Lv. 50	Electric / Flying	Ice, Rock
Galvantula	Lv. 50	Bug / Electric	Fire, Rock
Emolga	Lv. 50	Electric / Flying	Ice, Rock

Clay

Pokémon	Lv.	Type	Weak to
Excadrill	Lv. 50	Ground / Steel	Fire, Water, Fighting, Ground
Claydol	Lv. 50	Ground / Psychic	Water, Grass, Ice, Bug, Ghost, Dark
Krokorok	Lv. 50	Ground / Dark	Water, Grass, Ice, Fighting, Bug
Palpitoad	Lv. 50	Water / Ground	Grass
Krokorok	Lv. 50	Ground / Dark	Water, Grass, Ice, Fighting, Bug
Palpitoad	Lv. 50	Water / Ground	Grass

Bianca

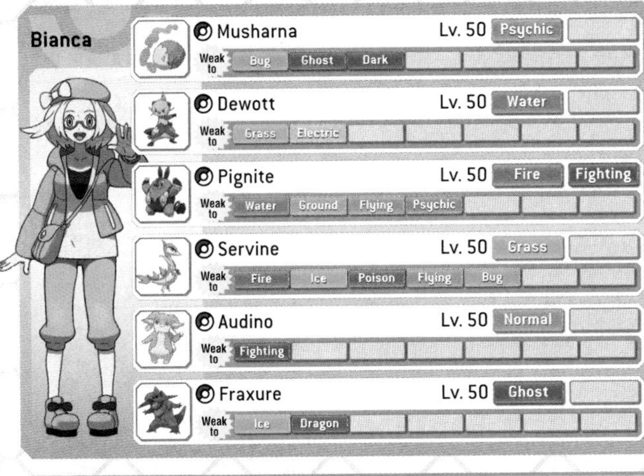

Pokémon	Lv.	Type	Weak to
Musharna	Lv. 50	Psychic	Bug, Ghost, Dark
Dewott	Lv. 50	Water	Grass, Electric
Pignite	Lv. 50	Fire / Fighting	Water, Ground, Flying, Psychic
Servine	Lv. 50	Grass	Fire, Ice, Poison, Flying, Bug
Audino	Lv. 50	Normal	Fighting
Fraxure	Lv. 50	Ghost	Ice, Dragon

Unova Leaders

Cheren

Pokémon	Lv.	Type	Weak to
Stoutland	Lv. 50	Normal	Fighting
Zangoose	Lv. 50	Normal	Fighting
Cinccino	Lv. 50	Normal	Fighting
Lopunny	Lv. 50	Normal	Fighting
Castform	Lv. 50	Normal	Fighting
Bouffalant	Lv. 50	Normal	Fighting

Unova Leaders (continued)

Roxie

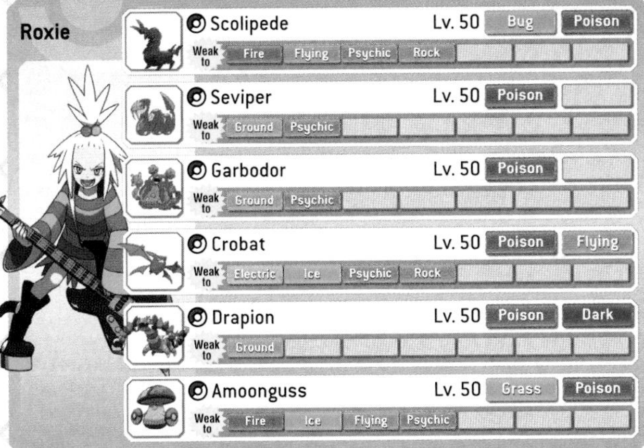

Pokémon	Lv.	Type	Weak to
Scolipede	Lv. 50	Bug / Poison	Fire, Flying, Psychic, Rock
Seviper	Lv. 50	Poison	Ground, Psychic
Garbodor	Lv. 50	Poison	Ground, Psychic
Crobat	Lv. 50	Poison / Flying	Electric, Ice, Psychic, Rock
Drapion	Lv. 50	Poison / Dark	Ground
Amoonguss	Lv. 50	Grass / Poison	Fire, Ice, Flying, Psychic

Burgh

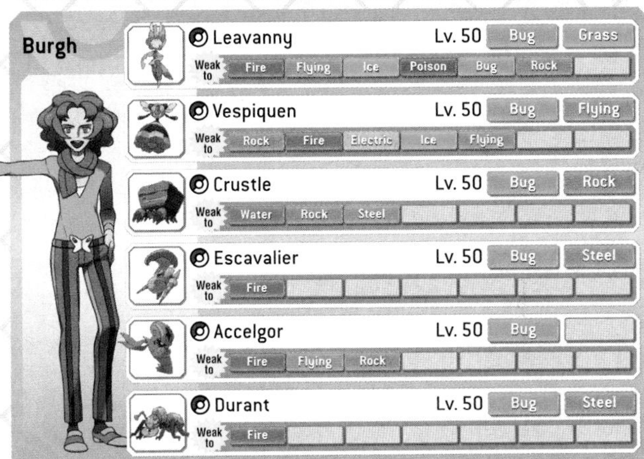

Pokémon	Lv.	Type	Weak to
Leavanny	Lv. 50	Bug / Grass	Fire, Flying, Ice, Poison, Bug, Rock
Vespiquen	Lv. 50	Bug / Flying	Rock, Fire, Electric, Ice, Flying
Crustle	Lv. 50	Bug / Rock	Water, Rock, Steel
Escavalier	Lv. 50	Bug / Steel	Fire
Accelgor	Lv. 50	Bug	Fire, Flying, Rock
Durant	Lv. 50	Bug / Steel	Fire

Elesa

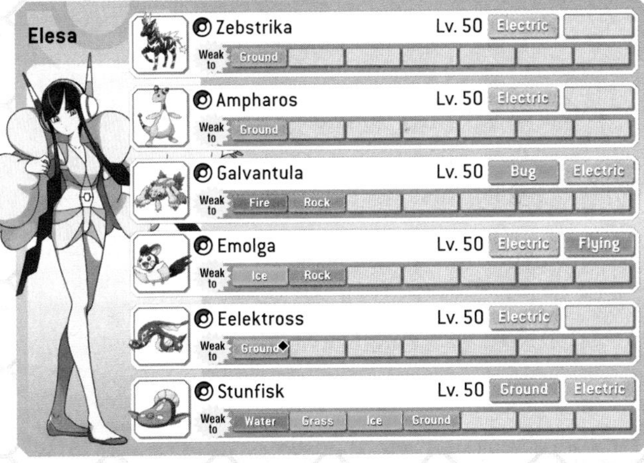

Pokémon	Lv.	Type	Weak to
Zebstrika	Lv. 50	Electric	Ground
Ampharos	Lv. 50	Electric	Ground
Galvantula	Lv. 50	Bug / Electric	Fire, Rock
Emolga	Lv. 50	Electric / Flying	Ice, Rock
Eelektross	Lv. 50	Electric	Ground◆
Stunfisk	Lv. 50	Ground / Electric	Water, Grass, Ice, Ground

Clay

Pokémon	Lv.	Type	Weak to
Excadrill	Lv. 50	Ground / Steel	Fire, Water, Fighting, Ground
Claydol	Lv. 50	Ground / Psychic	Water, Grass, Ice, Bug, Ghost, Dark
Krookodile	Lv. 50	Ground / Dark	Water, Grass, Ice, Fighting, Bug
Seismitoad	Lv. 50	Water / Ground	Grass
Mamoswine	Lv. 50	Ice / Ground	Fire◆, Water, Grass, Fighting, Steel
Golurk	Lv. 50	Ground / Ghost	Water, Grass, Ice, Ghost, Dark

◆ The damage may change depending on the effects of this Pokémon's Ability.

Unova Leaders (continued)

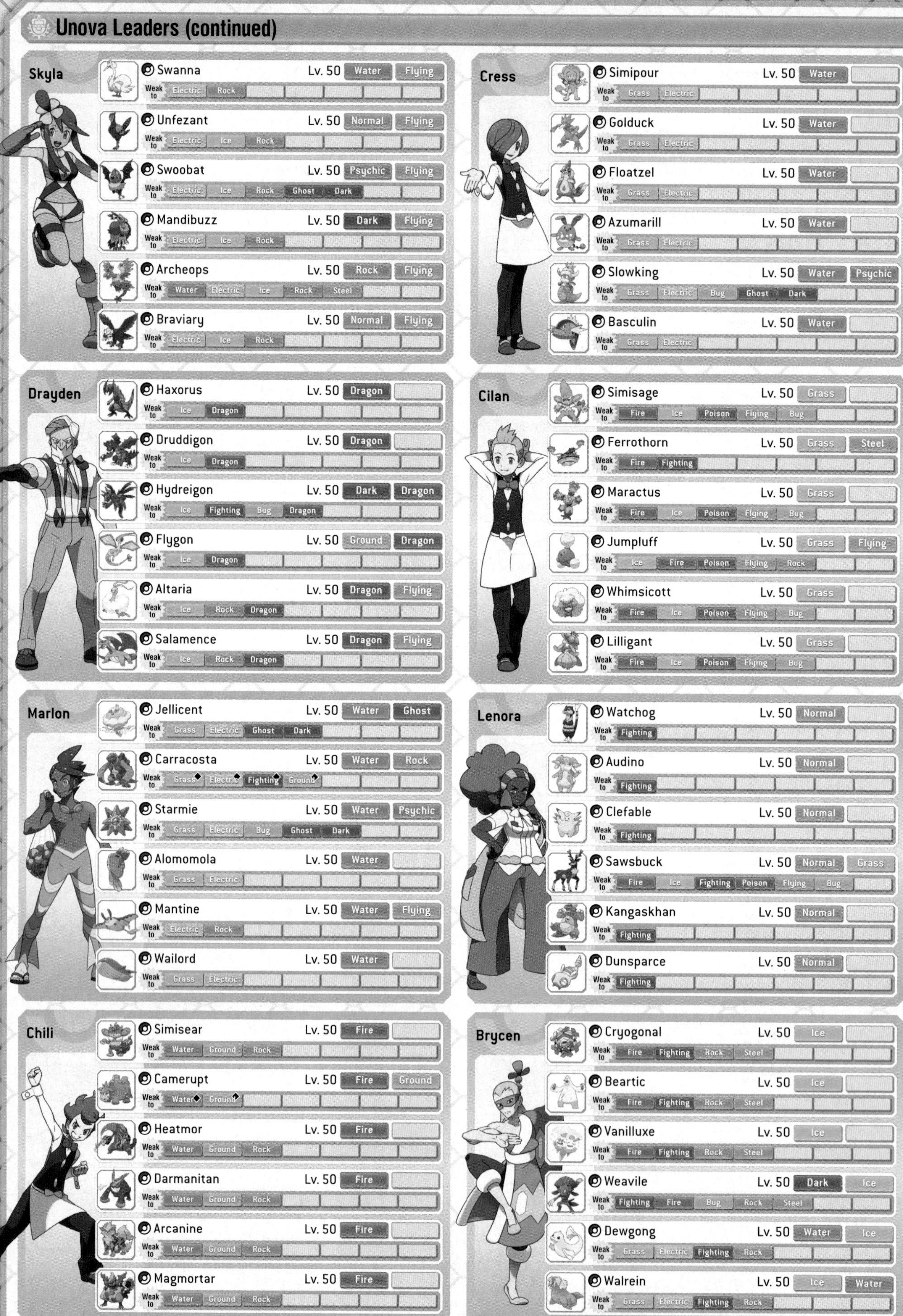

Skyla

Pokémon	Lv.	Type	Type	Weak to
Swanna	Lv. 50	Water	Flying	Electric, Rock
Unfezant	Lv. 50	Normal	Flying	Electric, Ice, Rock
Swoobat	Lv. 50	Psychic	Flying	Electric, Ice, Rock, Ghost, Dark
Mandibuzz	Lv. 50	Dark	Flying	Electric, Ice, Rock
Archeops	Lv. 50	Rock	Flying	Water, Electric, Ice, Rock, Steel
Braviary	Lv. 50	Normal	Flying	Electric, Ice, Rock

Cress

Pokémon	Lv.	Type	Type	Weak to
Simipour	Lv. 50	Water		Grass, Electric
Golduck	Lv. 50	Water		Grass, Electric
Floatzel	Lv. 50	Water		Grass, Electric
Azumarill	Lv. 50	Water		Grass, Electric
Slowking	Lv. 50	Water	Psychic	Grass, Electric, Bug, Ghost, Dark
Basculin	Lv. 50	Water		Grass, Electric

Drayden

Pokémon	Lv.	Type	Type	Weak to
Haxorus	Lv. 50	Dragon		Ice, Dragon
Druddigon	Lv. 50	Dragon		Ice, Dragon
Hydreigon	Lv. 50	Dark	Dragon	Ice, Fighting, Bug, Dragon
Flygon	Lv. 50	Ground	Dragon	Ice, Dragon
Altaria	Lv. 50	Dragon	Flying	Ice, Rock, Dragon
Salamence	Lv. 50	Dragon	Flying	Ice, Rock, Dragon

Cilan

Pokémon	Lv.	Type	Type	Weak to
Simisage	Lv. 50	Grass		Fire, Ice, Poison, Flying, Bug
Ferrothorn	Lv. 50	Grass	Steel	Fire, Fighting
Maractus	Lv. 50	Grass		Fire, Ice, Poison, Flying, Bug
Jumpluff	Lv. 50	Grass	Flying	Ice, Fire, Poison, Flying, Rock
Whimsicott	Lv. 50	Grass		Fire, Ice, Poison, Flying, Bug
Lilligant	Lv. 50	Grass		Fire, Ice, Poison, Flying, Bug

Marlon

Pokémon	Lv.	Type	Type	Weak to
Jellicent	Lv. 50	Water	Ghost	Grass, Electric, Ghost, Dark
Carracosta	Lv. 50	Water	Rock	Grass◆, Electric◆, Fighting◆, Ground◆
Starmie	Lv. 50	Water	Psychic	Grass, Electric, Bug, Ghost, Dark
Alomomola	Lv. 50	Water		Grass, Electric
Mantine	Lv. 50	Water	Flying	Electric, Rock
Wailord	Lv. 50	Water		Grass, Electric

Lenora

Pokémon	Lv.	Type	Type	Weak to
Watchog	Lv. 50	Normal		Fighting
Audino	Lv. 50	Normal		Fighting
Clefable	Lv. 50	Normal		Fighting
Sawsbuck	Lv. 50	Normal	Grass	Fire, Ice, Fighting, Poison, Flying, Bug
Kangaskhan	Lv. 50	Normal		Fighting
Dunsparce	Lv. 50	Normal		Fighting

Chili

Pokémon	Lv.	Type	Type	Weak to
Simisear	Lv. 50	Fire		Water, Ground, Rock
Camerupt	Lv. 50	Fire	Ground	Water◆, Ground◆
Heatmor	Lv. 50	Fire		Water, Ground, Rock
Darmanitan	Lv. 50	Fire		Water, Ground, Rock
Arcanine	Lv. 50	Fire		Water, Ground, Rock
Magmortar	Lv. 50	Fire		Water, Ground, Rock

Brycen

Pokémon	Lv.	Type	Type	Weak to
Cryogonal	Lv. 50	Ice		Fire, Fighting, Rock, Steel
Beartic	Lv. 50	Ice		Fire, Fighting, Rock, Steel
Vanilluxe	Lv. 50	Ice		Fire, Fighting, Rock, Steel
Weavile	Lv. 50	Dark	Ice	Fighting, Fire, Bug, Rock, Steel
Dewgong	Lv. 50	Water	Ice	Grass, Electric, Fighting, Rock
Walrein	Lv. 50	Ice	Water	Grass, Electric, Fighting, Rock

◆ The damage may change depending on the effects of this Pokémon's Ability.

Kanto Leaders

Brock

Pokémon	Lv.	Type	Weak to
Onix	Lv. 50	Rock, Ground	Water, Grass, Ice, Fighting, Ground, Steel
Golem	Lv. 50	Rock, Ground	Water, Grass, Ice, Fighting, Ground, Steel
Kabutops	Lv. 50	Rock, Water	Grass, Electric, Fighting, Ground
Omastar	Lv. 50	Rock, Water	Grass, Electric, Fighting, Ground
Aerodactyl	Lv. 50	Rock, Flying	Water, Electric, Ice, Rock, Steel
Relicanth	Lv. 50	Water, Rock	Grass, Electric, Fighting, Ground

Sabrina

Pokémon	Lv.	Type	Weak to
Alakazam	Lv. 50	Psychic	Bug, Ghost, Dark
Hypno	Lv. 50	Psychic	Bug, Ghost, Dark
Mr. Mime	Lv. 50	Psychic	Bug◆, Ghost◆, Dark◆
Slowking	Lv. 50	Water, Psychic	Grass, Electric, Bug, Ghost, Dark
Espeon	Lv. 50	Psychic	Bug, Ghost, Dark
Jynx	Lv. 50	Ice, Psychic	Fire◆, Bug, Rock, Ghost, Dark, Steel

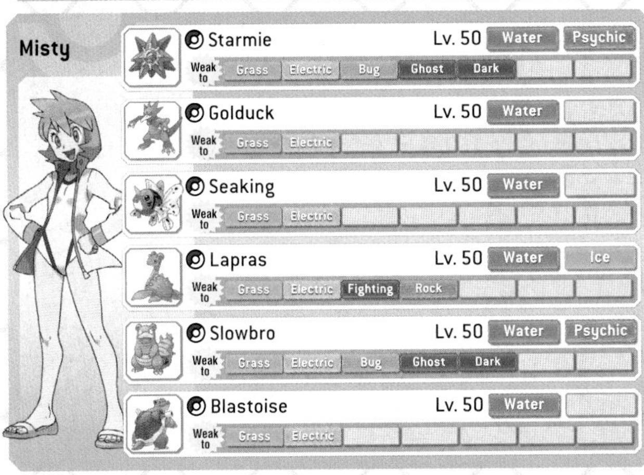

Misty

Pokémon	Lv.	Type	Weak to
Starmie	Lv. 50	Water, Psychic	Grass, Electric, Bug, Ghost, Dark
Golduck	Lv. 50	Water	Grass, Electric
Seaking	Lv. 50	Water	Grass, Electric
Lapras	Lv. 50	Water, Ice	Grass, Electric, Fighting, Rock
Slowbro	Lv. 50	Water, Psychic	Grass, Electric, Bug, Ghost, Dark
Blastoise	Lv. 50	Water	Grass, Electric

Blaine

Pokémon	Lv.	Type	Weak to
Arcanine	Lv. 50	Fire	Water, Ground, Rock
Ninetales	Lv. 50	Fire	Water, Ground, Rock
Charizard	Lv. 50	Fire, Flying	Rock, Water, Electric
Magmortar	Lv. 50	Fire	Water, Ground, Rock
Flareon	Lv. 50	Fire	Water, Ground, Rock
Rapidash	Lv. 50	Fire	Water, Ground, Rock

Lt. Surge

Pokémon	Lv.	Type	Weak to
Raichu	Lv. 50	Electric	Ground
Electrode	Lv. 50	Electric	Ground
Magnezone	Lv. 50	Electric, Steel	Ground, Fire, Fighting
Electivire	Lv. 50	Electric	Ground
Jolteon	Lv. 50	Electric	Ground
Ampharos	Lv. 50	Electric	Ground

Giovanni

Pokémon	Lv.	Type	Weak to
Rhyperior	Lv. 50	Ground, Rock	Water◆, Grass◆, Ice◆, Fighting◆, Ground◆, Steel◆
Golem	Lv. 50	Rock, Ground	Water, Grass, Ice, Fighting, Ground, Steel
Marowak	Lv. 50	Ground	Water, Grass, Ice
Sandslash	Lv. 50	Ground	Water, Grass, Ice
Nidoking	Lv. 50	Poison, Ground	Water, Ice, Ground, Psychic
Nidoqueen	Lv. 50	Poison, Ground	Water, Ice, Ground, Psychic

Erika

Pokémon	Lv.	Type	Weak to
Vileplume	Lv. 50	Grass, Poison	Fire, Ice, Flying, Psychic
Venusaur	Lv. 50	Grass, Poison	Fire, Ice, Flying, Psychic
Victreebel	Lv. 50	Grass, Poison	Fire, Ice, Flying, Psychic
Exeggutor	Lv. 50	Grass, Psychic	Bug, Fire, Ice, Poison, Flying, Ghost, Dark
Tangrowth	Lv. 50	Grass	Fire, Ice, Poison, Flying, Bug
Bellossom	Lv. 50	Grass	Fire, Ice, Poison, Flying, Bug

Janine

Pokémon	Lv.	Type	Weak to
Venomoth	Lv. 50	Bug, Poison	Fire, Flying, Psychic, Rock
Weezing	Lv. 50	Poison	Ground◆, Psychic
Ariados	Lv. 50	Bug, Poison	Fire, Flying, Psychic, Rock
Crobat	Lv. 50	Poison, Flying	Electric, Ice, Psychic, Rock
Arbok	Lv. 50	Poison	Ground, Psychic
Tentacruel	Lv. 50	Water, Poison	Electric, Ground, Psychic

Johto Leaders

Falkner

Pokémon	Lv.	Type	Type	Weak to
Pidgeot	Lv. 50	Normal	Flying	Electric, Ice, Rock
Fearow	Lv. 50	Normal	Flying	Electric, Ice, Rock
Dodrio	Lv. 50	Normal	Flying	Electric, Ice, Rock
Honchkrow	Lv. 50	Dark	Flying	Electric, Ice, Rock
Xatu	Lv. 50	Psychic	Flying	Electric, Ice, Rock, Ghost, Dark
Noctowl	Lv. 50	Normal	Flying	Electric, Ice, Rock

Chuck

Pokémon	Lv.	Type	Type	Weak to
Poliwrath	Lv. 50	Water	Fighting	Grass, Electric, Flying, Psychic
Machamp	Lv. 50	Fighting		Flying, Psychic
Hitmontop	Lv. 50	Fighting		Flying, Psychic
Hitmonchan	Lv. 50	Fighting		Flying, Psychic
Hitmonlee	Lv. 50	Fighting		Flying, Psychic
Primeape	Lv. 50	Fighting		Flying, Psychic

Bugsy

Pokémon	Lv.	Type	Type	Weak to
Scizor	Lv. 50	Bug	Steel	Fire
Shuckle	Lv. 50	Bug	Rock	Water, Rock, Steel
Heracross	Lv. 50	Bug	Fighting	Flying, Fire, Psychic
Pinsir	Lv. 50	Bug		Fire, Flying, Rock
Forretress	Lv. 50	Bug	Steel	Fire
Yanmega	Lv. 50	Bug	Flying	Rock, Fire, Electric, Ice, Flying

Jasmine

Pokémon	Lv.	Type	Type	Weak to
Steelix	Lv. 50	Steel	Ground	Fire, Water, Fighting, Ground
Magnezone	Lv. 50	Electric	Steel	Ground, Fire, Fighting
Forretress	Lv. 50	Bug	Steel	Fire
Skarmory	Lv. 50	Steel	Flying	Fire, Electric
Metagross	Lv. 50	Steel	Psychic	Fire, Ground
Mawile	Lv. 50	Steel		Fire, Fighting, Ground

Whitney

Pokémon	Lv.	Type	Type	Weak to
Miltank	Lv. 50	Normal		Fighting
Wigglytuff	Lv. 50	Normal		Fighting
Tauros	Lv. 50	Normal		Fighting
Ambipom	Lv. 50	Normal		Fighting
Ursaring	Lv. 50	Normal		Fighting
Clefable	Lv. 50	Normal		Fighting

Pryce

Pokémon	Lv.	Type	Type	Weak to
Mamoswine	Lv. 50	Ice	Ground	Fire◆, Water, Grass, Fighting, Steel
Jynx	Lv. 50	Ice	Psychic	Fire◆, Bug, Rock, Ghost, Dark, Steel
Dewgong	Lv. 50	Water	Ice	Grass, Electric, Fighting, Rock
Cloyster	Lv. 50	Water	Ice	Grass, Electric, Fighting, Rock
Lapras	Lv. 50	Water	Ice	Grass, Electric, Fighting, Rock
Weavile	Lv. 50	Dark	Ice	Fighting, Fire, Bug, Rock, Steel

Morty

Pokémon	Lv.	Type	Type	Weak to
Gengar	Lv. 50	Ghost	Poison	Ground◆, Psychic, Ghost, Dark
Mismagius	Lv. 50	Ghost		Ghost, Dark
Banette	Lv. 50	Ghost		Ghost, Dark
Dusknoir	Lv. 50	Ghost		Ghost, Dark
Sableye	Lv. 50	Dark	Ghost	
Froslass	Lv. 50	Ice	Ghost	Fire, Rock, Ghost, Dark, Steel

Clair

Pokémon	Lv.	Type	Type	Weak to
Dragonite	Lv. 50	Dragon	Flying	Ice, Rock, Dragon
Kingdra	Lv. 50	Water	Dragon	Dragon
Altaria	Lv. 50	Dragon	Flying	Ice, Rock, Dragon
Salamence	Lv. 50	Dragon	Flying	Ice, Rock, Dragon
Druddigon	Lv. 50	Dragon		Ice, Dragon
Garchomp	Lv. 50	Dragon	Ground	Ice, Dragon

◆ The damage may change depending on the effects of this Pokémon's Ability.

Hoenn Leaders

Roxanne

Pokémon	Lv.	Type	Type	Weak to
Probopass	Lv. 50	Rock	Steel	Fighting, Ground, Water
Armaldo	Lv. 50	Rock	Bug	Water, Rock, Steel
Cradily	Lv. 50	Rock	Grass	Ice, Fighting, Bug, Steel
Aggron	Lv. 50	Steel	Rock	Fighting, Ground, Water
Relicanth	Lv. 50	Water	Rock	Bug, Electric, Fighting, Ground
Golem	Lv. 50	Rock	Ground	Water, Grass, Ice, Fighting, Ground, Steel

Norman

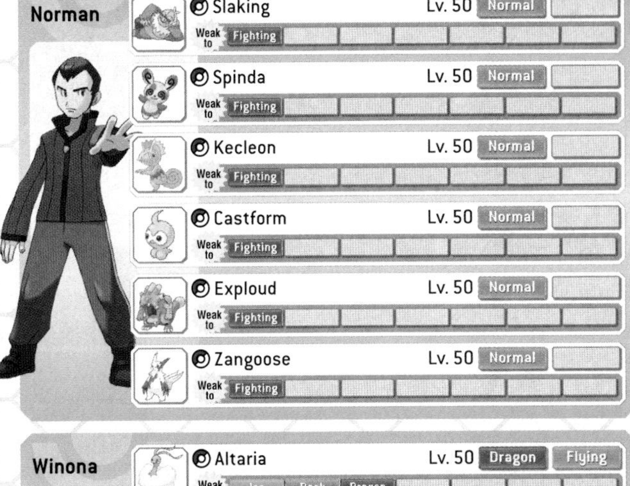

Pokémon	Lv.	Type	Type	Weak to
Slaking	Lv. 50	Normal		Fighting
Spinda	Lv. 50	Normal		Fighting
Kecleon	Lv. 50	Normal		Fighting
Castform	Lv. 50	Normal		Fighting
Exploud	Lv. 50	Normal		Fighting
Zangoose	Lv. 50	Normal		Fighting

Brawly

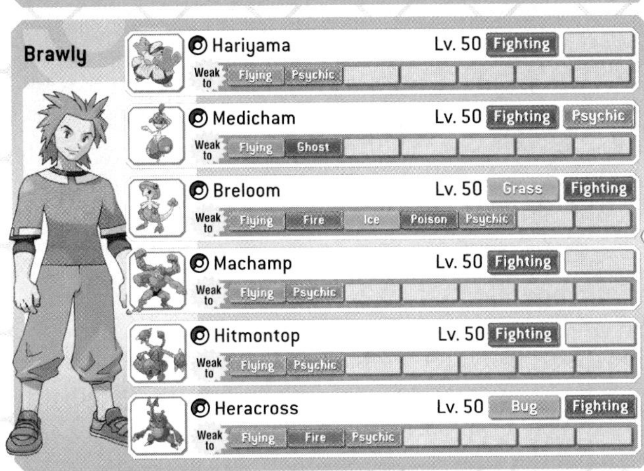

Pokémon	Lv.	Type	Type	Weak to
Hariyama	Lv. 50	Fighting		Flying, Psychic
Medicham	Lv. 50	Fighting	Psychic	Flying, Ghost
Breloom	Lv. 50	Grass	Fighting	Flying, Fire, Ice, Poison, Psychic
Machamp	Lv. 50	Fighting		Flying, Psychic
Hitmontop	Lv. 50	Fighting		Flying, Psychic
Heracross	Lv. 50	Bug	Fighting	Flying, Fire, Psychic

Winona

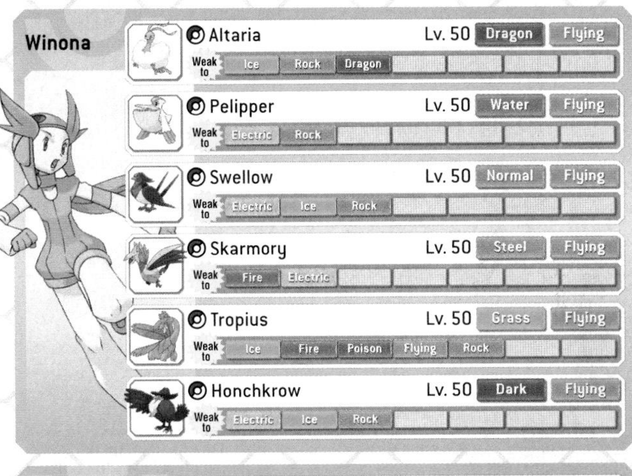

Pokémon	Lv.	Type	Type	Weak to
Altaria	Lv. 50	Dragon	Flying	Ice, Rock, Dragon
Pelipper	Lv. 50	Water	Flying	Electric, Rock
Swellow	Lv. 50	Normal	Flying	Electric, Ice, Rock
Skarmory	Lv. 50	Steel	Flying	Fire, Electric
Tropius	Lv. 50	Grass	Flying	Ice, Fire, Poison, Flying, Rock
Honchkrow	Lv. 50	Dark	Flying	Electric, Ice, Rock

Wattson

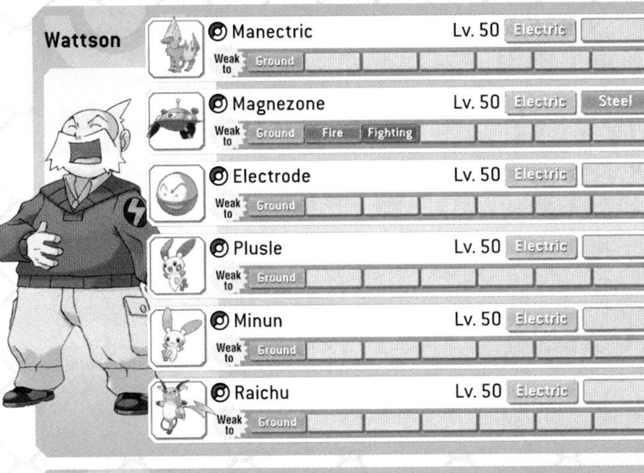

Pokémon	Lv.	Type	Type	Weak to
Manectric	Lv. 50	Electric		Ground
Magnezone	Lv. 50	Electric	Steel	Ground, Fire, Fighting
Electrode	Lv. 50	Electric		Ground
Plusle	Lv. 50	Electric		Ground
Minun	Lv. 50	Electric		Ground
Raichu	Lv. 50	Electric		Ground

Tate

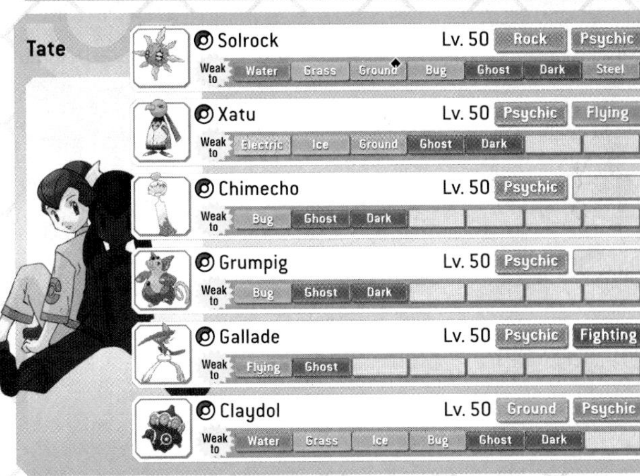

Pokémon	Lv.	Type	Type	Weak to
Solrock	Lv. 50	Rock	Psychic	Water, Grass, Ground◆, Bug, Ghost, Dark, Steel
Xatu	Lv. 50	Psychic	Flying	Electric, Ice, Ground, Ghost, Dark
Chimecho	Lv. 50	Psychic		Bug, Ghost, Dark
Grumpig	Lv. 50	Psychic		Bug, Ghost, Dark
Gallade	Lv. 50	Psychic	Fighting	Flying, Ghost
Claydol	Lv. 50	Ground	Psychic	Water, Grass, Ice, Bug, Ghost, Dark

Flannery

Pokémon	Lv.	Type	Type	Weak to
Torkoal	Lv. 50	Fire		Water, Ground, Rock
Camerupt	Lv. 50	Fire	Ground	Water◆, Ground◆
Magcargo	Lv. 50	Fire	Rock	Water, Ground, Fighting, Rock
Blaziken	Lv. 50	Fire	Fighting	Water, Ground, Flying, Psychic
Houndoom	Lv. 50	Dark	Fire	Water, Fighting, Ground, Rock
Magmortar	Lv. 50	Fire		Water, Ground, Rock

Liza

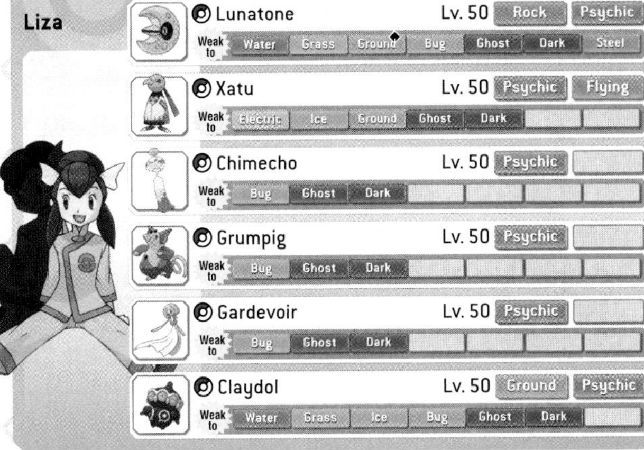

Pokémon	Lv.	Type	Type	Weak to
Lunatone	Lv. 50	Rock	Psychic	Water, Grass, Ground◆, Bug, Ghost, Dark, Steel
Xatu	Lv. 50	Psychic	Flying	Electric, Ice, Ground, Ghost, Dark
Chimecho	Lv. 50	Psychic		Bug, Ghost, Dark
Grumpig	Lv. 50	Psychic		Bug, Ghost, Dark
Gardevoir	Lv. 50	Psychic		Bug, Ghost, Dark
Claydol	Lv. 50	Ground	Psychic	Water, Grass, Ice, Bug, Ghost, Dark

Hoenn Leaders (continued)

Juan

Pokémon	Lv.	Type	Weak to
Kingdra	Lv. 50	Water / Dragon	Dragon
Walrein	Lv. 50	Ice / Water	Grass, Electric, Fighting, Rock
Crawdaunt	Lv. 50	Water / Dark	Grass, Electric, Fighting, Bug
Whiscash	Lv. 50	Water / Ground	Grass
Huntail	Lv. 50	Water	Grass, Electric
Gorebyss	Lv. 50	Water	Grass, Electric

Sinnoh Leaders

Roark

Pokémon	Lv.	Type	Weak to
Rampardos	Lv. 50	Rock	Water, Grass, Fighting, Ground, Steel
Probopass	Lv. 50	Rock / Steel	Fighting, Ground, Water
Sudowoodo	Lv. 50	Rock	Water, Grass, Fighting, Ground, Steel
Onix	Lv. 50	Rock / Ground	Water, Grass, Ice, Fighting, Ground, Steel
Golem	Lv. 50	Rock / Ground	Water, Grass, Ice, Fighting, Ground, Steel
Relicanth	Lv. 50	Water / Rock	Grass, Electric, Fighting, Ground

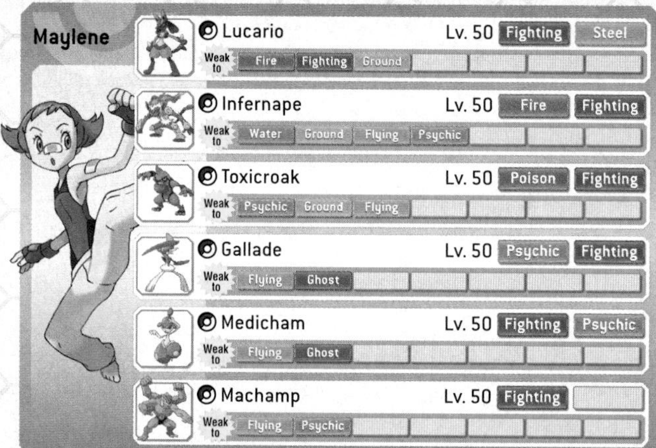

Maylene

Pokémon	Lv.	Type	Weak to
Lucario	Lv. 50	Fighting / Steel	Fire, Fighting, Ground
Infernape	Lv. 50	Fire / Fighting	Water, Ground, Flying, Psychic
Toxicroak	Lv. 50	Poison / Fighting	Psychic, Ground, Flying
Gallade	Lv. 50	Psychic / Fighting	Flying, Ghost
Medicham	Lv. 50	Fighting / Psychic	Flying, Ghost
Machamp	Lv. 50	Fighting	Flying, Psychic

Gardenia

Pokémon	Lv.	Type	Weak to
Roserade	Lv. 50	Grass / Poison	Fire, Ice, Flying, Psychic
Carnivine	Lv. 50	Grass	Fire, Ice, Poison, Flying, Bug
Cherrim	Lv. 50	Grass	Fire, Ice, Poison, Flying, Bug
Tangrowth	Lv. 50	Grass	Fire, Ice, Poison, Flying, Bug
Leafeon	Lv. 50	Grass	Fire, Ice, Poison, Flying, Bug
Torterra	Lv. 50	Grass / Ground	Ice, Fire, Flying, Bug

Crasher

Pokémon	Lv.	Type	Weak to
Floatzel	Lv. 50	Water	Grass, Electric
Empoleon	Lv. 50	Water / Steel	Electric, Fighting, Ground
Lumineon	Lv. 50	Water	Grass, Electric
Gastrodon	Lv. 50	Water / Ground	Grass
Quagsire	Lv. 50	Water / Ground	Grass
Gyarados	Lv. 50	Water / Flying	Electric, Rock

Fantina

Pokémon	Lv.	Type	Weak to
Mismagius	Lv. 50	Ghost	Ghost, Dark
Drifblim	Lv. 50	Ghost / Flying	Electric, Ice, Rock, Ghost, Dark
Spiritomb	Lv. 50	Ghost / Dark	
Dusknoir	Lv. 50	Ghost	Ghost, Dark
Rotom	Lv. 50	Electric / Ghost	Ground◆, Ghost, Dark
Gengar	Lv. 50	Ghost / Poison	Ground◆, Psychic, Ghost, Dark

Byron

Pokémon	Lv.	Type	Weak to
Bastiodon	Lv. 50	Rock / Steel	Fighting, Ground, Water
Steelix	Lv. 50	Steel / Ground	Fire, Fighting, Water, Ground
Bronzong	Lv. 50	Steel / Psychic	Fire◆, Ground◆
Magnezone	Lv. 50	Electric / Steel	Ground, Fire, Fighting
Aggron	Lv. 50	Steel / Rock	Fighting, Ground, Water
Forretress	Lv. 50	Bug / Steel	Fire

◆ The damage may change depending on the effects of this Pokémon's Ability.

Sinnoh Leaders (continued)

Candice

Pokémon	Lv.	Type	Weak to
Froslass	Lv. 50	Ice / Ghost	Fire, Rock, Ghost, Dark, Steel
Abomasnow	Lv. 50	Grass / Ice	Fire, Fighting, Flying, Poison, Bug, Rock, Steel
Weavile	Lv. 50	Dark / Ice	Fighting, Fire, Bug, Rock, Steel
Glaceon	Lv. 50	Ice	Fire, Fighting, Rock, Steel
Mamoswine	Lv. 50	Ice / Ground	Fire, Water, Grass, Fighting, Steel
Glalie	Lv. 50	Ice	Fire, Fighting, Rock, Steel

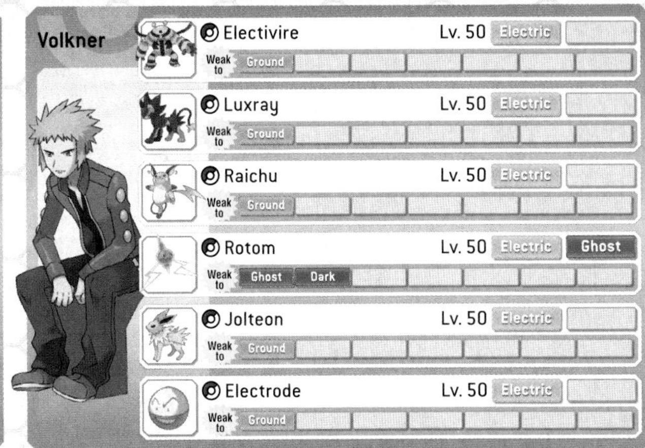

Volkner

Pokémon	Lv.	Type	Weak to
Electivire	Lv. 50	Electric	Ground
Luxray	Lv. 50	Electric	Ground
Raichu	Lv. 50	Electric	Ground
Rotom	Lv. 50	Electric / Ghost	Ghost, Dark
Jolteon	Lv. 50	Electric	Ground
Electrode	Lv. 50	Electric	Ground

World Leaders / Type Experts

Cheren (Normal Expert)

Pokémon	Lv.	Type	Weak to
Stoutland	Lv. 50	Normal	Fighting
Porygon-Z	Lv. 50	Normal	Fighting
Cinccino	Lv. 50	Normal	Fighting
Lickilicky	Lv. 50	Normal	Fighting
Castform	Lv. 50	Normal	Fighting
Bouffalant	Lv. 50	Normal	Fighting

Elesa (Electric Expert)

Pokémon	Lv.	Type	Weak to
Zebstrika	Lv. 50	Electric	Ground
Ampharos	Lv. 50	Electric	Ground
Luxray	Lv. 50	Electric	Ground
Emolga	Lv. 50	Electric / Flying	Ice, Rock
Eelektross	Lv. 50	Electric	Ground
Stunfisk	Lv. 50	Ground / Electric	Water, Grass, Ice, Ground

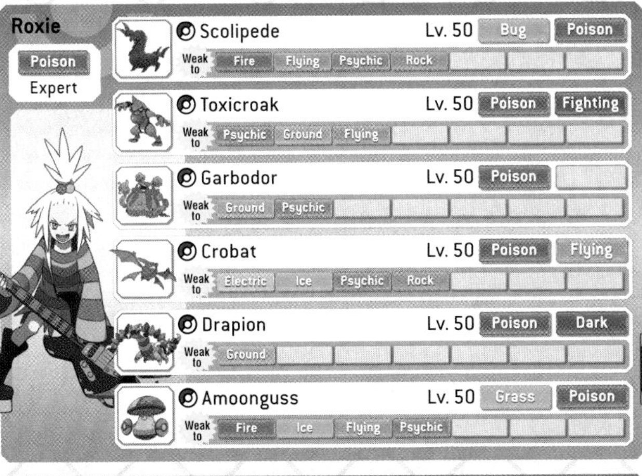

Roxie (Poison Expert)

Pokémon	Lv.	Type	Weak to
Scolipede	Lv. 50	Bug / Poison	Fire, Flying, Psychic, Rock
Toxicroak	Lv. 50	Poison / Fighting	Psychic, Ground, Flying
Garbodor	Lv. 50	Poison	Ground, Psychic
Crobat	Lv. 50	Poison / Flying	Electric, Ice, Psychic, Rock
Drapion	Lv. 50	Poison / Dark	Ground
Amoonguss	Lv. 50	Grass / Poison	Fire, Ice, Flying, Psychic

Clay (Ground Expert)

Pokémon	Lv.	Type	Weak to
Excadrill	Lv. 50	Ground / Steel	Fire, Water, Fighting, Ground
Flygon	Lv. 50	Ground / Dragon	Ice, Dragon
Krookodile	Lv. 50	Ground / Dark	Water, Grass, Ice, Fighting, Bug
Seismitoad	Lv. 50	Water / Ground	Grass
Mamoswine	Lv. 50	Ice / Ground	Fire, Water, Grass, Fighting, Steel
Golurk	Lv. 50	Ground / Ghost	Water, Grass, Ice, Ghost, Dark

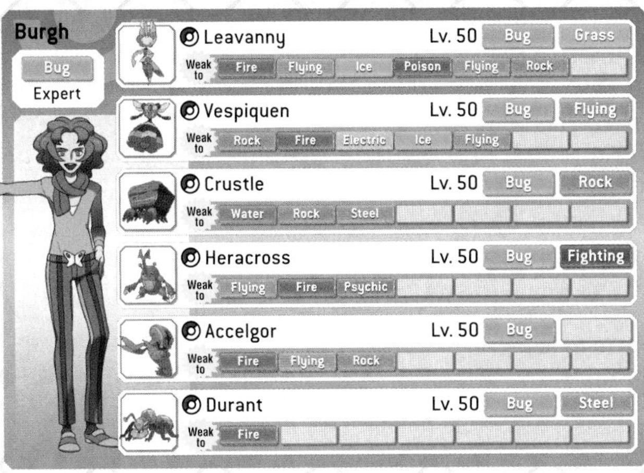

Burgh (Bug Expert)

Pokémon	Lv.	Type	Weak to
Leavanny	Lv. 50	Bug / Grass	Fire, Flying, Ice, Poison, Flying, Rock
Vespiquen	Lv. 50	Bug / Flying	Rock, Fire, Electric, Ice, Flying
Crustle	Lv. 50	Bug / Rock	Water, Rock, Steel
Heracross	Lv. 50	Bug / Fighting	Flying, Fire, Psychic
Accelgor	Lv. 50	Bug	Fire, Flying, Rock
Durant	Lv. 50	Bug / Steel	Fire

Skyla (Flying Expert)

Pokémon	Lv.	Type	Weak to
Swanna	Lv. 50	Water / Flying	Electric, Rock
Jumpluff	Lv. 50	Grass / Flying	Ice, Fire, Poison, Flying, Rock
Drifblim	Lv. 50	Ghost / Flying	Electric, Ice, Rock, Ghost, Dark
Mandibuzz	Lv. 50	Dark / Flying	Electric, Ice, Rock
Archeops	Lv. 50	Rock / Flying	Water, Electric, Ice, Rock, Steel
Braviary	Lv. 50	Normal / Flying	Electric, Ice, Rock

World Leaders / Type Experts (continued)

Drayden — Dragon Expert

Pokémon	Lv.	Type	Weak to
Haxorus	Lv. 50	Dragon	Ice, Dragon
Druddigon	Lv. 50	Dragon	Ice, Dragon
Hydreigon	Lv. 50	Dark / Dragon	Ice, Fighting, Bug, Dragon
Flygon	Lv. 50	Ground / Dragon	Ice, Dragon
Altaria	Lv. 50	Dragon / Flying	Ice, Rock, Dragon
Salamence	Lv. 50	Dragon / Flying	Ice, Rock, Dragon

Cilan — Grass Expert

Pokémon	Lv.	Type	Weak to
Simisage	Lv. 50	Grass	Fire, Ice, Poison, Flying, Bug
Ferrothorn	Lv. 50	Grass / Steel	Fire, Fighting
Serperior	Lv. 50	Grass	Fire, Ice, Poison, Flying, Bug
Jumpluff	Lv. 50	Grass / Flying	Fire, Ice, Poison, Flying, Rock
Whimsicott	Lv. 50	Grass	Fire, Ice, Poison, Flying, Bug
Lilligant	Lv. 50	Grass	Fire, Ice, Poison, Flying, Bug

Marlon — Water Expert

Pokémon	Lv.	Type	Weak to
Jellicent	Lv. 50	Water / Ghost	Grass, Electric, Ghost, Dark
Carracosta	Lv. 50	Water / Rock	Grass◆, Electric◆, Fighting◆, Ground◆
Starmie	Lv. 50	Water / Psychic	Grass, Electric, Bug, Ghost, Dark
Quagsire	Lv. 50	Water / Ground	Grass
Cloyster	Lv. 50	Water / Ice	Grass, Electric, Fighting, Rock
Wailord	Lv. 50	Water	Grass, Electric

Lenora — Normal Expert

Pokémon	Lv.	Type	Weak to
Watchog	Lv. 50	Normal	Fighting
Cinccino	Lv. 50	Normal	Fighting
Braviary	Lv. 50	Normal / Flying	Electric, Ice, Rock
Sawsbuck	Lv. 50	Normal / Grass	Fire, Ice, Fighting, Poison, Flying, Bug
Kangaskhan	Lv. 50	Normal	Fighting
Lickilicky	Lv. 50	Normal	Fighting

Chili — Fire Expert

Pokémon	Lv.	Type	Weak to
Simisear	Lv. 50	Fire	Water, Ground, Rock
Camerupt	Lv. 50	Fire / Ground	Water◆, Ground◆
Heatmor	Lv. 50	Fire	Water, Ground, Rock
Darmanitan	Lv. 50	Fire	Water, Ground, Rock
Arcanine	Lv. 50	Fire	Water, Ground, Rock
Emboar	Lv. 50	Fire / Fighting	Water, Ground, Flying, Psychic

Brycen — Ice Expert

Pokémon	Lv.	Type	Weak to
Cryogonal	Lv. 50	Ice	Fire, Fighting, Rock, Steel
Beartic	Lv. 50	Ice	Fire, Fighting, Rock, Steel
Vanilluxe	Lv. 50	Ice	Fire, Fighting, Rock, Steel
Weavile	Lv. 50	Dark / Ice	Fighting, Fire, Bug, Rock, Steel
Dewgong	Lv. 50	Water / Ice	Grass, Electric, Fighting, Rock
Walrein	Lv. 50	Ice / Water	Grass, Electric, Fighting, Rock

Cress — Water Expert

Pokémon	Lv.	Type	Weak to
Simipour	Lv. 50	Water	Grass, Electric
Crawdaunt	Lv. 50	Water / Dark	Grass, Electric, Fighting, Bug
Samurott	Lv. 50	Water	Grass, Electric
Azumarill	Lv. 50	Water	Grass, Electric
Slowking	Lv. 50	Water / Psychic	Grass, Electric, Bug, Ghost, Dark
Seismitoad	Lv. 50	Water / Ground	Grass

Brock — Rock Expert

Pokémon	Lv.	Type	Weak to
Onix	Lv. 50	Rock / Ground	Water, Grass, Ice, Fighting, Ground, Steel
Golem	Lv. 50	Rock / Ground	Water, Grass, Ice, Fighting, Ground, Steel
Kabutops	Lv. 50	Rock / Water	Grass, Electric, Fighting, Ground
Tyranitar	Lv. 50	Rock / Dark	Fighting, Water, Grass, Ground, Bug, Steel
Aerodactyl	Lv. 50	Rock / Flying	Water, Electric, Ice, Rock, Steel
Rhyperior	Lv. 50	Ground / Rock	Water◆, Grass◆, Ice◆, Fighting◆, Ground◆, Steel◆

◆ The damage may change depending on the effects of this Pokémon's Ability.

World Leaders / Type Experts (continued)

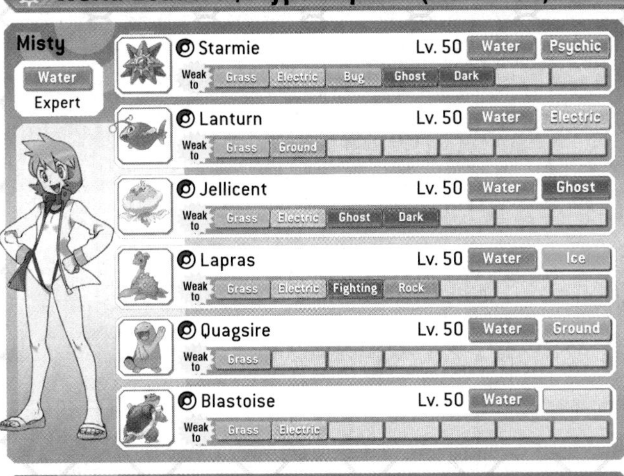

Misty — Water Expert

Pokémon	Lv.	Type	Weak to
Starmie	Lv. 50	Water / Psychic	Grass, Electric, Bug, Ghost, Dark
Lanturn	Lv. 50	Water / Electric	Grass, Ground
Jellicent	Lv. 50	Water / Ghost	Grass, Electric, Ghost, Dark
Lapras	Lv. 50	Water / Ice	Grass, Electric, Fighting, Rock
Quagsire	Lv. 50	Water / Ground	Grass
Blastoise	Lv. 50	Water	Grass, Electric

Lt. Surge — Electric Expert

Pokémon	Lv.	Type	Weak to
Raichu	Lv. 50	Electric	Ground
Electrode	Lv. 50	Electric	Ground
Magnezone	Lv. 50	Electric / Steel	Ground, Fire, Fighting
Electivire	Lv. 50	Electric	Ground
Jolteon	Lv. 50	Electric	Ground
Lanturn	Lv. 50	Water / Electric	Grass, Ground

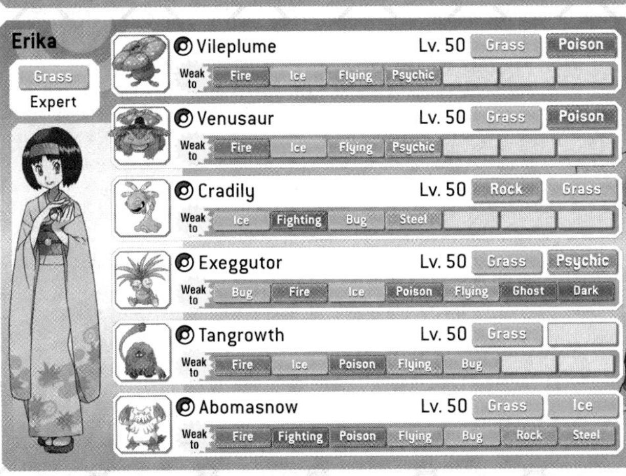

Erika — Grass Expert

Pokémon	Lv.	Type	Weak to
Vileplume	Lv. 50	Grass / Poison	Fire, Ice, Flying, Psychic
Venusaur	Lv. 50	Grass / Poison	Fire, Ice, Flying, Psychic
Cradily	Lv. 50	Rock / Grass	Ice, Fighting, Bug, Steel
Exeggutor	Lv. 50	Grass / Psychic	Bug, Fire, Ice, Poison, Flying, Ghost, Dark
Tangrowth	Lv. 50	Grass	Fire, Ice, Poison, Flying, Bug
Abomasnow	Lv. 50	Grass / Ice	Fire, Fighting, Poison, Flying, Bug, Rock, Steel

Sabrina — Psychic Expert

Pokémon	Lv.	Type	Weak to
Alakazam	Lv. 50	Psychic	Bug, Ghost, Dark
Metagross	Lv. 50	Steel / Psychic	Fire, Ground
Exeggutor	Lv. 50	Grass / Psychic	Bug, Fire, Ice, Poison, Flying, Ghost, Dark
Slowking	Lv. 50	Water / Psychic	Grass, Electric, Bug, Ghost, Dark
Espeon	Lv. 50	Psychic	Bug, Ghost, Dark
Sigilyph	Lv. 50	Psychic / Flying	Electric, Ice, Rock, Ghost, Dark

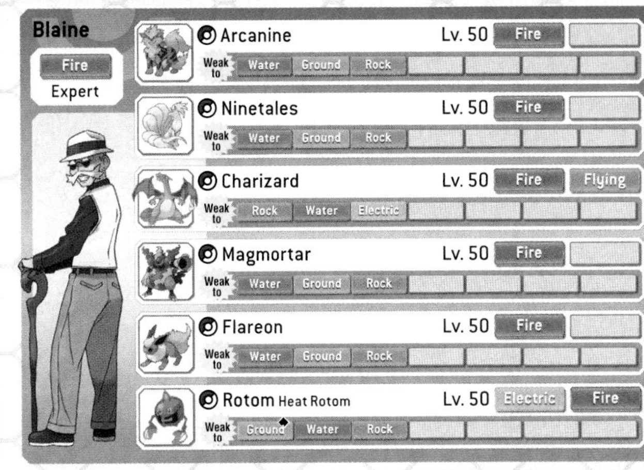

Blaine — Fire Expert

Pokémon	Lv.	Type	Weak to
Arcanine	Lv. 50	Fire	Water, Ground, Rock
Ninetales	Lv. 50	Fire	Water, Ground, Rock
Charizard	Lv. 50	Fire / Flying	Rock, Water, Electric
Magmortar	Lv. 50	Fire	Water, Ground, Rock
Flareon	Lv. 50	Fire	Water, Ground, Rock
Rotom Heat Rotom	Lv. 50	Electric / Fire	Ground◆, Water, Rock

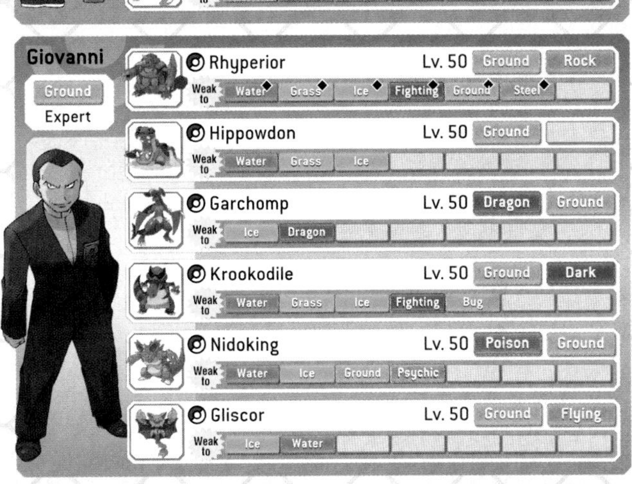

Giovanni — Ground Expert

Pokémon	Lv.	Type	Weak to
Rhyperior	Lv. 50	Ground / Rock	Water◆, Grass◆, Ice◆, Fighting◆, Ground◆, Steel◆
Hippowdon	Lv. 50	Ground	Water, Grass, Ice
Garchomp	Lv. 50	Dragon / Ground	Ice, Dragon
Krookodile	Lv. 50	Ground / Dark	Water, Grass, Ice, Fighting, Bug
Nidoking	Lv. 50	Poison / Ground	Water, Ice, Ground, Psychic
Gliscor	Lv. 50	Ground / Flying	Ice, Water

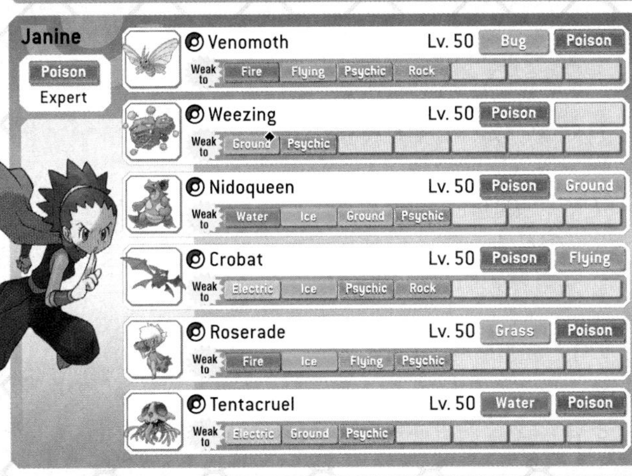

Janine — Poison Expert

Pokémon	Lv.	Type	Weak to
Venomoth	Lv. 50	Bug / Poison	Fire, Flying, Psychic, Rock
Weezing	Lv. 50	Poison	Ground◆, Psychic
Nidoqueen	Lv. 50	Poison / Ground	Water, Ice, Ground, Psychic
Crobat	Lv. 50	Poison / Flying	Electric, Ice, Psychic, Rock
Roserade	Lv. 50	Grass / Poison	Fire, Ice, Flying, Psychic
Tentacruel	Lv. 50	Water / Poison	Electric, Ground, Psychic

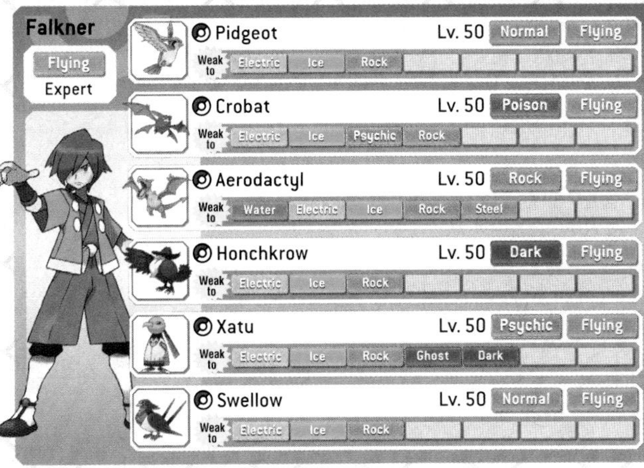

Falkner — Flying Expert

Pokémon	Lv.	Type	Weak to
Pidgeot	Lv. 50	Normal / Flying	Electric, Ice, Rock
Crobat	Lv. 50	Poison / Flying	Electric, Ice, Psychic, Rock
Aerodactyl	Lv. 50	Rock / Flying	Water, Electric, Ice, Rock, Steel
Honchkrow	Lv. 50	Dark / Flying	Electric, Ice, Rock
Xatu	Lv. 50	Psychic / Flying	Electric, Ice, Rock, Ghost, Dark
Swellow	Lv. 50	Normal / Flying	Electric, Ice, Rock

World Leaders / Type Experts (continued)

Bugsy — Bug Expert

Pokémon	Lv.	Type	Weak to
Scizor	Lv. 50	Bug / Steel	Fire
Shuckle	Lv. 50	Bug / Rock	Water, Rock, Steel
Heracross	Lv. 50	Bug / Fighting	Flying, Fire, Psychic
Pinsir	Lv. 50	Bug	Fire, Flying, Rock
Armaldo	Lv. 50	Rock / Bug	Water, Rock, Steel
Yanmega	Lv. 50	Bug / Flying	Rock, Fire, Electric, Ice, Flying

Jasmine — Steel Expert

Pokémon	Lv.	Type	Weak to
Steelix	Lv. 50	Steel / Ground	Fire, Water, Fighting, Ground
Magnezone	Lv. 50	Electric / Steel	Ground, Fire, Fighting
Forretress	Lv. 50	Bug / Steel	Fire
Skarmory	Lv. 50	Steel / Flying	Fire, Electric
Metagross	Lv. 50	Steel / Psychic	Fire, Ground
Lucario	Lv. 50	Fighting / Steel	Fire, Fighting, Ground

Whitney — Normal Expert

Pokémon	Lv.	Type	Weak to
Miltank	Lv. 50	Normal	Fighting
Blissey	Lv. 50	Normal	Fighting
Tauros	Lv. 50	Normal	Fighting
Ambipom	Lv. 50	Normal	Fighting
Ursaring	Lv. 50	Normal	Fighting
Lopunny	Lv. 50	Normal	Fighting

Pryce — Ice Expert

Pokémon	Lv.	Type	Weak to
Mamoswine	Lv. 50	Ice / Ground	Fire◆, Water, Grass, Fighting, Steel
Jynx	Lv. 50	Ice / Psychic	Fire◆, Bug, Rock, Ghost, Dark, Steel
Dewgong	Lv. 50	Water / Ice	Grass, Electric, Fighting, Rock
Cloyster	Lv. 50	Water / Ice	Grass, Electric, Fighting, Rock
Lapras	Lv. 50	Water / Ice	Grass, Electric, Fighting, Rock
Weavile	Lv. 50	Dark / Ice	Fighting, Fire, Bug, Rock, Steel

Morty — Ghost Expert

Pokémon	Lv.	Type	Weak to
Gengar	Lv. 50	Ghost / Poison	Ground◆, Psychic, Ghost, Dark
Mismagius	Lv. 50	Ghost	Ghost, Dark
Banette	Lv. 50	Ghost	Ghost, Dark
Dusknoir	Lv. 50	Ghost	Ghost, Dark
Chandelure	Lv. 50	Ghost / Fire	Water, Ground, Rock, Ghost, Dark
Froslass	Lv. 50	Ice / Ghost	Fire, Rock, Ghost, Dark, Steel

Clair — Dragon Expert

Pokémon	Lv.	Type	Weak to
Dragonite	Lv. 50	Dragon / Flying	Ice, Rock, Dragon
Kingdra	Lv. 50	Water / Dragon	Dragon
Altaria	Lv. 50	Dragon / Flying	Ice, Rock, Dragon
Salamence	Lv. 50	Dragon / Flying	Ice, Rock, Dragon
Druddigon	Lv. 50	Dragon	Ice, Dragon
Garchomp	Lv. 50	Dragon / Ground	Ice, Dragon

Chuck — Fighting Expert

Pokémon	Lv.	Type	Weak to
Poliwrath	Lv. 50	Water / Fighting	Grass, Electric, Flying, Psychic
Machamp	Lv. 50	Fighting	Flying, Psychic
Hitmontop	Lv. 50	Fighting	Flying, Psychic
Hitmonchan	Lv. 50	Fighting	Flying, Psychic
Hitmonlee	Lv. 50	Fighting	Flying, Psychic
Conkeldurr	Lv. 50	Fighting	Flying, Psychic

Roxanne — Rock Expert

Pokémon	Lv.	Type	Weak to
Probopass	Lv. 50	Rock / Steel	Fighting, Ground, Water
Armaldo	Lv. 50	Rock / Bug	Water, Rock, Steel
Cradily	Lv. 50	Rock / Grass	Ice, Fighting, Bug, Steel
Aggron	Lv. 50	Steel / Rock	Fighting, Ground, Water
Carracosta	Lv. 50	Water / Rock	Grass◆, Electric◆, Fighting◆, Ground◆
Golem	Lv. 50	Rock / Ground	Water, Grass, Ice, Fighting, Ground, Steel

◆ The damage may change depending on the effects of this Pokémon's Ability.

World Leaders / Type Experts (continued)

Brawly — Fighting Expert

Pokémon	Lv.	Type	Weak to
Hariyama	Lv. 50	Fighting	Flying, Psychic
Scrafty	Lv. 50	Dark / Fighting	Fighting, Flying
Breloom	Lv. 50	Grass / Fighting	Flying, Fire, Ice, Poison, Psychic
Machamp	Lv. 50	Fighting	Flying, Psychic
Mienshao	Lv. 50	Fighting	Flying, Psychic
Heracross	Lv. 50	Bug / Fighting	Flying, Fire, Psychic

Winona — Flying Expert

Pokémon	Lv.	Type	Weak to
Altaria	Lv. 50	Dragon / Flying	Ice, Rock, Dragon
Sigilyph	Lv. 50	Psychic / Flying	Electric, Ice, Rock, Ghost, Dark
Gyarados	Lv. 50	Water / Flying	Electric, Rock
Skarmory	Lv. 50	Steel / Flying	Fire, Electric
Tropius	Lv. 50	Grass / Flying	Ice, Fire, Poison, Flying, Rock
Honchkrow	Lv. 50	Dark / Flying	Electric, Ice, Rock

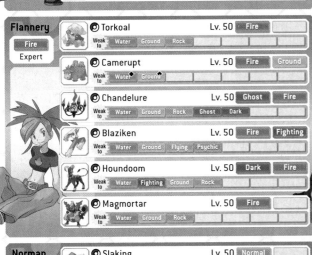

Wattson — Electric Expert

Pokémon	Lv.	Type	Weak to
Manectric	Lv. 50	Electric	Ground
Magnezone	Lv. 50	Electric / Steel	Ground, Fire, Fighting
Electrode	Lv. 50	Electric	Ground
Rotom Wash Rotom	Lv. 50	Electric / Water	Grass, Ground◆
Ampharos	Lv. 50	Electric	Ground
Raichu	Lv. 50	Electric	Ground

Tate — Psychic Expert

Pokémon	Lv.	Type	Weak to
Solrock	Lv. 50	Rock / Psychic	Water, Grass, Ground◆, Bug, Ghost, Dark, Steel
Xatu	Lv. 50	Psychic / Flying	Electric, Ice, Ground, Ghost, Dark
Bronzong	Lv. 50	Steel / Psychic	Fire◆, Ground◆
Reuniclus	Lv. 50	Psychic	Bug, Ghost, Dark
Gallade	Lv. 50	Psychic / Fighting	Flying, Ghost
Claydol	Lv. 50	Ground / Psychic	Water, Grass, Ice, Bug, Ghost, Dark

Flannery — Fire Expert

Pokémon	Lv.	Type	Weak to
Torkoal	Lv. 50	Fire	Water, Ground, Rock
Camerupt	Lv. 50	Fire / Ground	Water◆, Ground◆
Chandelure	Lv. 50	Ghost / Fire	Water, Ground, Rock, Ghost, Dark
Blaziken	Lv. 50	Fire / Fighting	Water, Ground, Flying, Psychic
Houndoom	Lv. 50	Dark / Fire	Water, Fighting, Ground, Rock
Magmortar	Lv. 50	Fire	Water, Ground, Rock

Liza — Psychic Expert

Pokémon	Lv.	Type	Weak to
Lunatone	Lv. 50	Rock / Psychic	Water, Grass, Ground◆, Bug, Ghost, Dark, Steel
Xatu	Lv. 50	Psychic / Flying	Electric, Ice, Ground, Ghost, Dark
Bronzong	Lv. 50	Steel / Psychic	Fire◆, Ground◆
Gothitelle	Lv. 50	Psychic	Bug, Ghost, Dark
Gardevoir	Lv. 50	Psychic	Bug, Ghost, Dark
Claydol	Lv. 50	Ground / Psychic	Water, Grass, Ice, Bug, Ghost, Dark

Norman — Normal Expert

Pokémon	Lv.	Type	Weak to
Slaking	Lv. 50	Normal	Fighting
Ambipom	Lv. 50	Normal	Fighting
Bouffalant	Lv. 50	Normal	Fighting
Staraptor	Lv. 50	Normal / Flying	Electric, Ice, Rock
Exploud	Lv. 50	Normal	Fighting
Sawsbuck	Lv. 50	Normal / Grass	Fire, Ice, Fighting, Poison, Flying, Bug

Juan — Water Expert

Pokémon	Lv.	Type	Weak to
Kingdra	Lv. 50	Water / Dragon	Dragon
Walrein	Lv. 50	Ice / Water	Grass, Electric, Fighting, Rock
Crawdaunt	Lv. 50	Water / Dark	Grass, Electric, Fighting, Bug
Whiscash	Lv. 50	Water / Ground	Grass
Relicanth	Lv. 50	Water / Rock	Grass, Electric, Fighting, Ground
Politoed	Lv. 50	Water	Grass, Electric

World Leaders / Type Experts (continued)

Roark — Rock Expert

Pokémon	Lv.	Type	Weak to
Rampardos	Lv. 50	Rock	Water, Grass, Fighting, Ground, Steel
Probopass	Lv. 50	Rock / Steel	Fighting, Ground, Water
Archeops	Lv. 50	Rock / Flying	Water, Electric, Ice, Rock, Steel
Crustle	Lv. 50	Bug / Rock	Water, Rock, Steel
Golem	Lv. 50	Rock / Ground	Water, Grass, Ice, Fighting, Ground, Steel
Relicanth	Lv. 50	Water / Rock	Grass, Electric, Fighting, Ground

Wake — Water Expert

Pokémon	Lv.	Type	Weak to
Floatzel	Lv. 50	Water	Grass, Electric
Empoleon	Lv. 50	Water / Steel	Electric, Fighting, Ground
Ludicolo	Lv. 50	Water / Grass	Poison, Flying, Bug
Gastrodon	Lv. 50	Water / Ground	Grass
Poliwrath	Lv. 50	Water / Fighting	Grass, Electric, Flying, Psychic
Gyarados	Lv. 50	Water / Flying	Electric, Rock

Gardenia — Grass Expert

Pokémon	Lv.	Type	Weak to
Roserade	Lv. 50	Grass / Poison	Fire, Ice, Flying, Psychic
Tropius	Lv. 50	Grass / Flying	Ice, Fire, Poison, Flying, Rock
Breloom	Lv. 50	Grass / Fighting	Flying, Fire, Ice, Poison, Psychic
Tangrowth	Lv. 50	Grass	Fire, Ice, Poison, Flying, Bug
Leafeon	Lv. 50	Grass	Fire, Ice, Poison, Flying, Bug
Torterra	Lv. 50	Grass / Ground	Ice, Fire, Flying, Bug

Byron — Steel Expert

Pokémon	Lv.	Type	Weak to
Bastiodon	Lv. 50	Rock / Steel	Fighting, Ground, Water
Excadrill	Lv. 50	Ground / Steel	Fire, Water, Fighting, Ground
Bronzong	Lv. 50	Steel / Psychic	Fire◆, Ground◆
Magnezone	Lv. 50	Electric / Steel	Ground, Fire, Fighting
Aggron	Lv. 50	Steel / Rock	Fighting, Ground, Water
Forretress	Lv. 50	Bug / Steel	Fire

Fantina — Ghost Expert

Pokémon	Lv.	Type	Weak to
Mismagius	Lv. 50	Ghost	Ghost, Dark
Drifblim	Lv. 50	Ghost / Flying	Electric, Ice, Rock, Ghost, Dark
Spiritomb	Lv. 50	Ghost / Dark	
Dusknoir	Lv. 50	Ghost	Ghost, Dark
Jellicent	Lv. 50	Water / Ghost	Grass, Electric, Ghost, Dark
Gengar	Lv. 50	Ghost / Poison	Ground◆, Psychic, Ghost, Dark

Candice — Ice Expert

Pokémon	Lv.	Type	Weak to
Froslass	Lv. 50	Ice / Ghost	Fire, Rock, Ghost, Dark, Steel
Abomasnow	Lv. 50	Grass / Ice	Fire, Fighting, Flying, Poison, Bug, Rock, Steel
Weavile	Lv. 50	Dark / Ice	Fighting, Fire, Bug, Rock, Steel
Glaceon	Lv. 50	Ice	Fire, Fighting, Rock, Steel
Mamoswine	Lv. 50	Ice / Ground	Fire◆, Water, Grass, Fighting, Steel
Glalie	Lv. 50	Ice	Fire, Fighting, Rock, Steel

Maylene — Fighting Expert

Pokémon	Lv.	Type	Weak to
Lucario	Lv. 50	Fighting / Steel	Fire, Fighting, Ground
Infernape	Lv. 50	Fire / Fighting	Water, Ground, Flying, Psychic
Toxicroak	Lv. 50	Poison / Fighting	Psychic, Ground, Flying
Gallade	Lv. 50	Psychic / Fighting	Flying, Ghost
Medicham	Lv. 50	Fighting / Psychic	Flying, Ghost
Machamp	Lv. 50	Fighting	Flying, Psychic

Volkner — Electric Expert

Pokémon	Lv.	Type	Weak to
Electivire	Lv. 50	Electric	Ground
Luxray	Lv. 50	Electric	Ground
Raichu	Lv. 50	Electric	Ground
Rotom Fan Rotom	Lv. 50	Electric / Flying	Ice, Rock
Jolteon	Lv. 50	Electric	Ground
Electrode	Lv. 50	Electric	Ground

◆ The damage may change depending on the effects of this Pokémon's Ability.

Champions

Blue

Pokémon	Level	Type	Weak to
Aerodactyl	Lv. 50	Rock, Flying	Water, Electric, Ice, Rock, Steel
Exeggutor	Lv. 50	Grass, Psychic	Bug, Fire, Ice, Poison, Flying, Ghost, Dark
Gyarados	Lv. 50	Water, Flying	Electric, Rock
Alakazam	Lv. 50	Psychic	Bug, Ghost, Dark
Arcanine	Lv. 50	Fire	Water, Ground, Rock
Machamp	Lv. 50	Fighting	Flying, Psychic

Cynthia

Pokémon	Level	Type	Weak to
Garchomp	Lv. 50	Dragon, Ground	Ice, Dragon
Spiritomb	Lv. 50	Ghost, Dark	
Togekiss	Lv. 50	Normal, Flying	Electric, Ice, Rock
Lucario	Lv. 50	Fighting, Steel	Fire, Fighting, Ground
Roserade	Lv. 50	Grass, Poison	Fire, Ice, Flying, Psychic
Glaceon	Lv. 50	Ice	Fire, Fighting, Rock, Steel

Lance

Pokémon	Level	Type	Weak to
Dragonite	Lv. 50	Dragon, Flying	Ice, Rock, Dragon
Salamence	Lv. 50	Dragon, Flying	Ice, Rock, Dragon
Kingdra	Lv. 50	Water, Dragon	Dragon
Hydreigon	Lv. 50	Dark, Dragon	Ice, Fighting, Bug, Dragon
Haxorus	Lv. 50	Dragon	Ice, Dragon
Flygon	Lv. 50	Ground, Dragon	Ice, Dragon

Alder

Pokémon	Level	Type	Weak to
Volcarona	Lv. 50	Bug, Fire	Rock, Water, Flying
Conkeldurr	Lv. 50	Fighting	Flying, Psychic
Reuniclus	Lv. 50	Psychic	Bug, Ghost, Dark
Krookodile	Lv. 50	Ground, Dark	Water, Grass, Ice, Fighting, Bug
Chandelure	Lv. 50	Ghost, Fire	Water, Ground, Rock, Ghost, Dark
Braviary	Lv. 50	Normal, Flying	Electric, Ice, Rock

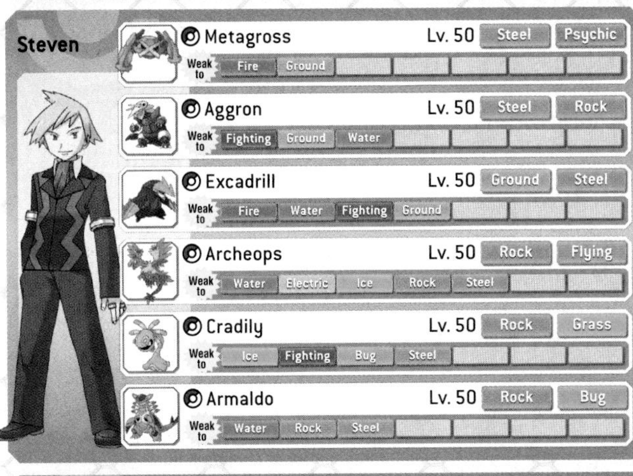

Steven

Pokémon	Level	Type	Weak to
Metagross	Lv. 50	Steel, Psychic	Fire, Ground
Aggron	Lv. 50	Steel, Rock	Fighting, Ground, Water
Excadrill	Lv. 50	Ground, Steel	Fire, Water, Fighting, Ground
Archeops	Lv. 50	Rock, Flying	Water, Electric, Ice, Rock, Steel
Cradily	Lv. 50	Rock, Grass	Ice, Fighting, Bug, Steel
Armaldo	Lv. 50	Rock, Bug	Water, Rock, Steel

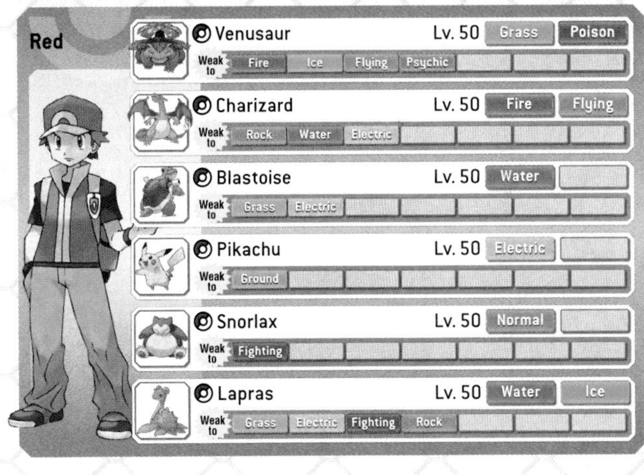

Red

Pokémon	Level	Type	Weak to
Venusaur	Lv. 50	Grass, Poison	Fire, Ice, Flying, Psychic
Charizard	Lv. 50	Fire, Flying	Rock, Water, Electric
Blastoise	Lv. 50	Water	Grass, Electric
Pikachu	Lv. 50	Electric	Ground
Snorlax	Lv. 50	Normal	Fighting
Lapras	Lv. 50	Water, Ice	Grass, Electric, Fighting, Rock

Wallace

Pokémon	Level	Type	Weak to
Milotic	Lv. 50	Water	Grass, Electric
Sharpedo	Lv. 50	Water, Dark	Grass, Electric, Fighting, Bug
Walrein	Lv. 50	Ice, Water	Grass, Electric, Fighting, Rock
Ludicolo	Lv. 50	Water, Grass	Poison, Flying, Bug
Swampert	Lv. 50	Water, Ground	Grass
Starmie	Lv. 50	Water, Psychic	Grass, Electric, Bug, Ghost, Dark

Mix Master

Cheren

Pokémon	Lv.	Type	Weak to
Stoutland	Lv. 50	Normal	Fighting
Porygon-Z	Lv. 50	Normal	Fighting
Cinccino	Lv. 50	Normal	Fighting
Lickilicky	Lv. 50	Normal	Fighting
Castform	Lv. 50	Normal	Fighting
Bouffalant	Lv. 50	Normal	Fighting

Clay

Pokémon	Lv.	Type	Weak to
Excadrill	Lv. 50	Ground / Steel	Fire, Water, Fighting, Ground
Flygon	Lv. 50	Ground / Dragon	Ice, Dragon
Krookodile	Lv. 50	Ground / Dark	Water, Grass, Ice, Fighting, Bug
Seismitoad	Lv. 50	Water / Ground	Grass
Mamoswine	Lv. 50	Ice / Ground	Fire◆, Water, Grass, Fighting, Steel
Golurk	Lv. 50	Ground / Ghost	Water, Grass, Ice, Ghost, Dark

Roxie

Pokémon	Lv.	Type	Weak to
Scolipede	Lv. 50	Bug / Poison	Fire, Flying, Psychic, Rock
Toxicroak	Lv. 50	Poison / Fighting	Psychic, Ground, Flying
Garbodor	Lv. 50	Poison	Ground, Psychic
Crobat	Lv. 50	Poison / Flying	Electric, Ice, Psychic, Rock
Drapion	Lv. 50	Poison / Dark	Ground
Amoonguss	Lv. 50	Grass / Poison	Fire, Ice, Flying, Psychic

Skyla

Pokémon	Lv.	Type	Weak to
Swanna	Lv. 50	Water / Flying	Electric, Rock
Jumpluff	Lv. 50	Grass / Flying	Ice, Fire, Poison, Flying, Rock
Drifblim	Lv. 50	Ghost / Flying	Electric, Ice, Rock, Ghost, Dark
Mandibuzz	Lv. 50	Dark / Flying	Electric, Ice, Rock
Archeops	Lv. 50	Rock / Flying	Water, Electric, Ice, Rock, Steel
Braviary	Lv. 50	Normal / Flying	Electric, Ice, Rock

Burgh

Pokémon	Lv.	Type	Weak to
Leavanny	Lv. 50	Bug / Grass	Fire, Flying, Ice, Poison, Bug, Rock
Vespiquen	Lv. 50	Bug / Flying	Rock, Fire, Electric, Ice, Flying
Crustle	Lv. 50	Bug / Rock	Water, Rock, Steel
Heracross	Lv. 50	Bug / Fighting	Flying, Fire, Psychic
Accelgor	Lv. 50	Bug	Fire, Flying, Rock
Durant	Lv. 50	Bug / Steel	Fire

Drayden

Pokémon	Lv.	Type	Weak to
Haxorus	Lv. 50	Dragon	Ice, Dragon
Druddigon	Lv. 50	Dragon	Ice, Dragon
Hydreigon	Lv. 50	Dark / Dragon	Ice, Fighting, Bug, Dragon
Flygon	Lv. 50	Ground / Dragon	Ice, Dragon
Altaria	Lv. 50	Dragon / Flying	Ice, Rock, Dragon
Salamence	Lv. 50	Dragon / Flying	Ice, Rock, Dragon

Elesa

Pokémon	Lv.	Type	Weak to
Zebstrika	Lv. 50	Electric	Ground
Ampharos	Lv. 50	Electric	Ground
Luxray	Lv. 50	Electric	Ground
Emolga	Lv. 50	Electric / Flying	Ice, Rock
Eelektross	Lv. 50	Electric	Ground◆
Stunfisk	Lv. 50	Ground / Electric	Water, Grass, Ice, Ground

Marlon

Pokémon	Lv.	Type	Weak to
Jellicent	Lv. 50	Water / Ghost	Grass, Electric, Ghost, Dark
Carracosta	Lv. 50	Water / Rock	Grass◆, Electric◆, Fighting◆, Ground◆
Starmie	Lv. 50	Water / Psychic	Grass, Electric, Bug, Ghost, Dark
Quagsire	Lv. 50	Water / Ground	Grass
Cloyster	Lv. 50	Water / Ice	Grass, Electric, Fighting, Rock
Wailord	Lv. 50	Water	Grass, Electric

◆ The damage may change depending on the effects of this Pokémon's Ability.

Pokémon Musical

At the Pokémon Musical

Have Your Pokémon Dance

You've got style! Use your sense of style to help your Pokémon stand out on stage!

The Pokémon Musical is a fun game where you put Props on one of your Pokémon. Which Props will you pick? How do you make your Pokémon stand out on stage? Test your stylin' skills!

Learn all about the Pokémon Musical

How to stand out in the Pokémon Musical 1 The Musical Theater is in Nimbasa City

The bright lights of the Pokémon Musical bring sparkle to the northern district of Nimbasa City. With the Prop Case you get from the owner at your first visit, your Pokémon can participate in the Pokémon Musical anytime you like.

Musical Theater

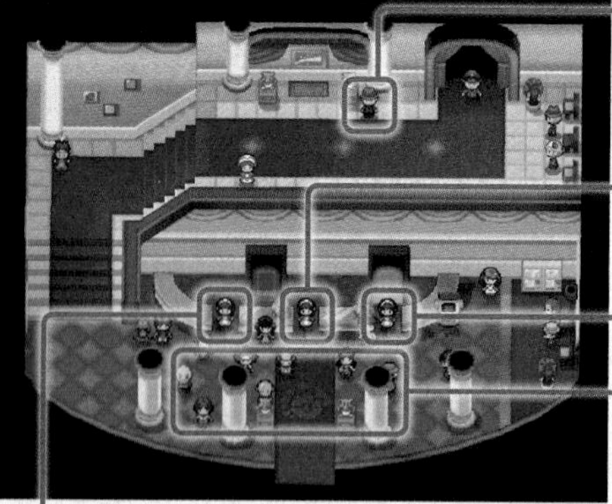

Musical Theater Owner

Talk to the owner and he'll give you new Props when you've met certain conditions, such as receiving the highest recognition five or 10 times.

Participating alone

When you want to participate in the Pokémon Musical by yourself, talk to the receptionist. Other participants will be selected automatically. The more you participate, the better the other participants become.

The changing room

You can play Dress Up with your Pokémon without having to participate in the Musical. Come here to see what Props you have and consider which Pokémon should participate.

Participating with your friends

Talk to this receptionist when you want to play the Pokémon Musical with your friends through IR or wireless communications.

Fans

After the show, your fans will gather in the reception area. Sometimes you'll receive a Prop when you talk to them. You can have up to 10 fans.

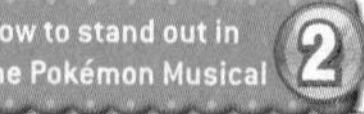

How to stand out in the Pokémon Musical 2 Get the Prop Case from the owner to participate

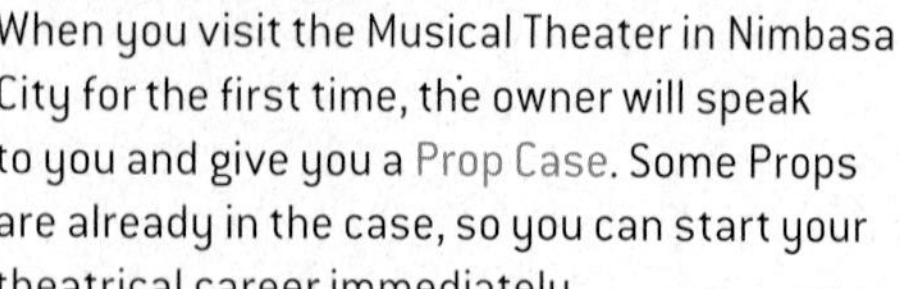

When you visit the Musical Theater in Nimbasa City for the first time, the owner will speak to you and give you a Prop Case. Some Props are already in the case, so you can start your theatrical career immediately.

Props that are already in the Prop Case

Top Hat	Square Glasses	Racket
Small Barrette	Red Parasol	Umber Belt
Pink Barrette	Cane	Hula Skirt
Blue Barrette	Microphone	Bow Tie
Green Barrette	Maraca	Tie

Memory Link lets you bring Props from your previous game

If you use Memory Link in Unova Link to carry over the data of *Pokémon Black Version* or *Pokémon White Version*, the owner will give you a Prop Case with the Props you collected in that game.

How to stand out in the Pokémon Musical 3

Pokémon Musical step-by-step guide

How you dress up your Pokémon with Props and how much it appeals to the audience will decide the overall performance rating. This step-by-step guide to the Pokémon Musical will show you what to do.

Step by step to the Pokémon Musical

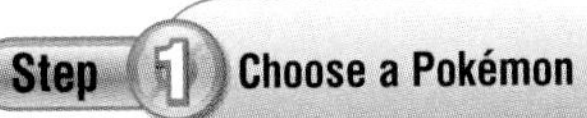

Step 1 Choose a Pokémon

Talk to the receptionist, and you can choose which Pokémon will participate in the musical. Choose one from your party.

Step 2 Choose a show

Choose one of the available shows, including any you've obtained from the Pokémon Global Link (p. 404).

Step 3 Dress up your Pokémon with Props

Dress up the Pokémon you selected by choosing the perfect Props for the show. Tap "OK!" when you're done with the Props. Check and make sure everything's good to go, because the show begins when you tap "OK!"

Step 4 Use Props that let your Pokémon make an appeal to the audience

Check the dancing Pokémon and the other participants after the show begins. You can make an appeal to the audience if your Pokémon wears a Prop on its arm. To take this action, tap the "APPEAL" icon on the Touch Screen.

How to stand out in the Pokémon Musical 4

Four shows, four styles

Style your Props to match each Pokémon Musical to make a mega impact on the audience!

Show Stardom

This stage is equipped with a huge monitor and searchlights like the ones for musicians. Up-tempo pop music plays.

Matching Style: Cool

Show Forest Stroll

Trees and colorful flowers cover the stage. The music is slow and calm, supporting the theme of taking a nice stroll. It might even remind you of a children's song.

Matching Style: Cute

Show A Sweet Soirée

Fancy furnishings along with windows of stained glass ornament the stage. Classical music creates a grown-up ambiance.

Matching Style: Elegant

Show Exciting Nimbasa

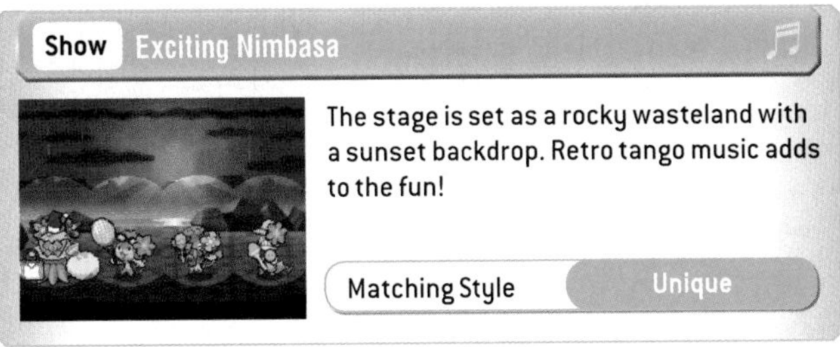

The stage is set as a rocky wasteland with a sunset backdrop. Retro tango music adds to the fun!

Matching Style: Unique

Download new shows at the Pokémon Global Link

Access the PGL and click "Customize," and you can download a Musical show.

Please check the PGL to check which shows are available for download.

How to stand out in the Pokémon Musical 5 Each Prop has its own style

You'll receive higher recognition when you use Props that match a show's style. Take a moment to check their styles as a guide in choosing the right Props.

Overall, totally cool!

Props and their styles

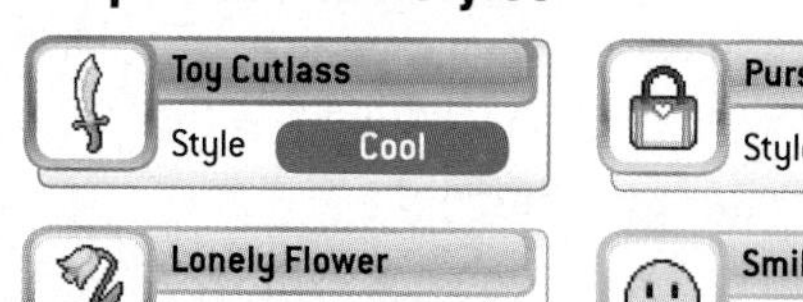

Prop	Style
Toy Cutlass	Cool
Purse	Cute
Lonely Flower	Elegant
Smiley-Face Mask	Unique

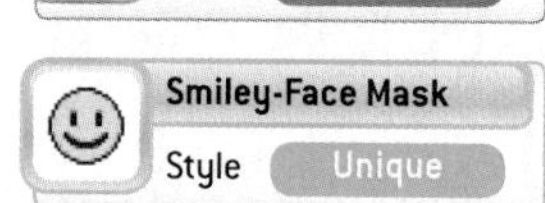

Check p. 452 for the Props list.

How to stand out in the Pokémon Musical 6 The more you try, the more Props you'll receive

The more Props you put on your Pokémon, the more fun it will be to watch. There are three main ways to get Props, though your fans will give you most of them. Try the Pokémon Musical often and collect all the Props!

Ways you can pick up new Props

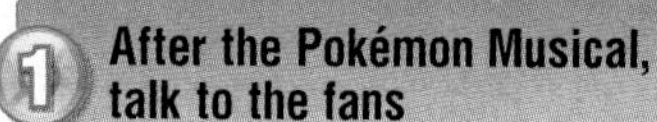

1 After the Pokémon Musical, talk to the fans

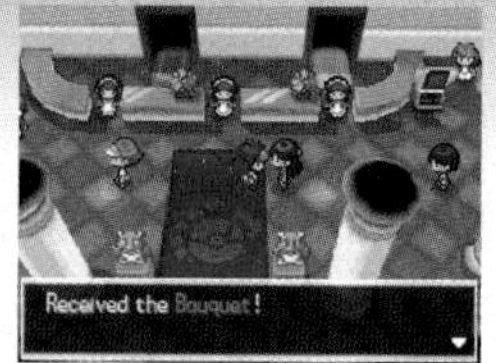

Received the Bouquet!

Talk to the fans in the reception area to receive a Prop. Talk to everyone! But you might not receive anything if the fans didn't like your Pokémon's performance.

2 Battle Musician Preston on Route 5

If you defeat Musician Preston, he'll give you the Electric Guitar Prop. If you've already obtained it by Memory Link, you won't receive it again.

3 Talk to the old man in a house in Opelucid City

Received the Gift Box!

Talk to the old man every day until you receive all four Props you can get from him. If you've already obtained them by Memory Link, you won't receive them again.

Tip: Receive special Props from the owner

Speak to the owner after meeting a certain condition, and he'll give you a special Prop. He will give you four different Props in total. Participate in the Pokémon Musical many times so you can get them all!

Received the Toy Cake!

Special Props and how to get them

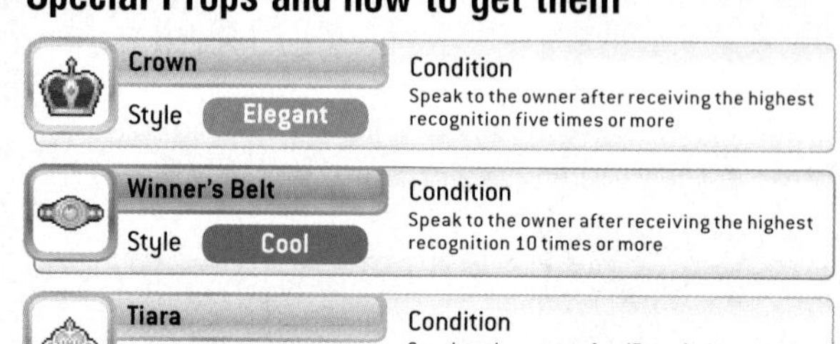

Prop	Style	Condition
Crown	Elegant	Speak to the owner after receiving the highest recognition five times or more
Winner's Belt	Cool	Speak to the owner after receiving the highest recognition 10 times or more
Tiara	Elegant	Speak to the owner after IR or wireless communications
Toy Cake	Cute	Speak to the owner on the birthday you set on your Nintendo DS system

How to stand out in the Pokémon Musical 7 Keep trying until you get all of the Medals from Mr. Medal

If you've received high recognition many times or collected all the Props, you'll receive seven Medals in total. To receive the 10 Followers Medal, you need to have 10 followers after a show. Show your mettle and gain every Medal!

Talented Cast Member

Rising Star

Big Star

Superstar

Musical Star

Trendsetter

10 Followers

Check p. 448 for the Medal list.

Dress up your Pokémon

Select just the right Props for each show

Dress Up is the most important part of the Pokémon Musical. The Props your Pokémon wears for each show greatly affect the overall performance. Check your look, and learn how to score high.

Dress Up Technique 1 Know how many Props you can put on a Pokémon and where

There are six body parts for Props: head, ear, face, arm, body, and waist. For ears and arms, you can put on two Props. Your Pokémon can wear a total of eight Props maximum. Generally, the more Props a Pokémon wears, the better its score will be.

Prop types and locations

1 Head

There are 23 different Props such as hats. All four styles are available.

2 Ears (two Props)

There are 10 different Props such as barrettes and flowers. No "Cool" Props are available.

3 Face

There are nine different Props such as glasses and masks. No "Cute" Props are available.

4 Arms (two Props)

There are 39 different Props such as a wand and a parasol. All four styles are available.

5 Body

There are 14 different Props such as a scarf and ties. No "Unique" Props are available.

6 Waist

There are five different Props such as belts and an apron. No "Cute" Props are available.

Tip: Use Props on its arms to make an appeal to the audience

The only way for the dancing Pokémon to make an appeal to the audience is with the Props on its arms. Make sure to put Props on each of your Pokémon's arms. Pokémon with four feet cannot hold arm Props.

Dress Up Technique 2 Learn how to put on Props

Pokémon Dress Up is done on a special screen where Props are displayed. Learn the screen layout and how to put on Props for a smooth start to the show. Be aware that the Prop styles are not shown on this screen. To see this, check the Prop list (p. 452).

Dress Up screen

Hula Skirt: A Prop that looks nice on the waist.
OK!

Prop name

Tap one of the Props, and you'll see its name and the body part it goes on.

Stash good candidates outside the ring

You can place Props freely outside the ring of Props. It can save time to keep some that you like outside the ring.

Sort your Props

Tap the body part to put a Prop on, and Props for the part will be displayed in front.

Props you have

A ring of Props you own appears around your Pokémon. Slide the ring to view them.

Newly obtained Props

When you dress up a Pokémon after you obtain a new Prop, "new" is displayed on it.

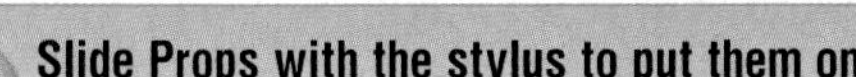

1 Slide Props with the stylus to put them on

Choose one Prop from the ring of Props and slide it onto your Pokémon with the stylus. It'll get put on the right body part. Some Pokémon cannot wear certain types of Props, depending on their body shape. Tap "OK" at the bottom of the screen when you are done adding Props.

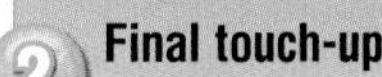

2 Final touch-up

You can do a final touch-up here to get all the Props just so. Slide the Props left-to-right and adjust their angles.

Tip

Try Props on different body parts

Each Prop has to be put on a certain location. However, some can be put on a different location, too. For example, the Top Hat can be put on an arm as well as on a head.

Dress Up Technique 3 A Prop's style determines how effective it is

When putting Props on your Pokémon, choose the matching Prop style and then pile on as many Props as you possibly can. Something else that affects your score is how other participants have dressed up their Pokémon.

Prop scoring rules

1. Props score high when their style matches the show.
2. Props don't score high when other participants use the same Props.
3. When the same Props are used, the Pokémon with more Props will score higher.
4. Props score high when no other Pokémon wears the same Prop.

Show Stardom

- Contestant 1 Eugene — Props: Cowboy Hat, Rose, Crimson Scarf
- Contestant 2 Hudson — Props: Fake Bone, Smiley-Face Mask, Football
- Contestant 3 Gilda — Props: Trident, Top Hat, Magic Wand

Show Forest Stroll

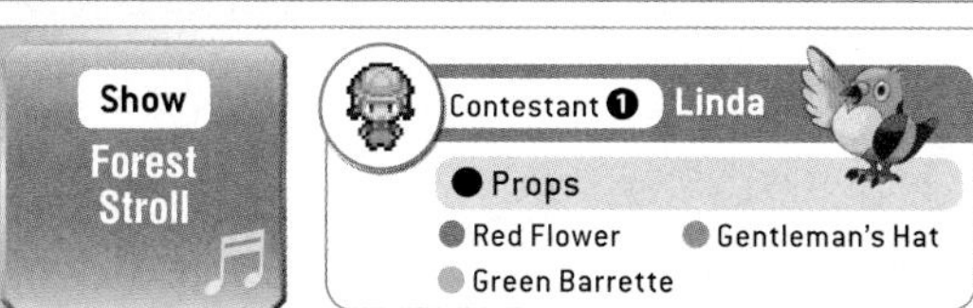

- Contestant 1 Linda — Props: Red Flower, Gentleman's Hat, Green Barrette

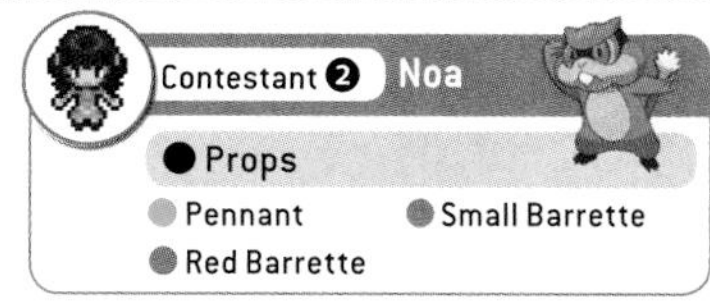

- Contestant 2 Noa — Props: Pennant, Small Barrette, Red Barrette

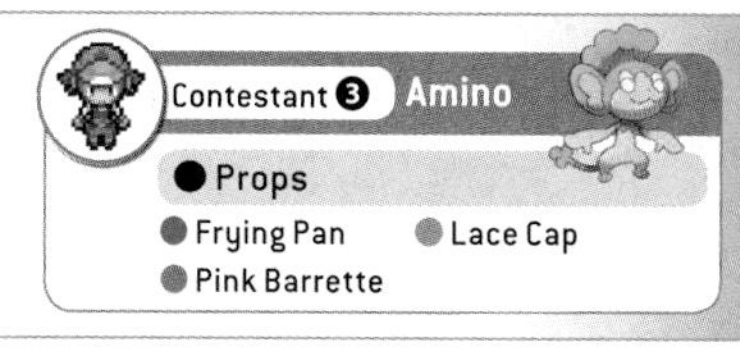

- Contestant 3 Amino — Props: Frying Pan, Lace Cap, Pink Barrette

Show A Sweet Soirée

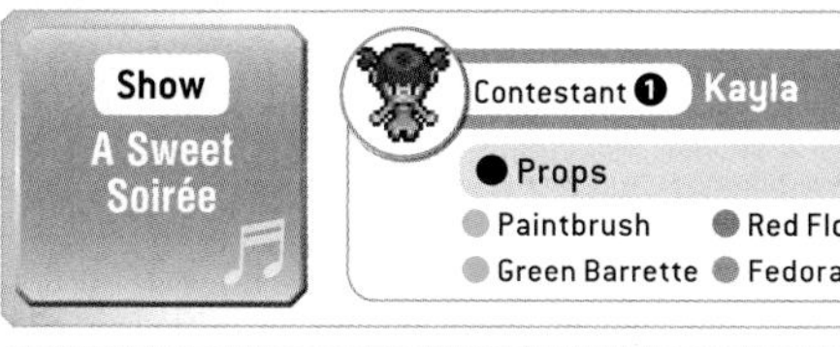

- Contestant 1 Kayla — Props: Paintbrush, Red Flower, Green Barrette, Fedora

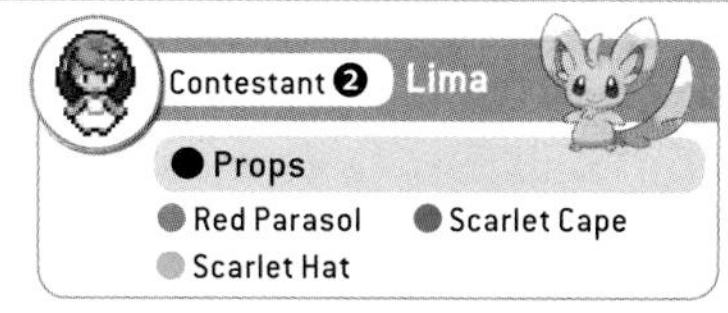

- Contestant 2 Lima — Props: Red Parasol, Scarlet Cape, Scarlet Hat

- Contestant 3 Leon — Props: Blue Flower, Lantern, Gorgeous Flower, Small Barrette

Show Exciting Nimbasa

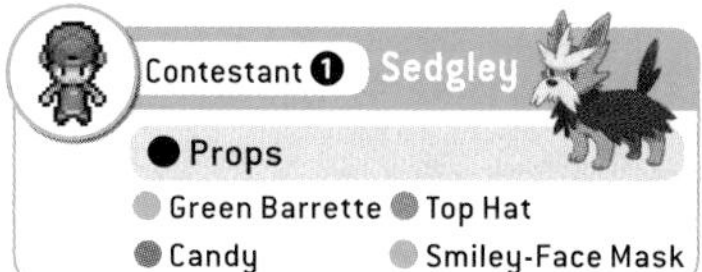

- Contestant 1 Sedgley — Props: Green Barrette, Top Hat, Candy, Smiley-Face Mask

- Contestant 2 Teljin — Props: Racket, Square Glasses, Blue Flower

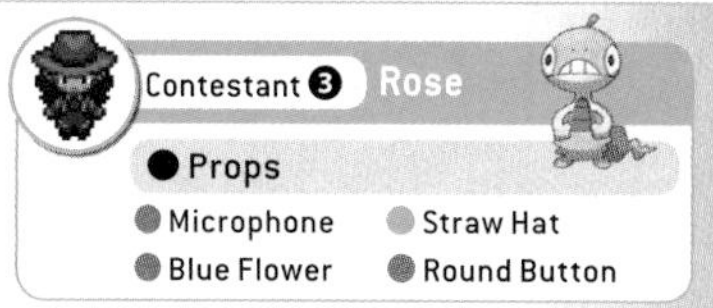

- Contestant 3 Rose — Props: Microphone, Straw Hat, Blue Flower, Round Button

Performances that get good reviews

Appeal to the audience at the perfect moment

After you're done dressing up your Pokémon, it will go on stage and perform in front of the audience. Your Pokémon can make an appeal to the audience if it has arm Props. When it gets the audience's attention, your Pokémon receives applause.

Musical Technique 1 Use Props on its arms to make an appeal to the audience

When on stage, Pokémon will perform and dance to musical accompaniment. Most of the time, you'll just watch your Pokémon dance, but there is one moment when your action is needed. If your Pokémon is wearing a Prop on its arm, "APPEAL" will be displayed. Tap it, and your Pokémon will rotate or throw its arm Prop to appeal to the audience. If your Pokémon makes an appeal at the right time, it can get the spotlight all to itself and receive applause from the audience.

Pokémon on stage
Pokémon on stage are under the spotlights. Sometimes only one Pokémon is spotlighted.

APPEAL
Tap these icons and your Pokémon will be the only one in the spotlight, scoring all the attention from the audience.

How to make an appeal

1. Your Pokémon can appeal to the audience using the Prop on its arm.
2. A successful appeal is rewarded with audience applause.
3. When no other Pokémon tries to appeal at the same time as your Pokémon, the appeal will succeed.

Interrupt another Pokémon's appeal

If your Pokémon tries to appeal at the same time as another Pokémon, it will cause the other Pokémon's appeal to fail. When you see another Pokémon starting to appeal, it's a good strategy to foil that appeal by quickly tapping "APPEAL."

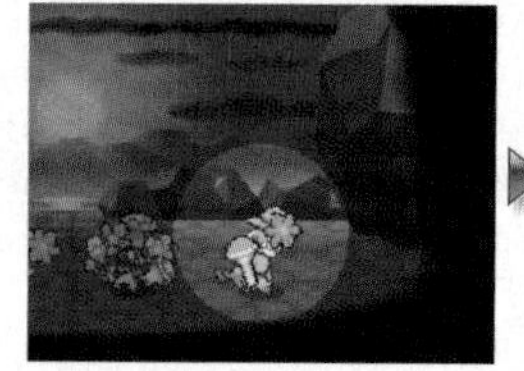

After the Pokémon Musical performance

Check the review with the Musical Photos and fan letters

When the Pokémon Musical ends, the Musical Photo is taken. You'll also receive a fan letter from the owner when you go backstage. Check these things to see how well your Pokémon did in the Musical.

After the Pokémon Musical

1 The Musical Photo

The Pokémon who received the highest recognition is in the air. The latest photo will be displayed in the hall.

2 A fan letter from the owner

Listen carefully to the owner reading the other fan letters so you can get your Pokémon better prepared for the next show.

3 Your fans gather in the reception area to give you Props

Talk to the fans in the reception area and you might receive Props. Not all fans give you Props, though.

Perform with your friends

Compete against your friends in the Pokémon Musical

You can participate in the Pokémon Musical with your friends and family members as well. Compete with each other using the Props you have and see who gets the most attention from the audience. You can receive Props from your fans just like when you participate alone.

How it works

1 Select one of your party Pokémon

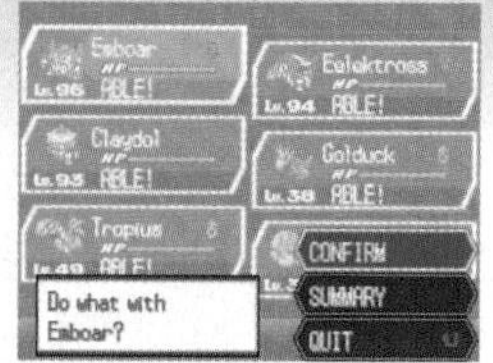

Select a Pokémon from your party to participate in the Pokémon Musical.

2 Select IR or wireless communications

You can select either Infrared Connection (IR) or wireless communications. Discuss among yourselves to see which communication mode works best for you.

3 Choose which contestant will be the leader

Choose one member to be the leader. The leader gets to pick the show.

Battle Subway

Win on the Battle Subway

Gather up your strongest Pokémon, and see the ones you raised with great care keep winning and winning!

The Battle Subway is a knockout competition where you'll face many Trainers one after another. Defeat seven Trainers, and you'll advance to face the next seven! Gather up your strongest Pokémon and best strategies to win every match.

Battle Subway Basics

Battle Subway Basics 1 The Battle Subway is in Nimbasa City

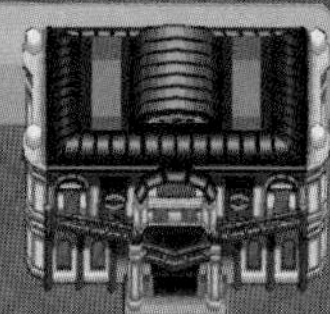

You'll find the Battle Subway at the Gear Station in the heart of Nimbasa City. Seven trains are available at the Gear Station, each with a different battle format. You'll battle while the train speeds to its next destination.

The Gear Station of the Battle Subway

Platform for Trains to Anville Town

You can get on the train between Nimbasa City and Anville Town.

Platform for Super Multi Trains

Platform for Multi Trains

Platform for Wi-Fi Trains

Platform for Super Double Trains

Platform for Double Trains

Platform for Super Single Trains

Platform for Single Trains

Exchange Service Corner

Keep winning to earn BP, and then exchange BP for items. You can exchange BP for TMs at the counter to your left.

Battle Subway Basics 2 Participate in seven different challenges

Seven different trains offer you different Pokémon battles. You can challenge the Super Single, Double, and Multi Trains if you have 21 straight wins in the Single, Double, or Multi Train.

Seven battle formats

Single Train	The Single Trains are for Single Battles. This is the most basic train.
Double Train	The Double Trains are for Double Battles.
Multi Train	The Multi Train is for Multi Battles, where you'll team up with another Trainer and use two Pokémon each.
Wi-Fi Train	The Wi-Fi-Train lets you challenge Trainers from all over the world through Nintendo Wi-Fi Connection.
Super Single Train	Trains for Single Battles with tougher Pokémon.
Super Double Train	Trains for Double Battles with tougher Pokémon.
Super Multi Train	Trains for Multi Battles with tougher Pokémon.

Common rules for all trains

1 Levels	• Pokémon of any level can participate. All Pokémon are set to Lv. 50 during a challenge. (After battles in the Battle Subway, their levels return to their original levels.)
2 Battle rules	• Each challenge consists of seven consecutive battles. You can decide to retire. • If you win against seven Trainers in a row, the train stops at a station.
3 Eligible Pokémon	• All participating Pokémon must be of different species, and they cannot hold duplicate items.
4 Ineligible Pokémon	Mewtwo, Mew, Ho-Oh, Lugia, Celebi, Kyogre, Groudon, Rayquaza, Jirachi, Deoxys, Palkia, Dialga, Giratina, Phione, Manaphy, Darkrai, Shaymin, Arceus, Victini, Reshiram, Zekrom, Kyurem, Keldeo, Meloetta, Genesect, and Eggs may not participate.

Battle Subway Basics 3 Achieve impressive records and collect Medals

You can earn up to seven Medals at the Battle Subway. Three of these Medals are from defeating the Subway Bosses, and you can pick up four more for challenging the Battle Subway many times.

Subway Low Gear

Subway Accelerator

Subway Top Gear

Runaway Express

Single Express

Double Express

Multi Express

Check p. 448 for the Medal list.

Battle Subway Basics  4 Extend your winning streak and get trophies

If you have 49 straight wins on Super Trains, you will receive a trophy for each battle format. Your trophies will be displayed in your house in Aspertia City.

A trophy proving you defeated the Single Master

A trophy proving you defeated the Double Master

A trophy proving you defeated the Multi Master

Battle Subway Basics  5 Exchange BP for items

Exchange BP for items at the Exchange Service Corner. At the counter to your left, you can choose TMs, while at the counter to your right, you can pick up items for Pokémon to hold in battle.

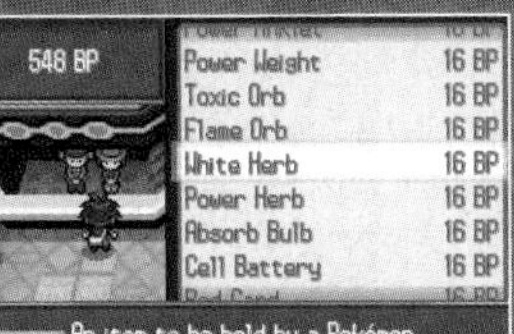

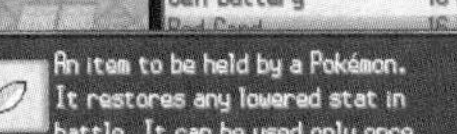

An item to be held by a Pokémon. It restores any lowered stat in battle. It can be used only once.

If you win against Ingo in the Single Train, you can get more BP

If you win against Emmet in the Double Train, you can get more BP

BP you earn from successful battles

Battle	1st round	2nd round	3rd round	4th round	5th round	6th round	7th round	8th round	9th round	10th round
Single Train	3 BP	3 BP	10 BP	—	—	—	—	—	—	—
Super Single Train	5 BP	6 BP	7 BP	8 BP	9 BP	10 BP	30 BP	10 BP	10 BP	10 BP
Double Train	3 BP	3 BP	10 BP	—	—	—	—	—	—	—
Super Double Train	5 BP	6 BP	7 BP	8 BP	9 BP	10 BP	30 BP	10 BP	10 BP	10 BP
Multi Train	3 BP	3 BP	10 BP	—	—	—	—	—	—	—
Super Multi Train	5 BP	6 BP	7 BP	8 BP	9 BP	10 BP	30 BP	10 BP	10 BP	10 BP

Battle	Rank 1	Rank 2	Rank 3	Rank 4	Rank 5	Rank 6	Rank 7	Rank 8	Rank 9	Rank 10
Wi-Fi Train	10 BP	10 BP	10 BP	10 BP	10 BP	10 BP	10 BP	10 BP	10 BP	10 BP
Wi-Fi Train (earlier train)	5 BP	5 BP	5 BP	5 BP	5 BP	5 BP	5 BP	5 BP	5 BP	5 BP

Items available at the Exchange Service Corner

Left Clerk

Prize	BP needed
TM17 Protect	6 BP
TM20 Safeguard	6 BP
TM32 Double Team	6 BP
TM59 Incinerate	6 BP
TM31 Brick Break	12 BP
TM79 Frost Breath	12 BP
TM89 U-turn	12 BP
TM10 Hidden Power	18 BP
TM23 Smack Down	18 BP
TM48 Round	18 BP
TM75 Swords Dance	18 BP
TM87 Swagger	18 BP
TM88 Pluck	18 BP
TM34 Sludge Wave	24 BP

Prize	BP needed
TM51 Ally Switch	24 BP
TM60 Quash	24 BP
TM64 Explosion	24 BP
TM77 Psych Up	24 BP

Right Clerk

Prize	BP needed
Calcium	1 BP
Carbos	1 BP
HP Up	1 BP
Iron	1 BP
Protein	1 BP
Zinc	1 BP
Fire Stone	3 BP
Leaf Stone	3 BP
Thunderstone	3 BP
Water Stone	3 BP
Binding Band	8 BP
Muscle Band	8 BP
Razor Claw	8 BP
Razor Fang	8 BP

Prize	BP needed
Scope Lens	8 BP
Wide Lens	8 BP
Wise Glasses	8 BP
Air Balloon	12 BP
BrightPowder	12 BP
Focus Band	12 BP
Iron Ball	12 BP
Zoom Lens	12 BP
Absorb Bulb	16 BP
Cell Battery	16 BP
Eject Button	16 BP
Flame Orb	16 BP
Power Anklet	16 BP
Power Band	16 BP

Prize	BP needed
Power Belt	16 BP
Power Bracer	16 BP
Power Herb	16 BP
Power Lens	16 BP
Power Weight	16 BP
Red Card	16 BP
Toxic Orb	16 BP
White Herb	16 BP
Choice Band	24 BP
Choice Scarf	24 BP
Choice Specs	24 BP
Focus Sash	24 BP
Life Orb	24 BP
Rare Candy	24 BP

Battle Subway Basics  6 Sometimes Trainers at stations give you items

In the Battle Subway, you arrive at a station every time you have seven straight wins. At some stations, you'll find Trainers who may give you items. Make sure to speak to one of them in the 4th round, because you'll get a Rare Candy to raise the level of a Pokémon.

Station Trainers for all Single, Double, and Multi Battles

Train	Number of rounds	Item
Normal Train	3rd round	PP Up
Super Train	3rd round	PP Up
	4th round	Rare Candy
	15th round	Lansat Berry
	29th round	Starf Berry

Take On the Single and Super Single Trains

The Single Train and the Super Single Train are the most basic trains, where you keep battling until you lose. To keep winning, prepare a group of strong Pokémon that can consistently dish out defeat to all opponents. Pokémon with high Speed and Attack or Sp. Atk are good choices, because you want to attack first to deal massive damage.

Current winning streak: 38!

Rules in the Single Train and the Super Single Train

1 Conditions for challenge	Single Train	You can challenge it anytime.
	Super Single Train	You can challenge it if you have 21 straight wins in the Single Train after finishing the main story.
2 Conditions for battles		• Choose three Pokémon from your party or Battle Box. • The battle format is one-on-one.

The opposing Trainers' Pokémon get stronger with each seven-win streak

Battles in trains are divided into seven-match challenges—and every time you notch seven straight wins, the opposing Trainers' Pokémon get stronger. If a Trainer is too strong for you, you may need to choose other Pokémon to participate in battles. Find the right combination of Pokémon for seven straight wins so you can extend your record!

Since you've won seven in a row,
I present you with these Battle Points!

If you have seven straight wins, you can pick up BP at a station. Win 32 times in a row to clear the Single Train challenge.

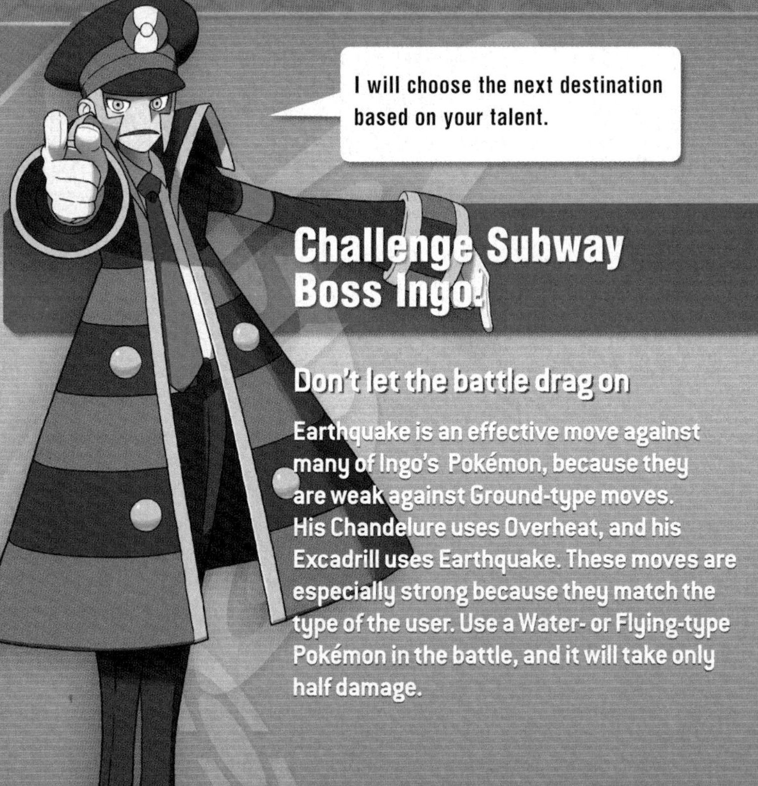

I will choose the next destination based on your talent.

Challenge Subway Boss Ingo!

Don't let the battle drag on

Earthquake is an effective move against many of Ingo's Pokémon, because they are weak against Ground-type moves. His Chandelure uses Overheat, and his Excadrill uses Earthquake. These moves are especially strong because they match the type of the user. Use a Water- or Flying-type Pokémon in the battle, and it will take only half damage.

Take On the Double and Super Double Trains

In the Double Train and the Super Double Train, you battle in two-on-two Double Battles. Your strategy will be different from Single Battles, because here your Pokémon need to cooperate and create combos. You'll also need to consider your opponent's combos and how to prevent them. Think ahead to foil the other Trainer's strategies.

What will Gigalith do?

Rules for the Double Train and the Super Double Train

1 Conditions for challenge	Double Train	You can challenge it anytime.
	Super Double Train	You can challenge it if you have 21 straight wins in the Double Train after finishing the main story.
2 Conditions for battles		• Choose four Pokémon from your party or Battle Box. • The battle format is two-on-two.

You need strategies specific to Double Battles

By using moves that attack multiple Pokémon at once—such as Rock Slide, Icy Wind, and Razor Leaf—you will dramatically increase your odds of winning. If you defeat even one opposing Pokémon before it has a chance to attack, your Pokémon will take less damage.

Pokémon with the Ability Water Absorb or Storm Drain can avoid taking damage from an ally's Surf.

Battle Subway Boss Emmet!

Double Train, 21st match

Pokémon	Lv.	Type	Weak to
Garbodor	Lv. 50	Poison	Ground, Psychic
Durant	Lv. 50	Bug, Steel	Fire
Crustle	Lv. 50	Bug, Rock	Water, Rock, Steel
Klinklang	Lv. 50	Steel	Fire, Fighting, Ground

Super Double Train, 49th match

Pokémon	Lv.	Type	Weak to
Chandelure	Lv. 50	Ghost, Fire	Water, Ground, Rock, Ghost, Dark
Eelektross	Lv. 50	Electric	Ground◆
Excadrill	Lv. 50	Ground, Steel	Fire, Water, Fighting, Ground
Haxorus	Lv. 50	Dragon	Ice, Dragon

◆ The damage may change depending on the effects of this Pokémon's Ability.

I like combinations of two Pokémon. And I like winning more than anything else.

Use moves with wide target ranges

Many of Emmet's Pokémon are weak against Ground or Water-type moves. Use moves such as Earth Power and Hydro Pump for massive damage.

Take On the Multi and Super Multi Trains

In the Multi Train and the Super Multi Train, two Trainers must cooperate and battle together. You'll have a partner for every challenge. Your own skills, plus your ability to coordinate with your partner, will determine the outcome of the battle. Correctly guess your partner's moves to choose your target carefully.

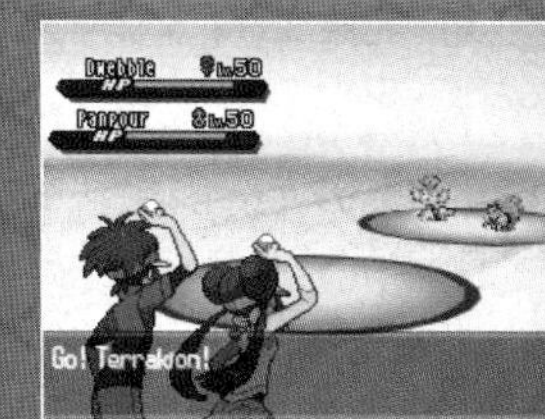

Rules for the Multi Train and the Super Multi Train

1 Conditions for challenge	Multi Train	You can challenge it any time.
	Super Multi Train	You can challenge it if you have 21 straight wins in the Multi Train after finishing the main story.
2 Conditions for battles		• Choose two Pokémon from your party or Battle Box. • Two Trainers team up for a two-on-two battle.

The battle depends on your teamwork

You cannot choose your partner's Pokémon moves, but sometimes you might pull off a combo by chance. (Or you might not!) If you can guess what your partner's Pokémon will do, try for the combo. If you cannot tell what it will do, rely on the solid moves of your Pokémon for sure damage.

At the station, you and your partner choose a strategy. Your partner can focus on attack, defense, or a balance between them.

Battle Subway Bosses Ingo and Emmet!

Read your partner's next move

If you focus on one of the bosses to knock his team out first, you can battle two-on-one afterward to get an edge in the battle.

Let's have the greatest battle, better than ever before.

Check safety. Everything's ready! Aim for victory! All aboard!

◆ The damage may change depending on the effects of this Pokémon's Ability.

Take On the Wi-Fi Train

In the Wi-Fi Train, you'll battle against Trainers from all over the world. Unlike other trains, you'll come back to the Gear Station after seven matches. If you keep winning, your Rank will go up. You'll face tougher Trainers as your Rank goes up. That's one way to know how good you're getting as a Trainer!

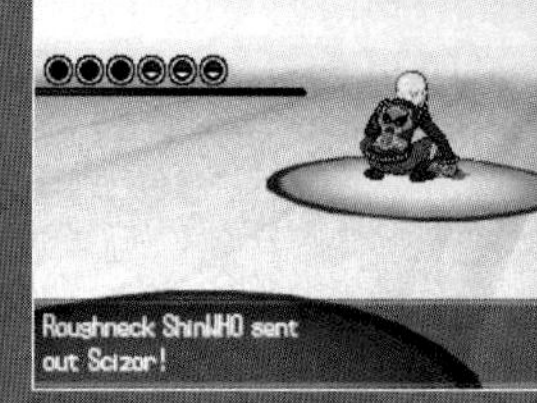

Roughneck ShinWHO sent out Scizor!

Rules for the Wi-Fi Train

1 Conditions for challenge	• You can participate whenever you are connected to Nintendo Wi-Fi Connection.
2 Conditions for battles	• You can choose three Pokémon from your party or Battle Box. • The battle format is one-on-one.

On the Wi-Fi Train  1 Trainers from all over the world will be your rivals

The battle format is the same as on the Single Trains, but on the Wi-Fi Train, you'll face Trainers from all over the world. As new Trainers show up one after another, a strategy that worked well before may not work on new Trainers. You must adapt your strategies depending on the opposing Trainers.

This is the end of the Wi-Fi Train line.

With the Wi-Fi Train, you'll come back to the Gear Station after seven matches.

The opposing Trainer changes every time. Sometimes, unfamiliar Pokémon will surprise you with their strength.

On the Wi-Fi Train  2 Keep winning and your Rank goes up

Your Rank improves if you win against seven Trainers in a row. You can battle strong Trainers who have prevailed in fierce battles to reach the same Rank as you. At Rank 9 or 10, one failed challenge could demote you. Keep winning without a loss to aim for Rank 10.

The higher your Rank gets, the stronger your rivals

You'll know your own Rank as you get on the Wi-Fi Train. Avoid consecutive failures so your Rank won't go down.

Conditions to change Ranks

Rank	Promotion	Demotion
Rank 1	A 7-win streak	—
Rank 2	A 7-win streak	5 consecutive failures in a 7-win streak
Rank 3	A 7-win streak	4 consecutive failures in a 7-win streak
Rank 4	A 7-win streak	4 consecutive failures in a 7-win streak
Rank 5	A 7-win streak	3 consecutive failures in a 7-win streak
Rank 6	A 7-win streak	3 consecutive failures in a 7-win streak
Rank 7	A 7-win streak	2 consecutive failures in a 7-win streak
Rank 8	A 7-win streak	2 consecutive failures in a 7-win streak
Rank 9	A 7-win streak	A failure in a 7-win streak
Rank 10	—	A failure in a 7-win streak

Special Events

The Dropped Item Event

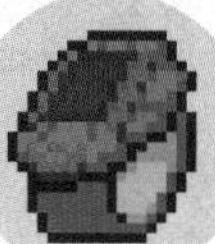

The Dropped Item you pick up in Nimbasa City is a Xtransceiver. If your character is a boy, the owner of the Dropped Item is Yancy; if your character is a girl, the item belongs to Curtis. Keep talking to Yancy or Curtis, and you'll find romance is in the air. Eventually, you'll be able to trade Pokémon.

Your interactions with Yancy or Curtis

Boy ▶ When your character is a boy

Girl ▶ When your character is a girl

1 Pick up the Dropped Item in Nimbasa City

Pick up the Dropped Item in Nimbasa City's amusement park. This is where the romance begins.

Boy

Girl

2 Talk to its owner on the Xtransceiver

You'll receive a call from the owner of the Dropped Item, Yancy (Curtis), and you'll end up holding on to it for now. When you go to one of the places listed below, you'll receive a call from Yancy (Curtis), and you can have a conversation. Talk with her (him) 10 times.

Boy

Girl

Places where you might get calls

Where	
Lacunosa Town	Route 7
Undella Town	Route 9
Mistralton City	Route 11
Driftveil City	Route 12
Lentimas Town	Route 13
Nimbasa City	Route 14
Route 5	Route 16
Route 6	

6 Meet up with Yancy (Curtis) at the Ferris wheel

Yancy (Curtis) will meet you at Nimbasa City's Ferris wheel.

Boy

Girl

7 Trade Pokémon in front of the Ferris wheel

You'll be able to go on one date at Nimbasa City's Ferris wheel each day. After you enter the Hall of Fame, you'll be able to trade Pokémon with Yancy (Curtis).

Boy

Girl

Will you trade me one of your Pokémon?

Pokémon that Yancy (Curtis) will trade you

Trade	When your character is a boy	When your character is a girl
1st	Meowth	Mankey
2nd	Wobbuffet	Wobbuffet
3rd	Ralts	Ralts
4th	Shieldon	Cranidos
5th	Rhyhorn	Rhyhorn
6th	Shellos (West Sea)	Shellos (East Sea)
7th	Mawile	Sableye
8th	Spiritomb	Spiritomb
9th	Snorlax	Snorlax
10th	Teddiursa	Phanpy
11th	Spinda	Spinda
12th	Togepi	Togepi

3 Return the Dropped Item

Meet Yancy (Curtis) in front of the Nimbasa City Ferris wheel and return the Dropped Item.

Boy

Girl

4 Have friendly conversations

You'll be able to call Yancy (Curtis) every now and again on the Xtransceiver. Yancy (Curtis) will call you as well.

Boy

Trainer
I'm kind of relieved that I can relax
from now on when we talk.

Girl

Trainer
I'm relieved that I can relax
from now on when we talk.

5 Accept the invitation

After 20 friendly conversations, Yancy (Curtis) will ask you to meet up at the Ferris wheel.

Boy

Trainer
I am off today, so
can we meet somewhere?

Girl

Trainer
I'm off work today, so
can we meet somewhere?

8 Will the real identity of Yancy (Curtis) be revealed?

The story continues and a certain conversation reveals the secret of Yancy (Curtis). If you blink, you might miss it, so pay close attention!

Boy

Girl

◆ Black Kyurem and White Kyurem can't be traded

Excitement at the Nimbasa City Ferris Wheel

You'll find some Trainers waiting in front of Nimbasa City's Ferris wheel. Battle them and then you can ride the Ferris wheel together. The Trainer waiting depends on the season and the day. Don't miss all the different tales they have to tell.

A Trainer for all seasons

Boy ▶ When your character is a boy

Girl ▶ When your character is a girl

Spring

Boy Lass Persephone

...Clunk!
...CLANG! Rumble-rumble-rumble!

Meet up with Nimbasa's Feral Liepard. She doesn't like to lose, and she'll challenge you to a test of courage in the Ferris wheel.

Girl Dancer Dirk

Oh! Look at that over there!
It's absolutely stunning...

Dancer Dirk is enjoying a rare day off. Looking at the scenery from the Ferris wheel reminds him of something that happened in the past.

Summer

Boy Nursery Aide June

Sweat is making my clothes stick to me...
I'll be fine. Check out the scenery.

June has something she wants to talk to you about. It's summer, so it's very hot and humid in the Ferris wheel. You should have worn more summer-appropriate clothes.

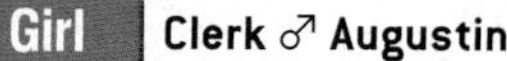

Girl Clerk ♂ Augustin

Clerk ♂ Augustin is slacking. Augustin's words reveal the shocking future in store for the Ferris wheel.

Autumn

Boy Clerk ♀ Trisha

Hee hee... My baby's kicking.
Maybe it's enjoying the view, too...

Trisha is carrying a child. She is very emotional about her development as a mother-to-be and the passage of time.

Girl Hiker Andy

Sniff... That's right...
I'm sure... But...

Andy cries as he reflects on the memory of a lost love. What could have happened to him two years ago?

Winter

Boy Beauty December

Don't move from that spot.
Be still... Just like that...

December doubts that you are who you say you are. She orders you to be still inside the Ferris wheel. What's December's true identity?

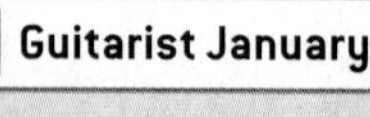

Girl Guitarist January

Ghost, oh my Ghost-type daaarling...
You can't feel my Normal-type touch! ♪

January thinks it's very rock 'n' roll how you wear light clothes even though it's winter. Even though you're riding the Ferris wheel, she sings songs for you. What she sings may surprise you!

Special Pokémon Trainers

Tuesday Rival

Wow! Awesome!
We're so high up!

Hugh says he wants to have his sister ride the Ferris wheel. He tries to act cool inside the Ferris wheel, but he gets really excited by the scenery from the window.

Wednesday Bianca

Wow!
This is sooo neat!!

Bianca shyly invites you to ride the Ferris wheel with her. She notices something from the window of the Ferris wheel. What could she have seen?

Friday N

Now that I think about it,
we both rode this Ferris wheel, too.

N loves Ferris wheels. N mentions that you remind him of a Trainer he met two years ago.

Saturday Cheren

That's the Skyarrow Bridge, and
that's Pinwheel Forest over there.

Cheren says he's never ridden the Ferris wheel. He reflects seriously on how he hasn't studied enough to understand what's fun about Ferris wheels.

Yancy or Curtis

Make a date with Yancy (Curtis) and ride the Ferris wheel together. Then you can trade for a Pokémon caught in a different region (p. 416). Each Pokémon you receive in these trades will have a Hidden Ability.

When your character is a boy

Yancy

It's strange...
Talking with you makes me feel so happy...

When your character is a girl

Curtis

When I'm with you,
I feel so relaxed somehow.

Unique Music Found in the Unova Region

Pokémon Black Version 2 and *Pokémon White Version 2* include many unique ways to play with sound. Listen carefully to discover all the fun music tricks in the game.

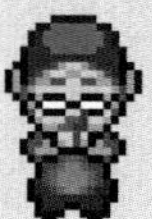

When you run, you can hear many sounds

When you run, drums are added to the music.

The intro to the music played on routes changes

The intro to the music that plays while you're on the routes changes with each season.

Tap your Gym Badges to play a song

Each Gym Badge plays a note (do re mi fa so la ti do) when you tap it.

The Virbank City Gym battle rocks along with Roxie

When you see Roxie in the Gym, the sound of her voice singing, "P-o-k-é-m-o-n, Pokémon!" reverberates through the Gym.

The Village Bridge music is performed more lavishly

Russo: La la la la la...

Talk to the four musicians around Village Bridge and they'll add something to the music.

The woman on Route 4 gives a quiz on Pokémon cries

A woman in a house will quiz you on the cries of the Pokémon in your party.

In Anville Town, a flute will sound

Approach the woman playing the flute on the bridge and you'll hear the sound of a flute added to the music.

In Opelucid City, you can hear a new instrument

In *Pokémon Black Version 2*, you'll hear a synthesizer, and in *Pokémon White Version 2*, you'll hear a string instrument.

The Tympole choir tunes up in Opelucid City

If you talk to the man in the house when you have a Tympole in your party, you can hear a chorus of Tympole!

Can you hear the dancers in Icirrus City?

Approach the four people who are dancing in a circle and the sound of clapping will be added to the music.

Something cool in a house in Icirrus City in winter

He's lost in the music...

You can reach the Sound Designer only when snow is piled up. He'll perform a song for you!

At the climax of Gym battles, the title theme rings out!

As a Gym Leader, I aim to be a wall for you to overcome!

When the Gym Leader's last Pokémon is sent out during each Gym battle, you'll hear a familiar tune—the theme song.

Adventure Data

Pokémon Moves

Explanations of the Move List

Move............ The move's name
Type............ The move's type
Kind............ Physical moves deal more damage when a Pokémon's Attack is high. Special moves deal more damage when a Pokémon's Sp. Atk is high. Status moves cause effects, such as status conditions.
Pow............ The move's attack power
Acc............ The move's accuracy
PP............ How many times the move can be used
Range......... The number and types of targets the move affects
Long........... Moves that can target the Pokémon on the other side during Triple Battles
DA............. Moves that require direct contact with the target

Range Guide

- Normal: The move affects the selected target.
- Self: The move affects only the user.
- 1 Ally: The move affects an adjacent ally in Double, Triple, and Multi Battles.
- Self/Ally: The move affects the user or one of its allies at random.
- Your Party: The move affects your entire party, including party Pokémon who are still in their Poké Balls.
- 1 Random: The move affects one of the opposing Pokémon at random.
- Many Others: The move affects multiple Pokémon at the same time.
- Adjacent: The move affects the surrounding Pokémon at the same time.
- Your Side: The move affects the side of the field where your Pokémon are.
- Other Side: The move affects the opponent's side of the field.
- Both Sides: The move affects the entire playing field without regard to opposing and ally Pokémon.
- Varies: The move is influenced by things like the opposing Pokemon's move or the user's type, so the effect and range are not fixed.

A

Move	Type	Kind	Pow.	Acc.	PP	Range	Long	DA	Effect
Absorb	Grass	Special	20	100	25	Normal	—	—	Restores HP by up to half of the damage dealt to the target.
Acid	Poison	Special	40	100	30	Many Others	—	—	A 10% chance of lowering the targets' Sp. Def by 1. Its power is weaker when it hits multiple Pokémon.
Acid Armor	Poison	Status	—	—	40	Self	—	—	Raises the user's Defense by 2.
Acid Spray	Poison	Special	40	100	20	Normal	—	—	Lowers the target's Sp. Def by 2.
Acrobatics	Flying	Physical	55	100	15	Normal	○	○	Attack's power is doubled if the user isn't holding an item.
Acupressure	Normal	Status	—	—	30	Self/Ally	—	—	Raises a random stat by 2.
Aerial Ace	Flying	Physical	60	—	20	Normal	○	○	A sure hit.
Aeroblast	Flying	Special	100	95	5	Normal	○	—	Critical hits land more easily.
After You	Normal	Status	—	—	15	Normal	—	—	The user helps the target and makes it use its move right after the user, regardless of its Speed. It fails if the target was going to use its move right after anyway, or if the target has already used its move this turn.
Agility	Psychic	Status	—	—	30	Self	—	—	Raises the user's Speed by 2.
Air Cutter	Flying	Special	55	95	25	Many Others	—	—	Critical hits land more easily. Its power is weaker when it hits multiple Pokémon.
Air Slash	Flying	Special	75	95	20	Normal	○	—	A 30% chance of making the target flinch (unable to use moves on that turn).
Ally Switch	Psychic	Status	—	—	15	Self	—	—	The user switches places with an ally. It fails if the user or target is in the middle (works only when the target is on the other end).
Amnesia	Psychic	Status	—	—	20	Self	—	—	Raises the user's Sp. Def by 2.
AncientPower	Rock	Special	60	100	5	Normal	—	—	A 10% chance of raising the user's Attack, Defense, Speed, Sp. Atk, and Sp. Def stats by 1.
Aqua Jet	Water	Physical	40	100	20	Normal	—	○	Always strikes first. The user with the higher Speed goes first if similar moves are used.
Aqua Ring	Water	Status	—	—	20	Self	—	—	Restores a little HP every turn.
Aqua Tail	Water	Physical	90	90	10	Normal	—	○	A regular attack.
Arm Thrust	Fighting	Physical	15	100	20	Normal	—	○	Attacks 2–5 times in a row in a single turn.
Aromatherapy	Grass	Status	—	—	5	Your Party	—	—	Heals status conditions of all your Pokémon, including those in your party.
Assist	Normal	Status	—	—	20	Self	—	—	Uses a random move from one of the Pokémon in your party that is not in battle.
Assurance	Dark	Physical	50	100	10	Normal	—	○	Attack's power is doubled if the target has already taken some damage in the same turn.
Astonish	Ghost	Physical	30	100	15	Normal	—	○	A 30% chance of making the target flinch (unable to use moves on that turn).
Attack Order	Bug	Physical	90	100	15	Normal	—	—	Critical hits land more easily.
Attract	Normal	Status	—	100	15	Normal	—	—	Leaves the target unable to attack 50% of the time. Only works if the user and the target are of different genders.
Aura Sphere	Fighting	Special	90	—	20	Normal	○	—	A sure hit.
Aurora Beam	Ice	Special	65	100	20	Normal	—	—	A 10% chance of lowering the target's Attack by 1.
Autotomize	Steel	Status	—	—	15	Self	—	—	Raises the user's Speed by 2 and lowers its weight by 220 lbs.
Avalanche	Ice	Physical	60	100	10	Normal	—	○	Attack's power is doubled if the user has taken damage from the target that turn.

B

Move	Type	Kind	Pow.	Acc.	PP	Range	Long	DA	Effect
Barrage	Normal	Physical	15	85	20	Normal	—	—	Attacks 2–5 times in a row in a single turn.
Barrier	Psychic	Status	—	—	30	Self	—	—	Raises the user's Defense by 2.
Baton Pass	Normal	Status	—	—	40	Self	—	—	User swaps out with an ally Pokémon and passes along any stat changes.
Beat Up	Dark	Physical	—	100	10	Normal	—	—	Attacks once for each Pokémon in your party, including the user. Does not count Pokémon that have fainted or have status conditions.
Belly Drum	Normal	Status	—	—	10	Self	—	—	The target loses half of its maximum HP but raises its Attack to the maximum.
Bestow	Normal	Status	—	—	15	Normal	—	—	If the target is not holding an item and the user is, the user can give that item to the target. Fails if the user is not holding an item or the target is holding an item.
Bide	Normal	Physical	—	—	10	Self	—	○	Inflicts twice the damage received during the next 2 turns. Cannot choose moves during those 2 turns.
Bind	Normal	Physical	15	85	20	Normal	—	○	Inflicts damage over 4–5 turns. The target cannot flee during that time.
Bite	Dark	Physical	60	100	25	Normal	—	○	A 30% chance of making the target flinch (unable to use moves on that turn).
Blast Burn	Fire	Special	150	90	5	Normal	—	—	The user can't move during the next turn. If the target is Frozen, it will be thawed.
Blaze Kick	Fire	Physical	85	90	10	Normal	—	○	A 10% chance of inflicting the Burned status condition on the target. If the target is Frozen, it will be thawed. Critical hits land more easily.
Blizzard	Ice	Special	120	70	5	Many Others	—	—	A 10% chance of inflicting the Frozen status condition on the targets. Is 100% accurate in the Hail weather condition. Its power is weaker when it hits multiple Pokémon.
Block	Normal	Status	—	—	5	Normal	—	—	The target can't escape. If used in a Trainer battle, it prevents the opposing Trainer from switching out a Pokémon.
Blue Flare	Fire	Special	130	85	5	Normal	—	—	A 20% chance of inflicting the Burned status condition on the target. If the target is Frozen, it will be thawed.
Body Slam	Normal	Physical	85	100	15	Normal	—	○	A 30% chance of inflicting the Paralysis status condition on the target.
Bolt Strike	Electric	Physical	130	85	5	Normal	—	○	A 20% chance of inflicting the Paralysis status condition on the target.
Bone Club	Ground	Physical	65	85	20	Normal	—	—	A 10% chance of making the target flinch (unable to use moves on that turn).
Bone Rush	Ground	Physical	25	90	10	Normal	—	—	Attacks 2–5 times in a row in a single turn.
Bonemerang	Ground	Physical	50	90	10	Normal	—	—	Attacks twice in a row in a single turn.
Bounce	Flying	Physical	85	85	5	Normal	○	○	The user flies into the air on the first turn and attacks on the second. A 30% chance of inflicting the Paralysis status condition on the target.

Move	Type	Kind	Pow.	Acc.	PP	Range	Long	DA	Effect
Brave Bird	Flying	Physical	120	100	15	Normal	○	○	The user takes 1/3 of the damage inflicted.
Brick Break	Fighting	Physical	75	100	15	Normal	—	○	This move is not affected by Reflect. It removes the effect of Reflect and Light Screen.
Brine	Water	Special	65	100	10	Normal	—	—	Attack's power is doubled if the target's HP is at half or below.
Bubble	Water	Special	20	100	30	Many Others	—	—	A 10% chance of lowering the targets' Speed by 1. Its power is weaker when it hits multiple Pokémon.
BubbleBeam	Water	Special	65	100	20	Normal	—	—	A 10% chance of lowering the target's Speed by 1.
Bug Bite	Bug	Physical	60	100	20	Normal	—	○	If the target is holding a Berry with a battle effect, the user eats that Berry and uses its effect.
Bug Buzz	Bug	Special	90	100	10	Normal	—	—	A 10% chance of lowering the target's Sp. Def by 1.
Bulk Up	Fighting	Status	—	—	20	Self	—	—	Raises the user's Attack and Defense by 1.
Bulldoze	Ground	Physical	60	100	20	Adjacent	—	—	Lowers the targets' Speed by 1. Its power is weaker when it hits multiple Pokémon.
Bullet Punch	Steel	Physical	40	100	30	Normal	—	○	Always strikes first. The user with the higher Speed goes first if similar moves are used.
Bullet Seed	Grass	Physical	25	100	30	Normal	—	—	Attacks 2–5 times in a row in a single turn.

C

Move	Type	Kind	Pow.	Acc.	PP	Range	Long	DA	Effect
Calm Mind	Psychic	Status	—	—	20	Self	—	—	Raises the user's Sp. Atk and Sp. Def by 1.
Camouflage	Normal	Status	—	—	20	Self	—	—	Changes the user's type to match the environment. Tall grass/Lawn: Grass type. Path/Sand/Entralink/Swamp: Ground type. Cave: Rock type. Water surface/Puddle/Shoal: Water type. Snow/Ice: Ice type. Indoors: Normal type.
Captivate	Normal	Status	—	100	20	Many Others	—	—	Raises the user's Sp. Atk by 2. Only works if the user and the target are of different genders.
Charge	Electric	Status	—	—	20	Self	—	—	Doubles the attack power of an Electric-type move used the next turn. Raises the user's Sp. Def by 1.
Charge Beam	Electric	Special	50	90	10	Normal	—	—	A 70% chance of raising the user's Sp. Atk by 1.
Charm	Normal	Status	—	100	20	Normal	—	—	Lowers the target's Attack by 2.
Chatter	Flying	Special	60	100	20	Normal	○	—	May inflict the Confused status condition on the target. Chance depends on the volume of the sound you recorded (Chatot only).
Chip Away	Normal	Physical	70	100	20	Normal	—	○	The target's stat changes don't affect this move.
Circle Throw	Fighting	Physical	60	90	10	Normal	—	○	Ends wild Pokémon battles after attacking. In a Double Battle with wild Pokémon or if the wild Pokémon's level is higher than the users, no additional effect takes place. In a battle with a Trainer, this move forces another Pokémon to switch in. If there is no Pokémon to switch in, no additional effect takes place.
Clamp	Water	Physical	35	85	15	Normal	—	○	Inflicts damage over 4–5 turns. The target cannot flee during that time.
Clear Smog	Poison	Special	50	—	15	Normal	—	—	Eliminates every stat change of the target.
Close Combat	Fighting	Physical	120	100	5	Normal	—	○	Lowers the user's Defense and Sp. Def by 1.
Coil	Poison	Status	—	—	20	Self	—	—	Raises the user's Attack, Defense, and accuracy by 1.
Comet Punch	Normal	Physical	18	85	15	Normal	—	○	Attacks 2–5 times in a row in a single turn.
Confuse Ray	Ghost	Status	—	100	10	Normal	—	—	Inflicts the Confused status condition on the target.
Confusion	Psychic	Special	50	100	25	Normal	—	—	A 10% chance of inflicting the Confused status condition on the target.
Constrict	Normal	Physical	10	100	35	Normal	—	○	A 10% chance of lowering the target's Speed by 1.
Conversion	Normal	Status	—	—	30	Self	—	—	Changes the user's type to that of one of its moves.
Conversion 2	Normal	Status	—	—	30	Normal	—	—	Changes the user's type to one that is strong against the last move the target used.
Copycat	Normal	Status	—	—	20	Self	—	—	Uses the last move used.
Cosmic Power	Psychic	Status	—	—	20	Self	—	—	Raises the user's Defense and Sp. Def by 1.
Cotton Guard	Grass	Status	—	—	10	Self	—	—	Raises the user's Defense by 3.
Cotton Spore	Grass	Status	—	100	40	Normal	—	—	Lowers the target's Speed by 2.
Counter	Fighting	Physical	—	100	20	Varies	—	○	If the user is attacked physically, this move inflicts twice the damage done to the user. Always strikes last.
Covet	Normal	Physical	60	100	40	Normal	—	○	When the target is holding an item and the user is not, the user can steal that item. A regular attack if the target is not holding an item.
Crabhammer	Water	Physical	90	90	10	Normal	—	○	Critical hits land more easily.
Cross Chop	Fighting	Physical	100	80	5	Normal	—	○	Critical hits land more easily.
Cross Poison	Poison	Physical	70	100	20	Normal	—	○	Critical hits land more easily. A 10% chance of inflicting the Poison status condition on the target.
Crunch	Dark	Physical	80	100	15	Normal	—	○	A 20% chance of lowering the target's Defense by 1.
Crush Claw	Normal	Physical	75	95	10	Normal	—	○	A 50% chance of lowering the target's Defense by 1.
Crush Grip	Normal	Physical	—	100	5	Normal	—	○	The more HP the target has left, the greater the attack's power (max 120).
Curse	Ghost	Status	—	—	10	Varies	—	—	Lowers the user's Speed by 1 and raises its Attack and Defense 1. If used by a Ghost-type Pokémon, the user loses half of its maximum HP, but the move lowers the target's HP by 1/4 of its maximum every turn.
Cut	Normal	Physical	50	95	30	Normal	—	○	A regular attack.

D

Move	Type	Kind	Pow.	Acc.	PP	Range	Long	DA	Effect
Dark Pulse	Dark	Special	80	100	15	Normal	○	—	A 20% chance of making the target flinch (unable to use moves on that turn).
Dark Void	Dark	Status	—	80	10	Many Others	—	—	Inflicts the Sleep status condition on the targets.
Defend Order	Bug	Status	—	—	10	Self	—	—	Raises the user's Defense and Sp. Def by 1.
Defense Curl	Normal	Status	—	—	40	Self	—	—	Raises the user's Defense by 1.
Defog	Flying	Status	—	—	15	Normal	—	—	Lowers the target's evasion by 1. Nullifies the effects of Light Screen, Reflect, Safeguard, Mist, Spikes, Toxic Spikes, and Stealth Rock on the target's side.
Destiny Bond	Ghost	Status	—	—	5	Self	—	—	If the user faints due to damage from a Pokémon, that Pokémon faints as well.
Detect	Fighting	Status	—	—	5	Self	—	—	The user evades all attacks that turn. If used in succession, its chance of failing rises.
Dig	Ground	Physical	80	100	10	Normal	—	○	The user burrows underground on the first turn and attacks on the second.
Disable	Normal	Status	—	100	20	Normal	—	—	The target can't use the move it just used for 4 turns.
Discharge	Electric	Special	80	100	15	Adjacent	—	—	A 30% chance of inflicting the Paralysis status condition on the targets. Its power is weaker when it hits multiple Pokémon.
Dive	Water	Physical	80	100	10	Normal	—	○	The user dives deep on the first turn and attacks on the second.
Dizzy Punch	Normal	Physical	70	100	10	Normal	—	○	A 20% chance of inflicting the Confused status condition on the target.
Doom Desire	Steel	Special	140	100	5	Normal	—	—	Attacks the target after 2 turns. This move is affected by the target's type.
Double Hit	Normal	Physical	35	90	10	Normal	—	○	Attacks twice in a row in a single turn.
Double Kick	Fighting	Physical	30	100	30	Normal	—	○	Attacks twice in a row in a single turn.
Double Team	Normal	Status	—	—	15	Self	—	—	Raises the user's evasion by 1.
Double-Edge	Normal	Physical	120	100	15	Normal	—	○	The user takes 1/3 of the damage inflicted.
DoubleSlap	Normal	Physical	15	85	10	Normal	—	○	Attacks 2–5 times in a row in a single turn.
Draco Meteor	Dragon	Special	140	90	5	Normal	—	—	Lowers the user's Sp. Atk by 2.
Dragon Claw	Dragon	Physical	80	100	15	Normal	—	○	A regular attack.

Pokémon Moves

D

Move	Type	Kind	Pow.	Acc.	PP	Range	Long	DA	Effect
Dragon Dance	Dragon	Status	—	—	20	Self	—	—	Raises the user's Attack and Speed by 1.
Dragon Pulse	Dragon	Special	90	100	10	Normal	○	—	A regular attack.
Dragon Rage	Dragon	Special	—	100	10	Normal	—	—	Deals a fixed 40 points of damage.
Dragon Rush	Dragon	Physical	100	75	10	Normal	—	○	A 20% chance of making the target flinch (unable to use moves on that turn).
Dragon Tail	Dragon	Physical	60	90	10	Normal	—	○	After attacking, it ends wild Pokémon battles. In a Double Battle with wild Pokémon or if the wild Pokémon's level is higher than the user's, no additional effect takes place. In a battle with a Trainer, this move forces another Pokémon to switch in. If there is no Pokémon to switch in, no additional effect takes place.
DragonBreath	Dragon	Special	60	100	20	Normal	—	—	A 30% chance of inflicting the Paralysis status condition on the target.
Drain Punch	Fighting	Physical	75	100	10	Normal	—	○	Restores HP by up to half of the damage dealt to the target.
Dream Eater	Psychic	Special	100	100	15	Normal	—	—	Only works when the target is asleep. Restores HP by up to half of the damage dealt to the target.
Drill Peck	Flying	Physical	80	100	20	Normal	○	○	A regular attack.
Drill Run	Ground	Physical	80	95	10	Normal	—	○	Critical hits land more easily.
Dual Chop	Dragon	Physical	40	90	15	Normal	—	○	Attacks twice in a row in a single turn.
DynamicPunch	Fighting	Physical	100	50	5	Normal	—	○	Inflicts the Confused status condition on the target.

E

Move	Type	Kind	Pow.	Acc.	PP	Range	Long	DA	Effect
Earth Power	Ground	Special	90	100	10	Normal	—	—	A 10% chance of lowering the target's Sp. Def by 1.
Earthquake	Ground	Physical	100	100	10	Adjacent	—	—	Does twice the damage if targets are underground due to using Dig. Its power is weaker when it hits multiple Pokémon.
Echoed Voice	Normal	Special	40	100	15	Normal	—	—	If this move is used every turn, no matter which Pokémon uses it, its power increases (max 200). If no Pokémon uses it in a turn, the power returns to normal.
Egg Bomb	Normal	Physical	100	75	10	Normal	—	—	A regular attack.
Electro Ball	Electric	Special	—	100	10	Normal	—	—	The faster the user is than the target, the greater the attack's power (max 150).
Electroweb	Electric	Special	55	95	15	Many Others	—	—	Lowers the targets' Speed by 1. Its power is weaker when it hits multiple Pokémon.
Embargo	Dark	Status	—	100	15	Normal	—	—	The target can't use items for 5 turns. The Trainer also can't use items on that Pokémon.
Ember	Fire	Special	40	100	25	Normal	—	—	A 10% chance of inflicting the Burned status condition on the target. If the target is Frozen, it will be thawed.
Encore	Normal	Status	—	100	5	Normal	—	—	The target is forced to keep using the last move it used. This effect lasts 3 turns.
Endeavor	Normal	Physical	—	100	5	Normal	—	○	Inflicts damage equal to the target's HP minus the user's HP.
Endure	Normal	Status	—	—	10	Self	—	—	Leaves the user with 1 HP when hit by a move that would KO it. If used in succession, its chance of failing rises.
Energy Ball	Grass	Special	80	100	10	Normal	—	—	A 10% chance of lowering the target's Sp. Def by 1.
Entrainment	Normal	Status	—	100	15	Normal	—	—	Makes the target's Ability the same as the user's. Fails with certain Abilities, however.
Eruption	Fire	Special	150	100	5	Many Others	—	—	If the user's HP is low, this move has lower attack power. If the targets are Frozen, they will be thawed. Its power is weaker when it hits multiple Pokémon.
Explosion	Normal	Physical	250	100	5	Adjacent	—	—	The user faints after using it. Its power is weaker when it hits multiple Pokémon.
Extrasensory	Psychic	Special	80	100	30	Normal	—	—	A 10% chance of making the target flinch (unable to use moves on that turn).
ExtremeSpeed	Normal	Physical	80	100	5	Normal	—	○	Always strikes first. Faster than other moves that strike first, except Fake Out. (If two Pokémon use this move, the one with the higher Speed goes first.)

F

Move	Type	Kind	Pow.	Acc.	PP	Range	Long	DA	Effect
Facade	Normal	Physical	70	100	20	Normal	—	○	Attack's power is doubled if the user has a Paralysis, Poison, or Burned status condition.
Faint Attack	Dark	Physical	60	—	20	Normal	—	○	A sure hit.
Fake Out	Normal	Physical	40	100	10	Normal	—	○	Always strikes first and makes the target flinch (unable to use moves on that turn). Only works on the first turn after the user is sent out. Faster than other moves that strike first.
Fake Tears	Dark	Status	—	100	20	Normal	—	—	Lowers the target's Sp. Def by 2.
False Swipe	Normal	Physical	40	100	40	Normal	—	○	Always leaves 1 HP, even if the damage would have made the target faint.
FeatherDance	Flying	Status	—	100	15	Normal	—	—	Lowers the target's Attack by 2.
Feint	Normal	Physical	30	100	10	Normal	—	—	Always strikes first. Faster than other moves that strike first, except Fake Out. If two Pokémon use this move, or the other Pokémon uses the ExtremeSpeed move, the one with the higher Speed goes first. Can hit targets using Protect, Detect, Quick Guard, or Wide Guard, and eliminates the effects of those moves.
Fiery Dance	Fire	Special	80	100	10	Normal	—	—	A 50% chance of raising the user's Sp. Atk by 1. If the target is Frozen, it will be thawed.
Final Gambit	Fighting	Special	—	100	5	Normal	—	○	Does damage to the target equal to the user's remaining HP. If the move lands, the user faints.
Fire Blast	Fire	Special	120	85	5	Normal	—	—	A 10% chance of inflicting the Burned status condition on the target. If the target is Frozen, it will be thawed.
Fire Fang	Fire	Physical	65	95	15	Normal	—	○	A 10% chance of inflicting the Burned status condition or making the target flinch (unable to use moves on that turn). If the target is Frozen, it will be thawed.
Fire Pledge	Fire	Special	50	100	10	Normal	—	—	When combined with Water Pledge or Grass Pledge, the power and effect change. If combined with Water Pledge, the power is 150 and it becomes a Water-type move. It will create a rainbow that turn which will last for the next 3 turns, making it more likely that your team's moves will have additional effects. If combined with Grass Pledge, the power is 150 and it remains a Fire-type move. The surrounding area becomes a sea of fire, which damages opposing Pokémon, except Fire types, that turn and the next 3 turns. If the target is Frozen, it will be thawed.
Fire Punch	Fire	Physical	75	100	15	Normal	—	○	A 10% chance of inflicting the Burned status condition on the target. If the target is Frozen, it will be thawed.
Fire Spin	Fire	Special	35	85	15	Normal	—	—	Inflicts damage over 4–5 turns. The target cannot flee during that time. If the target is Frozen, it will be thawed.
Fissure	Ground	Physical	—	30	5	Normal	—	—	The target faints with one hit if the user's level is equal to or greater than the target's level. The higher the user's level is compared to the target's, the more accurate the move is.
Flail	Normal	Physical	—	100	15	Normal	—	○	The lower the user's HP is, the more damage this move does to the target.
Flame Burst	Fire	Special	70	100	15	Normal	—	—	In Double and Triple Battles, it damages the Pokémon next to the target as well. If the target is Frozen, it will be thawed.
Flame Charge	Fire	Physical	50	100	20	Normal	—	○	Raises the user's Speed by 1. If the target is Frozen, it will be thawed.
Flame Wheel	Fire	Physical	60	100	25	Normal	—	○	A 10% chance of inflicting the Burned status condition on the target. If the target is Frozen, it will be thawed. This move can be used even if the user is Frozen. If the user is Frozen, this also thaws the user.
Flamethrower	Fire	Special	95	100	15	Normal	—	—	A 10% chance of inflicting the Burned status condition on the target. If the target is Frozen, it will be thawed.
Flare Blitz	Fire	Physical	120	100	15	Normal	—	○	The user takes 1/3 of the damage inflicted. A 10% chance of inflicting the Burned status condition. If the target is Frozen, it will be thawed. This move can be used even if the user is Frozen. If the user is Frozen, this also thaws the user.
Flash	Normal	Status	—	100	20	Normal	—	—	Lowers the target's accuracy by 1.
Flash Cannon	Steel	Special	80	100	10	Normal	—	—	A 10% chance of lowering the target's Sp. Def by 1.
Flatter	Dark	Status	—	100	15	Normal	—	—	Inflicts the Confused status condition on the target, but also raises its Sp. Atk by 1.
Fling	Dark	Physical	—	100	10	Normal	—	—	The user attacks by throwing its held item at the target. Power and effect vary depending on the item.
Fly	Flying	Physical	90	95	15	Normal	○	○	The user flies into the air on the first turn and attacks on the second.

Move	Type	Kind	Pow.	Acc.	PP	Range	Long	DA	Effect
Focus Blast	Fighting	Special	120	70	5	Normal	—	—	A 10% chance of lowering the target's Sp. Def by 1.
Focus Energy	Normal	Status	—	—	30	Self	—	—	Heightens the critical-hit ratio of the user's subsequent moves.
Focus Punch	Fighting	Physical	150	100	20	Normal	—	○	Always strikes last. The move misses if the user is hit before this move lands.
Follow Me	Normal	Status	—	—	20	Self	—	—	This move is given priority. Opposing Pokémon aim only at the user.
Force Palm	Fighting	Physical	60	100	10	Normal	—	○	A 30% chance of inflicting the Paralysis status condition on the target.
Foresight	Normal	Status	—	—	40	Normal	—	—	Attacks land easily regardless of the target's evasion. Makes Ghost-type Pokémon vulnerable to Normal- and Fighting-type moves.
Foul Play	Dark	Physical	95	100	15	Normal	—	○	The user turns the target's power against it. Damage varies depending on the target's Attack and Defense.
Freeze Shock	Ice	Physical	140	90	5	Normal	—	—	Builds power on the first turn and attacks on the second. A 30% chance of inflicting the Paralysis status condition on the target.
Frenzy Plant	Grass	Special	150	90	5	Normal	—	—	The user can't move during the next turn.
Frost Breath	Ice	Special	40	90	10	Normal	—	—	Always delivers a critical hit.
Frustration	Normal	Physical	—	100	20	Normal	—	○	The lower the user's friendship, the greater the attack's power.
Fury Attack	Normal	Physical	15	85	20	Normal	—	○	Attacks 2–5 times in a row in a single turn.
Fury Cutter	Bug	Physical	20	95	20	Normal	—	○	This move doubles in power with every successful hit (up to 5 hits). Power returns to normal once it misses.
Fury Swipes	Normal	Physical	18	80	15	Normal	—	○	Attacks 2–5 times in a row in a single turn.
Fusion Bolt	Electric	Physical	100	100	5	Normal	—	—	Attack's power is doubled if used immediately after Fusion Flare.
Fusion Flare	Fire	Special	100	100	5	Normal	—	—	Attack's power is doubled if used immediately after Fusion Bolt. If the target is Frozen, it will be thawed. This move can be used even if the user is Frozen. If the user is Frozen, this also thaws the user.
Future Sight	Psychic	Special	100	100	10	Normal	—	—	Attacks the target after 2 turns. This move is affected by the target's type.

G

Move	Type	Kind	Pow.	Acc.	PP	Range	Long	DA	Effect
Gastro Acid	Poison	Status	—	100	10	Normal	—	—	Disables the target's Ability.
Gear Grind	Steel	Physical	50	85	15	Normal	—	○	Attacks twice in a row in a single turn.
Giga Drain	Grass	Special	75	100	10	Normal	—	—	Restores HP by up to half of the damage dealt to the target.
Giga Impact	Normal	Physical	150	90	5	Normal	—	○	The user can't move during the next turn.
Glaciate	Ice	Special	65	95	10	Many Others	—	—	Lowers the targets' Speed by 1. Its power is weaker when it hits multiple Pokémon.
Glare	Normal	Status	—	90	30	Normal	—	—	Inflicts the Paralysis status condition on the target.
Grass Knot	Grass	Special	—	100	20	Normal	—	○	The heavier the target, the greater the attack's power.
Grass Pledge	Grass	Special	50	100	10	Normal	—	—	When combined with Water Pledge or Fire Pledge, the power and effect change. If combined with Water Pledge, the power is 150 and it remains a Grass-type move. The surrounding area will become a swamp, which lowers the Speed of opposing Pokémon that turn and the next 3 turns. If combined with Fire Pledge, the power is 150 and it becomes a Fire-type move. The surrounding area becomes a sea of fire, which damages opposing Pokémon, except Fire types, that turn and the next 3 turns. If the target is Frozen, it will be thawed.
GrassWhistle	Grass	Status	—	55	15	Normal	—	—	Inflicts the Sleep status condition on the target.
Gravity	Psychic	Status	—	—	5	Both Sides	—	—	Raises the accuracy of all Pokémon in battle for 5 turns. Ground-type moves will now hit a Pokémon with the Levitate Ability or a Flying-type Pokémon. Prevents the use of Bounce, Fly, Hi Jump Kick, Jump Kick, Magnet Rise, Splash, Sky Drop, and Telekinesis. Pulls any airborne Pokémon to the ground.
Growl	Normal	Status	—	100	40	Many Others	—	—	Lowers the targets' Attack by 1.
Growth	Normal	Status	—	—	40	Self	—	—	Raises the user's Attack and Sp. Atk by 1. Raises them by 2 when the weather condition is Sunny.
Grudge	Ghost	Status	—	—	5	Self	—	—	If the user faints because of a move, that move's PP drops to 0.
Guard Split	Psychic	Status	—	—	10	Normal	—	—	The user and the target's Defense and Sp. Def are added, then divided equally between them.
Guard Swap	Psychic	Status	—	—	10	Normal	—	—	Swaps Defense and Sp. Def changes between the user and the target.
Guillotine	Normal	Physical	—	30	5	Normal	—	○	The target faints with one hit if the user's level is equal to or greater than the target's level. The higher the user's level is compared to the target's, the more accurate the move is.
Gunk Shot	Poison	Physical	120	70	5	Normal	—	—	A 30% chance of inflicting the Poison status condition on the target.
Gust	Flying	Special	40	100	35	Normal	○	—	Does twice the damage if the target is in the sky due to using moves such as Fly or Bounce.
Gyro Ball	Steel	Physical	—	100	5	Normal	—	○	The faster the user is than the target, the greater the attack's power (max 150).

H

Move	Type	Kind	Pow.	Acc.	PP	Range	Long	DA	Effect
Hail	Ice	Status	—	—	10	Both Sides	—	—	Changes the weather condition to Hail for 5 turns, damaging all Pokémon except Ice types every turn.
Hammer Arm	Fighting	Physical	100	90	10	Normal	—	○	Lowers the user's Speed by 1.
Harden	Normal	Status	—	—	30	Self	—	—	Raises the user's Defense by 1.
Haze	Ice	Status	—	—	30	Both Sides	—	—	Eliminates every stat change of the targets.
Head Charge	Normal	Physical	120	100	15	Normal	—	○	The user takes 1/4 of the damage inflicted.
Head Smash	Rock	Physical	150	80	5	Normal	—	○	The user takes 1/2 of the damage inflicted.
Headbutt	Normal	Physical	70	100	15	Normal	—	○	A 30% chance of making the target flinch (unable to use moves on that turn).
Heal Bell	Normal	Status	—	—	5	Your Party	—	—	Heals status conditions of all your Pokémon, including those in your party.
Heal Block	Psychic	Status	—	100	15	Many Others	—	—	Targets cannot have HP restored by moves, etc. for 5 turns.
Heal Order	Bug	Status	—	—	10	Self	—	—	Restores HP by up to half of the user's maximum HP.
Heal Pulse	Psychic	Status	—	—	10	Normal	○	—	Restores the target's HP by up to half of its maximum HP.
Healing Wish	Psychic	Status	—	—	10	Self	—	—	The user faints, but fully heals the next Pokémon's HP and status conditions.
Heart Stamp	Psychic	Physical	60	100	25	Normal	—	○	A 30% chance of making the target flinch (unable to use moves on that turn).
Heart Swap	Psychic	Status	—	—	10	Normal	—	—	Swaps all stat changes between the user and the target.
Heat Crash	Fire	Physical	—	100	10	Normal	—	○	The heavier the user is than the target, the greater the attack's power (max 120).
Heat Wave	Fire	Special	100	90	10	Many Others	—	—	A 10% chance of inflicting the Burned status condition on the targets. If the targets are Frozen, they will be thawed. Its power is weaker when it hits multiple Pokémon.
Heavy Slam	Steel	Physical	—	100	10	Normal	—	○	The heavier the user is than the target, the greater the attack's power (max 120).
Helping Hand	Normal	Status	—	—	20	1 Ally	—	—	Strengthens the attack power of one ally's moves by 50%.
Hex	Ghost	Special	50	100	10	Normal	—	—	Deals twice the usual damage to a target affected by status conditions.
Hi Jump Kick	Fighting	Physical	130	90	10	Normal	—	○	If this move misses, the user loses half of its maximum HP.
Hidden Power	Normal	Special	—	100	15	Normal	—	—	Type and attack power change depending on the user.
Hone Claws	Dark	Status	—	—	15	Self	—	—	Raises Attack and accuracy by 1.
Horn Attack	Normal	Physical	65	100	25	Normal	—	○	A regular attack.

H

Move	Type	Kind	Pow.	Acc.	PP	Range	Long	DA	Effect
Horn Drill	Normal	Physical	—	30	5	Normal	—	○	The target faints with one hit if the user's level is equal to or greater than the target's level. The higher the user's level is compared to the target's, the more accurate the move is.
Horn Leech	Grass	Physical	75	100	10	Normal	—	○	Restores HP by up to half of the damage dealt to the target.
Howl	Normal	Status	—	—	40	Self	—	—	Raises the user's Attack by 1.
Hurricane	Flying	Special	120	70	10	Normal	○	—	A 30% chance of inflicting the Confused status condition on the target. Is 100% accurate in the Rain weather condition and 50% accurate in the Sunny weather condition. It hits even Pokémon that are in the sky due to using moves such as Fly and Bounce.
Hydro Cannon	Water	Special	150	90	5	Normal	—	—	The user can't move during the next turn.
Hydro Pump	Water	Special	120	80	5	Normal	—	—	A regular attack.
Hyper Beam	Normal	Special	150	90	5	Normal	—	—	The user can't move during the next turn.
Hyper Fang	Normal	Physical	80	90	15	Normal	—	○	A 10% chance of making the target flinch (unable to use moves on that turn).
Hyper Voice	Normal	Special	90	100	10	Many Others	—	—	Its power is weaker when it hits multiple Pokémon.
Hypnosis	Psychic	Status	—	60	20	Normal	—	—	Inflicts the Sleep status condition on the target.

I

Move	Type	Kind	Pow.	Acc.	PP	Range	Long	DA	Effect
Ice Ball	Ice	Physical	30	90	20	Normal	—	○	Attacks consecutively over 5 turns or until it misses. Cannot choose other moves during this time. Inflicts greater damage with every successful hit. Does twice the damage if used after Defense Curl.
Ice Beam	Ice	Special	95	100	10	Normal	—	—	A 10% chance of inflicting the Frozen status condition on the target.
Ice Burn	Ice	Special	140	90	5	Normal	—	—	Builds power on the first turn and attacks on the second. A 30% chance of inflicting the Burned status condition on the target.
Ice Fang	Ice	Physical	65	95	15	Normal	—	○	A 10% chance of inflicting the Frozen status condition or making the target flinch (unable to use moves on that turn).
Ice Punch	Ice	Physical	75	100	15	Normal	—	○	A 10% chance of inflicting the Frozen status condition on the target.
Ice Shard	Ice	Physical	40	100	30	Normal	—	—	Always strikes first. The user with the higher Speed goes first if similar moves are used.
Icicle Crash	Ice	Physical	85	90	10	Normal	—	—	A 30% chance of making the target flinch (unable to use moves on that turn).
Icicle Spear	Ice	Physical	25	100	30	Normal	—	—	Attacks 2–5 times in a row in a single turn.
Icy Wind	Ice	Special	55	95	15	Many Others	—	—	Lowers the targets' Speed by 1. Its power is weaker when it hits multiple Pokémon.
Imprison	Psychic	Status	—	—	10	Self	—	—	Opposing Pokémon cannot use a move if the user knows that move as well.
Incinerate	Fire	Special	30	100	15	Many Others	—	—	Burns up the Berry being held by each of the targets, which makes the Berries unusable. If the targets are Frozen, they will be thawed. Its power is weaker when it hits multiple Pokémon.
Inferno	Fire	Special	100	50	5	Normal	—	—	Inflicts the Burned status condition on the target. If the target is Frozen, it will be thawed.
Ingrain	Grass	Status	—	—	20	Self	—	—	Restores a little HP every turn. The user cannot be switched out after using this move. Ground-type moves will now hit the user even if it is a Flying-type Pokémon or has the Levitate Ability.
Iron Defense	Steel	Status	—	—	15	Self	—	—	Raises the user's Defense by 2.
Iron Head	Steel	Physical	80	100	15	Normal	—	○	A 30% chance of making the target flinch (unable to use moves on that turn).
Iron Tail	Steel	Physical	100	75	15	Normal	—	○	A 30% chance of lowering the target's Defense by 1.

J

Move	Type	Kind	Pow.	Acc.	PP	Range	Long	DA	Effect
Judgment	Normal	Special	100	100	10	Normal	—	—	A regular attack. This move's type changes according to the Plate that Arceus is holding.
Jump Kick	Fighting	Physical	100	95	10	Normal	—	○	If this move misses, the user loses half of its maximum HP.

K

Move	Type	Kind	Pow.	Acc.	PP	Range	Long	DA	Effect
Karate Chop	Fighting	Physical	50	100	25	Normal	—	○	Critical hits land more easily.
Kinesis	Psychic	Status	—	80	15	Normal	—	—	Lowers the target's accuracy by 1.
Knock Off	Dark	Physical	20	100	20	Normal	—	○	The target drops its held item. It gets the item back after the battle.

L

Move	Type	Kind	Pow.	Acc.	PP	Range	Long	DA	Effect
Last Resort	Normal	Physical	140	100	5	Normal	—	○	Fails unless the user has used each of its other moves at least once.
Lava Plume	Fire	Special	80	100	15	Adjacent	—	—	A 30% chance of inflicting the Burned status condition on the targets. If the targets are Frozen, they will be thawed. Its power is weaker when it hits multiple Pokémon.
Leaf Blade	Grass	Physical	90	100	15	Normal	—	○	Critical hits land more easily.
Leaf Storm	Grass	Special	140	90	5	Normal	—	—	Lowers the user's Sp. Atk by 2.
Leaf Tornado	Grass	Special	65	90	10	Normal	—	—	A 50% chance of lowering the target's accuracy by 1.
Leech Life	Bug	Physical	20	100	15	Normal	—	○	Restores HP by up to half of the damage dealt to the target.
Leech Seed	Grass	Status	—	90	10	Normal	—	—	Steals HP from the target every turn. Keeps working after the user switches out. Does not work on Grass types.
Leer	Normal	Status	—	100	30	Many Others	—	—	Lowers the targets' Defense by 1.
Lick	Ghost	Physical	20	100	30	Normal	—	○	A 30% chance of inflicting the Paralysis status condition on the target.
Light Screen	Psychic	Status	—	—	30	Your Side	—	—	Halves the damage to the Pokémon on your side from special moves. Effect lasts 5 turns even if the user is switched out. Effect is weaker in Double and Triple Battles.
Lock-On	Normal	Status	—	—	5	Normal	—	—	The user's next move will be a sure hit.
Lovely Kiss	Normal	Status	—	75	10	Normal	—	—	Inflicts the Sleep status condition on the target.
Low Kick	Fighting	Physical	—	100	20	Normal	—	○	The heavier the target, the greater the attack's power.
Low Sweep	Fighting	Physical	60	100	20	Normal	—	○	Lowers the target's Speed by 1.
Lucky Chant	Normal	Status	—	—	30	Your Side	—	—	The Pokémon on your side take no critical hits for 5 turns.
Lunar Dance	Psychic	Status	—	—	10	Self	—	—	The user faints, but fully heals the next Pokémon's HP, PP, and status conditions.
Luster Purge	Psychic	Special	70	100	5	Normal	—	—	A 50% chance of lowering the target's Sp. Def by 1.

M

Move	Type	Kind	Pow.	Acc.	PP	Range	Long	DA	Effect
Mach Punch	Fighting	Physical	40	100	30	Normal	—	○	Always strikes first. The user with the higher Speed goes first if similar moves are used.
Magic Coat	Psychic	Status	—	—	15	Self	—	—	Reflects moves with effects like Leech Seed or those that inflict the Sleep, Poison, Paralysis, or Confused status conditions.
Magic Room	Psychic	Status	—	—	10	Both Sides	—	—	No held items will have any effect for 5 turns. Fling cannot be used to throw items while Magic Room is in effect.

Move	Type	Kind	Pow.	Acc.	PP	Range	Long	DA	Effect
Magical Leaf	Grass	Special	60	—	20	Normal	—	—	A sure hit.
Magma Storm	Fire	Special	120	75	5	Normal	—	—	Inflicts damage over 4–5 turns. The target cannot flee during that time. If the target is Frozen, it will be thawed.
Magnet Bomb	Steel	Physical	60	—	20	Normal	—	—	A sure hit.
Magnet Rise	Electric	Status	—	—	10	Self	—	—	Nullifies Ground-type moves for 5 turns.
Magnitude	Ground	Physical	—	100	30	Adjacent	—	—	Attack power shifts between 10, 30, 50, 70, 90, 110, and 150. Does twice the damage to targets using Dig. Its power is weaker when it hits multiple Pokémon.
Me First	Normal	Status	—	—	20	Varies	—	—	Copies the target's chosen move and uses it with increased power. Fails if it does not strike first.
Mean Look	Normal	Status	—	—	5	Normal	—	—	The target can't escape. If used in a Trainer battle, it prevents the opposing Trainer from switching out a Pokémon.
Meditate	Psychic	Status	—	—	40	Self	—	—	Raises the user's Attack by 1.
Mega Drain	Grass	Special	40	100	15	Normal	—	—	Restores HP by up to half of the damage dealt to the target.
Mega Kick	Normal	Physical	120	75	5	Normal	—	○	A regular attack.
Mega Punch	Normal	Physical	80	85	20	Normal	—	○	A regular attack.
Megahorn	Bug	Physical	120	85	10	Normal	—	○	A regular attack.
Memento	Dark	Status	—	100	10	Normal	—	—	The user faints, but the target's Attack and Sp. Atk are lowered by 2.
Metal Burst	Steel	Physical	—	100	10	Varies	—	—	Targets the Pokémon that most recently damaged the user with a move. Inflicts 1.5 times the damage taken.
Metal Claw	Steel	Physical	50	95	35	Normal	—	○	A 10% chance of raising the user's Attack by 1.
Metal Sound	Steel	Status	—	85	40	Normal	—	—	Lowers the target's Sp. Def by 2.
Meteor Mash	Steel	Physical	100	85	10	Normal	—	○	A 20% chance of raising the user's Attack by 1.
Metronome	Normal	Status	—	—	10	Self	—	—	Uses one move randomly chosen from all possible moves.
Milk Drink	Normal	Status	—	—	10	Self	—	—	Restores HP by up to half of the user's maximum HP.
Mimic	Normal	Status	—	—	10	Normal	—	—	Copies the target's last-used move (copied move has a PP of 5). Fails if used before the opposing Pokémon uses a move.
Mind Reader	Normal	Status	—	—	5	Normal	—	—	The user's next move will be a sure hit.
Minimize	Normal	Status	—	—	20	Self	—	—	Raises the user's evasion by 2.
Miracle Eye	Psychic	Status	—	—	40	Normal	—	—	Attacks land easily regardless of the target's evasion. Makes Dark-type Pokémon vulnerable to Psychic-type moves.
Mirror Coat	Psychic	Special	—	100	20	Varies	—	—	If the user is attacked with a special move, this move inflicts twice the damage done to the user. Always strikes last.
Mirror Move	Flying	Status	—	—	20	Normal	—	—	Uses the last move that the target used.
Mirror Shot	Steel	Special	65	85	10	Normal	—	—	A 30% chance of lowering the target's accuracy by 1.
Mist	Ice	Status	—	—	30	Your Side	—	—	Protects against stat-lowering moves and additional effects for 5 turns.
Mist Ball	Psychic	Special	70	100	5	Normal	—	—	A 50% chance of lowering the target's Sp. Atk by 1.
Moonlight	Normal	Status	—	—	5	Self	—	—	Recovers HP. Recovers 1/2 of the user's maximum HP. In Sunny weather conditions, recovers 2/3 of the user's maximum HP. In Rain/Sandstorm/Hail weather, recovers 1/4 of the user's maximum HP.
Morning Sun	Normal	Status	—	—	5	Self	—	—	Recovers HP. Recovers 1/2 of the user's maximum HP. In Sunny weather conditions, recovers 2/3 of the user's maximum HP. In Rain/Sandstorm/Hail weather, recovers 1/4 of the user's maximum HP.
Mud Bomb	Ground	Special	65	85	10	Normal	—	—	A 30% chance of lowering the target's accuracy by 1.
Mud Shot	Ground	Special	55	95	15	Normal	—	—	Lowers the target's Speed by 1.
Mud Sport	Ground	Status	—	—	15	Both Sides	—	—	The power of Electric-type moves drops to 1/3 of normal as long as the user is in battle.
Muddy Water	Water	Special	95	85	10	Many Others	—	—	A 30% chance of lowering the targets' accuracy by 1. Its power is weaker when it hits multiple Pokémon.
Mud-Slap	Ground	Special	20	100	10	Normal	—	—	Lowers the target's accuracy by 1.

Move	Type	Kind	Pow.	Acc.	PP	Range	Long	DA	Effect
Nasty Plot	Dark	Status	—	—	20	Self	—	—	Raises the user's Sp. Atk by 2.
Natural Gift	Normal	Physical	—	100	15	Normal	—	—	Type and attack power change according to the Berry held by the user. The Berry is consumed when this move is used. This move fails if the user is not holding a Berry.
Nature Power	Normal	Status	—	—	20	Varies	—	—	Move varies depending on the environment. Tall grass/Lawn: Seed Bomb. Path/Sand/Entralink: Earthquake. Cave: Rock Slide. Swamp: Mud Bomb. Water surface/Puddle/Shoal: Hydro Pump. Snow: Blizzard. Ice: Ice Beam. Indoors: Tri Attack.
Needle Arm	Grass	Physical	60	100	15	Normal	—	○	A 30% chance of making the target flinch (unable to use moves on that turn).
Night Daze	Dark	Special	85	95	10	Normal	—	—	A 40% chance of lowering the target's accuracy by 1.
Night Shade	Ghost	Special	—	100	15	Normal	—	—	Deals a fixed amount of damage equal to the user's level.
Night Slash	Dark	Physical	70	100	15	Normal	—	○	Critical hits land more easily.
Nightmare	Ghost	Status	—	100	15	Normal	—	—	Lowers the target's HP by 1/4 of maximum every turn. Fails if the target is not asleep.

O

Move	Type	Kind	Pow.	Acc.	PP	Range	Long	DA	Effect
Octazooka	Water	Special	65	85	10	Normal	—	—	A 50% chance of lowering the target's accuracy by 1.
Odor Sleuth	Normal	Status	—	—	40	Normal	—	—	Attacks land easily regardless of the target's evasion. Makes Ghost-type Pokémon vulnerable to Normal- and Fighting-type moves.
Ominous Wind	Ghost	Special	60	100	5	Normal	—	—	A 10% chance of raising the user's Attack, Defense, Speed, Sp. Atk, and Sp. Def stats by 1.
Outrage	Dragon	Physical	120	100	10	1 Random	—	○	Attacks consecutively over 2–3 turns. Cannot choose other moves during this time. The user becomes Confused after using this move.
Overheat	Fire	Special	140	90	5	Normal	—	—	Lowers the user's Sp. Atk by 2. If the target is Frozen, it will be thawed.

Move	Type	Kind	Pow.	Acc.	PP	Range	Long	DA	Effect
Pain Split	Normal	Status	—	—	20	Normal	—	—	The user and target's HP are added, then divided equally between them.
Pay Day	Normal	Physical	40	100	20	Normal	—	—	Increases the amount of prize money received after battle (the user's level, multiplied by the number of attacks, multiplied by 5).
Payback	Dark	Physical	50	100	10	Normal	—	○	Attack's power is doubled if the user strikes after the target.
Peck	Flying	Physical	35	100	35	Normal	○	○	A regular attack.
Perish Song	Normal	Status	—	—	5	Adjacent	○	—	All adjacent Pokémon in battle will faint after 3 turns, unless switched out.
Petal Dance	Grass	Special	120	100	10	1 Random	—	○	Attacks consecutively over 2–3 turns. Cannot choose other moves during this time. The user becomes Confused after using this move.
Pin Missile	Bug	Physical	14	85	20	Normal	—	—	Attacks 2–5 times in a row in a single turn.
Pluck	Flying	Physical	60	100	20	Normal	○	○	If the target is holding a Berry with a battle effect, the user eats that Berry and uses its effect.
Poison Fang	Poison	Physical	50	100	15	Normal	—	○	A 30% chance of inflicting the Badly Poisoned status condition on the target. Damage from being Badly Poisoned increases with every turn.
Poison Gas	Poison	Status	—	80	40	Many Others	—	—	Inflicts the Poison status condition on the targets.
Poison Jab	Poison	Physical	80	100	20	Normal	—	○	A 30% chance of inflicting the Poison status condition on the target.

Move	Type	Kind	Pow.	Acc.	PP	Range	Long	DA	Effect
Poison Sting	Poison	Physical	15	100	35	Normal	—	—	A 30% chance of inflicting the Poison status condition on the target.
Poison Tail	Poison	Physical	50	100	25	Normal	—	○	A 10% chance of inflicting the Poison status condition on the target. Critical hits land more easily.
PoisonPowder	Poison	Status	—	75	35	Normal	—	—	Inflicts the Poison status condition on the target.
Pound	Normal	Physical	40	100	35	Normal	—	○	A regular attack.
Powder Snow	Ice	Special	40	100	25	Many Others	—	—	A 10% chance of inflicting the Frozen status condition on the targets. Its power is weaker when it hits multiple Pokémon.
Power Gem	Rock	Special	70	100	20	Normal	—	—	A regular attack.
Power Split	Psychic	Status	—	—	10	Normal	—	—	The user and the target's Attack and Sp. Atk are added, then divided equally between them.
Power Swap	Psychic	Status	—	—	10	Normal	—	—	Swaps Attack and Sp. Atk changes between the user and the target.
Power Trick	Psychic	Status	—	—	10	Self	—	—	Swaps original Attack and Defense stats (does not swap stat changes).
Power Whip	Grass	Physical	120	85	10	Normal	—	○	A regular attack.
Present	Normal	Physical	—	90	15	Normal	—	—	Attack power varies: 40 (40% chance), 80 (30% chance), or 120 (10% chance). A 20% chance of healing the target by 1/4 of its maximum HP.
Protect	Normal	Status	—	—	10	Self	—	—	The user evades all attacks that turn. If used in succession, its chance of failing rises.
Psybeam	Psychic	Special	65	100	20	Normal	—	—	A 10% chance of inflicting the Confused status condition on the target.
Psych Up	Normal	Status	—	—	10	Normal	—	—	Copies the target's stat changes to the user.
Psychic	Psychic	Special	90	100	10	Normal	—	—	A 10% chance of lowering the target's Sp. Def by 1.
Psycho Boost	Psychic	Special	140	90	5	Normal	—	—	Lowers the user's Sp. Atk by 2.
Psycho Cut	Psychic	Physical	70	100	20	Normal	—	—	Critical hits land more easily.
Psycho Shift	Psychic	Status	—	90	10	Normal	—	—	Shifts the user's Paralysis, Poison, Badly Poisoned, Burned, or Sleep status conditions to the target and heals the user.
Psyshock	Psychic	Special	80	100	10	Normal	—	—	Damage depends on the user's Sp. Atk and the target's Defense.
Psystrike	Psychic	Special	100	100	10	Normal	—	—	Damage depends on the user's Sp. Atk and the target's Defense.
Psywave	Psychic	Special	—	80	15	Normal	—	—	Inflicts damage equal to the user's level multiplied by a random value between 0.5 and 1.5.
Punishment	Dark	Physical	—	100	5	Normal	—	○	The higher the target's stat changes, the greater the attack's power.
Pursuit	Dark	Physical	40	100	20	Normal	—	○	Does twice the usual damage if the target is switching out.

Move	Type	Kind	Pow.	Acc.	PP	Range	Long	DA	Effect
Quash	Dark	Status	—	100	15	Normal	—	—	The user suppresses the target and makes it move last that turn. Fails if the target has already used its move that turn.
Quick Attack	Normal	Physical	40	100	30	Normal	—	○	Always strikes first. The user with the higher Speed goes first if similar moves are used.
Quick Guard	Fighting	Status	—	—	15	Your Side	—	—	The user protects itself and its allies from first-strike moves. If used in succession, its chance of failing rises.
Quiver Dance	Bug	Status	—	—	20	Self	—	—	Raises the user's Sp. Atk, Sp. Def, and Speed by 1.

Move	Type	Kind	Pow.	Acc.	PP	Range	Long	DA	Effect
Rage	Normal	Physical	20	100	20	Normal	—	○	Attack rises by 1 with each hit the user takes.
Rage Powder	Bug	Status	—	—	20	Self	—	—	This move goes first. Opposing Pokémon aim only at the user.
Rain Dance	Water	Status	—	—	5	Both Sides	—	—	Changes the weather condition to Rain for 5 turns, strengthening Water-type moves.
Rapid Spin	Normal	Physical	20	100	40	Normal	—	○	Releases the user from moves such as Bind, Wrap, Leech Seed, and Spikes.
Razor Leaf	Grass	Physical	55	95	25	Many Others	—	—	Critical hits land more easily. Its power is weaker when it hits multiple Pokémon.
Razor Shell	Water	Physical	75	95	10	Normal	—	○	A 50% chance of lowering the target's Defense by 1.
Razor Wind	Normal	Special	80	100	10	Many Others	—	—	Builds power on the first turn and attacks on the second. Critical hits land more easily. Its power is weaker when it hits multiple Pokémon.
Recover	Normal	Status	—	—	10	Self	—	—	Restores HP by up to half of the user's maximum HP.
Recycle	Normal	Status	—	—	10	Self	—	—	A held item that has been used can be used again.
Reflect	Psychic	Status	—	—	20	Your Side	—	—	Halves the damage to the Pokémon on your side from physical moves. Effect lasts 5 turns even if the user is switched out. Effect is weaker in Double and Triple Battles.
Reflect Type	Normal	Status	—	—	15	Normal	—	—	The user becomes the same type as the target.
Refresh	Normal	Status	—	—	20	Self	—	—	Heals Poison, Paralysis, and Burned conditions.
Rest	Psychic	Status	—	—	10	Self	—	—	Fully restores HP, but makes the user Sleep for 2 turns.
Retaliate	Normal	Physical	70	100	5	Normal	—	○	Attack's power is doubled if an ally fainted in the previous turn.
Return	Normal	Physical	—	100	20	Normal	—	○	The higher the user's friendship, the greater the attack's power.
Revenge	Fighting	Physical	60	100	10	Normal	—	○	Attack's power is doubled if the user has taken damage from the target that turn.
Reversal	Fighting	Physical	—	100	15	Normal	—	○	The lower the user's HP is, the more damage this move does to the target.
Roar	Normal	Status	—	100	20	Normal	—	—	Ends wild Pokémon battles. If the opposing Pokémon's level is higher than the user's, this move fails. In a Double Battle with wild Pokémon, this move fails. In a battle with a Trainer, this move forces the opposing Trainer to switch Pokémon. When there is no Pokémon to switch in, this move fails.
Roar of Time	Dragon	Special	150	90	5	Normal	—	—	The user can't move during the next turn.
Rock Blast	Rock	Physical	25	90	10	Normal	—	—	Attacks 2–5 times in a row in a single turn.
Rock Climb	Normal	Physical	90	85	20	Normal	—	○	A 20% chance of inflicting the Confused status condition on the target.
Rock Polish	Rock	Status	—	—	20	Self	—	—	Raises the user's Speed by 2.
Rock Slide	Rock	Physical	75	90	10	Many Others	—	—	A 30% chance of making the targets flinch (unable to use moves on that turn). Its power is weaker when it hits multiple Pokémon.
Rock Smash	Fighting	Physical	40	100	15	Normal	—	○	A 50% chance of lowering the target's Defense by 1.
Rock Throw	Rock	Physical	50	90	15	Normal	—	—	A regular attack.
Rock Tomb	Rock	Physical	50	80	10	Normal	—	—	Lowers the target's Speed by 1.
Rock Wrecker	Rock	Physical	150	90	5	Normal	—	—	The user can't move during the next turn.
Role Play	Psychic	Status	—	—	10	Normal	—	—	Copies the target's Ability. Fails with certain Abilities, however.
Rolling Kick	Fighting	Physical	60	85	15	Normal	—	○	A 30% chance of making the target flinch (unable to use moves on that turn).
Rollout	Rock	Physical	30	90	20	Normal	—	○	Attacks consecutively over 5 turns or until it misses. Cannot choose other moves during this time. Inflicts greater damage with every successful hit. Does twice the damage if used after Defense Curl.
Roost	Flying	Status	—	—	10	Self	—	—	Restores HP by up to half of the user's maximum HP, but brings Flying-type Pokémon to the ground for that turn.
Round	Normal	Special	60	100	15	Normal	—	—	When multiple Pokémon use this move in a turn, the first one to use it is followed immediately by the others. Attack's power is doubled when following another Pokémon using the same move.

Move	Type	Kind	Pow.	Acc.	PP	Range	Long	DA	Effect
Sacred Fire	Fire	Physical	100	95	5	Normal	—	—	A 50% chance of inflicting the Burned status condition on the target. If the target is Frozen, it will be thawed. This move can be used even if the user is Frozen. If the user is Frozen, this also thaws the user.
Sacred Sword	Fighting	Physical	90	100	20	Normal	—	◯	The target's stat changes don't affect this move.
Safeguard	Normal	Status	—	—	25	Your Side	—	—	Protects the Pokémon on your side from status conditions for 5 turns. Effects last even if the user switches out.
Sand Tomb	Ground	Physical	35	85	15	Normal	—	—	Inflicts damage over 4–5 turns. The target cannot flee during that time.
Sand-Attack	Ground	Status	—	100	15	Normal	—	—	Lowers the target's accuracy by 1.
Sandstorm	Rock	Status	—	—	10	Both Sides	—	—	Changes the weather condition to Sandstorm for 5 turns. The Sp. Def of Rock-type Pokémon increases. All Pokémon other than Rock, Steel, and Ground types take damage each turn.
Scald	Water	Special	80	100	15	Normal	—	—	A 30% chance of inflicting the Burned status condition on the target. This move can be used even if the user is Frozen. If the user is Frozen, this also thaws the user.
Scary Face	Normal	Status	—	100	10	Normal	—	—	Lowers the target's Speed by 2.
Scratch	Normal	Physical	40	100	35	Normal	—	◯	A regular attack.
Screech	Normal	Status	—	85	40	Normal	—	—	Lowers the target's Defense by 2.
Searing Shot	Fire	Special	100	100	5	Adjacent	—	—	A 30% chance of inflicting the Burned status condition on the targets. If the targets are Frozen, they will be thawed. Its power is weaker when it hits multiple Pokémon.
Secret Power	Normal	Physical	70	100	20	Normal	—	—	A 30% chance of one of the following additional effects, depending on the environment. Tall grass/Lawn: Sleep status condition. Path/Sand/Entralink: lowers accuracy by 1. Cave: the target flinches. Water surface/Puddle/Shoal: lowers Attack by 1. Swamp: lowers Speed by 1. Snow/Ice: Frozen status condition. Indoors: Paralysis status condition.
Secret Sword	Fighting	Special	85	100	10	Normal	—	—	Damage depends on the user's Sp. Atk and the target's Defense.
Seed Bomb	Grass	Physical	80	100	15	Normal	—	—	A regular attack.
Seed Flare	Grass	Special	120	85	5	Normal	—	—	A 40% chance of lowering the target's Sp. Def by 2.
Seismic Toss	Fighting	Physical	—	100	20	Normal	—	◯	Deals a fixed amount of damage equal to the user's level.
Selfdestruct	Normal	Physical	200	100	5	Adjacent	—	—	The user faints after using it. Its power is weaker when it hits multiple Pokémon.
Shadow Ball	Ghost	Special	80	100	15	Normal	—	—	A 20% chance of lowering the target's Sp. Def by 1.
Shadow Claw	Ghost	Physical	70	100	15	Normal	—	◯	Critical hits land more easily.
Shadow Force	Ghost	Physical	120	100	5	Normal	—	◯	Makes the user invisible on the first turn and attacks on the second. Strikes the target even if it is using Protect or Detect.
Shadow Punch	Ghost	Physical	60	—	20	Normal	—	◯	A sure hit.
Shadow Sneak	Ghost	Physical	40	100	30	Normal	—	◯	Always strikes first. The user with the higher Speed goes first if similar moves are used.
Sharpen	Normal	Status	—	—	30	Self	—	—	Raises the user's Attack by 1.
Sheer Cold	Ice	Special	—	30	5	Normal	—	—	The target faints with one hit if the user's level is equal to or greater than the target's level. The higher the user's level is compared to the target's, the more accurate the move is.
Shell Smash	Normal	Status	—	—	15	Self	—	—	Lowers the user's Defense and Sp. Def by 1 and raises the user's Attack, Sp. Atk, and Speed by 2.
Shift Gear	Steel	Status	—	—	10	Self	—	—	Raises the user's Speed by 2 and Attack by 1.
Shock Wave	Electric	Special	60	—	20	Normal	—	—	A sure hit.
Signal Beam	Bug	Special	75	100	15	Normal	—	—	A 10% chance of inflicting the Confused status condition on the target.
Silver Wind	Bug	Special	60	100	5	Normal	—	—	A 10% chance of raising the user's Attack, Defense, Speed, Sp. Atk, and Sp. Def stats by 1.
Simple Beam	Normal	Status	—	100	15	Normal	—	—	Changes the target's Ability to Simple. Fails with certain Abilities, however.
Sing	Normal	Status	—	55	15	Normal	—	—	Inflicts the Sleep status condition on the target.
Sketch	Normal	Status	—	—	1	Normal	—	—	Copies the last move used by the target. The user then forgets Sketch and learns the new move.
Skill Swap	Psychic	Status	—	—	10	Normal	—	—	Swaps Abilities between the user and target. Fails with certain Abilities, however.
Skull Bash	Normal	Physical	100	100	15	Normal	—	◯	Builds power on the first turn and attacks on the second. It raises the user's Defense stat by 1 on the first turn.
Sky Attack	Flying	Physical	140	90	5	Normal	◯	—	Builds power on the first turn and attacks on the second. Critical hits land more easily. A 30% chance of making the target flinch (unable to use moves on that turn).
Sky Drop	Flying	Physical	60	100	10	Normal	◯	◯	The user takes the target into the sky, then damages it by dropping it during the next turn. Does not damage Flying-type Pokémon.
Sky Uppercut	Fighting	Physical	85	90	15	Normal	—	◯	It hits even Pokémon that are in the sky due to using moves such as Fly and Bounce.
Slack Off	Normal	Status	—	—	10	Self	—	—	Restores HP by up to half of the user's maximum HP.
Slam	Normal	Physical	80	75	20	Normal	—	◯	A regular attack.
Slash	Normal	Physical	70	100	20	Normal	—	◯	Critical hits land more easily.
Sleep Powder	Grass	Status	—	75	15	Normal	—	—	Inflicts the Sleep status condition on the target.
Sleep Talk	Normal	Status	—	—	10	Self	—	—	Only works when the user is asleep. Randomly uses one of the user's moves.
Sludge	Poison	Special	65	100	20	Normal	—	—	A 30% chance of inflicting the Poison status condition on the target.
Sludge Bomb	Poison	Special	90	100	10	Normal	—	—	A 30% chance of inflicting the Poison status condition on the target.
Sludge Wave	Poison	Special	95	100	10	Adjacent	—	—	A 10% chance of inflicting the Poison status condition on the targets. Its power is weaker when it hits multiple Pokémon.
Smack Down	Rock	Physical	50	100	15	Normal	—	—	Ground-type moves will now hit a Pokémon with the Levitate Ability or a Flying-type Pokémon. They will also hit Pokémon that are in the sky due to using moves such as Fly and Bounce.
SmellingSalt	Normal	Physical	60	100	10	Normal	—	◯	Does twice the usual damage to targets with Paralysis, but heals that status condition.
Smog	Poison	Special	20	70	20	Normal	—	—	A 40% chance of inflicting the Poison status condition on the target.
SmokeScreen	Normal	Status	—	100	20	Normal	—	—	Lowers the target's accuracy by 1.
Snarl	Dark	Special	55	95	15	Many Others	—	—	Lowers the targets' Sp. Atk by 1. Its power is weaker when it hits multiple Pokémon.
Snatch	Dark	Status	—	—	10	Self	—	—	Steals the effects of recovery or stat-changing moves used by the target on that turn.
Snore	Normal	Special	40	100	15	Normal	—	—	Only works when the user is asleep. A 30% chance of making the target flinch (unable to use moves on that turn).
Soak	Water	Status	—	100	20	Normal	—	—	Changes the target's type to Water.
Softboiled	Normal	Status	—	—	10	Self	—	—	Restores HP by up to half of the user's maximum HP.
SolarBeam	Grass	Special	120	100	10	Normal	—	—	Builds power on the first turn and attacks on the second. In Sunny weather conditions, attacks on first turn. In Rain/Sandstorm/Hail weather conditions, the power is halved.
SonicBoom	Normal	Special	—	90	20	Normal	—	—	Deals a fixed 20 points of damage.
Spacial Rend	Dragon	Special	100	95	5	Normal	—	—	Critical hits land more easily.
Spark	Electric	Physical	65	100	20	Normal	—	◯	A 30% chance of inflicting the Paralysis status condition on the target.
Spider Web	Bug	Status	—	—	10	Normal	—	—	The target can't escape. If used in a Trainer battle, it prevents the opposing Trainer from switching out a Pokémon.
Spike Cannon	Normal	Physical	20	100	15	Normal	—	—	Attacks 2–5 times in a row in a single turn.
Spikes	Ground	Status	—	—	20	Other Side	—	—	Damages Pokémon as they are sent out to the opposing side. Power rises with each use, up to 3 times. Ineffective against Flying-type Pokémon and Pokémon with the Levitate Ability.
Spit Up	Normal	Special	—	100	10	Normal	—	—	Deals damage determined by how many times the user has used Stockpile. Fails if the user has not used Stockpile first. Nullifies Defense and Sp. Def stat increases caused by Stockpile.
Spite	Ghost	Status	—	100	10	Normal	—	—	Takes 4 points from the PP of the target's last used move.
Splash	Normal	Status	—	—	40	Self	—	—	No effect.

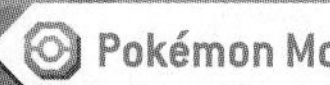

Move	Type	Kind	Pow.	Acc.	PP	Range	Long	DA	Effect
Spore	Grass	Status	—	100	15	Normal	—	—	Inflicts the Sleep status condition on the target.
Stealth Rock	Rock	Status	—	—	20	Other Side	—	—	Damages Pokémon as they are sent out to the opposing side. Damage is subject to type matchups.
Steamroller	Bug	Physical	65	100	20	Normal	—	○	A 30% chance of making the targets flinch (unable to use moves on that turn). Does twice the damage to a target using Minimize when it hits.
Steel Wing	Steel	Physical	70	90	25	Normal	—	○	A 10% chance of raising the user's Defense by 1.
Stockpile	Normal	Status	—	—	20	Self	—	—	Raises the user's Defense and Sp. Def by 1. Can be used up to 3 times.
Stomp	Normal	Physical	65	100	20	Normal	—	○	A 30% chance of making the target flinch (unable to use moves on that turn). Does twice the damage to a target using Minimize when it hits.
Stone Edge	Rock	Physical	100	80	5	Normal	—	—	Critical hits land more easily.
Stored Power	Psychic	Special	20	100	10	Normal	—	—	The higher the user's stat changes, the greater the attack's power.
Storm Throw	Fighting	Physical	40	100	10	Normal	—	○	Always delivers a critical hit.
Strength	Normal	Physical	80	100	15	Normal	—	○	A regular attack.
String Shot	Bug	Status	—	95	40	Many Others	—	—	Lowers the targets' Speed by 1.
Struggle	Normal	Physical	50	—	1	Normal	—	○	This move becomes available when all other moves are out of PP. The user takes damage equal to 1/4 of its maximum HP. Inflicts damage regardless of type matchup.
Struggle Bug	Bug	Special	30	100	20	Many Others	—	—	Lowers the targets' Sp. Atk by 1. Its power is weaker when it hits multiple Pokémon.
Stun Spore	Grass	Status	—	75	30	Normal	—	—	Inflicts the Paralysis status condition on the target.
Submission	Fighting	Physical	80	80	25	Normal	—	○	The user takes 1/4 of the damage inflicted.
Substitute	Normal	Status	—	—	10	Self	—	—	Uses 1/4 of maximum HP to create a copy of the user.
Sucker Punch	Dark	Physical	80	100	5	Normal	—	○	This move attacks first and deals damage only if the target's chosen move is an attack move.
Sunny Day	Fire	Status	—	—	5	Both Sides	—	—	Changes the weather condition to Sunny for 5 turns, strengthening Fire-type moves.
Super Fang	Normal	Physical	—	90	10	Normal	—	○	Halves the target's HP.
Superpower	Fighting	Physical	120	100	5	Normal	—	○	Lowers the user's Attack and Defense by 1.
Supersonic	Normal	Status	—	55	20	Normal	—	—	Inflicts the Confused status condition on the target.
Surf	Water	Special	95	100	15	Adjacent	—	—	Does twice the damage if the target is using Dive when attacked. Its power is weaker when it hits multiple Pokémon.
Swagger	Normal	Status	—	90	15	Normal	—	—	Inflicts the Confused status condition on the target, but also raises its Attack by 2.
Swallow	Normal	Status	—	—	10	Self	—	—	Restores HP, the amount of which is determined by how many times the user has used Stockpile. Fails if the user has not used Stockpile first. Nullifies Defense and Sp. Def stat increases caused by Stockpile.
Sweet Kiss	Normal	Status	—	75	10	Normal	—	—	Inflicts the Confused status condition on the target.
Sweet Scent	Normal	Status	—	100	20	Many Others	—	—	Lowers the targets' evasion by 1.
Swift	Normal	Special	60	—	20	Many Others	—	—	A sure hit. Its power is weaker when it hits multiple Pokémon.
Switcheroo	Dark	Status	—	100	10	Normal	—	—	Swaps items between the user and the target.
Swords Dance	Normal	Status	—	—	30	Self	—	—	Raises the user's Attack by 2.
Synchronoise	Psychic	Special	70	100	15	Adjacent	—	—	Inflicts damage on any Pokémon of the same type as the user. Its power is weaker when it hits multiple Pokémon.
Synthesis	Grass	Status	—	—	5	Self	—	—	Recovers HP. Recovers 1/2 of the user's maximum HP. In Sunny weather conditions, recovers 2/3 of the user's maximum HP. In Rain/Sandstorm/Hail weather, recovers 1/4 of the user's maximum HP.

Move	Type	Kind	Pow.	Acc.	PP	Range	Long	DA	Effect
Tackle	Normal	Physical	50	100	35	Normal	—	○	A regular attack.
Tail Glow	Bug	Status	—	—	20	Self	—	—	Raises the user's Sp. Atk by 3.
Tail Slap	Normal	Physical	25	85	10	Normal	—	○	Attacks 2–5 times in a row in a single turn.
Tail Whip	Normal	Status	—	100	30	Many Others	—	—	Lowers the targets' Defense by 1.
Tailwind	Flying	Status	—	—	30	Your Side	—	—	Doubles the Speed of the Pokémon on your side for 4 turns.
Take Down	Normal	Physical	90	85	20	Normal	—	○	The user takes 1/4 of the damage inflicted.
Taunt	Dark	Status	—	100	20	Normal	—	—	Prevents the target from using anything other than attack moves for 3 turns.
Teeter Dance	Normal	Status	—	100	20	Adjacent	—	—	Inflicts the Confused status condition on the targets.
Telekinesis	Psychic	Status	—	—	15	Normal	—	—	Makes the target float for 3 turns. All moves land regardless of their accuracy except for Ground-type moves and one-hit KO moves such as Sheer Cold and Horn Drill.
Teleport	Psychic	Status	—	—	20	Self	—	—	Ends wild Pokémon battles.
Thief	Dark	Physical	40	100	10	Normal	—	○	When the target is holding an item and the user is not, the user can steal that item.
Thrash	Normal	Physical	120	100	10	1 Random	—	○	Attacks consecutively over 2–3 turns. Cannot choose other moves during this time. The user becomes Confused after using this move.
Thunder	Electric	Special	120	70	10	Normal	—	—	A 30% chance of inflicting the Paralysis status condition on the target. Is 100% accurate in the Rain weather condition and 50% accurate in the Sunny weather condition. It hits even Pokémon that are in the sky due to using moves such as Fly and Bounce.
Thunder Fang	Electric	Physical	65	95	15	Normal	—	○	A 10% chance of making the target flinch (unable to use moves on that turn).
Thunder Wave	Electric	Status	—	100	20	Normal	—	—	Inflicts the Paralysis status condition on the target. Does not work on Ground types.
Thunderbolt	Electric	Special	95	100	15	Normal	—	—	A 10% chance of inflicting the Paralysis status condition on the target.
ThunderPunch	Electric	Physical	75	100	15	Normal	—	○	A 10% chance of inflicting the Paralysis status condition on the target.
ThunderShock	Electric	Special	40	100	30	Normal	—	—	A 10% chance of inflicting the Paralysis status condition on the target.
Tickle	Normal	Status	—	100	20	Normal	—	—	Lowers the target's Attack and Defense by 1.
Torment	Dark	Status	—	100	15	Normal	—	—	Makes the target unable to use the same move twice in a row.
Toxic	Poison	Status	—	90	10	Normal	—	—	Inflicts the Badly Poisoned status condition on the target. Damage from being Badly Poisoned increases with every turn.
Toxic Spikes	Poison	Status	—	—	20	Other Side	—	—	Lays a trap of poison spikes on the opposing side that inflict the Poison status condition on Pokémon that switch into battle. Using Toxic Spikes twice inflicts the Badly Poisoned condition. Toxic Spikes' effects end when a Poison-type Pokémon switches into battle. Ineffective against Flying-type Pokémon and Pokémon with the Levitate Ability.
Transform	Normal	Status	—	—	10	Normal	—	—	The user transforms into the target. The user has the same moves and Ability as the target (all moves have 5 PP).
Tri Attack	Normal	Special	80	100	10	Normal	—	—	A 20% chance of inflicting the Paralysis, Burned, or Frozen status condition on the target.
Trick	Psychic	Status	—	100	10	Normal	—	—	Swaps items between the user and the target.
Trick Room	Psychic	Status	—	—	5	Both Sides	—	—	For 5 turns, Pokémon with lower Speed go first. First-strike moves still go first. Self-canceling if used again while Trick Room is still in effect.
Triple Kick	Fighting	Physical	10	90	10	Normal	—	○	Attacks 3 times in a row in a single turn. Power raises from 10 to 20 to 30 as long as it continues to hit.
Trump Card	Normal	Special	—	—	5	Normal	—	○	A sure hit. The move's power increases as its PP decreases.
Twineedle	Bug	Physical	25	100	20	Normal	—	—	Attacks twice in a row in a single turn. A 20% chance of inflicting the Poison status condition on the target.
Twister	Dragon	Special	40	100	20	Many Others	—	—	A 20% chance of making the targets flinch (unable to use moves on that turn). Does twice the damage if the targets are in the sky due to using moves such as Fly or Bounce. Its power is weaker when it hits multiple Pokémon.

U

Move	Type	Kind	Pow.	Acc.	PP	Range	Long	DA	Effect
Uproar	Normal	Special	90	100	10	1 Random	—	—	The user makes an uproar for 3 turns. During that time, no Pokémon can fall asleep.
U-turn	Bug	Physical	70	100	20	Normal	—	○	After attacking, the user switches out with another Pokémon in the party.

V

Move	Type	Kind	Pow.	Acc.	PP	Range	Long	DA	Effect
Vacuum Wave	Fighting	Special	40	100	30	Normal	—	—	Always strikes first. The user with the higher Speed goes first if similar moves are used.
V-create	Fire	Physical	180	95	5	Normal	—	○	Lowers the user's Defense, Sp. Def, and Speed by 1. If the target is Frozen, it will be thawed.
Venoshock	Poison	Special	65	100	10	Normal	—	—	Does twice the damage to a target that has the Poison or Badly Poisoned status condition.
ViceGrip	Normal	Physical	55	100	30	Normal	—	○	A regular attack.
Vine Whip	Grass	Physical	35	100	15	Normal	—	○	A regular attack.
Vital Throw	Fighting	Physical	70	—	10	Normal	—	○	Always strikes later than normal, but has perfect accuracy.
Volt Switch	Electric	Special	70	100	20	Normal	—	—	After attacking, the user switches out with another Pokémon in the party.
Volt Tackle	Electric	Physical	120	100	15	Normal	—	○	The user takes 1/3 of the damage inflicted. A 10% chance of inflicting the Paralysis status condition on the target.

W

Move	Type	Kind	Pow.	Acc.	PP	Range	Long	DA	Effect
Wake-Up Slap	Fighting	Physical	60	100	10	Normal	—	○	Does twice the usual damage to a sleeping target, but heals that status condition.
Water Gun	Water	Special	40	100	25	Normal	—	—	A regular attack.
Water Pledge	Water	Special	50	100	10	Normal	—	—	When combined with Fire Pledge or Grass Pledge, the power and effect change. If combined with Fire Pledge, the power is 150 and it remains a Water-type move. It will create a rainbow that turn which will last for the next 3 turns, making it more likely that your team's moves will have additional effects. If combined with Grass Pledge, the power is 150 and it becomes a Grass-type move. The surrounding area will become a swamp, which lowers the Speed of opposing Pokémon that turn and the next 3 turns.
Water Pulse	Water	Special	60	100	20	Normal	○	—	A 20% chance of inflicting the Confused status condition on the target.
Water Sport	Water	Status	—	—	15	Both Sides	—	—	The power of Fire-type moves drops to 1/3 of normal as long as the user is in battle.
Water Spout	Water	Special	150	100	5	Many Others	—	—	If the user's HP is low, this move has lower attack power. Its power is weaker when it hits multiple Pokémon.
Waterfall	Water	Physical	80	100	15	Normal	—	○	A 20% chance of making the target flinch (unable to use moves on that turn).
Weather Ball	Normal	Special	50	100	10	Normal	—	—	In special weather conditions, this move's type changes and its attack power doubles. Sunny weather condition: Fire type. Rain weather condition: Water type. Hail weather condition: Ice type. Sandstorm weather condition: Rock type.
Whirlpool	Water	Special	35	85	15	Normal	—	—	Inflicts damage over 4–5 turns. The target cannot flee during that time. Does twice the damage if the target is using Dive when attacked.
Whirlwind	Normal	Status	—	100	20	Normal	—	—	Ends wild Pokémon battles. If the opposing Pokémon's level is higher than the user's, this move fails. In a Double Battle with wild Pokémon, this move fails. In a battle with a Trainer, this move forces the opposing Trainer to switch Pokémon. When there is no Pokémon to switch in, this move fails.
Wide Guard	Rock	Status	—	—	10	Your Side	—	—	Protects from special and physical moves that target multiple Pokémon. If used in succession, its chance of failing rises.
Wild Charge	Electric	Physical	90	100	15	Normal	—	○	The user takes 1/4 of the damage inflicted.
Will-O-Wisp	Fire	Status	—	75	15	Normal	—	—	Inflicts the Burned status condition on the target.
Wing Attack	Flying	Physical	60	100	35	Normal	○	○	A regular attack.
Wish	Normal	Status	—	—	10	Self	—	—	Restores 1/2 of maximum HP at the end of the next turn. Works even if the user has switched out.
Withdraw	Water	Status	—	—	40	Self	—	—	Raises the user's Defense by 1.
Wonder Room	Psychic	Status	—	—	10	Both Sides	—	—	Each Pokémon's Defense and Sp. Def stats are swapped for 5 turns.
Wood Hammer	Grass	Physical	120	100	15	Normal	—	○	The user takes 1/3 of the damage inflicted.
Work Up	Normal	Status	—	—	30	Self	—	—	Raises the user's Attack and Sp. Atk by 1.
Worry Seed	Grass	Status	—	100	10	Normal	—	—	Changes the target's Ability to Insomnia. Fails with certain Abilities, however.
Wrap	Normal	Physical	15	90	20	Normal	—	○	Inflicts damage over 4–5 turns. The target cannot flee during that time.
Wring Out	Normal	Special	—	100	5	Normal	—	○	The more HP the target has left, the greater the attack's power (max 120).

XYZ

Move	Type	Kind	Pow.	Acc.	PP	Range	Long	DA	Effect
X-Scissor	Bug	Physical	80	100	15	Normal	—	○	A regular attack.
Yawn	Normal	Status	—	—	10	Normal	—	—	Inflicts the Sleep status condition on the target at the end of the next turn unless the target switches out.
Zap Cannon	Electric	Special	120	50	5	Normal	—	—	Inflicts the Paralysis status condition on the target.
Zen Headbutt	Psychic	Physical	80	90	15	Normal	—	○	A 20% chance of making the target flinch (unable to use moves on that turn).

Field Moves

Move	Field Moves
Chatter	You can record your voice. It's played in battle.
Cut	Cuts down small trees so your party may pass.
Dig	Pulls you out of spaces like caves, returning you to the last entrance you went through.
Dive	In patches of darker water, you can dive to the bottom to explore the seafloor.
Flash	Illuminates dark caves.
Fly	Whisks you instantly to a town or city you've visited before.
Milk Drink	Distributes part of the user's own HP among teammates.
Softboiled	Distributes part of the user's own HP among teammates.
Strength	Moves large rocks and pushes them into holes to create a new path.
Surf	Allows you to move across water.
Sweet Scent	Attracts wild Pokémon and makes them appear.
Teleport	Transports you to the last Pokémon Center you used (cannot be used in caves or similar places).
Waterfall	Allows you to climb up and down waterfalls.

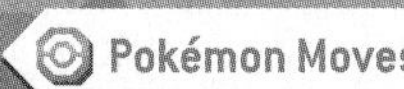

Where to find TMs and HMs and learn other moves

How to obtain TMs

No.	Move	How to obtain	Price
1	Hone Claws	Victory Road	—
2	Dragon Claw	Dragonspiral Tower	—
3	Psyshock	Giant Chasm Crater Forest	—
4	Calm Mind	Striaton City Poké Mart	80,000
5	Roar	Route 23	—
6	Toxic	Seaside Cave	—
7	Hail	Mistralton City Poké Mart	50,000
8	Bulk Up	Striaton City Poké Mart	80,000
9	Venoshock	Defeat Roxie at the Virbank City Pokémon Gym	—
10	Hidden Power	Receive for 18 BP at the Battle Subway or the Pokémon World Tournament	—
11	Sunny Day	Mistralton City Poké Mart	50,000
12	Taunt	Route 23	—
13	Ice Beam	Giant Chasm	—
14	Blizzard	Mistralton City Poké Mart	70,000
15	Hyper Beam	Shopping Mall 2F on Route 9	90,000
16	Light Screen	Nimbasa City Poké Mart	30,000
17	Protect	Receive for 6 BP at the Battle Subway or the Pokémon World Tournament	—
18	Rain Dance	Mistralton City Poké Mart	50,000
19	Telekinesis	Route 18	—
20	Safeguard	Receive for 6 BP at the Battle Subway or the Pokémon World Tournament	—
21	Frustration	From a Team Plasma Grunt at Floccesy Ranch	—
22	SolarBeam	Pinwheel Forest	—
23	Smack Down	Receive for 18 BP at the Battle Subway or the Pokémon World Tournament	—
24	Thunderbolt	From your rival on Victory Road (after you defeat him for the fifth time)	—
25	Thunder	Lacunosa Town Poké Mart	70,000
26	Earthquake	Route 15	—
27	Return	From Bianca in Aspertia City (after obtaining the Aspertia City Gym Badge)	—
28	Dig	Route 4	—
29	Psychic	Route 13	—
30	Shadow Ball	Reversal Mountain	—
31	Brick Break	Receive for 12 BP at the Battle Subway or the Pokémon World Tournament	—
32	Double Team	Receive for 6 BP at the Battle Subway or the Pokémon World Tournament	—
33	Reflect	Nimbasa City Poké Mart	30,000
34	Sludge Wave	Receive for 24 BP at the Battle Subway or the Pokémon World Tournament	—
35	Flamethrower	From an old man in a house on Route 23	—
36	Sludge Bomb	Route 8	—
37	Sandstorm	Mistralton City Poké Mart	50,000
38	Fire Blast	Lacunosa Town Poké Mart	70,000
39	Rock Tomb	Relic Castle	—
40	Aerial Ace	Talk to a boy in a house in Mistralton City and you'll find it in the field to the south of the runway (after obtaining the Mistralton City Gym Badge)	—
41	Torment	Castelia Sewers (spring and summer only)	—
42	Facade	From a Parasol Lady in the gate between the Marine Tube and Humilau City	—
43	Flame Charge	From a Battle Girl on the Tubeline Bridge	—
44	Rest	From a Guitarist in Castelia City	—
45	Attract	From a girl in Castelia City	—
46	Thief	Virbank Complex	—
47	Low Sweep	Wellspring Cave	—
48	Round	Receive for 18 BP at the Battle Subway or the Pokémon World Tournament	—
49	Echoed Voice	From a woman in the Musical Theater in Nimbasa City	—
50	Overheat	N's Castle	—
51	Ally Switch	Receive for 24 BP at the Battle Subway or the Pokémon World Tournament	—
52	Focus Blast	Wellspring Cave	—
53	Energy Ball	Aspertia City	—
54	False Swipe	From a man in Reversal Mountain (after completing the Reversal Mountain Habitat List)	—
55	Scald	Defeat Marlon at the Humilau City Pokémon Gym	—
56	Fling	Route 6	—
57	Charge Beam	From a Battle Girl in a house in Lentimas Town	—
58	Sky Drop	Mistralton City	—
59	Incinerate	Receive for 6 BP at the Battle Subway or the Pokémon World Tournament	—
60	Quash	Receive for 24 BP at the Battle Subway or the Pokémon World Tournament	—
61	Will-O-Wisp	Celestial Tower	—
62	Acrobatics	Defeat Skyla at the Mistralton City Pokémon Gym	—
63	Embargo	Driftveil City	—
64	Explosion	Receive for 24 BP at the Battle Subway or the Pokémon World Tournament	—
65	Shadow Claw	Celestial Tower	—
66	Payback	Route 16	—
67	Retaliate	Plasma Frigate	—
68	Giga Impact	Shopping Mall 2F on Route 9	90,000
69	Rock Polish	Reversal Mountain	—
70	Flash	From a man with sunglasses in Castelia City	—
71	Stone Edge	Twist Mountain	—
72	Volt Switch	Defeat Elesa at the Nimbasa City Pokémon Gym	—
73	Thunder Wave	Nimbasa City Poké Mart	10,000
74	Gyro Ball	Nimbasa City Poké Mart	10,000
75	Swords Dance	Receive for 18 BP at the Battle Subway or the Pokémon World Tournament	—
76	Struggle Bug	Defeat Burgh at the Castelia City Pokémon Gym	—
77	Psych Up	Receive for 24 BP at the Battle Subway or the Pokémon World Tournament	—
78	Bulldoze	Defeat Clay at the Driftveil City Pokémon Gym	—
79	Frost Breath	Receive for 12 BP at the Battle Subway or the Pokémon World Tournament	—
80	Rock Slide	Mistralton Cave	—
81	X-Scissor	Route 7	—
82	Dragon Tail	Defeat Drayden at the Opelucid City Pokémon Gym	—
83	Work Up	Defeat Cheren at the Aspertia City Pokémon Gym	—
84	Poison Jab	Moor of Icirrus	—
85	Dream Eater	Dreamyard	—
86	Grass Knot	Pinwheel Forest	—
87	Swagger	Receive for 18 BP at the Battle Subway or the Pokémon World Tournament	—
88	Pluck	Receive for 18 BP at the Battle Subway or the Pokémon World Tournament	—
89	U-turn	Receive for 12 BP at the Battle Subway or the Pokémon World Tournament	—
90	Substitute	Twist Mountain	—
91	Flash Cannon	Twist Mountain Outside	—
92	Trick Room	Abundant Shrine	—
93	Wild Charge	Victory Road	—
94	Rock Smash	From a man in Virbank Complex (after defeating three Workers)	—
95	Snarl	From a Backpacker in Lostlorn Forest	—

How to obtain HMs

No.	Move	How to obtain	Price
1	Cut	From Roxie in Virbank City (after defeating Team Plasma Grunts)	—
2	Fly	From Bianca on Route 5	—
3	Surf	From Cheren on Route 6	—
4	Strength	From your rival in the Castelia Sewers (after defeating Team Plasma Grunts)	—
5	Waterfall	From N on Victory Road	—
6	Dive	From your rival in Undella Town (after the Hall of Fame)	—

Moves taught in exchange for Shards

■ Moves taught by the master Move Tutor in Driftveil City in exchange for Red Shards

Move	No. of Red Shards needed
Bounce	4
Bug Bite	2
Covet	2
Drill Run	4
Dual Chop	6
Fire Punch	10
Gunk Shot	8
Ice Punch	10
Iron Head	4
Low Kick	8
Seed Bomb	6
Signal Beam	4
Super Fang	6
ThunderPunch	10
Uproar	6

■ Moves taught by the master Move Tutor in Lentimas Town in exchange for Blue Shards

Move	No. of Blue Shards needed
Aqua Tail	8
Block	6
Dark Pulse	10
Dragon Pulse	10
Earth Power	8
Electroweb	6
Foul Play	8
Gravity	10
Hyper Voice	6
Icy Wind	6
Iron Defense	2
Iron Tail	6
Last Resort	2
Magic Coat	4
Magnet Rise	4
Superpower	10
Zen Headbutt	8

■ Moves taught by the master Move Tutor in Humilau City in exchange for Yellow Shards

Move	No. of Yellow Shards needed
Bind	2
Drain Punch	10
Giga Drain	10
Heal Bell	4
Heat Wave	10
Knock Off	4
Pain Split	10
Role Play	8
Roost	6
Sky Attack	8
Snore	2
Synthesis	6
Tailwind	10
ThunderPunch	10

■ Moves taught by the master Move Tutor in Nacrene City in exchange for Green Shards

Move	No. of Green Shards needed
After You	8
Endeavor	12
Gastro Acid	6
Helping Hand	8
Magic Room	8
Outrage	10
Recycle	10
Skill Swap	12
Sleep Talk	12
Snatch	12
Spite	8
Stealth Rock	10
Trick	10
Wonder Room	8
Worry Seed	6

Moves taught by other people

Move	How to obtain
Blast Burn	Pokémon World Tournament (PWT)
Draco Meteor	Drayden's house in Opelucid City (talk to Drayden after the Hall of Fame)
Fire Pledge	Pokémon World Tournament (PWT)
Frenzy Plant	Pokémon World Tournament (PWT)
Grass Pledge	Pokémon World Tournament (PWT)
Hydro Cannon	Pokémon World Tournament (PWT)
Water Pledge	Pokémon World Tournament (PWT)

Pokémon Abilities

A

Ability	Effect in battle	Effect when the Pokémon is the lead in your party
Adaptability	Increases the power boost received by using a move of same type as the Pokémon.	—
Aftermath	Knocks off 1/4 of the attacking Pokémon's HP when a direct attack causes the Pokémon to faint.	—
Air Lock	Eliminates effects of weather on Pokémon.	—
Analytic	The power of its move is increased by 30% when the Pokémon moves last.	—
Anger Point	Raises the Pokémon's Attack to the maximum when hit by a critical hit.	—
Anticipation	Warns if your foe's Pokémon has supereffective moves or one-hit KO moves.	—
Arena Trap	Prevents the foe's Pokémon from fleeing or switching out. Ineffective against Flying-type Pokémon and Pokémon with the Levitate Ability.	It makes it easier to encounter wild Pokémon.

B

Ability	Effect in battle	Effect when the Pokémon is the lead in your party
Bad Dreams	Slightly lowers the HP of sleeping Pokémon every turn.	—
Battle Armor	Opposing Pokémon's moves will not hit critically.	—
Big Pecks	Prevents Defense from being lowered.	—
Blaze	Raises the power of Fire-type moves by 50% when the Pokémon's HP drops to 1/3 or less.	—

C

Ability	Effect in battle	Effect when the Pokémon is the lead in your party
Chlorophyll	Double Speed in the Sunny weather condition.	—
Clear Body	Protects against stat-lowering moves and Abilities.	—
Cloud Nine	Eliminates effects of weather on Pokémon.	—
Color Change	Changes the Pokémon's type into the type of the move that just hit it.	—
Compoundeyes	Raises accuracy by 30%.	Raises encounter rate with wild Pokémon holding items.
Contrary	Makes stat changes have an opposite effect (increase instead of decrease and vice versa).	—
Cursed Body	A 30% chance of inflicting Disable on the move the opponent used to hit the Pokémon.	—
Cute Charm	A 30% chance of inflicting the Infatuated condition when hit with a direct attack.	Raises encounter rate of wild Pokémon of the opposite gender.

D

Ability	Effect in battle	Effect when the Pokémon is the lead in your party
Damp	Pokémon on neither side can use Selfdestruct and Explosion. Nullifies the Aftermath Ability.	—
Defeatist	The Pokémon's Attack and Sp. Atk gets halved when HP becomes half or less.	—
Defiant	When an opponent's move or Ability lowers the Pokémon's stats, the Pokémon's Attack rises by 2.	—
Download	When the Pokémon enters battle, this Ability raises its Attack by 1 if the foe's Pokémon's Defense is lower than its Sp. Def, and raises it's Sp. Atk by 1 if the foe's Pokémon's Sp. Def is lower than its Defense.	—
Drizzle	Makes the weather Rain when the Pokémon enters battle.	—
Drought	Makes the weather Sunny when the Pokémon enters battle.	—
Dry Skin	Restores HP when the Pokémon is hit by a Water-type move. Restores HP in the Rain weather condition. However, the Pokémon receives increased damage from Fire-type moves. Takes damage every turn when in the Sunny weather condition.	—

E

Ability	Effect in battle	Effect when the Pokémon is the lead in your party
Early Bird	The Pokémon wakes quickly from the Sleep status condition.	—
Effect Spore	A 30% chance of inflicting the Poison, Paralysis, or Sleep status conditions when hit with a direct attack.	—

F

Ability	Effect in battle	Effect when the Pokémon is the lead in your party
Filter	Minimizes the damage received from supereffective moves.	—
Flame Body	A 30% chance of inflicting the Burned status condition when hit with a direct attack.	Facilitates hatching Eggs in your party.
Flare Boost	Increases the power of special moves by 50% when Burned.	—
Flash Fire	When the Pokémon is hit by a Fire-type move, its Fire-type moves increase Power by 50% rather than taking damage.	—
Flower Gift	Raises Attack and Sp. Def of the Pokémon in the Sunny weather condition.	—
Forecast	Changes Castform's form and type. Sunny weather condition: changes to Fire type. Rain weather condition: changes to Water type. Hail weather condition: changes to Ice type.	—
Forewarn	Reveals a move an opponent knows when the Pokémon enters battle. Damaging moves with high power are prioritized.	—
Friend Guard	Reduces damage done to allies by 25%.	—
Frisk	Checks an opponent's held item when the Pokémon enters battle.	—

G

Ability	Effect in battle	Effect when the Pokémon is the lead in your party
Gluttony	Allows the Pokémon to use its held Berry sooner when it has low HP.	—
Guts	Attack stat rises by 50% when the Pokémon is affected by a status condition.	—

H

Ability	Effect in battle	Effect when the Pokémon is the lead in your party
Harvest	A 50% chance of restoring the Berry the Pokémon used at turn end and 100% chance when the weather condition is Sunny.	—
Healer	A 33% chance every turn that an ally Pokémon's status condition will be healed.	—
Heatproof	Halves damage from Fire-type moves and from the Burned status condition.	—
Heavy Metal	Doubles the Pokémon's weight.	—
Honey Gather	If the Pokémon isn't holding an item, it will sometimes be left holding Honey after a battle (even if it didn't participate). Its chance of finding Honey increases with its level.	—
Huge Power	Doubles the Pokémon's Attack.	—
Hustle	Raises Attack by 50%, but lowers the accuracy of the Pokémon's physical moves by 20%.	Lowers encounter rate with high-level wild Pokémon.
Hydration	Cures status conditions at the end of the turn in the Rain weather condition.	—
Hyper Cutter	Prevents Attack from being lowered.	—

Ability	Effect in battle	Effect when the Pokémon is the lead in your party
Ice Body	Gradually restores HP in the Hail weather condition instead of taking damage.	—
Illuminate	No effect.	It makes it easier to encounter wild Pokémon.
Illusion	Appears in battle disguised as the last Pokémon in the party.	—
Immunity	Protects against the Poison status condition.	—
Imposter	Transforms itself into the Pokémon it is facing as it enters battle.	—
Infiltrator	Moves can hit even if the target used Reflect, Light Screen, Safeguard, or Mist.	—
Inner Focus	The Pokémon doesn't flinch by additional effect of a move.	—
Insomnia	Protects against the Sleep status condition.	—
Intimidate	Lowers opponents' Attack by 1 when the Pokémon enters battle.	Lowers encounter rate with low-level wild Pokémon.
Iron Barbs	Slightly reduces the HP of an opponent that hits the Pokémon with a direct attack.	—
Iron Fist	Increases the power of Ice Punch, Fire Punch, ThunderPunch, Mach Punch, Mega Punch, Comet Punch, Bullet Punch, Sky Uppercut, Drain Punch, Focus Punch, Dizzy Punch, DynamicPunch, Hammer Arm, Meteor Mash, and Shadow Punch.	—

Ability	Effect in battle	Effect when the Pokémon is the lead in your party
Justified	When the Pokémon is hit by a Dark-type move, Attack goes up by 1.	—

Ability	Effect in battle	Effect when the Pokémon is the lead in your party
Keen Eye	Prevents accuracy from being lowered.	Lowers encounter rate with low-level wild Pokémon.
Klutz	The Pokémon's held items have no effect.	—

Ability	Effect in battle	Effect when the Pokémon is the lead in your party
Leaf Guard	Protects the Pokémon from status conditions when in the Sunny weather condition.	—
Levitate	Gives full immunity to all Ground-type moves.	—
Light Metal	Halves the Pokémon's weight.	—
Lightningrod	Draws all Electric-type moves to the Pokémon. When the Pokémon is hit by an Electric-type move, Sp. Atk goes up by 1 rather than taking damage.	—
Limber	Protects against the Paralysis status condition.	—
Liquid Ooze	When an opposing Pokémon uses an HP-draining move, it damages the user instead.	—

Ability	Effect in battle	Effect when the Pokémon is the lead in your party
Magic Bounce	Reflects status moves.	—
Magic Guard	The Pokémon will not take damage from anything other than a direct attack. Nullifies the Liquid Ooze, Aftermath, Rough Skin, and Iron Barbs Abilities, the Sandstorm and Hail weather conditions, as well as status conditions such as Poison, Badly Poisoned, Burned, Nightmare, Curse, Leech Seed, Bind, Sand Tomb, Fire Spin, Clamp, and Magma Storm. The effects of Stealth Rock, Spikes, Wrap, Flame Burst, and Fire Pledge are negated as are the item effects from Black Sludge, Sticky Barb, Life Orb, and Rocky Helmet. The Pokémon also receives no recoil or move-failure damage from attacks.	—
Magma Armor	Prevents the Frozen status condition.	Facilitates hatching Eggs in your party.
Magnet Pull	Prevents Steel-type Pokémon from fleeing or switching out.	Raises encounter rate with wild Steel-type Pokémon.
Marvel Scale	Defense stat increases by 50% when the Pokémon is affected by a status condition.	—
Minus	Raises Sp. Atk by 50% when another ally has the Ability Plus or Minus.	—
Mold Breaker	Use moves on targets regardless of their Abilities. Does not nullify Abilities that have effects after an attack. For example, the Pokémon can score a critical hit against the target with Battle Armor, but it will still take damage from Rough Skin.	—
Moody	Raises one stat by 2 and lowers another by 1 at turn end.	—
Motor Drive	When the Pokémon is hit by an Electric-type move, Speed goes up by 1 rather than taking damage.	—
Moxie	When the Pokémon knocks out an opponent with a move, Attack goes up 1.	—
Multiscale	Halves damage when HP is full.	—
Multitype	Type changes according to the Plate Arceus is holding.	—
Mummy	Changes the Ability of the opponent that hits the Pokémon with a direct attack to Mummy.	—

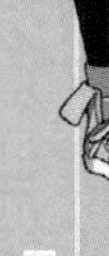

Ability	Effect in battle	Effect when the Pokémon is the lead in your party
Natural Cure	Cures the Pokémon's status conditions when it switches out.	—
No Guard	Moves used by or against the Pokémon always strike their targets.	It makes it easier to encounter wild Pokémon.
Normalize	All of the Pokémon's moves become Normal-type moves.	—

Ability	Effect in battle	Effect when the Pokémon is the lead in your party
Oblivious	Protects against the Infatuated status condition.	—
Overcoat	Protects the Pokémon from weather damage, such as Sandstorm and Hail.	—
Overgrow	Raises the power of Grass-type moves by 50% when the Pokémon's HP drops to 1/3 or less.	—
Own Tempo	Protects against the Confused status condition.	—

Ability	Effect in battle	Effect when the Pokémon is the lead in your party
Pickpocket	Steals an item when hit with a direct attack. It fails if the user is already holding an item.	—
Pickup	Picks up the item the foe's Pokémon used that turn at the end of the turn. Fails if the user is already holding an item.	If the Pokémon has no held item, it sometimes picks one up after battle (even if it didn't participate). It picks up different items depending on its level.
Plus	Raises Sp. Atk by 50% when another ally has the Ability Plus or Minus.	—
Poison Heal	Restores HP every turn if the Pokémon has the Poison status condition.	—

Pokémon Abilities

P

Ability	Effect in battle	Effect when the Pokémon is the lead in your party
Poison Point	A 30% chance of inflicting the Poison status condition when hit with a direct attack.	—
Poison Touch	A 30% chance of inflicting the Poison status condition when the Pokémon uses a direct attack.	—
Prankster	Gives priority to status moves.	—
Pressure	When the Pokémon is hit by an opponent's move, it depletes 1 additional PP from that move.	Lowers encounter rate with high-level wild Pokémon.
Pure Power	Doubles the Pokémon's Attack.	—

Q

Ability	Effect in battle	Effect when the Pokémon is the lead in your party
Quick Feet	Increases Speed by 50% when the Pokémon is affected with status conditions.	Lowers wild Pokémon encounter rate.

R

Ability	Effect in battle	Effect when the Pokémon is the lead in your party
Rain Dish	Gradually restores HP in the Rain weather condition.	—
Rattled	When the Pokémon is hit by a Ghost-, Dark-, or Bug-type move, Speed goes up by 1.	—
Reckless	Raises the power of moves with recoil damage.	—
Regenerator	Restores 1/3 its HP when withdrawn from battle.	—
Rivalry	If the target is the same gender, the Pokémon's Attack goes up. If the target is of the opposite gender, its Attack goes down. No effect when the gender is unknown.	—
Rock Head	No recoil damage from moves like Take Down and Double-Edge.	—
Rough Skin	Slightly reduces the HP of an opponent that hits the Pokémon with a direct attack.	—
Run Away	The Pokémon can always escape from a battle with a wild Pokémon .	—

S

Ability	Effect in battle	Effect when the Pokémon is the lead in your party
Sand Force	Raises the power of Ground-, Rock-, and Steel-type moves by 30% in the Sandstorm weather condition. Sandstorm does not damage the Pokémon.	—
Sand Rush	Doubles Speed in the Sandstorm weather condition. Sandstorm does not damage the Pokémon.	—
Sand Stream	Makes the weather Sandstorm when the Pokémon enters battle.	—
Sand Veil	Raises evasion in the Sandstorm weather condition. Sandstorm does not damage the Pokémon.	Lowers encounter rate with wild Pokémon in the Sandstorm weather condition.
Sap Sipper	When the Pokémon is hit by a Grass-type move, Attack goes up by 1 rather than taking damage.	—
Scrappy	Allows the Pokémon to hit Ghost-type Pokémon with Normal- and Fighting-type moves.	—
Serene Grace	Doubles chances of moves inflicting additional effects.	—
Shadow Tag	Prevents the opposing Pokémon from fleeing or switching out. If both your and the opposing Pokémon have this Ability, the effect is canceled.	—
Shed Skin	A 33% chance every turn of curing the Pokémon's status conditions.	—
Sheer Force	When moves with an additional effect are used, power increases by 30%, but the additional effect is lost.	—
Shell Armor	Opposing Pokémon's moves will not hit critically.	—
Shield Dust	Protects the Pokémon from additional effects of moves.	—
Simple	The effects of stat changes become more powerful.	—
Skill Link	Moves that strike successively strike the maximum number of times (2–5 times means it always strikes 5 times).	—
Slow Start	Halves Attack and Speed for 5 turns after the Pokémon enters battle.	—
Sniper	Moves that deliver a critical hit deal a great amount of damage.	—
Snow Cloak	Raises evasion in the Hail weather condition. Hail does not damage the Pokémon.	Lowers encounter rate with wild Pokémon in the Hail weather condition.
Snow Warning	Makes the weather Hail when the Pokémon enters battle.	—
Solar Power	Raises Sp. Atk by 50%, but takes damage every turn in the Sunny weather condition.	—
Solid Rock	Minimizes the damage received from supereffective moves.	—
Soundproof	Protects the Pokémon from sound-based moves: Snore, Heal Bell, Screech, Sing, Chatter, Metal Sound, GrassWhistle, Uproar, Supersonic, Growl, Hyper Voice, Roar, Perish Song, Bug Buzz, Round, and Echoed Voice.	—
Speed Boost	Raises Speed by 1 every turn.	—
Stall	The Pokémon's moves are used last in the turn.	—
Static	A 30% chance of inflicting the Paralysis status condition when hit with a direct attack.	Raises encounter rate with wild Electric-type Pokémon.
Steadfast	Raises Speed by 1 every time the Pokémon flinches.	—
Stench	A 10% chance of making the target flinch when the Pokémon uses a move to deal damage.	Lowers wild Pokémon encounter rate.
Sticky Hold	The Pokémon's held item cannot be stolen.	Makes Pokémon bite more often when fishing.
Storm Drain	Draws all Water-type moves to the Pokémon. When the Pokémon is hit by an Water-type move, Sp. Atk goes up by 1 rather than taking damage.	—
Sturdy	Protects the Pokémon against one-hit KO moves like Horn Drill and Sheer Cold. Leaves the Pokémon with 1 HP if hit by a move that would knock it out when its HP is full.	—
Suction Cups	Nullifies moves like Whirlwind, Roar, and Dragon Tail, which would force Pokémon to switch out.	Makes Pokémon bite more often when fishing.
Super Luck	Heightens the critical-hit ratio of the Pokémon's moves.	—
Swarm	Raises the power of Bug-type moves by 50% when the Pokémon's HP drops to 1/3 or less.	—
Swift Swim	Doubles Speed in the Rain weather condition.	—
Synchronize	When the Pokémon receives the Poison, Paralysis, or Burned status condition, this inflicts the same condition.	Raises encounter rate with wild Pokémon with the same Nature.

T

Ability	Effect in battle	Effect when the Pokémon is the lead in your party
Tangled Feet	Raises evasion when the Pokémon has the Confused status condition.	—
Technician	If the move's power is 60 or less, its power will increase by 50%. Also takes effect if a move's power is altered by itself or by another move.	—
Telepathy	Prevents damage from allies.	—
Teravolt	Use moves on targets regardless of their Abilities. Does not nullify Abilities that have effects after an attack. For example, the Pokémon can score a critical hit against the target with Battle Armor, but it will still take damage from Rough Skin.	—
Thick Fat	Halves damage from Fire- and Ice-type moves.	—
Tinted Lens	Nullifies the type disadvantage of the Pokémon's not-very-effective moves: 1/2 damage turns into regular damage, 1/4 damage turns into 1/2 damage.	—

T

Ability	Effect in battle	Effect when the Pokémon is the lead in your party
Torrent	Raises the power of Water-type moves by 50% when the Pokémon's HP drops to 1/3 or less.	—
Toxic Boost	Increases the power of physical moves by 50% when it has the Poison status condition.	—
Trace	Makes the Pokémon's Ability the same as the opponent's, except for certain Abilities like Forecast and Trace.	—
Truant	The Pokémon can use a move only once every other turn.	—
Turboblaze	Use moves on targets regardless of their Abilities. Does not nullify Abilities that have effects after an attack. For example, the Pokémon can score a critical hit against the target with Battle Armor, but it will still take damage from Rough Skin.	—

U

Ability	Effect in battle	Effect when the Pokémon is the lead in your party
Unaware	Ignores the stat changes of the opposing Pokémon, except Speed.	—
Unburden	Doubles Speed if the Pokémon loses or consumes a held item. Its Speed returns to normal if the Pokémon holds another item. No effect if the Pokémon starts out with no held item.	—
Unnerve	Prevent the opposing Pokémon from eating Berries.	—

V

Ability	Effect in battle	Effect when the Pokémon is the lead in your party
Victory Star	The accuracy of its allies and itself is 10% higher.	—
Vital Spirit	Protects against the Sleep status condition.	Lowers encounter rate with high-level wild Pokémon.
Volt Absorb	When the Pokémon is hit by an Electric-type move, HP is restored rather than taking damage.	—

W

Ability	Effect in battle	Effect when the Pokémon is the lead in your party
Water Absorb	When the Pokémon is hit by a Water-type move, HP is restored rather than taking damage.	—
Water Veil	Prevents the Burned status condition.	—
Weak Armor	When the Pokémon is hit by a physical attack, Defense goes down 1, but Speed goes up 1.	—
White Smoke	Protects against stat-lowering moves and Abilities.	Lowers wild Pokémon encounter rate.
Wonder Guard	Protects the Pokémon against all moves except supereffective ones.	—
Wonder Skin	Makes status moves more likely to miss.	—

Z

Ability	Effect in battle	Effect when the Pokémon is the lead in your party
Zen Mode	When over half its HP is lost, it changes form.	—

Items picked up with the Pickup Ability

Item	Level of Pokémon with Pickup Ability (Low → Lv. 100)									
	Low									Lv. 100
Potion	◎									
Antidote	○	◎								
Super Potion	○	○	◎							
Great Ball	○	○	○	◎						
Repel	○	○	○	○	◎					
Escape Rope	○	○	○	○	○	◎				
Full Heal	○	○	○	○	○	○	◎			
Hyper Potion	○	○	○	○	○	○	○	◎		
Ultra Ball	△	△	○	○	○	○	○	○	◎	
Revive		△	△	○	○	○	○	○	○	◎
Rare Candy			△	△	○	○	○	○	○	○
Sun Stone				△	△	○	○	○	○	○
Moon Stone					△	△	○	○	○	○
Heart Scale						△	△	○	○	○
Full Restore			▲	▲			△	△	○	○
Max Revive								△	△	○
PP Up									△	△
Max Elixir										△
Nugget	▲	▲								
King's Rock		▲	▲							
Ether				▲	▲					
Iron Ball					▲	▲				
Prism Scale						▲	▲	▲	▲	▲
Elixir							▲	▲		
Leftovers									▲	▲

◎ Often found ○ Sometimes found △ Rarely found ▲ Almost never found

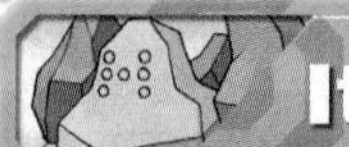

Items

A

Move	Explanation	Main Ways to obtain	Price
Absorb Bulb	Raises the holder's Sp. Atk by 1 when it is hit by a Water-type move. Goes away after use.	Exchange for 16 BP at the PWT or Battle Subway/Very rarely held by wild Roselia	—
Adamant Orb	When held by Dialga, it raises the power of Dragon- and Steel-type moves.	Dragonspiral Tower	—
Air Balloon	The holder floats and Ground-type moves will no longer hit the holder. The balloon pops when the holder is hit by an attack.	From the old man on 25F in the Driftveil Chateau Hotel/Exchange for 12 BP at the PWT or Battle Subway	—
Amulet Coin	Doubles prize money from a battle if the holding Pokémon joins in.	From a man on the first floor of a building in Castelia City	—
Antidote	Cures the Poison status condition.	Poké Mart (after obtaining one Gym Badge)/Route 9 Shopping Mall 1F	100
Armor Fossil	A Pokémon Fossil. When restored, it becomes Shieldon.	Receive from the Worker in Twist Mountain/Join Avenue Antique Shop (when the owner is from *Pokémon Black Version* or *Pokémon Black Version 2*)	300
Awakening	Cures the Sleep status condition.	Poké Mart (after obtaining one Gym Badge)/Route 9 Shopping Mall 1F	250

B

Move	Explanation	Main Ways to obtain	Price
BalmMushroom	A fragrant mushroom. Can be sold to the Maid on Route 5 for 25,000.	Very rarely held by wild Foongus and Amoonguss/From a man in a house in Accumula Town	—
Berry Juice	Restores the HP of one Pokémon by 20 points.	Undella Town/Held by wild Shuckle/Battle all three Trainers on the *Royal Unova* (Tuesday)	—
Big Mushroom	A big mushroom. Can be sold to the Poké Mart for 2,500. Can be sold to the Maid on Route 5 for 5,000.	Sometimes held by wild Foongus and Amoonguss/Prize for the correct answer in the Pansage, Pansear, or Panpour Show in Striaton City/Join Avenue Antique Shop	350
Big Nugget	A big nugget of pure gold. Can be sold to the old gentleman in Icirrus City for 30,000.	From the man in Chargestone Cave/Twist Mountain (winter)/Route 3/Nature Preserve/Very rarely held by wild Garbodor	500◆
Big Pearl	A big pearl. Can be sold to the Poké Mart for 3,750. Can be sold to the old gentleman in Icirrus City for 7,500.	Relic Passage/Route 14/Village Bridge/Sometimes held by wild Shellder and Cloyster	350◆
Big Root	Increases the amount of HP recovered when the holder uses an HP-draining move by 30%.	From the man on 25F of the Driftveil Continental Hotel	—
Binding Band	Doubles the damage done every turn by moves like Bind or Wrap when held.	Exchange for 8 BP at the PWT or Battle Subway	—
Black Belt	When held by a Pokémon, it boosts the power of Fighting-type moves.	From the woman in Icirrus City's Pokémon Center/Sometimes held by wild Throh and Sawk	—
Black Flute	A glass flute. Can be sold to the billionaire in Undella Town for 8,000.	From the sunglasses-wearing man on Route 13	—
Black Sludge	If the holder is a Poison-type Pokémon, it restores HP during battle. If the holder is any other type, it reduces HP during battle instead.	Castelia Sewers (spring, summer)/Sometimes held by wild Grimer and Trubbish, often held by Muk and Garbodor	—
BlackGlasses	When held by a Pokémon, it boosts the power of Dark-type moves.	Castelia City Back Street (spring, summer)	—
Blue Flute	A glass flute. Can be sold to the billionaire in Undella Town for 7,000.	From the sunglasses-wearing man on Route 13	—
Blue Shard	Give to the master Move Tutor in Lentimas Town to have him teach your Pokémon moves.	Desert Resort/Mistralton Cave/Village Bridge/Route 13/Route 17	500◆
BrightPowder	Lowers the accuracy of the holder's opponents.	Route 4 (*Pokémon White Version 2*)/From the girl in Anville Town (when you talk to her after finding her lost Pansage in Nimbasa City)	—
Bug Gem	When held by a Pokémon, it boosts the power of a Bug-type move by 50% one time. Goes away after use.	Found in dust clouds inside caves	—
Burn Heal	Cures the Burned status condition.	Poké Mart (after obtaining one Gym Badge)/Route 9 Shopping Mall 1F	250

C

Move	Explanation	Main Ways to obtain	Price
Calcium	Raises the base Sp. Atk stat of a Pokémon.	Route 9 Shopping Mall 3F/Exchange for 1 BP at the PWT or Battle Subway	9,800
Carbos	Raises the base Speed stat of a Pokémon.	Route 9 Shopping Mall 3F/Exchange for 1 BP at the PWT or Battle Subway	9,800
Casteliacone	Castelia City's famous ice cream. Cures all status conditions.	Castelia City's Casteliacone shop	100
Cell Battery	When the holder is hit by an Electric-type move, Attack goes up by 1. Goes away after use.	Exchange for 16 BP at the PWT or Battle Subway	—
Charcoal	When held by a Pokémon, it boosts the power of Fire-type moves.	Castelia City/From the woman on 1F of Castelia City's Battle Company	—
Choice Band	The holder can use only one of its moves, but Attack increases by 50%.	Exchange for 24 BP at the PWT or Battle Subway	—
Choice Scarf	The holder can use only one of its moves, but Speed increases by 50%.	Exchange for 24 BP at the PWT or Battle Subway	—
Choice Specs	The holder can use only one of its moves, but Sp. Atk increases by 50%.	Exchange for 24 BP at the PWT or Battle Subway	—
Claw Fossil	A Pokémon Fossil. When restored, it becomes Anorith.	Receive from the Worker in Twist Mountain/Join Avenue Antique Shop (when the owner is from *Pokémon White Version* or *Pokémon White Version 2*)	300
Cleanse Tag	Helps keep wild Pokémon away if the holder is the first one in the party.	From the chairman of Icirrus City's Pokémon Fan Club (when you show him a Pokémon you've raised 50 to 98 levels)	—
Clever Wing	Raises the base Sp. Def stat of a Pokémon by a little. Can be used until the stat reaches its maximum value.	Step on the shadows of flying Pokémon (Driftveil Drawbridge/Marvelous Bridge)/Reward for clearing Areas 6 through 9 of the Black Tower (White Treehollow)	—
Comet Shard	A shard that fell to the ground when a comet approached. Can be sold to the old gentleman in Icirrus City for 60,000.	Dragonspiral Tower/Very rarely held by wild Clefairy, Lunatone, and Solrock	—
Cover Fossil	A Pokémon Fossil. When restored, it becomes Tirtouga.	Receive from Lenora in Nacrene City/Join Avenue Antique Shop (when the owner is from *Pokémon White Version* or *Pokémon White Version 2*)	300

D

Move	Explanation	Main Ways to obtain	Price
Damp Mulch	A fertilizer to be spread on soft soil in regions where Berries are grown. The Pokémon Breeder in Mistralton City will buy it for 1,000.	Hidden Grottoes/Join Avenue Flower Shop (when the owner is from *Pokémon White Version 2*)	400
Damp Rock	Extends the duration of the move Rain Dance when held.	From the woman on Route 8 (talk to her during the morning)	—
Dark Gem	When held by a Pokémon, it boosts the power of a Dark-type move by 50% one time. Goes away after use.	Found in dust clouds inside caves	—
Dawn Stone	Evolves certain Pokémon.	Dreamyard/From the woman on Route 2 (show her a Pokémon with the Solid Rock Ability)/Found in dust clouds inside caves	60,000 ■
DeepSeaScale	When held by Clamperl, it doubles Sp. Def. Link Trade Clamperl while it holds the DeepSeaScale to evolve it into Gorebyss.	Sometimes held by wild Chinchou, Lanturn, and Gorebyss/White Forest (Saturdays and Sundays after clearing Area 5 of the White Treehollow)	2,000
DeepSeaTooth	When held by Clamperl, it doubles Sp. Atk. Link Trade Clamperl while it holds the DeepSeaScale to evolve it into Huntail.	Sometimes held by wild Carvanha, Sharpedo, and Huntail/White Forest (Saturdays and Sundays after clearing Area 2 of the White Treehollow)	1,000
Destiny Knot	When held, it shares the Infatuation status condition when it is afflicted by it.	From a woman in Castelia City	—
Dire Hit	Significantly raises the critical-hit ratio of the Pokémon on which it is used (can be used only once).	Route 9 Shopping Mall 3F/Nacrene City's store	650
Dome Fossil	A Pokémon Fossil. When restored, it becomes a Kabuto.	Receive from the Worker in Twist Mountain/Join Avenue Antique Shop (when the owner is from *Pokémon White Version* or *Pokémon White Version 2*)	300
Draco Plate	When held by a Pokémon, it boosts the power of Dragon-type moves. (When held by Arceus, it shifts Arceus's type to Dragon type.)	Undella Bay	—
Dragon Fang	When held by a Pokémon, it boosts the power of Dragon-type moves.	Victory Road/Sometimes held by wild Bagon and Druddigon	—
Dragon Gem	When held by a Pokémon, it boosts the power of a Dragon-type move by 50% one time. Goes away after use.	Found in dust clouds inside caves	—
Dragon Scale	Link Trade Seadra while it holds the Dragon Scale to evolve it into Kingdra.	Victory Road/Sometimes held by wild Horsea and Seadra/White Forest (Saturdays and Sundays after clearing Area 8 of the White Treehollow)	4,000
Dread Plate	When held by a Pokémon, it boosts the power of Dark-type moves. (When held by Arceus, it shifts Arceus's type to Dark type.)	Abyssal Ruins 1F	—
Dubious Disc	Link Trade Porygon2 while it holds the Dubious Disc to evolve it into Porygon-Z.	P2 Laboratory/Black City (Saturdays, Sundays after clearing Area 10 of the Black Tower)	60,000
Dusk Stone	Evolves certain Pokémon.	Strange House/Twist Mountain/Found in dust clouds inside caves/Black City (Monday through Friday after clearing Area 8 of the Black Tower)	40,000

E

Move	Explanation	Main Ways to obtain	Price
Earth Plate	When held by a Pokémon, it boosts the power of Ground-type moves. (When held by Arceus, it shifts Arceus's type to Ground type.)	Abyssal Ruins 1F	—
Eject Button	If the holder is hit by an attack, it switches places with a party Pokémon. Goes away after use.	Twist Mountain (winter)/Exchange for 16 BP at the PWT or Battle Subway	—
Electirizer	Link Trade Electabuzz while it holds the Electirizer to evolve it into Electivire.	Plasma Frigate (*Pokémon White Version 2*)/Join Avenue Antique Shop (when the owner is from *Pokémon White Version 2*)	350
Electric Gem	When held by a Pokémon, it boosts the power of an Electric-type move by 50% one time. Goes away after use.	Found in dust clouds inside caves	—
Elixir	Restores the PP of all of a Pokémon's moves by 10 points.	Route 6/Route 7/Route 9/Dragonspiral Tower	—
Energy Root	Restores the HP of one Pokémon by 200 points. Very bitter (lowers a Pokémon's friendship).	Driftveil Market/From a fan at Pokéstar Studios	800
EnergyPowder	Restores the HP of one Pokémon by 50 points. Very bitter (lowers a Pokémon's friendship).	Driftveil Market/From the man at the gate on the east side of Route 8/From a fan at Pokéstar Studios	500
Escape Rope	Use it to escape instantly from a cave or a dungeon.	Poké Mart (after obtaining one Gym Badge)/Route 9 Shopping Mall 1F	550
Ether	Restores the PP of a Pokémon's move by 10 points.	Talk to the man in Virbank Complex three times/Castelia City's Battle Company/Join Avenue Market	1,500
Everstone	Prevents Pokémon evolution when held.	From the man on 23F of the Driftveil Luxury Suites/Often held by wild Roggenrola and Boldore	200 ◆
Eviolite	Raises Defense and Sp. Def by 50% when held by a Pokémon that can still evolve.	From the man on 1F of a building in Castelia City (when the number of Seen Pokémon in the Pokédex is 40 or more)	—
Exp. Share	The holder earns Experience Points without even going into battle.	From the Janitor in Castelia City's Battle Company/From the chairman of Icirrus City's Pokémon Fan Club (show him a Pokémon you raised 25 to 49 levels)	—
Expert Belt	Raises the power of supereffective moves by 20%.	From the man in the Driftveil Market (when you have a Pokémon of Lv. 30 or higher in your party)/Very rarely held by wild Throh and Sawk	—

F

Move	Explanation	Main Ways to obtain	Price
Fighting Gem	When held by a Pokémon, it boosts the power of a Fighting-type move by 50% one time. Goes away after use.	Found in dust clouds inside caves	—
Fire Gem	When held by a Pokémon, it boosts the power of a Fire-type move by 50% one time. Goes away after use.	Found in dust clouds inside caves	—
Fire Stone	Evolves certain Pokémon.	Lentimas Town/Exchange for 3 BP at the PWT or Battle Subway/Found in dust clouds inside caves	20,000 ■
Fist Plate	When held by a Pokémon, it boosts the power of Fighting-type moves. (When held by Arceus, it shifts Arceus's type to Fighting type.)	Abyssal Ruins 1F	—
Flame Orb	Inflicts Burned status condition on the holder during battle.	Reversal Mountain (*Pokémon White Version 2*)/Exchange for 16 BP at the PWT or Battle Subway	—
Flame Plate	When held by a Pokémon, it boosts the power of Fire-type moves. (When held by Arceus, it shifts Arceus's type to Fire type.)	Abyssal Ruins 1F	—
Float Stone	Halves the holder's weight.	From the Linebacker on 2F of Drayden's house (Opelucid City)/Twist Mountain Outside/Join Avenue Antique Shop	200

◆ Cheapest price the item can be purchased for at a Join Avenue Antique Shop. ● Price when purchased at a Join Avenue Market. ■ Price when purchased at Black City (White Forest)

Items

F

Move	Explanation	Main Ways to obtain	Price
Fluffy Tail	Allows the holder to always run away from a wild Pokémon encounter.	Show the woman in Accumula Town a Pokémon with a height of 17 feet or more	—
Flying Gem	When held by a Pokémon, it boosts the power of a Flying-type move by 50% one time. Goes away after use.	Found in dust clouds inside caves	—
Focus Band	10% chance of leaving the holder with 1 HP when it receives damage that would KO it.	Exchange for 12 BP at the PWT or Battle Subway	—
Focus Sash	Leaves the holder with 1 HP when hit by a move that would KO it when its HP is full. Goes away after use.	Exchange for 24 BP at the PWT or Battle Subway	—
Fresh Water	Restores the HP of one Pokémon by 50 points.	Vending machines/Receive from Clyde at Pokémon Gyms	200
Full Heal	Cures all status conditions.	Poké Mart (after obtaining five Gym Badges)/Route 9 Shopping Mall 1F	600
Full Incense	When held by a Pokémon, it makes it move later.	Driftveil Market	9,600
Full Restore	Fully restores the HP and heals any status conditions of a single Pokémon.	Poké Mart (after obtaining eight Gym Badges)	3,000

G

Move	Explanation	Main Ways to obtain	Price
Genius Wing	Raises the base Sp. Atk stat of a Pokémon by a little. Can be used until the stat reaches its maximum value.	Step on the shadows of flying Pokémon (Driftveil Drawbridge/Marvelous Bridge)/Reward for clearing Areas 6 through 9 of the Black Tower (White Treehollow)	—
Ghost Gem	When held by a Pokémon, it boosts the power of a Ghost-type move by 50% one time. Goes away after use.	Found in dust clouds inside caves	—
Gooey Mulch	A fertilizer to be spread on soft soil in regions where Berries are grown. The Pokémon Breeder in Mistralton City will buy it for 1,000.	Hidden Grottoes/Join Avenue Flower Shop (when the owner is from *Pokémon White Version*)	400
Grass Gem	When held by a Pokémon, it boosts the power of a Grass-type move by 50% one time. Goes away after use.	Found in dust clouds inside caves	—
Green Shard	Give to the master Move Tutor in Nacrene City to have him teach your Pokémon moves.	Desert Resort/Route 12/Route 23/ Clay Tunnel/Moor of Icirrus/Join Avenue Antique Shop	500
Grip Claw	Extends the duration of moves like Bind and Wrap.	Route 4 (*Pokémon Black Version 2*)/Sometimes held by wild Sneasel	—
Griseous Orb	When held by Giratina, it changes it into its Origin Forme, and boosts the power of Dragon- and Ghost-type moves.	Dragonspiral Tower	—
Ground Gem	When held by a Pokémon, it boosts the power of a Ground-type move by 50% one time. Goes away after use.	Found in dust clouds inside caves	—
Growth Mulch	A fertilizer to be spread on soft soil in regions where Berries are grown. The Pokémon Breeder in Mistralton City will buy it for 1,000.	Hidden Grottoes/Join Avenue Flower Shop (when the owner is from *Pokémon Black Version 2*)	400
Guard Spec.	Prevents stat reduction among the Trainer's party Pokémon for five turns.	Route 9 Shopping Mall 3F/Nacrene City's store	700

H

Move	Explanation	Main Ways to obtain	Price
Hard Stone	When held by a Pokémon, it boosts the power of Rock-type moves.	Relic Passage/sometimes held by wild Corsola and Nosepass/Join Avenue Antique Shop	200
Heal Powder	Cures all status conditions. Very bitter (lowers a Pokémon's friendship).	Driftveil Market/From a boy on Driftveil Drawbridge (talk to him when Charizard is in your party)	450
Health Wing	Raises the base HP stat of a Pokémon by a little. Can be used until the stat reaches its maximum value.	Step on the shadows of flying Pokémon (Driftveil Drawbridge/Marvelous Bridge)/Reward for clearing Areas 6 through 9 of the Black Tower (White Treehollow)	—
Heart Scale	Give one to the reminder girl at the PWT, and she will have your Pokémon remember a move it has forgotten.	Desert Resort/Castelia City/Castelia Sewers (spring, summer)/By showing the woman in Driftveil City the Pokémon she wants to see/Route 6/Route 14	350◆
Heat Rock	Extends the duration of the move Sunny Day when held.	From the woman on Route 8 (talk to her during the afternoon)	—
Helix Fossil	A Pokémon Fossil. When restored, it becomes an Omanyte.	Receive from the Worker in Twist Mountain/Join Avenue Antique Shop (when the owner is from *Pokémon Black Version* or *Pokémon Black Version 2*)	300
Honey	Use in tall grass or in a cave to make wild Pokémon appear.	Sometimes held by wild Combee/Join Avenue Market	3,600 (for 12)
HP Up	Raises the base HP stat of a Pokémon.	Route 9 Shopping Mall 3F/Exchange for 1 BP at the PWT or Battle Subway	9,800
Hyper Potion	Restores the HP of one Pokémon by 200 points.	Poké Mart (after obtaining three Gym Badges)/Route 9 Shopping Mall 1F	1,200

I

Move	Explanation	Main Ways to obtain	Price
Ice Gem	When held by a Pokémon, it boosts the power of an Ice-type move by 50% one time. Goes away after use.	Found in dust clouds inside caves	—
Ice Heal	Cures the Frozen status condition.	Poké Mart (after obtaining one Gym Badge)/Route 9 Shopping Mall 1F	250
Icicle Plate	When held by a Pokémon, it boosts the power of Ice-type moves. (When held by Arceus, it shifts Arceus's type to Ice type.)	Abyssal Ruins 1F	—
Icy Rock	Extends the duration of the move Hail when held.	From the woman on Route 8 (talk to her at night or late night)	—
Insect Plate	When held by a Pokémon, it boosts the power of Bug-type moves. (When held by Arceus, it shifts Arceus's type to Bug type.)	Abyssal Ruins 1F	—
Iron	Raises the base Defense stat of a Pokémon.	Route 9 Shopping Mall 3F/Exchange for 1 BP at the PWT or Battle Subway	9,800
Iron Ball	Lowers the holder's Speed. If the holder has the Levitate Ability or is a Flying-type Pokémon, Ground-type moves now hit it.	Exchange for 12 BP at the PWT or Battle Subway	—
Iron Plate	When held by a Pokémon, it boosts the power of Steel-type moves. (When held by Arceus, it shifts Arceus's type to Steel type.)	Abyssal Ruins 1F	—

Move	Explanation	Main Ways to obtain	Price
King's Rock	When the holder hits a target with an attack, the is a 10% chance the target will flinch. Certain Pokémon evolve when Link Traded while holding this item.	Home of a famous Trainer in Nuvema Town/Sometimes held by wild Poliwhirl and Poliwrath/Join Avenue Antique Shop (when the owner is from *Pokémon Black Version*)	350

Move	Explanation	Main Ways to obtain	Price
Lagging Tail	When held by a Pokémon, it makes it move later.	Sometimes held by wild Slowpoke, Lickitung, and Lickilicky	—
Lava Cookie	Lavaridge Town's famous specialty. Cures all status conditions.	Battle all four Trainers on the *Royal Unova* (Monday, Wednesday, Friday)/From a fan at Pokéstar Studios	1,000 ●
Lax Incense	Lowers the accuracy of the holder's opponents.	Driftveil Market	9,600
Leaf Stone	Evolves certain Pokémon.	Route 7/Exchange for 3 BP at the PWT or Battle Subway/Found in dust clouds inside caves	1,000 ■
Leftovers	Restores the holder's HP by 1/16th of its maximum HP every turn.	Castelia Sewers	—
Lemonade	Restores the HP of one Pokémon by 80 points.	Vending machines/From the Waitress at Nacrene City's Café Warehouse (Saturdays)	350
Life Orb	Lowers the holder's HP by 10% of its max HP each time it attacks, but raises the power of moves by 30%.	Exchange for 24 BP at the PWT or Battle Subway	—
Light Clay	Extends the duration of moves like Reflect and Light Screen.	Route 4 (*Pokémon White Version 2*)/Sometimes held by wild Golurk	—
Luck Incense	Doubles prize money from a battle if the holding Pokémon joins in.	Driftveil Market	9,600
Lucky Egg	Increases the number of Experience Points received from battle by 50%.	From Professor Juniper in Celestial Tower	—
Lucky Punch	When held by Chansey, it raises the critical-hit ratio of its moves.	Successfully complete the Entralink Funfest Mission "Rock-Paper-Scissors Competition" with a double score	—
Lustrous Orb	When held by Palkia, it raises the power of Dragon- and Water-type moves.	Dragonspiral Tower	—

Move	Explanation	Main Ways to obtain	Price
Macho Brace	When held, it halves Speed, but makes it easier to raise base stats.	From the Infielder in the Nimbasa City gate	—
Magmarizer	Link Trade Magmar while it holds the Magmarizer to evolve it into Magmortar.	Plasma Frigate (*Pokémon Black Version 2*)/Join Avenue Antique Shop (when the owner is from *Pokémon Black Version 2*)	350
Magnet	When held by a Pokémon, it boosts the power of Electric-type moves.	Chargestone Cave	—
Max Elixir	Restores the PP of all of a Pokémon's moves completely.	Plasma Frigate/Victory Road/Icirrus City (winter)/Striaton City/Join Avenue Raffle Shop (6th prize)	—
Max Ether	Restores the PP of a Pokémon's move completely.	Desert Resort/Route 13/Join Avenue Raffle Shop (7th prize)	—
Max Potion	Completely restores the HP of a single Pokémon.	Poké Mart (after obtaining seven Gym Badges)/Route 9 Shopping Mall 1F	2,500
Max Repel	Prevents weak wild Pokémon from appearing for 250 steps after its use.	Poké Mart (after obtaining five Gym Badges)/Route 9 Shopping Mall 1F	700
Max Revive	Revives a fainted Pokémon and fully restores its HP.	Route 20 (autumn)/Plasma Frigate/From Rood in the Giant Chasm/Victory Road/From your mom after you enter the Hall of Fame	5,000 ●
Meadow Plate	When held by a Pokémon, it boosts the power of Grass-type moves. (When held by Arceus, it shifts Arceus's type to Grass type.)	Abyssal Ruins 1F	—
Mental Herb	The holder cures itself when moves like Taunt, Encore, Disable, Heal Block, or Attract make it unable to use moves freely. Goes away after use.	Sometimes held by wild Sewaddle, Swadloon, and Leavanny	—
Metal Coat	When held by a Pokémon, boosts the power of Steel-type moves. Link Trade certain Pokémon while they hold the Metal Coat to evolve them.	Chargestone Cave/Clay Tunnel/Sometimes held by wild Magnemite, Steelix, and Metang	350 ◆
Metal Powder	When held by Ditto, Defense doubles.	Sometimes held by wild Ditto	—
Metronome	Raises the power of a move used consecutively when held.	Lacunosa Town/From the woman in the house in Accumula Town (show her a Kricketot and then a Whismur)	—
Mind Plate	When held by a Pokémon, it boosts the power of Psychic-type moves. (When held by Arceus, it shifts Arceus's type to Psychic type.)	Abyssal Ruins 1F	—
Miracle Seed	When held by a Pokémon, it boosts the power of Grass-type moves.	Castelia City empty lot/From the woman on 1F of Castelia City's Battle Company (when you answer Snivy)/Sometimes held by wild Maractus	—
Moomoo Milk	Restores the HP of one Pokémon by 100 points.	Driftveil Market/From a fan at Pokéstar Studios/Join Avenue Market	500
Moon Stone	Evolves certain Pokémon.	Route 6/Giant Chasm Crater Forest/Dreamyard/Found in dust clouds inside caves	200 ◆
Muscle Band	When held by a Pokémon, it boosts the power of physical moves.	Exchange for 8 BP at the PWT or Battle Subway	—
Muscle Wing	Raises the base Attack stat of a Pokémon by a little. Can be used until the stat reaches its maximum value.	Step on the shadows of flying Pokémon (Driftveil Drawbridge/Marvelous Bridge)/Reward for clearing Areas 6 through 9 of the Black Tower (White Treehollow)	—
Mystic Water	When held by a Pokémon, it boosts the power of Water-type moves.	Route 4/From the woman on 1F of Castelia City's Battle Company (when you answer Oshawott)/Sometimes held by wild Castform	—

Move	Explanation	Main Ways to obtain	Price
NeverMeltIce	When held by a Pokémon, it boosts the power of Ice-type moves.	Dragonspiral Tower entrance (winter)/Sometimes held by wild Cryogonal	—
Normal Gem	When held by a Pokémon, it boosts the power of a Normal-type move by 50% one time. Goes away after use.	Found in dust clouds inside caves	—
Nugget	A nugget of pure gold. Can be sold to the Poké Mart for 5,000. Can be sold to the old gentleman in Icirrus City for 10,000.	Desert Resort/From the man in Chargestone Cave/Reversal Mountain/Route 9/Route 14	500 ◆

◆ Cheapest price the item can be purchased for at a Join Avenue Antique Shop. ● Price when purchased at a Join Avenue Market. ■ Price when purchased at Black City (White Forest).

Items

O

Move	Explanation	Main Ways to obtain	Price
Odd Incense	When held by a Pokémon, it boosts the power of Psychic-type moves.	Driftveil Market	9,600
Odd Keystone	A vital item that is needed to keep a stone tower from collapsing. Voices can be heard from it occasionally.	Join Avenue Antique Shop (when the owner is from *Pokémon White Version* or *Pokémon White Version 2*)	200
Old Amber	A piece of amber that contains genetic material. When restored, it becomes Aerodactyl.	Receive from the Worker in Twist Mountain/Join Avenue Antique Shop (when the owner is from *Pokémon Black Version* or *Pokémon Black Version 2*)	300
Old Gateau	Old Chateau's hidden specialty. Cures all status conditions.	Battle all five Trainers on the *Royal Unova* (Thursday)/From Cedric Juniper in Dragonspiral Tower	1,000 ●
Oval Stone	Level up Happiny while it holds the Oval Stone in the morning, afternoon, or evening to evolve it into Chansey.	Found in dust clouds inside caves/White Forest (Monday through Friday after clearing Area 10 of the White Treehollow)	6,000

P

Move	Explanation	Main Ways to obtain	Price
Parlyz Heal	Cures the Paralysis status condition.	Poké Mart (after obtaining one Gym Badge)/Route 9 Shopping Mall 1F	200
Pass Orb	A mysterious orb that generates Pass Powers.	Successfully complete Entralink Funfest Missions	—
Pearl	A pretty pearl. Can be sold to the Poké Mart for 700. Can be sold to the old gentleman in Icirrus City for 1,400.	Castelia Sewers/Walk Mienfoo in Humilau City/Join Avenue Antique Shop	350
Pearl String	Very large pearls that sparkle in a pretty silver color. Can be sold to the old gentleman in Icirrus City for 25,000.	Route 17/As a gift from Join Avenue guests	—
Plume Fossil	A Pokémon Fossil. When restored, it becomes Archen.	Receive from Lenora in Nacrene City/Join Avenue Antique Shop (when the owner is from *Pokémon White Version* or *Pokémon White Version 2*)	300
Poison Barb	When held by a Pokémon, it boosts the power of Poison-type moves.	Route 22/Sometimes held by wild Beedrill, Qwilfish, and Roselia	—
Poison Gem	When held by a Pokémon, it boosts the power of a Poison-type move by 50% one time. Goes away after use.	Found in dust clouds inside caves	—
Poké Doll	Allows the holder to always run away from a wild Pokémon encounter.	Route 9 Shopping Mall/Show the boy in Accumula Town a Pokémon with a height of eight inches or less	—
Poké Toy	Allows the holder to always run away from a wild Pokémon encounter.	Virbank City/Route 4 (guess the Pokémon cry imitation correctly)/Route 9 Shopping Mall 1F	1,000
Potion	Restores the HP of one Pokémon by 20 points.	Poké Mart (from the start)/Route 9 Shopping Mall 1F	300
Power Anklet	Halves the holder's Speed, but makes the Speed base stat easier to raise.	Exchange for 16 BP at the PWT or Battle Subway	—
Power Band	Halves the holder's Speed, but makes the Sp. Def base stat easier to raise.	Plasma Frigate (*Pokémon Black Version 2*)/From the girl in the house on Route 13 (*Pokémon White Version 2*)/Exchange for 16 BP at the PWT or Battle Subway	—
Power Belt	Halves the holder's Speed, but makes the Defense base stat easier to raise.	Plasma Frigate (*Pokémon White Version 2*)/Exchange for 16 BP at the PWT or Battle Subway	—
Power Bracer	Halves the holder's Speed, but makes the Attack base stat easier to raise.	Exchange for 16 BP at the PWT or Battle Subway	—
Power Herb	The holder can immediately use a move that requires a one-turn charge. Goes away after use.	Exchange for 16 BP at the PWT or Battle Subway	—
Power Lens	Halves the holder's Speed, but makes the Sp. Atk base stat easier to raise.	From the girl in the house on Route 13 (*Pokémon Black Version 2*)/Exchange for 16 BP at the PWT or Battle Subway	—
Power Weight	Halves the holder's Speed, but makes the HP base stat easier to raise.	Exchange for 16 BP at the PWT or Battle Subway	—
PP Max	Increases the max number of PP as high as it will go.	Victory Road/Pinwheel Forest/Dragonspiral Tower/Route 18/Join Avenue Raffle Shop (3rd prize)	—
PP Up	Increases the max number of PP by 1 level.	PWT/Route 6/ Celestial Tower/Reversal Mountain/Route 12/Route 21/Route 22/Giant Chasm	12,500 ●
Pretty Wing	A pretty wing. Sell to the Poké Mart for 100.	Step on the shadows of flying Pokémon (Driftveil Drawbridge/Marvelous Bridge)/From a fan at Pokéstar Studios	—
Prism Scale	Link Trade Feebas while it holds the Prism Scale to evolve it into Milotic.	From the man in Undella Town's Pokémon Center/Route 1/Join Avenue Antique Shop (when the owner is from *Pokémon White Version 2*)	350
Protector	Link Trade Rhydon while it holds the Protector to evolve it into Rhyperior.	Wellspring Cave/Black City (Saturdays, Sundays after clearing Area 2 of the Black Tower)	10,000
Protein	Raises the base Attack stat of a Pokémon.	Route 9 Shopping Mall 3F/Exchange for 1 BP at the PWT or Battle Subway	9,800
Psychic Gem	When held by a Pokémon, it boosts the power of a Psychic-type move by 50% one time. Goes away after use.	Found in dust clouds inside caves	—
Pure Incense	Helps keep wild Pokémon away if the holder is the first one in the party.	Driftveil Market	9,600

Q

Move	Explanation	Main Ways to obtain	Price
Quick Claw	Allows the holder to strike first sometimes.	From the woman in the east gate in Castelia City/Sometimes held by wild Sandshrew, Sandslash, and Sneasel	—
Quick Powder	When held by Ditto, Speed doubles.	Often held by wild Ditto	—

R

Move	Explanation	Main Ways to obtain	Price
RageCandyBar	Mahogany Town's famous snack. Restores the HP of one Pokémon by 20.	Battle all six Trainers on the *Royal Unova* (Saturday)/From a fan at Pokéstar Studios	2,000 ●
Rare Bone	A rare bone. Can be sold to the sunglasses-wearing man on Route 18 for 10,000.	Castelia Sewers (spring, summer)/Clay Tunnel/Twist Mountain/Very rarely held by wild Crustle	300 ◆
Rare Candy	Raises a Pokémon's level by 1.	Route 20 (autumn)/Virbank City/Relic Passage/Lostlorn Forest/Route 22/Seaside Cave	—

Move	Explanation	Main Ways to obtain	Price
Razor Claw	Boosts the holder's critical-hit ratio. Level up Sneasel while it holds the Razor Claw at night or late night to evolve it into Weavile.	Giant Chasm Crater Forest/Exchange for 8 BP at the PWT or Battle Subway	—
Razor Fang	When the holder hits a target with an attack, the is a 10% chance the target will flinch. Level up Gligar while it holds the Razor Fang in the evening or at night to evolve it into Gliscor.	Route 11/Exchange for 8 BP at the PWT or Battle Subway	—
Reaper Cloth	Link Trade Dusclops while it holds the Reaper Cloth to evolve it into Dusknoir.	Dreamyard/Join Avenue Antique Shop (when the owner is from *Pokémon Black Version 2*)	350
Red Card	If the holder is hit by an attack, the opposing Trainer is forced to switch out the attacking Pokémon. Goes away after use.	Exchange for 16 BP at the PWT or Battle Subway	—
Red Flute	A glass flute. Can be sold to the billionaire in Undella Town for 7,500.	From the sunglasses-wearing man on Route 13	—
Red Shard	Give to the master Move Tutor in Driftveil City to have him teach your Pokémon moves.	From the old man in Nimbasa City's Pokémon Center/Desert Resort/Route 13/Route 22/ Clay Tunnel	500◆
Relic Band	A bracelet made by a civilization about 3,000 years ago. The billionaire in Undella Town will buy it for 100,000.	Abyssal Ruins 2F, 3F	—
Relic Copper	A copper coin made by a civilization about 3,000 years ago. The billionaire in Undella Town will buy it for 1,000.	Abyssal Ruins 1F, 2F	—
Relic Crown	A crown made by a civilization about 3,000 years ago. The billionaire in Undella Town will buy it for 300,000.	Abyssal Ruins Top Floor	—
Relic Gold	A gold coin made by a civilization about 3,000 years ago. The billionaire in Undella Town will buy it for 100,000.	Abyssal Ruins 1F, 2F, 3F	—
Relic Silver	A silver coin made by a civilization about 3,000 years ago. The billionaire in Undella Town will buy it for 5,000.	Abyssal Ruins 1F, 2F, 3F	—
Relic Statue	A stone figure made by a civilization about 3,000 years ago. The billionaire in Undella Town will buy it for 200,000.	Abyssal Ruins 1F, 2F, 3F	—
Relic Vase	A vase made by a civilization about 3,000 years ago. The billionaire in Undella Town will buy it for 50,000.	Abyssal Ruins 1F, 2F, 3F	—
Repel	Prevents weak wild Pokémon from appearing for 100 steps after its use.	Poké Mart (after obtaining one Gym Badge)/Route 9 Shopping Mall 1F	350
Resist Wing	Raises the base Defense stat of a Pokémon by a little. Can be used until the stat reaches its maximum value.	Step on the shadows of flying Pokémon (Driftveil Drawbridge/Marvelous Bridge)/Reward for clearing Areas 6 through 9 of the Black Tower (White Treehollow)	—
Revival Herb	Revives a fainted Pokémon. Very bitter (lowers a Pokémon's friendship).	Driftveil Market	2,800
Revive	Revives a fainted Pokémon and restores half of its HP.	Poké Mart (after obtaining three Gym Badges)/Route 9 Shopping Mall 1F	1,500
Ring Target	Moves that would otherwise have no effect will hit the holder.	From the woman on 2F of Drayden's House in Opelucid City	—
Rock Gem	When held by a Pokémon, it boosts the power of a Rock-type move by 50% one time. Goes away after use.	Found in dust clouds inside caves	—
Rock Incense	When held by a Pokémon, it boosts the power of Rock-type moves.	Driftveil Market	9,600
Rocky Helmet	Does damage to the Pokémon that hit the holder with a direct attack.	From a man at the PWT/Relic Passage	—
Root Fossil	A Pokémon Fossil. When restored, it becomes Lileep.	Receive from the Worker in Twist Mountain/Join Avenue Antique Shop (when the owner is from *Pokémon Black Version* or *Pokémon Black Version 2*)	300
Rose Incense	When held by a Pokémon, it boosts the power of Grass-type moves.	Driftveil Market	9,600

S

Move	Explanation	Main Ways to obtain	Price
Sacred Ash	Revives all fainted Pokémon in your party and fully restores their HP.	Join Avenue Antique Shop	350
Scope Lens	Boosts the holder's critical-hit ratio.	From the man in Castelia City's Battle Company/Exchange for 8 BP at the PWT or Battle Subway	—
Sea Incense	When held by a Pokémon, it boosts the power of Water-type moves.	Driftveil Market	9,600
Sharp Beak	When held by a Pokémon, it boosts the power of Flying-type moves.	From the woman in Mistralton City's Cargo Service/Sometimes held by wild Fearow and Doduo	—
Shed Shell	The holder can always be switched out.	Sometimes held by wild Scraggy and Scrafty	—
Shell Bell	Restores the holder's HP by up to 1/8th of the damage dealt to the target.	From an old man on 1F of the Driftveil Grand Hotel (when the number of Seen Pokémon in the Pokédex is 70 or more)/Humilau City	—
Shiny Stone	Evolves certain Pokémon.	Abundant Shrine/Dragonspiral Tower/Found in dust clouds inside caves/White Forest (Monday through Friday after clearing Area 8 of the White Treehollow)	4,000
Shoal Salt	Salt found in the Shoal Cave. Can be sold to the Maid on Route 5 for 7,000.	Route 17 (use the Dowsing MCHN)	—
Shoal Shell	A seashell found in the Shoal Cave. Can be sold to the old gentleman in Icirrus City for 7,000.	Route 17 (use the Dowsing MCHN)	—
Silk Scarf	When held by a Pokémon, it boosts the power of Normal-type moves.	Virbank Complex	—
SilverPowder	When held by a Pokémon, it boosts the power of Bug-type moves.	Sometimes held by wild Butterfree and Masquerain/Held by wild Volcarona	—
Skull Fossil	A Pokémon Fossil. When restored, it becomes Cranidos.	Receive from the Worker in Twist Mountain/Join Avenue Antique Shop (when the owner is from *Pokémon White Version* or *Pokémon White Version 2*)	300
Sky Plate	When held by a Pokémon, it boosts the power of Flying-type moves. (When held by Arceus, it shifts Arceus's type to Flying type.)	Abyssal Ruins 1F	—
Smoke Ball	Allows the holder to always run away from wild Pokémon.	Reversal Mountain Outside/From the woman in a house in Opelucid City/Sometimes held by wild Koffing and Weezing	—
Smooth Rock	Extends the duration of the move Sandstorm when held.	From the woman on Route 8 (talk to her during the evening)	—
Soda Pop	Restores the HP of one Pokémon by 60 points.	Vending machines/From the Waitress at Nacrene City's Café Warehouse (Wednesdays)	300
Soft Sand	When held by a Pokémon, it boosts the power of Ground-type moves.	From the sunglasses-wearing man in Desert Resort/Sometimes held by wild Trapinch and Stunfisk	—

◆ Cheapest price the item can be purchased for at a Join Avenue Antique Shop. ● Price when purchased at a Join Avenue Market ■ Price when purchased at Black City (White Forest).

Items

S

Move	Explanation	Main Ways to obtain	Price
Soothe Bell	The holder's friendship improves more quickly.	From the old lady in the house in Nimbasa City (when the lead Pokémon in your party has high friendship)	—
Soul Dew	When held by Latios or Latias, it raises both the Sp. Atk and Sp. Def stats.	Dreamyard (after catching Latias or Latios)	—
Spell Tag	When held by a Pokémon, it boosts the power of Ghost-type moves.	From the old woman in Lentimas Town's Pokémon Center/Strange House/Sometimes held by wild Banette and Yamask	—
Splash Plate	When held by a Pokémon, it boosts the power of Water-type moves. (When held by Arceus, it shifts Arceus's type to Water type.)	Undella Bay	—
Spooky Plate	When held by a Pokémon, it boosts the power of Ghost-type moves. (When held by Arceus, it shifts Arceus's type to Ghost type.)	Abyssal Ruins 1F	—
Stable Mulch	A fertilizer to be spread on soft soil in regions where Berries are grown. The Pokémon Breeder in Mistralton City will buy it for 1,000.	Hidden Grottoes/Join Avenue Flower Shop (when the owner is from *Pokémon Black Version*)	400
Star Piece	A shard of a pretty gem that sparkles in a red color. Can be sold to the Poké Mart for 4,900. Can be sold to the old gentleman in Icirrus City for 9,800.	Route 13/Giant Chasm/Route 23/Sometimes held by wild Staryu and Starmie	—
Stardust	Lovely, red-colored sand. Can be sold to the Poké Mart for 1,000. Can be sold to the old gentleman in Icirrus City for 2,000.	Desert Resort/Route 4/Smash the challenge rock in Pinwheel Forest (when you have a Fighting-type Pokémon in your party)	—
Steel Gem	When held by a Pokémon, it boosts the power of a Steel-type move by 50% one time. Goes away after use.	Found in dust clouds inside caves	—
Stick	When held by Farfetch'd, it raises the critical-hit ratio of its moves.	Sometimes held by wild Farfetch'd	—
Sticky Barb	Damages the holder every turn. It can stick to an opponent that touches the holder with a direct attack.	Route 20 (autumn)/Sometimes held by wild Cacturne and Ferroseed	—
Stone Plate	When held by a Pokémon, it boosts the power of Rock-type moves. (When held by Arceus, it shifts Arceus's type to Rock type.)	Abyssal Ruins 1F	—
Sun Stone	Evolves certain Pokémon.	Giant Chasm Crater Forest/Pinwheel Forest/Found in dust clouds inside caves	200 ◆
Super Potion	Restores the HP of one Pokémon by 50 points.	Poké Mart (after obtaining one Gym Badge)/Route 9 Shopping Mall 1F	700
Super Repel	Prevents weak wild Pokémon from appearing for 200 steps after its use.	Poké Mart (after obtaining three Gym Badges)/Route 9 Shopping Mall 1F	500
Sweet Heart	Restores the HP of one Pokémon by 20 points.	Use the Feeling Check feature with Infrared Connection/From a fan in Pokéstar Studios	—
Swift Wing	Raises the base Speed stat of a Pokémon by a little. Can be used until the stat reaches its maximum value.	Step on the shadows of flying Pokémon (Driftveil Drawbridge/Marvelous Bridge)/Reward for clearing Areas 6 through 9 of the Black Tower (White Treehollow)	—

T

Move	Explanation	Main Ways to obtain	Price
Thick Club	When held by Cubone or Marowak, Attack is doubled.	Entralink Funfest Mission "Great Trade-Up"	—
Thunderstone	Evolves certain Pokémon.	Chargestone Cave/Exchange for 3 BP at the PWT or Battle Subway/Found in dust clouds inside caves	10,000 ■
TinyMushroom	A tiny mushroom. Can be sold to the Poké Mart for 250. Can be sold to the Maid on Route 5 for 500.	Often held by wild Foongus and Amoonguss/Hidden Grottoes/Join Avenue Antique Shop	350
Toxic Orb	Inflicts the Badly Poisoned status condition on the holder during battle.	Reversal Mountain (*Pokémon Black Version 2*)/Exchange for 16 BP at the PWT or Battle Subway	—
Toxic Plate	When held by a Pokémon, it boosts the power of Poison-type moves. (When held by Arceus, it shifts Arceus's type to Poison type.)	Abyssal Ruins 1F	—
TwistedSpoon	When held by a Pokémon, it boosts the power of Psychic-type moves.	Castelia Sewers	—

U

Move	Explanation	Main Ways to obtain	Price
Up-Grade	Link Trade Porygon while it holds the Up-Grade to evolve it into Porygon2.	From Cheren in Pinwheel Forest/Striaton City/Black City (Saturdays, Sundays after clearing Area 8 of the Black Tower)	40,000

W

Move	Explanation	Main Ways to obtain	Price
Water Gem	When held by a Pokémon, it boosts the power of a Water-type move by 50% one time. Goes away after use.	Found in dust clouds inside caves	—
Water Stone	Evolves certain Pokémon.	Route 19/Exchange for 3 BP at the PWT or Battle Subway/Found in dust clouds inside caves	2,000 ■
Wave Incense	When held by a Pokémon, it boosts the power of Water-type moves.	Driftveil Market	9,600
White Flute	A glass flute. Can be sold to the billionaire in Undella Town for 8,000.	From the sunglasses-wearing man on Route 13	—
White Herb	Restores lowered stats. Goes away after use.	Exchange for 16 BP at the PWT or Battle Subway	—
Wide Lens	Raises the holder's accuracy by 10%.	Route 4 (*Pokémon Black Version 2*)/Exchange for 8 BP at the PWT or Battle Subway/Sometimes held by wild Yanma and Yanmega	—
Wise Glasses	When held by a Pokémon, it boosts the power of special moves.	Exchange for 8 BP at the PWT or Battle Subway	—

XYZ

Move	Explanation	Main Ways to obtain	Price
X Accuracy	Raises the accuracy of a Pokémon on which it is used.	Route 9 Shopping Mall 3F/Nacrene City's store	950
X Attack	Raises the Attack stat of a Pokémon on which it is used by one level.	Route 9 Shopping Mall 3F/Nacrene City's store	500

Move	Explanation	Main Ways to obtain	Price
X Defend	Raises the Defense stat of a Pokémon on which it is used by one level.	Route 9 Shopping Mall 3F/Nacrene City's store	550
X Sp. Def	Raises the Sp. Def stat of a Pokémon on which it is used by one level.	Route 9 Shopping Mall 3F/Nacrene City's store	350
X Special	Raises the Sp. Atk of a Pokémon on which it is used by one level.	Route 9 Shopping Mall 3F/Nacrene City's store	350
X Speed	Raises the Speed of a Pokémon on which it is used by one level.	Route 9 Shopping Mall 3F/Nacrene City's store	350
Yellow Flute	A glass flute. Can be sold to the billionaire in Undella Town for 7,500.	From the sunglasses-wearing man on Route 13	—
Yellow Shard	Give to the master Move Tutor in Humilau City to have him teach your Pokémon moves.	Desert Resort/Mistralton Cave/Route 12/Striaton City/Join Avenue Antique Shop	500
Zap Plate	When held by a Pokémon, it boosts the power of Electric-type moves. (When held by Arceus, it shifts Arceus's type to Electric type.)	Abyssal Ruins 1F	—
Zinc	Raises the base Sp. Def stat of a Pokémon.	Route 9 Shopping Mall 3F/Exchange for 1 BP at the PWT or Battle Subway	9,800
Zoom Lens	Raises the holder's accuracy by 20% when it moves after the opposing Pokémon.	Exchange for 12 BP at the PWT or Battle Subway	—

◆ Cheapest price the item can be purchased for at a Join Avenue Antique Shop. ● Price when purchased at a Join Avenue Market. ■ Price when purchased at Black City (White Forest).

Key items

Move	Explanation	Main Ways to Obtain	Price
Bicycle	A folding Bicycle that lets you travel faster than running.	Receive from the Harlequin in Castelia City	—
Colress MCHN	A special device that brings out the potential of Pokémon. Use it on Crustle in Seaside Cave.	Receive from Colress on Route 22	—
Dark Stone	Zekrom's body was destroyed and changed into this stone. It waits for a hero to appear.	From N in N's Castle *(Pokémon Black Version 2)* after you defeat him	—
DNA Splicers	Use them once to fuse Kyurem with Zekrom (Reshiram). Use them again to separate the Pokémon.	Giant Chasm (after catching Kyurem)	—
Dowsing MCHN	A cutting-edge device that alerts you to hidden items.	Receive from Bianca in Castelia City	—
Dropped Item	When you find the Dropped Item in the amusement park in Nimbasa City, the Trainer who dropped it will give you a call.	Get in Nimbasa City	—
Gracidea	Shaymin can change Forme when holding this item (except at night).	Receive from the woman in Lacunosa Town's Pokémon Center (when Shaymin is in your party and you don't have the Gracidea)	—
Grubby Hanky	A handkerchief dropped by a regular customer at Café Warehouse in Nacrene City.	From the Waitress at Nacrene City's Café Warehouse (Sunday)	—
Light Stone	Reshiram's body was destroyed and changed into this stone. It waits for a hero to appear.	From N in N's Castle *(Pokémon White Version 2)* after you defeat him	—
Lunar Wing	Allows Cresselia to appear on Marvelous Bridge.	Strange House	—
Magma Stone	Allows Heatran to appear in Reversal Mountain.	Route 18	—
Medal Box	Holds the Medals you've obtained and records information about Medals.	Receive from Mr. Medal in Floccesy Town	—
Oval Charm	Eggs are discovered more easily at the Pokémon Day Care.	Receive from Professor Juniper when the number of Caught Pokémon in the Unova Pokédex reaches 297	—
Pal Pad	A useful pad that records friends and good times.	In the Bag from the start	—
Permit	A permit that grants access to the Nature Preserve from Mistralton City's Cargo Service.	Receive from Professor Juniper when the number of Seen Pokémon in the Unova Pokédex reaches 297	—
Plasma Card	A card key needed to enter the password in the Plasma Frigate.	Receive from a Team Plasma Grunt in the Plasma Frigate	—
Prop Case	A lovely case to store Props for your Pokémon to wear in the Musical.	Receive from the owner at the Musical Theater in Nimbasa City	—
Reveal Glass	Changes Tornadus, Thundurus, and Landorus's Formes.	Obtained when you go to the Abundant Shrine with the Landorus caught in *Pokémon Dream Radar* in your party	—
Shiny Charm	Raises encounter rate with Shiny Pokémon.	Receive from Professor Juniper in Nuvema Town when you catch every Pokémon in the National Pokédex	—
Super Rod	The best fishing rod. Use it to catch Pokémon from the waterside.	Receive from Cedric Juniper in Nuvema Town	—
Town Map	A very convenient map that can be viewed anytime.	Receive from Hugh's sister in Aspertia City	—
Vs. Recorder	Records your battles with friends and in battle facilities.	Get from the person you team up with in Nimbasa City (after defeating Ingo and Emmet)	—
Xtransceiver	A cutting-edge transceiver with a camera that lets you chat with up to three other people.	Get right away	—

Poké Balls

Move	Explanation	Main Ways to Obtain	Price
Poké Ball	An item for capturing wild Pokémon.	Poké Mart (from the start)/Route 9 Shopping Mall 2F	200
Dive Ball	A Poké Ball that makes it easier to catch Pokémon that live in the water.	Poké Marts in Undella Town and Humilau City	1,000
Dream Ball	A Poké Ball that magically appears in your Bag in the Entree Forest.	Only appears in your Bag when you are catching Pokémon in the Entree Forest	—
Dusk Ball	A Poké Ball that does better at night and in caves.	Poké Marts in Driftveil City, Lentimas Town, and Opelucid City/Route 9 Shopping Mall 2F	1,000
Great Ball	A Poké Ball that provides a higher Pokémon catch rate than a standard Poké Ball.	Poké Mart (after obtaining one Gym Badge)/Route 9 Shopping Mall 2F	600

Items

Poké Balls

Move	Explanation	Main Ways to Obtain	Price
Heal Ball	A gentle Poké Ball that heals the caught Pokémon's HP and status.	Poké Marts in Virbank City, Castelia City, Lentimas Town, and Victory Road/Route 9 Shopping Mall 2F	300
Luxury Ball	A Poké Ball that endears you to caught Pokémon.	Poké Marts in Undella Town, Humilau City, Victory Road, and the Pokémon League	1,000
Master Ball	It is the ultimate ball that will surely catch any wild Pokémon.	From Professor Juniper in Mistralton City/From Colress in the Plasma Frigate when it's by P2 Laboratory (after defeating him)	—
Nest Ball	A Poké Ball with a higher capture rate against weaker Pokémon.	Poké Marts in Castelia City, Driftveil City, and Lentimas Town/Route 9 Shopping Mall 2F	1,000
Net Ball	A Poké Ball with a high success rate against Bug- and Water-type Pokémon.	Poké Marts in Virbank City, Castelia City, and Driftveil City/Route 9 Shopping Mall 2F	1,000
Premier Ball	A rare Poké Ball made in commemoration of an event.	Buy 10 or more Poké Balls at once	—
Quick Ball	A Poké Ball with a good capture rate when thrown right at the start of battle.	Poké Marts in Opelucid City, Victory Road, and the Pokémon League/Route 9 Shopping Mall 2F	1,000
Repeat Ball	A Poké Ball that excels at catching Pokémon you've caught before.	Poké Marts in Victory Road, the Pokémon League, and Accumula Town	1,000
Timer Ball	A Poké Ball that does better after more turns have elapsed in battle.	Poké Marts in Opelucid City, Victory Road, and the Pokémon League/Route 9 Shopping Mall 2F	1,000
Ultra Ball	A Poké Ball that provides a higher Pokémon catch rate than a Great Ball.	Poké Mart (after obtaining five Gym Badges)/Route 9 Shopping Mall 2F	1,200

Berries

Move	Explanation	Main Ways to Obtain	Price
Aguav Berry	Holder restores some of its own HP when its HP falls to half or less, but if the holder dislikes Bitter flavors, it gains the Confused status condition.	Prize for Spin Trades in the Union Room	—
Apicot Berry	Holder's Sp. Def goes up 1 when its HP falls to half or less.	Join Avenue Flower Shop (when the owner is from *Pokémon White Version*)	2,000 (for 4)
Aspear Berry	Holder can heal itself of the Frozen status condition.	Show the Harlequin in Castelia City's Studio Castelia the Pokémon he wants to see/Route 11 (after defeating Pokémon Ranger Crofton or Thalia)	600 ▲ (for 4)
Babiri Berry	Halves damage the holder takes from supereffective Steel-type moves.	Join Avenue Flower Shop (when the owner is from *Pokémon White Version 2*)	2,000 (for 4)
Belue Berry	—	Not obtainable in these versions	—
Bluk Berry	—	From the man in Lacunosa Town's Pokémon Center (night/late night)/Join Avenue Flower Shop (when the owner is from *Pokémon White Version 2*)	600 (for 4)
Charti Berry	Halves damage the holder takes from supereffective Rock-type moves.	Sometimes held by wild Swellow/Join Avenue Flower Shop (when the owner is from *Pokémon White Version 2*)	2,000 (for 4)
Cheri Berry	Holder can heal itself of the Paralysis status condition.	Show the Harlequin in Castelia City's Studio Castelia the Pokémon he wants to see/Route 5 (after defeating Pokémon Ranger Lois)	600 ▲ (for 4)
Chesto Berry	Holder can heal itself of the Sleep status condition.	Show the Harlequin in Castelia City's Studio Castelia the Pokémon he wants to see/Chargestone Cave (after defeating Pokémon Ranger Louis or Briana)	600 ▲ (for 4)
Chilan Berry	Halves damage the holder takes from Normal-type moves.	Join Avenue Flower Shop (when the owner is from *Pokémon Black Version*)	2,000 (for 4)
Chople Berry	Halves damage the holder takes from supereffective Fighting-type moves.	Join Avenue Flower Shop (when the owner is from *Pokémon White Version*)	2,000 (for 4)
Coba Berry	Halves damage the holder takes from supereffective Flying-type moves.	Join Avenue Flower Shop (when the owner is from *Pokémon Black Version*)	2,000 (for 4)
Colbur Berry	Halves damage the holder takes from supereffective Dark-type moves.	Join Avenue Flower Shop (when the owner is from *Pokémon Black Version 2*)	2,000 (for 4)
Cornn Berry	—	Not obtainable in these versions	—
Custap Berry	The holder's move is more likely to strike first during the next turn when its HP becomes low.	Not obtainable in these versions	—
Durin Berry	—	Not obtainable in these versions	—
Enigma Berry	When the holder is damaged by a supereffective attack, some HP is restored.	Not obtainable in these versions	—
Figy Berry	Holder restores its own HP when its HP falls to half or less, but if the holder dislikes Spicy flavors, it gains the Confused status condition.	Prize for Spin Trades in the Union Room	—
Ganlon Berry	Holder raises its Defense stat by 1 when its HP becomes low.	Join Avenue Flower Shop (when the owner is from *Pokémon Black Version 2*)	2,000 (for 4)
Grepa Berry	Slightly raises the Pokémon's friendship, but lowers its base Sp. Def stat.	Buy from the woman on Route 5/Prize for Spin Trades in the Union Room	200 (for 5)
Haban Berry	Halves damage the holder takes from supereffective Dragon-type moves.	From Axew on 19F of the Grand Hotel Driftveil/Join Avenue Flower Shop (when the owner is from *Pokémon White Version*)	2,000 (for 4)
Hondew Berry	Slightly raises the Pokémon's friendship, but lowers its base Sp. Atk stat.	Buy from the woman on Route 5/Prize for Spin Trades in the Union Room	200 (for 5)
Iapapa Berry	Holder restores some of its own HP when its HP falls to half or less, but if the holder dislikes Sour flavors, it gains the Confused status condition.	Prize for Spin Trades in the Union Room	—
Jaboca Berry	When the holder takes damage from a physical attack, the Pokémon that landed the attack is also damaged.	Not obtainable in these versions	—
Kasib Berry	Halves damage the holder takes from supereffective Ghost-type moves.	Join Avenue Flower Shop (when the owner is from *Pokémon Black Version*)	2,000 (for 4)
Kebia Berry	Halves damage the holder takes from supereffective Poison-type moves.	Join Avenue Flower Shop (when the owner is from *Pokémon Black Version 2*)	2,000 (for 4)
Kelpsy Berry	Slightly raises the Pokémon's friendship, but lowers its base Attack stat.	Buy from the woman on Route 5/Prize for Spin Trades in the Union Room	200 (for 5)
Lansat Berry	Raises the critical-hit ratio of the holder's attacks when its HP falls to half or less.	From a Trainer on the 15th platform stop during a Battle Subway win streak	—
Leppa Berry	Holder restores 10 PP to a move when that move's PP reaches 0.	From a man in Lacunosa Town (night, late night)/Route 20 (after defeating Pokémon Ranger Bret or Malory in the autumn)	1,500 ▲

Move	Explanation	Main Ways to Obtain	Price
Liechi Berry	Holder raises its Attack stat by 1 when its HP becomes low.	Join Avenue Flower Shop (when the owner is from *Pokémon White Version*)	2,000 (for 4)
Lum Berry	Holder can heal itself of any status condition.	From the man in Lacunosa Town (night, late night)/From the Baker at Village Bridge (show her a Pokémon with the Honey Gather Ability)	800 ▲ (for 4)
Mago Berry	Holder restores some of its own HP when its HP falls to half or less, but if the holder dislikes Sweet flavors, it gains the Confused status condition.	Prize for Spin Trades in the Union Room	—
Magost Berry	—	Not obtainable in these versions	—
Micle Berry	Raises the accuracy of the holder's moves by 20% one time when its HP becomes low.	Not obtainable in these versions	—
Nanab Berry	—	Not obtainable in these versions	—
Nomel Berry	—	Not obtainable in these versions	—
Occa Berry	Halves damage the holder takes from supereffective Fire-type moves.	Join Avenue Flower Shop (when the owner is from *Pokémon Black Version*)/ Sometimes held by wild Pansage	2,000 (for 4)
Oran Berry	Holder restores its own HP by 10 when its HP falls to half or less.	From Alder on Route 19/Often held by wild Furret, Bibarel, Pansage, Pansear, and Panpour	600 ▲ (for 4)
Pamtre Berry	—	Not obtainable in these versions	—
Passho Berry	Halves damage the holder takes from supereffective Water-type moves.	Join Avenue Flower Shop (when the owner is from *Pokémon White Version*)/ Sometimes held by wild Pansear	2,000 for 4
Payapa Berry	Halves damage the holder takes from supereffective Psychic-type moves.	Join Avenue Flower Shop (when the owner is from *Pokémon White Version*)	2,000 (for 4)
Pecha Berry	Holder can heal itself of the Poison status condition.	Show the Harlequin in Castelia City's Studio Castelia the Pokémon he wants to see/ From the man in Lacunosa Town (night, late night)	600 ▲ (for 4)
Persim Berry	Holder can heal itself of the Confused status condition.	Seaside Cave (after defeating Pokémon Ranger Mikiko or Johan)/Often held by wild Spoink, Gothita, and Solosis	600 ▲ (for 4)
Petaya Berry	Raises the holder's Sp. Atk stat by 1 when its HP becomes low.	Join Avenue Flower Shop (when the owner is from *Pokémon Black Version*)	2,000 (for 4)
Pinap Berry	—	Not obtainable in these versions	—
Pomeg Berry	Slightly raises the Pokémon's friendship, but lowers its base HP stat.	Buy from the woman on Route 5/Prize for Spin Trades in the Union Room	200 (for 5)
Qualot Berry	Slightly raises the Pokémon's friendship, but lowers its base Defense stat.	Buy from the woman on Route 5/Prize for Spin Trades in the Union Room	200 (for 5)
Rabuta Berry	—	Not obtainable in these versions	—
Rawst Berry	Holder can heal itself of the Burned status condition.	Show the Harlequin in Castelia City's Studio Castelia the Pokémon he wants to see/ Desert Resort (after defeating Pokémon Ranger Anja or Jaden)	600 ▲ (for 4)
Razz Berry	—	Join Avenue Flower Shop (when the owner is from *Pokémon Black Version 2*)	600 (for 4)
Rindo Berry	Halves damage the holder takes from supereffective Grass-type moves.	Sometimes held by wild Finneon, Lumineon, and Panpour/Join Avenue Flower Shop (when the owner is from *Pokémon White Version 2*)	2,000 (for 4)
Rowap Berry	When the holder takes damage from a special attack, the Pokémon that landed the attack is also damaged.	Not obtainable in these versions	—
Salac Berry	Holder raises its Speed stat by 1 when its HP becomes low.	Join Avenue Flower Shop (when the owner is from *Pokémon White Version 2*)	2,000 (for 4)
Shuca Berry	Halves damage the holder takes from supereffective Ground-type moves.	Join Avenue Flower Shop (when the owner is from *Pokémon White Version 2*)	2,000 (for 4)
Sitrus Berry	Holder restores its own HP by 1/4 of its max HP when its HP falls to half or less.	Route 13 (after defeating Pokémon Ranger Dianne or Daryl)/From the woman on Village Bridge	800 ▲ (for 4)
Spelon Berry	—	Not obtainable in these versions	—
Starf Berry	Raises one of the holder's stats by 2 when its HP falls to half or less.	From a Trainer on the 29th platform stop during a Battle Subway win streak	—
Tamato Berry	Slightly raises the Pokémon's friendship, but lowers its base Speed stat.	Buy from the woman on Route 5/Prize for Spin Trades in the Union Room	200 (for 5)
Tanga Berry	Halves damage the holder takes from supereffective Bug-type moves.	Join Avenue Flower Shop (when the owner is from *Pokémon Black Version 2*)	2,000 (for 4)
Wacan Berry	Halves damage the holder takes from supereffective Electric-type moves.	Join Avenue Flower Shop (when the owner is from *Pokémon Black Version 2*)	2,000 (for 4)
Watmel Berry	—	Not obtainable in these versions	—
Wepear Berry	—	Not obtainable in these versions	—
Wiki Berry	Holder restores some of its own HP when its HP falls to half or less, but if the holder dislikes Dry flavors, it gains the Confused status condition.	Prize for Spin Trades in the Union Room	—
Yache Berry	Halves damage the holder takes from supereffective Ice-type moves.	Join Avenue Flower Shop (when the owner is from *Pokémon Black Version*)	2,000 (for 4)

▲ Price when purchased at a Join Avenue Flower Shop.

Mail

Greet Mail

Price 50

Sold in

Aspertia City, Virbank City, Floccesy Town, Castelia City

Favored Mail

Price 50

Sold in

Aspertia City, Virbank City, Floccesy Town, Castelia City

RSVP Mail

Price 50

Sold in

Aspertia City, Virbank City, Floccesy Town, Castelia City

Thanks Mail

Price 50

Sold in

Aspertia City, Virbank City, Floccesy Town, Castelia City

Inquiry Mail

Price 50

Sold in

Aspertia City, Virbank City, Floccesy Town, Castelia City

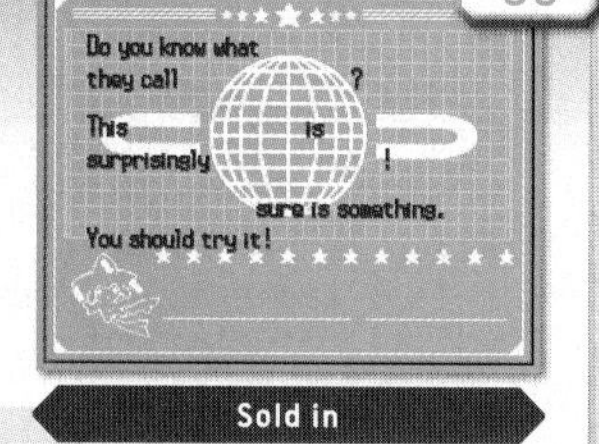

Like Mail

Price 50

Sold in

Aspertia City, Virbank City, Floccesy Town, Castelia City

Reply Mail

Price 50

Sold in

Aspertia City, Virbank City, Floccesy Town, Castelia City

BridgeMail S

Price 50

Sold in

Nacrene City

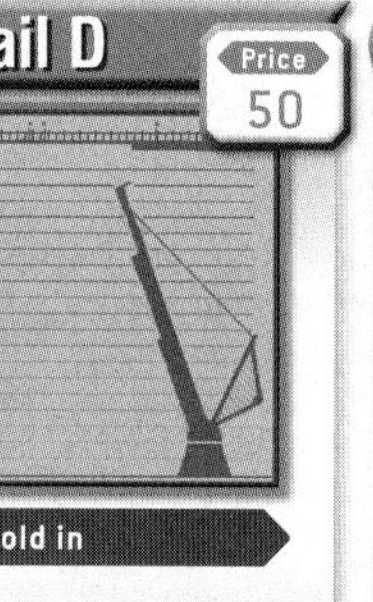

BridgeMail D

Price 50

Sold in

Driftveil City

BridgeMail T

Price 50

Sold in

Icirrus City

BridgeMail V

Price 50

Sold in

Opelucid City

BridgeMail M

Price 50

Sold in

Black City, White Forest

Medals

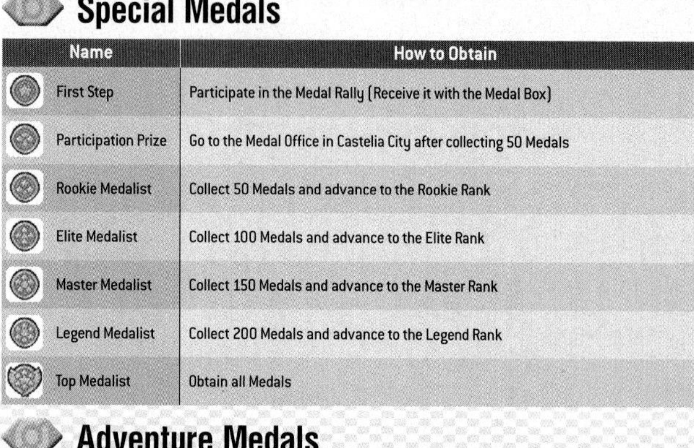

Special Medals

Name	How to Obtain
First Step	Participate in the Medal Rally (Receive it with the Medal Box)
Participation Prize	Go to the Medal Office in Castelia City after collecting 50 Medals
Rookie Medalist	Collect 50 Medals and advance to the Rookie Rank
Elite Medalist	Collect 100 Medals and advance to the Elite Rank
Master Medalist	Collect 150 Medals and advance to the Master Rank
Legend Medalist	Collect 200 Medals and advance to the Legend Rank
Top Medalist	Obtain all Medals

Adventure Medals

Name	How to Obtain
Light Walker	Take 5,000 steps
Middle Walker	Take 10,000 steps
Heavy Walker	Take 20,000 steps
Honored Footprints	Take 100,000 steps

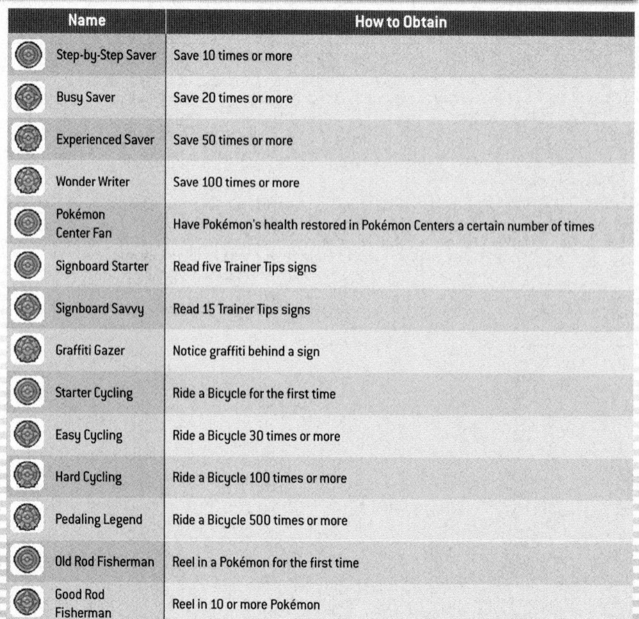

Name	How to Obtain
Step-by-Step Saver	Save 10 times or more
Busy Saver	Save 20 times or more
Experienced Saver	Save 50 times or more
Wonder Writer	Save 100 times or more
Pokémon Center Fan	Have Pokémon's health restored in Pokémon Centers a certain number of times
Signboard Starter	Read five Trainer Tips signs
Signboard Savvy	Read 15 Trainer Tips signs
Graffiti Gazer	Notice graffiti behind a sign
Starter Cycling	Ride a Bicycle for the first time
Easy Cycling	Ride a Bicycle 30 times or more
Hard Cycling	Ride a Bicycle 100 times or more
Pedaling Legend	Ride a Bicycle 500 times or more
Old Rod Fisherman	Reel in a Pokémon for the first time
Good Rod Fisherman	Reel in 10 or more Pokémon

Name	How to Obtain
Super Rod Fisherman	Reel in 50 or more Pokémon
Mighty Fisher	Reel in 100 or more Pokémon
Normal-type Catcher	Catch all the Normal-type Pokémon in the Unova Pokédex
Fire-type Catcher	Catch all the Fire-type Pokémon in the Unova Pokédex
Water-type Catcher	Catch all the Water-type Pokémon in the Unova Pokédex
Electric-type Catcher	Catch all the Electric-type Pokémon in the Unova Pokédex
Grass-type Catcher	Catch all the Grass-type Pokémon in the Unova Pokédex
Ice-type Catcher	Catch all the Ice-type Pokémon in the Unova Pokédex
Fighting-type Catcher	Catch all the Fighting-type Pokémon in the Unova Pokédex
Poison-type Catcher	Catch all the Poison-type Pokémon in the Unova Pokédex
Ground-type Catcher	Catch all the Ground-type Pokémon in the Unova Pokédex
Flying-type Catcher	Catch all the Flying-type Pokémon in the Unova Pokédex
Psychic-type Catcher	Catch all the Psychic-type Pokémon in the Unova Pokédex
Bug-type Catcher	Catch all the Bug-type Pokémon in the Unova Pokédex
Rock-type Catcher	Catch all the Rock-type Pokémon in the Unova Pokédex
Ghost-type Catcher	Catch all the Ghost-type Pokémon in the Unova Pokédex
Dragon-type Catcher	Catch all the Dragon-type Pokémon in the Unova Pokédex
Dark-type Catcher	Catch all the Dark-type Pokémon in the Unova Pokédex
Steel-type Catcher	Catch all the Steel-type Pokémon in the Unova Pokédex
Unova Catcher	Complete the Unova Pokédex and receive an award certificate from the Game Director in Castelia City
National Catcher	Complete the National Pokédex and receive an award certificate from the Game Director in Castelia City
30 Boxed	Deposit 30 or more Pokémon in the PC Boxes
120 Boxed	Deposit 120 or more Pokémon in the PC Boxes
360 Boxed	Deposit 360 or more Pokémon in the PC Boxes
Boxes Max	Deposit 720 Pokémon in the PC Boxes
Capturing Spree	Catch 50 or more Pokémon in a day
Vending Virtuoso	Buy 10 or more drinks at vending machines
Lucky Drink	Get a bonus at a vending machine
Evolution Hopeful	Evolve a Pokémon for the first time
Evolution Tech	Evolve Pokémon 10 times or more
Evolution Expert	Evolve Pokémon 50 times or more
Evolution Authority	Evolve Pokémon 100 times or more
Ace Pilot	Travel using Fly a certain number of times
Hustle Muscle	Drop a boulder using Strength a certain number of times
Trash Master	Check trash cans a certain number of times
Dowsing Beginner	Find a hidden item for the first time using the Dowsing MCHN
Dowsing Specialist	Find 10 or more hidden items using the Dowsing MCHN
Dowsing Collector	Find 50 or more hidden items using the Dowsing MCHN
Dowsing Wizard	Find 150 or more hidden items using the Dowsing MCHN
Naming Champ	Give Pokémon nicknames a certain number of times
Television Kid	Watch TV a certain number of times
Regular Customer	Shop a certain number of times

Name	How to Obtain
Moderate Customer	Spend 10,000 or more at shops
Great Customer	Spend 100,000 or more at shops
Indulgent Customer	Spend 1,000,000 or more at shops
Super Rich	Spend 10,000,000 or more at shops
Smart Shopper	Buy 10 Poké Balls at once and receive a Premier Ball
Sweet Home	Have your mom restore your Pokémon's HP at your home in Aspertia City
The First Passerby	Pass by a person for the first time with Tag Mode
30 Passersby	Pass by 30 or more people with Tag Mode
100 Passersby	Pass by 100 or more people with Tag Mode
Heavy Traffic	Pass by 1,000 or more people with Tag Mode
Pass Power ↑	Use a Pass Power for the first time
Pass Power ↑↑	Use 10 or more Pass Powers
Pass Power ↑↑↑	Use 50 or more Pass Powers
Pass Power MAX	Use 100 or more Pass Powers
Dozing Capture	Catch a Pokémon in the Entree Forest for the first time
Sleeping Capture	Catch 10 or more Pokémon in the Entree Forest
Deep Sleep Capture	Catch 50 or more Pokémon in the Entree Forest
Sweet Dreamer	Catch 100 or more Pokémon in the Entree Forest
Hidden Grotto Adept	Find all the Hidden Grottoes
Egg Beginner	Hatch a Pokémon Egg for the first time
Egg Breeder	Hatch 10 or more Pokémon Eggs
Egg Elite	Hatch 50 or more Pokémon Eggs
Hatching Aficionado	Hatch 100 or more Pokémon Eggs
Day-Care Faithful	Leave many Pokémon at the Pokémon Day Care on Route 3
Archeology Lover	Have a Pokémon Fossil restored in the Nacrene Museum in Nacrene City
Pure Youth	Catch N's Pokémon
Lucky Color	Catch a Shiny Pokémon
Pokérus Discoverer	Catch a Pokémon infected with the Pokérus
Castelia Boss	Defeat the three Trainers on the Back Street in Castelia City
Rail Enthusiast	Hear information on all the trains in Anville Town
Wailord Watcher	See a Wailord at the Marine Tube
Face Board Memorial	Take a photo at the face board in Humilau City
Heavy Machinery Pro	Give correct answers to five questions the Heavy Machinery Pro in Twist Mountain gives you
Ruins Raider	Reach the deepest part of the Abyssal Ruins in Undella Bay
Diamond Dust	See the Diamond Dust
Bridge Enthusiast	Visit all the bridges in the Unova region
Around Unova	Visit every city and town in the Unova region
Great Adventurer	Obtain all 97 Adventure Medals except this Medal

Medals

Battle Medals

Name	How to Obtain
Battle Learner	Go through 100 or more battles
Battle Teacher	Go through 200 or more battles
Battle Veteran	Go through 400 or more battles
Battle Virtuoso	Go through 2,000 or more battles
Link Battle Amateur	Have a Link Battle for the first time
Link Battle Pioneer	Have 10 or more Link Battles
Link Battle Expert	Have 50 or more Link Battles
Born to Battle	Have 100 or more Link Battles
Magikarp Award	Use the move Splash in a battle
Never Give Up	Use the move Struggle in a battle
Noneffective Artist	Use moves that aren't very effective because of a bad matchup
Supereffective Savant	Use supereffective moves a certain number of times
Subway Low Gear	Try the Battle Subway for the first time
Subway Accelerator	Try the Battle Subway 10 times or more
Subway Top Gear	Try the Battle Subway 50 times or more
Runaway Express	Try the Battle Subway 100 times or more
Single Express	Beat the Subway Boss in a Single Train in the Battle Subway
Double Express	Beat the Subway Boss in a Double Train in the Battle Subway
Multi Express	Beat the Subway Boss in a Multi Train in the Battle Subway
Test Novice	Take the first Battle Test in the Battle Institute in Nimbasa City
Test Fan	Take 10 Battle Tests in the Battle Institute in Nimbasa City
Test Enthusiast	Take 30 Battle Tests in the Battle Institute in Nimbasa City
Exam Genius	Take 50 Battle Tests in the Battle Institute in Nimbasa City
Exp. Millionaire	Earn 1,000,000 Exp. Points in a day
BP Wealthy	Earn 100 BP
Superb Locator	Meet a certain number of Pokémon who appear in special conditions such as rustling grass and dust clouds
Battle Repeater	Battle with 30 or more Trainers in Big Stadium and Small Court in Nimbasa City
Cruise Connoisseur	Take 10 or more cruises on the *Royal Unova* in Castelia City
Driftveil Mightiest	Win the Driftveil Tournament in the PWT
Rental Champ	Win the Rental Tournament in the PWT
Mix Champ	Win the Mix Tournament in the PWT
Unova Mightiest	Win the Unova Leaders Tournament in the PWT
Kanto Mightiest	Win the Kanto Leaders Tournament in the PWT
Johto Mightiest	Win the Johto Leaders Tournament in the PWT
Hoenn Mightiest	Win the Hoenn Leaders Tournament in the PWT
Sinnoh Mightiest	Win the Sinnoh Leaders Tournament in the PWT
Mightiest Leader	Win the World Leaders Tournament in the PWT
World's Mightiest	Win the Champions Tournament in the PWT
Rental Master	Win the Rental Master Tournament in the PWT
Mix Master	Win the Mix Master Tournament in the PWT
All Types Champ	Win all the Type Expert Tournaments in the PWT
Tower Junior	Explore up to Area 5 in the Black Tower in Black City
Tower Master	Explore up to Area 10 in the Black Tower in Black City
Treehollow Junior	Explore up to Area 5 in the White Treehollow in White Forest
Treehollow Master	Explore up to Area 10 in the White Treehollow in White Forest
20 Victories	Beat 20 Trainers in the Black Tower or the White Treehollow
50 Victories	Beat 50 Trainers in the Black Tower or the White Treehollow
100 Victories	Beat 100 Trainers in the Black Tower or the White Treehollow
1,000 Wins	Beat 1,000 Trainers in the Black Tower or the White Treehollow
Undefeated: Easy	Defeat all Trainers in Area 2, 3, 4 or 5 in the Black Tower or the White Treehollow
Undefeated: Hard	Defeat all Trainers in Area 6,7, 8, 9, or 10 in the Black Tower or the White Treehollow
Pinpoint: Easy	Clear Area 2, 3, 4 or 5 within four battles in the Black Tower or the White Treehollow
Pinpoint: Hard	Clear Area 6,7, 8, 9, or 10 within six battles in the Black Tower or the White Treehollow
Quick Clear: Easy	Clear Area 2, 3, 4 or 5 within 100 steps in the Black Tower or the White Treehollow
Quick Clear: Hard	Clear Area 6,7, 8, 9, or 10 within 1,000 steps in the Black Tower or the White Treehollow
Battle Guru	Obtain all 55 Battle Medals except this Medal

Entertainment Medals

Name	How to Obtain
Beginning Trader	Trade a Pokémon by Link Trade for the first time
Occasional Trader	Trade Pokémon 10 times or more by Link Trade
Frequent Trader	Trade Pokémon 50 times or more by Link Trade
Great Trade-Up	Trade Pokémon 100 times or more by Link Trade
Opposite Trader	Link Trade between *Pokémon Black 2* and *Pokémon White* or *Pokémon White 2*; or between *Pokémon White 2* and *Pokémon Black* or *Pokémon Black 2*
Pen Pal	Write Mail and have a Pokémon hold it
Talented Cast Member	Participate in Pokémon Musicals a certain number of times
Rising Star	Receive a good review for the first time in a Pokémon Musical
Big Star	Receive five good reviews in Pokémon Musicals
Superstar	Receive 10 good reviews in Pokémon Musicals
Musical Star	Receive 30 good reviews in Pokémon Musicals
Trendsetter	Collect all the Props used in Pokémon Musicals
10 Followers	Ten fans gather at the reception after a Pokémon Musical
First Friend	Register a Friend Code in your Pal Pad for the first time
Extensive Friendship	Register five or more Friend Codes in your Pal Pad
Broad Friendship	Register 10 or more Friend Codes in your Pal Pad
Global Connection	Register the maximum number of Friend Codes in your Pal Pad
Spin Trade Whiz	Play Spin Trade in the Union Room a certain number of times
Feeling Master	Play Feeling Check via Infrared Connection (IR) a certain number of times
Ace of Hearts	Score 80 points or more in Feeling Check via Infrared Connection (IR)
Ferris Wheel Fan	Meet a lot of people at the Ferris wheel in Nimbasa City
New Guide	Guide 10 or more customers in Join Avenue
Elite Guide	Guide 20 or more customers in Join Avenue
Veteran Guide	Guide 50 or more customers in Join Avenue
Guiding Champ	Guide 100 or more customers in Join Avenue

Name	How to Obtain
Shop Starter	Create five shops in Join Avenue
Shop Builder	Create 10 shops in Join Avenue
Shop Constructor	Create 20 shops in Join Avenue
Extreme Developer	Create 50 shops in Join Avenue
OK Souvenir Getter	Receive 10 or more souvenirs from visitors in Join Avenue
Good Souvenir Getter	Receive 30 or more souvenirs from visitors in Join Avenue
Great Souvenir Getter	Receive 50 or more souvenirs from visitors in Join Avenue
Tycoon of Souvenirs	Receive 100 or more souvenirs from visitors in Join Avenue
Avenue of Fame	Develop Join Avenue and earn the right to give it an original name
Minigame Fan	Play minigames on the Xtransceiver 10 times or more
Minigame Buff	Play minigames on the Xtransceiver 30 times or more
Minigame Expert	Play minigames on the Xtransceiver 50 times or more
Best Minigamer	Play minigames on the Xtransceiver 100 times or more
Balloon Rookie	Reach a total of 50 points in minigames on the Xtransceiver
Balloon Technician	Reach a total of 200 points in minigames on the Xtransceiver
Balloon Expert	Reach a total of 500 points in minigames on the Xtransceiver
Balloon Conqueror	Reach a total of 1,000 points in minigames on the Xtransceiver
New Face Hero	Release a starring movie for the first time in Pokéstar Studios
Hero Movie Star	Release the full series of *Brycen-Man Strikes Back* in Pokéstar Studios
Cop Movie Master	Release the full series of *Full Metal Cop* in Pokéstar Studios
UFO Movie Master	Release the full series of *Invaders* in Pokéstar Studios
Monster Movie Master	Release the full series of *Big Monster* in Pokéstar Studios
Sci-Fi Movie Master	Release the full series of *Timegate Traveler* in Pokéstar Studios
Romantic Movie Star	Release the full series of *Love and Battles* in Pokéstar Studios
Fantasy Movie Master	Release the full series of *Mystery Doors of the Magical Land* in Pokéstar Studios
Comedic Movie Star	Release the full series of *The Giant Woman* in Pokéstar Studios
Horror Movie Star	Release the full series of *Red Fog of Terror* in Pokéstar Studios
Robot Movie Master	Release the full series of *Everlasting Memories* in Pokéstar Studios
Ghost Movie Master	Release the full series of *Ghost Eraser* in Pokéstar Studios
Hero Ending	Release *Brycen-Man Strikes Back Harder* in Pokéstar Studios
Popular Movie Star	Release all movies in Pokéstar Studios
Masterpiece Star	Release all movies with happy endings in Pokéstar Studios
Blockbuster Star	Reach 100 billion box sales in Pokéstar Studios
First Cult Classic	Release a movie with a weird ending in Pokéstar Studios for the first time
Cult Classic Star	Release all movies with weird endings in Pokéstar Studios
10 People Funfest	Play an Entralink Funfest Mission with 10 people or more
30 People Funfest	Play an Entralink Funfest Mission with 30 people or more
Scored 100	Score 100 or more points in an Entralink Funfest Mission
Scored 1,000	Score 1,000 or more points in an Entralink Funfest Mission
Mission Host Lv. 1	Host 10 or more Entralink Funfest Missions
Mission Host Lv. 2	Host 50 or more Entralink Funfest Missions
Participant Lv. 1	Participate in an Entralink Funfest Mission for the first time
Participant Lv. 2	Participate in 10 or more Entralink Funfest Missions
Achiever Lv. 1	Clear 30 or more Entralink Funfest Missions
Achiever Lv. 2	Clear 100 or more Entralink Funfest Missions
Funfest Complete	Clear all Entralink Funfest Missions
Good Night	Use Game Sync to wake up a tucked-in Pokémon
Beginning of Memory	Use Memory Link and see a link event for the first time
Memory Master	Use Memory Link and see all the link events
Entertainment Master	Obtain the other 74 Entertainment Medals

Challenge Medals

Name	How to Obtain
Normal-type Champ	Win the Pokémon League and enter the Hall of Fame with only Normal-type Pokémon
Fire-type Champ	Win the Pokémon League and enter the Hall of Fame with only Fire-type Pokémon
Water-type Champ	Win the Pokémon League and enter the Hall of Fame with only Water-type Pokémon
Electric-type Champ	Win the Pokémon League and enter the Hall of Fame with only Electric-type Pokémon
Grass-type Champ	Win the Pokémon League and enter the Hall of Fame with only Grass-type Pokémon
Ice-type Champ	Win the Pokémon League and enter the Hall of Fame with only Ice-type Pokémon
Fighting-type Champ	Win the Pokémon League and enter the Hall of Fame with only Fighting-type Pokémon
Poison-type Champ	Win the Pokémon League and enter the Hall of Fame with only Poison-type Pokémon
Ground-type Champ	Win the Pokémon League and enter the Hall of Fame with only Ground-type Pokémon
Flying-type Champ	Win the Pokémon League and enter the Hall of Fame with only Flying-type Pokémon
Psychic-type Champ	Win the Pokémon League and enter the Hall of Fame with only Psychic-type Pokémon
Bug-type Champ	Win the Pokémon League and enter the Hall of Fame with only Bug-type Pokémon
Rock-type Champ	Win the Pokémon League and enter the Hall of Fame with only Rock-type Pokémon
Ghost-type Champ	Win the Pokémon League and enter the Hall of Fame with only Ghost-type Pokémon
Dragon-type Champ	Win the Pokémon League and enter the Hall of Fame with only Dragon-type Pokémon
Dark-type Champ	Win the Pokémon League and enter the Hall of Fame with only Dark-type Pokémon
Steel-type Champ	Win the Pokémon League and enter the Hall of Fame with only Steel-type Pokémon
One and Only	Win the Pokémon League and enter the Hall of Fame with only one Pokémon in your party
Supreme Challenger	Obtain the other 18 Challenge Medals

Pokémon Musical Props

Props for the Head

Prop	Style	How to obtain
Beret 	Unique	Receive from a fan after participating in a musical
Big Barrette 	Cute	Receive from a fan after participating in a musical
Chef's Hat 	Cool	Receive from a fan after participating in a musical
Cowboy Hat 	Cool	Receive from a fan after participating in a musical
Crown 	Elegant	Talk to the owner after getting the highest reviews five or more times
Decorative Ribbon 	Cute	Receive from a fan after participating in a musical
Fedora 	Cute	Receive from a fan after participating in a musical
Gentleman's Hat 	Elegant	Receive from a fan after participating in a musical
Headband 	Cute	Receive from a fan after participating in a musical
Helmet 	Unique	Receive from a fan after participating in a musical
Horned Helm 	Cool	Receive from a fan after participating in a musical
Jester's Cap 	Unique	Receive from a fan after participating in a musical
Lace Cap 	Elegant	Receive from a fan after participating in a musical
Laurel Wreath 	Elegant	Receive from a fan after participating in a musical
Pirate Hat 	Cool	Receive from a fan after participating in a musical
Professor Hat 	Unique	Receive from a fan after participating in a musical
Scarlet Hat 	Unique	Receive from the old man who loves musicals in Opelucid City
Straw Hat 	Unique	Receive from a fan after participating in a musical
Tiara 	Elegant	Talk to the owner after participating in a musical with friends via IR or wireless
Top Hat 	Elegant	Get right away
Wig 	Cool	Receive from a fan after participating in a musical
Windup Key 	Unique	Receive from a fan after participating in a musical
Witchy Hat 	Unique	Receive from a fan after participating in a musical

Props for the Ears

Prop	Style	How to obtain
Blue Barrette 	Cute	Get right away
Blue Flower 	Cute	Receive from a fan after participating in a musical
Gorgeous Flower 	Elegant	Receive from a fan after participating in a musical
Green Barrette 	Unique	Get right away
Pink Barrette 	Cute	Get right away
Red Barrette 	Cute	Receive from a fan after participating in a musical
Red Flower 	Cute	Receive from a fan after participating in a musical
Small Barrette 	Cute	Get right away
Snow Crystal 	Elegant	Receive from a fan after participating in a musical
Striped Barrette 	Cute	Receive from a fan after participating in a musical

Props for the Face

Prop	Style	How to obtain
Fluffy Beard	Elegant	Receive from the old man who loves musicals in Opelucid City
Germ Mask 	Unique	Receive from a fan after participating in a musical
Googly Specs 	Unique	Receive from a fan after participating in a musical
Gorgeous Specs 	Elegant	Receive from a fan after participating in a musical
Monocle 	Elegant	Receive from a fan after participating in a musical
Red Nose 	Unique	Receive from a fan after participating in a musical
Smiley-Face Mask 	Unique	Receive from a fan after participating in a musical
Square Glasses 	Elegant	Get right away
White Domino Mask 	Cool	Receive from a fan after participating in a musical

Props for the Arms

Prop	Style	How to obtain
Big Bag 	Unique	Receive from the old man who loves musicals in Opelucid City
Bouquet 	Elegant	Receive from a fan after participating in a musical
Candy 	Cute	Receive from a fan after participating in a musical
Cane 	Elegant	Get right away
Colorful Parasol 	Cute	Receive from a fan after participating in a musical
Electric Guitar 	Cool	Defeat Musician Preston on Route 5
Fake Bone 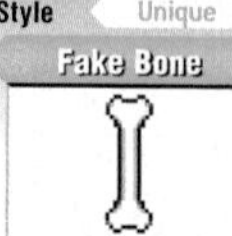	Unique	Receive from a fan after participating in a musical
Football 	Cool	Receive from a fan after participating in a musical
Frying Pan 	Cool	Receive from a fan after participating in a musical
Gift Box 	Cute	Receive from the old man who loves musicals in Opelucid City

Ladle
Style: Unique

How to obtain: Receive from a fan after participating in a musical

Lantern
Style: Cool

How to obtain: Receive from a fan after participating in a musical

Lonely Flower
Style: Elegant

How to obtain: Receive from a fan after participating in a musical

Magic Wand
Style: Unique

How to obtain: Receive from a fan after participating in a musical

Mallet
Style: Unique

How to obtain: Receive from a fan after participating in a musical

Maraca
Style: Unique

How to obtain: Get right away

Microphone
Style: Cute

How to obtain: Get right away

Paintbrush
Style: Unique

How to obtain: Receive from a fan after participating in a musical

Pennant
Style: Unique
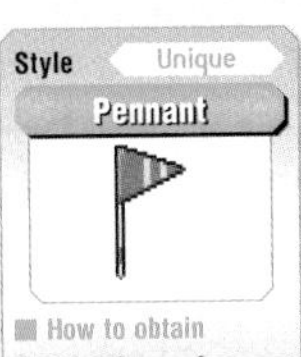
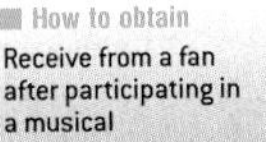
How to obtain: Receive from a fan after participating in a musical

Pocket Watch
Style: Elegant

How to obtain: Receive from a fan after participating in a musical

Purse
Style: Cute

How to obtain: Receive from a fan after participating in a musical

Racket
Style: Cool

How to obtain: Get right away

Red Parasol
Style: Cute

How to obtain: Get right away

Rigid Shield
Style: Cool

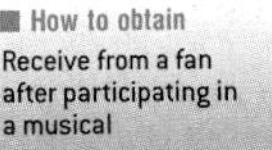
How to obtain: Receive from a fan after participating in a musical

Rose
Style: Elegant
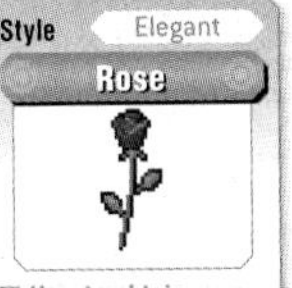
How to obtain: Receive from a fan after participating in a musical

Round Mushroom
Style: Unique

How to obtain: Receive from a fan after participating in a musical

Shuriken
Style: Cool

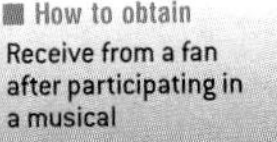
How to obtain: Receive from a fan after participating in a musical

Standing Mike
Style: Cool

How to obtain: Receive from a fan after participating in a musical

Tambourine
Style: Cute

How to obtain: Receive from a fan after participating in a musical

Thick Book
Style: Unique

How to obtain: Receive from a fan after participating in a musical

Toy Cake
Style: Cute

How to obtain: Talk to the owner on your birthday registered in your Nintendo DS system

Toy Cutlass
Style: Cool

How to obtain: Receive from a fan after participating in a musical

Toy Fishing Rod
Style: Cool

How to obtain: Receive from a fan after participating in a musical

Toy Sword
Style: Cool

How to obtain: Receive from a fan after participating in a musical

Trident
Style: Cool

How to obtain: Receive from a fan after participating in a musical

Trumpet
Style: Elegant

How to obtain: Receive from a fan after participating in a musical

Whisk
Style: Cute

How to obtain: Receive from a fan after participating in a musical

White Pompom
Style: Cute

How to obtain: Receive from a fan after participating in a musical

Wrench
Style: Cool

How to obtain: Receive from a fan after participating in a musical

Props for the Waist

Fake Bellybutton
Style: Unique
How to obtain: Receive from a fan after participating in a musical

Frilly Apron
Style: Elegant

How to obtain: Receive from a fan after participating in a musical

Hula Skirt
Style: Unique

How to obtain: Get right away

Umber Belt
Style: Cool

How to obtain: Get right away

Winner's Belt
Style: Cool

How to obtain: Talk to the owner after getting the highest reviews 10 or more times

Props for the Body

Bib
Style: Cute

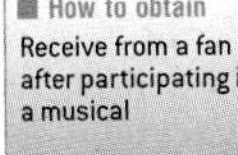
How to obtain: Receive from a fan after participating in a musical

Black Cape
Style: Elegant

How to obtain: Receive from a fan after participating in a musical

Black Tie
Style: Elegant

How to obtain: Receive from a fan after participating in a musical

Black Wings
Style: Cool

How to obtain: Receive from a fan after participating in a musical

Bow Tie
Style: Elegant

How to obtain: Get right away

Crimson Scarf
Style: Cute

How to obtain: Receive from a fan after participating in a musical

Dressy Tie
Style: Elegant

How to obtain: Receive from a fan after participating in a musical

Necklace
Style: Elegant

How to obtain: Receive from a fan after participating in a musical

Round Button
Style: Cute

How to obtain: Receive from a fan after participating in a musical

Scarlet Cape
Style: Cool

How to obtain: Receive from a fan after participating in a musical

Striped Tie
Style: Cool

How to obtain: Receive from a fan after participating in a musical

Tie
Style: Cool

How to obtain: Get right away

White Cape
Style: Elegant

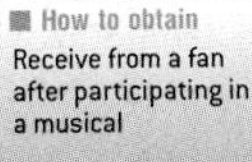
How to obtain: Receive from a fan after participating in a musical

White Wings
Style: Cute

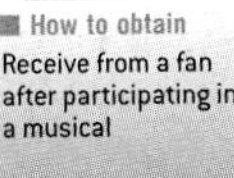
How to obtain: Receive from a fan after participating in a musical

How and Where to Meet Special Pokémon

How and Where to Meet Special Pokémon

National Pokédex No.	Pokémon	Level	Location	Item Needed	Conditions to Appear
377	Regirock	65	Clay Tunnel Rock Peak Chamber	—	—
378	Regice	65	Clay Tunnel Iceberg Chamber	—	Change the Key System setting to Iceberg Chamber with Unova Link's Key System.
379	Registeel	65	Clay Tunnel Iron Chamber	—	Change the Key System setting to Iron Chamber with Unova Link's Key System.
380	Latias	68	Dreamyard (*Pokémon White Version 2*)	—	—
381	Latios	68	Dreamyard (*Pokémon Black Version 2*)	—	—
480	Uxie	65	Nacrene City	—	After meeting it in the Cave of Being
481	Mesprit	65	Celestial Tower	—	After meeting it in the Cave of Being
482	Azelf	65	Route 23	—	After meeting it in the Cave of Being
485	Heatran	68	Reversal Mountain	Magma Stone	—
486	Regigigas	68	Twist Mountain	—	Put Regirock, Regice, and Registeel in your party
488	Cresselia	68	Marvelous Bridge	Lunar Wing	—
593	Jellicent ♂ (Hidden Ability)	40	Undella Bay (*Pokémon Black Version 2*)	—	Every Monday
593	Jellicent ♀ (Hidden Ability)	40	Undella Bay (*Pokémon White Version 2*)	—	Every Thursday
612	Haxorus (Shiny)	60	Nature Preserve	—	—
628	Braviary (Hidden Ability)	25	Route 4 (*Pokémon White Version 2*)	—	Every Monday
630	Mandibuzz (Hidden Ability)	25	Route 4 (*Pokémon Black Version 2*)	—	Every Thursday
637	Volcarona	35 (65)	Relic Castle Lowest floor, deepest room	—	—
638	Cobalion	45 (65)	Route 13	—	—
639	Terrakion	45 (65)	Route 22	—	—
640	Virizion	45 (65)	Route 11	—	—
643	Reshiram	70	Dragonspiral Tower Seventh Floor (*Pokémon White Version 2*)	—	—
644	Zekrom	70	Dragonspiral Tower Seventh Floor (*Pokémon Black Version 2*)	—	—
646	Kyurem	70	Giant Chasm Cave's Deepest Part	—	—

How to meet it again if you defeat it in battle	How to meet it again if you run from battle	How to meet it again if you lose the battle
Defeat the Elite Four and the Champion at the Pokémon League (comes back until you catch it)	Defeat the Elite Four and the Champion at the Pokémon League (comes back until you catch it)	Return for a rematch after being returned to the Pokémon Center
Defeat the Elite Four and the Champion at the Pokémon League (comes back until you catch it)	Defeat the Elite Four and the Champion at the Pokémon League (comes back until you catch it)	Return for a rematch after being returned to the Pokémon Center
Defeat the Elite Four and the Champion at the Pokémon League (comes back until you catch it)	Defeat the Elite Four and the Champion at the Pokémon League (comes back until you catch it)	Return for a rematch after being returned to the Pokémon Center
Defeat the Elite Four and the Champion at the Pokémon League (comes back until you catch it)	Defeat the Elite Four and the Champion at the Pokémon League (comes back until you catch it)	Return for a rematch after being returned to the Pokémon Center
Defeat the Elite Four and the Champion at the Pokémon League (comes back until you catch it)	Defeat the Elite Four and the Champion at the Pokémon League (comes back until you catch it)	Return for a rematch after being returned to the Pokémon Center
Defeat the Elite Four and the Champion at the Pokémon League (comes back until you catch it)	Defeat the Elite Four and the Champion at the Pokémon League (comes back until you catch it)	Return for a rematch after being returned to the Pokémon Center
Defeat the Elite Four and the Champion at the Pokémon League (comes back until you catch it)	Defeat the Elite Four and the Champion at the Pokémon League (comes back until you catch it)	Return for a rematch after being returned to the Pokémon Center
Defeat the Elite Four and the Champion at the Pokémon League (comes back until you catch it)	Defeat the Elite Four and the Champion at the Pokémon League (comes back until you catch it)	Return for a rematch after being returned to the Pokémon Center
Defeat the Elite Four and the Champion at the Pokémon League (comes back until you catch it)	Defeat the Elite Four and the Champion at the Pokémon League (comes back until you catch it)	Return for a rematch after being returned to the Pokémon Center
Defeat the Elite Four and the Champion at the Pokémon League (comes back until you catch it)	Defeat the Elite Four and the Champion at the Pokémon League (comes back until you catch it)	Return for a rematch after being returned to the Pokémon Center
Defeat the Elite Four and the Champion at the Pokémon League (comes back until you catch it)	Defeat the Elite Four and the Champion at the Pokémon League (comes back until you catch it)	Return for a rematch after being returned to the Pokémon Center
Go to Undella Bay on the next Monday	Go to Undella Bay on the next Monday	Return for a rematch after being returned to the Pokémon Center
Go to Undella Bay on the next Thursday	Go to Undella Bay on the next Thursday	Return for a rematch after being returned to the Pokémon Center
Defeat the Elite Four and the Champion at the Pokémon League (comes back until you catch it)	Defeat the Elite Four and the Champion at the Pokémon League (comes back until you catch it)	Return for a rematch after being returned to the Pokémon Center
Go to Route 4 on the next Monday	Go to Route 4 on the next Monday	Return for a rematch after being returned to the Pokémon Center
Go to Route 4 on the next Thursday	Go to Route 4 on the next Thursday	Return for a rematch after being returned to the Pokémon Center
Defeat the Elite Four and the Champion at the Pokémon League (comes back until you catch it) When it comes back, its level goes up to Lv. 65.	Defeat the Elite Four and the Champion at the Pokémon League (comes back until you catch it) When it comes back, its level goes up to Lv. 65.	Return for a rematch after being returned to the Pokémon Center
Defeat the Elite Four and the Champion at the Pokémon League (comes back until you catch it) When it comes back, its level goes up to Lv. 65.	Defeat the Elite Four and the Champion at the Pokémon League (comes back until you catch it) When it comes back, its level goes up to Lv. 65.	Return for a rematch after being returned to the Pokémon Center
Defeat the Elite Four and the Champion at the Pokémon League (comes back until you catch it) When it comes back, its level goes up to Lv. 65.	Defeat the Elite Four and the Champion at the Pokémon League (comes back until you catch it) When it comes back, its level goes up to Lv. 65.	Return for a rematch after being returned to the Pokémon Center
Defeat the Elite Four and the Champion at the Pokémon League (comes back until you catch it) When it comes back, its level goes up to Lv. 65.	Defeat the Elite Four and the Champion at the Pokémon League (comes back until you catch it) When it comes back, its level goes up to Lv. 65.	Return for a rematch after being returned to the Pokémon Center
Defeat the Elite Four and the Champion at the Pokémon League (comes back until you catch it)	Defeat the Elite Four and the Champion at the Pokémon League (comes back until you catch it)	Return for a rematch after being returned to the Pokémon Center
Defeat the Elite Four and the Champion at the Pokémon League (comes back until you catch it)	Defeat the Elite Four and the Champion at the Pokémon League (comes back until you catch it)	Return for a rematch after being returned to the Pokémon Center
Defeat the Elite Four and the Champion at the Pokémon League (comes back until you catch it)	Defeat the Elite Four and the Champion at the Pokémon League (comes back until you catch it)	Return for a rematch after being returned to the Pokémon Center

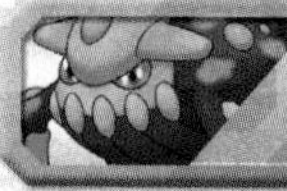

Pokémon Weakness Chart—National Pokédex

A

Pokémon	Type		Ability		Hidden Ability	Weak against these move types							X Immune to these move types		
Abomasnow	Grass	Ice	Snow Warning		Soundproof	★Fire	Fighting	Poison	Flying	Bug	Rock	Steel			
Abra	Psychic		Synchronize	Inner Focus	Magic Guard	Bug	Ghost	Dark							
Absol	Dark		Pressure	Super Luck	Justified	Fighting	Bug						Psychic		
Accelgor	Bug		Hydration	Sticky Hold	Unburden	Fire	Flying	Rock							
Aerodactyl	Rock	Flying	Rock Head	Pressure	Unnerve	Water	Electric	Ice	Rock	Steel			Ground		
Aggron	Steel	Rock	Sturdy	Rock Head	Heavy Metal	★Fighting	★Ground	Water					Poison		
Aipom	Normal		Run Away	Pickup		Fighting							Ghost		
Alakazam	Psychic		Synchronize	Inner Focus	Magic Guard	Bug	Ghost	Dark							
Alomomola	Water		Healer	Hydration	Regenerator	Grass	Electric								
Altaria	Dragon	Flying	Natural Cure		Cloud Nine	★Ice	Rock	Dragon					Ground		
Ambipom	Normal		Technician	Pickup		Fighting							Ghost		
Amoonguss	Grass	Poison	Effect Spore		Regenerator	Fire	Ice	Flying	Psychic						
Ampharos	Electric		Static		Plus	Ground									
Anorith	Rock	Bug	Battle Armor		Swift Swim	Water	Rock	Steel							
Arbok	Poison		Intimidate	Shed Skin		Ground	Psychic								
Arcanine	Fire		Intimidate	Flash Fire	Justified	Water	Ground	Rock					Fire♦2		
Arceus	Bug		Multitype			Fire	Flying	Rock							
Arceus	Dark		Multitype			Fighting	Bug						Psychic		
Arceus	Dragon		Multitype			Ice	Dragon								
Arceus	Electric		Multitype			Ground									
Arceus	Fighting		Multitype			Flying	Psychic								
Arceus	Fire		Multitype			Water	Ground	Rock							
Arceus	Flying		Multitype			Electric	Ice	Rock					Ground		
Arceus	Ghost		Multitype			Ghost	Dark						Normal	Fighting	
Arceus	Grass		Multitype			Fire	Ice	Poison	Flying	Bug					
Arceus	Ground		Multitype			Water	Grass	Ice					Electric		
Arceus	Ice		Multitype			Fire	Fighting	Rock	Steel						
Arceus	Normal		Multitype			Fighting							Ghost		
Arceus	Poison		Multitype			Ground	Psychic								
Arceus	Psychic		Multitype			Bug	Ghost	Dark							
Arceus	Rock		Multitype			Water	Grass	Fighting	Ground	Steel					
Arceus	Steel		Multitype			Fire	Fighting	Ground					Poison		
Arceus	Water		Multitype			Grass	Electric								
Archeops	Rock	Flying	Defeatist			Water	Electric	Ice	Rock	Steel			Ground		
Ariados	Bug	Poison	Swarm	Insomnia	Sniper	Fire	Flying	Psychic	Rock						
Armaldo	Rock	Bug	Battle Armor		Swift Swim	Water	Rock	Steel							
Aron	Steel	Rock	Sturdy	Rock Head	Heavy Metal	★Fighting	★Ground	Water					Poison		
Articuno	Ice	Flying	Pressure			★Rock	Fire	Electric	Steel				Ground		
Audino	Normal		Healer	Regenerator		Fighting							Ghost		
Axew	Dragon		Rivalry	Mold Breaker	Unnerve	Ice	Dragon								
Azelf	Psychic		Levitate			Bug	Ghost	Dark					Ground♦1		
Azumarill	Water		Thick Fat	Huge Power	Sap Sipper	Grass	Electric						Grass♦4		
Azurill	Normal		Thick Fat	Huge Power	Sap Sipper	Fighting							Ghost	Grass♦4	

B

Pokémon	Type		Ability		Hidden Ability	Weak against these move types							X Immune to these move types		
Bagon	Dragon		Rock Head		Sheer Force	Ice	Dragon								
Baltoy	Ground	Psychic	Levitate			Water	Grass	Ice	Bug	Ghost	Dark		Electric	Ground♦1	
Banette	Ghost		Insomnia	Frisk	Cursed Body	Ghost	Dark						Normal	Fighting	
Barboach	Water	Ground	Oblivious	Anticipation	Hydration	★Grass							Electric		
Basculin (Blue-Striped Form)	Water		Rock Head	Adaptability	Mold Breaker	Grass	Electric								
Basculin (Red-Striped Form)	Water		Reckless	Adaptability	Mold Breaker	Grass	Electric								
Bastiodon	Rock	Steel	Sturdy		Soundproof	★Fighting	★Ground	Water					Poison		
Bayleef	Grass		Overgrow			Fire	Ice	Poison	Flying	Bug					
Beartic	Ice		Snow Cloak		Swift Swim	Fire	Fighting	Rock	Steel						
Beautifly	Bug	Flying	Swarm			★Rock	Fire	Electric	Ice	Flying			Ground		
Beedrill	Bug	Poison	Swarm		Sniper	Fire	Flying	Psychic	Rock						
Beheeyem	Psychic		Telepathy	Synchronize	Analytic	Bug	Ghost	Dark							
Beldum	Steel	Psychic	Clear Body		Light Metal	Fire	Ground						Poison		
Bellossom	Grass		Chlorophyll		Healer	Fire	Ice	Poison	Flying	Bug					
Bellsprout	Grass	Poison	Chlorophyll		Gluttony	Fire	Ice	Flying	Psychic						
Bibarel	Normal	Water	Simple	Unaware	Moody	Grass	Electric	Fighting					Ghost		
Bidoof	Normal		Simple	Unaware	Moody	Fighting							Ghost		
Bisharp	Dark	Steel	Defiant	Inner Focus	Pressure	★Fighting	Fire	Ground					Poison	Psychic	
Blastoise	Water		Torrent		Rain Dish	Grass	Electric								
Blaziken	Fire	Fighting	Blaze		Speed Boost	Water	Ground	Flying	Psychic						
Blissey	Normal		Natural Cure	Serene Grace	Healer	Fighting							Ghost		
Blitzle	Electric		Lightningrod	Motor Drive	Sap Sipper	Ground							Electric♦1	Grass♦4	
Boldore	Rock		Sturdy		Sand Force	Water	Grass	Fighting	Ground	Steel					
Bonsly	Rock		Sturdy	Rock Head	Rattled	Water	Grass	Fighting	Ground	Steel					
Bouffalant	Normal		Reckless	Sap Sipper	Soundproof	Fighting							Ghost	Grass♦2	
Braviary	Normal	Flying	Keen Eye	Sheer Force	Defiant	Electric	Ice	Rock					Ground	Ghost	
Breloom	Grass	Fighting	Effect Spore	Poison Heal	Technician	★Flying	Fire	Ice	Poison	Psychic					
Bronzong	Steel	Psychic	Levitate	Heatproof	Heavy Metal	Fire	Ground♦3						Poison		
Bronzor	Steel	Psychic	Levitate	Heatproof	Heavy Metal	Fire	Ground♦3						Poison		
Budew	Grass	Poison	Natural Cure	Poison Point		Fire	Ice	Flying	Psychic						
Buizel	Water		Swift Swim		Water Veil	Grass	Electric								
Bulbasaur	Grass	Poison	Overgrow		Chlorophyll	Fire	Ice	Flying	Psychic						
Buneary	Normal		Run Away	Klutz	Limber	Fighting							Ghost		
Burmy	Bug		Shed Skin		Overcoat	Fire	Flying	Rock							
Butterfree	Bug	Flying	Compoundeyes		Tinted Lens	★Rock	Fire	Electric	Ice	Flying			Ground		

C

Pokémon	Type		Ability		Hidden Ability	Weak against these move types							X Immune to these move types		
Cacnea	Grass		Sand Veil		Water Absorb	Fire	Ice	Poison	Flying	Bug			Water♦4		
Cacturne	Grass	Dark	Sand Veil		Water Absorb	★Bug	Fire	Ice	Fighting	Poison	Flying		Psychic	Water♦4	
Camerupt	Fire	Ground	Magma Armor	Solid Rock	Anger Point	★Water	Ground						Electric		
Carnivine	Grass		Levitate			Fire	Ice	Poison	Flying	Bug			Ground♦1		
Carracosta	Water	Rock	Solid Rock	Sturdy	Swift Swim	★Grass	Electric	Fighting	Ground						
Carvanha	Water	Dark	Rough Skin		Speed Boost	Grass	Electric	Fighting	Bug				Psychic		
Cascoon	Bug		Shed Skin			Fire	Flying	Rock							
Castform (Normal)	Normal		Forecast			Fighting							Ghost		
Castform (Rainy Form)	Water		Forecast			Grass	Electric								
Castform (Snowy Form)	Ice		Forecast			Fighting	Rock	Steel							
Castform (Sunny Form)	Fire		Forecast			Water	Ground	Rock							
Caterpie	Bug		Shield Dust		Run Away	Fire	Flying	Rock							
Celebi	Psychic	Grass	Natural Cure			★Bug	Fire	Ice	Poison	Flying	Ghost	Dark			
Chandelure	Ghost	Fire	Flash Fire	Flame Body		Water	Ground	Rock	Ghost	Dark			Normal	Fighting	Fire♦2
Chansey	Normal		Natural Cure	Serene Grace	Healer	Fighting							Ghost		
Charizard	Fire	Flying	Blaze		Solar Power	★Rock	Water	Electric					Ground		
Charmander	Fire		Blaze		Solar Power	Water	Ground	Rock							
Charmeleon	Fire		Blaze		Solar Power	Water	Ground	Rock							
Chatot	Normal	Flying	Keen Eye	Tangled Feet	Big Pecks	Electric	Ice	Rock					Ground	Ghost	

★ Deals 4 times damage. ♦ 1 Ability prevents damage. ♦ 2 May deal damage depending on the Pokémon's Ability. ♦ 3 Damage may be prevented depending on the Pokémon's Ability. ♦ 4 Hidden Ability prevents damage.

Pokémon	Type		Ability		Hidden Ability	Weak against these move types							X Immune to these move types		
Cherrim	Grass		Flower Gift			Fire	Ice	Poison	Flying	Bug					
Cherubi	Grass		Chlorophyll			Fire	Ice	Poison	Flying	Bug					
Chikorita	Grass		Overgrow			Fire	Ice	Poison	Flying	Bug					
Chimchar	Fire		Blaze		Iron Fist	Water	Ground	Rock							
Chimecho	Psychic		Levitate			Bug	Ghost	Dark					Ground♦1		
Chinchou	Water	Electric	Volt Absorb	Illuminate	Water Absorb	Grass	Ground						Electric♦2	Water♦4	
Chingling	Psychic		Levitate			Bug	Ghost	Dark					Ground♦1		
Cinccino	Normal		Cute Charm	Technician	Skill Link	Fighting							Ghost		
Clamperl	Water		Shell Armor		Rattled	Grass	Electric								
Claydol	Ground	Psychic	Levitate			Water	Grass	Ice	Bug	Ghost	Dark		Electric	Ground♦1	
Clefable	Normal		Cute Charm	Magic Guard	Unaware	Fighting							Ghost		
Clefairy	Normal		Cute Charm	Magic Guard	Friend Guard	Fighting							Ghost		
Cleffa	Normal		Cute Charm	Magic Guard	Friend Guard	Fighting							Ghost		
Cloyster	Water	Ice	Shell Armor	Skill Link	Overcoat	Grass	Electric	Fighting	Rock						
Cobalion	Steel	Fighting	Justified			Fire	Fighting	Ground					Poison		
Cofagrigus	Ghost		Mummy			Ghost	Dark						Normal	Fighting	
Combee	Bug	Flying	Honey Gather		Hustle	★Rock	Fire	Electric	Ice	Flying			Ground		
Combusken	Fire	Fighting	Blaze		Speed Boost	Water	Ground	Flying	Psychic						
Conkeldurr	Fighting		Guts	Sheer Force		Flying	Psychic								
Corphish	Water		Hyper Cutter	Shell Armor	Adaptability	Grass	Electric								
Corsola	Water	Rock	Hustle	Natural Cure	Regenerator	★Grass	Electric	Fighting	Ground						
Cottonee	Grass		Prankster	Infiltrator	Chlorophyll	Fire	Ice	Poison	Flying	Bug					
Cradily	Rock	Grass	Suction Cups		Storm Drain	Ice	Fighting	Bug	Steel				Water♦4		
Cranidos	Rock		Mold Breaker		Sheer Force	Water	Grass	Fighting	Ground	Steel					
Crawdaunt	Water	Dark	Hyper Cutter	Shell Armor	Adaptability	Grass	Electric	Fighting	Bug				Psychic		
Cresselia	Psychic		Levitate			Bug	Ghost	Dark					Ground♦1		
Croagunk	Poison	Fighting	Anticipation	Dry Skin	Poison Touch	★Psychic	Ground	Flying					Water♦2		
Crobat	Poison	Flying	Inner Focus		Infiltrator	Electric	Ice	Psychic	Rock				Ground		
Croconaw	Water		Torrent			Grass	Electric								
Crustle	Bug	Rock	Sturdy	Shell Armor	Weak Armor	Water	Rock	Steel							
Cryogonal	Ice		Levitate			Fire	Fighting	Rock	Steel				Ground♦1		
Cubchoo	Ice		Snow Cloak		Rattled	Fire	Fighting	Rock	Steel						
Cubone	Ground		Rock Head	Lightningrod	Battle Armor	Water	Grass	Ice					Electric		
Cyndaquil	Fire		Blaze			Water	Ground	Rock							

D

Pokémon	Type		Ability		Hidden Ability	Weak against these move types							X Immune to these move types		
Darkrai	Dark		Bad Dreams			Fighting	Bug						Psychic		
Darmanitan (Standard Mode)	Fire		Sheer Force		Zen Mode	Water	Ground	Rock							
Darmanitan (Zen Mode)	Fire	Psychic			Zen Mode	Water	Ground	Rock	Ghost	Dark					
Darumaka	Fire		Hustle		Inner Focus	Water	Ground	Rock							
Deerling	Normal	Grass	Chlorophyll	Sap Sipper	Serene Grace	Fire	Ice	Fighting	Poison	Flying	Bug		Ghost	Grass♦2	
Deino	Dark	Dragon	Hustle			Ice	Fighting	Bug	Dragon				Psychic		
Delcatty	Normal		Cute Charm	Normalize	Wonder Skin	Fighting							Ghost		
Delibird	Ice	Flying	Vital Spirit	Hustle	Insomnia	★Rock	Fire	Electric	Steel				Ground		
Deoxys	Psychic		Pressure			Bug	Ghost	Dark							
Dewgong	Water	Ice	Thick Fat	Hydration	Ice Body	Grass	Electric	Fighting	Rock						
Dewott	Water		Torrent			Grass	Electric								
Dialga	Steel	Dragon	Pressure		Telepathy	Fighting	Ground						Poison		
Diglett	Ground		Sand Veil	Arena Trap	Sand Force	Water	Grass	Ice					Electric		
Ditto	Normal		Limber		Imposter	Fighting							Ghost		
Dodrio	Normal	Flying	Run Away	Early Bird	Tangled Feet	Electric	Ice	Rock					Ground	Ghost	
Doduo	Normal	Flying	Run Away	Early Bird	Tangled Feet	Electric	Ice	Rock					Ground	Ghost	
Donphan	Ground		Sturdy		Sand Veil	Water	Grass	Ice					Electric		
Dragonair	Dragon		Shed Skin		Marvel Scale	Ice	Dragon								
Dragonite	Dragon	Flying	Inner Focus		Multiscale	★Ice	Rock	Dragon					Ground		
Drapion	Poison	Dark	Battle Armor	Sniper	Keen Eye	Ground							Psychic		
Dratini	Dragon		Shed Skin		Marvel Scale	Ice	Dragon								
Drifblim	Ghost	Flying	Aftermath	Unburden	Flare Boost	Electric	Ice	Rock	Ghost	Dark			Normal	Fighting	Ground
Drifloon	Ghost	Flying	Aftermath	Unburden	Flare Boost	Electric	Ice	Rock	Ghost	Dark			Normal	Fighting	Ground
Drilbur	Ground		Sand Rush	Sand Force	Mold Breaker	Water	Grass	Ice					Electric		
Drowzee	Psychic		Insomnia	Forewarn	Inner Focus	Bug	Ghost	Dark							
Druddigon	Dragon		Rough Skin	Sheer Force	Mold Breaker	Ice	Dragon								
Ducklett	Water	Flying	Keen Eye	Big Pecks	Hydration	★Electric	Rock						Ground		
Dugtrio	Ground		Sand Veil	Arena Trap	Sand Force	Water	Grass	Ice					Electric		
Dunsparce	Normal		Serene Grace	Run Away	Rattled	Fighting							Ghost		
Duosion	Psychic		Overcoat	Magic Guard	Regenerator	Bug	Ghost	Dark							
Durant	Bug	Steel	Swarm	Hustle	Truant	★Fire							Poison		
Dusclops	Ghost		Pressure			Ghost	Dark						Normal	Fighting	
Dusknoir	Ghost		Pressure			Ghost	Dark						Normal	Fighting	
Duskull	Ghost		Levitate			Ghost	Dark						Normal	Fighting	Ground♦1
Dustox	Bug	Poison	Shield Dust			Fire	Flying	Psychic	Rock						
Dwebble	Bug	Rock	Sturdy	Shell Armor	Weak Armor	Water	Rock	Steel							

E

Pokémon	Type		Ability		Hidden Ability	Weak against these move types							X Immune to these move types		
Eelektrik	Electric		Levitate										Ground♦1		
Eelektross	Electric		Levitate										Ground♦1		
Eevee	Normal		Run Away	Adaptability	Anticipation	Fighting							Ghost		
Ekans	Poison		Intimidate	Shed Skin		Ground	Psychic								
Electabuzz	Electric		Static		Vital Spirit	Ground									
Electivire	Electric		Motor Drive		Vital Spirit	Ground							Electric♦1		
Electrike	Electric		Static	Lightningrod	Minus	Ground							Electric♦2		
Electrode	Electric		Soundproof	Static	Aftermath	Ground									
Elekid	Electric		Static		Vital Spirit	Ground									
Elgyem	Psychic		Telepathy	Synchronize	Analytic	Bug	Ghost	Dark							
Emboar	Fire	Fighting	Blaze			Water	Ground	Flying	Psychic						
Emolga	Electric	Flying	Static		Motor Drive	Ice	Rock						Ground	Electric♦4	
Empoleon	Water	Steel	Torrent		Defiant	Electric	Fighting	Ground					Poison		
Entei	Fire		Pressure			Water	Ground	Rock							
Escavalier	Bug	Steel	Swarm	Shell Armor	Overcoat	★Fire							Poison		
Espeon	Psychic		Synchronize		Magic Bounce	Bug	Ghost	Dark							
Excadrill	Ground	Steel	Sand Rush	Sand Force	Mold Breaker	Fire	Water	Fighting	Ground				Electric	Poison	
Exeggcute	Grass	Psychic	Chlorophyll		Harvest	★Bug	Fire	Ice	Poison	Flying	Ghost	Dark			
Exeggutor	Grass	Psychic	Chlorophyll		Harvest	★Bug	Fire	Ice	Poison	Flying	Ghost	Dark			
Exploud	Normal		Soundproof		Scrappy	Fighting							Ghost		

F

Pokémon	Type		Ability		Hidden Ability	Weak against these move types							X Immune to these move types		
Farfetch'd	Normal	Flying	Keen Eye	Inner Focus	Defiant	Electric	Ice	Rock					Ground	Ghost	
Fearow	Normal	Flying	Keen Eye		Sniper	Electric	Ice	Rock					Ground	Ghost	
Feebas	Water		Swift Swim		Adaptability	Grass	Electric								
Feraligatr	Water		Torrent			Grass	Electric								
Ferroseed	Grass	Steel	Iron Barbs			★Fire	Fighting						Poison		

Pokémon Weakness Chart—National Pokédex

F

Pokémon	Type		Ability		Hidden Ability	Weak against these move types							X Immune to these move types		
Ferrothorn	Grass	Steel	Iron Barbs			★Fire	Fighting						Poison		
Finneon	Water		Swift Swim	Storm Drain	Water Veil	Grass	Electric						Water♦2		
Flaaffy	Electric		Static		Plus	Ground									
Flareon	Fire		Flash Fire		Guts	Water	Ground	Rock					Fire♦1		
Floatzel	Water		Swift Swim		Water Veil	Grass	Electric								
Flygon	Ground	Dragon	Levitate			★Ice	Dragon						Electric	Ground♦1	
Foongus	Grass	Poison	Effect Spore		Regenerator	Fire	Ice	Flying	Psychic						
Forretress	Bug	Steel	Sturdy			★Fire							Poison		
Fraxure	Dragon		Rivalry	Mold Breaker	Unnerve	Ice	Dragon								
Frillish	Water	Ghost	Water Absorb	Cursed Body	Damp	Grass	Electric	Ghost	Dark				Normal	Fighting	Water♦2
Froslass	Ice	Ghost	Snow Cloak		Cursed Body	Fire	Rock	Ghost	Dark	Steel			Normal	Fighting	
Furret	Normal		Run Away	Keen Eye	Frisk	Fighting							Ghost		

G

Pokémon	Type		Ability		Hidden Ability	Weak against these move types							X Immune to these move types		
Gabite	Dragon	Ground	Sand Veil		Rough Skin	★Ice	Dragon						Electric		
Gallade	Psychic	Fighting	Steadfast		Justified	Flying	Ghost								
Galvantula	Bug	Electric	Compoundeyes	Unnerve	Swarm	Fire	Rock								
Garbodor	Poison		Stench	Weak Armor	Aftermath	Ground	Psychic								
Garchomp	Dragon	Ground	Sand Veil		Rough Skin	★Ice	Dragon						Electric		
Gardevoir	Psychic		Synchronize	Trace	Telepathy	Bug	Ghost	Dark							
Gastly	Ghost	Poison	Levitate			Psychic	Ghost	Dark					Normal	Fighting	Ground♦1
Gastrodon	Water	Ground	Sticky Hold	Storm Drain	Sand Force	★Grass							Electric	Water♦2	
Genesect	Bug	Steel	Download			★Fire							Poison		
Gengar	Ghost	Poison	Levitate			Psychic	Ghost	Dark					Normal	Fighting	Ground♦1
Geodude	Rock	Ground	Rock Head	Sturdy	Sand Veil	★Water	★Grass	Ice	Fighting	Ground	Steel		Electric		
Gible	Dragon	Ground	Sand Veil		Rough Skin	★Ice	Dragon						Electric		
Gigalith	Rock		Sturdy		Sand Force	Water	Grass	Fighting	Ground	Steel					
Girafarig	Normal	Psychic	Inner Focus	Early Bird	Sap Sipper	Bug	Dark						Ghost	Grass♦4	
Giratina (Altered Forme)	Ghost	Dragon	Pressure		Telepathy	Ice	Ghost	Dragon	Dark				Normal	Fighting	
Giratina (Origin Forme)	Ghost	Dragon	Levitate			Ice	Ghost	Dragon	Dark				Normal	Fighting	Ground♦1
Glaceon	Ice		Snow Cloak		Ice Body	Fire	Fighting	Rock	Steel						
Glalie	Ice		Inner Focus	Ice Body	Moody	Fire	Fighting	Rock	Steel						
Glameow	Normal		Limber	Own Tempo	Keen Eye	Fighting							Ghost		
Gligar	Ground	Flying	Hyper Cutter	Sand Veil	Immunity	★Ice	Water						Electric	Ground	
Gliscor	Ground	Flying	Hyper Cutter	Sand Veil	Poison Heal	★Ice	Water						Electric	Ground	
Gloom	Grass	Poison	Chlorophyll		Stench	Fire	Ice	Flying	Psychic						
Golbat	Poison	Flying	Inner Focus		Infiltrator	Electric	Ice	Psychic	Rock				Ground		
Goldeen	Water		Swift Swim	Water Veil	Lightningrod	Grass	Electric						Electric♦4		
Golduck	Water		Damp	Cloud Nine	Swift Swim	Grass	Electric								
Golem	Rock	Ground	Rock Head	Sturdy	Sand Veil	★Water	★Grass	Ice	Fighting	Ground	Steel		Electric		
Golett	Ground	Ghost	Iron Fist	Klutz	No Guard	Water	Grass	Ice	Ghost	Dark			Normal	Electric	Fighting
Golurk	Ground	Ghost	Iron Fist	Klutz	No Guard	Water	Grass	Ice	Ghost	Dark			Normal	Electric	Fighting
Gorebyss	Water		Swift Swim		Hydration	Grass	Electric								
Gothita	Psychic		Frisk			Bug	Ghost	Dark							
Gothitelle	Psychic		Frisk		Shadow Tag	Bug	Ghost	Dark							
Gothorita	Psychic		Frisk		Shadow Tag	Bug	Ghost	Dark							
Granbull	Normal		Intimidate	Quick Feet	Rattled	Fighting							Ghost		
Graveler	Rock	Ground	Rock Head	Sturdy	Sand Veil	★Water	★Grass	Ice	Fighting	Ground	Steel		Electric		
Grimer	Poison		Stench	Sticky Hold	Poison Touch	Ground	Psychic								
Grotle	Grass		Overgrow		Shell Armor	Fire	Ice	Poison	Flying	Bug					
Groudon	Ground		Drought			Water	Grass	Ice					Electric		
Grovyle	Grass		Overgrow		Unburden	Fire	Ice	Poison	Flying	Bug					
Growlithe	Fire		Intimidate	Flash Fire	Justified	Water	Ground	Rock					Fire♦2		
Grumpig	Psychic		Thick Fat	Own Tempo	Gluttony	Bug	Ghost	Dark							
Gulpin	Poison		Liquid Ooze	Sticky Hold		Ground	Psychic								
Gurdurr	Fighting		Guts	Sheer Force		Flying	Psychic								
Gyarados	Water	Flying	Intimidate		Moxie	★Electric	Rock						Ground		

H

Pokémon	Type		Ability		Hidden Ability	Weak against these move types							X Immune to these move types		
Happiny	Normal		Natural Cure	Serene Grace	Friend Guard	Fighting							Ghost		
Hariyama	Fighting		Thick Fat	Guts	Sheer Force	Flying	Psychic								
Haunter	Ghost	Poison	Levitate			Psychic	Ghost	Dark					Normal	Fighting	Ground♦1
Haxorus	Dragon		Rivalry	Mold Breaker	Unnerve	Ice	Dragon								
Heatmor	Fire		Gluttony	Flash Fire	White Smoke	Water	Ground	Rock					Fire♦2		
Heatran	Fire	Steel	Flash Fire			★Ground	Water	Fighting					Poison	Fire♦1	
Heracross	Bug	Fighting	Swarm	Guts	Moxie	★Flying	Fire	Psychic							
Herdier	Normal		Intimidate	Sand Rush	Scrappy	Fighting							Ghost		
Hippopotas	Ground		Sand Stream		Sand Force	Water	Grass	Ice					Electric		
Hippowdon	Ground		Sand Stream		Sand Force	Water	Grass	Ice					Electric		
Hitmonchan	Fighting		Keen Eye	Iron Fist	Inner Focus	Flying	Psychic								
Hitmonlee	Fighting		Limber	Reckless	Unburden	Flying	Psychic								
Hitmontop	Fighting		Intimidate	Technician	Steadfast	Flying	Psychic								
Ho-Oh	Fire	Flying	Pressure		Regenerator	★Rock	Water	Electric					Ground		
Honchkrow	Dark	Flying	Insomnia	Super Luck	Moxie	Electric	Ice	Rock					Ground	Psychic	
Hoothoot	Normal	Flying	Insomnia	Keen Eye	Tinted Lens	Electric	Ice	Rock					Ground	Ghost	
Hoppip	Grass	Flying	Chlorophyll	Leaf Guard	Infiltrator	★Ice	Fire	Poison	Flying	Rock			Ground		
Horsea	Water		Swift Swim	Sniper	Damp	Grass	Electric								
Houndoom	Dark	Fire	Early Bird	Flash Fire	Unnerve	Water	Fighting	Ground	Rock				Psychic	Fire♦2	
Houndour	Dark	Fire	Early Bird	Flash Fire	Unnerve	Water	Fighting	Ground	Rock				Psychic	Fire♦2	
Huntail	Water		Swift Swim		Water Veil	Grass	Electric								
Hydreigon	Dark	Dragon	Levitate			Ice	Fighting	Bug	Dragon				Psychic	Ground♦1	
Hypno	Psychic		Insomnia	Forewarn	Inner Focus	Bug	Ghost	Dark							

I

Pokémon	Type		Ability		Hidden Ability	Weak against these move types							X Immune to these move types		
Igglybuff	Normal		Cute Charm		Friend Guard	Fighting							Ghost		
Illumise	Bug		Oblivious	Tinted Lens	Prankster	Fire	Flying	Rock							
Infernape	Fire	Fighting	Blaze		Iron Fist	Water	Ground	Flying	Psychic						
Ivysaur	Grass	Poison	Overgrow		Chlorophyll	Fire	Ice	Flying	Psychic						

J

Pokémon	Type		Ability		Hidden Ability	Weak against these move types							X Immune to these move types		
Jellicent	Water	Ghost	Water Absorb	Cursed Body	Damp	Grass	Electric	Ghost	Dark				Normal	Fighting	Water♦2
Jigglypuff	Normal		Cute Charm		Friend Guard	Fighting							Ghost		
Jirachi	Steel	Psychic	Serene Grace			Fire	Ground						Poison		
Jolteon	Electric		Volt Absorb		Quick Feet	Ground							Electric♦1		
Joltik	Bug	Electric	Compoundeyes	Unnerve	Swarm	Fire	Rock								
Jumpluff	Grass	Flying	Chlorophyll	Leaf Guard	Infiltrator	★Ice	Fire	Poison	Flying	Rock			Ground		
Jynx	Ice	Psychic	Oblivious	Forewarn	Dry Skin	Fire	Bug	Rock	Ghost	Dark	Steel		Water♦4		

★ Deals 4 times damage. ♦ 1 Ability prevents damage. ♦ 2 May deal damage depending on the Pokémon's Ability. ♦ 3 Damage may be prevented depending on the Pokémon's Ability. ♦ 4 Hidden Ability prevents damage.

K

Pokémon	Type		Ability		Hidden Ability	Weak against these move types							X Immune to these move types		
Kabuto	Rock	Water	Swift Swim	Battle Armor	Weak Armor	★Grass	Electric	Fighting	Ground						
Kabutops	Rock	Water	Swift Swim	Battle Armor	Weak Armor	★Grass	Electric	Fighting	Ground						
Kadabra	Psychic		Synchronize	Inner Focus	Magic Guard	Bug	Ghost	Dark							
Kakuna	Bug	Poison	Shed Skin			Fire	Flying	Psychic	Rock						
Kangaskhan	Normal		Early Bird	Scrappy	Inner Focus	Fighting							Ghost		
Karrablast	Bug		Swarm	Shed Skin	No Guard	Fire	Flying	Rock							
Kecleon	Normal		Color Change			Fighting							Ghost		
Keldeo (Ordinary Form)	Water	Fighting	Justified			Grass	Electric	Flying	Psychic						
Keldeo (Resolute Form)	Water	Fighting	Justified			Grass	Electric	Flying	Psychic						
Kingdra	Water	Dragon	Swift Swim	Sniper	Damp	Dragon									
Kingler	Water		Hyper Cutter	Shell Armor	Sheer Force	Grass	Electric								
Kirlia	Psychic		Synchronize	Trace	Telepathy	Bug	Ghost	Dark							
Klang	Steel		Plus	Minus	Clear Body	Fire	Fighting	Ground					Poison		
Klink	Steel		Plus	Minus		Fire	Fighting	Ground					Poison		
Klinklang	Steel		Plus	Minus	Clear Body	Fire	Fighting	Ground					Poison		
Koffing	Poison		Levitate			Psychic							Ground♦1		
Krabby	Water		Hyper Cutter	Shell Armor	Sheer Force	Grass	Electric								
Kricketot	Bug		Shed Skin			Fire	Flying	Rock							
Kricketune	Bug		Swarm			Fire	Flying	Rock							
Krokorok	Ground	Dark	Intimidate	Moxie	Anger Point	Water	Grass	Ice	Fighting	Bug			Electric	Psychic	
Krookodile	Ground	Dark	Intimidate	Moxie	Anger Point	Water	Grass	Ice	Fighting	Bug			Electric	Psychic	
Kyogre	Water		Drizzle			Grass	Electric								
Kyurem	Dragon	Ice	Pressure			Fighting	Rock	Dragon	Steel						
Kyurem (Black Kyurem)	Dragon	Ice	Teravolt			Fighting	Rock	Dragon	Steel						
Kyurem (White Kyurem)	Dragon	Ice	Turboblaze			Fighting	Rock	Dragon	Steel						

L

Pokémon	Type		Ability		Hidden Ability	Weak against these move types							X Immune to these move types		
Lairon	Steel	Rock	Sturdy	Rock Head	Heavy Metal	★Fighting	★Ground	Water					Poison		
Lampent	Ghost	Fire	Flash Fire	Flame Body		Water	Ground	Rock	Ghost	Dark			Normal	Fighting	Fire♦2
Landorus (Incarnate Forme)	Ground	Flying	Sand Force		Sheer Force	★Ice	Water						Electric	Ground	
Landorus (Therian Forme)	Ground	Flying	Intimidate			★Ice	Water						Electric	Ground	
Lanturn	Water	Electric	Volt Absorb	Illuminate	Water Absorb	Grass	Ground						Electric♦2	Water♦4	
Lapras	Water	Ice	Water Absorb	Shell Armor	Hydration	Grass	Electric	Fighting	Rock				Water♦2		
Larvesta	Bug	Fire	Flame Body			★Rock	Water	Flying							
Larvitar	Rock	Ground	Guts		Sand Veil	★Water	★Grass	Ice	Fighting	Ground	Steel		Electric		
Latias	Dragon	Psychic	Levitate			Ice	Bug	Ghost	Dragon	Dark			Ground♦1		
Latios	Dragon	Psychic	Levitate			Ice	Bug	Ghost	Dragon	Dark			Ground♦1		
Leafeon	Grass		Leaf Guard		Chlorophyll	Fire	Ice	Poison	Flying	Bug					
Leavanny	Bug	Grass	Swarm	Chlorophyll	Overcoat	★Fire	★Flying	Ice	Poison	Bug	Rock				
Ledian	Bug	Flying	Swarm	Early Bird	Iron Fist	★Rock	Fire	Electric	Ice	Flying			Ground		
Ledyba	Bug	Flying	Swarm	Early Bird	Rattled	★Rock	Fire	Electric	Ice	Flying			Ground		
Lickilicky	Normal		Own Tempo	Oblivious	Cloud Nine	Fighting							Ghost		
Lickitung	Normal		Own Tempo	Oblivious	Cloud Nine	Fighting							Ghost		
Liepard	Dark		Limber	Unburden	Prankster	Fighting	Bug						Psychic		
Lileep	Rock	Grass	Suction Cups		Storm Drain	Ice	Fighting	Bug	Steel				Water♦4		
Lilligant	Grass		Chlorophyll	Own Tempo	Leaf Guard	Fire	Ice	Poison	Flying	Bug					
Lillipup	Normal		Vital Spirit	Pickup	Run Away	Fighting							Ghost		
Linoone	Normal		Pickup	Gluttony	Quick Feet	Fighting							Ghost		
Litwick	Ghost	Fire	Flash Fire	Flame Body		Water	Ground	Rock	Ghost	Dark			Normal	Fighting	Fire♦2
Lombre	Water	Grass	Swift Swim	Rain Dish	Own Tempo	Poison	Flying	Bug							
Lopunny	Normal		Cute Charm	Klutz	Limber	Fighting							Ghost		
Lotad	Water	Grass	Swift Swim	Rain Dish	Own Tempo	Poison	Flying	Bug							
Loudred	Normal		Soundproof		Scrappy	Fighting							Ghost		
Lucario	Fighting	Steel	Steadfast	Inner Focus	Justified	Fire	Fighting	Ground					Poison		
Ludicolo	Water	Grass	Swift Swim	Rain Dish	Own Tempo	Poison	Flying	Bug							
Lugia	Psychic	Flying	Pressure		Multiscale	Electric	Ice	Rock	Ghost	Dark			Ground		
Lumineon	Water		Swift Swim	Storm Drain	Water Veil	Grass	Electric						Water♦2		
Lunatone	Rock	Psychic	Levitate			Water	Grass	Bug	Ghost	Dark	Steel		Ground♦1		
Luvdisc	Water		Swift Swim		Hydration	Grass	Electric								
Luxio	Electric		Rivalry	Intimidate	Guts	Ground									
Luxray	Electric		Rivalry	Intimidate	Guts	Ground									

M

Pokémon	Type		Ability		Hidden Ability	Weak against these move types							X Immune to these move types		
Machamp	Fighting		Guts	No Guard	Steadfast	Flying	Psychic								
Machoke	Fighting		Guts	No Guard	Steadfast	Flying	Psychic								
Machop	Fighting		Guts	No Guard	Steadfast	Flying	Psychic								
Magby	Fire		Flame Body		Vital Spirit	Water	Ground	Rock							
Magcargo	Fire	Rock	Magma Armor	Flame Body	Weak Armor	★Water	★Ground	Fighting	Rock						
Magikarp	Water		Swift Swim		Rattled	Grass	Electric								
Magmar	Fire		Flame Body		Vital Spirit	Water	Ground	Rock							
Magmortar	Fire		Flame Body		Vital Spirit	Water	Ground	Rock							
Magnemite	Electric	Steel	Magnet Pull	Sturdy	Analytic	★Ground	Fire	Fighting					Poison		
Magneton	Electric	Steel	Magnet Pull	Sturdy	Analytic	★Ground	Fire	Fighting					Poison		
Magnezone	Electric	Steel	Magnet Pull	Sturdy	Analytic	★Ground	Fire	Fighting					Poison		
Makuhita	Fighting		Thick Fat	Guts	Sheer Force	Flying	Psychic								
Mamoswine	Ice	Ground	Oblivious	Snow Cloak	Thick Fat	Fire	Water	Grass	Fighting	Steel			Electric		
Manaphy	Water		Hydration			Grass	Electric								
Mandibuzz	Dark	Flying	Big Pecks	Overcoat	Weak Armor	Electric	Ice	Rock					Ground	Psychic	
Manectric	Electric		Static	Lightningrod	Minus	Ground							Electric♦2		
Mankey	Fighting		Vital Spirit	Anger Point	Defiant	Flying	Psychic								
Mantine	Water	Flying	Swift Swim	Water Absorb	Water Veil	★Electric	Rock						Ground	Water♦2	
Mantyke	Water	Flying	Swift Swim	Water Absorb	Water Veil	★Electric	Rock						Ground	Water♦2	
Maractus	Grass		Water Absorb	Chlorophyll	Storm Drain	Fire	Ice	Poison	Flying	Bug			Water♦2,4		
Mareep	Electric		Static		Plus	Ground									
Marill	Water		Thick Fat	Huge Power	Sap Sipper	Grass	Electric						Grass♦4		
Marowak	Ground		Rock Head	Lightningrod	Battle Armor	Water	Grass	Ice					Electric		
Marshtomp	Water	Ground	Torrent		Damp	★Grass							Electric		
Masquerain	Bug	Flying	Intimidate		Unnerve	★Rock	Fire	Electric	Ice	Flying			Ground		
Mawile	Steel		Hyper Cutter	Intimidate	Sheer Force	Fire	Fighting	Ground					Poison		
Medicham	Fighting	Psychic	Pure Power		Telepathy	Flying	Ghost								
Meditite	Fighting	Psychic	Pure Power		Telepathy	Flying	Ghost								
Meganium	Grass		Overgrow			Fire	Ice	Poison	Flying	Bug					
Meloetta (Aria Forme)	Normal	Psychic	Serene Grace			Bug	Dark						Ghost		
Meowth	Normal		Pickup	Technician	Unnerve	Fighting							Ghost		
Mesprit	Psychic		Levitate			Bug	Ghost	Dark					Ground♦1		
Metagross	Steel	Psychic	Clear Body		Light Metal	Fire	Ground						Poison		

Pokémon Weakness Chart—National Pokédex

M

Pokémon	Type		Ability		Hidden Ability	Weak against these move types							X Immune to these move types		
Metang	Steel	Psychic	Clear Body		Light Metal	Fire	Ground						Poison		
Metapod	Bug		Shed Skin			Fire	Flying	Rock							
Mew	Psychic		Synchronize			Bug	Ghost	Dark							
Mewtwo	Psychic		Pressure			Bug	Ghost	Dark							
Mienfoo	Fighting		Inner Focus	Regenerator	Reckless	Flying	Psychic								
Mienshao	Fighting		Inner Focus	Regenerator	Reckless	Flying	Psychic								
Mightyena	Dark		Intimidate	Quick Feet	Moxie	Fighting	Bug						Psychic		
Milotic	Water		Marvel Scale		Cute Charm	Grass	Electric								
Miltank	Normal		Thick Fat	Scrappy	Sap Sipper	Fighting							Ghost	Grass◆4	
Mime Jr.	Psychic		Soundproof	Filter	Technician	Bug	Ghost	Dark							
Minccino	Normal		Cute Charm	Technician	Skill Link	Fighting							Ghost		
Minun	Electric		Minus			Ground									
Misdreavus	Ghost		Levitate			Ghost	Dark						Normal	Fighting	Ground◆1
Mismagius	Ghost		Levitate			Ghost	Dark						Normal	Fighting	Ground◆1
Moltres	Fire	Flying	Pressure			★Rock	Water	Electric					Ground		
Monferno	Fire	Fighting	Blaze		Iron Fist	Water	Ground	Flying	Psychic						
Mothim	Bug	Flying	Swarm		Tinted Lens	★Rock	Fire	Electric	Ice	Flying			Ground		
Mr. Mime	Psychic		Soundproof	Filter	Technician	Bug	Ghost	Dark							
Mudkip	Water		Torrent		Damp	Grass	Electric								
Muk	Poison		Stench	Sticky Hold	Poison Touch	Ground	Psychic								
Munchlax	Normal		Pickup	Thick Fat	Gluttony	Fighting							Ghost		
Munna	Psychic		Forewarn	Synchronize	Telepathy	Bug	Ghost	Dark							
Murkrow	Dark	Flying	Insomnia	Super Luck	Prankster	Electric	Ice	Rock					Ground	Psychic	
Musharna	Psychic		Forewarn	Synchronize	Telepathy	Bug	Ghost	Dark							
Natu	Psychic	Flying	Synchronize	Early Bird	Magic Bounce	Electric	Ice	Rock	Ghost	Dark			Ground		
Nidoking	Poison	Ground	Poison Point	Rivalry	Sheer Force	Water	Ice	Ground	Psychic				Electric		

N

Pokémon	Type		Ability		Hidden Ability	Weak against these move types							X Immune to these move types		
Nidoqueen	Poison	Ground	Poison Point	Rivalry	Sheer Force	Water	Ice	Ground	Psychic				Electric		
Nidoran♀	Poison		Poison Point	Rivalry	Hustle	Ground	Psychic								
Nidoran♂	Poison		Poison Point	Rivalry	Hustle	Ground	Psychic								
Nidorina	Poison		Poison Point	Rivalry	Hustle	Ground	Psychic								
Nidorino	Poison		Poison Point	Rivalry	Hustle	Ground	Psychic								
Nincada	Bug	Ground	Compoundeyes			Fire	Water	Ice	Flying				Electric		
Ninetales	Fire		Flash Fire		Drought	Water	Ground	Rock					Fire◆1		
Ninjask	Bug	Flying	Speed Boost			★Rock	Fire	Electric	Ice	Flying			Ground		
Noctowl	Normal	Flying	Insomnia	Keen Eye	Tinted Lens	Electric	Ice	Rock					Ground	Ghost	
Nosepass	Rock		Sturdy	Magnet Pull	Sand Force	Water	Grass	Fighting	Ground	Steel					
Numel	Fire	Ground	Oblivious	Simple	Own Tempo	★Water	Ground						Electric		
Nuzleaf	Grass	Dark	Chlorophyll	Early Bird		★Bug	Fire	Ice	Fighting	Poison	Flying		Psychic		
Octillery	Water		Suction Cups	Sniper	Moody	Grass	Electric								
Oddish	Grass	Poison	Chlorophyll		Run Away	Fire	Ice	Flying	Psychic						

O

Pokémon	Type		Ability		Hidden Ability	Weak against these move types							X Immune to these move types		
Omanyte	Rock	Water	Swift Swim	Shell Armor	Weak Armor	★Grass	Electric	Fighting	Ground						
Omastar	Rock	Water	Swift Swim	Shell Armor	Weak Armor	★Grass	Electric	Fighting	Ground						
Onix	Rock	Ground	Rock Head	Sturdy	Weak Armor	★Water	★Grass	Ice	Fighting	Ground	Steel		Electric		
Oshawott	Water		Torrent			Grass	Electric								
Pachirisu	Electric		Run Away	Pickup	Volt Absorb	Ground							Electric◆4		
Palkia	Water	Dragon	Pressure		Telepathy	Dragon									

P

Pokémon	Type		Ability		Hidden Ability	Weak against these move types							X Immune to these move types		
Palpitoad	Water	Ground	Swift Swim	Hydration	Water Absorb	★Grass							Electric		
Panpour	Water		Gluttony			Grass	Electric								
Pansage	Grass		Gluttony			Fire	Ice	Poison	Flying	Bug					
Pansear	Fire		Gluttony			Water	Ground	Rock							
Paras	Bug	Grass	Effect Spore	Dry Skin		★Fire	★Flying	Ice	Poison	Bug	Rock		Water◆2		
Parasect	Bug	Grass	Effect Spore	Dry Skin		★Fire	★Flying	Ice	Poison	Bug	Rock		Water◆2		
Patrat	Normal		Run Away	Keen Eye	Analytic	Fighting							Ghost		
Pawniard	Dark	Steel	Defiant	Inner Focus	Pressure	★Fighting	Fire	Ground					Poison	Psychic	
Pelipper	Water	Flying	Keen Eye		Rain Dish	★Electric	Rock						Ground		
Persian	Normal		Limber	Technician	Unnerve	Fighting							Ghost		
Petilil	Grass		Chlorophyll	Own Tempo	Leaf Guard	Fire	Ice	Poison	Flying	Bug					
Phanpy	Ground		Pickup		Sand Veil	Water	Grass	Ice					Electric		
Phione	Water		Hydration			Grass	Electric								
Pichu	Electric		Static		Lightningrod	Ground							Electric◆4		
Pidgeot	Normal	Flying	Keen Eye	Tangled Feet	Big Pecks	Electric	Ice	Rock					Ground	Ghost	
Pidgeotto	Normal	Flying	Keen Eye	Tangled Feet	Big Pecks	Electric	Ice	Rock					Ground	Ghost	
Pidgey	Normal	Flying	Keen Eye	Tangled Feet	Big Pecks	Electric	Ice	Rock					Ground	Ghost	
Pidove	Normal	Flying	Big Pecks	Super Luck	Rivalry	Electric	Ice	Rock					Ground	Ghost	
Pignite	Fire	Fighting	Blaze			Water	Ground	Flying	Psychic						
Pikachu	Electric		Static		Lightningrod	Ground							Electric◆4		
Piloswine	Ice	Ground	Oblivious	Snow Cloak	Thick Fat	Fire	Water	Grass	Fighting	Steel			Electric		
Pineco	Bug		Sturdy			Fire	Flying	Rock							
Pinsir	Bug		Hyper Cutter	Mold Breaker	Moxie	Fire	Flying	Rock							
Piplup	Water		Torrent		Defiant	Grass	Electric								
Plusle	Electric		Plus			Ground									
Politoed	Water		Water Absorb	Damp	Drizzle	Grass	Electric						Water◆2		
Poliwag	Water		Water Absorb	Damp	Swift Swim	Grass	Electric						Water◆2		
Poliwhirl	Water		Water Absorb	Damp	Swift Swim	Grass	Electric						Water◆2		
Poliwrath	Water	Fighting	Water Absorb	Damp	Swift Swim	Grass	Electric	Flying	Psychic				Water◆2		
Ponyta	Fire		Run Away	Flash Fire	Flame Body	Water	Ground	Rock					Fire◆2		
Poochyena	Dark		Run Away	Quick Feet	Rattled	Fighting	Bug						Psychic		
Porygon	Normal		Trace	Download	Analytic	Fighting							Ghost		
Porygon-Z	Normal		Adaptability	Download	Analytic	Fighting							Ghost		
Porygon2	Normal		Trace	Download	Analytic	Fighting							Ghost		
Primeape	Fighting		Vital Spirit	Anger Point	Defiant	Flying	Psychic								
Prinplup	Water		Torrent		Defiant	Grass	Electric								
Probopass	Rock	Steel	Sturdy	Magnet Pull	Sand Force	★Fighting	★Ground	Water					Poison		
Psyduck	Water		Damp	Cloud Nine	Swift Swim	Grass	Electric								
Pupitar	Rock	Ground	Shed Skin			★Water	★Grass	Ice	Fighting	Ground	Steel		Electric		
Purrloin	Dark		Limber	Unburden	Prankster	Fighting	Bug						Psychic		
Purugly	Normal		Thick Fat	Own Tempo	Defiant	Fighting							Ghost		
Quagsire	Water	Ground	Damp	Water Absorb	Unaware	★Grass							Electric	Water◆2	
Quilava	Fire		Blaze			Water	Ground	Rock							

★ Deals 4 times damage. ◆ 1 Ability prevents damage. ◆ 2 May deal damage depending on the Pokémon's Ability. ◆ 3 Damage may be prevented depending on the Pokémon's Ability. ◆ 4 Hidden Ability prevents damage.

Q

Pokémon	Type		Ability		Hidden Ability	Weak against these move types							X Immune to these move types		
Qwilfish	Water	Poison	Poison Point	Swift Swim	Intimidate	Electric	Ground	Psychic							
Raichu	Electric		Static		Lightningrod	Ground							Electric◆4		
Raikou	Electric		Pressure			Ground									

R

Pokémon	Type		Ability		Hidden Ability	Weak against these move types							X Immune to these move types		
Ralts	Psychic		Synchronize	Trace	Telepathy	Bug	Ghost	Dark							
Rampardos	Rock		Mold Breaker		Sheer Force	Water	Grass	Fighting	Ground	Steel					
Rapidash	Fire		Run Away	Flash Fire	Flame Body	Water	Ground	Rock					Fire◆2		
Raticate	Normal		Run Away	Guts	Hustle	Fighting							Ghost		
Rattata	Normal		Run Away	Guts	Hustle	Fighting							Ghost		
Rayquaza	Dragon	Flying	Air Lock			★Ice	Rock	Dragon					Ground		
Regice	Ice		Clear Body			Fire	Fighting	Rock	Steel						
Regigigas	Normal		Slow Start			Fighting							Ghost		
Regirock	Rock		Clear Body			Water	Grass	Fighting	Ground	Steel					
Registeel	Steel		Clear Body			Fire	Fighting	Ground					Poison		
Relicanth	Water	Rock	Swift Swim	Rock Head	Sturdy	★Grass	Electric	Fighting	Ground						
Remoraid	Water		Hustle	Sniper	Moody	Grass	Electric								
Reshiram	Dragon	Fire	Turboblaze			Ground	Rock	Dragon							
Reuniclus	Psychic		Overcoat	Magic Guard	Regenerator	Bug	Ghost	Dark							
Rhydon	Ground	Rock	Lightningrod	Rock Head	Reckless	★Water	★Grass	Ice	Fighting	Ground	Steel		Electric		
Rhyhorn	Ground	Rock	Lightningrod	Rock Head	Reckless	★Water	★Grass	Ice	Fighting	Ground	Steel		Electric		
Rhyperior	Ground	Rock	Lightningrod	Solid Rock	Reckless	★Water	★Grass	Ice	Fighting	Ground	Steel		Electric		
Riolu	Fighting		Steadfast	Inner Focus	Prankster	Flying	Psychic								
Roggenrola	Rock		Sturdy		Sand Force	Water	Grass	Fighting	Ground	Steel					
Roselia	Grass	Poison	Natural Cure	Poison Point		Fire	Ice	Flying	Psychic						
Roserade	Grass	Poison	Natural Cure	Poison Point		Fire	Ice	Flying	Psychic						
Rotom	Electric	Grass	Levitate			Fire	Ice	Poison	Bug				Ground◆1		
Rotom (Fan Rotom)	Electric	Ghost	Levitate			Ghost	Dark						Normal	Fighting	Ground◆1
Rotom (Frost Rotom)	Electric	Ice	Levitate			Fire	Fighting	Rock					Ground◆1		
Rotom (Heat Rotom)	Electric	Fire	Levitate			Water	Rock						Ground◆1		
Rotom (Mow Rotom)	Electric	Water	Levitate			Grass							Ground◆1		
Rotom (Wash Rotom)	Electric	Flying	Levitate			Ice	Rock						Ground		
Rufflet	Normal	Flying	Keen Eye	Sheer Force		Electric	Ice	Rock					Ground	Ghost	
Sableye	Dark	Ghost	Keen Eye	Stall	Prankster								Normal	Fighting	Psychic
Salamence	Dragon	Flying	Intimidate		Moxie	★Ice	Rock	Dragon					Ground		

S

Pokémon	Type		Ability		Hidden Ability	Weak against these move types							X Immune to these move types		
Samurott	Water		Torrent			Grass	Electric								
Sandile	Ground	Dark	Intimidate	Moxie	Anger Point	Water	Grass	Ice	Fighting	Bug			Electric	Psychic	
Sandshrew	Ground		Sand Veil		Sand Rush	Water	Grass	Ice					Electric		
Sandslash	Ground		Sand Veil		Sand Rush	Water	Grass	Ice					Electric		
Sawk	Fighting		Sturdy	Inner Focus		Flying	Psychic								
Sawsbuck	Normal	Grass	Chlorophyll	Sap Sipper	Serene Grace	Fire	Ice	Fighting	Poison	Flying	Bug		Ghost	Grass◆2	
Sceptile	Grass		Overgrow		Unburden	Fire	Ice	Poison	Flying	Bug					
Scizor	Bug	Steel	Swarm	Technician	Light Metal	★Fire							Poison		
Scolipede	Bug	Poison	Poison Point	Swarm	Quick Feet	Fire	Flying	Psychic	Rock						
Scrafty	Dark	Fighting	Shed Skin	Moxie		Fighting	Flying						Psychic		
Scraggy	Dark	Fighting	Shed Skin	Moxie		Fighting	Flying						Psychic		
Scyther	Bug	Flying	Swarm	Technician	Steadfast	★Rock	Fire	Electric	Ice	Flying			Ground		
Seadra	Water		Poison Point	Sniper	Damp	Grass	Electric								
Seaking	Water		Swift Swim	Water Veil	Lightningrod	Grass	Electric						Electric◆4		
Sealeo	Ice	Water	Thick Fat	Ice Body	Oblivious	Grass	Electric	Fighting	Rock						
Seedot	Grass		Chlorophyll	Early Bird		Fire	Ice	Poison	Flying	Bug					
Seel	Water		Thick Fat	Hydration	Ice Body	Grass	Electric								
Seismitoad	Water	Ground	Swift Swim	Poison Touch	Water Absorb	★Grass							Electric		
Sentret	Normal		Run Away	Keen Eye	Frisk	Fighting							Ghost		
Serperior	Grass		Overgrow			Fire	Ice	Poison	Flying	Bug					
Servine	Grass		Overgrow			Fire	Ice	Poison	Flying	Bug					
Seviper	Poison		Shed Skin		Infiltrator	Ground	Psychic								
Sewaddle	Bug	Grass	Swarm	Chlorophyll	Overcoat	★Fire	★Flying	Ice	Poison	Bug	Rock				
Sharpedo	Water	Dark	Rough Skin		Speed Boost	Grass	Electric	Fighting	Bug				Psychic		
Shaymin (Land Forme)	Grass		Natural Cure			Fire	Ice	Poison	Flying	Bug					
Shaymin (Sky Forme)	Grass	Flying	Serene Grace			★Ice	Fire	Poison	Flying	Rock			Ground		
Shedinja	Bug	Ghost	Wonder Guard			Fire	Flying	Rock	Ghost	Dark			Type *1 outside of the five to the left		
Shelgon	Dragon		Rock Head		Overcoat	Ice	Dragon								
Shellder	Water		Shell Armor	Skill Link	Overcoat	Grass	Electric								
Shellos	Water		Sticky Hold	Storm Drain	Sand Force	Grass	Electric						Water◆2		
Shelmet	Bug		Hydration	Shell Armor	Overcoat	Fire	Flying	Rock							
Shieldon	Rock	Steel	Sturdy		Soundproof	★Fighting	★Ground	Water					Poison		
Shiftry	Grass	Dark	Chlorophyll	Early Bird		★Bug	Fire	Ice	Fighting	Poison	Flying		Psychic		
Shinx	Electric		Rivalry	Intimidate	Guts	Ground									
Shroomish	Grass		Effect Spore	Poison Heal	Quick Feet	Fire	Ice	Poison	Flying	Bug					
Shuckle	Bug	Rock	Sturdy	Gluttony	Contrary	Water	Rock	Steel							
Shuppet	Ghost		Insomnia	Frisk	Cursed Body	Ghost	Dark						Normal		
Sigilyph	Psychic	Flying	Wonder Skin	Magic Guard	Tinted Lens	Electric	Ice	Rock	Ghost	Dark			Ground		
Silcoon	Bug		Shed Skin			Fire	Flying	Rock							
Simipour	Water		Gluttony			Grass	Electric								
Simisage	Grass		Gluttony			Fire	Ice	Poison	Flying	Bug					
Simisear	Fire		Gluttony			Water	Ground	Rock							
Skarmory	Steel	Flying	Keen Eye	Sturdy	Weak Armor	Fire	Electric						Poison	Ground	
Skiploom	Grass	Flying	Chlorophyll	Leaf Guard	Infiltrator	★Ice	Fire	Poison	Flying	Rock			Ground		
Skitty	Normal		Cute Charm	Normalize	Wonder Skin	Fighting							Ghost		
Skorupi	Poison	Bug	Battle Armor	Sniper	Keen Eye	Fire	Flying	Psychic	Rock						
Skuntank	Poison	Dark	Stench	Aftermath	Keen Eye	Ground							Psychic		
Slaking	Normal		Truant			Fighting							Ghost		
Slakoth	Normal		Truant			Fighting							Ghost		
Slowbro	Water	Psychic	Oblivious	Own Tempo	Regenerator	Grass	Electric	Bug	Ghost	Dark					
Slowking	Water	Psychic	Oblivious	Own Tempo	Regenerator	Grass	Electric	Bug	Ghost	Dark					
Slowpoke	Water	Psychic	Oblivious	Own Tempo	Regenerator	Grass	Electric	Bug	Ghost	Dark					
Slugma	Fire		Magma Armor	Flame Body	Weak Armor	Water	Ground	Rock							
Smeargle	Normal		Own Tempo	Technician	Moody	Fighting							Ghost		
Smoochum	Ice	Psychic	Oblivious	Forewarn	Hydration	Fire	Bug	Rock	Ghost	Dark	Steel				
Sneasel	Dark	Ice	Inner Focus	Keen Eye	Pickpocket	★Fighting	Fire	Bug	Rock	Steel			Psychic		
Snivy	Grass		Overgrow			Fire	Ice	Poison	Flying	Bug					
Snorlax	Normal		Immunity	Thick Fat	Gluttony	Fighting							Ghost		
Snorunt	Ice		Inner Focus	Ice Body	Moody	Fire	Fighting	Rock	Steel						
Snover	Grass	Ice	Snow Warning		Soundproof	★Fire	Fighting	Poison	Flying	Bug	Rock	Steel			
Snubbull	Normal		Intimidate	Run Away	Rattled	Fighting							Ghost		

Pokémon Weakness Chart—National Pokédex

S

Pokémon	Type		Ability		Hidden Ability	Weak against these move types							X Immune to these move types		
Solosis	Psychic		Overcoat	Magic Guard	Regenerator	Bug	Ghost	Dark							
Solrock	Rock	Psychic	Levitate			Water	Grass	Bug	Ghost	Dark	Steel		Ground♦1		
Spearow	Normal	Flying	Keen Eye		Sniper	Electric	Ice	Rock					Ground	Ghost	
Spheal	Ice	Water	Thick Fat	Ice Body	Oblivious	Grass	Electric	Fighting	Rock						
Spinarak	Bug	Poison	Swarm	Insomnia	Sniper	Fire	Flying	Psychic	Rock						
Spinda	Normal		Own Tempo	Tangled Feet	Contrary	Fighting							Ghost		
Spiritomb	Ghost	Dark	Pressure		Infiltrator								Normal	Fighting	Psychic
Spoink	Psychic		Thick Fat	Own Tempo	Gluttony	Bug	Ghost	Dark							
Squirtle	Water		Torrent		Rain Dish	Grass	Electric								
Stantler	Normal		Intimidate	Frisk	Sap Sipper	Fighting							Ghost	Grass♦4	
Staraptor	Normal	Flying	Intimidate		Reckless	Electric	Ice	Rock					Ground	Ghost	
Staravia	Normal	Flying	Intimidate		Reckless	Electric	Ice	Rock					Ground	Ghost	
Starly	Normal	Flying	Keen Eye			Electric	Ice	Rock					Ground	Ghost	
Starmie	Water	Psychic	Illuminate	Natural Cure	Analytic	Grass	Electric	Bug	Ghost	Dark					
Staryu	Water		Illuminate	Natural Cure	Analytic	Grass	Electric								
Steelix	Steel	Ground	Rock Head	Sturdy	Sheer Force	Fire	Water	Fighting	Ground				Electric	Poison	
Stoutland	Normal		Intimidate	Sand Rush	Scrappy	Fighting							Ghost		
Stunfisk	Ground	Electric	Static	Limber	Sand Veil	Water	Grass	Ice	Ground				Electric		
Stunky	Poison	Dark	Stench	Aftermath	Keen Eye	Ground							Psychic		
Sudowoodo	Rock		Sturdy	Rock Head	Rattled	Water	Grass	Fighting	Ground	Steel					
Suicune	Water		Pressure			Grass	Electric								
Sunflora	Grass		Chlorophyll	Solar Power	Early Bird	Fire	Ice	Poison	Flying	Bug					
Sunkern	Grass		Chlorophyll	Solar Power	Early Bird	Fire	Ice	Poison	Flying	Bug					
Surskit	Bug	Water	Swift Swim		Rain Dish	Electric	Flying	Rock							
Swablu	Normal	Flying	Natural Cure		Cloud Nine	Electric	Ice	Rock					Ground	Ghost	
Swadloon	Bug	Grass	Leaf Guard	Chlorophyll	Overcoat	★Fire	★Flying	Ice	Poison	Bug	Rock				
Swalot	Poison		Liquid Ooze	Sticky Hold		Ground	Psychic								
Swampert	Water	Ground	Torrent		Damp	★Grass							Electric		
Swanna	Water	Flying	Keen Eye	Big Pecks	Hydration	★Electric	Rock						Ground		
Swellow	Normal	Flying	Guts		Scrappy	Electric	Ice	Rock					Ground	Ghost	
Swinub	Ice	Ground	Oblivious	Snow Cloak	Thick Fat	Fire	Water	Grass	Fighting	Steel			Electric		
Swoobat	Psychic	Flying	Unaware	Klutz	Simple	Electric	Ice	Rock	Ghost	Dark			Ground		
Taillow	Normal	Flying	Guts		Scrappy	Electric	Ice	Rock					Ground	Ghost	
Tangela	Grass		Chlorophyll	Leaf Guard	Regenerator	Fire	Ice	Poison	Flying	Bug					

T

Pokémon	Type		Ability		Hidden Ability	Weak against these move types							X Immune to these move types		
Tangrowth	Grass		Chlorophyll	Leaf Guard	Regenerator	Fire	Ice	Poison	Flying	Bug					
Tauros	Normal		Intimidate	Anger Point	Sheer Force	Fighting							Ghost		
Teddiursa	Normal		Pickup	Quick Feet	Honey Gather	Fighting							Ghost		
Tentacool	Water	Poison	Clear Body	Liquid Ooze	Rain Dish	Electric	Ground	Psychic							
Tentacruel	Water	Poison	Clear Body	Liquid Ooze	Rain Dish	Electric	Ground	Psychic							
Tepig	Fire		Blaze			Water	Ground	Rock							
Terrakion	Rock	Fighting	Justified			Water	Grass	Fighting	Ground	Psychic	Steel				
Throh	Fighting		Guts	Inner Focus		Flying	Psychic								
Thundurus (Incarnate Forme)	Electric	Flying	Prankster		Defiant	Ice	Rock						Ground		
Thundurus (Therian Forme)	Electric	Flying	Volt Absorb			Ice	Rock						Ground	Electric♦1	
Timburr	Fighting		Guts	Sheer Force		Flying	Psychic								
Tirtouga	Water	Rock	Solid Rock	Sturdy	Swift Swim	★Grass	Electric	Fighting	Ground						
Togekiss	Normal	Flying	Hustle	Serene Grace	Super Luck	Electric	Ice	Rock					Ground	Ghost	
Togepi	Normal		Hustle	Serene Grace	Super Luck	Fighting							Ghost		
Togetic	Normal	Flying	Hustle	Serene Grace	Super Luck	Electric	Ice	Rock					Ground	Ghost	
Torchic	Fire		Blaze		Speed Boost	Water	Ground	Rock							
Torkoal	Fire		White Smoke		Shell Armor	Water	Ground	Rock							
Tornadus (Incarnate Forme)	Flying		Prankster		Defiant	Electric	Ice	Rock					Ground		
Tornadus (Therian Forme)	Flying		Regenerator			Electric	Ice	Rock					Ground		
Torterra	Grass	Ground	Overgrow		Shell Armor	★Ice	Fire	Flying	Bug				Electric		
Totodile	Water		Torrent			Grass	Electric								
Toxicroak	Poison	Fighting	Anticipation	Dry Skin	Poison Touch	★Psychic	Ground	Flying					Water♦2		
Tranquill	Normal	Flying	Big Pecks	Super Luck	Rivalry	Electric	Ice	Rock					Ground	Ghost	
Trapinch	Ground		Hyper Cutter	Arena Trap	Sheer Force	Water	Grass	Ice					Electric		
Treecko	Grass		Overgrow		Unburden	Fire	Ice	Poison	Flying	Bug					
Tropius	Grass	Flying	Chlorophyll	Solar Power	Harvest	★Ice	Fire	Poison	Flying	Rock			Ground		
Trubbish	Poison		Stench	Sticky Hold	Aftermath	Ground	Psychic								
Turtwig	Grass		Overgrow		Shell Armor	Fire	Ice	Poison	Flying	Bug					
Tympole	Water		Swift Swim	Hydration	Water Absorb	Grass	Electric						Water♦4		
Tynamo	Electric		Levitate										Ground♦1		
Typhlosion	Fire		Blaze			Water	Ground	Rock							
Tyranitar	Rock	Dark	Sand Stream		Unnerve	★Fighting	Water	Grass	Ground	Bug	Steel		Psychic		
Tyrogue	Fighting		Guts	Steadfast	Vital Spirit	Flying	Psychic								
Umbreon	Dark		Synchronize		Inner Focus	Fighting	Bug						Psychic		
Unfezant	Normal	Flying	Big Pecks	Super Luck	Rivalry	Electric	Ice	Rock					Ground	Ghost	

U

Pokémon	Type		Ability		Hidden Ability	Weak against these move types							X Immune to these move types		
Unown	Psychic		Levitate			Bug	Ghost	Dark					Ground♦1		
Ursaring	Normal		Guts	Quick Feet	Unnerve	Fighting							Ghost		
Uxie	Psychic		Levitate			Bug	Ghost	Dark					Ground♦1		
Vanillish	Ice		Ice Body		Weak Armor	Fire	Fighting	Rock	Steel						

V

Pokémon	Type		Ability		Hidden Ability	Weak against these move types							X Immune to these move types		
Vanillite	Ice		Ice Body		Weak Armor	Fire	Fighting	Rock	Steel						
Vanilluxe	Ice		Ice Body		Weak Armor	Fire	Fighting	Rock	Steel						
Vaporeon	Water		Water Absorb		Hydration	Grass	Electric						Water♦1		
Venipede	Bug	Poison	Poison Point	Swarm	Quick Feet	Fire	Flying	Psychic	Rock						
Venomoth	Bug	Poison	Shield Dust	Tinted Lens	Wonder Skin	Fire	Flying	Psychic	Rock						
Venonat	Bug	Poison	Compoundeyes	Tinted Lens	Run Away	Fire	Flying	Psychic	Rock						
Venusaur	Grass	Poison	Overgrow		Chlorophyll	Fire	Ice	Flying	Psychic						
Vespiquen	Bug	Flying	Pressure		Unnerve	★Rock	Fire	Electric	Ice	Flying			Ground		
Vibrava	Ground	Dragon	Levitate			★Ice	Dragon						Electric	Ground♦1	
Victini	Psychic	Fire	Victory Star			Water	Ground	Rock	Ghost	Dark					
Victreebel	Grass	Poison	Chlorophyll		Gluttony	Fire	Ice	Flying	Psychic						
Vigoroth	Normal		Vital Spirit			Fighting							Ghost		
Vileplume	Grass	Poison	Chlorophyll		Effect Spore	Fire	Ice	Flying	Psychic						
Virizion	Grass	Fighting	Justified			★Flying	Fire	Ice	Poison	Psychic					
Volbeat	Bug		Illuminate	Swarm	Prankster	Fire	Flying	Rock							
Volcarona	Bug	Fire	Flame Body			★Rock	Water	Flying							

★ Deals 4 times damage. ♦ 1 Ability prevents damage. ♦ 2 May deal damage depending on the Pokémon's Ability. ♦ 3 Damage may be prevented depending on the Pokémon's Ability. ♦ 4 Hidden Ability prevents damage.

Pokémon	Type		Ability		Hidden Ability	Weak against these move types							X Immune to these move types		
Voltorb	Electric		Soundproof	Static	Aftermath	Ground									
Vullaby	Dark	Flying	Big Pecks	Overcoat	Weak Armor	Electric	Ice	Rock					Ground	Psychic	
Vulpix	Fire		Flash Fire		Drought	Water	Ground	Rock					Fire♦1		
Wailmer	Water		Water Veil	Oblivious	Pressure	Grass	Electric								

W

Pokémon	Type		Ability		Hidden Ability	Weak against these move types							X Immune to these move types		
Wailord	Water		Water Veil	Oblivious	Pressure	Grass	Electric								
Walrein	Ice	Water	Thick Fat	Ice Body	Oblivious	Grass	Electric	Fighting	Rock						
Wartortle	Water		Torrent		Rain Dish	Grass	Electric								
Watchog	Normal		Illuminate	Keen Eye	Analytic	Fighting							Ghost		
Weavile	Dark	Ice	Pressure		Pickpocket	★Fighting	Fire	Bug	Rock	Steel			Psychic		
Weedle	Bug	Poison	Shield Dust		Run Away	Fire	Flying	Psychic	Rock						
Weepinbell	Grass	Poison	Chlorophyll		Gluttony	Fire	Ice	Flying	Psychic						
Weezing	Poison		Levitate			Psychic							Ground♦1		
Whimsicott	Grass		Prankster	Infiltrator	Chlorophyll	Fire	Ice	Poison	Flying	Bug					
Whirlipede	Bug	Poison	Poison Point	Swarm	Quick Feet	Fire	Flying	Psychic	Rock						
Whiscash	Water	Ground	Oblivious	Anticipation	Hydration	★Grass							Electric		
Whismur	Normal		Soundproof		Rattled	Fighting							Ghost		
Wigglytuff	Normal		Cute Charm		Frisk	Fighting							Ghost		
Wingull	Water	Flying	Keen Eye		Rain Dish	★Electric	Rock						Ground		
Wobbuffet	Psychic		Shadow Tag		Telepathy	Bug	Ghost	Dark							
Woobat	Psychic	Flying	Unaware	Klutz	Simple	Electric	Ice	Rock	Ghost	Dark			Ground		
Wooper	Water	Ground	Damp	Water Absorb	Unaware	★Grass							Electric	Water♦2	
Wormadam (Plant Cloak)	Bug	Grass	Anticipation		Overcoat	★Fire	★Flying	Ice	Poison	Bug	Rock				
Wormadam (Sandy Cloak)	Bug	Ground	Anticipation		Overcoat	Fire	Water	Ice	Flying				Electric		
Wormadam (Trash Cloak)	Bug	Steel	Anticipation		Overcoat	★Fire							Poison		
Wurmple	Bug		Shield Dust			Fire	Flying	Rock							
Wynaut	Psychic		Shadow Tag		Telepathy	Bug	Ghost	Dark							
Xatu	Psychic	Flying	Synchronize	Early Bird	Magic Bounce	Electric	Ice	Rock	Ghost	Dark			Ground		

XYZ

Pokémon	Type		Ability		Hidden Ability	Weak against these move types							X Immune to these move types		
Yamask	Ghost		Mummy			Ghost	Dark						Normal	Fighting	
Yanma	Bug	Flying	Speed Boost	Compoundeyes	Frisk	★Rock	Fire	Electric	Ice	Flying			Ground		
Yanmega	Bug	Flying	Speed Boost	Tinted Lens	Frisk	★Rock	Fire	Electric	Ice	Flying			Ground		
Zangoose	Normal		Immunity		Toxic Boost	Fighting							Ghost		
Zapdos	Electric	Flying	Pressure			Ice	Rock						Ground		
Zebstrika	Electric		Lightningrod	Motor Drive	Sap Sipper	Ground							Electric♦1	Grass♦4	
Zekrom	Dragon	Electric	Teravolt			Ice	Ground	Dragon							
Zigzagoon	Normal		Pickup	Gluttony	Quick Feet	Fighting							Ghost		
Zoroark	Dark		Illusion			Fighting	Bug						Psychic		
Zorua	Dark		Illusion			Fighting	Bug						Psychic		
Zubat	Poison	Flying	Inner Focus		Infiltrator	Electric	Ice	Psychic	Rock				Ground		
Zweilous	Dark	Dragon	Hustle			Ice	Fighting	Bug	Dragon				Psychic		

Type Matchup Chart

Types are assigned both to moves and to the Pokémon themselves. These types can greatly affect the amount of damage dealt or received in battle, so learn how they line up against one another and give yourself the edge in battle.

Attacking Pokémon's Move Type \ Defending Pokémon's Type	Normal	Fire	Water	Grass	Electric	Ice	Fighting	Poison	Ground	Flying	Psychic	Bug	Rock	Ghost	Dragon	Dark	Steel
Normal													▲	×			▲
Fire		▲	▲	◉		◉						◉	▲		▲		◉
Water		◉	▲	▲					◉				◉		▲		
Grass		▲	◉	▲				▲	◉	▲		▲	◉		▲		▲
Electric			◉	▲	▲				×	◉					▲		
Ice		▲	▲	◉		▲			◉	◉					◉		▲
Fighting	◉					◉		▲		▲	▲	▲	◉	×		◉	◉
Poison				◉				▲	▲				▲	▲			×
Ground		◉		▲	◉			◉		×		▲	◉				◉
Flying				◉	▲		◉					◉	▲				▲
Psychic							◉	◉			▲					×	▲
Bug		▲		◉			▲	▲		▲	◉			▲		◉	▲
Rock		◉				◉	▲		▲	◉		◉					▲
Ghost	×										◉			◉		▲	▲
Dragon															◉		▲
Dark							▲				◉			◉		▲	▲
Steel		▲	▲		▲	◉							◉				▲

Legend

◉	Very effective "It's super effective!"	×2
	(No icon) Normal damage	×1
▲	Not too effective "It's not very effective"	×0.5
×	No effect "It doesn't affect..."	×0

- Fire-type Pokémon cannot be afflicted with the Burned condition.
- Grass-type Pokémon are immune to Leech Seed.
- Ice-type Pokémon are immune to the Frozen condition and take no damage from hail.
- Poison-type Pokémon are immune to the Poison and Badly Poisoned conditions, even when switching in with Toxic Spikes in play. Poison-type Pokémon nullify Toxic Spikes (unless these Pokémon are also Flying type or have the Levitate Ability).
- Ground-type Pokémon are immune to Thunder Wave and take no damage from a sandstorm.
- Flying-type Pokémon cannot be damaged by Spikes when switching in, or become afflicted with a Poison or Badly Poisoned condition due to switching in with Toxic Spikes in play.
- Rock-type Pokémon take no damage from a sandstorm. Their Sp. Def also goes up in a sandstorm.
- Steel-type Pokémon take no damage from a sandstorm. They are also immune to the Poison and Badly Poisoned conditions. Even if switched in with Toxic Spikes in play, they will not be afflicted by the Poison or Badly Poisoned condition.

CREDITS

The Pokémon Company
INTERNATIONAL

EDITOR-IN-CHIEF
Michael G. Ryan

PROJECT MANAGER
Emily Luty (Bridge Consulting Group)

TRANSLATORS
Hisato Yamamori
Tim Hove
David Numrich
Sayuri Munday
Jillian Nonaka

EDITORS
Kellyn Ballard
Blaise Selby
Hollie Beg
Wolfgang Baur

COVER DESIGNERS
Eric Medalle
Bridget O'Neill

ACKNOWLEDGEMENTS
Kenji Okubo
Mikako Fitzsimmons
Heather Dalgleish
Amy Levenson
Yasuhiro Usui
Mikiko Ryu
Rey Perez
Antoin Johnson
J.C. Smith
Hiromi Kimura (The Creative Group)
Sachiko Kimura
Kumiko Suzuki (Bridge Consulting Group)

COLLECTOR'S EDITION ACKNOWLEDGEMENTS
GAME FREAK inc.
Junichi Masuda
Shigeki Morimoto
Masafumi Saito

DESIGN & PRODUCTION
Prima Games
Donato Tica
Mark Hughes
Jamie Knight
Melissa Smith
Shaida Boroumand

99 Lives Design, LLC
Adam Crowell
Emily Crowell
Oliver Crowell
Sonja Morris

Standard Edition ISBN: 978-0-307-89561-5
Collector's Edition ISBN: 978-0-307-89562-2

Published in the United States by The Pokémon Company International.
333 108th Ave NE, Suite 1900, Bellevue, WA 98004 U.S.A.
1st Floor Block 5, Thames Wharf Studios, Rainville Road, London W6 9HA United Kingdom

Printed in the United States of America using materials from the *Pokémon Black Version 2 & Pokémon White Version 2: The Official Strategy Guide and Complete Walkthrough*. Original Japanese strategy guide published in Japan by OVERLAP, Inc.

ORIGINAL JAPANESE STRATEGY GUIDE:
Planning, Page Layout, Writing & Map Development: Shusuke Motomiya and ONEUP, Inc.
Art Direction, Design & Layout: RAGTIME CO., LTD., and SUZUKIKOUBOU, Inc.